FIFTH EDITION

ESSENTIALS *of* BUSINESS LAW

Jeffrey F. Beatty
Boston University

Susan S. Samuelson
Boston University

CENGAGE
Learning

Australia • Brazil • Japan • Korea • Mexico • Singapore • Spain • United Kingdom • United States

Essentials of Business Law, Fifth Edition
Jeffrey F. Beatty, Susan S. Samuelson

Senior Vice President, Global Product Manager,
Higher Education: Jack W. Calhoun

Vice President, General Manager, Social Science &
Qualitative Business: Erin Joyner

Product Director: Mike Worls

Sr. Product Manager: Vicky True Baker

Managing Developer: Jennifer King

Product Assistant: Tristann Jones

Sr. Content Project Manager: Holly Henjum

Sr. Media Developer: Kristen Meere

Manufacturing Planner: Kevin Kluck

Rights Acquisition Specialist: Anne Sheroff

Marketing Director: Kristen Hurd

Sr. Marketing Manager: Robin LeFevre

Marketing Coordinator: Christopher Walz

Production Service: Integra Software
Services Pvt. Ltd.

Sr. Art Director: Michelle Kunkler

Cover and Internal Designer: Lou Ann Thesing

Cover Image: Peter Pearson/Stockbyte/Getty

For product information and technology assistance, contact us at
Cengage Learning Customer & Sales Support, 1-800-354-9706

For permission to use material from this text or product,
submit all requests online at **www.cengage.com/permissions**
Further permissions questions can be emailed to
permissionrequest@cengage.com

Library of Congress Control Number: 2013952743

ISBN-13: 978-1-285-42700-3

ISBN-10: 1-285-42700-9

Cengage Learning
200 First Stamford Place, 4th Floor
Stamford, CT 06902
USA

Cengage Learning is a leading provider of customized learning solutions with office locations around the globe, including Singapore, the United Kingdom, Australia, Mexico, Brazil, and Japan. Locate your local office at: **www.cengage.com/global**

Cengage Learning products are represented in Canada by Nelson Education, Ltd.

To learn more about Cengage Learning Solutions, visit
www.cengage.com

Purchase any of our products at your local college store or at our preferred online store **www.cengagebrain.com**

Printed in the United States of America
2 3 4 5 6 19 18 17 16 15

CONTENTS: OVERVIEW

CONTENTS

Chapter 4 *Common Law, Statutory Law, and Administrative Law*   83

Chapter 5 *Constitutional Law*   109

UNIT 4
Employment, Business Organizations and Property   615

Chapter 26 *Employment and Labor Law*   616

Chapter 27 *Employment Discrimination*   644

Looking for more examples for class? Do you want the latest developments? Visit our blog at bizlawupdate.com or our Facebook page at Beatty Business Law. To be notified when we post updates, follow us on Twitter @bizlawupdate.

NOTE FROM THE AUTHORS

New to This Edition

A NEW CHAPTER: PRACTICAL CONTRACTS

In this textbook, as well as other business law texts, contracts chapters focus on the *theory* of contract law. And that theory is important. But our students tell us that theory, by itself, is not enough. They need to know how these abstract rules operate in *practice*. They want to understand the structure and content of a standard agreement. They have questions such as:

- Do I need a written agreement?
- What do these legal terms *really* mean?
- Are any important provisions missing?
- What happens if a term is unclear?
- Do I need to hire a lawyer? How can I use a lawyer most effectively?

We answer all these questions in Chapter 18, "Practical Contracts," which is new to this edition. As an illustration throughout the chapter, we use a real-life contract between a movie studio and an actor.

A NEW CHAPTER: EMPLOYMENT DISCRIMINATION

We have heard from faculty and students alike that employment law plays an increasingly important role in the life of a businessperson. At the same time, fewer and fewer workers belong to labor unions. Therefore, we have rewritten the labor law and employment law chapters from the previous edition. Instead of one chapter on labor law and one on employment law, we now have a new Chapter 26, "Employment and Labor Law," which covers both common law employment issues and labor law. In addition, Chapter 27, "Employment Discrimination," focuses solely on employment discrimination and includes, among other things, an expanded discussion of disparate impact cases, which have become increasingly common and important.

NEW MATERIAL: ETHICS CHAPTER

The Ethics chapter has been completely revised and is full of up-to-date examples, all either from the news or true stories provided by executives. The section on the Theories of Ethics has been enhanced and now includes, among others, John Rawls' theory of justice. This chapter also includes a discussion of the latest research on the ethics traps that prevent us from doing what we know to be right. Students are asked to develop their own list of Life

Principles that they can use to make ethical decisions and avoid ethics traps. The chapter also discusses the options that employees face when confronted with unethical behavior in the workplace. And, finally, the chapter concludes with a discussion of Corporate Social Responsibility—should companies practice it and, if so, how should they evaluate success?

LANDMARK CASES

As a general rule, we want our cases to be as current as possible, reporting on the world as it is now. However, sometimes students can benefit from reading vintage cases that are still good law and provide a deep understanding of how and why the law has developed as it has. Thus, for example, we have added a discussion about the famous Supreme Court case *Miranda v. Arizona*. Reading this case provides students with a much better understanding of why the Supreme Court created Miranda rights, and this context helps students follow the recent Supreme Court rulings on *Miranda*. Other landmark cases include *Hawkins v. McGee* (the case of the hairy hand), and *Griggs v. Duke Power Co.*

REORGANIZED AND REVISED MATERIAL

In response to requests from faculty, product liability is now covered in Chapter 6, "Torts and Product Liability." It seems that most people like to teach these two subjects together. The discussion of warranties is now found in the chapter on ownership and risk.

The new CPA exam no longer includes questions about banks and their customers, and much of that material (such as how long it takes checks to clear) is not very relevant to our students. Therefore we have deleted the chapter on Banks and Their Customers, and combined the remaining material on Negotiable Instruments into one chapter, which now covers how to create a negotiable instrument and liability.

The chapter on Securities Regulation has been expanded to include coverage of antitrust law, under the title, "Government Regulation." As the Justice Department increases its oversight of mergers and with price-fixing violations increasingly common, it is more important than ever for students to understand the basics of antitrust law.

In response to faculty requests, we have added a chapter on Consumer Protection. This material is critical for all of us—everyone from the experienced executive to the young adult with increasing financial responsibilities.

END OF CHAPTER MATERIAL

To facilitate class discussion and student learning, we have overhauled the study questions at the end of the chapters. They are now divided into three parts:

1. **Multiple-choice questions.** Because many instructors use this format in their tests, it seemed appropriate to provide practice questions. The answers to these multiple-choice questions are available to students online at **www.cengagebrain.com**.

2. **Essay questions.** Students can use these as study questions, and professors can also assign them as written homework problems.

3. **Discussion questions.** Instructors can use these questions to enhance class discussion. If assigned in advance, students will have a chance to think about the answers before class. This approach is similar to business cases, which often provide discussion questions in advance.

OTHER NEW MATERIAL

We have, of course, added substantial new material, with a particular focus on the Internet and social media. Chapter 26, "Employment and Labor Law," includes a section on social media. Chapter 29, "Corporations," uses Facebook as an example of how to organize a corporation. There are also new cases involving eBay and craigslist. In addition,

Chapter 28, "Starting a Business: LLCs and Other Options," includes a new section about socially conscious organizations.

STAYING CURRENT: OUR BLOG, FACEBOOK, AND TWITTER

To find out about new developments in business law, visit our blog at Bizlawupdate.com or our Facebook page at Beatty Business Law. If you follow us on Twitter @bizlawupdate, you will receive a notification automatically whenever we post to the blog.

The Beatty/Samuelson Difference

When we began work on the first edition of this textbook, our publisher warned us that our undertaking was risky because there were already so many law texts. Despite these warnings, we were convinced that there was a market for an Essentials book that was different from all the others. Our goal was to capture the passion and excitement—the sheer enjoyment—of the law. Business law is notoriously complex, and as authors we are obsessed with accuracy. Yet this intriguing subject also abounds with human conflict and hard-earned wisdom, forces that can make a law book sparkle.

Now, as this fifth edition goes to press, we look back over the intervening years and are touched by the many unsolicited comments from students, such as these posted on Amazon:

- "Glad I purchased this. It really helps put the law into perspective and allows me as a leader to make intelligent decisions. Thanks."

- "I enjoyed learning business law and was happy my college wanted this book. THUMBS UP!"

We think of the students who have emailed us to say, "In terms of clarity, comprehensiveness, and vividness of style, I think it's probably the best textbook I've ever used in any subject," and "I had no idea business law could be so interesting." Or the professor who said, "With your book, we have great class discussions." Comments such as these never cease to thrill us and to make us grateful that we persisted in writing an Essentials text like no other—a book that is precise and authoritative, yet a pleasure to read.

Comprehensive Staying comprehensive means staying current. This fifth edition contains over 25 new cases. Almost all were reported within the last two or three years. We never include a new court opinion merely because it is recent, but the law evolves continually, and our willingness to toss out old cases and add important new ones ensures that this book—and its readers—remain on the frontier of legal developments.

Look, for example, at the important field of corporate governance. All texts cover par value, and so do we. Yet a future executive is far likelier to face conflicts over Sarbanes-Oxley (SOX), executive compensation, and shareholder proposals. We present a clear path through this thicket of new issues. In Chapter 29, for example, read the section about the election and removal of directors. Typically, students (even those who are high-level executives) have a basic misconception about the process of removing a director from office. They think that it is easy. Once they understand the complexity of this process, their whole view of corporate governance—and compensation—changes. We want tomorrow's business leaders to anticipate the challenges that await them and then use their knowledge to avert problems.

Strong Narrative The law is full of great stories, and we use them. Your students and ours should come to class excited. Look at Chapter 3, "Dispute Resolution." No tedious list of next steps in litigation, this chapter teaches the subject by tracking a double-indemnity lawsuit. An executive is dead. Did he drown accidentally, obligating the insurance company to pay? Or did the businessman commit suicide, voiding the policy? The student follows the action from the discovery of the body, through each step of the lawsuit, to the final appeal.

Students read stories and remember them. Strong narratives provide a rich context for the remarkable quantity of legal material presented. When students care about the material they are reading, they persevere. We have been delighted to find that they also arrive in class eager to question, discuss, and learn more about issues.

Precise   The great joy of using English accurately is the power it gives us to attack and dissect difficult issues, rendering them comprehensible to any lay reader. This text takes on the most complex legal topics of the day, yet it is appropriate for *all college and graduate-level students*. Accessible prose goes hand in hand with legal precision. We take great pride in walking our readers through the most serpentine mazes this tough subject can offer.

As we explore this extraordinary discipline, we lure readers along with quirky anecdotes and colorful diagrams. (Notice that the chart on page 713 clarifies the complex rules of the duty of care in the business judgment rule.) However, before the trip is over, we insist that students:

- Gauge policy and political considerations,

- Grapple with legal and social history,

- Spot the nexus between disparate doctrines, and

- Confront tough moral choices.

Authoritative   We insist, as you do, on a law book that is indisputably accurate. A professor must teach with assurance, confident that every paragraph is the result of exhaustive research and meticulous presentation. Dozens of tough-minded people spent thousands of hours reviewing this book, and we are delighted with the stamp of approval we have received from trial and appellate judges, working attorneys, scholars, and teachers.

We reject the cloudy definitions and fuzzy explanations that can invade judicial opinions and legal scholarship. To highlight the most important rules, we use bold print, and then follow with vivacious examples written in clear, forceful English. (See, for example, the discussion of factual cause on page 149.) We cheerfully venture into contentious areas, relying on very recent appellate decisions. Can a creditor pierce the veil of an LLC? What are the rights of an LLC member in the absence of an operating agreement? (See pages 679–684.) Where there is doubt about the current (or future) status of a doctrine, we say so. In areas of particularly heated debate, we footnote our work: we want you to have absolute trust in this book.

A Book for Students   We have written this book as if we were speaking directly to our students. We provide black letter law, but we also explain concepts in terms that hook students. Over the years, we have learned how much more successfully we can teach when our students are intrigued. No matter what kind of a show we put on in class, *they are only learning when they want to learn*.

Every chapter begins with a story, either fictional or real, to illustrate the issues in the chapter and provide context. Chapter 32, "Cyberlaw," begins with the true story of a college student who discovers nude pictures of himself online. These photos had been taken in the locker room without his knowledge. What privacy rights do any of us have? Does the Internet jeopardize them? Students want to know—right away.

Many of our students were not yet born when Bill Clinton was elected president. They come to college with varying levels of preparation; many now arrive from other countries. We have found that to teach business law most effectively, we must provide its context. Chapter 26, on employment law, provides the historical setting for the employment-at-will doctrine. Chapter 33, on intellectual property, explains the difference between intellectual and other types of property.

At the same time, we enjoy offering "nuts-and-bolts" information that grabs students. For example, in Chapter 31, "Consumer Protection," we offer advice about how students can obtain a free credit report (page 768).

Students respond enthusiastically to this approach. One professor asked a student to compare our book with the one that the class was then using. This was the student's reaction: "I really enjoy reading the [Beatty & Samuelson] textbook and I have decided that I will give you this memo ASAP, but I am keeping the book until Wednesday so that I may continue reading. Thanks! :-)."

Along with other professors, we have used this text in courses for undergraduates, MBAs, and Executive MBAs, with the students ranging in age from 18 to 55. The book works, as some unsolicited comments indicate:

- An undergraduate wrote, "This is the best textbook I have had in college, on any subject."

- A business law professor stated that the "clarity of presentation is superlative. I have never seen the complexity of contract law made this readable."

- An MBA student commented, "I think the textbook is great. The book is relevant, easy to understand, and interesting."

- A state supreme court justice wrote that the book is "a valuable blend of rich scholarship and easy readability. Students and professors should rejoice with this publication."

- A Fortune 500 vice president, enrolled in an Executive MBA program, commented, "I really liked the chapters. They were crisp, organized and current. The information was easy to understand and enjoyable."

- An undergraduate wrote, "The textbook is awesome. A lot of the time I read more than what is assigned—I just don't want to stop."

Humor Throughout the text, we use humor—judiciously—to lighten and enlighten. Not surprisingly, students have applauded—but is it appropriate? How dare we employ levity in this venerable discipline? We offer humor because we take the law seriously. We revere the law for its ancient traditions; its dazzling intricacy; its relentless, though imperfect, attempt to give order and decency to our world. Because we are confident of our respect for the law, we are not afraid to employ some levity. Leaden prose masquerading as legal scholarship does no honor to the field.

Humor also helps retention. Research shows that the funnier or more bizarre the example, the longer students will remember it. Students are more likely to remember a contract problem described in a fanciful setting, and from that setting recall the underlying principle. By contrast, one widget is hard to distinguish from another.

Features

We chose the features for our book with great care. Each one supports an essential pedagogical goal. Here are some of those goals and the matching feature.

EXAM STRATEGY

GOAL: To help students learn more effectively and to prepare for exams. In preparing this fifth edition, we asked ourselves: What do students want? The short answer is—a good grade in the course. How many times a semester does a student ask you, "What can I do to study for the exam?" We are happy to help them study and earn a good grade because that means they are learning.

About six times per chapter, we stop the action and give students a two-minute quiz. In the body of the text, again in the end-of-chapter review, and also in the Instructor's Manual, we present a typical exam question. Here lies the innovation: We guide the student in analyzing the issue. We teach the reader—over and over—how to approach a question: To start with the overarching principle, examine the fine point raised in the question, apply the analysis that courts use, and deduce the right answer. This skill is second nature to lawyers, but not to students. Without practice, too many students panic, jumping at a convenient answer and leaving aside the tools that they have spent the course acquiring. Let's change that. Students tell us that they love the Exam Strategy feature.

YOU BE THE JUDGE

GOAL: Get students to think independently. When reading case opinions, students tend to accept the court's "answer." Judges, of course, try to reach decisions that appear indisputable, when in reality they may be controversial—or wrong. From time to time we want students to think through the problem and reach their own answer. Almost every chapter contains a You Be the Judge feature, providing the facts of the case and conflicting appellate arguments. The court's decision, however, appears only in the Instructor's Manual. Because students do not know the result, class discussions are more complex and lively.

ETHICS

GOAL: Make ethics real. We ask ethical questions about cases, legal issues, and commercial practices. Is it fair for one party to void a contract by arguing, months after the fact, that there was no consideration? What is a manager's ethical obligation when asked to provide a reference for a former employee? What is wrong with bribery? We believe that asking the questions and encouraging discussion reminds students that ethics is an essential element of justice and of a satisfying life.

CASES

GOAL: Bring Case Law Alive. Each case begins with a summary of the facts followed by a statement of both the issue and the decision. Next comes a summary of the court's opinion. We have written this summary ourselves to make the judges' reasoning accessible to all readers while retaining the court's focus and the decision's impact. We cite cases using a modified bluebook form. In the principal cases in each chapter, we provide the state or federal citation, the regional citation, and the LEXIS or Westlaw citation. We also give students a brief description of the court. Because many of our cases are so recent, some will have only a regional reporter and a LEXIS or Westlaw citation.

EXAM REVIEW

GOAL: Help students to remember and practice! At the end of every chapter, we provide a list of review points and several additional Exam Strategy exercises in a Question/Strategy/Result format. We also challenge the students with 15 or more problems—Multiple-Choice, Essay Questions, and Discussion Questions. The questions include the following:

- *You Be the Judge Writing Problem.* The students are given appellate arguments on both sides of the question and must prepare a written opinion.

- *Ethics.* This question highlights the ethical issues of a dispute and calls upon the student to formulate a specific, reasoned response.

- *CPA Questions.* Where relevant, practice tests include questions from previous CPA exams administered by the American Institute of Certified Public Accountants.

Answers to all the Multiple-Choice questions are available to students online through **www.cengagebrain.com**.

TEACHING MATERIALS

For more information about any of these ancillaries, contact your Cengage Learning/ SouthWestern Legal Studies Sales Representative for more details, or visit the Beatty & Samuelson *Essentials*, fifth edition web page, accessed through **www.cengagebrain.com.**

Instructor's Manual   Available through cengagebrain.com, this manual includes answers to the You Be the Judge cases and also to the questions at the end of each chapter. In addition, the Instructors' Manual provides additional cases to use as the basis of class discussion as well as other pedagogical features.

PowerPoint Lecture Review Slides   PowerPoint slides are available for instructors to use with their lectures, and can be accessed through cengagebrain.com.

Test Bank   The test bank offers hundreds of essay, short-answer, and multiple-choice problems. Editable files of the test bank are available at cengagebrain.com, and the test bank is also available through the Cognero Testing Software.

Cognero Testing Software—Computerized Testing Software   This online testing system contains all of the questions in the test bank. Instructors can add or edit questions, instructions, and answers; and select questions by previewing them on the screen, selecting them randomly, or selecting them by number. Instructors can also create and administer quizzes online.

CengageNOW   This robust, online course management system gives you more control in less time and delivers better student outcomes—NOW. CengageNOW for *Essentials* 5e includes six homework types that align with the six levels of Bloom's taxonomy: Knowledge: Chapter Review; Comprehension: Business Law Scenarios; Application: Legal Reasoning; Analysis: IRAC; Synthesis: Exam Strategy; and Evaluation: Business Wisdom. With all these elements used together, CengageNOW will ensure that students develop the higher-level thinking skills they need to reach an advanced understanding of the material.

Business Law CourseMate   Cengage Learning's Business Law CourseMate brings course concepts to life with interactive learning, study, and exam preparation tools— including an e-book—that supports the printed textbook. Designed to address a variety of learning styles, students will have access to flashcards, Learning Objectives, and the Key Terms for quick reviews. A set of auto-gradable, interactive quizzes will allow students to instantly gauge their comprehension of the material. For instructors, all quiz scores and student activity are mapped within Engagement Tracker, a set of intuitive student performance analytical tools that help identify at-risk students. An interactive blog helps connect book concepts to real-world situations happening now.

Business Law Digital Video Library   This dynamic online video library features over 90 video clips that spark class discussion and clarify core legal principles. The library is organized into six series:

- *Legal Conflicts in Business* includes specific modern business and e-commerce scenarios.

- *Ask the Instructor* contains straightforward explanations of concepts for student review.

- *Drama of the Law* features classic business scenarios that spark classroom participation.

- *Real World Legal* takes students out of the classroom and into real-life situations, encouraging them to consider the legal aspects of decision making in the business world.

- *Business Ethics in Action* challenges students to examine ethical dilemmas in the world of business.

Access to the Business Law Digital Video Library is available as an optional package with each new student text at no additional charge. Students with used books can purchase access to the video clips online. For more information about the Business Law Digital Video Library, visit **www.cengagebrain.com.**

A Handbook of Basic Law Terms, Blacks Law Dictionary Series   This paperback dictionary, prepared by the editor of the popular Black's Law Dictionary, can be packaged for a small additional cost with any new South-Western Legal Studies in Business text.

Student Guide to the SOX   This brief overview for business students explains SOX, what is required of whom, and how it might affect students in their business lives. Available as an optional package with the text.

Interaction with the Author   This is my standard: Every professor who adopts this book must have a superior experience. I am available to help in any way I can. Adopters of this text often call me or email me to ask questions, obtain a syllabus, offer suggestions, share pedagogical concerns, or inquire about ancillaries. One of the pleasures of working on this project has been this link to so many colleagues around the country. I value those connections, am eager to respond, and would be happy to hear from you.

Susan S. Samuelson
Phone: (617) 353-2033
Email: ssamuels@bu.edu

ACKNOWLEDGMENTS

We appreciate the thoughtful insights of the reviewers for this fifth edition:
Randall Berens
Ohio University-Lancaster

Machiavelli Chao
University of California, Irvine

Raven Davenport
Houston Community College System

Terry L. Dimmick
Lakeshore Technical College

Craig Dokken
Hamline University

Philip Ettman
Westfield State University

Sheryl Fitzpatrick
North Iowa Area Community College

Janet L. Grange
Chicago State University

John Gray
Faulkner University

Jack Green
MiraCosta College

Anne-Marie Hakstian
Salem State University

Nancy Johnson
Mt. San Jacinto Community College

Sandra Leigh King
Sullivan University

Ken Knox
Eastern Gateway Community
College

Joni Koegel
Cazenovia College

Greg Lauer
North Iowa Area Community College

Donald Letourneau
Pacific University

Magdalena Lorenz
State University of New York College of
Oneonta

Bill Mills
East Texas Baptist University

Jack Neveaux
Saint Mary's University of Minnesota

Brad Reid
Lipscomb University

Alan Rosenbloom
Baruch College

Tom Severance
MiraCosta College

Frank Wetterau
Delaware Technical Community College

Kim Wong
Central New Mexico Community College

Bruce Zucker
California State University, Northridge

And we are continually grateful to the following reviewers who gave such helpful comments on the first four editions of this book:

Manzoor Ahmad
Compton Educational Center, El Camino
College

Steven J. Arsenault
College of Charleston

Lois Beier
Kent State University

Martha Broderick
University of Maine

Amy Chataginer
Mississippi Gulf Coast Community
College

Burke Christensen
Eastern Kentucky University

Linda Christiansen
Indiana University Southeast

Michael Costello
University of Missouri, St. Louis

G. Howard Doty
Nashville State Technical Community
College

Teri Elkins
University of Houston

Lizbeth G. Ellis
New Mexico State University

Paul Fiorelli
Xavier University

Suzanne M. Gradisher
University of Akron

Gary Greene
Manatee Community College

Wendy Hind
Doane College

Elizabeth Grimm-Howell
University of Missouri—St. Louis

Richard Guarino
California State University, Sacramento

Stephen Hearn
Louisiana Tech University

Timothy Jackson
School of Business, California Baptist
University

William C. Kostner
Doane College

Ronald B. Kowalczyk
Elgin Community College

Colleen Arnott Less
Johnson & Wales University

Maurice J. McCann
Southern Illinois University Carbondale

Russ Meade
Gardner-Webb University

Michael Monhollon
Hardin-Simmons University

Carol Nielsen
Bemidji State University

Margaret A. Parker
Owens Community College

Barbara Redman
Gainesville State College

Bruce L. Rockwood
Bloomsburg University

Rebecca Rutz
Mississippi Gulf Coast Community
College—Jackson County Campus

Rachel Spooner
Boston University School
of Management

Cheryl Staley
Lake Land College

Paulette L. Stenzel
Michigan State University

Kenneth Ray Taurman, Jr.
Indiana University Southeast

Daphyne Saunders Thomas
James Madison University

Glen M. Vogel
Hofstra University

Deborah Walsh
Middlesex Community College

ABOUT THE AUTHORS

Jeffrey F. Beatty was an associate professor of business law at the Boston University School of Management. After receiving his B.A. from Sarah Lawrence and his J.D. from Boston University, he practiced with the Greater Boston Legal Services representing indigent clients. At Boston University, he won the Metcalf Cup and Prize, the university's highest teaching award. Professor Beatty also wrote plays and television scripts that were performed in Boston, London, and Amsterdam.

Susan S. Samuelson is a professor of business law at Boston University's School of Management. After earning her undergraduate and law degrees at Harvard University, Professor Samuelson practiced with the firm of Choate, Hall, and Stewart. She has written many articles on legal issues for scholarly and popular journals, including the *American Business Law Journal, Ohio State Law Journal, Boston University Law Review, Harvard Journal on Legislation, National Law Journal, Sloan Management Review, Better Homes and Gardens*, and *Boston Magazine*. At Boston University, she won the Broderick Prize for excellence in teaching. For 12 years, Professor Samuelson was the faculty director of the Boston University Executive MBA program.

The Legal Environment

CHAPTER 1

INTRODUCTION TO LAW

nuttakit/Shutterstock.com; © Stas Volik/Shutterstock.com

The Pagans were a motorcycle gang with a reputation for violence. Two of its rougher members, Rhino and Backdraft, entered a tavern called the *Pub Zone*, shoving their way past the bouncer. The pair wore gang insignia, in violation of the bar's rules. For a while, all was quiet, as the two sipped drinks at the bar. Then they followed an innocent patron toward the men's room, and things happened fast.

"Wait a moment," you may be thinking. "Are we reading a chapter on business law or one about biker crimes in a roadside tavern?" Both.

Law is powerful, essential, and fascinating. We hope this book will persuade you of all three ideas. Law can also be surprising. Later in the chapter we will return to the *Pub Zone* (with armed guards) and follow Rhino and Backdraft to the back of the pub. Yes, the pair engaged in street crime, which is hardly a focus of this text. However, their criminal acts will enable us to explore one of the law's basic principles, negligence. Should a pub owner pay money damages to the victim of gang violence? The owner herself did nothing aggressive. Should she have prevented the harm? Does her failure to stop the assault make her liable?

> For a while, all was quiet, as the two sipped drinks at the bar. Then they followed an innocent patron toward the men's room…

We place great demands on our courts, asking them to make our large, complex, and sometimes violent society into a safer, fairer, more orderly place. The *Pub Zone* case is a good example of how judges reason their way through the convoluted issues involved. What began as a gang incident ends up as a matter of commercial liability. We will traipse after Rhino and Backdraft because they have a lesson to teach anyone who enters the world of business.

1-1 THE ROLE OF LAW IN SOCIETY

1-1a Power

The strong reach of the law touches nearly everything we do, especially at work. Consider a mid-level manager at Sublime Corp., which manufactures and distributes video games.

During the course of a day's work, she might negotiate a deal with a game developer (contract law). Before signing any deals, she might research whether similar games already exist, which might diminish her ability to market the proposed new game (intellectual property law). One of her subordinates might complain about being harassed by a coworker (employment law). Another worker may complain about being required to work long hours (administrative law). And she may consider investing her own money in her company's stock, but she may wonder whether she will get into trouble if she invests based on inside information (securities law).

It is not only as a corporate manager that you will confront the law. As a voter, investor, juror, entrepreneur, and community member, you will influence and be affected by the law. Whenever you take a stance about a legal issue, whether in the corporate office, in the voting booth, or as part of local community groups, you help to create the fabric of our nation. Your views are vital. This book will offer you knowledge and ideas from which to form and continually reassess your legal opinions and values.

1-1b Importance

Law is also essential. *Every* society of which we have any historical record has had some system of laws. For example, consider the Visigoths, a nomadic European people who overran much of present-day France and Spain during the fifth and sixth centuries C.E. Their code admirably required judges to be "quick of perception, clear in judgment, and lenient in the infliction of penalties." It detailed dozens of crimes.

Our legal system is largely based upon the English model, but many societies contributed ideas. The Iroquois Native Americans, for example, played a role in the creation of our own government. Five major nations made up the Iroquois group: the Mohawk, Cayuga, Oneida, Onondaga, and Seneca. Each nation governed its own domestic issues. But each nation also elected "sachems" to a League of the Iroquois. The league had authority over any matters that were common to all, such as relations with outsiders. Thus, by the fifteenth century, the Iroquois had solved the problem of *federalism:* how to have two levels of government, each with specified powers. Their system impressed Benjamin Franklin and others and influenced the drafting of our Constitution, with its powers divided between state and federal governments.[1]

1-1c Fascination

In 1835, the young French aristocrat Alexis de Tocqueville traveled through the United States, observing the newly democratic people and the qualities that made them unique. One of the things that struck de Tocqueville most forcefully was the American tendency to file suit: "Scarcely any political question arises in the United States that is not resolved, sooner or later, into a judicial question."[2] De Tocqueville got it right: For better or worse, we do expect courts to solve many problems.

Not only do Americans litigate—they watch each other do it. Every television season offers at least one new courtroom drama to a national audience breathless for more cross-examination. Almost all of the states permit live television coverage of real trials. One of the most heavily viewed events in the history of courtroom television was the 1995

---

[1] Jack Weatherford, *Indian Givers* (New York: Fawcett Columbine, 1988), pp. 133–150.
[2] Alexis de Tocqueville, *Democracy in America* (1835), Vol. 1, Ch. 16.

murder trial of former football star O.J. Simpson: 150 million viewers tuned in. In most nations, coverage of judicial proceedings is not allowed.[3]

The law is a big part of our lives, and it is wise to know something about it. Within a few weeks, you will probably find yourself following legal events in the news with keener interest and deeper understanding. In this chapter, we develop the background for our study. We look at where law comes from: its history and its present-day institutions. In the section on jurisprudence, we examine different theories about what "law" really means. And finally we see how courts—and students—analyze a case.

1-2 ORIGINS OF OUR LAW

It would be nice if we could look up "the law" in one book, memorize it, and then apply it. But the law is not that simple, and *cannot* be that simple, because it reflects the complexity of contemporary life. In truth, there is no such thing as "the law." Principles and rules of law actually come from *many different* sources. Why is this so? In part because we inherited a complex structure of laws from England.

Additionally, ours is a nation born in revolution and created, in large part, to protect the rights of its people from the government. The Founding Fathers created a national government but insisted that the individual states maintain control in many areas. As a result, each state has its own government with exclusive power over many important areas of our lives. To top it off, the Founders guaranteed many rights to the people alone, ordering national *and* state governments to keep clear. This has worked, but it has caused a multilayered system, with 50 state governments and one federal government all creating and enforcing law.

1-2a English Roots

England in the tenth century was a rustic agricultural community with a tiny population and very little law or order. Vikings invaded repeatedly, terrorizing the Anglo-Saxon peoples. Criminals were hard to catch in the heavily forested, sparsely settled nation. The king used a primitive legal system to maintain a tenuous control over his people.

England was divided into shires, and daily administration was carried out by a "shire reeve," later called a sheriff. The shire reeve collected taxes and did what he could to keep peace, apprehending criminals and acting as mediator between feuding families. Two or three times a year, a shire court met; lower courts met more frequently. Today, this method of resolving disputes lives on as mediation, which we will discuss in Chapter 3.

Because there were so few officers to keep the peace, Anglo-Saxon society created an interesting method of ensuring public order. Every freeman belonged to a group of 10 freemen known as a "tithing," headed by a "tithingman." If anyone injured a person outside his tithing or interfered with the king's property, all 10 men of the tithing could be forced to pay. Today, we still use this idea of collective responsibility in business partnerships. All partners are personally responsible for the debts of the partnership. They could potentially lose their homes and all assets because of the irresponsible conduct of one partner. That liability has helped create new forms of business organization, including limited liability companies.

When cases did come before an Anglo-Saxon court, the parties would often be represented by a clergyman, by a nobleman, or by themselves. There were few professional lawyers. Each party produced "oath helpers," usually 12, who would swear that one version of events was correct. The Anglo-Saxon oath helpers were forerunners of our modern jury of 12 persons.

---

[3]Regardless of whether we allow cameras, it is an undeniable benefit of the electronic age that we can obtain information quickly. From time to time, we will mention websites of interest. Some of these are for nonprofit groups, while others are commercial sites. We do not endorse or advocate on behalf of any group or company; we simply wish to alert you to what is available.

In 1066, the Normans conquered England. William the Conqueror made a claim never before made in England: that he owned all of the land. The king then granted sections of his lands to his favorite noblemen, as his tenants in chief, creating the system of feudalism. These tenants in chief then granted parts of their land to *tenants in demesne,* who actually occupied a particular estate. Each tenant in demesne owed fidelity to his lord (hence, "landlord"). So what? Just this: land became the most valuable commodity in all of England, and our law still reflects that. One thousand years later, American law still regards land as special. The Statute of Frauds, which we study in the section on contracts, demands that contracts for the sale or lease of property be in writing. And landlord-tenant law, vital to students and many others, still reflects its ancient roots. Some of a landlord's rights are based on the 1,000-year-old tradition that land is uniquely valuable.

In 1250, Henry de Bracton (d. 1268) wrote a legal treatise that still influences us. *De Legibus et Consuetudinibus Angliae (On the Laws and Customs of England),* written in Latin, summarized many of the legal rulings in cases since the Norman Conquest. De Bracton was teaching judges to rule based on previous cases. He was helping to establish the idea of **precedent**. The doctrine of precedent, which developed gradually over centuries, requires that judges decide current cases based on previous rulings. This vital principle is the heart of American common law. Precedent ensures predictability. Suppose a 17-year-old student promises to lease an apartment from a landlord, but then changes her mind. The landlord sues to enforce the lease. The student claims that she cannot be held to the agreement because she is a minor. The judge will look for precedent, that is, older cases dealing with the same issue, and he will find many holding that a contract generally may not be enforced against a minor. That precedent is binding on this case, and the student wins. The accumulation of precedent, based on case after case, makes up the **common law**.

In the end, today's society is dramatically different from that of medieval English society. But interestingly, legal disputes from hundreds of years ago are often quite recognizable today. Some things have changed but others never do.

Here is an actual case from more than six centuries ago, in the court's own language. The plaintiff claims that he asked the defendant to heal his eye with "herbs and other medicines." He says the defendant did it so badly that he blinded the plaintiff in that eye.

Precedent
The tendency to decide current cases based on previous rulings.

Common law
Judge-made law.

THE OCULIST'S CASE (1329)

LI MS. Hale 137 (1), fo. 150, Nottingham[4]

CASE SUMMARY

Attorney Launde [for defendant]: Sir, you plainly see how [the plaintiff claims] that he had submitted himself to [the defendant's] medicines and his care; and after that he can assign no trespass in his person, inasmuch as he submitted himself to his care: but this action, if he has any, sounds naturally in breach of covenant. We demand [that the case be dismissed].

Excerpts from Judge Denum's Decision: I saw a Newcastle man arraigned before my fellow justice and me for the death of a man. I asked the reason for the indictment, and it was said that he had slain a man under his care, who died within four days afterwards. And because I saw that he was a [doctor] and that he had not done the thing feloniously but [accidentally] I ordered him to be discharged. And suppose a blacksmith, who is a man of skill, injures your horse with a nail, whereby you lose your horse: you shall never have recovery against him. No more shall you here.

Afterwards the plaintiff did not wish to pursue his case any more.

---

[4]J. Baker and S. Milsom, *Sources of English Legal History* (London: Butterworth & Co., 1986).

This case from 1329 is an ancient medical malpractice action. Attorney Launde does not deny that his client blinded the plaintiff. He claims that the plaintiff has brought the wrong kind of lawsuit. Launde argues that the plaintiff should have brought a case of "covenant"; that is, a lawsuit about a contract.

Judge Denum decides the case on a different principle. He gives judgment to the defendant because the plaintiff voluntarily sought medical care. He implies that the defendant would lose only if he had attacked the plaintiff. As we will see when we study negligence law, this case might have a different outcome today. Note also the informality of the judge's ruling. He rather casually mentions that he came across a related case once before and that he would stand by that outcome. The idea of precedent is just beginning to take hold.

1-2b Law in the United States

The colonists brought with them a basic knowledge of English law, some of which they were content to adopt as their own. Other parts, such as religious restrictions, were abhorrent to them. Many settlers had made the dangerous trip to America precisely to escape persecution, and they were not interested in recreating their difficulties in a new land. Finally, some laws were simply irrelevant or unworkable in a world that was socially and geographically so different. American law ever since has been a blend of the ancient principles of English common law and a zeal and determination for change.

During the nineteenth century, the United States changed from a weak, rural nation into one of vast size and potential power. Cities grew, factories appeared, and sweeping movements of social migration changed the population. Changing conditions raised new legal questions. Did workers have a right to form industrial unions? To what extent should a manufacturer be liable if its product injured someone? Could a state government invalidate an employment contract that required 16-hour workdays? Should one company be permitted to dominate an entire industry?

In the twentieth century, the rate of social and technological change increased, creating new legal puzzles. Were some products, such as automobiles, so inherently dangerous that the seller should be responsible for injuries even if no mistakes were made in manufacturing? Who should clean up toxic waste if the company that had caused the pollution no longer existed? If a consumer signed a contract with a billion-dollar corporation, should the agreement be enforced even if the consumer never understood it? New and startling questions arise with great regularity. Before we can begin to examine the answers, we need to understand the sources of contemporary law.

1-3 SOURCES OF CONTEMPORARY LAW

Throughout the text, we will examine countless legal ideas. But binding rules come from many different places. This section describes the significant *categories* of laws in the United States.

1-3a United States Constitution

America's greatest legal achievement was the writing of the United States Constitution in 1787. It is the supreme law of the land.[5] Any law that conflicts with it is void. This federal Constitution does three basic things. First, it establishes the national government of the United States, with its three branches. Second, it creates a system of checks and balances among the branches. And third, the Constitution guarantees many basic rights to the American people.

BRANCHES OF GOVERNMENT

The Founding Fathers sought a division of government power. They did not want all power centralized in a king or in anyone else. And so, the Constitution divides legal authority into three pieces: legislative, executive, and judicial power.

Legislative power gives the ability to create new laws. In Article I, the Constitution gives this power to the Congress, which is comprised of two chambers—a Senate and a House of Representatives. Voters in all 50 states elect representatives who go to Washington, D.C., to serve in the Congress and debate new legal ideas.

The House of Representatives has 435 voting members. A state's voting power is based on its population. Large states (Texas, California, and Florida) send dozens of representatives to the House. Some small states (Wyoming, North Dakota, and Delaware) send only one. The Senate has 100 voting members—two from each state.

Executive power is the authority to enforce laws. Article II of the Constitution establishes the President as commander in chief of the armed forces and the head of the executive branch of the federal government.

Judicial power gives the right to interpret laws and determine their validity. Article III places the Supreme Court at the head of the judicial branch of the federal government. Interpretive power is often underrated, but it is often every bit as important as the ability to create laws in the first place. For instance, the Supreme Court ruled that privacy provisions of the Constitution protect a woman's right to abortion, although neither the word "privacy" nor "abortion" appears in the text of the Constitution.[6]

At times, courts void laws altogether. For example, in 1995, the Supreme Court ruled that the Gun-Free School Zones Act of 1990 was unconstitutional because Congress did not have the authority to pass such a law.[7]

CHECKS AND BALANCES

Sidney Crosby might score 300 goals per season if checking were not allowed in the National Hockey League. But because opponents are allowed to hit Crosby and the rest of his teammates on the Penguins, he is held to a much more reasonable 50 goals per year.

Political checks work in much the same way. They allow one branch of the government to trip up another.

The authors of the Constitution were not content merely to divide government power three ways. They also wanted to give each part of the government some power over the other two branches. Many people complain about "gridlock" in Washington, but the government is slow and sluggish by design. The Founding Fathers wanted to create a system that, without broad agreement, would tend towards inaction.

The President can veto Congressional legislation. Congress can impeach the President. The Supreme Court can void laws passed by Congress. The President appoints judges to

---

[5]The Constitution took effect in 1788, when 9 of 13 colonies ratified it. Two more colonies ratified it that year, and the last of the 13 did so in 1789, after the government was already in operation. The complete text of the Constitution appears in Appendix A.

[6]*Roe v. Wade*, 410 U.S. 113 (1973).

[7]*United States v. Alfonso Lopez, Jr.*, 514 U.S. 549 (1995).

Sources of Law ⭐

50 State Governments

State Constitution
- establishes the state government
- guarantees the rights of state residents

One Federal Government

United States Constitution
- establishes limited federal government
- protects states' power
- guarantees liberty of citizens

Legislative Branch

State Legislature
- passes statutes on state law
- creates state agencies

Executive Branch

Governor
- proposes statutes
- signs or vetoes statutes
- oversees state agencies

Judicial Branch

State Courts
- create state common law
- interpret statutes
- review constitutionality of statutes and other acts

Administrative Agencies
oversee day-to-day application of law in dozens of commercial and other areas

Legislative Branch

Congress
- passes statutes
- ratifies treaties
- creates administrative agencies

Executive Branch

President
- proposes statutes
- signs or vetoes statutes
- oversees administrative agencies

Judicial Branch

Federal Courts
- interpret statutes
- create (limited) federal common law
- review the constitutionality of statutes and other legal acts

Administrative Agencies
oversee day-to-day application of law in dozens of commercial and other areas

© Cengage Learning

Federal Form of Government. Principles and rules of law come from many sources. The government in Washington creates and enforces law throughout the nation. But 50 state governments exercise great power in local affairs. And citizens enjoy constitutional protection from both state and federal government. The Founding Fathers wanted this balance of power and rights, but the overlapping authority creates legal complexity.

the federal courts, including the Supreme Court, but these nominees do not serve unless approved by the Senate. Congress (with help from the 50 states) can override the Supreme Court by amending the Constitution. The President and the Congress influence the Supreme Court by controlling who is placed on the court in the first place.

Many of these checks and balances will be examined in more detail later in this book, starting in Chapter 4.

FUNDAMENTAL RIGHTS

The Constitution also grants many of our most basic liberties. For the most part, they are found in the amendments to the Constitution. The First Amendment guarantees the rights of free speech, free press, and the free exercise of religion. The Fourth, Fifth, and Sixth Amendments protect the rights of any person accused of a crime. Other amendments ensure that the government treats all people equally and that it pays for any property it takes from a citizen.

By creating a limited government of three branches and guaranteeing basic liberties to all citizens, the Constitution became one of the most important documents ever written.

1-3b Statutes

The second important source of law is statutory law. The Constitution gave to the United States Congress the power to pass laws on various subjects. These laws are called **statutes**, and they can cover absolutely any topic, so long as they do not violate the Constitution.

Almost all statutes are created by the same method. An idea for a new law—on taxes, health care, texting while driving, or any other topic, big or small—is first proposed in the Congress. This idea is called a *bill*. The House and Senate then independently vote on the bill. To pass Congress, the bill must win a simple majority vote in each of these chambers.

If Congress passes a bill, it goes to the White House for the President's approval. If the President signs it, a new statute is created. It is no longer a mere idea; it is the law of the land. If the President refuses to approve, or *vetoes* a bill, it does not become a statute unless Congress overrides the veto. To do that, both the House and the Senate must approve the bill by a two-thirds majority. If this happens, it becomes a statute without the President's signature.

> **Statute**
> A law created by a legislative body.

1-3c Common Law

Binding legal ideas often come from the courts. Judges generally follow *precedent*. When courts decide a case, they tend to apply the legal rules that other courts have used in similar cases.

The principle that precedent is binding on later cases is called *stare decisis*, which means "let the decision stand." *Stare decisis* makes the law predictable, and this in turn enables businesses and private citizens to plan intelligently.

It is important to note that precedent is binding only on *lower* courts. For example, if the Supreme Court decided a case in one way in 1965, it is under no obligation to follow precedent if the same issue arises in 2015.

Sometimes, this ability to change is quite beneficial. In 1896, the Supreme Court decided (unbelievably) that segregation—separating people by race in schools, hotels, public transportation, and other public services—was legal under certain conditions.[8] In 1954, on the exact same issue, the court changed its mind.[9]

In other circumstances, it is more difficult to see the value in breaking with an established rule.

---

[8]*Plessy v. Ferguson*, 163 U.S. 537 (1896).
[9]*Brown v. Board of Education of Topeka*, 347 U.S. 483 (1954).

1-3d Court Orders

Judges have the authority to issue court orders that place binding obligations on specific people or companies. An injunction, for example, is a court order to stop doing something. A judge might order a stalker to stay more than 500 yards away from an ex-lover. Lindsay Lohan might be ordered to stop drinking and enter rehab. Courts have the authority to imprison or fine those who violate their orders.

1-3e Administrative Law

In a society as large and diverse as ours, the executive and legislative branches of government cannot oversee all aspects of commerce. Congress passes statutes about air safety, but United States senators do not stand around air traffic towers, serving coffee to keep everyone awake. The executive branch establishes rules concerning how foreign nationals enter the United States, but Presidents are reluctant to sit on the dock of the bay, watching the ships come in. Administrative agencies do this day-to-day work.

> **United States senators do not stand around air traffic towers, serving coffee to keep everyone awake.**

Most government agencies are created by Congress. Familiar examples are the Environmental Protection Agency (EPA), the Securities and Exchange Commission (SEC), and the Internal Revenue Service (IRS), whose feelings are hurt if it does not hear from you every April 15. Agencies have the power to create laws called *regulations*.

1-3f Treaties

The Constitution authorizes the President to make treaties with foreign nations. These agreements must then be ratified by the United States Senate by a two-thirds vote. When they are ratified, they are as binding upon all citizens as any federal statute. In 1994, the Senate ratified the North American Free Trade Agreement (NAFTA) with Mexico and Canada. NAFTA was controversial then and remains so today—but it is the law of the land.

1-4   CLASSIFICATIONS

We have seen where law comes from. Now we need to classify the various types of laws. First, we will distinguish between criminal and civil law. Then, we will take a look at the intersection between law and morality.

1-4a Criminal and Civil Law

Criminal law
Criminal law prohibits certain behavior.

It is a crime to embezzle money from a bank, to steal a car, to sell cocaine. **Criminal law** concerns behavior so threatening that society outlaws it altogether. Most criminal laws are statutes, passed by Congress or a state legislature. The government itself prosecutes the wrongdoer, regardless of what the bank President or car owner wants. A district attorney, paid by the government, brings the case to court. The injured party, for example the owner of the stolen car, is not in charge of the case, although she may appear as a witness. The government will seek to punish the defendant with a prison sentence, a fine, or both. If there is a fine, the money goes to the state, not to the injured party.

Civil law
Civil law regulates the rights and duties between parties.

Civil law is different, and most of this book is about civil law. **The civil law regulates the rights and duties between parties.** Tracy agrees in writing to lease you a 30,000-square-foot store in her shopping mall. She now has a *legal duty* to make the space available. But then another tenant offers her more money, and she refuses to let you move in. Tracy has violated her duty, but she has not committed a crime. The government will not prosecute the case. It is up to you to file a civil lawsuit. Your case will be based on the common law of contract. You will also seek equitable relief, namely, an injunction ordering Tracy not to lease to anyone else. You should win the suit, and you will get your injunction and some money damages. But Tracy will not go to jail.

Some conduct involves both civil and criminal law. Suppose Tracy is so upset over losing the court case that she becomes drunk and causes a serious car accident. She has committed the crime of driving while intoxicated, and the state will prosecute. Tracy may be fined or imprisoned. She has also committed negligence, and the injured party will file a lawsuit against her, seeking money. We will again see civil and criminal law joined together in the *Pub Zone* case, later in the chapter.

1-4b Law and Morality

Law is different from morality, yet the two are obviously linked. There are many instances when the law duplicates what all of us would regard as a moral position. It is negligent to drive too fast in a school zone, and few would dispute the moral value of seeking to limit harm to students. And the same holds with contract law: If the owner of land agrees in writing to sell property to a buyer at a stated price, both the buyer and the seller must go through with the deal, and the legal outcome matches our moral expectations.

On the other hand, we have had laws that we now clearly regard as immoral. At the turn of the century, a factory owner could typically fire a worker for any reason at all—including, for example, his religious or political views. It is immoral to fire a worker because she is Jewish—and today the law prohibits it.

Finally, there are legal issues where the morality is less clear. You are walking down a country lane and notice a three-year-old child playing with matches near a barn filled with hay. Are you obligated to intervene? No, says the law, though many think that is preposterous. (See Chapter 4, on common law, for more about this topic.) A company buys property and then discovers, buried under the ground, toxic waste that will cost $300,000 to clean up. The original owner has gone bankrupt. Should the new owner be forced to pay for the cleanup? If the new owner fails to pay for the job, who will?

Chapter 2 will further examine the bond between law and morality.

1-5 JURISPRUDENCE

We have had a glimpse of legal history and a summary of the present-day sources of American law. But what *is* law? That question is the basis of a field known as **jurisprudence**. What is the real nature of law? Can there be such a thing as an "illegal" law?

Jurisprudence
The philosophy of law.

1-5a Legal Positivism

This philosophy can be simply stated: Law is what the sovereign says it is. The **sovereign** is the recognized political power whom citizens obey, so in the United States, both state and federal governments are sovereign. A legal positivist holds that whatever the sovereign declares to be the law *is* the law, whether it is right or wrong.

The primary criticism of legal positivism is that it seems to leave no room for questions of morality. A law permitting a factory owner to fire a worker because she is Catholic is surely different from a law prohibiting arson. Do citizens in a democracy have a duty to consider such differences? Consider the following example.

Most states allow citizens to pass laws directly at the ballot box, a process called voter referendum. California voters often do this, and during the 1990s, they passed one of the

Sovereign
The recognized political power, whom citizens obey.

state's most controversial laws. Proposition 187 was designed to curb illegal immigration into the state by eliminating social spending for undocumented aliens. Citizens debated the measure fiercely but passed it by a large margin. One section of the new law forbade public schools from educating illegal immigrants. The law obligated a principal to inquire into the immigration status of all children enrolled in the school and to report undocumented students to immigration authorities. Several San Diego school principals rejected the new rules, stating that they would neither inquire into immigration status nor report undocumented aliens. Their statements produced a heated response. Some San Diego residents castigated the school officials as lawbreakers, claiming that:

- A school officer who knowingly disobeyed a law was setting a terrible example for students, who would assume they were free to do the same;

- The principals were advocating permanent residence and a free education for anyone able to evade our immigration laws; and

- The officials were scorning grass-roots democracy by disregarding a law passed by popular referendum.

Others applauded the principals' position, asserting that:

- The referendum's rules would transform school officials from educators into border police, forcing them to cross-examine young children and their parents;

- The new law was foolish because it punished innocent children for violations committed by their parents; and

- Our nation has long respected civil disobedience based on humanitarian ideals, and these officials were providing moral leadership to the whole community.

Ultimately, no one had to decide whether to obey Proposition 187. A federal court ruled that only Congress had the power to regulate immigration and that California's attempt was unconstitutional and void. The debate over immigration reform—and ethics—did not end, however. It continues to be a thorny issue.

1-5b Natural Law

St. Thomas Aquinas (1225–1274) answered the legal positivists even before they had spoken. In his *Summa Theologica*, he argued that an unjust law is no law at all and need not be obeyed. It is not enough that a sovereign makes a command. The law must have a moral basis.

Where do we find the moral basis that would justify a law? Aquinas says that "good is that which all things seek after." Therefore, the fundamental rule of all laws is that "good is to be done and promoted, and evil is to be avoided." This sounds appealing, but also vague. Exactly which laws promote good and which do not? Is it better to have a huge corporation dominate a market or many smaller companies competing? Did the huge company get that way by being better than its competitors? If Wal-Mart moves into a rural area, establishes a mammoth store, and sells inexpensive products, is that "good"? Yes, if you are a consumer who cares only about prices. No, if you are the owner of a Main Street store driven into bankruptcy. Maybe, if you are a resident who values small-town life but wants lower prices.

1-5c Legal Realism

Legal realists take a very different tack. They claim it does not matter what is written as law. What counts is who enforces that law and by what process. All of us are biased by issues such as income, education, family background, race, religion, and many other factors. These personal characteristics, they say, determine which contracts will be enforced and which ignored, why some criminals receive harsh sentences while others get off lightly, and so on.

Judge Jones hears a multimillion dollar lawsuit involving an airplane crash. Was the airline negligent? The law is the same everywhere, but legal realists say that Jones's background will determine the outcome. If she spent 20 years representing insurance companies, she will tend to favor the airline. If her law practice consisted of helping the "little guy," she will favor the plaintiff.

Other legal realists argue, more aggressively, that those in power use the machinery of the law to perpetuate their control. The outcome of a given case will be determined by the needs of those with money and political clout. A court puts "window dressing" on a decision, they say, so that society thinks there are principles behind the law. A problem with legal realism, however, is its denial that any lawmaker can overcome personal bias. Yet clearly some do act unselfishly.

SUMMARY OF JURISPRUDENCE	
Legal Positivism	Law is what the sovereign says.
Natural Law	An unjust law is no law at all.
Legal Realism	Who enforces the law counts more than what is in writing.

© Cengage Learning

No one school of jurisprudence is likely to seem perfect. We urge you to keep the different theories in mind as you read cases in the book.

1-6 WORKING WITH THE BOOK'S FEATURES

In this section, we introduce a few of the book's features and discuss how you can use them effectively. We will start with *cases*.

1-6a Analyzing a Case

A law case is the decision a court has made in a civil lawsuit or criminal prosecution. Cases are the heart of the law and an important part of this book. Reading them effectively takes practice. This chapter's opening scenario is based on a real case. Who can be held liable for the assault? Let's see.

KUEHN V. PUB ZONE

364 N.J. Super. 301, 835 A.2d 692
Superior Court of New Jersey, Appellate Division, 2003

CASE SUMMARY

Facts: Maria Kerkoulas owned the *Pub Zone* bar. She knew that several motorcycle gangs frequented the tavern. From her own experience tending bar, and conversations with city police, she knew that some of the gangs, including the Pagans, were dangerous and prone to attack customers for no reason. Kerkoulas posted a sign prohibiting any motorcycle gangs from entering the bar while wearing "colors," that is, insignia of their gangs. She believed that gangs without their colors were less prone to violence, and experience proved her right.

Rhino, Backdraft, and several other Pagans, all wearing colors, pushed their way past the tavern's bouncer and approached the bar. Although Kerkoulas saw their colors, she allowed them to stay for one drink. They later moved towards the back of the pub, and Kerkoulas believed they were departing. In fact, they followed a customer named Karl Kuehn to the men's room where, without any provocation, they savagely beat him. Kuehn was knocked unconscious and suffered brain hemorrhaging, disc herniation, and numerous fractures of facial bones. He was forced to undergo various surgeries, including eye reconstruction.

Although the government prosecuted Rhino and Backdraft for their vicious assault, our case does not concern that prosecution. Kuehn sued the *Pub Zone*, and that is the case we will read. The jury awarded him $300,000 in damages. However, the trial court judge overruled the jury's verdict. He granted a judgment for the *Pub Zone*, meaning that the tavern owed nothing. The judge ruled that the pub's owner could not have foreseen the attack on Kuehn, and had no duty to protect him from an outlaw motorcycle gang. Kuehn appealed, and the appeals court's decision follows.

Issue: *Did the Pub Zone have a duty to protect Kuehn from the Pagans' attack?*

Decision: Yes, the *Pub Zone* had a duty to protect Kuehn. The decision is reversed, and the jury's verdict is reinstated.

Reasoning: Whether a duty exists depends on the foreseeability of the harm, its potential severity, and the defendant's ability to prevent the injury. A court should also evaluate society's interest in the dispute.

A business owner generally has no duty to protect a customer from acts of a third party unless experience suggests that there is danger. However, if the owner could in fact foresee injury, she is obligated to take reasonable safety precautions.

Kerkoulas knew that the Pagans engaged in random violence. She realized that when gang members entered the pub, they endangered her customers. That is why she prohibited bikers from wearing their colors—a reasonable rule. Regrettably, the pub failed to enforce the rule. Pagans were allowed to enter wearing their colors, and the pub did not call the police. The pub's behavior was unreasonable and it is liable to Kuehn.

ANALYSIS

Plaintiff
The party who is suing.

Defendant
The party being sued.

Let's take it from the top. The case is called *Kuehn v. Pub Zone*. Karl Kuehn is the **plaintiff**, the person who is suing. The *Pub Zone* is being sued, and is called the **defendant**. In this example, the plaintiff's name happens to appear first, but that is not always true. When a defendant loses a trial and files an appeal, *some* courts reverse the names of the parties.

The next line gives the legal citation, which indicates where to find the case in a law library. We explain in the footnote how to locate a case if you plan to do research.[10]

The *Facts* section provides a background to the lawsuit, written by the authors of this text. The court's own explanation of the facts is often many pages long, and may involve complex matters irrelevant to the subject covered in this book, so we relate only what is necessary. This section will usually include some mention of what happened at the

---

[10]If you want to do legal research, you need to know where to find particular legal decisions. A case citation guides you to the correct volume(s). The full citation of our case is *Kuehn v. Pub Zone*, 364 N. J. Super. 301, 835 A. 2d 692. The string of numbers identifies two different books in which you can find the full text of this decision. The first citation is to "N. J. Super," which means the official court reporter of the state of New Jersey. New Jersey, like most states, reports its law cases in a series of numbered volumes. This case appears in volume 364 of the New Jersey Superior Court reporters. If you go to a law library and find that book, you can then turn to page 301 and—*voilà*!—you have the case. The decision is also reported in another set of volumes, called the regional reporters. This series of law reports is grouped by geographic region. New Jersey is included in the Atlantic region, so our case appears in reporters dedicated to that region. The "A" stands for Atlantic. After a series of reporters reaches volume 999, a second set begins. Our case appears in volume 835 of the second set of the Atlantic reporters ("A. 2d"), at page 692. In addition, cases are now available online, and your professor or librarian can show you how to find them electronically.

trial court. Lawsuits always begin in a trial court. The losing party often appeals to a court of appeals, and it is usually an appeals court decision that we are reading. The trial judge ruled in favor of *Pub Zone*, but later, in the decision we are reading, Kuehn wins.

The *Issue* section is very important. It tells you what the court had to decide—and also why you are reading the case. In giving its decision, a court may digress. If you keep in mind the issue and relate the court's discussion to it, you will not get lost.

The *Decision* is the court's answer to the issue posed. A court's decision is often referred to as its *holding*. The court rules that the *Pub Zone* did have a duty to Kuehn. The appellate court *reverses* the trial court's decision, meaning that it declares the trial judge's ruling wrong and void. The appellate judges also reinstate the jury verdict. The appellate court could have *remanded* the case if the judges had wished, meaning to send it back down to the lower court for a new trial. If the appeals court had agreed with the trial court's decision, the judges would have *affirmed* the lower court's ruling, meaning to uphold it.

The *Reasoning* section explains why the court reached its decision. The actual written decision may be three paragraphs or 75 pages. Some judges offer us lucid prose, while others seem intent on torturing the reader. Judges frequently digress and often discuss matters that are irrelevant to the issue on which this text is focusing. For those reasons, we have taken the court's explanation and recast it in our own words. If you are curious about the full opinion, you can always look it up.

Let us examine the reasoning. The court begins with a set of guidelines concerning a business owner's duty. Whether a defendant has such a duty depends on the foreseeability and severity of the harm, whether the business person could have prevented it, and society's interest. The court emphasizes that a bar owner is not an ensurer of its patrons' safety. Not every assault in a pub results in the defendant's liability. The judges are emphasizing that courts do not reach decisions arbitrarily. They attempt to make thoughtful choices, consistent with earlier rulings, which make good sense for the general public.

Having laid out the ground rules, the court describes the key facts, from this case, that it will use to decide whether the *Pub Zone* had a duty to Kuehn. The judges note that the bar's owner knew that gang members were dangerous. The rule against wearing colors made sense. When Pagans entered wearing their insignia, the pub had a duty to protect its patrons. The pub's owner was still not obligated to guarantee the safety of its patrons, but she had to do a reasonable job of reacting to the foreseeable danger. All Kerkoulas reasonably had to do was enforce the pub's no-colors rule and telephone the police if gang members refused to obey it. When she failed to take those steps, she violated her duty to Kuehn and became liable. The court reversed the trial judge's decision and reinstated the jury's verdict.

1-6b Devil's Advocate

Each chapter has several cases. After some of them, a "Devil's Advocate" feature offers you a contrasting view of the legal issue. This is not part of the case but is instead a suggestion of another perspective on the problem discussed. The authors take no position for or against the court's decision, but merely want you to consider an alternate view, and decide which analysis of the law makes more sense to you—that of the court or the Devil's Advocate. Is the following view persuasive?

Devil's Advocate   A court should not force small businesses to guarantee their customers' safety. Two or three violent men, whether motorcycle gang members or frustrated professors, could enter a grocery store or clothing retailer at anytime and mindlessly attack innocent visitors. Random attacks are just that—random, unforeseeable. No merchant should be required to anticipate them. Send the criminals to jail, but do not place the burden on honest businesspeople.

1-6c Exam Strategy

This feature gives you practice analyzing cases the way lawyers do—and the way *you* must on tests. Law exams are different from most others because you must determine the issue from the facts provided. Too frequently, students faced with a law exam forget that the questions relate to the issues in the text and those discussed in class. Understandably, students new to law may focus on the wrong information in the problem or rely on material learned elsewhere. Exam Strategies teach you to figure out exactly what issue is at stake, and then analyze it in a logical, consistent manner. Here is an example, relating to the element of "duty," which the court discussed in the *Pub Zone* case.

EXAM Strategy

The Big Red Traveling (BRT) Carnival is in town. Tony arrives at 8:00 p.m., parks in the lot—and is robbed at gunpoint by a man who beats him and escapes with his money. There are several police officers on the carnival grounds, but no officer is in the parking lot at the time of the robbery. Tony sues, claiming that brighter lighting and more police in the lot would have prevented the robbery. There has never before been any violent crime—robbery, beating, or otherwise—at any BRT carnival. BRT claims it had no duty to protect Tony from this harm. Who is likely to win?

Strategy: Begin by isolating the legal issue. What are the parties disputing? They are debating whether BRT had a duty to protect Tony from an armed robbery, committed by a stranger. Now ask yourself: How do courts decide whether a business has a duty to prevent this kind of harm? The *Pub Zone* case provides our answer. A business owner is not an ensurer of the visitor's safety. The owner generally has no duty to protect a customer from the criminal act of a third party, unless the owner knows the harm is occurring or could foresee it is about to happen. (In the *Pub Zone* case, the business owner knew of the gang's violent history, and could have foreseen the assault.) Now apply that rule to the facts of this case.

Result: There has never been a violent attack of any kind at a BRT carnival. BRT cannot foresee this robbery, and has no duty to protect against it. The carnival wins.

1-6d You Be the Judge

Many cases involve difficult decisions for juries and judges. Often both parties have legitimate, opposing arguments. Most chapters in this book will have a feature called "You Be the Judge," in which we present the facts of a case but not the court's holding.

We offer you two opposing arguments based on the kinds of claims the lawyers made in court. We leave it up to you to debate and decide which position is stronger or to add your own arguments to those given.

The following case is another negligence lawsuit, with issues that overlap those of the *Pub Zone* case. This time the court confronts a fight that resulted in a death. The victim's distraught family sued the owner of a bar, claiming that one of his employees was partly responsible for the death. Once again, the defendant asked the court to dismiss the case, claiming that he owed no duty to protect the victim—the same argument made by the *Pub Zone*.

But there is a difference here—this time the defendant owned the bar across the street, not the one where the fight took place. Could he be held legally responsible for the death? You be the judge.

You Be the Judge

SOLDANO V. O'DANIELS

141 Cal. App. 3d 443
Court of Appeal of California,
5th Appellate District, 1983

Facts: In the days before cell phones, a fight broke out at Happy Jack's Saloon. A good Samaritan ran across the street to the Circle Inn, where he asked the bartender to let him use the telephone to call the police. The bartender refused.

Back at Happy Jack's Saloon, the fight escalated, and a man shot and killed Soldano's father. Soldano sued the owner of the Circle Inn for negligence. He argued the bartender violated a legal duty when he refused to hand over the inn's telephone, and that, as the employer of the bartender, O'Daniels was partially liable for his father's death.

The lower court dismissed the case, citing the principle that generally, a person does not have a legal responsibility to help another unless he created the dangerous situation in the first place. Soldano appealed.

You Be the Judge: *Did the bartender have a duty to allow the use of the Circle Inn's telephone?*

Argument for the Defendant: Your honors, my client did not act wrongfully. He did nothing to create the danger. The fight was not even on his property. We sympathize with the plaintiff, but it is the shooter, and perhaps the bar where the fight took place, who are responsible for his father's death. Our client was not involved. Liability can be stretched only so far.

The court would place a great burden on the citizens of California by going against precedent. The Circle Inn is Mr. O'Daniel's private property. If the court imposes potential liability on him in this case, would citizens be forced to open the doors of their homes whenever a stranger claims an emergency?

Criminals would delight in their newfound ability to gain access to businesses and residences by simply demanding to use a phone to "call the police."

The law has developed sensibly. People are left to decide for themselves whether to help in a dangerous situation. They are not legally required to place themselves in harm's way.

Argument for the Plaintiff: Your honors, the Circle Inn's bartender had both a moral and a legal duty to allow the use of his establishment's telephone. The Circle Inn may be privately owned, but it is a business open to the public. Anyone in the world is invited to stop by and order a drink or a meal. The good Samaritan had every right to be there.

We do not argue that the bartender had an obligation to break up the fight or endanger himself in any way. We simply argue he had a responsibility to stand aside and allow a free call on his restaurant's telephone. Any "burden" on him or on the Circle Inn was incredibly slight. The potential benefits were enormous. The trial court made a mistake in concluding that a person *never* has a duty to help another. Such an interpretation makes for poor public policy.

There is no need to radically change the . Residences can be excluded from this ruling. People need not be required to allow strangers into their homes. This court can simply determine that businesses have a legal duty to allow the placement of emergency calls during normal business hours.

Chapter Conclusion

We depend upon the law to give us a stable nation and economy, a fair society, a safe place to live and work. These worthy goals have occupied ancient kings and twenty-first-century lawmakers alike. But while law is a vital tool for crafting the society we want, there are no easy answers about how to create it. In a democracy, we all participate in the crafting. Legal rules control us, yet *we* create *them*. A working knowledge of the law can help build a successful career—and a solid democracy.

EXAM REVIEW

1. **THE FEDERAL SYSTEM**   Our federal system of government means that law comes from a national government in Washington, D.C., and from 50 state governments. (pp. 7–9)

2. **LEGAL HISTORY**   The history of law foreshadows many current legal issues, including mediation, partnership liability, the jury system, the role of witnesses, the special value placed on land, and the idea of precedent. (pp. 4–5)

3. **PRIMARY SOURCES OF LAW**   The primary sources of contemporary law are:

   • United States Constitution and state constitutions;

   • Statutes, which are drafted by legislatures;

   • Common law, which is the body of cases decided by judges, as they follow earlier cases, known as precedent;

   • Court orders, which place obligations on specific people or companies;

   • Administrative law, the rules and decisions made by federal and state administrative agencies; and

   • Treaties, agreements between the United States and foreign nations. (pp. 6–10).

EXAM Strategy

Question: The stock market crash of 1929 and the Great Depression that followed were caused in part because so many investors blindly put their money into stocks they knew nothing about. During the 1920s, it was often impossible for an investor to find out what a corporation was planning to do with its money, who was running the corporation, and many other vital things. Congress responded by passing the Securities Act of 1933, which required a corporation to divulge more information about itself before it could seek money for a new stock issue. What kind of law did Congress create?

Strategy: What is the question seeking? The question asks you which *type* of law Congress created when it passed the 1933 Securities Act. What are the primary kinds of law? Administrative law consists of rules passed by agencies. Congress is not a federal agency. Common law is the body of cases decided by judges. Congress is not a judge. Statutes are laws passed by legislatures. Congress is a legislature. (See the "Result" at the end of this section.)

4. **CRIMINAL LAW**   Criminal law concerns behavior so threatening to society that it is outlawed altogether. Civil law deals with duties and disputes between parties, not with outlawed behavior. (pp. 10–11)

Question: Bill and Diane are hiking in the woods. Diane walks down a hill to fetch fresh water. Bill meets a stranger, who introduces herself as Katrina. Bill sells a kilo of cocaine to Katrina, who then flashes a badge and mentions how much she enjoys her job at the Drug Enforcement Agency. Diane, heading back to camp with the water, meets Freddy, a motorist whose car has overheated. Freddy is late for a meeting where he expects to make a $30 million profit; he's desperate for water for his car. He promises to pay Diane $500 tomorrow if she will give him the pail of water, which she does. The next day, Bill is in jail and Freddy refuses to pay for Diane's water. Explain the criminal law/civil law distinction and what it means to Bill and Diane. Who will do what to whom, with what results?

Strategy: You are asked to distinguish between criminal and civil law. What is the difference? The criminal law concerns behavior that threatens society and is therefore outlawed. The government prosecutes the defendant. Civil law deals with the rights and duties between parties. One party files a suit against the other. Apply those different standards to these facts. (See the "Result" at the end of this section.)

5. **JURISPRUDENCE**   Jurisprudence is concerned with the basic nature of law. Three theories of jurisprudence are

   1. Legal positivism: The law is what the sovereign says it is.
   2. Natural law: An unjust law is no law at all.
   3. Legal realism: Who enforces the law is more important than what the law says. (pp. 11–13)

3. Result: The Securities Act of 1933 is a statute.

4. Result: The government will prosecute Bill for dealing in drugs. If convicted, he will go to prison. The government will take no interest in Diane's dispute. However, if she chooses, she may sue Freddy for $500, the amount he promised her for the water. In that civil lawsuit, a court will decide whether Freddy must pay what he promised; however, even if Freddy loses, he will not go to jail.

MULTIPLE-CHOICE QUESTIONS

1. The United States Constitution is among the finest legal accomplishments in the history of the world. Which of the following influenced Benjamin Franklin, Thomas Jefferson, and the rest of the Founding Fathers?

   (a) English common law principles

   (b) the Iroquois's system of federalism

   (c) Both (a) and (b)

   (d) None of the above

2. Which of the following parts of the modern legal system are "borrowed" from medieval England?

   (a) Jury trials

   (b) Special rules for selling land

   (c) Following precedent

   (d) All of the above

3. Union organizers at a hospital wanted to distribute leaflets to potential union members, but hospital rules prohibited leafleting in areas of patient care, hallways, cafeterias, and any areas open to the public. The National Labor Relations Board, a government agency, ruled that these restrictions violated the law and ordered the hospital to permit the activities in the cafeteria and coffee shop. What kind of law was it creating?

   (a) A statute

   (b) Common law

   (c) A constitutional amendment

   (d) Administrative regulation

4. If the Congress creates a new statute with the President's support, it must pass the idea by a___majority vote in the House and the Senate. If the President vetoes a proposed statute and the Congress wishes to pass it without his support, the idea must pass by a___majority vote in the House and Senate.

   (a) simple; simple

   (b) simple; two-thirds

   (c) simple; three-fourths

   (d) two-thirds; three-fourths

5. What part of the Constitution addresses the most basic liberties?

   (a) Article I

   (b) Article II

   (c) Article III

   (d) Amendments

Essay Questions

1. Burglar Bob breaks into Vince Victim's house. Bob steals a flat-screen television and laptop and does a significant amount of damage to the property before he leaves. Fortunately, Vince has a state-of-the-art security system. It captures excellent images of Bob, who is soon caught by police. Assume that two legal actions follow, one civil and one criminal. Who will be responsible for bringing the civil case? What will be the outcome if the jury believes that Bob burgled Vince's house? Who will be responsible for bringing the criminal case? What will be the outcome if the jury believes that Bob burgled Vince's house?

2. As "The Oculist's Case" indicates, the medical profession has faced a large number of lawsuits for centuries. In Texas, a law provides that, so long as a doctor was not reckless and did not intentionally harm a patient, recovery for "pain and suffering" is limited to $750,000. In many other states, no such limit exists. If a patient will suffer a lifetime of pain after a botched operation, for example, he might recover millions in compensation. Which rule seems more sensible to you—the "Texas" rule or the alternative?

3. **YOU BE THE JUDGE WRITING PROBLEM** Should trials be televised? Here are a few arguments on both sides of the issue. You be the judge. **Arguments against live television coverage:** We have tried this experiment and it has failed. Trials fall into two categories: those that create great public interest and those that do not. No one watches dull trials, so we do not need to broadcast them. The few that are interesting have all become circuses. Judges and lawyers have shown that they cannot resist the temptation to play to the camera. Trials are supposed to be about justice, not entertainment. If a citizen seriously wants to follow a case, she can do it by reading the daily newspaper. **Arguments for live television coverage:** It is true that some televised trials have been unseemly affairs, but that is the fault of the presiding judges, not the media. Indeed, one of the virtues of television coverage is that millions of people now understand that we have a lot of incompetent people running our courtrooms. The proper response is to train judges to run a tight trial by prohibiting grandstanding by lawyers. Access to accurate information is the foundation on which a democracy is built, and we must not eliminate a source of valuable data just because some judges are ill-trained or otherwise incompetent.

4. Leslie Bergh and his two brothers, Milton and Raymond, formed a partnership to help build a fancy saloon and dance hall in Evanston, Wyoming. Later, Leslie met with his friend and drinking buddy, John Mills, and tricked Mills into investing in the saloon. Leslie did not tell Mills that no one else was investing cash or that the entire enterprise was already bankrupt. Mills mortgaged his home, invested $150,000 in the saloon—and lost every penny of it. Mills sued all three partners for fraud. Milton and Raymond defended on the grounds that they did not commit the fraud; only Leslie did. The defendants lost. Was that fair? By holding them liable, what general idea did the court rely on? What Anglo-Saxon legal custom did the ruling resemble?

5. *Kuehn v. Pub Zone* and *Soldano v. O'Daniels* both involve attacks in a bar. Should they have the same result? If so, in which way—in favor of the injured plaintiffs or owner-defendants? If not, why should they have different outcomes? What are the key facts that lead you to believe as you do?

DISCUSSION QUESTIONS

1. Do you believe that there are too many lawsuits in the United States? If so, do you place more blame for the problem on lawyers or on individuals who go to court? Is there anything that would help the problem, or will we always have large numbers of lawsuits?

2. In the 1980s, the Supreme Court ruled that it is legal for protesters to burn the American flag. This activity counts as free speech under the Constitution. If the Court hears a new flag-burning case in this decade, should it consider changing its ruling, or should it follow precedent? Is following past precedent something that seems sensible to you: always, usually, sometimes, rarely, or never?

3. When should a business be held legally responsible for customer safety? Consider the following statements, and consider the degree to which you agree or disagree:

- A business should keep customers safe from its own employees.
- A business should keep customers safe from other customers.
- A business should keep customers safe from themselves. (Example: an intoxicated customer who can no longer walk straight.)
- A business should keep people outside its own establishment safe if it is reasonable to do so.

4. In his most famous novel, *The Red and the Black*, the French author Stendhal (1783–1842) wrote: "There is no such thing as 'natural law': this expression is nothing but old nonsense. Prior to laws, what is natural is only the strength of the lion, or the need of the creature suffering from hunger or cold, in short, need." What do you think? Does legal positivism or legal realism seem more sensible to you?

5. At the time of this writing, voters are particularly disgruntled. A good many people seem to be disgusted with government. For this question, we intentionally avoid distinguishing between Democrats and Republicans, and we intentionally do not name any particular President. Consider the following statements, and consider the degree to which you agree or disagree:

- I believe that members of Congress usually try to do the right thing for America.
- I believe that Presidents usually try to do the right thing for America.
- I believe that Supreme Court justices usually try to do the right thing for America.

ETHICS AND CORPORATE SOCIAL RESPONSIBILITY

nuttakit/Shutterstock.com; © Stas Volik/Shutterstock.com

Eating is one of life's most fundamental needs and greatest pleasures. Yet all around the world many people go to bed hungry. Food companies have played an important role in reducing hunger by producing vast quantities of food cheaply. So much food, so cheaply that, in America, one in three adults and one in five children are obese. Some critics argue that food companies bear responsibility for this overeating because they make their products *too* alluring. Many processed food products are calorie bombs of fat (which is linked to heart disease), sugar (leading to diabetes), and salt (causing high blood pressure). What obligation do food producers and restaurants have to their customers? After all, no one is forcing anyone to eat. Do any of the following examples cross the line into unethical behavior?

1. Increasing Addiction. Food with high levels of fat, sugar, and salt not only taste better, they are also more addictive to consumers. Food processors hire neuroscientists who perform MRIs on consumers to gauge the precise level of fat, sugar, and salt that will create the most powerful cravings, the so-called bliss point. To take one example, in some Prego tomato sauces, sugar is the second most important ingredient after tomatoes. Did you know you were getting a large dose of sugar with your pasta?

> Food with high levels of fat, sugar and salt not only taste better, they are also more addictive to consumers.

2. Increasing Quantity. Food companies also work hard to create new categories of products that increase the number of times a day that people eat and the amount of calories in each session. For example, they have created a new category of food that is meant to be more than a snack but less than a meal, such as Hot Pockets. But some versions of this product have more than 700 calories, which

would be a lot for lunch, never mind for just a snack. And candy companies carefully package their products to encourage consumers to nibble all day. For example, when Hershey's learned that the wrappers on a Reese's Peanut Butter Cup act as a deterrent to nonstop eating, the company created Reese's minis, which are unwrapped candies in a resealable bag. Feel free to chow down!

Food executives argue that they are just providing what consumers want.

3. Increasing Calories. Uno Chicago Grill serves a macaroni and cheese dish that, by itself, provides more than two-thirds of the calories that a moderately active man should eat in one day, and almost three times the amount of saturated fat. But this dish is at least *food*. Dunkin Donuts offers a Frozen Caramel Coffee Coolatta with more than one-third the calories that a male should have in a day and 50 percent more saturated fat. Of course, these items are even worse choices for women and children. Should restaurants serve items such as these? If they do, what disclosure should they make?

4. Targeting Children. Kraft Food developed Lunchables, packaged food designed for children to take to school. The first version contained bologna, cheese, crackers, and candy—all of which delivered unhealthy levels of fat, sugar, and salt. The company lured children by advertising on Saturday morning cartoons.

5. Targeting the Poor. Traditionally, Coca Cola focused its marketing efforts on low-income areas in the United States. It then took this effort overseas, selling Coke in the slums of Brazil. One of its strategies is to provide small bottles that cost only 20 cents. Said Jeffrey Dunn, the former president and chief operating officer for Coca Cola in North and South America, "These people need a lot of things, but they don't need a Coke. I almost threw up."[1] When Dunn tried to develop more healthful strategies for Coke, he was fired.

2-1 INTRODUCTION

Ethics
How people should behave.

Ethics decision
Any choice that affects people or animals.

This text, for the most part, covers legal ideas. The law dictates how a person *must* behave. This chapter examines **ethics**, or how people *should* behave. Any choice that affects people or animals is an **ethics decision**. This chapter will explore ethical dilemmas that commonly arise in workplaces, and present tools for making decisions when the law does not require or prohibit any particular choice.

---

[1]Michael Moss, "The Extraordinary Science of Addictive Junk Food," *New York Times*, February 20, 2013.

If a person is intent on lying, cheating, and stealing his way through a career, then he is unlikely to be dissuaded by anything in this or any other course. But for the large majority of people who want to do the right thing, it is useful to study new ways of approaching difficult problems.

Laws represent society's view of basic ethical rules. And most people agree that certain activities such as murder, assault, and fraud are wrong. **However, laws may permit behavior that some feel is wrong, and it may criminalize acts that some feel are right.** For example, assisted suicide is legal in a few states. Some people believe that it is wrong under all circumstances, while others think that it is the right thing to do for someone suffering horribly from a terminal illness. Likewise, many people feel that it is ethical to record videos of farm animals being mistreated, although some states now prohibit secret videotaping on farms.

In this chapter, the usual legal cases are replaced by Ethics Cases with discussion questions. The goal of these scenarios is to generate classroom debates on right and wrong. It is important for everyone to hear a variety of different points of view. In your career, you will work with and manage diverse groups of people, so it is good to have insight into how different people perceive ethical issues.

We also hope that hearing these various points of view will help you develop your own Life Principles. These principles are the rules by which you live your life. As we will see, research shows that people who think about the right rules for living are less likely to do wrong. Developing your own Life Principles, based on your values, may be the most important outcome of reading this chapter and studying ethics.

How do you go about preparing a list of Life Principles? Think first of important categories. A list of Life Principles should include your rules on:

- Lying

- Stealing

- Cheating

- Applying the same or different standards at home and at work

- Your responsibility as a bystander when you see other people doing wrong

Specific is better than general. Many people say, for example, that they will maintain a healthy work life balance, but such a vow is not as effective as promising to set aside certain specific times each week for family activities. Many religions honor the Sabbath for this reason. Another common Life Principle is: "I will always put my family first." But what does that mean? That you are willing to engage in unethical behavior at work to make sure that you keep your job? Increase your income by cheating everyone you can? Or live your life so that you serve as a good example?

Some Life Principles focus not so much on right versus wrong but rather serve as a general guide for living a happier, more engaged life: I will keep promises, forgive those who harm me, say I'm sorry, appreciate my blessings every day, understand the other person's point of view, try to say "yes" when asked for a favor.

Remember that, no matter what you *say*, every ethics decision you make illustrates your *actual* Life Principles. For example, one MBA student told the story of how his boss had ordered him to cheat on his expense report. The company did not require any receipts for meals that cost less than $25. He and his fellow salespeople ate at fast food restaurants where it was almost impossible to spend $25. Everyone else was reporting a lot of $24 meals while he was submitting bills for $12. His boss told him he was making everyone else look bad and he needed to increase the amounts he claimed. What is your Life Principle in this case? Understand that if you cheat in this situation, your Life Principle is effectively: I am willing to cheat if it involves small sums or I am willing to cheat if I am unlikely to get caught. An alternative would be: I won't cheat even if my boss tells me to—I'll look for another job instead.

It is important to think through your Life Principles now, so that you will be prepared when facing ethical dilemmas in the future.

In this chapter, we will present eight topics:

1. The Role of Business in Society

2. Why Be Ethical?

3. Theories of Ethics

4. Ethics Traps

5. Lying

6. Applying the Principles

7. When the Going Gets Tough (responding to unethical behavior)

8. Corporate Social Responsibility

2-2 THE ROLE OF BUSINESS IN SOCIETY

Nobel Prize-winning economist Milton Friedman is famous for arguing that a corporate manager's primary responsibility is to the owners of the organization, that is, to shareholders. Unless the owners explicitly provide otherwise, managers should make the company as profitable as possible while also complying with the law.[2]

Others have argued that corporations should instead consider all company stakeholders, not just the shareholders. Stakeholders include employees, customers, and the communities and countries in which a company operates. This choice can create an obligation to such broad categories as "society" or "the environment." For example, after the shooting in Newtown, Connecticut, in which 20 first-graders and 6 educators were murdered, General Electric Co. stopped lending money to shops that sell guns. GE headquarters are near Newtown. Many of its employees lived in the area, and some had children in the Sandy Hook Elementary School where the shooting took place. In this case, GE was putting its employees ahead of its investors.

Every executive will treat employees well if she believes that doing so leads to increased profits. All executives are in favor of giving money to charity if the donation improves the company's image and thereby increases profits enough to pay for itself. But such win-win cases are not ethical dilemmas. In a true dilemma, a company considers an action that would not increase shareholder returns in any certain or measureable way but would benefit other stakeholders. Neither side is obviously right in the sense that everyone agrees or that the law requires one particular outcome.

As we will see in this chapter, managers face many choices in which the most profitable option is not the most ethical choice. For example, Michael Mudd, a former executive vice president of global corporate affairs for Kraft Foods, had this to say about his fellow executives:

> In so many other ways, these are good people. But, little by little, they strayed from the honorable business of feeding people appropriately to the deplorable mission of "increasing shareholder value" by enticing people to consume more and more high-margin, low-nutrition branded products.[3]

---

[2]He also mentions that managers should comply with "ethical custom" but never explains what that means. Milton Friedman, *New York Times Magazine*, September 13, 1970.

[3]Michael Moss, "How to Force Ethics on the Food Industry," *New York Times*, March 16, 2013.

Of course, when profitability increases and, with it, a company's stock price, managers also benefit because their compensation is often tied to corporate results, either explicitly or through ownership of stock and options. Thus, managers who say that they are just acting in the best interest of shareholders are also conveniently benefiting themselves. That connection creates an incentive to ignore stakeholders.

Conversely, doing the right thing will sometimes lead to a loss of profits or even one's job. For example, Hugh Aaron worked for a company that sold plastic materials.[4] One of the firm's major clients hired a new purchasing agent who refused to buy any product unless he was provided with expensive gifts, paid vacations, and sex. When Aaron refused to comply with these requests, the man bought from someone else. And that was that—the two companies never did business again. Aaron did not regret his choice—he believed that his employees' self-respect was as important as profits. But if your *only* concern is maximizing your company's profitability in the short run, you will find yourself in a position of making unethical choices.

2-3 WHY BE ETHICAL?

An ethical decision may not be the most profitable, but it does generate a range of benefits for employees, companies, and society.

2-3a Society as a Whole Benefits from Ethical Behavior

John Akers, the former chairman of IBM, argues that without ethical behavior, a society cannot be economically competitive. He puts it this way:

> Ethics and competitiveness are inseparable. We compete as a society. No society anywhere will compete very long or successfully with people stabbing each other in the back; with people trying to steal from each other; with everything requiring notarized confirmation because you can't trust the other fellow; with every little squabble ending in litigation; and with government writing reams of regulatory legislation, tying business hand and foot to keep it honest. That is a recipe not only for headaches in running a company, but for a nation to become wasteful, inefficient, and noncompetitive. There is no escaping this fact: the greater the measure of mutual trust and confidence in the ethics of a society, the greater its economic strength.[5]

In short, ethical behavior builds trust, which is important in all of our relationships. It is the ingredient that allows us to live and work together happily.

2-3b People Feel Better When They Behave Ethically

Every businessperson has many opportunities to be dishonest. But each of us must ask ourselves: What kind of person do we want to be? In what kind of world do we want to live? You might think about how you would like people who know you to describe you to others.

Managers want to feel good about themselves and the decisions they have made; they want to sleep well at night. Their decisions—to lay off employees, install safety devices in

---

[4]Virtually all of the examples in this chapter are true events involving real people. Only first names are used if the person prefers privacy. Full names are used when the individual has consented or the events are a matter of public record.

[5]David Grier, "Confronting Ethical Dilemmas," unpublished manuscript of remarks at the Royal Bank of Canada, September 19, 1989.

cars, burn a cleaner fuel—affect people's lives. And their unethical decisions are painful to remember.

To take an example, an executive, whom we will call "Hank," told a story that still haunts him. His boss had refused to pay his tuition for an MBA program so Hank went over his head and asked Sam, an executive several levels higher. Sam interceded immediately and personally approved the tuition reimbursement. He then took Hank under his wing, checking with him regularly to find out how the program and his work were going. Naturally, Hank felt grateful and indebted. Then one day, some other higher ups told him that they were planning a coup against Sam. They were trying to get him fired in a complete blindside. They offered Hank a big promotion in return for his help. All went according to plan and Sam was fired. When Sam found out about Hank's betrayal, he called to tell the younger man exactly what he thought of his character. Hank said that he will carry that phone call and his guilt forever. And because he was so untrustworthy, he finds it hard to trust others.

2-3c Unethical Behavior Can Be Very Costly

Unethical behavior is a risky business strategy—it can harm not only the bad actors but entire industries and even countries. For example, when VIPshop recently offered its shares publicly in the United States, they plummeted in price. This was the first Chinese company to go public in the United States in nine months, since a series of accounting frauds in other Chinese companies had caused billions of dollars in losses. Although VIPshop had done nothing wrong, investors were skeptical of *all* Chinese companies.

Although unethical decisions may increase short-term profits, they can create a lot of long-term harm. Johnson & Johnson (J&J) manufactured a new artificial hip that had more metal parts than the old version. In theory, the hip would last longer and thereby let the patient avoid difficult replacement surgery. But the theory turned out to be wrong. The two parts ground together, releasing microscopic bits of metal that not only failed quickly but also irreparably damaged the patient's bone and tissue. Even when Johnson & Johnson (J&J) had data from an English surgeon revealing these problems, it denied and stonewalled while continuing to sell the product. J&J now faces over 10,000 lawsuits. The company has not only taken a $3 billion charge in its financial statements to cover legal and medical costs, it finds its reputation sullied.

What is the cost of a lost reputation? Research indicates that consumers are willing to pay more for a product that they believe to be ethically produced. And much less if they believe it was made using shoddy ethical practices.[6] Unethical behavior can also cause other, subtler damage. In one survey, a majority of those questioned said that they had witnessed unethical behavior in their workplace and that this behavior had reduced productivity, job stability, and profits. Unethical behavior in an organization creates a cynical, resentful, and unproductive workforce.

Although there is no *guarantee* that ethical behavior pays in the short or long run, there is evidence that the ethical company is more *likely* to win financially. Ethical companies tend to have a better reputation, more creative employees, and higher returns than those that engage in wrongdoing.[7]

But if we decide that we want to behave ethically, how do we know what ethical behavior is?

2-4 THEORIES OF ETHICS

When making ethical decisions, people sometimes focus on the reason for the decision—they want to do what is right. Thus, if they think it is wrong to lie, then they will tell the truth no matter what the consequence. Other times, people think about the outcome

---

[6]Remi Trudel and June Cotte, "Does it Pay to Be Good," *Sloan Management Review*, January 8, 2009.
[7]For sources, see "Ethics: A Basic Framework," Harvard Business School case 9-307-059.

of their actions. They will do whatever it takes to achieve the right result, no matter what. This choice—between doing right and getting the right result—has been the subject of much philosophical debate.

2-4a Utilitarian Ethics

In 1863, Englishman John Stuart Mill wrote *Utilitarianism*. **To Mill, a correct decision was one that would maximize overall happiness and minimize overall pain, thereby producing the greatest net benefit.** As he put it, his goal was to produce the greatest good for the greatest number of people. Risk management and cost-benefit analyses are examples of utilitarian business practices.

Suppose that an automobile manufacturer could add a device to its cars that would reduce air pollution. As a result, the incidence of strokes and lung cancer would decline dramatically, saving society hundreds of millions of dollars over the life of the cars. But by charging a higher price to cover the cost of the device, the company would sell fewer cars and shareholders would earn lower returns. A utilitarian would argue that, despite the decline in profits, the company should install the device.

Consider this example that a student told us:

> During college, I used drugs—some cocaine, but mostly prescription painkillers. Things got pretty bad. At one point, I would wait outside emergency rooms hoping to buy drugs from people who were leaving. But that was three years ago. I went into rehab and have been clean ever since. I don't even drink. I've applied for a job, but the application asks if I have ever used drugs illegally. I am afraid that if I tell the truth, I will never get a job. What should I say on the application?

A utilitarian would ask: What harm will be caused if she tells the truth? She will be less likely to get that job, or maybe any job—a large and immediate harm. What if she lies? She might argue that no harm would result because she is now clean, and her past drug addiction will not have an adverse impact on her new employer.

There are many critics of utilitarian thought. Some argue that it is very difficult to *measure* utility accurately, at least in the way that one would measure distance or the passage of time. The car company does not really know how many lives will be saved or how much its profits might decline if the device is installed. It is also difficult to *predict* benefit and harm accurately. The recovered drug addict may relapse, or her employer may find out about her lie.

A focus on outcome can justify some really terrible behavior. Among other things, it can be used to legitimize torture. After the 9/11 terrorist attacks, Americans debated the acceptability of torture. Is it ethical to torture a terrorist with the hope of obtaining the details of an upcoming attack?

Or suppose that wealthy old Ebenezer has several chronic illnesses that cause him great suffering and prevent him from doing any of the activities that once gave meaning to his life. Also, he is such a nasty piece of work that everyone who knows him hates him. If he were to die, all his heirs would benefit tremendously from the money that they inherited from him, including a disabled grandchild who then could afford medical care that would improve his life dramatically. Would it be ethical to kill Ebenezer?

2-4b Deontological Ethics

The word **deontological** comes from the Greek word for *obligation*. **Proponents of deontological ethics believe that utilitarians have it all wrong and that the *results* of a decision are not as important as the *reason* for which it is made.** To a deontological thinker, the ends do not justify the means. Rather, it is important to do the right thing, no matter the result.

The best-known proponent of the deontological model was the eighteenth-century German philosopher Immanuel Kant. He believed in what he called the **categorical imperative**. He argued that you should not do something unless you would be willing to have everyone else do it, too. Applying this idea, he concluded that one should always tell

Deontological
From the Greek word for *obligation*. The duty to do the right thing, regardless of the result.

Kant's categorical imperative
An act is only ethical if it would be acceptable for everyone to do the same thing.

the truth because if *everyone* lied, the world would become an awful place. Thus, Kant would say that the drug user should tell the truth on job applications, even if that meant she could not find work. The truth should be told, no matter the outcome.

Kant also believed that human beings possess a unique dignity and that no decision that treats people as commodities could be considered just, even if the decision tended to maximize overall happiness, or profit, or any other quantifiable measure. Thus, Kant would argue against killing Ebenezer, no matter how unpleasant the man was.

Although many people disagree with some of Kant's specific ideas, most people do acknowledge that a utilitarian approach is incomplete, and that winning in the end does not automatically make a decision right.

2-4c Rawlsian Justice

How did you manage to get into college or graduate school? Presumably due to some combination of talent, hard work, and support from family and friends. Imagine that you had been born into different circumstances—say, a country where the literacy rate is only 25 percent and almost all of the population lives in desperate poverty. Would you be reading this book now? Most likely not. People are born with wildly different talents into very different circumstances, all of which dramatically affect their outcomes.

John Rawls (1921–2002) was an American philosopher who referred to these circumstances into which we are born as **life prospects.** In his view, hard work certainly matters, but so does luck. Rawls argued that we should think about what rules for society we would propose if we faced a **"veil of ignorance."** In other words, suppose that there is going to be a lottery tomorrow that would determine all our attributes. We could be a winner, ending up a hugely talented, healthy person in a loving family, or we could be the most miserable person on the face of the earth.

What type of society would we establish now, if we did not know whether we would be one of life's winners or losers? First, we would design some form of a democratic system that provided equal liberty to all and important rights such as freedom of speech and religion. Second, we would apply the **difference principle**. Under this principle we would *not* plan a system in which everyone received an equal income because society is better off if people have an incentive to work hard. But we would reward the type of work that provides the most benefit to the community as a whole. We might decide, for example, to pay doctors more than baseball players. But maybe not *all* doctors—perhaps just the ones who research cancer cures or provide care for the poor, not cosmetic surgeons operating on the affluent. Rawls argues that everyone should have the opportunity to earn great wealth so long as the tax system provides enough revenue to provide decent health, education, and welfare for all. In thinking about ethical decisions, it is worth remembering that many of us have been winners in life's lottery and that the unlucky are deserving of our compassion.

2-4d Front Page Test

There you are, trying to decide what to do in a difficult situation. How would you feel if your actions were going to be reported on the Huffington Post, your Facebook page, the front page of a national newspaper or would be tweeted to all of your followers? Would that help you decide what to do? Would such exposure have caused Hank to tell Sam about the planned coup? Make the Johnson & Johnson executives manage their hip implant differently?

The Front Page test is not completely foolproof—there are times you might want to do something private for legitimate reasons. You might, for example, think that having an abortion is completely ethical, but still not want everyone to know. Or, if you live in a state that prohibits the videotaping of mistreated farm animals, you would not want everyone to know that you had done so, even if you thought it the right thing to do.

Life prospects
The opportunities one has at birth, based on one's natural attributes and initial place in society.

"Veil of ignorance"
The rules for society that we would propose if we did not know how lucky we would be in life's lottery.

Difference principle
Rawls' suggestion that society should reward behavior that provides the most benefit to the community as a whole.

◆ Ethics Case: Lincoln at War ◆

In 1865, toward the end of the American civil war, President Abraham Lincoln had to choose between two rival goals: an immediate end to a devastating, bloody war or a change to the Constitution that would make slavery illegal. If he ended the war immediately, the Southern states would return to the Union and then be eligible to vote on the anti-slavery amendment. They would have enough votes to defeat it. He ultimately decided to delay peace with the South, a decision that cost thousands of lives.

To obtain the votes he needed, Lincoln did whatever it took. He figured out how to win over each individual Congressman, appealing to one man's sense of idealism, another's greed. He made threats and promises, handed out jobs and cash. And, in the end, he succeeded in ending the barbarous practice of slavery.[8]

QUESTIONS

- What would Mill, Kant, and Rawls have said about Lincoln's actions?

- What would have been the result if Lincoln had applied the Front Page test?

- Lincoln risked people's lives for his principles and made decisions that affected millions. Can you think of a similar scenario in a business context?

2-5 ETHICS TRAPS

Very few people wake up one morning and think, "Today I'll do something unethical." Then why do so many unethical things happen? Sometimes our brains trick us into believing wrong is right. It is important to understand the ethics traps that create great temptation to do what we know to be wrong or fail to do what we know to be right.

2-5a Money

Money is a powerful lure because most people believe that they would be happier if only they had more. But that is not necessarily true. Good health, companionship, and enjoyable leisure activities all contribute more to happiness than money does. And, regardless of income, 85 percent of Americans feel happy on a day-to-day basis anyway.

Money *can*, of course, provide some protection against the inevitable bumps in the road of life. Being hungry is no fun. If you lose your winter coat, you will be happier if you can replace it. It is easier to maintain friendships if you can afford to go out together occasionally. So money can contribute to happiness, but research indicates that this impact disappears when household income exceeds $75,000. Above that level, income seems to have no impact on day-to-day happiness. Indeed, there is some evidence that higher income levels actually *reduce* the ability to appreciate small pleasures. Interestingly, too, people who come into a windfall are happier if they spend it on others or save it rather than blowing it in a spree.[9]

Money is also a way of keeping score. If my company pays me more, that must mean I am a better employee. So although an increase in income above $75,000 does not affect

---

[8]The Steven Spielberg movie *Lincoln* illustrates this process.
[9]Elizabeth Dunn and Michael Norton, "Don't Indulge, Be Happy," *New York Times*, July 8, 2012; and Daniel Kahneman and Angus Deaton, "High Income Improves Evaluation of Life but not Emotional Well-Being," *Proceedings of the National Academy of Sciences of the United States of America*, August 4, 2010.

day-to-day happiness, higher pay can make people feel more satisfied with their lives. They consider themselves more successful and feel that their life is going better.

In short, the relationship between money and happiness is complicated. Above a certain level, more money does not make for more day-to-day happiness. Higher pay can increase general satisfaction with life but when people work so hard or so dishonestly that their health, friendships, and leisure activities suffer, it has the reverse effect.

2-5b Rationalization

A recent study found that more creative people tend to be less ethical. The reason? They are better at rationalizing their bad behavior. Virtually any foul deed can be rationalized. Some common rationalizations:

- If I don't do it, someone else will.

- I deserve this because...

- They had it coming.

- I am not harming a *person*—it is just a big company.

- This is someone else's responsibility.

For example, Dan Ariely has found in his ground-breaking research that almost everyone is willing to cheat, just a little. That is because we want to maximize results (and enhance our belief in how smart we are) but we also want to think of ourselves as being honest. If we cheat—just a little—then we can tell ourselves that it does not really count. Ariely did an experiment in which people were asked to solve math problems and he paid them for each correct answer. When participants knew that he was going to check their results, they averaged four correct answers. But when they were allowed to self-report the number they got correct, suddenly people averaged six correct answers.[10] You can imagine how they might have rationalized that behavior—"I was close on this one. I normally would have gotten that one right. Today was an off day for me." Surprisingly, when the participants were paid a lot for each correct answer ($10 as opposed to $0.50), they cheated *less*. Presumably, they would have felt worse about themselves if they stole a lot of money rather than a little.

To take a real example, the gift shop at the Kennedy Center for the Performing Arts in Washington, D.C., was mostly run by elderly volunteers. The shop had revenues of $400,000 a year, but someone was stealing $150,000 of that. It turned out there was not one thief. Instead, dozens of volunteers were each stealing a little bit, which added up. These people felt good about themselves for being volunteers so they thought that stealing a little was fine.[11]

Rationalization allows us to expect less of ourselves than we do other people. When we do something wrong, we are creative at explaining why it did not really count. For example, participants in a study were put in the position of deciding whether they or someone else got an easy assignment. When asked in the abstract what would be a fair method for assigning tasks, everyone said that the computer should make the assignments randomly. But when another group of people was actually given the authority to decide, three quarters ignored the computer option and just assigned themselves the easy jobs. And then they rated themselves high on a fairness scale.[12] In making a decision that affects you, it is important to remember that you are unlikely to be objective.

---

[10]Dan Ariely, "Why We Lie," *Wall Street Journal*, May 26, 2012.
[11]David Brooks, "The Moral Diet," *New York Times*, June 7, 2012.
[12]John Tierney, "Deep Down, We Can't Fool Even Ourselves," *New York Times*, July 1, 2008.

2-5c Conformity

Warren Buffett has been quoted as saying, "The five most dangerous words in business may be: 'Everybody else is doing it.'" Humans are social animals who are often willing to follow the leader, even to a place where they do not really want to go. If all the salespeople in a company cheat on their expense accounts, a new hire is much more likely to view this behavior as acceptable.

◆ Ethics Case: Diamonds in the Rough ◆

When Orlanda graduated from college, she got a job as a software engineer in Silicon Valley. After two years working in technical support, one of her customers offered her a job at his company. It turned out that her new firm was in shambles but, after months of killer hours, she managed to get the company on a better path. One of her biggest accomplishments was to help a major supplier solve its technical problems so that its product would work reliably. On her birthday, her contact at the supplier (who was a friend of her boss) gave her a diamond watch. Her company had no policy on accepting gifts, so she kept it. Afterwards, she realized that she was spending even more time working on this supplier's issues. But, she said to herself, this was good for her company, too. Also, no one at her company had high ethical standards anyway.

Some months later, the same supplier offered to buy her a diamond necklace if she would make his company a preferred supplier. He said the necklace would look just like the one he had given her boss.

QUESTIONS

1. What ethics traps is Orlanda facing?

2. Is there anything wrong with accepting these gifts?

2-5d Following Orders

When someone in authority issues orders, even to do something clearly wrong, it is very tempting to comply. Fear of punishment, the belief in authority figures, and the ability to rationalize all play a role. In a true story (with the facts disguised), Amanda worked at a private school that was struggling to pay its bills. As a result, it kept the lights turned off in the hallways. On a particularly cloudy day, a visitor tripped and fell in one of these darkened passages. When he sued, the principal told Amanda to lie on the witness stand and say that the lights had been on. The school's lawyer reinforced this advice. Amanda did as she was told. When asked why, she said, "I figured it must be the right thing to do if the lawyer said so. Also, if I hadn't lied, the principal would have fired me, and I might not have been able to get another job in teaching."

> "File sharing" sounds friendly and helpful—it has a very different ring than "stealing intellectual property," which is what it really is.

It seems likely that you will be faced many times with the dilemma of a boss who orders you to do something wrong. Executives have told us that they have been ordered to:

- Misrepresent data in a presentation to the board (so the boss could take on a project that was not as profitable as it should have been)

- Avoid hiring certain ethnic groups or pregnant women

- "Smooth" numbers, that is, report sales that had not, actually, taken place yet

- Support the boss' position, even if it was clearly wrong

Be aware, too, that setting goals for your subordinates carries risks. Especially if the goals are too narrowly focused. A law firm partner once said, "If we tell associates they have to bill 2,000 hours a year, they will bill 2,000 hours. Whether they will *work* 2,000 hours is another matter." Research supports this view. Participants in an experiment were more likely to cheat if they had been assigned specific goals, whether or not they were actually being paid for meeting the targets.[13]

As you might expect, employees who work for firms with a culture of blind obedience are twice as likely to report having seen unethical behavior as are workers at companies with a more collaborative environment.[14]

2-5e Euphemisms

To "smooth earnings" sounds a lot better than to "cook the books" or "commit fraud." And "file sharing" sounds friendly and helpful—it has a very different ring from "stealing intellectual property," which is what it really is. In making ethical decisions, it is important to use accurate terminology. Anything else is just a variation on rationalization.

2-5f Lost in a Crowd

After being struck by a car, a two-year-old child lies at the side of the road as people walk and ride by. No one stops to help, and the child dies. On a busy street, a man picks up a seven-year-old girl and carries her away while she screams, "You're not my dad—someone help me!" No one responds. The first incident was real; the second one was a test staged by a news station. It took hours and many repetitions before anyone tried to prevent the abduction.

When in a group, people are less likely to take responsibility, because they assume (hope?) that someone else will. They tend to check the reactions of others, and if everyone else seems calm, they assume that all is right. Bystanders are much more likely to react if they are alone and have to form an independent judgment.

Thus, in a business, if everyone is cheating on their expense accounts, smoothing earnings, or sexually harassing the staff, it is tempting to go with the flow rather than protest the wrongdoing. In the example about food companies that began this chapter, one former executive says that producers shrug off responsibility for obesity in America by pointing to all the "other" causes: a car culture; too much screen time; less outdoor play; fewer women at home to cook. And, Americans spend half of their food money outside the home anyway.

◆ Ethics Case: Train Spotting ◆

Wesley Autrey was standing on a train platform with his two young daughters and a man he did not know. Suddenly, this man had a seizure, causing him to fall on the tracks. Autrey could hear a train approaching so he knew he had only seconds to act. Leaping on to the track, he pulled the man between the rails and lay on top of him to protect him from the train. The train engineer tried to stop, but five cars passed over the two men. Both were unharmed.

Some years later in New York City, a homeless man pushed Ki-Suck Han onto subway tracks, in view of many people. No one reacted, except a photographer who took photos as Han was killed by a train.

---

[13]Alina Tugend, "Experts' Advice to the Goal-Oriented: Don't Overdo It," *New York Times*, October 5, 2012.
[14]"The view from the top and bottom," *The Economist*, September 24, 2011.

QUESTIONS

- Why was Autrey more likely to act than the crowds watching Han?

- What are your ethical obligations to respond when someone needs help? Or you observe wrongdoing?

- Imagine that, at your work, you know that someone is:
  - Lying on an expense account
  - Wrongly booking sales that have not yet occurred
  - Sexually harassing staff members

What is your ethical obligation? What would you do, under what circumstances?

2-5g Blind Spots

As Bob Dylan memorably sang, "How many times can a man turn his head and pretend that he just doesn't see?" The answer is: a whole lot. For example, Bernard Madoff will long be remembered for running one of the biggest frauds ever through his brokerage house. One of the mysteries yet unresolved is: Who else knew what was going on? His brother, Peter, was second in command at his brother's firm. He admitted that he had committed many crimes, including income tax evasion and filing false documents with regulators. But he has always insisted that he had no idea his brother was committing fraud.

And then there is the case of Barry Bonds, one of the greatest baseball players ever. Although he quickly gained tremendous weight and muscle mass that was consistent with the illegal use of steroids, neither his team nor baseball executives took any action against him until the federal government began an investigation. (To see the change in Bonds' physique, google "steroids, Barry Bonds.")

Or a partner in a law firm was consistently billing 2,000+ hours a year. Yet he seemed to have time to attend his children's school functions in the middle of the day and was rarely in the office early or late. Firm executives were shocked to discover that he had been over-billing clients.[15]

2-5h Avoiding Ethics Traps

As we see from these ethics traps, circumstances affect our decision making. You are, for example, more likely to act if alone rather than in a crowd.

Being in a hurry also makes a difference. A group of students at Princeton Theological Seminary (i.e., people in training to be ministers) were told to go to a location across campus to give a talk. On their walk over, they encountered a man lying in distress in a doorway. Only one-tenth of those participants who had been told they were late for their talk stopped to help the ill man while almost two-thirds of those who thought they had plenty of time did stop.[16]

The topic of the talk also mattered. Those who were speaking on the Parable of the Good Samaritan (in which a man offers aid to an injured person from a different clan) were twice as likely to provide help than those who were giving a talk on careers for seminarians.

---

[15]For more on this topic, see Max Bazerman and Ann Tenbrunsel, *Blind Spots: Why We Fail to Do What's Right and What to Do about It* (Princeton, NJ: Princeton University Press).

[16]John M. Darley and Daniel C. Batson, "From Jerusalem to Jericho": A study of situational and dispositional variables in helping behavior," *Journal of Personality and Social Psychology* 27, no.1 (July 1973): 100–108.

Two thoughts about how to avoid ethics traps:

1. **Do not trust your first instinct.** Being in a hurry, or in a crowd, being able to rationalize easily, using euphemisms, doing what every else does, receiving an order, being dazzled by money; these can all lead you to make a quick and wrong decision. Test your initial reaction by asking whether you have fallen into any of these traps.

2. **Remember your Life Principles.** In his research, Ariely found that participants were less likely to cheat if they were reminded of their school honor code or the Ten Commandments (the fundamental rules of both the Christian and Jewish religions). This result was true even if the participants were atheists.

2-6 Lying: A Special Case

We are taught from an early age to tell the truth. Yet research shows that we tell between one and two lies a day.[17] Is honesty the best policy? The consequences of lying can be severe: students are suspended, employees are fired, and witnesses are convicted of perjury. Sometimes the problems are subtler but still significant: a loss of trust or of opportunities.

When is lying acceptable? If poker players bluff their way through lousy hands, we consider them skilled because that is an accepted part of the game. What about white lies to make others feel better: I love your lasagna. You're not going bald. No, that sweater doesn't make you look fat. When Victoria McGrath suffered a terrible wound to her leg in the Boston Marathon bombing, Tyler Dodd comforted her at the scene by telling her that he had recovered from a shrapnel wound in Afghanistan. His story was not true—he had never been in combat or Afghanistan. McGrath was grateful to him for his lie because it gave her strength and hope. Was he right or wrong? What are your rules on lying?

Kant felt that any lie violated his principle of the categorical imperative. Because the world would be intolerable if everyone lied all the time, no one should lie ever. He gave the example of the murderer who knocks on your door and asks, "Where's Lukas?" You know Lukas is cowering just inside, but you might be tempted to lie and send the murderer off in the opposite direction. Kant preferred that you tell what is now called a **Kantian Evasion** or a **palter**. That is, you would make a truthful statement that is nonetheless misleading. So, you might say, truthfully, "I saw Lukas in the park just an hour ago." And off the murderer would go.

Kantian evasion or palter
A truthful statement that is nonetheless misleading.

Is a Kantian Evasion really more ethical than a lie? For example, when a candidate for the presidency, Bill Clinton was asked if he had ever smoked marijuana. He answered that he "never broke the laws of my state or of the United States." Later, it was revealed that he had used marijuana while a student in England. So, although technically correct, his statement was misleading. Was that really better than lying about marijuana use?

What are your Life Principles on this issue? There may indeed be good reasons to lie but what are they? Would it be right to say that you would only lie to benefit other people? Lukas hiding from the murderer? Children who believe in Santa Claus? It is useful to analyze this issue now rather than to rationalize later.

What about in business? Does the presence of *competition* make a difference? When do the ends justify the means?

---

[17]Bella M. DePaulo, Deborah A. Kashy, Susan E. Kirkendol, and Melissa M. Wyer, "Lying in Everyday Life," *Journal of Personality and Social Psychology* 70, no. 5, (1996): 979–995.

2 *Ethics and Corporate Social Responsibility* 37

◆ Ethics Case: Truth (?) in Borrowing ◆

Rob is in the business of buying dental practices. He finds solo practitioners, buys their assets, signs them to a long-term contract and then improves their management and billing processes so effectively that both he and the dentists are better off.

Rob has just found a great opportunity with a lot of potential profit. There is only *one* problem. The bank will not give him a loan to buy the practice without checking the dentist's financial record. Her credit rating is fine, but it turns out that she filed for bankruptcy twenty years ago. That event no longer appears on her credit rating, but the bank asked about bankruptcies on the form it required her to sign. She is perfectly willing to lie. Rob refused to turn in the form with a lie. But when the bank learned about the bankruptcy, it denied his loan even though *her* bankruptcy in no way affects *his* ability to pay the loan. And the incident is ancient history—the dentist's current finances are strong. Four other banks also refused to make the loan.

Rob is feeling pretty frustrated. He figures the return on this deal would be 20 percent. Everyone would benefit—the dentist would earn more, her patients would have better technology, he could afford a house in a better school district, and the bank would make a profit. There is one more bank he could try.

QUESTIONS

1. Should Rob file loan documents with the bank, knowing the dentist has lied?

2. Who would be harmed by this lie?

3. What if Rob pays back the loan without incident, as he knew he would? Was what he did wrong? Do the ends justify the means?

4. What is your Life Principle about telling lies? When is making a misrepresentation acceptable? To protect someone's life or physical safety? To protect a job? To protect another person's feelings? To gain an advantage? When others are doing the same?

5. Do you have the same rule when lying to protect yourself, as opposed to others?

2-7 APPLYING THE PRINCIPLES

Having thought about ethical principles and traps, let's now practice applying them to situations that are similar to those that you are likely to face in your life. Be aware that some of these ethical dilemmas illustrate the tradeoff between shareholders and stakeholders. Note also that sometimes the right decision will be obvious, but difficult to do because of the risk or expense. Other times, the right answer is unclear, because someone will be harmed no matter what choice you make. In both of these situations, it is important to recognize explicitly the forces that push or pull you when making a decision. Unless you are aware of these forces, you cannot make a truly informed decision.

2-7a Personal Ethics in the Workplace

Should you behave in the workplace the way you do at home, or do you have a separate set of ethics for each part of your life? What if your employees behave badly outside of work—should that affect their employment? Consider the following case.

◆ Ethics Case: No Sheen on Sheen ◆

Charlie Sheen, who starred in the hit CBS television show *Two and a Half Men*, admitted to using large quantities of cocaine. He was hospitalized with drug overdoses and had been charged with both misdemeanor and felony drug offenses, which led to probation several times. When asked about entering rehab, he said that only losers go to recovery programs and he could cure himself with his mind. He openly spent tens of thousands of dollars on prostitutes. His second wife filed a restraining order against him, alleging that he had pushed her down the stairs and threatened to kill her. He was also charged with a felony for threatening his third wife. She claimed that he held a knife to her throat and said, "You better be in fear. If you tell anybody, I'll kill you." Then there was the widely reported incident in the Plaza Hotel in New York City in which the police escorted him to the hospital after he trashed his room and threatened the prostitute whom he had hired—all while his ex-wife and children slept in a room across the hall. Five months later, the police removed his twin sons from his house after their mother obtained a restraining order. On a radio show, Sheen made anti-Semitic comments about his boss, called him a clown and a charlatan, and said that he "violently hated him." This boss was the most successful producer of comedy shows in the business.

QUESTIONS

1. If CBS fired Sheen from his television show, the network would lose tens of millions of dollars. At what point, if any, should CBS have fired him? If not for this, then for what?

2. Would you fire a warehouse worker who behaved this way? How much revenue does an employee have to bring in to be able to buy his way out of bad behavior?

3. What would you say to someone who argues that the goal at work is to make as much money as possible, but at home it is to be a kind and honorable human being?

4. What would Kant and Mill say is the right thing to do in this case? What result under the Front Page Test?

5. What ethics traps did Sheen's bosses face in this situation?

6. What is your Life Principle? What behavior are you willing to tolerate in the interest of profitability?

2-7b The Organization's Responsibility to Society

Many products can potentially cause harm to customers or employees. Does it matter if the customers and employees willingly accept exposure to these products? What constitutes informed agreement? What is the company's responsibility to those who are unwittingly harmed by its products?

◆ Ethics Case: Breathing the Fumes ◆

Every other year, the National Institutes of Health publish the "Report on Carcinogens," which lists products that cause cancer. Among those in the most recent report was formaldehyde, found in furniture, cosmetics, building products, carpets, and fabric softeners. Unless we take heroic efforts to avoid this chemical, we are all exposed to it when inside. Indeed, almost all homes have formaldehyde levels that exceed government safety rules. In an effort to shoot the messenger, the American Chemistry Council, which is an industry trade group, lobbied Congress to cut off funding for the "Report on Carcinogens"—not improve it, but defund it.

QUESTIONS

1. If you were one of the many companies using products that contain formaldehyde, what would you do? What would you be willing to pay to provide a safer product?

2. If you were an executive at Exxon, Dow, or DuPont, all members of the American Chemistry Council, what would you do?

3. What would Mill and Kant recommend?

4. What ethics traps would you face in making a decision?

5. What Life Principle would you apply?

2-7c The Organization's Responsibility to Its Employees

Organizations cannot be successful without good workers. In many circumstances, the shareholder and stakeholder models agree that employees should be treated well. Disgruntled workers are likely to be unmotivated and unproductive. But sometimes looking out for employees may not lead to higher profits. In these cases, does an organization have a duty to take care of its workers? The shareholder model says no; the stakeholder model takes the opposite view.

Corporate leaders are often faced with difficult decisions when the issue of layoffs arises. Choices can be particularly difficult to navigate when outsourcing is an option. *Outsourcing* refers to cutting jobs at home and relocating operations to another country. That is the issue in the following scenario.

◆ Ethics Case: The Storm After the Storm ◆

Yanni is the CEO of Cloud Farm, a company that provides online data centers for Internet companies. Because these data centers are enormous, they are located in rural areas where they are often the main employer. A series of tornados has just destroyed a data center near Farmfield, Arkansas, a town with a population of roughly 5,000 people. Farmfield is a three-hour drive from the nearest city, Little Rock.

Here is the good news: The insurance payout will cover the full cost of rebuilding. Indeed, the payout will be so generous that Cloud Farm could build a bigger and better facility than the one destroyed. The bad news? Data centers are much more expensive to build and operate in the United States than in Africa, Asia, or Latin America. Yanni could take the money from the insurance company and build three data centers overseas. He has asked Adam and Zoe to present the pros and cons of relocating.

Adam says, "If we rebuild overseas, our employees will never find equivalent jobs. We pay $20 an hour, and the other jobs in town are mostly minimum-wage. And remember how some of the guys worked right through Christmas to set up for that new client. They have been loyal to us—we owe them something in return. Going overseas is not just bad for Farmfield or Arkansas, it's bad for the country. We can't continue to ship jobs overseas."

Zoe responds, "That is the government's problem, not ours. We'll pay to retrain the workers, which, frankly, is a generous offer. Our investors get a return of 4 percent; the industry average is closer to 8 percent. If we act like a charity to support Farmfield, we could all lose our jobs. It is our obligation to do what's best for our shareholders— which, in this case, happens to be what's right for us, too."

QUESTIONS

1. Do you agree with Zoe's argument that it is the government's responsibility to create and protect American jobs, and that it is a CEO's job to increase shareholder wealth?

2. Imagine that you personally own $10,000 worth of shares in Cloud Farm. Would you be upset with a decision to rebuild the data center in the United States?

3. If you were in Yanni's position, would you rebuild the plant in Arkansas or relocate overseas?

4. If Cloud Farm decides to rebuild in Arkansas, should it pay the workers while the center is being rebuilt? If yes, should it apply to all the workers, or just the high-level ones who might leave if they were not paid?

5. What ethics traps does Yanni face in this situation?

6. What is your Life Principle on this issue? Would you be willing to risk your job to protect your employees?

2-7d An Organization's Responsibility to Its Customers

Customers are another group of essential stakeholders. A corporation must gain and retain loyal buyers if it is to stay in business for long. Treating customers well usually increases profits and helps shareholders.

But when, if ever, does an organization go too far? Is a leader acting appropriately when she puts customers first in a way that significantly diminishes the bottom line? The shareholder model says no. What do you say?

◆ Ethics Case: Mickey Weighs In ◆

As we have seen, many food companies manipulate products to maximize their appeal, without regard to the health of their customers. Disney is taking a different approach—announcing recently that only healthy foods can be advertised on its children's television channels, radio stations, and websites. Candy, fast food, and sugared cereals are banned from Mickey land. Kicked to the curb are such childhood favorites as Lunchables and Capri Sun drinks. In addition, sodium must be reduced by one quarter in food served at its theme parks. Nor does Disney permit its characters to associate with unhealthy foods. No more Mickey Pop-Tarts or Buzz Lightyear Happy Meals. Said Disney chairman, Robert Iger, "Companies in a position to help with solutions to childhood obesity should do just that."[18]

Disney will certainly lose advertising, but would not say how much. Food sales at its theme parks may decline if children find the options less appealing. Its licensing revenues are also affected by its decisions to remove Disney characters from the likes of Pop-Tarts and Happy Meals.

On the other hand, this healthy initiative will enhance its reputation, at least with parents, who increasingly seek healthy food options for their children. Disney will profit from license fees it receives for the use of a Mickey Check logo on healthy food in grocery aisles and restaurants. This food initiative may also help forestall more onerous government regulation.

---

[18]Brooks Barnes, "Promoting Nutrition, Disney to Restrict Junk-Food Ads," *New York Times*, June 5, 2012.

QUESTIONS

1. What obligation does Disney have to its young customers? Does it owe them anything other than entertainment?

2. How much advertising and licensing revenue would you be willing to give up to protect children from ads for unhealthy foods? Does your answer depend on how profitable the division is?

3. Does this information make you more likely to buy Disney products or allow your children to watch Disney TV?

4. What if this initiative had not come down from the highest levels in the company? Would you have been willing to fight for it?

5. What would Mill or Kant have said? What result with the Front Page Test?

6. What ethics traps does Disney face?

7. What is your Life Principle? How much profitability (or income) are you willing to give up to protect children you do not know?

2-7e Organization's Responsibility to Overseas Contract Workers

Do an American company's ethical obligations end at the border? What ethical duties does an American manager owe to stakeholders in countries where the culture and economic circumstances are very different? Should American companies (and consumers) buy goods that are produced in sweatshop factories?

Industrialization has always been the first stepping stone out of dire poverty—it was in England in centuries past, and it is now in the developing world. Eventually, higher productivity leads to higher wages. In China, factory managers have complained that their employees want to work even longer hours to earn more money. The results in China have been nothing short of remarkable. During the Industrial Revolution in England, per capita output doubled in 58 years; in China, it took only 10 years.

During the past 50 years, Taiwan and South Korea welcomed sweatshops. During the same period, India resisted what it perceived to be foreign exploitation. Although all three countries started at the same economic level, Taiwan and South Korea today have much lower levels of infant mortality and much higher levels of education than India.[19]

In theory, then, sweatshops might not be all bad. But are there limits? Consider the following case.

◆ Ethics Case: A Worm in the Apple ◆

"Riots, Suicides and More," blares an Internet headline about a FoxConn factory where iPhones and other Apple products are assembled. Apple is not alone in facing supplier scandals. So have Nike, Coca-Cola, and Gap, among many others. Do companies have an obligation to the employees of their suppliers? If so, how can they, or anyone, be sure what is really going on in a factory on the other side of the world? Professor Richard Locke of MIT has studied supply chain issues.[20] His conclusions:

---

[19]The data in this and the preceding paragraph are from Nicholas D. Kristof and Sheryl Wu Dunn, "Two Cheers for Sweatshops," *New York Times Magazine*, September 24, 2000, p. 70.
[20]"When the jobs inspector calls," *The Economist*, March 31, 2012.

- The first step that many companies took to improve working conditions overseas was to establish a code of conduct and then perform audits. Professor Locke found that these coercive practices do not work and that compliance is at best sporadic. For example, despite Hewlett-Packard's best efforts, only a handful of its 276 overseas factories consistently met its standards.

- A more collaborative approach worked better—when the auditors sent by multinationals saw their role as less of a police officer and more as a partner, committed to problem-solving and sharing of best practices.

- It can be hard to improve conditions without also changing a company's business model. One of the reasons that Apple uses Chinese manufacturers such as FoxConn is that its workers have fewer overtime restrictions. Just before the first iPhone was released, Steve Jobs decided that the screens had to be unscratchable glass instead of plastic. One Chinese company supplied a team of engineers that was housed in a dormitory and willing to work around the clock to design the right glass. When the glass arrived at FoxConn in the middle of the night, thousands of assemblers were put to work immediately.

What would you do in the following circumstances if you were in charge:

- In clothing factories, workers often remove the protective guards from their sewing machines, because the guards slow the flow of work. As a result, many workers suffer needle punctures. Factories resist the cost of buying new guards because the workers just take them off again. Is there a solution?

- In a factory in Central America, powerful chemicals were used to remove stains from clothing. The fumes from these chemicals were a health hazard but ventilation systems were too expensive. What could be done?[21]

- Timberland, Nike, and Hewlett-Packard have recognized that selling large numbers of new products creates great variation in demand and therefore pressure on factory workers to work overtime. What can a company do to reduce this pressure?

2-8 WHEN THE GOING GETS TOUGH

We have talked about the kinds of ethical issues that you are likely to face in your career. If you find yourself working for a company that tolerates an intolerable level of unethical behavior, you face three choices.

2-8a Loyalty

It is always important to pick one's battles. For example, a firm's accounting department must make many decisions about which reasonable people could disagree. Just because their judgment is different from yours does not mean that they are behaving unethically. Being a team player means allowing other people to make their own choices sometimes. However, the difference between being a team player and starting down the slippery slope can be very narrow. If you are carrying out a decision, or simply observing one, that makes you uncomfortable, then it is time to consult your Life Principles and review the section on ethics traps.

---

[21]These examples are from Richard Locke, Matthew Amengual, and Akshay Mangla, "Virtue out of Necessity?: Compliance, Commitment and the Improvement of Labor Conditions in Global Supply Chains," available at Princeton.edu.

2-8b Exit

When faced with the unacceptable, one option is to walk out the door quietly. You resign "to spend more time with your family," "to explore other opportunities," or "to accept an offer that is too good to refuse." This approach may be the safest for you because you are not ruffling any feathers or making any enemies. It is a small world, and you never know when someone you have offended will be in a position to do you harm. But a quiet exit leaves the bad guys in position to continue the unsavory behavior. For example, the CEO was sexually harassing Laura, but she left quietly for fear that if she reported him, he would harm her career. No one likes to hire a troublemaker. So the CEO proceeded to attack other women at the company until finally a senior man got wind of what was going on and confronted the chief. In short, the braver option is to exit loudly—reporting the wrong-doing on the way out the door.

2-8c Voice

As we saw in our discussion of conformity, wrong-doing often occurs because everyone just goes along to get along. One valiant soul with the courage to say, "This is wrong," can be a powerful force for the good. But confrontation may not be the only, or even the best, use of your voice. Learning to persuade, cajole, or provide better options are all important leadership skills. For example, Keith felt that the CEO of his company was about to make a bad decision, but he was unable to persuade the man to choose a different alternative. When Keith turned out to be correct, the CEO gave him no credit, saying, "You are equally responsible because your arguments weren't compelling enough." Keith thought the man had a point.

2-9 CORPORATE SOCIAL RESPONSIBILITY (CSR)

So far, we have largely been talking about a company's duty not to cause harm. But do companies have a **corporate social responsibility**—that is, an obligation to contribute positively to the world around it? Do businesses have an affirmative duty to do good? You remember Milton Friedman's view that a manager's obligation is to make the company as profitable as possible while also complying with the law. Harvard Professor Michael Porter has written that CSR often benefits a company. For example, improving economic and social conditions overseas can create new customers with money to spend. Educational programs may provide a better workforce. However, Porter observes:

> The acid test of good corporate philanthropy is whether the desired social change is so beneficial to the company that the organization would pursue the change even if no one ever knew about it.[22]

Thus, for example, Yoplait has periodically run a "Save Lids to Save Lives" campaign. For every Yoplait lid mailed in, the company makes a donation to the Susan G. Komen breast cancer charity. During these campaigns, Yoplait gains market share. Should companies be willing to improve the world even if their efforts *reduce* profitability?

◆ Ethics Case: The Beauty of a Well-Fed Child ◆

Cosmetic companies often use gift-with-purchase offers to promote their products. For example, with any $45 Estee Lauder purchase at Bloomingdale's, you can choose a free

Corporate social responsibility
An organization's obligation to contribute positively to the world around it.

---

[22]Michael E. Porter and Mark R. Kramer, "The Competitive Advantage of Corporate Philanthropy," *Harvard Business Review* (December 2002).

seven piece gift of creams and makeup valued at over $165, plus a special-edition Lily Pulitzer cosmetic bag.

But Clarins has put a new spin on these offers with what it calls "gift with purpose." Buy two Clarins items at Macy's and you will receive six trial-size products *and* the company will pay the United Nations World Food Program enough for 10 school meals.

Because so many cosmetic companies do gift-with-purchase offers, it is difficult for any one company to stand out from the crowd. That is Clarins' goal with this offer. The company hopes that cosmetic buyers, many of whom are women with children, will find this opportunity to feed children particularly compelling. Says the Macy's vice president for national media relations and cause marketing, "With no energy or lift on the customers' part, they get this really feel-good element with the shopping experience."[23]

QUESTIONS

1. If you were an executive at Clarins or Macy's, what would you want to know before approving this promotion?

2. How important is it to improve the image of these two companies? Would this promotion do so?

3. Would you approve this promotion if it were not profitable on its own account? How much of a subsidy would you be willing to grant?

Chapter Conclusion

Many times in your life, you will be tempted to do something that you know in your heart of hearts is wrong. Referring to your own Life Principles, being aware of potential traps, will help you to make the right decisions. But it is also important that you be able to afford to do the right thing. Having a reserve fund to cover six months' living expenses makes it easier for you to leave a job that does not agree with your personal ethics. Too many times, people make the wrong, and sometimes the illegal decision, for financial reasons.

Managers wonder what they can do to create an ethical environment in their companies. In the end, the surest way to infuse ethics throughout an organization is for top executives to behave ethically themselves. Few will bother to do the right thing unless they observe that their bosses value and support such behavior. Even employees who are ethical in their personal lives may find it difficult to uphold their standards at work if those around them behave differently. To ensure a more ethical world, managers must be an example for others, both within and outside their organizations.

EXAM REVIEW

1. **ETHICS**   The law dictates how a person *must* behave. Ethics governs how people *should* behave. Any decision that affects people or animals is an ethics decision. (p. 24)

2. **LIFE PRINCIPLES**   Life Principles are the rules by which you live your life. If you develop these Life Principles now, you will be better prepared when facing ethics dilemmas in the future. (pp. 25–26)

---

[23]Adam Andrew Newman, "A Cosmetic Freebie with a Cause," *New York Times*, April 7, 2013.

3. **THE ROLE OF BUSINESS IN SOCIETY**   An ongoing debate about whether managers should focus only on what is best for shareholders or whether they should consider the interests of other stakeholders as well. (pp. 26–27)

4. **WHY BE ETHICAL?**

   - Society as a whole benefits from ethical behavior.

   - People feel better when they behave ethically.

   - Unethical behavior can be very costly. (pp. 27–28)

5. **THEORIES OF ETHICS**

   - Utilitarian thinkers such as John Stuart Mill believe that the right decision maximizes overall happiness and minimizes overall pain.

   - Deontological thinkers such as Immanuel Kant believe that the ends do not justify the means. Rather, it is important to do the right thing, no matter the result.

   - With his categorical imperative, Kant argued that you should not do something unless you would be willing to have everyone else do it, too.

   - John Rawls asked us to consider what type of society we would establish if we did not know whether we would be one of life's winners or losers. He called this situation "the veil of ignorance."

   - Under the Front Page Test, you ask yourself what you would do if your actions were going to be reported publicly on or offline. (pp. 28–30)

6. **ETHICS TRAPS**

   - Money

   - Rationalization

   - Conformity

   - Following orders

   - Euphemisms

   - Lost in a crowd

   - Blind spots (pp. 31–34)

7. **TO AVOID ETHICS TRAPS:**

   - Do not trust your first instinct.

   - Remember your Life Principles. (pp. 35–36)

8. **KANTIAN EVASION**   A truthful statement that is nonetheless misleading. (p. 34)

9. **MANAGING AN UNETHICAL ENVIRONMENT**   When faced with unethical behavior, you have three choices:

   - Loyalty

   - Exit (either quiet or noisy)

   - Voice (pp. 42–43)

10. **CORPORATE SOCIAL RESPONSIBILITY**   An organization's obligation to contribute positively to the world around it. (p. 43)

MULTIPLE-CHOICE QUESTIONS

1. Milton Friedman was a strong believer in the _____ model. He _____ argue that a corporate leader's sole obligation is to make money for the company's owners.

   (a) shareholder; did

   (b) shareholder; did not

   (c) stakeholder; did

   (d) stakeholder; did not

2. Which of the following wrote the book *Utilitarianism* and believed that moral actions should "generate the greatest good for the greatest number"?

   (a) Milton Friedman

   (b) John Stuart Mill

   (c) Immanuel Kant

   (d) John Rawls

3. Which of the following believed that the dignity of human beings must be respected, and that the most ethical decisions are made out of a sense of obligation?

   (a) Milton Friedman

   (b) John Stuart Mill

   (c) Immanuel Kant

   (d) John Rawls

4. Kant believed that:

   (a) It is ethical to tell a lie if necessary to protect an innocent person from great harm.

   (b) It is ethical to tell a lie if the benefit of the lie outweighs the cost.

   (c) It is ethical to make a true, but misleading, statement.

   (d) It is wrong to tell an outright lie or to mislead.

5. The following statement is true:

   (a) Most people are honest most of the time.

   (b) Even people who do not believe in God are more likely to behave honestly after reading the Ten Commandments.

   (c) When confronted with wrong-doing, most people immediately recognize what is happening.

   (d) People make their best ethical decisions when in a hurry.

ESSAY QUESTIONS

1. The Senate recently released a report on wrongdoing at JP Morgan Chase. It found that bank executives lied to investors and the public. Also, traders, with the knowledge of top management, changed risk limits to facilitate more trading and then violated even these higher limits. Executives revalued the bank's investment portfolio to reduce apparent losses. JP Morgan's internal investigation failed to find this wrongdoing. Into what ethics traps did these JP Morgan employees fall? What options did the executives and traders have for dealing with this wrongdoing?

2. Located in Bath, Maine, Bath Iron Works builds high tech warships for the Navy. Winning Navy contracts is crucial to the company's success—it means jobs for the community and profits for the shareholders. Navy officials held a meeting at Bath's offices with its executives and those of a competitor to review the specs for an upcoming bid. Both companies desperately wanted to win the contract. After the meeting, a Bath worker realized that one of the Navy officials had left a folder on a chair labeled: "Business Sensitive." It contained information about the competitors' bid that would be a huge advantage to Bath. William Haggett, the Bath CEO, was notified about the file just as he was walking out the door to give a luncheon speech. What should he do? What pitfalls did he face? What result if he considered Mill, Kant, or the Front Page test?

3. A group of medical schools conducted a study on very premature babies—those born between 24 and 27 weeks of gestation (instead of the normal 40 weeks). These children face a high risk of blindness and death. The goal of the study was to determine which level of oxygen in a baby's incubator produced the best results. Before enrolling families in the study, the investigators did not tell them that being in the study could increase their child's risk of blindness or death. The study made some important discoveries: the level at which too much oxygen increased the risk of blindness and level at which too little increased the risk of death. What would Mill and Kant say about this decision *not* to tell the families?

4. Because Raina processes payroll at her company, she knows how much everyone earns, including the top executives. This information could make for some good gossip, but she has kept it all completely secret. She just found out, however, that her boss knew that it is against company policy for her to do payroll for C-level employees. Yesterday, the CEO went to her boss to confirm that he, the boss, was personally doing the processing for top management. Her boss lied to the CEO and said that he was. Then he begged Raina not to tell the truth if the CEO checked with her. Raina just got a message that the CEO wants to see her. What does she say if he asks about the payroll?

5. Each year, the sale of Girl Scout cookies is the major fund-raiser for local troops. But because the organization was criticized for promoting such unhealthy food, it introduced a new cookie, Mango Cremes with Nutrifusion. It promotes this cookie as a vitamin-laden, natural whole food. "A delicious way to get your vitamins." But these vitamins are a minuscule part of the cookie. The rest has more bad saturated fat than an Oreo. The Girl Scouts do much good for many girls. And to do this good, they need to raise money. What would Kant and Mill say? What about the Front Page test? What do you say?

6. When James Kilts became CEO of Gillette Co., the consumer products giant had been a mainstay of the Boston community for a hundred years. But the organization was going through hard times: its stock was trading at less than half its peak price, and

some of its established brands of razors were suffering under intense competitive pressure. In four short years, Kilts turned Gillette around—strengthening its core brands, cutting jobs, and paying off debt. With the company's stock up 61 percent, Kilts had added $20 billion in shareholder value.

Then Kilts suddenly sold Gillette to Procter & Gamble (P&G) for $57 billion. So short was Kilts's stay in Boston that he never moved his family from their home in Rye, New York. The deal was sweet for Gillette shareholders—the company's stock price went up 13 percent in one day. And tasty also for Kilts—his payoff was $153 million, including a $23.9 million reward from P&G for having made the deal and for a "change in control" clause in his employment contract that was worth $12.6 million. In addition, P&G agreed to pay him $8 million a year to serve as vice chairman after the merger. When he retired, his pension would be $1.2 million per year. Moreover, two of his top lieutenants were offered payments totaling $57 million.

Any downside to this deal? Four percent of the Gillette workforce—6,000 employees—were fired. If the payouts to the top three Gillette executives were divided among these 6,000, each unemployed worker would receive $35,000. The loss of this many employees (4,000 of whom lived in New England) had a ripple effect throughout the area's economy. Although Gillette shareholders certainly benefited in the short run from the sale, their profit would have been even greater without this $210 million payout to the executives. Moreover, about half the increase in Gillette revenues during the time that Kilts was running the show were attributable to currency fluctuations. A cheaper dollar increased revenue overseas. If the dollar had moved in the opposite direction, there might not have been any increase in revenue. Indeed, for the first two years after Kilts joined Gillette, the stock price declined. It was not until the dollar turned down that the stock price improved.

Do CEOs who receive sweeteners have too strong an incentive to sell their companies? Is it unseemly for them to be paid so much when many employees will lose their jobs?

DISCUSSION QUESTIONS

1. While waiting in line in a supermarket, you observe a woman trying to pay with food stamps. Under the law, food stamps cannot be used to pay for prepared items so the register would not accept the stamps in payment for a $6 container of chicken noodle soup from the deli counter. The woman explained that she was sick and did not have the energy to cook. She just wanted to go home and go to bed. In general, you agree that this law is reasonable—people on limited budgets should not be buying more expensive prepared food. But the woman is sick. Would it be ethical for you to pay for her chicken soup if she agreed to pay for $6 worth of your grocery items?

2. In Japan, automobile GPS systems come equipped with an option for converting them into televisions so that drivers can watch their favorite shows, yes, while driving. "We can't help but respond to our customers' needs," says a company spokesperson.[24] Although his company does not recommend the practice of watching while driving, he explained that it is the driver's responsibility to make this decision. Is it right to sell a product that could cause great harm to innocent bystanders? Where does the company's responsibility end and the consumer's begin? What would Mill and Kant say?

---

[24]Chester Dawson, "Drivers Use Navigation Systems to Tune In," *Wall Street Journal*, April 23, 2013.

3. Darby has been working for 14 months at Holden Associates, a large management consulting firm. She is earning $75,000 a year, which *sounds* good but does not go very far in New York City. It turns out that her peers at competing firms are typically paid 20 percent more and receive larger annual bonuses. Darby works about 60 hours a week—more if she is traveling. A number of times, she has had to reschedule her vacation or cancel personal plans to meet client deadlines. She hopes to go to business school in a year and has already begun the application process.

   Holden has a policy that permits any employee who works as late as 8:00 p.m. to eat dinner at company expense. The employee can also take a taxi home. Darby is in the habit of staying until 8:00 p.m. every night, whether or not her workload requires it. Then she orders enough food for dinner, with leftovers for lunch the next day. She has managed to cut her grocery bill to virtually nothing. Sometimes she invites her boyfriend to join her for dinner. As a student, he is always hungry and broke. Darby often uses the Holden taxi to take them back to his apartment, although the cab fare is twice as high as to her own place.

   Sometimes Darby stays late to work on her business school applications. Naturally, she uses Holden equipment to print out and photocopy the finished applications. Darby has also been known to return online purchases through the Holden mailroom on the company dime. Many employees do that, and the mailroom workers do not seem to mind.

   Is Darby doing anything wrong? What ethics traps is she facing? What would your Life Principle be in this situation?

4. Steve supervises a team of account managers. One night at a company outing, Lawrence, a visiting account manager, made some wildly inappropriate sexual remarks to Maddie, who is on Steve's team. When she told Steve, he was uncertain what to do, so he asked his boss. She was concerned that if Steve took the matter further and Lawrence was fired or even disciplined, her whole area would suffer. Lawrence was one of the best account managers in the region, and everyone was overworked as it was. She told Steve to get Maddie to drop the matter. Just tell her that these things happen, and Lawrence did not mean anything by it.

   What should Steve do? What ethics traps does he face? What would be your Life Principle in this situation?

5. David has just spoken with a member of his sales team who has not met her sales goals for some months. She has also missed 30 days of work in the past six months. It turns out that she is in the process of getting a divorce, and her teenage children are reacting very badly. Some of the missed days have been for court, others because the children have refused to go to school. If David's team does not meet its sales goals, no one will get a bonus, and his job may be at risk. What should he do?

6. Many people enjoy rap music at least in part because of its edgy, troublemaking vibe. The problem is that some of this music could cause real trouble, Thus, Ice-T's song "Cop Killer" generated significant controversy when it was released. Among other things, its lyrics celebrated the idea of slitting a policeman's throat. Rick Ross rapped about drugging and raping a woman. Time Warner Inc. did not withdraw Ice T's song, but Reebok fired Ross over his lyrics. One difference: Time Warner was struggling with a $15 billion debt and a depressed stock price. Reebok at first refused to take action but then singing group UltraViolet began circulating an online petition against the song and staged a protest at the main Reebok store in New York.

   What obligation do media companies have to their audience? What factors matter when making a decision about content?

7. You are negotiating a new labor contract with union officials. The contract covers a plant that has experienced operating losses over the past several years. You want to negotiate concessions from labor to reduce the losses. However, labor is refusing any compromises. You could tell them that, without concessions, the plant will be closed, although that is not true.

   Is bluffing ethical? Under what circumstances? What would Kant and Mill say? What result under the Front Page test? What is your Life Principle?

8. Craig Newmark and Jim Buckmaster founded craigslist, the most popular website in the country for classified ads. Rather than maximizing its profits, craigslist instead focused on developing a community among its users. It was a place to find an apartment, a pet, a job, a couch, a date, a babysitter and, it turned out, a prostitute. Most of the ads on craigslist were free, but blatant ads for sex were not. Much of the company's revenue was from these illegal services. Many of the prostitutes available on craigslist were not independent

entrepreneurs; they were women and girls bought and sold against their will. To fight sex trafficking, craigslist required credit cards and phone numbers, and it reported any suspicious ads. Law enforcement officials pressured craigslist to close the sex section of its website. But some people argued that blocking these ads was a violation of free speech and would just drive this business more underground where law enforcement officials were less likely to be able to find it. Others said that banning these ads made the business model of selling children for sex less profitable. Does it seem that trafficking women and children was in keeping with the founders' personal ethics code? What were their options? Could they have had any real impact on this thriving industry? What pitfalls did they face?

9. You are a president of a small, highly rated, liberal college in California. Many of the dining hall workers are Latino. Some of these workers are trying to organize a union, which would dramatically increase the college's costs at a time of budget pressure. One of your vice presidents suggests hiring a law firm to review the college's employment records to make sure all employees are in the United States legally. What would you do?

10. Many socially responsible funds are now available to investors who want to make ethical choices. For example, the Appleseed Fund avoids tobacco products, alcoholic beverages, gambling, weapons systems, or pornography while the TIAA-CREF Social Choice Equity Premier Fund invests in companies that are "strong stewards of the environment," devoted to serving local communities and committed to high labor standards. Are socially responsible funds attractive to you? Does it matter if they are less profitable than other alternatives? How much less profitable? Do you now, or will you in the future, use them in saving for your own retirement?

CHAPTER 3

DISPUTE RESOLUTION

nuttakit/Shutterstock.com; © Stas Volik/Shutterstock.com

Tony Caruso had not returned for dinner, and his wife, Karen, was nervous. She put on some sandals and hurried across the dunes, a half mile to the ocean shore. She soon came upon Tony's dog, Blue, tied to an old picket fence. Tony's shoes and clothing were piled neatly nearby. Karen and friends searched frantically throughout the evening.

A little past midnight, Tony's body washed ashore, his lungs filled with water. A local doctor concluded he had accidentally drowned.

Karen and her friends were not the only ones who were distraught. Tony had been partners with Beth Smiles in an environmental consulting business, Enviro-Vision. They were good friends, and Beth was emotionally devastated. When she was able to focus on business issues, Beth filed an insurance claim with the Coastal Insurance Group. Beth hated to think about Tony's death in financial terms, but she was relieved that the struggling business would receive $2 million on the life insurance policy.

> A little past midnight, Tony's body washed ashore, his lungs filled with water.

Several months after filing the claim, Beth received this reply from Coastal: "Under the policy issued to Enviro-Vision, we are conditionally liable in the amount of $1 million in the event of Mr. Caruso's death. If his death is accidental, we are conditionally liable to pay double indemnity of $2 million. But pursuant to section H(5), death by suicide is not covered.

"After a thorough investigation, we have concluded that Anthony Caruso's death was an act of suicide, as defined in section B(11) of the policy. Your claim is denied in its entirety." Beth was furious. She was convinced Tony was incapable of suicide. And her company could not afford the $2 million loss. She decided to consult her lawyer, Chris Pruitt.

3-1 THREE FUNDAMENTAL AREAS OF LAW

This case is a fictionalized version of several real cases based on double indemnity insurance policies. In this chapter, we follow Beth's dispute with Coastal from initial interview through appeal, using it to examine three fundamental areas of law: the structure of our court systems, civil lawsuits, and alternative dispute resolution.

When Beth Smiles meets with her lawyer, Chris Pruitt brings a second attorney from his firm, Janet Booker, who is an experienced **litigator;** that is, a lawyer who handles court cases. If they file a lawsuit, Janet will be in charge, so Chris wants her there for the first meeting. Janet probes about Tony's home life, the status of the business, his personal finances, everything. Beth becomes upset that Janet doesn't seem sympathetic, but Chris explains that Janet is doing her job: she needs all the information, good and bad.

3-1a Litigation versus Alternative Dispute Resolution

Janet starts thinking about the two methods of dispute resolution: litigation and alternative dispute resolution. **Litigation** refers to lawsuits, the process of filing claims in court, and ultimately going to trial. **Alternative dispute resolution** is any other formal or informal process used to settle disputes without resorting to a trial. It is increasingly popular with corporations and individuals alike because it is generally cheaper and faster than litigation, and we will focus on this topic in the last part of this chapter.

3-2 COURT SYSTEMS

The United States has over 50 *systems* of courts. One nationwide system of *federal* courts serves the entire country. In addition, each individual state—such as California, Florida, and Texas—has its court system. The state and federal courts are in different buildings, have different judges, and hear different kinds of cases. Each has special powers and certain limitations.

3-2a State Courts

The typical state court system forms a pyramid, as Exhibit 3.1 shows. Some states have minor variations on the exhibit. For example, Texas has two top courts: a Supreme Court for civil cases and a Court of Criminal Appeals for criminal cases.

TRIAL COURTS

Almost all cases start in trial courts, which are endlessly portrayed on television and in film. There is one judge, and there will often (but not always) be a jury. This is the only court to hear testimony from witnesses and receive evidence. **Trial courts** determine the facts of a particular dispute and apply to those facts the law given by statutes or earlier court decisions.

In the Enviro-Vision dispute, the trial court will decide all important facts that are in dispute. How did Tony Caruso die? Did he drown? Assuming he drowned, was his death accidental or suicide? Once the jury has decided the facts, it will apply the law to those facts. If Tony Caruso died accidentally, contract law provides that Beth Smiles is entitled to double indemnity benefits. If the jury decides he killed himself, Beth gets nothing.

Facts are critical. That may sound obvious, but in a course devoted to legal principles, it is easy to lose track of the key role that factual determinations play in the resolution of any dispute. In the Enviro-Vision case, we will see that one bit of factual evidence goes undetected, with costly consequences.

Jurisdiction refers to a court's power to hear a case. In state or federal court, a plaintiff may start a lawsuit only in a court that has jurisdiction over that kind of case. Some courts have very limited jurisdiction, while others have the power to hear almost any case.

Litigator
A lawyer who handles court cases.

Litigation
The process of filing claims in court and ultimately going to trial.

Alternative dispute resolution
Any other formal or informal process used to settle disputes without resorting to a trial.

Trial courts
Determine the facts of a particular dispute and apply to those facts the law given by earlier appellate court decisions.

Jurisdiction
A court's power to hear a case.

State Supreme Court

Appellate Courts

Appeal Courts

General Civil Division

General Criminal Division

Small Claims Division

Juvenile Division

Land Division

Municipal Division

Probate Division

Domestic Relations Division

■ **Trial Courts of General Jurisdiction**   ■ **Trial Courts of Limited Jurisdiction**

EXHIBIT 3.1   A trial court determines facts, while an appeals court ensures that the lower court correctly applied the law to those facts.

SUBJECT MATTER JURISDICTION

Subject matter jurisdiction means that a court has the authority to hear a particular type of case.

Trial Courts of Limited Jurisdiction   These courts may hear only certain types of cases. Small claims court has jurisdiction only over civil lawsuits involving a maximum of, say, $5,000 (the amount varies from state to state). A juvenile court hears only cases involving minors. Probate court is devoted to settling the estates of deceased persons, though in some states it will hear certain other cases as well.

> **Subject matter jurisdiction**
> A court has the authority to hear a particular type of case.

Trial Courts of General Jurisdiction   Trial courts of general jurisdiction, however, can hear a very broad range of cases. The most important court, for our purposes, is the general civil division. This court may hear virtually any civil lawsuit. In one day it might hear a $450 million shareholders' derivative lawsuit, an employment issue involving freedom of religion, and a foreclosure on a mortgage. Most of the cases we study start in this court.[1] If Enviro-Vision's case against Coastal goes to trial in a state court, it will begin in the trial court of general jurisdiction.

PERSONAL JURISDICTION

Personal jurisdiction

The legal authority to require the defendant to stand trial, pay judgments, and the like.

In addition to subject matter jurisdiction, courts must also have **personal jurisdiction** over the defendant. Personal jurisdiction is the legal authority to require the defendant to stand trial, pay judgments, and the like. When plaintiffs file lawsuits, defendants sometimes make *a special appearance* to challenge a court's personal jurisdiction. If the court agrees with the defendant's argument, the lawsuit will be dismissed.

Personal jurisdiction generally exists, if one or more of the following occur:

1. For individuals, the defendant is a resident of the state in which a lawsuit is filed. For companies, the defendant is doing business in that state.

2. The defendant takes a formal step to defend a lawsuit. Most papers filed with a court count as formal steps, but special appearances do not.

Summons

The court's written notice that a lawsuit has been filed against the defendant.

3. A **summons** is *served* on a defendant. A summons is the court's written notice that a lawsuit has been filed against the defendant. The summons must be delivered to the defendant when she is physically within the state in which the lawsuit is filed.

For example, Texarkana straddles the Texas/Arkansas border. If a lawsuit is filed in a Texas court, a defendant who lives in Arkansas can be served if, when walking down the street in Texarkana, she steps across the state line into Texas. Corporations are required to hire a registered agent in any state in which they do business. If a registered agent receives a summons, then the corporation is served.

Long-arm statute

A statute that gives a court jurisdiction over someone who commits a tort, signs a contract, or conducts "regular business activities" in the state.

4. A **long-arm statute** applies. If all else fails—the defendant does not reside in the state, does not defend the lawsuit, and has not been served with a summons while in the state—a court still can obtain jurisdiction under long-arm statutes. These statutes typically claim jurisdiction over someone who commits a tort, signs a contract, or conducts "regular business activities" in the state.

As a general rule, courts tend to apply long-arm statutes aggressively, hauling defendants into their courtrooms. However, the due process guarantees in the United States Constitution require fundamental fairness in the application of long-arm statutes. Therefore, courts can claim personal jurisdiction only if a defendant has had *minimum contacts* with a state. In other words, it is unfair to require a defendant to stand trial in another state if he has had no meaningful interaction with that state.

In the following Landmark Case, the Supreme Court explains its views on this important constitutional issue.

---

[1]Note that the actual name of the court will vary from state to state. In many states, it is called *superior court* because it has power superior to the courts of limited jurisdiction. In New York, it is called *supreme court* (anything to confuse the layperson); in some states, it is called *court of common pleas;* in Oregon and other states, it is a *circuit court.* They are all civil trial courts of general jurisdiction. Within this branch, some states are beginning to establish specialized business courts to hear complex commercial disputes. At least one state has created a cybercourt for high-tech cases. Lawyers will argue their cases by teleconference and present evidence via streaming video.

Landmark Case

INTERNATIONAL SHOE CO. v. STATE OF WASHINGTON
326 U.S. 310
Supreme Court of the United States, 1945

CASE SUMMARY

Facts: Although International Shoe manufactured footwear only in St. Louis, Missouri, it sold its products nationwide. It did not have offices or warehouses in the state of Washington, but it did send about a dozen salespeople there. The salespeople rented space in hotels and businesses, displayed sample products, and took orders. They were not authorized to collect payment from customers.

When the State of Washington sought contributions to the state's unemployment fund, International Shoe refused to pay. Washington sued. The company argued that it was not engaged in business in the state and, therefore, that Washington courts had no jurisdiction over it.

The Supreme Court of Washington ruled that International Shoe did have sufficient contacts with the state to justify a lawsuit there. International Shoe appealed to the United States Supreme Court.

operated continuously in Washington for many years. Their presence has been more than occasional or casual. And the agents' activities have generated a significant number of sales for the company. Washington's collection action is directly related to commercially valuable activities that took place within the state's borders.

Due Process merely requires reasonable fairness. International Shoe has benefitted greatly from activities in Washington, and it faces no injustice if this suit proceeds. The minimum contacts doctrine is satisfied.

Affirmed.

Issue: *Did International Shoe have sufficient minimum contacts in the state of Washington to permit jurisdiction there?*

Decision: Yes, the company had minimum contacts with the state.

Reasoning: Agents for International Shoe have

APPELLATE COURTS

Appellate courts are entirely different from trial courts. Three or more judges hear the case. There are no juries, ever. These courts do not hear witnesses or take new evidence. They hear appeals of cases already tried below. **Appeals courts** generally accept the facts given to them by trial courts and review the trial record to see if the court made errors of law.

Higher courts generally defer to lower courts on factual findings. Juries and trial court judges see all evidence as it is presented, and they are in the best position to evaluate it. An appeals court will accept a factual finding unless there was *no evidence at all* to support it. If the jury decides that Tony Caruso committed suicide, the appeals court will normally accept that fact, even if the appeals judges consider the jury's conclusion dubious. On the other hand, if a jury concluded that Tony had been murdered, an appeals court would overturn that finding if neither side had introduced any evidence of murder during the trial.

An appeals court reviews the trial record to make sure that the lower court correctly applied the law to the facts. If the trial court made an **error of law**, the appeals court may require a new trial. Suppose the jury concludes that Tony Caruso committed suicide but votes to award Enviro-Vision $1 million because it feels sorry for Beth Smiles. That is an error of law: If Tony committed suicide, Beth is entitled to nothing. An appellate court will reverse the decision. Or suppose that the trial judge permitted a friend of Tony's to state that he was certain Tony would never commit suicide.

Appeals courts
Generally accept the facts given to them by trial courts and review the trial record to see if the court made errors of law.

Error of law
Because of this, the appeals court may require a new trial.

Normally, such opinions are not permissible at trial, and it was a legal error for the judge to allow the jury to hear it.

Court of Appeals   The party that loses at the trial court may appeal to the intermediate court of appeals. The party filing the appeal is the **appellant**. The party opposing the appeal (because it won at trial) is the **appellee**.

This court allows both sides to submit written arguments on the case, called **briefs**. Each side then appears for oral argument, usually before a panel of three judges. The appellant's lawyer has about 15 minutes to convince the judges that the trial court made serious errors of law, and that the decision should be **reversed**; that is, nullified. The appellee's lawyer has the same time to persuade the court that the trial court acted correctly, and that the result should be **affirmed;** that is, permitted to stand.

State Supreme Court   This is the highest court in the state, and it accepts some appeals from the court of appeals. In most states, there is no absolute right to appeal to the Supreme Court. If the high court regards a legal issue as important, it accepts the case. It then takes briefs and hears oral argument just as the appeals court did. If it considers the matter unimportant or the law well-established, it refuses to hear the case, meaning that the court of appeals' ruling is the final word on the case.[2]

In most states, seven judges, often called *justices*, sit on the Supreme Court. They have the final word on state law.

3-2b Federal Courts

As discussed in Chapter 1, federal courts are established by the United States Constitution, which limits what kinds of cases can be brought in any federal court. See Exhibit 3.2. For our purposes, two kinds of civil lawsuits are permitted in federal court: federal question cases and diversity cases.

FEDERAL QUESTION CASES

A claim based on the United States Constitution, a federal statute, or a federal treaty is called a **federal question** case.[3] Federal courts have jurisdiction over these cases. If the Environmental Protection Agency (a part of the federal government) orders Logging Company not to cut in a particular forest, and Logging Company claims that the agency has wrongly deprived it of its property, that suit is based on a federal statute and is thus a federal question. If Little Retailer sues Mega Retailer, claiming that Mega has established a monopoly, that claim is also based on a statute—the Sherman Antitrust Act—and creates federal question jurisdiction. Enviro-Vision's potential suit merely concerns an insurance contract. The federal district court has no federal question jurisdiction over the case.

DIVERSITY CASES

Even if no federal law is at issue, federal courts have **diversity jurisdiction** when (1) the plaintiff and defendant are citizens of different states *and* (2) the amount in dispute exceeds $75,000. The theory behind diversity jurisdiction is that courts of one state might be biased against citizens of another state. To ensure fairness, the parties have the option to use a federal court as a neutral playing field.

---

[2]In some states with smaller populations, there is no intermediate appeals court. All appeals from trial courts go directly to the state supreme court.

[3]28 U.S.C. §1331 governs federal question jurisdiction, and 28 U.S.C. §1332 covers diversity jurisdiction.

Appellant
The party filing the appeal.

Appellee
The party opposing the appeal.

Briefs
Written arguments on the case.

Reversed
Nullified.

Affirmed
Permitted to stand.

Federal question
A case in which the claim is based on the United States Constitution, a federal statute, or a federal treaty.

Diversity jurisdiction
(1) When the plaintiff and defendant are citizens of different states and (2) When the amount in dispute exceeds $75,000.

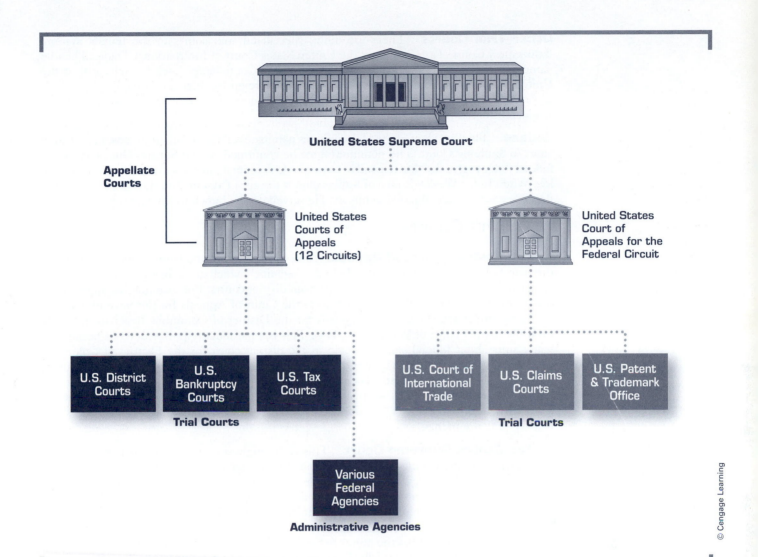

United States Supreme Court

Appellate Courts

United States Courts of Appeals (12 Circuits)

United States Court of Appeals for the Federal Circuit

U.S. District Courts	U.S. Bankruptcy Courts	U.S. Tax Courts

Trial Courts

U.S. Court of International Trade	U.S. Claims Courts	U.S. Patent & Trademark Office

Trial Courts

Various Federal Agencies

Administrative Agencies

© Cengage Learning

EXHIBIT 3.2   The Fedral Court System

Enviro-Vision is located in Oregon and Coastal Insurance is incorporated in Georgia.[4] They are citizens of different states and the amount in dispute far exceeds $75,000. Janet could file this case in a United States District Court based on diversity jurisdiction.

TRIAL COURTS

United States District Court   This is the primary trial court in the federal system. The nation is divided into about 94 districts, and each has a district court. States with smaller populations have one district. States with larger populations have several; Florida is divided geographically into three districts.

---

[4]For diversity purposes, a corporation is a citizen of the state in which it is incorporated and the state in which it has its principal place of business.

Other Trial Courts   There are other, specialized trial courts in the federal system. Bankruptcy Court, Tax Court, and the United States Court of International Trade all handle name-appropriate cases. The United States Claims Court hears cases brought against the United States, typically on contract disputes. The Foreign Intelligence Surveillance Court is a very specialized, secret court, which oversees requests for surveillance warrants against suspected foreign agents.

Judges   The President of the United States nominates all federal court judges, from district court to Supreme Court. The nominees must be confirmed by the Senate. Once confirmed, federal judges serve for "life in good behavior." Many federal judges literally stay on the job for life. When Judge Wesley Brown of Kansas died at the age of 104 in 2012, he held the record as the oldest active federal judge in history. He served on the bench for five decades.

APPELLATE COURTS

United States Courts of Appeals   These are the intermediate courts of appeals. As the map below shows, they are divided into "circuits," which are geographical areas. There are 11 numbered circuits, hearing appeals from district courts. For example, an appeal from the Northern District of Illinois would go to the Court of Appeals for the Seventh Circuit.

A twelfth court, the Court of Appeals for the District of Columbia, hears appeals only from the district court of Washington, D.C. This is a particularly powerful court because so many suits about federal statutes begin in the district court for the District of Columbia. Also in Washington is the Thirteenth Court of Appeals, known as the Federal Circuit. It hears appeals from specialized trial courts, as shown in Exhibit 3.2.

Within one circuit there are many circuit judges, up to about 50 judges in the largest circuit, the Ninth. When a case is appealed, three judges hear the appeal, taking briefs and hearing oral arguments.

United States Supreme Court   This is the highest court in the country. There are nine justices on the Court. One justice is the chief justice and the other eight are associate justices. When they decide a case, each justice casts an equal vote. The chief justice's special power comes from his authority to assign opinions to a given justice. The justice assigned to write an opinion has an opportunity to control the precise language and thus to influence the voting by other justices.

The Supreme Court has the power to hear appeals in any federal case, and in certain cases that began in state courts. Generally, it is up to the Court whether or not it will accept a case. A party that wants the Supreme Court to review a lower court ruling must file a petition for a **writ of *certiorari***, asking the Court to hear the case. Four of the nine justices must vote in favor of hearing a case before a writ will be granted. The Court receives several thousand requests every year but usually accepts fewer than 100. Most cases accepted involve either an important issue of constitutional law or an interpretation of a major federal statute.

Writ of *certiorari*
A petition asking the Supreme Court to hear a case.

EXAM Strategy

Question: Mark has sued his neighbor, Janelle, based on the state common law of negligence. He is testifying in court, explaining how Janelle backed a rented truck out of her driveway and slammed into his Lamborghini, causing $82,000 in damages. Where would this take place?

(a) State appeals court

(b) United States Court of Appeals

(c) State trial court

(d) Federal District Court

(e) Either state trial court or Federal District Court

Strategy: The question asks about trial and appellate courts, and also about state versus federal courts. One issue at a time, please. What are the different functions of trial and appellate courts? *Trial* courts use witnesses, and often juries, to resolve factual disputes. *Appellate* courts never hear witnesses and never have juries. Applying that distinction to these facts tells us whether we are in a trial or appeals court.

Next Issue: *State* trial courts may hear lawsuits on virtually any issue. *Federal District Courts* may only hear two kinds of cases: federal question (those involving a statute or constitutional provision); or diversity (where the parties are from different states *and* the amount at issue is $75,000 or higher). Apply what we know to the facts here.

Result: We are in a trial court because Mark is testifying. Could we be in Federal District Court? No. The suit is based on state common law. This is not a diversity case because the parties live in the same state. We are in a state trial court.

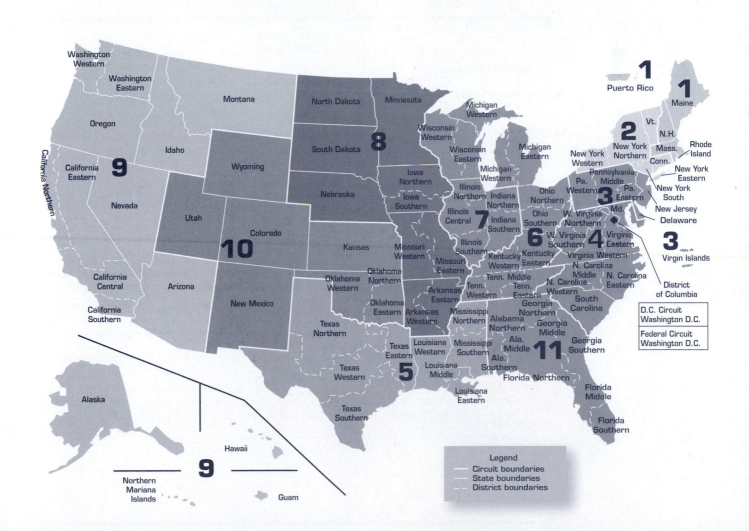

3-3 LITIGATION

Janet Booker decides to file the Enviro-Vision suit in the Oregon trial court. She thinks that a state court judge may take the issue more seriously than a federal district court judge.

3-3a Pleadings

Pleadings

The documents that begin a lawsuit, consisting of the complaint, the answer, and sometimes a reply.

Complaint

A short, plain statement of the facts alleged and the legal claims made.

The documents that begin a lawsuit are called the **pleadings**. These consist of the complaint, the answer, and sometimes a reply.

COMPLAINT

The plaintiff files in court a **complaint**, which is a short, plain statement of the facts she is alleging and the legal claims she is making. The purpose of the complaint is to inform the defendant of the general nature of the claims and the need to come into court and protect his interests.

Janet Booker files the complaint, as shown below. Since Enviro-Vision is a partnership, she files the suit on behalf of Beth personally.

STATE OF OREGON
CIRCUIT COURT

Multnomah County
_____

Elizabeth Smiles,
Plaintiff

v.

Coastal Insurance Company, Inc.,
Defendant

_____

Civil Action No. _____

JURY TRIAL DEMANDED

COMPLAINT

Plaintiff Elizabeth Smiles states that:

1. She is a citizen of Multnomah County, Oregon.
2. Defendant Coastal Insurance Company, Inc., is incorporated under the laws of Georgia and has as its usual place of business 148 Thrift Street, Savannah, Georgia.
3. On or about July 5, 2012, plaintiff Smiles ("Smiles"), Defendant Coastal Insurance Co, Inc. ("Coastal") and Anthony Caruso entered into an insurance contract ("the contract"), a copy of which is annexed hereto as Exhibit "A." This contract was signed by all parties or their authorized agents, in Multnomah County, Oregon.
4. The contract obligates Coastal to pay to Smiles the sum of two million dollars ($2 million) if Anthony Caruso should die accidentally.
5. On or about September 20, 2012, Anthony Caruso accidentally drowned and died while swimming.
6. Coastal has refused to pay any sum pursuant to the contract.
7. Coastal has knowingly, willingly and unreasonably refused to honor its obligations under the contract.

WHEREFORE, plaintiff Elizabeth Smiles demands judgment against defendant Coastal for all monies due under the contract; demands triple damages for Coastal's knowing, willing, and unreasonable refusal to honor its obligations; and demands all costs and attorney's fees, with interest.
ELIZABETH SMILES,
By her attorney,
[Signed]
Janet Booker
Pruitt, Booker & Bother
983 Joy Avenue
Portland, OR
October 18, 2012

SERVICE

When she files the complaint in court, Janet gets a summons, which is a paper ordering the defendant to answer the complaint within 20 days. A sheriff or constable then *serves* the two papers by delivering them to the defendant. Coastal's headquarters are in Georgia, so the state of Oregon has required Coastal to specify someone as its agent for receipt of service in Oregon.

ANSWER

Once the complaint and summons are served, Coastal has 20 days in which to file an answer. Coastal's answer, shown below, is a brief reply to each of the allegations in the complaint. The answer tells the court and the plaintiff exactly what issues are in dispute. Since Coastal admits that the parties entered into the contract that Beth claims they did, there is no need for her to prove that in court. The court can focus its attention on the disputed issue: whether Tony Caruso died accidentally.

STATE OF OREGON
CIRCUIT COURT

Multnomah County   Civil Action No. 09-5626

Elizabeth Smiles,
Plaintiff
v.
Coastal Insurance Company, Inc.,
Defendant

ANSWER

Defendant Coastal Insurance Company, Inc., answers the complaint as follows:

1. Admit.
2. Admit.
3. Admit.
4. Admit.
5. Deny.
6. Admit.
7. Deny.

COASTAL INSURANCE COMPANY, INC.,
By its attorney,
[Signed]
Richard B. Stewart
Kiley, Robbins, Stewart & Glote
333 Victory Boulevard
Portland, OR
October 30, 2012

If the defendant fails to answer in time, the plaintiff will ask for a **default judgment**. In granting a default judgment, the judge accepts every allegation in the complaint as true and renders a decision that the plaintiff wins without a trial.

Recently, two men sued PepsiCo, claiming that the company stole the idea for Aquafina water from them. They argued that they should receive a portion of the profits for every bottle of Aquafina ever sold.

PepsiCo failed to file a timely answer, and the judge entered a default judgment in the amount of $1.26 billion. On appeal, the default judgment was overturned and PepsiCo was able to escape paying the massive sum, but other defendants are sometimes not so lucky.

It is important to respond to courts on time.

Default judgment

A decision that the plaintiff wins without trial because the defendant failed to answer in time.

COUNTER-CLAIM

Counter-claim
A second lawsuit by the defendant against the plaintiff.

Sometimes a defendant does more than merely answer a complaint and files a **counter-claim**, meaning a second lawsuit by the defendant against the plaintiff. Suppose that after her complaint was filed in court, Beth had written a letter to the newspaper, calling Coastal a bunch of "thieves and scoundrels who spend their days mired in fraud and larceny." Coastal would not have found that amusing. The company's answer would have included a counterclaim against Beth for libel, claiming that she falsely accused the insurer of serious criminal acts. Coastal would have demanded money damages.

Reply
An answer to a counter-claim.

If Coastal counter-claimed, Beth would have to file a **reply**, which is simply an answer to a counter-claim. Beth's reply would be similar to Coastal's answer, admitting or denying the various allegations.

CLASS ACTIONS

Class action
An individual represents the entire group of plaintiffs, including those who are unaware of the lawsuit or even unaware they were harmed.

Suppose Janet uncovers evidence that Coastal denies 80 percent of all life insurance claims, calling them suicide. She could ask the court to permit a **class action**. If the court granted her request, she would represent the entire group of plaintiffs, including those who are unaware of the lawsuit or even unaware they were harmed. Class actions can give the plaintiffs much greater leverage, since the defendant's potential liability is vastly increased. In the back of her mind, Janet has thoughts of a class action, *if* she can uncover evidence that Coastal has used a claim of suicide to deny coverage to a large number of claimants.

Notice how potent a class action can be. From his small town in Maine, Ernie decides to get rich quickly. On the Internet, he advertises "Energy Breakthrough! Cut your heating costs 15 percent for only $25." In response, 100,000 people send him their money, and they receive a photocopied graph, illustrating that if you wear two sweaters instead of one, you will feel 15 percent warmer. Ernie has deceitfully earned $2,500,000 in pure profit. What can the angry homeowners do? Under the laws of fraud and consumer protection, they have a legitimate claim to their $25, and perhaps even to treble damages ($75). But few will sue, because the time and effort required would be greater than the money recovered.

Economists analyze such legal issues in terms of *efficiency*. The laws against Ernie's fraud are clear and well-intended, but they will not help in this case because it is too expensive for 100,000 people to litigate such a small claim. The effort would be hugely *inefficient*, both for the homeowners and for society generally. The economic reality may permit Ernie to evade the law's grasp.

That is one reason we have class actions. A dozen or so "heating plan" buyers can all hire the same lawyer. This attorney will file court papers in Maine on behalf of *everyone*, nationwide, who has been swindled by Ernie—including the 99,988 people who have yet to be notified that they are part of the case. Now the con artist, instead of facing a few harmless suits for $25, must respond to a multimillion-dollar claim being handled by an experienced lawyer. Treble damages become menacing: three times $25 times 100,000 is no joke, even to a cynic like Ernie. He may also be forced to pay for the plaintiffs' attorney, as well as all costs of notifying class members and disbursing money to them. With one lawyer representing an entire class, the legal system has become fiercely efficient.

Congress recently passed a statute designed to force large, multi-state class actions out of state courts, into federal. Proponents of the new law complained that state courts often gave excessive verdicts, even for frivolous lawsuits. They said the cases hurt businesses while enriching lawyers. Opponents argued that the new law was designed to shield large corporations from paying for the harm they caused by sending the cases into a federal system that is often hostile to such suits.

JUDGMENT ON THE PLEADINGS

A party can ask the court for a judgment based simply on the pleadings themselves, by filing a motion to dismiss. A **motion** is a formal request to the court that the court take some step or issue some order. During a lawsuit, the parties file many motions. A **motion to dismiss** is a request that the court terminate a case without permitting it to go further. Suppose that a state law requires claims on life insurance contracts to be filed within three years, and Beth files her claim four years after Tony's death. Coastal would move to dismiss based on this late filing. The court might well agree, and Beth would never get into court.

DISCOVERY

Few cases are dismissed on the pleadings. Most proceed quickly to the next step. **Discovery** is the critical, pre-trial opportunity for both parties to learn the strengths and weaknesses of the opponent's case.

   The theory behind civil litigation is that the best outcome is a negotiated settlement and that parties will move toward agreement if they understand the opponent's case. That is likeliest to occur if both sides have an opportunity to examine the evidence the other side will bring to trial. Further, if a case does go all the way to trial, efficient and fair litigation cannot take place in a courtroom filled with surprises. On television dramas, witnesses say astonishing things that amaze the courtroom (and keep viewers hooked through the next commercial). In real trials, the lawyers know in advance the answers to practically all questions asked because discovery has allowed them to see the opponent's documents and question its witnesses. The following are the most important forms of discovery.

Interrogatories   These are written questions that the opposing party must answer, in writing, under oath.

Depositions   These provide a chance for one party's lawyer to question the other party, or a potential witness, under oath. The person being questioned is the **deponent**. Lawyers for both parties are present. During depositions, and in trial, good lawyers choose words carefully and ask questions calculated to advance their cause. A fine line separates ethical, probing questions from those that are tricky, and a similar line divides answers that are merely unhelpful from perjury.

Production of Documents and Things   Each side may ask the other side to produce relevant documents for inspection and copying; to produce physical objects, such as part of a car alleged to be defective; and for permission to enter on land to make an inspection, for example, at the scene of an accident.

Physical and Mental Examination   A party may ask the court to order an examination of the other party, if his physical or mental condition is relevant, for example, in a case of medical malpractice.

   Janet Booker begins her discovery with interrogatories. Her goal is to learn Coastal's basic position and factual evidence and then follow up with more detailed questioning during depositions. Her interrogatories ask for every fact Coastal relied on in denying the claim. She asks for the names of all witnesses, the identity of all documents, including electronic records, the description of all things or objects that they considered. She requests the names of all corporate officers who played any role in the decision and of any expert witnesses Coastal plans to call. Interrogatory No. 18 demands extensive information on all *other* claims in the past three years that Coastal has denied based on alleged suicide. Janet is looking for evidence that would support a class action.

   Beth remarks on how thorough the interrogatories are. "This will tell us what their case is." Janet frowns and looks less optimistic: she has done this before.

Motion
A formal request to the court that the court take some step or issue some order.

Motion to dismiss
A request that the court terminate a case without permitting it to go further.

Discovery
The pre-trial opportunity for both parties to learn the strengths and weaknesses of the opponent's case.

Deponent
The person being questioned in a deposition.

Coastal has 30 days to answer Janet's interrogatories. Before it responds, Coastal mails to Janet a notice of deposition, stating its intention to depose Beth Smiles. Beth and Janet will go to the office of Coastal's lawyer, and Beth will answer questions under oath. But at the same time Coastal sends this notice, it sends *25 other notices of deposition*. The company will depose Karen Caruso as soon as Beth's deposition is over. Coastal also plans to depose all seven employees of Enviro-Vision; three neighbors who lived near Tony and Karen's beach house; two policemen who participated in the search; the doctor and two nurses involved in the case; Tony's physician; Jerry Johnson, Tony's tennis partner; Craig Bergson, a college roommate; a couple who had dinner with Tony and Karen a week before his death; and several other people.

Beth is appalled. Janet explains that some of these people might have relevant information. But there may be another reason that Coastal is doing this: the company wants to make this litigation hurt. Janet will have to attend every one of these depositions. Costs will skyrocket.

Motion for a protective order
Request that the court limit discovery.

Janet files a **motion for a protective order**. This is a request that the court limit Coastal's discovery by decreasing the number of depositions. Janet also calls Coastal's lawyer, Rich Stewart, and suggests that they discuss what depositions are really necessary. Rich insists that all of the depositions are important. This is a $2 million case, and Coastal is entitled to protect itself. As both lawyers know, **the parties are entitled to discover anything that could reasonably lead to valid evidence.**

> **But there may be another reason that Coastal is doing this: the company wants to make this litigation hurt.**

Before Beth's deposition date arrives, Rich sends Coastal's answers to Enviro-Vision's interrogatories. The answers contain no useful information whatsoever. For example, Interrogatory No. 10 asked, "If you claim that Anthony Caruso committed suicide, describe every fact upon which you rely in reaching that conclusion." Coastal's answer simply says, "His state of mind, his poor business affairs, and the circumstances of his death all indicate suicide."

Janet calls Rich and complains that the interrogatory answers are a bad joke. Rich disagrees, saying that it is the best information they have so early in the case. After they debate it for 20 minutes, Rich offers to settle the case for $100,000. Janet refuses and makes no counteroffer.

Janet files a **motion to compel answers to interrogatories,** in other words, a formal request that the court order

Memorandum
A document detailing the arguments in support of a motion.

Coastal to supply more complete answers. Janet submits a **memorandum** with the motion, which is a supporting argument. Although it is only a few pages long, the memorandum takes several hours of online research and writing to prepare—more costs. Janet also informs Rich Stewart that Beth will not appear for the deposition, since Coastal's interrogatory answers are inadequate.

Rich now files *his* motion to compel, asking the court to order Beth Smiles to appear for her deposition. The court hears all of the motions together. Janet argues that Coastal's interrogatory answers are hopelessly uninformative and defeat the whole purpose of discovery. She claims that Coastal's large number of depositions creates a huge and unfair expense for a small firm.

Rich claims that the interrogatory answers are the best that Coastal can do thus far and that Coastal will supplement the answers when more information becomes available. He argues against Interrogatory No. 18, the one in which Janet asked for the names of other policyholders whom Coastal considered suicides. He claims that Janet is engaging in a fishing expedition that would violate the privacy of Coastal's insurance customers and provide no information relevant to this case. He demands that Janet make Beth available for a deposition.

In camera inspection
A judge's private review of evidence to determine whether it should be provided to the opposing party.

These discovery rulings are critical because they will color the entire lawsuit. A trial judge has to make many discovery decisions before a case reaches trial. At times, the judge must weigh the need of one party to see documents against the other side's need for privacy. One device a judge can use in reaching a discovery ruling is an **in camera inspection**, meaning that the judge views the requested documents alone, with no lawyers present, and decides whether the other side is entitled to view them.

E-Discovery   The biggest change in litigation in the last decade is the explosive rise of electronic discovery. Companies send hundreds, or thousands, or millions of emails—every day. Many have attachments, sometimes hundreds of pages long. In addition, businesses large and small have vast amounts of data stored electronically. All of this information is potentially subject to discovery.

It is enormously time-consuming and expensive for companies to locate all of the relevant material, separate it from irrelevant or confidential matter, and furnish it. A firm may be obligated to furnish *millions* of emails to the opposing party. In one recent case, a defendant had to pay 31 lawyers full time, for six months, just to wade through the e-ocean of documents and figure out which had to be supplied and how to produce it. Not surprisingly, this data eruption has created a new industry: high-tech companies that assist law firms in finding, sorting, and delivering electronic data.

Who is to say what must be supplied? What if an email string contains individual emails that are clearly privileged (meaning a party need not divulge them), but others that are not privileged? May a company refuse to furnish the entire string? Many will try. However, some courts have ruled that companies seeking to protect email strings must create a log describing every individual email and allow the court to determine which are privileged.[5]

When the cost of furnishing the data becomes burdensome, who should pay, the party seeking the information or the one supplying it? In one million-dollar corporate lawsuit, the defendant turned over 3,000 emails and 211,000 other documents. But the trial judge noted that many of the email attachments—sometimes 12 to an email—had gone missing, and required the company to produce them. The defendant protested that finding the attachments would cost an additional $206,000. The judge ordered the company to do it, and bear the full cost.

Both sides in litigation sometimes use gamesmanship during discovery. Thus, if an individual sues a large corporation, for example, the company may deliberately make discovery so expensive that the plaintiff cannot afford the legal fees. And if a plaintiff has a poor case, he might intentionally try to make the discovery process more expensive for the defendant than his settlement offer. Even if a defendant expects to win at trial, an offer to settle a case for $50,000 can look like a bargain if discovery alone will cost $100,000. Some defendants refuse, but others are more pragmatic.

The following case illustrates another common discovery problem: refusal by one side to appear for deposition. Did the defendant cynically believe that long delay would win the day, given that the plaintiff was 78 years old? What can a court do in such a case?

STINTON V. ROBIN'S WOOD, INC.

45 A.D. 3d 203, 842 NYS2d 477
New York App. Div., 2007

CASE SUMMARY

Facts: Ethel Flanzraich, 78 years old, slipped and fell on the steps of property owned by Robin's Wood. She broke her left leg and left arm. Flanzraich sued, claiming that Robin's Wood caused her fall by negligently painting the stairs. The defendant's employee, Anthony Monforte, had painted the steps. In its answer to the complaint, Robin's Wood denied all the significant allegations.

---

[5]*Universal Service Fund Telephone Billing Practices Litigation*, 232 F.R.D. 669 (D. Kan. 2005).

During a preliminary conference with the trial judge, the parties agreed to hold depositions of both parties on August 4. Flanzraich appeared for deposition, but Robin's Wood did not furnish its employee, Monforte, nor did it offer any other company representative. The court then ordered the deposition of the defendant to take place the following April 2. Again, Robin's Wood produced neither Monforte nor anyone else. On July 16, the court ordered the defendant to produce its representative within 30 days. Once more, no one showed up for deposition.

On August 18—over *one year* after the original deposition date—Flanzraich moved to strike the defendant's answer, meaning that the plaintiff would win by default. The company argued that it had made diligent efforts to locate Monforte and force him to appear. However, all the letters sent to Monforte were addressed care of Robin's Wood. Finally, the company stated that it no longer employed Monforte.

The trial judge granted the motion to strike the answer. That meant that Robin's Wood was liable for Flanzraich's fall. The only remaining issue was damages. The court determined that Robin's Wood owed $22,631 for medical expenses, $150,000 for past pain and suffering, and $300,000 for future pain and suffering. One day later, Flanzraich died of other causes. Robin's Wood appealed.

Issue: *Did the trial court abuse its discretion by striking the defendant's answer?*

Decision: No, the trial court did not abuse its discretion. Affirmed.

Reasoning: Normally, a lawsuit must be decided on the evidence and reasonable conclusions. However, if a defendant fails to respond to discovery requests, and its failure is willful, extreme, and disrespectful of the court, a trial judge may strike the defendant's answer altogether.

Robin's Wood failed to comply with three orders to appear for deposition. The company never produced Monforte while he worked there. It failed to notify the plaintiff when Monforte left, and it made no effort to produce another employee for deposition. The company did everything it could to ensure that Flanzraich would never speak with its worker. Had the company at least produced another representative, Flanzraich could have learned where Monforte had gone because the record indicates Robin's Wood knew his whereabouts.

These delays were particularly menacing to Flanzraich's case because she was elderly—a fact well known to the company. A trial judge may respond to such offensive conduct with appropriate orders.

In the Enviro-Vision case, the judge rules that Coastal must furnish more complete answers to the interrogatories, especially as to why the company denied the claim. However, he rules against Interrogatory No. 18, the one concerning other claims Coastal has denied. This simple ruling kills Janet's hope of making a class action of the case. He orders Beth to appear for the deposition. As to future depositions, Coastal may take any 10 but then may take additional depositions only by demonstrating to the court that the deponents have useful information.

Rich proceeds to take Beth's deposition. It takes two full days. He asks about Enviro-Vision's past and present. He learns that Tony appeared to have won their biggest contract ever from Rapid City, Oregon, but that he then lost it when he had a fight with Rapid City's mayor. He inquires into Tony's mood, learns that he was depressed, and probes in every direction he can to find evidence of suicidal motivation. Janet and Rich argue frequently over questions and whether Beth should have to answer them. At times, Janet is persuaded and permits Beth to answer; other times, she instructs Beth not to answer. For example, toward the end of the second day, Rich asks Beth whether she and Tony had been sexually involved. Janet instructs Beth not to answer. This fight necessitates another trip into court to determine whether Beth must answer. The judge rules that Beth must discuss Tony's romantic life only if Coastal has some evidence that he was involved with someone outside his marriage. The company lacks any such evidence.

Now limited to 10 depositions, Rich selects his nine other deponents carefully. For example, he decides to depose only one of the two nurses; he chooses to question Jerry Johnson, the tennis partner, but not Craig Bergson, the former roommate; and so forth. When we look at the many legal issues this case raises, his choices seem minor. In fact, unbeknownst to Rich or anyone else, his choices may determine the outcome of the case. As we will see later, Craig Bergson has evidence that is possibly crucial to the lawsuit. If Rich decides not to depose him, neither side will ever learn the evidence and the jury will never hear it. A jury can decide a case only based on the evidence presented to it. *Facts are elusive—and often controlling.*

In each deposition, Rich carefully probes with his questions, sometimes trying to learn what he actually does not know, sometimes trying to pin down the witness to a specific version of facts so that Rich knows how the witness will testify at trial. Neighbors at the beach testify that Tony seemed tense; one testifies about seeing Tony, unhappy, on the beach with his dog. Another testifies he had never before seen Blue tied up on the beach. Karen Caruso admits that Tony had been somewhat tense and unhappy the last couple of months. She reluctantly discusses their marriage, admitting there were problems.

Other Discovery   Rich sends Requests to Produce Documents, seeking medical records about Tony. Once again, the parties fight over which records are relevant, but Rich gets most of what he wants. Janet does less discovery than Rich because most of the witnesses she will call are friendly witnesses. She can interview them privately without giving any information to Coastal. With the help of Beth and Karen, Janet builds her case just as carefully as Rich, choosing the witnesses who will bolster the view that Tony was in good spirits and died accidentally.

She deposes all the officers of Coastal who participated in the decision to deny insurance coverage. She is particularly aggressive in pinning them down as to the limited information they had when they denied Beth's claim.

SUMMARY JUDGMENT

When discovery is completed, both sides may consider seeking summary judgment. **Summary judgment** is a ruling by the court that no trial is necessary because no essential facts are in dispute. The purpose of a trial is to determine the facts of the case; that is, to decide who did what to whom, why, when, and with what consequences. If there are no relevant facts in dispute, then there is no need for a trial.

In the following case, the defendant won summary judgment, meaning that the case never went to trial. And yet, this was only the beginning of trouble for that defendant, Bill Clinton.

Summary judgment
A ruling by the court that no trial is necessary because no essential facts are in dispute.

JONES V. CLINTON

990 F. Supp. 657, 1998 U.S. Dist. LEXIS 3902
United States District Court for the Eastern District of Arkansas, 1998

CASE SUMMARY

Facts: In 1991, Bill Clinton was governor of Arkansas. Paula Jones worked for a state agency, the Arkansas Industrial Development Commission (AIDC). When Clinton became president, Jones sued him, claiming that he had sexually harassed her. She alleged that in May 1991, the governor arranged for her to meet him in a hotel room in Little Rock, Arkansas. When they were alone, he put his hand on her leg and slid it toward her pelvis. She escaped from his grasp, exclaimed, "What are you doing?" and said she was "not that kind of girl." Upset and confused, she sat on a sofa near the door. She claimed that Clinton approached her, "lowered his trousers and underwear, exposed his penis, and told her to kiss it." Jones was horrified, jumped up, and said she had to leave. Clinton responded by saying, "Well, I don't want to make you do anything you don't want to do," and pulled his pants up. He

added that if she got in trouble for leaving work, Jones should "have Dave call me immediately and I'll take care of it." He also said, "You are smart. Let's keep this between ourselves." Jones remained at AIDC until February 1993, when she moved to California because of her husband's job transfer.

President Clinton denied all the allegations. He also filed for summary judgment, claiming that Jones had not alleged facts that justified a trial. Jones opposed the motion for summary judgment.

Issue: *Was Clinton entitled to summary judgment, or was Jones entitled to a trial?*

Decision: Jones failed to make out a claim of sexual harassment. Summary judgment was granted for the president.

Reasoning: To establish this type of sexual harassment case, a plaintiff must show that her refusal to submit to unwelcome sexual advances resulted in specific harm to her job.

Jones received every merit increase and cost-of-living allowance for which she was eligible. Her only job transfer involved a minor change in working conditions, with no reduction in pay or benefits. Jones claims that she was obligated to sit in a less private area, often with no work to do, and was the only female employee not to receive flowers on Secretary's Day. However, even if these allegations are true, all are trivial and none is sufficient to create a sexual harassment suit. Jones has demonstrated no specific harm to her job.

In other words, the court acknowledged that there were factual disputes, but concluded that even if Jones proved each of her allegations, she would *still* lose the case, because her allegations fell short of a legitimate case of sexual harassment. Jones appealed the case. Later the same year, as the appeal was pending and the House of Representatives was considering whether to impeach President Clinton, the parties settled the dispute. Clinton, without acknowledging any of the allegations, agreed to pay Jones $850,000 to drop the suit.

Janet and Rich each consider moving for summary judgment, but both correctly decide that they would lose. There is one major fact in dispute: did Tony Caruso commit suicide? Only a jury may decide that issue. As long as there is *some evidence* supporting each side of a key factual dispute, the court may not grant summary judgment.

EXAM Strategy

Question: You are a judge. Mel has sued Kevin, claiming that while Kevin was drunk, he negligently drove his car down Mel's street, and destroyed rare trees on a lot that Mel owns, next to his house. Mel's complaint stated that three witnesses at a bar saw Kevin take at least eight drinks less than an hour before the damage was done. In Kevin's answer, he denied causing the damage and denied being in the bar that night.

Kevin's lawyer has moved for summary judgment. He proves that three weeks before the alleged accident, Mel sold the lot to Tatiana.

Mel's lawyer opposes summary judgment. He produces a security camera tape proving that Kevin was in the bar, drinking beer, 34 minutes before the damage was done. He produces a signed statement from Sandy, a landscape gardener who lives across the street from the scene. Sandy states that she heard a crash, hurried to the windows, and saw Kevin's car weaving away from the damaged trees. She is a landscape gardener and estimates the tree damage at $30,000 to $40,000. How should you rule on the motion?

Strategy: Do not be fooled by red herrings about Kevin's drinking or the value of the trees. Stick to the question: should you grant summary judgment? Trials are necessary to resolve disputes about essential factual issues. Summary judgment is appropriate when there are no essential facts in dispute. Is there an essential fact not in dispute? Find it. Apply the rule. Being a judge is easy!

Result: There are facts in dispute, but none of them are essential. It makes no difference whether Kevin was drunk or sober, whether he caused the harm or was at home in bed. Because Mel does not own the property, he cannot recover for the damage to it. He cannot win. You should grant Kevin's summary judgment motion.

FINAL PREPARATION

Well over 90 percent of all lawsuits are settled before trial. But the parties in the Enviro-Vision dispute are unable to compromise, so each side gears up for trial. The attorneys make lists of all witnesses they will call. They then prepare each witness very carefully, rehearsing the questions they will ask. It is considered ethical and proper to rehearse the questions, provided the answers are honest and come from the witness. It is unethical and illegal for a lawyer to tell a witness what to say. It also makes for a weaker presentation of evidence—witnesses giving scripted answers are often easy to spot. The lawyers also have colleagues cross-examine each witness, so that the witnesses are ready for the questions the other side's lawyer will ask.

This preparation takes hours and hours, for many days. Beth is frustrated that she cannot do the work she needs to for Enviro-Vision because she is spending so much time preparing the case. Other employees have to prepare as well, especially for cross- examination by Rich Stewart, and it is a terrible drain on the small firm. More than a year after Janet filed her complaint, they are ready to begin trial.

3-4 TRIAL

3-4a Adversary System

Our system of justice assumes that the best way to bring out the truth is for the two contesting sides to present the strongest case possible to a neutral factfinder. Each side presents its witnesses and then the opponent has a chance to cross-examine. The adversary system presumes that by putting a witness on the stand and letting both lawyers question her, the truth will emerge.

The judge runs the trial. Each lawyer sits at a large table near the front. Beth, looking tense and unhappy, sits with Janet. Rich sits with a Coastal executive. In the back of the courtroom are benches for the public. On one bench sits Craig Bergson. He will watch the entire proceeding with intense interest and a strange feeling of unease. He is convinced he knows what really happened.

Janet has demanded a jury trial for Beth's case, and Judge Rowland announces that they will now impanel the jury.

3-4b Right to Jury Trial

Not all cases are tried to a jury. As a general rule, both plaintiff and defendant have a right to demand a jury trial when the lawsuit is one for money damages. For example, in a typical contract lawsuit, such as Beth's insurance claim, both plaintiff and defendant have a jury trial right whether they are in state or federal court. Even in such a case, though, the parties may *waive* the jury right, meaning they agree to try the case to a judge. Also, if the plaintiff is seeking an equitable remedy such as an injunction or other court-ordered enforcement, there is no jury right for either party.

3-4c Voir Dire

The process of selecting a jury is called **voir dire**, which means "to speak the truth."[6] The court's goal is to select an impartial jury; the lawyers will each try to get a jury as favorable to their side as possible. A court sends letters to potential jurors who live in its county. Those who do not report for jury duty face significant consequences.

Voir dire
The process of selecting a jury.

---

[6]Students of French note that *voir* means "to see" and assume that *voir dire* should translate as "to see, to speak." However, the legal term is centuries old and derives not from modern French but from Old French, in which *voir* meant "truth."

Challenges for cause
A claim that a juror has demonstrated probable bias.

Peremptory challenges
The right to excuse a juror for virtually any reason.

When voir dire begins, potential jurors are questioned individually, sometimes by the judge and sometimes by the two lawyers, as each side tries to ferret out potential bias. Each lawyer may make any number of **challenges for cause**, claiming that a juror has demonstrated probable bias. For example, if a prospective juror in the Enviro-Vision case works for an insurance company, the judge will excuse her on the assumption that she would be biased in favor of Coastal. If the judge perceives no bias, the lawyer may still make a limited number of **peremptory challenges**, entitling him to excuse that juror for virtually any reason, which need not be stated in court. For example, if Rich believes that a juror seems hostile to him personally, he will use a peremptory challenge to excuse that juror, even if the judge sensed no animosity. The process continues until 14 jurors are seated. Twelve will comprise the jury; the other two are alternates who hear the case and remain available in the event one of the impaneled jurors becomes ill or otherwise cannot continue.

Although jury selection for a case can sometimes take many days, in the Enviro-Vision case, the first day of the hearing ends with the jury selected. In the hallway outside the court, Rich offers Janet $200,000 to settle. Janet reports the offer to Beth and they agree to reject it. Craig Bergson drives home, emotionally confused. Only three weeks before his death, Tony had accidentally met his old roommate and they had had several drinks. Craig believes that what Tony told him answers the riddle of this case.

PEREDA V. PARAJON

957 So.2d 1194
Florida Court of Appeals, 2007

CASE SUMMARY

Facts: Maria Parajon sued Diana Pereda for injuring her in a car accident. During *voir dire*, Parajon's lawyer asked the panel of prospective jurors these questions: "Is there anybody sitting on this panel now that has ever been under the care of a physician for personal injuries, whether you had a lawsuit or not? In other words, you may not have had any sort of lawsuit, but you slipped and fell—you had any accidents?"

Several of the prospective jurors raised their hands, allowing the lawyers to question more deeply into possible bias. However, Lisa Berg, a prospective juror who happened to be a lawyer, did not respond. Berg and others were seated as jurors, and ultimately awarded Parajon $450,000 for medical damages and pain and suffering.

After the trial, questioned in court by the judge, Berg admitted that three years earlier she had been injured in a car accident, hired a lawyer to sue, and settled out of court for $4,000. Asked about the settlement, Berg replied, "I think everyone always wants more money."

Parajon moved for a new trial but the judge denied the motion. Parajon appealed.

Issue: *Is Parajon entitled to a new trial based on Berg's failure to disclose her own personal injury lawsuit?*

Decision: Yes, Parajon is entitled to a new trial. Reversed and remanded for a new trial.

Reasoning: When a juror does not accurately answer questions during voir dire, a new trial is called for if the following three criteria are met:

First, the information is relevant and material to the case. Second, the juror concealed it. Third, the lawyers made a diligent effort to seek the information.

Berg's own car accident was relevant and material because it might have influenced her opinion in the case. As a lawyer herself, Berg knew that the question applied to her, and she deliberately chose not to answer it. The fact that other prospective jurors answered the question indicated that Parajon's lawyers made a diligent and reasonable attempt to get the information.

3-4d Opening Statements

The next day, each attorney makes an opening statement to the jury, summarizing the proof he or she expects to offer, with the plaintiff going first. Janet focuses on Tony's successful life, his business and strong marriage, and the tragedy of his accidental death.[7]

Rich works hard to establish a friendly rapport with the jury. If members of the jury like him, they will tend to pay more attention to his presentation of evidence. He expresses regret about the death. Nonetheless, suicide is a clear exclusion from the policy. If insurance companies are forced to pay claims never bargained for, everyone's insurance rates will go up.

3-4e Burden of Proof

In civil cases, the plaintiff has the burden of proof. That means that the plaintiff must convince the jury that its version of the case is correct; the defendant is not obligated to disprove the allegations.

The plaintiff's burden in a civil lawsuit is to prove its case by a **preponderance of the evidence**. It must convince the jury that its version of the facts is at least *slightly more likely* than the defendant's version. Some courts describe this as a "51-49" persuasion; that is, that plaintiff s proof must "just tip" credibility in its favor. By contrast, in a criminal case, the prosecution must demonstrate **beyond a reasonable doubt** that the defendant is guilty. The burden of proof in a criminal case is much tougher because the likely consequences are, too. See Exhibit 3.3.

Preponderance of the evidence
The plaintiff's burden in a civil lawsuit.

Beyond a reasonable doubt
The government's burden in a criminal prosecution.

3-4f Plaintiff's Case

Because the plaintiff has the burden of proof, Janet puts in her case first. She wants to prove two things. First, that Tony died. That is easy because the death certificate clearly demonstrates it and Coastal does not seriously contest it. Second, in order to win double

© Cengage Learning

EXHIBIT 3.3   Burden of Proof. In a civil lawsuit, a plaintiff wins with a mere preponderance of the evidence. But the prosecution must persuade a jury beyond a reasonable doubt in order to win a criminal conviction.

---

[7]Janet Booker has dropped her claim for triple damages against Coastal. To have any hope of such a verdict, she would have to show that Coastal had no legitimate reason at all for denying the claim. Discovery has convinced her that Coastal will demonstrate some rational reasons for what it did.

Direct examination

When a lawyer questions her own witness.

Cross-examine

To ask questions of an opposing witness.

indemnity damages, she must show that the death was accidental. She will do this with the testimony of the witnesses she calls, one after the other. Her first witness is Beth. When a lawyer asks questions of her own witness, it is **direct examination.** Janet brings out all the evidence she wants the jury to hear: that the business was basically sound, though temporarily troubled, that Tony was a hard worker, why the company took out life insurance policies, and so forth.

Then Rich has a chance to **cross-examine** Beth, which means to ask questions of an opposing witness. He will try to create doubt in the jury's mind. He asks Beth only questions for which he is certain of the answers, based on discovery. Rich gets Beth to admit that the firm was not doing well the year of Tony's death; that Tony had lost the best client the firm ever had; that Beth had reduced salaries; and that Tony had been depressed about business.

3-4g Rules of Evidence

The lawyers are not free simply to ask any question they want. The law of evidence determines what questions a lawyer may ask and how the questions are to be phrased, what answers a witness may give, and what documents may be introduced. The goal is to get the best evidence possible before the jurors so they can decide what really happened. In general, witnesses may only testify about things they saw or heard.

These rules are complex, and a thorough look at them is beyond the scope of this chapter. However, they can be just as important in resolving a dispute as the underlying substantive law. Suppose that a plaintiff's case depends upon the jury hearing about a certain conversation, but the rules of evidence prevent the lawyer from asking about it. That conversation might just as well never have occurred.

Janet calls an expert witness, a marine geologist, who testifies about the tides and currents in the area where Tony's body was found. The expert testifies that even experienced swimmers can be overwhelmed by a sudden shift in currents. Rich objects strenuously that this is irrelevant, because there is no testimony that there *was* such a current at the time of Tony's death. The judge permits the testimony.

Karen Caruso testifies that Tony was in "reasonably good" spirits the day of his death, and that he often took Blue for walks along the beach. Karen testifies that Blue was part Newfoundland. Rich objects that testimony about Blue's pedigree is irrelevant, but Janet insists it will show why Blue was tied up. The judge allows the testimony. Karen says that whenever Blue saw them swim, he would instinctively go into the water and pull them to shore. Does that explain why Blue was tied up? Only the jury can answer.

Cross-examination is grim for Karen. Rich slowly but methodically questions her about Tony's state of mind and brings out the problems with the company, his depression, and tension within the marriage. Janet's other witnesses testify essentially as they did during their depositions.

3-4h Motion for Directed Verdict

At the close of the plaintiff's case, Rich moves for a directed verdict; that is, a ruling that the plaintiff has entirely failed to prove some aspect of her case. Rich is seeking to win without even putting in his own case. He argues that it was Beth's burden to prove that Tony died accidentally and that she has entirely failed to do that.

Directed verdict

A ruling that the plaintiff has entirely failed to prove some aspect of her case.

A **directed verdict is permissible only if the evidence so clearly favors the defendant that reasonable minds could not disagree on it.** If reasonable minds could disagree, the motion must be denied. Here, Judge Rowland rules that the plaintiff has put in enough evidence of accidental death that a reasonable person could find in Beth's favor. The motion is denied.

There is no downside for Rich to ask for a directed verdict. The trial continues as if he had never made such a motion.

3-4i Defendant's Case

Rich now puts in his case, exactly as Janet did, except that he happens to have fewer witnesses. He calls the examining doctor, who admits that Tony could have committed suicide by swimming out too far. On cross-examination, Janet gets the doctor to acknowledge that he has no idea whether Tony intentionally drowned. Rich also questions several neighbors as to how depressed Tony had seemed and how unusual it was that Blue was tied up. Some of the witnesses Rich deposed, such as the tennis partner Jerry Johnson, have nothing that will help Coastal's case, so he does not call them.

Craig Bergson, sitting in the back of the courtroom, thinks how different the trial would have been had he been called as a witness. When he and Tony had the fateful drink, Tony had been distraught: business was terrible, he was involved in an extramarital affair that he could not end, and he saw no way out of his problems. He had no one to talk to and had been hugely relieved to speak with Craig. Several times Tony had said, "I just can't go on like this. I don't want to, anymore." Craig thought Tony seemed suicidal and urged him to see a therapist Craig knew and trusted. Tony had said that it was good advice, but Craig is unsure whether Tony sought any help.

This evidence would have affected the case. Had Rich known of the conversation, he would have deposed Craig and the therapist. Coastal's case would have been far stronger, perhaps overwhelming. But Craig's evidence will never be heard. Facts are critical. Rich's decision to depose other witnesses and omit Craig may influence the verdict more than any rule of law.

3-4j Closing Arguments

Both lawyers sum up their case to the jury, explaining how they hope the jury will interpret what they have heard. Janet summarizes the plaintiff's version of the facts, claiming that Blue was tied up so that Tony could swim without worrying about him. Rich claims that business and personal pressures had overwhelmed Tony. He tied up his dog, neatly folded his clothes, and took his own life.

3-4k Jury Instructions

Judge Rowland instructs the jury as to its duty. He tells them that they are to evaluate the case based only on the evidence they heard at trial, relying on their own experience and common sense.

He explains the law and the burden of proof, telling the jury that it is Beth's obligation to prove that Tony died. If Beth has proven that Tony died, she is entitled to $1 million; if she has proven that his death was accidental, she is entitled to $2 million. However, if Coastal has proven suicide, Beth receives nothing. Finally, he states that if they are unable to decide between accidental death and suicide, there is a legal presumption that it was accidental. Rich asks Judge Rowland to rephrase the "legal presumption" part, but the judge declines.

3-4l Verdict

The jury deliberates informally, with all jurors entitled to voice their opinion. Some deliberations take two hours; some take two weeks. Many states require a unanimous verdict; others require only, for example, a 10–2 vote in civil cases.

This case presents a close call. No one saw Tony die. Yet even though they cannot know with certainty, the jury's decision will probably be the final word on whether he took his own life. After a day and a half of deliberating, the jury notifies the judge that it has reached a verdict. Rich quickly makes a new offer: $350,000. (The two sides have the right to settle a case until the moment when the last appeal is decided.) Beth hesitates but turns it down.

The judge summons the lawyers to court, and Beth goes as well. The judge asks the foreman if the jury has reached a decision. He states that it has: The jury finds that Tony Caruso drowned accidentally, and awards Beth Smiles $2 million.

3-4m Motions after the Verdict

Rich immediately moves for a **judgment *non obstante veredicto*** (JNOV), meaning a judgment notwithstanding the jury's verdict. He is asking the judge to overturn the jury's verdict. Rich argues that the jury's decision went against all of the evidence. He also claims that the judge's instructions were wrong and misled the jury.

Judge Rowland denies the JNOV. Rich immediately moves for a new trial, making the same claim, and the judge denies the motion. Beth is elated that the case is finally over—until Janet says she expects an appeal. Craig Bergson, leaving the courtroom, wonders if he did the right thing. He felt sympathy for Beth and none for Coastal. Yet now he is neither happy nor proud.

3-5 APPEALS

Two days later, Rich files an appeal to the court of appeals. The same day, he phones Janet and increases his settlement offer to $425,000. Beth is tempted but wants Janet's advice. Janet says the risks of an appeal are that the court will order a new trial, and they would start all over. But to accept this offer is to forfeit over $1.5 million. Beth is unsure what to do. The firm desperately needs cash now, and appeals may take years. Janet suggests they wait until oral argument, another eight months.

Rich files a brief arguing that there were two basic errors at the trial: first, that the jury's verdict is clearly contrary to the evidence; and second, that the judge gave the wrong instructions to the jury. Janet files a reply brief, opposing Rich on both issues. In her brief, Janet cites many cases that she claims are **precedent**: earlier decisions by the state appellate courts on similar or identical issues.

Eight months later, the lawyers representing Coastal and Enviro-Vision appear in the court of appeals to argue their case. Rich, the appellant, goes first. The judges frequently interrupt his argument with questions. They show little sympathy for his claim that the verdict was against the facts. They seem more sympathetic with his second point, that the instructions were wrong.

When Janet argues, all of their questions concern the judge's instructions. It appears they believe the instructions were in error. The judges take the case under advisement, meaning they will decide some time in the future—maybe in two weeks, maybe in five months.

3-5a Appeals Court Options

The court of appeals can **affirm** the trial court, allowing the decision to stand. The court may **modify** the decision, for example, by affirming that the plaintiff wins but decreasing the size of the award. (That is unlikely here; Beth is entitled to $2 million or nothing.) The court might **reverse and remand**, nullifying the lower court's decision and returning the case to the lower court for a new trial. Or it could simply **reverse**, turning the loser (Coastal) into the winner, with no new trial.

What will it do here? On the factual issue, it will probably rule in Beth's favor. There *was* evidence from which a jury could conclude that Tony died accidentally. It is true that there was also considerable evidence to support Coastal's position, but that is probably not enough to overturn the verdict. If reasonable people could disagree on what the evidence proves, an appellate court generally refuses to change the jury's factual findings. The court of appeals is likely to rule that a reasonable jury *could* have found accidental death, even if the appellate judges personally suspect that Tony may have killed himself.

The judge's instructions raise a more difficult problem. Some states would require a more complex statement about "presumptions."[8]

What does a court of appeals do if it decides the trial court's instructions were wrong? If it believes the error rendered the trial and verdict unfair, it will remand the case; that is, send it back to the lower court for a new trial. However, the court may conclude that the mistake was **harmless error**. A trial judge cannot do a perfect job, and not every error is fatal. The court may decide the verdict was fair in spite of the mistake.

Janet and Beth talk. Beth is very anxious and wants to settle. She does not want to wait four or five months, only to learn that they must start all over. Janet urges that they wait a few weeks to hear from Rich: They don't want to seem too eager.

A week later, Rich telephones and offers $500,000. Janet turns it down, but says she will ask Beth if she wants to make a counter-offer. She and Beth talk. They agree that they will settle for $1 million. Janet then calls Rich and offers to settle for $1.7 million. Rich and Janet debate the merits of the case. Rich later calls back and offers $750,000, saying he doubts that he can go any higher. Janet counters with $1.4 million, saying she doubts she can go any lower. They argue, both predicting that they will win on appeal.

Rich calls, offers $900,000 and says, "That's it. No more." Janet argues for $1.2 million, expecting to nudge Rich up to $1 million. He doesn't nudge, instead saying, "Take it or leave it." Janet and Beth talk it over. Janet telephones Rich and accepts $900,000 to settle the case.

If they had waited for the court of appeals decision, would Beth have won? It is impossible to know. It is certain, though, that whoever lost would have appealed. Months would have passed waiting to learn if the state supreme court would accept the case. If that court had agreed to hear the appeal, Beth would have endured another year of waiting, brief writing, oral argument, and tense hoping. The high court has all of the options discussed: to affirm, modify, reverse and remand, or simply reverse.

Harmless error
A mistake by the trial judge that was too minor to affect the outcome.

3-6 ALTERNATIVE DISPUTE RESOLUTION

As we have seen in the previous section, trials can be trying. Lawsuits can cause prolonged periods of stress, significant legal bills, and general unpleasantness. Many people and companies prefer to settle cases out of court. Alternative dispute resolution (ADR) provides several semi-formal methods of resolving conflicts. We will look at different types of ADR and analyze their strengths and weaknesses.

3-6a Negotiation

In most cases, the parties negotiate, whether personally or through lawyers. Fortunately, the great majority of disputes are resolved this way. Negotiation often begins as soon as a dispute arises and may last a few days or several years.

---

[8]Judge Rowland probably should have said, "The law presumes that death is accidental, not suicide. So if there were no evidence either way, the plaintiff would win because we presume accident. But if there is competing evidence, the presumption becomes irrelevant. If you think that Coastal Insurance has introduced some evidence of suicide, then forget the legal presumption. You must then decide what happened based on what you have seen and heard in court, and on any inferences you choose to draw." Note that the judge's instructions were different, though similar.

3-6b Mediation

Mediation is the fastest growing method of dispute resolution in the United States. Here, a neutral person, called a **mediator**, attempts to guide the two disputing parties toward a voluntary settlement. (In some cases, there may be two or more mediators, but we will use the singular.) Generally, the two disputants voluntarily enter mediation, although some judges order the parties to try this form of ADR before allowing a case to go to trial.

A mediator does not render a decision in the dispute, but uses a variety of skills to move the parties toward agreement. Often a mediator will shuttle between the antagonists, hearing their arguments, sorting out the serious issues from the less important, prompting the parties and lawyers alike to consider new perspectives, and looking for areas of agreement. Mediators must earn the trust of both parties, listen closely, try to diffuse anger and fear, and build the will to settle. Good mediators do not need a law degree, but they must have a sense of humor and low blood pressure.

Mediation has several major advantages. Because the parties maintain control of the process, the two antagonists can speak freely. They need not fear conceding too much, because no settlement takes effect until both parties sign. All discussions are confidential, further encouraging candid talk. This is particularly helpful in cases involving proprietary information that might be revealed during a trial.

Of all forms of dispute resolution, mediation probably offers the strongest "win-win" potential. Since the goal is voluntary settlement, neither party needs to fear that it will end up the loser. This is in sharp contrast to litigation, where one party is very likely to lose. Removing the fear of defeat often encourages thinking and talking that are more open and realistic than negotiations held in the midst of a lawsuit. Studies show that over 75 percent of mediated cases do reach a voluntary settlement. Such an agreement is particularly valuable to parties that wish to preserve a long-term relationship. Consider two companies that have done business successfully for 10 years but now are in the midst of a million-dollar trade dispute. A lawsuit could last three or more years and destroy any chance of future trade. However, if the parties mediate the disagreement, they might reach an amicable settlement within a month or two and could quickly resume their mutually profitable business.

This form of ADR works for disputes both big and small. Two college roommates who cannot get along may find that a three-hour mediation session restores tranquility in the apartment. On a larger scale, consider the work of former U.S. Senator George Mitchell, who mediated the Anglo-Irish peace agreement, setting Northern Ireland on the path to peace for the first time in three centuries. Like most good mediators, Mitchell was remarkably patient. In an early session, Mitchell permitted the head of one militant party to speak without interruption—for seven straight hours. The diatribe yielded no quick results, but Mitchell believed that after Northern Ireland's tortured history, any nonviolent discussions represented progress.

3-6c Arbitration

In this form of ADR, the parties agree to bring in a neutral third party, but with a major difference: The arbitrator has the power to impose an award. The arbitrator allows each side equal time to present its case and, after deliberation, issues a binding decision, generally without giving reasons. Unlike mediation, arbitration ensures that there will be a final result, although the parties lose control of the outcome.

Judge Judy and similar TV court shows are examples of arbitration. Before the shows are taped, people involved in a real dispute sign a contract in which they give up the right to go to court over the incident and agree to be bound by the judge's decision.

Parties in arbitration give up many additional rights that litigants retain, including discovery and class action. In arbitration, as already discussed as applied to trials, discovery allows the two sides in a lawsuit to obtain documentary and other evidence from the opponent before the dispute is decided. Arbitration permits both sides to keep secret many files that would have to be divulged in a court case, potentially depriving the opposing side of valuable evidence. A party may have a stronger case than it realizes, and the absence of discovery may permanently deny it that knowledge. As discussed earlier in this chapter, a class action is a suit in which one injured party represents a large group of people who have suffered similar harm. Arbitration eliminates this possibility, since injured employees face the employer one at a time. Finally, the fact that an arbitrator may not provide a written, public decision bars other plaintiffs, and society generally, from learning what happened.

Traditionally, parties sign arbitration agreements *after* some incident takes place. A car accident would happen first, and the drivers would agree to arbitration second. But today, many parties agree *in advance* to arbitrate any disputes that may arise in the future. For example, a new employee may sign an agreement requiring arbitration of any future disputes with his employer; a customer opening an account with a stockbroker or bank— or health plan—may sign a similar form, often without realizing it. The good news is fewer lawsuits; the bad news is you might be the person kept out of court.

Assume that you live in Miami. Using the Internet, you order a $1,000 ThinkLite laptop computer, which arrives in a carton loaded with six fat instructional manuals and many small leaflets. You read some of the documents and ignore others. For four weeks, you struggle to make your computer work, to no avail. Finally, you call ThinkLite and demand a refund, but the company refuses. You file suit in your local court, at which time the company points out that buried among the hundreds of pages it mailed you was a *mandatory arbitration form*. This document prohibits you from filing suit against the company and states that if you have any complaint with the company, you must fly to Chicago, pay a $2,000 arbitrator's fee, plead your case before an arbitrator selected by the Laptop Trade Association of America, and, should you lose, pay ThinkLite's attorneys' fees, which could be several thousand dollars. Is that mandatory arbitration provision valid? It is too early to say with finality, but thus far, the courts that have faced such clauses have enforced them.[9]

Chapter Conclusion

No one will ever know for sure whether Tony Caruso took his own life. Craig Bergson's evidence might have tipped the scales in favor of Coastal. But even that is uncertain, since the jury could have found him unpersuasive. After two years, the case ends with a settlement and uncertainty—both typical lawsuit results. The missing witness is less common but not extraordinary. The vaguely unsatisfying feeling about it all is only too common and indicates why most parties settle out of court.

---

[9]See, for example, *Hill v. Gateway* 2000, 105 F.3d 1147, 1997 U.S. App. LEXIS 1877 (7th Cir. 1997), upholding a similar clause.

EXAM REVIEW

1. **COURT SYSTEMS**   There are many *systems* of courts, one federal and one in each state. A federal court will hear a case only if it involves a federal question or diversity jurisdiction. (pp. 52–57)

2. **TRIAL AND APPELLATE COURTS**   Trial courts determine facts and apply the law to the facts; appeals courts generally accept the facts found by the trial court and review the trial record for errors of law. (pp. 55–59)

EXAM Strategy

Question: Jade sued Kim, claiming that Kim promised to hire her as an in-store model for $1,000 per week for eight weeks. Kim denied making the promise, and the jury was persuaded: Kim won. Jade has appealed, and now she offers Steve as a witness. Steve will testify to the appeals court that he saw Kim hire Jade as a model, exactly as Jade claimed. Will Jade win on appeal?

Strategy: Before you answer, make sure you know the difference between trial and appellate courts. What is the difference? Apply that distinction here. (See the "Result" at the end of this section.)

3. **PLEADINGS**   A complaint and an answer are the two most important pleadings; that is, documents that start a lawsuit. (p. 60)

4. **DISCOVERY**   Discovery is the critical pre-trial opportunity for both parties to learn the strengths and weaknesses of the opponent's case. Important forms of discovery include interrogatories, depositions, production of documents and objects, physical and mental examinations, and requests for admission. (pp. 63–66)

5. **MOTIONS**   A motion is a formal request to the court. (p. 63)

6. **SUMMARY JUDGMENT**   Summary judgment is a ruling by the court that no trial is necessary because there are no essential facts in dispute. (pp. 67–68)

7. **JURY TRIALS**   Generally, both plaintiff and defendant may demand a jury in any lawsuit for money damages. (p. 69)

8. **VOIR DIRE**   Voir dire is the process of selecting jurors in order to obtain an impartial panel. (p. 69)

Question: You are a lawyer, representing the plaintiff in a case of alleged employment discrimination. The court is selecting a jury. Based on questions you have asked, you believe that juror number 3 is biased against your client. You explain this to the judge, but she disagrees. Is there anything you can do?

Strategy: The question focuses on your rights during voir dire. If you believe that a juror will not be fair, you may make two different types of challenge. What are they? (See the "Result" at the end of this section.)

9. **BURDEN OF PROOF**   The plaintiff's burden of proof in a civil lawsuit is preponderance of the evidence, meaning that its version of the facts must be at least slightly more persuasive than the defendant's. In a criminal prosecution, the government must offer proof beyond a reasonable doubt in order to win a conviction. (p. 71)

10. **RULES OF EVIDENCE**   The rules of evidence determine what questions may be asked during trial, what testimony may be given, and what documents may be introduced. (p. 72)

11. **VERDICTS**   The verdict is the jury's decision in a case. The losing party may ask the trial judge to overturn the verdict, seeking a JNOV or a new trial. Judges seldom grant either. (pp. 73–74)

12. **APPEALS**   An appeals court has many options. The court may affirm, upholding the lower court's decision; modify, changing the verdict but leaving the same party victorious; reverse, transforming the loser into the winner; and/or remand, sending the case back to the lower court. (pp. 74–75)

13. **ADR**   Alternative dispute resolution is any formal or informal process to settle disputes without a trial. Mediation, arbitration, and other forms of ADR are growing in popularity. (pp. 75–77)

2. Result: Trial courts use witnesses to help resolve factual disputes. Appellate courts review the record to see if there have been errors of law. Appellate courts never hear witnesses, and they will not hear Steve. Jade will lose her appeal.

8. Result: You have already made a challenge for cause, claiming bias, but the judge has rejected your challenge. If you have not used up all of your peremptory challenges, you may use one to excuse this juror, without giving any reason.

MULTIPLE-CHOICE QUESTIONS

1. The burden of proof in a civil trial is to prove a case _____. The burden of proof rests with the _____.
   (a) beyond a reasonable doubt; plaintiff
   (b) by a preponderance of the evidence; plaintiff
   (c) beyond a reasonable doubt; defendant
   (d) by a preponderance of the evidence; defendant

2. Alice is suing Betty. After the discovery process, Alice believes that no relevant facts are in dispute, and that there is no need for a trial. She should move for:
   (a) a judgment on the pleadings
   (b) a directed verdict
   (c) a summary judgment
   (d) a JNOV

3. Glen lives in Illinois. He applies for a job with a Missouri company, and he is told, amazingly, that the job is open only to white applicants. He will now sue the Missouri company under the Civil Rights Act, a federal statute. Can Glen sue in federal court?
   (a) Yes, absolutely.
   (b) Yes, but only if he seeks damages of at least $75,000. Otherwise, he must sue in a state court.
   (c) Yes, but only if the Missouri company agrees. Otherwise, he must sue in a state court.
   (d) No, absolutely not. He must sue in a state court.

4. A default judgment can be entered if which of the following is true?
   (a) A plaintiff presents her evidence at trial and clearly fails to meet her burden of proof.
   (b) A defendant loses a lawsuit and does not pay a judgment within 180 days.
   (c) A defendant fails to file an answer to a plaintiff's complaint on time.
   (d) A citizen fails to obey an order to appear for jury duty.

5. Barry and Carl are next-door neighbors. Barry's dog digs under Carl's fence and does $500 worth of damage to Carl's garden. Barry refuses to pay for the damage, claiming that Carl's cats "have been digging up my yard for years."

   The two argue repeatedly, and the relationship turns frosty. Of the following choices, which has no outside decision maker and is most likely to allow the neighbors to peacefully coexist after working out the dispute?
   (a) Trial
   (b) Arbitration
   (c) Mediation

ESSAY QUESTIONS

1. You plan to open a store in Chicago, specializing in rugs imported from Turkey. You will work with a native Turk who will purchase and ship the rugs to your store. You are wise enough to insist on a contract establishing the rights and obligations of both parties and would prefer an ADR clause. But you do not want a clause that will alienate your overseas partner. What kind of ADR clause should you include, and why?

2. Which court(s) have jurisdiction over each of these lawsuits—state or federal? Explain your reasoning for each answer.

   - Pat wants to sue his next-door neighbor, Dorothy, claiming that Dorothy promised to sell him the house next door.

   - Paula, who lives in New York City, wants to sue Dizzy Movie Theatres, whose principal place of business is Dallas. She claims that while she was in Texas on holiday, she was injured by their negligent maintenance of a stairway. She claims damages of $30,000.

   - Phil lives in Tennessee. He wants to sue Dick, who lives in Ohio. Phil claims that Dick agreed to sell him 3,000 acres of farmland in Ohio, worth over $2 million.

   - Pete, incarcerated in a federal prison in Kansas, wants to sue the United States government. He claims that his treatment by prison authorities violates three federal statutes.

3. British discovery practice differs from that in the United States. Most discovery in Britain concerns documents. The lawyers for the two sides, called *solicitors*, must deliver to the opposing side a list of all relevant documents in their possession. Each side may then request to look at and copy those it wishes. Depositions are rare. What advantages and disadvantages are there to the British practice?

4. Trial practice also is dramatically different in Britain. The parties' solicitors do not go into court. Courtroom work is done by different lawyers, called *barristers*. The barristers have very limited rights to interview witnesses before trial. They know the substance of what each witness intends to say but do not rehearse questions and answers, as in the United States. Which approach do you consider more effective? More ethical? What is the purpose of a trial? Of pre-trial preparation?

5. Claus Scherer worked for Rockwell International and was paid over $300,000 per year. Rockwell fired Scherer for alleged sexual harassment of several workers, including his secretary, Terry Pendy. Scherer sued in United States District Court, alleging that Rockwell's real motive in firing him was his high salary.

   Rockwell moved for summary judgment, offering deposition transcripts of various employees. Pendy's deposition detailed instances of harassment, including comments about her body, instances of unwelcome touching, and discussions of extramarital affairs. Another deposition, from a Rockwell employee who investigated the allegations, included complaints by other employees as to Scherer's harassment. In his own deposition, which he offered to oppose summary judgment, Scherer testified that he could not recall the incidents alleged by Pendy and others. He denied generally that he had sexually harassed anyone. The district court granted summary judgment for Rockwell. Was its ruling correct?

DISCUSSION QUESTIONS

1. In the Tony Caruso case described throughout this chapter, the defendant offers to settle the case at several stages. Knowing what you do now about litigation, would you have accepted any of the offers? If so, which one(s)? If not, why not?

2. The burden of proof in civil cases is fairly low. A plaintiff wins a lawsuit if he is 51 percent convincing, and then he collects 100 percent of his damages. Is this result reasonable? Should a plaintiff in a civil case be required to prove his case beyond a reasonable doubt? Or, if a plaintiff is only 51 percent convincing, should he get only 51 percent of his damages?

3. Large numbers of employees have signed mandatory arbitration agreements in employment contracts. Courts usually uphold these clauses. Imagine that you signed a contract with an arbitration agreement, that the company later mistreated you, and that you could not sue in court. Would you be upset? Or would you be relieved to go through the faster and cheaper process of arbitration?

4. Imagine a state law that allows for residents to sue "spammers"—those who send uninvited commercial messages through email—for $30. One particularly prolific spammer sends messages to hundreds of thousands of people.

   John Smith, a lawyer, signs up 100,000 people to participate in a class-action lawsuit. According to the agreements with his many clients, Smith will keep one-third of any winnings. In the end, Smith wins a $3 million verdict and pockets $1 million. Each individual plaintiff receives a check for $20.

   Is this lawsuit a reasonable use of the court's resources? Why or why not?

5. Higher courts are reluctant to review a lower court's *factual* findings. Should this be so? Would appeals be fairer if appellate courts reviewed *everything*?

nuttakit/Shutterstock.com; © Stas Volik/Shutterstock.com

COMMON LAW, STATUTORY LAW, AND ADMINISTRATIVE LAW

Jason observes a toddler wander onto the railroad tracks and hears a train approaching. He has plenty of time to pull the child from the tracks with no risk to himself, but chooses to do nothing. The youngster is killed. The child's family sues Jason for his callous behavior, and a court determines that Jason owes—nothing.

"Why can't they just fix the law?" students and professionals often ask, in response to Jason's impunity and countless other legal oddities. Their exasperation is understandable. This chapter cannot guarantee intellectual tranquility, but it should diminish the sense of bizarreness that law can instill. We will look at three sources of law: common law, statutory law, and administrative law. Most of the law you learn in the course comes from one of these sources. The substantive law will make more sense when you have a solid feel for how it was created.

4-1 COMMON LAW

Jason and the toddler present a classic legal puzzle: What, if anything, must a bystander do when he sees someone in danger? We will examine this issue to see how the common law works.

Common law
Judge-made law.

The **common law** is judge-made law. It is the sum total of all the cases decided by appellate courts. The common law of Pennsylvania consists of all cases decided by appellate courts in that state. The Illinois common law is made up of all of the cases decided by Illinois appellate courts. Two hundred years ago, almost all of the law was common law. Today, common law still predominates in tort, contract, and agency law, and it is very important in property, employment, and some other areas.

4-1a Stare Decisis

Stare decisis
"Let the decision stand," that is, the ruling from a previous case.

Precedent
An earlier case that decided the issue.

A law course is not a law course without random Latin phrases. **Stare decisis** means "let the decision stand." It is the essence of the common law. Once a court has decided a particular issue, it will generally apply the same rule in similar cases in the future. Suppose the highest court of Arizona must decide whether a contract signed by a 16-year-old can be enforced against him. The court will look to see if there is **precedent**; that is, whether the high court of Arizona has already decided a similar case. The Arizona court looks and finds several earlier cases, all holding that such contracts may not be enforced against a minor. The court will probably apply that precedent and refuse to enforce the contract in this case. Courts do not always follow precedent, but they generally do: *stare decisis*.

A desire for predictability created the doctrine of *stare decisis*. The value of predictability is apparent: People must know what the law is. If contract law changed daily, an entrepreneur who leased factory space and then started buying machinery would be uncertain if the factory would actually be available when she was ready to move in. Will the landlord slip out of the lease? Will the machinery be ready on time? The law must be knowable. Yet there must also be flexibility in the law, some means to respond to new problems and a changing social climate. Sometimes, we are better off if we are not encumbered by ironclad rules established before electricity was discovered. These two ideas are in conflict: The more flexibility we permit, the less predictability we enjoy. We will watch the conflict play out in the bystander cases.

4-1b Bystander Cases

This country inherited from England a simple rule about a **bystander's obligations: You have no duty to assist someone in peril unless you created the danger.** In *Union Pacific Railway Co. v. Cappier*,[1] through no fault of the railroad, a train struck a man. Railroad employees saw the incident happen but did nothing to assist him. By the time help arrived, the victim had died. The court held that the railroad had no duty to help the injured man:

> With the humane side of the question courts are not concerned. It is the omission or negligent discharge of legal duties only which come within the sphere of judicial cognizance. For withholding relief from the suffering, for failure to respond to the calls of worthy charity, or for faltering in the bestowment of brotherly love on the unfortunate, penalties are found not in the laws of men but in [the laws of God].

As harsh as this judgment might seem, it was an accurate statement of the law at that time in both England and the United States: Bystanders need do nothing. Contemporary writers found the rule inhumane and cruel, and even judges criticized it. But—*stare decisis*—they

---

[1]66 Kan. 649, 72 P. 281 (1903).

followed it. With a rule this old and well established, no court was willing to scuttle it. What courts did do was seek openings for small changes.

Eighteen years after the Kansas case of *Cappier*, a court in nearby Iowa found the basis for one exception. Ed Carey was a farm laborer, working for Frank Davis. While in the fields, Carey fainted from sunstroke and remained unconscious. Davis simply hauled him to a nearby wagon and left him in the sun for an additional four hours, causing serious permanent injury. The court's response:

> It is unquestionably the well-settled rule that the master is under no legal duty to care for a sick or injured servant for whose illness or injury he is not at fault. Though not unjust in principle, this rule, if carried unflinchingly and without exception to its logical extreme, is sometimes productive of shocking results. To avoid this criticism [we hold that where] a servant suffers serious injury, or is suddenly stricken down in a manner indicating the immediate and emergent need of aid to save him from death or serious harm, the master, if present is in duty bound to take such reasonable measures as may be practicable to relieve him, even though such master be not chargeable with fault in bringing about the emergency.[2]

And this is how the common law often changes: bit by tiny bit. In Iowa, a bystander could now be liable *if* he was the employer and *if* the worker was suddenly stricken and *if* it was an emergency and *if* the employer was present. That is a small change but an important one.

For the next 50 years, changes in bystander law came very slowly. Consider *Osterlind v. Hill*, a case from 1928.[3] Osterlind rented a canoe from Hill's boatyard, paddled into the lake, and promptly fell into the water. For *30 minutes*, he clung to the side of the canoe and shouted for help. Hill heard the cries but did nothing; Osterlind drowned. Was Hill liable? No, said the court: A bystander has no liability. Not until half a century later did the same court reverse its position and begin to require assistance in extreme cases. Fifty years is a long time for the unfortunate Osterlind to hold on.[4]

In the 1970s, changes came more quickly.

TARASOFF V. REGENTS OF THE UNIVERSITY OF CALIFORNIA

17 Cal.3d 425, 551 P.2d 334, 131 Cal. Rptr. 14
Supreme Court of California, 1976

CASE SUMMARY

Facts: On October 27, 1969, Prosenjit Poddar killed Tatiana Tarasoff. Tatiana's parents claimed that two months earlier Poddar had confided his intention to kill Tatiana to Dr. Lawrence Moore, a psychologist employed by the University of California at Berkeley. They sued the university, claiming that Dr. Moore should have warned Tatiana and/or should have arranged for Poddar's confinement.

Issue: *Did Dr. Moore have a duty to Tatiana Tarasoff, and did he breach that duty?*

Decision: Yes, Dr. Moore had a duty to Tatiana Tarasoff.

Reasoning: Under the common law, one person generally owes no duty to control the conduct of another or to warn anyone who is in danger. However, courts make an

---

[2]*Carey v. Davis*, 190 Iowa 720, 180 N.W. 889 (1921).
[3]263 Mass. 73, 160 N.E. 301 (1928).
[4]*Pridgen v. Boston Housing Authority*, 364 Mass. 696, 308 N.E.2d 467 (Mass. 1974).

exception when the defendant has a special relationship to a dangerous person or potential victim. A therapist is someone who has just such a special relationship with a patient.

It is very difficult to predict whether a patient presents a serious danger of violence, and no one can be expected to do a perfect job. A therapist must exercise only the reasonable degree of skill, knowledge, and care ordinarily possessed by others in the field. In this case, however, there is no dispute about whether Dr. Moore could have foreseen violence or predicted that Poddar would kill Tatiana. Once a therapist determines, or reasonably should determine, that a patient poses a serious danger of violence to someone, he must make reasonable efforts to protect the potential victim. The Tarasoffs have stated a legitimate claim against Dr. Moore.

The *Tarasoff* exception applies when there is some special relationship, such as therapist–patient. What if there is no such relationship? Remember the *Soldano v. O'Daniels* case from Chapter 1, in which the bartender refused to call the police.

As in the earlier cases we have seen, this lawsuit presented an emergency. But the exception created in *Carey v. Davis* applied only if the bystander was an employer, and that in *Tarasoff* only for a doctor. In *Soldano*, the bystander was neither. Should the law require him to act, that is, should it carve a new exception? Here is what the California court decided:

> Many citizens simply "don't want to get involved." No rule should be adopted [requiring] a citizen to open up his or her house to a stranger so that the latter may use the telephone to call for emergency assistance. … [S]uch an action may be fraught with danger. It does not follow, however, that use of a telephone in a public portion of a business should be refused for a legitimate emergency call.
>
> We conclude that the bartender owed a duty to [Soldano] to permit the patron from Happy Jack's to place a call to the police or to place the call himself. It bears emphasizing that the duty in this case does not require that one must go to the aid of another. That is not the issue here. The employee was not the good samaritan intent on aiding another. The patron was.

And so, courts have made several subtle changes to the common law rule. Let's apply them to the opening scenario. If the toddler's family sues Jason, will they be successful? Probably not.

Jason did not have a duty or a special relationship of trust with the toddler. Jason did not stand in the way of someone else trying to call the police. He may be morally culpable for refusing to save a life, but he will not be legally liable unless an entirely new change to the common law occurs.

The bystander rule, that hardy oak, is alive and well. Various initials have been carved into its bark—the exceptions we have seen and a variety of others—but the trunk is strong and the leaves green. Perhaps someday the proliferating exceptions will topple it, but the process of the common law is slow, and that day is nowhere in sight.

EXAM Strategy

Question: When Rachel is walking her dog, Bozo, she watches a skydiver float to earth. He lands in an enormous tree, suspended 45 feet above ground. "Help!" the man shouts. Rachel hurries to the tree and sees the skydiver bleeding profusely. She takes out her cell phone to call 911 for help, but just then Bozo runs away. Rachel darts after the dog, afraid that he will jump in a nearby pond and emerge smelling of mud. She forgets about the skydiver and takes Bozo home. Three hours later, the skydiver expires.

The victim's family sues Rachel. She defends by saying she feared that Bozo would have an allergic reaction to mud, and that in any case she could not have climbed 45 feet up a tree to save the man. The family argues that the dog is not allergic to mud, that even if he is, a pet's inconvenience pales compared to human life, and that Rachel could have phoned for emergency help without climbing an inch. Please rule.

Strategy: The family's arguments might seem compelling, but are they relevant? Rachel is a bystander, someone who perceives another in danger. What is the rule concerning a bystander's obligation to act? Apply the rule to the facts of this case.

Result: A bystander has no duty to assist someone in peril unless she created the danger. Rachel did not create the skydiver's predicament. She had no obligation to do anything. Rachel wins.

4-2 STATUTORY LAW

More law is created by statute than by the courts. Statutes affect each of us every day, in our business, professional, and personal lives. When the system works correctly, this is the one part of the law over which "we the people" have control. We elect the legislators who pass state statutes; we vote for the senators and representatives who create federal statutes.

Every other November, voters in all 50 states cast ballots for members of Congress. The winners of congressional elections convene in Washington, D.C., and create statutes. In this section, we look at how Congress does its work creating statutes.[5] Using the Civil Rights Act as a backdrop, we will follow a bill as it makes its way through Congress and beyond.

4-2a Bills

Congress is organized into two houses, the House of Representatives and the Senate. Either house may originate a proposed statute, that is called a **bill**. To become law, the bill must be voted on and approved by both houses. Once both houses pass it, they will send it to the President. If the President signs the bill, it becomes law and is then a statute. If the President opposes the bill, he will **veto** it, in which case it is not law.[6]

If you visit either house of Congress, you will probably find half a dozen legislators on the floor, with one person talking and no one listening. This is because most of the work is done in committees. Both houses are organized into dozens of committees, each with special functions. The House currently has about 25 committees (further divided into about 150 subcommittees), and the Senate has approximately 20 committees (with about 86 subcommittees). For example, the Armed Services Committee of each house oversees the huge defense budget and the workings of the armed forces. Labor committees handle legislation concerning organized labor and working conditions. Banking committees develop expertise on financial institutions. Judiciary committees review nominees to the federal courts. There are dozens of other committees, some very powerful, because they control vast amounts of money, and some relatively weak. Few of us ever think about the House Agricultural Subcommittee on Specialty Crops. But if we owned a family peanut farm, we would pay close attention to the subcommittee's agenda, because those members of Congress would pay close attention to us.

Bill
A proposed statute, submitted to Congress or a state legislature.

Veto
The power of the President to reject legislation passed by Congress.

---

[5]State legislatures operate similarly in creating state laws.
[6]Congress may, however, attempt to override the veto. See the discussion following.

When a bill is proposed in either house, it is referred to the committee that specializes in that subject. Why are bills proposed in the first place? For any of several reasons:

- **New Issue, New Worry.** If society begins to focus on a new issue, Congress may respond with legislation. We consider below, for example, the congressional response in the 1960s to employment discrimination.

- **Unpopular Judicial Ruling.** If Congress disagrees with a judicial interpretation of a statute, the legislators may pass a new statute to modify or "undo" the court decision. For example, if the Supreme Court misinterprets a statute about musical copyrights, Congress may pass a new law correcting the Court's error. However, the legislators have no such power to modify a court decision based on the Constitution. When the Supreme Court ruled that lawyers had a right *under the First Amendment* to advertise their services, Congress lacked the power to change the decision.

- **Criminal Law.** Statutory law, unlike common law, is prospective. Legislators are hoping to control the future. And that is why almost all criminal law is statutory. A court cannot retroactively announce that it *has been* a crime for a retailer to accept kickbacks from a wholesaler. Everyone must know the rules in advance because the consequences—prison, a felony record, etc.—are so harsh.

4-2b Discrimination: Congress and the Courts

The civil rights movement of the 1950s and 1960s convinced most citizens that African Americans suffered significant and unacceptable discrimination in jobs, housing, voting, schools, and other basic areas of life. Demonstrations and boycotts, marches and counter-marches, church bombings and killings persuaded the nation that the problem was vast and urgent.

In 1963, President Kennedy proposed legislation to guarantee equal rights in these areas. The bill went to the House Judiciary Committee, which heard testimony for weeks. Witnesses testified that blacks were often unable to vote because of their race, that landlords and home sellers adamantly refused to sell or rent to African Americans, that education was grossly unequal, and that blacks were routinely denied good jobs in many industries. Eventually, the Judiciary Committee approved the bill and sent it to the full House.

The bill was dozens of pages long and divided into "titles," with each title covering a major issue. Title VII concerned employment. We will consider the progress of Title VII in Congress and in the courts. Here is one section of Title VII, as reported to the House floor:[7]

> Sec. 703(a). It shall be an unlawful employment practice for an employer—to fail or refuse to hire or to discharge any individual, or otherwise to discriminate against any individual with respect to his compensation, terms, conditions, or privileges of employment, because of such individual's race, color, religion, or national origin; or
>
> to limit, segregate, or classify his employees in any way which would deprive or tend to deprive any individual of employment opportunities or otherwise adversely affect his status as an employee, because of such individual's race, color, religion, or national origin.

---

[7]The section number in the House bill was actually 704(a); we use 703 here because that is the number of the section when the bill became law and the number to which the Supreme Court refers in later litigation.

4-2c Debate

The proposed bill was intensely controversial and sparked argument throughout Congress. Here are some excerpts from one day's debate on the House floor, on February 8, 1964:[8]

> MR. WAGGONNER. I speak to you in all sincerity and ask for the right to discriminate if I so choose because I think it is my right. I think it is my right to choose my social companions. I think it is my right if I am a businessman to run it as I please, to do with my own as I will. I think that is a right the Constitution gives to every man. I want the continued right to discriminate and I want the other man to have the right to continue to discriminate against me, because I am discriminated against every day. I do not feel inferior about it.
>
> I ask you to forget about politics, forget about everything except the integrity of the individual, leaving to the people of this country the right to live their lives in the manner they choose to live. Do not destroy this democracy for a Socialist government. A vote for this bill is no less.
>
> MR. CONTE. If the serious cleavage which pitted brother against brother and citizen against citizen during the tragedy of the Civil War is ever to be justified, it can be justified in this House and then in the other body with the passage of this legislation which can and must reaffirm the rights to all individuals which are inherent in our Constitution.
>
> The distinguished poet Mark Van Doren has said that "equality is absolute or no, nothing between can stand," and nothing should now stand between us and the passage of strong and effective civil rights legislation. It is to this that we are united in a strong bipartisan coalition today, and when the laws of the land proclaim that the 88th Congress acted effectively, judiciously, and wisely, we can take pride in our accomplishments as free men.

Other debate was less rhetorical and aimed more at getting information. The following exchange anticipates a 30-year controversy on quotas:

> MR. JOHANSEN. I have asked for this time to raise a question and I would ask particularly for the attention of the gentleman from New York [Mr. Goodell] because of a remark he made—and I am not quarreling with it. I understood him to say there is no plan for balanced employment or for quotas in this legislation I am raising a question as to whether in the effort to eliminate discrimination—and incidentally that is an undefined term in the bill—we may get to a situation in which employers and conceivably union leaders, will insist on legislation providing for a quota system as a matter of self-protection.
>
> Now let us suppose this hypothetical situation exists with 100 jobs to be filled. Let us say 150 persons apply and suppose 75 of them are Negro and 75 of them are white. Supposing the employer hires 75 white men. [Does anyone] have a right to claim they have been discriminated against on the basis of color?
>
> MR. GOODELL. It is the intention of the legislation that if applicants are equal in all other respects there will be no restriction. One may choose from among equals. So long as there is no distinction on the basis of race, creed, or color it will not violate the act.

The debate on racial issues carried on. Later in the day, Congressman Smith of Virginia offered an amendment that could scarcely have been smaller—or more important:

> Amendment offered by Mr. Smith of Virginia: On page 68, line 23, after the word "religion," insert the word "sex."

In other words, Smith was asking that discrimination on the basis of sex also be outlawed, along with the existing grounds of race, color, national origin, and religion. Congressman Smith's proposal produced the following comments:

---

[8]The order of speakers is rearranged, and the remarks are edited.

MR. CELLER. You know, the French have a phrase for it when they speak of women and men. They say "vive la différence." I think the French are right. Imagine the upheaval that would result from adoption of blanket language requiring total equality. Would male citizens be justified in insisting that women share with them the burdens of compulsory military service? What would become of traditional family relationships? What about alimony? What would become of the crimes of rape and statutory rape? I think the amendment seems illogical, ill timed, ill placed, and improper.

MRS. ST. GEORGE. Mr. Chairman, I was somewhat amazed when I came on the floor this afternoon to hear the very distinguished chairman of the Committee on the Judiciary [Mr. Celler] make the remark that he considered the amendment at this point illogical. I can think of nothing more logical than this amendment at this point.

There are still many States where women cannot serve on juries. There are still many States where women do not have equal educational opportunities. In most States and, in fact, I figure it would be safe to say, in all States—women do not get equal pay for equal work. That is a very well known fact. And to say that this is illogical. What is illogical about it? All you are doing is simply correcting something that goes back, frankly to the Dark Ages.

The debate continued. Some supported the "sex" amendment because they were determined to end sexual bias. But politics are complex. Some *opponents* of civil rights supported the amendment because they believed that it would make the legislation less popular and cause Congress to defeat the entire Civil Rights bill.

That strategy did not work. The amendment passed, and sex was added as a protected trait. And, after more debate and several votes, the entire bill passed the House. It went to the Senate, where it followed a similar route from the Judiciary Committee to the full Senate. Much of the Senate debate was similar to what we have seen. But some senators raised a new issue, concerning §703(2), which prohibited *segregating or classifying* employees based on any of the protected categories (race, color, national origin, religion, or sex). Senator Tower was concerned that §703(2) meant that an employee in a protected category could never be given any sort of job test. So the Senate amended §703 to include a new subsection:

> Sec. 703(h). Notwithstanding any other provision of this title, it shall not be an unlawful employment practice for an employer … to give and to act upon the results of any professionally developed ability test provided that such test is not designed, intended or used to discriminate because of race, color, religion, sex or national origin.

With that amendment, and many others, the bill passed the Senate.

CONFERENCE COMMITTEE

Civil rights legislation had now passed both houses, but the bills were no longer the same due to the many amendments. This is true with most legislation. The next step is for the two houses to send representatives to a House-Senate Conference Committee. This committee examines all of the differences between the two bills and tries to reach a compromise. With the Civil Rights bill, Senator Tower's amendment was left in; other Senate amendments were taken out. When the Conference Committee had settled every difference between the two versions, the new, modified bill was sent back to each house for a new vote.

The House of Representatives and the Senate again angrily debated the compromise language reported from the Conference Committee. Finally, after years of violent public demonstrations and months of debate, each house passed the same bill. President Johnson promptly signed it. The Civil Rights Act of 1964 was law. See Exhibit 4.1.

EXHIBIT 4.1 The two houses of Congress are organized into dozens of committees, a few of which are shown here. The path of the 1964 Civil Rights Act (somewhat simplified) was as follows: [1] The House Judiciary Committee approved the bill and sent it to the full House; [2] the full House passed the bill and sent it to the Senate, where it was assigned to the Senate Judiciary Committee; [3] the Senate Judiciary Committee passed an amended version of the bill and sent it to the full Senate; [4] the full Senate passed the bill with additional amendments. Since the Senate version was now different from the bill the House passed, the bill went to a Conference Committee. The Conference Committee [5] reached a compromise and sent the new version of the bill back to both houses. Each house passed the compromise bill (6 and 7) and sent it to the President, who signed it into law (8).

But the passing of a statute is not always the end of the story. Sometimes courts must interpret congressional language and intent.

4-2d Statutory Interpretation

Title VII of the Civil Rights Act obviously prohibited an employer from saying to a job applicant, "We don't hire minorities." In some parts of the country, that had been common practice; after the Civil Rights Act passed, it became rare. Employers who routinely hired whites only, or promoted only whites, found themselves losing lawsuits. A new group of cases arose, those in which some job standard was set that appeared to be racially neutral, yet had a discriminatory effect. In North Carolina, the Duke Power Co. required that applicants for higher paying, promotional positions meet two requirements: They must have a high school diploma and they must pass a standardized written test. There was no evidence that either requirement related to successful job performance. Blacks met the requirements in lower percentages than whites, and consequently whites obtained a disproportionate share of the good jobs.

Title VII did not precisely address this kind of case. It clearly outlawed overt discrimination. Was Duke Power's policy overt discrimination, or was it protected by Senator Tower's amendment, §703(h)? The case went all the way to the Supreme Court, where the Court had to interpret the new law.

Courts are often called upon to interpret a statute, that is, to explain precisely what the language means and how it applies in a given case. There are three primary steps in a court's statutory interpretation:

- **Plain Meaning Rule.** When a statute's words have ordinary, everyday significance, the court will simply apply those words. Section 703(a)(1) of the Civil Rights Act prohibits firing someone because of her religion. Could an employer who had fired a Catholic because of her religion argue that Catholicism is not really a religion, but more of a social group? No. The word "religion" has a plain meaning, and courts apply its commonsense definition.

- **Legislative History and Intent.** If the language is unclear, the court must look deeper. Section 703(a)(2) prohibits classifying employees in ways that are discriminatory. Does that section prevent an employer from requiring high school diplomas, as Duke Power did? The explicit language of the statute does not answer the question. The court will look at the law's history to determine the intent of the legislature. The court will examine committee hearings, reports, and the floor debates that we have seen.

- **Public Policy.** If the legislative history is unclear, courts will rely on general public policies, such as reducing crime, creating equal opportunity, and so forth. They may include in this examination some of their own prior decisions. Courts assume that the legislature is aware of prior judicial decisions, and if the legislature did not change those decisions, the statute will be interpreted to incorporate them.

Here is how the Supreme Court interpreted the 1964 Civil Rights Act.

Landmark Case

GRIGGS V. DUKE POWER CO.
401 U.S. 424, 91 S. Ct. 849, 1971 U.S. LEXIS 134
United States Supreme Court, 1971

CASE SUMMARY

Facts: See the discussion of the Duke Power Company's job requirements in the "Statutory Interpretation" section above.

Issue: *Did Title VII of the 1964 Civil Rights Act require that employment tests be job-related?*

Decision: Yes, employment tests must be job-related.

Reasoning: Congress's goal in enacting Title VII is plain from its language: to achieve equality of opportunity and remove barriers that have favored whites. An employer may not use any practice, procedure, or test that perpetuates discrimination. This is true not only for overtly discriminatory behavior but also for conduct that appears fair yet has a discriminatory effect. The key is business necessity. An employment test or restriction that excludes blacks is prohibited unless it is required to do the particular job. In this case, neither the high school completion requirement nor the general intelligence test is related to job performance, and therefore neither is permissible.

And so the highest Court ruled that if a job requirement had a discriminatory impact, the employer could use that requirement only if it was related to job performance. Many more cases arose. For almost two decades courts held that, once workers showed that a job requirement had a discriminatory effect, the employer had the burden to prove that the requirement was necessary for the business. The requirement had to be essential to achieve an important goal. If there was any way to achieve that goal without discriminatory impact, the employer had to use it.

4-2e Changing Times

But things changed. In 1989, a more conservative Supreme Court decided *Wards Cove Packing Co. v. Atonio*.[9] The plaintiffs were nonwhite workers in salmon canneries in Alaska. The canneries had two types of jobs: skilled and unskilled. Nonwhites (Filipinos and Alaska Natives) invariably worked as low-paid, unskilled workers, canning the fish. The higher paid, skilled positions were filled almost entirely with white workers, who were hired during the off-season in Washington and Oregon.

There was no overt discrimination. But plaintiffs claimed that various practices led to the racial imbalances. The practices included failing to promote from within the company, hiring through separate channels (cannery jobs were done through a union hall, skilled positions were filled out of state), nepotism, and an English language requirement. Once again the case reached the Supreme Court, where Justice White wrote the Court's opinion.

If the plaintiffs succeeded in showing that the job requirements led to racial imbalance, said the Court, the employer now only had to demonstrate that the requirement or practice "serves, in a significant way, the legitimate employment goals of the employer [T]here is no requirement that the challenged practice be 'essential' or 'indispensable' to the employer's business." In other words, the Court removed the "business necessity" requirement of *Griggs* and replaced it with "legitimate employment goals."

4-2f Voters' Role

The response to *Wards Cove* was quick. Liberals decried it; conservatives hailed it. Everyone agreed that it was a major change that would make it substantially harder for plaintiffs to bring successful discrimination cases. Democrats introduced bills to reverse the interpretation of *Wards Cove*. President George H. W. Bush strongly opposed any new bill. He said it would lead to "quotas," that is, that employers would feel obligated to hire a certain percentage of workers from all racial categories to protect themselves from suits. This was the issue that Congressman Johansen had raised in the original House debate in 1964.

Both houses passed bills restoring the "business necessity" holding of *Griggs*. Again there were differences, and a Conference Committee resolved them. After acrimonious debate, both houses passed the compromise bill in October 1990. Was it therefore law? No. President Bush immediately vetoed the bill. He said it would compel employers to adopt quotas.

4-2g Congressional Override

When the President vetoes a bill, Congress has one last chance to make it law: an override. If both houses repass the bill, each by a two-thirds margin, it becomes law over the President's veto. Congress attempted to pass the 1990 Civil Rights bill over the Bush veto, but it fell short in the Senate by one vote.

---

[9] 490 U.S. 642, 109 S. Ct. 2115, 1989 U.S. LEXIS 2794 (1989).

Civil rights advocates tried again, in January 1991, introducing a new bill to reverse the *Wards Cove* rule. Again both houses debated and bargained. The new bill stated that, once an employee proves that a particular employment practice causes a discriminatory impact, the employer must "demonstrate that the challenged practice is job related for the position in question and consistent with business necessity."

Now the two sides fought over the exact meanings of two terms: "job related" and "business necessity." Each side offered definitions, but they could not reach agreement. It appeared that the entire bill would founder over those terms. So Congress did what it often does when faced with a problem of definition: It dropped the issue. Liberals and conservatives agreed not to define the troublesome terms. They would leave that task to courts to perform through statutory interpretation.

With the definitions left out, the new bill passed both houses. In November 1991, President Bush signed the bill into law. The President stated that the new bill had been improved and no longer threatened to create racial quotas. His opponents charged he had reversed course for political reasons, anticipating the 1992 presidential election.

And so, the Congress restored the "business necessity" interpretation to its own 1964 Civil Rights Act. No one would say, however, that it had been a simple process.

EXAM Strategy

Question: Kelly Hackworth took a leave of absence from her job at Progressive Insurance to care for her ailing mother. When she offered to return, Progressive refused to give her the same job or one like it. She sued based on the Family Medical Leave Act, a federal statute that requires firms to give workers returning from family leave their original job or an equivalent one. However, the statute excludes from its coverage workers whose company employs "fewer than 50 people within 75 miles" of the worker's jobsite. Between Ms. Hackworth's jobsite in Norman, Oklahoma, and the company's Oklahoma City workplace (less than 75 miles away), Progressive employed 47 people. At its Lawton, Oklahoma facility, Progressive employed three more people—but Lawton was 75.6 miles (wouldn't you know it) away from Norman. Progressive argued that the job was not covered by the statute. Hackworth claimed that this distance should be considered "within 75 miles," thereby rendering her eligible for FMLA leave. Even if it were not, she urged, it would be absurd to disqualify her from important rights based on a disparity of six-tenths of a mile. Please rule.

Strategy: The question asks you to interpret a statute. How do courts do that? There are three steps: the plain meaning rule; legislative history; and public policy. Apply those steps to these facts.

Result: In this real case, the court ruled that the plain meaning of "within 75 miles" was *75 miles or less*. Lawton was not 75 miles or less from Norman. The statute did not apply and Ms. Hackworth lost.[10]

---

[10]*Hackworth v. Progressive Casualty Ins. Co.*, 468 F.3d 722 (10th Cir. 2006).

4-3 ADMINISTRATIVE LAW

Before beginning this section, please return your seat to its upright position. Stow the tray firmly in the seatback in front of you. Turn off any laptops, cell phones, or other electronic devices. Sound familiar? Administrative agencies affect each of us every day in hundreds of ways. They have become the fourth branch of government. Supporters believe that they provide unique expertise in complex areas; detractors regard them as unelected government run amok.

Many administrative agencies are familiar. The Federal Aviation Administration, which requires all airlines to ensure that your seats are upright before takeoff and landing, is an administrative agency. The Internal Revenue Service expects to hear from us every April 15. The Environmental Protection Agency regulates the water quality of the river in your town. The Federal Trade Commission oversees the commercials that shout at you from your television set.

Before beginning this section, please return your seat to its upright position. Stow the tray firmly in the seatback in front of you.

Other agencies are less familiar. You may never have heard of the Bureau of Land Management, but if you go into the oil and gas industry, you will learn that this powerful agency has more control over your land than you do. If you develop real estate in Palos Hills, Illinois, you will tremble every time the Appearance Commission of the City of Palos Hills speaks, since you cannot construct a new building without its approval. If your software corporation wants to hire an Argentine expert on databases, you will get to know the complex workings of Immigration and Customs Enforcement: No one lawfully enters this country without its nod of approval.

4-3a Background

By the 1880s, trains crisscrossed America. But this technological miracle became an economic headache. Congress worried that the railroads' economic muscle enabled a few powerful corporations to reap unfair profits. The railroad industry needed closer regulation. Who would do it? Courts decide individual cases; they do not regulate industries. Congress itself passes statutes, but it has no personnel to oversee the day-to-day working of a huge industry. For example, Congress lacks the expertise to establish rates for freight passing from Kansas City to Chicago, and it has no personnel to enforce rates once they are set.

A new entity was needed. Congress passed the Interstate Commerce Act, creating the Interstate Commerce Commission (ICC), the first administrative agency. The ICC began regulating freight and passenger transportation over the growing rail system and continued to do so for over 100 years. Congress gave the ICC power to regulate rates and investigate harmful practices, to hold hearings, issue orders, and punish railroads that did not comply.

The ICC was able to hire and develop a staff that was expert in the issues that Congress wanted controlled. The agency had enough flexibility to deal with the problems in a variety of ways: by regulating, investigating, and punishing. And that is what has made administrative agencies an attractive solution for Congress: One entity, focusing on one industry, can combine expertise and flexibility. However, the ICC also developed great power, which voters could not reach, and thereby started the great and lasting conflict over the role of agencies.

During the Great Depression of the 1930s, the Roosevelt administration and Congress created dozens of new agencies. Many were based on social demands, such as the need of the elderly population for a secure income. Political and social conditions dominated again in the 1960s, as Congress created agencies, such as the Equal Employment Opportunity Commission, to combat discrimination.

Then during the 1980s, the Reagan administration made an effort to decrease the number and strength of the agencies. For several years some agencies declined in influence, though others did not. Today, there is still controversy about how much power agencies should have.

4-3b Classification of Agencies

Agencies exist at the federal, state, and local level. We will focus on federal agencies because they have national impact and great power. Most of the principles discussed apply to state and local agencies as well. Virtually any business or profession you choose to work in will be regulated by at least one administrative agency, and it may be regulated by several.

EXECUTIVE-INDEPENDENT

Some federal agencies are part of the executive branch, while others are independent agencies. This is a major distinction. The President has much greater control of executive agencies for the simple reason that he can fire the agency head at any time. An executive agency will seldom diverge far from the President's preferred policies. Some familiar executive agencies are the Internal Revenue Service (part of the Treasury Department); the Federal Bureau of Investigation (Department of Justice); the Food and Drug Administration (Department of Health and Human Services); and the Nuclear Regulatory Commission (Department of Energy).

The President has no such removal power over independent agencies. The Federal Communications Commission (FCC) is an independent agency. For many corporations involved in broadcasting, the FCC has more day-to-day influence on their business than Congress, the courts, and the President combined. Other powerful independent agencies are the Federal Trade Commission, the Securities and Exchange Commission, the National Labor Relations Board, and the Environmental Protection Agency.

ENABLING LEGISLATION

Enabling legislation
Laws passed by Congress that establish federal agencies and define their powers.

Congress creates a federal agency by passing **enabling legislation**. The Interstate Commerce Act was the enabling legislation that established the ICC. Typically, the enabling legislation describes the problems that Congress believes need regulation, establishes an agency to do it, and defines the agency's powers.

Critics argue that Congress is delegating to another body powers that only the legislature or courts are supposed to exercise. This puts administrative agencies above the voters. But legal attacks on administrative agencies have consistently failed for several decades. Courts acknowledge that agencies have become an integral part of a complex economy, and so long as there are some limits on an agency's discretion, courts will generally uphold its powers.

4-4 POWER OF AGENCIES

Administrative agencies use three kinds of power to do the work assigned to them: They make rules, they investigate, and they adjudicate.

4-4a Rulemaking

One of the most important functions of an administrative agency is to make rules. In making rules, the agency attempts, prospectively, to establish fair and uniform behavior for all businesses in the affected area. **To create a new rule is to promulgate it.** Agencies promulgate two types of rules: legislative and interpretive.

Types of Rules: Legislative and Interpretive

Legislative rules are the most important agency rules, and they are much like statutes. Here, an agency creates law by requiring businesses or private citizens to act in a certain way. Suppose you operate a website for young shoppers, aged 10 to 18. Like most online merchants, you consider yourself free to collect as much data as possible about consumers. Wrong. The Federal Trade Commission, a federal agency, has promulgated detailed rules governing any site directed to young children. Before obtaining private data from these immature consumers, you must let them know exactly who you are, how to contact site operators, precisely what you are seeking, and how it will be used. You must also obtain verifiable parental consent before collecting, using, or disclosing any personal information. Failure to follow the rules can result in a substantial civil penalty. This modest legislative rule, in short, will be more important to your business than most statutes passed by Congress.

Interpretive rules do not change the law. They are the agency's interpretation of what the law already requires. But they can still affect all of us. For example, in 1977, Congress amended the Clean Air Act in an attempt to reduce pollution from factories. The act required the Environmental Protection Agency (EPA) to impose emission standards on "stationary sources" of pollution. But what did "stationary source" mean? It was the EPA's job to define that term. Obscure work, to be sure, yet the results could be seen and even smelled, because the EPA's definition would determine the quality of air entering our lungs every time we breathe. Environmentalists wanted the term defined to include every smokestack in a factory so that the EPA could regulate each one. The EPA, however, developed the "bubble concept," ruling that "stationary source" meant an entire factory, but not the individual smokestacks. As a result, polluters could shift emission among smokestacks in a single factory to avoid EPA regulation. Environmentalists howled that this interpretation gutted the purpose of the statute, but to no avail. The agency had spoken, merely by interpreting a statute.[11]

How Rules Are Made

Corporations fight many a court battle over whether an agency has the right to issue a particular rule and whether it was promulgated properly. The critical issue is this: How much participation is the public entitled to before an agency issues a rule? There are two basic methods of rulemaking.[12]

Informal Rulemaking   On many issues, agencies may use a simple "notice and comment" method of rulemaking. The agency must publish a proposed rule in advance and permit the public a comment period. During this period, the public may submit any objections and arguments, with supporting data. The agency will make its decision and publish the final rule.

For example, the Department of Transportation may use the informal rulemaking procedure to require safety features for all new automobiles. The agency must listen to objections from interested parties, notably car manufacturers, and it must give a written response to the objections. The agency is required to have rational reasons for the final choices it makes. However, it is not obligated to satisfy all parties or do their bidding.

Formal Rulemaking   In the enabling legislation, Congress may require that an agency hold a hearing before promulgating rules. Congress does this to make the agency more accountable to the public. After the agency publishes its proposed rule, it must hold a public

---

[11]An agency's interpretation can be challenged in court, and this one was.

[12]Certain rules may be made with no public participation at all. For example, an agency's internal business affairs and procedures can be regulated without public comment, as can its general policy statements. None of these directly affect the public, and the public has no right to participate.

hearing. Opponents of the rule, typically affected businesses, may cross-examine the agency experts about the need for the rule and may testify against it. When the agency makes its final decision about the rule, it must prepare a formal, written response to everything that occurred at the hearing.

When used responsibly, these hearings give the public access to the agency and can help formulate sound policy. When used irresponsibly, hearings can be manipulated to stymie needed regulation. The most famous example concerns peanut butter. The Food and Drug Administration (FDA) began investigating peanut butter content in 1958. It found, for example, that Jif peanut butter, made by Procter & Gamble (P&G), had only 75 percent peanuts and 20 percent of a Crisco-type base. P&G fought the investigation, and any changes, for years. Finally, in 1965, the FDA proposed a minimum of 90 percent peanuts in peanut butter; P&G wanted 87 percent. The FDA wanted no more than 3 percent hydrogenated vegetable oil; P&G wanted no limit.

The hearings dragged on for months. One day, the P&G lawyer objected to the hearing going forward because he needed to vote that day. Another time, when an FDA official testified that consumer letters indicated the public wanted to know what was really in peanut butter, the P&G attorney demanded that the official bring in and identify the letters—all 20,000 of them. Finally, in 1968, a decade after beginning its investigation, the FDA promulgated final rules requiring 90 percent peanuts but eliminating the 3 percent cap on vegetable oil.[13]

4-4b Investigation

Agencies do a wide variety of work, but they all need broad factual knowledge of the field they govern. Some companies cooperate with an agency, furnishing information and even voluntarily accepting agency recommendations. For example, the U.S. Consumer Product Safety Commission investigates hundreds of consumer products every year and frequently urges companies to recall goods that the agency considers defective. Many firms comply.

Other companies, however, jealously guard information, often because corporate officers believe that disclosure would lead to adverse rules. To force disclosure, agencies use *subpoenas* and *searches*.

SUBPOENAS

Subpoena

An order to appear at a particular place and time. A **subpoena *duces tecum*** requires the person to produce certain documents or things.

A **subpoena** is an order to appear at a particular time and place to provide evidence. A **subpoena *duces tecum*** requires the person to appear and bring specified documents. Businesses and other organizations intensely dislike subpoenas and resent government agents plowing through records and questioning employees. What are the limits on an agency's investigation? The information sought:

- Must be *relevant* to a lawful agency investigation. The FCC is clearly empowered to investigate the safety of broadcasting towers, and any documents about tower construction are obviously relevant. Documents about employee racial statistics might indicate discrimination, but the FCC lacks jurisdiction on that issue and thus may not demand such documents.

- Must not be *unreasonably burdensome*. A court will compare the agency's need for the information with the intrusion on the corporation.

- Must not be *privileged*. The Fifth Amendment privilege against self-incrimination means that a corporate officer accused of criminal securities violations may not be compelled to testify about his behavior.

---

[13]For an excellent account of this high-fat hearing, see Mark J. Green, *The Other Government* (New York: W. W. Norton & Co., 1978), pp. 136–150.

Search and Seizure   At times an agency will want to conduct a surprise search of an enterprise and seize any evidence of wrongdoing. May an agency do that? Yes, although there are limitations. When a particular industry is *comprehensively regulated*, courts will assume that companies know they are subject to periodic, unannounced inspections. In those industries, an administrative agency may conduct a search without a warrant and seize evidence of violations. For example, the mining industry is minutely regulated, with strict rules covering equipment, mining depths, and air quality. Mining executives understand that they are closely watched. Accordingly, the Bureau of Mines may make unannounced, warrantless searches to ensure safety.[14]

The following case established many of the principles just described.

Landmark Case

UNITED STATES V. BISWELL

406 U.S. 311
United States Supreme Court, 1972

CASE SUMMARY

Facts: Biswell's pawnshop had a license to sell "sporting weapons." Treasury agents demanded to inspect his locked storeroom without a warrant, claiming that the Gun Control Act of 1968 gave them that right. Under this law, Treasury agents had permission to inspect firearm dealers' business records, firearms, and ammunition during business hours.

Biswell voluntarily opened the storeroom, where an agent found two sawed-off rifles. Because these guns did not remotely meet the definition of "sporting weapons," Biswell was convicted on firearms charges.

The appellate court found that, because the search violated the Fourth Amendment, the rifles could not be admitted as evidence. It reversed the conviction, and the government appealed to the Supreme Court.

Issue: *Did the agent's warrantless search violate the Constitution?*

Decision: No, the agent had a right to search the firearm dealer's premises without a warrant.

Reasoning: The Gun Control Act of 1968 was a valid statute aimed at regulating firearms and preventing violent crime. As part of this effort, it gave the Treasury agents the right to perform frequent and unannounced inspections of firearm dealers' premises. What good is a firearm inspection that is announced ahead of time? A warrant requirement would certainly frustrate the statute's purpose of controlling illegal guns.

Warrants protect an individual's expectation of privacy. Biswell had no justifiable expectation of privacy in his storeroom, since he, like all firearms dealers, knew that his business records, firearms, and ammunition were subject to inspection. Biswell accepted these rules when he obtained his license. Also he received annual reminders.

Since inspections furthered the Gun Control Act's important purpose and Biswell could not reasonably expect his storeroom to be private, the seizure of the sawed-off rifles was permissible. They should have been admitted into evidence.

4-4c Adjudication

To **adjudicate** a case is to hold a hearing about an issue and then decide it. Agencies adjudicate countless cases. The FCC adjudicates which applicant for a new television license is best qualified. The Occupational Safety and Health Administration (OSHA) holds adversarial hearings to determine whether a manufacturing plant is dangerous.

Adjudicate
To hold a formal hearing about an issue and then decide it.

---

[14]*Donovan v. Dewey*, 452 U.S. 594, 101 S. Ct. 2534, 1980 U.S. LEXIS 58 (1981).

Administrative law judge (ALJ)

An agency employee who acts as an impartial decision maker.

Most adjudications begin with a hearing before an **administrative law judge (ALJ)**. There is no jury. An ALJ is an employee of the agency but is expected to be impartial in her rulings. All parties are represented by counsel. The rules of evidence are informal, and an ALJ may receive any testimony or documents that will help resolve the dispute.

After all evidence is taken, the ALJ makes a decision. The losing party has a right to appeal to an appellate board within the agency. The appellate board may ignore the ALJ's decision. If it does not, an unhappy party may appeal to federal court.

4-5 LIMITS ON AGENCY POWER

There are four primary methods of reining in these powerful creatures: statutory, political, judicial, and informational.

4-5a Statutory Control

As discussed, the enabling legislation of an agency provides some limits. It may require that the agency use formal rulemaking or investigate only certain issues. The Administrative Procedure Act imposes additional controls by requiring basic fairness in areas not regulated by the enabling legislation.

4-5b Political Control

The President's influence is greatest with executive agencies. Congress, though, "controls the purse." No agency, executive or independent, can spend money it does not have. An agency that angers Congress risks having a particular program defunded or its entire budget cut. Further, Congress may decide to defund an agency as a cost-cutting measure. In its effort to balance the budget, Congress abolished the Interstate Commerce Commission, transferring its functions to the Transportation Department.

Congress has additional control because it must approve presidential nominees to head agencies. Before approving a nominee, Congress will attempt to determine her intentions. And, finally, Congress may amend an agency's enabling legislation, limiting its power.

4-5c Judicial Review

An individual or corporation directly harmed by an administrative rule, investigation, or adjudication may generally have that action reviewed in federal court.[15] The party seeking review, for example, a corporation, must have suffered direct harm; the courts will not listen to theoretical complaints about an agency action.[16] And that party must first have taken all possible appeals within the agency itself.[17]

---

[15] In two narrow groups of cases, a court may not review an agency action. In a few cases, courts hold that a decision is "committed to agency discretion," a formal way of saying that courts will keep hands off. This result occurs only with politically sensitive issues, such as international air routes. In some cases, the enabling legislation makes it absolutely clear that Congress wanted no court to review certain decisions. Courts will honor that.

[16] The law describes this requirement by saying that a party must have standing to bring a case. A college student who has a theoretical belief that the EPA should not interfere with the timber industry has no standing to challenge an EPA rule that prohibits logging in a national forest. A lumber company that was ready to log that area has suffered a direct economic injury: It has standing to sue.

[17] This is the doctrine of exhaustion of remedies. A lumber company may not go into court the day after the EPA publishes a proposed ban on logging. It must first exhaust its administrative remedies by participating in the administrative hearing and then pursuing appeals within the agency before venturing into court.

STANDARD ON REVIEW

Suppose OSHA promulgates a new rule limiting the noise level within steel mills. Certain mill operators are furious because they will have to retool their mills in order to comply. After exhausting their administrative appeals, they file suit seeking to force OSHA to withdraw the new rule. How does a court decide the case? Or, in legal terms, what standard does a court use in reviewing the case? Does it simply substitute its own opinion for that of the agency? No, it does not. The standard a court uses must take into account:

Facts   Courts generally defer to an agency's fact finding. If OSHA finds that human hearing starts to suffer when decibels reach a particular level, a court will probably accept that as final. The agency is presumed to have expertise on such subjects. As long as there is *substantial evidence* to support the fact decision, it will be respected.

Law   Courts often—but not always—defer to an agency's interpretation of the law. This is due in part to the enormous range of subjects that administrative agencies monitor. Consider the following example. "Chicken catchers" work in large poultry operations, entering coops, manually capturing broilers, loading them into cages, and driving them to a processing plant, where they ... well, never mind. On one farm, the catchers wanted to organize a union, but the company objected, pointing out that *agricultural* workers had no right to do so. Were chicken catchers "agricultural workers"? The National Labor Relations Board, an administrative agency, declared that chicken catchers were in fact *ordinary* workers, entitled to organize. The Supreme Court ruled that courts were obligated to give deference to the agency's decision about chicken catchers. If the agency's interpretation was *reasonable*, it was binding, even if the court itself might not have made the same analysis. The workers were permitted to form a union—though the chickens were not.

In the following case, however, the Supreme Court disagreed with the FCC's standards about profanity on TV. The high court ruled that these standards were too vague to be enforceable. The case contains vulgar language, so *please do not read it.*

FEDERAL COMMUNICATIONS COMMISSION v. FOX TELEVISION STATIONS, INC.

132 S. Ct. 2307
United States Supreme Court, 2012

CASE SUMMARY

Facts: "People have been telling me I'm on the way out every year, right? So f*** 'em," said Cher, on a televised Billboard Music Awards ceremony. A year later, on the same program, Nicole Richie asked, "Have you ever tried to get cow s*** out of a Prada purse? It's not so f****** simple."

U.S. law bans the broadcast of "any obscene, indecent, or profane language." The Federal Communications Commission (FCC), which regulates the broadcast industry, had issued guidelines indicating that the utterance of an isolated vulgarity was acceptable so long as it was not repeated at length. After Nicole Richie explained the difficulties of cleaning a Prada purse, the FCC declared a more stringent indecency policy. This stricter standard made a single fleeting expletive punishable if the word was, "patently offensive." But the FCC failed to give a clear definition of the term, and it enforced the new rule unevenly. For example, it allowed bad language during news interviews and films, but condemned the same words in other contexts.

When the FCC found that Fox had violated the agency's standards by broadcasting Cher and Nicole Richie's three words, Fox argued that the new policy was too vague and arbitrary. The appeals court agreed with Fox. The Supreme Court granted *certiorari.*

Issue: *Was the FCC's indecency policy unacceptably vague and arbitrary?*

Decision: Yes, the FCC had failed to give broadcasters fair notice of what kind of conduct could be punished. And it did not apply the rules equally to everyone.

Reasoning: The FCC has the right to set and change its policies. However, laws must provide a person of ordinary intelligence with reasonable notice of what behavior is prohibited. How could Fox have known that a fleeting F-word on live TV was forbidden when at other times such words were not? It could not and it did not.

Clear rules also ensure that government agencies do not act in an arbitrary or discriminatory fashion. To be fair, they must treat the same behavior in the same way. Never before had the FCC penalized this conduct. In fact, even after its stricter indecency standard was set, the FCC allowed the utterance of the F-word in other contexts. The FCC cannot penalize Fox if it then ignores the same behavior in others.

4-5d Informational Control and the Public

We started this section describing the pervasiveness of administrative agencies. We should end it by noting one way in which all of us have some direct control over these ubiquitous authorities: information.

> A popular government, without popular information, or the means of acquiring it, is but a Prologue to a Farce or a Tragedy—or perhaps both. Knowledge will forever govern ignorance, and a people who mean to be their own Governors must arm themselves with the power which knowledge gives.
>
> *James Madison, President, 1809–1817*

Two federal statutes arm us with the power of knowledge.

FREEDOM OF INFORMATION ACT

Congress passed the landmark Freedom of Information Act (known as "FOIA") in 1966. It is designed to give all of us, citizens, businesses, and organizations alike, access to the information that federal agencies are using. The idea is to avoid government by secrecy.

Any citizen or executive may make a "FOIA request" to any federal government agency. It is simply a written request that the agency furnish whatever information it has on the subject specified. Two types of data are available under FOIA. Anyone is entitled to information about how the agency operates, how it spends its money, and what statistics and other information it has collected on a given subject. People routinely obtain records about agency policies, environmental hazards, consumer product safety, taxes and spending, purchasing decisions, and agency forays into foreign affairs. A corporation that believes that OSHA is making more inspections of its textile mills than it makes of the competition could demand all relevant information, including OSHA's documents on the mill itself, comparative statistics on different inspections, OSHA's policies on choosing inspection sites, and so forth.

Second, all citizens are entitled to any records the government has *about them*. You are entitled to information that the Internal Revenue Service, or the Federal Bureau of Investigation, has collected about you.

FOIA does not apply to Congress, the federal courts, or the executive staff at the White House. Note also that, since FOIA applies to federal government agencies, you may not use it to obtain information from state or local governments or private businesses.

Exemptions   An agency officially has 10 days to respond to the request. In reality, most agencies are unable to meet the deadline but are obligated to make good faith efforts. FOIA exempts altogether nine categories from disclosure. The most important exemptions permit an agency to keep confidential information that relates to national security, criminal investigations, internal agency matters such as personnel or policy discussions, trade secrets or financial institutions, or an individual's private life.

PRIVACY ACT

This 1974 statute prohibits federal agencies from giving information about an individual to other agencies or organizations without written consent. There are exceptions, but overall this act has reduced the government's exchange of information about us "behind our back."

EXAM Strategy

Question: Builder wants to develop 1,000 acres in rural Montana, land that is home to the Kite Owl. The EPA rules that the Kite Owl is an endangered species, and prohibits development of the property. The developer appeals to the court. The EPA based its decision on five statistical studies, and the opinions of three out of seven experts. The court looks at the same evidence and acknowledges that the EPA decision is carefully reasoned and fair. However, the judges believe that the other four experts were right: The owl is *not* endangered. Should the court permit development?

Strategy: What is the legal standard for deciding whether a court should affirm or reverse an agency decision? As long as there is *substantial evidence* to support the factual conclusions, and a *reasonable basis* for the legal conclusion, the court should not impose its judgment. Agencies are presumed to have special expertise in their areas. As the *Fox Television* case tells us, an agency ruling should generally be affirmed unless it is arbitrary and capricious. Apply that standard here.

Result: The EPA made a careful, reasoned decision. The court may disagree, but it should not impose its views. The court must affirm the agency's ruling and prohibit development.

Chapter Conclusion

"Why can't they just fix the law?" They can, and sometimes they do—but it is a difficult and complex task. "They" includes a great many people and forces, from common law courts to members of Congress to campaign donors to administrative agencies. The courts have made the bystander rule slightly more humane, but it has been a long and bumpy road. Congress managed to restore the legal interpretation of its own 1964 Civil Rights Act, but it took months of debate and compromising. The FDA squeezed more peanuts into a jar of Jif, but it took nearly a decade to get the lid on.

A study of law is certain to create some frustrations. This chapter cannot prevent them all. However, an understanding of how law is made is the first step toward controlling that law.

EXAM REVIEW

1. **COMMON LAW**   The common law evolves in awkward fits and starts because courts attempt to achieve two contradictory purposes: predictability and flexibility. (p. 84)

2. **STARE DECISIS**   *Stare decisis* means "let the decision stand" and indicates that once a court has decided a particular issue, it will generally apply the same rule in future cases. (p. 84)

3. **BYSTANDER RULE**   The common law bystander rule holds that, generally, no one has a duty to assist someone in peril unless the bystander himself created the danger. Courts have carved some exceptions during the last 100 years, but the basic rule still stands. (pp. 84–85)

4. **LEGISLATION**   Bills originate in congressional committees and go from there to the full House of Representatives or Senate. If both houses pass the bill, the legislation normally must go to a Conference Committee to resolve differences between the two versions. The compromise version then goes from the Conference Committee back to both houses, and if passed by both, to the President. If the President signs the bill, it becomes a statute; if he vetoes it, Congress can pass it over his veto with a two-thirds majority in each house. (pp. 87–94)

5. **STATUTORY INTERPRETATION**   Courts interpret a statute by using the plain meaning rule; then, if necessary, legislative history and intent; and finally, if necessary, public policy. (pp. 91–93)

EXAM Strategy

Question: Whitfield, who was black, worked for Ohio Edison. Edison fired him, but then later offered to rehire him. Another employee argued that Edison's original termination of Whitfield had been race discrimination. Edison rescinded its offer to rehire Whitfield. Whitfield sued Edison, claiming that the company was retaliating for the other employee's opposition to discrimination. Edison pointed out that Title VII of the 1964 Civil Rights Act did not explicitly apply in such cases. Among other things, Title VII prohibits an employer from retaliating against *an employee* who has opposed illegal discrimination. But it does not say anything about retaliation based on *another employee's* opposition to discrimination. Edison argued that the statute did not protect Whitfield.

Strategy: What three steps does a court use to interpret a statute? First, we apply the plain meaning rule. Does that rule help us here? The statute neither allows nor prohibits Edison's conduct. The law does not mention this situation, and the plain meaning rule is of no help. Second step: Legislative history and intent. What did Congress intend with Title VII generally? With the provision that bars retaliation against a protesting employee? Resolving those issues should give you the answer to this question.

---

6. **ADMINISTRATIVE AGENCIES**   Congress creates federal administrative agencies with enabling legislation. The Administrative Procedure Act controls how agencies do their work. (pp. 95–96)

7. **RULEMAKING**   Agencies may promulgate legislative rules, which generally have the effect of statutes, or interpretive rules, which merely interpret existing statutes. (pp. 97–98)

8. **INVESTIGATION**   Agencies have broad investigatory powers and may use subpoenas and, in some cases, warrantless searches to obtain information. (pp. 98–99)

EXAM Strategy

Question: When Hiller Systems, Inc., was performing a safety inspection on board the M/V *Cape Diamond*, an ocean-going vessel, an accident killed two men. The Occupational Safety and Health Administration (OSHA), a federal agency, attempted to investigate, but Hiller refused to permit any of its employees to speak to OSHA investigators. What could OSHA do to pursue the investigation? What limits would there have been on OSHA's actions?

Strategy: Agencies make rules, investigate, and adjudicate. Which is involved here? Investigation. During an investigation, what power has an agency to force a company to produce data? What are the limits on that power?

9. **ADJUDICATION**   Agencies adjudicate cases, meaning that they hold hearings and decide issues. Adjudication generally begins with a hearing before an administrative law judge and may involve an appeal to the full agency or ultimately to federal court. (pp. 99–100)

10. **AGENCY LIMITATIONS**   The four most important limitations on the power of federal agencies are statutory control in the enabling legislation and the APA; political control by Congress and the President; judicial review; and the informational control created by the FOIA and the Privacy Act. (pp. 100–103)

5. Result: Congress passed Title VII as a bold, aggressive move to end race discrimination in employment. Further, by specifically prohibiting retaliation against an employee, Congress indicated it was aware that companies might punish those who spoke in favor of the very goals of Title VII. Protecting an employee from anti-discrimination statements made by a coworker is a very slight step beyond that, and appears consistent with the goals of Title VII and the anti-retaliation provision. Whitfield should win, and in the real case, he did.[18]

8. Result: OSHA can issue a subpoena *duces tecum*, demanding that those on board the ship, and their supervisors, appear for questioning, and bring with them all relevant documents. OSHA may ask for anything that is (1) relevant to the investigation, (2) not unduly burdensome, and (3) not privileged. Conversations between one of the ship inspectors and his supervisor are clearly relevant; a discussion between the supervisor and the company's lawyer is privileged.

---

[18]*EEOC v. Ohio Edison*, 7 F.3d 541 (6th Cir. 1993).

MULTIPLE-CHOICE QUESTIONS

1. A bill is vetoed by _____ .

   (a) the Speaker of the House

   (b) a majority of the voting members of the Senate

   (c) the President

   (d) the Supreme Court

2. If a bill is vetoed, it may still become law if it is approved by_____ .

   (a) two-thirds of the Supreme Court

   (b) two-thirds of registered voters

   (c) two-thirds of the Congress

   (d) the President

   (e) an independent government agency

3. Which of the following Presidents was most influential in the passing of the Civil Rights Act?

   (a) Franklin D. Roosevelt

   (b) Ronald Reagan

   (c) Abraham Lincoln

   (d) John F. Kennedy

   (e) George W. Bush

4. Under FOIA, any citizen may demand information about.

   (a) how an agency operates

   (b) how an agency spends its money

   (c) files that an agency has collected on the citizen herself

   (d) all of the above

5. If information requested under FOIA is not exempt, an agency has _____ to comply with the request.

   (a) 10 days

   (b) 30 days

   (c) 3 months

   (d) 6 months

ESSAY QUESTIONS

1. Until 1989 every state had a statute outlawing the burning of American flags. But in *Texas v. Johnson*,[19] the Supreme Court declared such statutes unconstitutional, saying that flag burning is symbolic speech protected by the First Amendment. Does Congress have the power to overrule the Court's decision?

2. In 1988, terrorists bombed Pan Am Flight 103 over Lockerbie, Scotland, killing all passengers on board. Congress sought to remedy security shortcomings by passing the Aviation Security Improvement Act of 1990, which, among other things, ordered the Federal Aviation Authority (FAA) to prescribe minimum training requirements and staffing levels for airport security. The FAA promulgated rules according to the informal rulemaking process. However, the FAA refused to disclose certain rules concerning training at specific airports. A public interest group called Public Citizen, Inc., along with family members of those who had died at Lockerbie, wanted to know the details of airport security. What steps should they take to obtain the information? Are they entitled to obtain it?

3. The Aviation Security Improvement Act states that the FAA can refuse to divulge information about airport security. The FAA interprets this statement to mean that it can withhold data in spite of the FOIA. Public Citizen and the Lockerbie family members interpret FOIA as being the controlling statute, requiring disclosure. Is the FAA interpretation binding?

4. An off-duty, out-of-uniform police officer and his son purchased some food from a 7-Eleven convenience store and were still in the parking lot when a carload of teenagers became rowdy. The officer went to speak to them, and the teenagers assaulted him. The officer shouted to his son to get the 7-Eleven clerk to call for help. The son entered the store, told the clerk that a police officer needed help, and instructed the clerk to call the police. He returned 30 seconds later and repeated the request, urging the clerk to say it was a Code 13. The son claimed that the clerk laughed at him and refused to do it. The policeman sued the store. **Argument for the Store:** We sympathize with the policeman and his family, but the store has no liability. A bystander is not obligated to come to the aid of anyone in distress unless the bystander created the peril, and obviously the store did not do so. The policeman should sue those who attacked him. **Argument for the Police Officer:** We agree that in general a bystander has no obligation to come to the aid of one in distress. However, when a business that is open to the public receives an urgent request to call the police, the business should either make the call or permit someone else to do it.

5. Federal antitrust statutes are complex, but the basic goal is straightforward: To prevent a major industry from being so dominated by a small group of corporations that they destroy competition and injure consumers. Does Major League Baseball violate the antitrust laws? Many observers say that it does. A small group of owners not only dominate the industry, but actually *own* it, controlling the entry of new owners into the game. This issue went to the United States Supreme Court in 1922. Justice Holmes ruled, perhaps surprisingly, that baseball is exempt from the antitrust laws, holding that baseball is not "trade or commerce." Suppose that members of Congress dislike this ruling and the current condition of baseball. What can they do?

---

[19]491 U.S. 397, 109 S. Ct. 2533, 1989 U.S. LEXIS 3115 (1989).

DISCUSSION QUESTIONS

1. Courts generally follow precedent, but in the *Tarasoff* and *Soldano* cases discussed earlier, they did not. Consider this chapter's opening scenario . *Should* Jason bear any *legal* responsibility for the toddler's untimely end; or should a court follow precedent and hold Jason blameless?

2. Revisit the *Fox Television Stations* case. Do you agree with the opinion? What would a sensible broadcast obscenity policy contain? When (if ever) should a network face fines for airing bad language?

3. Revisit *United States v. Biswell.* Do you agree with the Court's decision? Is it reasonable that government agencies can conduct searches more freely if a business is in an industry that is comprehensively regulated? Should a pawnshop face more searches than other kinds of enterprises, or should the rules be the same for all companies?

4. FOIA applies to government agencies, but it exempts Congress. Should top lawmakers be obligated to comply with FOIA requests, or would that create more problems than it would solve?

5. Suppose you were on a state supreme court and faced with a restaurant-choking case. Should you require restaurant employees to know and employ the Heimlich maneuver to assist a choking victim? If they do a bad job, they could cause additional injury. Should you permit them to do nothing at all? Is there a compromise position? What social policies are most important?

CHAPTER 5

CONSTITUTIONAL LAW

nuttakit/Stutterstock.com; © Stas Volik/Shutterstock.com

The consultant started his presentation to the energy company's board of directors. "So I don't have to tell you that if the Smith-Jones Bill ever passes Congress, it will be an utter disaster for your company. The House has already passed it. The President wants it. The only thing that kept it from becoming law this summer is that the Senate was too chicken to bring it up for a vote in an election year.

"Here's the bottom line: To be comfortable, you need three candidates who see things your way to beat current senators who support the bill."

> ## In state #3, we go negative. Really negative.

The next slide showed a large map of the United States with three states highlighted in red. "These are your best bets. Attempting wins here would cost $ 60 million total—not so much for a billion-dollar-a-year operation like yours.

"The money would go to saturation advertising from Labor Day to Election Day. I want to buy TV ads during local news programs all day, and during most primetime shows. I want the viewers to see your ads at least a dozen times before they go to the polls.

"In state #1, the challenger—your candidate—is a squeaky-clean state representative, but no one knows much about her outside her own district. She carries herself well, has a nice family. People will like her if they see her. Your money makes sure people will see her.

"In state #2, your guy hasn't really done much. But his grandfather was a hero at Normandy, and his dad was a coal miner. Great-grandparents were immigrants who came through New York with nothing in their pockets—I can see the ad with the Statue of Liberty already. A lot of voters will appreciate his family's story. This strategy will work if we have the funds to tell the story often enough.

"In state #3, we go negative. Really negative. Our opponent has been in the Senate a long time, and he's taken maybe 100,000 photos. We have three of them showing him with world leaders who have become unpopular of late. We're going to use them to tell a story about the senator putting foreign interests above American jobs and national security. People are angry—they think America is losing its place in the world. Our polling shows that this kind of campaign will be highly effective.

"You need to get into this election. All of your stakeholders benefit if the Smith-Jones Bill dies—your workers stay on the job, your shareholders make more money, and your customers pay lower prices. Corporations are nothing more or less than the people who work for them, and they have the right to express their political opinions. These ads would simply give your workers the chance to exercise their right to free speech."

The CFO interrupted, "Look, we're all against the Smith-Jones Bill. But is this plan *legal*?"

5-1 GOVERNMENT POWER

5-1a One in a Million

The Constitution of the United States is the greatest legal document ever written. No other written constitution has lasted so long, governed so many, or withstood such challenge. This amazing work was drafted in 1787, when two weeks were needed to make the horseback ride from Boston to Philadelphia, a pair of young cities in a weak and disorganized nation. Yet today, when that trip requires less than two hours by jet, that same Constitution successfully governs the most powerful country on earth. This longevity is a tribute to the wisdom and idealism of the Founding Fathers. The Constitution is not perfect, but overall, it has worked astonishingly well and has become the model for many constitutions around the world.

The Constitution sits above everything else in our legal system. No law can conflict with it. The chapter opener raises a constitutional issue: Does Congress have the right to prohibit corporations from spending money to affect elections, or are these actions protected as free speech under the First Amendment? We will explore this question later in the chapter when we discuss the *Citizens United* case.

The Constitution is short and relatively easy to read. This brevity is potent. The Founding Fathers, or Framers, wanted it to last for centuries, and they understood that would happen only if the document permitted interpretation and "fleshing out" by later generations. The Constitution's versatility is striking. In this chapter, the first part provides an overview of the Constitution, discussing how it came to be and how it is organized. The second part describes the power given to the three branches of government. The third part explains the individual rights the Constitution guarantees to citizens.

5-2 OVERVIEW

Thirteen American colonies declared independence from Great Britain in 1776 and gained it in 1783. The new status was exhilarating. Ours was the first nation in modern history founded on the idea that the people could govern themselves, democratically. The idea was daring, brilliant, and fraught with difficulties. The states were governing themselves under the Articles of Confederation, but these articles gave the central government no real power. The government could not tax any state or its citizens and had no way to raise money. The national government also lacked the power to regulate commerce between the states or between foreign nations and any state. This state of governance was disastrous. States began to impose taxes on goods entering from other states. The young "nation" was a collection of poor relations, threatening to squabble themselves to death.

In 1787, the states sent a group of 55 delegates to Philadelphia. Rather than amend the old articles, the Framers set out to draft a new document and to create a government that had never existed before. It was hard going. What structure should the government have? How much power? Representatives like Alexander Hamilton, a *federalist*, urged a strong central government. The new government must be able to tax and spend, regulate commerce, control the borders, and do all things that national governments routinely do. But Patrick Henry and other *antifederalists* feared a powerful central government. They had fought a bitter war precisely to get rid of autocratic rulers; they had seen the evil that a distant government could inflict. The antifederalists insisted that the states retain maximum authority, keeping political control closer to home.

The debate continues to this day, and periodically it plays a key role in elections. The "tea party" movement, for example, is a modern group of antifederalists.

Another critical question was how much power the *people* should have. Many of the delegates had little love for the common people and feared that extending this idea of democracy too far would lead to mob rule. Antifederalists again disagreed. The British had been thrown out, they insisted, to guarantee individual liberty and a chance to participate in the government. Power corrupted. It must be dispersed among the people to avoid its abuse.

How to settle these basic differences? By compromise, of course. **The Constitution is a series of compromises about power.** We will see many provisions granting power to one branch of the government while at the same time restraining the authority given.

5-2a Separation of Powers

The Framers did not want to place too much power in any single place. One method of limiting power was to create a national government divided into three branches, each independent and equal. Each branch would act as a check on the power of the other two. Article I of the Constitution created a Congress, which was to have legislative, or lawmaking, power. Article II created the office of President, defining the scope of executive, or enforcement, power. Article III established judicial, or interpretive, power by creating the Supreme Court and permitting additional federal courts.

Consider how the three separate powers balance one another: Congress was given the power to pass statutes, a major grant of power. But the President was permitted to veto, or block, proposed statutes, a nearly equal grant. Congress, in turn, had the right to override the veto, ensuring that the President would not become a dictator. The President was allowed to appoint federal judges and members of his cabinet, but only with a consenting vote from the Senate.

5-2b Individual Rights

The original Constitution was silent about the rights of citizens. This void alarmed many who feared that the new federal government would have unlimited power over their lives. So in 1791, the first 10 amendments, known as the **Bill of Rights**, were added to the Constitution, guaranteeing many liberties directly to individual citizens.

In the next two sections, we look in more detail at the two sides of the great series of compromises: power granted and rights protected.

Bill of Rights
The first 10 amendments to the Constitution outlining the rights of citizens.

5-3 POWER GRANTED

5-3a Congressional Power

To recap two key ideas from Chapter 1:

1. Voters in all 50 states elect representatives who go to Washington, D.C., to serve in Congress.

2. The Congress is comprised of the House of Representatives and the Senate. The House has 435 voting members, and states with large populations send more representatives. The Senate has 100 members—two from each state.

Congress wields tremendous power. Its members create statutes that influence our jobs, money, health care, military, communications, and virtually everything else. But can Congress create *any* kind of law that it wishes? No.

Article I, section 8 is a critically important part of the Constitution. It lists the 18 types of statutes that Congress is allowed to pass, such as imposing taxes, declaring war, and coining money. Thus, only the national government may create currency. The state of Illinois cannot print $20 bills with Barack Obama's profile.

States *are* allowed to create all other kinds of laws for themselves because the Tenth Amendment says, "All powers not delegated to the United States by the Constitution … are reserved to the States."

Commerce Clause

The part of Article I, Section 8, that gives Congress the power to regulate commerce with foreign nations and among states.

The **Commerce Clause** is the specific item in Article I, section 8, most important to your future as a businessperson. It calls upon Congress "to regulate commerce among the several States," and its impact is described in the next section.

INTERSTATE COMMERCE

With the Commerce Clause, the Framers sought to accomplish several things in response to the commercial chaos that existed under the Articles of Confederation. They wanted the federal government to speak with one voice when regulating commercial relations with foreign governments.[1] The Framers also wanted to give Congress the power to bring coordination and fairness to trade among the states, and to stop the states from imposing the taxes and regulations that were wrecking the nation's domestic trade.

Virtually all of the numerous statutes that affect businesses are passed under the Commerce Clause. But what does it mean to regulate interstate commerce? Are all business transactions "interstate commerce," or are there exceptions? In the end, the courts must interpret what the Constitution means.

SUBSTANTIAL EFFECT RULE

An important test of the Commerce Clause came in the Depression years of the 1930s, in *Wickard v. Filburn*.[2] The price of wheat and other grains had fluctuated wildly, severely harming farmers and the national food market. Congress sought to stabilize prices by limiting the bushels per acre that a farmer could grow. Filburn grew more wheat than federal law allowed and was fined. In defense, he claimed that Congress had no right to regulate him because none of his wheat went into *interstate* commerce. He sold some locally and used the rest on his own farm as food for livestock and as seed. The Commerce Clause, Filburn claimed, gave Congress no authority to limit what he could do.

The Supreme Court disagreed and held that **Congress may regulate any activity that has a substantial economic effect on interstate commerce.** Filburn's wheat *affected* interstate commerce because the more he grew for use on his own farm, the less he would need to buy in the open market of interstate commerce. In the end, "interstate commerce" does not require that things travel from one state to another.

In *United States v. Lopez*,[3] however, the Supreme Court ruled that Congress *had* exceeded its power under the Commerce Clause. Congress had passed a criminal statute called the "Gun-Free School Zones Act," which forbade any individual from possessing a firearm in

---

[1] *Michelin Tire Corp. v. Wages, Tax Commissioner*, 423 U.S. 276, 96 S. Ct. 535, 1976 U.S. LEXIS 120 (1976).

[2] 317 U.S. 111, 63 S. Ct. 82, 1942 U.S. LEXIS 1046 (1942).

[3] 514 U.S. 549, 115 S. Ct. 1624, 1995 U.S. LEXIS 3039 (1995).

a school zone. The goal of the statute was obvious: to keep schools safe. Lopez was convicted of violating the act and appealed his conviction all the way to the high Court, claiming that Congress had no power to pass such a law. The government argued that the Commerce Clause gave it the power to pass the law, but the Supreme Court was unpersuaded.

> The possession of a gun in a local school zone is in no sense an economic activity that might, through repetition elsewhere, substantially affect any sort of interstate commerce. [Lopez] was a local student at a local school; there is no indication that he had recently moved in interstate commerce, and there is no requirement that his possession of the firearm have any concrete tie to interstate commerce. To uphold the Government's contentions here, we would have to pile inference upon inference in a manner that would bid fair to convert congressional authority under the Commerce Clause to a general police power of the sort retained by the States. [The statute was unconstitutional and void.]

Congress's power is great—but still limited.

Current Application: The Patient Protection and Affordable Healthcare Act

In 2010, Congress passed the Patient Protection and Affordable Healthcare Act and President Barack Obama signed it into law. The wide-ranging legislation was aimed at reducing the number of uninsured Americans and also the cost of health care. Almost immediately after it passed, many states sued and argued that the law violated the Constitution by exceeding Congress's power to regulate interstate commerce.

The challenge centered on a provision (which the press refers to as the "individual mandate") in the Act that required many people to purchase health insurance or face fines. The states argued that requiring people to buy something was fundamentally different from regulating people who *voluntarily* decide to participate in commerce.

Amidst contentious political debate, the lower courts were divided on whether this healthcare statute was constitutional. In 2012, the Supreme Court had the final word in *National Federation of Independent Business v. Sebelius*.[4] The Justices agreed in part with the states: Requiring individuals to obtain health insurance was not within Congress's power under the Commerce Clause. Nevertheless, the Court held that the individual mandate was a constitutional exercise of another one of Congress's powers, its *taxing* power. The Court reasoned that the fines imposed on individuals without health insurance could reasonably be characterized as a tax and were therefore constitutional.

STATE LEGISLATIVE POWER

The "dormant" or "negative" aspect of the Commerce Clause governs state efforts to regulate interstate commerce. **The dormant aspect holds that a state statute that discriminates against interstate commerce is almost always unconstitutional.** Here is an example, but please do not read it if you plan to drive later today. Michigan and New York permitted in-state wineries to sell directly to consumers. They both denied this privilege to out-of-state producers, who were forced to sell to wholesalers, who offered the wine to retailers, who sold to consumers. This provision created an impossible barrier for many small vineyards, which did not produce enough wine to attract wholesalers. Even if they did, the multiple resales drove their prices prohibitively high.

Local residents and out-of-state wineries sued, claiming that the state regulations violated the dormant Commerce Clause. The Supreme Court ruled that these statutes obviously discriminated against out-of-state vineyards; the schemes were illegal unless Michigan and New York could demonstrate an important goal that could not be met any other way. The states' alleged motive was to prevent minors from purchasing wine over the Internet. However, Michigan and New York offered no evidence that such purchases were really a problem. The Court said that minors seldom drink wine, and when they do, they seek instant

[4]648 F.3d 1235 (2012).

gratification, not a package in the mail. States that allowed direct shipment to consumers reported no increase in purchases by minors. This discrimination against interstate commerce, like most, was unconstitutional.[5]

> **Devil's Advocate**   Underage drinking is a serious problem. The Court should allow states wide leeway in their efforts to limit alcohol consumption by minors. Even if the state regulations are imperfect, they may help reduce underage drinking.

SUPREMACY CLAUSE

What happens when both the federal and state governments pass regulations that are permissible, but conflicting? For example, Congress passed the federal Occupational Safety and Health Act (OSHA) establishing many job safety standards, including those for training workers who handle hazardous waste. Congress had the power to do so under the Commerce Clause. Later, Illinois passed its own hazardous waste statutes, seeking to protect both the general public and workers. The state statute did not violate the Commerce Clause because it imposed no restriction on interstate commerce.

Each statute specified worker training and employer licensing. But the requirements differed. Which statute did Illinois corporations have to obey? Article VI of the Constitution contains the answer. The **Supremacy Clause** states that the Constitution, and federal statutes and treaties, shall be the supreme law of the land.

Supremacy Clause
Makes the Constitution, and federal statutes and treaties, the supreme law of the land.

- If there is a conflict between federal and state statutes, the federal law **preempts** the field, meaning it controls the issue. The state law is void.

- Even in cases where there is no conflict, if Congress demonstrates that it intends to exercise exclusive control over an issue, federal law preempts.

Thus state law controls only when there is no conflicting federal law *and* Congress has not intended to dominate the issue. In the Illinois case, the Supreme Court concluded that Congress intended to regulate the issue exclusively. Federal law therefore preempted the field, and local employers were obligated to obey only the federal regulations.

EXAM Strategy

Question: Dairy farming was more expensive in Massachusetts than in other states. To help its farmers, Massachusetts taxed all milk sales, regardless of where the milk was produced. The revenues went into a fund that was then distributed to in-state dairy farmers. Discuss.

Strategy: By giving a subsidy to local farmers, the state is treating them differently from out-of-state dairies. This discrepancy raises Commerce Clause issues. The dormant aspect applies. What does it state? Apply that standard to these facts.

Result: The dormant aspect holds that a state statute that discriminates against interstate commerce is almost always invalid. Massachusetts was subsidizing its farmers at the expense of those from other states. The tax violates the Commerce Clause and is void.

---

[5]*Granholm v. Heald*, 544 U.S. 460, 1255 S. Ct. 1885 (2005).

5-3b Executive Power

Article II of the Constitution defines executive power. The President's most basic job function is to enforce the nation's laws. Three of his key powers concern appointment, legislation, and foreign policy.

APPOINTMENT

Administrative agencies play a powerful role in business regulation, and the President nominates the heads of most of them. These choices dramatically influence what issues the agencies choose to pursue and how aggressively they do it. For example, a President who seeks to expand the scope of regulations on air quality may appoint a forceful environmentalist to run the Environmental Protection Agency (EPA), whereas a President who dislikes federal regulations will choose a more passive agency head.[6]

LEGISLATION

The President and his advisers propose bills to Congress. During the last 50 years, a vast number of newly proposed bills have come from the executive branch. Some argue that *too many* proposals come from the President and that Congress has become overly passive. When a President proposes controversial legislation on a major issue, such as Social Security reform, the bill can dominate the news—and Congress—for months or even years. The President, of course, also has the power to veto bills.[7]

FOREIGN POLICY

The President conducts the nation's foreign affairs, coordinating international efforts, negotiating treaties, and so forth. The President is also the commander in chief of the armed forces, meaning that he heads the military. But Article II does not give him the right to declare war—only the Senate may do that. A continuing tension between the President and Congress has resulted from the President's use of troops overseas *without* a formal declaration of war.

5-3c Judicial Power

Article III of the Constitution creates the Supreme Court and permits Congress to establish lower courts within the federal court system.[8] Federal courts have two key functions: adjudication and judicial review.

ADJUDICATING CASES

The federal court system hears criminal and civil cases. Generally, prosecutions of federal crimes begin in United States District Court. That same court has limited jurisdiction to hear civil lawsuits, a subject discussed in Chapter 3, on dispute resolution.

JUDICIAL REVIEW

One of the greatest "constitutional" powers appears nowhere in the Constitution. In 1803, the Supreme Court decided *Marbury v. Madison*.[9] Congress had passed a relatively minor statute that gave certain powers to the Supreme Court, and Marbury wanted the Court to use those powers. The Court refused. In an opinion written by Chief Justice John Marshall, the Court held that the statute violated the Constitution because Article III of the Constitution

---

[6] For a discussion of administrative agency power, see Chapter 4, on administrative law.

[7] For a discussion of the President's veto power and Congress's power to override a veto, see Chapter 4, on statutory law.

[8] For a discussion of the federal court system, see Chapter 3, on dispute resolution.

[9] 5 U.S. 137, 1 Cranch 137 (1803).

did not grant the Court those powers. The details of the case were insignificant, but the ruling was profound: Because the statute violated the Constitution, said the Court, it was void. **Judicial review refers to the power of federal courts to declare a statute or governmental action unconstitutional and void.**

This formidable grab of power has produced two centuries of controversy. The Court was declaring that it alone had the right to evaluate acts of the other two branches of government—the Congress and the executive—and to decide which were valid and which were void. The Constitution nowhere grants this power. Undaunted, Marshall declared that "[I]t is emphatically the province and duty of the judicial department to say what the law is." In later cases, the Supreme Court expanded on the idea, holding that it could also nullify state statutes, rulings by state courts, and actions by federal and state officials. In this chapter, we have already encountered an example of judicial review in the *Lopez* case, where the justices declared that Congress lacked the power to pass local gun regulations.

Is judicial review good for the nation? Those who oppose it argue that federal court judges are all appointed, not elected, and that we should not permit judges to nullify a statute passed by elected officials because that diminishes the people's role in their government. Those who favor judicial review insist that there must be one cohesive interpretation of the Constitution and the judicial branch is the logical one to provide it. The following example of judicial review shows how immediate and emotional the issue can be. It is a criminal prosecution for a brutal crime. Cases like this force us to examine two questions about judicial review. What is the proper punishment for such a horrible crime? Just as important, *who should make that decision— appointed judges, or elected legislators?*

KENNEDY V. LOUISIANA

554 U.S. 407
United States Supreme Court, 2008

CASE SUMMARY

Facts: Patrick Kennedy raped his eight-year-old stepdaughter, referred to as L.H. A forensic expert testified that L.H.'s physical injuries were the most severe he had ever witnessed from a sexual assault. The jury also heard evidence that the defendant had raped another eight-year-old. Kennedy was convicted of aggravated rape, because the victim was under 12 years of age.

The jury voted to sentence Kennedy to death, which was permitted by the Louisiana statute. The state supreme court affirmed the death sentence, and Kennedy appealed to the United States Supreme Court. He argued that the Louisiana statute was unconstitutional. The Eighth Amendment prohibits cruel and unusual punishment, which includes penalties that are out of proportion to the crime. Kennedy claimed that capital punishment was out of proportion to rape, and violated the Eighth Amendment.

Issue: *Did the Louisiana statute violate the Constitution by permitting the death penalty in a case of child rape?*

Decision: Yes, the Louisiana statute violated the Eighth Amendment. Reversed.

Reasoning: Constitutional liberties create limits. States may define crimes and set punishments, but the penalties must not be excessive in light of evolving standards of decency in modern society. The death penalty requires special attention.

Only six states (Louisiana, Georgia, Montana, Oklahoma, South Carolina, and Texas) allowed for a death sentence in cases of child rape. The other 44 states either did not have capital crimes or allow for the death penalty only when a defendant takes a life.

The majority of the Justices determined that the crime in this case, while horrific, was nonetheless not equivalent to murder in its "severity and irrevocability." It concluded that Louisiana's statute amounted to cruel and unusual punishment.

Dissent by Justice Alito: The court is wrong about the evolving standards of decency. In recent years, five states have passed laws that impose capital punishment in capital rape cases. They have acted in response to a significant increase in reports of the sexual abuse of children. These laws did not violate the Eighth Amendment.

Judicial Activism/Judicial Restraint   The power of judicial review is potentially dictatorial. The Supreme Court nullifies statutes passed by Congress (*Marbury v. Madison*, *United States v. Lopez*) and executive actions. May it strike down any law it dislikes? In theory, no—the Court should nullify only laws that violate the Constitution. But in practice, yes—the Constitution means whatever the majority of the current justices says that it means, since it is the Court that tells us which laws are violative.

Judicial activism refers to a court's willingness, or even eagerness, to become involved in major issues and to decide cases on constitutional grounds. Activists are sometimes willing to "stretch" laws beyond their most obvious meaning. **Judicial restraint** is the opposite, an attitude that courts should leave lawmaking to legislators and nullify a law only when it unquestionably violates the Constitution. Some justices believe that the Founding Fathers never intended the judicial branch to take a prominent role in sculpting the nation's laws and its social vision.

From the 1950s through the 1970s, the Supreme Court took an activist role, deciding many major social issues on constitutional grounds. The landmark 1954 decision in *Brown v. Board of Education* ordered an end to racial segregation in public schools, not only changing the nation's educational systems, but altering forever its expectations about race.[10] The Court also struck down many state laws that denied minorities the right to vote. Beginning with *Miranda v. Arizona*, the Court began a sweeping reappraisal of the police power of the state and the rights of criminal suspects during searches, interrogations, trials, and appeals.[11] And in *Roe v. Wade*, the Supreme Court established certain rights to abortion, most of which remain after nearly 40 years of continuous litigation.[12]

Beginning in the late 1970s, and lasting to the present, the Court has pulled back from its social activism. Exhibit 5.1 illustrates the balance among Congress, the President, and the Court.

The Constitution established a federal government of checks and balances. Congress may propose statutes; the President may veto them; and Congress may override the veto. The President nominates cabinet officers, administrative heads, and Supreme Court justices, but the Senate must confirm his nominees. Finally, the Supreme Court (and lower federal courts) exercise judicial review over statutes and executive actions. Unlike the other checks and balances, judicial review is not provided for in the Constitution, but is a creation of the Court itself in *Marbury v. Madison*.

Judicial activism
A court's willingness to decide issues on constitutional grounds.

Judicial restraint
A court's attitude that it should leave lawmaking to legislators.

5-4 PROTECTED RIGHTS

The amendments to the Constitution protect the people of this nation from the power of state and federal government. The First Amendment guarantees rights of free speech, free press, and religion; the Fourth Amendment protects against illegal searches; the Fifth Amendment ensures due process; the Sixth Amendment demands fair treatment for defendants in criminal prosecutions; and the Fourteenth Amendment guarantees equal protection of the law. We consider the First, Fifth, and Fourteenth Amendments in this chapter and the Fourth, Fifth, and Sixth Amendments in Chapter 7, on crime.

The "people" who are protected include citizens and, for most purposes, corporations. Corporations are considered persons and receive most of the same protections. The great majority of these rights also extends to citizens of other countries who are in the United States.

---

[10]347 U.S. 483, 74 S. Ct. 686, 1954 U.S. LEXIS 2094 (1954).
[11]384 U.S. 436, 86 S. Ct. 1602, 1966 U.S. LEXIS 2817 (1966).
[12]410 U.S. 113, 93 S. Ct. 705, 1973 U.S. LEXIS 159 (1973).

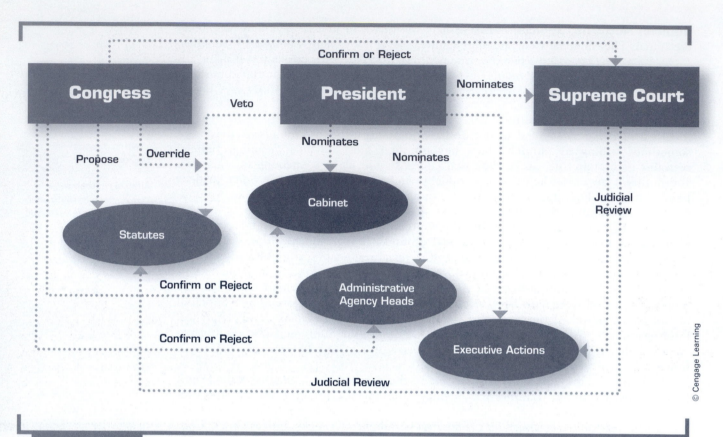

EXHIBIT 5.1   The Path of Legislation: The Balance among the President, the Congress, and the Court

Constitutional rights generally protect only against governmental acts. The Constitution generally does not protect us from the conduct of private parties, such as corporations or other citizens.

5-4a Incorporation

A series of Supreme Court cases has extended virtually all of the important constitutional protections to *all levels* of national, state, and local government. This process is called **incorporation** because rights explicitly guaranteed at one level are incorporated into rights that apply at other levels.

5-4b First Amendment: Free Speech

The First Amendment states that "Congress shall make no law ... abridging the freedom of speech ...." In general, we expect our government to let people speak and hear whatever they choose. The Founding Fathers believed democracy would work only if the members of the electorate were free to talk, argue, listen, and exchange viewpoints in any way they wanted. The people could only cast informed ballots if they were informed. "Speech" also includes symbolic conduct, as the following case flamingly illustrates.

TEXAS V. JOHNSON

491 U.S. 397
United States Supreme Court, 1989

CASE SUMMARY

Facts: Outside the Republican National Convention in Dallas, Gregory Johnson participated in a protest against policies of the Reagan administration. Participants gave speeches and handed out leaflets. Johnson burned an American flag. He was arrested and convicted under a Texas statute that prohibited desecrating the flag, but the Texas Court of Criminal Appeals reversed on the grounds that the conviction violated the First Amendment. Texas appealed to the United States Supreme Court.

Issue: *Does the First Amendment protect flag burning?*

Decision: Affirmed. The First Amendment protects flag burning.

Reasoning: The First Amendment literally applies only to "speech," but the Supreme Court had already ruled that the Amendment also protects written words and other conduct that conveys a specific message. For example, earlier decisions protected a student's right to wear a black armband in protest against American military actions. Judged by this standard, flag burning is symbolic speech.

Texas argued that its interest in honoring the flag justified its prosecution of Johnson, since he knew that his action would be deeply offensive to many citizens. However, if there is a bedrock principle underlying the First Amendment, it is that the government may not prohibit the expression of an idea simply because society finds it offensive.

The best way to preserve the flag's special role in our lives is not to punish those who feel differently but to persuade them that they are wrong. We do not honor our flag by punishing those who burn it, because in doing so we diminish the freedom that this cherished emblem represents.

POLITICAL SPEECH

Because the Framers were primarily concerned with enabling democracy to function, political speech has been given an especially high degree of protection. Such speech may not be barred even when it is offensive or outrageous. A speaker, for example, could accuse a U.S. senator of being insane and could use crude, violent language to describe him. The speech is still protected. **Political speech is protected unless it is intended and likely to create imminent lawless action.**[13] For example, suppose the speaker said, "The senator is inside that restaurant. Let's get some matches and burn the place down." Speech of this sort is not protected. The speaker could be arrested for attempted arson or attempted murder.

One of the most important recent developments in constitutional law concerns the ability of *organizations* to engage in political speech. In the case that follows, a sharply divided Supreme Court weighed in on the issue raised in this chapter's opening scenario.

---

[13]*Brandenburg v. Ohio*, 395 U.S. 444, 89 S. Ct. 1827, 1969 U.S. LEXIS 1367 (1969).

CITIZENS UNITED v. FEDERAL ELECTION COMMISSION

558 U.S. 310
Supreme Court of the United States, 2010

CASE SUMMARY

Facts: Citizens United, a nonprofit organization, produced a documentary on presidential candidate Hillary Clinton. The group wanted to run television ads promoting *Hillary: the Movie*. The Bipartisan Campaign Reform Act of 2002 banned "electioneering communication" by corporations and unions for the 30 days before a presidential primary. Citizens United challenged the Act.

Issue: *Did the Bipartisan Campaign Reform Act violate the First Amendment?*

Decision: Yes, the law violated the First Amendment.

Reasoning: Prohibiting organizations from "electioneering communications" amounts to censorship. Speech is vital to a democracy, and it must not be suppressed.

Corporations are protected by the First Amendment, and therefore, they have the right to express their political views. Yet, under this statute, any negative portrayal of a politician on television, radio, or YouTube, that takes place near an election could be a felony.

Corruption should be curbed, but not at the expense of free speech. Americans must be allowed to decide for themselves which ideas are worthy of discussion. The government cannot make the decision for them.

TIME, PLACE, AND MANNER

Even when speech is protected, the government may regulate the *time*, *place*, and *manner* of such speech. A town may require a group to apply for a permit before using a public park for a political demonstration. The town may insist that the demonstration take place during daylight hours and that there be adequate police supervision and sanitation provided. However, the town may not prohibit such demonstrations outright.

Many public universities have designated "free speech zones" located in high-traffic areas of campus that are not immediately adjacent to a large number of classrooms. The zones allow for debates to proceed and reach many students, but they minimize the chances that noisy demonstrations will interfere with lectures.

MORALITY AND OBSCENITY

The regulation of morality and obscenity presents additional problems. Obscenity has never received constitutional protection. The Supreme Court has consistently held that it does not play a valued role in our society and has refused to give protection to obscene works. That is well and good, but it merely forces the question: What is obscene?

In *Miller v. California*,[14] the Court created a three-part test to determine if a creative work is obscene. The basic guidelines for the factfinder are:

- Whether the average person, applying contemporary community standards, would find that the work, taken as a whole, appeals to the prurient interest;

- Whether the work depicts or describes, in a patently offensive way, sexual conduct specifically defined by the applicable state law; and

- Whether the work, taken as a whole, lacks serious literary, artistic, political, or scientific value.

---

[14]413 U.S. 15, 93 S. Ct. 2607, 1973 U.S. LEXIS 149 (1973).

If the trial court finds that the answer to all three of those questions is "yes," it may judge the material obscene; the state may then prohibit the work. If the state fails to prove any one of the three criteria, though, the work is not obscene.[15] A United States District Court ruled that "As Nasty As They Wanna Be," recorded by 2 Live Crew, was obscene. The appeals court, however, reversed, finding that the state had failed to prove lack of artistic merit.[16]

COMMERCIAL SPEECH

Commercial speech refers to speech that has a dominant theme to propose a commercial transaction. For example, most advertisements on television and in the newspapers are **commercial speech**. This sort of speech is protected by the First Amendment, but the government is permitted to regulate it more closely than other forms of speech. Commercial speech that is false or misleading may be outlawed altogether. **The government may regulate other commercial speech, provided that the rules are reasonable and directed to a legitimate goal.** The following case demonstrates the very different treatment given to this type of speech.

Commercial speech
Communication, such as advertisements, that has the dominant theme of proposing a business transaction.

SALIB V. CITY OF MESA

133 P.3d 756 212 Ariz. 446
Arizona Court of Appeals, 2006

CASE SUMMARY

Facts: Edward Salib owned a Winchell's Donut House in Mesa, Arizona. To attract customers, he displayed large signs advertising his products in his store window. The city ordered him to remove the signs because they violated its Sign Code, which prohibited covering more than 30% of a store's windows with signs. Salib sued, claiming that the Sign Code violated his First Amendment free speech rights. The trial court gave summary judgment for Mesa, and the store owner appealed.

Issue: *Did Mesa's Sign Code violate the First Amendment?*

Decision: No, the Code placed a reasonable limit on commercial speech. Affirmed.

Reasoning: The First Amendment guarantees free speech rights to people and to organizations. The government, though, can restrict commercial speech in some circumstances. Regulators, for example, can ban false and misleading messages. They may also place limits on other advertisements if they pass the following three-part test:

First, the government has a substantial interest. Second, a restriction directly advances this interest. Third, the restriction is narrowly tailored to meet its goal.

In the case, the City of Mesa claimed a substantial interest in making its business district aesthetically pleasing. It argued that the Sign Code did in fact make the city more attractive. Mesa also claimed that its 30% standard was a narrow and reasonable compromise between its interest in city beautification and the rights of business owners.

The court agreed with Mesa's arguments and declined to second-guess the standard.

[15]*Penthouse Intern Ltd. v. McAuliffe*, 610 F.2d 1353 (5th Cir. 1980).
[16]960 F.2d 134 (1992).

EXAM Strategy

Question: Maria owns a lot next to a freeway that passes through Tidyville. She has rented a billboard to Huge Mart, a nearby retailer, and a second billboard to Green, a political party. However, Tidyville prohibits off-premises signs (those not on the advertiser's property) that are visible from the freeway. Tidyville's rule is designed to make the city more attractive, to increase property values, and to eliminate distractions that may cause freeway accidents. Huge Mart and Green sue, claiming that Tidyville's law violates their First Amendment rights. Who wins?

(a) Huge Mart is likely to win; Green is likely to lose.

(b) Green is likely to win; Huge Mart is likely to lose.

(c) Huge Mart and Green are both likely to win.

(d) Huge Mart and Green are both likely to lose.

Strategy: What is the difference between the two cases? Huge Mart wants the billboard for commercial speech; Green wants it for a political message. What are the legal standards for commercial and political free speech? Apply those standards.

Result: The government may regulate commercial speech, provided that the rules are reasonable and directed to a legitimate goal. Political speech is given much stronger protection, and can be prohibited only if it is intended and likely to create imminent lawless action. The regulation outlawing *advertising* will be upheld, but Tidyville will not be allowed to block political messages.

Four years of work and your entire career are suddenly on the line.

5-4c Fifth Amendment: Due Process and the Takings Clause

You are a senior at a major state university. You feel great about a difficult exam you took in Professor Watson's class. The Dean's Office sends for you, and you enter curiously, wondering if your exam was so good that the dean is awarding you a prize. Not quite. The exam proctor has accused you of cheating. Based on the accusation, Watson has flunked you. You protest that you are innocent and demand to know what the accusation is. The dean says that you will learn the details at a hearing, if you wish to have one. She reminds you that if you lose the hearing, you will be expelled from the university. Four years of work and your entire career are suddenly on the line.

The hearing is run by Professor Holmes, who will make the final decision. Holmes is a junior faculty member in Watson's department. (Next year, Watson will decide Holmes's tenure application.) At the hearing, the proctor accuses you of copying from a student sitting in front of you. Both Watson and Holmes have already compared the two papers and concluded that they are strongly similar. Holmes tells you that you must convince him the charge is wrong. You examine the papers, acknowledge that there are similarities, but plead as best you can that you never copied. Holmes doesn't buy it. The university expels you, placing on your transcript a notation of cheating.

Have you received fair treatment? To answer that, we must look to the Fifth Amendment, which provides several vital protections. We will consider two related provisions, the Due Process Clause and the Takings Clause. Together, they state: "No person shall be …

deprived of life, liberty, or property without due process of law; nor shall private property be taken for public use, without just compensation." These clauses prevent the government from arbitrarily taking the most valuable possessions of a citizen or corporation. The government has the right to take a person's liberty or property. But there are three important limitations:

- **Procedural Due Process.** Before depriving anyone of liberty or property, the government must go through certain steps, or procedures, to ensure that the result is fair.

- **The Takings Clause**. When the government takes property for public use, such as to build a new highway, it has to pay a fair price.

- **Substantive Due Process.** Some rights are so fundamental that the government may not take them from us at all. The substance of any law or government action may be challenged on fundamental fairness grounds.

PROCEDURAL DUE PROCESS

The government deprives citizens or corporations of their property in a variety of ways. The Internal Revenue Service may fine a corporation for late payment of taxes. The Customs Service may seize goods at the border. As to liberty, the government may take it by confining someone in a mental institution or by taking a child out of the home because of parental neglect. The purpose of **procedural due process** is to ensure that before the government takes liberty or property, the affected person has a fair chance to oppose the action. There are two steps in analyzing a procedural due process case:

- Is the government attempting to take liberty or property?

- If so, how much process is due? (If the government is *not* attempting to take liberty or property, there is no due process issue.)

Is the Government Attempting to Take Liberty or Property?   Liberty interests are generally easy to spot: Confining someone in a mental institution and taking a child from her home are both deprivations of liberty. A property interest may be obvious. Suppose that, during a civil lawsuit, the court **attaches** a defendant's house, meaning it bars the defendant from selling the property at least until the case is decided. This way, if the plaintiff wins, the defendant will have assets to pay the judgment. The court has clearly deprived the defendant of an important interest in his house, and the defendant is entitled to due process. However, a property interest may be subtler than that. A woman holding a job with a government agency has a "property interest" in that job, because her employer has agreed not to fire her without cause, and she can rely on it for income. If the government does fire her, it is taking away that property interest, and she is entitled to due process. A student attending any public school has a property interest in her education. If a public university suspends a student as described above, it is taking her property, and she, too, should receive due process.

How Much Process Is Due?   Assuming that a liberty or property interest is affected, a court must decide how much process is due. Does the person get a formal trial, or an informal hearing, or merely a chance to reply in writing to the charges against her? If she gets a hearing, must it be held before the government deprives her of her property, or is it enough that she can be heard shortly thereafter? **What sort of hearing the government must offer depends upon how important the property or liberty interest is and on whether the government has a competing need for efficiency.** The more important the interest, the more formal the procedures must be.

Neutral Factfinder   Regardless of how formal the hearing, one requirement is constant: The factfinder must be neutral. Whether it is a superior court judge deciding a multimillion-dollar contract suit or an employment supervisor deciding the fate of a government employee,

Takings Clause
A clause in the Fifth Amendment that ensures that when any governmental unit takes private property for public use, it must compensate the owner.

Procedural due process
The doctrine that ensures that before the government takes liberty or property, the affected person has a fair chance to oppose the action.

Attachment
The process by which a court bars a defendant from selling property.

the factfinder must have no personal interest in the outcome. In *Ward v. Monroeville*,[17] the plaintiff was a motorist who had been stopped for traffic offenses in a small town. He protested his innocence and received a judicial hearing. But the "judge" at the hearing was the town mayor. Traffic fines were a significant part of the town's budget. The motorist argued that the town was depriving him of procedural due process because the mayor had a financial interest in the outcome of the case. The United States Supreme Court agreed and reversed his conviction.

Attachment of Property   As described earlier, a plaintiff in a civil lawsuit often seeks to *attach* the defendant's property. Attachment protects the plaintiff, but it may also harm the defendant if, for example, he is about to close a profitable real estate deal. Attachments used to be routine. In *Connecticut v. Doehr*, the Supreme Court required more caution.[18] Based on *Doehr*, when a plaintiff seeks to attach at the beginning of the trial, a court must look at the plaintiff's likelihood of winning. Generally, the court must grant the defendant a hearing *before* attaching the property. The defendant, represented by a lawyer, may offer evidence as to how attachment would harm him and why it should be denied.

Government Employment   A government employee must receive due process before being fired. Generally, this means some kind of hearing, but not necessarily a formal court hearing. The employee is entitled to know the charges against him, to hear the employer's evidence, and to have an opportunity to tell his side of the story. He is not entitled to have a lawyer present. The hearing "officer" need only be a neutral employee. Further, in an emergency, where the employee is a danger to the public or the organization, the government may suspend with pay, before holding a hearing. It then must provide a hearing before the decision becomes final.

Academic Suspension   There is still a property interest here, but it is the least important of those discussed. When a public school concludes that a student has failed to meet its normal academic standards, such as by failing too many courses, it may dismiss him without a hearing. Due process is served if the student receives notice of the reason and has some opportunity to respond, such as by writing a letter contradicting the school's claims.

In cases of disciplinary suspension or expulsion, courts generally require schools to provide a higher level of due process. In the hypothetical at the beginning of this section, the university has failed to provide adequate due process.[19] The school has accused the student of a serious infraction. The school must promptly provide details of the charge and cannot wait until the hearing to do so. The student should see the two papers and have a chance to rebut the charge. Moreover, Professor Holmes has demonstrated bias. He appears to have made up his mind in advance. He has placed the burden on the student to disprove the charges. And he probably feels obligated to support Watson's original conclusion, since Watson will be deciding his tenure case next year.

THE TAKINGS CLAUSE

Florence Dolan ran a plumbing store in Tigard, Oregon. She and her husband wanted to enlarge it on land they already owned. But the city government said that they could expand only if they dedicated some of their own land for use as a public bicycle path and for other public use. Does the city have the right to make them do that? For an answer, we must look to a different part of the Fifth Amendment.

The Takings Clause prohibits a state from taking private property for public use without just compensation. A town wishing to build a new football field may boot you out of your

---

[17]409 U.S. 57, 93 S. Ct. 80, 1972 U.S. LEXIS 11 (1972).

[18]501 U.S. 1, 111 S. Ct. 2105, 1991 U.S. LEXIS 3317 (1991).

[19]See, for example, *University of Texas Medical School at Houston v. Than*, 901 S.W.2d 926, 1995 Tex. LEXIS 105 (Tex. 1995).

house. But the town must compensate you. The government takes your land through the power of **eminent domain**. Officials must notify you of their intentions and give you an opportunity to oppose the project and to challenge the amount the town offers to pay. But when the hearings are done, the town may write you a check and level your house, whether you like it or not.

More controversial issues arise when a local government does not physically take the property but passes regulations that restrict its use. Tigard is a city of 30,000 in Oregon. The city developed a comprehensive land use plan for its downtown area in order to preserve green space, to encourage transportation other than autos, and to reduce its flooding problems. Under the plan, when a property owner sought permission to build in the downtown section, the city could require some of her land to be used for public purposes. This has become a standard method of land use planning throughout the nation. States have used it to preserve coastline, urban green belts, and many environmental features.

When Florence Dolan applied for permission to expand, the city required that she dedicate a 15-foot strip of her property to the city as a bicycle pathway and that she preserve, as greenway, a portion of her land within a floodplain. She sued, and though she lost in the Oregon courts, she won in the United States Supreme Court. The Court held that Tigard City's method of routinely forcing all owners to dedicate land to public use violated the Takings Clause. The city was taking the land, even though title never changed hands.[20]

The Court did not outlaw all such requirements. What it required was that, **before a government may require an owner to dedicate land to a public use, it must show that this owner's proposed building requires this dedication of land.** In other words, it is not enough for Tigard to have a general plan, such as a bicycle pathway, and to make all owners participate in it. Tigard must show that it needs *Dolan's* land *specifically for a bike path and greenway*. This argument will be much harder for local governments to demonstrate than merely showing a city-wide plan. A related issue arose in the following controversial case. A city used eminent domain to take property on behalf of *private developers*. Was this a valid public use?

The *Kelo* decision was controversial, and in response, some states passed statutes prohibiting eminent domain for private development.

Eminent domain

The power of the government to take private property for public use.

KELO V. CITY OF NEW LONDON, CONNECTICUT

545 U.S. 469
United States Supreme Court, 2005

CASE SUMMARY

Facts: New London, Connecticut, was declining economically. The city's unemployment rate was double that of the state generally, and the population was at its lowest in 75 years. In response, state and local officials targeted a section of the city, called Fort Trumbull, for revitalization. Located on the Thames River, Fort Trumbull comprised 115 privately owned properties and 32 additional acres of an abandoned naval facility. The development plan included one section for a waterfront conference hotel and stores; a second one for 80 private residences; and one for research facilities.

The state bought most of the properties from willing sellers. However, 9 owners of 15 properties refused to sell, and filed suit. The owners claimed that the city was trying to take land for private use, not public, in violation of the Takings Clause. The case reached the United States Supreme Court.

Issue: *Did the city's plan violate the Takings Clause?*

Decision: No, the plan was constitutional. Affirmed.

Reasoning: The Takings Clause allows for some transfers of real property from one private party to another, so

---

[20] *Dolan v. City of Tigard*, 512 U.S. 374, 114 S. Ct. 2309, 1994 U.S. LEXIS 4826 (1994).

long as the land will be used by the public. For example, land may be taken to allow for the construction of a railroad, even if private railroad companies will be the primary beneficiaries of the transfer.

New London's economic development plan aims to create jobs and increase the city's tax receipts. The Supreme Court has not previously considered this type of public use, but now determines that economic development is a

legitimate public purpose. New London did not violate the Takings Clause.

Dissent by Justice O'Connor: Any public benefit in this case would be incidental and secondary. Under the majority's opinion, the government can now take private property *for any* purpose. This case will most likely benefit those with inside access to government officials, at the expense of small property owners.

SUBSTANTIVE DUE PROCESS

This doctrine is part of the Due Process Clause, but it is entirely different from procedural due process and from government taking. During the first third of the twentieth century, the Supreme Court frequently nullified state and federal laws, asserting that they interfered with basic rights. For example, in a famous 1905 case, *Lochner v. New York*,[21] the Supreme Court invalidated a New York statute that had limited the number of hours that bakers could work in a week. New York had passed the law to protect employee health. But the Court declared that private parties had a basic constitutional right to contract. In this case, the statute interfered with the rights of the employer and the baker to make any bargain they wished. Over the next three decades, the Court struck down dozens of state and federal laws that were aimed at working conditions, union rights, and social welfare generally. This was called **substantive due process**[22] because the Court was looking at the underlying rights being affected, such as the right to contract, not at any procedures.

Substantive due process
A form of due process that holds that certain rights are so fundamental that the government may not eliminate them.

Critics complained that the Court was interfering with the desires of the voting public by nullifying laws that the justices personally disliked (judicial activism). During the Great Depression, however, things changed. Beginning in 1934, the Court completely reversed itself and began to uphold the types of laws it earlier had struck down.

The Supreme Court made an important substantive due process ruling in the case of *BMW v. Gore*.[23] A BMW dealership sold Gore a car that had sustained water damage. Instead of telling him of the damage, they simply repainted the car and sold it as new.

In Chapter 6, we will examine two different types of cash awards that juries may make in tort cases. For now, let's call them "ordinary" and "punitive" damages. When plaintiffs win tort cases, juries may always award ordinary damages to offset real, measureable losses. In addition, juries are sometimes allowed to add to an award to further punish a defendant for bad behavior.

In the *BMW* case, the jury awarded Gore $4,000 in ordinary damages as the difference in value between a flawless new car and a water-damaged car. The jury then awarded a delighted Gore $4 *million* in punitive damages. In the end, the Supreme Court decided that the punitive award was so disproportionate to the harm actually caused that it violated substantive due process rights.

5-4d Fourteenth Amendment: Equal Protection Clause

Shannon Faulkner wanted to attend The Citadel, a state-supported military college in South Carolina. She was a fine student who met every admission requirement that The Citadel set except one: She was not a man. The Citadel argued that its long and distinguished history demanded that it remain all male. Faulkner responded that she was a citizen

---

[21]198 U.S. 45, 25 S. Ct. 539, 1905 U.S. LEXIS 1153 (1905).

[22]Be the first on your block to pronounce this word correctly. The accent goes on the first syllable: *sub*stantive.

[23]517 U.S. 559 (1996).

of the state and ought to receive the benefits that others got, including the right to a military education. Could the school exclude her on the basis of gender?

The Fourteenth Amendment provides that "No State shall ... deny to any person within its jurisdiction the equal protection of the laws." This is the **Equal Protection Clause**, and it means that, generally speaking, **governments must treat people equally.** Unfair classifications among people or corporations will not be permitted. A notorious example of unfair classification would be race discrimination: Permitting only white children to attend a public school violates the Equal Protection Clause.

Yet clearly, governments do make classifications every day. People with high incomes pay a higher tax rate than those with low incomes; some corporations are permitted to deal in securities, while others are not. To determine which classifications are constitutionally permissible, we need to know what is being classified. There are three major groups of classifications. The outcome of a case can generally be predicted by knowing which group it is in.

- **Minimal Scrutiny: Economic and Social Relations.** Government actions that classify people or corporations on these bases are almost always upheld.

- **Intermediate Scrutiny: Gender.** Government classifications are sometimes upheld.

- **Strict Scrutiny: Race, Ethnicity, and Fundamental Rights.** Classifications based on any of these are almost never upheld.

> **Equal Protection Clause**
> A clause in the Fourteenth Amendment that generally requires the government to treat people equally.

MINIMAL SCRUTINY: ECONOMIC AND SOCIAL REGULATION

Just as with the Due Process Clause, laws that regulate economic or social issues are presumed valid. They will be upheld if they are *rationally related to a legitimate goal*. This means a statute may classify corporations and/or people, and the classifications will be upheld if they make any sense at all. The New York City Transit Authority excluded all methadone users from any employment. The United States District Court concluded that this practice violated the Equal Protection Clause by unfairly excluding all those who were on methadone. The court noted that even those who tested free of any illegal drugs and were seeking non-safety-sensitive jobs, such as clerks, were turned away. That reasoning, said the district court, was irrational.

Not so, said the United States Supreme Court. The Court admitted that the policy might not be the wisest. It would probably make more sense to test individually for illegal drugs rather than automatically exclude methadone users. But, said the Court, it was not up to the justices to choose the best policy. They were only to decide if the policy was rational. Excluding methadone users related rationally to the safety of public transport and therefore did not violate the Equal Protection Clause.[24]

INTERMEDIATE SCRUTINY: GENDER

Classifications based on sex must meet a tougher test than those resulting from economic or social regulation. Such laws must *substantially relate to important government objectives*. Courts have increasingly nullified government sex classifications as societal concern with gender equality has grown.

At about the same time Shannon Faulkner began her campaign to enter The Citadel, another woman sought admission to the Virginia Military Institute (VMI), an all-male state school. The Supreme Court held that Virginia had violated the Equal Protection Clause by excluding women from VMI. The Court ruled that gender-based

---

[24]*New York City Transit Authority v. Beazer*, 440 U.S. 568, 99 S. Ct. 1355, 1979 U.S. LEXIS 77 (1979).

government discrimination requires an "exceedingly persuasive justification," and that Virginia had failed that standard of proof. The Citadel promptly opened its doors to women as well.[25]

STRICT SCRUTINY: RACE, ETHNICITY, AND FUNDAMENTAL RIGHTS

Any government action that intentionally discriminates against racial or ethnic minorities, or interferes with a fundamental right, is presumed invalid. In such cases, courts will look at the statute or policy with *strict scrutiny;* that is, courts will examine it very closely to determine whether there is compelling justification for it. The law will be upheld only if it is *necessary to promote a compelling state interest.* Very few meet that test.

- **Racial and Ethnic Minorities.** Any government action that intentionally discriminates on the basis of race, or ethnicity is presumed invalid. For example, in *Palmore v. Sidoti,*[26] the state had refused to give child custody to a mother because her new spouse was racially different from the child. The practice was declared unconstitutional. The state had made a racial classification, it was presumed invalid, and the government had no *compelling need* to make such a ruling.

Fundamental rights
Rights so basic that any governmental interference with them is suspect and likely to be unconstitutional.

- **Fundamental Rights**. A government action interfering with a fundamental right also receives strict scrutiny and will likely be declared void. For example, New York State gave an employment preference to any veteran who had been a state resident when he entered the military. Newcomers who were veterans were less likely to get jobs, and therefore this statute interfered with the right to travel, a fundamental right. The Supreme Court declared the law invalid.[27]

EXAM Strategy

Question: Megan is a freshman at her local public high school; her older sister Jenna attends a nearby private high school. Both girls are angry because their schools prohibit them from joining their respective wrestling teams, where only boys are allowed. The two girls sue based on the U.S. Constitution. Discuss the relevant law and predict the outcomes.

Strategy: One girl goes to private school and one to public school. Why does that matter? Now ask what provision of the Constitution is involved, and what legal standard it establishes.

Result: The Constitution offers protection from the *government.* A private high school is not part of the government, and Jenna has no constitutional case. Megan's suit is based on the Equal Protection Clause. This is gender discrimination, meaning that Megan's school must convince the court that keeping girls off the team *substantially relates to an important government objective.* The school will probably argue that wrestling with stronger boys will be dangerous for girls. However, courts are increasingly suspicious of any gender discrimination and are unlikely to find the school's argument persuasive.

---

[25]*United States v. Virginia*, 518 U.S. 515, 116 S. Ct. 2264, 1996 U.S. LEXIS 4259 (1996).
[26]466 U.S. 429, 104 S. Ct. 1879, 1984 U.S. LEXIS 69 (1984).
[27]*Attorney General of New York v. Soto-Lopez*, 476 U.S. 898, 106 S. Ct. 2317, 1986 U.S. LEXIS 59 (1986).

Chapter Conclusion

The legal battle over power never stops. The obligation of a state to provide equal educational opportunity for both genders relates to whether Tigard, Oregon, may demand some of Ms. Dolan's store lot for public use. Both issues are governed by one amazing document. That same Constitution determines what tax preferences are permissible and even whether a state may require you to wear clothing. As social mores change in step with broad cultural developments, as the membership of the Supreme Court changes, the balance of power between federal government, state government, and citizens will continue to evolve. There are no easy answers to these constitutional questions because there has never been a democracy so large, so diverse, or so powerful.

EXAM REVIEW

1. **CONSTITUTION**   The Constitution is a series of compromises about power. (p. 111)

2. **ARTICLES I, II, AND III**   Article I of the Constitution creates the Congress and grants all legislative power to it. Article II establishes the office of President and defines executive powers. Article III creates the Supreme Court and permits lower federal courts; the article also outlines the powers of the federal judiciary. (p. 111)

3. **COMMERCE CLAUSE**   Under the Commerce Clause, Congress may regulate any activity that has a substantial effect on interstate commerce. (p. 112)

4. **INTERSTATE COMMERCE**   A state may not regulate commerce in any way that will interfere with interstate commerce. (p. 112)

EXAM Strategy

Question: Maine exempted many charitable institutions from real estate taxes but denied this benefit to a charity that primarily benefited out-of-state residents. Camp Newfound was a Christian Science organization, and 95 percent of its summer campers came from other states. Camp Newfound sued Maine. Discuss.

Strategy: The state was treating organizations differently depending on what states their campers come from. This raised Commerce Clause issues. Did the positive aspect or dormant aspect of that clause apply? The dormant aspect applied. What does it state? Apply that standard to these facts. (See the "Result" at the end of this section.)

5. **SUPREMACY CLAUSE**   Under the Supremacy Clause, if there is a conflict between federal and state statutes, the federal law preempts the field. Even without a conflict, federal law preempts if Congress intended to exercise exclusive control. (p. 114)

6. **PRESIDENTIAL POWERS**   The President's key powers include making agency appointments, proposing legislation, conducting foreign policy, and acting as commander in chief of the armed forces. (p. 111)

7. **FEDERAL COURTS**   The federal courts adjudicate cases and also exercise judicial review, which is the right to declare a statute or governmental action unconstitutional and void. (pp. 115–117)

8. **FREEDOM OF SPEECH**   Freedom of speech includes symbolic acts. Political speech by both people and organizations is protected unless it is intended and likely to create imminent lawless action. (pp. 118–122)

9. **REGULATION OF SPEECH**   The government may regulate the time, place, and manner of speech. (p. 120)

10. **COMMERCIAL SPEECH**   Commercial speech that is false or misleading may be outlawed; otherwise, regulations on this speech must be reasonable and directed to a legitimate goal. (pp. 121–122)

EXAM Strategy

Question: A federal statute prohibits the broadcasting of lottery advertisements, except by stations that broadcast in states permitting lotteries. The purpose of the statute is to support efforts of states that outlaw lotteries. Truth Broadcasting operates a radio station in State A (a nonlottery state) but broadcasts primarily in State B (a lottery state). Truth wants to advertise State A's lottery but is barred by the statute. Does the federal statute violate Truth's constitutional rights?

Strategy: This case involves a particular kind of speech. What kind? What is the rule about that kind of speech? (See the "Result" at the end of this section.)

---

11. **PROCEDURAL DUE PROCESS**   Procedural due process is required whenever the government attempts to take liberty or property. The amount of process that is due depends upon the importance of the liberty or property threatened. (pp. 123–124)

EXAM Strategy

Question: Fox's Fine Furs claims that Ermine owes $68,000 for a mink coat on which she has stopped making payments. Fox files a complaint and also asks the court clerk to *garnish* Ermine's wages. A garnishment is a court order to an employer to withhold an employee's wages, or a portion of them, and pay the money into court so that there will be money for the plaintiff, if it wins. What constitutional issue does Fox's request for garnishment raise?

Strategy: Ermine is in danger of losing part of her income, which is property. The Due Process Clause prohibits the government (the court) from taking life, liberty, or property without due process. What process is Ermine entitled to? (See the "Result" at the end of this section.)

---

12. **TAKINGS CLAUSE**   The Takings Clause prohibits a state from taking private property for public use without just compensation. (pp. 124–126)

13. **SUBSTANTIVE DUE PROCESS**   A substantive due process analysis presumes that any economic or social regulation is valid, and presumes invalid any law that infringes upon a fundamental right. (p. 126)

14. **EQUAL PROTECTION CLAUSE**   The Equal Protection Clause generally requires the government to treat people equally. Courts apply strict scrutiny in any equal protection case involving race, ethnicity, or fundamental rights; intermediate scrutiny to any case involving gender; and minimal scrutiny to an economic or social regulation. (pp. 126–128)

4. Result: The dormant aspect holds that a state statute that discriminates against interstate commerce is almost always invalid. Maine was subsidizing charities that served in-state residents and penalizing those that attracted campers from elsewhere. The tax rules violated the Commerce Clause and were void.[28]

10. Result: An advertisement is *commercial* speech. The government may regulate this speech so long as the rules are reasonable and directed to a legitimate goal. The goal of supporting nonlottery states is reasonable, and there is no violation of Truth's free speech rights.[29]

11. Result: Ermine is entitled to notice of Fox's claim and to a hearing *before* the court garnishes her wages.[30]

MULTIPLE-CHOICE QUESTIONS

1. Greenville College, a public community college, has a policy of admitting only male students. If the policy is challenged under the Fourteenth Amendment, _____ scrutiny will be applied.

   (a) strict

   (b) intermediate

   (c) rational

   (d) none of the above

2. You begin work at Everhappy Corp. at the beginning of November. On your second day at work, you wear a political button on your overcoat, supporting your choice for governor in the upcoming election. Your boss glances at it and says, "Get that stupid thing out of this office or you're history, chump." Your boss _____ violated your First Amendment rights. After work, you put the button back on and start walking home. You pass a police officer who blocks your path and says, "Take off that stupid button or you're going to jail, chump." The officer _____ violated your First Amendment rights.

   (a) has; has

   (b) has; has not

   (c) has not; has

   (d) has not; has not

---

[28]*Camps Newfound/Owatonna, Inc. v. Town of Harrison, Maine,* 520 U.S. 564, 117 S. Ct. 1590 (1997).
[29]*United States v. Edge Broadcasting,* 509 U.S. 418, 113 S. Ct. 2696 (1993).
[30]*Sniadach v. Family Finance Corp.,* 395 U.S. 337 (1969).

3. Which of the following statements accurately describes statutes that Congress and the President may create?

   (a) Statutes must be related to a power listed in Article I, section 8, of the Constitution.

   (b) Statutes must not infringe on the liberties in the Bill of Rights.

   (c) Both (a) and (b)

   (d) None of the above

4. Which of the following is true of the origin of judicial review?

   (a) It was created by Article II of the Constitution.

   (b) It was created by Article III of the Constitution.

   (c) It was created in the *Marbury v. Madison* case.

   (d) It was created by the Fifth Amendment.

   (e) It was created by the Fourteenth Amendment.

5. Consider *Kelo v. City of New London*, in which a city with a revitalization plan squared off against property owners who did not wish to sell their property. The key constitutional provision was the Takings Clause in the _____ Amendment. The Supreme Court decided the city _____ use eminent domain and take the property from the landowners.

   (a) Fifth; could

   (b) Fifth; could not

   (c) Fourteenth; could

   (d) Fourteenth; could not

Essay Questions

1. **YOU BE THE JUDGE WRITING PROBLEM** Scott Fane was a CPA licensed to practice in New Jersey and Florida. He built his New Jersey practice by making unsolicited phone calls to executives. When he moved to Florida, the Board of Accountancy there prohibited him (and all CPAs) from personally soliciting new business. Fane sued. Does the First Amendment force Florida to forgo foreclosing Fane's phoning? **Argument for Fane:** The Florida regulation violates the First Amendment, which protects commercial speech. Fane was not saying anything false or misleading, but was just trying to secure business. This is an unreasonable regulation, designed to keep newcomers out of the marketplace and maintain steady business and high prices for established CPAs. **Argument for the Florida Board of Accountancy:** Commercial speech deserves—and gets—a lower level of protection than other speech. This regulation is a reasonable method of ensuring that the level of CPA work in our state remains high. CPAs who personally solicit clients are obviously in need of business. They are more likely to bend legal and ethical rules to obtain clients and keep them happy, and will lower the standards throughout the state.

2. President George H. W. Bush insisted that he had the power to send American troops into combat in the Middle East, without congressional assent. Yet before authorizing force in Operation Desert Storm, he secured congressional authorization. President Bill Clinton stated that he was prepared to invade Haiti without a congressional vote. Yet he bargained hard to avoid an invasion, and ultimately American troops entered without the use of force. Why the seeming doubletalk by both Presidents?

3. In the landmark 1965 case of *Griswold v. Connecticut*, the Supreme Court examined a Connecticut statute that made it a crime for any person to use contraception. The majority declared the law an unconstitutional violation of the right of privacy. Justice Black dissented, saying, "I do not to any extent whatever base my view that this Connecticut law is constitutional on a belief that the law is wise or that its policy is a good one. [It] is every bit as offensive to me as it is to the majority. [There is no criticism by the majority of this law] to which I cannot subscribe—except their conclusion that the evil qualities they see in the law make it unconstitutional." What legal doctrines are involved here? Why did Justice Black distinguish between his personal views on the statute and the power of the Court to overturn it?

4. Gilleo opposed American participation in the war in the Persian Gulf. She displayed a large sign on her front lawn that read, "Say No to War in the Persian Gulf, Call Congress Now." The city of Ladue prohibited signs on front lawns and Gilleo sued. The city claimed that it was regulating "time, place, and manner." Explain that statement, and decide who should win.

5. David Lucas paid $975,000 for two residential lots on the Isle of Palms near Charleston, South Carolina. He intended to build houses on them. Two years later, the South Carolina legislature passed a statute that prohibited building seaward of a certain line, and Lucas's property fell in the prohibited zone. Lucas claimed that his land was now useless and that South Carolina owed him its value. Explain his claim. Should he win?

DISCUSSION QUESTIONS

1. Return to the opening scenario and the *Citizens United* case. Is political advertising purchased by corporations appropriate? Do you agree with the five members of the Supreme Court who voted to allow it, or with the four who dissented and would have drawn distinctions between free speech by individuals and organizations? Why?

2. **Ethics** Is political advertising by a nonprofit political organization like Citizens United any more or less appropriate than advertising by for-profit corporations like the one described in the opening scenario? If you were a board member in the opening scenario, which (if any) of the three ads would you vote to authorize?

3. Consider the "tea party" movement. Do you believe that the federal government should be able to create whatever laws it deems to be in the country's best interests, or do you believe that individual states, like Florida and California,

should have more control over the laws within their own borders?

4. This chapter is filled with examples of statutes that have been struck down by the courts. A Texas law banning flag burning was rejected by the Supreme Court, as was a Louisiana death penalty statute. The Affordable Healthcare Act was voided by multiple lower court judges before the Supreme Court ultimately upheld the law.

   Do you like the fact that courts can void laws which they determine to be in violation of the Constitution? Or is it wrong for appointed judges to overrule "the will of the majority," as expressed by elected members of Congress and state legislatures?

5. Gender discrimination currently receives "intermediate" Fourteenth Amendment scrutiny. Is this right? Should gender receive "strict" scrutiny as does race? Why or why not?

CHAPTER 6

TORTS AND PRODUCT LIABILITY

In a small Louisiana town, Don Mashburn ran a restaurant called Maison de Mashburn. The *New Orleans States-Item* newspaper reviewed his eatery, and here is what the article said:

'Tain't Creole, 'tain't Cajun, 'tain't French, 'tain't country American, 'tain't good. I don't know how much real talent in cooking is hidden under the mélange of hideous sauces which make this food and the menu a travesty of pretentious amateurism, but I find it all quite depressing. Put a yellow flour sauce on top of the duck, flame it for drama, and serve it with some horrible multiflavored rice in hollowed-out fruit and what have you got? A well-cooked duck with an ugly sauce that tastes too sweet and thick and makes you want to scrape off the glop to eat the plain duck. [The stuffed eggplant was prepared by emptying] a shaker full (more or less) of paprika on top of it. [One sauce created] trout à la green plague [while another should have been called] yellow death on duck.

Mashburn sued, claiming that the newspaper had committed libel, damaging his reputation and hurting his business.[1] Trout à la green plague will be the first course on our menu of tort law. Mashburn learned, as you will, why filing such a lawsuit is easier than winning it.

> 'Tain't Creole, 'tain't Cajun, 'tain't French, 'tain't country American, 'tain't good.

---

[1]*Mashburn v. Collin*, 355 So.2d 879 (La. 1977).

The odd word "tort" is borrowed from the French, meaning "wrong." And that is what it means in law: a wrong. More precisely, a **tort** is a violation of a duty imposed by the civil law. When a person breaks one of those duties and injures another, it is a tort. The injury could be to a person or her property. Libel, which the restaurant owner in the opening scenario alleged, is one example of a tort. A surgeon who removes the wrong kidney from a patient commits a different kind of tort, called negligence. A business executive who deliberately steals a client away from a competitor, interfering with a valid contract, commits a tort called interference with a contract. A con artist who tricks you out of your money with a phony offer to sell you a boat commits fraud, yet another tort.

Because tort law is so broad, it takes a while to understand its boundaries. To start with, we must distinguish torts from two other areas of law: criminal law and contract law.

It is a *crime* to steal a car, to embezzle money from a bank, to sell cocaine. As discussed in Chapter 1, society considers such behavior so threatening that the government itself will prosecute the wrongdoer, whether or not the car owner or bank president wants the case to go forward. A district attorney, who is paid by the government, will bring the case to court, seeking to send the defendant to prison, fine him, or both. If there is a fine, the money goes to the state, not to the victim.

In a tort case, it is up to the injured party to seek compensation. She must hire her own lawyer, who will file a lawsuit. Her lawyer must convince the court that the defendant breached some legal duty and ought to pay money damages to the plaintiff. The plaintiff has no power to send the defendant to jail. Bear in mind that a defendant's action might be both a crime and a tort. A man who punches you in the face for no reason commits the tort of battery. You may file a civil suit against him and will collect money damages if you can prove your case. He has also committed a crime, and the state may prosecute, seeking to imprison and fine him.

Tort

A violation of a duty imposed by the civil law.

Differences between Contract, Tort, and Criminal Law			
Type of Obligation	**Contract**	**Tort**	**Criminal Law**
How the obligation is created	The parties agree on a contract, which creates duties for both.	The civil law imposes duties of conduct on all persons.	The criminal law prohibits certain conduct.
How the obligation is enforced	Suit by plaintiff.	Suit by plaintiff.	Prosecution by government.
Possible result	Money damages for plaintiff.	Money damages for plaintiff.	Punishment for defendant, including prison and/or fine.
Example	Raul contracts to sell Deirdre 5,000 pairs of sneakers at $50 per pair, but fails to deliver them. Deirdre buys the sneakers elsewhere for $60 per pair and receives $50,000, her extra expense.	A newspaper falsely accuses a private citizen of being an alcoholic. The plaintiff sues and wins money damages to compensate for her injured reputation.	Leo steals Kelly's car. The government prosecutes Leo for grand theft, and the judge sentences him to two years in prison. Kelly gets nothing.

© Cengage Learning

A tort is also different from a contract dispute. A contract case is based on an agreement two people have already made. For example, Deirdre claims that Raul promised to sell her 10,000 pairs of sneakers at a good price but has failed to deliver them. She files a contract lawsuit. In a tort case, there is usually no "deal" between the parties. Don Mashburn had never met the restaurant critic who attacked his restaurant and obviously had never made any kind of contract. The plaintiff in a tort case claims that the law itself creates a duty that the defendant has breached.

Intentional torts

Harm caused by a deliberate action.

Tort law is divided into categories. In the first part of this chapter, we consider **intentional torts**; that is, harm caused by a deliberate action. The newspaper columnist who wrongly accuses someone of being a drunk has committed the intentional tort of libel. In the last sections, we examine negligence and strict liability, which involve injuries and losses caused by neglect and oversight rather than by deliberate conduct.

A final introductory point: When we speak of intentional torts, we do not necessarily mean that the defendant intended to harm the plaintiff. If the defendant does something deliberately and it ends up injuring somebody, she is probably liable even if she meant no harm. For example, intentionally throwing a snowball at a friend is a deliberate act. If the snowball permanently damages his eye, the *harm* is unintended, but the defendant is liable for the intentional tort of battery because the *act* was intentional.

We look first at the most common intentional torts and then at the most important intentional torts that are related to business.

6-1 INTENTIONAL TORTS

6-1a Defamation

The First Amendment guarantees the right to free speech, a vital freedom that enables us to protect other rights. But that freedom is not absolute.

Libel

Written defamation.

Slander

Oral defamation.

The law of defamation concerns false statements that harm someone's reputation. Defamatory statements can be written or spoken. Written defamation is called **libel**. Suppose a newspaper accuses a local retail store of programming its cash registers to overcharge customers when the store has never done so. That is libel. Oral defamation is **slander**. If Professor Wisdom, in class, refers to Sally Student as a drug dealer when she has never sold drugs, he has slandered her. Exhibit 6.1 maps the tension in every defamation case—between an individual's right to protect his reputation and the public's right to know.

There are four elements to a defamation case. An element is something that a plaintiff must prove to win a lawsuit. The plaintiff in any kind of lawsuit must prove *all* of the elements to prevail. The elements in a defamation case are:

- **Defamatory statement.** This is a statement likely to harm another person's reputation. Professor Wisdom's accusation will clearly harm Sally's reputation.

- **Falseness.** The statement must be false. If Sally Student actually sold marijuana to a classmate, then Professor Wisdom has a defense to slander.

- **Communicated.** The statement must be communicated to at least one person *other than the plaintiff.* If Wisdom speaks privately to Sally and accuses her of dealing drugs, there is no slander.

- **Injury.** In many slander cases, the plaintiff generally must show some injury. Sally's injury would be lower reputation in the school, embarrassment, and humiliation. But in slander cases that involve false statements about sexual behavior, crimes, contagious diseases, and professional abilities, the law is willing to assume injury without requiring the plaintiff to prove it. Lies in these four categories amount to **slander per se**.

Libel cases are treated like cases of slander per se, and courts award damages without proof of injury.[2]

Slander per se

Slander involving false statements about sexual behavior, crimes, contagious diseases, and professional abilities.

OPINION

Thus far, what we have seen is uncontroversial. If a television commentator refers to Frank Landlord as a "vicious slumlord who rents uninhabitable units," and Frank actually maintains his buildings perfectly, Frank will be compensated for the harm. But what if the television commentator states a harsh *opinion* about Frank? Remember that the plaintiff must demonstrate a "false" statement. Opinions generally cannot be proven true or false, and so they do not usually amount to defamation.

Suppose that the television commentator says, "Frank Landlord certainly does less than many rich people do for our community." Is that defamation? Probably not. Who are the "rich people"? How much do they do? How do we define "does less"? These vague assertions indicate the statement is one of opinion. Even if Frank works hard feeding homeless families, he will probably lose a defamation case.

A related defense involves cases where a supposed statement of fact clearly should not be taken literally. Mr. Mashburn, who opened the chapter suing over his restaurant review, lost his case. The court held that a reasonable reader would have understood the statements to be opinion only. "A shaker full of paprika" and "yellow death on duck" were not to be taken literally but were merely the author's expression of his personal dislike.

PUBLIC PERSONALITIES

The rules of the game change for those who play in the open. Government officials and other types of public figures such as actors and athletes receive less protection from defamation. In the landmark case *New York Times Co. v. Sullivan*,[3] the Supreme Court ruled that the free exchange of information is vital in a democracy and is protected by the First Amendment to the Constitution.

The rule from the *New York Times* case is that a public official or public figure can win a defamation case only by proving **actual malice** by the defendant. Actual malice means that the defendant knew the statement was false or acted with reckless disregard of the truth. If the plaintiff merely shows that the defendant newspaper printed incorrect statements, even very damaging ones, that will not suffice to win the suit. In the *New York Times* case, the police chief of Birmingham, Alabama, claimed that the *Times* falsely accused him of racial violence in his job. He lost because he could not prove that the *Times* had acted with actual malice. If he had shown that the *Times* knew the accusation was false, he would have won.

---

[2]When defamation by radio and television became possible, the courts chose to consider it libel, analogizing it to newspapers because of the vast audience. This means that in broadcasting cases, a plaintiff generally does not have to prove damages.

[3]376 U.S. 254, 84 S. Ct. 710, 1964 U.S. LEXIS 1655 (1964).

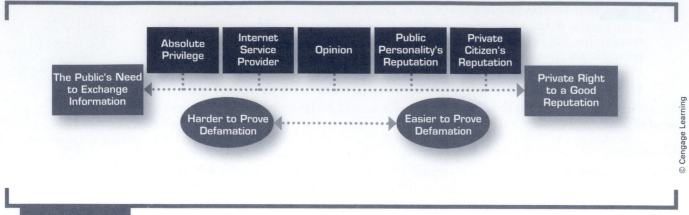

© Cengage Learning

EXHIBIT 6.1   Defamation cases show a tension between the public's need for information and a citizen's right to protect his reputation.

ONLINE DEFAMATION

Kenneth Zeran awoke one day to learn he had become notorious. An unidentified person had posted a message on an AOL bulletin board advertising "Naughty Oklahoma T-Shirts." The shirts featured deeply offensive slogans relating to the 1995 bombing of a federal building in Oklahoma City, in which hundreds of innocent people died. Those interested in purchasing such a T-shirt were instructed to call "Ken" at Zeran's home telephone number. In fact, Zeran had nothing to do with the posting or the T-shirts. He was quickly inundated with phone messages from furious callers, some of whom made death threats.

Zeran could not conveniently change his number because he ran his business from his home. A radio talk show host in Oklahoma City angrily urged its listeners to call Zeran, which they did. Before long, Zeran was receiving an abusive call every two minutes. He sued AOL for defamation—and lost.

The court held that AOL was immune from a defamation suit based on a third-party posting, based on the Communications Decency Act (CDA). Section 230 of the CDA creates this immunity for any Internet service provider, the court declared, adding:

> It would be impossible for service providers to screen each of their millions of postings for possible problems. Faced with potential liability for each message republished by their services, interactive computer service providers might choose to severely restrict the number and type of messages posted. Congress considered the weight of the speech interests implicated and chose to immunize service providers to avoid any such restrictive effect.[4]

PRIVILEGE

Absolute privilege

A witness testifying in a court or legislature may never be sued for defamation.

Defendants receive additional protection from defamation cases when it is important for them to speak freely. **Absolute privilege** exists in courtrooms and legislative hearings. Anyone speaking there, such as a witness in court, can say anything at all and never be sued for defamation. (Deliberately false testimony would be *perjury*, but still not *slander*.)

---

[4]*Zeran v. America Online, Inc.*, 129 F.3d 327, 1997 U.S. App. LEXIS 31791 (4th Cir. 1997).

6-1b False Imprisonment

False imprisonment is the intentional restraint of another person without reasonable cause and without consent. Suppose that a bank teller becomes seriously ill and wants to go to the doctor, but the bank will not permit her to leave until she makes a final tally of her accounts. Against her wishes, company officials physically bar her from leaving the bank. That is false imprisonment. The restraint was unreasonable because her accounts could have been verified later.[5]

False imprisonment cases most commonly arise in retail stores, which sometimes detain employees or customers for suspected theft. Most states now have statutes governing the detention of suspected shoplifters. **Generally, a store may detain a customer or worker for alleged shoplifting provided there is a reasonable basis for the suspicion and the detention is done reasonably.** To detain a customer in the manager's office for 20 minutes and question him about where he got an item is lawful. To chain that customer to a display counter for three hours and humiliate him in front of other customers is unreasonable and constitutes false imprisonment.

False imprisonment
Is the intentional restraint of another person without reasonable cause and without consent.

6-1c Intentional Infliction of Emotional Distress

What should happen when a defendant's conduct hurts a plaintiff emotionally but not physically? Historically, not much did happen. Courts once refused to allow recovery, assuming that if they awarded damages for mere emotional injury, they would be inviting a floodgate of dubious claims. But gradually judges reexamined their thinking and reversed this tendency. Today, most courts allow a plaintiff to recover for emotional injury that a defendant intentionally caused. Some courts will also permit recovery when a defendant's negligent conduct caused the emotional injury.

The **intentional infliction of emotional distress** results from extreme and outrageous conduct that causes serious emotional harm. A credit officer was struggling vainly to locate Sheehan, who owed money on his car. The officer phoned Sheehan's mother, falsely identified herself as a hospital employee, and said she needed to find Sheehan because his children had been in a serious auto accident. The mother provided Sheehan's whereabouts, which enabled the company to seize his car. But Sheehan spent seven hours frantically trying to locate his supposedly injured children, who in fact were fine. The credit company was liable for the intentional infliction of emotional distress.[6]

By contrast, a muffler shop, trying to collect a debt from a customer, made six phone calls over three months, using abusive language. The customer testified that this caused her to be upset, to cry, and to have difficulty sleeping. The court ruled that the muffler shop's conduct was neither extreme nor outrageous.[7]

The following case arose in a setting that guarantees controversy—an abortion clinic.

Intentional infliction of emotional distress
An intentional tort in which the harm results from extreme and outrageous conduct that causes serious emotional harm.

[5]*Kanner v. First National Bank of South Miami*, 287 So.2d 715, 1974 Fla. App. LEXIS 8989 (Fla. Dist. Ct. App. 1974).
[6]*Ford Motor Credit Co. v. Sheehan*, 373 So.2d 956, 1979 Fla. App. LEXIS 15416 (Fla. Dist. Ct. App. 1979).
[7]*Midas Muffler Shop v. Ellison*, 133 Ariz. 194, 650 P.2d 496, 1982 Ariz. App. LEXIS 488 (Ariz. Ct. App. 1982).

JANE DOE AND NANCY ROE V. LYNN MILLS

212 Mich. App. 73
Michigan Court of Appeals, 1995

CASE SUMMARY

Facts: Late one night, an anti-abortion protestor named Robert Thomas climbed into a dumpster located behind the Women's Advisory Center, an abortion clinic. He found documents indicating that the plaintiffs were soon to have abortions at the clinic. Thomas gave the information to Lynn Mills. The next day, Mills and Sister Lois Mitoraj created signs, using the women's names, indicating that they were about to undergo abortions and urging them not to "kill their babies."

Doe and Roe (not their real names) sued, claiming intentional infliction of emotional distress (as well as breach of privacy, discussed later in this chapter). The trial court dismissed the lawsuit before trial, ruling that the defendants' conduct was not extreme and outrageous. The plaintiffs appealed.

Issue: *Did the plaintiffs make a valid claim of intentional infliction of emotional distress?*

Decision: Yes. The plaintiffs made a valid claim of intentional infliction of emotional distress.

Reasoning: A defendant is liable for the intentional infliction of emotional distress only when his conduct is outrageous in character, extreme in degree, and utterly intolerable in a civilized community. A good test is whether the average member of the community would respond to the defendant's conduct by exclaiming, "Outrageous!"

These defendants had a constitutional right to protest against abortions, but they had no such right to publicize private matters. Their behavior here might well have caused the average person to say, "Outrageous!" The plaintiffs were entitled to a trial, so that a jury could decide whether the defendants inflicted emotional distress.

6-1d Additional Intentional Torts

Battery

An intentional touching of another person in a way that is harmful or offensive.

Battery is an intentional touching of another person in a way that is unwanted or offensive. There need be no intention to *hurt* the plaintiff. If the defendant intended to do the physical act, and a reasonable plaintiff would be offended by it, battery has occurred.

Suppose an irate parent throws a chair at a referee during his daughter's basketball game, breaking the man's jaw. It is irrelevant that the father did not intend to injure the referee. But a parent who cheerfully slaps the winning coach on the back has not committed battery because a reasonable coach would not be offended.

Assault

An act that makes a person reasonably fear an imminent battery.

Assault occurs when a defendant does some act that makes a plaintiff fear an imminent battery. It is assault even though the battery never occurs. Suppose Ms. Wilson shouts "Think fast!" at her husband and hurls a toaster at him. He turns and sees it flying at him. His fear of being struck is enough to win a case of assault, even if the toaster misses.

Fraud

Injuring another person by deliberate deception.

Fraud is injuring another person by deliberate deception. It is fraud to sell real estate knowing that there is a large toxic waste deposit underground of which the buyer is ignorant. Fraud is a tort that typically occurs during contract negotiation, and it is discussed in more detail in Unit 2, on contracts.

6-2 DAMAGES

6-2a Compensatory Damages

Mitchel Bien, who is deaf and mute, enters the George Grubbs Nissan dealership, where folks sell cars aggressively. Very aggressively. Maturelli, a salesman, and Bien communicate by writing messages back and forth. Maturelli takes Bien's own car keys, and the two then test drive a 300ZX. Bien says he does not want the car, but Maturelli escorts him back inside and fills out a sales sheet. Bien repeatedly asks for his keys, but Maturelli only laughs, pressuring him to buy the new car. Minutes pass. Hours pass. Bien becomes frantic, writing a dozen notes, begging to leave, threatening to call the police. Maturelli mocks Bien and his physical disabilities. Finally, after four hours, the customer escapes.

Bien sues for the intentional infliction of emotional distress. Two former salesmen from Grubbs testify they have witnessed customers cry, yell, and curse as a result of the aggressive tactics. Doctors state that the incident has traumatized Bien, dramatically reducing his confidence and self-esteem and preventing his return to work even three years later.

The jury awards Bien damages. But how does a jury calculate the money? For that matter, why should a jury even try? Money can never erase pain or undo a permanent injury. The answer is simple: Money, however inexact, is often the only thing a court has to give.

A successful plaintiff generally receives **compensatory damages**, meaning an amount of money that the court believes will restore him to the position he was in before the defendant's conduct caused injury. Here is how damages are calculated.

First, a plaintiff receives money for medical expenses that he has proven by producing bills from doctors, hospitals, physical therapists, and psychotherapists. Bien receives all the money he has paid. If a doctor testifies that he needs future treatment, Bien will offer evidence of how much that will cost. The **single recovery principle** requires a court to settle the matter once and for all, by awarding a lump sum for past *and future* expenses, if there will be any. A plaintiff may not return in a year and say, "Oh, by the way, there are some new bills."

Second, the defendants are liable for lost wages. The court takes the number of days or months that Bien missed work and multiplies that by his salary. If Bien is currently unable to work, a doctor estimates how many more months he will miss work, and the court adds that to his damages.

Third, a plaintiff is paid for pain and suffering. Bien testifies about how traumatic the four hours were and how the experience has affected his life. He may state that he now fears shopping, suffers nightmares, and seldom socializes. To bolster the case, a plaintiff uses expert testimony, such as the psychiatrists who testified for Bien. Awards for pain and suffering vary enormously, from a few dollars to many millions, depending on the injury and depending on the jury. In some lawsuits, physical and psychological pain are momentary and insignificant; in other cases, the pain is the biggest part of the verdict. In this case, the jury awarded Bien $573,815, calculated as in the table that follows.[8]

Awards for future harm (such as future pain and suffering) involve the court making its best estimate of the plaintiff's hardship in the years to come. This is not an exact science. If the judgment is reasonable, it will rarely be overturned. Ethel Flanzraich, aged 78, fell on stairs that had been badly maintained. In addition to her medical expense, the court awarded her $150,000 for future pain and suffering. The day after the court gave its award, Ms. Flanzraich died of other causes. Did that mean her family must forfeit that money? No. The award was reasonable when made and had to be paid.[9]

Compensatory damages
Money intended to restore a plaintiff to the position he was in before the injury.

Single recovery principle
Requires a court to settle the matter once and for all, by awarding a lump sum for past and future expenses.

> Bien becomes frantic, writing a dozen notes, begging to leave, threatening to call the police.

---

[8]The compensatory damages are described in *George Grubbs Enterprises v. Bien*, 881 S.W.2d 843, 1994 Tex. App. LEXIS 1870 (Tex. Ct. App. 1994). In addition to the compensatory damages described, the jury awarded $5 million in punitive damages. The Texas Supreme Court reversed the award of punitive damages, but not the compensatory. *Id.*, 900 S.W.2d 337, 1995 Tex. LEXIS 91 (Tex. 1995). The high court did not dispute the appropriateness of punitive damages, but reversed because the trial court failed to instruct the jury properly as to how it should determine the assets actually under the defendants' control, an issue essential to punitive damages but not compensatory.

[9]We looked at discovery issues from this case in Chapter 3. *Stinton v. Robin's Wood*, 45 A.D.3d 203, 842 N.Y.S.2d 477 (N.Y.App.Div. 2007).

Past medical	$ 70.00
Future medical	6,000.00
Past rehabilitation	3,205.00
Past lost earning capacity	112,910.00
Future lost earning capacity	34,650.00
Past physical symptoms and discomfort	50,000.00
Future physical symptoms and discomfort	50,000.00
Past emotional injury and mental anguish	101,980.00
Future emotional injury and mental anguish	200,000.00
Past loss of society and reduced ability to socially interact with family, former fiancee, and friends, and hearing (i.e., nondeaf) people in general	10,000.00
Future loss of society and reduced ability to socially interact with family, former fiancee, and friends, and hearing people	5,000.00
TOTAL	**$573,815.00**

© Cengage Learning

6-2b Punitive Damages

Punitive damages

Damages that are intended to punish the defendant for conduct that is extreme and outrageous.

Here we look at a different kind of award, one that is more controversial and potentially more powerful: punitive damages. The purpose is not to compensate the plaintiff for harm, because compensatory damages will have done that. **Punitive damages** are intended to punish the defendant for conduct that is extreme and outrageous. Courts award these damages in relatively few cases. The idea behind punitive damages is that certain behavior is so unacceptable that society must make an example of it. A large award of money should deter the defendant from repeating the mistake and others from ever making it. Some believe punitive damages represent the law at its most avaricious, while others attribute to them great social benefit.

Although a jury has wide discretion in awarding punitive damages, the Supreme Court has ruled that, if a verdict is unreasonable, it violates the Due Process clause of the Constitution. Ira Gore purchased a new BMW automobile from an Alabama dealer and then discovered that the car had been repainted. He sued. At trial, BMW acknowledged a nationwide policy of not informing customers of predelivery repairs when the cost was less than 3% of the retail price. The company had sold about 1,000 repainted cars nationwide. The jury concluded that BMW had engaged in gross, malicious fraud and awarded Gore $4,000 in compensatory damages and $4 million in punitive damages. The Alabama Supreme Court reduced the award to $2 million, but the United States Supreme Court ruled that even that amount was grossly excessive. The Court held that in awarding punitive damages, a court must consider three "guideposts":

- The reprehensibility of the defendant's conduct;
- The ratio between the harm suffered and the award; and
- The difference between the punitive award and any civil penalties used in similar cases.

The Court concluded that BMW had shown no evil intent and that Gore's harm had been purely economic (as opposed to physical). Further, the Court found the ratio of 500 to 1, between punitive and compensatory damages, to be excessive, although it offered no definitive rule about a proper ratio. On remand, the Alabama Supreme Court reduced the punitive damages award to $50,000.[10]

The U.S. Supreme Court gave additional guidance on punitive damages in the following landmark case.

Landmark Case

STATE FARM V. CAMPBELL
538 U.S. 408
Supreme Court of the United States (2003)

Facts: While attempting to pass several cars on a two-lane road, Campbell drove into oncoming traffic. An innocent driver swerved to avoid Campbell and died in a collision with a third driver. The family of the deceased driver and the surviving third driver both sued Campbell.

As Campbell's insurer, State Farm represented him in the lawsuit. It turned down an offer to settle the case for $50,000, the limit of Campbell's policy. The company had nothing to gain by settling because even if Campbell lost big at trial, State Farm's liability was capped at $50,000.

A jury returned a judgment against Campbell for $185,000. He was responsible for the $135,000 that exceeded his policy limit. He argued with State Farm, claiming that it should have settled the case. Eventually, State Farm paid the entire $185,000, but Campbell still sued the company, alleging fraud and intentional infliction of emotional distress.

His lawyers presented evidence that State Farm had deliberately acted in its own best interests rather than his. The jury was convinced, and in the end, awarded $1 million in compensatory damages and $145 million in punitive damages. State Farm appealed.

Issue: *Did the punitive damages violate the Due Process Clause?*

Decision: Yes. A ratio of punitive to compensatory damages of 145-to-1 was excessive, especially where the plaintiff suffered limited harm.

Reasoning: The goal of punitive damages is to prevent and punish wrongdoing. However, the Due Process Clause requires that people have fair warning about what conduct will be punished and how severe the penalty will be. When punitive damages are grossly excessive, they violate this provision of the Constitution.

Punitive damages are reasonable only if they are proportionate both to the amount of harm suffered by the plaintiff and to the compensatory damages awarded. We do not impose any precise limit on punitive damages awards, because results will depend on the particular facts of each case. However, we are skeptical of any awards in which the ratio between punitive and compensatory damages is greater than nine. Awards at this level are unlikely to satisfy due process, while still achieving the State's goals of prevention and punishment. Double-digit ratios could be possible, but only in cases of extreme harm.

The Campbells' award had a *triple*-digit ratio of 145-to-1. That is, the lower court awarded the Campbells $145 million in punitive damages and $1 million in compensatory damages. What was the extent of their harm? The Campbells suffered a year and a half of emotional distress. They had no physical injuries or trauma. Their economic damage was not significant either, since State Farm paid the excess verdict. One million dollars was adequate compensation for their stress and hurt feelings.

We reverse the judgment and remand this case to the lower court.

---

[10]*BMW of North America, Inc. v. Gore*, 517 U.S. 559, 116 S. Ct. 1589, 1996 U.S. LEXIS 3390 (1996)

6-3 BUSINESS TORTS

In this section, we look at several intentional torts that occur almost exclusively in a commercial setting: interference with a contract, interference with a prospective advantage, and the rights to privacy and publicity. Note that several business torts are discussed elsewhere in the book:

- Patents, copyrights, and trademarks are discussed in Chapter 33, on intellectual property.

- False advertising, discussed in part under the Lanham Act section (later in this chapter), is considered more broadly in Chapter 31, on consumer law.

- Consumer issues are also covered in Chapter 31. The material in the present chapter focuses not on consumer claims but on disputes between businesses.

6-3a Tortious Interference with Business Relations

Competition is the essence of business. Successful corporations compete aggressively, and the law permits and expects them to. But there are times when healthy competition becomes illegal interference. This is called tortious interference with business relations. It can take one of two closely related forms—interference with a contract or interference with a prospective advantage.

TORTIOUS INTERFERENCE WITH A CONTRACT

**Tortious interference
with a contract**

An intentional tort in which the defendant improperly induced a third party to breach a contract with the plaintiff.

Tortious interference with a contract exists if the plaintiff can establish the following four elements:

- There was a contract between the plaintiff and a third party;

- The defendant knew of the contract;

- The defendant improperly *induced* the third party to breach the contract or made performance of the contract impossible; and

- There was injury to the plaintiff.

Because businesses routinely compete for customers, employees, and market share, it is not always easy to identify tortious interference. There is nothing wrong with two companies bidding against each other to buy a parcel of land, and nothing wrong with one corporation doing everything possible to convince the seller to ignore all competitors. But once a company has signed a contract to buy the land, it is improper to induce the seller to break the deal. The most commonly disputed issues in these cases concern elements one and three: Was there a contract between the plaintiff and another party? Did the defendant improperly induce a party to breach it? Defendants will try to show that the plaintiff had no contract.

A defendant may also rely on the defense of **justification;** that is, a claim that special circumstances made its conduct fair. To establish justification, a defendant must show that:

- It was acting to protect an existing economic interest, such as its own contract with the third party;

- It was acting in the public interest, for example, by reporting to a government agency that a corporation was overbilling for government services; or

- The existing contract could be terminated at will by either party, meaning that although the plaintiff had a contract, the plaintiff had no long-term assurances because the other side could end it at any time.

Texaco v. Pennzoil   One of the largest verdicts in the history of American law came in a case of contract interference. Pennzoil made an unsolicited bid to buy 20 percent of Getty Oil at $112.50 per share, and the Getty board approved the agreement. Before the lawyers for both sides could complete the paperwork, Texaco appeared and offered Getty stockholders $128 per share for the entire company. Getty officers turned their attention to Texaco, but Pennzoil sued, claiming tortious interference. Texaco replied that it had not interfered because there was no binding contract.

The jury bought Pennzoil's argument, and they bought it big: $7.53 billion in actual damages, and $3 billion more in punitive damages. After appeals and frantic negotiations, the two parties reached a settlement. Texaco agreed to pay Pennzoil $3 billion as settlement for having wrongfully interfered with Pennzoil's agreement to buy Getty.

TORTIOUS INTERFERENCE WITH A PROSPECTIVE ADVANTAGE

Interference with a prospective advantage is an awkward name for a tort that is simply a variation on interference with a contract. The difference is that, for this tort, there need be no contract; the plaintiff is claiming outside interference with an expected economic relationship. Obviously, the plaintiff must show more than just the hope of a profit.

A plaintiff who has a definite and reasonable expectation of obtaining an economic advantage may sue a corporation that maliciously interferes and prevents the relationship from developing.

Suppose that Jump Co. and Block Co. both hope to purchase a professional basketball team. The team's owners reject the offer from Block. They informally agree to a price with Jump but refuse to make a binding deal until Jump leases a stadium. Block owns the only stadium in town and refuses to lease to Jump, meaning that Jump cannot buy the team. Block has interfered with Jump's prospective advantage.

> **Tortious interference with a prospective advantage**
> Malicious interference with a developing econimic relationship.

6-3b Privacy and Publicity

We live in a world of dazzling technology, and it is easier than ever—and more profitable— to spy on someone. Does the law protect us? What power do we have to limit the intrusion of others into our lives and to prohibit them from commercially exploiting information about us?

INTRUSION

Intrusion into someone's private life is a tort if a reasonable person would find it offensive. Peeping through someone's windows or wiretapping his telephone are obvious examples of intrusion. In a famous case involving a "paparazzo" photographer and Jacqueline Kennedy Onassis, the court found that the photographer had invaded her privacy by making a career out of photographing her. He had bribed doormen to gain access to hotels and restaurants she visited, had jumped out of bushes to photograph her young children, and had driven power boats dangerously close to her. The court ordered him to stop.[11] Nine years later, the paparazzo was found in contempt of court for again taking photographs too close to Ms. Onassis. He agreed to stop once and for all—in exchange for a suspended contempt sentence.

> **Intrusion**
> A tort in which a reasonable person would find the invasion of her private life offensive.

COMMERCIAL EXPLOITATION

The right to commercial exploitation prohibits the use of someone's likeness or voice for commercial purposes without permission. This business tort is the flip side of privacy and covers the right to make money from publicity. For example, it would be illegal to run a magazine ad showing Keira Knightley holding a can of soda without her permission. The ad would imply that she endorses the product. Someone's identity is her own, and it cannot be used for commercial gain unless she permits it.

---

[11]*Galella v. Onassis*, 487 F. 2d 986.

Ford Motor Co. hired a singer to imitate Bette Midler's version of a popular song. The imitation was so good that most listeners were fooled into believing that Ms. Midler was endorsing the product. That, ruled a court, violated her right to commercial exploitation.

6-4 NEGLIGENCE

Party time! A fraternity at the University of Arizona welcomed new members, and the alcohol flowed freely. Several hundred people danced and shrieked and drank, and no one checked for proof of age. A common occurrence—but one that ended tragically. A minor student drove away, intoxicated, and slammed into another car. The other driver, utterly innocent of wrongdoing, was gravely injured.

The drunken student was obviously liable, but his insurance did not cover the huge medical bills. The injured man also sued the fraternity. Should that organization be legally responsible? The question leads to other similar issues. Should a restaurant that serves an intoxicated adult be liable for resulting harm? If *you* give a party, should you be responsible for any damage caused by your guests?

These are moral questions—but very practical ones, as well. They are typical issues of negligence law. In this contentious area, courts continually face one question: *When someone is injured, how far should responsibility extend?*

We might call negligence the "unintentional" tort because it concerns harm that arises by accident. A person, or perhaps an organization, does some act, neither intending nor expecting to hurt anyone, yet someone is harmed. Should a court impose liability? The fraternity members who gave the party never wanted—or thought—that an innocent man would suffer terrible damage. But he did. Is it in society's interest to hold the fraternity responsible?

Before we can answer this question, we need some background knowledge. Things go wrong all the time, and society needs a means of analyzing negligence cases consistently and fairly.

To win a negligence case, a plaintiff must prove five elements. Much of the remainder of this chapter will examine them in detail. They are:

- **Duty of Due Care.** The defendant had a legal responsibility *to the plaintiff*.

- **Breach.** The defendant breached her duty of care or failed to meet her legal obligations.

- **Factual Cause.** The defendant's conduct actually caused the injury.

- **Proximate Cause.** It was *foreseeable* that conduct like the defendant's might cause *this type of harm*.

- **Damages.** The plaintiff has actually been hurt or has actually suffered a measureable loss.

To win a case, a plaintiff must prove all the elements listed above. If a defendant eliminates only one item on the list, there is no liability.

6-4a Duty of Due Care

Each of us has a duty to behave as a reasonable person would under the circumstances.

If you are driving a car, you have a duty to all the other people near you to drive like a reasonable person. If you drive while drunk, or send text messages while behind the wheel, then you fail to live up to your duty of care.

But how *far* does your duty extend? Judges draw an imaginary line around the defendant and say that she owes a duty to the people within the circle, but not to those outside it. The test is generally "foreseeability." If the defendant could have foreseen injury to a particular person, she has a duty to him. Suppose that one of your friends posts a YouTube video of you texting behind the wheel and her father is so upset from watching it that he falls down the stairs. You would not be liable for the father's downfall because it was not foreseeable that he would be harmed by your texting.

Let us apply these principles to the case described in the scenario that opened this section.

HERNANDEZ V. ARIZONA BOARD OF REGENTS

177 Ariz. 244, 866 P.2d 1330, 1994 Ariz.
LEXIS 6 Arizona Supreme Court, 1994

CASE SUMMARY

Facts: At the University of Arizona, the Epsilon Epsilon chapter of Delta Tau Delta fraternity gave a welcoming party for new members. The fraternity's officers knew that the majority of its members were under the legal drinking age, but they permitted everyone to consume alcohol. John Rayner, who was under 21 years of age, left the party. He drove negligently and caused a collision with an auto driven by Ruben Hernandez. At the time of the accident, Rayner's blood alcohol level was 0.15, exceeding the legal limit. The crash left Hernandez blind, severely brain damaged, and quadriplegic.

Hernandez sued Rayner, who settled the case, based on the amount of his insurance coverage. The victim also sued the fraternity, its officers and national organization, all fraternity members who contributed money to buy alcohol, the university, and others. The trial court granted summary judgment for all defendants, and the court of appeals affirmed. Hernandez appealed to the Arizona Supreme Court.

Issue: *Did the fraternity and the other defendants have a duty of due care to Hernandez?*

Decision: The defendants did have a duty of due care to Hernandez. Reversed and remanded.

Reasoning: Yes. Historically, Arizona and most states have considered that *consuming* alcohol led to liability, but *not furnishing* it. However, the common law also has had a longstanding rule that a defendant could be liable for supplying some object to a person who is likely to endanger others. Giving a car to an intoxicated youth would be an example of such behavior; the youth might easily use the object (the car) to injure other people.

There is little difference between giving a car to an intoxicated youth and giving alcohol to a young person with a car. Both acts involve minors who, because of their age and inexperience, are likely to endanger third parties. Moreover, furnishing alcohol to a minor violates several state statutes. As a result, most states have concluded that a defendant who serves intoxicating drinks to a minor is legally responsible for resulting harm to third parties. Arizona now joins that majority. The defendants did have a duty of due care to Hernandez and to the public in general.

In several circumstances, people have special duties to others. Three of them are outlined below.

SPECIAL DUTY: LANDOWNERS

The common law applies special rules to a landowner for injuries occurring on her property. In most states, the owner's duty depends on the type of person injured.

Lowest Liability: Trespassing Adults   A **trespasser** is anyone on another's property without consent. A landowner is liable to a trespasser only for intentionally injuring him or for some other gross misconduct. The landowner has no liability to a trespasser for mere negligence. Jake is not liable if a vagrant wanders onto his land and is burned by defective electrical wires.

Trespasser

A person on another's property without consent.

Mid-level Liability: Trespassing Children   The law makes exceptions when the trespassers are **children** If there is some manmade thing on the land *that may be reasonably expected to attract children*, the landowner is probably liable for any harm. Daphne lives next door to a day-care center and builds a treehouse on her property. Unless she has fenced off the dangerous area, she is probably liable if a small child wanders onto her property and injures himself when he falls from the rope ladder to the treehouse.

Licensee
A person on another's land for her own purposes but with the owner's permission.

Higher Liability: Licensee   A **licensee** is anyone on the land for her own purposes but with the owner's permission. A social guest is a typical licensee. A licensee is entitled to a warning of hidden dangers that the owner knows about. If Juliet invites Romeo for a late supper on the balcony and fails to mention that the wooden railing is rotted, she is liable when her hero plunges to the courtyard.

But Juliet is liable only for injuries caused by *hidden* dangers—she has no duty to warn guests of obvious dangers. She need not say, "Romeo, oh Romeo, don't place thy hand in the toaster, Romeo."

Invitee
A person who has a right to enter another's property because it is a public place or a business open to the public.

Highest Liability: Invitee   An **invitee** is someone who has a right to be on the property because it is a public place or a business open to the public. The owner has a duty of reasonable care to an invitee. Perry is an invitee when he goes to the town beach. If riptides have existed for years and the town fails to post a warning, it is liable if Perry drowns. Perry is also an invitee when he goes to Dana's coffee shop. Dana is liable if she ignores spilled coffee that causes Perry to slip.

With social guests, you must have *actual knowledge* of some specific hidden danger to be liable. Not so with invitees. You are liable even if you had *no idea* that something on your property posed a hidden danger. Therefore, if you own a business, you must conduct inspections of your property on a regular basis to make sure that nothing is becoming dangerous.

The courts of some states have modified these distinctions, and a few have eliminated them altogether. California, for example, requires "reasonable care" as to all people on the owner's property, regardless of how or why they got there. But most states still use the classifications outlined above.

Special Duty: Professionals

A person at work has a heightened duty of care. While on the job, she must act as a reasonable person *in her profession*. A taxi driver must drive as a reasonable taxi driver would. A heart surgeon must perform bypass surgery with the care of a trained specialist in that field.

Two medical cases illustrate the reasonable person standard. A doctor prescribes a powerful drug without asking his patient about other medicines she is currently taking. The patient suffers a serious drug reaction from the combined medications. The physician is liable for the harm. A reasonable doctor *always* checks current medicines before prescribing new ones.

On the other hand, assume that a patient dies on the operating table in an emergency room. The physician followed normal medical procedures at every step of the procedure and acted with reasonable speed. In fact, the man had a fatal stroke. The surgeon is not liable. A doctor must do a reasonable professional job, but she cannot guarantee a happy outcome.

Special Duty: Hiring and Retention

Employers also have special responsibilities.

In a recent one-year period, more than 1,000 homicides and 2 million attacks occurred in the workplace. Companies must beware because they can be liable for hiring or retaining violent employees. A mailroom clerk with a previous rape and robbery conviction followed a secretary home after work and killed her. Even though the murder took place off the company premises, the court held that the defendant would be liable if it knew or should have known of the mail clerk's criminal history.[12] In other cases, companies have been found liable for failing to check an applicant's driving record, contact personal references, or search criminal records.

Courts have also found companies negligent for *retaining* dangerous workers. If an employee threatens a coworker, the organization is not free to ignore the menacing conduct. If the employee acts on his threats, the company may be liable.[13]

6-4b Breach of Duty

The second element of a plaintiff's negligence case is **breach of duty**. If a legal duty of care exists, then a plaintiff must show that the defendant did not meet it. Did the defendant act as a reasonable person, or as a reasonable professional? Did she warn social guests of hidden dangers she knew to exist in her apartment?

Normally, a plaintiff proves this part of a negligence case by convincing a jury that they would not have behaved as the defendant did—indeed, that no reasonable person would.

NEGLIGENCE PER SE

In certain areas of life, courts are not free to decide what a "reasonable" person would have done because the state legislature has made the decision for them. **When a legislature sets a minimum standard of care for a particular activity, in order to protect a certain group of people, and a violation of the statute injures a member of that group, the defendant has committed negligence per se.** A plaintiff who can show negligence per se need not prove breach of duty.

In Minnesota, the state legislature became alarmed about children sniffing glue, which they could easily purchase in stores. The legislature passed a statute prohibiting the sale to a minor of any glue containing toluene or benzene. About one month later, 14-year-old Steven Zerby purchased Weldwood Contact Cement from the Coast-to-Coast Store in his hometown. The glue contained toluene. Steven inhaled the glue and died from injury to his central nervous system.

The store clerk had not realized that the glue was dangerous. Irrelevant: He was negligent per se because he violated the statute. Perhaps a reasonable person would have made the same error. Irrelevant. The legislature had passed the statute to protect children, the sale of the glue violated the law, and a child was injured. The store was automatically liable.

6-4c Causation

We have seen that a plaintiff must show that the defendant owed him a duty of care and that the defendant breached the duty. To win, the plaintiff must also show that the defendant's breach of duty *caused* the plaintiff's harm. Courts look at two separate causation issues: Was the defendant's behavior the *factual cause* of the harm? Was it the *proximate cause?*

FACTUAL CAUSE

If the defendant's breach led to the ultimate harm, it is the factual cause. Suppose that Dom's Brake Shop tells a customer his brakes are now working fine, even though Dom knows that is false. The customer drives out of the shop, cannot stop at a red light, and hits a bicyclist crossing the intersection. Dom is liable to the cyclist. Dom's unreasonable behavior was the factual cause of the harm. Think of it as a row of dominoes. The first domino (Dom's behavior) knocked over the next one (failing brakes), which toppled the last one (the cyclist's injury).

---

[12]*Gaines v. Monsanto*, 655 S.W.2d 568, 1983 Mo. LEXIS 3439 (Mo. Ct. App. 1983).
[13]*Yunker v. Honeywell*, 496 N.W.2d 419, 1993 Minn. App. LEXIS 230 (Minn. Ct. App. 1993).

Suppose, alternatively, that just as the customer is exiting the repair shop, the cyclist hits a pothole and tumbles off her cycle. Dom has breached his duty to his customer, but he is not liable to the cyclist—she would have been hurt anyway. This is a row of dominoes that veers off to the side, leaving the last domino (the cyclist's injury) untouched. No factual causation.

PROXIMATE CAUSE

For the defendant to be liable, the *type of harm* must have been reasonably *foreseeable*. In the first example just discussed, Dom could easily foresee that bad brakes would cause an automobile accident. He need not have foreseen *exactly* what happened. He did not know there would be a cyclist nearby. What he could foresee was this *general type* of harm involving defective brakes. Because the accident that occurred was of the type he could foresee, he is liable.

By contrast, assume the collision of car and bicycle produces a loud crash. Two blocks away, a pet pig, asleep on the window ledge of a twelfth-story apartment, is startled by the noise, awakens with a start, and plunges to the sidewalk, killing a veterinarian who was making a house call. If the vet's family sues Dom, should it win? Dom's negligence was the factual cause: It led to the collision, which startled the pig, which flattened the vet. Most courts would rule, though, that Dom is not liable. The type of harm is too bizarre. Dom could not reasonably foresee such an extraordinary chain of events, and it would be unfair to make him pay for it. See Exhibit 6.2. Another way of stating that Dom is not liable to the vet's family is by calling the falling pig a *superseding cause*. When one of the "dominoes" in the row is entirely unforeseeable, courts will call that event a superseding cause, letting the defendant off the hook.

EXHIBIT 6.2

© Cengage Learning

EXAM Strategy

Question: Jenny asked a neighbor, Tom, to water her flowers while she was on vacation. For three days, Tom did this without incident, but on the fourth day, when he touched the outside faucet, he received a violent electric shock that shot him through the air, melted his sneakers and glasses, set his clothes on fire, and seriously burned him. Tom sued, claiming that Jenny had caused his injuries by negligently repairing a second-floor toilet. Water from the steady leak had flooded through the walls, soaking wires and eventually causing the faucet to become electrified. You are Jenny's lawyer. Use one (and only one) element of negligence law to move for summary judgment.

Strategy: The four elements of negligence we have examined thus far are duty to this plaintiff, breach, factual cause, and proximate cause. Which element seems to be most helpful to Jenny's defense? Why?

Result: Jenny is entitled to summary judgment because this was not a foreseeable type of injury. Even if she did a bad job of fixing the toilet, she could not reasonably have anticipated that her poor workmanship could cause *electrical* injuries to anyone.[14]

RES IPSA LOQUITUR

Normally, a plaintiff must prove factual cause and a foreseeable type of harm in order to establish negligence. But in a few cases, a court may be willing to *infer* that the defendant caused the harm under the doctrine of ***res ipsa loquitur*** ("the thing speaks for itself"). Suppose a pedestrian is walking along a sidewalk when an air conditioning unit falls on his head from a third-story window. The defendant, who owns the third-story apartment, denies any wrongdoing, and it may be difficult or impossible for the plaintiff to prove why the air conditioner fell. In such cases, many courts will apply *res ipsa loquitur* and declare that **the facts imply that the defendant's negligence caused the accident.** If a court uses this doctrine, then the defendant must come forward with evidence establishing that it did *not* cause the harm.

Because *res ipsa loquitur* dramatically shifts the burden of proof from plaintiff to defendant, it applies only when (1) the defendant had exclusive control of the thing that caused the harm, (2) the harm normally would not have occurred without negligence, and (3) the plaintiff had no role in causing the harm. In the air conditioner example, most states would apply the doctrine and force the defendant to prove that she did nothing wrong.

Res ipsa loquitur
The facts *imply* that the defendant's negligence caused the accident.

6-4d Damages

Finally, a plaintiff must prove that he has been injured or that he has had some kind of measureable losses. In some cases, injury is obvious. For example, Ruben Hernandez suffered grievous harm when struck by the drunk driver. But in other cases, injury is unclear. **The plaintiff must persuade the court that he has suffered harm that is genuine, not speculative.**

Some cases raise tough questions. Among the most vexing are suits involving *future* harm. Exposure to toxins or trauma may lead to serious medical problems down the road— or

---

[14]Based on *Hebert v. Enos*, 60 Mass. App. Ct. 817, 806 N.E.2d 452 (Mass. Ct. App. 2004).

it may not. A woman's knee is damaged in an auto accident, causing severe pain for two years. She is clearly entitled to compensation for her suffering. After two years, all pain may cease for a decade—or forever. Yet there is also a chance that in 15 or 20 years, the trauma will lead to painful arthritis. A court must decide today the full extent of present *and future* damages; a plaintiff cannot return to court years later and demand compensation for newly arisen ailments. The challenge to our courts is to weigh the possibilities and percentages of future suffering and decide whether to compensate a plaintiff for something that might never happen.

6-5 DEFENSES

6-5a Contributory and Comparative Negligence

Sixteen-year-old Michelle Wightman was out driving at night, with her friend Karrie Wieber in the passenger seat. They came to a railroad crossing, where the mechanical arm had descended and warning bells were sounding. They had been sounding for a long time. A Conrail train had suffered mechanical problems and was stopped 200 feet from the crossing, where it had stalled for roughly an hour. Michelle and Karrie saw several cars ahead of them go around the barrier and cross the tracks. Michelle had to decide whether she would do the same.

Long before Michelle made her decision, the train's engineer had seen the heavy Saturday night traffic crossing the tracks and realized the danger. The conductor and brakeman also understood the peril, but rather than posting a flagman, who could have stopped traffic when a train approached, they walked to the far end of their train to repair the mechanical problem. A police officer had come upon the scene, told his dispatcher to notify the train's parent company Conrail of the danger, and left.

Michelle decided to cross the tracks. She slowly followed the cars ahead of her. Seconds later, both girls were dead. A freight train traveling at 60 miles per hour struck the car broadside, killing both girls instantly.

Michelle's mother sued Conrail for negligence. The company claimed that it was Michelle's foolish risk that led to her death. Who wins when both parties are partly responsible? It depends on whether the state uses a legal theory called contributory negligence. **Under contributory negligence, if the plaintiff is even slightly negligent, she recovers nothing.** If Michelle's death occurred in a contributory negligence state, and the jury considered her even minimally responsible, her estate would receive no money.

Critics attacked this rule as unreasonable. A plaintiff who was 1 percent negligent could not recover from a defendant who was 99 percent responsible. So most states threw out the contributory negligence rule, replacing it with comparative negligence. **In a comparative negligence state, a plaintiff may generally recover even if she is partially responsible.** The jury will be asked to assess the relative negligence of the two parties.

Michelle died in Ohio, which is a comparative negligence state. The jury concluded that reasonable compensatory damages were $1 million. It also concluded that Conrail was 60 percent responsible for the tragedy and Michelle 40 percent. See Exhibit 6.3. The girl's mother received $600,000 in compensatory damages.

Today, most but not all states have adopted some form of comparative negligence. Critics claim that this principle rewards a careless plaintiff. If Michelle had obeyed the law, she would still be alive. In response to this complaint, many comparative negligence states do *not* permit a plaintiff to recover anything if he was more than 50 percent responsible for his own injury.

EXHIBIT 6.3   Defendant's negligence injures plaintiff, who suffers $1 million in damages.

In the Conrail case, the jury decided that the rail company was extraordinarily negligent. Expert witnesses testified that similar tragedies occurred every year around the nation and the company knew it. Conrail could easily have prevented the loss of life by posting a flagman on the road. The jury awarded the estate $25 million in punitive damages. The trial judge reduced the verdict by 40 percent to $15 million. The state supreme court affirmed the award.[15]

6-5b Assumption of the Risk

Good Guys, a restaurant, holds an ice-fishing contest on a frozen lake to raise money for accident victims. Margie grabs a can full of worms and strolls to the middle of the lake to try her luck, but slips on the ice and suffers a concussion. If she sues Good Guys, how will she fare? She will fall a second time. Wherever there is an obvious hazard, a special rule applies. **Assumption of the risk: A person who voluntarily enters a situation that has an obvious danger cannot complain if she is injured.** Ice is slippery, and we all know it. If you venture onto a frozen lake, any falls are your own tough luck.

However, the doctrine does not apply if someone is injured in a way that is not an inherent part of the dangerous activity. NFL players assume substantial risks each time they take the field, but some injuries fall outside the rule. In a game between the Jets and the Dolphins, Jets assistant coach Sal Alosi, standing on the sideline, tripped Dolphins player Nolan Carroll during a punt return. The trip was not a "normal" part of a football game, and the "assumption of the risk" doctrine would not prevent Carroll from recovering damages.

The following case involves a lake, jet skis—and a great tragedy.

---

[15]*Wightman v. Consolidated Rail Corporation*, 86 Ohio St. 3d 431, 715 N.E.2d 546, 1999 Ohio LEXIS 2924 (Ohio 1999).

TRUONG V. NGUYEN

67 Cal. Rptr.3d 675, 156 Cal.App.4th 865
California Court of Appeals, 2007

CASE SUMMARY

Facts: On a warm California day, there were about 30 personal watercraft (jet skis) operating on Coyote Lake. The weather was fair and visibility good. Anthony Nguyen and Rachael Truong went for a ride on Anthony's Polaris watercraft. Cu Van Nguyen and Chuong Nguyen (neither of whom were related to Anthony) were both riding a Yamaha Waverunner. Both jet skis permitted a driver and passenger, each seated. The two watercraft collided near the middle of the lake. Rachael was killed, and the others were injured.

Rachael's parents sued Anthony, Cu Van, and Chuong, alleging that negligent operation of their watercraft caused their daughter's death. The court granted defendants' motion for summary judgment, on the grounds that Rachel had assumed the risk of riding on a jet ski. Her parents appealed, arguing that jet skiing was not a sport and Rachael never assumed any risk.

Issue: *Does assumption of the risk apply to jet skiing?*

Decision: Yes. Jet skiing is a sport and its participants assume certain risks of injury.

Reasoning: A "sport" is an activity (1) that is done for enjoyment or thrill, (2) requires physical skill, and (3) involves challenges that create some risk of injury. When people choose to participate in a sport, they assume that sport's inherent risks. The doctrine of assumption of the risk bars liability when a participant suffers an injury that is "part of the game," even if conduct that caused the injury violates the rules of the game.

For example, in baseball, a batter is not supposed to carelessly throw the bat after getting a hit. However, assumption of the risk recognizes that this activity is part of the game—and a risk players assume when they choose to play baseball. An umpire cannot sue a batter when injured by a *carelessly* thrown bat. He can recover only if the batter *intentionally* harmed him or engaged in reckless conduct that was not reasonably or foreseeably part of the game. So, the umpire is justified in complaining if the batter repeatedly whacked him with the bat, because this conduct is not part of baseball as we know it.

The question in this case was whether assumption of the risk applied to jet skiing. Rachael's parents contended that assumption of risk did not apply, because jet skiing is not a sport. But jet skiing fits into the definition of a sport. It is done for enjoyment or thrill, not for transportation. It involves skill and risk. Jet skiers race each other and jump the wakes of other jet skis in an open-hulled vehicle. An activity does not have to be a competitive or spectator sport for assumption of risk to apply.

The plaintiffs also argued that Rachael did not assume the risk as an active participant because she was not driving the jet ski. However, a passenger on a personal watercraft is enjoying the same thrills, taking on the same challenges, and facing the same risks as the operator. Rachael was an active participant who assumed the risks inherent in jet skiing.

For these reasons, the summary judgment is affirmed.

6-6 STRICT LIABILITY

Strict liability

A branch of tort law that imposes a much higher level of liability when harm results from ultrahazardous acts or defective products.

Some activities are so naturally dangerous that the law places an especially high burden on anyone who engages in them. A corporation that produces toxic waste can foresee dire consequences from its business that a stationery store cannot. This higher burden is **strict liability**. There are two main areas of business that incur strict liability: *ultrahazardous activity* and *defective products*.

6-6a Ultrahazardous Activity

Ultrahazardous activities include using harmful chemicals, operating explosives, keeping wild animals, bringing dangerous substances onto property, and a few similar activities where the danger to the general public is especially great. **A defendant engaging in an ultrahazardous activity is almost always liable for any harm that results.** Plaintiffs do not have to prove duty or breach or foreseeable harm. Recall the deliberately bizarre case we posed earlier of the pig falling from a window ledge and killing a veterinarian. Dom, the mechanic whose negligence caused the car crash, could not be liable for the veterinarian's death because the plunging pig was a superseding cause.

But now imagine that the pig is jolted off the window ledge by a company engaged in an ultrahazardous activity. Sam's Blasting Co. sets off a perfectly lawful blast to clear ground for a new building down the street. When the pig is startled and falls, the blasting company is liable. Even if Sam took extraordinary care, it will do him no good at trial. The "reasonable person" rule is irrelevant in a strict liability case.

Because "strict liability" translates into "defendant is liable," parties in tort cases often fight over whether the defendant was engaged in an ultrahazardous activity. If the court rules that the activity was ultrahazardous, the plaintiff is assured of winning. If the court rules that it was not ultrahazardous, the plaintiff must prove all elements of negligence.

The line is often hazy. A lawful fireworks display does not incur strict liability, but crop dusting does. Cutting timber is generally not abnormally dangerous, but hauling logs might be. The enormous diversity of business activities in our nation ensures continual disputes over this important principle.

6-6b Product Liability

Defective products can also create strict liability. Most states have adopted the following model:

1. One who sells any product in a defective condition unreasonably dangerous to the user or consumer or to his property is subject to liability for physical harm thereby caused to the ultimate user or consumer, or to his property, if

   a. the seller is engaged in the business of selling such a product, and

   b. it is expected to and does reach the user or consumer without substantial change in the condition in which it is sold.

2. The rule stated in Subsection (1) applies although

   a. the seller has exercised all possible care in the preparation and sale of his product, and

   b. the user or consumer has not bought the product from or entered into any contractual relation with the seller.[16]

These are the key terms in subsection (1):

- **Defective condition unreasonably dangerous to the user.** The defendant is liable only if the product is defective when it leaves his hands. There must be something wrong with the goods. If they are reasonably safe and the buyer's mishandling of the goods causes the harm, there is no strict liability. If you attempt to open a soda bottle by knocking the cap against a counter, and the glass shatters and cuts you, the manufacturer owes nothing. A carving knife can produce a lethal wound, but everyone knows that, and a sharp knife is not unreasonably dangerous. On the other hand, prescription drugs may harm in ways that neither a layperson nor a doctor would anticipate. The manufacturer *must provide adequate warnings* of any dangers that are not apparent.

---

[16]Restatement (Second) of Torts Section 402A.

- **In the business of selling.** The seller is liable only if she normally sells this kind of product. Suppose your roommate makes you a peanut butter sandwich and, while eating it, you cut your mouth on a sliver of glass that was in the jar. The peanut butter manufacturer faces strict liability, as does the grocery store where your roommate bought the goods. But your roommate is not strictly liable because he is not in the food business.

- **Reaches the user without substantial change.** Obviously, if your roommate put the glass in the peanut butter thinking it was funny, neither the manufacturer nor the store is liable.

And here are the important phrases in subsection (2).

- **Has exercised all possible care.** This is the heart of strict liability, which makes it a potent claim for consumers. *It is no defense that the seller used reasonable care.* If the product is dangerously defective and injures the user, the seller is liable even if it took every precaution to design and manufacture the product safely. Suppose the peanut butter jar did in fact contain a glass sliver when it left the factory. The manufacturer proves that it uses extraordinary care in keeping foreign particles out of the jars and thoroughly inspects each container before it is shipped. The evidence is irrelevant. The manufacturer has shown that it was not *negligent* in packaging the food, but reasonable care is irrelevant in strict liability cases.

- **No contractual relation.** When two parties contract, they are in privity. Privity only exists between the user and the person from whom she actually bought the goods, but in strict liability cases, *privity is not required.* Suppose the manufacturer that made the peanut butter sold it to a distributor, which sold it to a wholesaler, which sold it to a grocery store, which sold it to your roommate. You may sue the manufacturer, distributor, wholesaler, and store, even though you had no privity with any of them.

CONTEMPORARY TRENDS

If the steering wheel on a brand new car falls off, and the driver is injured, that is a clear case of defective manufacturing, and the company will be strictly liable. Those are the easy cases. But defective design cases have been more contentious. Suppose a vaccine that prevents serious childhood illnesses inevitably causes brain damage in a very small number of children because of the nature of the drug. Is the manufacturer liable? What if a racing sailboat, designed only for speed, is dangerously unstable in the hands of a less-experienced sailor? Is the boat's maker responsible for fatalities? Suppose an automobile made of light-weight metal uses less fuel but exposes its occupants to more serious injuries in an accident. How is a court to decide whether the design was defective? Often, these design cases also involve issues of warnings: Did the drug designer diligently detail dangers to doctors? Should a sailboat seller sell speedy sailboats solely to seasoned sailors?

Over the years, most courts have adopted one of two tests for design and warning cases. The first is *consumer expectation*. Here, a court finds the manufacturer liable for defective design if the product is less safe than a reasonable consumer would expect. If a smoke detector has a 3 percent failure rate and the average consumer has no way of anticipating that danger, effective cautions must be included, though the design may be defective anyway.

Many other states use a *risk-utility test*. Here, a court must weigh the benefits for society against the dangers that the product poses. Principal factors in the risk-utility test include:

- The *value* of the product,

- The *gravity*, or seriousness, of the danger,

- The *likelihood* that such danger will occur,

- The mechanical feasibility of a *safer alternative* design, and

- The *adverse consequences* of an alternative design.

Chapter Conclusion

This chapter has been a potpourri of misdeeds, a bubbling cauldron of conduct best avoided.
Although tortious acts and their consequences are diverse, two generalities apply. First, the boundaries are imprecise, the outcome of a particular case depending to a considerable extent upon the factfinder who analyzes it. Second, the thoughtful executive and the careful citizen, aware of the shifting standards and potentially vast liability, will strive to ensure that his or her conduct never provides that factfinder an opportunity to give judgment.

EXAM REVIEW

1. TORT   A tort is a violation of a duty imposed by the civil law. (p. 135)

Question: Keith is driving while intoxicated. He swerves into the wrong lane and causes an accident, seriously injuring Caroline. Which statement is true?

(a) Caroline could sue Keith, who might be found guilty in her suit.

(b) Caroline and the state could start separate criminal cases against Keith.

(c) Caroline could sue Keith, and the state could prosecute Keith for drunk driving.

(d) The state could sue Keith but only with Caroline's consent.

(e) The state could prosecute Keith and sue him at the same time, for drunk driving.

Strategy: What party prosecutes a criminal case? The government does, not the injured party. What is the result in a criminal case? Guilt or innocence. What about a tort lawsuit? The injured party brings a tort suit. The defendant may be found liable but never guilty. (See the "Result" at the end of this section.)

2. DEFAMATION   Defamation involves a defamatory statement that is false, uttered to a third person, and causes an injury. Opinion and privilege are valid defenses. (pp. 136–138)

Question: Benzaquin had a radio talk show. On the program, he complained about an incident in which state trooper Fleming had stopped his car, apparently for lack of a proper license plate and safety sticker. Benzaquin explained that the license plate had been stolen and the sticker fallen onto the dashboard, but Fleming refused to let him drive away. Benzaquin and two young grandsons had to find other transportation. On the show, Benzaquin angrily recounted the incident, then described Fleming and troopers generally: "We're not paying them to be dictators and Nazis"; "this man is an absolute barbarian, a lunkhead, a meathead." Fleming sued Benzaquin for defamation. Comment.

Strategy: Review the elements of defamation. Can these statements be proven true or false? If not, what is the result? Look at the defenses. Does one apply? (See the "Result" at the end of this section.)

3. **MALICE**   Public personalities can win a defamation suit only by proving actual malice. (p. 137)

4. **FALSE IMPRISONMENT**   False imprisonment is the intentional restraint of another person without reasonable cause and without consent. (p. 139)

5. **EMOTIONAL DISTRESS**   The intentional infliction of emotional distress involves extreme and outrageous conduct that causes serious emotional harm. (p. 139)

6. **ADDITIONAL INTENTIONAL TORTS**   Battery is an intentional touching of another person in a way that is unwanted or offensive. Assault involves an act that makes the plaintiff fear an imminent battery. Fraud is injuring another person by intentional deception. (p. 140)

7. **DAMAGES**   Compensatory damages are the normal remedy in a tort case. In unusual cases, the court may award punitive damages, not to compensate the plaintiff but to punish the defendant. (pp. 140–143)

8. **TORTIOUS INTERFERENCE**   Tortious interference with business relations involves the defendant harming an existing contract or a prospective relationship that has a definite expectation of success. (pp. 144–145)

9. **PRIVACY AND PUBLICITY**   The related torts of privacy and publicity involve unreasonable intrusion into someone's private life and unfair commercial exploitation by using someone's name, likeness, or voice without permission. (pp. 145–146)

10. **NEGLIGENCE ELEMENTS**   The five elements of negligence are duty of due care, breach, factual causation, proximate causation, and damage. (p. 146)

11. **DUTY OF DUE CARE**   If the defendant could foresee that misconduct would injure a particular person, he probably has a duty to her. Special duties exist for people on the job, landowners, and employers. (pp. 146–149)

EXAM Strategy

Question: A supervisor reprimanded an employee for eating in a restaurant when he should have been at work. Later, the employee showed up at the supervisor's office and shot him. Although the employee previously had been violent, management withheld this information from supervisory personnel. Is the company liable for the supervisor's injury?

Strategy: An employer must do a *reasonable* job of hiring and retaining employees. (See the "Result" at the end of this section.)

12. **BREACH OF DUTY**   A defendant breaches his duty of due care by failing to meet his duty of care. (p. 149)

13. **NEGLIGENCE PER SE**   If a legislature sets a minimum standard of care for a particular activity in order to protect a certain group of people, and a violation of the statute injures a member of that group, the defendant has committed negligence per se. (p. 149)

14. **FACTUAL CAUSE**   If one event directly led to the ultimate harm, it is the factual cause. (pp. 149–150)

15. **PROXIMATE CAUSE**   For the defendant to be liable, the type of harm must have been reasonably foreseeable. (p. 150)

16. **DAMAGES**   The plaintiff must persuade the court that he has suffered a harm that is genuine, not speculative. Damages for emotional distress, without a physical injury, are awarded only in select cases. (pp. 151–152)

EXAM Strategy

Question: Marko owned a cat and allowed it to roam freely outside. In the three years he had owned the pet, the animal had never bitten anyone. The cat entered Romi's garage. When Romi attempted to move it outside, the cat bit her. Romi underwent four surgeries, was fitted with a plastic finger joint, and spent more than $39,000 in medical bills. She sued Marko, claiming both strict liability and ordinary negligence. Assume that state law allows a domestic cat to roam freely. Evaluate both of Romi's claims.

Strategy: Negligence requires proof that the defendant breached a duty to the plaintiff by behaving unreasonably, and that the resulting harm was foreseeable. Was it? When would harm by a domestic cat be foreseeable? A defendant can be strictly liable for keeping a wild animal. Apply that rule as well. (See the "Result" at the end of this section.)

1. Result: (a) is wrong because a defendant cannot be found guilty in a civil suit. (b) is wrong because a private party has no power to prosecute a criminal case. (c) is correct. (d) is wrong because the state will prosecute Keith, not sue him. (e) is wrong for the same reason.

2. Result: The court ruled in favor of Benzaquin because a reasonable person would understand the words to be opinion and ridicule. They are not statements of fact because most of them could not be proven true or false. A statement like "dictators and Nazis" is not taken literally by anyone.[17]

11. Result: This employer may have been liable for negligently hiring a previously violent employee, and it certainly did an unreasonable job in retaining him without advising his supervisor of the earlier violence. The assault was easily foreseeable, and the employer is liable.[18]

17. Result: If Marko's cat had bitten or attacked people in the past, this harm was foreseeable and Marko is liable. If the cat had never done so, and state law allows domestic animals to roam, Romi probably loses her suit for negligence. Her strict liability case definitely fails: A housecat is not a wild animal.

[17]*Fleming v. Benzaquin*, 390 Mass. 175, 454 N.E.2d 95 (1983).
[18]*Caudle v. Betts*, 512 So.2d 389 (La. 1987).

MULTIPLE-CHOICE QUESTIONS

1. Jane writes an article for a newspaper reporting that Ann was arrested for stealing a car. The story is entirely false. Ann is not a public figure. Which of the following torts has Jane committed?
   (a) Ordinary slander
   (b) Slander per se
   (c) Libel
   (d) None of the above

2. Refer back to Question 1. If Ann decides to sue, she _____ have to show evidence that she suffered an injury. If she ultimately wins her case, a jury _____ have the option to award punitive damages.
   (a) will; will
   (b) will; will not
   (c) will not; will
   (d) will not; will not

3. Sam sneaks up on Tom, hits him with a baseball bat, and knocks him unconscious. Tom never saw Sam coming. He wakes up with a horrible headache. Which of the following torts has Sam committed?
   (a) Assault
   (b) Battery
   (c) Both (a) and (b)
   (d) None of the above

4. Al runs a red light and hits Carol's car. She later sues, claiming the following losses:

   $10,000—car repairs

   $10,000—medical expenses

   $10,000—lost wages (she could not work for two months after the accident)

   $10,000—pain and suffering

   If the jury believes all of Carol's evidence and she wins her case, how much will she receive in *compensatory* damages?
   (a) $40,000
   (b) $30,000
   (c) $20,000
   (d) $10,000
   (e) $0

5. Zack lives in a state that prohibits factory laborers from working more than 12 hours in any 24-hour period. The state legislature passed the law to cut down on accidents caused by fatigued workers.

   Ignoring the law, Zack makes his factory employees put in 14-hour days. Eventually, a worker at the end of a long shift makes a mistake and severely injures a coworker. The injured worker sues Zack.

Which of the following terms will be most relevant to the case?

(a) *Res ipsa loquitur*

(b) Assumption of the risk

(c) Negligence per se

(d) Strict liability

Essay Questions

1. Caldwell was shopping in a K-Mart store, carrying a large purse. A security guard observed her looking at various small items such as stain, hinges, and antenna wire. On occasion, she bent down out of sight of the guard. The guard thought he saw Caldwell put something in her purse. Caldwell removed her glasses from her purse and returned them a few times. After she left, the guard approached her in the parking lot and said that he believed she had store merchandise in her pocketbook, but he could not say what he thought was put there. Caldwell opened the purse, and the guard testified that he saw no K-Mart merchandise in it. The guard then told Caldwell to return to the store with him. They walked around the store for approximately 15 minutes, while the guard said six or seven times that he saw her put something in her purse. Caldwell left the store after another store employee indicated she could go. Caldwell sued. What kind of suit did she file, and what should the outcome be?

2. Tata Consultancy of Bombay, India, is an international computer consulting firm. It spends considerable time and effort recruiting the best personnel from India's leading technical schools. Tata employees sign an initial three-year employment commitment, often work overseas, and agree to work for a specified additional time when they return to India. Desai worked for Tata, but then he quit and formed a competing company, which he called Syntel. His new company contacted Tata employees by phone, offering higher salaries, bonuses, and assistance in obtaining permanent resident visas in the United States if they would come work for Syntel. At least 16 former Tata employees left their jobs without completing their contractual obligations and went to work for Syntel. Tata sued. What did it claim, and what should be the result?

3. **YOU BE THE JUDGE WRITING PROBLEM** Johnny Carson was for many years the star of a well-known television show, *The Tonight Show*. For about 20 years, he was introduced nightly on the show with the phrase, "Here's Johnny!" A large segment of the television watching public associated the phrase with Carson.

   A Michigan corporation was in the business of renting and selling portable toilets. The company chose the name "Here's Johnny Portable Toilets," and coupled the company name with the marketing phrase, "The World's Foremost Commodian." Carson sued, claiming that the company's name and slogan violated his right to commercial exploitation.

   ARGUMENT FOR CARSON: The toilet company is deliberately taking advantage of Johnny Carson's good name. He worked hard for decades to build a brilliant career and earn a reputation as a creative, funny, likable performer.

No company has the right to use his name, his picture, or anything else closely identified with him, such as the phrase "Here's Johnny." The pun is personally offensive and commercially unfair.

ARGUMENT FOR HERE'S JOHNNY PORTABLE TOILETS: Johnny Carson doesn't own his first name. It is available for anyone to use for any purpose. Further, the popular term "john," meaning toilet, has been around much longer than Carson or even television. We are entitled to make any use of it we want. Our corporate name is amusing to customers who have never heard of Carson, and we are entitled to profit from our brand recognition.

4. At approximately 7:50 p.m, bells at the train station rang and red lights flashed, signaling an express train's approach. David Harris walked onto the tracks, ignoring a yellow line painted on the platform instructing people to stand back. Two men shouted to Harris, warning him to get off the tracks. The train's engineer saw him too late to stop the train, which was traveling at approximately 55 mph. The train struck and killed Harris as it passed through the station. Harris's widow sued the railroad, arguing that the railroad's negligence caused her husband's death. Evaluate her argument.

5. A new truck, manufactured by General Motors Corp. (GMC), stalled in rush hour traffic on a busy interstate highway because of a defective alternator, which caused a complete failure of the truck's electrical system. The driver stood nearby and waved traffic around his stalled truck. A panel truck approached the GMC truck, and immediately behind the panel truck, Davis was driving a Volkswagen fastback. Because of the panel truck, Davis was unable to see the stalled GMC truck. The panel truck swerved out of the way of the GMC truck, and Davis drove straight into it. The accident killed him. Davis's widow sued GMC. GMC moved for summary judgment, alleging (1) no duty to Davis, (2) no factual causation, and (3) no foreseeable harm. Comment.

DISCUSSION QUESTIONS

1. You have most likely heard of the *Liebeck v. McDonalds* case. Liebeck spilled hot McDonald's coffee in her lap and suffered third-degree burns. At trial, evidence showed that her cup of coffee was brewed at 190 degrees, and that, more typically, a restaurant's "hot coffee" is in the range of 140 to 160 degrees. A jury awarded Liebeck $160,000 in compensatory damages and $2.7 million in punitive damages. The judge reduced the punitive award to $480,000, or three times the compensatory award. Comment on the case and whether the result was reasonable.

2. Celebrities often have problems with tabloids and the paparazzi. It is difficult for public figures to win libel lawsuits because they must show actual malice. Intrusion lawsuits are also tricky, and flocks of photographers often stalk celebrities at all hours. Is this right? Should the law change to offer more privacy to famous people? Or is a loss of privacy just the price of success?

3. Many retailers have policies that instruct employees *not* to attempt to stop shoplifters. Some store owners fear false imprisonment lawsuits and possible injuries to workers more than losses related to stolen merchandise. Are these "don't be a hero" policies reasonable? Would you put one in place if you owned a retail store?

4. Imagine an undefeated high school football team on which the average lineman weighs 300 pounds. Also, imagine an 0–10 team on which the average lineman weighs 170 pounds. The undefeated team sets out to hit as hard as they can on every play and to run up the score as much as possible. Before the game is over, 11 players from the lesser team have been carried off the field with significant injuries. All injuries were the result of "clean hits"—none of the plays resulted in a penalty. Even late in the game, when the score is 70–0, the undefeated team continues to deliver devastating hits that are far beyond what would be required to tackle and block. The assumption of the risk doctrine exempts the undefeated team from liability. Is this reasonable?

5. People who serve alcohol to others take a risk. In some circumstances, they can be held legally responsible for the actions of the people they serve. Is this fair? Should an intoxicated person be the only one liable if harm results? If not, in what specific circumstances is it fair to stretch liablility to other people?

CHAPTER 7

CRIME

Crime can take us by surprise. Stacey tucks her nine-year-old daughter, Beth, into bed. Promising her husband, Mark, that she will be home by 11:00 p.m., she jumps into her car and heads back to Be Patient, Inc. She plugs her iPhone into the player of her $85,000 sedan and tries to relax by listening to music. Be Patient is a healthcare organization that owns five geriatric hospitals. Most of its patients use Medicare, and Stacey supervises all billing to their largest client, the federal government.

nuttakit/Shutterstock.com; © Stas Volik/Shutterstock.com

She parks in a well-lighted spot on the street and walks to her building, failing to notice two men, collars turned up, watching from a parked truck. Once in her office, she goes straight to her computer and works on billing issues. Tonight's work goes more quickly than she expected, thanks to new software she helped develop. At 10:30 she emerges from the building with a quick step and a light heart, walks to her car—and finds it missing.

A major crime has occurred during the 90 minutes Stacey was at her desk, but she will never report it to the police. It is a crime that costs Americans countless dollars each year, yet Stacey will not even mention it to friends or family. Stacey is the criminal.

> **A major crime has occurred during the 90 minutes Stacey was at her desk, but she will never report it to the police.**

When we think of crime, we imagine the drug dealers and bank robbers endlessly portrayed on television. We do not picture corporate executives sitting at polished desks. "Street crimes" are indeed serious threats to our security and happiness. They deservedly receive the attention of the public and the law. But when measured only in dollars, street crime takes second place to white-collar crime, which costs society *tens of billions* of dollars annually.

The hypothetical about Stacey is based on many real cases and is used to illustrate that crime does not always dress the way we expect. Her car was never stolen; it was simply towed. Two parking bureau employees, watching from their truck, saw Stacey park illegally and did their job. It is Stacey who committed a crime—Medicare fraud. Every month, she has billed the government about $10 million for work that her company has not performed. Stacey's scheme was quick and profitable—and a distressingly common crime.

Crime, whether violent or white-collar, is detrimental to all society. It imposes a huge cost on everyone. Just the *fear* of crime is expensive—homeowners buy alarm systems and businesses hire security guards. But the anger and fear that crime engenders sometimes tempt us to forget that not all accused people are guilty. Everyone suspected of a crime should have the protections that you yourself would want in that situation. As the English jurist William Blackstone said, "Better that ten guilty persons escape than that one innocent suffer."

Thus, criminal law is a balancing act—between making society safe and protecting us all from false accusations and unfair punishment.

This chapter has four parts:

1. The differences between a civil and criminal case;

2. **Criminal procedure**—the *process* by which criminals are accused, tried, and sentenced;

3. Crimes that *harm* businesses;

4. Crimes committed *by* businesses.

Criminal procedure
The process by which criminals are accused, tried, and sentenced.

7-1 THE DIFFERENCES BETWEEN A CIVIL AND CRIMINAL CASE

Most of this book focuses on civil law, so we begin with a discussion of the differences between a civil and criminal case.

Civil law involves the rights and liabilities that exist between private parties. As we have seen, if one person claims that another has caused her a civil injury, she must file a lawsuit and convince a court of her damages.

Criminal law is different. Conduct is criminal when society outlaws it. When a state legislature or Congress concludes that certain behavior threatens public safety and welfare, it passes a statute forbidding that behavior; in other words, declaring it criminal. Medicare fraud, which Stacey committed, is a crime because Congress has outlawed it. Money laundering is a crime because Congress concluded that it was a fundamental part of the drug trade and prohibited it.

Criminal law
Prohibits and punishes conduct that threatens public safety and welfare.

7-1a Prosecution

Suppose the police arrest Roger and accuse him of breaking into a store and stealing 50 computers. The owner of the store is the one harmed, and he has the right to sue the thief in civil court to recover money damages. **But only the government can prosecute a**

crime and punish Roger by sending him to prison. The government may also impose a fine on Roger, but it keeps the fine and does not share it with the victim. (However, the court will sometimes order **restitution**, meaning that the defendant must reimburse the victim for harm suffered.) The local prosecutor has total discretion in deciding whether to bring Roger to trial on criminal charges.

Restitution
A court order that a guilty defendant reimburse the victim for the harm suffered.

7-1b Burden of Proof

In a civil case, the plaintiff must prove her case only by a preponderance of the evidence.[1] But because the penalties for conviction in a criminal case are so serious, the government must prove its case **beyond a reasonable doubt**. Also, the stigma of a criminal conviction would stay with Roger forever, making it more difficult to obtain work and housing. Therefore, in all criminal cases, if the jury has any significant doubt at all that Roger stole the computers, it *must* acquit him.

Beyond a reasonable doubt
The very high burden of proof in a criminal trial, demanding much more certainty than required in a civil trial.

7-1c Right to a Jury

The facts of a case are decided by a judge or jury. A criminal defendant has a right to a trial by jury for any charge that could result in a sentence of six months or longer. The defendant may demand a jury trial or may waive that right, in which case the judge will be the factfinder.

7-1d Felony/Misdemeanor

A **felony** is a serious crime, for which a defendant can be sentenced to one year or more in prison. Murder, robbery, rape, drug dealing, money laundering, wire fraud, and embezzlement are felonies. A **misdemeanor** is a less serious crime, often punishable by a year or less in a county jail. Public drunkenness, driving without a license, and simple possession of a single marijuana cigarette are considered misdemeanors in most states.

Felony
A serious crime, for which a defendant can be sentenced to one year or more in prison.

Misdemeanor
A less serious crime, often punishable by less than a year in a county jail.

7-2 CRIMINAL PROCEDURE

The title of a criminal case is usually the government versus someone: *The United States of America v. Simpson* or *The State of Texas v. Simpson*, for example. This name illustrates a daunting thought—if you are Simpson, the vast power of the government is against you. Because of the government's great power and the severe penalties it can impose, criminal procedure is designed to protect the accused and ensure that the trial is fair. Moreover, a criminal defendant is often engaged in an uphill climb from the beginning because people often assume that anyone accused of a crime must be guilty. Many of the protections for those accused of a crime are found in the first 10 amendments to the United States Constitution, known as the Bill of Rights.

7-2a Conduct Outlawed

Crimes are created by statute. The prosecution must demonstrate to the court that the defendant's conduct is indeed outlawed by a statute. Returning to Roger, the alleged computer thief, the state charges that he stole computer equipment from a store, a crime clearly defined by statute as larceny.

---

[1] See the earlier discussion in Chapter 3, on dispute resolution.

The Fifth and Fourteenth Amendments to the Constitution require that the language of criminal statutes be clear and definite enough that (1) ordinary people can understand what conduct is prohibited and (2) the police are discouraged from arbitrary and discriminatory enforcement. Thus, for example, the Supreme Court ruled that a statute that prohibited loitering was unconstitutionally vague because it did not clarify exactly what behavior was prohibited and it tended to be enforced arbitrarily.[2]

7-2b State of Mind

VOLUNTARY ACT

A defendant is not guilty of a crime if she was forced to commit it. In other words, she is not guilty if she acted under duress. However, the defendant bears the burden of proving by a preponderance of the evidence that she did act under duress. In 1974, a terrorist group kidnapped heiress Patricia Hearst from her apartment near the University of California at Berkeley. After being tortured for two months, she participated in a bank robbery with the group. Despite opportunities to escape, she stayed with the criminals until her capture by the police a year later. The State of California put on her on trial for bank robbery. One question for the jury was whether she had voluntarily participated in the crime. This was an issue on which many people had strong opinions. Ultimately Hearst was convicted, sent to prison, and then later pardoned.

Guilty

A judge or jury's finding that a defendant has committed a crime.

ENTRAPMENT

When the government induces the defendant to break the law, the prosecution must prove beyond a reasonable doubt that the defendant was predisposed to commit the crime. The goal is to separate the cases where the defendant was innocent before the government tempted him from those where the defendant was only too eager to break the law.

Kalchinian and Sherman met in the waiting room of a doctor's office where they were both being treated for drug addiction. After several more meetings, Kalchinian told Sherman that the treatment was not working for him and he was desperate to buy drugs. Could Sherman help him? Sherman repeatedly refused, but ultimately agreed to help end Kalchinian's suffering by providing him with drugs. Little did Sherman know that Kalchinian was a police informant. Sherman sold drugs to Kalchinian a number of times. Kalchinian rewarded this act of friendship by getting Sherman hooked again and then turning him in to the police. A jury convicted Sherman of drug dealing, but the Supreme Court overturned the conviction on the grounds that Sherman had been entrapped.[3] The court felt there was no evidence that Sherman was predisposed to commit the crime.

7-2c Gathering Evidence: The Fourth Amendment

If the police suspect that a crime has been committed, they will need to obtain evidence. **The Fourth Amendment to the Constitution prohibits the government from making illegal searches and seizures of individuals, corporations, partnerships, and other organizations.** The goal of the Fourth Amendment is to protect the individual from the powerful state.

WARRANT

As a general rule, the police must obtain a warrant before conducting a search. A warrant is written permission from a neutral official, such as a judge or magistrate, to conduct a search.[4] **The warrant must specify with reasonable certainty the place to be searched and the items**

---

[2]*Kolender v. Lawson*, 461 U.S. 352 (S. Ct. 1983).
[3]*Sherman v. United States*, 356 U.S. 369 (S. Ct. 1958).
[4]A magistrate is a judge who tries minor criminal cases or undertakes primarily administrative responsibilities.

to be seized. Thus, if the police say they have reason to believe that they will find bloody clothes in the suspect's car in his garage, they cannot also look through his house and confiscate file folders.

If the police search without a warrant, they have, in most cases, violated the Fourth Amendment. **But even a search conducted with a warrant violates the Fourth Amendment if:**

- There was no probable cause to issue the warrant;

- The warrant does not specify the place to be searched and the things sought; or

- The search extends beyond what is specified in the warrant.

PROBABLE CAUSE

Probable cause

It is likely that evidence of crime will be found in the place to be searched.

The magistrate will issue a warrant only if there is probable cause. **Probable cause** means that based on all the information presented, **it is likely that evidence of a crime will be found in the place to be searched.** Often, the police base their applications for a warrant on data provided by an informant. The magistrate will want evidence to support the informant's reliability. If it turns out that this informant has been wrong the last three times he gave evidence to the police, the magistrate will probably refuse the request for a warrant.

SEARCHES WITHOUT A WARRANT

There are seven circumstances under which police may **search without a warrant:**

1. **Plain View.** Police may search if they see a machine gun, for example, sticking out from under the front seat of a parked car.

2. **Stop and Frisk.** None of us wants to live in a world in which police can randomly stop and frisk us on the street anytime they feel like it. The police do have the right to stop and frisk, but *only if* they have a clear and specific reason to suspect that criminal activity may be afoot and that the person may be armed and dangerous.[5]

3. **Emergencies.** If, for example, the police believe that evidence is about to be destroyed, they can search.

4. **Automobiles.** If police have lawfully stopped a car and observe evidence of other crimes in the car, such as burglary tools, they may search.

5. **Lawful Arrest.** Police may always search a suspect they have arrested. The goal is to protect the officers and preserve evidence.

6. **Consent.** Anyone lawfully living in a dwelling can allow the police in to search without a warrant. If your roommate gives the police permission to search your house, that search is legal.

7. **No Expectation of Privacy.** The police have a right to search any area in which the defendant does not have a reasonable expectation of privacy. For example, Rolando Crowder was staying at his friend Bobo's apartment. Hearing the police in the hallway, he ran down to the basement. The police found Crowder in the basement with drugs nearby. Crowder argued that the police should have obtained a warrant, but the court ruled that Crowder had no expectation of privacy in Bobo's basement.[6]

Apart from these seven exceptions, a warrant is required.

---

[5]*Terry v. Ohio*, 392 U.S. 1 (S. Ct. 1968).
[6]*Ohio v. Crowder*, 2010 Ohio 3766; 2010 Ohio App. LEXIS 3210 (2010).

EXCLUSIONARY RULE

Under the exclusionary rule, evidence obtained illegally may not be used at trial. The Supreme Court created the exclusionary rule to ensure that police conduct legal searches. The theory is simple: If police know in advance that illegally obtained evidence cannot be used in court, they will not be tempted to make improper searches. Is the exclusionary rule a good idea?

Opponents of the rule argue that a guilty person may go free because one police officer bungled. They are outraged by cases like *Coolidge v. New Hampshire*.[7] Pamela Mason, a 14-year-old babysitter, was brutally murdered. Citizens of New Hampshire were furious, and the state's attorney general personally led the investigation. Police found strong evidence that Edward Coolidge had done it. They took the evidence to the attorney general, who personally issued a search warrant. A search of Coolidge's car uncovered incriminating evidence, and he was found guilty of murder and sentenced to life in prison. But the United States Supreme Court reversed the conviction. The warrant had not been issued by a neutral magistrate. A law officer may not lead an investigation and simultaneously decide what searches are permissible.

After the Supreme Court reversed Coolidge's conviction, New Hampshire scheduled a new trial, attempting to convict him with evidence lawfully obtained. Before the trial began, Coolidge pleaded guilty to second degree murder. He was sentenced and remained in prison until his release years later.

In fact, very few people do go free because of the exclusionary rule. One study showed that evidence is actually excluded in only 1.3 percent of all prosecutions; and in about one-half of *those* cases, the court convicted the defendant on other evidence. Only in 0.7 percent of all prosecutions did the defendant go free after the evidence was suppressed.[8]

There are two exceptions to the exclusionary rule:

1. **Inevitable Discovery.** The inevitable discovery exception permits the use of evidence that would inevitably have been discovered even without the illegal search. If an informant was about to tell the police about Coolidge's car, then the evidence found there would have been admissible, so long as the court believed the testimony was true.

2. **Good Faith Exception.** Suppose the police use a search warrant believing it to be proper, but it later proves to have been defective. Is the search therefore illegal? No, so long as the police reasonably believed the warrant was valid, the search is legal.[9]

Should the exclusionary rule apply in the following case? You be the judge.

Exclusionary rule
Evidence obtained illegally may not be used at trial.

---

[7]403 U.S. 443, 91 S. Ct. 2022, 1971 U.S. LEXIS 25 (S. Ct. 1971).
[8]See the discussion in *United States v. Leon* (Justice Brennan, dissenting), 468 U.S. 897, 1985 U.S. LEXIS 153 (S. Ct. 1984).
[9]Ibid.

You Be the Judge

Facts: Wendy Northern was hospitalized for a drug overdose. When police questioned her in the hospital, she identified her drug dealer as Antwaun Smith. She then called him to arrange for the purchase of crack cocaine at her house that evening. When Smith arrived at her house, the police

OHIO V. SMITH

2009 Ohio 6426; 920 N.E.2d 949;
2009 Ohio Lexis 3496
Supreme Court of Ohio, 2009

arrested him, searched him, and confiscated his cell phone. When the police looked at the phone some time later, they discovered call records and phone numbers confirming that this phone had been used to speak with Northern.

The police had neither a warrant nor Smith's consent to search the phone. Smith filed a motion requesting that the evidence from his cell phone be excluded because it had been obtained without a warrant. After the judge denied this motion, Smith was found guilty and sentenced to 12 years in prison. The appeals court upheld his conviction. He appealed to the Ohio Supreme Court.

You Be the Judge: *Was the search of Smith's cell phone legal? Should the evidence found on the phone be excluded?*

Argument for the Police: The police have the right to search anyone they arrest. During a perfectly legal search, they discovered Smith's cell phone. Prior courts have ruled that defendants have a low expectation of privacy in address books and that police can search them without a warrant. A cell phone is an electronic address book. Therefore, the search of Smith and the subsequent search of the contents of the phone were both legal. The evidence was properly admitted in court.

Argument for Smith: Police have the right to search someone they have arrested so that they can protect themselves and prevent evidence from being destroyed.

A search of the cell phone's contents was not necessary to ensure officer safety, and there was no evidence that the call records and phone numbers were in danger of being destroyed. Once the police had the phone, they had plenty of time to ensure that the data were preserved. In addition, they might have been able to obtain Smith's phone records from his service provider.

The police were entitled to search Smith and discover his cell phone. But they did not have the right to search the phone without a warrant. Modern cell phones are much more similar to a laptop than to an old-fashioned address book—they have the ability to transmit large amounts of personal data in various forms. Courts have ruled that defendants have a high expectation of privacy in laptop computers and that the police must obtain a warrant before searching one. It would be a terrible precedent to declare that the police could search cell phones without a warrant.

THE PATRIOT ACT

In response to the devastating attacks of September 11, 2001, Congress passed a sweeping antiterrorist law known as the Patriot Act. The statute was designed to give law enforcement officials greater power to investigate and prevent potential terrorist assaults. The bill raced through Congress nearly unopposed. Proponents hailed it as a vital weapon for use against continuing lethal threats. Opponents argued that the hastily passed law would not provide serious benefits but did threaten the liberties of the very people it purported to shield.

In an early legal test, a federal judge permitted the government to use secret evidence in its effort to freeze the assets of Global Relief Foundation, a religious organization suspected of terrorist activity. The group, which claimed to be purely humanitarian, asserted that it could hardly defend itself against unseen evidence. Finding "acute national security concerns," the judge allowed the government to introduce the evidence in private, without the foundation ever seeing it.[10]

The law also permitted the FBI to issue a **national security letter** (NSL) to communications firms such as Internet service providers (ISPs) and telephone companies. An NSL typically demanded that the recipient furnish to the government its customer records, *without ever divulging* to anyone what it had done. NSLs could be used to obtain access to subscriber billing records, phone, financial, credit, and other information—even records of books taken from libraries. However, an appeals court ruled that a secret NSL could be issued only if the government first demonstrated to a court's satisfaction that disclosure of the NSL would risk serious harm.[11]

---

[10]*Global Relief Found., Inc. v. O'Neill*, 315 F.3d 748, 2002 U.S. App. LEXIS 27172 (7th Cir. 2002).
[11]*Doe v. Mukasey*, 549 F.3d 861, 2008 U.S. App. LEXIS 25193 (2d Cir. 2008).

EXAM Strategy

Question: Police bang down the door of Mary Beth's apartment, enter without her permission, and search the apartment. They had no warrant. When the officers discover that she is smoking marijuana, they arrest her. What motion will the defense lawyer make before trial? Please rule on the defendant's motion. Are there any facts that would make you change your ruling?

Strategy: The defendant's motion is based on the police conduct. What was wrong with that conduct, and what are the consequences?

Result: The defense lawyer will argue that the police violated the Fourth Amendment because they lacked a warrant for the search. He will ask that the court suppress the drug evidence. Ordinarily, the court would grant that motion unless there was other evidence—for example, the police smelled marijuana from the hallway, and Mary Beth would have smoked it all if the police had taken the time to obtain a warrant.

7-2d The Case Begins

The trial is now ready to begin. But, the government may not be able to use all the evidence it has gathered.

THE FIFTH AMENDMENT

The Fifth Amendment to the Constitution protects criminal defendants—both the innocent and the guilty—in several ways.

Due Process   **Due process** requires fundamental fairness at all stages of the case. The basic elements of due process are discussed in Chapter 5, on constitutional law. In the context of criminal law, due process sets additional limits. The requirement that the prosecution disclose evidence favorable to the defendant is a due process rule. Similarly, if a witness says that a tall white male robbed the liquor store, it would violate due process for the police to place the male suspect in a lineup with four short women.

Due process
Requires fundamental fairness at all stages of the case.

Self-Incrimination   The Fifth Amendment bars the government from forcing any person to provide evidence against himself. In other words, the police may not use mental or physical coercion to force a confession or any other information out of someone. Society does not want a government that engages in torture. Such abuse might occasionally catch a criminal, but it would grievously injure innocent people and make all citizens fearful of the government that is supposed to represent them. Also, coerced confessions are inherently unreliable. The defendant may confess simply to end the torture. (The protection against self-incrimination applies only to people; corporations and other organizations are not protected and may be required to provide incriminating information.)

Exclusionary Rule (Again)   If the police do force a confession, the exclusionary rule prohibits the prosecution from using it or any information they obtain as a result of what the defendant has said. (This secondary information is referred to as "the fruit of the poisonous tree.") For example, when the police illegally arrest Alice, she tells them that she has bought drugs from Beau. The police go to Beau's house, where they find drugs. He tells them that Caitlyn is his dealer and, indeed, the police find drugs in Caitlyn's bedroom. None of this evidence—neither the confessions nor the drugs—is admissible in court because it all stemmed from Alice's illegal arrest.

The rationale is the same as for Fourth Amendment searches: Suppressing the evidence means that police will not attempt to get it illegally. But remember that the confession is void only if it results from custodial questioning. Suppose a policeman, investigating a bank robbery, asks a pedestrian if he noticed anything peculiar. The pedestrian says, "You mean after I robbed the bank?" Result? There was no custodial questioning, and the confession *may* be used against him.

Miranda Rights   The police cannot legally force a suspect to provide evidence against himself. But sometimes, under forceful interrogation, he might forget his constitutional rights. In the following landmark case, the Supreme Court established the requirement that police remind suspects of their rights—with the very same warning that we have all heard so many times on television shows.

Landmark Case

MIRANDA V. ARIZONA
384 U.S. 436; 1966 U.S. LEXIS 2817
Supreme Court of the United States, 1966

CASE SUMMARY

Facts: Ernesto Miranda was a mentally ill, indigent citizen of Mexico. The Phoenix police arrested him at his home and brought him to a police station, where a rape victim identified him as her assailant. The police did not tell him that he had a right to have a lawyer present during questioning. After two hours of interrogation, Miranda signed a confession which said that it had been made voluntarily.

At Miranda's trial, the judge admitted this written confession into evidence over the objection of defense counsel. The officers testified that Miranda had also made an oral confession during the interrogation. The jury found Miranda guilty of kidnapping and rape. After the Supreme Court of Arizona affirmed the conviction, the U.S. Supreme Court agreed to hear his case.

Issues: *Was Miranda's confession admissible at trial? Should his conviction be upheld?*

Decision: Neither his written nor his oral confession was admissible. His conviction was overturned.

Reasoning: To maintain a fair balance between state power and individual rights, to respect human dignity, our system of criminal justice demands that the government seeking to punish an individual produce the evidence against him by its own independent labors rather than by the cruel, simple expedient of compelling it from his own mouth.

Therefore, once the police take a suspect into custody or otherwise deprive him of his freedom, they are required to protect his constitutional right to avoid self-incrimination. To do so, they must warn him that he has a right to remain silent, that any statement he does make may be used as evidence against him, and that he has a right to the presence of an attorney, either retained or appoi-nted. If the police do not inform the accused of these rights, then nothing he says or writes can be admitted in court.

The defendant may waive these rights, provided the waiver is made voluntarily, knowingly, and intelligently. If, however, he indicates in any manner and at any stage of the process that he does not want to be interrogated or wishes to consult with an attorney before speaking, then the police cannot question him. The mere fact that he may have answered some questions or volunteered some statements on his own does not deprive him of the right to refrain from answering any further inquiries until he has consulted with an attorney.

7-2e Right to a Lawyer

As *Miranda* made clear, a criminal defendant has the right to a lawyer before being interrogated by the police. The Sixth Amendment guarantees the **right to a lawyer** at all important stages of the criminal process. Because of this right, the government must **appoint a lawyer** to represent, free of charge, any defendant who cannot afford one.

7-2f After Arrest

INDICTMENT

Once the police provide the local prosecutor with evidence, he presents this evidence to a **grand jury** and asks its members to indict the defendant. The grand jury is a group of ordinary citizens, like a trial jury, but the grand jury holds hearings for several weeks at a time, on many different cases. It is the grand jury's job to determine whether there is probable cause that this defendant committed the crime with which she is charged. At the hearing in front of the grand jury, only the prosecutor presents evidence, not the defense attorney because it is better for the defendant to save her evidence for the trial jury. After all, the defense attorney may want to see what evidence the prosecution has before deciding how to present the case.

If the grand jury determines that there is probable cause, an **indictment** is issued. An indictment is the government's formal charge that the defendant has committed a crime and must stand trial.

Grand jury
A group of ordinary citizens who decides whether there is probable cause the defendant committed the crime with which she is charged.

Indictment
The government's formal charge that the defendant has committed a crime and must stand trial.

ARRAIGNMENT

At an arraignment, a clerk reads the formal charges of the indictment. The judge asks whether the defendant has a lawyer. If she does not, the judge urges her to get one quickly. If a defendant cannot afford a lawyer, the court will appoint one to represent her free of charge. The judge now asks the lawyer how the defendant pleads to the charges. At this stage, most defendants plead not guilty.

DISCOVERY

During the months before trial, both prosecution and defense will prepare the most effective case possible. There is less formal discovery than in civil trials. The prosecution is obligated to hand over any evidence favorable to the defense that the defense attorney requests. The defense has a more limited obligation to inform the prosecution of its evidence. In most states, for example, if the defense will be based on an alibi, counsel must reveal the alibi to the government before trial.

PLEA BARGAINING

Sometime before trial, the two attorneys will meet to try to negotiate a plea bargain. A **plea bargain** is an agreement between prosecution and defense that the defendant will plead guilty to a reduced charge, and the prosecution will recommend to the judge a relatively lenient sentence. In the federal court system, about 75 percent of all prosecutions end in a plea bargain. In state court systems, the number is often higher. A judge need not accept the bargain but usually does.

For example, astronaut Lisa Nowak drove across country dressed in a wig and trench coat to attack fellow astronaut Colleen Shipman, whom she viewed as a romantic rival. After Nowak's arrest, police found in her car a BB gun, a knife, and surgical tubing, which was thought to be evidence of her violent intent. Nowak was charged with attempted murder and attempted kidnapping, but much of the evidence was thrown out of court under the exclusionary rule because of police misconduct. Nowak ultimately pleaded guilty to battery and burglary of a car. At that point, she had served two days in jail. She did not receive further jail time, but she was required to complete 50 hours of community service and to attend anger-management classes.

Plea bargain
An agreement in which the defendant pleads guilty to a reduced charge, and the prosecution recommends to the judge a relatively lenient sentence.

TRIAL AND APPEAL

When there is no plea bargain, the case must go to trial. The mechanics of a criminal trial are similar to those for a civil trial, described in Chapter 3, on dispute resolution. It is the prosecution's job to convince the jury beyond a reasonable doubt that the defendant committed every element of the crime charged. The defense counsel will do everything possible to win an acquittal. In federal courts, prosecutors obtain a conviction in about 80 percent of cases; in state courts, the percentage is slightly lower. Convicted defendants have a right to appeal, and again, the appellate process is similar to that described in Chapter 3.

DOUBLE JEOPARDY

Double jeopardy

A criminal defendant may be prosecuted only once for a particular criminal offense.

The prohibition against **double jeopardy** means that a defendant may be prosecuted only once for a particular criminal offense. The purpose is to prevent the government from destroying the lives of innocent citizens with repetitive prosecutions. Imagine that Rod and Lucy are accused of murdering a taxi driver. Rod is tried first and wins an acquittal. At Lucy's trial, Rod testifies that he is, indeed, the murderer. The jury acquits Lucy. The Double Jeopardy Clause prohibits the state from retrying Rod again for the same offense, even though he has now confessed to it.

PUNISHMENT

The Eighth Amendment prohibits cruel and unusual punishment. The most dramatic issue litigated under this clause is the death penalty. The Supreme Court has ruled that capital punishment is not inherently unconstitutional. Most state statutes divide a capital case into two parts, so that the jury first considers only guilt or innocence, and then, if the defendant is found guilty, deliberates on the death penalty. As part of that final decision, the jury must consider aggravating and mitigating circumstances that may make the ultimate penalty more or less appropriate.[12]

As you might expect from the term "cruel and unusual," courts are generally unsympathetic to such claims unless the punishment is truly outrageous. For example, Mickle pleaded guilty to rape. The judge sentenced him to prison for five years and also ordered that he undergo a vasectomy. The appeals court ruled that this sentence was cruel and unusual. Although the operation in itself is not cruel (indeed, many men voluntarily undergo it), when imposed as punishment, it is degrading and in that sense cruel. It is also an unusual punishment.[13]

In the following case, the Supreme Court was not moved to overturn a harsh punishment.

EWING V. CALIFORNIA

538 U.S. 11, 123 S. Ct. 1179, 155 L.Ed.2d 108
United States Supreme Court, 2003

CASE SUMMARY

Facts: California passed a "three strikes" law, dramatically increasing sentences for repeat offenders. A defendant with two or more serious convictions, who was convicted of a third felony, had to receive an indeterminate sentence of life imprisonment. Such a sentence required the defendant to actually serve a minimum of 25 years, and in some cases much more. Gary Ewing, on parole from a nine-year prison term, stole three golf clubs worth $399 each, and was prosecuted. Because he had prior convictions, the crime, normally a misdemeanor,

---

[12]*Gregg v. Georgia*, 428 U.S. 153, 96 S. Ct. 2909, 1976 U.S. LEXIS 82 (S. Ct. 1976).
[13]*Mickle v. Henrichs*, 262 F. 687 (1918).

was treated as a felony. Ewing was convicted and sentenced to 25 years to life. He appealed, claiming that the sentence violated the Eighth Amendment.

Issue: *Did Ewing's sentence violate the Eighth Amendment?*

Decision: No, the sentence did not violate the Eighth Amendment. Affirmed.

Reasoning: States have a valid interest in deterring and jailing habitual criminals. Nothing in the Eighth Amendment prohibits the California legislature from choosing this method of protecting the public. Recidivism is a serious public safety concern nationwide. According to a recent report, 67 percent of former inmates released from state prison were charged with a serious new crime within three years. Property offenders like Ewing were even likelier to commit a new crime than those who served time for violent crimes.

Ewing had already been convicted of numerous misdemeanors and felonies, and he had served nine terms of incarceration. He committed most of his crimes while on parole or probation. His previous convictions included serious crimes, such as robbery and residential burglary. By imposing a three strikes sentence, the State is not merely punishing the "triggering" offense. The State is also deciding to treat more harshly someone whose repeated criminal acts demonstrate that he is incapable of conforming to the norms of society.

Unquestionably the sentence is a long one, and the three strikes law has generated controversy. But criticism of the statute should be directed to the State legislature. Federal courts do not sit as a "super-legislature," second-guessing policy choices made by elected officials. The three strikes law represents a rational legislative judgment, entitled to judicial deference, that repeat offenders who have committed serious crimes must be incapacitated.

Ewing's sentence of 25 years to life is not grossly disproportionate and therefore does not violate the Eighth Amendment.

Devil's Advocate

Are we really going to send Ewing to prison for a minimum of 25 years—for *shoplifting?* It is true that Ewing is a recidivist, and undoubtedly a state is entitled to punish chronic troublemakers more harshly than first-time offenders. However, this still seems excessive. In California, a first-time offense of "arson causing *great bodily injury*" incurs a maximum nine-year sentence. A first-time offender convicted of voluntary manslaughter receives a sentence of no more than 11 years. Only a first-time murderer receives a penalty equal to Ewing's—25 years to life. It is unfair to Ewing to equate his property crimes with a homicide, and foolish for society to spend this much money locking him up.

The Eighth Amendment also outlaws excessive fines. Forfeiture is the most controversial topic under this clause. **Forfeiture** is a *civil* law proceeding that is permitted by many different *criminal* statutes. Once a court has convicted a defendant under certain criminal statutes—such as a controlled substance law—the government may seek forfeiture of property associated with the criminal act. *How much* property can the government take? To determine if forfeiture is fair, courts generally look at three factors: whether the property was used in committing the crime, whether it was purchased with proceeds from illegal acts, and whether the punishment is disproportionate to the defendant's wrongdoing. Neal Brunk pleaded guilty to selling 2.5 ounces of marijuana, and the government promptly sought forfeiture of his house on 90 acres, worth about $99,000. The court found that forfeiture was legitimate because Brunk had used drug money to buy the land and then sold narcotics from the property.[14] By contrast, Hosep Bajakajian attempted to leave the United States without reporting $375,000 cash to customs officials as the law requires.

---

[14]*U.S. v. Brunk,* 2001 U.S. App. LEXIS 7566 (4th Cir. 2001).

The government demanded forfeiture of the full sum, but the Supreme Court ruled that seizure of the entire amount was grossly disproportionate to the minor crime of failing to report cash movement.[15]

7-3 CRIMES THAT HARM BUSINESS

Businesses must deal with four major crimes: larceny, fraud, arson, and embezzlement.

7-3a Larceny

It is holiday season at the mall, the period of greatest profits—and the most crime. At the Foot Forum, a teenager limps in wearing ragged sneakers and sneaks out wearing Super Sneakers, valued at $145. Down the aisle at a home furnishing store, a man is so taken by a $375 power saw that he takes it. Sweethearts swipe sweaters, pensioners pocket produce. All are committing larceny.

Larceny
The trespassory taking of personal property with the intent to steal it.

Larceny is the trespassory taking of personal property with the intent to steal it. "Trespassory taking" means that someone else originally has the property. The Super Sneakers are personal property (not real estate), they were in the possession of the Foot Forum, and the teenager deliberately left without paying, intending never to return the goods. That is larceny. By contrast, suppose Fast Eddie leaves Bloomingdale's in New York, descends to the subway system, and jumps over a turnstile without paying. Larceny? No. He has "taken" a service—the train ride—but not personal property.

Each year, about $10 billion in merchandise is stolen from retail stores in the United States. Economists estimate that *12 cents out of every dollar* spent in retail stores covers the cost of shoplifting. Some criminal experts believe that drug addicts commit over half of all shoplifting to support their habits. Stores have added electronic surveillance, security patrols, and magnetic antitheft devices, but the problem will not disappear.

> **Economists estimate that *12 cents out of every dollar* spent in retail stores covers the cost of shoplifting.**

7-3b Fraud

Robert Dorsey owned Bob's Chrysler in Highland, Illinois. When he bought cars, the First National Bank of Highland paid Chrysler, and Dorsey—supposedly—repaid the bank as he sold the autos. Dorsey, though, began to suffer financial problems, and the bank suspected he was selling cars without repaying his loans. A state investigator notified Dorsey that he planned to review all dealership records. One week later, a fire engulfed the dealership. An arson investigator discovered that an electric iron, connected to a timer, had been placed on a pile of financial papers doused with accelerant.

The saddest part of this true story is that it is all too common. Some experts suggest that 1 percent of corporate revenues are wasted on fraud alone. Dorsey was convicted and imprisoned for committing two crimes that cost business billions of dollars annually—fraud (for failing to repay the loans) and arson (for burning down the dealership).[16]

Fraud
Deception for the purpose of obtaining money or property.

Fraud refers to various crimes, all of which have a common element: **the deception of another person for the purpose of obtaining money or property from him.** Robert Dorsey's

---

[15] *U.S. v. Bajakajian*, 524 U.S. 321, 118 S. Ct. 2028, 1998 U.S. LEXIS 4172 (S. Ct. 1998).
[16] *United States v. Dorsey*, 27 F.3d 285, 1994 U.S. App. LEXIS 15010 (7th Cir. 1994).

precise violation was bank fraud, a federal crime.[17] It is bank fraud to use deceit to obtain money, assets, securities, or other property under the control of any financial institution.

WIRE FRAUD AND MAIL FRAUD

Wire and mail fraud are additional federal crimes, involving the use of interstate mail, telegram, telephone, radio, or television to obtain property by deceit.[18] For example, if Marsha makes an interstate phone call to sell land that she does not own, that is wire fraud.

THEFT OF HONEST SERVICES

Under traditional standards, a culprit could only be convicted of fraud if he had deceived the victim to get something of value from *her*. But what if a CEO manipulates the financial results of his company and otherwise misleads investors to keep the stock price high? He has not committed fraud under this traditional definition because he did not personally obtain money from the investors—they bought their stock either from other shareholders or from the company.

To find a way to punish these wrongdoers, prosecutors looked to a federal statute that prohibits the **theft of honest services**.[19] Originally, this law was used to prosecute public officials who took bribes or kickbacks. But then prosecutors began to apply it to employees in the private sector as well. Prosecutors took the view that an employee violated this law if she did not fully perform the job for which she was paid. Thus, the CEO could be charged for not having done his job properly. But under this standard, the scope of the statute became enormous. In theory, an employee who called in sick so that he could watch his son's play has violated this statute. The scope of the statute permitted enormous discretion on the part of prosecutors.

The Supreme Court has stepped in to limit its scope. As the following case reveals, **the theft of honest services statute prohibits public and private employees from taking bribes or kickbacks.**

SKILLING v. UNITED STATES

130 S. Ct. 2896, 2010 U.S. LEXIS 5259
Supreme Court of the United States, 2010

Facts: Enron Corporation was an energy company in Houston that hired a young Harvard Business School graduate named Jeffrey Skilling to run one of its subsidiaries. Eleven years later, Skilling was promoted to president and chief operating officer. At that time, only six companies in the United States had higher revenues than Enron. Ten months after Skilling's promotion, Enron filed for bankruptcy protection.

The company's stock, which had been trading at $90 per share, became virtually worthless. A government investigation uncovered an elaborate conspiracy to prop up Enron's stock prices by overstating the company's finances.

Skilling was convicted of violating the honest services statute, sentenced to more than 24 years in prison, and ordered to pay $45 million in restitution. Skilling appealed, arguing that the honest services statute only applied to bribery and kickback schemes. The Fifth Circuit affirmed his conviction. The Supreme Court granted *certiorari*.

Issue: *Did Skilling violate the honest services statute?*

Decision: No, Skilling was not in violation.

Reasoning: The due process clause of the Constitution provides that a criminal statute must define a violation so

---

[17]18 U.S.C. §1344.
[18]18 U.S.C. §§1341–1346.
[19]18 U.S.C. §1346.

precisely that an ordinary person knows what activities are illegal. Skilling argued that the honest services statute did not meet this standard because it was too vague. It could apply to a very wide range of behavior, including some that is quite innocent.

Traditionally this statute was used against people who took bribes or kickbacks. That is a clear standard everyone can understand. Therefore, we hold that the honest services statute is constitutional, but only when applied to someone who has taken bribes or kickbacks.

The government did not allege that Skilling took bribes to misstate Enron's financials. The wrong-doing was for his own benefit. Therefore, he was not in violation of the honest services statute.

Skilling had been found guilty of three crimes: honest services fraud, wire fraud, and securities fraud. Although the Supreme Court ruled that Skilling had not violated the honest services statute, they remanded the case to the appeals court to determine if the other two convictions were independent enough to stand on their own without the honest services element. If not, he would have to be retried. The appeals court did uphold Skilling's two other convictions.

INSURANCE FRAUD

Insurance fraud is another common crime. A Ford suddenly swerves in front of a Toyota, causing it to brake hard. A Mercedes, unable to stop, slams into the Toyota, as the Ford races away. Regrettable accident? No: a "swoop and squat" fraud scheme. The Ford and Toyota drivers were working together, hoping to cause an accident with someone else. The "injured" Toyota driver now goes to a third member of the fraud team—a dishonest doctor—who diagnoses serious back and neck injuries and predicts long-term pain and disability. The driver files a claim against the Mercedes's driver, whose insurer may be forced to pay tens or even hundreds of thousands of dollars for an accident that was no accident. Insurance companies investigate countless cases like this each year, trying to distinguish the honest victim from the criminal.

EXAM Strategy

Question: Eric mails glossy brochures to 25,000 people, offering to sell them a one-month time-share in a stylish apartment in Las Vegas. The brochure depicts an imposing building, an opulent apartment, and spectacular pools. To reserve a space, customers need only send in a $2,000 deposit. Three hundred people respond, sending in the money. In fact, there is no such building. Eric, planning to flee with the cash, is arrested and prosecuted. His sentence could be as long as 20 years. (1) With what crime is he charged? (2) Is this a felony or misdemeanor prosecution? (3) Does Eric have a right to a jury trial? (4) What is the government's burden of proof?

Strategy: (1) Eric is deceiving people, and that should tell you the *type* of crime. (2, 3) The potential 20-year sentence determines whether Eric's crime is a misdemeanor or felony, and whether or not he is entitled to a jury trial. (4) We know that the government has the burden of proof in criminal prosecutions—but *how much* evidence must it offer?

Result: Eric has committed fraud. A felony is one in which the sentence could be a year or more. The potential penalty here is 20 years, so the crime is a felony. Eric has a right to a jury, as does any defendant whose sentence could be six months or longer. The prosecution must prove its case beyond a reasonable doubt, a much higher burden than that in a civil case.

7-3c Arson

Robert Dorsey, the Chrysler dealer, committed a second serious crime. **Arson** is the malicious use of fire or explosives to damage or destroy any real estate or personal property. It is both a federal and a state crime. Dorsey used arson to conceal his bank fraud. Most arsonists hope to collect on insurance policies. Every year thousands of buildings burn, particularly in economically depressed neighborhoods, as owners try to make a quick kill or extricate themselves from financial difficulties. Everyone who purchases insurance ends up paying higher premiums because of this immorality.

Arson

The malicious use of fire or explosives to damage or destroy real estate or personal property.

7-3d Embezzlement

This crime also involves illegally obtaining property, but with one big difference: The culprit begins with legal possession. **Embezzlement** is the fraudulent conversion of property already in the defendant's possession.

This is a story without romance: For 15 years, Kristy Watts worked part-time as a bookkeeper for romance writer Danielle Steele, handling payroll and accounting. During that time, Watts stole $768,000 despite earning a salary of $200,000 a year. Watts said that she had been motivated by envy and jealousy. She was sentenced to three years in prison and agreed to pay her former boss almost $1 million.

Embezzlement

The fraudulent conversion of property already in the defendant's possession.

7-4 CRIMES COMMITTED BY BUSINESS

A corporation can be found guilty of a crime based on the conduct of any of its **agents,** who include anyone undertaking work on behalf of the corporation. An agent can be a corporate officer, an accountant hired to audit financial statements, a sales clerk, or almost any other person performing a job at the company's request.

If an agent commits a criminal act within the scope of his employment and with the intent to benefit the corporation, the company is liable.[20] This means that the agent himself must first be guilty. If the agent is guilty, the corporation is, too.

Critics believe that the criminal law has gone too far. It is unfair, they argue, to impose *criminal* liability on a corporation, and thus penalize the shareholders, unless high-ranking officers were directly involved in the illegal conduct. The following case concerns a corporation's responsibility for a death caused by its employee.

COMMONWEALTH v. ANGELO TODESCA CORP.

446 Mass. 128, 842 N.E. 2d 930
Supreme Judicial Court of Massachusetts, 2006

CASE SUMMARY

Facts: Brian Gauthier, an experienced truck driver, worked for Todesca, a paving company. After about a year driving a particular 10-wheel tri-axle dump truck, Gauthier noticed that its back-up alarm had stopped working. When he reported this, the company mechanic realized that the old alarm needed replacement. The mechanic had none in stock, so the company instructed Gauthier to drive the truck without the alarm.

About a month later, Gauthier and other Todesca drivers were delivering asphalt to a work site on a highway

---

[20]*New York Central & Hudson River R.R. Co. v. United States,* 212 U.S. 481, 29 S. Ct. 304, 1909 U.S. LEXIS 1832 (S. Ct. 1909). Note that what counts is the intention to benefit, not actual benefit. A corporation will not escape liability by showing that the scheme failed.

at the entrance to a shopping mall. A police officer directed the construction vehicles and the routine mall traffic. A different driver asked the officer to "watch our backs" as the trucks backed through the intersection. All of the other trucks were equipped with back-up alarms. When it was Gauthier's turn to back up, he struck the police officer, killing him.

The state charged the Todesca Corporation with motor vehicle homicide, and the jury found the company guilty. The trial judge imposed a fine—of $2,500. The court of appeals reversed the conviction, and the prosecution appealed to the state's highest court.

Issue: *Could the company be found guilty of motor vehicle homicide?*

Decision: Yes, the company was guilty of motor vehicle homicide.

Reasoning: The defendant maintains that a corporation never can be criminally liable for motor vehicle homicide because a corporation cannot "operate" a vehicle. We disagree. A corporation can act only through its agents. By the defendant's reasoning, a corporation never could be liable for any crime. A corporation can no more serve alcohol to minors, or bribe government officials, than operate a vehicle negligently. Only human agents are capable of these actions. Nevertheless, we consistently have held that a corporation may be criminally liable for such acts when performed by corporate employees, acting within the scope of their employment and on behalf of the corporation.

Gauthier's truck was not equipped with a functioning back-up alarm, and he knew the alarm was missing. The defendant had a written safety policy mandating that all its trucks be equipped with such alarms. An employee's violation of his employer's rules, intended to protect the safety of third persons, is evidence of the employee's negligence, for which the employer may be held liable.

Gauthier never informed the victim that his truck did not have an alarm. The jury could have inferred that the victim, a veteran police officer, knew that the defendant routinely equipped its trucks with backup alarms. The victim expected to hear a backup alarm and would have, almost right in his ear, had the truck been properly maintained.

Affirmed.

7-4a Selected Crimes Committed by Business
WORKPLACE CRIMES

The workplace can be dangerous. Working on an assembly line exposes factory employees to fast-moving machinery. For a roofer, the first slip may be the last. The invisible radiation in a nuclear power plant can be deadlier than a bullet. The most important statute regulating the workplace is the federal **Occupational Safety and Health Act of 1970 (OSHA),**[21] which sets safety standards for many industries.[22] May a state government go beyond standards set by OSHA and use the criminal law to punish dangerous conditions? In *People v. O'Neill* [23] courts of Illinois answered that question with a potent "yes," permitting a *murder prosecution* against corporate executives themselves.

Film Recovery Systems was an Illinois corporation in business to extract silver from used X-ray film and then resell it. Steven O'Neill was president of Film Recovery, Charles Kirschbaum was its plant manager, and Daniel Rodriguez the foreman. To extract the silver, workers at Film Recovery soaked the X-ray film in large, open, bubbling vats that contained sodium cyanide.

A worker named Stefan Golab became faint. He left the production area and walked to the lunchroom, where workers found him trembling and foaming at the mouth. He lost consciousness. Rushed to a hospital, he was pronounced dead on arrival. The medical examiner determined that Golab died from acute cyanide poisoning caused by inhalation of cyanide fumes in the plant.

---

[21] 29 U.S.C. §§651 et seq. (1982).
[22] See Chapter 26 on employment law.
[23] 23194 Ill. App. 3d 79, 550 N.E.2d 1090, 1990 Ill. App. LEXIS 65 (Ill. App. Ct. 1990).

Illinois indicted Film Recovery and several of its managers for murder. The indictment charged that O'Neill and Kirschbaum committed murder by failing to disclose to Golab that he was working with cyanide and other potentially lethal substances and by failing to provide him with appropriate and necessary safety equipment.

The case was tried to a judge without a jury. Workers testified that O'Neill, Kirschbaum, and other managers never told them they were using cyanide or that the fumes they inhaled could be harmful; that management made no effort to ventilate the factory; that Film Recovery gave the workers no goggles or protective clothing; that the chemicals they worked with burned their skin; that breathing was difficult in the plant because of strong, foul orders; and that workers suffered frequent dizziness, nausea, and vomiting.

The trial judge found O'Neill, Kirschbaum, and others guilty of murder. Illinois defines murder as performing an act that the defendant *knows will create a strong probability of death* in the victim, and the judge found they had done that. He found Film Recovery guilty of involuntary manslaughter. Involuntary manslaughter is *recklessly* performing an act that causes death. He sentenced O'Neill, Kirschbaum, and Rodriguez to 25 years in prison.

The defendants appealed, contending that the verdicts were inconsistent. They argued, and the Illinois Court of Appeals agreed, that the judge had made contradictory findings. Murder required the specific intent of *knowing there was a strong probability of death*, whereas the manslaughter conviction required *reckless* conduct. The appeals court reversed the convictions and remanded for a new trial.

Moments before the new trial was to start, O'Neill, Kirschbaum, and Rodriguez all pleaded guilty to involuntary manslaughter. They received sentences of three years, two years, and four months, respectively.

HIRING ILLEGAL WORKERS

Employers are required to verify their workers' eligibility for employment in the United States. It is illegal to knowingly employ unauthorized workers. Within three days of hiring a worker, the employer must complete an I-9 form, which lists the items that can be used as documentation of eligibility. The government has the right to arrest illegal employees, and it can also bring charges against the business that hired them.

RICO

The **Racketeer Influenced and Corrupt Organizations Act (RICO)** is one of the most powerful and controversial statutes ever written.[24] Congress passed the law primarily to prevent gangsters from taking money they earned illegally and investing it in legitimate businesses. But RICO has expanded far beyond the original intentions of Congress and is now used more often against ordinary businesses than against organized criminals. Some regard this wide application as a tremendous advance in law enforcement, but others view it as an oppressive weapon used to club ethical companies into settlements they should never have to make.

What is a violation of this law? **RICO prohibits using two or more racketeering acts to accomplish any of these goals: (1) investing in or acquiring legitimate businesses with criminal money; (2) maintaining or acquiring businesses through criminal activity; or (3) operating businesses through criminal activity.**

What does that mean in English? It is a two-step process to prove that a person or an organization has violated RICO.

Racketeer Influenced and Corrupt Organizations Act (RICO)

A powerful federal statute, originally aimed at organized crime, now used in many criminal prosecutions and civil lawsuits.

---

[24]18 U.S.C. §§1961–1968.

Racketeering acts
Any of a long list of specified crimes, such as embezzlement, arson, mail fraud, wire fraud, and so forth.

1. The prosecutor must show that the defendant committed two or more **racketeering acts,** which are any of a long list of specified crimes: embezzlement, arson, mail fraud, wire fraud, and so forth. Thus, if a gangster ordered a building torched in January and then burned a second building in October, that would be two racketeering acts. If a stockbroker told two customers that Bronx Gold Mines was a promising stock, when she knew that it was worthless, that would be two racketeering acts.

2. The prosecutor must then show that the defendant used these racketeering acts to accomplish one of the three *purposes* listed above. If the gangster committed two arsons and then used the insurance payments to buy a dry cleaning business, that would violate RICO. If the stockbroker gave fraudulent advice and used the commissions to buy advertising for her firm, that would also violate RICO.

The government may prosecute both individuals and organizations for violating RICO. For example, the government prosecuted financier Michael Milken for manipulating stock prices. It also threatened to prosecute his employer, Drexel Burnham Lambert. If the government proves its case, the defendant can be hit with large fines and a prison sentence of up to 20 years. RICO also permits the government to seek forfeiture of the defendant's property. A court may order a convicted defendant to hand over any property or money used in the criminal acts or derived from them. Courts often freeze a defendant's assets once charges are brought to ensure that he will not hide the assets. If all his assets are frozen, he will have a hard time paying his defense lawyer, so a freeze often encourages a defendant to plea bargain on a lesser charge. Both Milken and Drexel entered into plea agreements with the government, rather than face a freeze on their assets, or in Milken's case, a long prison sentence.

In addition to criminal penalties, RICO also creates civil law liabilities. The government, organizations, and individuals all have the right to file civil lawsuits, seeking damages and, if necessary, injunctions. For example, a physician sued State Farm Insurance, alleging that the company had hired doctors to produce false medical reports that the company used to cut off claims by injured policy holders. As a result of these fake reports, the company refused to pay the plaintiff for legitimate services he performed on the policy holders. RICO is powerful (and for defendants, frightening) in part because a civil plaintiff can recover **treble damages;** that is, a judgment for three times the harm actually suffered, as well as attorney's fees.

Money Laundering

Money laundering
Using the proceeds of criminal acts and either promoting crime or concealing the source of the money.

Money laundering consists of taking the proceeds of certain criminal acts and either (1) using the money to promote crime, or (2) attempting to conceal the source of the money.[25]

Money laundering is an important part of major criminal enterprises. Successful criminals earn enormous sums, which they must filter back into the flow of commerce so that their crimes go undetected. Laundering is an essential part of the corrosive traffic in drugs. Profits, all in cash, may mount so swiftly that dealers struggle to use the money without attracting the government's attention. For example, Colombian drug cartels set up a sophisticated system in which they shipped money to countries such as Dubai that do not keep records on cash transactions. This money was then transferred to the U.S. disguised as offshore loans. Prosecution by the U.S. government led to the demise of some of the banks involved.

But drug money is not the only or even major component of so-called flight capital. Criminals also try to hide the vast sums they earn from arms dealing and tax evasion. Some of this money is used to support terrorist organizations.

---

[25]18 U.S.C. §§1956 et seq.

EXAM Strategy

Question: Explain the difference between embezzlement and money laundering. Give an example of each.

Strategy: Both crimes involve money illegally obtained, but they are very different. As to embezzlement, how did the criminal obtain the funds? In a laundering case, to what use is the criminal trying to put the cash?

Result: Embezzlement refers to fraudulently taking money that is already in the defendant's possession. For example, if a financial advisor, *lawfully entrusted* with his client's funds for investing, uses some of the cash to buy himself a luxurious yacht, he has embezzled the client's money. Money laundering consists of taking *illegally obtained* money and either using the funds to promote additional crimes or attempting to *conceal* the source of the cash. Thus, an arms dealer might launder money so that he can use it to finance a terrorist organization.

OTHER CRIMES

Additional crimes that affect business appear elsewhere in the text. Antitrust violations, in which a corporation fixes prices, can lead to criminal prosecutions. Securities fraud is a crime and can lead to severe prison sentences. (See Chapter 30, on securities and antitrust.)

7-4b Punishing a Corporation

FINES

The most common punishment for a corporation is a fine, as demonstrated in the Todesca case. This makes sense in that the purpose of a business is to earn a profit, and a fine, theoretically, hurts. But most fines are modest by the present standards of corporate wealth. In the Todesca prosecution, does a $2,500 fine force corporate leaders to be more cautious, or does it teach them that cutting corners makes economic sense, because the penalties will be a tolerable cost of doing business?

Sometimes the fines are stiffer. British Petroleum (BP) was found guilty of two serious environmental violations. In Alaska, the company's failure to inspect and clean pipelines caused 200,000 gallons of crude oil to spill onto the tundra. In Texas, the company's failure to follow standard procedures for ensuring safe refineries caused a catastrophic explosion that killed 15 people and injured 170 more. The total fine for both criminal violations was $62 million.[26] Is that enough to change BP's practices? Evidently not. In the spring of 2010, a BP well called Deepwater Horizon exploded, killing 11 workers and releasing into the Gulf of Mexico the largest marine oil spill ever. The Deepwater rig had violated many safety requirements.

COMPLIANCE PROGRAMS

The **Federal Sentencing Guidelines** are the detailed rules that judges must follow when sentencing defendants convicted in federal court of crimes. The guidelines instruct judges to determine whether, at the time of the crime, the corporation had in place a serious

Federal Sentencing Guidelines
The detailed rules that judges must follow when sentencing defendants convicted of crimes in federal court.

---

[26]Source: http://epa.gov/

Compliance program
A plan to prevent and detect criminal conduct at all levels of the company.

compliance program; that is, a plan to prevent and detect criminal conduct at all levels of the company. A company that can point to a detailed, functioning compliance program may benefit from a dramatic reduction in the fine or other punishment meted out. Indeed, a tough compliance program may even convince federal investigators to curtail an investigation and to limit any prosecution to those directly involved, rather than attempting to get a conviction against high-ranking officers or the company itself.

For a compliance plan to be deemed effective:

- The program must be reasonably capable of reducing the prospect of criminal conduct.

- Specific, high-level officers must be responsible for overseeing the program.

- The company must not place in charge any officers it knows or should have known, from past experience, are likely to engage in illegal conduct.

- The company must effectively communicate the program to all employees and agents.

- The company must ensure compliance by monitoring employees in a position to cheat and by promptly disciplining any who break the law.

Chapter Conclusion

Crime has an enormous impact on business. Companies are victims of crimes, and sometimes they also commit criminal actions. Successful business leaders are ever-vigilant to protect their company from those who wish to harm it, whether from the inside or the outside.

EXAM REVIEW

EXAM Strategy

1. **BURDEN OF PROOF**   In all prosecutions, the government must prove its case beyond a reasonable doubt. (p. 166)

Question: Arnie owns a two-family house in a poor section of the city. A fire breaks out, destroying the building and causing $150,000 damage to an adjacent store. The state charges Arnie with arson. Simultaneously, Vickie, the store owner, sues Arnie for the damage to her property. Both cases are tried to juries, and the two juries hear identical evidence of Arnie's actions. But the criminal jury acquits Arnie, while the civil jury awards Vickie $150,000. How did that happen?

Strategy: The opposite outcomes are probably due to the different burdens of proof in a civil and criminal case. Make sure you know that distinction. (See the "Result" at the end of this section.)

2. **RIGHT TO A JURY**   A criminal defendant has a right to a trial by jury for any charge that could result in a sentence of six months or longer. (p. 166)

3. **DURESS**   A defendant is not guilty of a crime if she committed it under duress. However, the defendant bears the burden of proving by a preponderance of the evidence that she acted under duress. (p. 167)

4. **ENTRAPMENT**   When the government induces the defendant to break the law, the prosecution must prove beyond a reasonable doubt that the defendant was predisposed to commit the crime. (p. 167)

5. **FOURTH AMENDMENT**   The Fourth Amendment to the Constitution prohibits the government from making illegal searches and seizures of individuals, corporations, partnerships, and other organizations. (pp. 167–171)

6. **WARRANT**   As a general rule, the police must obtain a warrant before conducting a search, but there are seven circumstances under which the police may search without a warrant. (pp. 167–168)

7. **THE EXCLUSIONARY RULE**   Under the exclusionary rule, a prosecutor may not use evidence obtained illegally. (p. 169)

8. **FIFTH AMENDMENT**   The Fifth Amendment requires due process in all criminal procedures and prohibits double jeopardy and self-incrimination. (pp. 167 and 171)

9. **SIXTH AMENDMENT**   The Sixth Amendment guarantees criminal defendants the right to a lawyer. (p. 173)

10. **EIGHTH AMENDMENT**   The Eighth Amendment prohibits excessive fines and cruel and unusual punishments. (p. 174)

11. **LARCENY**   Larceny is the trespassory taking of personal property with the intent to steal. (p. 176)

12. **FRAUD**   Fraud refers to a variety of crimes, all of which involve the deception of another person for the purpose of obtaining money or property. (pp. 176–178)

<h2>EXAM Strategy</h2>

Question: Chuck is a DJ on a radio station. A music company offers to pay him every time he plays one of its songs. Soon enough, Chuck is earning $10,000 a week in these extra payments, and his listeners love the music. In Chuck's view, this is a win-win situation. Is Chuck right?

Strategy: This is not traditional fraud because Chuck is not getting money from the people he is cheating—his listeners. Indeed, they are happy. Is there another type of fraud that applies in this situation? (See the "Result" at the end of this section.)

13. **ARSON**   Arson is the malicious use of fire or explosives to damage or destroy real estate or personal property. (p. 179)

14. **EMBEZZLEMENT**   Embezzlement is the fraudulent conversion of property already in the defendant's possession. (p. 179)

15. **CORPORATE LIABILITY**   If a company's agent commits a criminal act within the scope of her employment and with the intent to benefit the corporation, the company is liable. (p. 179)

16. **RICO**　RICO prohibits using two or more racketeering acts to invest in legitimate business or carry on certain other criminal acts. RICO permits civil lawsuits as well as criminal prosecutions. (pp. 181–182)

Question: Cheryl is a bank teller. She figures out a way to steal $99.99 per day in cash without getting caught. She takes the money daily for eight months and invests it in a catering business she is starting with Floyd, another teller. When Floyd learns what she is doing, he tries it, but is caught in his first attempt. He and Cheryl are both prosecuted.

(a) Both are guilty only of larceny.

(b) Both are guilty of larceny and violating RICO.

(c) Both are guilty of embezzlement; Cheryl is also guilty of violating RICO.

(d) Both are guilty of embezzlement and violating RICO.

Strategy: You need to know the difference between larceny and embezzlement. What is it? Once you have that figured out, focus on RICO. The government must prove two things: First, that the defendant committed crimes more than once—how many times? Second, that the defendant used the criminal proceeds for a specific purpose—what? (See the "Result" at the end of this section.)

17. **MONEY LAUNDERING**　Money laundering consists of taking profits from a criminal act and either using them to promote crime or attempting to conceal their source. (p. 182)

1. Result:　The plaintiff offered enough proof to convince a jury by a preponderance of the evidence that Arnie had damaged her store. However that same evidence, offered in a criminal prosecution, was not enough to persuade the jury beyond a reasonable doubt that Arnie had lit the fire.

12. Result:　Chuck has committed a theft of honest services because he has taken a bribe.

16. Result:　Cheryl and Floyd both committed embezzlement, which refers to fraudulently taking money that was properly in their possession. Floyd did it once, but a RICO conviction requires two or more racketeering acts—Floyd has not violated RICO. Cheryl embezzled dozens of times and invested the money in a legitimate business. She is guilty of embezzlement and RICO; the correct answer is (c).

MULTIPLE-CHOICE QUESTIONS

1. In a criminal case, which statement is true?
   (a) The prosecution must prove the government's case by a preponderance of the evidence.
   (b) The criminal defendant is entitled to a lawyer even if she cannot afford to pay for it herself.
   (c) The police are never allowed to question the accused without a lawyer present.
   (d) All federal crimes are felonies.

2. The police are not required to obtain a warrant before conducting a search if:

   (a) a reliable informant has told them they will find evidence of a crime in a particular location.

   (b) they have a warrant for part of a property and another section of the property is in plain view.

   (c) they see someone on the street who could possibly have committed a criminal act.

   (d) someone living on the property has consented to the search.

3. Under the exclusionary rule, which statement is true?

   (a) Evidence must be excluded from trial if the search warrant is defective, even if the police believed at the time of the search that it was valid.

   (b) The prosecution cannot use any evidence the police found at the site of the illegal search, but it can use any evidence the police discover elsewhere as a result of the illegal search.

   (c) Any statements a defendant makes after arrest are inadmissible if the police do not read him his *Miranda* rights.

   (d) If a conviction is overturned because of the exclusionary rule, the prosecution is not allowed to retry the defendant.

4. Benry asks his girlfriend, Alina, to drive his car to the repair shop. She drives his car all right—to Las Vegas, where she hits the slots. Alina has committed:

   (a) fraud.

   (b) embezzlement.

   (c) larceny.

   (d) a RICO violation.

5. Which of the following elements is *required* for a RICO conviction?

   (a) Investment in a legitimate business

   (b) Two or more criminal acts

   (c) Maintaining or acquiring businesses through criminal activity

   (d) Operating a business through criminal activity

ESSAY QUESTIONS

1. **YOU BE THE JUDGE WRITING PROBLEM** An undercover drug informant learned from a mutual friend that Philip Friedman "knew where to get marijuana." The informant asked Friedman three times to get him some marijuana, and Friedman agreed after the third request. Shortly thereafter, Friedman sold the informant a small amount of the drug. The informant later offered to sell Friedman three pounds of marijuana. They negotiated the price and then made the sale. Friedman was tried for trafficking in drugs. He argued entrapment. Was Friedman entrapped? **Argument for Friedman:** The undercover agent had to ask three times before Friedman sold him a small amount of drugs. A real drug dealer, predisposed to commit the crime, leaps at an opportunity to sell. If the government spends time and money luring innocent people into the commission of crimes, all of us are the losers. **Argument for the Government:** Government officials suspected Friedman

of being a sophisticated drug dealer, and they were right. When he had a chance to buy three pounds, a quantity only a dealer would purchase, he not only did so, but he bargained with skill, showing a working knowledge of the business. Friedman was not entrapped—he was caught.

2. Conley owned video poker machines. Although they are outlawed in Pennsylvania, he placed them in bars and clubs. He used profits from the machines to buy more machines. Is he guilty of money laundering?

3. Karin made illegal firearm purchases at a gun show. At her trial, she alleged that she had committed this crime because her boyfriend had threatened to harm her and her two daughters if she did not. Her lawyer asked the judge to instruct the jury that the prosecution had an obligation to prove beyond a reasonable doubt that Karin had acted freely. Instead, the judge told the jury that Karin had the burden of proving duress by a preponderance of the evidence. Who is correct?

4. An informant bought drugs from Dorian. The police obtained a search warrant to search Dorian's house. But before they acted on the warrant, they sent the informant back to try again. This time, Dorian said he did not have any drugs. The police then acted on the warrant and searched his house. Did the police have probable cause?

5. Shawn was caught stealing letters from mailboxes. After pleading guilty, he was sentenced to two months in prison and three years supervised release. One of the supervised release conditions required him to stand outside a post office for eight hours wearing a signboard stating, "I stole mail. This is my punishment." He appealed this requirement on the grounds that it constituted cruel and unusual punishment. Do you agree?

DISCUSSION QUESTIONS

1. Under British law, a police officer must now say the following to a suspect placed under arrest: "You do not have to say anything. But if you do not mention now something which you later use in your defense, the court may decide that your failure to mention it now strengthens the case against you. A record will be made of anything you say and it may be given in evidence if you are brought to trial." What is the goal of this British law? What does a police officer in the United States have to say, and what difference does it make at the time of an arrest? Which approach is better?

2. **Ethics** You are a prosecutor who thinks it is possible that Naonka, in her role as CEO of a brokerage firm, has stolen money from her customers, many of whom are not well off. If you charge her and her company with RICO violations, you know that she is likely to plea bargain because otherwise her assets and those of the company may be frozen by the court. As part of the plea bargain, you might be able to get her to disclose evidence about other people who might have taken part in this criminal activity. But you do not have any hard evidence at this point. Would such an indictment be ethical? Do the ends justify the means? Is it worth it to harm Naonka for the chance of protecting thousands of innocent investors?

3. Van is brought to the police station for questioning about a shooting at a mall. The police read him his *Miranda* rights. For the rest of the three-hour interrogation, he remains silent except for a few one-word responses. Has he waived his right to remain silent? Can those few words be used against him in court?

4. Police arrested Hank on a warrant issued in a neighboring county. When they searched him, the police found drugs and a gun. Only later did the police discover that when they had used the warrant, it was not valid because it had been recalled months earlier. The notice of recall had not been entered into the database. Should the evidence of drugs and a gun be suppressed under the exclusionary rule?

5. Andy was arrested for driving under the influence of alcohol (DUI). He had already been convicted of another driving offense. The court in the *first* offense was notified of this later DUI charge and took that information into consideration when determining Andy's sentence. Did the state violate Andy's protection against double jeopardy when it subsequently tried and convicted him for the DUI offense?

CHAPTER 8

INTERNATIONAL LAW

nuttakit/Shutterstock.com; © Stas Volik/Shutterstock.com

The month after Anfernee graduates from business school, he opens a clothing store. Sales are brisk, but Anfernee is making little profit because his American-made clothes are expensive. Then an Asian company offers to sell him identical merchandise for 45 percent less than the American suppliers charge. Anfernee is elated, but quickly begins to wonder: Why is the new price so low? The sales representative expects Anfernee to sell no clothes except his. Is that legal? He also requests a $50,000 cash "commission" to smooth the export process in his country. That sounds suspicious, too. The questions multiply. Will the contract be written in English or a foreign language? Must Anfernee pay in dollars or some other currency? The foreign company wants a letter of credit. What does that mean? What law will govern the agreement? If the clothes are defective, how will disputes be resolved—and where?

> **The world is now one vast economy, and deals can cross borders quickly.**

Transnational business grows with breathtaking speed. The United States now exports more than $1 trillion worth of goods and services. Leading exports include industrial machinery, computers, aircraft, agricultural products, electronic equipment, and chemicals. Anfernee should put this lesson under his cap: The world is now one vast economy, and deals can cross borders quickly.

8-1 TRADE REGULATION: THE BIG PICTURE

Nations regulate international trade in many ways. In this section, we look at export and import controls that affect trade out of and into the United States. **Exporting** is shipping goods or services out of a country. The United States, with its huge farms, is the world's largest exporter of agricultural products. **Importing** is shipping goods and services into a country. The United States suffers trade deficits every year because the value of its imports exceeds that of its exports, as the following table demonstrates.

Exporting

Shipping goods or services out of a country.

Importing

Shipping goods or services into a country.

Rank	Country	Exports (in billions of U.S. dollars)	Imports (in billions of U.S. dollars)
	Total, All Countries	1,278	1,912
1	Canada	249	277
2	China	92	365
3	Mexico	163	230

© Cengage Learning

8-1a Export Controls

You and a friend open an electronics business, intending to purchase goods in this country for sale abroad. A representative of Interlex stops in to see you. Interlex is a Latin American electronics company, and the firm wants you to help it acquire a certain kind of infrared dome, that helps helicopters identify nearby aircraft. You find a Pennsylvania company that manufactures the domes, and you realize that you can buy and sell them to Interlex for a handsome profit. Any reason not to? As a matter of fact, there is.

All nations limit what may be exported. In the United States, several statutes do this. The **Export Administration Act of 1985**[1] is one. This statute balances the need for free trade, which is essential in a capitalist society, with important requirements of national security. The statute permits the federal government to restrict exports if they endanger national security, harm foreign policy goals, or drain scarce materials.

The Secretary of Commerce makes a Controlled Commodities List of those items that meet any of these criteria. No one may export any commodity on the list without a license.

A second major limitation comes from the **Arms Export Control Act**.[2] This statute permits the President to create a second list of controlled goods, all related to military weaponry. Again, no person may export any listed item without a license.

The AECA will prohibit you from exporting the infrared domes. They are used in the guidance system of one of the most sophisticated weapons in the American defense arsenal. Foreign governments have attempted to obtain the equipment through official channels, but the federal government has placed the domes on the list of restricted military items. When one U.S. citizen sent such goods overseas, he was convicted and imprisoned.[3]

---

[1] 50 U.S.C. §2402 (1994).
[2] 22 U.S.C. §2778 (1994).
[3] *United States v. Tsai*, 954 F.2d 155, 1992 U.S. App. LEXIS 601 (3d Cir. 1992).

8-1b Import Controls

TARIFFS

Tariff

A tax imposed on goods when they enter a country.

Tariffs are the most widespread method of limiting what may be imported into a nation. A **tariff** is a tax imposed on goods when they enter a country. Tariffs are also called *duties*. Nations use tariffs primarily to protect their domestic industries. Because the company importing the goods must pay this duty, the importer's costs increase, making the merchandise more expensive for consumers. This renders domestic products more attractive. High tariffs unquestionably help local industry, but they may harm local buyers. Consumers often benefit from zero tariffs because the unfettered competition drives down prices.

Tariffs change frequently and vary widely from one country to another. For manufactured goods, the United States imposes an average tariff of less than 4 percent, about the same as that in the European Union. However, some major trading partners around the world set tariffs of 10 percent to 30 percent for identical items, with those duties generally being highest in developing countries. Foodstuffs show even greater diversity. For agricultural products, average tariffs are about 25 percent in North America, but over 100 percent in South Asia. As we will see later in the chapter, regional trade treaties have changed the tariff landscape. The majority of all U.S. products entering Mexico are duty free. Almost all trade between Canada and the United States is done with zero tariffs, which is partly why the two nations do more bilateral commerce than any others in the world.

Classification   The U.S. Customs Service[4] imposes tariffs at the point of entry into the United States. A customs official inspects the merchandise as it arrives and classifies it, in other words, decides precisely what the goods are. This decision is critical because tariffs can vary greatly depending on the classification. Disputes at this stage typically involve an importer claiming that the Customs Service has imposed the wrong classification. Companies will often go to great lengths to convince a court to lower tariffs on their products.

In the following case, Isotoner claimed that a tariff violated the Constitution. Did the company make a sensible argument? You be the judge.

---

[4]The Customs Service is part of the United States Customs and Border Protection, which is itself a division of the Department of Homeland Security.

You Be the Judge

Facts: Isotoner imports gloves for sale in the United States. The United States imposes a higher tariff on "men's" leather gloves than it does on gloves manufactured "for other persons." Isotoner argued that this difference violated the Constitution's Equal Protection Clause and amounted to illegal gender discrimination. The lower court dismissed the complaint, and Isotoner appealed.

TOTES-ISOTONER CO. V. UNITED STATES

594 F.3d 1346
United States Court of Appeals for the Federal Circuit, 2010

Issue: *Did higher tariff rates for men's gloves amount to illegal gender discrimination?*

Argument for Isotoner: Because the Constitution requires equal protection under the law, the government must treat people the same. In this instance, the government treats men worse than women—with the result that men will have to pay more for gloves. This is unacceptable. Surely this court would not allow a special tax on yarmulkes, or higher tariffs linked to race. Distinctions that disfavor an entire group of people cannot stand.

Argument for the United States: To be in violation of the Equal Protection Clause, the government must intend to discriminate. That is not the case here. Tariff rates are set for a variety of reasons. Men's and women's gloves may be made by different companies, in different countries, with different impacts on American industry. Surely the government has the discretion to set different tariff rates for gloves or any other kind of imported goods.

Valuation   After classifying the imported goods, customs officials impose the appropriate duty *ad valorem*, meaning "according to the value of the goods." In other words, the service must determine the value of the merchandise before it can tax a percentage of that value. This step can be equally contentious, since goods will have different prices at each stage of manufacturing and delivery. The question is supposed to be settled by the **transaction value** of the goods, meaning the price actually paid for the merchandise when sold for export to the United States (plus shipping and other minor costs). But there is often room for debate, so importers and their agents try to negotiate the most favorable valuation.

> **Ad valorem**
> Customs officials impose duties "according to the value of the goods."

DUTIES FOR DUMPING AND SUBSIDIZING

Dumping means selling merchandise at one price in the domestic market and at a cheaper, unfair price in an international market. Suppose a Singapore company, CelMaker, makes cellular telephones for $20 per unit and sells them in the United States for $12 each, vastly undercutting domestic American competitors. CelMaker may be willing to suffer short-term losses in order to bankrupt competitors. Once it has gained control of that market, it will raise its prices, more than compensating for its initial losses. And CelMaker may get help from its home government. Suppose the Singapore government prohibits foreign cellular phones from entering Singapore. CelMaker may sell its phones for $75 at home, earning such high profits that it can afford the temporary losses in America.

In the United States, the Commerce Department investigates suspected dumping. If the department concludes that the foreign company is selling items at less than fair value, and that this harms an American industry, it will impose a dumping duty that is sufficiently high to put the foreign goods back on fair footing with domestic products.

Subsidized goods are also unfair. Suppose the Singapore government permits CelMaker to pay no taxes for 10 years. This enormous benefit will enable the company to produce cheap phones and undersell competitors. Again, the United States imposes a tariff on subsidized goods, called **countervailing duties**. If CelMaker sells phones for $15 that would cost an unsubsidized competitor $21 to make, it will pay a $6 countervailing duty on every phone entering the United States.

> **Dumping**
> Selling merchandise at one price in the domestic market and at a cheaper, unfair price in an international market.

> **Subsidized goods**
> Goods that benefit from government financial assistance, which artificially lower their price.

> **Countervailing duties**
> Duties imposed on subsidized imports.

8-1c Treaties

Recall from Chapter 1 that the President makes treaties with foreign nations. To take effect, treaties must then be approved by at least two-thirds of the United States Senate. This section will examine three significant trade agreements.

GENERAL AGREEMENT ON TARIFFS AND TRADE (GATT)

What is GATT? The greatest boon to American commerce in a century—or perhaps it is the worst assault on the American economy in 200 years. It depends on whom you ask. Let's start where everyone agrees.

GATT is the General Agreement on Tariffs and Trade. This massive international treaty has been negotiated on and off since the 1940s as nations have sought to eliminate

> **GATT**
> The General Agreement on Tariffs and Trade.

trade barriers and bolster commerce. GATT has already had a considerable effect. In 1947, the worldwide average tariff on industrial goods was about 40 percent. Now it is about 4 percent. The world's economies have exploded over the past six decades. Leading supporters of GATT suggest that its lower tariffs vastly increase world trade. The United States is one of the biggest beneficiaries because for decades this country has imposed lower duties than most other nations. A typical American family's annual income has increased due to the more vigorous domestic economy, and at the same time, many goods are less expensive because they enter with low duties.

But opponents claim that the United States now competes against nations with unlimited pools of exploited labor. These countries dominate labor-intensive industries such as textiles, clothing, and manufacturing, and are steadily taking jobs from millions of American workers. Because domestic job losses come in low-end employment, those put out of work are precisely those least able to find a new job.

World Trade Organization (WTO)

Organization created by GATT to stimulate international commerce and resolve trade disputes.

GATT created the **World Trade Organization (WTO)** to stimulate international commerce and resolve trade disputes. The WTO is empowered to hear arguments from any signatory nation about tariff violations or nontariff barriers. This international "court" may order compliance from any nation violating GATT and may penalize countries by imposing trade sanctions.

Here is how the WTO decides a trade dispute. Suppose that the United States believes that Brazil is unfairly restricting trade. The United States uses the WTO offices to request a consultation with Brazil's trade representative. In the majority of cases, these discussions lead to a satisfactory settlement. If the consultation does not resolve the problem, the United States asks the WTO's Dispute Settlement Body (DSB) to form a panel, which consists of three nations uninvolved in the dispute. After the panel hears testimony and arguments from both countries, it releases its report. The DSB generally approves the report, unless either nation appeals. If there is an appeal, the WTO Appellate Body hears the dispute and generally makes the final decision, subject to approval by the entire WTO. No single nation has the power to block final decisions. If a country refuses to comply with the WTO's ruling, affected nations may retaliate by imposing punitive tariffs. The following case forced the WTO to weigh the merits of two important, competing goals: environmental protection and trade growth.

UNITED STATES—IMPORT PROHIBITION OF CERTAIN SHRIMP AND SHRIMP PRODUCTS

AB-1998-4
WTO Appellate Body, 1998

CASE SUMMARY

Facts: Sea turtles are migratory animals that live throughout the world. The United States recognizes the animals as an endangered species. Studies showed that the greatest threat to the turtles, around the world, came from shrimp fishermen inadvertently catching the animals in their nets. The U.S. government responded by requiring any importers to certify that shrimp entering the country had been caught using Turtle Excluder Devices (TEDs), which keep the animals out of the nets.

India, Pakistan, Malaysia, and Thailand filed complaints with the WTO, claiming that the United States had no right to impose its environmental concerns on world trade. The United States argued that Article XX of the WTO Agreement permitted trade restrictions based on environmental concerns. Article XX states in part:

Nothing in this Agreement shall be construed to prevent the adoption or enforcement by any Member of measures: … (b) necessary to protect human, animal or plant life or health; … (g) relating to the conservation of exhaustible natural resources if such measures are made effective in conjunction with restrictions on domestic production or consumption;

The Dispute Settlement Body declared that the United States had no right to impose its policies on shrimp importers, and the United States appealed.

Issue: *Did the WTO Agreement permit the United States to impose environmental restrictions on shrimp importers?*

Decision: No. The restrictions discriminated against other WTO Members.

Reasoning: To protect sea turtles, the United States required that its domestic, commercial shrimp trawl vessels use TEDs. Protecting the environment is a legitimate and noble objective. The United States, like all other Members of the WTO, has the right to adopt strict standards for its citizens.

However, the United States does *not* have the right to arbitrarily impose its own standards on other WTO Member nations. The United States was requiring foreign countries to adopt the same regulatory program for their shrimp trawl vessels as it had for its own without taking into consideration the different conditions that may occur in other countries.

If the United States' primary objective was to save sea turtles, it should have persuaded other Members to sign an environmental treaty for their protection. Instead, it tried to achieve this goal in a backdoor manner.

Although the United States' policy served a legitimate environmental objective, its application constituted arbitrary and unjustifiable discrimination between Members of the WTO.

Environmental groups attacked the ruling, declaring that the WTO paid lip service to the environment but ensured further killing of an important endangered species. Trade supporters applauded it. In addition to the trade versus environment tension, there is a second conflict: rich versus poor. Critics of the shrimp regulations claim that it is unseemly for a wealthy nation to punish subsistence fishermen because of environmental concerns. Their opponents argue that we all share this planet, and long-term growth for each of us depends upon living in harmony with limited resources and fragile ecosystems. Which of the competing goals is more important to you?

Ethics

Child labor is a wrenching issue. The practice exists to some degree in all countries and is common throughout the developing world. The International Labor Organization estimates that more than 250 million children under the age of 14 work full or part time. As the world generally becomes more prosperous, this ugly problem has actually increased. Children in developing countries typically work in agriculture and domestic work, but many toil in mines and factories.

The rug industry illustrates the international nature of this tragedy. In the 1970s, the Shah of Iran banned child labor in rug factories, but many manufacturers simply packed up and moved to southern Asia. Today, tens of millions of children, some as young as four, toil in rug workrooms, seven days a week, 12 hours a day. Child labor raises compelling moral questions—and economic ones as well. In 1997, Congress passed a statute prohibiting the import of goods created by forced or indentured child labor. The first suit under the new law targeted the carpet factories of southern Asia and sought an outright ban on most rugs from that area. Is this statute humane legislation or cultural imperialism dressed as a nontariff barrier? Should the voters of this country or the WTO decide the issue? In answering such difficult questions, we must bear in mind that child labor is truly universal. The United Farm Workers union estimates that 800,000 underage children help their migrant parents harvest U.S. crops.

Our response to such a troubling moral issue need not take the form of a statute or lawsuit. Duke University is one of the most popular names in sports apparel, and the school sells millions of dollars worth of T-shirts, sweatshirts, jackets, caps, and other sportswear bearing its logo. In response to the troubling issue of child labor, Duke adopted a code of conduct that prohibits its manufacturers from using forced or child labor and requires all of the firms to pay a minimum wage, permit union organizing, and maintain a safe workplace. The university plans to monitor the companies producing its apparel and terminate the contract for any firm that violates its rules.

REGIONAL AGREEMENTS: NAFTA AND THE EUROPEAN UNION

North American Free Trade Agreement (NAFTA)
A treaty eliminating almost all trade barriers, tariff and nontariff, between the United States, Canada, and Mexico.

In 1993, the United States, Canada, and Mexico signed the **North American Free Trade Agreement (NAFTA)**. The principal goal was to eliminate almost all trade barriers between the three nations. Like GATT, this treaty has been controversial. Unquestionably, trade between the three nations has increased enormously. Mexico now exports more goods to the United States than do Germany, Britain, and Korea combined. Opponents of the treaty argue that NAFTA costs the United States jobs and lowers the living standards of American workers by forcing them to compete with low-paid labor. For example, Swingline Staplers closed a factory in Queens, New York, after 75 years of operation and moved to Mexico. Instead of paying its American workers $11.58 per hour, Swingline decided to pay Mexican workers 50 cents an hour to do the same job.

Proponents contend that although some jobs are lost, many others are gained, especially in fields with a bright future, such as high technology. They claim that as new jobs invigorate the Mexican economy, consumers there will be able to afford American goods for the first time, providing an enormous new market.

EXAM Strategy

Question: California producers of sea salt protest to the American government that they cannot compete with the same product imported from China. How do the California producers want the United States government to respond? May the U.S. government legally oblige?

Strategy: Domestic producers who cannot compete with foreign competition typically ask their government to impose higher tariffs on the imported goods. However, the whole point of GATT, and the WTO, is to avoid trade wars. There are two instances in which the U.S. government is free to levy increased duties on the Chinese goods. What are they?

Result: When a company *dumps* goods, it sells them overseas at an artificially low price, generally to destroy competition and gain a foothold. That is illegal, and the domestic (U.S.) government may impose dumping duties to protect local producers. Subsidized goods—those supported by the foreign company's government—are also illegal. If the United States government can demonstrate illegal subsidies, it will impose countervailing duties designed to give all producers an equal chance.

Euro
The common currency of most EU countries.

Twenty-eight countries belong to the European Union (EU), including Great Britain, Germany, France, Italy, and Spain, as well as Latvia and Slovakia.

The EU is one of the world's most powerful associations, with a population of nearly half a billion people. Its sophisticated legal system sets EU-wide standards for tariffs, dumping, subsidies, antitrust, transportation, and many other issues. The first goals of the EU were to eliminate trade barriers between member nations, establish common tariffs with respect to external countries, permit the free movement of citizens across its borders, and coordinate its agricultural and fishing policies for the collective good. The EU has largely achieved these goals. Seventeen of the EU countries have adopted a common currency, the **euro**. Participating countries comprise what is known as the eurozone. Following the recent global financial crisis, the future of the euro was called into question, as the the debts of the weaker member nations burdened the eurozone's financial stability.

8-2 INTERNATIONAL SALES AGREEMENTS

Overseas markets offer tremendous growth potential. Foreign customers have an astonishing desire for some kinds of American goods and services.

Cowboy boots are hot in France. Imagine that you own and operate Big Heel, Inc., a small Texas company that makes superb boots. You realize that France could be a bonanza. What should you consider as you proceed? Several things.

8-2a The Sales Contract

Le Pied d'Or, a new, fast-growing French chain of shoe stores, is interested in buying 10,000 pairs of your boots at about $300 per pair. You are wise enough to know that you must have a written contract—$3 million is a lot of money for Big Heel.

WHAT LAW GOVERNS?

Potentially, three conflicting laws could govern your boot contract: Texas law, French law, and an international treaty. Each is different, and it is therefore essential to negotiate which law will control.

Texas lawyers are familiar with the Texas law and will generally prefer that it govern. French law is obviously different, and French lawyers and business executives are naturally partial to it. How to compromise? Perhaps by using a neutral law.

The **United Nations Convention on Contracts for the International Sale of Goods (CISG)** is the result of 50 years of work by various international groups, all seeking to create a uniform, international law on this important subject. The United States and most of its principal trading partners have adopted this important treaty.

The CISG applies automatically to any contract for the sale of goods between two parties from different countries if each operates in a country that is a **signatory**. (Goods are moveable objects like boots.) France and the United States have both signed. Thus, the CISG automatically applies to the Big Heel–Pied d'Or deal unless the parties *specifically opt out*. If the parties want to be governed by other law, their contract must state very clearly that they exclude the CISG and elect, for example, French law.

CISG
United Nations treaty governing the international sale of goods.

Signatory
A nation that signs a treaty.

CHOICE OF FORUM

The parties must decide not only what law governs, but also where disagreements will be resolved. This can be a significant part of a contract, because the French and American legal systems are dramatically different. In a French civil lawsuit, generally neither side is entitled to depose the other or to obtain interrogatories or even documents. This is in sharp contrast to the American system, where such discovery methods dominate litigation. American lawyers, accustomed to discovery to prepare a case and advance settlement talks, are sometimes frankly unnerved by the French system. Similarly, French lawyers are dismayed at the idea of spending two years taking depositions, exchanging paper, and arguing motions, all at great expense. At trial, the contrasts grow. In a French civil trial, there is generally no right to a jury. The rules of evidence are more flexible (and unpredictable), neither side employs its own expert witnesses, and the parties themselves never appear as witnesses.

CHOICE OF LANGUAGE AND CURRENCY

The parties must select a language for the contract and a currency for payment. Language counts because legal terms seldom translate literally. Currency is vital because the exchange rate may alter between the signing and payment. Suppose the Argentine peso falls

30 percent against the dollar in one week. An Argentine company that contracted on Monday to pay $1 million for U.S. aircraft engines will suddenly have to pay 30 percent more in pesos to meet its contractual obligations. To avoid such calamities, companies engaged in international commerce often purchase from currency dealers a guarantee to obtain the needed currency at a future date for a guaranteed price. Assuming that Big Heel insists on being paid in U.S. dollars, Pied d'Or could obtain a quote from a currency dealer as to the present cost of obtaining $3 million at the time the boots are to be delivered. Pied d'Or might pay a 5 percent premium for this guarantee, but it will have insured itself against disastrous currency swings.

Choices Made   The parties agree that the contract price will be paid in U.S. dollars. Pied d'Or is unfamiliar with U.S. law and absolutely refuses to make a deal unless either French law or the CISG governs. Your lawyer, Susan Fisher, recommends accepting the CISG, provided that the contract is written in English and that any disputes will be resolved in Texas courts. Pied d'Or balks at this, but Fisher presses hard, and ultimately those are the terms agreed upon. Fisher is delighted with the arrangement, pointing out that the CISG provisions can all be taken into account as the contract is written, and that by using Texas courts to settle any dispute, Big Heel has an advantage in terms of familiarity and location.

LETTER OF CREDIT

Because Pied d'Or is new and fast growing, you are not sure it will be able to foot the bill. Pied d'Or provides a letter of reference from its bank, La Banque Bouffon, but this is a small bank and it is unfamiliar to you. You need greater assurance of payment, and your lawyer recommends that payment be made by **letter of credit**. Here is how the letter will work.

Letter of credit
A commercial device used to guarantee payment in international trade.

Big Heel demands that the contract include a provision requiring payment by confirmed, irrevocable letter of credit. Le Pied d'Or agrees. The French company now contacts its bank, La Banque Bouffon, and instructs Bouffon to issue a letter of credit to Big Heel. The letter of credit is a promise *by the bank itself* to pay Big Heel if Big Heel presents certain documents. Banque Bouffon, of course, expects to be repaid by Pied d'Or. The bank is in a good position to assess Pied d'Or's creditworthiness since it is local and can do any investigating it wants before issuing the credit. It may also insist that Pied d'Or give Bouffon a mortgage on property, or that Pied d'Or deposit money in a separate Bouffon account. Pied d'Or is the **account party** on the letter of credit, and Big Heel is the **beneficiary**.

Account party
Party that applies for the letter of credit from its bank.

Beneficiary
Party that will be paid by the issuing bank pursuant to a letter of credit.

But at Big Heel, you are still not entirely satisfied. You feel that a bank is unlikely to default on its promises, but still, you do not know anything about Bouffon. That is why you have required a *confirmed* letter of credit. Bouffon will forward its letter of credit to Big Heel's own bank, Wells Fargo. Wells Fargo examines the letter and then *confirms* the letter. This is *Wells Fargo's own legal guarantee* that it will pay Big Heel. Wells Fargo will do this only if it knows, through international banking contacts, that Bouffon is a sound and trustworthy bank. The risk has now been spread to two banks, and at Big Heel, you are finally confident of payment.

You get busy, make excellent boots, and pack them. When they are ready, you truck them to Galveston, where they are taken alongside a ship, *Le Fond de la Mer*. Your agent presents the goods to the ship's officials, along with customs documents that describe the goods. *Le Fond de la Mer's* officer in turn issues your agent a **negotiable bill of lading**. This document describes *exactly* the goods received—their quantity, color, quality, and anything else important.

Negotiable bill of lading
A document of title that describes the goods received by the common carrier.

You now take the negotiable bill of lading to Wells Fargo. You also present to Wells Fargo a **draft**, which is simply a formal order to Wells Fargo to pay, based on the letter of credit.

Draft
A formal order to pay.

Wells Fargo will look closely at the bill of lading, which must specify *precisely* the goods described in the letter of credit. Why so cautious? Because the bank is dealing only in paper. It never sees the boots. Wells Fargo is exchanging $3 million of its own money based on instructions in the letter of credit. The bank should pay only if the bill of lading indicates that *Le Fond de la Mer* received exactly what is described in the letter of credit. Wells Fargo will decide whether the bill of lading is *conforming* or *nonconforming*. If the terms of both documents are identical, the bill of lading is conforming and Wells Fargo must pay. If the terms vary, the bill of lading is nonconforming and Wells Fargo will deny payment. Thus, if the bill of lading indicated 9,000 pairs of boots and 1,000 pairs of sneakers, it is nonconforming and Big Heel would get no money.

Wells Fargo concludes that the documents are conforming, so it issues a check to Big Heel for $3 million. In return, you endorse the bill of lading and other documents over to Wells Fargo, which endorses the same documents and sends them to Banque Bouffon. Bouffon makes the same minute inspection and then writes a check to Wells Fargo. Bouffon then demands payment from Le Pied d'Or. Pied d'Or pays its bank, receiving in exchange the bill of lading and customs documents. Note that payment in all stages is now complete, though the boots are still rolling on the high seas. Finally, when the boots arrive in Le Havre, Pied d'Or trucks roll up to the wharf and, using the bill of lading and customs documents, collect the boots. See Exhibit 8.1.

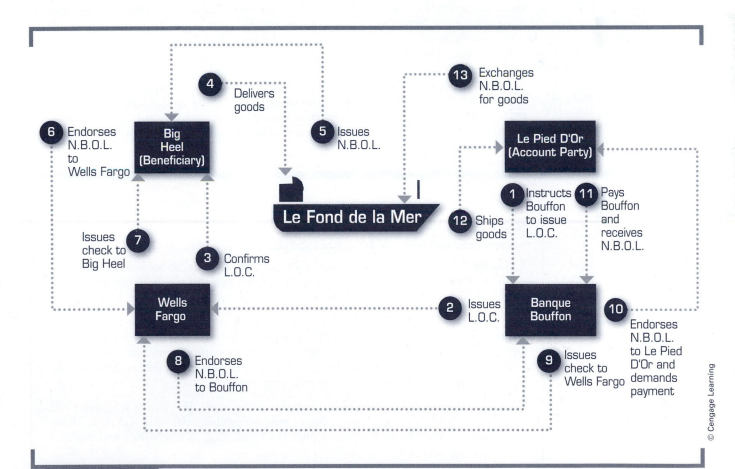

© Cengage Learning

EXHIBIT 8.1 A Typical International Letter of Credit Transaction for the Sale of Goods

CENTRIFUGAL CASTING MACHINE CO., INC. V. AMERICAN BANK & TRUST CO.

966 F.2d 1348, 1992 U.S. App. LEXIS 13089
United States Court of Appeals for the Tenth Circuit, 1992

CASE SUMMARY

Facts: Centrifugal Casting Machine Co. (CCM) entered into a contract with the State Machinery Trading Co. (SMTC), an agency of the Iraqi government. CCM agreed to manufacture cast-iron pipe plant equipment for a total price of $27 million. The contract specified payment of the full amount by confirmed irrevocable letter of credit. The Central Bank of Iraq then issued the letter, on behalf of SMTC (the "account party") to be paid to CCM (the "beneficiary"). The Banca Nazionale del Lavoro (BNL) confirmed the letter.

Following Iraq's invasion of Kuwait on August 2, 1990, President George H. W. Bush issued two executive orders blocking the transfer of property in the United States in which Iraq held any interest. In other words, no one could use, buy, or sell any Iraqi property or cash. When CCM attempted to draw upon the letter of credit, the United States government intervened. The government claimed that like all Iraqi money in the United States, this money was frozen by the executive order. The United States District Court rejected the government's claim, and the government appealed.

Issue: *Was CCM entitled to be paid pursuant to the letter of credit?*

Decision: Yes, CCM was entitled to payment. Affirmed.

Reasoning: The United States claimed that it froze Iraqi assets to punish international aggression. That is a legitimate foreign policy argument. However, no court has the power to rewrite basic principles of international trade.

A letter of credit has unique value for two reasons. First, the bank that issues the letter is substituting its credit for that of the buyer. Because the bank is promising to pay with its own funds, the seller is confident of receiving its money.

Second, the bank's obligation to pay on the letter of credit is entirely separate from the underlying bargain between buyer and seller. The bank must pay even if the seller has breached the contract or the buyer has gone bankrupt. The money in this case came from the bank that issued the letter; the government may not seize it. Any other ruling would undermine all letters of credit.

EXAM Strategy

Question: In an international contract for the sale of goods, Seller is to be paid by a confirmed irrevocable letter of credit. Buyer claims that the goods are defective and threatens to sue. If the parties are going to end up in court anyway, why bother with a letter of credit?

Strategy: A confirmed letter of credit is unique because the seller is assured of payment as soon as it presents a proper bill of lading to the appropriate local bank— regardless of the quality of the goods. Seller would much rather defend this lawsuit against Buyer than sue for its money in foreign courts.

Result: There *may* be a lawsuit, but Seller is not worried. It is Buyer who must sue, probably in Seller's home country. Buyer now risks substantial time and cash for an uncertain outcome. When the parties discuss a settlement, as surely they will, Seller is holding a big advantage—the cash.

8-3 INTERNATIONAL TRADE ISSUES

Assume that Ambux is an American communications corporation that decides to invest in a growing overseas market. The president of Ambux is particularly interested in building telephone systems in the former republics of the Soviet Union, reasoning that these economies offer great opportunity for growth. She hires a consultant to advise her on the most important issues concerning possible investment in Uzbekistan and other former Soviet republics. The consultant presents several related issues:

- Repatriation of profits
- Expropriation
- Sovereign immunity
- Act of State doctrine
- The Foreign Corrupt Practices Act (FCPA)
- Extraterritoriality

8-3a Repatriation of Profits

Repatriation of profits occurs when an investing company pulls its earnings out of a foreign country and takes them back home. If Ambux builds a telephone system in Uzbekistan, it will plan to make money and then repatriate the profit to its headquarters in the United States. But Ambux must not assume an automatic right to do so. Many countries impose a much higher tax on repatriated profits than on normal income in order to keep the money in domestic commerce. Others bar repatriation altogether. Developing countries in particular want the money to "stay home." Thus, before Ambux invests anywhere, it must ensure that it can repatriate profits or live with any limitations the foreign country might impose.

> **Repatriation of profits**
> The act of bringing profits earned in a foreign country back to a company's home country.

Fortunately, investing in Uzbekistan is relatively secure. Uzbekistan and the United States have signed a trade treaty guaranteeing unlimited repatriation for American investors. This treaty should suffice. But Ambux might still feel cautious. Uzbekistan is a relatively new nation, and the mechanisms for actually getting the money out of Uzbekistan banks may be slow or faulty. The solution is to get a written agreement from the Minister of Commerce explicitly permitting Ambux to repatriate all profits and providing a clear mechanism to do it through the local banks.

> **Many countries impose a much higher tax on normal income in order to keep the money in domestic commerce.**

8-3b Expropriation

Many nations, both developed and developing, **nationalize** property, meaning that they declare the national government to be the new owner. For example, during the 1940s and 1950s, Great Britain nationalized its coal, steel, and other heavy industries. The state assumed ownership and paid compensation to the previous owners. In the United States, nationalization is rare, but local governments often take land by eminent domain, to be used for roads or other public works. As we have seen, the United States Constitution requires that the owners be fairly compensated.

When a government takes property owned by *foreign* investors, it is called **expropriation**. The U.S. government historically has acknowledged that the expropriation of American

> **Nationalize**
> Action in which a government assumes ownership of property.

> **Expropriation**
> The government's seizure of property owned by foreign investors.

interests is legal, provided the host government pays the owners *promptly and fully, in dollars*. But if compensation is inadequate or long delayed, or made in a local currency that is hard to exchange, the taking is a **confiscation**.

Confiscation
The government takes property without fair payment.

The courts of almost all nations agree that confiscation is illegal. But it can be difficult or impossible to prevent because courts of a host country may be partial to their own government.

SOVEREIGN IMMUNITY

Sovereign immunity holds that the courts of one nation lack the jurisdiction (power) to hear suits against foreign governments. Most nations respect this principle. In the United States, the **Foreign Sovereign Immunities Act (FSIA)** states that American courts generally cannot entertain suits against foreign governments.[5] This is a difficult hurdle for a company to overcome when seeking compensation for foreign expropriation, but there are three possible exceptions.

Foreign Sovereign Immunities Act (FSIA)
A statute providing that American courts generally cannot entertain suits against foreign governments.

Waiver   A lawsuit is permitted against a foreign country that waives its immunity, that is, voluntarily gives up this protection. Suppose the Czech government wishes to buy fighter planes from an American manufacturer. The manufacturer might insist on a waiver in the sales contract, and the Czech Republic might be willing to grant one to get the weapons it desires. If the planes land safely but the checks bounce, the manufacturer may sue.

Commercial Activity   A plaintiff in the United States can sue a foreign country engaged in commercial, but not political, activity. Suppose the government of Iceland hires an American ecology-consulting firm to help its fishermen replenish depleted fishing grounds. Since fishing is a for-profit activity, the contract is commercial, and if Iceland refuses to pay, the company may sue in American courts.

Violation of International Law   A plaintiff in this country may sue a foreign government that has confiscated property in violation of international law, provided that the property either ends up in the United States or is involved in commercial activity that affects someone in the United States. Suppose a foreign government confiscates a visiting American ship, with no claim of right, and begins to use it for shipping goods for profit. Later, the ship carries some American produce. The taking was illegal, and it now affects American commerce. The original owner may sue.

INVESTMENT INSURANCE

Companies eager to do business abroad but anxious about expropriation should consider publicly funded insurance. In 1971, Congress established the Overseas Private Investment Corporation (OPIC) to insure U.S. investors against overseas losses due to political violence and expropriation. OPIC insurance is available to investors at relatively low rates for investment in almost any country.

Should Ambux investigate OPIC insurance before investing in Uzbekistan? Absolutely. While the Uzbekistan government has the best of intentions with respect to foreign investment, the nation is young and the government has no track record. A government can change course quickly. Why take unnecessary risks?

8-3c Foreign Corrupt Practices Act

The **Foreign Corrupt Practices Act (FCPA)**[6] makes it illegal for an American businessperson to give "anything of value" to any foreign official in order to influence an official decision. It is sad but true that in many countries, bribery is routine and widely accepted. When Congress investigated foreign bribes to see how common they were, more than 450 U.S. companies admitted paying hundreds of millions of dollars in bribes to foreign officials.

Foreign Corrupt Practices Act
A statute that illegalizes bribes to foreign officials by U.S. individuals or businesses.

---

[5] 28 U.S.C. Sec. §330, §332(a), §39(f) and §§60–6.
[6] 15 U.S.C. §§78 et seq.

Legislators concluded that such massive payments distorted competition among American companies for foreign contracts, interfered with the free market system, and undermined confidence everywhere in our way of doing business. In response, Congress passed the FCPA.

American executives have long complained that the FCPA puts their companies at a competitive disadvantage. Of the more than 200 nations in the world, very few aggressively prevent their nationals from bribing foreign officials. (In some countries, a bribe paid to a foreign official may even be treated as a tax deduction!) Others argue that the United States should not try to affect the way other countries do business by creating laws that apply outside its own borders.

The FCPA has two principal requirements:

- **Bribes.** The statute makes it illegal for U.S. companies and citizens to bribe foreign officials to influence a governmental decision. The statute prohibits giving anything of value and also bars using third parties as a conduit for such payments. Interestingly, the bribe need not be actually paid. A *promise* to pay bribes violates the Act. Also, the bribe need not be successful. If an American company makes an unauthorized payment but never gains any benefit, the company has still violated the law.

- **Recordkeeping.** All publicly traded companies—whether they engage in international trade or not—must keep detailed records that prevent hiding or disguising bribes. These records must be available for inspection by U.S. officials.

Not all payments violate the FCPA. A **grease or facilitating payment is legal.** Grease payments are common in many foreign countries to obtain a permit, process governmental papers, or obtain utility service. For example, the cost of a permit to occupy an office building might be $100, but the government clerk suggests that you will receive the permit faster (within this lifetime) if you pay $150, one-third of which he will pocket. Such small payments are legal. You cannot bribe the high-level decision makers who award contracts in the first place. But, once a contract has been secured, you may often bribe lower-level government workers to encourage them to speed things along.

Further, a payment does not violate the FCPA if it was legal under the written laws of the country in which it was made. Since few countries establish written codes *permitting* officials to receive bribes, this defense is unlikely to help many Americans who hand out gifts.

Punishments can be severe. A company may face large fines and the loss of profits earned as a result of illegal bribes. In 2011, Johnson & Johnson agreed to pay $77 million to settle an FCPA action. In addition to financial penalties, individuals who violate the FCPA can face up to five years in prison.

The following case is a classic example of bribery. Not much loyalty within Owl Securities. Why is that? What does it teach us?

United States v. King

351 F.3d 859
Eighth Circuit Court of Appeals, 2003

Case Summary

Facts: Owl Securities and Investments, Ltd., hoped to develop a large port in Limon, Costa Rica. The project included docks, housing, recreational facilities, an airport, and more. Richard King was one of Owl's largest inves-

tors, and Stephen Kingsley its CEO. The government charged King with attempting to pay a $1 million bribe (also known as a "kiss payment" or "toll" or "closing cost") to senior Costa Rican officials to obtain land and other concessions needed for the project. At trial, several of Owl's officers, including Kingsley, testified against King. A jury convicted King of violating the FCPA. He received a 30-month sentence and a fine of $60,000. He appealed.

Issue: *Did King violate the FCPA?*

Decision: Yes. Taped conversations proved that King knowingly violated the FCPA.

Reasoning: The FCPA prohibits making an offer, payment, promise to pay, or authorization of the payment of anything of value to any foreign official for purposes of influencing an official act or decision. There was ample evidence to prove King's knowledge and authorization of the proposed payment to the Costa Rican officials.

For example, the following taped exchanges are just a small sample of what the jury heard.

Kingsley: Yeah, what, um, what Pablo had said, was why just pay, pay off the current politicians. Pay off the future ones.
King: That's right. Because we're gonna have to work with them anyway.
Kingsley: And so what he was saying was double, you know, give them more money. Buy the opposition. If you buy the current party and the opposition, then it doesn't matter who's in because there's only two parties.

King: The thing that really worries me is that, uh, if the Justice Department gets a hold of. Finds out how many people we've been paying off down there. Uh, or even if they don't. Are we gonna have to spend the rest of our lives paying off these petty politicians to keep them out of our hair? I can just see us, every, every day some politician on our doorstep down there wanting a hand out for this or that … . Think we could pay the top people enough, that the rest of the people won't bother us any. That's what I'm hoping this million dollars does. I'm hoping it pays enough top people …

[A later recording:]

Kingsley: Now Pablo's continued to talk to the politicians. They know about the toll, closing costs call it what you will.
King: Does everybody agree to what we talked about recently?
Kingsley: Yeah, a million into escrow for the toll.
King: And then we get the property … ?
Kingsley: Um hum. Yeah now let me I'll, I'll, I'll come on to that because I'll explain how we work through that. Uh, essentially once the politicians see the money in escrow, they'll move. That's what it comes down to. Pablo's gonna send a list, an e-mail with a list of politicians already paid off and the ones he's gonna pay off.
King: Isn't that awfully dangerous?

Based on this evidence, King's conviction was affirmed.

Ethics
What's wrong with bribery, anyway? Many businesspeople think it is relatively harmless—just a cost of doing business, like New York City's high taxes or Germany's high labor costs. Corruption is not a victimless crime. Poor people in poor countries are the losers when officials are on the take; corruption means that good projects are squeezed out by bad ones. And corruption can reduce a country's entire administration to a state of decay. Honest officials give up. Bribes grow ever bigger and more ubiquitous. The trough becomes less well stocked; the snouts plunge deeper. Worldwide about $400 billion is lost each year to corruption in government procurement. The anticorruption czar in Mexico estimated that bribes reduce Mexico's gross domestic product annually by 9.5 percent. This sum is twice the country's education budget.[7]

[7] *"Who Will Listen to Mr. Clean?" The Economist,* August 2, 1997, p. 52.

EXAM Strategy

Question: Splash is a California corporation that develops resorts. Lawrence, a Splash executive, is hoping to land a $700 million contract with a developing country in Southeast Asia. He seeks your advice. "I own a beach house in Australia, worth about $2 million. If I give it to a certain government official in the Asian country, I know that will close the resort deal. If I don't, someone else will, and my company loses out. Do you think that's wrong? Should I do it?" Please advise him.

Strategy: Lawrence has phrased his question in terms of ethics, but there is more involved. What law governs his proposed conduct? Is Lawrence legally safe, given that the land is foreign and the contract will be signed overseas?

Result: If Lawrence gives anything of value (such as a house) to secure a government contract, he has violated the FCPA. It makes no difference where the property is located or the deal signed. He could go to jail, and his company could be harshly penalized. Ethically, his gift would exacerbate corruption in a developing nation and mean that the agreement was determined by a bribe, not the merits of Splash. Other companies might do a superior job employing local workers, constructing an enduring resort, and protecting the environment, all for less money.

8-3d Extraterritoriality

The United States has many statutes designed to protect employees, such as those that prohibit discrimination on race, religion, gender, and so forth. Do these laws apply overseas? This is an issue of **extraterritoriality**—the power of one nation to impose its laws in other countries.[8] Many American companies do business through international **subsidiaries**— foreign companies that they control. The subsidiary may be incorporated in a nation that denies workers the protection they would receive in the United States. What should happen when an employee of a foreign subsidiary argues that his rights under an American statute have been violated? You make the call.

Extraterritoriality
The power of one nation to impose its laws in other countries.

---

[8]Extraterritoriality can also refer to exemption from local laws. For example, ambassadors are generally exempt from the law of the nation in which they serve.

You Be the Judge

CARNERO V. BOSTON SCIENTIFIC CORPORATION

433 F.3d 1
First Circuit Court of Appeals, 2006

Facts: Boston Scientific (BSC) was an American company that manufactured medical equipment. The company had its headquarters in Massachusetts but did business around the world through foreign subsidiaries. One of the company's subsidiaries was Boston Scientific Argentina (BSA), and it was there that Ruben Carnero began working. His employment contract stated he would work at BSA's headquarters in Buenos Aires and be paid in pesos. Argentine law was to govern the contract. Four years later, Carnero took an assignment to work as country manager for a different BSC subsidiary, Boston Scientific Do Brasil (BSB). Carnero frequently traveled to Massachusetts to meet with company executives, but he did most of his work in South America.

About a year later, BSB fired Carnero, and BSA soon did the same. Carnero claimed that the companies terminated him in retaliation for his reporting to BSC executives that the Argentine and Brazilian subsidiaries inflated sales figures and engaged in other accounting fraud. Carnero filed suit in Massachusetts, alleging that his firing violated an American statute, the Sarbanes-Oxley Act of 2002 (SOX).

Congress passed that law in response to the massive fraud cases involving Enron, Arthur Andersen, and others. The law was passed primarily to protect investors, but included a "whistleblower" provision. That section was designed to guard employees who informed superiors or investigating officials of fraud within the company. The law allows injured employees reinstatement and back pay.

BSC argued that SOX did not apply overseas and the District Court agreed, dismissing the case. Carnero appealed.

Issue: *Did SOX protect a whistleblower employed overseas by a subsidiary of an American company?*

Argument for Carnero: Congress passed SOX because the American people were appalled by the massive fraud in major corporations, and the resulting harm to employees, investors, the community, and the economy. The whistleblower protection is designed to encourage honest employees to come forward and report wrongdoing—an act that no employee wants to do, and one which has historically led to termination. Mr. Carnero knew his report would be poorly received, but believed he had an ethical obligation to protect his company. For that effort, he was fired, and now Boston Scientific attempts to avoid liability using the technicality of corporate hierarchy.

Yes, Mr. Carnero was employed by BSB and BSA. But both of those companies are owned and operated by Boston Scientific. It is the larger company, with headquarters in the United States, which calls the shots. That is why executives in Massachusetts frequently asked Mr. Carnero to report to them—and why he brought them his unhappy news.

A whistleblower deserves gratitude and a pay raise. Mr. Carnero may well have saved his employer from massive losses and public disgrace. Would Boston Scientific like to wind up as Enron did—the company in bankruptcy court, its executives in prison? If Boston Scientific is too petty to acknowledge Mr. Carnero's contribution, the company should at least honor the purpose and intent of SOX by protecting his job.

Argument for Boston Scientific: First, we do not know whether there have been any accounting irregularities or not. Second, the fact that Mr. Carnero is employed by companies incorporated in Argentina and Brazil is more than a technicality. He is asking an American court to go into two foreign countries—sovereign nations with good ties to the United States—and investigate accounting and employment practices of companies incorporated and operating there. The very idea is offensive. No nation can afford to treat its allies and trading partners with such contempt.

If the United States can impose its whistleblowing law in foreign countries, may those nations impose their rules and values here? Suppose that a country forbids women to do certain work. May companies in those nations direct American subsidiaries to reject all female job applicants? Neither the citizens nor courts of this country would tolerate such interference for a moment.

Mr. Carnero's idea is also impractical. How would an American court determine why he was fired? Must the trial judge here subpoena Brazilian witnesses and demand documentary evidence from that country?

Finally, the SOX law does not apply overseas because Congress never said it did. The legislators—well aware that American corporations operate subsidiaries abroad—made no mention of those companies when they passed this statute.

Chapter Conclusion

Overseas investment, like sales abroad, offers potentially great rewards but significant pitfalls. A working knowledge of international law is essential to any entrepreneur or executive seriously considering foreign commerce. Issues such as choice of law, repatriation of profits, and expropriation can mean the difference between profit and loss. As the WTO lowers barriers, international trade will only increase, and your awareness of these principles will grow still more valuable.

EXAM REVIEW

1. **EXPORT RESTRICTIONS** Several statutes restrict exports from the United States that would harm national security, foreign policy, or certain other goals. (p. 191)

2. **TARIFFS** A tariff is a tax imposed on goods entering a country. The Customs Service classifies goods when they enter the United States and imposes appropriate tariffs. (pp. 192–193)

EXAM Strategy

Question: Sports Graphics, Inc. imports "Chill" brand coolers from Taiwan. Chill coolers have an outer shell of vinyl, with handles and pockets, and an inner layer of insulation. In one lawsuit, the issue was whether "Chill" coolers were "luggage" or "articles used for preparing, serving, or storing food or beverages," as Sports Graphics claimed. Who was the other party to the dispute, why did the two sides care about this, and what arguments did they make?

Strategy: The Customs Service (the other party) classifies goods and then imposes an appropriate *ad valorem* tax. What is at stake, of course, is money. (See the "Result" at the end of this section.)

3. **DUMPED AND SUBSIDIZED IMPORTS** Most countries, including the United States, impose duties for goods that have been dumped (sold at an unfairly low price in the international market) and for subsidized goods (those benefiting from government financial assistance in the country of origin). (p. 193)

4. **GATT** The General Agreement on Tariffs and Trade (GATT) is lowering the average duties worldwide. Proponents see it as a boon to trade; opponents see it as a threat to workers. (pp. 193–195)

5. **WTO** GATT created the WTO, which resolves disputes between signatories to the treaty. (pp. 194–195)

EXAM Strategy

Question: In a recent WTO case, several nations claimed that American laws concerning shrimp fishing were unfair and illegal. The case demonstrated a conflict between two important values. What were the values? In your view, which is more important? Who won and why?

Strategy: Make sure you understand the *Shrimp Products* case in the text. (See the "Result" at the end of this section.)

6. **CISG** A sales agreement between an American company and a foreign company may be governed by American law, by the law of the foreign country, or by the CISG. (p. 197)

7. **LETTERS OF CREDIT**   A confirmed, irrevocable letter of credit is an important means of facilitating international sales contracts, because the seller is assured of payment by a local bank so long as it delivers the specified goods. (pp. 198–200)

EXAM Strategy

Question: Flyby Knight (FK) contracts to sell 12 helicopters to Air Nigeria for $8 million each. Payment is to be made by letter of credit, issued by the Bank of Nigeria, confirmed by Citibank in New York, and due when the confirming bank receives a bill of lading indicating all helicopters are on board ship, ready for sailing to Nigeria. FK loads the aircraft on board ship, and the next day delivers the bill of lading to Citibank. The same day, Air Nigeria informs FK that its inspectors onboard ship have discovered serious flaws in the rotator blades and the fuel lines. Air Nigeria states it will neither accept nor pay for the helicopters. Is FK entitled to its $96 million?

(a) FK is entitled to no money.

(b) FK is entitled to no money *provided* Air Nigeria can prove the helicopters are defective.

(c) Air Nigeria is obligated to pay FK the full price.

(d) Bank of Nigeria is obligated to pay FK the full price.

(e) Citibank is obligated to pay FK the full price.

Strategy: Payment is to be made by confirmed letter of credit. Ask yourself what that means. In such a case, the confirming bank is obligated to pay the seller when the bank receives a bill of lading indicating that conforming goods have been delivered. What about the fact that the goods seem defective? That is irrelevant. It is precisely to avoid long-distance arguments over such problems that sellers insist on these letters. (See the "Result" at the end of this section.)

---

8. **REPATRIATION**   A foreign government may restrict repatriation of profits. (p. 201)

9. **EXPROPRIATION**   Expropriation refers to a government taking property owned by foreign investors. U.S. courts regard this as lawful, provided the country pays the American owner promptly and fully in dollars. (pp. 201–202)

10. **SOVEREIGN IMMUNITY**   Sovereign immunity means that, in general, American courts lack jurisdiction to hear suits against foreign governments unless the foreign nation has waived immunity, is engaging in commercial activity, or has violated international law. (p. 202)

11. **FOREIGN CORRUPT PRACTICES ACT (FCPA)**   The FCPA makes it illegal for an American businessperson to bribe foreign officials. (pp. 202–204)

12. **EXTRATERRITORIALITY**   The principle that refers to the power of one nation to impose its laws in other ountries. (pp. 205–206)

2. Result: Customs evidently claimed the goods were luggage, with a higher tariff than food storage articles. Customs argued that the handles and portability made the articles luggage. But Sports Graphics prevailed, convincing the court that the primary purpose of the containers was the storage of food. The lawsuit reduced the company's tariff from 20 percent to 3.4 percent.

5. Result: Small nations sued, claiming that American regulations made it difficult or impossible for them to fish, devastating their economic growth. The United States argued that vital environmental concerns mandated such rules. The WTO found in favor of the small nations, ruling that before the United States imposed its environmental standards on other countries, it must engage in multinational negotiations, seeking an acceptable compromise. Environmentalists argued that the decision was short-sighted, and contributed to the destruction of an endangered species. Supporters of the decision responded that long-term environmental concerns sound patronizing and hollow to people with empty stomachs.

7. Result: When Citibank receives the bill of lading, indicating delivery of the helicopters, it is obligated to pay. The correct answer is (e).

MULTIPLE-CHOICE QUESTIONS

1. A letter of credit is issued by a _____.
  (a) buyer
  (b) seller
  (c) shipping company
  (d) bank

2. Tariffs are a tax on _____. Treaties like NAFTA seek to _____ tariffs.
  (a) imports; increase
  (b) imports; decrease
  (c) exports; increase
  (d) exports; decrease

3. The President negotiates a defense agreement with a foreign government. To take effect, the agreement must be ratified by which of the following?
  (a) Two-thirds of the House of Representatives
  (b) Two-thirds of the Senate
  (c) The Supreme Court
  (d) (a) and (b)
  (e) (a), (b), and (c)

4. Lynn owns a small printing company in Nevada. She makes a contract with a company in France to print custom children's books and ship them to France. The contract does not say anything about which body of law will be used to resolve any disputes that arise. If there is a conflict, which body of law will actually be applied to the case?

    (a) Nevada law

    (b) French law

    (c) The CISG

    (d) None of the above

5. Countervailing duties are imposed when _____.

    (a) dumping occurs

    (b) goods are unreasonably subsidized

    (c) Both (a) and (b)

    (d) None of the above

ESSAY QUESTIONS

1. Arnold Mandel exported certain high-technology electronic equipment. Later, he was in court arguing that the equipment he shipped should not have been on the Department of Commerce's Commodity Control List. What items may be on that list, and why does Mandel care?

2. **YOU BE THE JUDGE WRITING PROBLEM** Continental Illinois National Bank issued an irrevocable letter of credit on behalf of Bill's Coal Co. for $805,000, with the Allied Fidelity Insurance Co. as beneficiary. Bill's Coal Co. then went bankrupt. Allied then presented to Continental documents that were complete and conformed to the letter of credit. Continental refused to pay. Since Bill's Coal was bankrupt, there was no way Continental would collect once it had paid on the letter. Allied filed suit. Who should win? **Argument for Allied Fidelity:** An irrevocable letter of credit serves one purpose: to assure the seller that it will be paid if it performs the contract. Allied has met its obligation. The company furnished documents demonstrating compliance with the agreement. Continental *must* pay. Continental's duty to pay is an independent obligation, unrelated to the status of Bill's Coal. The bank issued this letter knowing the rules of the game and expecting to make a profit. It is time for Continental to honor its word. **Argument for Continental Bank:** In this transaction, the bank was merely a middleman, helping to facilitate payment of a contract. Allied has fulfilled its obligations under the contract, and we understand the company's desire to be paid. Regrettably, Bill's Coal is bankrupt. No one is going to be paid on this deal. Allied should have researched Bill's financial status more thoroughly before entering into the agreement. While we sympathize with Allied's dilemma, it has only itself to blame and cannot expect the bank to act as some sort of insurance company for a deal gone awry.

3. Jean-François, a French wine exporter, sues Bobby Joe, a Texas importer, claiming that Bobby Joe owes him $2 million for wine. Jean-François takes the witness stand to describe how the contract was created. Where is the trial taking place?

4. The Kyrgyz Republic is one of the new nations that broke away from the old Soviet Union. In September 1994, the government of Kyrgyzstan made two independent announcements; (1) It was abolishing all taxes on repatriation; and (2) the government was resigning and would shortly be replaced. Explain the significance of these announcements for an American company considering a major investment in Kyrgyzstan.

5. The Instituto de Auxilios y Viviendas is a government agency of the Dominican Republic. Dr. Marion Fernandez, the general administrator of the Instituto and Secretary of the Republic, sought a loan for the Instituto. She requested that Charles Meadows, an American citizen, secure the Instituto a bank loan of $12 million. If he obtained a loan on favorable terms, he would receive a fee of $240,000. Meadows secured a loan on satisfactory terms, which the Instituto accepted. He then sought his fee, but the Instituto and the Dominican government refused to pay. He sued the government in United States District Court. The Dominican government claimed immunity. Comment.

DISCUSSION QUESTIONS

1. The United States consistently imports much more than it exports. The annual gap is consistently several hundred billion dollars. Does this concern you? If so, what should be done about it? If not, why not?

2. Does the FCPA seem sensible? Is fighting corruption the right thing to do, or does the statute place American companies at an unacceptable competitive disadvantage?

3. Generally speaking, should the United States pass laws that seek to control behavior outside its borders? Or, when in Rome, should our companies and subsidiaries be allowed to do as the Romans do?

4. Do you favor free trade agreements like NAFTA? Do you believe that free trade benefits everyone in the long run, or are you more concerned that American jobs may be lost?

5. Imagine that you read an article that reports the maker of your favorite brand of clothing uses child labor in its overseas factories. Being realistic, would you avoid buying that kind of clothing in the future? Why or why not?

Contracts

CHAPTER 9

INTRODUCTION TO CONTRACTS

nuttakit/Shutterstock.com; neelsky/Shutterstock.com

Chris always knew that he would propose to his girlfriend Alissa at Chez Luc, a ritzy, reservations-only restaurant. When it came time to pop the question, Chris went on Chez Luc's website to reserve a special table. But the website would not grant him a seating time unless he agreed not to use his cell phone at the restaurant. Chris clicked on "I agree" and was issued a booking at his waterfront table of choice.

After Alissa's exuberant "yes" during the appetizer, the newly-engaged couple could not contain their excitement. With their iPhones, Chris and Alissa took pictures of themselves, which they immediately posted on Facebook. They each called their parents from the table to share the good news ... only to be stopped in their tracks by the angry *maître d'*, who asked the couple to leave the dining room for breaching their contract with the restaurant.

> The website would not grant him a seating time unless he agreed not to use his cell phone at the restaurant.

We make promises and agreements all the time—from the casual "*I will call you later*" to the more formal employment contracts. Some agreements are in writing; some are not. Some we can negotiate; some we cannot. One of the aims of contract law is to sort those agreements that are "worthy" of legal enforcement from those that are not. How do we know if an agreement is "worthy"? The answer might surprise you. Most people assume that contracts must always be long, unintelligible documents written by lawyers, or that they are necessarily hefty agreements of great financial significance.

In reality, contract law is based on the notion that you are the best judge of your own welfare. This means that you have the freedom to enter into relationships and agree to the rules that will govern them. However, this freedom is not limitless: The law imposes certain formalities. Your agreements must meet seven requirements, which we will analyze in detail in upcoming chapters.

Contract law is a story of freedom and power, rules and relationships—with drama to spare. It is important to study this story to avoid your own contract drama. Let's start with an introduction to contracts.

9-1 CONTRACTS

9-1a Elements of a Contract

A contract is merely a legally enforceable agreement. People regularly make promises, but only some of them are enforceable. For a contract to be enforceable, seven key characteristics *must* be present. We will study this "checklist" at length in the next several chapters.

- **Offer.** All contracts begin when a person or a company proposes a deal. It might involve buying something, selling something, doing a job, or anything else. But only proposals made in certain ways amount to a legally recognized offer.

- **Acceptance.** Once a party receives an offer, he must respond to it in a certain way. We will examine the requirements of both offers and acceptances in the next chapter.

- **Consideration.** There has to be bargaining that leads to an *exchange* between the parties. Contracts cannot be a one-way street; both sides must receive some measureable benefit.

- **Legality.** The contract must be for a lawful purpose. Courts will not enforce agreements to sell cocaine, for example.

- **Capacity.** The parties must be adults of sound mind.

- **Consent.** Certain kinds of trickery and force can prevent the formation of a contract.

- **Writing.** While verbal agreements often amount to contracts, some types of contracts must be in writing to be enforceable.

9-1b Other Important Issues

Once we have examined the essential parts of contracts, the unit will turn to other important issues:

- **Third-Party Interests.** If Jerome and Tara have a contract, and if the deal falls apart, can Kevin sue to enforce the agreement? It depends.

- **Performance and Discharge.** If a party fully accomplishes what the contract requires, his duties are discharged. But what if his obligations are performed poorly, or not at all?

- **Remedies.** A court will award money or other relief to a party injured by a breach of contract.

Contracts Checklist

☐ Offer
☐ Acceptance
☐ Consideration
☐ Legality
☐ Capacity
☐ Consent
☐ Writing

© Cengage Learning

Let's apply these principles to the opening scenario.

Is the "contract" between Chris and Chez Luc legally binding? Can Chez Luc kick out—or even *sue*—Chris for using his cell phone? In deciding this issue, a judge would consider whether the parties intentionally made an agreement, which included a valid offer and acceptance. The restaurant's website set forth its terms, to which Chris agreed by clicking "I agree"—so there is no question there. A judge would then carefully examine whether the parties exchanged something of value that proved that they both meant to be bound by this agreement. And there was. The restaurant gave up a coveted reservation time in exchange for Chris's promise to stay away from his phone. A judge would also verify that the parties were adults of sound mind and that the subject matter of the contract was legal. Assuming Chris was of legal age (and we certainly hope he was, since he was getting engaged), the agreement was valid and enforceable. Whether kicking out a newly-engaged couple is good business practice for a restaurant … now, that's a different story!

9-1c All Shapes and Sizes

Some contracts—like those in the opener—are small. But contracts can also be large. Lockheed Martin and Boeing spent years of work and millions of dollars competing for a U.S. Defense Department aircraft contract. Why the fierce effort? The deal was potentially good for 25 years and *$200 billion*. Lockheed won. The company earned the right to build the next generation of fighter jets—3,000 planes, with different varieties of the aircraft to be used by each of the American defense services and some allied forces as well.

Many contracts involve public issues. The Lockheed agreement concerns government agencies deciding how to spend taxpayer money for national defense. Other contracts concern intensely private matters. Mary Beth Whitehead signed a contract with William and Elizabeth Stern, of New Jersey. For a fee of $10,000, Whitehead agreed to act as a surrogate mother, and then deliver the baby to the Sterns for adoption after she carried it to term. But when little Melissa was born, Whitehead changed her mind and fled to Florida with the baby. The Sterns sued for breach of contract. Surrogacy contracts now lead to hundreds of births per year. Are the contracts immoral? Should they be illegal? Are there limits to what one person may pay another to do? The New Jersey Supreme Court, the first to rule on the issue, declared the contract illegal and void. The court nonetheless awarded Melissa to the Sterns, saying that it was in the child's best interest to live with them. Inevitably, legislators disagree about this emotional issue. Some states have passed statutes permitting surrogacy, while others prohibit it.

At times, we even enter contracts without knowing it. Suppose you try to book a flight using your frequent-flyer miles, but the airline tells you the terms of the frequent-flyer program have changed and you must earn more mileage. According to the Supreme Court, you may well have an enforceable agreement based on the terms the airline quoted when you earned the miles.[1]

9-1d Contracts Defined

Contract

A legally enforceable agreement.

We have seen that a **contract** is a promise that the law will enforce. As we look more closely at the elements of contract law, we will encounter some intricate issues. This is partly because we live in a complex society, which conducts its business in a wide variety of ways. Remember, though, that we are usually interested in answering three basic questions, all relating to promises:

- Is it certain that the defendant promised to do something?

- If she did promise, is it fair to make her honor her word?

- If she did not promise, are there unusual reasons to hold her liable anyway?

---

[1]*American Airlines, Inc. v. Wolens*, 513 U.S. 219, 115 S. Ct. 817, 1995 U.S. LEXIS 690 (1995).

9-1e Development of Contract Law

Courts have not always assumed that promises are legally significant. In the twelfth and thirteenth centuries, promises were not binding unless a person made them *in writing and affixed a seal* to the document. This was seldom done, and therefore most promises were unenforceable.

The common law changed very slowly, but by the fifteenth century, courts began to allow some suits based on a broken promise. There were still major limitations. Suppose a merchant hired a carpenter to build a new shop, and the carpenter failed to start the job on time. Now courts would permit the suit, but only if the merchant had paid some money to the carpenter. If the merchant made a 10 percent down payment, the contract would be enforceable. But if the merchant merely *promised* to pay when the building was done, and the carpenter never began work, the merchant could recover nothing.

In 1602, English courts began to enforce mutual *promises;* that is, deals in which neither party gave anything to the other but both promised to do something in the future. Thus, if a farmer promised to deliver a certain quantity of wheat to a merchant and the merchant agreed on the price, both parties were now bound by their promise, even though there had been no down payment. This was a huge step forward in the development of contract law, but many issues remained. Consider the following employment case from 1792, which raises issues of public policy that still challenge courts today.

Davis v. Mason

Court of King's Bench
Michaelmas Term, 33d George III , p. 118 (1792)

Case Summary

Facts: Mason was a surgeon/apothecary in the English town of Thetford. Davis wished to apprentice himself to Mason. The two agreed that Davis would work for Mason and learn his profession. They further agreed that if Davis left Mason's practice, he would not set up a competing establishment within 10 miles of Thetford at any time within 14 years. Davis promised to pay £200 if he violated the agreement not to compete.

Davis began working for Mason in July 1789. In August 1791, Mason dismissed Davis, claiming misconduct, though Davis denied it. Davis then established his own practice within 10 miles of Thetford. Mason sued for the £200.

Davis admitted promising to pay the money. But he claimed that the agreement should be declared illegal and unenforceable. He argued that 14 years was unreasonably long to restrict him from the town of Thetford, and that 10 miles was too great a distance. (Ten miles in those days might take the better part of a day to travel.) He added an additional policy argument, saying that it was harmful to the public health to restrict a doctor from practicing his profession: If the people needed his service, they should have it. Finally, he said that his "consideration" was too great for this deal. In other words, it was unfair that he should pay £200, because he did not receive anything of that value from Mason.

Issue: *Was the contract too unreasonable to enforce?*

Decision: No. The parties made a reasonable agreement. Judgment for the plaintiff.

Reasoning: Both Mason and Davis made promises, and each expected to benefit from the agreement. Davis stood to learn a trade, and Mason secured protection from competition in the future. Davis alleges that the contract was unreasonable, but how long is too long? How far is too far? This line is difficult to draw, and I will not even try. The people of Thetford will suffer no harm because other doctors have the right to practice medicine there without restriction.

Davis must pay the £200.

Noncompetition agreement

A contract in which one party agrees not to compete with another.

The contract between Davis and Mason is called a **noncompetition agreement**. Today they are more common than ever, and frequently litigated. The policy issues that Davis raised have never gone away. You may well be asked to sign a noncompetition agreement sometime in your professional life. We look at the issue in detail in Chapter 11, on consideration. That outcome was typical of contract cases for the next 100 years. Courts took a *laissez-faire* approach, declaring that parties had *freedom to contract* and would have to live with the consequences. Lord Kenyon saw Davis and Mason as equals, entering a bargain that made basic sense, and he had no intention of rewriting it. After 500 years of evolution, courts had come to regard promises as almost sacred. The law had gone from ignoring most promises to enforcing nearly all.

By the early twentieth century, bargaining power in business deals had changed dramatically. Farms and small businesses were yielding place to huge corporations in a trend that accelerated throughout the century. In the twenty-first century, multinational corporations span many continents, wielding larger budgets and more power than many of the nations in which they do business. When such a corporation contracts with a small company or an individual consumer, the latter may have little or no leverage. Courts increasingly looked at the basic fairness of contracts. Noncompetition agreements are no longer automatically enforced. Courts may alter them or ignore them entirely because the parties have such unequal power and because the public may have an interest in letting the employee go on to compete. Davis's argument—that the public is entitled to as many doctors as it needs—is frequently more successful in court today than it was in the days of Lord Kenyon.

Legislatures and the courts limit the effect of promises in other ways. Suppose you purchase a lawn mower with an attached tag, warning you that the manufacturer is not responsible in the event of any malfunction or injury. You are required to sign a form acknowledging that the manufacturer has no liability of any kind. That agreement is clear enough—but a court will not enforce it. The law holds that the manufacturer *has* warranted the product to be good for normal purposes, regardless of any language included in the sales agreement. If the blade flies off and injures a child, the manufacturer is liable. This is socially responsible, even though it interferes with a private agreement.

The law has not come full circle back to the early days of the common law. Courts still enforce the great majority of contracts. But the possibility that a court will ignore an agreement means that any contract is a little less certain than it would have been a century ago.

9-2 TYPES OF CONTRACTS

Before undertaking a study of contracts, you need to familiarize yourself with some important vocabulary. This section will present five sets of terms.

9-2a Bilateral and Unilateral Contracts

Bilateral contract

A promise made in exchange for another promise.

In a **bilateral contract**, both parties make a promise. A producer says to Gloria, "I'll pay you $2 million to star in my new romantic comedy, which we are shooting three months from now in Santa Fe." Gloria says, "It's a deal." That is a bilateral contract. Each party has made a promise to do something. The producer is now bound to pay Gloria $2 million, and Gloria is obligated to show up on time and act in the movie. The vast majority of contracts are bilateral contracts. They can be for services, such as this acting contract; they can be for the sale of goods, such as 1,000 tons of steel, or for almost any other purpose. When the bargain is a promise for a promise, it is a bilateral agreement.

In a unilateral contract, one party makes a promise that the other party can accept only by *actually doing* something. These contracts are less common. Suppose the movie producer tacks a sign to a community bulletin board. It has a picture of a dog with a phone number, and it reads, "I'll pay $100 to anyone who returns my lost dog." If Leo sees the sign, finds the producer, and merely promises to find the dog, he has not created a contract. Because of the terms on the sign, Leo must actually find and return the dog to stake a claim to the $100.

9-2b Executory and Executed Contracts

A contract is **executory** when it has been made, but one or more parties has not yet fulfilled its obligations. Recall Gloria, who agrees to act in the producer's film beginning in three months. The moment Gloria and the producer strike their bargain, they have an executory bilateral express contract.

A contract is **executed** when all parties have fulfilled their obligations. When Gloria finishes acting in the movie and the producer pays her final fee, their contract will be fully executed.

Executory contract

An agreement in which one or more parties has not yet fulfilled its obligations.

Executed contract

An agreement in which all parties have fulfilled their obligations.

EXAM Strategy

Question: Abby has long coveted Nicola's designer handbag because she saw one of them in a movie. Finally, Nicola offers to sell her friend the bag for $350 in cash. "I don't have the money right now," Abby replies, "but I'll have it a week from Friday. Is it a deal?" Nicola agrees to sell the bag. Use two terms to describe the contract.

Strategy: In a bilateral contract, both parties make a promise, but in a unilateral agreement, only one side does so. An executory contract is one with unfulfilled obligations, while an executed agreement is one with nothing left to be done.

Result: Nicola promised to sell the bag for $350 cash, and Abby agreed to pay. Because both parties made a promise, this a bilateral agreement. The deal is not yet completed, meaning that they have an executory contract.

9-2c Valid, Unenforceable, Voidable, and Void Agreements

A **valid contract** is one that satisfies all of the law's requirements. It has no problems in any of the seven areas listed at the beginning of this chapter, and a court will enforce it. The contract between Gloria and the producer is a valid contract, and if the producer fails to pay Gloria, she will win a lawsuit to collect the unpaid fee.

An **unenforceable agreement** occurs when the parties intend to form a valid bargain, but a court declares that some rule of law prevents enforcing it. Suppose Gloria and the producer orally agree that she will star in his movie, which he will start filming in 18 months. The law, as we will see in Chapter 14, requires that this contract be in writing because it cannot be completed within one year. If the producer signs up another actress two months later, Gloria has no claim against him.

A **voidable contract** occurs when the law permits one party to terminate the agreement. This happens, for example, when an agreement has been signed under duress, or when the other party has committed fraud. Assume that in negotiations, the producer lies to Gloria about an important fact, which leads her to accept the contract. The producer tells her that Steven Spielberg has signed on to be the film's director. As we will learn in Chapter 13, this fraudulent agreement is voidable at Gloria's option. If Gloria later decides that another director is acceptable, she may choose to stay in the contract. But if she decides that she wants to cancel the agreement and sue, she can do that as well.

A **void agreement** is one that neither party can enforce, usually because the purpose of the deal is illegal or because one of the parties had no legal authority to make a contract.

The following case illustrates the difference between voidable and void agreements.

Valid contract

An agreement that satisfies all of the law's requirements and is enforceable in court.

Unenforceable agreement

An agreement that a court will not enforce.

Voidable contract

An agreement that may be terminated by one of the parties.

Void agreement

A contract that neither party can enforce, because the bargain is illegal or one of the parties had no legal authority to make it.

MR. W FIREWORKS, INC. V. OZUNA

2009 Tex. App. LEXIS 8237
Court of Appeals of Texas, Fourth District, San Antonio, 2009

CASE SUMMARY

Facts: Mr. W sold fireworks. Under Texas law, retailers could only sell fireworks to the public during the two weeks immediately before the Fourth of July and during the two weeks immediately before New Year's Day. And so, fireworks sellers like Mr. W tended to lease property.

Mr. W leased a portion of Ozuna's land. The lease contract contained two key terms:

"In the event the sale of fireworks on the aforementioned property is or shall become unlawful during the period of this lease and the term granted, this lease shall become void.

"Lessor(s) agree not to sell or lease any part of said property including any adjoining, adjacent, or contiguous property to any person(s) or corporation for the purpose of selling fireworks in competition to the Lessee during the term of this lease, *and for a period of ten years after lease is terminated*." [Emphasis added.]

A longstanding San Antonio city ordinance banned the sale of fireworks inside city limits, and also within 5,000 feet of city limits. Like all growing cities, San Antonio sometimes annexed new land, and its city limits changed. One annexation caused the Ozuna property to fall within 5,000 feet of the new city limit, and it became illegal to sell fireworks from the property. Mr. W stopped selling fireworks and paying rent on Ozuna's land.

Two years later, San Antonio's border shifted again. This time, the city *disannexed* some property and *shrank*.

The new city limits placed Ozuna's property just beyond the 5,000-foot no-fireworks zone. Ozuna then leased a part of his land to Alamo Fireworks, a competitor of Mr. W.

Then the real fireworks began. Mr. W sued for breach of contract, arguing that Ozuna had no right to lease to a competitor for a period of 10 years. The trial court granted Ozuna's motion for summary judgment. Mr. W appealed.

Issue: *Did Ozuna breach his contract with Mr. W by leasing his land to a competitor?*

Decision: No, the entire contract was void and therefore no provisions were enforceable.

Reasoning: Contracts that require an illegal act are void, which means that neither party can enforce any provision. It is as if the contract never existed. Thus, Ozuna argued that when the law made the sale of fireworks illegal, the lease became *void* and the entire agreement was unenforceable.

In contrast, Mr. W wanted to enforce the provision that prevented Ozuna from renting the land to competitors but not the one that required him to pay rent. Mr. W's could not have it both ways. He could not choose to keep the benefits of the contract while rejecting its obligations. When selling fireworks became illegal, the entire lease was extinguished, which released Ozuna from the noncompete restriction.

9-2d Express and Implied Contracts

Express contract
An agreement with all the important terms explicitly stated.

In an **express contract**, the two parties explicitly state all the important terms of their agreement. The vast majority of contracts are express contracts. The contract between the producer and Gloria is an express contract because the parties explicitly state what Gloria will do, where and when she will do it, and how much she will be paid. Some express contracts are oral, as that one was, and some are written. They might be bilateral express contracts, as Gloria's was, or unilateral express contracts, as Leo's was. Obviously, it is wise to make express contracts, and to put them in writing. We emphasize, however, that many oral contracts are fully enforceable.

Implied contract
A contract may be formed when words or conduct suggest that the parties intended a binding agreement.

In an **implied contract**, the words and conduct of the parties indicate that they intended an agreement. Suppose every Friday, for two months, the producer asks Lance to mow his lawn, and loyal Lance does so each weekend. Then, for three more weekends, Lance simply shows up without the producer asking, and the producer continues to pay for the work done. But on the 12th weekend, when Lance rings the doorbell to collect, the producer suddenly says, "I never asked you to mow it. Scram." The producer is correct that there was no express contract because the parties had not spoken for several weeks. But a court will probably rule that the conduct of the parties has *implied* a contract. Not only did Lance mow the lawn every weekend, but the producer even paid on three weekends when they had not spoken. It was reasonable for Lance to assume that he had a weekly deal to mow and be paid.

Today, the hottest disputes about implied contracts continue to arise in the employment setting. Many corporate employees have at-will relationships with their companies. This means that the employees are free to quit at any time and the company has the right to fire them, for virtually any reason. But often a company provides its workers with personnel manuals that lay out certain rights. Does a handbook create a contract guaranteeing those rights? What is your opinion?

You Be the Judge

DeMasse v. ITT Corporation

194 Ariz. 500, 984 P.2d 1138
Supreme Court of Arizona, 1999

Facts: Roger DeMasse and five others were employees-at-will at ITT Corporation, where they started working at various times between 1960 and 1979. Each was paid an hourly wage.

ITT issued an employee handbook, which it revised four times over two decades.

The first four editions of the handbook stated that within each job classification, any layoffs would be made in reverse order of seniority. The fifth handbook made two important changes. First, the document stated that "nothing contained herein shall be construed as a guarantee of continued employment. ITT does not guarantee continued employment to employees and retains the right to terminate or lay off employees."

Second, the handbook stated that "ITT reserves the right to amend, modify, or cancel this handbook, as well as any or all of the various policies [or rules] outlined in it." Four years later, ITT notified its hourly employees that layoff guidelines for hourly employees would be based not on seniority, but on ability and performance. About 10 days later, the six employees were laid off, though less-senior employees kept their jobs. The six employees sued.

You Be The Judge: *Did ITT have the right to unilaterally change the layoff policy?*

Argument for the workers: It is true that all of the plaintiffs were originally employees-at-will, subject to termination at the company's whim. However, things changed when the company issued the first handbook. ITT chose to include a promise that layoffs would be based on seniority. Long-term workers and new employees all understood the promise and relied on it. The company put it there to attract and retain good workers. The policy worked. Responsible employees understood that the longer they remained at ITT, the safer their job was. Company and employees worked together for many years with a common understanding, and that is a textbook definition of an implied contract.

Once a contract is formed, whether express or implied, it is binding on both sides. That is the whole point of a contract. If one side could simply change the terms of an agreement on its own, what value would any contract have? The company's legal argument is a perfect symbol of its arrogance: It believes that because these workers are mere hourly workers, they have no rights, even under contract law. The company is mistaken. Implied contracts are binding, and ITT should not make promises it does not intend to keep.

Argument for ITT: Once an at-will employee, always one. ITT had the right to fire any of its employees at any time—just as the workers had the right to quit whenever they wished. That never changed, and in case any workers forgot it, the company reiterated the point in its most recent handbook. If the plaintiffs thought layoffs would happen in any particular order, that is their error, not ours.

All workers were bound by the terms of whichever handbook was then in place. For many years, the company had made a seniority-layoff promise. Had we fired a senior worker during that period, he or she would have had a legitimate complaint—and that is why we did not do it. Instead, we gave everyone four years' notice that things would change. Any workers unhappy with the new policies should have left to find more congenial work.

Why should an employee be allowed to say, "I prefer to rely on the old, outdated handbooks, not the new one"? The plaintiffs' position would mean that no company is ever free to change its general work policies and rules. Since when does an at-will employee have the right to dictate company policy? That would be disastrous for the whole economy—but fortunately it is not the law.

9-2e Promissory Estoppel and Quasi-Contracts

Now we turn away from "true" contracts and consider two unusual circumstances. Sometimes, courts will enforce agreements even if they fail to meet the usual requirement of a contract. We emphasize that these remedies are uncommon exceptions to the general rules. Most of the agreements that courts enforce are the express contracts that we have already studied. Nonetheless, the next two remedies are still pivotal in some lawsuits. In each case, a sympathetic plaintiff can demonstrate an injury but *there is no contract.* The plaintiff cannot claim that the defendant breached a contract, because none ever existed. The plaintiff must hope for more "creative" relief.

The two remedies can be confusingly similar. The best way to distinguish them is the following:

- In promissory estoppel cases, the defendant made a promise that the plaintiff relied on.

- In quasi-contract cases, the defendant received a *benefit* from the plaintiff.

PROMISSORY ESTOPPEL

A fierce fire swept through Dana and Derek Andreason's house in Utah, seriously damaging it. The good news was that agents for Aetna Casualty promptly visited the Andreasons and helped them through the crisis. The agents reassured the couple that all of the damage was covered by their insurance, instructed them on which things to throw out and replace, and helped them choose materials for repairing other items. The bad news was that the agents were wrong: The Andreasons' policy had expired six weeks before the fire. When Derek Andreason presented a bill for $41,957 worth of meticulously itemized work that he had done under the agents' supervision, Aetna refused to pay.

The Andreasons sued—but not for breach of contract. There *was* no contract—they allowed their policy to expire. They sued Aetna under the legal theory of promissory estoppel: Even when there is no contract, a plaintiff may use **promissory estoppel** to enforce the defendant's promise if he can show that:

Promissory estoppel

A *possible* remedy for an injured plaintiff in a case with no valid contract, where the plaintiff can show a promise, reasonable reliance, and injustice.

- The defendant made a promise knowing that the plaintiff would likely rely on it;

- The plaintiff did rely on the promise; and

- The only way to avoid injustice is to enforce the promise.

Aetna made a promise to the Andreasons—namely, its assurance that all of the damage was covered by insurance. The company knew that the Andreasons would rely on that promise, which they did by ripping up a floor that might have been salvaged, throwing out some furniture, and buying materials to repair the house.

> **Is enforcing the promise the only way to avoid injustice?**

out some furniture, and buying materials to repair the house. Is enforcing the promise the only way to avoid injustice? Yes, ruled the Utah Court of Appeals.[2] The Andreasons' conduct was reasonable and based entirely on what the Aetna agents told them. Under promissory estoppel, the Andreasons received virtually the same amount they would have obtained had the insurance contract been valid.

There was plenty of romance in the following case. Was there an enforceable promise?

---

[2]*Andreason v. Aetna Casualty & Surety Co.*, 848 P.2d 171, 1993 Utah App. LEXIS 26 (Utah App. 1993).

NORTON V. HOYT

278 F.Supp.2d 214
United States District Court for the District of Rhode Island, 2003

CASE SUMMARY

Facts: Gail Norton sued Russell Hoyt, and this is what she alleged. The two met when Norton, who was single, worked as an elementary school teacher. Hoyt told her he was also single, and they began an affair. She later learned that he was married, but he assured her he was getting a divorce, and they continued their relationship.

Six years later, Hoyt, who was rich, convinced Norton to quit her job so that they could travel together. The couple lived lavishly, spending time in Newport, Rhode Island, where Hoyt was part of the yachting crowd, in London, the Bahamas, and other agreeable places. Hoyt rented Norton an apartment, bought her cars, and repeated his promises to divorce his wife and marry his lover. He never did either.

After 23 years, Hoyt ended the relationship. Norton became ill and saw various doctors for anxiety, depression, headaches, stomach maladies, and weight loss. During one joint therapy session, Hoyt told Norton and the psychiatrist that he would continue to support her with $80,000 a year. But he did not.

Norton sued, claiming promissory estoppel. Hoyt moved for summary judgment. In ruling on the motion, the court assumed that Norton's allegations were true.

Issue: *Was Norton entitled to support, based on promissory estoppel?*

Decision: No. Norton failed to establish promissory estoppel.

Reasoning: Norton did not establish a clear, unambiguous promise. She claimed that Hoyt promised to take care of her for life. But what does "take care of for life" mean? It could refer to emotional closeness, social pleasures, or financial support.

Even assuming, for the sake of argument, that there was a clear, unconditional promise, Norton's reliance was unreasonable. It is true that the couple discussed wedding plans, but Norton knew that Hoyt was married and that he spent time with his wife and children. She and Hoyt never presented themselves as husband and wife. Friends and family knew of their complicated living arrangement. Further, Norton knew that Hoyt had lied to her about his marital status, had never fulfilled his promise of marriage, and was committing adultery by spending time with her. At some point between year 1 of their affair and year 23, she should have grasped that reliance on Hoyt's promises was badly misplaced. Her conduct was unreasonable, and she cannot establish promissory estoppel.

Hoyt's motion for summary judgment is granted.

Devil's Advocate

Why should one person be able to make repeated promises over two decades and escape all responsibility? Even if Hoyt's precise words varied, each of his promises involved long-term emotional and financial security for Norton. Norton was naïve, but Hoyt was dishonest. The law should be a tool for teaching people like him a lesson.

Why have we chosen to illustrate an important point of law—promissory estoppel—with a case that fails? Because that is the typical outcome. Plaintiffs allege promissory estoppel very frequently, but seldom succeed. They do occasionally win, as the Andreasons demonstrated earlier, but courts are skeptical of these claims. The lesson is clear: Before you rely on a promise, negotiate a binding contract.

QUASI-CONTRACT

Don Easterwood leased over 5,000 acres of farmland in Jackson County, Texas, from PIC Realty for one year. The next year, he obtained a second one-year lease. During each year, Easterwood farmed the land, harvested the crops, and prepared the land for the following year's planting. Toward the end of the second lease, after Easterwood had harvested his crop, he and PIC began discussing the terms of another lease. While they negotiated, Easterwood prepared the land for the following year, cutting and plowing the soil. But the negotiations for a new lease failed, and Easterwood moved off the land. He sued PIC Realty for the value of his work preparing the soil.

Easterwood had neither an express nor an implied contract for the value of his work. How could he make any legal claim? By relying on the legal theory of a quasi-contract: Even when there is no contract, a court may use **quasi-contract** to compensate a plaintiff who can show that:

- The plaintiff gave some benefit to the defendant;

- The plaintiff reasonably expected to be paid for the benefit and the defendant knew this; and

- The defendant would be unjustly enriched if he did not pay.

Quasi-contract

A *possible* remedy for an injured plaintiff in a case with no valid contract, where the plaintiff can show benefit to the defendant, reasonable expectation of payment, and unjust enrichment.

If a court finds all of these elements present, it will generally award the value of the goods or services that the plaintiff has conferred. The damages awarded are called *quantum meruit*, meaning that the plaintiff gets "as much as he deserves." The court is awarding money that it believes the plaintiff *morally ought to have*, even though there was no valid contract entitling her to it. This again is judicial activism, with the courts inventing a "quasi" contract where no true contract exists. The purpose is justice, the term is contradictory.

Quantum meruit

"As much as he deserves"—the damages awarded in a quasi-contract case.

Don Easterwood testified that in Jackson County, it was quite common for a tenant farmer to prepare the soil for the following year but then be unable to farm the land. In those cases, he claimed, the landowner compensated the farmer for the work done. Other witnesses agreed that this was the local custom. The court ruled that indeed there was no contract, but that all elements of quasi-contract had been satisfied. Easterwood gave a benefit to PIC because the land was ready for planting. Jackson County custom caused Easterwood to assume he would be paid, and PIC Realty knew it. Finally, said the court, it would be unjust to let PIC benefit without paying anything. The court ordered PIC to pay the fair market value of Easterwood's labors.

FOUR THEORIES OF RECOVERY

Theory	Did the Defendant Make a Promise?	Is There a Contract?	Description
Express Contract	Yes	Yes	The parties intend to contract and agree on explicit terms.
Implied Contract	Not explicitly	Yes	The parties do not formally agree, but their words and conduct indicate an intention to create a contract.
Promissory Estoppel	Yes	No	There is no contract, but the defendant makes a promise that she can foresee will induce reliance; the plaintiff relies on it; and it would be unjust not to enforce the promise.
Quasi-Contract	No	No	There is no intention to contract, but the plaintiff gives some benefit to the defendant, who knows that the plaintiff expects compensation; it would be unjust not to award the plaintiff damages.

© Cengage Learning

EXAM Strategy

Question: The table above lists the different theories a plaintiff may use to recover damages in a contract dispute. In the following examples, which one will each plaintiff use in trying to win the case?

1. Company pays all employees 10 percent commission on new business they develop. Company compensates each employee when the new customer pays its first bill. After Leandro obtains three new clients, Company fires him. When the new customers pay their bill, Company refuses to pay Leandro a commission because he is no longer an employee. Leandro sues.

2. Burt agrees in writing to sell Red 100 lobsters for $15 each, payable by credit card, in exactly 30 days. When the lobsters fail to arrive, Red sues.

3. Company handbook, given to all new hires, states that no employee will be fired without a hearing and an appeal. Company fires Delores without a hearing or appeal. She sues.

Strategy: In (1), the Company never promised to pay a commission to nonemployees, so there is no contract. However, the Company *benefited* from Leandro's work. In (2), the parties have *clearly stated all terms* to a simple sales agreement. In (3), the Company and Delores never negotiated termination, but *the handbook suggests* that all employees have certain rights.

Result: (1) is a case of quasi-contract because the company benefited and should reasonably expect to pay. (2) is an express contract because all terms are clearly stated. (3) is an implied contract, similar to the *DeMasse* case, based on the handbook.

9-3 SOURCES OF CONTRACT LAW

9-3a Common Law

We have seen the evolution of contract law from the twelfth century to the present. Express and implied contracts, promissory estoppel, and quasi-contract were all crafted, over centuries, by courts deciding one contract lawsuit at a time. Many contract lawsuits continue to be decided using common law principles developed by courts.

9-3b Uniform Commercial Code

Business methods changed quickly during the first half of the last century. Transportation sped up. Corporations routinely conducted business across state borders and around the world. These developments presented a problem. Common law principles, whether related to contracts, torts, or anything else, sometimes vary from one state to another. New York and California courts often reach similar conclusions when presented with similar cases, but they are under no obligation to do so. Business leaders became frustrated that, to do business across the country, their companies had to deal with many different sets of common law rules.

Executives, lawyers, and judges wanted a body of law for business transactions that reflected modern commercial methods and provided uniformity throughout the United States. It would be much easier, they thought, if some parts of contract law were the same in every state. That desire gave birth to the Uniform Commercial Code (UCC), created in 1952. The drafters intended the UCC to facilitate the easy formation and enforcement of contracts in a fast-paced world. The Code governs many aspects of commerce, including the sale and leasing of goods, negotiable instruments, bank deposits, letters of credit, investment securities, secured transactions, and other commercial matters. Every state has adopted at least part of the UCC to govern commercial transactions within that state. For our purposes in studying contracts, the most important part of the Code is Article 2, which governs the sale of goods. **"Goods" means anything movable, except for money, securities, and certain legal rights.** Goods include pencils, commercial aircraft, books, and Christmas trees. Goods do not include land or a house because neither is movable, nor do they include a stock certificate. A contract for the sale of 10,000 sneakers is governed by the UCC; a contract for the sale of a condominium in Marina del Rey is governed by the California common law.

When analyzing any contract problem as a student or businessperson, you must note whether the agreement concerns the sale of goods. For many issues, the common law and the UCC are reasonably similar. But sometimes, the law is quite different under the two sets of rules.

And so, the UCC governs contracts for a sale of goods, while common law principles govern contracts for sales of services and everything else. Most of the time, it will be clear whether the UCC or the common law applies. But what if a contract involves both goods and services? When you get your oil changed, you are paying in part for the new oil and oil filter (goods) and in part for the labor required to do the job (services). In a mixed contract, Article 2 governs only if the *primary purpose* was the sale of goods. In the following case, the court had to decide the primary purpose.

FALLSVIEW GLATT KOSHER CATERERS, INC. V. ROSENFELD

2005 WL 53623
Civil Court, City of New York, 2005

CASE SUMMARY

Facts: During the Jewish holidays, Fallsview Glatt Kosher Caterers organized programs at Kutcher's Country Club, where it provided all accommodations, food, and entertainment.

Fallsview sued Willie Rosenfeld, alleging that he had requested accommodations for 15 members of his family, agreeing to pay $24,050, and then failed to appear or pay.

Rosenfeld moved to dismiss, claiming that even if there had been an agreement, it was never put in writing. Under UCC Section 2-201, any contract for the sale of goods worth $500 or more can be enforced only if it is in writing and signed. Fallsview argued that the agreement was not for the sale of goods, but for services. The company claimed that because the contract was not governed by the UCC, it should be enforced even with no writing.

Issue: *Was the agreement one for the sale of goods, requiring a writing, or for services, enforceable with no writing?*

Decision: The agreement was for services. The defendant's motion to dismiss is denied.

Reasoning: Rosenfeld contends that the predominant purpose of the contract was the service of Kosher food. He urges that the hotel accommodations and entertainment were merely incidental benefits. This conclusion is compelled, he suggests, by the very nature of the Passover holiday. The essential religious obligation during this eight-day period is to eat only food that is "Kosher for Passover." It is the desire to obtain acceptable nourishment that causes customers to participate in such programs.

Fallsview countered by offering the court a schedule of activities available during the Passover program. These included tennis, racquetball, swimming, Swedish massage, "make over face lift show," "trivia time," aerobics, bingo, ice skating, dancing, "showtime," "power walk," arts and crafts, day camp, ping-pong, Yiddish theater, board games, horse racing, horseback riding, wine tasting, and indoor bocce. The activities were provided, along with accommodation and food, for an all-inclusive price. It is apparent that the activities and accommodations were a major part of the program, and that services were a more important aspect of the agreement than were goods.

Fallsview also argues that if, as Rosenfeld claims, hotel reservations are for the sale of goods, then all such contracts made via telephone or the Internet would be unenforceable, leaving the hospitality industry in an impossible situation. That may or may not be true, but it does indicate how important it is not to carelessly apply a statutory provision to contracts beyond its scope. UCC Section 2-201 was never meant to cover an agreement involving such a full slate of accommodations and activities.

EXAM Strategy

Question: Leila agrees to pay Kendrick $35,000 to repair windmills. Confident of this cash, Kendrick contracts to buy Derrick's used Porsche for $33,000. Then Leila informs Kendrick she does not need his help and will not pay him. Kendrick tells Derrick that he no longer wants the Porsche. Derrick sues Kendrick, and Kendrick files suit against Leila. What law or laws govern these lawsuits?

Strategy: Always be conscious of whether a contract is for services or the sale of goods. Different laws govern. To make that distinction, you must understand the term "goods." If you are clear about that, the question is answered easily.

Result: *Goods* means anything movable, and a Porsche is movable—one might say "super-movable." The UCC will control Derrick's suit. Repairing windmills is primarily a service. Kendrick's lawsuit is governed by the common law of contracts.

Chapter Conclusion

Contracts govern countless areas of our lives, from intimate family issues to multibillion-dollar corporate deals. Understanding contract principles is essential for a successful business or professional career and is invaluable in private life. This knowledge is especially important because courts no longer rubber-stamp any agreement that two parties have made. If we know the issues that courts scrutinize, the agreement we draft is likelier to be enforced. We thus achieve greater control over our affairs—the very purpose of a contract.

EXAM REVIEW

1. **CONTRACTS: DEFINITION AND ELEMENTS**   A contract is a legally enforceable promise. Analyzing whether a contract exists involves inquiring into these issues: offer, acceptance, consideration, capacity, legal purpose, consent, and sometimes, whether the deal is in writing. (pp. 215–216)

2. **DEVELOPMENT**   The development of contract law stretches into the distant past. Before the fifteenth century, courts rarely enforced promises at all. By the 1600s, courts enforced many mutual promises, and by 1900, most promises containing the seven elements of a contract were strictly enforced. (pp. 217–218)

3. **UNILATERAL AND BILATERAL CONTRACTS**   In bilateral contracts, the parties exchange promises. In a unilateral contract, only one party makes a promise, and the other must take some action—his return promise is insufficient to form a contract. (pp. 218 –219)

4. **EXECUTORY AND EXECUTED CONTRACTS**   In an executory contract, one or both of the parties have not yet have not done everything that they promised to do. In an executed contract, all parties have fully performed. (p. 219)

5. **ENFORCEABILITY**

   • Valid contracts are fully enforceable.

   • An unenforceable agreement is one with a legal defect.

   • A voidable contract occurs when one party has an option to cancel the agreement.

   • A void agreement means that the law will ignore the deal regardless of what the parties want. (pp. 219–220)

EXAM Strategy

Question: Yasmine is negotiating to buy Stewart's house. She asks him what condition the roof is in.

"Excellent," he replies. "It is only 2 years old, and should last 25 more." In fact, Stewart knows that the roof is 26 years old and has had a series of leaks. The parties sign a sales contract for $600,000. A week before Yasmine is to pay for the house and take possession, she discovers the leaks and learns that the mandatory new roof will cost $35,000. At the same time, she learns that the house has increased in value by $60,000 since she signed the agreement. What options does Yasmine have?

Strategy: You know intuitively that Stewart's conduct is as shabby as his roof. What is the legal term for his deception? Fraud. Does fraud make an agreement void or voidable? Does it matter? (See the "Result" at the end of this section.)

---

6. **EXPRESS AND IMPLIED CONTRACTS**   If the parties formally agreed and stated explicit terms, there is probably an express contract. If the parties did not formally agree but their conduct, words, or past dealings indicate they intended a binding agreement, there may be an implied contract. (pp. 220–221)

7. **OTHER REMEDIES**   If there is no contract, are there other reasons to give the plaintiff damages?

   • A claim of promissory estoppel requires that the defendant made a promise knowing that the plaintiff would likely *rely*, and the plaintiff did so. It would be wrong to deny recovery.

   • A claim of quasi-contract requires that the defendant received a benefit, knowing that the plaintiff would expect compensation, and it would be unjust not to grant it. (pp. 222–224)

EXAM Strategy

Question: The Hoffmans owned and operated a successful small bakery and grocery store. They spoke with Lukowitz, an agent of Red Owl Stores, who told them that for $18,000, Red Owl would build a store and fully stock it for them. The Hoffmans sold their bakery and grocery store and purchased a lot on which Red Owl was to build the store. Lukowitz then told Hoffman that the price had gone up to $26,000. The Hoffmans borrowed the extra money from relatives, but then Lukowitz informed them that the cost would be $34,000. Negotiations broke off, and the Hoffmans sued. The court determined that there was no contract because too many details had not been worked out—the size of the store, its design, and the cost of constructing it. Can the Hoffmans recover any money?

Strategy: Because there is no contract, the Hoffmans must rely on either promissory estoppel or quasi-contract. Promissory estoppel focuses on the defendant's promise and the plaintiff's reliance. Those suing in quasi-contract must show that the defendant received a benefit for which it should reasonably expect to pay. Does either fit here? (See the "Result" at the end of this section.)

8. **SOURCES OF CONTRACT LAW**   If a contract is for the sale of goods, the UCC is the relevant body of law. For anything else, the common law governs. If a contract involves both goods and services, a court will determine the agreement's primary purpose. (pp. 225–227)

EXAM Strategy

Question: Honeywell, Inc. and Minolta Camera Co. had a contract providing that Honeywell would give to Minolta various technical information on the design of a specialized camera lens. Minolta would have the right to use the information in its cameras, provided that Minolta also used certain Honeywell parts in its cameras. Honeywell delivered to Minolta numerous technical documents, computer software, and test equipment, and Honeywell engineers met with Minolta engineers at least 20 times to discuss the equipment. Several years later, Honeywell sued, claiming that Minolta had taken the design information but failed to use Honeywell parts in its cameras. Minolta moved to dismiss, claiming that the UCC required lawsuits concerning the sale of goods to be filed within four years of the breach and that this lawsuit was too late. Honeywell answered that the UCC did not apply, and that therefore, Minnesota's six-year statute of limitations governed. Who is right?

Strategy: Like many contracts, this one involves both goods, which are governed by the UCC, and services, controlled by the common law. We decide which of those two laws governs by using the predominant purpose test. Was this contract primarily about selling goods or about providing services? (See the "Result" at the end of this section.)

5. Result: Indeed, it does matter. Stewart's fraud makes the contract voidable by Yasmine. She has the right to terminate the agreement and pay nothing. However, she may go through with the contract if she prefers. The choice is hers—but not Stewart's.

7. Result: Red Owl received no benefit from the Hoffmans' sale of their store or purchase of the lot. However, Red Owl did make a promise and expected the Hoffmans to rely on it, which they did. The Hoffmans won their claim of promissory estoppel.

8. Result: The primary purpose of this agreement was not the sale of goods, but rather the exchange of technical data, ideas, designs, and so forth. The common law governs the contract, and Honeywell's suit may go forward.

MULTIPLE-CHOICE QUESTIONS

1. A sitcom actor, exhausted after his 10-hour workweek, agrees to buy a briefcase full of cocaine from Lewis for $12,000. Lewis and the actor have a _____ contract.

(a) valid

(b) unenforceable

(c) voidable

(d) void

2. Carol says, "Pam, you're my best friend in the world. I just inherited a million bucks, and I want you to have some of it. Come with me to the bank tomorrow, and I'll give you $10,000." "Sweet!" Pam replies. Later that day, Carol has a change of heart. She is allowed to do so. Examine the list of the elements of a contract, and cite the correct reason.

(a) The agreement was not put into writing.

(b) The agreement lacks a legal purpose.

(c) Pam did not give consideration.

(d) Pam does not have the capacity to make a contract.

3. On the first day of the baseball season, Dean orders a new Cardinals hat from Amazon.com. At the moment he submits his order, Dean and Amazon have an _____ contract. Two days later, Amazon delivers the hat to Dean's house. At this point, Dean and Amazon have an _____ contract.

(a) executory; executory

(b) executory; executed

(c) executed; executory

(d) executed; executed

4. Linda goes to an electronics store and buys a high-definition TV. Lauren hires a company to clean her swimming pool once a week. The _____ governs Linda's contract with the store, and the _____ governs Lauren's contract with the cleaning company.

    (a) common law; common law

    (b) common law; UCC

    (c) UCC; common law

    (d) UCC; UCC

5. Consider the following scenarios:

    I. Madison says to a group of students, "I'll pay $35 to the first one of you who shows up at my house and mows my lawn."

    II. Lea posts a flyer around town that reads, "Reward: $500 for information about the person who keyed my truck last Saturday night in the Wag-a-Bag parking lot. Call Lea at 555-5309."

Which of these proposes a *unilateral* contract?

    (a) I only

    (b) II only

    (c) Both I and II

    (d) None of the above

ESSAY QUESTIONS

1. Pennsylvania contracted with Envirotest Systems, Inc., an Arizona company, to build 86 automobile emissions inspection stations in 25 counties and operate them for seven years. This contract is worth hundreds of millions of dollars to Envirotest. But Pennsylvania legislators suddenly opposed the entire system, claiming that it would lead to long delays and high expenses for motorists. These lawmakers urged that Pennsylvania simply stop construction of the new system. Was Pennsylvania allowed to get out of the contract because its legislators concluded the whole system is unwise?

2. Central Maine Power Co. made a promotional offer in which it promised to pay a substantial sum to any homeowner or builder who constructed new housing heated with electricity. Motel Services, Inc., which was building a small housing project for the city of Waterville, Maine, decided to install electrical heat in the units in order to qualify for the offer. It built the units and requested payment for the full amount of the promotional offer. Is Central Maine obligated to pay? Why or why not?

3. Interactive Data Corp. hired Daniel Foley as an assistant product manager at a starting salary of $18,500. Over the next six years, Interactive steadily promoted Foley until he became Los Angeles branch manager at a salary of $56,116. Interactive's officers repeatedly told Foley that he would have his job as long as his performance was adequate. In addition, Interactive distributed an employee handbook that specified "termination guidelines," including a mandatory seven-step pre-termination procedure. Two years later, Foley learned that his recently hired supervisor, Robert Kuhne, was under investigation by the FBI for embezzlement at his previous job. Foley reported this to Interactive officers. Shortly thereafter, Interactive fired Foley. He sued, claiming that Interactive could fire him only for good cause, after the seven-step procedure. What kind of a claim is he making? Should he succeed?

4. **ETHICS** You want to lease your automobile to a friend for the summer but do not want to pay a lawyer to draw up the lease. Joanna, a neighbor, is in law school. She is not licensed to practice law. She offers to draft a lease for you for $100, and you unwisely accept. Later, you refuse to pay her fee, and she sues to collect. Who will win the lawsuit, and why? Apart from the law, was it morally right for the law student to try to help you by drafting the lease? Was she acting helpfully, or foolishly, or fraudulently? Is it just for you to agree to her fee and then refuse to pay it? What is society's interest in this dispute? Should a court be more concerned with the ethical issue raised by the conduct of the two parties or with the social consequences of this agreement?

5. **YOU BE THE JUDGE WRITING PROBLEM** John Stevens owned a dilapidated apartment that he rented to James and Cora Chesney for a low rent. The Chesneys began to remodel and rehabilitate the unit. Over a four-year period, they installed two new bathrooms, carpeted the floors, installed new septic and heating systems, and rewired, replumbed, and painted. Stevens periodically stopped by and saw the work in progress. The Chesneys transformed the unit into a respectable apartment. Three years after their work was done, Stevens served the Chesneys with an eviction notice. The Chesneys counterclaimed, seeking the value of the work they had done. Are they entitled to it? **Argument for Stevens:** Mr. Stevens is willing to pay the Chesneys exactly the amount he agreed to pay: nothing. The parties never contracted for the Chesneys to fix up the apartment. In fact, they never even discussed such an agreement. The Chesneys are making the absurd argument that anyone who chooses to perform certain work, without ever discussing it with another party, can finish the job and then charge it to the other person. If the Chesneys expected to get paid, obviously they should have said so. If the court were to allow this claim, it would be inviting other tenants to make improvements and then bill the landlord. The law has never been so foolish. **Argument for the Chesneys:** The law of quasi-contract was crafted for cases exactly like this. The Chesneys have given an enormous benefit to Stevens by transforming the apartment and enabling him to rent it at greater profit for many years to come. Stevens saw the work being done and understood that the Chesneys expected some compensation for these major renovations. If Stevens never intended to pay the fair value of the work, he should have stopped the couple from doing the work or notified them that there would be no compensation. It would be unjust to allow the landlord to seize the value of the work, evict the tenants who did it, and pay nothing.

DISCUSSION QUESTIONS

1. Have you ever made an agreement that mattered to you, only to have the other person refuse to follow through on the deal? Looking at the list of elements in the chapter, did your agreement amount to a contract? If not, which element did it lack?

2. Consider promissory estoppel and quasi-contracts. Do you like the fact that these doctrines exist? Should courts have "wiggle room" to enforce deals that fail to meet formal contract requirements? Or, should the rule be "If it's not an actual contract, too bad. No deal."

3. Is it sensible to have two different sets of contract rules—one for sales of goods and another for everything else? Would it be better to have a single set of rules for all contracts?

4. In the case *Davis v. Mason*, a court considered an early non-compete agreement. Did the court in that case reach a proper conclusion? What should courts say in similar cases in modern times?

5. Return to the opening scenario. Chris made a valid agreement with Chez Luc, which is enforceable in court. Does the thought of a restaurant suing a patron for using his phone seem odd? Why? If the restaurant does not plan to take the patrons to court, why bother to have a contract at all?

CHAPTER 10

AGREEMENT

Interior. A glitzy café, New York. Evening. Bob, a famous director, and Katrina, a glamorous actress, sit at a table, near a wall of glass looking onto a New York sidewalk that is filled with life and motion. Bob sips a margarita while carefully eyeing Katrina. Katrina stares at her wine glass.

BOB *(smiling confidently)*: *Body Work* is going to be huge—for the right actress. I know a film that's gonna gross a hundred million when I'm holding one. I'm holding one.

KATRINA *(perking up at the mention of money)*: It is quirky. It's fun. And she's very strong, very real.

BOB: She's you. That's why we're sitting here. We start shooting in seven months.

KATRINA *(edging away from the table)*: I have a few questions. That nude scene.

BOB: The one on the toboggan run?

KATRINA: *That* one was O.K. But the one in the poultry factory—very explicit. I don't work nude.

BOB: It's not really nude. Think of all those feathers fluttering around.

KATRINA: It's nude.

nuttakit/Shutterstock.com; neelsky/Shutterstock.com

> I should talk with my agent. I'd need something in writing about the nude scene …

BOB: We'll work it out. This is a romantic comedy, not tawdry exploitation. Katrina, we're talking $2.5 million. A little accommodation, please. We'll give you $600,000 up front, and the rest deferred, the usual percentages.

KATRINA: Bob, my fee is $3 million. As you know. That hasn't changed.

Katrina picks up her drink, doesn't sip it, places it on the coaster, using both hands to center it perfectly. He waits, as she stares silently at her glass.

BOB: We're shooting in Santa Fe, the weather will be perfect. You have a suite at the Excelsior, plus a trailer on location.

KATRINA: I should talk with my agent. I'd need something in writing about the nude scene, the fee, percentages—all the business stuff. I never sign without talking to her.

Bob shrugs and sits back.

KATRINA *(made anxious by the silence)*: I love the character, I really do.

BOB: You and several others love her. *(That jolts her.)* Agents can wait. I have to put this together fast. We can get you the details you want in writing. *Body Work* is going to be bigger than *Sex in the City*.

That one hooks her. She looks at Bob. He nods reassuringly. Bob sticks out his hand, smiling. Katrina hesitates, lets go of her drink, and SHAKES HANDS, looking unsure. Bob signals for the check.

Do Bob and Katrina have a deal? *They* seem to think so. But is her fee $2.5 million or $3 million? What if Katrina demands that all nude scenes be taken out, and Bob refuses? Must she still act in the film? Or suppose her agent convinces her that *Body Work* is no good even with changes. Has Katrina committed herself? What if Bob auditions another actress the next day, likes her, and signs her? Does he owe Katrina her fee? Or suppose Bob learns that the funding has fallen apart and there will be no film. Is Katrina entitled to her money?

Bob and Katrina have acted out a classic problem in *agreement,* one of the basic issues in contract law. Their lack of clarity means that disputes are likely and lawsuits possible. Similar bargaining goes on every day around the country and around the world, and the problems created are too frequently resolved in court. Some negotiating is done in person; more is done over the phone, by fax, by email—or all of them combined. This chapter highlights the most common sources of misunderstanding and litigation so that you can avoid making contracts you never intended—or deals that you cannot enforce.

There almost certainly is no contract between Bob and Katrina. Bob's offer was unclear. Even if it was valid, Katrina counteroffered. When they shook hands, it is impossible to know what terms each had in mind.

Contracts Checklist

☑ Offer
☑ Acceptance
☐ Consideration
☐ Legality
☐ Capacity
☐ Consent
☐ Writing

© Cengage Learning

10-1 MEETING OF THE MINDS

Remember from the last chapter that contracts have seven key characteristics. Agreements that have a problem in any of the areas do not amount to valid contracts. In this chapter, we examine the first two items on the checklist.

Parties form a contract only if they have a meeting of the minds. For this to happen, one side must make an **offer** and the other must make an **acceptance**. An offer proposes definite terms, and an acceptance unconditionally agrees to them.

Throughout the chapter, keep in mind that courts make *objective* assessments when evaluating offers and acceptances. A court will not try to get inside Katrina's head and decide what she was thinking as she shook hands. It will look at the handshake *objectively,* deciding how a reasonable person would interpret her words and conduct. Katrina may honestly have meant to conclude a deal for $3 million with no nude scenes, while Bob might in good faith have believed he was committing himself to $2.5 million and absolute control of the script. Neither belief will control the outcome.

Offer

An act or statement that proposes definite terms and permits the other party to create a contract by accepting those terms.

10-2 OFFER

Offeror
The person who makes an offer.

Offeree
The person to whom an offer is made.

Bargaining begins with an offer. The person who makes an offer is the **offeror**. The person to whom he makes that offer is the **offeree**. The terms are annoying but inescapable because, like handcuffs, all courts use them

Two questions determine whether a statement is an offer:

- Do the offeror's words and actions indicate an *intention* to make a bargain?
- Are the terms of the offer reasonably definite?

Zachary says to Sharon, "Come work in my English language center as a teacher. I'll pay you $800 per week for a 35-hour week, for six months starting Monday." This is a valid offer. Zachary's words seem to indicate that he intends to make a bargain and his offer is definite. If Sharon accepts, the parties have a contract that either one can enforce.

In the section below, we present several categories of statements that are generally *not* valid offers.

10-2a Statements That Usually Do Not Amount to Offers

INVITATIONS TO BARGAIN

An invitation to bargain is not an offer. Suppose Martha telephones Joe and leaves a message on his answering machine, asking if Joe would consider selling his vacation condo on Lake Michigan. Joe faxes a signed letter to Martha saying, "There is no way I could sell the condo for less than $150,000." Martha promptly sends Joe a cashier's check for that amount. Does she own the condo? No. Joe's fax was not an offer. It is merely an invitation to negotiate. Joe is indicating that he might well be happy to receive an offer from Martha, but he is not promising to sell the condo for $150,000 or for any amount.

PRICE QUOTES

A price quote is generally not an offer. If Imperial Textile sends a list of fabric prices for the new year to its regular customers, the list is not an offer. Once again, the law regards it merely as a solicitation of offers. Suppose Ralph orders 1,000 yards of fabric, quoted in the list at $40 per yard. *Ralph* is making the offer, and Imperial may decline to sell at $40, or at any price, for that matter.

This can be an expensive point to learn. Leviton Manufacturing makes electrical fixtures and switches. Litton Microwave manufactures ovens. Leviton sent a price list to Litton, stating what it would charge for specially modified switches for use in Litton's microwaves. The price letter included a statement greatly limiting Leviton's liability in the event of any problem with the switches. Litton purchased thousands of the switches and used them in manufacturing its microwaves. But consumers reported fires due to defects in the switches. Leviton claimed that under the contract it had no liability. But the court held that the price letter was not an offer. It was a request to receive an offer. Thus the contract ultimately formed did not include Leviton's liability exclusion. Litton won over $4 million.[1] See Exhibit 10.1.

LETTERS OF INTENT

In complex business negotiations, the parties may spend months bargaining over dozens of interrelated issues. Because each party wants to protect itself during the discussions, ensuring that the other side is serious without binding itself to premature commitments,

---

[1]*Litton Microwave Cooking Products v. Leviton Manufacturing Co., Inc.*, 15 F.3d 790, 1994 U.S. App. LEXIS 1876 (8th Cir. 1994).

EXHIBIT 10.1 The Litton case demonstrates why it is important to distinguish a valid offer from a mere price quote. Leviton's price list (including a limited warranty) was *not* an offer. When Litton ordered goods (with no limit to the warranty), it was making an offer, which Leviton accepted by delivering the goods. The resulting contract did not contain the limited warranty that Leviton wanted, costing that company a $4 million judgment.

it may be tempting during the negotiations to draft a **letter of intent**. The letter *might* help distinguish a serious party from one with a casual interest, summarize the progress made thus far, and assist the parties in securing necessary financing. Usually, letters of intent do not create any legal obligation. They merely state what the parties are considering, not what they have actually agreed to. But note that is possible for a letter of intent to bind the parties if its language indicates that the parties *intended* to be bound.

Letter of intent
A letter that summarizes negotiating progress.

ADVERTISEMENTS

Mary Mesaros received a notice from the United States Bureau of the Mint, announcing a new $5 gold coin to commemorate the Statue of Liberty. The notice contained an order form stating:

> VERY IMPORTANT—PLEASE READ: YES, Please accept my order for the U.S. Liberty Coins I have indicated. I understand that all sales are final and not subject to refund. Verification of my order will be made by the Department of the Treasury, U.S. Mint. If my order is received by December 31, I will be entitled to purchase the coins at the Pre-Issue Discount price shown.

Mesaros ordered almost $2,000 worth of the coins. But the Mint was inundated with so many requests for the coin that the supply was soon exhausted. Mesaros and thousands of others never got their coins. This was particularly disappointing because the market value of the coins doubled shortly after their issue. Mesaros sued on behalf of the entire class of disappointed purchasers. Like most who sue based on an advertisement, she lost.[2] **An advertisement is generally not an offer.** An advertisement is merely a request for offers. The consumer makes the offer, whether by mail, as above, or by arriving at a merchant's store ready to buy. The seller is free to reject the offer.

Advertisers should be careful, however, not to be too specific in their ads. Some ads do count as offers, as the following case illustrates.

---

[2]*Mesaros v. United States*, 845 F.2d 1576, 1988 U.S. App. LEXIS 6055 (Fed. Cir. 1988).

Landmark Case

CARLILL V. CARBOLIC SMOKE BALL COMPANY

1 QB 256
Court of Appeal, 1892

Facts: In the early 1890s, English citizens greatly feared the Russian flu. The Carbolic Smoke Ball Company ran a newspaper ad that contained two key passages:

"£100 reward will be paid by the Carbolic Smoke Ball Company to any person who contracts the influenza after having used the ball three times daily for two weeks according to the printed directions supplied with each ball.

"£1000 is deposited with the Alliance Bank, shewing our sincerity in the matter."

The product was a ball that contained carbolic acid. Users would inhale vapors from the ball through a long tube.

Carlill purchased a smoke ball and used it as directed for two months. She then caught the flu. She sued, arguing that because her response to the ad had created a contract with the company, she was entitled to £100.

The trial court agreed, awarding Carlill the money. The company appealed.

Issues: *Did the advertisement amount to an offer? If so, was the offer accepted?*

Decision: Yes. The ad was an offer that only required performance to become a binding contract.

Reasoning: The Carbolic Smoke Ball Company made an express and unmistakable promise to pay £100 under certain circumstances. Did the company intend to make this statement a *promise*? It sure sounded like a promise. The company mentioned its bank deposit of £1000 as proof of its sincerity and intention to comply.

Was this promise a binding offer? Generally, acceptance should be communicated to the offeror. But some offers, like this one, do not require notice of acceptance. It was obvious by the company's words and the nature of the transaction that it did not expect notice of acceptance, just performance. Carlill's use of the smoke ball was her acceptance. Because she got the flu despite her efforts, the company must pay her.

It is possible that many people who use the Carbolic Smoke Ball will get the flu. Too bad for the company; it must pay them all.

Carlill lived 50 years more, dying at the age of 96—of the flu.

This case serves as a cautionary tale. Running a "normal" ad which describes a product, its features, and its price does not amount to an offer. But, if a company proposes to take an action—like pay $100 to customers who take certain, specific actions—then it may find itself contractually obligated to follow through on its promises. The acceptance of the offer makes a unilateral contract.

Note also that, regardless of whether an ad counts as an offer, consumers have protection from those shopkeepers who are intent upon deceit. Almost every state has some form of consumer protection statute, which outlaws false advertising. For example, an automobile dealer who advertises a remarkably low price but then has only one automobile at that price has probably violated a consumer protection statute because the ad was published in bad faith, to trick consumers into coming to the dealership. In the *Mesaros* case, the United States Mint did not violate any consumer protection statute because it acted in good faith and simply ran out of coins.

AUCTIONS

It is the property you have always dreamed of owning—and it is up for auction! You arrive bright and early, stand in front, bid early, bid often, bid higher, bid highest of all—it's yours! For five seconds. Then, to your horror, the auctioneer announces that none of the bids were juicy enough and he is withdrawing the property. Robbery! Surely he cannot do that? But he can. Auctions are exciting and useful, but you must understand the rules.

Every day, auctions are used to sell exquisite works of art, real estate, and many other things. **Placing an item up for auction is *not* an offer—it is merely a request for an offer.** The *bids* are the offers. If and when the hammer falls, the auctioneer has accepted the offer.

The important thing to know about a particular auction is whether it is conducted with or without reserve. Most auctions are *with reserve,* meaning that the items for sale have a minimum price. The law assumes that an auction is with reserve unless the auctioneer clearly states otherwise. The auctioneer will not sell anything for less than its reserve (minimum price). So when the bidding for your property failed to reach the reserve, the auctioneer was free to withdraw it.

The rules are different in an auction *without reserve.* Here, there is no minimum. Once the first bid is received, the auctioneer *must* sell the merchandise to the highest bidder.

EXAM Strategy

Question: Ahn and Chet are both unhappy. (1) Ahn, an interior designer, is working on a hotel project. In the annual catalog of a furniture wholesaler, she sees that sofa beds cost $3,000. Based on the catalog, she sends an order for 100 sofa beds to the wholesaler. The wholesaler notifies Ahn that the price has gone up to $4,000. (2) At an estate auction, held without reserve, Chet is the highest bidder on a rare violin. The seller considers Chet's bid too low and refuses to sell. Both Ahn and Chet sue, but only one will win. Which plaintiff will win, and why?

Strategy: (1) A contract requires an offer and an acceptance. When the furniture wholesaler sent out its catalog, did it make an offer that Ahn could accept? (2) Chet was high bidder. At some auctions, the high bidder is merely making an offer, but at others, he wins the item. Which kind of auction was this?

Result: (1) A price quote is generally not an offer. Ahn's order for 100 sofas was the offer, and the company was free to reject it. Ahn loses. (2) Most auctions are with reserve, meaning that the high bidder is merely making an offer. However, this one was without reserve. Chet gets the violin.

10-2b Problems with Definiteness

It is not enough that the offeror indicates that she intends to enter into an agreement. **The terms of the offer must also be definite.** If they are vague, then even if the offeree agrees to the deal, a court does not have enough information to enforce it and there is no contract.

You want a friend to work in your store for the holiday season. This is a definite offer: "I offer you a job as a sales clerk in the store from November 1 through December 29, 40 hours per week at $10 per hour." But suppose, by contrast, you say: "I offer you a job as a sales clerk in the store during the holiday season. We will work out a fair wage once we see how busy things get." Your friend replies, "That's fine with me." This offer is indefinite, and there is no contract. What is a fair wage? $15 per hour? Or $20 per hour? What is the "holiday season"? How will the determinations be made? There is no binding agreement.

The following case, which concerns a famous television show, presents a problem with definiteness.

BAER V. CHASE

392 F.3d 609
Third Circuit Court of Appeals, 2004

CASE SUMMARY

Facts: David Chase was a television writer-producer with many credits, including a detective series called *The Rockford Files*. He became interested in a new program, set in New Jersey, about a "mob boss in therapy," a concept he eventually developed into *The Sopranos*. Robert Baer was a prosecutor in New Jersey who wanted to write for television. He submitted a *Rockford Files* script to Chase, who agreed to meet with Baer.

When they met, Baer pitched a different idea, concerning "a film or television series about the New Jersey Mafia." He did not realize Chase was already working on such an idea. Later that year, Chase visited New Jersey. Baer arranged meetings for Chase with local detectives and prosecutors, who provided the producer with information, material, and personal stories about their experiences with organized crime. Detective Thomas Koczur drove Chase and Baer to various New Jersey locations and introduced Chase to Tony Spirito. Spirito shared stories about loan sharking, power struggles between family members connected with the mob, and two colorful individuals known as Big Pussy and Little Pussy, both of whom later became characters on the show.

Back in Los Angeles, Chase wrote and sent to Baer a draft of the first *Sopranos* teleplay. Baer called Chase and commented on the script. The two spoke at least four times that year, and Baer sent Chase a letter about the script.

When *The Sopranos* became a hit television show, Baer sued Chase. He alleged that on three separate occasions, Chase had agreed that if the program succeeded, Chase would "take care of Baer, and would "remunerate Baer in a manner commensurate to the true value of his services." This happened twice on the phone, Baer claimed, and once during Chase's visit to New Jersey.

The understanding was that if the show failed, Chase would owe nothing. Chase never paid Baer anything.

The district court dismissed the case, holding that the alleged promises were too vague to be enforced. Baer appealed.

Issue: *Was Chase's promise definite enough to be enforced?*

Decision: No. The promise was too indefinite to be enforced. Affirmed.

Reasoning: To create a binding agreement, the offer and acceptance must be definite enough that a court can tell what the parties were obligated to do. The parties need to agree on all the essential terms; if they do not, there is no enforceable contract.

One of the essential terms is price. The agreement must either specify the compensation to be paid or describe a method by which the parties can calculate it. The duration of the contract is also basic: How long do the mutual obligations last?

There is no evidence that the parties agreed on how much Chase would pay Baer, or when, or for what period. The parties never defined what they meant by the "true value" of Baer's services, or how they would determine it. The two never discussed the meaning of "success" as applied to *The Sopranos*. They never agreed on how "profits" were to be calculated. The parties never discussed when the alleged agreement would begin or end.

Baer argues that the courts should make an exception to the principle of definiteness when the agreement concerns an "idea submission." The problem with his contention is that there is not the slightest support for it in the law. There is no precedent whatsoever for ignoring the definiteness requirement, in this type of contract or any other.

 Ethics   Was it fair for Chase to use Baer's services without compensation? Did Baer really *expect* to get paid, or was he simply hoping that his work would land him a job?

EXAM Strategy

Question: Niels owned three adjoining parcels of land in Arizona ranging from 60 to 120 acres. Hannah wanted to buy one. The two had dinner in Chicago and then sketched this agreement: "Binding Contract: Niels agrees to sell one of his three Arizona lots to Hannah. Within 14 days, the parties will meet on the land, decide which lot Hannah is buying, and settle on a price. If they cannot agree on a price, they will decide a fair method of doing so. Both parties agree to be bound by this contract." Each signed. When they meet in Arizona, Niels refuses to sell any land, and Hannah sues. What will happen?

Strategy: Do not be fooled by wording such as "Binding Contract." Focus on the legal issues: Was there a meeting of the minds? Niels and Hannah *thought* they had a contract—but courts make an objective assessment, not subjective. Did Niels make an offer? Were the terms definite?

Result: Both parties believed they had a binding deal, and both parties were wrong. There are two primary issues—which lot is being sold and how much will it cost—and neither is specified. How are they to select a lot? What is a "fair method" of determining price? Other issues are not touched upon: When will the deal close, how will payment be made, what happens if Hannah cannot finance the purchase? The terms are too vague. The parties never reached a meeting of the minds, and Hannah will lose her suit.

10-2c The UCC and Open Terms

In the last chapter, we introduced the Uniform Commercial Code (UCC). Article 2 of the UCC governs contracts when the primary purpose is a sale of goods. Remember that goods are moveable, tangible objects. Usually, UCC provisions are not significantly different from common law rules. But on occasion, the UCC modifies the common law rule in some major way. In such cases, we will present a separate description of the key UCC provision. The UCC as a whole is covered in Unit 3. Depending on the class time available, some instructors prefer to discuss the UCC separately, while others like to include it in the general discussion of contracts. This book is designed to work with either approach.

We have just seen that, under the common law, the terms of an offer must be definite. But under the UCC, many indefinite contracts are allowed to stand. Throughout this unit, we witness how the UCC makes the law of sales more flexible. There are several areas of contract law where imperfect negotiations may still create a binding agreement under the Code, even though the same negotiations under the common law would have yielded no contract. "Open terms" is one such area.

Yuma County Corp. produced natural gas. Yuma wanted a long-term contract to sell its gas so that it could be certain of recouping the expenses of exploration and drilling. Northwest Central Pipeline, which operated an interstate pipeline, also wanted a deal for 10 or more years so it could make its own distribution contracts, knowing it would have a steady supply of natural gas in a competitive market. But neither Yuma nor Northwest wanted to make a long-term *price* commitment, because over a period of years the price of natural gas could double—or crash. Each party wanted a binding agreement without a definitive price. If their negotiations had been governed by the common law, they would have run smack into the requirement of definiteness— no price, no contract. But because this was a sale of goods, it was governed by the UCC.

Under UCC §2-204(3), even though one or more terms are left open, a contract does not fail for indefiniteness if the parties have intended to make a contract and there is a reasonably certain basis for giving an appropriate remedy. Thus, a contract for the sale of goods may be enforced when a key term is missing. Business executives may have many reasons to leave open a delivery date, a price, or some other term. But note that the parties must still have *intended* to create a contract. The UCC will not create a contract where the parties never intended one.

In some cases, the contract will state how the missing term is to be determined. Yuma County and Northwest drafted a contract with alternative methods of determining the price. In the event that the price of natural gas was regulated by the Federal Energy Regulatory Commission (FERC), the price would be the highest allowed by the FERC. If the FERC deregulated the price (as it ultimately did), the contract price would be the average of the two highest prices paid by different gas producers in a specified geographic area.

GAP-FILLER PROVISIONS

Gap-filler provisions

UCC rules for supplying missing terms.

Even if a UCC contract lacks a specific method for determining missing terms, the Code itself contains **gap-filler provisions**, which are rules for *supplying* missing terms. Some of the most important gap-filler provisions of the Code follow.

Open Price   In general, if the parties do not settle on a price, the Code establishes that the goods will be sold for a reasonable price. This will usually be the market value or a price established by a neutral expert or agency. (UCC §2-305.)

Output contract

Obligates the seller to sell all of his output to the buyer, who agrees to accept it.

Output and Requirements Provisions   An **output contract** obligates the seller to sell all of his output to the buyer, who agrees to accept it. For example, a cotton grower might agree to sell all of his next crop to a textile firm. A **requirements contract** obligates a buyer to obtain all of his needed goods from the seller. A vineyard might agree to buy all of its wine bottles from one supplier. Output and requirements contracts are by definition incomplete, since the exact quantity of the goods is unspecified. The Code requires that in carrying out such contracts, both parties act in good faith. Neither party may suddenly demand a quantity of goods (or offer a quantity of goods) that is disproportionate to their past dealings or their reasonable estimates. (UCC §2-306.)

Requirements contract

Obligates a buyer to obtain all of his needed goods from the seller.

10-2d Termination of Offers

Once an offer has been made, it faces only two possible fates—it can be terminated or accepted. If an offer is terminated, it can never be accepted. If it is accepted, and if there are no problems with any of the five remaining elements on the Contracts Checklist, then a valid contract is created. Offers can be terminated in four ways: revocation, rejection, expiration, and by operation of law.

TERMINATION BY REVOCATION

An offer is **revoked** when the offeror "takes it back" before the offeree accepts. In general, the offeror may revoke the offer any time before it has been accepted. Imagine that I call you and say, "I'm going out of town this weekend. I'll sell you my ticket to this weekend's football game for $75." You tell me that you'll think it over and call me back. An hour later, my plans change. I call you a second time and say, "Sorry, but the deal's off—I'm going to the game after all." I have revoked my offer, and you can no longer accept it.

In the next case, this rule was worth $100,000 to one of the parties.

NADEL V. TOM CAT BAKERY

2009 N.Y. Misc. LEXIS 5105
Supreme Court of New York, New York County, 2009

CASE SUMMARY

Facts: A Tom Cat Bakery delivery van struck Elizabeth Nadel as she crossed a street. Having suffered significant injuries, Nadel filed suit. Before the trial began, the attorney representing the bakery's owner offered a $100,000 settlement, which Nadel refused.

While the jury was deliberating, the bakery's lawyer again offered Nadel the $100,000 settlement. She decided to think about it during lunch. Later that day, the jury sent a note to the judge. The bakery owner told her lawyer that if the note indicated the jury had reached a verdict, that he should revoke the settlement offer.

Back in the courtroom, the bakery's lawyer said, "My understanding is that there's a note …. I was given an instruction that if the note is a verdict, my client wants to take the verdict."

Nadel's lawyer then said, "My client will take the settlement. My client will take the settlement."

The trial court judge allowed the forewoman to read the verdict, which awarded Nadel—nothing. She appealed, claiming that a $100,000 settlement had been reached.

Issue: *Did Nadel's lawyer accept the settlement offer in time?*

Decision: No, the bakery owner's lawyer revoked the offer before acceptance.

Reasoning: An offer definitely existed. And the twice-repeated statement, "My client will take the settlement," indicates a clear desire to accept the proposal. The problem is that the acceptance came too late.

Analyzing the timeline, the bakery owner's attorney indicated that if a verdict had been returned, he revoked the offer. This notice was given before the attempted acceptance. And so, since a verdict had in fact been returned, the offer was no longer open.

The parties did not reach a binding settlement agreement.

Making Contracts Temporarily Irrevocable

Some offers cannot be revoked, at least for a time. Often, people and businesses need time to evaluate offers. If a car dealer offers you a green sedan for $25,000, you may want to shop around for a few days to try to find a better price. In the meantime, you may want to make sure that the green sedan is still available if you decide to return. Can you legally prevent the car dealer from selling the car to anyone else while you ponder the offer? In some circumstances, yes.

Option Contract (All Types of Contracts) With an option contract, an interested purchaser *buys* the right to have the offer held open. **The offeror may not revoke an offer during the option period.** Suppose you pay the car dealer $250 to hold open its offer until February 2. Later that day, the dealership notifies you that it is selling to someone else. Result? You can enforce *your* contract. The car dealer had no power to revoke because you purchased an option.

Firm Offers (UCC Contracts Only) Once again, the UCC has changed the law on the sale of goods. If a promise made in writing is signed by a *merchant*, and if it agrees to hold open an offer for a stated period, then an offer may not be revoked. The open period may not exceed three months. So, if the car dealer gives you a piece of paper that reads, "The offer on the green sedan is open at $25,000 until Friday at noon," he cannot revoke the offer before Friday at noon, even though you have not paid him anything. (UCC §2-205.)

Termination by Rejection

If an offeree clearly indicates that he does not want to take the offer, then he has **rejected** it. **If an offeree rejects an offer, the rejection immediately terminates the offer.** Suppose a major accounting firm telephones you and offers a job, starting at $80,000. You respond, "Nah. I'm gonna work on my surfing for a year or two." The next day, you come to your senses and write the firm, accepting its offer. No contract. Your rejection terminated the offer and ended your power to accept it.

Counteroffer A party makes a **counteroffer** when it responds to an offer with a new and different proposal. Frederick faxes Kim, offering to sell a 50 percent interest in the Fab Hotel in New York for only $135 million. Kim faxes back and says, "That's too much, but I'll pay $115 million." Moments later, Kim's business partner convinces her that Frederick's offer was a bargain, and she faxes an acceptance of his $135 million offer. Does Kim have a binding deal? No. **A counteroffer is a rejection.** When Kim offered $115 million, she rejected Frederick's offer. Her original fax created a new offer, for $115 million, which Frederick never accepted. The parties have no contract at any price.

Counteroffer
A return offer and a rejection of the original offer.

TERMINATION BY EXPIRATION

An offeror may set a time limit. Quentin calls you and offers you a job in his next motion picture. He tells you, "I've got to know by tomorrow night." If you call him in three days to accept, you are out of the picture. **When an offer specifies a time limit for acceptance, that period is binding.**

If the offer specifies no time limit, the offeree has a *reasonable* **period in which to accept.** A reasonable period varies, depending upon the type of offer, previous dealings between the parties, and any normal trade usage or customary practices in a particular industry.

TERMINATION BY OPERATION OF LAW

In some circumstances, the law itself terminates an offer. **If an offeror dies or becomes mentally incapacitated, the offer terminates automatically and immediately.** Arnie offers you a job as an assistant in his hot-air balloon business. Before you can even accept, Arnie tumbles out of a balloon at 3,000 feet. The offer terminates along with Arnie.

Destruction of the subject matter terminates the offer. A car dealer offers to sell you a rare 1938 Bugatti for $7,500,000 if you bring cash the next day. You arrive, suitcase stuffed with cash, just in time to see Arnie drop 3,000 feet through the air and crush the Bugatti. The dealer's offer is terminated.

10-3 ACCEPTANCE

As we have seen, when there is a valid offer outstanding, it remains effective until it is terminated or accepted. An offeree accepts by saying or doing something that a reasonable person would understand to mean that he definitely wants to take the offer. Assume that Ellie offers to sell Gene her old iPod for $50. If Gene says, "I accept your offer," then he has indeed accepted, but there is no need to be so formal. He can accept the offer by saying, "It's a deal," or, "I'll take it," or any number of things. He need not even speak. If he hands her a $50 bill, he also accepts the offer.

It is worth noting that **the offeree must say or do** *something* **to accept.** Marge telephones Vick and leaves a message on his answering machine: "I'll pay $75 for your business law textbook from last semester. I'm desperate to get a copy, so I will assume you agree unless I hear from you by 6:00 tonight." Marge hears nothing by the deadline and assumes she has a deal. She is mistaken. Vick neither said nor did anything to indicate that he accepted.

10-3a Mirror Image Rule

If only he had known! A splendid university, an excellent position as department chair— gone. And all because of the mirror image rule.

> Was it sensible to deny the professor a job over a mere 14-day difference? Sensible or not, that is the law.

Ohio State University wrote to Philip Foster offering him an appointment as a professor and chair of the art history department. His position was to begin July 1, and he had until June 2 to accept the job. On June 2, Foster telephoned the dean and left a message accepting the position, *effective July 15*. Later, Foster thought better of it and wrote the university, accepting the school's starting date of July 1. Too late! Professor Foster never did occupy that chair at Ohio State. The court held that since his acceptance varied the starting date, it was a counteroffer. And a counteroffer, as we know, is a rejection.[3]

---

[3] *Foster v. Ohio State University*, 41 Ohio App. 3d 86, 534 N.E.2d 1220, 1987 Ohio App. LEXIS 10761 (Ohio Ct. App. 1987).

Was it sensible to deny the professor a job over a mere 14-day difference? Sensible or not, that is the law. The common law **mirror image rule** requires that acceptance be on *precisely* the same terms as the offer. If the acceptance contains terms that add or contradict the offer, even in minor ways, courts generally consider it a counteroffer. The rule worked reasonably well in the 19th century, when parties would write an original contract and exchange it, penciling in any changes. But now that businesses use standardized forms to purchase most goods and services, the rule creates enormous difficulties. Sellers use forms they have prepared, with all conditions stated to their advantage, and buyers employ their own forms, with terms they prefer. The forms are exchanged in the mail or electronically, with neither side clearly agreeing to the other party's terms.

The problem is known as the "battle of forms." Once again, the UCC has entered the fray, attempting to provide flexibility and common sense for those contracts involving the sale of goods. But for contracts governed by the common law, such as Professor Foster's, the mirror image rule is still the law.

Mirror image rule

Requires that acceptance be on precisely the same terms as the offer.

10-3b UCC and the Battle of Forms

UCC §2-207 dramatically modifies the mirror image rule for the sale of goods. Under this provision, an acceptance that adds additional or different terms often will create a contract.

ADDITIONAL OR DIFFERENT TERMS

One basic principle of the common law of contracts remains unchanged: The key to creation of a contract is a valid offer that the offeree *intends* to accept. If there is no intent to accept, there is no contract. The big change brought about by UCC §2-207 is this: **An offeree who accepts may include in the acceptance terms that are additional to or different from those in the offer.** Thus, even with additional or different terms, the acceptance may well create a contract.

> *Example A*. Wholesaler writes to Manufacturer, offering to buy "10,000 wheelbarrows at $50 per unit. Payable on delivery, 30 days from today's date." Manufacturer writes back, "We accept your offer of 10,000 wheelbarrows at $50 per unit, payable on delivery. *Interest at normal trade rates for unpaid balances*." Manufacturer clearly intends to form a contract. The company has added a new term, but there is still a valid contract.

However, if the offeree states that her acceptance is *conditioned on the offeror's assent* to the new terms, there is no contract.

> *Example B*. Same offer as above. Manufacturer adds the interest rate clause and states, "Our acceptance is conditional upon your agreement to this interest rate." Manufacturer has made a counteroffer. There is no contract, yet. If Wholesaler accepts the counteroffer, there is a contract; if Wholesaler does not accept it, there is no contract.

Additional terms are those that bring up *new* issues, such as interest rates, not contained in the original offer. Additional terms in the acceptance are considered proposals to add to the contract. Assuming that both parties are merchants, the additional terms *will generally become part of the contract*. Thus, in Example A, the interest rate will become a part of the binding deal. If Wholesaler is late in paying, it must pay whatever interest rate is current.

In three circumstances, the additional terms in the acceptance *do not* become part of the contract:

- If the original offer *insisted on its own terms*. In other words, if Wholesaler wrote, "I offer to buy them on the following terms and *no other terms*," then the Manufacturer is not free to make additions.

- If the additional terms *materially alter* the original offer. Suppose Manufacturer wrote back, "We accept your offer for 10,000 wheelbarrows. Delivery will be made within

180 days, unless we notify you of late delivery." Manufacturer has changed the time from 30 days to 180 days, with a possible extension beyond that. That is a material alteration, and it will not become part of the contract. By contrast, Manufacturer's new language concerning "interest at normal trade rates" was not a material alteration, and therefore that interest rate becomes part of the contract.

- If the offeror receives the additional terms and *promptly objects* to them.

Different terms are those that contradict terms in the offer. For example, if the seller's form clearly states that no warranty is included, and the buyer's form says the seller warrants all goods for three years, the acceptance contains different terms. An acceptance may contain different terms and still create a contract. But in these cases, courts have struggled to decide what the terms of the contract are. **The majority of states hold that different (contradictory) terms cancel each other out.** Neither term is included in the contract. Instead, the neutral terms from the Code itself are "read into" the contract. These are the gap-filler terms discussed above. If, for example, the forms had contradictory warranty clauses (as they almost always do), the different terms would cancel each other out, and the warranty clauses from the UCC would be substituted.[4]

EXAM Strategy

Question: Elaine faxes an offer to Raoul. Raoul writes, "I accept. Please note, I will charge 2 percent interest per month for any unpaid money." He signs the document and faxes it back to Elaine. Do the two have a binding contract?

Strategy: Slow down, this is trickier than it seems. Raoul has added a term to Elaine's offer. We must take two steps to decide whether there is a contract. In a contract for services, acceptance must mirror the offer, but not so in an agreement for the sale of goods.

Result: If this is an agreement for services, there is no contract. However, if this agreement is for goods, the additional term *may* become part of an enforceable contract.

Question: Assume that Elaine's offer concerns goods. Is there an agreement?

Strategy: Under UCC §2-207, an additional term will become part of a binding agreement for goods except in three instances. What are the three exceptions?

Result: Raoul's extra term will be incorporated in a binding contract unless (1) Elaine's offer made clear she would accept no other terms; (2) Raoul's interest rate is a material alteration of the offer (almost never the case for interest rates); or (3) Elaine promptly rejects the interest rate.

---

[4]Not all states follow this rule, however. Some courts have held that when the acceptance contains terms that contradict those in the offer, the language in the offer should be final. A few courts have ruled that the terms in the acceptance should control.

10-3c Clickwraps and Shrinkwraps

You want to purchase Attila brand software and download it to your computer. You type in your credit card number and other information, agreeing to pay $99. Attila also requires that you "read and agree to" all of the company's terms. You click "I agree," without having read one word of the terms. Three frustrating weeks later, tired of trying to operate defective Attilaware, you demand a refund and threaten to sue. The company replies that you are barred from suing because the terms you agreed to included an arbitration clause. To resolve any disputes, you must travel to Attila's hometown, halfway across the nation, use an arbitrator that the company chooses, pay one-half the arbitrator's fee, and also pay Attila's legal bills if you should lose. The agreement makes it financially impossible for you to get your money back. Is that contract enforceable?

You have entered into a "clickwrap" agreement. Similar agreements, called "shrinkwraps," are packaged inside many electronic products. A shrinkwrap notice might require that before inserting a purchased CD into your computer, you must read and agree to all terms in the brochure. Clickwraps and shrinkwraps often include arbitration clauses. They frequently limit the seller's liability if anything goes wrong, saying that the manufacturer's maximum responsibility is to refund the purchase price (even if the software destroys your hard drive).

Many courts that have analyzed these issues have ruled that clickwrap and shrinkwrap agreements are indeed binding, even against consumers. The courts have emphasized that sellers are entitled to offer a product on any terms they wish, and that shrinkwrap and clickwrap are the most efficient methods of including complicated terms in a small space. Think before you click![5]

However, some courts have *refused* to enforce such contracts against a consumer, stating that the buyer never understood or agreed to the shrinkwrapped terms. The court in the following case works hard to balance the competing interests, and in the process demonstrates that this new area of law is very much in flux.

SPECHT V. NETSCAPE COMMUNICATIONS CORPORATION

306 F.3d 17
Second Circuit Court of Appeals, 2002

CASE SUMMARY

Facts: A group of plaintiffs sued Netscape, claiming that two of the company's products illegally captured private information about files that they downloaded from the Internet. The plaintiffs alleged that this was electronic eavesdropping, in violation of two federal statutes.

From Netscape's Web page, the plaintiffs had downloaded SmartDownload, a software plug-in that enabled them to download the company's Communicator software. The Web page advertised the benefits of Smart-Download, and near the bottom of the screen was a tinted button labeled "Download." The plaintiffs clicked to download. If, instead of downloading, they had scrolled further down, they would have seen an invitation to "review and agree to the terms of the Netscape SmartDownload software license agreement." By clicking the appropriate button, they would have been sent to a series of linked pages, and finally arrived at a license

---

[5] *ProCD, Inc. v. Zeidenberg*, 86 F.3d 1447 (7th Cir. 1996), is the leading case to enforce shrinkwrap agreements (and, by extension, clickwraps). *Klocek v. Gateway*, 104 F. Supp. 1332 (D. Kan. 2000), is one of the few cases to reject such contracts. *Klocek*, however, was dismissed for failure to reach the federal court $75,000 jurisdictional level.

agreement. Among the terms was an agreement to arbitrate any dispute. In other words, a consumer downloading Smart-Download was in theory giving up the right to file suit if anything went wrong, and agreeing to settle the dispute by arbitration. However, the plaintiffs never reviewed the license terms.

In the district court, Netscape moved to dismiss the case and compel arbitration. Netscape claimed that the plaintiffs had forfeited any right to sue based on the license agreement. The district court denied the company's motion, ruling that the plaintiffs had not agreed to the terms of the license. Netscape appealed.

Issue: *Had the plaintiffs agreed to arbitrate their claims?*

Decision: No, the plaintiffs did not agree to arbitration.

Reasoning: Netscape contends that if the plaintiffs had scrolled down to the next screen, they would have discovered the license terms. This means that they were on notice of those terms and effectively agreed to them.

When a contract is based on paper documents, courts often find that notice like this does bind the parties. If one document adequately advises a party that the agreement includes terms detailed in a *second* document, the terms can be enforceable. The same principle sometimes applies in the world of e-commerce, when pages contain pop-up screens and hyperlinks to other sites. The question in this case is whether the plaintiffs received sufficient notice of the licensing terms. Did they give real consent to those terms?

What the plaintiffs saw was a screen filled with praise for a fast, free plug-in called SmartDownload. The plaintiffs were urged to "Download Now!" At the very bottom was a "Download" button. There was no immediately visible notice that license terms were detailed elsewhere, or that the company required assent to the terms.

The company claims that the position of the scroll bar notified the plaintiffs that there was additional information below the download button. This is unrealistic. A reasonable person would not conclude from the scroll bar position that important licensing terms were referred to farther down. When consumers are urged to download free software at the click of a button, a reference to license terms placed on a submerged screen is not enough to put them on notice of those terms. The plaintiffs never assented to the terms.

The lower court denied the motion to compel arbitration. That order is affirmed.

The plaintiffs in *Specht* won because they knew nothing about the arbitration clause and were unlikely to discover it on the company's website. Notice what happens when a user *does* know about terms posted online. Register.com was a registrar of Internet domain names, meaning that it issued domain names to people and companies establishing a new website. The company was legally obligated to make available to the public, for free, the names and contact information of its customers. Register was also in the business of assisting owners, for a fee, to develop their websites.

Verio, Inc., competed in the site development business. Verio's automated software program (robot) would search Register.com daily, seeking information about new sites. *After* Verio obtained contact information, a notice would appear on the Register site, stating:

> By submitting a query, you agree that under no circumstances will you use this data to support the transmission of mass unsolicited, commercial advertising or solicitation via email.

In fact, though, Verio used the contact information for exactly that purpose, sending mass emailings to owners of new websites, soliciting their development business. Register sued. Verio defended by stating it was not bound by the notice because the notice did not appear until after it had obtained the information. Verio argued that when it sent the queries, it was unaware of any restrictions on use of the data. The court was unpersuaded, and explained its reasoning with a simple but telling metaphor:

> The situation might be compared to one in which plaintiff P maintains a roadside fruit stand displaying bins of apples. A visitor, defendant D, takes an apple and bites into it. As D turns to leave, D sees a sign, visible only as one turns to exit, which says "Apples—50 cents apiece." D does not pay for the apple. D believes he has no obligation to pay because he had no notice when he bit into the apple that 50 cents was expected in return. D's view is that he never agreed to pay for the apple. Thereafter, each day, several times a day, D revisits the stand, takes an apple, and eats it. D never leaves money.

P sues D in contract for the price of the apples taken. D defends on the ground that on no occasion did he see P's price notice until after he had bitten into the apples. D may well prevail as to the first apple taken. D had no reason to understand upon taking it that P was demanding the payment. In our view, however, D cannot continue on a daily basis to take apples for free, knowing full well that P is offering them only in exchange for 50 cents in compensation, merely because the sign demanding payment is so placed that on each occasion D does not see it until he has bitten into the apple.

Register.com won its case. Verio was prohibited from using the contact information for mass emailings because it had actual knowledge of the restrictions placed on its use.[6]

10-3d Communication of Acceptance

The offeree must communicate his acceptance for it to be effective. The questions that typically arise concern the method, the manner, and the time of acceptance.

METHOD AND MANNER OF ACCEPTANCE

The term "method" refers to whether acceptance is done in person or by mail, telephone, email, or fax. The term "manner" refers to whether the offeree accepts by promising, by making a down payment, by performing, and so forth. **If an offer demands acceptance in a particular method or manner, the offeree must follow those requirements.** An offer might specify that it be accepted in writing, or in person, or before midnight on June 23. An offeror can set any requirements she wishes. Omri might say to Oliver, "I'll sell you my bike for $200. You must accept my offer by standing on a chair in the lunchroom tomorrow and reciting a poem about a cow." Oliver can only accept the offer in the exact manner specified if he wants to form a contract.

If the offer does not specify a type of acceptance, the offeree may accept in any reasonable manner and method. An offer generally may be accepted by performance or by a promise, unless it specifies a particular method. The same freedom applies to the method. If Masako faxes Eric an offer to sell 1,000 acres in Montana for $800,000, Eric may accept by mail or fax. Both are routinely used in real estate transactions, and either is reasonable.

TIME OF ACCEPTANCE: THE MAILBOX RULE

An acceptance is generally effective upon dispatch, meaning the moment it is out of the offeree's control. Terminations, on the other hand, are effective when received. When Masako faxes her offer to sell land to Eric, and he mails his acceptance, the contract is binding the moment he puts the letter into the mail. In most cases, this **mailbox rule** is just a detail. But it becomes important when the offeror revokes her offer at about the same time the offeree accepts. Who wins? Suppose Masako's offer has one twist:

Mailbox rule
Acceptance is generally effective upon dispatch. Terminations are effective when received.

- On Monday morning, Masako faxes her offer to Eric.

- On Monday afternoon, Eric writes, "I accept" on the fax, and Masako mails a revocation of her offer.

- On Tuesday morning, Eric mails his acceptance.

- On Thursday morning, Masako's revocation arrives at Eric's office.

- On Friday morning, Eric's acceptance arrives at Masako's office.

Outcome? Eric has an enforceable contract. Masako's offer was effective when it reached Eric. His acceptance was effective on Tuesday morning, when he mailed it. Nothing that happens later can "undo" the contract.

---

[6]*Register.com v. Verio, Inc.*, 353 F.3d 393 (2d Cir. 2004).

SOLDAU V. ORGANON, INC.

860 F.2d 355, 1988 U.S. App. LEXIS 14757
Ninth Circuit Court of Appeals, 1988

CASE SUMMARY

Facts: Organon fired John Soldau. Then the company sent to him a letter offering to pay him double the normal severance pay, provided Soldau would sign a full release, that is, a document giving up any and all claims he might have against Organon. The release was included with the letter. Soldau signed it, dated it, and took it to the nearest post office, where he deposited it in the mailbox. When he returned home, Soldau discovered in the mail a check from Organon for the double severance pay. He hustled back to the post office, where he persuaded a postal clerk to open the mailbox and retrieve the release he had posted. He then cashed Organon's check and finally filed a suit against the company, alleging that his firing was age discrimination.

The federal district court gave summary judgment for Organon, ruling that Soldau's acceptance of the proposed release was effective when he mailed it, creating a contract. He appealed.

Issue: *Did Soldau create a contract by mailing the release?*

Decision: Yes. Soldau created an enforceable contract. Affirmed.

Reasoning: Soldau argues that federal law should govern this case, not California law. In fact, it makes no difference because both court systems use the "mailbox" rule. Acceptance is effective when dispatched. The U.S. Supreme Court adopted the rule almost 100 years ago. Since then, every court, treatise, and commentator has approved the rule, both in the United States and most common law countries. The mailbox rule offers a reasonable method of balancing the risks between two parties. Leaving it as a settled principle creates certainty in contract formation.

The moment Soldau put the envelope in the mailbox, the company became obligated to give him double severance pay, and he gave up any right to file suit.

Chapter Conclusion

The law of offer and acceptance can be complex. Yet for all its faults, the law is not the principal source of dispute between parties unhappy with negotiations. Most litigation concerning offer and acceptance comes from *lack of clarity* on the part of the people negotiating. The many examples discussed are all understandable given the speed and fluidity of the real world of business. But the executive who insists on clarity is likelier in the long run to spend more time doing business and less time in court.

EXAM REVIEW

1. **MEETING OF THE MINDS** The parties can form a contract only if they have a meeting of the minds, which requires that they understand each other and show that they intend to reach an agreement. (p. 235)

Question: Norv owned a Ford dealership and wanted to expand by obtaining a BMW outlet. He spoke with Jackson and other BMW executives on several occasions. Norv now claims that those discussions resulted in an oral contract that requires BMW to grant him a franchise, but the company disagrees. Norv's strongest evidence of a contract is the fact that Jackson gave him forms on which to order BMWs. Jackson answered that it was his standard practice to give such forms to prospective dealers, so that if the franchise were approved, car orders could be processed quickly. Norv states that he was "shocked" when BMW refused to go through with the deal. Is there a contract?

Strategy: A court makes an *objective* assessment of what the parties did and said to determine whether they had a meeting of the minds and intended to form a contract. Norv's "shock" is irrelevant. Do the order forms indicate a meeting of the minds? Was there additional evidence that the parties had reached an agreement? (See the "Result" at the end of this section.)

2. **OFFER**   An offer is an act or statement that proposes definite terms and permits the other party to create a contract by accepting those terms. (p. 235)

3. **OTHER STATEMENTS**   Invitations to bargain, price quotes, letters of intent, and advertisements are generally not offers. However, an ad in which a company proposes to take a specific action when a customer takes a specific action can amount to an offer. And letters of intent that indicate the parties intended to be bound can also count as offers. (pp. 236–239)

Question: "Huge selection of Guernsey sweaters," reads a newspaper ad from Stuffed Shirt, a clothing retailer. "Regularly $135, today only $65." Waldo arrives at Stuffed Shirt at 4:00 that afternoon, but the shop clerk says there are no more sweaters. He shows Waldo a newly arrived Shetland sweater that sells for $145. Waldo sues, claiming breach of contract and violation of a consumer protection statute. Who will prevail?

(a) Waldo will win the breach of contract suit and the consumer protection suit.

(b) Waldo will lose the breach of contract suit but might win the consumer protection suit.

(c) Waldo will lose the consumer protection suit but should win the breach of contract suit.

(d) Waldo will win the consumer protection suit only if he wins the contract case.

(e) Waldo will lose both the breach of contract suit and the consumer protection suit.

Strategy: Waldo assumes that he is accepting the store's offer. But did Stuffed Shirt make an offer? If not, there cannot be a contract. Does the consumer protection statute help him? (See the "Result" at the end of this section.)

4. **DEFINITENESS**   The terms of the offer must be definite, although under the UCC the parties may create a contract that has open terms. (pp. 239–240)

5. **TERMINATION**   An offer may be terminated by revocation, rejection, expiration, or operation of law. (pp. 242–244)

EXAM Strategy

Question: Rick is selling his Espresso Coffee Maker. He sends Tamara an email, offering to sell the machine for $350. Tamara promptly emails back, offering to buy the item for $300. She hears nothing from Rick, so an hour later Tamara stops by his apartment, where she learns that he just sold the machine to his roommate for $250. She sues Rick. Outcome?

(a) Tamara will win because her offer was higher than the roommate's.

(b) Tamara will win because Rick never responded to her offer.

(c) Tamara will win because both parties made clear offers, in writing.

(d) Tamara will lose because she rejected Rick's offer.

(e) Tamara will lose because her offer was not definite.

Strategy: A valid contract requires a definite offer and acceptance. Rick made a valid offer. When Tamara said she would buy the machine for a lower amount, was that acceptance? If not, what was it? (See the "Result" at the end of this section.)

6. **MIRROR IMAGE RULE AND UCC §2-207**   The common law mirror image rule requires acceptance on precisely the same terms as the offer. Under the UCC, an offeree may often create a contract even when the acceptance includes terms that are additional to or different from those in the offer. (pp. 244–245)

7. **CLICKWRAPS**   Clickwrap and shrinkwrap agreements are generally enforceable. (pp. 247–249)

8. **MANNER OF ACCEPTANCE**   If an offer demands acceptance in a particular method or manner, the offeree must follow those requirements. If the offer does not specify a type of acceptance, the offeree may accept in any reasonable manner and medium. (p. 249)

9. **MAILBOX RULE**   An acceptance is generally effective upon dispatch, meaning from the moment it is out of the offeree's control. Terminations usually are not effective until received. (pp. 249–250)

1. Result: The order forms are neither an offer nor an acceptance. Norv has offered no evidence that the parties agreed on price, date of performance, or any other key terms. There is no contract. Norv allowed eagerness and optimism to replace common sense.[7]

---

[7]Based on *Arnold Pontiac-GMC, Inc. v. General Motors Co.*, 786 F.2d 564 (3d Cir. 1986).

3. Result: An advertisement is usually not an offer, but merely a solicitation of one. It is Waldo who is making the offer, which the store may reject. Waldo loses his contract case, but he may win under the consumer protection statute. The correct answer is (b). If Stuffed Shirt proclaimed "Huge selection" when there were only five sweaters, the store was deliberately misleading consumers, and Waldo wins. However, if there was indeed a large selection, and Waldo arrived too late, he is out of luck.

5. Result: Tamara made a counteroffer of $300. A counteroffer is a rejection. Tamara rejected Rick's offer and simultaneously offered to buy the coffee maker at a lower price. Rick was under no obligation to sell to Tamara at any price. He will win Tamara's suit.

MULTIPLE-CHOICE QUESTIONS

1. Rebecca, in Honolulu, faxes a job offer to Spike, in Pittsburgh, saying, "We can pay you $55,000 per year, starting June 1." Spike faxes a reply, saying, "Thank you! I accept your generous offer, though I will also need $3,000 in relocation money. See you June 1. Can't wait!" On June 1, Spike arrives, to find that his position is filled by Gus. He sues Rebecca.

   (a) Spike wins $55,000.

   (b) Spike wins $58,000.

   (c) Spike wins $3,000.

   (d) Spike wins restitution.

   (e) Spike wins nothing.

2. Arturo hires Kate to work in his new sporting goods store. "Look," he explains, "I can only pay you $9 an hour. But if business is good a year from now, and you're still here, I'm sure I can pay you a healthy bonus." Four months later, Arturo terminates Kate. She sues.

   (a) Kate will win her job back, plus the year's pay and the bonus.

   (b) Kate will win the year's pay and the bonus.

   (c) Kate will win only the bonus.

   (d) Kate will win only her job back.

   (e) Kate will win nothing.

3. Manny offers to sell Gina his TV for $100 on January 1. On January 2, Gina writes out a letter of acceptance. On January 3, Gina drops the letter in a mailbox. On January 4, a postal worker gets the letter out of the mailbox and takes it to the post office. On January 5, the letter arrives in Manny's mailbox. When (if ever) was a contract formed?

   (a) January 2

   (b) January 3

   (c) January 4

   (d) January 5

   (e) None of the above—a contract has not been formed.

4. Frank, an accountant, says to Missy, "I'll sell you my laptop for $100." Missy asks, "Will you give me until tomorrow to make up my mind?" "Sure," Frank replies. Which of the following is true?

   (a) Frank cannot revoke his offer, no matter what.

   (b) Frank cannot revoke his offer, but only if Missy pays him to keep the offer open until tomorrow.

   (c) Frank can revoke his offer no matter what, because he is not a merchant.

   (d) Frank can revoke his offer no matter what, because he did not promise Missy anything in writing.

5. Which of the following amounts to an offer?

   (a) Ed says to Carmen, "I offer to sell you my pen for $1."

   (b) Ed says to Carmen, "I'll sell you my pen for $1."

   (c) Ed writes, "I'll sell you my pen for $1," and gives the note to Carmen.

   (d) All of the above.

   (e) (a) and (c) only.

ESSAY QUESTIONS

1. The town of Sanford, Maine, decided to auction off a lot it owned. The town advertised that it would accept bids through the mail, up to a specified date. Arthur and Arline Chevalier mailed in a bid that turned out to be the highest. When the town refused to sell them the lot, they sued. Result?

2. The Tufte family leased a 260-acre farm from the Travelers Insurance Co. Toward the end of the lease, Travelers mailed the Tuftes an option to renew the lease. The option arrived at the Tuftes' house on March 30, and gave them until April 14 to accept. On April 13, the Tuftes signed and mailed their acceptance, which Travelers received on April 19. Travelers claimed there was no lease and attempted to evict the Tuftes from the farm. May they stay?

3. Consolidated Edison Co. of New York (Con Ed) sought bids from General Electric Co. (GE) and others to supply it with two huge transformers. Con Ed required that the bids be held open for 90 days. GE submitted a written bid and included a clause holding the bid open for 90 days. During that period, Con Ed accepted GE's bid, but GE refused to honor it. Is there a contract?

4. The Dukes leased land from Lillian Whatley. Toward the end of their lease, they sent Ms. Whatley a new contract, renewing the lease for three years and giving themselves the option to buy the land at any time during the lease for $50,000. Ms. Whatley crossed out the clause giving them an option to buy. She added a sentence at the bottom, saying, "Should I, Lillian Whatley, decide to sell at end [*sic*] of three years, I will give the Dukes the first chance to buy." Then she signed the lease, which the Dukes accepted in the changed form. They continued to pay the rent until Ms. Whatley sold the land to another couple for $35,000. The Dukes sued. Are the Dukes entitled to the land at $50,000? At $35,000?

5. **YOU BE THE JUDGE WRITING PROBLEM** Academy Chicago Publishers (Academy) approached the widow of author John Cheever about printing some of his unpublished stories. She signed a contract, which stated:

> The Author will deliver to the Publisher on a mutually agreeable date one copy of the manuscript of the Work as finally arranged by the editor and satisfactory to the Publisher in form and content …. Within a reasonable time and a mutually agreeable date after delivery of the final revised manuscript, the Publisher will publish the Work at its own expense, in such style and manner and at such price as it deems best, and will keep the Work in print as long as it deems it expedient.

Within a year, Academy had located and delivered to Mrs. Cheever more than 60 unpublished stories. But she refused to go ahead with the project. Academy sued for the right to publish the book. The trial court ruled that the agreement was valid; the appeals court affirmed; and the case went to the Illinois Supreme Court. Was Academy's offer valid, and was the contract enforceable? **Argument for Mrs. Cheever:** The agreement is too vague to be enforceable. None of the essential terms are specified: the number of stories, their length, who selects them, the date of publication, the size or cost of the book, or anything else. There is no contract. **Argument for Academy:** Mrs. Cheever wanted to publish this book and agreed in writing to help Academy do so. Both parties understood the essential nature of the book and were willing to permit some flexibility, to ensure a good edition. She has no right to back out now.

DISCUSSION QUESTIONS

1. Advertisements usually do not amount to offers. Is this fair? Should businesses have legal obligations to sell items at an advertised price?

2. Most auctions are held "with reserve." If you place the highest bid at such an auction, and if your bid is below the reserve, then you do not get the item. Is this fair? Should the law award you the item at the price you bid?

3. Someone offers to sell you a concert ticket for $50, and you reply, "I'll give you $40," The seller refuses to sell at the lower price, and you say, "OK, OK, I'll pay you $50." Clearly, no contract has been formed, because you made a counteroffer. If the seller has changed her mind and no longer wants to sell for $50, she doesn't have to. But is this fair? If it is all part of the same conversation,

should you be able to accept the $50 offer and get the ticket?

4. If you click an "I agree" box, odds are that its terms are binding on you, even if the box contains dozens or even hundreds of lines of dense text. Is this fair? Should the law change to limit the enforceability of clickwraps?

5. Courts stick to objective (reasonable person) standards when evaluating offers and acceptances. Juries are not asked to "get inside someone's head"; they are instructed to determine what a reasonable person would think of offerors' and offerees' statements. Is this practice reasonable? Would it be better if the law directly considered whether people *wanted* to make contracts?

CHAPTER 11

CONSIDERATION

Have you ever rented a movie that you did not want every one of your friends to know about? Cathryn Harris did. Imagine her shock when she rented a movie online from Blockbuster, only to find out that this news was automatically transmitted to her Facebook page and then broadcast to all her "friends." Just think how bad that could be.

Harris sued Blockbuster for this violation of her privacy, only to find out she had clicked away her right to sue. To rent the movie, she had had to click that little box saying she agreed to all the terms and conditions. And one of those terms and conditions was an agreement to arbitrate, not litigate. Can Blockbuster get away with this?

It turns out that this movie has a happy ending. The court ruled that the contract between Harris and Blockbuster was unenforceable because there was no *consideration*.

nuttakit/Shutterstock.com; © neelsky/Shutterstock.com

> To rent the movie, she had to click that little box saying she agreed to all the terms and conditions.

Consideration is our next step on the road to understanding contracts. In the last chapter, we learned what it takes to create an agreement. But an agreement is not necessarily a legally enforceable contract.

This is the first of four chapters that will examine problems that can prevent an agreement from becoming a contract. A lack of consideration is one of them. Without it, a promise is "just a promise" and nothing more.

11-1 WHAT IS CONSIDERATION?

The central idea of consideration is simple: Contracts must be a two-way street. If one side gets all the benefit and the other side gets nothing, then an agreement lacks consideration and is not an enforceable contract.

There are three rules of consideration:

1. Both parties must get something of *measureable value* from the contract. That thing can be money, boots, an agreement not to sue, or anything else that has real value.

2. A *promise* to give something of value counts as consideration. A *promise* to mow someone's lawn next week is the equivalent of actually *doing* the yard work when evaluating whether consideration exists.

3. The two parties must have *bargained for* whatever was exchanged and struck a deal: "If you do this, I'll do that." If you just decide to deliver a cake to your neighbor's house without her knowing, that may be something of value, but since you two did not bargain for it, there is no contract, and she does not owe you the price of the cake.

Let's take an example: Sally's Shoe Store and Baker Boots agree that she will pay $20,000 for 100 pairs of boots. They both get something of value—Sally gets the boots, Baker gets the money. A contract is formed when the promises are made because a promise to give something of value counts. The two have bargained for this deal, so there is valid consideration.

Now for an example where there is no consideration. Marvin works at Sally's. At 9 a.m., he is in a good mood and promises to buy his coworker a Starbucks latte during the lunch hour. The delighted coworker agrees. Later that morning, the coworker is rude to Marvin, who then changes his mind about buying the coffee. He is free to do so. His promise created a one-way street: The coworker stood to receive all the benefit of the agreement, while Marvin got nothing. Because Marvin received no value, there is no contract.

Contracts Checklist

☐ Offer
☐ Acceptance
☑ Consideration
☐ Legality
☐ Capacity
☐ Consent
☐ Writing

© Cengage Learning

11-1a What Is Value?

As we have seen, an essential part of consideration is that both parties must get something of value. That item of value can be either an "act" or a "forbearance."

ACT

A party commits an **act** when she does something she was not legally required to do in the first place. She might do a job, deliver an item, or pay money, for example. An act does not count if the party was simply complying with the law or fulfilling her obligations under an existing contract. Thus, for example, suppose that your professor tells the university that she will not post final grades unless she is paid an extra $5,000. Even if the university agrees to this outrageous demand, that agreement is not a valid contract because the professor is already under an obligation to post final grades.

Act

Any action that a party was not legally required to take in the first place.

FORBEARANCE

Forbearance
Refraining from doing something that one has a legal right to do.

A **forbearance** is, in essence, the opposite of an act. A plaintiff forbears if he agrees *not* to do something he had a legal right to do. An entrepreneur might promise a competitor not to open a competing business, or an elderly driver (with a valid driver's license) might promise concerned family members that he will not drive at night.

Let's apply these ideas to the most famous of all consideration lawsuits. Our story begins in 1869, when a well-meaning uncle makes a promise to his nephew. Ever since *Hamer v. Sidway* appeared, generations of American law students have dutifully inhaled the facts and sworn by its wisdom; now you, too, may drink it in.

Landmark Case

HAMER V. SIDWAY
**124 N.Y. 538, 27 N.E. 256, 1891 N.Y. LEXIS 1396
New York Court of Appeals, 1891**

CASE SUMMARY

Facts: This is a story with two Stories. William Story wanted his nephew to grow up healthy and prosperous. In 1869, he promised the 15-year-old boy (also William Story) $5,000 if the lad would refrain from drinking liquor, using tobacco, swearing, and playing cards or billiards for money until his twenty-first birthday. (In that wild era—can you believe it?—the nephew had a legal right to do all those things.) The nephew agreed and, what is more, he kept his word. When he reached his twenty-first birthday, the nephew notified his uncle that he had honored the agreement. The uncle congratulated the young man and promised to give him the money, but he said he would wait a few more years before handing over the cash, until the nephew was mature enough to handle such a large sum. The uncle died in 1887 without having paid, and his estate refused to honor the promise. Because the nephew had transferred his rights in the money, it was a man named Hamer who eventually sought to collect from the uncle's estate. The estate argued that since the nephew had given no consideration for the uncle's promise, there was no enforceable contract. The trial court found for the plaintiff, and the uncle's estate appealed.

Issue: *Did the nephew give consideration for the uncle's promise?*

Decision: Yes, the nephew's conduct was valid consideration and the contract must be enforced.

Reasoning: The uncle's estate argues that the conduct, far from harming the boy, actually aided him. Because it is wise to avoid tobacco, alcohol, and gambling, the nephew's decision to give up those vices could never be consideration for a contract. The agreement could be enforced only if the behavior somehow benefited the uncle—which it did not. The estate's argument, however, is unpersuasive. Courts do not and should not ask whether agreed-on behavior actually helps anyone. What matters is simply this: Did one party do something or refrain from doing something at the request of the other party? If so, that conduct or forbearance is consideration, and the contract is enforceable.

Before making the agreement, the nephew had lawfully used alcohol and tobacco. When his uncle promised him $5,000, the nephew gave up the various activities, restricting his freedom of action for several years. Because the nephew did what his uncle requested, the contract must be enforced whether or not anyone benefited.

The issue of value in a contract is an important one, so let's look at another case. In the movies, when a character wants to get serious about keeping a promise—*really* serious—he sometimes signs an agreement in blood. As it turns out, this kind of thing actually happens in real life. In the following case, did the promise of forbearance have value? Did a contract signed in blood count? You be the judge.

You Be the Judge

KIM v. SON
2009 Cal. App. LEXIS 2011
Court of Appeal of California, 2009

Facts: Stephen Son was a part owner and operator of two corporations. Because the businesses were corporations, Son was not personally liable for the debts of either one.

Jinsoo Kim invested a total of about $170,000 in the companies. Eventually, both of them failed, and Kim lost his investment. Son felt guilty over Kim's losses.

Later, Son and Kim met in a sushi restaurant and drank heroic quantities of alcohol. At one point, Son pricked his finger with a safety pin and wrote the following in his own blood: "Sir, please forgive me. Because of my deeds, you have suffered financially. I will repay you to the best of my ability." In return, Kim agreed not to sue him for the money owed.

Son later refused to honor the bloody document and pay Kim the money. Kim filed suit to enforce their contract.

The judge determined that the promise did not create a contract because there had been no consideration.

You Be the Judge: *Was there consideration?*

Argument for Kim: As a part of the deal made at the sushi restaurant, Kim agreed not to sue Son. What could be more of a forbearance than that? Kim had a right to sue at any time, and he gave the right up. Even if Kim was unlikely to win, Son would still prefer not to be sued.

Besides, the fact that Son signed the agreement in blood indicates how seriously he took the obligation to repay his loyal investor. At a minimum, Son eased his guilty conscience by making the agreement, and surely that is worth something.

Argument for Son: Who among you has not at one point or another become intoxicated, experienced emotions more powerful than usual, and regretted them the next morning? Whether calling an ex-girlfriend and professing endless love or writing out an agreement in your own blood, it is all the same.

A promise not to file a meritless lawsuit has no value at all. It did not matter to Son whether or not Kim filed suit because Kim could not possibly win. If this promise counts as value, then the concept of consideration is meaningless because anyone can promise not to sue anytime. Son had no obligation to pay Kim. And the bloody napkin does not change that fact because it was made without consideration of any kind. It is an ordinary promise, not a contract that creates any legal obligation.

11-1b Adequacy of Consideration

Gold can make people crazy. At the turn of the 20th century, John Tuppela joined the gold rush to Alaska. He bought a mine and worked it hard, a disciplined man in an unforgiving enterprise. Sadly, his prospecting proved futile and mental problems overwhelmed him. In 1914, a court declared him insane and locked him in an institution in Portland, Oregon. Four years later, Tuppela emerged and learned to his ecstasy that gold had been discovered in his mine, now valued at over half a million dollars. Then the bad news hit: A court-appointed guardian had sold the mine for pennies while Tuppela was institutionalized. Destitute and forlorn, Tuppela turned to his lifelong friend, Embola, saying, "If you will give me $50 so I can go to Alaska and get my property back, I will pay you $10,000 when I win my property." Embola accepted the offer, advancing the $50.

After a long and bitter fight, Tuppela won back his mine, though a guardian would still supervise his assets. Tuppela asked the guardian to pay the full $10,000 to Embola, but the guardian refused. Embola sued, and the issue was whether his $50 was *adequate consideration* to support Tuppela's promise of $10,000. A happy ending: Embola won and recovered his money.

Courts seldom inquire into the *adequacy* of consideration. Although the difference between Embola's $50 and Tuppela's $10,000 was huge, it was not for a court to decide whether the parties had made an intelligent bargain. Embola undertook a risk, and his $50 was valid consideration. The question of adequacy is for the parties as they bargain, not for the courts.

Law professors often call this the "peppercorn rule," a reference to a Civil War–era case in which a judge mused, "What is a valuable consideration? A peppercorn."[1] Even the tiniest benefit to a plaintiff counts, so long as it has a measureable value.

EXAM Strategy

Question: 50 Cent has been rapping all day, and he is very thirsty. He pulls his Ferrari into the parking lot of a convenience store. The store turns out to be closed, but luckily for him, a PepsiCo machine sits outside. While walking over to it, he realizes that he has left his wallet at home. Frustrated, he whistles to a 10-year-old kid who is walking by. "Hey kid!" he shouts. "I need to borrow fifty cents!" "I know who you are!" the kid replies. Fiddy tries again. "No, no, I need to *borrow* fifty cents!" The kid walks over. "Well, I'm not going to just give you my last fifty cents. But maybe you can sell me something." 50 Cent cannot believe it, but he really is very thirsty. He takes off a Rolex, which is his least expensive bling. "How about this?" "Deal," the kid says, handing over two quarters. Is the kid entitled to keep the watch?

Strategy: Even in extreme cases, courts rarely take an interest in *how much* consideration is given, or whether everyone got a "good deal." Even though the Rolex is worth thousands of times more than the quarters, the quarters still count under the peppercorn rule.

Result: After this transaction, 50 Cent may have second thoughts, but they will be too late. The kid committed an act by handing over his money—he was under no legal obligation to do so. And 50 Cent received something of small but measureable value. So there is consideration to support this deal, and 50 Cent would not get his watch back.

11-1c Illusory Promises

Annabel calls Jim and says, "I'll sell you my bicycle for 325 bucks. Interested?" Jim says, "I'll look at it tonight in the bike rack. If I like what I see, I'll pay you in the morning." At sunrise, Jim shows up with the $325, but Annabel refuses to sell. Can Jim enforce their deal? No. He said he would buy the bicycle *if he liked it*, keeping for himself the power to get out of the agreement for any reason at all. He is not *committing* himself to do anything, and the law considers his promise illusory—that is, not really a promise at all. **An illusory promise is not consideration.** Because he has given no consideration, there is no contract, and *neither party* can enforce the deal.

Let's revisit the Blockbuster case from the opening scenario. Blockbuster's clickwrap box read, in part:

> Blockbuster may at any time, and at its sole discretion, modify these Terms and Conditions of Use, including without limitation the Privacy Policy, with or without notice. Such modifications will be effective immediately upon posting.

---

[1]*Hobbs v. Duff*, 23 Cal. 596 (1863).

Because Blockbuster had the ability to change the rules at any time for any reason, the court determined that the contract was illusory and that Harris was not bound by Blockbuster's arbitration clause.[2]

11-2 APPLICATIONS OF CONSIDERATION

We will spend the remainder of the chapter looking at specific situations in which consideration plays a central role.

11-2a The UCC: Consideration in Requirements and Output Contracts

In a requirements contract, the buyer agrees to purchase 100 percent of her goods from one seller. The seller agrees to sell the buyer whatever quantity she reasonably needs. The quantity is not stated in the contract, though it may be estimated based on previous years or best calculations. The common law regarded requirements contracts as void because the buyer held all the power. She could purchase a vast quantity or none at all. She was making no commitment, and hence was giving no consideration. Common law courts refused to enforce requirements contracts, as well as their counterpart, output contracts.

In an output contract, the seller guarantees to sell 100 percent of its output to one buyer, and the buyer agrees to accept the entire quantity. For example, a timber company might agree to sell all of its wood products to a lumber wholesaler. The common law frowned on this because now it was the seller who was making no real commitment.

The problem with the common law rule was that many merchants valued these contracts. Consider the utility of requirements contracts. From the buyer's viewpoint, a requirements contract provides flexibility. The buyer can adjust purchases based on consumer demands. The agreement also guarantees her a source of goods in a competitive market. For a seller, the requirements agreement will ensure him at least this one outlet and will prevent competitors from selling to this buyer. The contract should enable the seller to spend less on marketing and may enable him to predict sales more accurately. Output contracts have similar value.

The UCC responded in a forthright fashion: **Section 2-306 expressly allows output and requirements contracts in the sale of goods**.[3] However, the Code places one limitation on how much the buyer may demand (or the seller may offer):

> A term which measures the quantity by the output of the seller or the requirements of the buyer means such actual output or requirements as may occur *in good faith*, ...

The "good faith" phrase is critical. In requirements contracts, courts have ruled that it is the "good faith" that a buyer brings to the deal that represents her consideration.[4] In other words, by agreeing to act in good faith, she actually is limiting her options. Because she is obligating herself, the deal becomes binding. Beware that this is not just wordplay. A buyer *must make its requirement demands in good faith*, based on the expectations the parties had when they signed the deal.

---

[2]*Harris v. Blockbuster Inc.*, 622 F. Supp. 2d 396 (N.D. Tex. 2009).

[3]UCC §2-306(2) permits a related type of contract, the exclusive dealing agreement. Here, either a buyer or a seller of goods agrees to deal exclusively with the other party. The results are similar to an output or requirements agreement. Once again, one party is receiving a guarantee in exchange for a promise that the common law would have considered illusory. Under the Code, such a deal is enforceable.

[4]*Famous Brands, Inc. v. David Sherman Corp.*, 814 F.2d 517, 1987 U.S. App. LEXIS 3634 (8th Cir. 1987).

Suppose that you operate a T-shirt business. You and a wholesaler agree on a two-year requirements contract with a fixed price of $3 per T-shirt and an estimate of 150 T-shirts per week. If business is slow the first two months, you are permitted to purchase only 25 T-shirts per week if that is all you are selling. Should sales suddenly boom and you need 200 per week, you may also require that many. Both of those demands are made in good faith. But suppose the price of cotton skyrockets and the wholesale cost of T-shirts everywhere suddenly doubles. You have a two-year guaranteed price of $3 per T-shirt. Could you demand 2,000 T-shirts per week, knowing that you will be able to resell the shirts to other retailers for a big profit? No. That is not acting in good faith based on the original expectations of the parties. The wholesaler is free to ignore your exorbitant demand. The legal requirement has come full circle: Your good faith is valid consideration and makes the deal enforceable—but it is binding on you, too.

EXAM Strategy

Question: Will bought simple wood furniture and custom-painted it for sale to interior designers. He entered into a written agreement to buy all the furniture he needed, for two years, from Wood Knot, Inc. Wood Knot agreed to supply Will with all the furniture he requested. During the second year, Will's business grew, and he requested 28 percent more furniture than in the first year. Wood Knot would not deliver unless Will would pay a higher price per unit, which Will would not. Will sued. What kind of a contract was this? Will Will win? Why or why not?

Strategy: Because this agreement did not specify the quantity of goods being sold, we know that it was either a requirements contract or an output contract. Review the difference between the two. Which was this agreement? These contracts are now legal, with one major limitation. What is that limitation? Apply it here.

Result: This was a requirements contract because Will agreed to purchase all his furniture from Wood Knot. Under the UCC, requirements contracts are enforceable, provided the buyer makes his demands in good faith. Will's increased order was a result of his booming business. Indeed, he entered into this agreement to protect his ability to grow his company. He made the request in good faith, the contract is enforceable, and yes—Will *will* win.

> Of course, exceptions are the spice of law …

11-2b Preexisting Duty

As we have seen, **a promise to do something that a party is already obligated to do is not consideration.** Of course, exceptions are the spice of law, and the preexisting duty rule provides us with a rackful. Courts have created these exceptions because a rigid application of the rule might interfere with legitimate business goals.

EXCEPTION: ADDITIONAL WORK

When a party agrees to do something above and beyond what he is obligated to do, his promise is generally valid consideration. Cecil has promised to build a fabulous swimming pool/cabana for Nathalie for $250,000. When the work is half complete, he offers to build the cabana out of seashells rather than pine wood. If Nathalie agrees to a new price of $300,000 for the pool complex, she is obligated to pay because Cecil's extra work is valid consideration for her promise.

EXCEPTION: MODIFICATION

If both parties agree that a modification is necessary, the surest way to accomplish that is to rescind the original contract and draft a new one. **To rescind means to cancel.** Thus, if neither party has completed its obligations, the agreement to rescind will terminate each party's rights and obligations under the old contract. This should be done in writing. Then the parties sign the new agreement. Courts will *generally* enforce a rescission and modification provided both parties voluntarily entered into it, in good faith. If one side, determined to earn greater profits, unfairly coerces the other into the changes, the modification is invalid.

Once again, the UCC has changed the common law, making it easier for merchants to modify agreements for the sale of goods. UCC §2-209 provides:

- An agreement modifying a contract within this Article needs no consideration to be binding.

- A signed agreement which excludes modification or rescission except by a signed writing cannot be otherwise modified or rescinded.

Here is how these two provisions work together. Mike's Magic Mania (MMM) agrees to deliver 500 rabbits and 500 top hats to State University for the school's Sleight of Hand 101 course. The goods, including 100 cages and 1,000 pounds of rabbit food, are to arrive no later than September 1, in time for the new semester, with payment on delivery. By September 20, no rabbits have appeared, in or out of hats. The university buys similar products from another supply house at a 25 percent steeper price and sues MMM for the difference. Mike claims that in early September, the dean had orally agreed to permit delivery in October. The dean is on sabbatical in Tahiti and cannot be reached for comment. Is the alleged modification valid?

Under the common law, the modification would have been void because MMM gave no consideration for the extended delivery date. However, this is a sale of goods, and under UCC §2-209, an oral modification may be valid even without consideration. Unfortunately for Mike, though, the original agreement included a clause forbidding oral modification. Any changes had to be in writing, signed by both parties. Mike never obtained such a document. Even if the dean did make the oral agreement, the university wins.

The following case arose in a setting that is traumatic and lamentably common: A homeowner could not make his mortgage payments. Foreclosure loomed. Did the parties agree to save the home?

You Be the Judge

CITIZENS TRUST BANK v. WHITE

274 Ga.App.508, 618 S.E.2d 9
Georgia Court of Appeals, 2005

Facts: Herbert White owned a house in Atlanta. He refinanced his home through Citizens Trust Bank, but fell behind on his loan payments. He owed about $43,000. The bank notified White that it intended to foreclose. After some delays, the bank sent White a formal notice that it would sell his house at a foreclosure sale on the courthouse steps, on May 7. The finance agreement provided that if the bank foreclosed, White owed the full amount.

On that date, White arrived and offered the bank $35,000 to stop the foreclosure. The bank's collection manager, D.J. Hughlett, accepted the money and drafted a letter, which he and White signed:

Citizens Trust Bank agrees to postpone the foreclosure [based on] a payment of $33,000 in certified funds and a possible $2,000 from the account of Cora White Cummings on the above-referenced property. Our Attorney, William A. Broughman, will forward to you a written agreement, for your signature, to consummate this transaction. The payoff balance as of 11:05 a.m. is $7,986.43. If his sister pays the $2,000, the balance will be $5,986.43.

White did pay the extra $2,000. Hughlett decided that the signed letter was a forbearance agreement with White, so he did not bother to send an additional document. Hughlett believed that White would pay the balance within 30 days, but White never did so. The bank sent a new foreclosure notice and did in fact sell the house.

White sued the bank, claiming that it had breached its agreement not to foreclose. The jury agreed, awarding White $250,000 in compensatory damages. The bank appealed, arguing that White gave no consideration for the agreement because he was already obligated to pay the full balance.

You Be the Judge: *Was the signed letter an enforceable contract?*

Argument for the Bank: Mr. White fell behind on his mortgage payments. As soon as the bank notified him that it was foreclosing, his full debt became due. When he offered to pay a percentage of that debt, he was fulfilling a preexisting duty. He was *legally obligated* to pay the $35,000 that he "offered," along with the full balance due. A promise to do what a party is required to do is never consideration. Without consideration, there is no contract.

The jury made an emotional decision based on sympathy for the debtor. That type of decision leads to bad policy and bad law. The policy is poor because if everyone were allowed to default without suffering a loss, no bank would lend money and most citizens could never buy a house. The law is even worse because the case should not have gone to a jury. The trial judge should have dismissed the suit based on the preexisting duty rule.

Argument for Mr. White: There were two parties to this agreement, and both believed they had a binding agreement. The bank's officer agreed to postpone foreclosure. He also promised to forward a formal document confirming the understanding but did not do so. And why did he send no other document? Because he believed the bank had already agreed to halt any foreclosure effort. He was right.

Mr. White paid 80 percent of the balance due. It is wrong for the bank to take the money and then break its promise. Furthermore, it is absurd to foreclose based on such a modest debt. The legal argument about consideration is nonsense. Mr. White's consideration was a check for $35,000.

The jury award indicates a group of average citizens who were angry about what the bank did. The verdict should be affirmed.

EXAM Strategy

Question: Star Struck, a Hollywood talent agency, employs Puneet as one of its young agents and Max as a part-time delivery boy. Puneet's contract is for one year. She earns $5,000 per month, payable on the last day of each month. After she has worked at the firm for four months, a Star Struck executive says to her, "We are having cash flow problems. We cannot pay you this month, and will probably fall about two months behind. However, if you will agree to do Max's job for the next few months, we can pay you on time." Puneet cheerfully agrees to the deal. However, after a few weeks of the extra labor, Puneet confesses that she is overwhelmed and can no longer do Max's job. Star Struck fires her. Puneet sues. Was there a binding agreement for Puneet to do Max's work?

Strategy: Star Struck made an offer to Puneet and she accepted it. But a contract needs more than offer and acceptance. Both parties must give consideration. Had they done more than they were required to do under their preexisting duty?

Result: A promise to do what a party is already obligated to do is not consideration. Star Struck was required to pay Puneet every month, so its "offer" included no consideration. Without consideration, there can be no agreement. Puneet was not obligated to do Max's job, and she will win this lawsuit.

EXCEPTION: UNFORESEEN CIRCUMSTANCES

Hugo has a deal to repair major highways. Hugo hires Hal's Hauling to cart soil and debris. Hal's trucks begin work, but after crossing the work site several times, they sink to their axles in sinister, sucking slime. Hal demands an additional 35 percent payment from Hugo to complete the job, pointing out that the surface was dry and cracked and that neither Hal nor Hugo was aware of the subsurface water. Hal howls that he must use different trucks with different tires and work more slowly to permit the soil to dry. Hugo hems and haws and finally agrees. But when the hauling is finished, Hugo refuses to pay the extra money. Is Hugo liable?

   Yes. When unforeseen circumstances cause a party to make a promise regarding an unfinished project, that promise is generally valid consideration. Even though Hal is only promising to finish what he was already obligated to do, his promise is valid consideration because neither party knew of the subsoil mud. Hal was facing a situation quite different from what the parties anticipated. It is almost as though he were undertaking a new project. Hal has given consideration, and Hugo is bound by his promise to pay extra money.

11-3 SETTLEMENT OF DEBTS

You claim that your friend Felicity owes you $90,000, but she refuses to pay. Finally, when you are desperate, Felicity offers you a cashier's check for $60,000—provided you accept it as full settlement. To get your hands on some money, you agree and cash the check. The next day, you sue Felicity for $30,000. Who wins? It will depend principally upon one major issue: Was Felicity's debt liquidated or unliquidated?

11-3a Liquidated Debt

A **liquidated debt** is one in which there is no dispute about the amount owed. A loan is a typical example. If a bank lends you $10,000, and the note obligates you to repay that amount on June 1 of the following year, you clearly owe that sum. The debt is liquidated.

   In cases of liquidated debt, if the creditor agrees to take less than the full amount as full payment, her agreement is not binding. The debtor has given no consideration to support the creditor's promise to accept a reduced payment, and therefore the creditor is not bound by her word. The reasoning is simply that the debtor is already obligated to pay the full amount, so no bargaining could reasonably cause the creditor to accept less. If Felicity's debt to you is liquidated, your agreement to accept $60,000 is not binding, and you will successfully sue for the balance.

Liquidated debt
A debt in which there is no dispute about the amount owed.

EXCEPTION: DIFFERENT PERFORMANCE

There is one important exception to this rule. If the debtor offers a *different performance* to settle the liquidated debt, and the creditor agrees to take it as full settlement, the agreement is binding. Suppose that Felicity, instead of paying $60,000, offers you five acres in Alaska, and you accept. When you accept the deed to the land, you have given up your entire claim, regardless of the land's precise value.

11-3b Unliquidated Debt: Accord and Satisfaction

A debt is **unliquidated** for either of two reasons: (1) the parties dispute whether any money is owed, or (2) the parties agree that some money is owed but dispute how much. When a debt is unliquidated for either reason, the parties may enter into a binding agreement to settle for less than what the creditor demands.

Unliquidated debt
A debt that is disputed because the parties disagree over its existence or amount.

Such a compromise will be enforced if:

- The debt is unliquidated;
- The parties agree that the creditor will accept as full payment a sum less than she has claimed; and
- The debtor pays the amount agreed upon.

Accord and satisfaction
A completed agreement to settle a debt for less than the sum claimed.

This agreement is called an **accord and satisfaction**. The accord is the agreement to settle for less than the creditor claims. The satisfaction is the actual payment of that compromised sum. An accord and satisfaction is valid consideration to support the creditor's agreement to drop all claims. Each party is giving up something: The creditor gives up her full claim, and the debtor gives up his assertion that he owed little or nothing.

Accord and Satisfaction by Check

Most accord and satisfaction agreements involve payment by check. UCC §3-311 governs these agreements, using the same common law rules described above.[5] The Code specifies that when the debtor writes "full settlement" on the check, a creditor who cashes the check generally has entered into an accord and satisfaction. If Felicity's debt is unliquidated, and she gives you a check with "full payment of all debts" written on the face in bold letters, the moment you deposit the check, you lose any claim to more money. What happens if the debtor makes such a notation but the creditor changes it? A massage therapist learned the answer and felt sore for days.

HENCHES V. TAYLOR

138 Wash. App. 1026, 2007 WL 1241525
Washington Court of Appeals, 2007

CASE SUMMARY

Facts: Jim Henches, a licensed massage therapist, treated Benjamin Taylor after he was injured in a car accident. When all treatments were finished, Henches billed Taylor for more than $7,000. Taylor's insurance company claimed the bill was exorbitant, and paid only $2,625, for 24 massage treatments.

Henches continued to send bills to Taylor, not only for the balance due, but for additional time spent consulting with Taylor's other health care providers, preparing to testify in Taylor's personal injury lawsuit, and attempting to collect his debts. In response to a bill for $11,945.86, Taylor's lawyer James Harris sent Henches a letter, stating:

I have reviewed your billing statements and am having a difficult time understanding a number of charges you included. By my calculations, the amount owed to you is approximately $5,243.45. I have enclosed a check for that amount as payment in full to settle Mr. Taylor's account with you.

The letter was accompanied by a check with "final payment" written on the notation line. Henches filed suit, seeking the full balance. Then he wrote "attorney/fee" on the check, over the word "final," and deposited the check.

The trial court gave summary judgment to Taylor, ruling that deposit of the check constituted accord and satisfaction. Henches appealed.

Issue: *Was there an accord and satisfaction, discharging the debt?*

Decision: Yes, depositing the check created an accord and satisfaction.

Reasoning: An accord and satisfaction exists when three circumstances arise. Parties have a legitimately disputed debt. They agree that a partial payment of the debt will settle the dispute. Finally, the defendant accepts the partial payment.

---

[5]A check is legally an instrument, which is why this section comes from Article 3 of the Code. For a full discussion of instruments, see Chapter 22.

In this case, the defendant easily established the first and third elements. The parties had a genuine dispute over the costly treatments, and Henches deposited the check. But Henches claimed that he had not agreed to accept the check as full payment of the debt. In the end, his own actions contradicted his argument.

When he wrote "attorney/fee" over the word "final," Henches indicated that he knew that Taylor intended for the check to be a final settlement. If an amount is in dispute and the defendant offers partial payment as full settlement, then accepting this money counts as full satisfaction, no matter what else the plaintiff may do. When Henches deposited the check, he lost the ability to seek any further payment.

UCC Exceptions

The Code creates two exceptions for accord and satisfaction cases involving checks. The first exception concerns "organizations," which typically are businesses. The general rule of §3-311 is potentially calamitous to them because a company that receives thousands of checks every day is unlikely to inspect all notations. A consumer who owes $12,000 on a credit card might write "full settlement" on a $200 check, potentially extinguishing the entire debt through accord and satisfaction. Under the exception, if an organization notifies a debtor that any offers to settle for less than the debt claimed must be made to a particular official, and the check is sent to anyone else in the organization, depositing the check generally does *not* create an accord and satisfaction. Thus a clerk who deposits 900 checks daily for payment of MasterCard debts will not have inadvertently entered into dozens of accord and satisfaction agreements.

The second exception allows a way out to most creditors who have inadvertently created an accord and satisfaction. If, within 90 days of cashing a "full payment" check, the creditor offers repayment of the same amount to the debtor, there is no accord and satisfaction. Homer claims that Virgil owes him $7 million but foolishly cashes Virgil's check for $3 million, without understanding that "paid in full" means just what it says. Homer has created an accord and satisfaction. But if he promptly sends Virgil a check for $3 million, he has undone the agreement and may sue for the full amount.

11-4 Consideration: Trends

11-4a Employment Agreements

In a noncompete agreement, an employee promises not to work for a competitor for some time after leaving the company. It used to be that these covenants were rare and reserved for top officers, but they have now become commonplace throughout many organizations. We will talk about them more in the next chapter, but often these covenants raise an issue of consideration: What consideration does the employee receive for signing a covenant not to compete? After all, the company is already under an obligation to pay the employee for working. What additional value does the employee receive in return for signing the agreement?

Although this area of law is developing and is a bit murky, the following case reflects the current majority view. Sometimes consideration issues can drive you nuts.

SNIDER BOLT & SCREW V. QUALITY SCREW & NUT

2009 U.S. Dist. LEXIS 50797
United States District Court for the Western District of Kentucky, 2009

CASE SUMMARY

Facts: James Scott began working for Snider Bolt & Screw in 1999. In 2002, Scott signed an employment agreement with Snider, which included a covenant not to compete. The covenant prohibited him from taking a job with a competitor for one year after leaving Snider. Three years later, Scott quit his job at Snider and immediately went to work for Quality Screw & Nut.

Snider obtained a temporary restraining order that banned Scott from working at his new job. Quality argued that the covenant not to compete was void for lack of consideration. It asked the court to lift the temporary restraining order.

Issue: *Was there consideration for the covenant not to compete?*

Decision: Yes, the covenant was supported by adequate consideration.

Reasoning: The central question here is whether the 2002 covenant had consideration—that is, whether both Snider and Scott received new benefits.

From 1999 to 2002, Scott worked for Snider without a contract. Snider could have fired him at any time. Upon signing the employment agreement, Scott promised not to compete with Snider in the future, a new promise. Snider got the benefit of that promise of loyalty. After going to work for Quality in 2005, Scott argued that the covenant was void for lack of consideration because he got nothing in return for his promise.

But that was not true: The employment contract *did* bind Snider in a new way. In the contract, Snider implicitly promised continued employment. Snider could have fired Scott, but did not. Kentucky courts have found that an implied promise to continue employment counts as consideration, whether the employee is at will or has a contract.

The covenant was supported by adequate consideration. The motion to lift the temporary restraining order is denied.

11-4b Promissory Estoppel and "Moral Consideration"

Judges have a tool by which they can enforce agreements even if there is no consideration. Under the doctrine of promissory estoppel, a judge has the discretion to "ignore" the fact that consideration does not exist if a promise causes foreseeable reliance by a plaintiff and a great injustice would be done if the promise were broken. Some courts will use the phrase "moral consideration" to describe this basic idea.

For example, consider a pledge to charity. If Dave promises to give money to charity and then fails to make the donation, there is no consideration because he has received nothing in return. If the charity sues to enforce the promise, it cannot show that it has committed an act or forbearance.[6]

Nevertheless, some courts will force donors to make good on their donations anyway. Especially in the case of large donations, courts will often cite the "grave injustices" that can follow from this kind of promise breaking. "If you don't give the 'Coats for Kids' program the $100,000 you've pledged, then thousands of children will go without a coat this winter," a judge might say. Also, it may be that the charity has relied on the pledge to open another

---

[6]An exception to this, of course, would be if the charity agreed to give Dave something at the time he made the pledge. As a "fix" for consideration problems, many charities send donors something of trivial value when pledges are made—maybe a water bottle or a tote bag. Under the peppercorn rule, even something of small value counts as a legal act, and it converts a mere promise of a donation into an enforceable contract.

storefront or undertake a new program. Courts are likely to enforce the pledge in these circumstances.

It is unwise to make charitable pledges, especially large pledges, if you might change your mind.

EXAM Strategy

Question: In an Alabama case, Webb saved McGowin's life by preventing a giant block of wood from falling on his head.[7] Webb was permanently disabled in the accident and was never able to work again. Later, McGowin promised to give Webb money every two weeks for the rest of his life. McGowin made the payments for awhile but then stopped. Webb sued.

Strategy: No consideration exists here. McGowin made the promise to pay the money *after* Webb's heroic act. Webb did not give McGowin anything of value *in return for* the promise to pay money. But what about promissory estoppel?

Result: In the case, the court found that "moral consideration" was present, and that Webb was entitled to the payments to prevent substantial injustice.

It is important to note that applications of promissory estoppel and similar doctrines are rare. Ordinarily, if there is no consideration, then there is no contract. However, in extreme cases, it is possible for a court to enforce a deal even without consideration. But this is not something you can count on.

Chapter Conclusion

This ancient doctrine of consideration is simple to state but subtle to apply. The parties must bargain and enter into an exchange of promises or actions. If they do not, there is no consideration and the courts are unlikely to enforce any promise made. A variety of exceptions modify the law, but a party wishing to render its future more predictable—the purpose of a contract—will rely on a solid bargain and exchange.

EXAM REVIEW

1. **CONSIDERATION**   There are three rules of consideration:

   1. Both parties must get something of *measureable value* from the contract.
   2. A *promise* to give something of value counts as consideration.
   3. The two parties must have *bargained for* whatever was exchanged. (p. 257)

---

[7]*Webb v. McGowin*, 168 So. 196 (Ala.1935).

2. **ACT OR FORBEARANCE**   The item of value can be either an act or a forbearance. (pp. 258–259)

EXAM Strategy

Question: An aunt saw her eight-year-old nephew enter the room, remarked what a nice boy he was, and said, "I would like to take care of him now." She promptly wrote a note, promising to pay the boy $3,000 upon her death. Her estate refused to pay. Is it obligated to do so?

Strategy: A contract is enforceable only if the parties have given consideration. The consideration might be an act or a forbearance. Did the nephew give consideration? (See the "Result" at the end of this section.)

3. **ADEQUACY**   The courts will seldom inquire into the adequacy of consideration. This is the "peppercorn rule." (pp. 259–260)

4. **ILLUSORY PROMISES**   An illusory promise is not consideration. (pp. 260–261)

Question: Eagle ran convenience stores. He entered into an agreement with Commercial Movie in which Commercial would provide Eagle with DVDs for rental. Eagle would pay Commercial 50 percent of the rental revenues. If Eagle stopped using Commercial's service, Eagle could not use a competitor's services for 18 months. The agreement also provided: "Commercial shall not be liable for compensation or damages of any kind, whether on account of the loss by Eagle of profits, sales or expenditures, or on account of any other event or cause whatsoever." Eagle complied with the agreement for two years but then began using a competitor's service, and Commercial sued. Eagle claimed that the agreement was unenforceable for lack of consideration. Please rule.

Strategy: In this case, both parties seem to have given consideration. But there is a flaw in the "promise" that Commercial made. Commercial can never be liable to Eagle—no matter what happens. (See the "Result" at the end of this section.)

5. **REQUIREMENT AND OUTPUT CONTRACTS**   Under sales law, requirement and output contracts are valid. Although one side controls the quantity, its agreement to make demands *in good faith* is consideration. (pp. 261–262)

6. **PREEXISTING DUTY**   Under the doctrine of preexisting duty, a promise to do something that the party is already legally obligated to perform is generally not consideration. (p. 262)

7. **LIQUIDATED DEBT**   A liquidated debt is one in which there is no dispute about the amount owed. For a liquidated debt, a creditor's promise to accept less than the full amount is not binding. (p. 265)

8. **UNLIQUIDATED DEBT**   For an unliquidated debt, if the parties agree that the creditor will accept less than the full amount claimed and the debtor performs, there is an accord and satisfaction and the creditor may not claim any balance. (pp. 265–266)

9. **"FULL PAYMENT"**   Notations In most states, payment by a check that has a "full payment" notation will create an accord and satisfaction unless the creditor is an organization that has notified the debtor that full payment offers must go to a certain officer. (p. 267)

EXAM Strategy

Question: When White's wife died, he filed a claim with Boston Mutual for $10,000 death benefits under her insurance policy. The insurer rejected the claim, saying that his wife had misrepresented her medical condition in the application form. The company sent White a check for $478.75, which it said represented "a full refund of all applicable premiums paid" for the coverage. White deposited the check. Had the parties reached an accord and satisfaction?

Strategy: The UCC permits parties to enter into an accord and satisfaction by check. The debtor must make clear that the check is offered in full payment of a disputed debt. Debtors generally do that by writing "Final Settlement," "Accepted as Full Payment of All Debts," or some similar notation on the check. Had the insurance company complied with that requirement? (See the "Result" at the end of this section.)

10. **PROMISSORY ESTOPPEL**   Sometimes, to prevent injustice, courts will enforce agreements even if no consideration is present. These deals are still not formal contracts, but the courts will enforce a promise nonetheless. (pp. 268–269)

EXAM Strategy

Question: Phil Philanthropist called PBS during a fund drive and pledged to donate $100,000. PBS then planned and began to produce a Fourth of July *Sesame Street* special, counting on the large donation to fund it. Later, Phil changed his mind and said he had decided not to donate the money after all. PBS sued because without the money, it would not be able to complete the show. Will PBS win the lawsuit?

Strategy: Analyze the promise to donate the $100,000. Does it contain consideration? If not, is there any other legal possibility? (See the "Result" at the end of this section.)

2. Result: The nephew gave no consideration. He did not promise to do anything. He committed no act or forbearance. Without consideration, there is no enforceable contract. The estate wins.

4. Result: Commercial's promise was illusory. The company was free to walk away from the deal at any time. Commercial could never be held liable. Commercial gave no consideration, and there was no binding contract for either party to enforce.

9. Result: The insurer merely stated that its check was a refund of premiums. Nowhere did the company indicate that the check was full payment of its disputed obligation. The company should have made it clear that it would not pay any benefits and that this payment was all that it would offer. There was no accord and satisfaction.

10. Result: There is no "regular" consideration here because Phil received no measureable benefit and PBS did not act or forbear. But PBS can likely make a strong case that a great injustice will be done if the money is not paid. A judge might well decide to apply the doctrine of promissory estoppel and require Phil to make the donation.

Multiple-Choice Questions

1. For consideration to exist, there must be:
   (a) A bargained-for exchange
   (b) A manifestation of mutual assent
   (c) Genuineness of assent
   (d) Substantially equal economic benefits to both parties

2. Which of the following requires consideration in order to be binding on the parties?
   (a) Modification of a contract involving the sale of real estate
   (b) Modification of a sale of goods contract under the UCC
   (c) Both (a) and (b)
   (d) None of the above

3. Ted's wallet is as empty as his bank account, and he needs $3,500 immediately. Fortunately, he has three gold coins that he inherited from his grandfather. Each is worth $2,500, but it is Sunday, and the local rare coins store is closed. When approached, Ted's neighbor Andrea agrees to buy the first coin for $2,300. Another neighbor, Cami, agrees to buy the second for $1,100. A final neighbor, Lorne, offers "all the money I have on me"—$100—for the last coin. Desperate, Ted agrees to the proposal. Which of the deals is supported by consideration?
   (a) Ted's agreement with Andrea only
   (b) Ted's agreements with Andrea and Cami only
   (c) All three of the agreements
   (d) None of the agreements

4. In a(n) _____ contract, the seller guarantees to sell 100 percent of its output to one buyer, and the buyer agrees to accept the entire quantity. This kind of arrangement _____ acceptable under the UCC.
   (a) output; is
   (b) output; is not
   (c) requirements; is
   (d) requirements; is not

5. Noncompete agreements are common features of employment contracts. Currently, courts _____ enforce these clauses.

(a) always

(b) usually

(c) rarely

(d) never

ESSAY QUESTIONS

1. American Bakeries had a fleet of over 3,000 delivery trucks. Because of the increasing cost of gasoline, the company was interested in converting the trucks to propane fuel. It signed a requirements contract with Empire Gas, in which Empire would convert "approximately 3,000" trucks to propane fuel, as American Bakeries requested, and would then sell all the required propane fuel to run the trucks. But American Bakeries changed its mind and never requested a single conversion. Empire sued for lost profits. Who won?

2. CeCe Hylton and Edward Meztista, partners in a small advertising firm, agreed to terminate the business and split assets evenly. Meztista gave Hylton a two-page document showing assets, liabilities, and a bottom line of $35,235.67, with half due to each partner. Hylton questioned the accounting and asked to see the books. Meztista did not permit Hylton to see any records and refused to answer her phone calls. Instead, he gave her a check in the amount of $17,617.83, on which he wrote "Final payment/payment in full." Hylton cashed the check, but she wrote on it, "Under protest—cashing this check does not constitute my acceptance of this amount as payment in full." Hylton then filed suit, demanding additional monies. Meztista claimed that the parties had made an accord and satisfaction. What is the best argument for each party? Who should win?

3. ETHICS Melnick built a house for Gintzler, but the foundation was defective. Gintzler agreed to accept the foundation if Melnick guaranteed to make future repairs caused by the defects. Melnick agreed but later refused to make any repairs. Melnick argued that his promise to make future repairs was unsupported by consideration. Who will win the suit? Is either party acting unethically? Which one, and why?

4. Sami walks into a restaurant. She is given a menu, which indicates that lobster is $30. Sami orders the lobster. It arrives, and Sami thinks it is very tasty. When the bill arrives, Sami tries to execute a clever ploy she learned about in her business law class. She writes a check to the restaurant for $20 and writes "full settlement" across the top. The waiter accepts the check without looking at it, and the restaurant manager later deposits it in the restaurant's bank account. Is this a liquidated or an unliquidated debt? Is Sami off the hook for the last $10?

5. In the bleachers …

"You're a prince, George!" Mike exclaimed. "Who else would give me a ticket to the big game?"

"No one, Mike, no one."

"Let me offer my thanks. I'll buy you a beer!"

"Ah," George said. "A large beer would hit the spot right now."

"Small. Let me buy you a small beer."

"Ah, well, good enough."

Mike stood and took his wallet from his pocket. He was distressed to find a very small number of bills inside. "There's bad news, George!" he said.

"What's that?"

"I can't buy you the beer, George."

George considered that for a moment. "I'll tell you what, Mike," he said. "If you march to the concession stand right this minute and get me my beer, I won't punch you in the face."

"It's a deal!" Mike said.

Discuss the consideration issues raised by this exchange.

6. Jack Tallas came to the United States from Greece in 1914. He lived in Salt Lake City for nearly 70 years, achieving great success in insurance and real estate. During the last 14 years of his life, his friend Peter Dementas helped him with numerous personal and business chores. Two months before his death, Tallas dictated a memorandum to Dementas, in Greek, stating:

> PETER K. DEMENTAS is my best friend I have in this country, and since he came to the United States, he treats me like a father and I think of him as my own son. He takes me in his car grocery shopping. He drives me to the doctor and also takes me every week to Bingham to pick up my mail, collect the rents, and manage my properties. For all the services Peter has given me all these years, I owe to him the amount of $50,000 (Fifty Thousand Dollars). I will shortly change my will to include him as my heir.

Tallas signed the memorandum, but he did not in fact alter his will to include Dementas. The estate refused to pay, and Dementas sued. Was there consideration? Please rule.

DISCUSSION QUESTIONS

Apply the following material to the next three questions.

Some view consideration as a technicality that allows people to make promises and then back out of them. Perhaps all promises should be enforced. In Japan, for example, promises to give gifts are enforceable without consideration.[8]

In the United States, if I promise to give you a gift merely because I feel like being nice, I can freely change my mind as far as contract law is concerned.

A court will not make me follow through because there is no consideration.

In Japan, I would be obligated to buy the gift if all other elements of a contract were present—an offer, an acceptance, and so forth.

Some argue that consideration in U.S. law is a doctrine left over from centuries long past, that it lacks any reasonable modern purpose, and that it should be abolished.

---

[8]See Japan's Civil Code, Article 549.

1. Do you agree with this statement: "A person should always keep his or her word."

2. When it comes to giving gifts, which is better—the Japanese or American rule?

3. Are there any specific types of agreements (perhaps high-value, long-term, extremely time-consuming ones) that should definitely require consideration?

4. In the gold rush example, Embola gave Tuppela $50 in exchange for a promise of $10,000 later. Under the peppercorn rule, the deal was a contract. Is the peppercorn rule sensible? Should courts require a more *even* exchange of value?

5. In the last two chapters, we have examined clickwrap boxes. Sometimes courts refuse to enforce clickwrap terms because of problems with acceptance or consideration, but usually the terms are enforced. Is there a way to make clickwraps fair to both sides? Would it be better to ban clickwrap boxes altogether?

CHAPTER 12

LEGALITY

Soheil Sadri, a California resident, did some serious gambling at Caesar's Tahoe casino in Nevada. And lost. To keep gambling, he wrote checks to Caesar's and then signed two memoranda pledging to repay all money advanced. After two days, with his losses totaling more than $22,000, he went home. Back in California, Sadri stopped payment on the checks and refused to pay any of the money he owed Caesar's. The casino sued. In defense, Sadri claimed that California law considered his agreements illegal and unenforceable. He was unquestionably correct about one thing: a contract that is illegal is void and unenforceable.

nuttakit/Shutterstock.com; © neelsky/Shutterstock.com

> **A contract that is illegal is void and unenforceable.**

12-1 Contracts That Violate A Statute

In this chapter, we examine a variety of contracts that courts will not enforce. Illegal agreements fall into two groups: those that violate a statute, and those that violate public policy.

12-1a Wagers

Gambling is big business. Almost all states now permit some form of wagering, from casinos to racetracks to lotteries, and they eagerly collect the billions of dollars in revenue generated. Supporters urge that casinos create jobs and steady income, boost state coffers, and take business away from organized crime. Critics argue that naive citizens inevitably lose money they can ill afford to forfeit, and that addicted gamblers destroy their families and weaken the fabric of communities. With citizens and states divided over the ethics of gambling, it is inevitable that we have conflicts such as the dispute between Sadri and Caesar's. The basic rule, however, is clear: **A gambling contract is illegal unless it is a type of wagering *specifically authorized* by state statute**.

In California, as in many states, gambling on credit is not allowed. In other words, it is illegal to lend money to help someone wager. But in Nevada, gambling on credit is legal, and debt memoranda such as Sadri's are enforceable contracts. Caesar's sued Sadri in California (where he lived). The result? The court admitted that California's attitude toward gambling had changed, and that bingo, poker clubs, and lotteries were common. Nonetheless, the court denied that the new tolerance extended to wagering on credit:

> There is a special reason for treating gambling on credit differently from gambling itself. Having lost his or her cash, the pathological gambler will continue to play on credit, if extended, in an attempt to win back the losses. This is why enforcement of gambling debts has always been against public policy in California and should remain so, regardless of shifting public attitudes about gambling itself. If Californians want to play, so be it. But the law should not invite them to play themselves into debt. The judiciary cannot protect pathological gamblers from themselves, but we can refuse to participate in their financial ruin.[1]

Caesar's lost and Sadri kept his money. However, do not become too excited at the prospect of risk-free wagering. Casinos responded to cases like *Sadri* by changing their practices. Most now extend credit only to a gambler who agrees that disputes about repayment will be settled in *Nevada* courts. Because such contracts are legal in that state, the casino is able to obtain a judgment against a defaulting debtor and—yes—enforce that judgment in the gambler's home state.

Despite these more restrictive casino practices, Sadri's dispute is a useful starting place from which to examine contract legality because it illustrates two important themes.

First, morality is a significant part of contract legality. In refusing to enforce an obligation that Sadri undeniably had made, the California court relied on the human and social consequences of gambling and on the ethics of judicial enforcement of gambling debts. Second, "void" really means just that: A court will not intercede to assist either party to an illegal agreement, even if its refusal leaves one party shortchanged.

---

[1]*Metropolitan Creditors Service of Sacramento v. Sadri*, 15 Cal. App. 4th 1821, 1993 Cal. App. LEXIS 559, 19 Cal. Rptr. 2d 646 (Cal. Ct. App. 1993).

12-1b Insurance

Another market in which "wagering" unexpectedly pops up is that of insurance. You may certainly insure your own life for any sum you choose. But may you insure someone else's life? **Anyone taking out a policy on the life of another must have an insurable interest in that person.** The most common insurable interest is family connection, such as spouses or parents. Other valid interests include creditor-debtor status (the creditor wants payment if the debtor dies) and business association (an executive in the company is so valuable that the firm will need compensation if something happens to him). If there is no insurable interest, there is generally no contract.

EXAM Strategy

Question: Jimenez sold Breton a used motorcycle for $5,500, payable in weekly installments. Jimenez then purchased an insurance policy on Breton's life, worth $320,000 if Breton died in an accident. Breton promptly died in a collision with an automobile. The insurance company offered only $5,500, representing the balance due on the motorcycle. Jimenez sued, demanding $320,000. Make an argument that the insurance company should win.

Strategy: The issue is whether Jimenez had an insurable interest in Breton's life. If he had no interest, he cannot collect on an insurance policy. If he had an interest, what was it? For how much money?

Result: Jimenez's had an interest in Breton's life to insure payment of the motorcycle debt—$5,500. Beyond that, this policy represented a wager by Jimenez that Breton was going to die. Contracts for such wagers are unenforceable. Jimenez is entitled only to $5,500.[2]

12-1c Licensing Statutes

You sue your next-door neighbor in small claims court, charging that he keeps a kangaroo in his backyard and that the beast has disrupted your family barbecues by leaping over the fence, demanding salad, and even kicking your cousin in the ear. Your friend Foster, a graduate student from Melbourne, offers to help you prepare the case, and you agree to pay him 10 percent of anything you recover. Foster proves surprisingly adept at organizing documents and arguments. You win $1,200, and Foster demands $120. Must you pay? The answer is determined by the law of licensing.

States require licenses for anyone who practices a profession, such as law or medicine, works as a contractor or plumber, and for many other kinds of work. These licenses are required in order to protect the public. States demand that an electrician be licensed because the work is potentially dangerous to a homeowner: The person doing the work must know an amp from a watt. **When a licensing requirement is designed to protect the public, any contract made by an unlicensed worker is unenforceable.** Your friend Foster is unlicensed to practice law. Even though Foster did a fine job with your small claims case, he cannot enforce his contract for $120.

States use other licenses simply to raise money. For example, most states require a license to open certain kinds of retail stores. This requirement does not protect the public because the state will not investigate the store owner the way it will examine a prospective

---

[2]*Jimenez v. Protective Life Insurance Co.*, 8 Cal. App. 4th 528 (Cal. App. 1992).

lawyer or electrician. The state is simply raising money. **When a licensing requirement is designed merely to raise revenue, a contract made by an unlicensed person is generally enforceable.** Thus, if you open a stationery store and forget to pay the state's licensing fee, you can still enforce a contract to buy 10,000 envelopes from a wholesaler at a bargain price.

Many cases, such as the following one, involve contractors seeking to recover money for work they did without a license.

AUTHENTIC HOME IMPROVEMENTS V. MAYO

2006 WL 2687533
District of Columbia Superior Court, 2006

CASE SUMMARY

Facts: Authentic Home Improvements performed work on Diane Mayo's home, but she sued for return of the money she had paid. In court, Authentic's owner acknowledged that he did not have a contractor's license when the company began the work, but expected to obtain it soon. The court ordered Authentic to refund Mayo the entire sum she had paid, and the company agreed. Later, however, Authentic returned to court, stating that things had changed. The license had in fact been issued soon after work began. Authentic argued that it should not be obligated to return Mayo's money, and was in fact entitled to its full fee for the work accomplished.

Issue: *Did the new license entitle Authentic to its fee?*

Decision: No. The new license did not change the outcome.

Reasoning: Consumers lose billions each year on fraudulent home improvement schemes. For this reason, courts strictly interpret licensing requirements for contractors. Even when homeowners knowingly hire a contractor who lacks a license and then benefit from his work, they are not required to pay him.

Authentic lacked a license when the work on Mayo's home started. The relevant statute plainly requires a license in hand before a job begins. A driver cannot drive a car without license plates merely because she expects delivery of her plates soon, and the same principle applies here.

Authentic remains obligated to refund Mayo's money.

12-1d Usury

It pays to understand usury.

Henry Paper and Anthony Pugliese were real estate developers. They bought property in Florida, intending to erect an office building. Walter Gross, another developer, agreed to lend them $200,000 at 15 percent interest. Gross knew the partners were desperate for the money, so at the loan closing, he demanded 15 percent equity (ownership) in the partnership, in addition to the interest. Paper and Pugliese had no choice but to sign the agreement. The two partners never repaid the loan, and when Gross sued, the court ruled that they need never pay a cent.

Usury laws prohibit charging excess interest on loans. Some states, such as New York, set very strict limits. Others, like Utah, allow for virtually any rate. A lender who charges a usurious rate of interest may forfeit the illegal interest, all interest, or, in some states, the entire loan.

Florida law requires a lender who exceeds 25 percent interest to forfeit the entire debt. Where was the usury in Gross's case? Just here: When Gross insisted on a 15 percent share of the partnership, he was simply extracting additional interest and disguising it as partnership equity. The Paper-Pugliese partnership had equity assets of $600,000. A 15 percent equity, plus interest payments of 15 percent over 18 months, was the equivalent of a per annum interest rate of 45 percent. Gross probably thought he had made a deal that was too good to be true. And in the state of Florida, it was. He lost the entire debt.[3]

---

[3]*Jersey Palm-Gross, Inc. v. Paper*, 639 So.2d 664, 1994 Fla. App. LEXIS 6597 (Fla. Ct. App. 1994).

CREDIT CARD DEBT

Many consumers are desperate to obtain credit cards on any terms. When First Premier Bank launched a credit card with a 79.9 percent rate of interest, 700,000 people applied for it within the next two years.

How can such a rate exist?

Even if a state's usury statute applies to credit cards, savvy lenders can often avoid limits on interest rates. For example, national banks can choose the interest rate either in the state where they are located or where the consumer lives. Of course, they choose the higher one. Also, many card issuers require borrowers to sign contracts that say the laws of a lender-friendly state will be applied to all future disputes. New York customers might agree to live by Utah laws, for example.

Most courts continue to enforce these contracts that impose high out-of-state rates. But since the financial meltdown of 2008, some courts have started to express distaste for this practice. In the following case, a New York court addressed the issue.

AMERICAN EXPRESS TRAVEL RELATED SERVICES COMPANY, INC. v. ASSIH

893 N.Y.S.2d 438
Civil Court of the City of New York, Richmond County, 2009

Facts: When Titus Assih missed a payment on his American Express card, his interest rate ballooned from 12.24% to 21%, and eventually to 27.99%. Assih, a New York resident, made small payments for a time, but soon he stopped paying altogether.

American Express sued Assih in New York. It asked the court to apply Utah law, as provided in the credit card agreement. But the agreement's only connection to Utah was that American Express had assigned its interest to a one-branch bank in Utah.

Assih argued that New York law, which sets strict limits on the maximum interest rate for credit cards, should apply instead.

Issues: *Should New York or Utah law apply? Did the increased rates violate usury statutes?*

Decision: New York law should apply and the increased rates were illegal.

Reasoning: Have you ever *seen* the *Wizard of Oz*? The answer is probably yes and no. You may have seen the film, but no one *in* the movie has ever actually *seen* the Wizard himself, leaving Dorothy to wonder whether the ruler of Oz really exists.

Like the Land of Oz, run by the mysterious Wizard, the Land of Credit Cards binds consumers to agreements they never see or sign. These contracts may change without notice and are subject to the interest rate of a faraway state. And the consumers may have no idea!

Utah law permits *any* rate of interest so long as the parties agree to it. No wonder American Express chose Utah law. But New York courts will not enforce a contract if they have to apply the law of a state that has no relationship to the parties.

Utah had nothing to do with this transaction. American Express was a New York corporation whose principal place of business was New York. Assih lived in New York. He used his American Express card in New York. He sent his credit card payments to a New York address. Therefore, New York, not Utah, law must apply.

New York's civil usury statute sets the legal rate of interest at 16%; New York's criminal usury rate is 25%. Except for Assih's initial 12.24% rate, all of the interest rates American Express charged violated the New York civil usury statutes. Assih's last billings at 27.99% even exceeded New York's criminal rate.

The Wizard of Oz warned Dorothy against arousing "the wrath of the great and powerful Oz." At risk of arousing the wrath of American Express, this court held that under New York law, the usurious contract between American Express and Assih was void.

12-2 CONTRACTS THAT VIOLATE PUBLIC POLICY

In the preceding section, we saw that courts refuse to enforce contracts that violate a *statute*. However, a judge may declare a contract illegal even if it does not violate a statute. In this section, we examine cases in which a *public policy* prohibits certain contracts. In other words, we focus primarily on common law rules.

12-2a Restraint of Trade: Noncompete Agreements

In a noncompete agreement (sometimes called a *covenant not to compete)*, an employee promises not to work for a competitor for some time after leaving his company. For example, an anchorwoman for an NBC news affiliate in Miami might agree that she will not anchor any other Miami station's news show for one year after she leaves her present employer. Noncompetes are often valid, but the common law places some restrictions on them.

It was once true that these covenants were rare and reserved for top corporate officers, but they have now become commonplace in many organizations at virtually all levels. Employers have legitimate concerns that employees might go to work for a competitor and take with them valuable information about doing business in that industry. Some employers, though, attempt to place harsh restrictions on their employees simply to discourage them from leaving.

Employees often view noncompetes as unfair and unduly burdensome. Nonetheless, noncompete agreements are enforceable, so long as they are reasonable in time, activity, and territory. In other words, a noncompete providing that you cannot work in the same industry in the same city for one year is likely to be valid, but not an agreement that essentially prevents you from working at all, such as one that prohibits you from doing any job, anywhere, for ten years.

Was the noncompete in the following case styled fairly, or was the employee clipped?

KING V. HEAD START FAMILY HAIR SALONS, INC.

886 So.2d 769
Supreme Court of Alabama, 2004

CASE SUMMARY

Facts: Kathy King was a single mother supporting a college-age daughter. For 25 years, she had worked as a hairstylist. For the most recent 16 years, she had worked at Head Start, which provided haircuts, coloring, and styling for men and women. King was primarily a stylist, though she had also managed one of the Head Start facilities.

King quit Head Start and began working as manager of a Sports Clips shop, located in the same mall as the store she just left. Sports Clip offered only haircuts, and primarily served men and boys. Head Start filed suit, claiming that King was violating the noncompetition agreement that she had signed. The agreement prohibited King from working at a competing business within a two-mile radius of any Head Start facility for 12 months after leaving the company. The trial court issued an injunction enforcing the noncompete. King appealed.

Issue: *Was the noncompetition agreement valid?*

Decision: The agreement was only partly valid.

Reasoning: Head Start does business in 30 locations throughout Jefferson and Shelby counties. Virtually every hair-care facility in those counties is located within 2 miles of a Head Start business, and is thus covered by the noncompetition agreement. The contract is essentially a blanket restriction, entirely barring King from this business.

King works to support herself and her daughter. She is 40 years old and has worked in the hair-care industry for 25 years. She cannot be expected at this stage in life to learn new job skills.

Enforcing the noncompetition agreement would inflict a grave hardship on her. It would be unfair to permit the contract to impoverish King and her daughter. On the other hand, Head Start is entitled to some of the protection that it sought in this agreement. The company has a valid concern: if King is permitted to work anywhere she wants, she could take away many customers from Head Start. The trial court should fashion a more reasonable geographic restriction, one that will permit King to ply her trade while ensuring that Head Start does not unfairly lose customers. For example, the lower court could prohibit King from working within 2 miles of the Head Start salon where she previously worked, or some variation on that idea.

Reversed and remanded.

SALE OF A BUSINESS

Kory has operated a real estate office, Hearth Attack, in a small city for 35 years, building an excellent reputation and many ties with the community. She offers to sell you the business and its goodwill for $300,000. But you need assurance that Kory will not take your money and promptly open a competing office across the street. With her reputation and connections, she would ruin your chances of success. Also, you have paid her a significant sum, so even if she does not work, she is unlikely to go hungry any time soon. You insist on a noncompete clause in the sale contract. In this clause, Kory promises that for one year, she will not open a new real estate office or go to work for a competing company within a 10-mile radius of Hearth Attack. Suppose, six months after selling you the business, Kory goes to work for a competing real estate agency two blocks away. You seek an injunction to prevent her from working. Who wins?

> **With her reputation and connections, she would ruin your chances of success.**

Noncompete agreements related to the sale of a business are also enforceable if reasonable in time, activity, and territory. Courts are generally stricter in enforcing agreements related to the sale of a business than they are ones that are based simply on employment. Kory is almost certainly bound by her agreement. One year is a reasonable time to allow you to get your new business started. A 10-mile radius is probably about the area that Hearth Attack covers, and realty is obviously a fair business from which to prohibit Kory. A court will probably grant the injunction, barring Kory from her new job.

EXAM Strategy

Question: Caf-Fiend is an expanding chain of coffeehouses. The company offers to buy Bessie's Coffee Shop, in St. Louis, on these terms: Bessie will manage the store, as Caf-Fiend's employee, for one year after the sale. For four years after the sale, Bessie will not open a competing restaurant anywhere within 12 miles. For the same four years, she will not work anywhere in the United States for a competing coffee retailer. Are the last two terms enforceable against Bessie?

Strategy: This contract includes two noncompete clauses. In the first, Bessie agrees not to open a competing business. Courts generally enforce such clauses if they are reasonable in time, geography, and scope of activity. Is this clause reasonable? The second clause involves employment. Courts take a dimmer view of these agreements. Is this clause essential to protect the company's business? Is it unduly harsh for Bessie?

Result: The first restriction is reasonable. Caf-Fiend is entitled to prevent Bessie from opening her own coffeehouse around the corner and drawing her old customers. The second clause is unfair to Bessie. If she wants to move from St. Louis to San Diego and work as a store manager, she is prohibited. It is impossible to see how such employment would harm Caf-Fiend—but it certainly takes away Bessie's career options. The first restriction is valid, the second one unenforceable.

THE CALIFORNIA EXCEPTION

In California, the law on noncompetes is different from the rest of the country. In this important state, noncompete agreements are *not* enforceable in employment contracts. In other words, a noncompete is valid only if (1) the employee signs it at the same time she is selling her share of a company and (2) it is reasonable in time, activity, and territory.

12-2b The Legality of Noncompetition Clauses (Noncompetes)

Type of Noncompetition Agreement	When Enforceable	
Not ancillary to a sale of business or employment	Never	
Ancillary to a sale of business	If reasonable in time, geography, and scope of activity	
Ancillary to employment	Contract is *more* likely to be enforced when it involves: • Trade secrets or confidential information: These are almost always protected • Customer lists developed over extended period of time and carefully protected • Limited time and geographical scope • Terms essential to protect the employer's business	Contract is *less* likely to be enforced when it involves: • Employee who already had the skills when he arrived, or merely developed general skills on the job • Customer lists that can be derived from public sources • Excessive time or geographical scope • Terms that are unduly harsh on the employee or contrary to public interest

© Cengage Learning

12-2c Exculpatory Clauses

You decide to capitalize on your expert ability as a skier and open a ski school in Colorado, "Pike's Pique." But you realize that skiing sometimes causes injuries, so you require anyone signing up for lessons to sign this form:

> I agree to hold Pike's Pique and its employees entirely harmless in the event that I am injured in any way or for any reason or cause, including but not limited to any acts, whether negligent or otherwise, of Pike's Pique or any employee or agent thereof.

The day your school opens, Sara Beth, an instructor, deliberately pushes Toby over a cliff because Toby criticized her clothes. Eddie, a beginning student, "blows out" his knee attempting an advanced racing turn. And Maureen, another student, reaches the bottom of a steep run and slams into a snowmobile that Sara Beth parked there. Maureen, Eddie, and Toby's families all sue Pike's Pique. You defend based on the form you had them sign. Does it save the day?

Exculpatory clause

A contract provision that attempts to release one party from liability in the event the other is injured.

The form on which you are relying is an **exculpatory clause**, that is, one that attempts to release you from liability in the event of injury to another party. Exculpatory clauses are common. Ski schools use them, and so do parking lots, landlords, warehouses, sports franchises, and day-care centers. All manner of businesses hope to avoid large tort judgments by requiring their customers to give up any right to recover. Is such a clause valid? Sometimes. Courts frequently—but do not always—ignore exculpatory clauses, finding that one party was forcing the other party to give up legal rights that no one should be forced to surrender.

An exculpatory clause is generally unenforceable when it attempts to exclude an intentional tort or gross negligence. When Sara Beth pushes Toby over a cliff, that is the intentional tort of battery. A court will not enforce the exculpatory clause. Sara Beth is clearly liable.[4] As to the snowmobile at the bottom of the run, if a court determines that was gross negligence (carelessness far greater than ordinary negligence), then the exculpatory clause will again be ignored. If, however, it was ordinary negligence, then we must continue the analysis.

An exculpatory clause is usually unenforceable when the affected activity is in the public interest, such as medical care, public transportation, or some essential service. Suppose Eddie goes to a doctor for surgery on his damaged knee, and the doctor requires him to sign an exculpatory clause. The doctor negligently performs the surgery, accidentally leaving his cuff links in Eddie's left knee. The exculpatory clause will not protect the doctor. Medical care is an essential service, and the public cannot give up its right to demand reasonable work.

But what about Eddie's suit against Pike's Pique? Eddie claims that he should never have been allowed to attempt an advanced maneuver. His suit is for ordinary negligence, and the exculpatory clause probably *does* bar him from recovery. Skiing is a recreational activity. No one is obligated to do it, and there is no strong public interest in ensuring that we have access to ski slopes.

An exculpatory clause is generally unenforceable when the parties have greatly unequal bargaining power. When Maureen flies to Colorado, suppose that the airline requires her to sign a form contract with an exculpatory clause. Because the airline almost certainly has much greater bargaining power, it can afford to offer a "take it or leave it" contract. The bargaining power is so unequal, though, that the clause is probably unenforceable. Does Pike's Pique have a similar advantage? Probably not. Ski schools are not essential and are much smaller enterprises. A dissatisfied customer might refuse to sign such an agreement and take her business elsewhere. A court probably will not see the parties as *grossly* unequal.

---

[4]Note that Pike's Pique is probably not liable under agency law principles that preclude an employer's liability for an employee's intentional tort.

An exculpatory clause is generally unenforceable unless the clause is clearly written and readily visible. If Pike's Pique gave all ski students an eight-page contract, and the exculpatory clause was at the bottom of page seven in small print, the average customer would never notice it. The clause would be void.

In the following case, the court focused on the public policy concerns of exculpatory clauses used in a very common setting. Should the exculpatory clause stop the tenant from suing the landlord? You be the judge.

You Be the Judge

RANSBURG V. RICHARDS
770 N.E.2d 393
Indiana Court of Appeals, 2002

Facts: Barbara Richards leased an apartment at Twin Lakes, a complex owned by Lenna Ransburg. The written lease declared that:

- Twin Lakes would "gratuitously" maintain the common areas.
- Richards's use of the facilities would be "at her own risk."
- Twin Lakes was not responsible for any harm to the tenant or her guests, anywhere on the property (including the parking lot), even if the damage was caused by Twin Lakes' negligence.

It snowed. As Richards walked across the parking lot to her car, she slipped and fell on snow-covered ice. Richards sued Ransburg, who moved for summary judgment based on the exculpatory clause. The trial court denied Ransburg's motion, and she appealed.

You Be the Judge: *Was the exculpatory clause valid?*

Argument for Tenant: An exculpatory clause in a contract for an essential service violates public policy. When an ill person seeks medical care, his doctor cannot require him to sign an exculpatory clause. In the same way, a person has to live somewhere. Her landlord cannot force her to sign a waiver.

Landlords tend to be wealthy and powerful. There is generally no equality of bargaining power between them. The tenants are not freely agreeing to the exculpatory language.

Moreover, if a landlord fails to maintain property, not just the tenant is at risk. Visitors, the mail carrier, and the general public could all walk through the Twin Lakes parking lot. The public's interest is served when landlords maintain their properties. They must be held liable when they negligently fail to maintain common areas and injuries result.

Argument for Landlord: Ms. Richards does indeed have to live somewhere, but she does not have to live on the plaintiff's property. Surely there are many dozens of properties nearby. If Richards had been dissatisfied with any part of the proposed lease—excessive rent, strict rules, or an exculpatory clause—she was free to take her business to another landlord.

Landlords may generally be wealthier than their tenants, but that fact alone does not mean that a landlord is so powerful that leases are offered on a "take it or leave it" basis. Here, the landlord stated the exculpatory clause plainly. This is a clear contract between adults, and it should stand in its entirety.

BAILMENT CASES

Exculpatory clauses are very common in bailment cases. **Bailment** means giving possession and control of personal property to another person. The person giving up possession is the **bailor**, and the one accepting possession is the **bailee**. When you leave your laptop computer with a dealer to be repaired, you create a bailment. The same is true when you check your coat at a restaurant or lend your Matisse to a museum. Bailees often try to limit their liability for damage to property by using an exculpatory clause.

Judges are slightly more apt to enforce an exculpatory clause in a bailment case because any harm is to *property* and not persons. But courts will still look at many of the

Bailment
Giving possession and control of personal property to another person.

Bailor
One who creates a bailment by delivering goods to another.

Bailee
A person who rightfully possesses goods belonging to another.

same criteria we have just examined to decide whether a bailment contract is enforceable. In particular, when the bailee is engaged in an important public service, a court is once again likely to ignore the exculpatory clause. The following contrasting cases illustrate this.

In *Weiss v. Freeman*,[5] Weiss stored personal goods in Freeman's self-storage facility. Freeman's contract included an exculpatory clause relieving it of any and all liability. Weiss's goods were damaged by mildew, and she sued. The court held the exculpatory clause valid. The court considered self-storage to be a significant business, but not as vital as medical care or housing. It pointed out that a storage facility would not know what each customer stored and therefore could not anticipate the harm that might occur. Freedom of contract should prevail, the clause was enforceable, and Weiss got no money.

But in *Gardner v. Downtown Porsche Audi*,[6] Gardner left his Porsche 911 at Downtown for repairs. He signed an exculpatory clause saying that Downtown was "Not Responsible for Loss or Damage to Cars or Articles Left in Cars in Case of Fire, Theft, or Any Other Cause Beyond Our Control." Due to Downtown's negligence, Gardner's Porsche was stolen. The court held the exculpatory clause void. It ruled that contemporary society is utterly dependent upon automobile transportation and Downtown was therefore in a business of great public importance. No repair shop should be able to contract away liability, and Gardner won. (This case also illustrates that using 17 uppercase letters in one sentence does not guarantee legal victory.)

EXAM Strategy

Facts: Shauna flew a World War II fighter aircraft as a member of an exhibition flight team. While the team was performing in a delta formation, another plane collided with Shauna's aircraft, causing her to crash-land and leaving her permanently disabled. Shauna sued the other pilot and the team. The defendants moved to dismiss based on an exculpatory clause that Shauna had signed. The clause was one paragraph long, and it stated that Shauna knew team flying was inherently dangerous and could result in injury or death. She agreed not to hold the team or any members liable in case of an accident. Shauna argued that the clause should not be enforced against her if she could prove the other pilot was negligent. Please rule.

Strategy: The issue is whether the exculpatory clause is valid. Courts are likely to declare such clauses void if they concern vital activities like medical care, exclude an intentional tort or gross negligence, or if the parties had unequal bargaining power.

Result: This is a clear, short clause, between parties with equal bargaining power, and does not exclude an intentional tort or gross negligence. The activity is unimportant to the public welfare. The clause is valid. Even if the other pilot was negligent, Shauna will lose, meaning the court should dismiss her lawsuit.

---

[5]1994 Tenn. App. LEXIS 393 (Tenn. Ct. App. 1993).
[6]180 Cal. App. 3d 713, 225 Cal. Rptr. 757, 1986 Cal. App. LEXIS 1542 (Cal. Ct. App. 1986).

12-2d Unconscionable Contracts

Gail Waters was young, naive, and insecure. A serious injury when she was 12 years old left her with an annuity, that is, a guaranteed annual payment for many years. When Gail was 21, she became involved with Thomas Beauchemin, an ex-convict, who introduced her to drugs. Beauchemin suggested that Gail sell her annuity to some friends of his, and she agreed. Beauchemin arranged for a lawyer to draw up a contract, and Gail signed it. She received $50,000 for her annuity, which at that time had a cash value of $189,000 and was worth, over its remaining 25 years, $694,000. Gail later decided this was not a wise bargain. Was the contract enforceable? That depends on the law of unconscionability.

An unconscionable contract is one that a court refuses to enforce because of fundamental unfairness. Even if a contract does not violate any specific statute or public policy, it may still be void if it "shocks the conscience" of the court.

Historically, a contract was considered unconscionable if it was "such as no man in his senses and not under delusion would make on the one hand, and as no honest and fair man would accept on the other."[7] The two factors that most often led a court to find unconscionability were (1) **oppression**, meaning that one party used its superior power to force a contract on the weaker party, and (2) **surprise**, meaning that the weaker party did not fully understand the consequences of its agreement.

These cases have always been controversial because it is not easy to define oppression and unfair surprise. Further, anytime a court rejects a contract as unconscionable, it diminishes freedom of contract. If one party can escape a deal based on something as hard to define as unconscionability, then no one can rely as confidently on any agreement. As an English jurist said in 1824, "public policy is a very unruly horse, and when once you get astride it, you never know where it will carry you."[8]

Gail Waters won her case. The Massachusetts high court ruled:

> Beauchemin introduced the plaintiff to drugs, exhausted her credit card accounts to the sum of $6,000, unduly influenced her, suggested that the plaintiff sell her annuity contract, initiated the contract negotiations, was the agent of the defendants, and benefited from the contract between the plaintiff and the defendants. The defendants were represented by legal counsel; the plaintiff was not. The cash value of the annuity policy at the time the contract was executed was approximately four times greater than the price to be paid by the defendants. For payment of not more than $50,000 the defendants were to receive an asset that could be immediately exchanged for $189,000, or they could elect to hold it for its guaranteed term and receive $694,000.
>
> The defendants assumed no risk and the plaintiff gained no advantage. We are satisfied that the disparity of interests in this contract is so gross that the court cannot resist the inference that it was improperly obtained and is unconscionable.[9]

ADHESION CONTRACTS

A related issue concerns **adhesion contracts**, which are standard form contracts prepared by one party and given to the other on a "take it or leave it" basis. We have all encountered them many times when purchasing goods or services. When a form contract is vigorously negotiated between equally powerful corporations, the resulting bargain is generally enforced. However, when the contract is simply presented to a consumer who has no ability to bargain, it is an adhesion contract and subject to an unconscionability challenge.

Oppression
One party uses its superior power to force a contract on the weaker party.

Adhesion contracts
Standard form contracts prepared by one party and presented to the other on a "take it or leave it" basis.

---

[7] *Hume v. United States*, 132 U.S. 406, 411, 10 S. Ct. 134, 1889 U.S. LEXIS 1888 (1889), quoting *Earl of Chesterfield v. Janssen*, 38 Eng. Rep. 82, 100 (Ch. 1750).
[8] *Richardson v. Mellish*, 2 Bing. 229, 103 Eng. Rep. 294, 303 (1824).
[9] *Waters v. Min Ltd.*, 412 Mass. 64, 587 N.E.2d 231, 1992 Mass. LEXIS 66 (1992).

WORLDWIDE INSURANCE V. KLOPP

603 A.2d 788, 1992 Del. LEXIS 13
Supreme Court of Delaware, 1992

CASE SUMMARY

Facts: Ruth Klopp had auto insurance with Worldwide. She was injured in a serious accident that left her with permanent neck and back injuries. The other driver was uninsured, so Klopp filed a claim with Worldwide under her "uninsured motorist" coverage. Her policy required arbitration of such a claim, and the arbitrators awarded Klopp $90,000. But the policy also stated that if the arbitrators awarded more than the statutory minimum amount of insurance ($15,000), either side could appeal the award and request a full trial. Worldwide appealed and demanded a trial.

In the trial court, Klopp claimed that the appeal provision was unconscionable and void. The trial court agreed and entered judgment for the full $90,000. Worldwide appealed.

Issue: *Was the provision that required arbitration and then permitted appeal by either party void as unconscionable?*

Decision: Yes. The contract provision was unconscionable. Affirmed.

Reasoning: Worldwide contended that the arbitration provision was clear and unambiguous, but Klopp argued that it was grossly unfair. State policy favors the use of arbitration to resolve disputes, but it rejects any part of a contract of adhesion that is unconscionable.

This contract bound both parties to a low award, one that an insurance company would be unlikely to appeal anyway. Either party may appeal a high award, but common sense suggests that only the insurer would do so. The policy enabled the insurer to avoid a high arbitration award that may have been perfectly fair.

This policy promoted litigation and provided an arbitration "escape hatch" that favored insurance companies. The provision was unconscionable and void.

THE UCC: UNCONSCIONABILITY AND SALES LAW

With the creation of the Uniform Commercial Code (UCC), the law of unconscionability got a boost. The Code explicitly adopts unconscionability as a reason to reject a contract.[10] Although the Code directly applies only to the sale of goods, its unconscionability section has proven to be influential in other cases as well, and courts today are more receptive than they were 100 years ago to a contract defense of fundamental unfairness.

The drafters of the UCC reinforced the principle of unconscionability by including it in §2-302:

> If the court as a matter of law finds the contract or any clause of the contract to have been unconscionable at the time it was made the court may refuse to enforce the contract, or it may enforce the remainder of the contract without the unconscionable clause, or it may so limit the application of any unconscionable clause as to avoid any unconscionable result.

In Code cases, the issue of unconscionability often arises when a company attempts to limit the normal contract law remedies. Yet the Code itself allows such limitations, provided they are reasonable.

Section 2-719 provides in part:

> [A contract] may provide for remedies in addition to or in substitution for those provided [by the Code itself] *and may limit or alter the measure of damages recoverable* ... as by limiting the buyer's remedies to return of the goods and repayment of the price ....

---

[10]UCC §2-302.

In other words, the Code includes two potentially competing sections: §2-719 permits a seller to insist that the buyer's only remedy for defective goods is return of the purchase price, but §2-302 says that *any unconscionable* provision is unenforceable. In lawsuits concerning defective goods, the seller often argues that the buyer's only remedies are those stated in the agreement, and the buyer responds that the contract limitation is unconscionable.

Electronic Data Systems (EDS) agreed to create complex software for Chubb Life America at a cost of $21 million. Chubb agreed to make staggered payments over many months as the work proceeded. The contract included a limitation on remedies, stating that if EDS became liable to Chubb, its maximum liability would be equal to two monthly payments.

EDS's work was woefully late and unusable, forcing Chubb to obtain its software elsewhere. Chubb sued, claiming $40 million in damages based on the money paid to EDS and additional funds spent purchasing alternative goods. EDS argued that the contract limited its liability to two monthly payments, a fraction of Chubb's damage. Chubb, of course, responded that the limitation was unconscionable.

The court noted that both parties were large, sophisticated corporations. As they negotiated the agreement, the companies both used experienced attorneys and independent consultants. This was no contract of adhesion presented to a meek consumer, but an allocation of risk resulting from hard bargaining. The court declared that the clause was valid, and EDS owed no more than two monthly payments.[11]

Chapter Conclusion

It is not enough to bargain effectively and obtain a contract that gives you exactly what you want. You must also be sure that the contract is legal. What appears to be an insurance contract might legally be an invalid wager. Unintentionally forgetting to obtain a state license to perform a certain job could mean you will never be paid for it. Bargaining a contract with a noncompete or exculpatory clause that is too one-sided may lead a court to ignore it. Legality is multifaceted, sometimes subtle, and always important.

Exam Review

Illegal contracts are void and unenforceable. Illegality most often arises in these settings:

1. **WAGERING**   A purely speculative contract—whether for gambling or insurance—is likely to be unenforceable. (p. 277)

2. **LICENSING**   When the licensing statute is designed to protect the public, a contract by an unlicensed plaintiff is generally unenforceable. When such a statute is designed merely to raise revenue, a contract by an unlicensed plaintiff is generally enforceable. (pp. 278–279)

---

[11]*Colonial Life Insurance Co. v. Electronic Data Systems Corp.*, 817 F. Supp. 235, 1993 U.S. Dist. LEXIS 4123 (D.N.H. 1993).

EXAM Strategy

Question: James Wagner agreed to build a house for Nancy Graham. Wagner was not licensed as a contractor, and Graham knew it. When the house was finished, Graham refused to pay the final $23,000, and Wagner sued. Who will prevail?

Strategy: A licensing statute designed to protect the public is strictly enforced, but that is not true for one intended only to raise revenue. What was the purpose of this statute? (See the "Result" at the end of this section.)

3. **USURY**   Excessive interest is generally unenforceable and may be fatal to the entire debt. Credit card debt is often exempt from usury laws. (pp. 279–280)

EXAM Strategy

Question: McElroy owned 104 acres worth about $230,000. He got into financial difficulties and approached Grisham, asking to borrow $100,000. Grisham refused, but ultimately the two reached this agreement: McElroy would sell Grisham his property for $80,000, and the contract would include a clause allowing McElroy to repurchase the land within two years for $120,000. McElroy later claimed the contract was void. Is he right?

Strategy: Loans involving usury do not always include a clearly visible interest rate. You may have to do some simple math to see the interest being charged. McElroy wanted to borrow $100,000, but instead sold his property, with the right to repurchase. If he did repurchase, how much interest would he have effectively paid? (See the "Result" at the end of this section.)

4. **NONCOMPETE**   A noncompete clause in the sale of a business must be limited to a reasonable time, geographic area, and scope of activity. In an employment contract, such a clause is considered reasonable—and enforceable—only to protect trade secrets, confidential information, and customer lists. (pp. 281–283)

EXAM Strategy

Question: The purchaser of a business insisted on putting this clause in the sales contract: The seller would not compete, for five years, "anywhere in the United States, the continent of North America, or anywhere else on earth." What danger does that contract represent *to the purchaser?*

Strategy: This is a noncompete clause based on the sale of a business. Such clauses are valid if reasonable. Is this clause reasonable? If it is unreasonable, what might a court do? (See the "Result" at the end of this section.)

5. **EXCULPATORY CLAUSES**   These clauses are generally void if the activity involved is in the public interest, the parties are greatly unequal in bargaining power, or the clause is unclear. In other cases, they are generally enforced. (pp. 284–286)

6. **UNCONSCIONABILITY** Oppression and surprise may create an unconscionable bargain. An adhesion contract is especially suspect when it is imposed by a corporation on a consumer or small company. Under the UCC, a limitation of liability is less likely to be unconscionable when both parties are sophisticated corporations. (pp. 287–289)

---

2. Result: This statute was designed to protect the public. Wagner was unlicensed and cannot enforce the contract. Graham wins.

3. Result: By selling at $80,000 and repurchasing at $120,000, McElroy would be paying $40,000 in interest on an $80,000 loan. The 50 percent rate is usurious. The court prohibited Graham from collecting the interest.

4. Result: "Anywhere else on earth"? This is almost certainly unreasonable. It is hard to imagine a purchaser who would legitimately need such wide-ranging protection. In some states, a court might rewrite the clause, limiting the effect to the seller's state, or some reasonable area. However, in other states, a court finding a clause unreasonable will declare it void in its entirety—enabling the seller to open a competing business next door.

MULTIPLE-CHOICE QUESTIONS

1. At a fraternity party, George mentions that he is going to learn to hang-glide during spring break. Vicki, a casual friend, overhears him, and the next day she purchases a $100,000 life insurance policy on George's life. George has a happy week of hang-gliding. But on the way home, he is bitten by a parrot and dies of a rare tropical illness. Vicki files a claim for $100,000. The insurance company refuses to pay.

    (a) Vicki will win $100,000, but only if she mentioned animal bites to the insurance agent.
    (b) Vicki will win $100,000 regardless of whether she mentioned animal bites to the insurance agent.
    (c) Vicki will win $50,000.
    (d) Vicki will win nothing.

2. Now assume that Vicki has loaned George $50,000. George again mentions that he is going to learn to hang-glide during spring break, so Vicki purchases the $100,000 life insurance policy on George's life. If George dies and the insurance company refuses to pay …

    (a) Vicki will win $100,000, but only if she mentioned animal bites to the insurance agent.
    (b) Vicki will win $100,000 regardless of whether she mentioned animal bites to the insurance agent.
    (c) Vicki will win $50,000.
    (d) Vicki will win nothing.

3. KwikFix, a Fortune 500 company, contracts with Allied Rocket, another huge company, to provide the software for Allied's new Jupiter Probe rocket for $14 million. The software is negligently designed, and when the rocket blasts off from Cape Kennedy, it travels only as far as Fort Lauderdale before crashing to Earth. Allied Rocket sues for $200 million and proves that as a result of the disaster, it lost a huge government contract, worth at least that much, which KwikFix was aware of. KwikFix responds that its contract with Allied included a clause limiting its liability to the value of the contract. Is the contract clause valid?

(a) The clause is unenforceable because it is unconscionable.

(b) The clause is unenforceable because it is exculpatory.

(c) The clause is enforceable because both parties are sophisticated corporations.

(d) The clause is enforceable because $200 million is an unconscionable claim.

4. Ricki goes to a baseball game. The back of her ticket clearly reads: "Fan agrees to hold team blameless for all injuries _____ pay attention to the game at all times for your own safety!" In the first inning, a foul ball hits Ricki in the elbow. She _____ sue the team over the foul ball. Ricki spends the next several innings riding the opposing team's first baseman. The *nicest* thing she says to him is, "You suck, Franklin!" In the eighth inning, Franklin has had enough. He grabs the ballboy's chair and throws it into the stands, injuring Ricki's other elbow. Ricki _____ sue the team over the thrown chair.

(a) can; can

(b) can; cannot

(c) cannot; can

(d) cannot; cannot

5. Jim, about to start a pickup soccer game, asks Desiree if she will hold his wallet while he plays. Desiree, a law student, says, "Sure, if you'll sign this exculpatory clause holding me blameless for negligence." Jim is very surprised, but he signs the paper that Desiree holds out for him. A bailment _____ been created. If Desiree is careless and loses the wallet, she _____ be liable to Jim.

(a) has; will

(b) has; will not

(c) has not; will

(d) has not; will not

ESSAY QUESTIONS

1. For 20 years, Art's Flower Shop relied almost exclusively on advertising in the yellow pages to bring business to its shop in a small West Virginia town. One year, the yellow pages printer accidentally did not print Art's ad, and Art's suffered an enormous drop in business. Art's sued for negligence and won a judgment of $50,000 from the jury, but the printing company appealed, claiming that under an exculpatory clause in the contract, the company could not be liable to Art's for more than the cost of the ad, about $910. Art's claimed that the exculpatory clause was unconscionable. Please rule.

2. Brockwell left his boat to be repaired at Lake Gaston Sales. The boat contained electronic equipment and other personal items. Brockwell signed a form stating that Lake Gaston had no responsibility for any loss to any property in or on the boat. Brockwell's electronic equipment was stolen and other personal items were damaged, and he sued. Is the exculpatory clause enforceable?

3. Guyan Machinery, a West Virginia manufacturing corporation, hired Albert Voorhees as a salesman and required him to sign a contract stating that if he left Guyan, he would not work for a competing corporation anywhere within 250 miles of West Virginia for a two-year period. Later, Voorhees left Guyan and began working at Polydeck Corp., another West Virginia manufacturer. The only product Polydeck made was urethane screens, which comprised half of 1 percent of Guyan's business. Is Guyan entitled to enforce its noncompete clause?

4. 810 Associates owned a 42-story skyscraper in midtown Manhattan. The building had a central station fire alarm system, which was monitored by Holmes Protection. A fire broke out and Holmes received the signal. But Holmes's inexperienced dispatcher misunderstood the signal and failed to summon the fire department for about nine minutes, permitting tremendous damage. 810 sued Holmes, which defended based on an exculpatory clause that relieved Holmes of any liability caused in any way. Holmes's dispatcher was negligent. Does it matter *how* negligent he was?

5. **YOU BE THE JUDGE WRITING PROBLEM** Oasis Waterpark, located in Palm Springs, California, sought out Hydrotech Systems, Inc., a New York corporation, to design and construct a surfing pool. Hydrotech replied that it could design the pool and sell all the necessary equipment to Oasis, but it could not build the pool because it was not licensed in California. Oasis insisted that Hydrotech do the construction work because Hydrotech had unique expertise in these pools. Oasis promised to arrange for a licensed California contractor to "work with" Hydrotech on the construction; Oasis also assured Hydrotech that it would pay the full contract price of $850,000, regardless of any licensing issues. Hydrotech designed and installed the pool as ordered. But Oasis failed to make the final payment of $110,000. Hydrotech sued. Can Hydrotech sue for either breach of contract or fraud (trickery)? **Argument for Oasis:** The licensing law protects the public from incompetence and dishonesty. The legislature made the section strict: no license, no payment. If the court were to start picking and choosing which unlicensed contractors could win a suit, it would be inviting incompetent workers to endanger the public and then come into court and try their luck. That is precisely the danger the legislature seeks to avoid. **Argument for Hydrotech:** This is not the kind of case the legislature was worried about. Hydrotech has never solicited work in California. Hydrotech went out of its way to avoid doing any contracting work, informing Oasis that it was unlicensed in the state. Oasis insisted on bringing Hydrotech into the state to do work. If Oasis has its way, word will go out that any owner can get free work done by hiring an *unlicensed* builder. Make any promises you want, get the work done to your satisfaction, and then stiff the contractor—you'll never have to pay.

DISCUSSION QUESTIONS

1. **ETHICS** Richard and Michelle Kommit traveled to New Jersey to have fun in the casinos. While in Atlantic City, they used their MasterCard to withdraw cash from an ATM conveniently located in the "pit"—the gambling area of a casino. They ran up debts of $5,500 on the credit card and did not pay. The Connecticut National Bank sued for the money. Law aside, who has the moral high ground? Is it acceptable for the *casino* to offer ATM services in the gambling pit? If a *credit card* company allows customers to withdraw cash in a casino, is it encouraging them to lose money? Do the Kommits have any ethical right to use the ATM, attempt to win money by gambling, and then seek to avoid liability?

2. The Justice Department shut down three of the most popular online poker websites (Poker Stars, Absolute Poker, and Full Tilt Poker). State agencies take countless actions each year to stop illegal gaming operations. Do you believe that gambling by adults *should* be regulated? If so, which types? Rate the following types of gambling from most acceptable to least acceptable:

   - online poker
   - casino gambling
   - state lotteries
   - bets on pro sports
   - horse racing
   - bets on college sports

3. Van hires Terri to add an electrical outlet to his living room for his new HDTV. Terri does an excellent job, and the new outlet works perfectly. She presents Van with a bill for $200. But Terri is not a licensed electrician. Her state sets licensing standards in the profession to protect the public. And so, Van can refuse to pay Terri's bill. Is this reasonable? *Should* he be able to avoid payment?

4. Should noncompete agreements in employment contracts be illegal altogether? Is there equality of bargaining power between the company and the employee? Should non-competes be limited to top officers of a company? Would you be upset if a prospective employer asked *you* to agree to a one year covenant not to compete?

5. Revisit the Gail Waters example on page **287**. Imagine now that Beauchemin was not her boyfriend, and that he had not introduced her to the drugs to which she became addicted. If all other facts in the case remain the same, would the purchase of the annuity for $50,000 still be unconscionable, in your opinion?

CHAPTER 13

CAPACITY AND CONSENT

Katie, age 17, visits her local electronics store to buy a new laptop. At the register, she pays $400 in cash for the machine. No one is with her, and the cashier does not ask her to show her ID.

Out in the parking lot, Katie's cell phone rings. As she fumbles for it, she loses her grip on the new laptop. It falls to the pavement—crack!—bounces once, and comes to rest a few feet away from her.

Just then, a Hummer rounds the corner. It runs over Katie's new laptop. "Ugg ..." she says, feeling nauseous. The SUV stops, and the reverse lights come on. It backs slowly over the laptop again. The driver, oblivious, rolls down his window and asks Katie, "Say, is there a gas station around here?"

"That way," a shocked Katie says, pointing to a sign in the distance. "But you just ..."

"Oh, I see it! Thanks a million!" The driver puts the Hummer in gear and drives over the laptop a third time. The small jolt loosens the one lug nut securing the spare tire to the back of the SUV. The heavy spare falls directly on top of what remains of Katie's new laptop.

> **Just then, a Hummer rounds the corner. It runs over Katie's new laptop.**

Scooping up wires, bits of plastic, and pieces of metal, she goes back inside the store. Dumping the pieces on the customer service desk, she says, "I've changed my mind about this computer."

The clerk looks at the collection of laptop parts, shakes his head, and points to a sign behind him. "Look, I can't take merchandise back if it's damaged. And this laptop is definitely damaged."

"Too bad," Katie says. "I want my money back. Now."

Is Katie entitled to a full refund? In most states, the answer is *yes*.

This chapter examines **voidable contracts**. When a contract is voidable, one party has the option either to enforce or terminate the agreement. Two specific issues are presented.

Capacity concerns the legal ability of a party to enter a contract in the first place. Someone may lack capacity because of his young age or mental infirmity. **Consent refers to whether a contracting party truly understood what she was getting into and whether she made the agreement voluntarily.** Consent issues arise in cases of fraud, mistake, duress, and undue influence.

13-1 CAPACITY

Contracts Checklist
- ☐ Offer
- ☐ Acceptance
- ☐ Consideration
- ☐ Legality
- ☑ Capacity
- ☐ Consent
- ☐ Writing

© Cengage Learning

Capacity is the legal ability to enter into a contract. An adult of sound mind has capacity. Generally, any deal she enters into will be enforced if all elements on the Contracts Checklist—agreement, consideration, and so forth—are present. But two groups of people usually lack legal capacity: minors and those with a mental impairment.

13-1a Minors

In contract law, a minor is someone under the age of 18. Because a minor lacks legal capacity, she normally can create only a voidable contract. **A voidable contract may be canceled by the party who lacks capacity.** Notice that *only the party lacking capacity* may cancel the agreement. So a minor who enters into a contract generally may choose between enforcing the agreement or negating it. The other party—an adult, or perhaps a store—has no such right. Voidable contracts are very different from those that are void, which we examined in Chapter 12, on legality. A *void* contract is illegal from the beginning and may not be enforced by either party. A *voidable* contract is legal but permits one party to escape, if he so wishes.

DISAFFIRMANCE

Disaffirm
To give notice of refusal to be bound by an agreement.

A minor who wishes to escape from a contract generally may **disaffirm** it; that is, he may notify the other party that he refuses to be bound by the agreement. There are several ways a minor may disaffirm a contract. He may simply tell the other party, orally or in writing, that he will not honor the deal. Or he may disaffirm a contract by refusing to perform his obligations under it. A minor may go further—he can undo a contract that has already been completed by filing a suit to **rescind** the contract; that is, to have a court formally cancel it.

Rescind
To cancel a contract.

Kevin Green was 16 when he signed a contract with Star Chevrolet to buy a used Camaro. Because he was a minor, the deal was voidable. When the Camaro blew a gasket and Kevin informed Star Chevrolet that he wanted his money back, he was disaffirming the contract. He happened to do it because the car suddenly seemed a poor buy, but he could have disaffirmed for any reason at all, such as deciding that he no longer liked Camaros. When Kevin disaffirmed, he was entitled to his money back.

RESTITUTION

A minor who disaffirms a contract must return the consideration he has received, to the extent he is able. Restoring the other party to its original position is called **restitution.** The consideration that Kevin Green received in the contract was, of course, the Camaro.

Restitution
Restoring an injured party to its original position.

What happens if the minor is not able to return the consideration because he no longer has it or it has been destroyed? Most states hold that the minor is *still* entitled to his money back. A minority of states follow the **status quo rule**, which provides that, if a minor cannot return the consideration, the adult or store is only required to return its *profit margin* to the minor.

In the opening scenario, Katie attempted to return a destroyed laptop for the full purchase price of $400. Assume that the store paid a computer manufacturer $350 for the laptop and then marked it up $50.

In most states, Katie would be entitled to the full $400 purchase price, even though the laptop is now worthless. The sign at the customer service desk would have no effect, and the store would have to absorb the loss. But, if Katie lives in a state with the status quo rule, then the store will have to refund only $50 to Katie. It is permitted to keep the other $350 so that it breaks even on the transaction, or is "returned to the status quo."

Ethics   The rule permitting a minor to disaffirm a contract is designed to discourage adults from making deals with innocent children, and it is centuries old. Is this rule still workable in our modern consumer society? There are entire industries devoted to (and dependent upon) minors. Think of children's films, music, sneakers, and toys. Does this rule imperil retailers? Is it *right* to give a 17-year-old high school senior so much power to cancel agreements? In the opening scenario, is it reasonable for Katie to seek a full refund, or is she taking advantage of the system?

TIMING OF DISAFFIRMANCE/RATIFICATION

A minor may disaffirm a contract anytime before she reaches age 18. She also may disaffirm within a reasonable time *after* turning 18. Suppose that 17-year-old Betsy signs a contract to buy a $3,000 stereo. The following week, she picks up the system and pays for it in full. Four months later, she turns 18, and two months after that, she disaffirms the contract. Her disaffirmance is effective. In most states, she gets 100 percent of her money back. In some cases, minors have been entitled to disaffirm a contract several *years* after turning 18. But the minor's right to disaffirm ends if she ratifies the contract. **Ratification** is made by any words or action indicating an intention to be bound by the contract. Suppose Betsy, age 17, buys her stereo on credit, promising to pay $150 per month. She has made only four payments by the time she turns 18, but after reaching her majority, she continues to pay every month for six more months. Then she attempts to disaffirm. Too late. Her actions—payment of the monthly bill for six months as an adult—ratified the contract she entered into as a minor. She is now fully obligated to pay the entire $3,000, on the agreed-upon schedule.

Ratification
Words or actions indicating an intention to be bound by a contract.

EXCEPTION: NECESSARIES

A necessary is something essential to the minor's life and welfare. **On a contract for necessaries, a minor must pay for the value of the benefit received.** In other words, the minor may still disaffirm the contract and return whatever is unused. But he is liable to pay for whatever benefit he obtained from the goods while he had them. Food, clothing, housing, and medical care are necessaries. Thus a 16-year-old who buys and eats a 99-cent cheeseburger cannot later seek his 99 cents from the fast food restaurant.

EXCEPTION: MISREPRESENTATION OF AGE

The rules change somewhat if a minor lies about his age. Sixteen-year-old Dan is delighted to learn from his friend Betsy that a minor can buy a fancy stereo system, use it for a year or so, and then get his money back. Dan drops into SoundBlast and asks to buy a $4,000 surround-sound system. The store clerk says that the store no longer sells expensive systems to underage customers. Dan produces a fake driver's license indicating that he is 18, and the clerk sells him the system. A year later, Dan drives up to SoundBlast and unloads the system, now in shambles. He asks for his $4,000 back. Is he still permitted to disaffirm?

States have been troubled by this problem, and there is no clear rule. A few states will still permit Dan to disaffirm the contract entirely. The theory is that a minor must be saved from his own poor judgment, including his foolish lie. Many states, though, will prohibit

Dan from disaffirming the contract. They take the reasonable position that the law was intended to protect childhood innocence, not calculated deceit.

13-1b Mentally Impaired Persons

You are a trial court judge. Don wants you to rule that his father, Cedric, is mentally incompetent and, on behalf of Cedric, to terminate a contract he signed.

Here is the evidence.

Cedric is a 75-year-old millionaire who keeps $300,000 stuffed in pillow cases in the attic. He lives in a filthy house with a parrot whom he calls the Bishop, an iguana named Orlando, and a tortoise known as Mrs. Sedgely. All of the pets have small beds in Cedric's grungy bedroom, and each one eats at the dining table with its master. Cedric pays college students $50 an hour to read poetry to the animals, but he forbids the reading of sonnets, which he regards as "the devil's handiwork."

Don has been worried about Cedric's bizarre behavior for several years and has urged his father to enter a nursing home. Last week, when Don stopped in to visit, Cedric became angry at him, accusing his son of disrespecting the Bishop and Mrs. Sedgely, who were enjoying a 15th-century Castilian poem that Jane, a college student, was reading. Don then blurted out that Cedric was no longer able to take care of himself. Cedric snapped back, "I'll show you how capable I am." On the back of a 40-year-old menu, he scratched out a contract promising to give Jane "$100,000 today and $200,000 one year from today if she agrees to feed, house, and care for the Bishop, Orlando, and Mrs. Sedgely for the rest of their long lives." Jane *quickly* signed the agreement. Don urges that the court, on Cedric's behalf, declare the contract void. How will you rule? Courts often struggle when deciding cases of mental competence.

A person suffers from a mental impairment if, by reason of mental illness or defect, he is unable to understand the nature and consequences of the transaction.[1] The mental impairment can be due to some mental illness, such as schizophrenia, or to mental retardation, brain injury, senility, or any other cause that renders the person unable to understand the nature and consequences of the contract.

A party suffering a mental impairment usually creates only a voidable contract. The impaired person has the right to disaffirm the contract just as a minor does. But again, the contract is voidable, not void. The mentally impaired party generally has the right to full performance if she wishes.

The law creates an exception: If a person has been adjudicated insane, then all of his future agreements are void. "Adjudicated insane" means that a judge has made a formal finding that a person is mentally incompetent and has assigned the person a guardian.

How will a court evaluate Cedric's mental status? Of course, if there had already been a judicial determination that he was insane, any contract he signed would be void. Since no judge has issued such a ruling about Cedric, the court will listen to doctors or therapists who have evaluated him and to anyone else who can testify about Cedric's recent conduct. The court may also choose to look at the contract itself, to see if it is so lopsided that no competent person would agree to it.

How will Don fare in seeking to preserve Cedric's wealth? Poorly. Unless Don has more evidence than we have heard thus far, he is destined to eat canned tuna while Jane and the Bishop dine on caviar. Cedric is decidedly eccentric, and perhaps unwise. But those characteristics do not prove mental impairment. Neither does leaving a fortune to a poetry reader. If Don could produce evidence from a psychiatrist that Cedric, for example, was generally delusional or could not distinguish a parrot from a religious leader, that would persuade a court of mental impairment. But on the evidence presented thus far, Mrs. Sedgely and friends will be living well.[2]

---

[1] Restatement (Second) of Contracts §15.

[2] For a similar case, see *Harwell v. Garrett,* 239 Ark. 551, 393 S.W.2d 256, 1965 Ark. LEXIS 1033 (1965).

INTOXICATION

Similar rules apply in cases of drug or alcohol intoxication. When one party is so intoxicated that he cannot understand the nature and consequences of the transaction, the contract is voidable.

We wish to stress that courts are *highly* skeptical of intoxication arguments. If you go out drinking and make a foolish agreement, you are probably stuck with it. Even if you are too drunk to drive, you are probably not nearly too drunk to make a contract. If your blood alcohol level is, say, .08, your coordination and judgment are poor. Driving in such a condition is dangerous. But you probably have a fairly clear awareness of what is going on around you.

To back out of a contract on the grounds of intoxication, you must be able to provide evidence that you did not understand the "nature of the agreement," or the basic deal that you made.

The following landmark case is a rare exception, and the defendant was able to escape the deal. The defendant had lots of witnesses who testified that he had no idea what he was doing.

> Did he understand what he was doing? Did he know where and who he was?

Landmark Case

BABCOCK V. ENGEL
58 Mont. 597; 194 P. 137
Supreme Court of Montana, 1920

Facts: While Charles Engel's wife was out of town, he sat home alone, drinking mightily. During this period, he made the following agreement with G. M. Babcock: Engel traded his 320-acre farm and $2,000 worth of personal property for Babcock's hotel. Engel's property was worth approximately twice the value of the hotel. Engel later refused to honor the deal on the grounds that he had been intoxicated when he made the agreement. Babcock sued, but the jury sided with Engel and dismissed the complaint. Babcock appealed.

Issue: *Did Engel's intoxication make his agreement with Babcock voidable?*

Decision: Yes. Engel's inability to understand the nature and consequences of his act made the contract voidable.

Reasoning: The main question here was not whether Engel was drunk. The facts indicated that he was completely wasted and the jury agreed. Engel testified that as soon as his wife left town, he binged on whisky for two days. (Let's just say he missed her …) After stumbling into town, he downed four or five more drinks of whisky and blackberry before negotiating a bad deal with Babcock.

The law was only concerned with the ugly details of Engel's drunkenness because they described his mental capacity when he entered into the contract. Could Engel have freely consented in his condition? Did he understand what he was doing? Did he know where and who he was? Four credible witnesses testified that the befuddled Engel had no idea what he was doing and did not look qualified to transact business.

Traditionally, the law refused to give a "free pass" to the drunk, opting instead to make them liable for the consequences of their overindulgence. But alcohol intoxication is just one of many causes of incapacity, all of which are subject to the same rule. If a party is unable to understand the nature and consequences of his act, the resulting contract is voidable at his option when he regains capacity. The trial court's decision was affirmed.

Restitution

A mentally infirm party who seeks to void a contract must make restitution. If a party succeeds with a claim of mental impairment, the court will normally void the contract but will require the impaired party to give back whatever she got. Suppose Danielle buys a Rolls-Royce and promises in writing to pay $4,000 per month for five years. Three weeks later, she seeks to void the contract on the grounds of mental impairment. She must return the Rolls. If the car has depreciated, Danielle normally will have to pay for the decrease in value. What happens if restitution is impossible? Generally, courts require a mentally infirm person to make full restitution if the contract is to be rescinded. If restitution is impossible, the court will not rescind the agreement unless the infirm party can show bad faith by the other. This is because, unlike minority, which is generally easy to establish, mental competence may not be so apparent to the other person negotiating.

Contracts Checklist
- ☐ Offer
- ☐ Acceptance
- ☐ Consideration
- ☐ Legality
- ☐ Capacity
- ☑ Consent
- ☐ Writing

© Cengage Learning

13-2 Reality of Consent

Smiley offers to sell you his house for $300,000, and you agree in writing to buy it. After you move in, you discover that the house is sinking into the earth at the rate of six inches per week. In twelve months, your only access to the house may be through the chimney. You sue, seeking to rescind. You argue that when you signed the contract, you did not truly consent because you lacked essential information. In this section we look at four claims that parties make in an effort to rescind a contract based on lack of valid consent: (1) fraud, (2) mistake, (3) duress, and (4) undue influence.

13-2a Fraud

Fraud begins when a party to a contract says something that is factually wrong. "This house has no termites," says a homeowner to a prospective buyer. If the house is swarming with the nasty pests, the statement is a misrepresentation. But does it amount to fraud? An injured person must show the following:

1. The defendant knew that his statement was false, or that he made the statement recklessly and without knowledge of whether it was false.

2. The false statement was material.

3. The injured party justifiably relied on the statement.

Element One: Intentional or Reckless Misrepresentation of Fact

The injured party must show a false statement of fact. Notice that this does not mean the statement was a necessarily a "lie." If a homeowner says that the famous architect Stanford White designed her house, but Bozo Loco actually did the work, it is a false statement.

Now, if the owner knows that Loco designed the house, she has committed the first element of fraud. And, if she has no idea who designed the house, her assertion that it was "Stanford White" also meets the first element.

But the owner might have a good reason for the error. Perhaps a local history book identifies the house as a Stanford White. If she makes the statement with a reasonable belief that she is telling the truth, she has made an innocent misrepresentation (discussed in the next section) and not fraud.

Opinions and "puffery" do not amount to fraud. An opinion is not a statement of fact. A seller says, "I think land values around here will be going up 20 or 30 percent for the foreseeable future." That statement is pretty enticing to a buyer, but it is not a false statement of fact. The maker is clearly stating her own opinion, and the buyer who relies on it does so at his peril. A close relative of opinion is something called "puffery."

Get ready for one of the most astonishing experiences you've ever had! This section on puffery is going to be the finest section of any textbook you have ever read! You're going to find the issue intriguing, the writing dazzling, and the legal summary unforgettable!

"But what happens," you might wonder, "if this section fails to astonish? What if I find the issue dull, the writing mediocre, and the legal summary incomprehensible? Can I sue for fraud?" No. The promises we made were mere puffery. A statement is puffery when a reasonable person would realize that it is a sales pitch, representing the exaggerated opinion of the seller. Puffery is not a statement of fact. Because puffery is not factual, it is never a basis for rescission.

Consumers filed a class action against Intel Corporation, claiming fraud. They asserted that Intel advertised its "Pentium 4" computer chip as the "best" in the market when in fact it was no faster than the Pentium III chip. The Illinois Supreme Court dismissed the claims, asserting that no reasonable consumer would make a purchase relying solely on the name "Pentium 4." Even if the consumers could show that Intel plotted to persuade the market that the Pentium 4 was the finest processor, they are demonstrating nothing but puffery.

Saying that the Pentium 4 is "better" or "best" could mean that the Pentium 4 is cheaper, smaller, more reliable, of higher quality, better for resale, more durable, creates less heat, uses less electricity, is more compatible with some versions of software, or is simply the latest in a temporal line of processors. Because the term "better" as a mere suggestion in the name "Pentium 4" is not capable of precise measuring, it is mere puffery and therefore not actionable. That is true even if Intel specifically set out to show the market that the Pentium 4 was the best processor to date.[3]

Courts have found many similar phrases to be puffery, including "high-quality," "expert workmanship," and "you're in good hands with us."

ELEMENT TWO: MATERIALITY

The injured party must demonstrate that the statement was material, or important. A minor misstatement does not meet this second element of fraud. Was the misstatement likely to influence the decision of the misled party significantly? If so, it was material.

Imagine a farmer selling a piece of his land. He measures the acres himself, and calculates a total of 200. If the actual acreage is 199, he has almost certainly not made a *material* misstatement. But if the actual acreage is 150, he has.

ELEMENT THREE: JUSTIFIABLE RELIANCE

The injured party also must show that she actually did rely on the false statement and that her reliance was reasonable. Suppose the seller of a gas station lies through his teeth about the structural soundness of the building. The buyer believes what he hears but does not much care because he plans to demolish the building and construct a day-care center. There was a material misstatement but no reliance, and the buyer may not rescind.

The reliance must be justifiable—that is, reasonable. If the seller of wilderness land tells Lewis that the area is untouched by pollution, but Lewis can see a large lake on the property covered with six inches of oily red scum, Lewis is not justified in relying on the seller's statements. If he goes forward with the purchase, he may not rescind.

No Duty to Investigate   In the previous example, Lewis must act reasonably and keep his eyes open if he walks around the "wilderness" property. But he has no duty to undertake an investigation of what he is told. In other words, if the seller states that the countryside is pure and the lake looks crystal clear, Lewis is not obligated to take water samples and have them tested by a laboratory. A party to a contract has no obligation to investigate the other party's factual statements.

---

[3]*Barbara's Sales, Inc. v. Intel Corp.*, 879 N.E.2d 910 (Ill. 2007).

PLAINTIFF'S REMEDIES FOR FRAUD

In the case of fraud, the injured party generally has a choice of rescinding the contract or suing for damages or, in some cases, doing both. The contract is voidable, which meant that injured party is not *forced* to rescind the deal but may if he wants. Fraud *permits* the injured party to cancel. Alternatively, the injured party can sue for damages—the difference between what the contract promised and what it delivered.

Nancy learns that the building she bought has a terrible heating system. A new one will cost $12,000. If the seller told her the system was "like new," Nancy may rescind the deal. But it may be economically harmful for her to do so. She might have sold her old house, hired a mover, taken a new job, and so forth. What are her other remedies? She could move into the new house and sue for the difference between what she got and what was promised, which is $12,000, the cost of replacing the heating system.

In some states, a party injured by fraud may both rescind *and* sue for damages. In these states, Nancy could rescind her contract, get her deposit back, and then sue the seller for any damages she has suffered. Her damages might be, for example, a lost opportunity to buy another house or wasted moving expenses.

In fact, this last option—rescinding and still suing for damages—is available in all states when a contract is for the sale of goods. **UCC §2-721 permits a party to rescind a contract and then sue for damages when fraud is committed.**

INNOCENT MISREPRESENTATION

If all elements of fraud are present except the misrepresentation of fact was not made intentionally or recklessly, then **innocent misrepresentation** has occurred. So, if a person misstates a material fact and induces reliance, but he had good reason to believe that his statement was true, then he has not committed fraud. Most states allow rescission of a contract, but not damages, in such a case.

SPECIAL PROBLEM: SILENCE

We know that a party negotiating a contract may not misrepresent a material fact. The house seller may not say that "the roof is in great shape" when she sleeps under an umbrella to avoid rain. But what about silence? Suppose the seller knows the roof is in dreadful condition but the buyer never asks. Does the seller have an affirmative obligation to disclose what she knows?

This is perhaps the hottest topic today in the law of misrepresentation. In 1817, the United States Supreme Court laid down the general rule that a party had no duty to disclose, even when he knew that the other person was negotiating under a mistake.[4] In other words, the Court was reinforcing the old rule of *caveat emptor*, "let the buyer beware." But social attitudes about fairness have changed. Today, a seller who knows something that the buyer does not know is often required to divulge it.

Nondisclosure of a fact amounts to misrepresentation in these four cases: (1) where disclosure is necessary to *correct a previous assertion*; (2) where disclosure would correct a *basic mistaken assumption* that the other party is relying on; (3) where disclosure would correct the other party's *mistaken understanding about a writing*; or (4) where there is *a relationship of trust* between the two parties.[5]

To Correct a Previous Assertion   During the course of negotiations, one party's perception of the facts may change. When an earlier statement later appears inaccurate, the change generally must be reported.

---

[4]*Laidlaw v. Organ*, 15 U.S. 178, 1817 U.S. LEXIS 396 (1817).
[5]Restatement (Second) of Contracts §161.

W. R. Grace & Co. wanted to buy a natural-gas field in Mississippi. An engineer's report indicated the presence of large gas reserves. On the basis of the engineering report, the Continental Illinois National Bank committed to a $75 million nonrecourse production loan. A "nonrecourse loan" meant that Continental would be repaid only with revenues from the gas field. After Continental committed, but before it had closed on the loan, Grace had an exploratory well drilled and struck it rich—with water. The land would never produce any gas. Without informing Continental of the news, Grace closed the $75 million loan. When Grace failed to repay, Continental sued and won. A party who learns new information indicating that a previous statement is inaccurate must disclose the bad news.[6]

To Correct a Basic Mistaken Assumption   When one party knows that the other is negotiating with a mistaken assumption about an important fact, the party who knows of the error must correct it. Jeffrey Stambovsky agreed to buy Helen Ackley's house in Nyack, New York, for $650,000. Stambovsky signed a contract and made a $32,500 down payment. Before completing the deal, he learned that in several newspaper articles, Ackley had publicized the house as being haunted. Ackley had also permitted the house to be featured in a walking tour of the neighborhood as "a riverfront Victorian (*with ghost*)." Stambovsky refused to go through with the deal and sued to rescind. He won. The court ruled that Ackley sold the house knowing Stambovsky was ignorant of the alleged ghosts. She also knew that a reasonable buyer might avoid a haunted house, fearing grisly events—or diminished resale value. Stambovsky could not have discovered the apparitions himself, and Ackley's failure to warn permitted him to rescind the deal.[7]

A seller generally must report any latent defect he knows about that the buyer should not be expected to discover himself. As social awareness of the environment increases, a buyer potentially worries about more and more problems. We now know that underground toxic waste, carelessly dumped in earlier decades, can be dangerous or even lethal. Accordingly, any property seller who realizes that there is toxic waste underground, or any other hidden hazard, must reveal that fact.

> She also knew that a reasonable buyer might avoid a haunted house, fearing grisly events ...

To Correct a Mistaken Understanding about a Writing   Suppose the potential buyer of a vacation property has a town map showing that the land he wants to buy has a legal right of way to a beautiful lake. If the seller of the land knows that the town map is out of date and that there is no such right of way, she must disclose her information.

A Relationship of Trust   Maria is planning to sell her restaurant to her brother Ricardo. Maria has a greater duty to reveal problems in the business because Ricardo assumes she will be honest. **When one party naturally expects openness and honesty, based on a close relationship, the other party must act accordingly.** If the building's owner has told Maria he will not renew her lease, she must pass that information on to Ricardo.

What happens if an owner, rather than disclosing hidden defects, sells the property "as is"? The following case provides insight.

---

[6]*FDIC v. W.R. Grace & Co.*, 877 F.2d 614, 1989 U.S. App. LEXIS 8905 (7th Cir. 1989).

[7]*Stambovsky v. Ackley*, 169 A.D.2d 254, 572 N.Y.S.2d 672, 1991 N.Y. App. Div. LEXIS 9873 (N.Y. App. Div. 1991).

HESS V. CHASE MANHATTAN BANK, USA, N.A.

220 S.W.3d 758
Missouri Supreme Court, 2007

CASE SUMMARY

Facts: Billy Stevens owned a paint company. On several occasions, he ordered employees to load a trailer with 55-gallon paint drums, and pallets of old paint cans, and dump them on property he owned. This illegal dumping saved Stevens the cost of proper disposal. Later, employees notified the Environmental Protection Agency of what Stevens had done, and the EPA began an investigation. (Stevens later served time for environmental crimes.)

Stevens defaulted on his mortgage to the land. While Chase Manhattan Bank was in the process of foreclosing, it learned that the EPA was investigating the property for contamination. Chase foreclosed and put the property up for sale "as is." Several buyers expressed interest. The bank did not inform any of them of the ongoing EPA investigation. Dennis Hess bought the property for $52,000.

After Hess bought the land, he discovered the illegal waste and sued Chase for failing to disclose the EPA's investigation. The jury awarded Hess $52,000 and Chase appealed.

Issue: *Did Chase have a duty to disclose to Hess the ongoing investigation?*

Decision: Yes. Chase had a duty to disclose the investigation. Affirmed.

Reasoning: Buyers of "as-is" properties must exercise ordinary diligence before making the purchase. Sellers of such properties need not disclose anything that buyers could discover during a reasonable inspection. Chase argued that because old paint cans were strewn about the property, Hess should have known that the previous owner had dumped hazardous waste there.

Hess responded that even though the paint cans were visible, he had no way of knowing that the EPA was investigating the land. He claimed that he would not have purchased the property if Chase had notified him of the government inquiry. Hess also presented evidence that two other potential buyers who were aware of the paint cans had made offers on the land. But both testified that they would not have done so if they had known about the EPA investigation.

Chase was wrong to conceal its superior knowledge because Hess had no reasonable chance to discover *the EPA action* during his inspection of the property. Chase's silence amounted to fraud, and Missouri law does not allow a disclaimer like "as is" to protect a defendant from liability for fraud.

Hess may rescind the contract and recover the $52,000 purchase price.

EXAM Strategy

Question: Mako is selling his country house for $400,000. Guppy, an interested buyer, asks whether there is sufficient water from the property's well. Mako replies, "Are you kidding? Watch this." He turns on the tap, and the water flows bountifully. Mako then shows Guppy the well, which is full. Guppy buys the property, but two weeks later, the well runs dry. In fact, Mako knew the water supply was inadequate, and he had the well filled by a tanker truck while the property was being sold. A hydrologist tells Guppy it will cost $100,000 to dig a better well, with no guarantee of success. Guppy sues Mako. What remedy should Guppy seek? Who will win?

Strategy: Is this a case of innocent misrepresentation or fraud? Fraud. Therefore, Guppy may seek two remedies: damages or rescission. Make sure that you understand the difference. To win, Guppy must show he relied on a fact that was both false and material.

Result: When Mako responded to Guppy's question by demonstrating the apparent abundance of water, he made a false statement. This was fraud (not innocent misrepresentation), because Mako knew the well was inadequate. That was a material fact. Guppy reasonably relied on the demonstration. Guppy will win. He can elect to rescind the contract (return the property to Mako and get his money back) or choose damages (the cost of digging a proper well). Given the uncertain nature of well digging, he would be wise to rescind.

13-2b Mistake

Contract law principles come from many sources, and in the area of "legal mistake," a cow significantly influenced the law. The cow was named Rose. She was a gentle animal that lived in Michigan in 1886. Rose's owner, Hiram Walker & Sons, bought her for $850. After a few years, the company concluded that Rose could have no calves. As a barren cow, she was worth much less than $850, so Walker contracted to sell her to T. C. Sherwood for a mere $80. But when Sherwood came to collect Rose, the parties realized that (surprise!) she was pregnant. Walker refused to part with the happy mother, and Sherwood sued. Walker defended, claiming that both parties had made a *mistake* and that the contract was voidable.

A mistake can take many forms. It may be a basic error about an essential characteristic of the thing being sold, as in Rose's case. It could be an erroneous prediction about future prices, such as an expectation that oil prices will rise. It might be a mechanical error, such as a builder offering to build a new home for $300 when he clearly meant to bid $300,000. Some mistakes lead to voidable contracts, others create enforceable deals. The first distinction is between bilateral and unilateral mistakes.

BILATERAL MISTAKE

A **bilateral mistake** occurs when both parties negotiate based on the same factual error. Sherwood and Walker both thought Rose was barren, both negotiated accordingly, and both were wrong. The Michigan Supreme Court gave judgment for Walker, the seller, permitting him to rescind the contract because the parties were *both* wrong about the essence of what they were bargaining for.

Bilateral mistake
Occurs when both parties assume the same factual error.

If the parties contract based on an important factual error, the contract is voidable by the injured party. Sherwood and Walker were both wrong about Rose's reproductive ability, and the error was basic enough to cause a tenfold difference in price. Walker, the injured party, was entitled to rescind the contract. Note that the error must be *factual*. Suppose Walker sold Rose thinking that the price of beef was going to drop, when in fact the price rose 60 percent in five months. That would be simply a *prediction* that proved wrong, and Walker would have no right to rescind.

Conscious Uncertainty No rescission is permitted where one of the parties knows he is taking on a risk; that is, he realizes there is uncertainty about the quality of the thing being exchanged. Rufus offers 10 acres of mountainous land to Priscilla. "I can't promise you anything about this land," he says, "but they've found gold on every adjoining parcel." Priscilla, eager for gold, buys the land, digs long and hard, and discovers—mud. She may not rescind the contract. She understood the risk she was assuming, and there was no mutual mistake.

UNILATERAL MISTAKE

Sometimes only one party enters a contract under a mistaken assumption, a situation called **unilateral mistake**. In these cases, it is more difficult for the injured party to rescind a contract. This makes sense since in a bilateral error, neither side really knew what it was getting into, and rescission seems a natural remedy. But with unilateral mistakes, one side

Unilateral mistake
Occurs when only one party enters a contract under a mistaken assumption.

may simply have made a better bargain than the other. As we have seen throughout this unit on contracts, courts are unwilling to undo an agreement merely because someone made a foolish deal. Nonetheless, if her proof is strong, the injured party in a case of unilateral mistakes still may sometimes rescind a contract.

To rescind for unilateral mistake, a party must demonstrate that she entered the contract because of a basic factual error and that *either* (1) enforcing the contract would be *unconscionable* or (2) the nonmistaken party *knew* of the error.[8]

A town obtains five bids for construction of a new municipal swimming pool. Four are between $100,000 and $111,000. Fred's bid is for $82,000. His offer includes a figure of $2,000 for excavation work, while the others have allotted about $20,000 for that work. Fred has inadvertently dropped a zero, resulting in a bid that is $18,000 too low. Town officials accept Fred's offer. When he sues to rescind, Fred wins. Town officials knew that the work could not be done that cheaply, and it would be unfair to hold Fred to a mathematical error that the other side perceived.[9]

In contrast, suppose that Rebecca sues Pierce, whose bad driving caused an accident, and Amy, who owned the car that Pierce was driving. While the case is pending, Amy's insurance company, Risknaught, pays Rebecca a $70,000 settlement. Later, the state supreme court rules that Pierce was an unauthorized driver, and an owner's insurer is never liable in such a case. Risknaught seeks to rescind its settlement, claiming unilateral mistake as to its liability. The company loses. Risknaught was aware that an appellate ruling might establish new precedent. The insurer settled based on a decision calculated to minimize its risk.[10]

In the following case an automobile dealer made a mistake—how often does *this* happen?—in the customer's favor.

DONOVAN v. RRL CORPORATION

26 Cal. 4th 261, 27 P.3d 702, 109 Ca. Rptr. 2d 807
Supreme Court of California, 2001

CASE SUMMARY

Facts: Brian Donovan was in the market for a used car. As he scanned the Costa Mesa *Daily Pilot*, he came upon a "Pre-Owned Coup-A-Rama Sale!" at Lexus of Westminster. Of the 16 cars listed in the ad (with vehicle identification numbers), one was a sapphire blue Jaguar XJ6 Vanden Plas, priced at $25,995.

Brian drove to a Jaguar dealership to do some comparison shopping. Jaguars of the same year and mileage cost about $8,000 to $10,000 more than the auto at the Lexus agency. The next day, Brian and his wife hurried over to the Coup-A-Rama event, spotted the Jaguar (which had the correct VIN) and asked a salesperson if they might test drive it. Pleased with the ride, Brian said to the salesman, "O.K. We will take it at your price, $26,000." This figure startled the sales representative, who glanced at the newspaper ad Brian showed him, and responded, "That's a mistake."

As indeed it was. The Lexus agency had paid $35,000 for the Jaguar and intended to sell it for about $37,000. Brian was adamant. "No, I want to buy it at your advertised price, and I will write you a check right now." The sales manager was called in, and he refused to sell the car for less than $37,000.

It turned out that the *Daily Pilot's* typographical and proofreading errors had caused the mistake, although the Lexus dealership had failed to review the proof sheet, which would have revealed the error before the ad went to press.

Brian sued. The trial court found that unilateral mistake prevented enforcement of the contract. The appellate court reversed, and Donovan appealed to the state's highest court.

The state supreme court first ruled that there *was* in fact a contract between the parties. Generally, a newspaper

---

[8]Restatement (Second) of Contracts §153.
[9]See examples provided in Restatement (Second) of Contracts §153.
[10]See, for example *AID Hawai'i Ins. Co. v. Bateman*, 82 Haw. 453, 923 P.2d 395 (Haw. 1996).

advertisement is merely a solicitation for an offer, and does not permit the customer to form a contract by accepting. (See Chapter 10, on agreement.) However, a California statute generally holds automobile dealers to the terms of their offers. The court then went on to examine the mistake.

Issue: *Did the Lexus dealer's mistake entitle it to rescind the contract?*

Decision: Yes, the mistake entitled the dealership to rescind.

Reasoning: The price is a "basic assumption" of a contract. A significant mistake about that price may permit one party to rescind an agreement. The injured party must show that the error is so severe that it would be unfair to enforce the bargain.

Measured by this standard, the Lexus dealership's price error was a material mistake. A sales price of $25,995 would require the dealer to sell the Lexus for $12,000 less than it intended. That is a 32% error, creating a bonanza for Donovan and a large loss for the seller.

Donovan argues that a dealer is able to monitor its ads and must be strictly held to the terms that it publishes. However, if a court were to enforce this rule, it would mean that a dealer who inadvertently advertised a $75,000 car for $75 would be stuck with the bargain. That is too harsh.

There is no evidence that the Lexus dealership knew of the misprint or intended to mislead customers. Nothing indicated that the dealer routinely permitted such errors to appear in the press. It was the *Daily Pilot* that made the mistake. The dealership should not suffer a large loss because of that error. The judgment in favor of the dealership is affirmed.

EXAM Strategy

Question: Joe buys an Otterhound named Barky, from Purity Dog Shop. He pays $2,500 for the puppy. The high cost is a result of the certificate Purity gives him, indicating that the puppy's parents were both AKC champions (elite dogs). Two months later, Joe sells the hound to Emily for $2,800. Joe and Emily both believe that Barky is descended from champions. Then a state investigation reveals that Purity has been cheating and its certificates are fakes. Barky is just a regular dog, worth about $100. Emily sues Joe. Who wins?

Strategy: Both parties are mistaken about the kind of dog Joe is selling, so this is an instance of bilateral mistake. What is the rule in such cases?

Result: If the two sides agree based on an important factual error, the contract is voidable by the injured party. A mutt is entirely different from a dog that might become a champion. The parties erred about the essence of their deal. Joe's good faith does not save him, and Emily is entitled to rescind.

13-2c Duress

True consent is also lacking when one party agrees to a contract under **duress**. If kindly Uncle Hugo signs over the deed to the ranch because Niece Nelly is holding a gun to his head, Hugo has not consented in any real sense, and he will have the right to rescind the contract. **If one party makes an improper threat that causes the victim to enter into a contract, and the victim had no reasonable alternative, the contract is voidable.**[11]

On a Sunday morning, Bancroft Hall drove to pick up his daughter Sandra, who had slept at a friend's house. The Halls are black and the neighborhood was white. A suspicious

Duress
An improper threat made to force another party to enter into a contract.

---
[11]Restatement (Second) of Contracts §175(1).

neighbor called the police, who arrived, aggressively prevented the Halls from getting into their own car, and arrested the father. The Halls had not violated any law or done anything wrong whatsoever. Later an officer told Hall that he could leave immediately if he signed a full release (stating that he had no claims of any kind against the police), but that if he refused to sign it, he would be detained for a bail hearing. Hall signed the release but later filed suit. The police defended based on the release.

The court held that the release was voidable because Hall had signed it under duress. The threat to detain Hall for a bail hearing was clearly improper because he had committed no crime. He also had no reasonable alternative to signing. A jury awarded the Halls over half a million dollars.[12]

Can "improper threats" take other forms? Does *economic* intimidation count? Many plaintiffs have posed that question over the last half century, and courts have grudgingly yielded.

Today, in most states, economic duress *can* also be used to void a contract. But economic duress sounds perilously close to hard bargaining—in other words, business. The free market system is expected to produce tough competition. A smart, aggressive executive may bargain fiercely. How do we distinguish economic duress from legal, successful business tactics? Courts have created no single rule to answer the question, but they do focus on certain issues.

In analyzing a claim of economic duress, courts look at these factors:

- Acts that have no legitimate business purpose
- Greatly unequal bargaining power
- An unnaturally large gain for one party
- Financial distress to one party

Is the following case one of duress or hard bargaining?

---

[12]*Halls v. Ochs*, 817 F.2d 920, U. S. App. LEXIS 5822 (1st Cir. 1987).

You Be the Judge

Facts: Amy Maida sued her employer, RLS Legal Solutions, for various claims relating to her job. RLS asked that the case be dismissed because Maida had signed an arbitration agreement. Maida had in fact signed the contract while already working at RLS. However, she responded that the agreement should not be enforced because she had signed it under economic duress. At trial, she was asked whether she had found the agreement acceptable:

> I did not. The arbitration clause was going to allow me not to be able to be in a position that I needed to be in now, and that is, to have someone represent me to help me where I feel like the company did me wrong.

IN RE RLS LEGAL SOLUTIONS, LLC
2005 WL 171381
Texas Court of Appeals, 2005

would not be paid until I signed the agreement. I had received my paychecks by direct deposit for three years. [RLS did in fact stop the direct deposit payment of Maida's salary.]

I needed my paycheck to meet my financial responsibilities since I am a single family income household provider. I had no way to pay my mortgage, vehicle note, car and homeowner's insurance as well as any household bills.

Maida testified that after signing and returning the agreement, she received a manual check. Maida said

After I refused to agree to this arbitration clause, I was told that my payroll checks would not be direct deposited into my account until I signed the agreement and that I that when she asked why she had not been paid by direct deposit as usual, she was told her paycheck would be held until she signed the agreement.

RLS argued that Maida had eventually received every paycheck to which she was entitled, had suffered no losses, and was free to leave RLS at any time if she found her employment terms unacceptable.

The trial court refused to dismiss the case or order arbitration, and RLS appealed.

You Be the Judge: *Did Maida sign the arbitration under economic duress?*

Argument for RLS: Your honors, it is hard to take seriously a claim of economic duress when the plaintiff has not lost one cent and was never forced to sign anything. RLS runs a business, not a community center. To stay competitive, we constantly revise our commercial practices, and this was one such change. We did not ask for a bizarre or inappropriate change: Arbitration is a widely favored method of settling disputes, quicker and cheaper *for all parties.*

Maida signed. Yes, we stopped direct deposit of her check, but in the end, we paid her all she was due. We were not obligated to pay her in any particular fashion, or even to continue her employment. If she wanted to stay with us, she had to play by our rules.

Argument for Maida: The company could offer an arbitration contract to all workers. But that is distinct from forcing such agreements down employee throats, which is what they did here. RLS knows that its workers depend on prompt payment of payroll checks to avoid falling quickly into debt. The company offered Maida the arbitration agreement, she rejected it, and they responded by stopping direct deposit of her check. Knowing that she was the sole provider for her family, the firm intended to subject her to intolerable economic pressure. It worked. However, the court should have no part of this coercion. The two sides had hugely differing bargaining power, and RLS attempted to use financial distress to obtain what it could not by persuasion.

13-2d Undue Influence

She was single and pregnant. A shy young woman in a large city with no family nearby, she needed help and support. She went to the Methodist Mission Home of Texas where she found room and board, support—and a lot of counseling. Her discussions with a minister and a private counselor stressed one point: that she should give up her baby for adoption. She signed the adoption papers, but days later, she decided she wanted the baby after all. Was there any ground to rescind? She claimed *undue influence,* in other words, that the Mission Home so dominated her thinking that she never truly consented. Where one party has used undue influence, the contract is voidable at the option of the injured party. There are two elements to the plaintiff's case. **To prove undue influence, the injured party must demonstrate:**

- A relationship between the two parties either of trust or of domination, and

- Improper persuasion by the stronger party.[13]

In the Methodist Mission case, the court held that the plaintiff had been young and extremely vulnerable during the days following the birth of her child. The mission's counselor, to whom she turned for support, had spent day after day forcefully insisting that the young woman had no moral or legal right to keep her child. This amounted to undue influence. The court voided the adoption agreement.[14] In the following case, the age difference is reversed.

---

[13]Restatement (Second) of Contracts §177.

[14]*Methodist Mission Home of Texas v. N A B*, 451 S.W.2d 539, 1970 Tex. App. LEXIS 2055 (Tex. Civ. App. 1970).

SEPULVEDA V. AVILES

762 N.Y.S.2d 358, 308 A.D.2d 1
New York Supreme Court, Appellate Division, 2003

CASE SUMMARY

Facts: Agnes Seals owned and lived in a ten-unit apartment building on East 119th Street in New York City. When she was 80 years old, a fire damaged much of the building's interior, leaving Seals physically and mentally unable to care for the property. Shortly after the fire, she met David Aviles, a 35-year-old neighbor. Aviles convinced Seals to sell him the building, promising to care for her for the rest of her life. She sold him the building for $50,000, taking a down payment of $10,000, with the rest to be paid over time. At the closing, Seals was represented by an attorney, Martin Freedman, whom she had never met before, and who had been referred to her by Aviles's lawyer (with whom he shared office space).

Three years later, Seals died. Her will left her entire estate to Elba and Victor Sepulveda, but the building had been Seals's principal asset. The Sepulvedas sued Aviles, asking the court to set aside the sale of the building, claiming that Aviles had used undue influence to trick Seals into a sale that was not in her interest. The jury found that Aviles had not used undue influence, and the Sepulvedas appealed.

Issue: *Did Aviles use undue influence to obtain the apartment building?*

Decision: Yes, Aviles used undue influence.

Reasoning: The jury's verdict was completely at odds with the evidence. A social worker testified that at the time of the sale, Seals was traumatized by the fire, housebound, and utterly dependent on others for her daily needs. Sister Lachapelle, a second neutral witness, confirmed this. They both stated that Aviles promised to take care of Seals if she would sell him the building. At the closing, Seals was represented by a lawyer she had never met before, recommended to her by Aviles.

A medical expert testified that in his opinion, Seals suffered from severe Alzheimer's disease at the time of the sale. Aviles testified that at the time of the sale, Seals was coherent and lucid, but the expert testimony is far more persuasive than Aviles's self-serving, lay opinion.

At trial, Aviles admitted that he made unfettered use of Seals's funds and credit cards. In a particularly brazen example, he wrote Seals monthly checks for payment on the house, and then had her endorse the checks back to him. Aviles deposited the checks in his account, having effectively paid nothing for the house. The sale was a sham.

Aviles clearly and repeatedly used undue influence to bring about the sale and then avoid his payments for the building. The jury's verdict that there was no undue influence was based on a wildly unreasonable interpretation of the evidence. The case is reversed and remanded for a new trial.

Chapter Conclusion

An agreement between two parties may not be enough to make a contract enforceable. A minor or a mentally impaired person may generally disaffirm contracts. Even if both parties are adults of sound mind, courts will insist that consent be genuine. Misrepresentation, mistake, duress, and undue influence all indicate that at least one party did not truly consent. As the law evolves, it imposes an increasingly greater burden of *good faith negotiating* on the party in the stronger position.

EXAM REVIEW

1. **VOIDABLE CONTRACT**   Capacity and consent are different contract issues that can lead to the same result: a voidable contract. A voidable agreement is one that can be canceled by a party who lacks legal capacity or who did not give true consent. (p. 296)

2. **MINORS**   A minor (someone under the age of 18) generally may disaffirm any contract while she is still a minor or within a reasonable time after reaching age 18. (pp. 296–298)

EXAM Strategy

Question: John Marshall and Kirsten Fletcher decided to live together. They leased an apartment, each agreeing to pay one-half of the rent. When he signed the lease, Marshall was 17. Shortly after signing the lease, Marshall turned 18, and two weeks later, he moved into the apartment. He paid his half of the rent for two months and then moved out because he and Fletcher were not getting along. Fletcher sued Marshall for one-half of the monthly rent for the remainder of the lease. Who wins?

Strategy: Marshall was clearly a minor when he signed the lease, and he could have rescinded the agreement at that time. However, after he turned 18, he moved in and began to pay rent. What effect did that have on his contract obligation? (See the "Result" at the end of this section.)

3. **MENTAL IMPAIRMENT**   A mentally impaired person may generally disaffirm a contract. In such a case, though, he generally must make restitution. (pp. 298–299)

4. **INTOXICATION**   A person who is so intoxicated that he fails to understand the nature of an agreement may disaffirm a contract. (p. 299)

5. **FRAUD**   Fraud is grounds for rescinding a contract. The injured party must prove all of the following:

   a. A false statement of fact made intentionally or recklessly

   b. Materiality

   c. Justifiable reliance (pp. 300–305)

6. **INNOCENT MISREPRESENTATION**   Innocent misrepresentation also allows an injured party to rescind a contract, but it does not allow a plaintiff to sue for damages. It has the same elements as fraud, but it does not require intent or recklessness. (p. 302)

EXAM Strategy

Question: Ron buys 1,000 "Smudgy Dolls" for his toy store. Karen, the seller, tells him the dolls are in perfect condition, even though she knows their heads are defectively attached. Ron sells all of the products, but then he has to face 1,000 angry customers with headless dolls. Ron sues Karen seeking rescission. What is the likely outcome?

(a) This is fraud, and Ron will be able to rescind.

(b) This is an innocent misrepresentation, and Ron will be able to rescind.

(c) This is fraud, but Ron will not be able to rescind.

d. This is an innocent misrepresentation, but Ron will not be able to rescind.

e. This is neither fraud nor an innocent misrepresentation.

Strategy: Karen knew her statement was false, so this is a case of fraud if all elements can be met. Ron must prove a false statement of fact, materiality, and reliance. Can he do so? (See the "Result" at the end of this section.)

7. **SILENCE**   Silence amounts to misrepresentation only in four instances:

- Where disclosure is necessary to *correct a previous assertion*;

- Where disclosure would correct a *basic mistaken assumption* on which the other party is relying;

- Where disclosure would correct the other party's *mistaken understanding about a writing*; or

- Where there is a *relationship of trust* between the two parties. (pp. 302–305)

8. **MISTAKE**   In a case of bilateral mistake, either party may rescind the contract. In a case of unilateral mistake, the injured party may rescind only upon a showing that enforcement would be unconscionable or that the other party knew of her mistake. (pp. 302–304)

9. **DURESS**   If one party makes an improper threat that causes the victim to enter into a contract, and the victim had no reasonable alternative, the contract is voidable. (pp. 307–309)

EXAM Strategy

Question: Andreini's nerve problem diminished the use of his hands. Dr. Beck operated, but the problem grew worse. A nurse told the patient that Beck might have committed a serious error that exacerbated the problem. Andreini returned for a second operation, which Beck assured him would correct the problem. But after Andreini had been placed in a surgical gown, shaved, and prepared for surgery, the doctor insisted that he sign a release relieving Beck of liability for the first operation. Andreini did not want to sign it, but Beck refused to operate until he did. Later, Andreini sued Beck for malpractice. A trial court dismissed Andreini's suit based on the release. You are on the appeals court. Will you affirm the dismissal or reverse?

Strategy: Andreini is claiming physical duress. Did Beck act *improperly* in demanding a release? Did Andreini have a *realistic alternative?* (See the "Result" at the end of this section.)

10. **UNDUE INFLUENCE**   Once again the injured party may rescind a contract, but only upon a showing of a special relationship and improper persuasion. (pp. 309–310)

2. Result: A minor can disaffirm a contract. However, if he turns 18 and then ratifies the agreement, he is fully liable. When he paid the rent, Marshall ratified the contract, and thus he is fully liable.

5. Result: Karen made a false statement of fact, knowing it was wrong. It was material, and Ron reasonably relied on her. Karen has committed fraud. Ron is entitled to rescind the agreement. The correct answer is "a."

8. Result: The Utah Supreme Court reversed the trial court, so you probably should as well. Beck forced Andreini to sign under duress. The threat to withhold surgery was improper, and Andreini had no reasonable alternative.

MULTIPLE-CHOICE QUESTIONS

1. Kerry finds a big green ring in the street. She shows it to Leroy, who says, "Wow. That could be valuable." Neither Kerry nor Leroy knows what the ring is made of or whether it is valuable. Kerry sells the ring to Leroy for $100, saying, "Don't come griping if it turns out to be worth two dollars." Leroy takes the ring to a jeweler who tells him it is an unusually perfect emerald, worth at least $75,000. Kerry sues to rescind.

   (a) Kerry will win based on fraud.

   (b) Kerry will win based on mutual mistake.

   (c) Kerry will win based on unilateral mistake.

   (d) Kerry will lose.

2. Veronica has a beer and then makes a contract. She continues drinking, and her blood alcohol level eventually rises to .09, which is just above her state's threshold for drunk driving. She makes a second contract while in this condition. Veronica's first contract is _____, and her second contract is _____.

   (a) valid; valid

   (b) valid; voidable

   (c) voidable; voidable

   (d) voidable; void

3. Jerry is so mentally ill that he is unable to understand the nature and consequences of his transactions, but he has not been adjudicated insane. Penny has been adjudicated insane, and a court has appointed a guardian to handle her affairs. Jerry's contracts are _____, and Penny's contracts are _____.

   (a) valid; valid

   (b) valid; voidable

   (c) valid; void

   (d) voidable; voidable

   (e) voidable; void

4. Angela makes a material misstatement of fact to Lance, which he relies on when he signs Angela's contract. Fraud exists if Angela made the misstatement _____.

   (a) intentionally

   (b) recklessly

(c) carelessly

(d) (a) and (b) only

(e) (a), (b), and (c)

5. Scarborough's Department Store opens for business on a busy shopping day just before Christmas. A hurried clerk places a sign in the middle of a table piled high with red cashmere sweaters. The sign reads, "SALE—100% Cashmere—$0.99 Each." The sign, of course, was supposed to read "$99 each."

This is a _____ mistake, and customers _____ be able to demand that Scarborough's sell the sweaters for 99 cents.

(a) unilateral; will

(b) unilateral; will not

(c) bilateral; will

(d) bilateral; will not

ESSAY QUESTIONS

1. Raymond Barrows owned a 17-acre parcel of undeveloped land in Seaford, Delaware. For most of his life, Mr. Barrows had been an astute and successful businessman, but by the time he was 85 years old, he had been diagnosed as "very senile and confused 90 percent of the time." Glenn Bowen offered to buy the land. Barrows had no idea of its value, so Bowen had it appraised by a friend, who said it was worth $50,000. Bowen drew up a contract, which Barrows signed. In the contract, Barrows agreed to sell the land for $45,000, of which Bowen would pay $100 at the time of closing; the remaining $44,900 was due whenever Bowen developed the land and sold it. There was no time limit on Bowen's right to develop the land nor any interest due on the second payment. Comment.

2. On television and in magazines, Maurine and Mamie Mason saw numerous advertisements for Chrysler Fifth Avenue automobiles. The ads described the car as "luxurious," "quality-engineered," and "reliable." When they went to inspect the car, the salesman told them the warranty was "the best … comparable to Cadillacs and Lincolns." After the Masons bought a Fifth Avenue, they began to have many problems with it. Even after numerous repairs, the car was unsatisfactory and required more work. The Masons sued, seeking to rescind the contract based on the ads and the dealer's statement. Will they win?

3. The McAllisters had several serious problems with their house, including leaks in the ceiling, a buckling wall, and dampness throughout. They repaired the buckling wall by installing I-beams to support it. They never resolved the leaks and the dampness. When they decided to sell the house, they said nothing to prospective buyers about the problems. They stated that the I-beam had been added for reinforcement. The Silvas bought the house for $60,000. Soon afterwards, they began to have problems with leaks, mildew, and dampness. Are the Silvas entitled to any money damages? Why or why not?

4. Roy Newburn borrowed money and bought a $49,000 truck from Treadwell Ford. A few months later, the truck developed transmission problems. Newburn learned that the truck had 170,000 more miles on it than the odometer indicated. The company admitted the mileage error and promised to install a new transmission for free.

Treadwell did install the new transmission, but when Newburn came to pick up the truck, Treadwell demanded that he sign a general release absolving the dealership of any claims based on the inaccurate mileage. Treadwell refused to turn over the truck until Newburn finally signed. The truck broke down again, and delays cost Newburn so much income that he fell behind on his loan payments and lost the truck. He sued Treadwell, which defended based on the release. Is the release valid?

5. Morell bought a security guard business from Conley, including the property on which the business was located. Neither party knew that underground storage tanks were leaking and contaminating the property. After the sale, Morell discovered the tanks and sought to rescind the contract. Should he be allowed to do so?

Discussion Questions

1. Sixteen-year-old Travis Mitchell brought his Pontiac GTO into M&M Precision Body and Paint for body work and a paint job. M&M did the work and charged $1,900, which Travis paid. When Travis later complained about the quality of the work, M&M did some touching up, but Travis was still dissatisfied. He demanded his $1,900 back, but M&M refused to refund it because all of the work was "in" the car and Travis could not return it to the shop. The state of Nebraska, where this occurred, follows the majority rule on this issue. Does Travis get his money? Is this a *fair* result?

2. Contract law gives minors substantial legal protection. But does a modern high school student *need* so much protection? Older teens may have been naive in the 1700s, but today, they are quite savvy. Should the law change so that only younger children—perhaps those aged 14 and under—have the ability to undo agreements?

3. In the old Michigan case featuring Rose the Cow, the court refused to enforce the agreement. Was this a fair result? Should bilateral mistakes create voidable contracts, or should Walker have been required to sell the cow for $80?

4. Susan drops by Dean's garage sale. She buys a painting for $10. Both she and Dean think that the painting is a copy of a Matisse. Later, Susan is delighted to discover that the painting is actually a Matisse and is worth $50,000,000. Dean hears the news, and wants the painting back. Will he get it? Why or why not?

5. Do you have sympathy for intoxicated people who make agreements? Should the law ever let them back out of deals when they sober up? After all, no one forced them to get drunk. Should the law be more lenient, or is it reasonable as it currently exists?

CHAPTER 14

WRITTEN CONTRACTS

Oliver and Perry were college roommates, two sophomores with contrasting personalities. They were sitting in the cafeteria with some friends, Oliver chatting away, Perry slumped on a plastic bench. Oliver suggested that they buy a lottery ticket, as the prize for that week's drawing was $13 million. Perry muttered, "Nah. You never win if you buy just one ticket." Oliver bubbled up, "O.K., we'll buy a ticket every week. We'll keep buying them from now until we graduate. Come on, it'll be fun. This month, I'll buy the tickets. Next month, you will, and so on." Other students urged Perry to do it and, finally, he agreed.

The two friends carefully reviewed their deal. Each party was providing consideration—namely, the responsibility for purchasing tickets during his month. The amount of each purchase was clearly defined at one dollar. They would start that week and continue until graduation day, two and a half years down the road. Finally, they would share equally any money won. As three witnesses looked on, they shook hands on the bargain. That month, Oliver bought a ticket every week, randomly choosing numbers, and won nothing. The next month, Perry bought a ticket with equally random numbers—and won $52 million. Perry moved out of their dorm room into a suite at the Ritz and refused to give Oliver one red cent. Oliver sued, seeking $26 million, and the return of his Nintendo Wii U console. If the former friends had understood the Statute of Frauds, they would never have gotten into this mess.[1]

> **Perry moved out of their dorm room into a suite at the Ritz and refused to give Oliver one red cent.**

nuttakit/Shutterstock.com; © neelsky/Shutterstock.com

---

[1]Based loosely on *Lydon v. Beauregard* (Middlesex Sup. Ct., Mass., Dec. 22, 1989), reported in Paul Langher, "Couple Lose Suit to Share $2.8M Prize," *Boston Globe*, December 23, 1989, p. 21.

The rule we examine in this chapter is not exactly news. Originally passed by the British Parliament in 1677, the Statute of Frauds has changed little over the centuries. The purpose was to prevent lying (fraud) in civil lawsuits. Jury trials of that era invited perjury. Neither the plaintiff nor the defendant was permitted to testify, meaning that the jury never heard from the people who really knew what had happened. Instead, the court heard testimony from people who claimed to have witnessed the contract being created. Knowing that he would never be subjected to aggressive cross-examination, a plaintiff might easily allege that a fake contract was real, and then bribe witnesses to support his case. A powerful earl, seeking to acquire 300 acres of valuable land owned by a neighboring commoner, might claim that the neighbor had orally promised to sell his land. Although the claim was utterly false, the earl would win if he could bribe enough "reputable" witnesses to persuade the jury.

To provide juries with more reliable evidence that a contract did or did not exist, Parliament passed the Statute of Frauds. It required that in several types of cases, a contract would be enforced only if it was in writing. Contracts involving interests in land were first on the list.

In the days before the Revolutionary War, when Pennsylvania was still a British possession, the colony's supreme court heard the following case, which centered on the Statute of Frauds. Notice the case citation. This is very nearly the first case reported in United States history, further evidence that the Statute of Frauds is not news. Back then, rulings were expressed quite differently (and they seemed to enjoy capitalization), but you will be able to see Judge Coleman's point.

Landmark Case

THE LESSEE OF RICHARDSON V. CAMPBELL
1 U.S. 10
Supreme Court of Pennsylvania, 1764

Facts: A tenant had rented land from Richardson. However, Campbell claimed the property was really his. To stay there, the tenant had to prove that Richardson owned the land.

Richardson's tenant offered a deed (which was then called a *patent*) to support his claim; Campbell provided receipts as evidence that he had bought the property years prior.

To prove that the receipts were for the disputed property, Campbell wanted to introduce statements from an important person—Thomas Penn, whose father, William, had founded the Pennsylvania colony. Obviously, the tenant did not want that evidence admitted in court.

Issue: *Was oral evidence about the ownership of land admissible in court?*

Decision: No. Oral evidence was not admissible in court to prove ownership of land.

Excerpts from Justice Coleman's Decision: PLAINTIFF supported his Title by a Patent. The Defendant produced Receipts several Years prior to Plaintiff's Patent; but the Plaintiff contend[ed] that the Receipts were only for Money paid on an adjacent Tract; the Defendant produced a Witness to prove a parol Declaration of Mr. Thomas Penn that the Land in dispute was sold to Defendant.

This piece of Evidence was opposed by the Plaintiff, and refused BY THE COURT.

Almost all states of this country have passed their own version of the Statute of Frauds. It is important to remember, as we examine the rules and exceptions, that Parliament and the state legislatures all had a commendable, straightforward purpose in passing their respective statutes of fraud: *to provide a court with the best possible evidence of whether the parties intended to make a contract*. Ironically, the British government has repealed the writing requirement for most contracts. Parliament concluded that the old statute, far from preventing wrongdoing, was *helping* people commit fraud. A wily negotiator could orally agree to terms and then, if the deal turned unprofitable, walk away from the contract, knowing it was unenforceable without written evidence.

Thus far, no state in this country has entirely repealed its Statute of Frauds. Instead, courts have carved exceptions into the original statute to prevent unfairness. Some scholars have urged state legislatures to go further and repeal the law altogether. Other commentators defend the Statute of Frauds as a valuable tool for justice. They argue that, among other benefits, the requirement of a writing cautions people to be careful before making—or relying on—a promise. For now, the Statute of Frauds is a vital part of law. Sadly, Oliver from the opening scenario will learn this the hard way.

According to the Statute of Frauds, a plaintiff may not enforce any of the following agreements unless the agreement, or some memorandum of it, is in writing and signed by the defendant.

The agreements that must be in writing are those:

- For any interest in **land**;

- That **cannot be performed within one year**;

- To pay the **debt of another**;

- Made by an **executor of an estate**;

- Made **in consideration of marriage**; and

- For the **sale of goods worth** $500 **or more**.

In other words, when two parties make an agreement covered by any one of these six topics, it must be in writing to be enforceable. Oliver and Perry made a definite agreement to purchase lottery tickets during alternate months and share the proceeds of any winning ticket. But their agreement was to last two and a half years. As the second item on the list indicates, a contract must be in writing if it cannot be performed within one year. The good news is that Oliver gets back his Wii U. The bad news is he gets none of the lottery money. Even though three witnesses saw the deal made, it is unlikely to be enforced in any state. Perry will walk away with all $52 million.

Note that although the Oliver-Perry agreement is unenforceable, it is not void. Suppose that Perry does the right thing, agreeing to share the winnings with Oliver. Over the next 20 years, as he receives the winnings, Perry gives one-half to his friend. But then, having squandered his own fortune, Perry demands the money back from Oliver, claiming that the original contract violated the Statute of Frauds. Perry loses. **Once a contract is fully executed, it makes no difference that it was unwritten.** The Statute of Frauds prevents the enforcement of an executory contract; that is, one in which the parties have not fulfilled their obligations. But the contract is not *illegal*. Once both parties have fully performed, neither party may demand rescission. The Statute of Frauds allows a party to cancel future obligations but not undo past actions.

Ethics The *law* permits Perry to keep all of the lottery money. But does Perry have a *moral* right to deny Oliver his half-share? Is the Statute of Frauds serving a useful purpose here? Remember that Parliament passed the original Statute of Frauds believing that a written document would be more reliable than the testimony of alleged witnesses. If we permitted Oliver to enforce the oral contract, based on his testimony and that of the witnesses, would we simply be inviting other plaintiffs to invent lottery "contracts" that had never been made?

14-1 COMMON LAW STATUTE OF FRAUDS: CONTRACTS THAT MUST BE IN WRITING

14-1a Agreements for an Interest in Land

A contract for the sale of any interest in land must be in writing to be enforceable. Notice the phrase "interest in land." This means *any legal right* regarding land. A house on a lot is an interest in land. A mortgage, an easement, and a leased apartment are all interests in land. As a general rule, leases must therefore be in writing, although most states have created an exception for short-term leases. A short-term lease is often one for a year or less, although the length varies from state to state.

Kary Presten and Ken Sailer were roommates in a rental apartment in New Jersey that had a view of the Manhattan skyline. The lease was in Sailer's name, but the two split all expenses. Then the building became a "cooperative," meaning that each tenant would have the option of buying the apartment.[2] Sailer learned he could buy his unit for only $55,800 if he promptly paid a $1,000 fee to maintain his rights. He mentioned to Presten that he planned to buy the unit, and Presten asked if he could become half-owner. Sailer agreed and borrowed the $1,000 from Presten to pay his initial fee. But as the time for closing on the purchase came nearer, Sailer realized that he could sell the apartment for a substantial profit. He placed an ad in a paper and promptly received a firm offer for $125,000. Sailer then told Presten that their deal was off, and that he, Sailer, would be buying the unit alone. He did exactly that, and Presten filed suit. Regrettably, the outcome of Presten's suit was only too easy to predict.

A cooperative apartment is an interest in land, said the court. This agreement could be enforced only if put in writing and signed by Sailer. The parties had put nothing in writing, and therefore Presten was out of luck. He was entitled to his $1,000 back, but nothing more. The apartment belonged to Sailer, who could live in it or sell it for a large, quick profit.[3]

Suppose that you are interested in buying five expensive acres in a fast-growing rural area. There is no water on the property, and the only way to bring public water to it is through land owned by the neighbor, Joanne, who agrees to sell you an easement through her property. An **easement** is a legal right that an owner gives to another person to make some use of the owner's land. In other words, Joanne will permit you to dig a 200-foot trench through her land and lay a water pipe there in exchange for $15,000. May you now safely purchase the five acres? Not until Joanne has signed the written easement. You might ignore this "technicality," since Joanne seems friendly and honest. But you could then spend $300,000 buying your property only to learn that Joanne has changed her mind. She might refuse to go through with the deal unless you pay $150,000 for the easement. Without her permission to lay the pipe, your new land is worthless. Avoid such nightmares: Get it in writing.

EXCEPTION: FULL PERFORMANCE BY THE SELLER

If the seller completely performs her side of a contract for an interest in land, a court is likely to enforce the agreement even if it was oral. Adam orally agrees to sell his condominium to Maggie for $150,000. Adam delivers the deed to Maggie and expects his money a week later, but Maggie fails to pay. Most courts will allow Adam to enforce the oral contract and collect the full purchase price from Maggie.

---

[2]Technically, the residents of a "co-op" do not own their apartments. They own a share of the corporation that owns the building. Along with their ownership shares, residents obtain a right to occupy their units for a modest fee.

[3]*Presten v. Sailer*, 225 N.J. Super. 178, 542 A.2d 7, 1988 N.J. Super. LEXIS 151 (N.J. Super. Ct. App. Div. 1988).

EXCEPTION: PART PERFORMANCE BY THE BUYER

The buyer of land may be able to enforce an oral contract if she paid part of the purchase price *and either* entered upon the land *or* made improvements to it. Suppose that Eloise sues Grover to enforce an alleged oral contract to sell a lot in Happydale. She claims they struck a bargain in January. Grover defends based on the Statute of Frauds, saying that even if the two did reach an oral agreement, it is unenforceable. Eloise proves that she paid 10 percent of the purchase price, that she began excavating on the lot in February to build a house, and that Grover knew of the work. Eloise has established part performance and will be allowed to enforce her contract.

This exception makes sense if we recall the purpose of the Statute of Frauds: to provide the best possible evidence of the parties' intentions. The fact that Grover permitted Eloise to enter upon the land and begin building on it is compelling evidence that the two parties had reached an agreement. But be aware that most claims of part performance fail. Merely paying a deposit on a house is not part performance. A plaintiff seeking to rely on part performance must show partial payment *and* either entrance onto the land *or* physical improvements to it.

EXCEPTION: PROMISSORY ESTOPPEL

The other exception to the writing requirement is our old friend promissory estoppel. **If a promisor makes an oral promise that should reasonably cause the promisee to rely on it, and the promisee does rely, the promisee may be able to enforce the promise,** despite the Statute of Frauds, if that is the only way to avoid injustice. This exception potentially applies to any contract that must be written, such as those for land, those that cannot be performed within one year, and so forth.

Maureen Sullivan and James Rooney lived together for seven years, although they never married. They decided to buy a house. The two agreed that they would be equal owners, but Rooney told Sullivan that in order to obtain Veterans Administration financing, he would have to be the sole owner on the deed. They each contributed to the purchase and maintenance of the house, and Rooney repeatedly told Sullivan that he would change the deed to joint ownership. He never did. When the couple split up, Sullivan sued, seeking a 50 percent interest in the house. She won. The agreement was for an interest in land and should have been in writing, said the court. But Rooney had clearly promised Sullivan that she would be a half-owner, and she had relied by contributing to the purchase and maintenance. The Statute of Frauds was passed to *prevent* fraud, not to enable one person to mislead another and benefit at her expense.[4]

EXAM Strategy

Question: Aditi and Danielle, MBA students, need an apartment for next September. They find a lovely two-bedroom unit that the owner is rehabbing. The students can see that the owner is honest, his workmanship excellent. The owner agrees to rent them the apartment beginning September 1, for $1,200 per month for one year. "Come back at the end of August. By then, my work will be done and I'll have the papers to sign." Aditi asks, "Should we sign something now, to be sure?" The landlord laughs and replies, "I trust you. You don't trust me?" They both trust him, and they shake hands on the deal. When the students return in August, the landlord has rented it to Danielle's former boyfriend for $1,400 per month. Aditi and Danielle sue. Who wins?

Strategy: Under the Statute of Frauds, a contract for the sale of any interest in land must be in writing to be enforceable. What does "any interest" mean? Does the Statute of Frauds apply to this case?

---

[4]*Sullivan v. Rooney*, 404 Mass. 160, 533 N.E.2d 1372, 1989 Mass. LEXIS 49 (1989).

> **Result:** An "interest" means any legal right. A lease is an interest in land, meaning that the students cannot enforce this agreement unless it is in writing, signed by the owner—and it is not. The students need to look for a new apartment.

14-1b Agreements That Cannot Be Performed within One Year

Contracts that cannot be performed within one year are unenforceable unless they are in writing. This one-year period begins on the date the parties make the agreement. The critical word here is "cannot." If a contract *could possibly* be completed within one year, it need not be in writing. Betty gets a job at Burger Brain, throwing fries in oil. Her boss tells her she can have Fridays off for as long as she works there. That oral contract is enforceable whether Betty stays one week or twenty years. "As long as she works there" *could* last for less than one year. Betty might quit the job after six months. Therefore, it does not need to be in writing.[5]

If an agreement will *necessarily* take longer than one year to finish, it must be in writing to be enforceable. If Betty is hired for a term of three years as manager of Burger Brain, the agreement is unenforceable unless put in writing. She cannot perform three years of work in one year.

Or, if you hire a band to play at your wedding 15 months from today, the agreement must be in writing. The gig may take only a single day, but that day will definitely not fall in the next 12 months.

The following case starts with a notorious diet pill and ends with a paralegal suing her boss. Which argument carries greater weight?

---

[5] This is the majority rule. In most states, for example, if a company hires an employee "for life," the contract need not be in writing because the employee could die within one year. "Contracts of uncertain duration are simply excluded [from the Statute of Frauds]; the provision covers only those contracts whose performance cannot possibly be completed within a year." Restatement (Second) of Contracts §130, Comment a, at 328 (1981). See, for example *Mackay v. Four Rivers Packing Co.*, 2008 WL 427789 (Id. 2008). However, a few states disagree. The Illinois Supreme Court ruled that a contract for lifetime employment is enforceable only if written. *McInerney v. Charter Golf, Inc.*, 176 Ill. 2d 482, 680 N.E.2d 1347, 1997 Ill. LEXIS 56 (Ill. 1997).

You Be the Judge

SAWYER V. MILLS
2007 WL 1113038
Kentucky Court of Appeals, 2007

Facts: Barbara Sawyer, a paralegal, worked for attorney Melbourne Mills, assisting him in a class action lawsuit against the makers of a popular diet drug called Fen-Phen. Mills promised Sawyer a large bonus "when the ship comes in," but he never specified how much he would pay her. Mills successfully settled the Fen-Phen case for millions of dollars, and he later met with Sawyer and her husband to discuss her bonus. The Sawyers secretly recorded the conversation.

The Sawyers asked Mills for a $1 million bonus, to be paid as a lump sum. Mills refused. However, the parties kept talking and Mills eventually agreed to pay Sawyer $1 million, plus $65,000 for a luxury automobile. Payments were to be made in monthly installments of $10,000, for 10 years. Mills also agreed to sign a document confirming his promise. Sawyer's lawyer drafted the writing, but Mills never signed it. He did pay nine monthly installments, along with an extra payment of $100,000.

At trial, jurors heard the tape recording, which confirmed the oral agreement. The jury concluded that the parties had reached a binding agreement and awarded Sawyer $900,000. However, the court granted a judgment notwithstanding the verdict for Mills. He ruled that the agreement was barred by the Statute of Frauds. Sawyer appealed.

You Be the Judge: *Does the Statute of Frauds prevent enforcement of Mills's promise?*

Argument for Sawyer: The Statute of Frauds exists to make sure that a plaintiff does not come into court and allege an oral promise that never existed. The fear of fraudulent claims is legitimate, but obviously it does not apply in this case. We *know* that Mills agreed to pay a million dollars because we can *hear* him make the promise. We know the exact terms of the agreement, and we know it was a reasonable arrangement based on years of work and a massive settlement. We even hear Mills agree to sign a document confirming his promise.

The Statute of Frauds was designed to prevent fraud—not encourage it. Mills's tiresome, technical arguments did not fool the jurors. After hearing—literally—the evidence, the jury knew there had been a deal and awarded Sawyer her fair share. Let's stop playing legal games, start doing justice, and restore the verdict.

Argument for Mills: This is a simple case. The plaintiffs allege an oral contract for 10 years' worth of installment payments. In other words, *if* there was an agreement, it was for 10 years' duration. Sawyer's own lawyer drafted a contract—never signed—for compensation lasting a full decade. Under the Statute of Frauds, an agreement that cannot be performed within one year is unenforceable unless written and signed. End of case.

If our legislature wanted to encourage secret tape recordings and deception, it could have included an exception to the Statute of Frauds, giving tricky plaintiffs a reward for bad-faith negotiating. However, the legislators wisely have made no such exception. The alleged oral contract is worthless.

14-1c Promise to Pay the Debt of Another

When one person agrees to pay the debt of another as a favor to that debtor, it is called a collateral promise, and it must be in writing to be enforceable. D. R. Kemp was a young entrepreneur who wanted to build housing in Tuscaloosa, Alabama. He needed $25,000 to complete a project he was working on, so he went to his old college professor, Jim Hanks, for help. The professor said he would see what he could do about getting Kemp a loan. Professor Hanks spoke with his good friend Travis Chandler, telling him that Kemp was highly responsible and would be certain to repay any money loaned. Chandler trusted Professor Hanks but wanted to be sure of his money. Professor Hanks assured Chandler that if for any reason Kemp did not repay the loan, he, Hanks, would pay Chandler in full. With that assurance, Chandler wrote out a check for $25,000, payable to Kemp, never having met the young man.

Kemp, of course, never repaid the loan. (Thank goodness he did not; this textbook has no use for people who do what they promise.) Kemp exhausted the cash trying to sustain his business, which failed anyway, so he had nothing to give his creditor. Chandler approached Professor Hanks, who refused to pay, and Chandler sued. The outcome was easy to predict. Professor Hanks had agreed to repay Kemp's debt *as a favor to Kemp*, making it a collateral promise. Chandler had nothing in writing, and that is exactly what he got from his lawsuit—nothing.

EXCEPTION: THE LEADING OBJECT RULE

There is one major exception to the collateral promise rule. When the promisor guarantees to pay the debt of another and *the leading object of the promise is some benefit to the promisor himself*, then the contract will be enforceable even if unwritten. In other words, if the promisor makes the guarantee not as a favor to the debtor, but primarily out of *self-interest*, the Statute of Frauds does not apply.

Robert Perry was a hog farmer in Ohio. He owed $26,000 to Sunrise Cooperative, a supplier of feed. Because Perry was in debt, Sunrise stopped giving him feed on credit and began selling him feed on a cash-only basis. Perry also owed money to Farm Credit Services, a loan agency. Perry promised Farm Credit he would repay his loans as soon as his hogs were big enough to sell. But Perry couldn't raise hogs without feed, which he lacked the money to purchase. Farm Credit was determined to bring home the bacon, so it asked Sunrise Cooperative to give Perry the feed on credit. Farm Credit orally promised to pay any debt that Perry did not take care of. When Perry defaulted on his payments to Sunrise, the feed supplier sued Farm Credit based on its oral guarantee. Farm Credit claimed the promise was unenforceable, based on the Statute of Frauds. But the court found in favor of Sunrise. The *leading object* of Farm Credit's promise to Sunrise was self-interest, and the oral promise was fully enforceable.[6]

14-1d Promise Made by an Executor of an Estate

This rule is merely a special application of the previous one, concerning the debt of another person. An executor is the person who is in charge of an estate after someone dies. The executor's job is to pay debts of the deceased, obtain money owed to him, and disburse the assets according to the will. In most cases, the executor will use only the estate's assets to pay those debts. The Statute of Frauds comes into play when an executor promises to pay an estate's debts with her own funds. An executor's promise to use her own funds to pay a debt of the deceased must be in writing to be enforceable.

Suppose Esmeralda dies penniless, owing Tina $35,000. Esmeralda's daughter, Sapphire, is the executor of her estate. Tina comes to Sapphire and demands her $35,000. Sapphire responds, "There is no money in mamma's estate, but don't worry, I'll make it up to you with my own money." Sapphire's oral promise is unenforceable. Tina should get it in writing while Sapphire is feeling generous.

14-1e Promise Made in Consideration of Marriage

Barney is a multimillionaire with the integrity of a gangster and the charm of a tax collector. He proposes to Li-Tsing, who promptly rejects him. Barney then pleads that if Li-Tsing will be his bride, he will give her an island he owns off the coast of California. Li-Tsing begins to see his good qualities and accepts. After they are married, Barney refuses to deliver the deed. Li-Tsing will get nothing from a court either, because **a promise made in consideration of marriage must be in writing to be enforceable**.

14-2 THE COMMON LAW STATUTE OF FRAUDS: WHAT THE WRITING MUST CONTAIN

Each of the types of contract described above must be in writing in order to be enforceable. What must the writing contain? It may be a carefully typed contract, using precise legal terminology, or an informal memo scrawled on the back of a paper napkin at a business lunch. The writing may consist of more than one document, written at different times, with

---

[6]*Sunrise Cooperative v. Robert Perry*, 1992 Ohio App. LEXIS 3913 (Ohio Ct. App. 1992).

each document making a piece of the puzzle. But there are some general requirements: the writing

- **Must be signed by the defendant, and**
- **Must state with reasonable certainty the name of each party, the subject matter of the agreement, and all of the essential terms and promises.**[7]

14-2a Signature

A state's Statute of Frauds typically requires that the writing be "signed by the party to be charged therewith"; that is, the party who is resisting enforcement of the contract. Throughout this chapter, we refer to that person as the defendant because when these cases go to court, it is the defendant who is disputing the existence of a contract.

Judges define "signature" very broadly. Using a pen to write one's name certainly counts, but it is not required. A secretary who stamps an executive's signature on a letter fulfills this requirement. In fact, any mark or logo placed on a document to indicate acceptance, even an "X," will generally satisfy the Statute of Frauds. And electronic commerce, as we discuss below, creates new methods of signing.

14-2b Reasonable Certainty

Suppose Garfield and Hayes are having lunch, discussing the sale of Garfield's vacation condominium. They agree on a price and want to make some notation of the agreement even before their lawyers work out a detailed purchase and sales agreement. A perfectly adequate memorandum might say, "Garfield agrees to sell Hayes his condominium at 234 Baron Boulevard, Apartment 18, for $350,000 cash, payable on June 18, 2015, and Hayes promises to pay the sum on that day." They should make two copies of their agreement and sign both. Notice that although Garfield's memo is short, it is *certain* and *complete*. This is critical because problems of vagueness and incompleteness often doom informal memoranda.

Vagueness

Ella Hayden owned valuable commercial property on a highway called Route 9. She wrote a series of letters to her stepson Mark, promising that several of the children, including Mark, would share the property. One letter said, "We four shall fairly divide the Route 9 property." Other letters said, "When the Route 9 Plaza is sold, you can take a long vacation," and "The property will be sold. You and Dennis shall receive the same amount." Ella Hayden died without leaving Mark anything. He sued, but got nothing. The court ruled:

> The above passages written by Ms. Hayden do not recite the essential elements of the alleged contract with reasonable certainty. The writings do not state unequivocally or with sufficient particularity the subject matter to which the writings relate, nor do they provide the terms and conditions of alleged promises made which constitute a contract. The alleged oral contract between Ms. Hayden and Mr. Hayden cannot be identified from the passages from Ms. Hayden's letters quoted above when applied to existing facts. In sum, Mr. Hayden's cause of action seeking an interest in the Route 9 property is foreclosed by the Statute of Frauds.[8]

Incompleteness

During Ronald McCoy's second interview with Spelman Memorial Hospital, the board of directors orally offered him a three-year job as assistant hospital administrator. McCoy accepted. Spelman's CEO, Gene Meyer, sent a letter confirming the offer, which said:

---

[7]Restatement (Second) of Contracts §131.
[8]*Hayden v. Hayden*, Mass. Lawyers Weekly No. 12-299-93 (Middlesex Sup. Ct. 1994).

To reconfirm the offer, it is as follows: (1) We will pay for your moving expenses. (2) I would like you to pursue your Master's Degree at an area program. We will pay 100 percent tuition reimbursement. (3) Effective September 26, you will be eligible for all benefits. (4) A starting salary of $48,000 annually with reviews and eligibility for increases at 6 months, 12 months, and annually thereafter. (5) We will pay for the expenses of 3 trips, if necessary, in order for you to find housing. (6) Vacation will be for 3 weeks a year after one year; however, we do allow for this to be taken earlier. [Signed] Gene Meyer.

Spelman Hospital fired McCoy less than a year after he started work, and McCoy sued. The hospital's letter seems clear, and it is signed by an authorized official. The problem is, it is incomplete. Can you spot the fatal omission? The court did.

McCoy wanted to hold the hospital's board to its spoken promise that he would have a job for a term of three years. To be enforceable, a contract for a term of over one year must be in writing under the Statute of Frauds.

To satisfy the Statute of Frauds, an employment contract—[or] its memorandum or note—must contain *all* essential terms, including *duration of the employment relationship*. Without a statement of duration, an employment-at-will arrangement is created, which is terminable at any time by either party with no liability for breach of contract. McCoy's argument that the letter constituted a memorandum of an oral contract fails because the letter does not state an essential element: duration. The letter did not state that Spelman was granting McCoy employment for any term—only that his salary would be reviewed at 6 months, 12 months, and "annually thereafter."[9]

The lawsuits in this section demonstrate the continuing force of the Statute of Frauds. If the promisor had truly wanted to make a binding commitment, he or she could have written the appropriate contract or memorandum in a matter of minutes. Great formality and expense are unnecessary. But the written document *must be clear and complete*, or it will fail.

EXAM Strategy

Question: Major Retailer and Owner negotiated a lease of a strip mall, the tenancy to begin August 1. Retailer's lawyer then drafted a lease accurately reflecting all terms agreed to, including the parties, exact premises, condition of the store, dates of the lease, and monthly rent of $18,000. Retailer signed the lease and delivered it to Owner on July 1. On July 20, Owner leased the same space to a different tenant for $23,000 per month. Retailer sued, claiming that the parties had a binding deal, and the Owner had breached his agreement in order to obtain higher rent. Who will win?

Strategy: To comply with the Statute of Frauds, a writing must state all essential terms. This lease appears to do that. However, the writing must contain one other thing. What is it?

Result: The writing must be *signed* by the party claiming that there is no contract; that is, by the defendant. Owner never signed the lease. This lease does not comply with the Statute of Frauds, and the Retailer will lose his case.

---

[9]*McCoy v. Spelman Memorial Hospital*, 845 S.W.2d 727, 1993 Mo. App. LEXIS 105 (Mo. Ct. App. 1993).

14-2c Electronic Contracts and Signatures

E-commerce has grown at a dazzling rate—each year, U.S. enterprises buy and sell tens of billions of dollars worth of goods and services over the Internet. What happens to the writing requirement, though, when there is no paper? The present Statute of Frauds requires some sort of "signature" to ensure that the defendant committed to the deal. Today, an "electronic signature" could mean a name typed (or automatically included) at the bottom of an email message, a retinal or vocal scan, or a name signed by electronic pen on a writing tablet, among others.

E-signatures are valid in all 50 states. Almost all states have adopted the **Uniform Electronic Transactions Act (UETA)**.[10] UETA declares that *electronic* contracts and signatures are as enforceable as those on paper. In other words, the normal rules of contract law apply, and neither party can avoid such a deal merely because it originated in cyberspace. A federal statute, the **Electronic Signatures in Global and National Commerce Act (E-SIGN)**, also declares that contracts cannot be denied enforcement simply because they are in electronic form, or signed electronically. It applies in states that have not adopted UETA.

Note that, in many states, certain documents still require a traditional (non-electronic) signature. Wills, adoptions, court orders, and notice of foreclosure are common exceptions. If in doubt, get a hard copy, signed in ink.

14-3 THE UCC'S STATUTE OF FRAUDS

We have reached another section dedicated to the Uniform Commercial Code (UCC). Remember that UCC rules govern only contracts involving a sale of goods. Because some merchants make dozens or even hundreds of oral contracts every year, the drafters of the UCC wanted to make the writing requirement less onerous for the sale of goods.

> The key difference between the common law rule and the UCC rule is that the Code does *not* require *all* of the terms of the agreement to be in writing.

The UCC requires a writing for the sale of goods worth $500 or more. The Code's requirements are easier to meet than those of the common law. **UCC §**2-201, the Statute of Frauds section, has three important elements:

1. The basic rule

2. The merchants' exception

3. Special circumstances

14-3a UCC §2-201(1)—The Basic Rule

A contract for the sale of goods worth $500 or more is not enforceable unless there is some writing, signed by the defendant, indicating that the parties reached an agreement. The key difference between the common law rule and the UCC rule is that the Code does *not* require *all* of the terms of the agreement to be in writing. The Code looks for something simpler: *an indication that the parties reached an agreement.* Only two things are required: the signature of the defendant and the quantity of goods being sold. Suppose a short memorandum between

---

[10]The states that have not adopted the Uniform Electronic Transactions Act, at the time of this writing, are Illinois, New York, and Washington.

textile dealers indicates that Seller will sell to Buyer "grade AA 100 percent cotton, white athletic socks." If the writing does not state the price, the parties can testify at court about what the market price was at the time of the deal. If the writing says nothing about the delivery date, the court will assume a reasonable delivery date, say, 60 days. But how many socks were to be delivered? 100 pairs or 100,000? The court will have no objective evidence, and so, the quantity must be written.

Writing	Result
"Confirming phone conversation today, I will send you 1,000 reams of paper for laser printing, usual quality & price. [Signed,] Seller."	This memorandum satisfies UCC §2-201(1), and the contract may be enforced against the seller. The buyer may testify as to the "usual" quality and price between the two parties, and both sides may rely on normal trade usage.
"Confirming phone conversation today, I will send you best quality paper for laser printing, $3.25 per ream, delivery date next Thursday.[Signed,] Seller."	This memorandum is not enforceable because it states no quantity.

14-3b UCC §2-201(2)—The Merchants' Exception

When both parties are "merchants," that is, businesspeople who routinely deal in the goods being sold, the Code will accept an even more informal writing. **Within a reasonable time of making an oral contract, if a merchant sends a written confirmation to another, and if the confirmation is definite enough to bind the *sender herself*, then the merchant who receives the confirmation will *also* be bound by it unless he objects in writing within 10 days.** This exception dramatically changes the rules from the common law, but it applies only between two merchants. The drafters of the Code assumed that experienced merchants are able to take care of themselves in fast-moving negotiations. The critical difference is this: A writing may create a binding contract *even when it is not signed by the defendant.*

Madge manufactures "beanies," that is, silly caps with plastic propellers on top. Rachel, a retailer, telephones her, and they discuss the price of the beanies, shipping time, and other details. Madge then faxes Rachel a memo: "This confirms your order for 2,500 beanies at $12.25 per beanie. Colors: blue, green, black, orange, red. Delivery date: 10 days. [Signed] Madge." Rachel receives the fax, reads it while negotiating with another manufacturer, and throws it in the wastebasket. Rachel buys her beanies elsewhere, and Madge sues. Rachel defends, claiming there is no written contract because she, Rachel, never signed anything. Madge wins under UCC §2-201(2). Both parties were merchants because they routinely dealt in these goods. Madge signed and sent a confirming memo that could have been used to hold her, Madge, to the deal. When Rachel read it, she was not free to disregard it. Obviously, the intelligent business practice would have been to promptly fax a reply saying, "I disagree. We do not have any deal for beanies." Since Rachel failed to respond within 10 days, Madge has an enforceable contract.

For a confirming memo to count, a merchant must send it within a *reasonable* time. But how long is that? A few days certainly qualifies. Could 13 months be quick enough?

SETON CO. V. LEAR CORP.

198 Fed. Appx. 496, 2006 WL 2860774
Sixth Circuit Court of Appeals, 2006

CASE SUMMARY

Facts: General Motors hired Lear Corporation to supply all of the leather seats for its trucks and SUVs. In October 1998, Lear reached an agreement with Seton Company to provide Lear with the actual cut-to-pattern leather, which Lear would then assemble. Seton agreed to give Lear certain rebates, based on the size of the orders. Despite the great value of this contract, the parties initially put nothing in writing. (Note to students: Later in life, if you negotiate a multimillion dollar deal and fail to put it in writing, your grade in this course will be *retroactively lowered!*)

Both parties performed the contract satisfactorily for about a year. Then they agreed to a slight modification in the rebates. All was still well. In the fall of 1999, Lear asked Seton to send a written summary of the agreement, including the modified rebates. In November 1999, Seton sent a one-page memorandum to Lear, summarizing the agreement. It stated: "Lear is to award Seton the entire [truck and SUV program] cut to pattern business for the life of the program." The letter ended with a request that Lear "kindly return with acknowledgement signature," but Lear did not do so.

For two more years, the parties worked together amicably. Then Seton became anxious that Lear was planning to take its business elsewhere. In January 2002, Seton sent a letter, requesting that Lear affirm its commitment to deal exclusively with Seton for the life of the GMC program. Lear responded that there had never been any such agreement. Seton filed suit.

At trial, Lear claimed that no contract had ever been signed. Seton replied that its memo summarizing the agreement created a valid contract, under the "merchant exception" rule. The jury agreed with Seton and awarded the company $34 million. Lear appealed.

Issue: *Did Seton's memorandum create a contract under the merchant exception?*

Decision: Yes, the confirming memo between merchants created a contract under the UCC. Affirmed.

Reasoning: Lear argued that the November letter was not a written confirmation of an existing contract, but rather an offer of a new contract. The company emphasized that the phrase "kindly return with acknowledgement signature" was evidence that there was no final agreement. But the jury disagreed. It was clearly influenced by Seton's argument that the letter referred to a prior agreement between Lear and Seton executives. Also, although the letter asked for a signature, it did not require one. For these reasons, the letter amounted to more than a mere offer.

The UCC does require, however, that merchants send any confirmatory memo within a reasonable length of time. Lear contended that the letter could not count as a written confirmation because it arrived 13 months after the first discussion of the deal with Seton, but the jury disagreed, probably because the relationship between the companies had been casual and friendly for a long time.

14-3c UCC §2-201(3)—Special Circumstances

An oral contract *may* be enforceable, even without a written memorandum, if:

- The seller is specially manufacturing the goods for the buyer, *or*

- The defendant admits in court proceedings that there was a contract, *or*

- The goods have been delivered or they have been paid for.

SPECIALLY MANUFACTURED GOODS

If a seller, specially manufacturing goods for the buyer, begins work on them before the buyer cancels, and the goods cannot be sold elsewhere, the oral contract is binding. Bernice manufactures solar heating systems. She phones Jason and orders 75 special electrical converter units designed for her heating system, at $150 per unit. Jason begins manufacturing the units, but then Bernice phones again and says she no longer needs them. Bernice is bound by the contract. The goods are being manufactured for her and cannot be sold elsewhere. Jason had already begun work when she attempted to cancel. If the case goes to court, Jason will win.

ADMISSIONS IN COURT

When the defendant admits in court proceedings that the parties made an oral contract, the agreement is binding. Rex sues Sophie, alleging that she orally agreed to sell him five boa constrictors that have been trained to stand in a line and pass a full wine glass from one snake to the next. Sophie defends the lawsuit, but during a deposition, she says, "OK, we agreed verbally, but nothing was ever put in writing, and I knew I didn't have to go through with it. When I went home, the snakes made me feel really guilty, and I decided not to sell." Sophie's admission under oath dooms her defense.

GOODS DELIVERED OR PAID FOR

If the seller has delivered the goods, or the buyer has paid for them, the contract may be enforced even with nothing in writing. Malik orally agrees to sell 500 plastic chairs to a university for use in its cafeteria. Malik delivers 300 of the chairs, but then the university notifies him that it will not honor the deal. Malik is entitled to payment for the 300 chairs, though not for the other 200. Conversely, if the university had sent a check for one-half of the chairs, it would be entitled to 250 chairs.

EXAM Strategy

Question: Beasley is a commercial honey farmer. He orally agrees to sell 500,000 pounds of honey to Grizzly at $1 per pound. Grizzly immediately faxes Beasley a signed confirmation, summarizing the deal. Beasley receives the fax but ignores it, and he never responds to Grizzly. Five days later, Beasley sells his honey to Brown for $1.15 per pound. Grizzly sues Beasley for breach of contract. Beasley claims that he signed nothing and was free to sell his honey anywhere he wanted. Who will win?

Strategy: Honey is a moveable thing, meaning that this contract is governed by the UCC. Under the Code, contracts for the sale of goods worth $500 or more must be in writing. However, the merchant exception changes things when both parties are merchants. Beasley and Grizzly are both merchants. Apply the merchant exception.

Result: Beasley breached the contract. Within a reasonable time after making the agreement, Grizzly sent a memo to Beasley confirming it. Beasley had 10 days either to object in writing or be held to the agreement. Beasley will lose this lawsuit because he ignored the faxed confirmation.

14-4 PAROL EVIDENCE

Tyrone agrees to buy Martha's house for $800,000. The contract obligates Tyrone to make a 10 percent down payment immediately and pay the remaining $720,000 in 45 days. As the two parties sign the deal, Tyrone discusses his need for financing. Unfortunately, at the end of 45 days, he has been unable to get a mortgage for the full amount. He claims that the parties orally agreed that he would get his deposit back if he could not obtain financing. But the written agreement says no such thing, and Martha disputes the claim. Who will win? Probably Martha, because of the parol evidence rule.

Parol evidence refers to anything (apart from the written contract itself) that was said, done, or written *before* the parties signed the agreement or *as they signed it*. Martha's conversation with Tyrone about financing the house was parol evidence because it occurred as they were signing the contract. Another important term is **integrated contract**, which means a writing that the parties intend as the final, complete expression of their agreement. Now for the rule.

Integrated contract

A writing that the parties intend as the final, complete expression of their agreement.

The parol evidence rule: When two parties make an integrated contract, neither one may use parol evidence to contradict, vary, or add to its terms. Negotiations may last for hours, weeks, or even months. Almost no contract includes everything that the parties said. When parties consider their agreement integrated, any statements they made before or while signing are irrelevant. If a court determines that Martha and Tyrone intended their agreement to be integrated, it will prohibit testimony about Martha's oral promises. One way to avoid parol evidence disputes is to include an *integration clause*. That is a statement clearly proclaiming that this writing is the "full and final expression" of the parties' agreement, and that anything said before signing or while signing is irrelevant. In the following case, learned people learned about parol evidence the hard way.

MAYO V. NORTH CAROLINA STATE UNIVERSITY

608 S.E.2d 116
North Carolina Court of Appeals, 2005

CASE SUMMARY

Facts: Dr. Robert Mayo was a tenured faculty member of the engineering department at North Carolina State University (NCSU), and director of the school's nuclear engineering program. In July, he informed his department chair, Dr. Paul Turinsky, that he was leaving NCSU effective September 1. Turinsky accepted the resignation.

In October, after Mayo had departed, Phyllis Jennette, the university's payroll coordinator, informed him that he had been overpaid. She explained that for employees who worked 9 months but were paid over 12 months, the salary checks for July and August were in fact prepayments for the period beginning that September. Because Mayo had not worked after September 1, the checks for July and August were overpayment. When he refused to refund the money, NCSU sought to claim it in legal proceedings. The first step was a hearing before an administrative agency.

At the hearing, Turinsky and Brian Simet, the university's payroll director, explained that the "prepayment" rule was a basic part of every employee's contract. However, both acknowledged that the prepayment rule was not included in any of the documents that formed Mayo's contract, including his appointment letter, annual salary letter, and policies adopted by the university's trustees. The university officials used other evidence, outside the written documents, to establish the prepayment policy.

Based on the additional evidence, the agency ruled that NCSU was entitled to its money. However, Mayo appealed to court, and the trial judge declared that he owed nothing, ruling that the university was not permitted to rely on parol evidence to establish its policy. NCSU appealed.

Issue: *Could NCSU have relied on parol evidence to establish its prepayment rule?*

Decision: No, neither party could have used parol evidence to explain the terms of the agreement. Affirmed.

Reasoning: When the parties intend a written document to be the final, integrated expression of their agreement, neither side may introduce parol evidence that changes, adds to, or contradicts any of the written terms. However, if the writing is not intended as a full integration of the agreement, or if the writing is ambiguous, then parol evidence is allowed.

Brian Simet, the university's payroll director, argued that the prepayment rule was a basic part of every employee's contract. However, during the agency hearing, he acknowledged that the rule was "not stated anywhere specifically."

The department chair, Dr. Turinsky, testified that Professor Mayo's employment agreement consisted only of his appointment letter, his annual salary letter, and the policies adopted and amended by the school's Board of Governors and its Board of Trustees. The language in each of these documents was unambiguous and said nothing about the supposed "prepayment rule." Dr. Turinsky also stated that he had never heard of the prepayment rule until September, after Professor Mayo left the school.

It appeared that the parties intended these documents to be the final, integrated expression of Professor Mayo's employment agreement. Because the documents were complete and unambiguous, parol evidence was excluded.

Professor Mayo owed the university nothing based on the alleged overpayment.

14-4a Exception: An Incomplete or Ambiguous Contract

If a court determines that a written contract is incomplete or ambiguous, it will permit parol evidence. Suppose that an employment contract states that the company will provide "full health coverage for Robert Watson and his family," but does not define *family*. Three years later, Watson divorces and remarries, acquiring three stepchildren, and a year later, his second wife has a baby. Watson now has two children by his first marriage and four by the second. The company refuses to insure Watson's first wife or his stepchildren. A court will probably find a key clause in his health care contract—"coverage for ... *his family*"—is ambiguous. A judge cannot determine exactly what the clause means from the contract itself, so the parties will be permitted to introduce parol evidence to prove whether or not the company must insure Watson's extended family.[11]

14-4b Fraud, Misrepresentation, or Duress

A court will permit parol evidence of fraud, misrepresentation, or duress. To encourage Annette to buy his house, Will assures her that no floodwaters from the nearby river have ever come within two miles of the house. Annette signs a contract that is silent about flooding and includes an integration clause stating that neither party is relying on any oral statements made during negotiations. When Annette moves in, she discovers that the foundation is collapsing due to earlier flooding and that Will knew of the flooding and the damage. Despite the integration clause, a court will probably allow Annette to testify about Will's misrepresentations.[12]

Chapter Conclusion

Some contracts must be in writing to be enforceable, and the writing must be clear and unambiguous. Drafting the contract need not be arduous. The disputes illustrated in this chapter could all have been prevented with a few carefully crafted sentences. It is worth the time and effort to write them.

---

[11]See, for example *Eure v. Norfolk Shipbuilding & Drydock Corp., Inc.*, 561 S.E.2d 663 (Va. 2002).
[12]*Lindberg v. Roseth*, 137 Idaho 222, 46 P.3d 518 (Idaho 2002).

EXAM REVIEW

1. **THE STATUTE OF FRAUDS**   Several types of contract are enforceable only if written:

- **LAND**   The sale of any interest in land. (pp. 319–320)

- **ONE YEAR**   An agreement that *cannot* be performed within one year. (pp. 321–322)

EXAM Strategy

CPA Question: Able hired Carr to restore Able's antique car for $800. The terms of their oral agreement provided that Carr had 18 months to complete the work. Actually, the work could be completed within one year. The agreement is:

(a) Unenforceable because it covers services with a value in excess of $500

(b) Unenforceable because it covers a time period in excess of one year

(c) Enforceable because personal service contracts are exempt from the Statute of Frauds

(d) Enforceable because the work could be completed within one year

Strategy: This is a subtle question. Notice that the contract is for a sum greater than $500. But that is a red herring. Why? The contract also might take 18 months to perform. But it *could* be finished in less than a year. (See the "Result" at the end of this section.)

- **DEBT OF ANOTHER**   A promise to pay the debt of another, including promises made by executors to pay an estate's debts. (pp. 322–323)

EXAM Strategy

Question: Donald Waide had a contracting business. He bought most of his supplies from Paul Bingham's supply center. Waide fell behind on his bills, and Bingham told Waide that he would extend no more credit to him. That same day, Donald's father, Elmer Waide, came to Bingham's store, and said to Bingham that he would "stand good" for any sales to Donald made on credit. Based on Elmer's statement, Bingham again gave Donald credit, and Donald ran up $10,000 in goods before Bingham sued Donald and Elmer. What defense did Elmer make, and what was the outcome?

Strategy: This was an oral agreement, so the issue is whether the promise had to be in writing to be enforceable. Review the list of six contracts that must be in writing. Is this agreement there? (See the "Result" at the end of this section.)

- **EXECUTORS**   A promise made by an executor of an estate. (p. 323)
- **MARRIAGE**   A promise made in consideration of marriage. (p. 323)
- **GOODS**   The sale of goods worth $500 or more. (p. 326)

EXAM Strategy

Question: James River-Norwalk, Inc., was a paper and textile company that needed a constant supply of wood. James River orally contracted with Gary Futch to supply wood for the company, and Futch did so for several years. The deal was worth many thousands of dollars, but nothing was put in writing. Futch actually purchased the wood for his own account and then resold it to James River. After a few years, James River refused to do more business with Futch. Did the parties have a binding contract?

Strategy: If this is a contract for services, it is enforceable without anything in writing. However, if it is one for the sale of goods, it must be in writing. Clearly what James River wanted was the wood, and it did not care where Futch found it. (See the "Result" at the end of this section.)

2. **CONTENTS**   The writing must be signed by the defendant and must state the name of all parties, the subject matter of the agreement, and all essential terms and promises. Electronic signatures usually are valid. (pp. 323–326)

3. **UNIFORM COMMERCIAL CODE (UCC)**   A contract or memorandum for the sale of goods may be less complete than those required by the common law.

- The basic UCC rule requires only a memorandum signed by the defendant, indicating that the parties reached an agreement and specifying the quantity of goods.

- Between merchants, even less is required. If one merchant sends written confirmation of a contract, the merchant who receives the document must object within 10 days or be bound by the writing.

- In the following special circumstances, no writing may be required: the goods are specially manufactured, one party admits in litigation that there was a contract, or one party pays for part of the goods or delivers some of the goods. (pp. 326–329)

4. **PAROL EVIDENCE**   When an integrated contract exists, neither party may generally use parol evidence to contradict, vary, or add to its terms. Parol evidence refers to anything (apart from the written contract itself) that was said, done, or written before the parties signed the agreement or as they signed it. (pp. 329–331)

1. **"One Year" Result:**   (d) A contract for the sale of goods worth $500 or more must be in writing—but this is a contract for services, not the sale of goods, so the $800 price is irrelevant. The contract can be completed within one year, and thus it falls outside the Statute of Frauds. This is an enforceable agreement.

1. **"Debt of Another" Result:**   Elmer made a promise to pay the debt of another. He did so as a favor to his son. This is a collateral promise. Elmer never signed any such promise, and the agreement cannot be enforced against him.

1. **"Goods" Result:**   James River was buying wood, and this is a contract for the sale of goods. With nothing in writing, signed by James River, Futch has no enforceable agreement.

MULTIPLE-CHOICE QUESTIONS

1. **CPA QUESTION** Two individuals signed a contract that was intended to be their entire agreement. The parol evidence rule will prevent the admission of evidence offered to:

    (a) Explain the meaning of an ambiguity in the written contract

    (b) Establish that fraud had been committed in the formation of the contract

    (c) Prove the existence of a contemporaneous oral agreement modifying the contract

    (d) Prove the existence of a subsequent oral agreement modifying the contract

2. Raul wants to plant a garden, and he agrees to buy a small piece of land for $300. Later, he agrees to buy a table for $300. Neither agreement is put in writing. The agreement to buy the land _____ enforceable, and the agreement to buy the table _____ enforceable.

    (a) is; is

    (b) is; is not

    (c) is not; is

    (d) is not; is not

3. The common law Statute of Frauds requires that to be "in writing," an agreement must be signed by ...

    (a) the plaintiff

    (b) the defendant

    (c) both (a) and (b)

    (d) none of the above

4. Mandy verbally tells a motorcycle dealer that she will make her son's motorcycle payments if he falls behind on them. Will Mandy be legally required to live up to this agreement?

    (a) Yes, absolutely

    (b) Yes, if her son is under 18

    (c) Yes, if Mandy will be the primary driver of the motorcycle

    (d) Yes, if the motorcycle is worth less than $500

    (e) No, absolutely not

5. In December 2012, Eric hires a band to play at a huge graduation party he is planning to hold in May, 2014. The deal is never put into writing. In January 2014, if he wanted to cancel the job, Eric _____ be able to do so. If he does not cancel, and if the band shows up and plays at the party in May 2014, Eric _____ have to pay them.

    (a) will; will

    (b) will; will not

    (c) will not; will

    (d) will not; will not

ESSAY QUESTIONS

1. Richard Griffin and three other men owned a grain company called Bearhouse, Inc., which needed to borrow money. First National Bank was willing to loan $490,000, but it insisted that the four men sign personal guaranties on the loan, committing themselves to repaying up to 25 percent of the loan each if Bearhouse defaulted. Bearhouse went bankrupt. The bank was able to collect some of its money from Bearhouse's assets, but it sued Griffin for the balance. At trial, Griffin wanted to testify that before he signed his guaranty, a bank officer assured him that he would only owe 25 percent of *whatever balance was unpaid*, not 25 percent of the total loan. How will the court decide whether Griffin is entitled to testify about the conversation?

2. When Deana Byers married Steven Byers, she was pregnant with another man's child. Shortly after the marriage, Deana gave birth. The marriage lasted only two months, and the couple separated. In divorce proceedings, Deana sought child support. She claimed that Steven had orally promised to support the child if Deana would marry him. Steven claims he never made the promise. Comment on the outcome.

3. Lonnie Hippen moved to Long Island, Kansas, to work in an insurance company owned by Griffiths. After he moved there, Griffiths offered to sell Hippen a house he owned, and Hippen agreed in writing to buy it. He did buy the house and moved in, but two years later, Hippen left the insurance company. He then claimed that at the time of the sale, Griffiths had orally promised to buy back his house at the selling price if Hippen should happen to leave the company. Griffiths defended based on the Statute of Frauds. Hippen argued that the Statute of Frauds did not apply because the repurchase of the house was essentially part of his employment with Griffiths. Comment.

4. Landlord owned a clothing store and agreed in writing to lease the store's basement to another retailer. The written lease, which both parties signed, (1) described the premises exactly, (2) identified the parties, and (3) stated the monthly rent clearly. But an appeals court held that the lease did not satisfy the Statute of Frauds. Why not?

5. **YOU BE THE JUDGE WRITING PROBLEM** Harrison Epperly operated United Brake Systems in Indianapolis, Indiana, and wanted to open a similar store in Nashville. He offered Kenneth Jarrett a job as manager, promising six months' severance pay if the store was not profitable in six months, and 49 percent ownership if he managed the new store for 10 years. Jarrett agreed, but the two men never put the deal in writing. Under Jarrett's management, the Nashville branch grew dramatically. After four years of renting space, the company purchased the land and buildings it used. Epperly periodically acknowledged his promise to make Jarrett 49 percent owner of the Nashville branch, and from time to time, he mentioned the arrangement to other workers. But after 10 years, Epperly sold United Brake, which had grown to 23 branches, to another company for $11 million. Jarrett sued Epperly for 49 percent of the Nashville branch. The trial court awarded Jarrett $812,000. Epperly appealed. Is Jarrett's contract with Epperly barred by the Statute of Frauds? **Argument for Epperly:** This alleged contract is unenforceable for two reasons. First, the agreement includes real estate; namely, the valuable land and buildings the company uses. A contract for the sale of any interest in land is unenforceable unless written. Second, the contract could not have been performed

within 1 year. If there was a deal, then by Jarrett's own words, the parties intended it to last 10 years. And 10 years' work cannot be performed in 1 year. **Argument for Jarrett:** The agreement had nothing to do with land. Jarrett and Epperly agreed that Mr. Jarrett would obtain a 49 percent ownership of the *Nashville branch*. At the time they made that agreement, the Nashville branch had no real estate. There is no rule saying that a valid contract becomes invalid because a corporation acquires some land. The "not in one year" argument also misses the point. The primary obligation was to open the branch and manage it for six months. If it was not profitable, Mr. Jarrett would immediately receive six months' severance pay, and the contract would be fully performed by both parties in less than a year. Finally, Epperly made a binding commitment, and Mr. Jarrett relied. Promissory estoppel prohibits Mr. Epperly from using deceit to profit.

DISCUSSION QUESTIONS

1. **ETHICS** Jacob Deutsch owned commercial property. He orally agreed to rent it for six years to Budget Rent-A-Car. Budget took possession, began paying monthly rent, and, over a period of several months, expended about $6,000 in upgrading the property. Deutsch was aware of the repairs. After a year, Deutsch attempted to evict Budget. Budget claimed it had a six-year oral lease, but Deutsch claimed that such a lease was worthless. Please rule. Is it ethical for Deutsch to use the Statute of Frauds in attempting to defeat the lease? Assume that, as landlord, you had orally agreed to rent premises to a tenant, but then for business reasons, you preferred not to carry out the deal. Would you evict a tenant if you thought the Statute of Frauds would enable you to do so? How should you analyze the problem? What values are most important to you?

2. Mast Industries and Bazak International were two textile firms. Mast orally offered to sell certain textiles to Bazak for $103,000. Mast promised to send documents confirming the agreement, but it never did. Finally, Bazak sent a memorandum to Mast confirming the agreement, describing the goods, and specifying their quantity and the price. Bazak's officer signed the memo. Mast received the memo but never agreed to it in writing. When Mast failed to deliver the goods, Bazak sued. Who will win? Why?

3. Is the Statute of Frauds reasonable, or does it unacceptably allow people to escape their obligations on a mere technicality?

4. Does the coverage of the Statute of Frauds make sense as it currently stands? Would it be better to expand the law and require that all contracts be in writing? Or should the law be done away with altogether?

5. Compare the common law Statute of Frauds to the UCC version. What are the specific differences? Which is more reasonable? Why?

nuttakit/Shutterstock.com; © neelsky/Shutterstock.com

THIRD PARTIES

Morty is 80, and a back injury makes it impossible for him to keep up with his yard work. The weeds in his front yard are knee-high by the Fourth of July, when his son John comes to visit for a week.

Surprised at the condition of the lawn, John gets the old mower out of the garage and mows it himself. Later in the visit, John calls a local landscaping company. He agrees to pay $500 for the company to send workers to mow Morty's lawn every two weeks for the rest of the year.

The company bills John's credit card, but it never sends anyone to cut the grass. As the summer wears on, John and Morty make several angry phone calls to the landscaper, without result. The owner of the company seems not to care, and it may take a lawsuit to motivate him to refund John's money so that he can hire someone else to do the job.

But if John is too busy to take legal action, can *Morty* do so?

[
If John is too busy to take legal action, can *Morty* do so?
]

The last five chapters examined the Contracts Checklist, so you now know all the elements that must be present for a valid contract to exist. In this chapter and the next three, we turn our attention to other contracts issues.

15-1 THIRD PARTY BENEFICIARY

The two parties who make a contract always intend to gain some benefit for themselves. Often, though, their bargain will also benefit *someone else*. **A third party beneficiary is someone who was not a party to the contract but stands to benefit from it.** Many contracts create third party beneficiaries. In the opening scenario, Morty is a third party beneficiary of John's agreement with the landscaping company. As another example, suppose a Major League Baseball team contracts to purchase from Seller 20 acres of an abandoned industrial site to be used for a new stadium. The owner of a pizza parlor on the edge of Seller's land might benefit enormously, since 40,000 hungry fans in the neighborhood for 81 home games every season could turn her once-marginal operation into a gold mine of cheese and pepperoni.

But what if the contract falls apart? What if the team backs out of the deal to buy the land? Seller can certainly sue because it is a party to the contract. But what about the pizza parlor owner? Can she sue to enforce the deal and recover lost profits for unsold sausage and green pepper?

The outcome in cases like these depends upon the intentions of the two contracting parties. If they *intended* to benefit the third party, she will probably be permitted to enforce their contract. If they did not intend to benefit her, she probably has no power to enforce the agreement.

15-1a Intended Beneficiaries

Intended beneficiary

Someone who may enforce a contract made between two other parties.

Promisor

Makes the promise that a third party seeks to enforce.

Promisee

The contract party *to whom* a promise is made.

A person is an **intended beneficiary** and may enforce a contract if the parties intended her to benefit and if either (a) enforcing the promise will satisfy a *duty* of the promisee to the beneficiary or (b) the promisee intended to make a *gift* to the beneficiary. (The **promisor** is the one who makes the promise that the third party beneficiary is seeking to enforce. The **promisee** is the other party to the contract.)

In other words, a third party beneficiary must show two things in order to enforce a contract that two other people created. First, she must show that the two contracting parties were aware of her situation and knew that she would receive something of value from their deal. Second, she must show that the promisee wanted to benefit her for one of two reasons: either to satisfy some duty owed or to make her a gift.

If the promisee is fulfilling some duty, the third party beneficiary is called a **creditor beneficiary**. Most often, the duty that a promisee will be fulfilling is a debt already owed to the beneficiary. If the promisee is making a gift, the third party is a **donee beneficiary**.[1] So long as the third party is either a creditor or a donee beneficiary, she may enforce the contract. If she is only an incidental beneficiary, she may not.

We will apply this rule to the dispute over Morty's lawn. Like most contracts, the deal between John and the landscaping company had two promises: the company's promise to mow the lawn every two weeks and John's agreement to pay $500. The one that interests us is the promise to mow the lawn. The company is the promisor and John is the promisee.

Did the two parties intend to benefit Morty? Yes, they did. John wanted his father's property maintained. Did John owe Morty a legal duty? No. Did John intend to make a gift to Morty? Yes. So, Morty is an intended, donee beneficiary, and he can sue the landscaping company to enforce the contract himself.

By contrast, the pizza parlor owner will surely lose. A stadium is a multimillion-dollar investment, and it is most unlikely that the baseball team and the seller of the land were even

---

[1]"Donee" comes from the word "donate."

aware of the owner's existence, let alone that they intended to benefit her. She probably cannot prove either the first element or the second element, and certainly not both.

In the following case, a dazzling diamond loses its luster. Who is entitled to sue?

SCHAUER V. MANDARIN GEMS OF CALIFORNIA, INC.

2005 WL 5730
Court of Appeal of California, 2005

CASE SUMMARY

Facts: Sarah Schauer and her fiancé, Darin Erstad, went shopping for an engagement ring, first at Tiffany and Cartier, then at Mandarin Gems, where they were captivated by a 3.01 carat diamond with a clarity grading of "S11." Erstad bought the ring the same day for $43,121. Later, Mandarin supplied Erstad with a written appraisal, again rating the ring as an S11 and valuing it at $45,500. Paul Lam, a certified gemologist, signed the appraisal.

Diamonds may last forever, but this marriage was short-lived. The divorce decree gave each party the right to keep whatever personal property they currently held, meaning that Schauer could keep the ring. She had the ring appraised by the Gem Trade Laboratory, which gave it a poorer clarity rating and a value of $20,000.

Schauer sued Mandarin for misrepresentation and breach of contract, but the jeweler defended by saying that it had never contracted with her, and that she was not a third party beneficiary of the company's agreement with Erstad. The trial court dismissed Schauer's suit, and she appealed.

Issue: *Did Schauer have any right to sue for breach of contract?*

Decision: Yes, she was entitled to sue. Reversed and remanded.

Reasoning: A true third party beneficiary may enforce a contract made by others unless they rescinded the agreement. Persons who expect to incidentally or remotely benefit from a bargain may not enforce it.

A plaintiff claiming status as a third party beneficiary must demonstrate that the promisor understood that the promisee intended to benefit the third party. It is not necessary that both parties intended to benefit the third party.

Schauer alleged that she and Erstad went shopping for an engagement ring. They were together when they looked at the ring, and they explained to the jeweler that Erstad was buying the diamond to give to Schauer as an engagement ring. The jeweler *must* have understood that Erstad was entering into a sales contract intending to benefit Schauer.

Schauer alleged facts that, if found to be true, established her as a third party beneficiary. She was entitled to proceed with her contract claim against Mandarin Gems.

EXAM Strategy

Question: Mr. Inspector examines houses and gives its reports to potential buyers. Mr. Inspector contracts with Greenlawn, a real estate agent, to furnish reports on houses that Greenlawn is selling. The agreement allows the agent to give the reports to potential buyers. Greenlawn gives Molly one of Mr. Inspector's reports and, relying upon it, she buys a house. Although the report states that the house is structurally sound, it turns out that chronic roof leaks have caused water to seep into the walls. Molly sues Mr. Inspector. The inspector requests summary judgment, claiming that he had no contract with Molly.

Strategy: Mr. Inspector is right in saying he had no agreement with Molly. To prevail, Molly must demonstrate she is a third party beneficiary of the contract between the other two. A third party beneficiary may enforce a contract if the parties intended to benefit her and either (a) enforcing the promise will satisfy a duty of the promisee to the beneficiary or (b) the promisee intended to make a gift to the beneficiary.

> **Result:** Greenlawn used the inspection summaries as sales tools. When Greenlawn assured a potential buyer that she could rely upon a report, the real estate agent took on a duty to deliver reliable information. Mr. Inspector understood that. The two parties intended to benefit Greenlawn's buyers. Molly may sue Mr. Inspector for breach of his contract with the agent. Mr. Inspector's motion for summary judgment is denied.

15-1b Incidental Beneficiaries

Incidental beneficiary
Someone who might have benefited from a contract between two others but has no right to enforce that agreement.

A person who fails to qualify as a donee beneficiary or a creditor beneficiary is merely an **incidental beneficiary** and may not enforce the contract. The pizza parlor owner is an incidental beneficiary.

In an effort to persuade courts, many plaintiffs make creative arguments that they are intended beneficiaries with enforcement rights. Is every taxpayer an intended beneficiary of a government contract? Do labor unions have rights if a contract refers to them in general terms? Or are these plaintiffs incidental beneficiaries? The following case answers these questions.

UNITE HERE LOCAL 30 v. CALIFORNIA DEPARTMENT OF PARKS AND RECREATION

2011 Cal. App. LEXIS 510
Court of Appeal of California, 2011

CASE SUMMARY

Facts: The California Department of Parks and Recreation and Delaware North Companies entered into a contract giving Delaware North the right to operate a concession stand at a state park in San Diego for 10 years. Four years into the contract, Delaware North assigned its rights to operate the stand to another company.

Delaware North fired many of its employees, and the new operator did not rehire them. Some of these workers were members of the union Unite Here Local 30. Local 30 sued to block the assignment. It was joined in the suit by Bridgette Browning, who lived in the area and seemed to care who provided her hot dogs.

The trial court rejected the plaintiffs' claims, and the plaintiffs appealed.

Issue: *Did the plaintiffs have the right to enforce the contract between the state and the concession stand company?*

Decision: No. The plaintiffs were not intended beneficiaries.

Reasoning: To enforce someone else's contract, a party does not have to be specifically named in it. Third parties may enforce a contract if they are an intended beneficiary, that is, a member of a class of persons for whose benefit it was made. But intended beneficiaries must prove that the contract was actually made for their benefit, not just that they happened to benefit from the deal.

The plaintiffs argued that they had a right to sue for breach of contract and block the assignment because the concession contract was indeed intended for their benefit.

Did the terms of the concession contract reveal an intent to benefit Bridgette Browning? She argued that state contracts intend to benefit the general public and the taxpayers and that as a hot-dog-eating, park-going taxpayer of California, she had a right to sue. However, the fact that members of the public benefit from the contract—a hot pretzel or friendly service at the park's concession stand—does not make them *intended beneficiaries*. Browning would be an intended beneficiary only if the point of the contract was to make a gift to her. That was not the goal of this contract.

Did the terms of the concession contract reveal an intent to benefit Local 30? To prove this intent, Local 30 pointed to a clause in the contract that prohibited Delaware North from promoting or deterring union organizing. But that provision hardly revealed an intent to benefit Local 30, or any union for that matter. At best, it showed an intent to remain neutral to union organizing, hardly a gift. Local 30 was no more than an incidental beneficiary.

Since the plaintiffs were not intended beneficiaries, they had no right to sue to enforce the contract.

15-2 Assignment and Delegation

After a contract is made, one or both parties may wish to substitute someone else for themselves. Six months before Maria's lease expires, an out-of-town company offers her a new job at a substantial increase in pay. After taking the job, she wants to sublease her apartment to her friend Sarah.

A contracting party may transfer his rights under the contract, which is called an **assignment** of rights. Or a party may transfer her obligations under the contract, which is a **delegation** of duties. Frequently, a party will make an assignment and delegation simultaneously, transferring both rights (such as the right to inhabit an apartment) and duties (like the obligation to pay monthly rent) to a third party.

Assignment
Transferring contract *rights*.

Delegation
Transferring contract *duties*.

15-2a Assignment

Lydia needs 500 bottles of champagne. Bruno agrees to sell them to her for $10,000, payable 30 days after delivery. He transports the wine to her.

Bruno owes Doug $8,000 from a previous deal. He says to Doug, "I don't have your money, but I'll give you my claim to Lydia's $10,000." Doug agrees. Bruno then *assigns* to Doug his rights to Lydia's money, and in exchange Doug gives up his claim against Bruno for $8,000. Bruno is the **assignor, the one making an assignment**, and Doug is the **assignee, the one receiving an assignment**.

Why would Bruno offer $10,000 when he owed Doug only $8,000? Because all he has is a *claim* to Lydia's money. Cash in hand is often more valuable. Doug, however, is willing to assume some risk for a potential $2,000 gain.

Bruno notifies Lydia of the assignment. Lydia, who owes the money, is called the **obligor**; that is, the one obligated to do something. At the end of 30 days, Doug arrives at Lydia's doorstep, asks for his money, and gets it, since Lydia is obligated to him. Bruno has no claim to any payment. See Exhibit 15.1.

Obligor
The party obligated to do something.

EXAM Strategy

Question: Hasannah, an art dealer, signs a contract with Jason. Hasannah will deliver a David Hockney painting to Jason's house. Jason may keep it for 30 days and then either return it or pay Hasannah $2 million. Hasannah delivers the painting. Hasannah finds a better building to house her gallery and agrees to buy it from Shannon. She and Shannon sign a contract allowing Shannon to receive Jason's payment if he keeps the picture. Hasannah then notifies Jason to pay Shannon the $2 million. Identify the obligor, the assignor, and the assignee.

Strategy: The obligor is the one obligated to do something. The assignor makes an assignment and the assignee receives it.

Result: Jason is obligated either to return the picture or pay $2 million for it. He is the obligor. Hasannah is entitled to the money, but she assigns her right to Shannon. Hasannah is the assignor and Shannon the assignee.

The Parties Make a Contract:

Bruno (Assignor) — Agrees to Sell Champagne — 2 — Agrees to Pay $10,000 for Champagne — **Lydia** (Obligor)

Delivers Champagne — 3

Has a Previous Debt of $8,000 — 1

4 — Assigns All Rights to the Contract

5

Doug (Assignee)

Makes Payment of $10,000 — 5

© Cengage Learning

EXHIBIT 15.1   The Anatomy of an Assignment

WHAT RIGHTS ARE ASSIGNABLE?

Most contract rights are assignable, but not all. Disputes sometimes arise between the two contracting parties about whether one of the parties could legally assign her rights to a third party. Any **contractual right may be assigned unless assignment**

(a) would substantially change the obligor's rights or duties under the contract;

(b) is forbidden by law or public policy; or

(c) is validly precluded by the contract itself.[2]

Substantial Change   An assignment is prohibited if it would substantially change the obligor's situation. For example, Bruno is permitted to assign to Doug his rights to payment from Lydia because it makes no difference to Lydia whether she writes a check to one person or another. But suppose that, before delivery, Lydia had wanted to assign her rights to the shipment of 500 bottles of champagne to a business in another country. In this example, Bruno would be the obligor, and his duties would substantially change. Shipping heavy items over long distances adds substantial costs, so Lydia would not be able to make the assignment.

Assignment is also prohibited when the obligor is agreeing to perform personal services. The close working relationship in such agreements makes it unfair to expect the obligor to work with a stranger. Warner, a feature film director, hires Mayer to be his assistant on a film

---

[2]Restatement (Second) of Contracts §317(2). And note that UCC §2-210 is, for our purposes, nearly identical.

to be shot over the next 10 weeks. Warner may not assign his right to Mayer's work to another director.

Public Policy   Some assignments are prohibited by public policy. For example, someone who has suffered a personal injury may not assign her claim to a third person. Vladimir is playing the piano on his roof deck when the instrument rolls over the balustrade and drops 35 stories before smashing Wanda's foot. Wanda has a valid tort claim against Vladimir, but she may not assign the claim to anyone else. As a matter of public policy, all states have decided that the sale of personal injury claims could create an unseemly and unethical marketplace.

Contract Prohibition   Finally, one of the contracting parties may try to prohibit assignment in the agreement itself. For example, most landlords include in the written lease a clause prohibiting the tenant from assigning the tenancy without the landlord's written permission.

Subleasing disputes between landlord and tenant are common. How much leeway does a landlord have in rejecting a proposed assignment? The following case provides the answer.

TENET HEALTHSYSTEM SURGICAL, L.L.C. V. JEFFERSON PARISH HOSPITAL SERVICE DISTRICT NO. 1

426 F.3d 738
Fifth Circuit Court of Appeals, 2005

CASE SUMMARY

Facts: MSC, Inc., owned the Marrero Shopping Center, and leased space to Tenet HealthSystem for use in outpatient surgery and general medical practice. The lease allowed Tenet to assign the lease with the consent of the lessor and stated that consent would not be unreasonably withheld.

Two years later, Marrero sold the shopping center to West Jefferson Medical Center, which owned an adjacent hospital and wanted the space for expansion. A few months after that, Tenet went out of business and requested permission from West Jefferson to assign its lease to Pelican Medical, which intended to use the space for an occupational medicine clinic. Pelican's clinic would offer workmen's compensation-related medical services, including physical examinations, drug and alcohol testing, and minor surgical procedures. West Jefferson denied permission, stating that Pelican would be performing work not permitted under the original lease, and also because Pelican would compete with West Jefferson.

Tenet sued, claiming that West Jefferson was unreasonably withholding permission to assign. The trial court granted summary judgment for West Jefferson. Tenet appealed.

Issue: *Did West Jefferson unreasonably withhold permission to assign the lease?*

Decision: Yes, West Jefferson withheld consent for an improper reason. Reversed and remanded.

Reasoning: Tenet, the tenant, used the office space for nothing more than minor surgery. Pelican proposed to offer many medical services in the space, but none were unusual. West Jefferson objected primarily because it did not want to lose patients to Pelican. This is a reasonable economic concern, but nonetheless it is not a factor that a landlord may consider in approving a lease assignment. In this situation, a landlord must make an objective assessment that is not related to its own personal circumstances. Thus, it may consider only whether the new tenant is financially responsible, will adequately maintain the property, and will use the premises for a legal business.

Tenet's lease allowed for "general medical and physician's offices." Pelican did not propose to provide any services not covered by that definition. There was no indication that Pelican would miss lease payments or damage the property. West Jefferson may have acted as a reasonable business in defending its own interests, but it acted wrongfully in its role as landlord.

How Rights Are Assigned

Writing   In general, an assignment may be written or oral, and no particular formalities are required. However, when someone wants to assign rights governed by the Statute of Frauds, she must do it in writing. Suppose City contracts with Seller to buy Seller's land and then brings in Investor to complete the project. If City wants to assign to Investor its rights to the land, it must do so in writing.

Consideration   An assignment can be valid with or without consideration, but the lack of consideration may have consequences. Two examples should clarify this. Recall Bruno, who sells champagne to Lydia and then assigns to Doug his right to payment. In that case, there *is* consideration for the assignment. Bruno assigns his rights only because Doug cancels the old debt, and his agreement to do that is valid consideration. **An assignment for consideration is irrevocable.** Once the two men agree, Bruno may not telephone Doug and say, "I've changed my mind, I want Lydia to pay me after all." Lydia's $10,000 now belongs to Doug.

But suppose that Bruno assigns his contract rights to his sister Brunhilde as a birthday present. This is a **gratuitous assignment**; that is, one made as a gift, for no consideration. **A gratuitous assignment is generally revocable if it is oral and generally irrevocable if it is written.** If Bruno verbally assigns his rights to Brunhilde, but then changes his mind, telephones Lydia, and says, "I want you to pay me after all," that revocation is effective, and Brunhilde gets nothing. But if Bruno puts his assignment in writing and Brunhilde receives it, Bruno has given up his right to receive Lydia's payment.

Gratuitous assignment
An assignment made as a gift, for no consideration.

Notice to Obligor   The assignment is valid from the moment it is made, regardless of whether the assignor notifies the obligor. But an assignor with common sense will immediately inform the obligor of the assignment. Suppose Maude has a contract with Nelson, who is obligated to deliver 700 live frogs to her shop. If Maude (assignor) assigns her rights to Obie (assignee), Maude should notify Nelson (obligor) the same day. If she fails to inform Nelson, he may deliver the frogs to Maude. Nelson will have no further obligations under the contract, and Maude will owe Obie 700 frogs.

Rights of the Parties After Assignment

Once the assignment is made and the obligor notified, the assignee may enforce her contractual rights against the obligor. If Lydia fails to pay Doug for the champagne she gets from Bruno, Doug may sue to enforce the agreement. The law will treat Doug as though he had entered into the contract with Lydia.

But if a lawsuit arises, the reverse is also true. **The obligor may generally raise all defenses against the assignee that she could have raised against the assignor.** Suppose Lydia opens the first bottle of champagne—silently. "Where's the pop?" she wonders. There is no pop because all 500 bottles have gone flat. Bruno has failed to perform his part of the contract, and Lydia may use Bruno's nonperformance as a defense against Doug. If the champagne was indeed worthless, Lydia owes Doug nothing.

Assignor's Warranty   The law implies certain warranties, or assurances, on the part of the assignor. Unless the parties expressly agree to exclude them, the assignor warrants that (1) the rights he is assigning actually do exist, and (2) there are no defenses to the rights other than those that would be obvious, like nonperformance. But the assignor *does not* warrant that the obligor is solvent. Bruno is impliedly warranting to Doug that Lydia has no defenses to the contract, but he is not guaranteeing Doug that she has the money to pay, or that she will pay.

SPECIAL ISSUE: THE UNIFORM COMMERCIAL CODE AND ASSIGNMENTS OF SECURITY INTERESTS

The provisions of the Uniform Commercial Code (UCC) regarding assignments in contracts for the sale of goods are very similar to common law rules.[3] However, Article 9 of the Code has special rules about the assignment of **security interests**, which are the legal rights in personal property that assure payment. When an automobile dealer sells you a new car on credit, the dealer will keep a security interest in your car. If you do not make your monthly payments, the dealer retains a right to repossess the vehicle. That authority is called a *security interest*. (See Chapter 23 for a full discussion.)

Companies that sell goods often prefer to assign their security interests to some other firm, such as a bank or finance company. The bank is the assignee. Just as we saw with the common law, the assignee of a security interest generally has all of the rights that the assignor had. And the obligor (the buyer) may also raise all of the defenses against the assignee that she could have raised against the assignor.

Under UCC §9-404, the obligor on a sales contract may generally assert any defenses against the assignee that arise from the contract, and any other defenses that arose before notice of assignment. The Code's reference to any defenses that arise from the contract means that if the assignor breached his part of the deal, the obligor may raise that as a defense. Suppose a dealer sells you a new Porsche on credit, retaining a security interest. He assigns the security interest to the bank. The car is great for the first few weeks, but then the roof slides onto the street and both doors fall off. You refuse to make any more monthly payments. When the bank sues you, you may raise the automobile's defects as a defense, just as you could have raised them against the dealer itself. Where the Code talks about other defenses that arose before notice of assignment, it refers, for example, to fraud. Suppose the dealer knew that before you bought the Porsche, it had been smashed up and rebuilt. If the dealer told you it was fresh from the factory, that would be fraud, and you could raise the defense against the bank.

A contract may prohibit an obligor from raising certain defenses against an assignee. Sometimes a seller of goods will require the buyer to sign a contract that permits the seller to assign *and* prohibits the buyer from raising defenses against the assignee that he could have raised against the seller. University wants to buy a computer system on credit from Leland for $85,000. Leland agrees to the deal but insists that the contract permit him to assign his rights to anyone he chooses. He also wants this clause: "University agrees that it will not raise against an assignee any defenses that it may have had against Leland." This clause is sometimes called a **waiver clause** because the obligor is waiving (giving up) rights. Courts may also refer to it as an **exclusion clause** since the parties are excluding potential defenses. Leland wants a waiver clause because it makes his contract more valuable. As soon as University signs the agreement, Leland can take his contract to Krushem Collections, a finance company. Krushem might offer Leland $70,000 cash for the contract. Leland can argue, "You have to pay $85,000 for this. You are guaranteed payment by University since they cannot raise any defenses against you, even if the computer system collapses in the first half-hour." Leland gets cash and need not worry about collecting payments. Krushem receives the full value of the contract, with interest, spread out over several years.

Under UCC §9-403, an agreement by a buyer (or lessee) that he will not assert against an assignee any claim or defense that he may have against the seller (or lessor) is generally enforceable by the assignee if he took the assignment in good faith, for value, without notice of the potential defenses. In other words, Leland's waiver clause with University is enforceable. If Leland assigns the contract to Krushem Collections and the system proves worthless, Krushem

Security interests
Rights in personal property that assure payment or the performance of some obligation.

---

[3]UCC §2-210.

is still entitled to its monthly payments from University. The school must seek its damages against Leland—a far more arduous step than simply withholding payment.

These waiver clauses are generally *not* valid in consumer contracts. If Leland sold a computer system to a consumer (an individual purchasing it for her personal use), the waiver would generally be unenforceable.

In the following case, one side pushes the waiver rule to its extreme. Can an assignee recover for money advanced … when the money was never advanced? You be the judge.

You Be the Judge

WELLS FARGO BANK MINNESOTA V. BROOKSAMERICA MORTGAGE CORPORATION

419 F.3d 107
Second Circuit Court of Appeals, 2005

Facts: Michael Brooks desperately needed financing for his company, BrooksAmerica, so he agreed to a sale-leaseback agreement with Terminal Marketing Company. Terminal would pay BrooksAmerica $250,000, and in exchange it would obtain title to BrooksAmerica's computers and office equipment. BrooksAmerica would then lease the equipment for three years, for $353,000. The equipment would never leave BrooksAmerica's offices.

The contract included a "hell or high water clause" stating that BrooksAmerica's obligation to pay was "absolute and unconditional." Another clause permitted Terminal to assign its rights without notice to BrooksAmerica and stated that the assignee took its rights "free from all defenses, setoffs, or counterclaims."

Brooks also signed a "Delivery and Acceptance Certificate" stating that BrooksAmerica had received the $250,000 (even though no money had yet changed hands) and reaffirming BrooksAmerica's absolute obligation to pay an assignee, despite any defenses BrooksAmerica might have.

Terminal assigned its rights to Wells Fargo, which had taken about 2,000 other equipment leases from Terminal. Terminal never paid any portion of the promised $250,000. Brooks refused to make the required payments (about $10,000 per month) and Wells Fargo sued. Brooks acknowledged that Wells Fargo paid Terminal for the assignment.

Both parties moved for summary judgment. The trial court ruled in favor of Wells Fargo, and Brooks appealed.

You Be the Judge: *Is Wells Fargo entitled to its monthly lease payments despite the fact that BrooksAmerica never received financing?*

Argument for BrooksAmerica: We acknowledge the general validity of UCC §9-403. However, in this case, "Good faith" required Wells Fargo to make sure that Terminal had performed. A simple inquiry would have informed Wells Fargo that Terminal was entitled to no money. This entire transaction is a sham, and §9-403 was never drafted to encourage financial swindles.

The trial court *penalized* BrooksAmerica for acting in good faith. Mr. Brooks signed the Delivery Certificate assuming that any reasonable company would promptly deliver the money it had promised. Unfortunately, Terminal does not operate at the same ethical level—a fact that Wells Fargo should know from its earlier assignments.

Argument for Wells Fargo: Under UCC §9-403, an assignee such as Wells Fargo may enforce a waiver of defenses clause if the assignment was taken in good faith, for value, and free of knowledge of any claims or defenses. Wells Fargo meets that test.

The "simple inquiry" argument has two flaws. First, §9-403 does not require one. The UCC requires good faith, not an investigation. Second, Wells Fargo *did* investigate by checking the contract and the Delivery Certificate. We have done more than required. We have taken thousands of equipment leases as assignees. In this case, we examined the contract and the Delivery Certificate, and assumed that BrooksAmerica had received its money. If Terminal had not paid, why did Mr. Brooks sign a certificate stating he had received his cash? We are entitled to payment. Any dispute between BrooksAmerica and Terminal is for those parties to resolve.

Wells Fargo makes an absurd argument. Neither Terminal nor any assignee has a right to enforce a financing contract when Terminal failed to deliver the financing. There is no valid contract to enforce here because Terminal never paid the $250,000 owed to BrooksAmerica.

15-2b Delegation of Duties

Garret has always dreamed of racing stock cars. He borrows $250,000 from his sister, Maybelle, in order to buy a car and begin racing. He signs a promissory note, which is a document guaranteeing that he will repay Maybelle the full amount, plus interest, on a monthly basis over 10 years. Regrettably, during his first race, Garret discovers that he has a speed phobia and quits the business. Garret transfers the car and all of his equipment to Brady, who agrees in writing to pay all money owed to Maybelle. Brady sends a check for a few months, but then the payments stop. Maybelle sues Garret, who defends based on the transfer to Brady. Will his defense work?

Garret has assigned his rights in the car and business to Brady, and that is entirely legal. But more important, he has *delegated his duties* to Brady. Garret was the **delegator** and Brady was the **delegatee**. In other words, the promissory note he signed was a contract, and the agreement imposed certain *duties* on Garret, primarily the obligation to pay Maybelle $250,000 plus interest. Garret had a right to delegate his duties to Brady, but delegating those duties did not relieve Garret of *his own* obligation to perform them. When Maybelle sues, she will win. Garret, like many debtors, would have preferred to wash his hands of his debt, but the law is not so obliging.

Most duties are delegable. But delegation does not by itself relieve the delegator of his own liability to perform the contract.

Garret's delegation to Brady was typical in that it included an assignment at the same time. If he had merely transferred ownership, that would have been only an assignment. If he had convinced Brady to pay off the loan without getting the car, that would have been merely a delegation. He did both at once. See Exhibit 15.2.

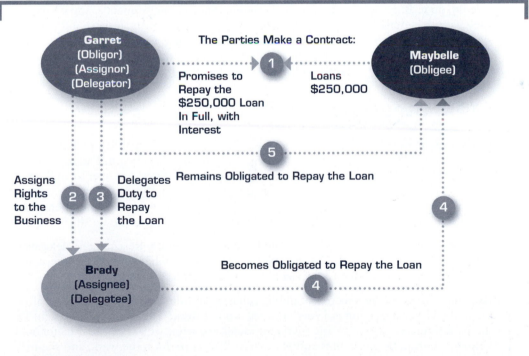

EXHIBIT 15.2   The Anatomy of a Delegation

© Cengage Learning

WHAT DUTIES ARE DELEGABLE?

The rules concerning what duties may be delegated mirror those about the assignment of rights. And once again, the common law agrees with the UCC. An obligor may delegate his duties unless:

1. delegation would violate public policy, or

2. the original contract prohibits delegation, or

3. the obligee has a substantial interest in personal performance by the obligor.[4]

Public Policy   Delegation may violate public policy, such as in a public works contract. If City hires Builder to construct a subway system, state law may prohibit Builder from delegating his duties to Beginner. The theory is that a public agency should not have to work with parties that it never agreed to hire.

Contract Prohibition   It is very common for a contract to prohibit delegation. We saw in the "Assignment" section that courts may refuse to enforce a clause that limits one party's ability to assign its contract rights. That does not hold true with delegation. The parties may forbid almost any delegation, and the courts will enforce the agreement. Hammer, a contractor, is building a house and hires Spot as his painter, including in his contract a clause prohibiting delegation. Just before the house is ready for painting, Spot gets a better job elsewhere and wants to delegate his duties to Brush. Hammer may refuse the delegation, even if Brush is equally qualified.

Substantial Interest in Personal Performance   Suppose Hammer had omitted the "nondelegation" clause from his contract with Spot. Could Hammer still refuse the delegation on the grounds that he has a substantial interest in having Spot do the work? No. Most duties are delegable, so long as they do not violate public policy or a clause in a contract. There is nothing so special about painting a house that one particular painter is required to do it. But some kinds of work do require personal performance, and obligors may not delegate these tasks. The services of lawyers, doctors, dentists, artists, and performers are considered too personal to be delegated. There is no single test that will perfectly define this group, but generally when the work will test the *character, skill, discretion, and good faith of the obligor*, she may *not* delegate her job.

EXAM Strategy

Question: Parker is a well-known actress. She agrees to act in Will's play for four weeks, for $30,000 per week. A week before rehearsals are to begin, Parker notifies Will that she cannot appear because a film producer has offered her over $1 million to start shooting immediately. She has arranged for Claire, another well-known actress, to appear in her place. Will objects. Parker claims, correctly, that their agreement does not prohibit her from making this substitution. Is Parker allowed to do this?

Strategy: Parker is attempting to delegate her duties. Under the Restatement, delegation is allowed unless (1) it would violate public policy, (2) it is prohibited by the contract, or (3) the obligee has a substantial interest in the obligor's personal performance.

Result: This is hardly a matter of public concern, and the contract does not speak to the issue. However, acting is a very personal kind of work. The actor must be right for the part, interact smoothly with other cast members, work well with the director, and help draw the audience. Will is entitled to have Parker perform the work, and she may not delegate her role.

---

[4]Restatement (Second) of Contracts §318. And see UCC §2-210, establishing similar limits.

Improper Delegation and Repudiation Sometimes parties delegate duties they should not. Suppose Spot, having agreed not to delegate his painting job, is so tempted by the higher offer from another contractor that he delegates the work anyway. Hammer informs Spot he will not allow Brush on the job site. If Spot still refuses to work, he has **repudiated** the agreement; in other words, he has formally notified the other side that he will not perform his side of the contract. Hammer will probably sue him. On the other hand, if Hammer allows Brush up the ladder and Brush completes the job, Hammer has no claim against anybody.

NOVATION

As we have seen, a delegator does not automatically get rid of his duties merely by delegating them. But there is one way a delegator *can* do so. A **novation** is a three-way agreement in which the obligor transfers all rights and duties to a third party. The obligee agrees to look only to that third party for performance.

> **Novation**
> A three-way agreement in which the obligor transfers all rights and duties to a third party.

Recall Garret, the forlorn race car driver. When he wanted to get out of his obligations to Maybelle, he should have proposed a novation. Were one created, he would assign all rights and delegate all duties to Brady, and Maybelle would agree that *only Brady* was obligated by the promissory note, releasing Garret from his responsibility to repay. Why would Maybelle do this? She might conclude that Brady was a better bet than Garret and that this was the best way to get her money. Maybelle would prefer to have both people liable. But Garret might refuse to bring Brady into the deal until Maybelle permits a novation. In the example given, Garret failed to obtain a novation, and hence he and Brady were *both* liable on the promissory note.

Since a novation has the critical effect of releasing the obligor from liability, you will not be surprised to learn that two parties to a contract sometimes fight over whether some event was a simple delegation of duties or a novation. Here is one such contest.

It appears that Mary Pratt, moving to Arizona, honestly thought she was not only out of the ice cream business but relieved of any debt to the Rosenbergs. This lawsuit undoubtedly came as a cold shock. What should she have done to avoid the dispute?

ROSENBERG V. SON, INC.

491 N.W.2d 71, 1992 N.D. LEXIS 202
Supreme Court of North Dakota, 1992

CASE SUMMARY

Facts: The Rosenbergs owned a Dairy Queen in Grand Forks, North Dakota. They agreed in writing to sell the Dairy Queen to Mary Pratt. The contract required her to pay $10,000 down and $52,000 over 15 years, at 10 percent interest. Two years later, Pratt assigned her rights and delegated her duties under the sales contract to Son, Inc. The agreement between Pratt and Son contained a "Consent to Assignment" clause that the Rosenbergs signed. Pratt then moved to Arizona and had nothing further to do with the Dairy Queen. The Rosenbergs never received full payment for the Dairy Queen. They sued Mary Pratt.

The trial court gave summary judgment for Pratt, finding that she was no longer obligated on the original contract. The Rosenbergs appealed.

Issue: *Did Pratt obtain a novation relieving her of her duties under the original sales contract?*

Decision: No. Pratt did not obtain a novation. Reversed and remanded.

Reasoning: One party to a contract does not escape liability simply by delegating duties and assigning rights. To relieve itself of all responsibility, a party must obtain a novation, meaning an agreement from the other side that all liability has now passed on to a third person.

It was apparent from the language of this agreement that the parties intended only an assignment, not a novation. The document made no mention of discharging Pratt from her duties. In fact, the agreement included a clause in which Son indemnified Pratt; the only reason for such a provision was that Pratt remained liable to the Rosenbergs.

The assignment did not become a novation merely because Rosenberg signed it. A creditor may permit assignment without releasing the original obligor. That is what happened here, and Pratt remained liable to the Rosenbergs.

Chapter Conclusion

A moment's caution! It is important to remember that the parties to a contract may not have the right to substitute someone else into the contract. The parties to a contract always have legal rights themselves, but when outsiders enter the picture, subtle differences in key areas determine whether additional rights exist.

EXAM REVIEW

1. **THIRD PARTY BENEFICIARY**   A third party beneficiary is an intended beneficiary and may enforce a contract if the parties intended her to benefit from the agreement and if either (1) enforcing the promise will satisfy a debt of the promisee to the beneficiary, or (2) the promisee intended to make a gift to the beneficiary. The intended beneficiary described in (1) is a creditor beneficiary, while (2) describes a donee beneficiary. Any beneficiary who meets neither description is an incidental beneficiary and has no right to enforce the contract. (pp. 338–340)

2. **ASSIGNMENT AND DELEGATION**   An assignment transfers the assignor's contract rights to the assignee. A delegation transfers the delegator's duties to the delegatee. (pp. 341–350)

3. **RIGHTS ASSIGNABLE**   A party generally may assign contract rights unless doing so would substantially change the obligor's rights or duties, is forbidden by law, or is validly precluded by the contract. (pp. 342–344)

EXAM Strategy

Question: Angelo Zavarella and Yvette Rodrigues were injured in an automobile accident allegedly caused by a vehicle belonging to Truck Equipment of Boston. Travelers Insurance Co. paid insurance benefits to Zavarella and Rodrigues, who then assigned to Travelers their claims against Truck Equipment. Travelers sued Truck Equipment, which moved to dismiss. What is Truck Equipment's claim that the case should be dismissed, and how would you rule?

Strategy: Travelers is claiming to be the assignee of the plaintiffs' claims. Any contractual right may be assigned except in the three instances listed above. Does one of those prohibitions apply? (See the "Result" at the end of this section.)

4. **ENFORCEMENT**   Once the assignment is made and the obligor notified, the assignee may enforce her contractual rights against the obligor. The obligor, in turn, may generally raise all defenses against the assignee that she could have raised against the assignor. (p. 344)

5. **THE UCC AND SECURITY INTERESTS**   Article 9 of the UCC governs security interests, which are the legal rights to personal property that assure payment of a debt. Under Article 9, obligors may assert defenses against assignees that arise from contracts, and agreements not to enforce such defenses are generally valid. (pp. 345–346)

6. **DUTIES DELEGABLE**   Duties are delegable unless delegation would violate public policy, the contract prohibits delegation, or the obligee has a substantial interest in personal performance by the obligor. (pp. 347–350)

EXAM Strategy

Question: Pizza of Gaithersburg, Maryland, owned five pizza shops. Pizza arranged with Virginia Coffee Service to install soft drink machines in each of its stores and maintain them. The contract made no mention of the rights of either party to delegate. Virginia Coffee delegated its duties to the Macke Co., leading to litigation between Pizza and Macke. Pizza claimed that Virginia Coffee was barred from delegating because Pizza had a close working relationship with the president of Virginia Coffee, who personally kept the machines in working order. Was the delegation legal?

Strategy: Any contractual duty may be delegated except in the three instances listed above. Does one of those prohibitions apply? (See the "Result" at the end of this section.)

7. **DISCHARGE**   Unless the obligee agrees otherwise, delegation does not discharge the delegator's duty to perform. (p. 347)

8. **NOVATION**   A *novation* is a three-way agreement in which the obligor delegates all duties to the delegatee and the obligee agrees to hold only the delegatee responsible. (pp. 349–350)

EXAM Strategy

Question: Mardy, a general contractor, is building a house. He contracts with Plumbco to do all plumbing work for $120,000. Before Plumbco begins the work, it notifies Mardy in writing that Leo will be doing the work instead. Mardy does not respond. When Leo fails to perform, Mardy sues Plumbco. Plumbco is

(a) Liable

(b) Liable only if Plumbco agreed to remain responsible for the job

(c) Not liable because Mardy failed to repudiate the delegation

(d) Not liable because Plumbco validly delegated its duties

(e) Not liable because the parties entered into a novation

Strategy: Delegation does not by itself relieve the delegator of his own liability to perform the contract. In a novation, the obligee agrees to look only to the third party for performance. Was this a delegation or a novation? (See the "Result" at the end of this section.)

3. Result: Truck Equipment's winning argument was one sentence long: Claims for personal injury may not be assigned. Such assignments would transform accident claims into commercial commodities and encourage assignees to exaggerate the gravity of the harm.

6. Result: There is no public policy issue involved. The contract is silent as to delegation. And Pizza's only legitimate interest was in seeing that installation and maintenance were adequate. There is no reason to believe that Virginia Coffee would perform the work better than others. The duty was delegable, and Virginia Coffee wins.

8. Result: When Plumbco announced that Leo would do the work, Mardy did not respond. Mardy certainly did not agree to look exclusively to Leo for performance. There has not been a novation, and Plumbco remains liable on the contract. The correct answer is (a).

MULTIPLE-CHOICE QUESTIONS

1. **CPA QUESTION** Yost contracted with Egan for Yost to buy certain real property. If the contract is otherwise silent, Yost's rights under the contract are:

(a) Assignable only with Egan's consent

(b) Nonassignable because they are personal to Yost

(c) Nonassignable as a matter of law

(d) Generally assignable

2. **CPA QUESTION** One of the criteria for a valid assignment of a sales contract to a third party is that the assignment must:

   (a) Not materially increase the other party's risk or duty

   (b) Not be revocable by the assignor

   (c) Be supported by adequate consideration from the assignee

   (d) Be in writing and signed by the assignor

3. Amanda agrees to pay Jennifer $300 for a pair of tickets to see Jerry Seinfeld. "Seinfeld is my boyfriend Octavio's favorite comedian, and the tickets will be a great birthday present for him," she tells Jennifer. Amanda pays up and tells a delighted Octavio about the tickets, but Jennifer never delivers them. Octavio is a(n) _____ beneficiary of the agreement, and as such, he _____ have a right to enforce the contract himself.

   (a) donee; does

   (b) donee; does not

   (c) incidental; does

   (d) incidental; does not

4. A novation completely releases an _____ from any further liability. To be effective, it _____ require the agreement of both the obligor and obligee.

   (a) obligor; does

   (b) obligor; does not

   (c) obligee; does

   (d) obligee; does not

5. Will misses three straight payments on his SUV, and his bank repossesses it. The right to repossess _____ a security interest. Security interests are governed by Article _____ of the Uniform Commercial Code.

   (a) is; 2

   (b) is; 9

   (c) is not; 2

   (d) is not; 9

ESSAY QUESTIONS

1. Intercontinental Metals Corp. (IMC) contracted with the accounting firm of Cherry, Bekaert, & Holland to perform an audit. Cherry issued its opinion about IMC, giving all copies of its report directly to the company. IMC later permitted Dun & Bradstreet to examine the statements, and Raritan River Steel Co. saw a report published by Dun & Bradstreet. Relying on the audit, Raritan sold IMC $2.2 million worth of steel on credit, but IMC promptly went bankrupt. Raritan sued Cherry, claiming that IMC was not as sound as Cherry had reported and that the accounting firm had breached its contract with IMC. Comment on Raritan's suit.

2. Woodson Walker and Associates leased computer equipment from Park Ryan Leasing. The lease said nothing about assignment. Park Ryan then assigned the lease to TCB as security for a loan. Park Ryan defaulted on its loan, and Walker failed to make several payments on the lease. TCB sued Walker for the lease payments. Was the assignment valid, given the fact that the original lease made no mention of it? If the assignment was valid, may Walker raise defenses against TCB that it could have raised against Park Ryan?

3. C. Gaston Whiddon owned Gaston's LP Gas Co., Inc. Curtis Dufour purchased the company. Since Whiddon had personally operated the company for many years, Dufour was worried about competition from him and insisted on a noncompetition clause in the sales contract. The clause stated that Whiddon would not "compete with Gaston's LP Gas Co. anywhere south of Interstate Highway 20 for nine years." Three years later, the Herring Gas Co. offered to buy all of Dufour's gas business, assuming that Whiddon would not be a competitor for six more years. Dufour sold all of the assets to Herring, keeping the actual corporation "Gaston's LP Gas Co." for himself. What mistake in drafting have Dufour and Herring made?

4. **YOU BE THE JUDGE WRITING PROBLEM** David Ricupero suspected his wife Polly of having an affair, so he taped her phone conversations and, based on what he heard, sued for divorce. David's lawyer, William Wuliger, had the recorded conversations transcribed for use at trial. The parties settled the divorce out of court and signed an agreement that included this clause:

   > Except as herein otherwise provided, each party hereto completely and forever releases the other and his attorneys from any and all rights each has or may have … to any property, privileges, or benefits accruing to either by virtue of their marriage, or conferred by the Statutory or Common Law of Ohio or the United States of America.

   After the divorce was final, Polly sued William Wuliger for invasion of privacy and violation of federal wiretapping law. Wuliger moved to dismiss the case based on the clause quoted. Polly argued that Wuliger was not a party to the divorce settlement and had no right to enforce it. May Wuliger enforce the waiver clause from the Ricuperos' divorce settlement? **Argument for Wuliger:** The contract language demonstrates that the parties intended to release one another and their attorneys from any claims. That makes Wuliger an intended third party beneficiary, and he is entitled to enforce the agreement. If Polly did not want to release Wuliger from such claims, she was free not to sign the agreement. **Argument for Polly Ricupero:** A divorce agreement settles the affairs between the couple. That is all it is ever intended to do, and the parties here never intended to benefit a lawyer. Wuliger is only an incidental beneficiary and cannot use this contract to paper over his violation of federal wiretapping law.

5. Judith and John Brooks hired Wayne Hayes to build a house. The contract required Hayes to "provide all necessary labor and materials and perform all work of every nature whatsoever to be done in the erection of the residence." Hayes hired subcontractors to do all of the work. One of Hayes's employees checked on the work site daily, but neither Hayes nor any of his employees actively supervised the building. The Brookses were aware of this working arrangement and consented to it. The mason negligently installed the fireplace, ultimately leading to a serious fire. The Brookses sued Hayes for breach of contract. Hayes contended that when the Brookses approved of his hiring of subcontractors to do all work, that created a novation relieving him of any liability. Discuss.

Discussion Questions

1. A century and a half ago, an English judge stated: "All painters do not paint portraits like Sir Joshua Reynolds, nor landscapes like Claude Lorraine, nor do all writers write dramas like Shakespeare or fiction like Dickens. Rare genius and extraordinary skill are not transferable." What legal doctrine is the judge describing? What is the ethical basis of this rule?

2. Nationwide Discount Furniture hired Rampart Security to install an alarm in its warehouse. A fire would set off an alarm in Rampart's office, and the security company was then supposed to notify Nationwide immediately. A fire did break out, but Rampart allegedly failed to notify Nationwide, causing the fire to spread next door and damage a building owned by Gasket Materials Corp. Gasket sued Rampart for breach of contract, and Rampart moved for summary judgment. Comment.

3. If a person promises to give you a gift, there is usually no consideration. The person can change his mind and decide not to give you the present, and there is nothing you can do about it. But if a person makes a contract with *someone else* and intends that you will receive a gift under the agreement, you are a donee beneficiary and you *do* have rights to enforce the deal. Are these rules unacceptably inconsistent? If so, which rule should change?

4. Imagine that you hire your trusted friend, Fran, to paint your house, and that you do not include a nondelegation clause in the agreement. Fran delegates the job to Sam, who is a stranger to you. The delegation is legal, but should it be? Is it reasonable that you must accept the substitute painter?

5. In our society, a person can buy and sell almost anything. But as this chapter describes, you cannot sell personal injury claims. Should you be able to? Imagine that you are injured in a car wreck. You are told that you might win $100,000 in a lawsuit eventually, but that you might not receive payment for years, and you might also lose the case and recover nothing. If someone is willing to pay you $20,000 cash-on-the-barrelhead today for the rights to your claim, is it fair that public policy concerns prohibit you from taking the money?

CHAPTER 16

PERFORMANCE AND DISCHARGE

nuttakit/Shutterstock.com; © neelsky/Shutterstock.com

Polly was elated. It was the grand opening of her new restaurant, Polly's Folly, and everything was bubbling. The wait staff hustled, and Caesar, the chef, churned out succulent dishes. Polly had signed a contract promising him $1,500 per week for one year, "provided Polly is personally satisfied with his cooking." Polly was determined that her restaurant would be glorious. Her three-year lease would cost $6,000 per month, and she had signed an advertising deal with Billboard Bonanza for the same period. Polly had also promised Eddie, a publicity agent, a substantial monthly fee, to begin as soon as the restaurant was 80 percent booked for one month. Tonight, with candles flickering at packed tables, Polly beamed.

After a week, Polly's smiles were a bit forced. Some of Caesar's new dishes had been failures, including a grilled swordfish that was hard to pierce and shrimp jambalaya that was too spicy. The restaurant was only 60 percent full, and the publicity agent yelled at Caesar for costing him money. Later that month, Polly disliked a veal dish and gagged on one of Caesar's soups. She fired her chef.

> Polly disliked a veal dish and gagged on one of Caesar's soups. She fired her chef.

Then troubles gushed forth—literally. A water main burst in front of Polly's restaurant, flooding the street. The city embarked on a two-month repair job that ultimately took four times that long. The street was closed to traffic, and no one could park within blocks of Polly's restaurant. Patronage dropped steadily as hungry customers refused to deal with the bad parking and construction noise. After several months, behind on the rent and in debt to everyone, Polly closed her doors for good.

Shortly, the court doors swung open, offering a full menu of litigation. Polly's landlord sued for three years' rent, and Billboard Bonanza demanded its money for the same period. Caesar claimed his year's pay. Eddie, the agent, insisted on some money for his hard work. Polly defended vigorously, seeking to be *discharged* from her various contracts.

If a party is **discharged**, she is "finished," and has no more duties under a contract. In each lawsuit, Polly asked a court to declare that her obligations were terminated and that she owed no money.

Most contracts are discharged by full performance. In other words, the parties generally do what they promise. Suppose, before the restaurant opened, Walter had promised to deliver 100 sets of cutlery to Polly and she had promised to pay $20 per set. Walter delivered the goods on time, and Polly paid $2,000 on delivery. The parties got what they expected, and that contract was fully discharged.

Sometimes the parties discharge a contract by agreement. For example, the parties may agree to **rescind** their contract, meaning that they terminate it by mutual agreement.[1] If Polly's landlord believed he could get more rent from a new tenant, he might agree to rescind her lease. But he was dubious about the rental market and refused to rescind.

At times, a court may discharge a party who has not performed. When things have gone amiss, a judge must interpret the contract and issues of public policy to determine who in fairness should suffer the loss. In the lawsuits brought by the landlord and Billboard Bonanza, Polly argued a defense called "commercial impracticability," claiming that she should not be forced to rent space that was useless to her or buy advertising for a restaurant that had closed. From Polly's point of view, the claim was understandable. But we can also respect the arguments made by the landlord and the advertiser, that they did not cause the burst water main. Claims of commercial impracticability are difficult to win, and Polly lost against both of these opponents. Though she was making no money at all from the restaurant, the court found her liable in full for the lease and the advertising contract.[2]

Polly's argument against Caesar raised another issue of discharge. Caesar claimed that his cooking was good professional work and that all chefs have occasional disasters, especially in a new restaurant. But Polly responded that they had a "personal satisfaction" contract. Under such contracts, "good" work may not suffice if it fails to please the promisee. Polly won this argument, and Caesar recovered nothing.

As to Eddie's suit, Polly raised a defense called "condition precedent," meaning that some event had to occur before she was obligated to pay. Polly claimed that she owed Eddie money only if and when the restaurant was

Discharged

A party is discharged when she has no more duties under the contract.

Rescind

To terminate a contract by mutual agreement.

---

[1]The parties could also decide that one party's duties will be performed by someone else, a modification called a **novation**. Alternatively, they could create an **accord and satisfaction**, in which they agree that one party will substitute a new kind of performance in place of his contract obligations. See Chapter 15, on third parties, and Chapter 11, on consideration.

[2]Based on *Luminous Neon v. Parscale*, 17 Kan. App. 2d 241, 836 P.2d 1201, 1992 Kan. App. LEXIS 572 (Kan. Ct. App. 1992).

80 percent full for a month, and that had never happened. The court agreed and discharged Polly on Eddie's claim.

We will analyze each of these issues, and begin with a look at conditions.

16-1 CONDITIONS

Condition

An event that must occur before a party becomes obligated under a contract.

Parties often put conditions in a contract. A **condition** is an event that must occur before a party becomes obligated under a contract. "I'll agree to do something, but only if something else happens first." Polly agreed to pay Eddie, the agent, a percentage of her profits, but with an important condition: 80 percent of the tables had to be booked for a month. Unless and until those tables were occupied, Polly owed Eddie nothing. That never happened, or, in contract language, the *condition failed*, and so Polly was discharged.

Conditions can take many forms. Alex would like to buy Kevin's empty lot and build a movie theater on it, but the city's zoning law will not permit that kind of business in that location. Alex signs a contract to buy Kevin's empty lot in 120 days, *provided that* within 100 days, the city re-zones the area to permit a movie theater. If the city fails to re-zone the area by day 100, Alex is discharged and need not complete the deal.

Another example: Friendly Insurance issues a policy covering Vivian's house, promising to pay for any loss due to fire, but only if Vivian furnishes proof of her losses within 60 days of the damage. If the house burns down, Friendly becomes liable to pay. But if Vivian arrives with her proof 70 days after the fire, she collects nothing. Friendly, though it briefly had a duty to pay, was discharged when Vivian failed to furnish the necessary information on time.

16-1a How Conditions Are Created

EXPRESS CONDITIONS

The parties may expressly state a condition. Alex's contract with Kevin expressly discharged all obligations if the city failed to re-zone within the stated period. Notice that **no special language is necessary to create the condition**. Phrases such as "provided that" frequently indicate a condition, but neither those nor any other specific words are essential. So long as the contract's language indicates that the parties *intended* to create a condition, a court will enforce it.

Because informal language can create a condition, the parties may dispute whether they intended one or not. Sand Creek Country Club, in Indiana, was eager to expand its clubhouse facilities and awarded the design work to CSO Architects. The club wanted the work done quickly but had not secured financing. The architects sent a letter confirming their agreement:

> It was our intent to allow Mr. Dan Moriarty of our office to start work on your project as early as possible in order to allow you to meet the goals that you have set for next fall. Also, it was the intent of CSO to begin work on your project and delay any billings to you until your financing is in place. As I explained to you earlier, we will continue on this course until we reach a point where we can no longer continue without receiving some payment.

The club gave CSO the go-ahead to begin design work, and the architects did their work and billed Sand Creek for $33,000. But the club, unable to obtain financing, refused to pay. Sand Creek claimed that CSO's letter created a *condition* in their agreement; namely, that the club would have to pay only if and when it obtained financing. The court was unpersuaded and ruled that the parties had never intended to create an express condition. The architects were merely delaying their billing as a convenience to the club. It would be absurd, said the court, to assume that CSO intended to perform $33,000 worth of work for free.[3]

---

[3] *Sand Creek Country Club, Ltd. v. CSO Architects, Inc.*, 582 N.E.2d 872, 1991 Ind. App. LEXIS 2151 (Ind. Ct. App. 1991).

Professional sports contracts are often full of conditions. Assume that the San Francisco Giants want to sign Tony Fleet to play center field. The club considers him a fine defensive player but a dubious offensive performer. The many conditional clauses in his contract reflect hard bargaining over an athlete who may or may not become a star. The Giants guarantee Fleet only $500,000, a very modest salary by Major League Baseball standards. If the speedy outfielder appears in at least 120 games, his pay increases to $1 million. Winning a Gold Glove award is worth an extra $200,000 to him. The Giants insist on a team option to re-sign Fleet for the following season at a salary of $800,000, but if the center-fielder plays in fewer than 100 games, the team loses that right, leaving Fleet free to negotiate for higher pay with other teams.

IMPLIED CONDITIONS

At other times, the parties say nothing about a condition, but it is clear from their agreement that they have implied one. Charlotte orally rents an apartment to Hakan for one year and promises to fix any problems in the unit. It is an implied condition that Hakan will promptly notify Charlotte of anything needing repair. Although the parties have not said anything about notice, it is only common sense that Hakan must inform his landlord of defects since she will have no other way to learn of them.

16-1b Types of Conditions

Courts divide conditional clauses into three categories: (1) condition precedent, (2) condition subsequent, and (3) concurrent conditions.[4] But what they have in common is more important than any of their differences. The key to all conditional clauses is this: **If the condition does not occur, one party will probably be discharged without having to perform his obligations under a contract**.

CONDITION PRECEDENT

In this kind of condition, an event must occur *before* a duty arises. Polly's contract with Eddie concerned a condition precedent. Polly had no obligation to pay Eddie anything *unless and until* the restaurant was 80 percent full for a month. Since that never happened, she was discharged. If the parties agreed to a condition precedent, the *plaintiff* has the burden to prove that the condition happened and that the defendant was obligated to perform.

In the following case, the plaintiff claimed that it had met a condition precedent and was entitled to a payment. Not surprisingly, the defendant had a different point of view.

AMERICAN ELECTRONIC COMPONENTS, INC. v. AGERE SYSTEMS, INC.

2009 U.S. App. LEXIS 12763
Third Circuit Court of Appeals, 2009

CASE SUMMARY

Facts: American Electronic Components, Inc. (AECI), agreed to a three-year contract under which it would act as a non-exclusive sales representative for Agere Systems's surplus equipment. The contract said in part, "AECI shall

---

[4]The Restatement (Second) of Contracts has officially abandoned the terms *condition precedent* and *condition subsequent*. See Restatement §§224 et seq. But courts routinely use the terms, so it is difficult to avoid the old distinctions.

receive a percentage of the sale price for each item of equipment sold to a third party by AECI." The contract allowed Agere to sell its own equipment.

Agere announced that it planned to close a subsidiary in Madrid and sell off its surplus equipment. AECI found potential buyers for the Madrid equipment, but Agere ultimately sold the items to a different buyer.

AECI sued, arguing that it should be paid a commission because of its effort in trying to sell the Madrid equipment. It also argued that when Agere sold the equipment on its own, it had interfered with AECI's ability to fulfill the contract's condition precedent.

The trial court dismissed the complaint, and AECI appealed.

Issues: *Was a completed sale a condition precedent in this agreement? Was Agere liable for interfering with AECI's sales efforts?*

Decision: Yes, a completed sale was a condition precedent for earning a sales commission and no, Agere did not improperly interfere with AECI's sales efforts.

Reasoning: AECI relied on two arguments to prove it deserved a commission on the sale of the Madrid equipment.

First, AECI contended that because it spent substantial time and energy looking for a buyer, it was somehow owed something. The contract did not support this argument. The contract clearly set forth when AECI was owed a commission: when AECI consummated a sale of equipment. Thus, whether or not AECI expended resources to find a buyer for the Madrid equipment, simply does not matter. The contract's condition precedent was finalizing the sale, not *trying really hard* to finalize it.

Second, AECI argued that Agere improperly prevented it from fulfilling the contract's condition precedent—consummating the sale. A party may not escape its contractual duties by wrongfully preventing the performance of a condition precedent. There was no evidence that Agere engaged in subterfuge to prevent AECI from earning a commission. Agere was free to sell its own equipment.

Agere won. It did not owe a commission to AECI on the sale of the Madrid equipment.

CONDITION SUBSEQUENT

This type of condition must occur *after* a particular duty arises. If the condition does not occur, the duty is discharged. Vivian's policy with Friendly Insurance contains a condition subsequent. As soon as the fire broke out, Friendly became obligated to pay for the damage. But if Vivian failed to produce her proof of loss on time, Friendly's obligation ended—it was discharged. Note that, with a condition subsequent, it is the *defendant* who must prove that the condition occurred, relieving him of any obligation.

Condition Precedent and Condition Subsequent Compared				
	Condition Created	**Does Condition Occur?**	**Duty Is Determined**	**Result**
Condition Precedent	"Fee to be paid when restaurant is filled to 80% capacity for one month."	Condition DOES occur: restaurant is packed. Condition DOES NOT occur: Restaurant is empty.	Duty arises: Polly owes Eddie his fee. Duty never arises: Polly is discharged.	Polly pays the fee. Polly pays nothing.
	Condition Created	**Duty Is Determined**	**Does Condition Occur?**	**Result**
Condition Subsequent	"Vivian must give proof of loss within 60 days."	Fire damages property, and Friendly Insurance becomes obligated to pay Vivian.	Condition DOES occur: Vivian proves her losses within 60 days. Condition DOES NOT occur: Vivian fails to prove her losses within 60 days.	Friendly pays Vivian for her losses. Friendly is discharged and owes nothing.

© Cengage Learning

CONCURRENT CONDITIONS

Here, both parties have a duty to perform *simultaneously*. Renee agrees to sell her condominium to Tim on July 5. Renee agrees to furnish a valid deed and clear title to the property on that date, and Tim promises to present a cashier's check for $200,000. The parties have agreed to concurrent conditions. Each performance is the condition for the other's performance. If Renee arrives at the Registry of Deeds and can say only, "Don't worry. I'm totally sure I own this property," Tim need not present his check; similarly, if Tim arrives with only an "IOU" scribbled on the back of a candy wrapper, Renee has no duty to hand over a valid deed.

EXAM Strategy

Question: Roberto wants to buy Naomi's house for $350,000 and is willing to make a 20 percent down payment, which satisfies Naomi. However, he needs a $280,000 mortgage in order to complete the purchase, and he is not certain he can obtain one. Naomi is worried that Roberto might change his mind about buying the house and then use alleged financing problems to skip out of the deal. How can the two parties protect themselves?

Strategy: Both parties should use conditional clauses in the sales agreement. Naomi must force Roberto to do his best to obtain a mortgage. How? Roberto's clause should protect him if he cannot obtain a sufficient mortgage. How?

Result: Naomi should demand the 20 percent down payment. Further, her conditional clause should state that Roberto forfeits the down payment unless he demonstrates that, within two weeks, he has applied in good faith for a mortgage to at least three banks. Roberto should insist that if he promptly and fully applies to three banks but fails to obtain a mortgage, his down payment is refunded.

PUBLIC POLICY

At times, a court will refuse to enforce an express condition on the grounds that it is unfair and harmful to the general public. In other words, a court might agree that the parties created a conditional clause but conclude that permitting its enforcement would hurt society. Did the insurance contract in the following case harm society? You be the judge.

You Be the Judge

Facts: On November 26, a Country Life Insurance agent went to the house of Donald and Anna Mae Anderson. He persuaded the Andersons to buy a life insurance policy and accepted a check for $1,600. He gave the Andersons a "conditional receipt for medical policy," dated that day. The form stated that the Andersons would have a valid

ANDERSON V. COUNTRY LIFE INSURANCE CO.

180 Ariz. 625, 886 P.2d 1381, 1994 Ariz. App. LEXIS 240 Arizona Court of Appeals, 1994

life insurance policy with Country Life, effective November 26, but only when all conditions were met. The most important of these conditions was that the Country Life home office accepts the Andersons as medical risks. The Andersons were pleased with the new policy and glad that it was effective that same day.

It was not. Donald Anderson died of a heart attack a few weeks later. Country Life declined the Andersons as medical risks and refused to issue a policy. Anna Mae Anderson sued. Country Life pointed out that medical approval was a condition precedent. In other words, the company argued that the policy would be effective as of November 26, but only if it later decided to make the policy effective. Based on this argument, the trial court gave summary judgment for Country Life. Ms. Anderson appealed, claiming that the conditional clause was a violation of public policy.

You Be the Judge: *Did the conditional clause violate public policy?*

Argument for Ms. Anderson: Your honors, this policy is a scam. This so-called "conditional receipt for medical policy" is designed to trick customers and then steal their money. The company leads people to believe they are covered as of the day they write the check. But they aren't covered until *much later*, when the insurer gets around to deciding the applicant's medical status.

The company gets the customer's money right away and gives nothing in exchange. If the company, after taking its time, decides the applicant is not medically fit, it returns the money, having used it for weeks or even months to earn interest. If, on the other hand, the insurance company decides the applicant is a good bet, it then issues the policy effective for weeks or months *in the past, when coverage is of no use.* No one can die retroactively, your honors. The company is being paid for a period during which it had no risk. This is a fraud and a disgrace, and the company should pay the benefits it owes.

Argument for Country Life: Your honors, is Country Life supposed to issue life insurance policies without doing a medical check? That is the road to bankruptcy and would mean that no one could obtain this valuable coverage. Of course we do a medical inquiry, as quickly as possible. It's in our interest to get the policy decided one way or the other.

The policy clearly stated that coverage was effective *only when approved by the home office,* after all inquiries were made. The Andersons knew that as well as the agent. If they were covered immediately, why would the company do a medical check? Country Life resents suggestions that this policy is a scam, when in reality it is Ms. Anderson who is trying to profit from a tragedy that the company had nothing to do with.

The facts of this case are unusual. Obviously, most insureds do not die between application and acceptance. It would be disastrous for society to rewrite every insurance policy in this state based on one very sad fact pattern. The contract was clear and it should be enforced as written.

16-2 PERFORMANCE

Caitlin has an architect draw up plans for a monumental new house, and Daniel agrees to build it by September 1. Caitlin promises to pay $900,000 on that date. The house is ready on time, but Caitlin has some complaints. The living room was supposed to be 18 feet high, but it is only 17 feet; the pool was to be azure, yet it is aquamarine; the maid's room was not supposed to be wired for cable television, but it is. Caitlin refuses to pay anything for the house. Is she justified? Of course not, it would be absurd to give her a magnificent house for free when it has only tiny defects. But in this easy answer lurks a danger. Technically, Daniel did breach the contract, and yet the law allows him to recover the full contract price, or virtually all of it. Once that principle is established, how far will a court stretch it? Suppose the living room is only 14 feet high, or 12 feet, or 5 feet? What if the foundation has a small crack? A vast and dangerous split? What if Daniel finishes the house a month late? Six months late? Three years late? At some point, a court will conclude that Daniel has so thoroughly botched the job that he deserves little or no money. But where, exactly, is that point? This is a question that businesses—and judges—face often.

The more complex a contract, the more certain that at least one party will perform imperfectly. Nearly every house ever built has at least some small defects. A delivery of a thousand bushels of apples is sure to include a few rotten ones. A custom-designed computer system for a huge airline is likely to have some glitches. The cases raise several related doctrines, all concerning *how well* a party performed its contractual obligations.

16-2a Strict Performance and Substantial Performance

STRICT PERFORMANCE

When Daniel built Caitlin's house with three minor defects, she refused to pay, arguing that he had not *strictly performed* his obligations. Her assertion was correct, yet she lost anyway. Courts dislike strict performance because it enables one party to benefit without paying and sends the other one home empty-handed. A party is generally not required to render **strict performance** unless the contract expressly demands it *and* such a demand is reasonable. Caitlin's contract never suggested that Daniel would forfeit all payment if there were minor problems. Even if Caitlin had insisted on such a clause, few courts would have enforced it because the requirement would be unreasonable for a project as complicated as the construction of a $900,000 home.

There are some cases where strict performance does make sense. Marshall agrees to deliver 500 sweaters to Leo's store, and Leo promises to pay $20,000 cash on delivery. If Leo has only $19,000 cash and a promissory note for $1,000, he has failed to perform, and Marshall need not give him the sweaters. Leo's payment represents 95 percent of what he promised, but there is a big difference between getting the last $1,000 in cash and receiving a promissory note for that amount.

Strict performance
Requires one party to perform its obligations precisely, with no deviation from the contract terms.

SUBSTANTIAL PERFORMANCE

Daniel, the house builder, won his case against Caitlin because he fulfilled *most* of his obligations, even though he did an imperfect job. Courts often rely on the substantial performance doctrine, especially in cases involving services as opposed to those concerning the sale of goods or land. In a contract for services, a party that **substantially performs** its obligations will generally receive the full contract price, minus the value of any defects. Daniel receives $900,000, the contract price, minus the value of a ceiling that is 1 foot too low, a pool the wrong color, and so forth. It will be for the trial court to decide how much those defects are worth. If the court decides the low ceiling is a $10,000 defect, the pool color is worth $5,000, and the cable television wiring error is worth $500, then Daniel receives $884,500

On the other hand, a **party that fails to perform substantially receives nothing on the contract itself and will recover only the value of the work, if any.** If the foundation cracks in Caitlin's house and the walls collapse, Daniel will not receive his $900,000. In such a case, he collects only the market value of the work he has done, which, since the house is a pile of rubble, is probably zero.

When is performance substantial? There is no perfect test, but courts look at these issues:

Substantially performs
Occurs when one party fulfills enough of its contract obligations to warrant payment.

- How much benefit has the promisee received?

- If it is a construction contract, can the owner use the thing for its intended purpose?

- Can the promisee be compensated with money damages for any defects?

- Did the promisor act in good faith?

EXAM Strategy

Question: Jade owns a straight track used for drag racing. She hires Trevor to resurface it, for $180,000, paying $90,000 down. When the project is completed, Jade refuses to pay the balance and sues Trevor for her down payment. He counterclaims for the $90,000 still due. At trial, Trevor proves that all of the required materials were applied by trained workers in an expert fashion, the dimensions were perfect, and his profit margin very modest. The head of the national drag racing association testifies that his group considers the strip unsafe. He noticed puddles in both asphalt lanes, found the concrete starting pads unsafe, and believed the racing surface needed to be ground off and reapplied. His organization refuses to sanction races at the track until repairs are made. Who wins the suit?

Strategy: When one party has performed imperfectly, we have an issue of substantial performance. To decide whether Trevor is entitled to his money, we apply four factors: (1) How much benefit did Jade receive? (2) Can she use the racing strip for its intended purpose? (3) Can Jade be compensated for defects? (4) Did Trevor act in good faith?

Result: Jade has received no benefit whatsoever. She cannot use her drag strip for racing. Compensation will not help Jade—she needs a new strip. Trevor's work must be ripped up and replaced. Trevor may have acted in good faith, but he failed to deliver what Jade bargained for. Jade wins all of the money she paid. (As we will see in the next chapter, she may also win additional sums for her lost profits.)

16-2b Personal Satisfaction Contracts

Sujata, president of a public relations firm, hires Ben to design a huge multimedia project for her company, involving computer software, music, and live actors, all designed to sell frozen bologna sandwiches to supermarkets. His contract guarantees him two years' employment, provided all of his work "is acceptable in the sole judgment of Sujata." Ben's immediate supervisor is delighted with his work and his colleagues are impressed, but Sujata is not. Three months later, she fires him, claiming that his work is "uninspired." Does she have the right to do that?

Personal satisfaction contract

Permits the promisee to make a subjective evaluation of the promisor's performance.

This is a **personal satisfaction contract**, in which the promisee makes a personal, subjective evaluation of the promisor's performance. Employment contracts may require personal satisfaction of the employer; agreements for the sale of goods may demand that the buyer be personally satisfied with the product; and deals involving a credit analysis of one party may insist that his finances be satisfactory to the other party. In resolving disputes like Ben and Sujata's, judges must decide: When is it *fair* for the promisee to claim that she is not satisfied? May she make that decision for any reason at all, even on a whim?

A court applies a subjective standard only if assessing the work involves personal feelings, taste, or judgment and the contract explicitly demanded personal satisfaction. A "subjective standard" means that the promisee's personal views will greatly influence her judgment, even if her decision is foolish and unfair. Artistic or creative work, or highly specialized tasks designed for a particular employer, may involve subtle issues of quality and personal preference. Ben's work combines several media and revolves around his judgment. Accordingly, the law applies a subjective standard to Sujata's decision. Since she concludes that his work is uninspired, she may legally fire him, even if her decision is irrational.

> ## Either the system works or it does not.

Note that the promisee, Sujata, has to show two things: that assessing Ben's work involves her personal judgment *and* that their contract explicitly demands personal satisfaction. If the contract were vague on this point, Sujata would lose. Had the agreement merely said, "Ben will at all times make his best efforts," Sujata could not fire him.

In all other cases, a court applies an *objective* standard to the promisee's decision. In other words, the objective standard will be used if assessing the work does not involve personal judgment *or* if the contract failed to explicitly demand personal satisfaction. An objective standard means that the promisee's judgment of the work must be reasonable.

Suppose Sujata hires Leila to install an alarm system for her company, and the contract requires that Sujata be "personally satisfied." Leila's system passes all tests, but Sujata claims, "It just doesn't make me feel secure. I know that someday it's going to break down." May Sujata refuse to pay? No. Even though the contract used the phrase "personally satisfied," a mechanical alarm system does not involve personal judgment and taste. Either the system works or it does not. A reasonable person would find that Leila's system is just fine and therefore, under the objective standard, Sujata must pay. The law strongly favors the objective standard because the subjective standard gives unlimited power to the promisee.

16-2c Good Faith

The parties to a contract must carry out their obligations in good faith. The difficulty, of course, is applying this general rule to the wide variety of problems that may arise when people or companies do business. How far must one side go to meet its good faith burden? Marvin Shuster was a physician in Florida. Three patients sued him for alleged malpractice. Shuster denied any wrongdoing and asked his insurer to defend the claims. But the insurance company settled all three claims without defending and with a minimum of investigation. Shuster paid nothing out of his own pocket, but he sued the insurance company, claiming that it acted in bad faith. The doctor argued that the company's failure to defend him caused emotional suffering and meant that it would be impossible for him to obtain new malpractice insurance. The Florida Supreme Court found that the insurer acted in good faith. The contract clearly gave all control of malpractice cases to the company. It could settle or defend as it saw fit. Here, the company considered it more economical to settle quickly, and Shuster should have known, from the contract language, that the insurer might choose to do so.[5]

In the following case, one party to a contract played its cards very close to its chest. Too close?

BRUNSWICK HILLS RACQUET CLUB INC. v. ROUTE 18 SHOPPING CENTER ASSOCIATES

182 N.J. 210 864 A.2d 387
Supreme Court of New Jersey, 2005

CASE SUMMARY

Facts: Brunswick Hills Racquet Club (Brunswick) owned a tennis club on property that it leased from Route 18 Shopping Center Associates (Route 18). The lease ran for 25 years, and Brunswick had spent about $1 million in capital improvements. The lease expired March 30, 2002. Brunswick had the option of either buying the property or purchasing a 99-year lease, both on very favorable terms. To exercise its option, Brunswick had to notify Route 18 no later than September 30, 2001, and had to pay the option price of $150,000. If Brunswick failed to exercise its options, the existing lease automatically renewed as of September 30, for 25 more years, but at more than triple the current rent.

In February, 2000—19 months before the option deadline—Brunswick's lawyer, Gabriel Spector, wrote to Rosen Associates, the company that managed Route 18, stating that Brunswick intended to exercise the option for a 99-year lease. He requested that the lease be sent well in advance so that he could review it. He did not make the required payment of $150,000.

---

[5]*Shuster v. South Broward Hospital Dist. Physicians' Prof. Liability Ins. Trust*, 591 So. 2d 174, 1992 Fla. LEXIS 20 (Fla. 1992).

In March, Rosen replied that it had forwarded Spector's letter to its attorney, who would be in touch. In April, Spector again wrote, asking for a reply from Rosen or its lawyer.

Over the next six months, Spector continually asked for a copy of the lease, or information, but neither Route 18's lawyer nor anyone else provided any data. In January 2001, Spector renewed his requests for a copy of the lease. Route 18's lawyer never replied. Sadly, in May 2001, after a long illness, Spector died. In August 2001, Spector's law partner, Arnold Levin, wrote to Rosen, again stating Brunswick's intention to buy the 99-year lease and requesting a copy of all relevant information. He received no reply, and the September deadline passed.

In February 2002, Route 18's lawyer dropped the hammer, notifying Levin that Brunswick could not exercise its option to lease because it had failed to pay the $150,000 by September 30, 2001.

Brunswick sued, claiming that Route 18 had breached its duty of good faith and fair dealing. The trial court found that Route 18 had no duty to notify Brunswick of impending deadlines and gave summary judgment for Route 18. The appellate court affirmed, and Brunswick appealed to the state supreme court.

Issue: *Did Route 18 breach its duty of good faith and fair dealing?*

Decision: Yes, Route 18 breached its duty of good faith and fair dealing.

Reasoning: Courts generally should not tinker with precisely drafted agreements entered into by experienced businesspeople. Nonetheless, every party to a contract is bound by a duty of good faith and fair dealing in its performance. Good faith is conduct that conforms to community standards of decency and reasonableness. Neither party may do anything that will prevent the other from receiving the contract benefits.

Route 18 and its agents acted in bad faith. Nineteen months before the deadline, Brunswick Hills notified the landlord that it intended to exercise its option to purchase a 99-year lease. Brunswick Hills mistakenly believed that its payment was not due until closing. During that year and a half, Route 18 engaged in a pattern of evasion, sidestepping every request by Brunswick Hills to move forward on closing the lease. After Spector's death, Route 18's lawyer continued to play possum despite the obvious risk to Brunswick Hills. Route 18 acknowledged that it did not want the lease payment because the long-term lease was not in its financial interest.

Neither a landlord nor its attorney is required to act as his brother's keeper. However, there are ethical norms that apply even in the harsh world of commercial transactions. All parties must behave in good faith and deal fairly with the other side. Brunswick Hills' repeated letters and calls to close the lease placed an obligation on Route 18 to respond in a timely, honest manner. The company failed to do that, and Brunswick Hills is entitled to exercise the 99-year lease.

EXAM Strategy

Question: Sun operates an upscale sandwich shop in New Jersey, in a storefront that she leases from Ricky for $18,000 per month. The lease, which expires soon, allows Sun to renew for five years at $22,000 per month. Ricky knows, but Sun does not, that in a year, Prada will open a store on the same block. The dramatic increase in pedestrian traffic will render Sun's space more valuable. Ricky says nothing about Prada, Sun declines to renew, and Ricky leases the space for $40,000 a month. Sun sues Ricky, claiming he breached his duty of good faith and fair dealing. Based on the *Brunswick Hills* case, how would the New Jersey Supreme Court rule?

Strategy: In the *Brunswick Hills* case, the court, on the one hand, criticized the defendant for cynically evading the plaintiff's efforts to renew. However, the court also said, "We do not expect a landlord or even an attorney to act as his brother's keeper in a commercial transaction." Using those opposing themes as guidelines, examine the court's decision and predict the ruling in Sun's suit.

Result: *Brunswick Hills* begins: "Courts generally should not tinker with a finely drawn and precise contract entered into by experienced business people." Sun's lease imposes no responsibility on Ricky to report on neighborhood changes or forecast profitability. Further, Sun made no requests to Ricky about the area's future. Sun is asking Ricky to be "her brother's keeper," and neither this court nor any other will do that. She loses.

16-2d Time of the Essence Clauses

Go, sir, gallop, and don't forget that the world was made in six days. You can ask me for anything you like, except time.

Napoleon, to an aide, 1803

Generals are not the only ones who place a premium on time. Ask Gene LaSalle. The Seabreeze Restaurant agreed to sell him all of its assets. The parties signed a contract stating the price and closing date. Seabreeze insisted on a clause saying, "Seabreeze considers that time is of the essence in consummating the proposed transaction." Such clauses are common in real estate transactions and in any other agreement where a delay would cause serious damage to one party. LaSalle was unable to close on the date specified and asked for an extension. Seabreeze refused and sold its assets elsewhere. A Florida court affirmed that Seabreeze acted legally.

A **time of the essence clause** will generally make contract deadlines strictly enforceable. Seabreeze regarded a timely sale as important, and LaSalle agreed to the provision. There was nothing unreasonable about the clause, and LaSalle suffered the consequences of his delay.[6]

Suppose the contract had named a closing date but included no time of the essence clause. If LaSalle offered to close three days late, could Seabreeze sell elsewhere? No. **Merely including a date for performance does not make time of the essence.** Courts dislike time of the essence arguments because even a short delay may mean that one party forfeits everything it expected to gain from the bargain. If the parties do not *clearly* state that prompt performance is essential, then both are entitled to reasonable delays.

Time of the essence clauses
Generally make contract dates strictly enforceable.

16-3 BREACH

When one party breaches a contract, the other party is discharged. The discharged party has no obligation to perform and may sue for damages. Edwin promises that on July 1, he will deliver 20 tuxedos, tailored to fit male chimpanzees, to Bubba's circus for $300 per suit. After weeks of delay, Edwin concedes he hasn't a cummerbund to his name. Bubba is discharged and owes nothing. In addition, he may sue Edwin for damages.

16-3a Material Breach

As we know, parties frequently perform their contract duties imperfectly, which is why courts accept substantial performance rather than strict performance, particularly in contracts involving services. In a more general sense, **courts will discharge a contract only if a party**

---

[6]*Seabreeze Restaurant, Inc. v. Paumgardhen*, 639 So. 2d 69, 1994 Fla. App. LEXIS 4546 (Fla. Dist. Ct. App. 1994).

committed a *material* **breach.** A material breach is one that substantially harms the innocent party and for which it would be hard to compensate without discharging the contract. Suppose Edwin fails to show up with the tuxedos on June 1 but calls to say they will arrive under the big top the next day. He has breached the agreement. Is his breach material? No. This is a trivial breach, and Bubba is not discharged. When the tuxedos arrive, he must pay. The following case raises the issue in the context of a major college sports program.

O'BRIEN v. OHIO STATE UNIVERSITY

2007 WL 2729077
Ohio Court of Appeals, 2007

CASE SUMMARY

Facts: The Ohio State University (OSU), experiencing a drought in its men's basketball program, brought in Coach Jim O'Brien to turn things around. He did. In only his second year, he guided the OSU Buckeyes to its best record ever. The team played in the most prestigious postseason tournament, run by the National Collegiate Athletic Association (NCAA), and won a berth in the "final four." O'Brien was named national coach of the year. OSU's athletic director promptly offered O'Brien a multi-year contract worth about $800,000 per year.

Section 5.1 of the contract included termination provisions. OSU could fire O'Brien *for cause* if (a) there was a material breach of the contract by the coach, or (b) O'Brien's conduct subjected the school to NCAA sanctions. OSU could also terminate O'Brien *without cause*, but in that case it had to pay him the full salary owed.

O'Brien began recruiting a talented 21-year-old Serbian player named Alex Radojevic. While getting to know the young man, O'Brien discovered two things. First, it appeared that Radojevic had been paid to play briefly for a Yugoslavian team, meaning that he was ineligible to play in the NCAA. Second, it was clear that Radojevic's family had suffered terribly during the strife in the Balkans.

O'Brien concluded that Radojevic would never play for OSU or any major college. He also decided to loan Radojevic's mother some money. Any such loan would violate an NCAA rule if done to recruit a player, but

O'Brien believed the loan was legal since Radojevic could not play in the NCAA anyway. Several years later, OSU learned of the loan and realized that O'Brien had never reported it. Hoping to avoid trouble with the NCAA, OSU imposed sanctions on itself. The university also fired the coach, claiming he had lied, destroyed the possibility of postseason play, and harmed the school's reputation.

O'Brien sued, claiming he had not materially breached the contract. The trial court awarded the coach $2.5 million, and OSU appealed.

Issue: *Did O'Brien materially breach the contract?*

Decision: No, he did not materially breach his contract. Affirmed.

Reasoning: OSU suffered no substantial damage. The Buckeyes played poorly in the weeks leading up to the announcement of the ban on postseason play, and they were unlikely to receive an NCAA bid.

The university's reputation was not significantly harmed because Radojevic never played for the school. Also, OSU promptly recruited a top coach to replace O'Brien. Moreover, OSU presented no evidence that O'Brien lied about the payment, tried to conceal it, or even knew that it was wrong.

Violations of NCAA rules are common. A minor violation is not necessarily a material breach. Coach O'Brien remained entitled to his $2.5 million award.

16-3b Anticipatory Breach

Sally will receive her bachelor's degree in May and already has a job lined up for September. She has signed a two-year contract to work as window display designer for Surebet Department Store. The morning of graduation, she reads in the paper that Surebet is going out of business that very day. Surebet has told Sally nothing about her status. Sally need not wait until September to learn her fate. Surebet has committed an **anticipatory breach by making it**

unmistakably clear that it will not honor the contract. Sometimes a promisor will actually inform the promisee that it will not perform its duties. At other times, as here, the promisor takes some step that makes the breach evident. Sally is discharged and may immediately seek other work. She is also entitled to file suit for breach of contract. The court will treat Surebet's anticipatory breach just as though the store had actually refused to perform on September 1.

16-3c Statute of Limitations

A party injured by a breach of contract should act promptly. A **statute of limitations** begins to run at the time of injury and will limit the time within which the injured party may file suit. These laws set time limits for filing lawsuits. Statutes of limitation vary from state to state and from issue to issue within a state. Failure to file suit within the time limits discharges the party who breached the contract. Always consult a lawyer promptly in the case of a legal injury.

Statute of limitations
A statutory time limit within which an injured party must file suit.

16-4 IMPOSSIBILITY

"Your honor, my client wanted to honor the contract. He just couldn't. *Honest*." This plea often echoes around courtrooms as one party seeks discharge without fulfilling his contract obligations. Does the argument work? It depends. If performing a contract was truly impossible, a court will discharge the agreement. But if honoring the deal merely imposed a financial burden, the law will generally enforce the contract.

16-4a True Impossibility

These cases are easy—and rare. **True impossibility means that something has happened making it literally impossible to do what the promisor said he would do.** Francoise owns a vineyard that produces Beaujolais Nouveau wine. She agrees to ship 1,000 cases of her wine to Tyrone, a New York importer, as soon as this year's vintage is ready. Tyrone will pay $50 per case. But a fungus wipes out her entire vineyard. Francoise is discharged. It is theoretically impossible for Francoise to deliver wine from her vineyard, and she owes Tyrone nothing.

Meanwhile, though, Tyrone has a contract with Jackson, a retailer, to sell 1,000 cases of Beaujolais Nouveau wine at $70 per case. Tyrone has no wine from Francoise, and the only other Beaujolais Nouveau available will cost him $85 per case. Instead of earning $20 per case, Tyrone will lose $15. Does this discharge Tyrone's contract with Jackson? No. It is possible for him to perform—it's just more expensive. He must fulfill his agreement.

True impossibility is generally limited to these three causes:

- *Destruction of the Subject Matter,* as happened with Francoise's vineyard.

- **Death of the promisor in a personal services contract.** When the promisor agrees personally to render a service that cannot be transferred to someone else, her death discharges the contract. Producer hires Josephine to write the lyrics for a new Broadway musical, but Josephine dies after writing only two words: "Act One." The contract was personal to Josephine and is now discharged. Neither Josephine's estate nor Producer has any obligation to the other. But notice that most contracts are not for personal services. Suppose that Tyrone, the wine importer, dies. His contract to sell wine to Jackson is not discharged because anyone can deliver the required wine. Tyrone's estate remains liable on the deal with Jackson.

- **Illegality.** Chet, a Silicon Valley entrepreneur, wants to capitalize on his computer expertise. He contracts with Construction Co. to build a factory in Iran that will manufacture computers for sale in that country. Construction Co. fails to build the factory on time, and Chet sues. Construction Co. defends by pointing out that the President of the United States has issued an executive order barring trade between the United States and Iran. Construction Co. wins; the executive order discharged the contract.

16-4b Commercial Impracticability and Frustration of Purpose

It is rare for contract performance to be truly impossible but very common for it to become a financial burden to one party. Suppose Bradshaw Steel in Pittsburgh agrees to deliver 1,000 tons of steel beams to Rice Construction in Saudi Arabia at a given price, but a week later, the cost of raw ore increases 30 percent. A contract once lucrative to the manufacturer is suddenly a major liability. Does that change discharge Bradshaw? Absolutely not. Rice signed the deal *precisely to protect itself against price increases.* As we have seen, the primary purpose of contracts is to enable the parties to control their future.

Yet there may be times when a change in circumstances is so extreme that it would be unfair to enforce a deal. What if a strike made it impossible for Bradshaw to ship the steel to Saudi Arabia, and the only way to deliver would be by air, at *five times* the sea cost? Must Bradshaw fulfill its deal? What if a new war meant that any ships or planes delivering the goods might be fired upon? Other changes could make the contract undesirable for *Rice.* Suppose the builder wanted steel for a major public building in Riyadh, but the Saudi government decided not to go forward with the construction. The steel would then be worthless to Rice. Must the company still accept it?

None of these hypotheticals involves true impossibility. It is physically possible for Bradshaw to deliver the goods and for Rice to receive. But in some cases, it may be so dangerous, costly, or pointless to enforce a bargain that a court will discharge it instead. Courts use the related doctrines of commercial impracticability and frustration of purpose to decide when a change in circumstances should permit one side to escape its duties.

Commercial impracticability means some event has occurred that neither party anticipated and *fulfilling the contract would now be extraordinarily difficult and unfair to one party.* If a shipping strike forces Bradshaw to ship by air, the company will argue that neither side expected the strike and that Bradshaw should not suffer a fivefold increase in shipping costs. Bradshaw will probably win the argument.

Frustration of purpose means some event has occurred that neither party anticipated and *the contract now has no value for one party.* If Rice's building project is canceled, Rice will argue that the steel now is useless to the company. Frustration cases are hard to predict. Some states would agree with Rice, but others would hold that it was Rice's obligation to protect itself with a government guarantee that the project would be completed. Courts consider the following factors in deciding impracticability and frustration claims:

- **Mere financial difficulties will never suffice to discharge a contract.** Barbara and Michael Luber divorced, and Michael agreed to pay alimony. He stopped making payments and claimed that it was impracticable for him to do so because he had hit hard times and simply did not have the money. The court dismissed his argument, noting that commercial impracticability requires some objective event that neither party anticipated, not merely the financial deterioration of one party.[7]

- **The event must have been truly unexpected.** Wayne Carpenter bought land from the state of Alaska, intending to farm it and agreeing to make monthly payments. The sales contract stated that Alaska did not guarantee the land for agriculture or any other purpose. Carpenter struggled to farm the land but failed; as soon as the ground thawed, the water

---

[7]*Luber v. Luber*, 418 Pa. Super. 542, 614 A.2d 771, 1992 Pa. Super. LEXIS 3338 (Pa. Super. Ct. 1992).

table rose too high for crops. Carpenter abandoned the land and stopped making payments. Alaska sued and won. The high court rejected Carpenter's claim of impracticability since the "event"—bad soil—was not unexpected. Alaska had warned that the land might prove unworkable, and Carpenter had no claim for commercial impracticability.[8]

- **If the promisor must use a different means to accomplish her task, at a greatly increased cost, she probably does have a valid claim of impracticability.** If a shipping strike forces Bradshaw to use a different means of delivery—say, air—and this multiplies its costs several times, the company is probably discharged. But a mere increase in the cost of raw materials, such as a 30 percent rise in the price of ore, will almost never discharge the promisor.

- **A *force majeure* clause is significant but not necessarily dispositive.** To protect themselves from unexpected events, companies sometimes include a *force majeure* clause, allowing cancellation of the agreement in case of extraordinary and unexpected events. A typical clause might permit the seller of goods to delay or cancel delivery in the event of "acts of God, fire, labor disputes, accidents, or transportation difficulties." A court will always consider a *force majeure* clause, but it may not enforce it if one party is trying to escape from routine financial problems.

Chapter Conclusion

Negotiate carefully. A casually written letter may imply a condition precedent that the author never intended. The term *personal satisfaction* should be defined so that both parties know whether one party may fire the other on a whim. Never assume that mere inconvenience or financial loss will discharge contractual duties.

EXAM REVIEW

1. **CONDITION** A condition is an event that must occur before a party becomes obligated. It may be stated expressly or implied, and no formal language is necessary to create one. (pp. 358–362)

EXAM Strategy

Question: Stephen Krogness, a real estate broker, agreed to act as an agent for Best Buy Co., which wanted to sell several of its stores. The contract provided that Best Buy would pay Krogness a commission of 2 percent for "a sale to any prospect submitted directly to Best Buy by Krogness." Krogness introduced Corporate Realty Capital (CRC) to Best Buy, and the parties negotiated but could not reach agreement. CRC then introduced Best Buy to BB Properties (BB). Best Buy sold several properties to BB for $46 million. CRC acted as the broker. Krogness sought a commission of $528,000. Is he entitled to it?

Strategy: This contract contains a conditional clause. What is it? What must occur before Best Buy is obligated to pay Krogness? Did that event happen? (See the "Result" at the end of this section.)

---

[8] *State v. Carpenter*, 869 P.2d 1181, 1994 Alaska LEXIS 23 (Alaska 1994).

2. **SUBSTANTIAL PERFORMANCE** Strict performance, which requires one party to fulfill its duties perfectly, is unusual. In construction and service contracts, substantial performance is generally sufficient to entitle the promisor to the contract price, minus the cost of defects in the work. (pp. 363–364)

3. **PERSONAL SATISFACTION** Personal satisfaction contracts are interpreted under an objective standard, requiring reasonable ground for dissatisfaction, unless the work involves personal judgment *and* the parties intended a subjective standard. (pp. 364–365)

4. **GOOD FAITH** Good faith performance is required in all contracts. (pp. 365–366)

5. **TIME OF THE ESSENCE** Time of the essence clauses result in strict enforcement of contract deadlines. (p. 367)

EXAM Strategy

Question: Colony Park Associates signed a contract to buy 44 acres of residential land from John Gall. The contract stated that closing would take place exactly one year later. The delay was to enable Colony Park to obtain building permits to develop condominiums. Colony Park worked diligently to obtain all permits, but delays in sewer permits forced Colony Park to notify Gall it could not close on the agreed date. Colony Park suggested a date exactly one month later. Gall refused the new date and declined to sell. Colony Park sued. Gall argued that since the parties specified a date, time was of the essence and Colony Park's failure to buy on time discharged Gall. Please rule.

Strategy: A time of the essence clause generally makes a contract date strictly enforceable. Was there one in this agreement? (See the "Result" at the end of this section.)

6. **MATERIAL BREACH** A material breach is the only kind that will discharge a contract; a trivial breach will not. (pp. 367–368)

7. **IMPOSSIBILITY** True impossibility means that some event has made it impossible to perform an agreement. It is typically caused by destruction of the subject matter, the death of an essential promisor, or intervening illegality. (pp. 369–371)

EXAM Strategy

Question: Omega Concrete had a gravel pit and factory. Access was difficult, so Omega contracted with Union Pacific Railroad (UP) for the right to use a private road that crossed UP property and tracks. The contract stated that use of the road was solely for Omega employees and that Omega would be responsible for closing a gate that UP planned to build where the private road joined a public highway. In fact, UP never constructed the gate; Omega had no authority to construct the gate. Mathew Rogers, an Omega employee, was killed by a train while using the private road. Rogers's family sued Omega, claiming that Omega failed to keep the gate closed as the contract required. Is Omega liable?

Strategy: True impossibility means that the promisor cannot do what he promised to do. Is this such a case? (See the "Result" at the end of this section.)

8. **COMMERCIAL IMPRACTICABILITY** Commercial impracticability means that some unexpected event has made it extraordinarily difficult and unfair for one party to perform its obligations. (pp. 370–371)

9. **FRUSTRATION OF PURPOSE** Frustration of purpose may occur when an unexpected event render/s a contract completely useless to one party. (pp. 370–371)

> **1. Result:** The conditional clause requires Best Buy to pay a commission for "a sale to any prospect submitted directly to Best Buy by Krogness." Krogness did not in fact introduce BB Properties to Best Buy. The condition has not occurred, and Best Buy is under no obligation to pay.
>
> **5. Result:** Merely including a date for performance does not make time of the essence. A party that considers a date critical must make that clear. This contract did not indicate that the closing date was vital to either party, so a short delay was reasonable. Gall was ordered to convey the land to Colony Park.
>
> **7. Result:** There was no gate, and Omega had no right to build one. This is a case of true impossibility. Omega was not liable.

MULTIPLE-CHOICE QUESTIONS

1. **CPA QUESTION** Nagel and Fields entered into a contract in which Nagel was obligated to deliver certain goods by September 10. On September 3, Nagel told Fields that he had no intention of delivering the goods. Prior to September 10, Fields may successfully sue Nagel under the doctrine of:

   (a) promissory estoppel

   (b) accord and satisfaction

   (c) anticipatory breach

   (d) substantial performance

2. Most contracts are discharged by _____.

   (a) agreement of the parties

   (b) full performance

   (c) failure of conditions

   (d) commercial impracticability

   (e) a material breach

3. If a contract contains a condition precedent, the _____ has the burden of proving that the condition actually happened. If a condition subsequent exists, the _____ has the burden of showing that the condition occurred.

   (a) plaintiff; plaintiff

   (b) plaintiff; defendant

   (c) defendant; plaintiff

   (d) defendant; defendant

4. Big Co., a construction company, builds a grocery store. The contract calls for a final price of $5 million. Big Co. incurred $4.5 million in costs and stands to make a profit of $500,000. On a final inspection, the grocery store owner is upset. His blueprints called for 24 skylights, but the finished building has only 12. Installing the additional skylights would cost $100,000. Big Co. made no other errors. How much must the grocery store owner pay Big Co.?

(a) $5,000,000

(b) $4,900,000

(c) $4,500,000

(d) $0

5. Lenny makes K2, a synthetic form of marijuana, in his basement. He signs an agreement with the Super Smoke Shop to deliver 1,000 cans of K2 for $10,000. After the contract is signed, but before the delivery, Super Smoke Shop's state legislature makes the sale of K2 illegal. Lenny's contract will be discharged because of _____.

(a) true impossibility

(b) commercial impracticability

(c) frustration of purpose

(d) None of the above

ESSAY QUESTIONS

1. **ETHICS** Commercial Union Insurance Co. (CU) insured Redux, Ltd. The contract made CU liable for fire damage but stated that the insurer would not pay for harm caused by criminal acts of any Redux employees. Fire destroyed Redux's property. CU claimed that the "criminal acts" clause was a condition precedent, but Redux asserted it was a condition subsequent. What difference does it make, and who is legally right? Does the insurance company's position raise any ethical issues? Who drafted the contract? How clear were its terms?

2. Stephen Muka owned U.S. Robotics. He hired his brother Chris to work in the company. His letter promised Chris $1 million worth of Robotics stock at the end of one year, "provided you work reasonably hard & smart at things in the next year." (We should all have such brothers.) Chris arrived at Robotics and worked the full year, but toward the end of the year, Stephen died. His estate refused to give Chris the stock, claiming their agreement was a personal satisfaction contract and only Stephen could decide whether Chris had earned the reward. Comment.

3. Ken Ward was an Illinois farmer who worked land owned by his father-in-law, Frank Ruda. To finance his operation, he frequently borrowed money from Watseka First National Bank, paying back the loans with farming profits. But Ward fell deeper and deeper into debt, and Watseka became concerned. When Ward sought additional loans, Watseka insisted that Ruda become a guarantor on all of the outstanding debt, and the father-in-law agreed. The new loans had an acceleration clause, permitting the bank to demand payment of the entire debt if it believed itself "insecure"; that is, at risk of a default. Unfortunately, just as Ward's debts reached more than $120,000, Illinois suffered a severe drought, and Ward's crops failed. Watseka asked Ruda to sell

some of the land he owned to pay back part of the indebtedness. Ruda reluctantly agreed but never did so. Meanwhile, Ward decreased his payments to the bank because of the terrible crop. Watseka then "accelerated" the loan, demanding that Ruda pay off the entire debt. Ruda defended by claiming that Watseka's acceleration at such a difficult time was bad faith. Who should win?

4. Loehmann's clothing stores, a nationwide chain with headquarters in New York, was the anchor tenant in the Lincoln View Plaza Shopping Center in Phoenix, Arizona, with a 20-year lease from the landlord, Foundation Development, beginning in 1978. Loehmann's was obligated to pay rent the first of every month and to pay common-area charges four times a year. The lease stated that if Loehmann's failed to pay on time, Foundation could send a notice of default, and that if the store failed to pay all money due within 10 days, Foundation could evict. On February 23, 1987, Foundation sent to Loehmann's the common-area charges for the quarter ending January 31, 1987. The balance due was $3,500. Loehmann's believed the bill was in error and sent an inquiry on March 18, 1987. On April 10, 1987, Foundation insisted on payment of the full amount within 10 days. Foundation sent the letter to the Loehmann's store in Phoenix. On April 13, 1987, the Loehmann's store received the bill and, since it was not responsible for payments, forwarded it to the New York office. Because the company had moved offices in New York, a Loehmann's officer did not see the bill until April 20. Loehmann's issued a check for the full amount on April 24 and mailed it the following day. On April 28, Foundation sued to evict; on April 29, the company received Loehmann's check. Please rule.

5. **YOU BE THE JUDGE WRITING PROBLEM** Kuhn Farm Machinery, a European company, signed an agreement with Scottsdale Plaza Resort, of Arizona, to use the resort for its North American dealers' convention during March 1991. Kuhn agreed to rent 190 guest rooms and spend several thousand dollars on food and beverages. Kuhn invited its top 200 independent dealers from the United States and Canada and about 25 of its own employees from the United States, Europe, and Australia, although it never mentioned those plans to Scottsdale.

On August 2, 1990, Iraq invaded Kuwait, and on January 16, 1991, the United States and allied forces were at war with Iraq. Saddam Hussein and other Iraqi leaders threatened terrorist acts against the United States and its allies. Kuhn became concerned about the safety of those traveling to Arizona, especially its European employees. By mid-February, 11 of the top 50 dealers with expense-paid trips had either canceled their plans to attend or failed to sign up. Kuhn postponed the convention. The resort sued. The trial court discharged the contract under the doctrines of commercial impracticability and frustration of purpose. The resort appealed. Did commercial impracticability or frustration of purpose discharge the contract? **Argument for Scottsdale Plaza Resort:** The resort had no way of knowing that Kuhn anticipated bringing executives from Europe, and even less reason to expect that if anything interfered with their travel, the entire convention would become pointless. Most of the dealers could have attended the convention, and the resort stood ready to serve them. **Argument for Kuhn:** The parties never anticipated the threat of terrorism. Kuhn wanted this convention so that its European executives, among others, could meet top North American dealers. That is now impossible. No company would risk employee lives for a meeting. As a result, the contract has no value at all to Kuhn, and its obligations should be discharged by law.

DISCUSSION QUESTIONS

1. Evans built a house for Sandra Dyer, but the house had some problems. The garage ceiling was too low. Load-bearing beams in the "great room" cracked and appeared to be steadily weakening. The patio did not drain properly. Pipes froze. Evans wanted the money promised for the job, but Dyer refused to pay. Comment.

2. Krug International, an Ohio corporation, had a contract with Iraqi Airways to build aeromedical equipment for training pilots. Krug then contracted for Power Engineering, an Iowa corporation, to build the specialized gearbox to be used in the training equipment for $150,000. Power did not know that Krug planned to resell the gearbox to Iraqi Airways. When Power had almost completed the gearbox, the Gulf War broke out and the United Nations declared an embargo on all shipments to Iraq. Krug notified Power that it no longer wanted the gearbox. Power sued. Please rule.

3. The death of a promisor in a *personal services* contract discharges an agreement. But if a promisor dies, other kinds of contracts live on. Is this sensible? Would it be better to discharge all kinds of agreements if one of the parties passes away?

4. Is commercial impracticability (such as the shipping strike described earlier in the chapter) a good reason for discharge? What about frustration of purpose (such as the cancellation of the construction project in Saudi Arabia)? Is one more justified than the other? Are parties who back out of contracts on these grounds acting reasonably?

5. Franklin J. Moneypenny hires Angela to paint his portrait. She is to be paid $50,000 if the painting is acceptable "in Franklin's sole judgment." At the big unveiling, 99 of 100 attendees think that Angela has done a masterful job. Franklin disagrees. He thinks the painting makes him look like a toad. (He does in fact look like a toad, but he does not like to contemplate this fact.) Franklin refuses to pay, and, because he signed a personal satisfaction contract, Angela gets nothing. Is this fair? Should the law allow personal satisfaction contracts?

nuttakit/Shutterstock.com; © neelsky/Shutterstock.com

REMEDIES

Ben is the general manager of an NFL football team. Driving home in his truck, he is in a sour humor. Spencer, the team's best running back, under contract to play for one more year at $2.5 million, has announced he is leaving the team to act in a new sitcom. Ben wonders whether he can stop Spencer from leaving the team. Even if it is possible, would it be worthwhile to make a disgruntled, out-of-condition athlete carry (and fumble) the ball? If Spencer leaves, it will cost at least $5 million to hire a runner with equal speed and power.

Ben's phone rings. Louise, a dealer in rare autos, has bad news.

"I hate to tell you, Ben, but the deal just fell through."

"What are you talking about? We both signed! That's a binding contract!" A seller in Florida had agreed in writing to sell Ben a 1955 Ferrari for $900,000.

"*I* know it's true, and *you* know it," Louise murmurs soothingly. "But the seller has decided he just can't part with it."

Ben slams his cell phone down, turns into his driveway—and notices that the back door is open. Did he leave it that way? No. The burglar did. Ben has lost about $100,000 worth of jewelry, clothing, and sports memorabilia. Why didn't the alarm sound? When he demands an explanation from Alarmist, his home security provider, the quality assurance representative assures Ben that he will receive the full compensation due under his contract—$600. Later that night, Ben will have a long talk with his lawyer about breached contracts and remedies.

> Ben slams his cell phone down, turns into his driveway—and notices that the back door is open. Did he leave it that way? No. The burglar did.

17-1 BREACHING A CONTRACT

Someone breaches a contract when he fails to perform a duty without a valid excuse. Spencer is legally committed to play for the team for one more year and is clearly breaching his contract when he informs the team that in the future, he will be playing for laughs. But what can the team do about the runner's breach? In other words, what is the team's *remedy?* **A remedy is the method a court uses to compensate an injured party.**

Should a court stop Spencer from performing in his new sitcom? Force him to carry the ball instead? An order forcing someone to refrain from doing something is an **injunction**. Courts frequently grant injunctions to an employer, blocking an employee from *leaving* to work elsewhere. However, courts almost never use an order to force an employee to *complete* a contract with his employer because that would force two antagonistic parties to work together. In other words, Ben can probably stop Spencer from working in television, but no court will order the running back to suit up and play.

Courts also award **expectation damages**, meaning the money required to put one party in the position he would have been in had the other side performed the contract. If Spencer's team is forced to hire another running back for double the money they expected to pay Spencer, the team will probably recover the difference between the two players' salaries.

The Ferrari seller has breached his deal with Ben. What is Ben's remedy? He does not want money damages; he wants that lovely red car. In cases of property that is rare or difficult to replace, courts often award **specific performance**, forcing both parties to complete the deal. Ben should get his car.

Finally, the alarm company is trying to *insist* upon a remedy—a very limited one, which will leave Ben largely uncompensated for the burglary. Alarmist is relying on a **liquidated damages clause**, meaning a provision in the contract that declares in advance what one party will receive if the other side breaches. Courts sometimes enforce these clauses. But as we will see later, Alarmist's liquidated damages clause may be too harsh, and thus unenforceable.

How to best help an injured party, without unfairly harming the other person, is the focus of remedies. The questions and issues created by Ben's Bad Day are typical remedy problems. Courts have struggled with remedies for centuries, but we will master the subject in one chapter.

Injunction

A court order that requires someone to do something or refrain from doing something.

Expectation damages

The money required to put one party in the position he would have been in had the other side performed the contract.

Specific performance

Forces both parties to complete the deal.

Liquidated damages clause

A provision in a contract that declares in advance what one party will receive if the other party breaches.

Ethics
Though a court may have several alternative remedies available, it is important to note that most have one thing in common: The focus is on compensating the injured party rather than punishing the party in breach. A court must decide whether to prevent Spencer from leaving the gridiron for the television studio, but it will not consider fining or jailing him.

Some critics argue that someone who willfully breaches a contract should pay a penalty. The Ferrari seller knows he is obligated to part with his car but tries to keep it anyway. Spencer blithely ignores his obligations to the team. Should a remedy reflect morality? In this chapter, we will see very few instances in which a court *punishes* unethical conduct. Is this right? Should contract law exact a price for bad behavior?

17-1a Identifying the "Interest" to Be Protected

The first step that a court takes in choosing a remedy is to decide what interest it is trying to protect. An **interest** is a legal right in something. Someone can have an interest in property, for example, by owning it, or renting it to a tenant, or lending money so someone else may

Interest

A legal right in something.

buy it. He can have an interest in a *contract* if the agreement gives him some benefit. There are four principal contract interests that a court may seek to protect:

- **Expectation interest.** This refers to what the injured party reasonably thought she would get from the contract. The goal is to put her in the position she would have been in if both parties had fully performed their obligations.

- **Reliance interest.** The injured party may be unable to demonstrate expectation damages, perhaps because it is unclear he would have profited. But he may still prove that he *spent money* in reliance on the agreement and that in fairness, he should receive compensation.

- **Restitution interest.** The injured party may be unable to show an expectation interest or reliance. But perhaps she has conferred a benefit *on the other party*. Here, the objective is to restore to the injured party the benefit she has provided.

- **Equitable interest.** In some cases, money damages will not suffice to help the injured party. Something more is needed, such as an order to transfer property to the injured party (specific performance) or an order forcing one party to stop doing something (an injunction).

In this chapter, we look at all four interests.

17-2 EXPECTATION INTEREST

This is the most common remedy that the law provides for a party injured by a breach of contract. **The expectation interest is designed to put the injured party in the position she would have been in had both sides fully performed their obligations.** A court tries to give the injured party the money she would have made from the contract. If accurately calculated, this should take into account all the gains she reasonably expected and all the expenses and losses she would have incurred. The injured party should not end up better off than she would have been under the agreement, nor should she suffer a loss.

If you ever go to law school, you will almost certainly encounter the following case during your first weeks of classes. It has been used to introduce the concept of damages in contract lawsuits for generations. Enjoy the famous "case of the hairy hand."

Landmark Case

HAWKINS V. MCGEE
84 N.H. 114, 146 A. 641
Supreme Court of New Hampshire, 1929

CASE SUMMARY

Facts: Hawkins suffered a severe electrical burn on the palm of his right hand. After years of living with disfiguring scars, he went to visit Dr. McGee, who was well known for his early attempts at skin-grafting surgery. The doctor told Hawkins "I will guarantee to make the hand a hundred percent perfect hand." Hawkins hired him to perform the operation.

McGee cut a patch of healthy skin from Hawkins's chest and grafted it over the scar tissue on Hawkins' palm. Unfortunately, the chest hair on the skin graft was very thick, and it continued to grow after the surgery. The operation resulted in a hairy palm for Hawkins. Feeling embarrassed, Hawkins sued Dr. McGee.

The trial court judge instructed the jury to consider two factors in calculating damages: (1) pain and suffering from the operation, and (2) the difference in Hawkins's condition before (with the burned palm) and after the surgery (with the hairy hand). The jury awarded Hawkins $3,000, but the court reduced the award to $500. Harried, Hawkins appealed.

Issue: *Did the jury calculate Hawkins' damages correctly?*

Decision: No. The court's instructions were wrong on both counts.

Reasoning: The jury found that the doctor's promise of "a hundred percent perfect hand" created an enforceable contract. Contract damages are intended to put the plaintiff in the position he would have been in had the defen-dant kept his part of the bargain. What would Hawkins's hand have looked like if Dr. McGee's had kept his promise? It certainly would not have had chest hair on it. As such, the court concluded that the correct calculation of contract damages was the difference in value between the promised perfect hand and the resulting hairy paw. The pain and suffering Hawkins experienced in the operation had nothing to do with this calculation because it was part of the price he was willing to pay for the promise of a good hand.

The case was remanded for a new trial.

Now let's consider a more modern example.

William Colby was a former director of the CIA. He wanted to write a book about his 15 years in Vietnam. He paid James McCarger $5,000 for help in writing an early draft and promised McCarger another $5,000 if the book was published. Then he hired Alexander Burnham to cowrite the book. Colby's agent secured a contract with Contemporary Books, which included a $100,000 advance. But Burnham was hopelessly late with the manuscript and Colby missed his publication date. Colby fired Burnham and finished the book without him. Contemporary published *Lost Victory* several years late, and the book flopped, earning no significant revenue. Because the book was so late, Contemporary paid Colby a total of only $17,000. Colby sued Burnham for his lost expectation interest. The court awarded him $23,000, calculated as follows:

	$100,000	advance, the only money Colby was promised
	− 10,000	agent's fee
	= 90,000	Fee for the two authors, combined
divided by 2	= 45,000	Colby's fee (the other half went to the coauthor)
	− 5,000	owed to McCarger under the earlier agreement
	= 40,000	Colby's expectation interest
	− 17,000	Fee Colby eventually received from Contemporary
	= 23,000	Colby's expectation damages; that is, the additional amount he would have received had Burnham finished on time

© Cengage Learning

The *Colby* case[1] presented a relatively easy calculation of damages. Other contracts are complex. Courts typically divide the expectation damages into three parts: (1) direct (or "compensatory") damages, which represent harm that flowed directly from the contract's breach; (2) consequential (or "special") damages, which represent harm caused by the injured party's unique situation; and (3) incidental damages, which are minor costs such as storing or returning defective goods, advertising for alternative goods, and so forth. The first two, direct and consequential, are the important ones.

Note that punitive damages are absent from our list. The golden rule in contracts cases is to give successful plaintiffs "the benefit of the bargain" and not to punish defendants.

---

[1]*Colby v. Burnham*, 31 Conn. App. 707, 627 A.2d 457, 1993 Conn. App LEXIS 299 (Conn. App. Ct. 1993).

Punitive damages are occasionally awarded in lawsuits that involve both a contract *and* either an intentional tort (such as fraud) or a breach of fiduciary duty, but they are not available in "simple" cases involving only a breach of contract.

17-2a Direct Damages

Direct damages are those that flow directly from the contract. They are the most common monetary award for the expectation interest. These are the damages that inevitably result from the breach. Suppose Ace Productions hires Reina to star in its new movie, *Inside Straight*. Ace promises Reina $3 million, providing she shows up June 1 and works until the film is finished. But in late May, Joker Entertainment offers Reina $6 million to star in its new feature, and on June 1, Reina informs Ace that she will not appear. Reina has breached her contract, and Ace should recover direct damages.

What are the damages that flow directly from the contract? Ace has to replace Reina. If Ace hires Kayla as its star and pays her a fee of $4 million, Ace is entitled to the difference between what it expected to pay ($3 million) and what the breach forced it to pay ($4 million), or $1 million in direct damages.

Direct damages
Are those that flow directly from the contract.

17-2b Consequential Damages

In addition to direct damages, the injured party may seek consequential damages or, as they are also known, "special damages." **Consequential damages reimburse for harm that results from the *particular* circumstances of the plaintiff.** These damages are only available if they are a *foreseeable consequence* of the breach. Suppose, for example, Raould breaches two contracts—he is late picking both Sharon and Paul up for a taxi ride. His breach is the same for both parties, but the consequences are very different. Sharon misses her flight to San Francisco and incurs a substantial fee to rebook the flight. Paul is simply late for the barber, who manages to fit him in anyway. Thus, Raould's damages would be different for these two contracts. The rule concerning this remedy comes from a famous 1854 case, *Hadley v. Baxendale*. This is another case that all American law students read. Now it is your turn.

Consequential damages
Are those resulting from the unique circumstances of a particular injured party.

HADLEY V. BAXENDALE

9 EX. 341, 156 Eng. Rep. 145
Court of Exchequer, 1854

CASE SUMMARY

Facts: The Hadleys operated a flour mill in Gloucester. The crankshaft broke, causing the mill to grind to a halt. The Hadleys employed Baxendale to cart the damaged part to a foundry in Greenwich, where a new one could be manufactured. Baxendale promised to make the delivery in one day, but he was late transporting the shaft, and as a result, the Hadleys' mill was shut for five extra days. They sued, and the jury awarded damages based in part on their lost profits. Baxendale appealed.

Issue: *Was the defendant liable for profits lost because of his delay in delivering the shaft?*

Decision: No. The defendant was not liable for lost profits.

Reasoning: When one side breaches a contract, the other party's damages should be those that arise inevitably from the breach or those that both parties reasonably anticipated when they made the agreement. If the contract involves special circumstances and the plaintiff tells the defendant about them when they make the deal, then the defendant is liable for all injuries. On the other hand, if the plaintiff never informed the defendant about the unique situation, then the defendant should be liable only for harm that might occur in the normal course of events.

The Hadleys told Baxendale only that the article to be carried was a broken shaft from their mill. How could Baxendale have realized that a delay in delivery would prevent the mill from operating? He might have assumed, very reasonably, that the Hadleys owned a second shaft and were sending this one for repairs while the mill ground on. It would be unfair to presume that Baxendale realized that delay would halt the mill. The case should be retried, and the jury may not consider the Hadleys' lost profits.

The rule from *Hadley v. Baxendale* has been unchanged ever since: **The injured party may recover consequential damages only if the *breaching party* should have *foreseen* them when the two sides formed the contract**.

Let us return briefly to *Inside Straight*. Suppose that, long before shooting began, Ace had sold the film's soundtrack rights to Spinem Sound for $2 million. Spinem believed it would make a profit only if Reina appeared in the film, so it demanded the right to discharge the agreement if Reina dropped out. When Reina quit, Spinem terminated the contract. Now, when Ace sues Reina, it will also seek $2 million in consequential damages for the lost music revenue.

The $2 million is not a direct damage. The contract between Reina and Act has nothing directly to do with selling soundtrack rights. But the loss is nonetheless a consequence of Reina bailing out on the project. And so, if Reina knew about Ace's contract with Spinem when she signed to do the film, the loss would be foreseeable to her, and she would be liable for $2 million. If she never realized she was an essential part of the music contract, and if a jury determines that she had no reason to expect the $2 million loss, she owes nothing for the lost soundtrack profits.

Injured plaintiffs often try to recover lost profits. Courts will generally award these damages if (1) the lost profits were foreseeable and (2) plaintiff provides enough information so that the factfinder can reasonably estimate a fair amount. The calculation need not be done with mathematical precision. In the following case, the plaintiffs lost not only profits—but their entire business. Can they recover for harm that is so extensive? You decide.

You Be the Judge

BI-ECONOMY MARKET, INC. v. HARLEYSVILLE INS. CO. OF NEW YORK

2008 WL 423451
New York Court of Appeals, 2008

Facts: Bi-Economy Market was a family-owned meat market in Rochester, New York. The company was insured by Harleysville Insurance. The "Deluxe Business Owner's" policy provided replacement cost for damage to buildings and inventory. Coverage also included "business interruption insurance" for one year, meaning the loss of pretax profit plus normal operating expenses, including payroll.

The company suffered a disastrous fire, which destroyed its building and all inventory. Bi-Economy immediately filed a claim with Harleysville, but the insurer responded slowly. Harleysville eventually offered a settlement of $163,000. A year later, an arbitrator awarded the Market $407,000. During that year, Harleysville paid for seven months of lost income but declined to pay more. The company never recovered or reopened.

Bi-Economy sued, claiming that Harleysville's slow, inadequate payments destroyed the company. The company also sought consequential damages for the permanent destruction of its business. Harleysville claimed that it was only responsible for damages specified in the contract: the building, inventory, and lost income. The trial court granted summary judgment for Harleysville. The appellate court affirmed, claiming that when they entered into the contract, the parties did not contemplate damages for termination of the business. Bi-Economy appealed to the state's highest court.

You Be the Judge: *Is Bi-Economy entitled to consequential damages for the destruction of its business?*

Argument for Bi-Economy: Bi-Economy is a small, family business. We paid for business interruption insurance for an obvious reason: In the event of a disaster, we lacked the resources to keep going while buildings were constructed and inventory purchased. We knew that in such a calamity, we would need prompt reimbursement—compensation covering the immediate damage and our ongoing lost income. Why else would we pay the premiums?

At the time we entered into the contract, Harleysville could easily foresee that if it responded slowly, with insufficient payments, we could not survive. They knew that is what we wanted to avoid—and it is just what happened. The insurer's bad faith offer of a low figure, and its payment of only seven months' lost income, ruined a fine family business. When the insurance company agreed to business interruption coverage, it was declaring that it would act fast and fairly to sustain a small firm in crisis. The insurer should now pay for the full harm it has wrought.

Argument for Harleysville: We contracted to insure the Market for three losses: its building, inventory, and lost income. After the fire, we performed a reasonable, careful evaluation and made an offer we considered fair. An arbitrator later awarded Bi-Market additional money, which we paid. However it is absurd to suggest that in addition to that, we are liable for an open-ended commitment for permanent destruction of the business.

Consequential damages are appropriate in cases where a plaintiff suffers a loss that was not covered in the contract. In this case, though, the parties bargained over exactly what Harleysville would pay in the event of a major fire. If the insurer has underpaid for lost income, let the court award a fair sum. However, the parties never contemplated an additional, enormous payment for cessation of the business. There is almost no limit as to what that obligation could be. If Bi-Market was concerned that a fire might put the company permanently out of business, it should have said so at the time of negotiating for insurance. The premium would have been dramatically higher.

Neither Bi-Market nor Harleysville ever imagined such an open-ended insurance obligation, and the insurer should not pay an extra cent.

17-2c Incidental Damages

Incidental damages are the relatively minor costs that the injured party suffers when *responding to* the breach. When Reina, the actress, breaches the film contract, the producers may have to leave the set and fly back to Los Angeles to hire a new actress. The travel cost is an incidental damage. In another setting, suppose Maud, a manufacturer, has produced 5,000 pairs of running shoes for Foot The Bill, a retail chain, but Foot The Bill breaches the agreement and refuses to accept the goods. Maud will have to store the shoes and advertise for alternate buyers. The storage and advertising costs are incidental expenses, and Maud will recover them.

Incidental damages
Relatively minor costs that the injured party suffers when responding to the breach.

17-2d The UCC and Damages

Under the Uniform Commercial Code (UCC), remedies for breach of contract in the sale of goods are similar to the general rules discussed throughout this chapter. UCC §§2-703 through 2-715 govern the remedies available to buyers and sellers.[2]

---

[2]We discuss these remedies in greater detail in Unit 3, on commercial transactions.

SELLER'S REMEDIES

If a buyer breaches a sale of goods contract, the seller generally has at least two remedies. She may resell the goods elsewhere. If she acts in good faith, she will be awarded **the difference between the original contract price and the price she was able to obtain in the open market**. Assume that Maud, the manufacturer, had a contract to sell her shoes to Foot The Bill for $55 per pair and Foot The Bill's breach forces her to sell them on the open market, where she gets only $48 per pair. Maud will win $7 per pair times 5,000 pairs, or $35,000, from Foot The Bill.

Alternatively, the buyer may choose not to resell and settle for the difference between the contract price and the market value of the goods. Maud, in other words, may choose to keep the shoes. If she can prove that their market value is $48 per pair, for example, by showing what other retailers would have paid her for them, she will still get her $7 each, representing the difference between what the contract promised her and what the market would support. In either case, the money represents direct damages. Maud is also entitled to incidental damages, such as the storage and advertising expenses described above. But there is one significant difference under the UCC: **Most courts hold that the seller of goods is *not* entitled to consequential damages**. Suppose Maud hired two extra workers to inspect, pack, and ship the shoes for Foot The Bill. Those are consequential damages, but Maud will not recover them because she is the seller and the contract is for the sale of goods.

BUYER'S REMEDIES

The buyer's remedies in sale of goods contracts (which are, as always, governed by the Uniform Commercial Code) are similar to those we have already considered. She typically has two options. First, the buyer can "cover" by purchasing substitute goods. To **cover** means to make a good faith purchase of goods similar to those in the contract. The buyer may then obtain **the difference between the original contract price and her cover price**. Alternatively, if the buyer chooses not to cover, she is entitled to the difference between the original contract price and the market value of the goods.

Cover

To make a good faith purchase of goods similar to those in the contract.

Suppose Mary has contracted to buy 1,000 six-foot Christmas trees at $25 per tree from Elmo. The market suddenly rises, and not feeling the spirit of the season, Elmo breaches his deal and sells the trees elsewhere. If Mary makes a good faith effort to cover but is forced to pay $40 per tree, she may recover the difference from Elmo, meaning $15 per tree times 1,000 trees, or $15,000. Similarly, if she chooses not to cover but can prove that $40 is now the market value of the trees, she is entitled to her $15 per tree.

Under the UCC, **the buyer *is* entitled to consequential damages, provided that the seller could reasonably have foreseen them**. If Mary tells Elmo, when they sign their deal, that she has a dozen contracts to resell the trees for an average price of $50 per tree, she may recover $25 per tree, representing the difference between her contract price with Elmo and the value of the tree *to her*, based on her other contracts.[3] If she failed to inform Elmo of the other contracts, she would not receive any money based on them. The buyer is also entitled to whatever incidental damages may have accrued.

---

[3]As we discuss in the section on mitigation later in the chapter, Mary will get only her consequential damages if she attempts to cover.

EXAM Strategy

Question: Chloe is a fashion designer. Her recent collection of silk-velvet evening gowns was gobbled up by high-end retailers, who now clamor for more. Chloe needs 300 yards of the same fabric by August 15. Mill House, which has supplied fabric to Chloe for many years, agrees to sell her 300 yards at $100 per yard, delivered on August 15. The market value of the fabric is $125, but Mill House gives Chloe a break because she is a major customer.

Chloe contracts with Barneys and Neiman Marcus to sell a total of 50 dresses, at an *additional* profit to Chloe of $800 per dress. On August 15, Mill House delivers defective fabric. Chloe cannot make her dresses in time, and the retailers cancel their orders. Chloe sues Mill House and wins—but what are her damages?

Strategy: To determine damages, first ask whether the contract is governed by the common law or the UCC. This agreement concerns goods, so the Code applies. The UCC permits a buyer to recover damages for the difference between the contract price and the market value of the goods. The Code also allows consequential damages if the seller could have foreseen them. Apply those standards.

Result: Because Chloe's contract enabled her to save $25 per yard for 300 yards, she is entitled to $7,500. Chloe has also lost profits of $40,000. Mill House could easily have foreseen those losses because the supplier knew that Chloe was a designer who fabricated and sold dresses. Chloe is entitled to $47,500.

We turn now to instances where the injured party cannot prove expectation damages.

17-3 RELIANCE INTEREST

To win expectation damages, the injured party must prove the breach of contract caused damages that can be *quantified with reasonable certainty*. This rule sometimes presents plaintiffs with a problem.

George plans to manufacture and sell silk scarves during the holiday season. In the summer, he contracts with Cecily, the owner of a shopping mall, to rent a high-visibility stall for $100 per day. George then buys hundreds of yards of costly silk and gets to work cutting and sewing. But in September, Cecily refuses to honor the contract. George sues and proves Cecily breached a valid contract. But what is his remedy?

George cannot establish an expectation interest in his scarf business. He *hoped* to sell each scarf for a $40 gross profit. He *planned* on making $2,000 per day. But how much would he *actually* have earned? Enough to retire on? Enough to buy a salami sandwich for lunch? He has no way of proving his profits, and a court cannot give him his expectation interest.

Instead, George will ask for *reliance damages*. The **reliance interest** is designed to put an injured party in the position he would have been in had the parties never entered into a contract. This remedy focuses on the time and money the injured party spent performing his part of the agreement.

George should be able to recover reliance damages from Cecily. Assuming he is unable to sell the scarves to a retail store, which is probable since retailers will have made purchases long ago, George should be able to recover the cost of the silk fabric he bought and perhaps something for the hours of labor he spent cutting and sewing. But reliance damages can be difficult to win because *they are harder to quantify*. Courts prefer to compute damages using

Reliance interest
Puts the injured party in the position he would have been in had the parties never entered into a contract.

the numbers provided in a contract. If a contract states a price of $25 per Christmas tree and one party breaches, the arithmetic is easy. Judges can become uncomfortable when asked to base damages on vague calculations. How much was George's time worth in making the scarves? How good was his work? How likely were the scarves to sell? If George has a track record in the industry, he will be able to show a market price for his services. Without such a record, his reliance claim becomes a tough battle.

17-3a Promissory Estoppel

We have seen in earlier chapters that a plaintiff may sometimes recover damages based on promissory estoppel even when there is no valid contract. The plaintiff must show that the defendant made a promise knowing that the plaintiff would likely rely on it, that the plaintiff did rely, and that the only way to avoid injustice is to enforce the promise. **In promissory estoppel cases, a court will generally award** *reliance damages.* It would be unfair to give expectation damages for the full benefit of the bargain when, legally speaking, there has been no bargain.

In the following case, the victorious plaintiff demonstrates how unreliable reliance damages are and how winning can be hard to distinguish from losing.

TOSCANO v. GREENE MUSIC

124 Ca. App. 4th 685, 21 Ca.Rptr.3d 732
Court of Appeal of California, 2004

CASE SUMMARY

Facts: Joseph Toscano was the general manager of Fields Pianos (Fields) in Santa Ana, California. He was unhappy with his job and decided to seek other employment. Toscano contacted Michael Greene, who owned similar stores. In July, Greene offered Toscano a sales management job, starting September 1. Relying on that offer, Toscano resigned from Fields on August 1. However, in mid-August, Greene withdrew his employment offer. Toscano later found lower-paying jobs in other cities.

Toscano sued Greene for breach of contract and promissory estoppel. Greene argued that Toscano was not entitled to any expectation damages because his employment with Greene would have been at will, meaning he could lose the job at any time. Greene also urged that because Toscano was an at-will employee at Fields, he could recover at most one month's lost wage.

The trial court ruled that Toscano was entitled to reliance damages for all lost wages at Fields, starting from the day he resigned, going forward until his anticipated retirement in 2017. Toscano's expert accountant calculated his past losses (until the time of trial) at $119,061, and his future lost earnings at $417,772. The trial court awarded Toscano $536,833, and Greene appealed.

Issue: *Was Toscano entitled to reliance damages?*

Decision: Yes, Toscano was entitled to reliance damages, but only as recalculated after a new trial.

Reasoning: Toscano gave up his job with Fields, relying on Greene's promise of employment, but was then denied his new position. Toscano made a claim of promissory estoppel. Because this is an equitable doctrine, a court applying it must make a particular effort to do what is right and just.

A plaintiff such as Toscano, lured away by a job promise that goes unfulfilled, should be allowed to recover the wages he lost at his former employment. That is basic fairness. Further, Toscano should not be denied compensation merely because he was an at-will employee at his former job. Any other holding would contradict the basic equitable principles mentioned. However, when the lower court awarded Toscano lost *future* earnings from the time of trial to his retirement, it went too far.

Toscano's expert on damages was Roberta Spoon. In calculating Toscano's lost future wages, she assumed that without the job offer from Greene, he would have remained with Fields until he retired. She made this assumption based on the fact that, in the past, Toscano had never changed jobs for any reason except an increase in pay. Her assumption, however, missed the basic point of at-will employment. Whether Toscano intended to remain with Fields until retirement was irrelevant. What counts was whether the Fields company itself wanted Toscano to remain. Because he was an at-will employee, Fields could have terminated him any time it wanted, for virtually any reason.

For an expert witness to assume that Toscano would remain at the same job for nearly a decade and a half was sheer speculation. Toscano should have presented testimony from Jerry Goldman, Toscano's boss at Fields, or some other evidence indicating that he would have been permitted to remain at the company until he retired.

The lower court award of past losses, until the time of trial, was affirmed. The award of lost future earnings was vacated, and the case was remanded for a new trial on those damages only. The judgment was otherwise affirmed.

Notice that the court never even mentions that Toscano acted in good faith, relying on Greene's promise, while the latter offered no excuse for suddenly withdrawing his offer. Is it fair to permit Greene to escape all liability? This court, like most, simply will not award significant damages where there is no contract permitting a clear calculation of losses.

The judges, though, have not entirely closed the door on Toscano. What is the purpose of the remand? What might Toscano demonstrate on remand? What practical difficulties will he encounter?

17-4 RESTITUTION INTEREST

Lillian and Harold Toews signed a contract to sell 1,500 acres of Idaho farmland to Elmer Funk. (No, not *that* one—the Bugs Bunny character you are thinking of is Elmer Fudd.) He was to take possession immediately, but he would not receive the deed until he finished paying for the property, in 10 years. This arrangement enabled him to enroll in a government program that would pay him "set-asides" for *not* farming. Funk kept most aspects of his agreement. He did move onto the land and did receive $76,000 from the government for a year's worth of inactivity. (Nice work if you can get it.) The only part of the bargain Funk did not keep was his promise to pay. Lillian and Harold sued. Funk had clearly breached the deal. But what remedy?

> He did move onto the land and did receive $76,000 from the government for a year's worth of inactivity. (Nice work if you can get it.)

The couple still owned the land, so they did not need it reconveyed. Funk had no money to pay for the farm, so they would never get their expectation interest. And they had expended almost no money based on the deal, so they had no reliance interest. What they had done, though, was to *confer a benefit* on Funk. They had enabled him to obtain $76,000 in government money. Harold and Lillian wanted a return of the benefit they had conferred on Funk, a remedy called *restitution*. The **restitution interest** is designed to return to the injured party a benefit that he has conferred on the other party, which it would be unjust to leave with that person. The couple argued that they had bestowed a $76,000 benefit on Funk and that it made absolutely no sense for him to keep it. The Idaho Court of Appeals agreed. It ruled that the couple had a restitutionary interest in the government set-aside money and ordered Funk to pay them the money.[4]

Restitution interest
Is designed to return to the injured party a benefit he has conferred on the other party.

---

[4] *Toews v. Funk*, 129 Idaho 316, 924 P.2d 217, 1994 Idaho App. LEXIS 75 (Idaho Ct. App. 1994).

Restitution is awarded in two types of cases. First, the law allows restitution when the parties have reached a contract and one of them breaches, as Funk did. In such cases, a court may choose restitution because no other remedy is available or because no other remedy would be as fair. Second, courts may award restitution in cases of quasi-contract, which we examined in Chapter 9. In quasi-contract cases, the parties never made a contract, but one side did benefit the other. We consider each kind of restitution interest in turn.

17-4a Restitution in Cases of a Voidable Contract

Rescission

To "undo" a contract and put the parties where they were before they made the agreement.

Restitution is a common remedy in contracts involving fraud, misrepresentation, mistake, and duress. In these cases, restitution often goes hand in hand with **rescission**, which means to "undo" a contract and put the parties where they were before they made the agreement. Courtney sells her favorite sculpture to Adam for $95,000, both parties believing the work to be a valuable original by Barbara Hepworth. Two months later, Adam learns that the sculpture is a mere copy, worth very little. A court will permit Adam to rescind the contract on the ground of mutual mistake. At the same time, Adam is entitled to restitution of the purchase price. Courtney gets the worthless carving, and Adam receives his money back.

The following case involved fraud in the sale of a valuable property.

PUTNAM CONSTRUCTION & REALTY CO. V. BYRD

632 So.2d 961, 1992 Ala. LEXIS 1289
Supreme Court of Alabama, 1992

CASE SUMMARY

Facts: Putnam Construction & Realty Co. owned the University Square Business Center (USBC), an office complex with several major tenants, including McDonnell-Douglas, TRW, and the Army Corps of Engineers. William Byrd and some partners (the "buyers") entered into a contract to buy USBC for slightly over $17 million. They financed the purchase with a $16.2 million loan from Northwestern Mutual Life. Northwestern's loan was secured with a mortgage on the USBC, meaning that if the borrowers failed to repay the loan, Northwestern would own the property. Shortly after the sale closed, Byrd learned that several of the major tenants were leaving. The buyers sued Putnam, seeking rescission of the contract and restitution of their money. The trial court found that Putnam (the "sellers") had committed fraud. It rescinded the sales contract, returning the property to the sellers. It ordered the sellers to assume full liability for the mortgage. The trial court did not, however, order restitution of the buyers' expenses, such as the closing costs. The sellers appealed—which proved to be a big mistake.

Issue: *Were the buyers entitled to rescission and/or restitution?*

Decision: Yes. The buyers were entitled to both rescission and restitution.

Reasoning: The sellers knew that the Corps of Engineers planned to build its own facility and vacate the USBC, yet they told the buyers that the Corps would be staying. They also knew that McDonnell-Douglas was leaving but failed to inform the buyers. The sellers clearly committed fraud.

Money damages would be speculative and would leave the buyers saddled with a property that operates at a steadily increasing loss. The fairest way to compensate them was by rescinding the contract, and the trial court's ruling on that issue was affirmed. However, the buyers also incurred substantial out-of-pocket expenses because of the sellers' fraud. To compensate them for these losses, they were entitled to receive restitution damages of $483,006.75 in closing costs, $121,000 in mortgage interest payments, and $500,000 in nonrefundable fees paid to Northwestern to obtain the loan. The case was remanded for the trial court to impose all of these remedies.

Ethics   Imagine that you are the officer from Putnam in charge of negotiating the sale of USBC to the buyers. You learn that several major tenants are soon to depart and realize that if the buyers learn this, they will lower their offer or reject the deal altogether. Your boss insists you tell the buyers that all tenants will be staying. What will you do? What Life Principles will you apply?

17-4b Restitution in Cases of a Quasi-Contract

George Anderson owned a valuable 1936 Plymouth. He took it to Ronald Schwegel's repair shop, and the two orally agreed that Schwegel would restore the car for $6,000. Unfortunately, they never agreed on the meaning of the word *restore*. Anderson thought the term meant complete restoration, including body work and engine repairs, whereas Schwegel intended body work but no engine repairs. After doing some of the work, Schwegel told Anderson that the car needed substantial engine work, and he asked for Anderson's permission to allow an engine shop to do it. Anderson agreed, believing the cost was included in the original estimate. When the car was finished and running smoothly, Schwegel demanded $9,800. Anderson refused to pay more than the $6,000 agreed price, and Schwegel sued.

The court held that there was no valid contract between the parties. A contract requires a meeting of the minds. Here, said the court, there was no meeting of the minds on what *restore* included, and hence Schwegel could not recover either his expectation or his reliance interest since both require an enforceable agreement. Schwegel then argued that a quasi-contract existed. In other words, he claimed that even if there had been no valid agreement, he had performed a service for Anderson and that it would be unjust for Anderson to keep it without paying. **A court may award restitution, even in the absence of a contract, where one party has conferred a benefit on another and it would be unjust for the other party to retain the benefit.** The court ruled that Schwegel was entitled to the full $3,800 above and beyond the agreed price because that was the fair market value of the additional work. Anderson had asked for the repairs and now had an auto that was substantially improved. It would be unjust, ruled the court, to permit him to keep that benefit for free.[5]

17-5 OTHER REMEDIES

In contract lawsuits, plaintiffs are occasionally awarded the remedies of specific performance, injunction, and reformation.

17-5a Specific Performance

Leona Claussen owned Iowa farmland. She sold some of it to her sister-in-law, Evelyn Claussen, and, along with the land, granted Evelyn an option to buy additional property at $800 per acre. Evelyn could exercise her option anytime during Leona's lifetime or within six months of Leona's death. When Leona died, Evelyn informed the estate's executor that she was exercising her option. But other relatives wanted the property, and the executor refused to sell. Evelyn sued and asked for *specific performance*. She did not want an award of damages; she wanted *the land itself*. The remedy of specific performance forces the two parties to perform their contract.

---

[5]*Anderson v. Schwegel*, 118 Idaho 362, 796 P.2d 1035, 1990 Idaho App. LEXIS 150 (Idaho Ct. App. 1990).

A court will award specific performance, ordering the parties to perform the contract, only in cases involving the sale of land or some other asset that is considered "unique." Courts use this remedy when money damages would be inadequate to compensate an injured party. If the subject is unique and irreplaceable, money damages will not put the injured party in the same position she would have been in had the agreement been kept. So a court will order the seller to convey the rare object and the buyer to pay for it.

Historically, every parcel of land has been regarded as unique, and therefore specific performance is always available in real estate contracts. Family heirlooms and works of art are also often considered unique. Evelyn Claussen won specific performance. The Iowa Supreme Court ordered Leona's estate to convey the land to Evelyn for $800 per acre.[6] Generally speaking, either the seller or the buyer may be granted specific performance. One limitation in land sales is that a buyer may obtain specific performance only if she was ready, willing, and able to purchase the property on time. If Evelyn had lacked the money to buy Leona's property for $800 per acre within the six-month time limit, the court would have declined to order the sale.

EXAM Strategy

Question: The Monroes, a retired couple who live in Illinois, want to move to Arizona to escape the northern winter. In May, the Monroes contract in writing to sell their house to the Temples for $450,000. Closing is to take place June 30. The Temples pay a deposit of $90,000. However, in early June, the Monroes travel through Arizona and discover it is too hot for them. They promptly notify the Temples they are no longer willing to sell, and return the $90,000, with interest. The Temples sue, seeking the house. In response, the Monroes offer evidence that the value of the house has dropped from about $450,000 to about $400,000. They claim that the Temples have suffered no loss. Who will win?

Strategy: Most contract lawsuits are for money damages, but not this one. The Temples want the house. Because they want the house itself, and not money damages, the drop in value is irrelevant. What legal remedy are the Temples seeking? They are suing for specific performance. When will a court grant specific performance? Should it do so here?

Result: In cases involving the sale of land or some other unique asset, a court will grant specific performance, ordering the parties to perform the agreement. All houses are regarded as unique. The court will force the Monroes to sell their house, provided the Temples have sufficient money to pay for it.

Other unique items, for which a court will order specific performance, include such things as secret formulas, patents, and shares in a closely held corporation. Money damages would be inadequate for all these things since the injured party, even if she got the cash, could not go out and buy a substitute item. By contrast, a contract for a new Cadillac Escalade is not enforceable by specific performance. If the seller breaches, the buyer is entitled to the difference between the contract price and the market value of the car. The buyer can take his money elsewhere and purchase a virtually identical SUV.

17-5b Injunction

In the opening scenario, the NFL team's general manager considered whether to seek an injunction against his running back who wanted to leave the team and act in a TV show. An **injunction** is a court order that requires someone to refrain from doing something.

---

[6]*In re Estate of Claussen*, 482 N.W.2d 381, 1992 Iowa Sup. LEXIS 52 (Iowa 1992).

In the increasingly litigious world of professional sports, injunctions are commonplace. In the following basketball case, the trial court issued a **preliminary injunction;** that is, an order issued early in a lawsuit prohibiting a party from doing something *during the course of the lawsuit.* The court attempts to protect the interests of the plaintiff immediately. If, after trial, it appears that the plaintiff has been injured and is entitled to an injunction, the trial court will make its order a **permanent injunction**. If it appears that the preliminary injunction should never have been issued, the court will terminate the order.

MILICIC v. BASKETBALL MARKETING COMPANY, INC.

2004 Pa.SUPER. 333, 857 A.2d 689
Superior Court of Pennsylvania, 2004

CASE SUMMARY

Facts: The Basketball Marketing Company (BMC) marketed, distributed, and sold basketball apparel and related products. BMC signed a long-term endorsement contract with a 16-year-old Serbian player, Darko Milicic, who was virtually unknown in the United States. Two years later, Milicic became the second pick in the National Basketball Association's draft, making him an immensely marketable young man.

Four days after his 18th birthday, Milicic made a buyout offer to BMC, seeking release from his contract so that he could arrange a more lucrative one elsewhere. BMC refused to release him. A week later, Milicic notified BMC in writing that he was disaffirming the contract, and he returned all money and goods he had received from the company. BMC again refused to release Milicic.

Believing that Milicic was negotiating an endorsement deal with either Reebok or Adidas, BMC sent both companies letters informing them it had an enforceable endorsement deal with Milicic that was valid for several more years. Because of BMC's letter, Adidas ceased negotiating with Milicic just short of signing a contract. Milicic sued BMC, seeking a preliminary injunction that would prohibit BMC from sending such letters to competitors. The trial court granted the preliminary injunction and BMC appealed.

Issue: *Was Milicic entitled to a preliminary injunction?*

Decision: Yes, Milicic was entitled to a preliminary injunction. Affirmed.

Reasoning: Like any plaintiff seeking a preliminary injunction, Milicic had to prove four elements.

First, Milicic had to prove his case had a strong likelihood of success on the merits. Under Pennsylvania law, a minor may void a contract by disaffirming it within a reasonable time of turning 18 years old. Milicic sent BMC a letter only 11 days after his 18th birthday, unequivocally stating that he disavowed the agreement made when he was a minor. In all likelihood, Milicic will succeed in nullifying the contract with BMC.

Second, he had to prove injunctive relief was necessary to prevent immediate and irreparable harm for which money damages would not adequately compensate Milicic. Top NBA picks negotiate and secure endorsements quickly, to take advantage of the excitement and publicity generated by the draft. BMC blocked Milicic's efforts to conclude an agreement with Adidas. Continued obstruction would have caused Milicic irreparable harm.

Third, denying the injunction would cause greater injury than granting it. BMC violated important public policy by refusing to acknowledge a minor's power to disaffirm. The law presumes that a minor lacks the maturity to negotiate such an important agreement. When a company wants to conclude a contract with a minor, it is well-established practice to ask that a court appoint a guardian for the minor. It is astonishing that BMC, a company whose business was based entirely on contract law, failed to protect Milicic's interest—and its own—by requesting a guardian.

Finally, Milicic had to prove that a preliminary injunction would restore the parties to the status quo that existed when he turned 18, by preventing BMC from further interfering with Milicic's negotiations. The lower court properly granted injunctive relief.

17-5c Reformation

The final remedy, and perhaps the least common, is **reformation**, a process in which a court will partially rewrite a contract. Courts seldom do this because the whole point of a contract is to enable the parties to control their own futures. But a court may reform a contract if it believes a written agreement includes a simple mistake. Suppose that Roger orally agrees to sell 35 acres to Hannah for $600,000. The parties then draw up a written agreement, accidentally describing the land as including 50 additional acres that neither party considered part of the deal. Roger refuses to sell. Hannah sues for specific performance but asks the court to *reform* the written contract to reflect the true agreement. Most but not all courts would reform the agreement and enforce it.

A court may also reform a contract to save it. If Natasha sells her advertising business to Joseph and agrees not to open a competing agency in the same city anytime in the next 10 years, a court may decide that it is unfair to force her to wait a decade. It could reform the agreement and permit Natasha to compete, say, 3 years after the sale. But some courts are reluctant to reform contracts and would throw out the entire noncompetition agreement rather than reform it. Parties should never settle for a contract that is sloppy or overbroad, assuming that a court will later reform errors. They may find themselves stuck with a bargain they dislike, or with no contract at all.

17-6 Special Issues

Finally, we consider some special issues of damages, beginning with a party's obligation to minimize its losses.

17-6a Mitigation of Damages

A party injured by a breach of contract may not recover for damages that he could have avoided with reasonable efforts. In other words, when one party perceives that the other has breached or will breach the contract, the injured party must try to prevent unnecessary loss. A party is expected to **mitigate** his damages; that is, to keep damages as low as he reasonably can.

Malcolm agrees to rent space in his mall to Zena, for a major department store. As part of the lease, Malcolm agrees to redesign the interior to meet her specifications. After Malcolm has spent $20,000 in architect and design fees, Zena informs Malcolm that she is renting other space and will not occupy his mall. Malcolm nonetheless continues the renovation work, spending an additional $50,000 on materials and labor. Malcolm will recover the lost rental payments and the $20,000 expended in reliance on the deal. He will *not* recover the extra $50,000. He should have stopped work when he learned of Zena's breach.

17-6b Nominal Damages

Nominal damages are a token sum, such as one dollar, given to a plaintiff who demonstrates that the defendant breached the contract but cannot prove serious injury. A school board unfairly fires Gemma, a teacher. If she obtains a teaching job at a better school for identical pay the very next day, she probably can show no damages at all. Nonetheless, the school wrongfully terminated her, and a court may award nominal damages. Nominal damages provide plaintiff with a "moral victory."

17-6c Liquidated Damages

It can be difficult or even impossible to prove how much damage the injured party has suffered. So lawyers and executives negotiating a deal may include in the contract a **liquidated damages** clause, a provision stating in advance how much a party must pay if it breaches. Assume that Laurie has hired Bruce to build a five-unit apartment building for $800,000. Bruce promises to complete construction by May 15. Laurie insists on a liquidated damages clause providing that if Bruce finishes late, Laurie's final price is reduced by $3,000 for each week of delay. Bruce finishes the apartment building June 30, and Laurie reduces her payment by $18,000. Is that fair? The answer depends on two factors: **A court will generally enforce a liquidated damages clause if (1) at the time of creating the contract, it was very difficult to estimate actual damages, and (2) the liquidated amount is reasonable.** In any other case, the liquidated damage will be considered a mere penalty and will prove unenforceable.

We will apply the two factors to Laurie's case. When the parties made their agreement, would it have been difficult to estimate actual damages caused by delay? Yes. Laurie could not prove that all five units would have been occupied or how much rent the tenants would have agreed to pay. Was the $3,000 per week reasonable? Probably. To finance an $800,000 building, Laurie will have to pay at least $6,000 interest per month. She must also pay taxes on the land and may have other expenses. Laurie does not have to prove that every penny of the liquidated damages clause is justified, but only that the figure is reasonable. A court will probably enforce her liquidated damages clause.

On the other hand, suppose Laurie's clause demanded $3,000 per day. There is no basis for such a figure, and a court will declare it a penalty clause and refuse to enforce it. Laurie will be back to square one, forced to prove in court any damages she claims to have suffered from Bruce's delay.

In the chapter's opening scenario, the alarm company tries to invoke a liquidated damages clause that would leave Ben largely uncompensated. Depending on what the parties knew when they made the agreement, a court may well find the clause too harsh and permit Ben to sue for his actual losses.

EXAM Strategy

Question: In March, James was accepted into the September ninth-grade class at the Brookstone Academy, a highly competitive private school. To reserve his spot, James's father, Rex, sent in a deposit of $2,000 and agreed in writing to pay the balance due, $19,000. If James withdrew in writing from the school by August 1, Rex owed nothing more to Brookstone. However, once that date passed, Rex was obliged to pay the full $19,000, whether or not James attended. On August 5, Rex hand-delivered to Brookstone a letter stating that James would not attend. Brookstone demanded the full tuition and, when Rex refused to pay, sued for $19,000. Analyze the case.

Strategy: When one party seeks contract damages that are specified in the agreement, it is relying on a liquidated damages clause. A court will generally enforce a liquidated damages clause provided the plaintiff can prove two things. What are those two things? Can this plaintiff meet that standard?

Result: Brookstone must prove that at the time of creating the contract it was difficult to estimate actual damages and that the liquidated amount is reasonable. Rex will probably argue that the liquidated amount is unreasonable, contending that a competitive school can quickly fill a vacancy with another eager applicant. Brookstone will counter that budgeting, which begins in January, is difficult and imprecise. Tuition money goes toward staff salaries, maintenance, utilities, and many other expenses. If the school cannot not rely in January on a certain income, the calculation becomes impossible. Rex had four months to make up his mind, and by August 1, the school was firmly committed to its class size and budget. In a similar case, the court awarded the full tuition to the school, concluding that the sum was a reasonable estimate of the damages.

Chapter Conclusion

The powers of a court are broad and flexible and may suffice to give an injured party what it deserves. But problems of proof and the uncertainty of remedies demonstrate that the best solution is a carefully drafted contract and socially responsible behavior.

EXAM REVIEW

1. **BREACH**   Someone breaches a contract when he fails to perform a duty without a valid excuse. (pp. 378–379)

2. **REMEDY**   A remedy is the method a court uses to compensate an injured party. (p. 378)

3. **INTERESTS**   An interest is a legal right in something, such as a contract. The first step that a court takes in choosing a remedy is to decide what interest it is protecting. (pp. 378–379)

4. **EXPECTATION**   The expectation interest puts the injured party in the position she would have been in had both sides fully performed. It has three components:

   (a) Direct damages, which flow directly from the contract.
   (b) Consequential damages, which result from the unique circumstances of the particular injured party. The injured party may recover consequential damages only if the breaching party should have foreseen them.
   (c) Incidental damages, which are the minor costs an injured party incurs responding to a breach. (pp. 379–385)

EXAM Strategy

Question: Mr. and Ms. Beard contracted for Builder to construct a house on property he owned and sell it to the Beards for $785,000. The house was to be completed by a certain date, and Builder knew that the Beards were selling their own home in reliance on the completion date. Builder was late with construction, forcing the Beards to spend $32,000 in rent. Ultimately, Builder never finished the house, and the Beards moved elsewhere. They sued. At trial, expert testimony indicated the market value of the house as promised would have been $885,000. How much money are the Beards entitled to, and why?

Strategy: Normally, in cases of property, an injured plaintiff may use specific performance to obtain the land or house. However, there *is* no house, so there will be no specific performance. The Beards will seek their expectation interest. Under the contract, what did they reasonably expect? They anticipated a finished house, on a particular date, worth $885,000. They did not expect to pay rent while waiting. Calculate their losses. (See the "Result" at the end of this section.)

5. **RELIANCE**   The reliance interest puts the injured party in the position he would have been in had the parties never entered into a contract. It focuses on the time and money that the injured party spent performing his part of the agreement. If there was

no valid contract, a court might still award reliance damages under a theory of promissory estoppel. (pp. 385–387)

Question: Bingo is emerging as a rock star. His last five concerts have all sold out. Lucia signs a deal with Bingo to perform two concerts in one evening in Big City for a fee of $50,000 for both shows. Lucia then rents the Auditorium for that evening, guaranteeing to pay $50,000. Bingo promptly breaks the deal before any tickets are sold. Lucia sues, pointing out that the Auditorium seats 3,000 and she anticipated selling all tickets for an average of $40 each, for a total gross of $120,000. How much will Lucia recover, if anything?

Strategy: The parties created a valid contract, and Lucia relied on it. She claims two losses: the payment to rent the hall and her lost profits. A court may award reliance damages if the plaintiff can quantify them, provided the damages are not speculative. Can Lucia quantify either of those losses? Both of them? Were they speculative? (See the "Result" at the end of this section.)

6. **RESTITUTION**   The restitution interest returns to the injured party a benefit that she has conferred on the other party which would be unjust to leave with that person. Restitution can be awarded in the case of a contract created, for example, by fraud, or in a case of quasi-contract, where the parties never created a binding agreement. (pp. 387–389)

7. **SPECIFIC PERFORMANCE**   Specific performance, ordered only in cases of land or a unique asset, requires both parties to perform the contract. (pp. 389–390)

8. **INJUNCTION**   An injunction is a court order that requires someone to do something or refrain from doing something. (pp. 390–391)

9. **REFORMATION**   Reformation is the process by which a court will—occasionally— rewrite a contract to ensure that it accurately reflects the parties' agreement and/or to maintain the contract's viability. (p. 392)

10. **MITIGATION**   The duty to mitigate means that a party injured by a breach of contract may not recover for damages that he could have avoided with reasonable efforts. (p. 392)

Question: Ambrose hires Bierce for $25,000 to supervise the production of Ambrose's crop, but then breaks the contract by firing Bierce at the beginning of the season. A nearby grower offers Bierce $23,000 for the same growing season, but Bierce refuses to take such a pay cut. He stays home and sues Ambrose. How much money, if any, will Bierce recover from Ambrose, and why?

Strategy: Ambrose has certainly breached the contract. The injured party normally receives the difference between his expectation interest and what he actually received. Bierce expected $25,000 and received nothing. However, Bierce made no effort to minimize his losses. How much would Bierce have lost had he mitigated?

11. **NOMINAL DAMAGES**   Nominal damages are a token sum, such as one dollar, given to an injured plaintiff who cannot prove damages. (p. 392)

12. **LIQUIDATED DAMAGES**   A liquidated damages clause will be enforced if and only if, at the time of creating the contract, it was very difficult to estimate actual damages and the liquidated amount is reasonable. (pp. 392–393)

> **4. Result:**   The Beards' direct damages represent the difference between the market value of the house and the contract price. They expected a house worth $100,000 more than their contract price, and they are entitled to that sum. They also suffered consequential damages. The Builder knew they needed the house as of the contract date, and he could foresee that his breach would force them to pay rent. He is liable for a total of $132,000.
>
> **5. Result:**   Lucia can easily demonstrate that Bingo's breach cost her $50,000—the cost of the hall. However, it is uncertain how many tickets she would have sold. Unless Lucia has a strong track record selling tickets to concerts featuring Bingo, a court is likely to conclude that her anticipated profits were speculative. She will probably receive nothing for that claim.
>
> **10. Result:**   Even if he had mitigated, Bierce would have lost $2,000. He is entitled to that sum. However, he cannot recover the remaining $23,000. After Ambrose breached, Bierce had identical work available to him, but he failed to take it. His failure to mitigate is fatal.

MULTIPLE-CHOICE QUESTIONS

1. **CPA QUESTION**   Master Mfg., Inc., contracted with Accur Computer Repair Corp. to maintain Master's computer system. Master's manufacturing process depends on its computer system operating properly at all times. A liquidated damages clause in the contract provided that Accur would pay $1,000 to Master for each day that Accur was late responding to a service request. On January 12, Accur was notified that Master's computer system had failed. Accur did not respond to Master's service request until January 15. If Master sues Accur under the liquidated damage provision of the contract, Master will:

   (a) Win, unless the liquidated damages provision is determined to be a penalty

   (b) Win, because under all circumstances liquidated damage provisions are enforceable

   (c) Lose, because Accur's breach was not material

   (d) Lose, because liquidated damage provisions violate public policy

2. **CPA QUESTION**   Kaye contracted to sell Hodges a building for $310,000. The contract required Hodges to pay the entire amount at closing. Kaye refused to close the sale of the building. Hodges sued Kaye. To what relief is Hodges entitled?

   (a) Punitive damages and direct damages

   (b) Specific performance and direct damages

   (c) Consequential damages or punitive damages

   (d) Direct damages or specific performance

3. A manufacturer delivers a new tractor to Farmer Ted on the first day of the harvest season. But, the tractor will not start. It takes two weeks for the right parts to be delivered and installed. The repair bill comes to $1,000. During the two weeks, some acres of Farmer Ted's crops die. He argues in court that his lost profit on those acres is $60,000. If a jury awards $1,000 for tractor repairs, it will be in the form of _____ damages. If it awards $60,000 for the lost crops, it will be in the form of _____ damages.

(a) direct; direct

(b) direct; consequential

(c) consequential; direct

(d) consequential; consequential

(e) direct; incidental

4. Julie signs a contract to buy Nick's 2002 Mustang GT for $5,000. Later, Nick changes his mind and refuses to sell his car. Julie soon buys a similar 2002 Mustang GT for $5,500. She then sues Nick and wins $500. The $500 represents her _____.

(a) expectation interest

(b) reliance interest

(c) restitution interest

(d) None of the above

5. Under the Uniform Commercial Code, a seller _____ generally entitled to recover consequential damages, and a buyer _____ generally entitled to recover consequential damages.

(a) is; is

(b) is; is not

(c) is not; is

(d) is not; is not

ESSAY QUESTIONS

1. Lewis signed a contract for the rights to all timber located on Nine-Mile Mine. He agreed to pay $70 per thousand board feet ($70/mbf). As he began work, Nine-Mile became convinced that Lewis lacked sufficient equipment to do the job well and forbade him to enter the land. Lewis sued. Nine-Mile moved for summary judgment. The mine offered proof that the market value of the timber was exactly $70/mbf, and Lewis had no evidence to contradict Nine-Mile. The evidence about market value proved decisive. Why? Please rule on the summary judgment motion.

2. Twin Creeks Entertainment signed a deal with U.S. JVC Corp. in which JVC would buy 60,000 feature-film videocassettes from Twin Creeks over a three-year period. JVC intended to distribute the cassettes nationwide. Relying on its deal with JVC, Twin Creeks signed an agreement with Paramount Pictures, agreeing to purchase a minimum of $600,000 worth of Paramount cassettes over a two-year period. JVC breached its deal with Twin Creeks and refused to accept the cassettes it had agreed upon. Twin Creeks sued and claimed, among other damages, the money it owed to Paramount. JVC moved to dismiss the claim based on the Paramount contract, on the ground that Twin Creeks, the seller of goods, was not entitled to such damages. What kind of damages is Twin Creeks seeking? Please rule on the motion to dismiss.

3. Racicky was in the process of buying 320 acres of ranchland. While that sale was being negotiated, Racicky signed a contract to sell the land to Simon. Simon paid $144,000, the full price of the land. But Racicky went bankrupt before he could complete the *purchase* of the land, let alone its sale. Which of these remedies should Simon seek: expectation, restitution, specific performance, or reformation?

4. Parkinson was injured in an auto accident by a driver who had no insurance. Parkinson filed a claim with her insurer, Liberty Mutual, for $2,000 under her "uninsured motorist" coverage. Liberty Mutual told her that if she sought that money, her premiums would go "sky high," so Parkinson dropped the claim. Later, after she had spoken with an attorney, Parkinson sued. What additional claim was her attorney likely to make?

5. **YOU BE THE JUDGE WRITING PROBLEM** John and Susan Verba sold a Vermont lakeshore lot to Shane and Deborah Rancourt for $115,000. The Rancourts intended to build a house on the property, but after preparing the land for construction, they learned that a wetland protection law prevented building near the lake. They sued, seeking rescission of the contract. The trial court concluded that the parties had reached their agreement under a "mutual, but innocent, misunderstanding." The trial judge gave the Verbas a choice: They could rescind the contract and refund the purchase price, or they could give the Rancourts $55,000, the difference between the sales price and the actual market value of the land. The Rancourts appealed. Were the Rancourts entitled to rescission of the contract? **Argument for the Rancourts:** When the parties have made a mutual mistake about an important factual issue, either party is entitled to rescind the contract. The land is of no use to us and we want our money back. **Argument for the Verbas:** Both sides were acting in good faith and both sides made an honest mistake. We are willing to acknowledge that the land is worth somewhat less than we all thought, and we are willing to refund $55,000. The buyers should not complain—they are getting the property at about half the original price, and the error was as much their fault as ours.

DISCUSSION QUESTIONS

1. **ETHICS** The National Football League owns the copyright to the broadcasts of its games. It licenses local television stations to telecast certain games and maintains a "blackout rule," which prohibits stations from broadcasting home games that are not sold out 72 hours before the game starts. Certain home games of the Cleveland Browns team were not sold out, and the NFL blocked local broadcast. But several bars in the Cleveland area were able to pick up the game's signal by using special antennas. The NFL wanted the bars to stop showing the games. What did it do? Was it unethical of the bars to broadcast the games that they were able to pick up? Apart from the NFL's legal rights, do you think it had the moral right to stop the bars from broadcasting the games?

2. Consequential damages can be many times higher than direct damages. Consider the "Farmer Ted" scenario raised in multiple-choice question 3, which is based on a real case.[7] Is it fair for consequential damages to be 60 times higher than direct damages? The Supreme Court is skeptical that *punitive* damages should be more than 9 times compensatory damages in a tort case. Should a similar "soft limit" apply to consequential damages in contract cases?

3. Is reformation ever a reasonable remedy? Should courts be in the business of rewriting contracts, or should they stick to determining whether agreements are enforceable?

4. If someone breaks a contract, the other party can generally sue and win some form of damages. But for centuries, the law has considered land to be unique. And so, a lawsuit that involves a broken agreement for a sale of land will usually result in an order of specific performance. Is this ancient rule still reasonable? If someone backs out of an agreement to sell an acre of land, should he be ordered to turn over the land itself? Why not just require him to pay an appropriate number of dollars in damages?

5. Is it reasonable to require the mitigation of damages? If a person is wronged because the other side breached a contract, should she have any obligations at all? For example, suppose that a tenant breaches a lease by leaving early. Should the landlord have an obligation to try to find another tenant before the end of the lease?

---

[7] *Prutch v. Ford*, 574 P.2d 102 (Colo. 1977).

CHAPTER 18

PRACTICAL CONTRACTS

nuttakit/Shutterstock.com; © neelsky/Shutterstock.com

Two true stories:

One

Holly (on the phone to her client, Judd): Harry's lawyer just emailed me a letter that Harry says he got from you last year. I'm reading from the letter now: "Each year that you meet your revenue goals, you'll get a 1 percent equity interest." Is it possible you sent that letter?

Judd: I don't remember the exact wording, but probably something like that.

Holly: You told me, absolutely, positively, you had never promised Harry any stock. That he was making the whole thing up.

Judd: He was threatening to leave unless I gave him some equity, so I said what he wanted to hear. But that letter didn't *mean* anything. This is a family business, and no one but my children will ever get stock.

> **I don't know what the *contract* says—that's just the legal stuff.**

Two

Grace (on the phone with her lawyer): Providential has raised its price to $12 a pound. I can't afford to pay that! We had a deal that the price would never go higher than 10 bucks. I've talked to Buddy over there, but he is refusing to back down. We need to do something!

Lawyer: Let me look at the contract.

Grace (her voice rising): I don't know what the *contract* says—that's just the legal stuff. Our *business* deal was no more than $10 a pound!

You have been studying the theory of contract law. This chapter is different—its purpose is to demonstrate how that theory operates in practice. We will look at the structure and content of a standard agreement and answer questions such as: Do you need a written agreement? What do all these legal terms mean? Are any important provisions missing? By the end of the chapter, you will have a road map for understanding a written contract.[1] (Note that we do not repeat here what you have learned in prior chapters about the *substantive* law of contracts.) This chapter has another goal, too: We will look at the relationship between lawyers and their clients and their different roles in creating a contract.

Businesspeople, not surprisingly, tend to focus more on business than on the technicalities of contract law. However, *ignoring* the role of a written agreement can lead to serious trouble. Both of the clients in the opening scenario ended up being bound by a contract they did not want.

To illustrate our discussion of specific contract provisions, we will use a real contract between an actor and a producer to make a movie. For reasons of confidentiality, however, we have changed the names.

Before we begin our discussion of written contracts, let's ask: **Do you need a written agreement at all?** Some years ago, this author was with a group of lawyers, all of whom had done a major home renovation and *none of whom* had signed a contract with the builder. All of the projects had turned out well. The lawyers had not prepared a written contract because they trusted their builders, who all had good recommendations from prior clients. Also, a building project by its very nature requires regular negotiations because it is impossible to predict all the potential changes: How much would it cost to move that door? How much do we save if we use Caesarstone instead of granite?

These cases worked out well without a written contract, but there are times when you should *definitely* sign an agreement:

1. The Statute of Frauds requires it.

2. The deal is crucial to your life or the life of your business.

3. The terms are complex.

4. You do not have an ongoing relationship of trust with the other party.

Once you decide you need a written contract, then what?

18-1 THE LAWYER

The American Bar Association commissioned a study to find out what people think of lawyers. Survey participants responded with these words: greedy, corrupt, manipulative, snakes, and sharks.[2] Businesspeople refer to their lawyers with terms like *business prevention department*. They are reluctant to ask an attorney to draft a contract for fear of the time and expense that lawyers can inject into the process. And they worry that the lawyers will interfere in the business deal itself, at best causing unnecessary hindrance, at worst killing the deal. Part of the problem is that lawyers and clients have different views of the future.

---

[1]For further reading on practical contracts, see Scott Burnham, *Drafting and Analyzing Contracts* (Lexis/Nexis, 2003); Charles M. Fox, *Working with Contracts* (Practical Law Institute, 2008); George W. Kuney, *The Elements of Contract Drafting* (Thomson/West, 2006).
[2]Robert Clifford, *Opening Statement: Now More than Ever*, 28 Litigation 1, Spring 2002.

18-1a Lawyers and Clients

Businesspeople are optimists—they believe that they have negotiated a great deal and everything is going to go well—sales will boom, the company will prosper. **Lawyers have a different perspective—their primary goal is to protect their clients by avoiding litigation, now and in the future.** For this reason, lawyers are trained to be pessimists—they try to foresee and protect against everything that can possibly go wrong. Businesspeople sometimes view this lawyering as a waste of time and a potential deal-killer. What if the two parties cannot agree about what to do in the event of a very unlikely circumstance? The deal might just collapse.

To take one example of this lawyerly perspective, a couple happily married nigh on 40 years went to see a lawyer about changes in their will. The husband wanted to transfer some assets to his wife. The lawyer advised against it—after all, the couple might divorce. They became angry and indignant because *they would never get divorced*. And they may very well be right. However, just that week, the lawyer had seen another couple who did divorce after 41 years of marriage. He thought it better to be on the safe side and consider the possibility that such events might happen.

Lawyers also prefer to negotiate touchy subjects at the beginning of a relationship, when everyone is on friendly terms and eager to make a deal, rather than waiting until trouble strikes. In the long run, nothing harms a relationship more than unpleasant surprises. For example, the Artist in the movie contract we will refer to throughout this chapter did not know in advance what conditions on the set would be, how grueling the shooting schedule, or how many friends and family would visit him. So his lawyer negotiated a deal in which the Producer agreed to provide a driver, a "first-class star trailer (which shall be a double pop-out)," a luxury hotel suite, and an adjacent room for visitors. In the end, because the role called for the Artist to live in the wilderness, he ultimately slept in a tent on the set to experience his part more fully, so he did not need the double pop-out trailer or the luxury suite. He also dispensed with the driver. But, under different circumstances, he might have wanted those luxuries, and his lawyer's goal was to protect his interests. It is a lot easier to forgo an expense than to add one to a movie budget.

Another advantage of using lawyers to conduct these negotiations is that they can serve as the bad guys. Instead of the client raising tough issues, the lawyers do. Many a client has said, "but my lawyer insists … " If the lawyer takes the blame, the client is able to maintain a better relationship with the other party. And hiring a lawyer communicates to the other parties that you are taking the deal seriously, and they will not be able to take advantage of you.

Of course, this lawyerly protection comes at a cost—legal fees, time spent bargaining, the hours used to read complex provisions, and the potential for good will to erode during negotiations.

Do you need a lawyer? The answer largely depends on the complexity of the deal. Most people do not hire a lawyer to review an apartment lease—the language is standard, and the prospective tenant has little power to change the terms of the deal. On the other hand, you should not undertake a significant acquisition or purchase agreement on your own.

18-1b Hiring a Lawyer

If you do hire a lawyer, be aware of certain warning signs. Although the lawyer's goal is to protect you, a good attorney should be a dealmaker, not a deal-breaker. She should help you do what you want and, therefore, should never (or, at least, hardly ever) say, "You cannot do this." Instead, she should say, "Here are the risks to this approach" or "Here is another way to achieve your goal."

Moreover, your lawyer's goal should not be to annihilate the other side. In the end, the contract will be more beneficial to everyone if the parties' relationship is harmonious. Trying to exact every last ounce of flesh, using whatever power you have to an abusive extreme, is not a sound long-term strategy. In the end, the best deals are those in which all the parties' incentives are aligned. Success for one means success for all—or at least, success for one party does not *prohibit* a positive outcome for the other side. If either side in the movie contract behaved unreasonably, word would quickly spread in the insular Hollywood world, damaging the troublemaker's ability to make other deals.

Now either you have a lawyer or you do not. The next step is to think about developing the contract.

18-2 THE CONTRACT

In this section, we discuss how a contract is prepared and what provisions it should include.

18-2a Who Drafts It?

Once businesspeople have agreed to the terms of the deal, it is time to prepare a draft of the contract. Generally, both sides would prefer to *control the pen* (i.e., to prepare the first draft of the contract) because the drafter has the right to choose a structure and wording that best represents his interests. Typically, the party with the most bargaining power prepares the drafts. In the movie contract, Producer's lawyer prepared the first draft. The contract then went to Artist's lawyer, who added the provisions that mattered to his client.

18-2b How to Read a Contract

Reading a contract is not like cracking open a novel. Instead, it should be a focused, multi-step process:

- **Pre-reading.** Before you begin reading the first draft of a contract, spend some time thinking about the provisions that are important to you. If you skip this step, you may find that as you read, your attention is so focused on the specific language of the contract that you lose sight of the larger picture.

- **The first read.** Read through once, just to get the basic idea of the contract—its structure and major provisions.

- **What-ifs.** This is the time to think about various outcomes, good and bad. Under the terms of the contract, what happens if all goes according to your plan? Also consider worst-case scenarios. In both situations, does the contract produce the result that you want? What happens if sales are higher than you expect, or if the product causes unexpected harm?

- **The second read.** Now read the contract to make sure that it handles the what-ifs in a manner that is satisfactory to you. Think about the relationship between various provisions—does it make sense?

Following this approach will help you avoid mistakes.

18-2c Mistakes

This author once worked with a lawyer who made a mistake in a contract. "No problem," he said. "I can win that one in court." Not a helpful attitude, given that one purpose of a contract is to *avoid* litigation. In this section, we look at the most common types of mistakes and how to avoid them.

VAGUENESS

Businesspeople sometimes *deliberately* choose vagueness. They do not want the terms of the contract to be clear. It may be that they are not sure what they can get from the other side, or in some cases, even what they really want. So they try to create a contract that leaves their options open. However, as the following case illustrates: **Vagueness is your enemy.**

You Be the Judge

Facts: Jones Brothers Construction was the general contractor on a job to expand American Airlines' facilities at O'Hare International Airport. After Quake bid on the project, Jones Brothers orally informed Quake that it had won the project and would receive a contract soon. Jones Brothers wanted the license numbers of the subcontractors that Quake would be using, but Quake could not furnish those numbers until it had assured its subcontractors that they had the job. Quake did not want to give that assurance until *it* was certain of its own work. So Jones Brothers sent a letter of intent that stated, among other things:

> We have elected to award the contract for the subject project to your firm as we discussed on April 15. A contract agreement outlining the detailed terms and conditions is being prepared and will be available for your signature shortly.
>
> Your scope of work includes the complete installation of expanded lunchroom, restaurant, and locker facilities for American Airlines employees, as well as an expansion of American Airlines' existing Automotive Maintenance Shop. A sixty (60) calendar day period shall be allowed for the construction of the locker room, lunchroom, and restaurant area beginning the week of April 22. The entire project shall be completed by August 15.
>
> This notice of award authorizes the work set forth in the attached documents at a lump sum price of $1,060,568.00.

QUAKE CONSTRUCTION, INC. v. AMERICAN AIRLINES, INC.

141 Ill. 2d 281, 565 N.E.2d 990, 1990 Ill. LEXIS 151
Supreme Court of Illinois, 1990

Jones Brothers Construction Corporation reserves the right to cancel this letter of intent if the parties cannot agree on a fully executed subcontract agreement.

The parties never signed a more detailed written contract, and ultimately Jones Brothers hired another company. Quake sued, seeking to recover the money it spent in preparation and its loss of anticipated profit.

You Be the Judge: *Was the letter of intent a valid contract?*

Argument for Quake: This letter was a valid contract. It explicitly stated that Jones awarded the contract to Quake. It also said, "This notice of award authorizes the work." The letter included significant detail about the scope of the contract, including the specific facilities Quake would be working on. Furthermore, the work was to commence approximately 4 to 11 days after the letter was written. This short period of time indicates that the parties intended to be bound by the letter so that work could begin quickly. And, the letter contained a cancellation clause. If it was not a contract, why would anyone need to cancel it?

Argument for Jones: This letter was not a contract. It referred several times to the execution of a formal contract by the parties, thus indicating that they did not intend to be bound by the letter. Look at the cancellation clause carefully: It could also be interpreted to mean that the parties did not intend to be bound by any agreement until they entered into a formal contract.

What a disaster for both parties that they have to litigate the meaning of this letter of intent! The problem is that they agreed to something so vague. Sometimes parties adopt vagueness as a *strategy*. One party may be trying to get a commitment from the other side without obligating itself. A party may feel *almost* ready to commit and yet still have reservations. It wants the *other* party to make a commitment so that planning can go forward. This is understandable but dangerous.

If you were negotiating for Jones Brothers and wanted to clarify negotiations without committing your company, how could you do it? State in the letter that it is *not a contract*, and that *neither side is bound by it*. State that it is a memorandum summarizing negotiations thus far, but that neither party will be bound until a full written contract is signed.

But what if Quake cannot get a commitment from its subcontractors until they are certain that it has the job? Quake should take the initiative and present Jones Brothers with its own letter of intent, stating that the parties *do* have a binding agreement for $1 million worth of work. Insist that Jones Brothers sign it. Jones Brothers would then be forced to decide whether it is willing to make a binding commitment. If Jones Brothers is not willing to commit, let it openly say so. At least both parties will know where they stand.

The movie contract provides another example of deliberate vagueness. In these contracts, nudity is always a contentious issue. Producers believe that nudity sells movie tickets; actors are afraid that it may tarnish their reputation. In the first draft of our contract, Artist's lawyer specified:

> Artist may not be photographed and shall not be required to render any services nude below the waist or in simulated sex scenes without Artist's prior written consent.

(This clause also applied to any double depicting Artist.) However, the script called for a scene in which Artist was swimming nude and the director wanted the option of showing him below the waist from the back. Ultimately, the nudity clause read as follows:

> Producer has informed Artist that Artist's role in the Picture might require Artist to appear and be photographed (a) nude, which nudity may include only above-the-waist nudity and rear below-the-waist nudity, but shall exclude frontal below-the-waist nudity; and (b) in simulated sex scenes. Artist acknowledges and agrees that Artist has accepted such employment in the Picture with full knowledge of Artist's required participation in nude scenes and/or in simulated sex scenes and Artist's execution of the Agreement constitutes written consent by Artist to appear in the nude scenes and simulated sex scenes and to perform therein as reasonably required by Producer. A copy of the scenes from the screenplay requiring Artist's nudity and/or simulated sex are attached hereto. Artist shall have a right of meaningful prior consultation with the director of the Picture regarding the manner of photography of any scenes in which Artist appears nude or engaged in simulated sex acts.
>
> Artist may wear pants or other covering that does not interfere with the shooting of the nude scenes or simulated sex scenes. Artist's buttocks and/or genitalia shall not be shown, depicted, or otherwise visible without Artist's prior written consent. Artist shall have the absolute right to change his mind and not perform in any nude scene or simulated sex scene, notwithstanding that Artist had prior thereto agreed to perform in such scene.

What does this provision mean? Has Artist agreed to perform in nude scenes or not? He has acknowledged that the script calls for nude scenes and he has agreed, in principle, that he will appear in them. However, he did not want to agree categorically, before shooting had even started and he had experience working with this director. Actor has a number of options—he can refuse to shoot nude scenes altogether, or he can shoot them and then, after viewing them, decide not to allow them in the movie. With a clause such as this one, the director shot different versions of the scene—some with nudity and some without—so that if Artist rejected the nude scene, the director still had options.

The true test of whether a vague clause belongs in a contract is this: Would you sign the contract if you knew that the other side's interpretation would prevail in litigation? In this example, each side was staking out its position, and deferring a final negotiation until there was an actual disagreement about a nude scene. If you would be happy enough with the other side's position in the end, the vague clause simply defers a fight that you can afford to lose. But if the point is really important to you, it may be wiser to resolve the issue before you sign the contract by writing the clause in a way that clearly reflects your desired outcome.

EXAM Strategy

Question: The nudity provision in the movie contract is vague. Rewrite it so that it accurately expresses the agreement between the parties.

Strategy: This is easy! Just say what the parties intended the deal to be.

Result: "The script for the Picture includes scenes showing Artist (a) with frontal nudity from the waist up and with rear below-the-waist nudity (but no frontal below-the-waist nudity); and (b) in simulated sex scenes. However, no scenes shall be shot in which Artist's buttocks and/or genitalia are shown, depicted, or otherwise visible without Artist's prior written consent. Artist shall have the absolute right not to perform in any nude scene or simulated sex scene. If shot, no nude or sex scenes may appear in the Picture without Artist's prior written consent."

AMBIGUITY

Vagueness occurs when the parties do not want the contract to be clear. Ambiguity is different—it means that the provision is *accidentally* unclear. It occurs in contracts when the parties think only about what *they* want a provision to mean, without considering the literal meaning or the other side's perspective. When reading a contract, try to imagine all the different ways a clause can be interpreted. Because you think it means one thing does not mean that the other side will share your view. For example, suppose that an employment contract says, "Employee agrees not to work for a competitor for a period of three years from employment." Does that mean three years from the date of hiring or the date of termination? Unclear, so who knows?

To take another example, the dictionary defines vandalism as *deliberately mischievous or malicious destruction or damage of property*. Arson is *the malicious burning of a house or property*. Seems clear enough—but does arson count as vandalism? In the following case, no one thought about this question until a house burned down.

CIPRIANO v. PATRONS MUTUAL INSURANCE COMPANY OF CONNECTICUT

2005 Conn. Super. LEXIS 3577
Superior Court of Connecticut, 2005

CASE SUMMARY

Facts: Juacikino Cipriano purchased an insurance policy on his house from Patrons Mutual Insurance Company. The policy stated that the company would not pay for any damage to the *residence* caused by vandalism or burglary if the residence was vacant for more than 30 days in a row just before the loss. Furthermore, the company would not pay for damage to *personal property* caused by fire, lightning, or vandalism.

After Cipriano's house had been vacant for more than 30 days, an arsonist burned it down. Patrons denied his claim on the grounds that arson is vandalism, which his policy did not cover. Cipriano filed suit against Patrons. The insurance company filed a motion for summary judgment.

Issues: *Does arson count as vandalism? Must Patrons pay Cipriano's claim?*

Decision: Arson does not count as vandalism. Patrons' motion for summary judgment is denied. It will have to pay Cipriano.

Reasoning: Patrons would not have to pay Cipriano if his house was damaged by vandalism. Does vandalism include arson? The policy never defined this important term. But the policy did list fire and vandalism as two different dangers. Is arson fire or vandalism? Or both?

In the case of ambiguity, two rules apply:

- Language in an insurance policy is interpreted as an ordinary person would understand it.
- A term is interpreted in favor of the party that did *not* draft the contract.

The term "arson" can reasonably mean "fire," "vandalism," or both. There is no way to know which definition the parties meant. Because the insurance company drafted the policy, this term must be interpreted in favor of Cipriano. Therefore, we rule that the term "vandalism" does not include "arson."

Patrons' motion for summary judgment is denied.

This case illustrates an important rule of contract drafting: **Any ambiguity is interpreted against the drafter of the contract.** (The *Cipriano* policy is a good example of how incomprehensible insurance policies can be. This complexity tends to erode judicial sympathy for the perpetrator.) Although both sides need to be careful in reading a contract—litigation benefits no one—the side that prepares the documents bears a special burden. This rule is meant to:

1. Protect laypeople from the dangers of form contracts that they have little power to change. Even if the insured in this case had read the contract carefully, it is unlikely that an insurance company would change its form contract for him.

2. Protect people who are unlikely to be represented by a lawyer. Most people do not hire a lawyer to read insurance contracts (or any form contract). And without an experienced lawyer, it is highly unlikely that an insured would ask, "So is arson included in the vandalism clause?"

3. Encourage those who prepare contracts to do so carefully.

Typos

The bane of a lawyer's existence! This author worked on a securities offering in which the sales document almost went out with part of the company's name spelled *Pertoleum* instead of *Petroleum*. (And legend has it that a United Airlines securities offering once featured "Untied Airlines.") Although clients tend not to have a sense of humor about such errors, at least there would be no adverse legal result. That is not always the case with typos.

A group of condominium buyers ended up in litigation over a tiny typo in their purchase agreements: an "8" instead of a "9." What difference could that possibly make? A lot, it turns out. Extell Development Corporation built the Rushmore, a luxury condominium complex in Manhattan. When Extell began selling the units, it agreed to refund any buyer's down payment if the first closing did not occur by September 1, 2009. (The goal was to protect buyers who might not have any place to live if the building was not finished on time.) In the end, the first closing occurred in February 2009. No problem, right? No problem except that, by accident, the purchase contract said September 1, *2008* rather than *2009*. In the meantime, the Manhattan real estate market tumbled, and many purchasers of Rushmore condominiums wanted to back out. After litigation all the way to the Federal Court of Appeals, Extell was required to refund the deposits.

What is the law of typos? First of all, the law has a fancier word than *typo*—it is **scrivener's error**. A scrivener is a clerk who copies documents. **In the case of a scrivener's error, a court will reform a contract if there is clear and convincing evidence that the mistake does not reflect the true intent of the parties.** In the Rushmore case, an arbitrator refused to reform the contract, ruling that there was no clear and convincing evidence that the parties intended something other than the contract term as written.

In the following case, even more money was at stake. What would you do if you were the judge?

Scrivener's error
A typo.

You Be the Judge

HERITAGE TECHNOLOGIES V. PHIBRO-TECH

2008 U.S. Dist. LEXIS 329
United States District Court for the Southern District
of Indiana, 2008

Facts: Heritage wanted to buy a substance called tribasic copper chloride (TBCC) from Phibro but, because of uncertainty in the industry, the two companies could not agree on a price for future years. It turned out, though, that the price of TBCC tended to rise and fall with that of copper sulfate, so Heritage proposed that the amount it paid for TBCC would increase an additional $15 per ton for each $0.01 increase in the cost of copper sulfate over $0.38 per pound.

Two top officers of Heritage and Phibro met in the Delta Crown Room at LaGuardia Airport to negotiate the purchase contract. At the end of their meeting, the Phibro officer hand wrote a document stating the terms of their deal and agreeing to the Heritage pricing proposal.

Negotiations between the two companies continued, leading to some changes and additions to their Crown Room agreement. In a draft prepared by Phibro, the $.01 number was changed to $0.1—that is, from 1 cent to 10 cents. In other words, in the original draft, Heritage agreed to a first increase if copper sulfate went above 39 cents per pound, an additional price rise at 40 cents, and so on. But in the Phibro draft, Heritage's first increase would not occur until the price of copper sulfate went to 48 cents a pound, with a second rise at 58 cents. In short, the Phibro draft was much more favorable to Heritage than the Heritage proposal had been.

At some point during the negotiations, the lawyer for Heritage asked his client if the $0.1 figure was accurate. The Heritage officer said that the increase in this amount was meant to be payment for other provisions that favored Phibro. There is no evidence that this statement was true. The contract went through eight drafts and numerous changes, but after the Crown Room meeting, the two sides never again discussed the $0.1 figure.

After the execution of the agreement, Heritage discovered a different mistake. When Heritage brought the error to Phibro's attention, Phibro agreed to make the change even though it was to Phibro's disadvantage to do so.

All was peaceful until the price of copper sulfate went to $0.478 per pound. Phibro believed that because the price was above $0.38 per pound, it was entitled to an increased payment. Heritage responded that the increase would not occur until the price went above $0.48. Phibro then looked at the agreement and noticed the $0.1 term for the first time. Phibro contacted Heritage to say that the $0.1 term was a typo and not what the two parties had originally agreed in the Delta Crown Room. Heritage refused to amend the agreement and Phibro filed suit.

You Be the Judge: *Should the court enforce the contract as written, or as the parties agreed in their Crown Room meeting? Which number is correct—$0.10 or $0.01*

Argument for Phibro: In the Delta Crown Room, the two negotiators agreed to a $15 per ton increase in the price of TBCC for each 1-cent increase in copper sulfate price. Then by mistake, the contract said 10 cents. The two parties never negotiated the 10-cent provision, and there is no evidence that they had agreed to it. The court should revise this contract to be consistent with the parties' agreement, which was 1 cent.

Also, the 10-cent figure makes no economic sense. The point of the provision was that the price of TBCC would go up at the same rate as copper sulfate, and 1 cent for each ton is a much more accurate reflection of the relationship between these two commodities than 10 cents per ton.

Argument for Heritage: The Delta Crown Room agreement was nothing more than a draft. The contract went through eight rounds of changes. The change in price was in return for other provisions that benefited Phibro.

The parties conducted negotiations by sending drafts back and forth rather than by talking on the phone. Both parties were represented by a team of lawyers, the agreement went through eight drafts, and this pricing term was never altered despite several other changes and additions. There is no clear and convincing evidence that both parties were mistaken about what the document actually said. Ultimately, the parties agreed to 10 cents, and that is what the court should enforce.

Ethics   When Heritage found a different mistake in the contract, Phibro agreed to correct it, even though the correction was unfavorable to Phibro. But when a mistake occurred in Heritage's favor, it refused to honor the intended terms of the agreement. Is Heritage behaving ethically? Does Heritage have an obligation to treat Phibro as well as Phibro behaved towards Heritage? Is it right to take advantage of other people's mistakes? What Life Principle would you apply in this situation?

PREVENTING MISTAKES

Here are ways to prevent mistakes in a contract.

Let your lawyer draft the contract   As a general rule, your lawyer is less likely to make mistakes than you are. Of all the players in the *Heritage* case, only one person noticed the error—Heritage's lawyer.

Resist overlawyering   Yes, your lawyer should draft the contract, but that does not mean she should have free rein, no matter what. This author once worked with a real estate attorney who had developed his own standard mortgage contract, of which he was immensely proud. Whenever he saw a provision in another contract that was missing from his own, he immediately added it. His standard form contract soon topped 100 pages. That contract was painful to read and did no service to his clients.

> As a general rule, your lawyer is less likely to make mistakes than you are.

Read the important terms carefully   Before signing a contract, check carefully and thoughtfully the names of the parties, the dates, dollar amounts, and interest rates. If all these elements are correct, you are unlikely to go too far wrong. And, of course, having read this chapter, you will never mistake $0.10 for $0.01.

Finally, when your lawyer presents you with a written contract, you should follow these rules:

1. Complain if your lawyer gives you a contract with provisions that are irrelevant to your situation.
2. If you do not know what a provision means, ask. If you still do not know (or if your lawyer does not know), ask her to take it out. Lawyers rarely draft from scratch; they tend to use other contracts as templates. Just because a provision was in another agreement does not mean that it is appropriate for you.
3. Remember that a contract is also a reference document. During the course of your relationship with the other party, you may need to refer to the contract regularly. That will be difficult if you do not understand portions of it, or if the contract is so disorganized you cannot find a provision when you need it.

Which brings us to our next topic—the structure of a contract. Once you understand the standard outline of a contract, it will be much easier for you to find your way through the thicket of provisions.

18-2d The Structure of a Contract

Traditional contracts tended to use archaic words—*whereas* and *heretofore* were common. Modern contracts are more straightforward, without as many linguistic flourishes. Our movie contract takes the modern approach.

TITLE

Contracts have a title, which generally is in capital letters, underlined, and centered at the top of the page. The title should be as descriptive as possible—a generic title such as AGREEMENT does not distinguish one contract from another. Much better to entitle it EMPLOYMENT AGREEMENT or CONFIDENTIALITY AGREEMENT. The title of our movie contract is MEMORANDUM OF AGREEMENT (not a particularly useful name), but in the upper right-hand corner, there is space for the date of the contract and the subject. Let's say the subject is "Dawn Rising/Clay Parker." It would have been even better if the title of the movie had been: Agreement between Clay Parker and Winterfield Productions for Dawn Rising.

INTRODUCTORY PARAGRAPH

The introductory paragraph includes the date, the names of the parties, and the nature of the contract. The names of the parties and the movie are defined terms, for example, Clay Parker ("Artist"). By defining the names, the actual names do not have to be repeated throughout the agreement. In this way, a standard form contract can be used in different deals without worrying about whether the names of the parties are correct throughout the document.

The introductory paragraph should also include specific language indicating that the parties entered into an agreement. In our contract, the opening paragraph states:

> This shall confirm the agreement ("Agreement") between WINTERFIELD PRODUCTIONS ("Producer") and CLAY PARKER ("Artist") regarding the acting services of Artist in connection with the theatrical motion picture tentatively entitled "DAWN RISING" (the "Picture"),[3] as follows:

This introductory paragraph is not numbered.

It is here that traditional contracts included their "Whereas" provisions. Thus, for example, a traditional movie contract might say the following:

> WHEREAS, Producer desires to retain the services of Artist for the purpose of making a theatrical motion picture; and
>
> WHEREAS, Artist desires to work for Producer on the terms and subject to the conditions set forth herein;
>
> NOW, THEREFORE, in consideration of the mutual covenants contained herein, and for other good and valuable consideration, the receipt and adequacy of which are hereby acknowledged, the parties agree as follows:

None of these flourishes are necessary, but some people prefer them.

DEFINITIONS

Most contracts have some definitions. As we have seen in the movie contract, *Artist*, *Producer*, and *Movie* were defined in the introductory paragraph. Sometimes, definitions are included in a separate section. Alternatively, they can appear throughout the contract. The movie contract does not have a definitions section, but many terms, such as *fixed compensation* and *teaser*, are defined within it.

COVENANTS

Covenant

A promise in a contract.

Now we get to the heart of the contract: What are the parties agreeing to do? Failure to perform these obligations constitutes a breach of the contract and damages will result. **Covenant** is a legal term that means a promise in a contract.

At this stage, the relationship between lawyer and client is particularly important. They will obtain the best result if they work well together. And to achieve a successful outcome, both need to contribute. Clients should figure out what they need for the agreement to be successful. It is at this point that they have the most control over the deal, and they should exercise it. *It is a mistake to assume that everything will work itself out.* Instead, clients need to protect themselves now as best they can. Lawyers can help in this process because they have worked on other similar deals and they know what can go wrong. Listen to them—they are on your side.

Imagine you are an actor about to sign a contract to make a movie. What provisions would you want? Begin by asking what your goals are for the project. Certainly, to make a movie that gets good reviews and good box office. So you will ask for as much control over the process and product as you can get—selection of the director and costars, for instance. Maybe influence on

---

[3]These are not the parties' real names but are offered to illustrate the concepts.

the editing process. But you also want to make sure that the movie does not hurt your career. What provisions would you need to achieve that goal? And shooting a movie can be grueling work, so you want to ensure that your physical and emotional needs are met, particularly when you are on location away from home. Try to think of all the different events that could happen and how they would affect you. The contract should make provisions for these occurrences.

Now take the other side and imagine what you would want if you were the producer. The producer's goal is to make money—which means creating a quality movie while spending as little as possible and maintaining control over the process and final product. As you can see, some of the goals conflict—both Artist and Producer want control over the final product. Who will win that battle?

Here are the terms of the movie contract.

The Artist negotiated:

1. A fixed fee of $1,800,000, to be paid in equal installments at the end of each week of filming

2. Extra payment if the filming takes longer than 10 weeks

3. 7.5 percent of the gross receipts of the movie

4. A royalty on any product merchandising, the rate to be negotiated in good faith

5. Approval over (but approval shall not be unreasonably withheld):

   a. the director, costars, hairdresser, makeup person, costume designer, stand-ins, and the look of his role (although he lists one director and costar whom he has preapproved)

   b. any changes in the script that materially affect his role

   c. all product placements, but he preapproves the placement of Snickers candy bars

   d. locations where the filming takes place

   e. all videos, photos, and interviews of him

   f. the translation of the script for French subtitles (he is fluent in French)

6. Approval (at his sole discretion) over the release of any blooper videos

7. His name to be listed first in the movie credits, on a separate card (i.e., alone on the screen)

8. That the producer not give any photographs from the set to a tabloid (such as, the *National Enquirer* or the *Star*)

9. At least 12 hours off duty from the end of each day of filming to the start of the next day

10. That he fly first class to any locations outside of Los Angeles

11. That the producer pay for 10 first-class airline tickets for his friends to visit him on location

12. A luxury hotel suite for himself and a room for his friends

13. A driver and four-wheel-drive SUV to transport him to the set

14. The right to keep some wardrobe items

The Producer negotiated:

1. All intellectual property rights to the movie

2. The right not to make the movie, although he would still have to pay Artist the fixed fee

3. Control over the final cut of the movie

4. That the Artist will show up on a certain date and work in good faith for

   a. 2 weeks in pre-production (wardrobe and rehearsals)
   b. 10 weeks shooting the movie
   c. 2 free weeks after the shooting ends, in case the director wants to reshoot some scenes. The Artist must in good faith make himself available whenever the director needs him

5. The right to fire Artist if his appearance or voice materially changes before or during the filming of the movie

6. That the Artist help promote the movie on dates subject to Artist's approval, which shall not be unreasonably withheld

BREACH

So now we have the covenants in the movie contract. What happens if one of the parties breaches a covenant? Throughout the life of a contract, there could be many small breaches. Say, Artist shows up one day late for filming or he gains five pounds. Maybe Producer deposits Artist's paycheck a few days late. Perhaps a pop-out trailer is not available. Although these events may technically be violations, a court would not impose sanctions over such minor issues. To constitute a violation of the contract, the breach must be material. A **material breach** is important enough to defeat an essential purpose of the contract. Although a court would probably not consider one missed day to be a material breach, if Artist repeatedly failed to show up, that would be material.

> **Material breach**
> A violation of a contract that defeats an essential purpose of the agreement.

Given that the goal of a contract is to avoid litigation, it is can be useful to define what a breach is. The movie contract uses this definition:

> Artist fails or refuses to perform in accordance with Producer's instructions or is otherwise in material breach or material default hereof," and "Artist's use of drugs [other than prescribed by a medical doctor]."

The contract goes on, however, to give Artist one free pass:

> It being agreed that with regard to one instance of default only, Artist shall have 24 hours after receipt of notice during principal photography, or 48 hours at all other times, to cure any alleged breach or default hereof.

Sometimes, you will recall, contracts state the consequences of a breach, such as the amount of damages. A damages clause can specify a certain amount, a limitation on the total, or other variations. In other words, the contract could say, "If Artist breaches, Producer is entitled to $1 million in damages." (You remember from prior chapters that these are called *liquidated damages*.) Alternatively, a damage clause could say, "Damages will not exceed $1 million." But the vast majority of contracts have neither liquidated damages nor damage caps.

> **Sole discretion**
> A party to a contract has the absolute right to make a decision on that issue.
>
> **Reasonable**
> Ordinary or usual under the circumstances.
>
> **Good faith**
> An honest effort to meet both the spirit and letter of a contract.

Good Faith   Note that many of the covenants in the movie contract provide that the right must be exercised reasonably or that a decision must be made in good faith (except for the right to approve blooper videos, over which Artist has sole discretion). A party with **sole discretion** has the *absolute* right to make any decision on that issue. Sole discretion clauses are not entered into lightly. **Reasonable** means ordinary or usual under the circumstances. **Good faith** means an honest effort to meet both the spirit and letter of the contract. These are the technical definitions. What do material, reasonably, and in good faith mean in practice?

In the following case, a famous athlete felt that the other party had committed a material breach of their contract, behaved unreasonably, and acted in bad faith. Do you agree?

LeMond Cycling, Inc. v. PTI Holding, Inc.

2005 U.S. Dist. LEXIS 742
United States District Court for the District of Minnesota, 2005

Facts: American Greg LeMond was a three-time winner of the Tour de France, cycling's most prestigious race. In 1994, *Sports Illustrated* named him one of the 40 most influential people in sports during the prior 40 years. Protective Technologies International, Inc. (Protective) sold cycling accessories under brand names like Barbie, Playskool, and Tonka to retailers such as Target, Wal-Mart, and Toys R Us.

LeMond and Protective signed a contract giving Protective the right to market LeMond cycling accessories. In return, Protective promised to:

- pay LeMond $500,000 a year plus royalties on annual sales exceeding $8.33 million

- use commercially reasonable efforts to produce and market the LeMond products

- keep LeMond informed of Protective's efforts

Protective tried to sell LeMond products to its regular customers, but only Target was interested and then only in a minor way. It agreed to allocate just 6 feet of shelf space to LeMond items. Protective did not tell LeMond about this deal.

Few of the LeMond accessories sold at Target, perhaps because Protective did not promote or advertise the products. Protective argued that it was Target's job to do the marketing. Because of poor sales, Target reduced the LeMond shelf space to just 4 feet and, ultimately, discontinued the products altogether. In neither instance did Protective inform LeMond.

Protective began to sell Schwinn bicycle accessories to the retailers that had rejected LeMond products, earning over $30 million in the process. Protective then abandoned all efforts to sell LeMond items.

LeMond filed suit against Protective for breach of contract. Protective filed a motion for summary judgment.

Issue: *Did Protective breach its contract with LeMond?*

Decision: The court granted part of the summary judgment motion, but not all. Protective may have breached the contract.

Reasoning: LeMond argued that Protective violated the contract by acting unreasonably and in bad faith.

To win, LeMond must first prove that Protective breached a *material* term of the contract. "Material" means a term so fundamental that its violation frustrates an essential purpose of the contract. Protective's failure to keep LeMond informed of its efforts was not material. The essential purpose of the contract was to sell bicycle accessories, not to send reports. More reports would not have meant more sales.

However, Protective's promise to use commercially reasonable efforts to sell products was material because that was the primary purpose of the contract. Although the contract does not define this term, it is well established that in evaluating commercial reasonableness, courts consider two factors:

1. standard practice in the licensing industry.

2. the financial resources, business expertise and practices of Protective.

Whether Protective met this standard must be determined at trial.

In addition, LeMond argued that Protective violated the contract's implied covenant of good faith and fair dealing by contracting with Schwinn. Bad faith means that a party has acted dishonestly or out of some ulterior motive. LeMond has produced some evidence that Protective effectively abandoned LeMond and focused solely on Schwinn. That factual dispute is another matter that must be determined at trial.

In drafting covenants, there are two issues to keep in mind.

Reciprocal Promises and Conditions   Suppose that a contract provides that:

1. Actor shall take part in the principal photography of Movie for 10 weeks, commencing on March 1.

2. Producer shall pay Artist $180,000 per week.

Reciprocal promises
Promises that are each enforceable independently.

Conditional promises
Promises that a party agrees to perform only if the other side has first done what it promised.

In this case, even if Artist does not show up for shooting, Producer is still required to pay him. These provisions are **reciprocal promises, which means that they are each enforceable independently.** Producer must make payment and then sue Artist, hoping to recover damages in court.

The better approach is for the covenants to be **conditional**—a party agrees to perform them only if the other side has first done what it promised. For example, in the real movie contract, Producer promises to pay Artist "On the condition that Artist fully performs all of Artist's services and obligations and agreements hereunder and is not in material breach or otherwise in material default hereof." And Artist has the right to attend any premieres of the movie and invite three friends, "On the condition that Artist fully performs all services and material obligations hereunder."

In short, if you do not expect to perform under the contract until the other side has met its obligations, be sure to say so.

Language of the Covenants   To clarify who exactly is doing what, covenants in a contract should use the active, not passive voice. In other words, a contract should say "Producer shall pay Artist $1.8 million," not "Artist shall be paid $1.8 million."

For important issues where disputes are likely to arise, the language should be precise, detailed, and complete. The movie contract uses 453 words to define the Artist's services just for shooting the movie, not including promotional efforts once the film is released. These acting services include, "dubbing, retakes, reshoots, and added scenes."

REPRESENTATIONS AND WARRANTIES

Representations and warranties
Statements of fact about the past or present.

Covenants are the promises the parties make about what they will do in the future. Representations and warranties are statements of fact about the past or present: They are true when the contract is signed (or at some other specific, designated time).[4] Representations and warranties are important—without them, the other party might not have agreed to the contract. For example, in the movie contract, Artist warrants that he is a member of the Screen Actors Guild. This provision is important because, if it were not true, Producer would either have to obtain a waiver or pay a substantial penalty.

In a contract between two companies, each side will generally represent and warrant facts such as: They legally exist, they have the authority to enter into the contract, their financial statements are accurate, they have revealed all material litigation, and they own all relevant assets. In a contract for the sale of goods, the contract will include warranties about the condition of the goods being sold.

EXAM Strategy

Question: Producer does not want Artist to pilot an airplane during the term of the contract. Would that provision be a warranty and representation or a covenant? How would you phrase it?

Strategy: Warranties and representations are about events in the past or present. A covenant is a promise for the future. If, for example, Producer wanted to know that Artist had never used drugs in the past, that provision would be a warranty and representation.

---

[4]Although, technically, there is a slight difference between a representation and a warranty, many lawyers confuse the two terms, and the distinction is not important. We will treat them as synonyms, as many lawyers do.

Result: A promise not to pilot an airplane is a covenant. The contract could say, "Until Artist completes all services required hereunder, he shall not pilot an airplane."

BOILERPLATE

These standard previsions are typically placed in a section entitled *Miscellaneous*. Many people think that *boilerplate* is a synonym for *boring and irrelevant*, but it is worth remembering that the term comes from the iron or steel that protects the hull of a ship—something that shipbuilders ignore to the passengers' peril. A contract without boilerplate is valid and enforceable—so it can be tempting to skip these provisions, but they do play an important protective role. In essence, boilerplate creates a private law that governs disputes between the parties. Courts can also play this role and, indeed, in the absence of boilerplate they will. But remember that an important goal of a contract is to avoid court involvement.

Here are some standard, and important, boilerplate provisions.

Choice of Law and Forum
Choice of law provisions determine which state's laws will be used to interpret the contract. **Choice of forum** determines the state in which any litigation would take place. (One state's courts can apply another state's laws.) Lawyers often view these two provisions as the most important boilerplate. Individual states might have dramatically different laws. Even the so-called uniform statutes, such as the Uniform Commercial Code, can vary widely from state to state. Variations are even more pronounced in other areas of the law, in particular in the common law, which is created by state courts. As for forum, it is a lot more convenient and cheaper to litigate a case in one's home courts.

When resolving a dispute, the choice of law and forum can strongly influence the outcome. For this reason, sometimes parties are reluctant to negotiate the provision and instead decide not to designate a forum and just take their chances. Or they may choose a neutral, equally inconvenient forum like Delaware. Without a choice of forum clause, the parties may well end up litigating where to litigate, or they may find themselves even worse off—with parallel cases filed by each in his preferred forum.

The movie contract states: "This Agreement shall be deemed to have been made in the State of California and shall be construed and enforced in accordance with the law of the State of California." The contract did not, but might have, also specified the forum—that any litigation would be tried in California.

Modification
Contracts should contain a provision governing modification. The movie contract states: "This Agreement may not be amended or modified except by an instrument in writing signed by the party to be charged with such amendment or modification."

"Charged with such amendment" means the party who is adversely affected by the change. For example, if Producer agrees to pay Artist more, then Producer must sign the amendment. Without this provision, a conversation over beers between Producer and Artist about a change in pay might turn out to be an enforceable amendment.

The original version of the movie contract said that Artist would be photographed nude only above the waist. He ultimately agreed to rear-below-the-waist photography. That amendment (which the parties called a *rider*—another term for amendment or addition) took the form of a letter from Artist agreeing to the change. Producer then signed the letter, acknowledging receipt and acceptance. The amendment would have been valid even without Producer's signature because Artist was "charged with such Amendment."

Choice of law provisions
Determine which state's laws will be used to interpret the contract.

Choice of forum provisions
Determine the state in which any litigation would take place.

Rider
An amendment or addition to a contract.

If a contract has a provision requiring that amendments be in writing, there are three ways to amend it:

1. Signing an amendment (or rider).
2. Crossing out by hand the wrong language and replacing it with the correct terms. It is good practice for both parties to initial each change. This method is typically used before the document is signed—say, at the closing if the parties notice a mistake.
3. Rewriting the entire contract to include the changed provisions. In this case, the contract is typically renamed: The Amended and Restated Agreement. This method is most appropriate if there are many complex alterations.

Note that amending a contract may raise issues of consideration, a topic discussed in Chapter 11.

Assignment of rights

A transfer of benefits under a contract to another person.

Delegation of duties

A transfer of obligations in a contract.

Assignment of Rights and Delegation of Duties

An **assignment of rights** is a transfer of your benefits under a contract to another person, while **delegation of duties** is a transfer of your obligations. In the movie contract, Producer has the right to assign the contract, but he must stay secondarily liable on it. In other words, someone else can take over the contract for him, but if that person fails to live up to his obligations, Producer is liable. Artist might be unhappy if another production company takes over the movie, but he is still required under the contract to perform his acting services. At least he knows that Producer is liable for his paycheck.

Delegation means that someone else performs the duties under the contract. It certainly matters to Producer which actor shows up to do the shooting. Artist cannot say, "I'm too busy—here's my cousin Jack." So the movie contract provides:

> It is expressly understood and agreed that the services to be rendered by Artist hereunder are of the essence of this Agreement and that such services shall not be delegated to any other person or entity, nor shall Artist assign the right to receive compensation hereunder.

In essence, Producer not only cares who shows up for shooting, but he also wants to make sure that no one else cashes the checks. He wants to deal only with Artist. And he worries that if Artist assigns the right to receive payment, he will feel less motivated to do his job well.

Arbitration

Some contracts prohibit the parties from suing in court and require that disputes be settled by an arbitrator. The parties to a contract do not have to arbitrate a dispute unless the contract specifically requires it. Arbitration has its advantages—flexibility and savings in time and money—but it also has disadvantages. For example, most contracts between consumers and brokerage houses require arbitration. Consumer advocates argue that the arbitrators in these disputes are biased in favor of the brokerage houses—who engage in many arbitrations—over consumers who are likely to be one-time customers. And many believe that employees receive a less favorable result when they arbitrate, rather than litigate, disputes with their employer. Also, if a court makes a mistake in applying the law, an appellate court can correct the error. But if an arbitrator makes a mistake, there is generally no appeal. The movie contract does not include an arbitration provision.

Attorney's Fees

As a general rule, parties to a contract must pay their own legal fees, no matter who is in the wrong. But contracts may override this general rule and provide that the losing party in a dispute must pay the attorney's fees for both sides. Such a provision tends to discourage the poorer party from litigating with a rich opponent for fear of having to pay two sets of attorney's fees. The movie contract provides:

> Artist hereby agrees to indemnify Producer from and against any and all losses, costs (including, without limitation, reasonable attorneys' fees), liabilities, damages, and claims of any nature arising from or in connection with any breach by Artist of any agreement, representation, or warranty made by Artist under this Agreement.

There is no equivalent provision for breaches by Producer. What does that omission tell you about the relative bargaining power of the two parties?

Integration   During contract negotiations, the parties may discuss many ideas that are not ultimately included in the final version. The point of an integration clause is to prevent either side from later claiming that the two parties had agreed to additional provisions. The movie contract states:

> This Agreement, along with the exhibits attached hereto, shall constitute a binding contract between the parties hereto and shall supersede any and all prior negotiations and communications, whether written or oral, with respect hereto.

Without this clause, even a detailed written contract can be amended by an undocumented conversation—a dangerous situation since the existence and terms of the amendment will depend on what a court *thinks* was said and intended, which may or may not be what actually happened.

EXAM Strategy

Question: Daniel and Annie signed a contract providing that Daniel would lend $50,000 to Annie's craft beer business at an interest rate of 8 percent. During negotiations, Daniel and Annie agreed that the interest rate would go down to 5 percent once she had sold 25,000 cases. This provision never made it into the contract. After the contract had been signed, Daniel agreed to reduce the interest rate to 6 percent once volume exceeded 25,000 cases. The contract had an integration provision but no modification clause. What interest rate must Annie pay once she has sold 25,000 cases?

Strategy: If a contract has an integration provision, then side agreements made during negotiations are unenforceable unless included in the written contract. Without a modification provision, oral agreements made after the contract was signed may be enforceable.

Result: A court would not enforce the side agreement that reduced the interest rate to 5 percent. However, it is possible that a court would enforce the 6 percent agreement.

Severability   If, for whatever reason, some part of the contract turns out to be unenforceable, a severability provision asks the court simply to delete the offending clause and enforce the rest of the contract. For example, courts will not enforce unreasonable noncompete clauses. (California courts will not enforce any noncompetes, unless made in connection with the sale of a business.) In one case, a consultant signed an employment contract that prohibited him from engaging in his occupation "anyplace in the world." The court struck down this noncompete provision but ruled that the rest of the contract (which contained trade secret clauses) was valid. The movie contract states:

> In the event that there is any conflict between any provision of this Agreement and any statute, law, or regulation, the latter shall prevail; provided, however, that in such event, the provision of this Agreement so affected shall be curtailed and limited only to the minimum extent necessary to permit compliance with the minimum requirement, and no other provision of this Agreement shall be affected thereby and all other provisions of this Agreement shall continue in full force and effect.

Force majeure event

A disruptive, unexpected occurrence for which neither party is to blame that prevents one or both parties from complying with a contract.

Force Majeure   A *force majeure* **event** is a disruptive, unexpected occurrence for which neither party is to blame that prevents one or both parties from complying with the contract. *Force majeure* events typically include war, terrorist attack, fire, flood, or general acts of God. If, for example, a major terrorist event were to halt air travel, Artist might not be able to appear on set as scheduled. The movie contract defines *force majeure* events thus:

> fire, war, governmental action or proceeding, third-party breach of contract, injunction, or other material interference with the production or distribution of motion pictures by Producer, or any other unexpected or disruptive event sufficient to excuse performance of this Agreement as a matter of law or other similar causes beyond Producer's control or by reason of the death, illness, or incapacity of the producer, director, or a member of the principal cast or other production personnel.

Notices   After a contract is signed, there may be times when the parties want to send each other official notices—of a breach, an objection, or an approval, for example. In this section, the parties list the addresses where these notices may be sent. For Producer, it is company headquarters. For Artist, there are three addresses: his agent, his manager, and his lawyer. The notice provision also typically specifies when the notice is effective: when sent, when it would normally be expected to arrive, or when it actually does arrive.

Closing   To indicate that the parties have agreed to the terms of the contract, they must sign it. A simple signature is sufficient, but contracts often contain flourishes. The movie contract, for example, states:

> IN WITNESS WHEREOF, the parties hereto have executed this Agreement as of the date first written above.

With clauses like this, it is important to make sure that there is an (accurate) date on the first page. If not otherwise provided in the "Notices" section, it is a good idea to include the parties' addresses. The movie contract also listed Artist's social security number.

When a party to the contract is a corporation, the signature lines should read like this:

Winterfield Productions, Inc.
By:_____
Name:
Title:

If an individual signs her own name without indicating that she is doing so in her role as an employee of Winterfield Productions, Inc., she would be personally liable.

In the end, both parties signed the contract, and the movie was made. According to Rotten Tomatoes, the online movie site, professional reviewers rated it 7.9 out of 10.

Chapter Conclusion

You will undoubtedly sign many contracts in your life. Their length and complexity can be daunting. (In the movie contract, one of the paragraphs is 1,000 words.) The goal of this chapter is to help you understand the structure and meaning of the most important provisions so that you can read and analyze contracts more effectively.

EXAM REVIEW

1. **AMBIGUITY**   Any ambiguity in a contract is interpreted against the party who drafted the agreement. (pp. 406–407)

2. **SCRIVENER'S ERROR**   A scrivener's error is a typographical mistake. In the case of a scrivener's error, a court will reform a contract if there is clear and convincing evidence that the mistake does not reflect the true intent of the parties. (p. 407)

EXAM Strategy

Question: Martha intended to transfer a piece of land to Paul. By mistake, she signed a contract transferring two parcels of land. Each piece was accurately described in the contract. Will the court reform this contract and transfer one piece of land back to her?

Strategy: Begin by asking if this was a scrivener's error. Then consider whether the court will correct the mistake.

3. **BEFORE SIGNING A CONTRACT**   Before signing a contract, check carefully and thoughtfully the names of the parties, the dates, dollar amounts, and interest rates. (p. 409)

4. **MATERIAL BREACH**   A material breach is important enough to defeat an essential purpose of the contract. (p. 412)

EXAM Strategy

Question: Laurie's contract to sell her tortilla chip business to Hudson contained a provision that she must continue to work at the business for five years. One year later, she quit. Hudson refused to pay her the amounts still owing under the contract. Laurie alleged that he is liable for the full amount because her breach was not material. Is Laurie correct?

Strategy: What was the essential purpose of the contract? Was Laurie's breach important enough to defeat it?

5. **SOLE DISCRETION**   A party with sole discretion has the absolute right to make any decision on that issue. (p. 412)

EXAM Strategy

Question: A tenant rented space from a landlord for a seafood restaurant. Under the terms of the lease, the tenant could assign the lease only if the landlord gave her consent, which she had the right to withhold "for any reason whatsoever, at her sole discretion." The tenant grew too ill to run the restaurant and asked permission to assign the lease. The landlord refused. In court, the tenant argued that the landlord could not unreasonably withhold her consent. Is the tenant correct?

Strategy: A sole discretion clause grants the absolute right to make a decision. Are there any exceptions?

6. **REASONABLE**   Reasonable means ordinary or usual under the circumstances. (p. 412)

7. **GOOD FAITH**   Good faith means an honest effort to meet both the spirit and letter of the contract. (p. 412)

8. **STRUCTURE OF A CONTRACT**   The structure of a contract looks like this:

1. Title
2. Introductory Paragraph
3. Definitions
4. Covenants
5. Breach
6. Conditions
7. Representations and Warranties
   i. Covenants are the promises the parties make about what they will do in the future.
   ii. Representations and warranties are statements of fact about the present or past—they are true when the contract is signed (or at some other specific, designated time).

8. Boilerplate

   i.   Choice of Law and Forum
   ii.   Modification
   iii. Assignment of Rights and Delegation of Duties
   iv.   Arbitration
   v.   Attorney's Fees
   vi.   Integration
   vii. Severability
   viii. *Force Majeure*
   ix.   Notices
   x.   Closing (pp. 409–412)

2. Result: The court ruled that it was not a scrivener's error because it was not a typo or clerical error. Therefore, the court did not reform the contract, and the land was not transferred back to Martha.

4. Result: The purpose of the contract was for Hudson to build up the business and make a profit. Laurie's departure interfered with that goal. The court ruled that the breach was material and Hudson did not have to pay the sums still owing under the contract.

5. Result: The court ruled for the landlord. She had the absolute right to make any decision so long as the decision was not illegal. The moral: Sole discretion clauses are serious business. Do not enter into one lightly.

MULTIPLE-CHOICE QUESTIONS

1. Which of the following statements is true?

(a) Vagueness occurs when the parties do not want the contract to be clear.

(b) Ambiguity occurs when the parties do not want the contract to be clear.

(c) Vagueness in a contract is often appropriate as a way to clinch a deal.

(d) Ambiguity is an appropriate tactic, particularly by the party drafting the contract.

2. In the *Cipriano* case, what happened?

(a) The jury decided in favor of Cipriano because arson is vandalism.

(b) The jury decided against Cipriano because arson is not vandalism.

(c) The judge dismissed the motion for summary judgment because the contract was ambiguous.

(d) The judge granted the motion for summary judgment because the contract was not ambiguous.

3. In the case of a scrivener's error, what happens?

(a) A court will not reform the contract. The parties must live with the document they signed.

(b) A court will reform the contract if there is clear and convincing evidence that the clause in question does not reflect the true intent of the parties.

(c) A court will reform the contract if a preponderance of the evidence indicates that that the clause in question does not reflect the true intent of the parties.

(d) A court will invalidate the contract in its entirety.

4. In the *LeMond* case, the court ruled:

(a) Protective's failure to supply marketing and media plans was a material breach of the contract because without those plans, LeMond could not monitor sales.

(b) Protective's failure to supply marketing and media plans was a material breach of the contract because Protective had agreed to supply the plans.

(c) The requirement that Protective use commercially reasonable means to promote the product line was not enforceable because the term was ambiguous.

(d) Protective's failure to supply marketing and media plans was not a material breach of the contract.

5. A contract states (1) that Buzz Co. legally exists and (2) will provide 2,000 pounds of wild salmon each week. Which of the following statements is true?

(a) Clause 1 is a covenant and Clause 2 is a representation.

(b) Clause 1 is a representation and Clause 2 is a covenant.

(c) Both clauses are representations.

(d) Both clauses are covenants.

ESSAY QUESTIONS

1. List three types of contracts that should definitely be in writing, and one that probably does not need to be.

2. Make a list of provisions that you would expect in an employment contract.

3. List three provisions in a contract that would be material, and three that would not be.

4. Slimline and Distributor signed a contract providing that Distributor would use reasonable efforts to promote and sell Slimline's diet drink. Slimline was already being sold in Warehouse Club. After the contract was signed, Distributor stopped conducting in-store demos of Slimline. It did not repackage the product as Slimline and Warehouse requested. Sales of Slimline continued to increase during the term of the contract. Slimline sued Distributor, alleging a violation of the agreement. Who should win?

5. **YOU BE THE JUDGE WRITING PROBLEM** Chip bought an insurance policy on his house from Insurance Co. The policy covered damage from fire but explicitly excluded coverage for harm caused "by or through an earthquake." When an earthquake struck, Chip's house suffered no fire damage, but the earthquake caused a building some blocks away to catch on fire. That fire ultimately spread to Chip's house, burning it down. Is Insurance Co. liable to Chip? **Argument for Insurance Co.:** The policy could not have been clearer or more explicit. If there had been no earthquake, Chip's house would still be standing. The policy does not cover his loss. **Argument for Chip:** His house was not damaged by an earthquake; it burned down. The policy covered fire damage. If a contract is ambiguous, it must be interpreted against the drafter of the contract.

DISCUSSION QUESTIONS

1. In the movie contract, which side was the more successful negotiator? Can you think of any terms that either party left out? Are any of the provisions unreasonable?

2. What are the advantages and disadvantages of hiring a lawyer to draft or review a contract?

3. What are the penalties if Artist breaches the movie contract? Are these reasonable? Too heavy? Too light?

4. **ETHICS** In the *Heritage* case, the two companies had agreed to a price change of $0.01. When Heritage's lawyer pointed out to his client the change to $0.10, the Heritage officer did not tell Phibro. The change was subtle in appearance but important in its financial impact. Was Heritage's behavior ethical? When the opposing side makes a mistake in a contract, do you have an ethical obligation to tell them? What Life Principles would you apply in this situation?

5. Blair Co.'s top officers approached an investment bank to find a buyer for the company. The bank sent an engagement letter to Blair with the following language:

> If, within 24 months after the termination of this agreement, Blair is bought by anyone with whom Bank has had substantial discussions about such a sale, Blair must pay Bank its full fee.

Is there any problem with the drafting of this provision? What could be done to clarify the language?

Commercial Transactions

CHAPTER 19

INTRODUCTION TO SALES

He Sued, She Sued. Harold and Maude made a great couple because both were compulsive entrepreneurs. One evening they sat on their penthouse roof deck, overlooking the twinkling Chicago skyline. Harold sipped a decaf coffee while negotiating, over the phone, with a real estate developer in San Antonio. Maude puffed a cigar as she bargained on a different line with a toy manufacturer in Cleveland. They hung up at the same time. "I did it!" shrieked Maude, "I made an incredible deal for the robots—five bucks each!" "No, *I* did it!" trumpeted Harold, "I sold the 50 acres in Texas for $300,000 more than it's worth." They dashed indoors.

Maude quickly scrawled a handwritten memo, which said, "Confirming our deal—100,000 Psychopath Robots—you deliver Chicago—end of summer." She did not mention a price, or an exact delivery date, or when payment would be made. She signed her memo and faxed it to the toy manufacturer. Harold took more time. He typed a thorough contract, describing precisely the land he was selling, the $2.3 million price, how and when each payment would be made and the deed conveyed. He signed the contract and faxed it, along with a plot plan showing the surveyed land. Then the happy couple grabbed a bottle of champagne, returned to the deck—and placed a side bet on whose contract would prove more profitable. The loser would have to cook and serve dinner for six months.

Neither Harold nor Maude ever heard again from the other parties. The toy manufacturer sold the Psychopath Robots to another retailer at a higher price. Maude was forced to buy comparable toys elsewhere for $9 each. She sued. And the Texas property buyer changed his mind, deciding to develop a Club Med in Greenland and refusing to pay Harold for his land. He sued. Only one of the two plaintiffs succeeded. Which one?

> Confirming our deal—100,000 Psychopath Robots—you deliver Chicago—end of summer.

The adventures of Harold and Maude illustrate the Uniform Commercial Code (UCC) in action. The Code is the single most important source of law for people engaged in commerce and controls the vast majority of contracts made every day in every state. The Code is ancient in origin, contemporary in usage, admirable in purpose, and flawed in application. "Yeah, yeah, that's fascinating," snaps Harold, "but who wins the bet?" Relax, Harold, we'll tell you in a minute.

19-1 DEVELOPMENT OF COMMERCIAL LAW

In England in the 1500s, it was far more important to hold land than it was to have money. Large landowners—barons, earls, and dukes—stood in excellent positions. They had access to the king or queen, they were exempt from many kinds of arrest, and, if they did get into trouble, they generally were tried before other members of the nobility in special courts. It is not surprising that law was then centered squarely upon *real property*, which mainly consists of land and permanent structures. But society changes, and so do businesses. When this happens, the law may fall behind the times.

In the 1500s, merchants in England began to have problems using existing law to resolve commercial disputes. There were many laws about land, but few for contracts. English judges were only beginning to acknowledge that an exchange of mere promises, with no money or property changing hands, might lead to an enforceable agreement. But merchants dealt in the sale of goods, not real estate. Their livelihood depended upon promises, on the rapid movement of their wares, and on their ability to enforce bargains. Dissatisfied with the few remedies that courts offered, businessmen throughout England and the Continent began to treat their own customs as law and to settle disputes in trade organizations rather than civil courts. The body of rules they relied on became known as the *lex mercatoria*, or **law merchant**. The law merchant was thus a "custom made" law, created by the merchants who used it. The new doctrine focused on promises, the sale and exchange of goods, and payment.

In the middle of the 20th century, contract law again required a reinvention. Two problems had become apparent in the United States:

1. Old contract law principles often did not reflect modern business practices.

2. Laws had become different from one state to another.

On many legal topics, contract law included, the national government has had little to say and has allowed the states to act individually. Texas decides what kinds of agreements count as contracts in Texas, and next door in Oklahoma, the rules may be very different. On many issues, states reached essentially similar conclusions, so contract law developed in the same direction. But sometimes, the states disagreed, and contract law took on the aspect of a patchwork quilt.

The UCC was created as an attempt to solve these two problems. It was a proposal written by legal scholars and not a law drafted by members of Congress or state legislatures. The scholars at the American Law Institute and the National Conference of Commissioners on Uniform State Laws had great ideas, but they had no legal authority to make anyone do anything.

Over time, lawmakers in all 50 states were persuaded to adopt many parts of the UCC. They responded to these persuasive arguments:

1. Businesses will benefit if most commercial transactions are governed by the modern and efficient contract law principles that are outlined in the UCC.

2. Businesses everywhere will be able to operate more efficiently, and transactions will be more convenient, if the law surrounding most of their transactions is the same in all 50 states.

This chapter will focus on Article 2 of the UCC, which applies to the sale of goods. A **good** is a moveable physical object except for money and securities (like stock certificates). A house is not a good, but the *stuff* in the house—the car in the garage, the televisions, the furniture, and almost everything else—is. Article 2 applies to contracts that sell goods, as well as to contracts that sell a mix of goods and services if the *predominant purpose* of the deal is to sell goods.

It is worth noting that the UCC is not a total replacement for older principles in contract law. Contract lawsuits not involving goods are still resolved using the older common law rules. The table below outlines the UCC and the types of contracts that it does govern.

The entire Code is available online at **http://www.law.cornell.edu/ucc/ucc.table.html**.

Article 1:	
General Provisions	The purpose of the code, general guidance in applying it, and definitions.
Article 2:	
Sale of Goods	The sale of *goods,* such as a new car, 20,000 pairs of gloves, or 101 dalmatians. This is one of the two most important articles in the UCC.
Article 2A:	
Leases	A temporary exchange of goods for money, such as renting a car.
Article 3:	
Negotiable Instruments	The use of checks, promissory notes, and other negotiable instruments.
Article 4:	
Bank Deposits and Collections	The rights and obligations of banks and their customers.
Article 4A:	
Funds Transfers	An instruction, given by a bank customer, to credit a sum of money to another's account.
Article 5:	
Letters of Credit	The use of credit, extended by two or more banks, to facilitate a contract between two parties who do not know each other and require guarantees by banks they trust.
Article 6:	
Bulk Transfers	The sale of a major part of a company's inventory or equipment. This article has been repealed in all but a few states.
Article 7:	
Warehouse Receipts, Bills of Lading, and Other Documents of Title	Documents proving ownership of goods that are being transported or stored.

(continued)

Article 8:	
Investment Securities	Rights and liabilities concerning shares of stock or other ownership of an enterprise.
Article 9:	
Secured Transactions	A sale of goods in which the seller keeps a financial stake in the goods he has sold, such as a car dealer who may repossess the car if the buyer fails to make payments. This is one of the two most important articles in the Code.

© Cengage Learning

19-1a Harold and Maude, Revisited

Harold and Maude each negotiated what they believed was an enforceable agreement, and both filed suit: Harold for the sale of his land, Maude for the purchase of toy robots. Only one prevailed. The difference in outcome demonstrates one of the changes that the UCC has wrought in the law of commercial contracts and illustrates why everyone in business needs a working knowledge of the Code. As we revisit the happy couple, Harold is clearing the dinner dishes. Maude sits back in her chair, lights a cigar, and compliments her husband on the apple tart. Harold, scowling and spilling coffee, wonders what went wrong.

Harold's contract was for the sale of land and governed by the common law of contracts. The common law Statute of Frauds requires any agreement for the sale of land to be in writing and *signed by the defendant*, in this case the buyer in Texas. Harold signed it, but the buyer never did, so Harold's meticulously detailed document was worth less than a five-cent cigar.

Maude's quickly scribbled memorandum concerning psychotic robot toys was for the sale of goods and was governed by Article 2 of the UCC. The Code requires less detail and formality in a writing. Because Maude and the seller were both merchants, the document she scribbled could be enforced *even against the defendant*, who had never signed anything. The fact that Maude left out the price and other significant terms was not fatal to a contract under the UCC, although under the common law such omissions would have made the bargain unenforceable. We will look in greater detail at these UCC changes. For now it is enough to see that the Code has carved major changes into the common law of contracts, alterations that Harold is beginning to appreciate.

19-1b This Unit and This Chapter

This unit covers three principal subjects, all relating to commercial transactions that the Code governs. The first chapters concern the sale of goods and focus primarily on Article 2. In the present chapter we emphasize how Code provisions work together to change the common law. In the following chapters we examine title to goods and warranties (Chapter 20) and performance and remedies (Chapter 21).

A future chapter (Chapter 22) surveys the law of negotiable instruments. Checks are the most common kind of negotiable instrument, but we will see that there are many other varieties and that each creates different rights and obligations. We include in the unit a chapter devoted to secured transactions (Chapter 23), that is, a sale of goods in which the seller keeps a financial stake in the goods he has sold, and a later chapter that analyzes bankruptcy law (Chapter 24).

The remainder of this chapter examines contract formation under Article 2 of the UCC. When an agreement is struck, the first fundamental question of contract law is this: Has an enforceable contract been formed? As you read the chapter, keep the following ideas in mind:

1. *The UCC is pro-business.* The whole point of the UCC is to make business transactions more reliable, convenient, and predictable.

2. *Tie goes to the contract.* In baseball, a tie goes to the runner. Under the UCC, the preference is to declare an agreement to be a contract if no clear reason exists to declare it invalid.

19-2 UCC Basics

19-2a Code's Purpose

The UCC proclaims its purposes clearly:

UCC §1-102(2): Underlying purposes and policies of this Act are

(a) to simplify, clarify and modernize the law governing commercial transactions;
(b) to permit the continued expansion of commercial practices through custom, usage and agreement of the parties;
(c) to make uniform the law among the various jurisdictions.

This is not mere boilerplate. To "modernize," in (a), requires a focus on the needs of contemporary businesspeople, not on rules developed when judges rode horseback. Suppose a court must decide whether a writing is detailed enough to satisfy the Code's Statute of Frauds. The judge may rely on §1-102 to decide that because modern commerce is so fast, even the skimpiest of writings is good enough to demonstrate that the parties had reached a bargain. In doing so, the judge would deliberately be turning away from legal history to accommodate business practices in an electronic age.

Section 1-102 also states that "[t]his Act shall be liberally construed and applied to promote its underlying purposes," meaning that when in doubt, courts should focus on the goals described. The Code emphasizes *getting the right results* rather than following rigid rules of contract law.

19-2b Scope of Article 2

Because the UCC changes the common law, it is essential to know whether the Code applies in a given case. Negotiations may lead to an enforceable agreement when the UCC applies, even though the same bargaining would create no contract under the common law.

Good

Are things that are moveable, other than money and investment securities.

UCC §2-102: Article 2 applies to the sale of goods.[1] **Goods** are things that are moveable, other than money and investment securities. Hats are goods, and so are railroad cars, lumber, books, and bottles of wine. Land is not a good, nor is a house. So an agreement for the delivery of 10,000 board feet of white pine is a contract for the sale of goods, and Article 2 governs it. But the article does not apply to a contract for the sale of an office building. A skyscraper is not moveable (although an entire city *may* be[2]).

---

[1]Officially, Article 2 tells us that it applies to *transactions* in goods, which is a slightly broader category than sale of goods. But most sections of Article 2, and most court decisions, focus exclusively on sales, and so shall we.

[2]"If you are lucky enough to have lived in Paris as a young man, then wherever you go for the rest of your life, it stays with you, for Paris is a moveable feast." (Ernest Hemingway, 1950).

Article 2 regulates **sales**, which means that one party transfers title to the other in exchange for money. If you sell your motorcycle to a friend, that is a sale of goods. If you lend the bike to your friend for the weekend, that is not a sale, and Article 2 does not apply. Article 2 also does not apply to the leasing of goods, for example, when you rent a car. A sale involves a permanent change in ownership whereas a lease concerns a temporary change in possession.

19-2c Mixed Contracts

To determine whether the UCC governs, we need to know what kind of an agreement the parties made. Was it one for the sale of goods (UCC) or one for services (common law)? In fact the agreement combined both goods and services and was therefore a *mixed contract*. **In a mixed contract involving sales and services, the UCC will govern if the *predominant purpose* is the sale of goods, but the common law will control if the predominant purpose is providing services.**

For example, assume that you take your car to a mechanic for repairs and that there are problems with the work. If a lawsuit ensues, a court will have to determine whether the predominant purpose of the contract was the parts (goods) which were replaced or the labor (service) involved in the work.

19-2d Merchants

UCC §2-104: A **merchant** is someone who routinely deals in the particular goods involved, *or* who appears to have special knowledge or skill in those goods, *or* who uses agents with special knowledge or skill in those goods. A used car dealer is a "merchant" when it comes to selling autos, because he routinely deals in them. A man selling his own car to someone who responded to his classified ad is not acting as a merchant.

The UCC frequently holds a merchant to a higher standard of conduct than a non-merchant. For example, a merchant may be held to an oral contract if she received written confirmation of it, even though the merchant herself never signed the confirmation. That same confirmation memo, arriving at the house of a non-merchant, would *not* create a binding deal. We will see many instances of this dual level of responsibility, one for a merchant and the other for a non-merchant.

Merchant
Generally, someone who routinely deals in the particular goods involved.

19-2e Good Faith and Unconscionability

The UCC imposes a duty of good faith in the performance of all contracts. For *non-merchants*, good faith means honesty in fact. For a *merchant,* good faith means honesty in fact *plus* the exercise of reasonable commercial standards of fair dealing.[3] Thus, when parties perform a contract, or in certain cases when they negotiate, neither side may lie or mislead. Further, a party who is a merchant must act as fairly as the business community routinely expects.

The UCC employs a second principle to encourage fair play and just results: the doctrine of unconscionability. UCC §2-302: A contract may be **unconscionable** if it is shockingly one-sided and fundamentally unfair. If a court concludes that some part of a contract is unconscionable, it will refuse to enforce that provision. Courts seldom find a contract unconscionable if the two parties are businesses, but they are quicker to apply the doctrine when one party is a consumer.

The doctrine of good faith focuses on a party's behavior as it performs an agreement: Was it attempting to carry out its obligations in a reasonable manner and do what both sides expected when they made the deal? Unconscionability looks primarily at the contract itself. Are any terms so grossly unfair that a court should reform or ignore them?

Unconscionable
A contract that is shockingly one-sided and fundamentally unfair.

---

[3]UCC §§1-201(19), 1-203, and 2-103.

19-3 CONTRACT FORMATION

The common law expected the parties to form a contract in a fairly predictable and traditional way: The offeror made a clear offer that included all important terms, and the offeree agreed to all terms. Nothing was left open. The drafters of the UCC recognized that businesspeople frequently do not think or work that way and that the law should reflect business reality.

19-3a Formation Basics: §2-204

UCC §2-204 provides three important rules that enable parties to make a contract quickly and informally:

1. *Any Manner That Shows Agreement.* The parties may make a contract in any manner sufficient to show that they reached an agreement. They may show the agreement with words, writings, or even their conduct. Lisa negotiates with Ed to buy 300 barbecue grills. The parties agree on a price, but other business prevents them from finishing the deal. Then six months later, Lisa writes, "Remember our deal for 300 grills? I still want to do it if you do." Ed does not respond, but a week later, a truck shows up at Lisa's store with the 300 grills and Lisa accepts them. The combination of their original discussion, Lisa's subsequent letter, Ed's delivery, and her acceptance all adds up to show that they reached an agreement. The court will enforce their deal, and Lisa must pay the agreed-upon price.

2. *Moment of Making Is Not Critical.* The UCC will enforce a deal even though it is difficult, in common law terms, to say exactly when it was formed. Was Lisa's deal formed when they orally agreed? When he delivered? She accepted? The Code's answer: It does not matter. The contract is enforceable.

3. *One or More Terms May Be Left Open.* The common law insisted that the parties clearly agree on all important terms. If they did not, there was no meeting of minds and no enforceable deal. The Code changes that. **Under the UCC, a court may enforce a bargain even though one or more terms were left open.** Lisa's letter never said when she required delivery of the barbecues or when she would pay. Under the UCC, the omission is not fatal. As long as there is some certain basis for giving damages to the injured party, the court will do just that. Suppose Lisa refused to pay, claiming that the agreement included no date for her payment. A court would rule that the parties assumed she would pay within a commercially reasonable time, such as 30 days.

In the following case, we can almost see the roller coasters, smell the cotton candy—and hear the carnival owners arguing. Because the cases in this chapter involve more than one Code section, we will outline the relevant provisions at the outset.

Code Provisions Discussed in This Case	
Issue	**Relevant Code Section**
1. What law governs?	UCC §2-102: Article 2 applies to the sale of goods.
2. Did the parties form a contract?	UCC §2-204: The parties may make a contract in any manner sufficient to show agreement.

© Cengage Learning

Jannusch v. Naffziger

2008 WL 540877
Illinois Court of Appeals, 2008

Case Summary

Facts: Festival Foods prepared and sold prepared food at carnivals in the Midwest. Owners Gene and Martha Jannusch made a verbal agreement to sell the business to the Naffzigers for $150,000. They paid $10,000 and took possession of the Festival Foods truck and trailer. They paid taxes and employees, bought supplies, and sold food at six events.

Because they had earned less at the carnivals than they had expected, the Naffzigers returned the truck and trailer and refused to pay the remaining $140,000. At trial, they argued that no definite agreement had been reached.

The common law requires a meeting of the minds for a contract to be created. Under the UCC, parties may form a contract in "any manner sufficient to show agreement."

The Naffzigers argued that the UCC did not apply to their agreement. The trial court agreed and ruled that a contract did not exist because there had never been a meeting of the minds. The Jannuschs appealed.

Issues: *Did the common law or the UCC govern this agreement? Did the parties form a contract?*

Decision: The UCC applied to the contract. Under the UCC, an enforceable agreement existed. Reversed and remanded.

Reasoning: The defendants argued that the purchase of a business was not a sale of goods. However, Article 2 of the UCC applies to an agreement so long as the *predominant purpose* of the deal is a sale of goods. The truck and trailer were valuable assets, and those goods were the core of the contract. Thus, the UCC did apply.

Therefore, we must next ask whether the parties had shown agreement. They set the price at $150,000. They discussed which items were to be included. The defendants took and used the items at six different carnivals. Under the UCC, these exchanges were enough to create an enforceable contract. The Naffzigers breached the contract when they returned the truck and trailer.

Based on the UCC, the Jannuschs won a case they would have lost under the common law. Next we look at changes the Code has made in the centuries-old requirement of a writing.

19-3b Statute of Frauds

UCC §2-201 requires a writing for any sale of goods worth $500 or more. However, under the UCC, the writing need not summarize the agreement completely, and it need not even be entirely accurate. Once again, the Code is modifying the common law rule, permitting parties to enforce deals with less formality. In some cases, the court grants an exception and enforces an agreement with no writing at all. Here are the rules.

Contracts for Goods Worth $500 or More

Section 2-201 demands a writing for any contract of goods over this limit, meaning that virtually every significant sale of goods has some writing requirement. Remember that a contract for goods costing less than $500 is still covered by the UCC, but it may be oral.

Writing Sufficient to Indicate a Contract

The Code only requires a writing *sufficient to indicate* that the parties made a contract. In other words, the writing need not *be* a contract. A simple memo is enough, or a letter or informal note, mentioning that the two sides reached an agreement, is enough. **In general, the writing must be signed by the defendant,** that is, whichever party is claiming there was no deal. Dick signs and sends to Shirley a letter saying, "This is to acknowledge your agreement to buy all 650 books in my rare book collection for $188,000." Shirley signs nothing. A day later, Louis offers Dick $250,000. Is Dick free to sell? No. He signed the memo, it indicates a contract, and Shirley can enforce it against him.

Now reverse the problem. Suppose that after Shirley receives Dick's letter, she decides against rare books in favor of original scripts from the *South Park* television show. Dick sues. Shirley wins because *she* signed nothing.

INCORRECT OR OMITTED TERMS

If the writing demonstrates the two sides reached an agreement, it satisfies §2-201 even if it omits important terms or states them incorrectly. Suppose Dick writes "$1888,000," indicating almost $2 million, when he meant to write "$188,000." The letter still shows that the parties made a deal, and the court will enforce it, relying on oral testimony to determine the correct price.

ENFORCEABLE ONLY TO THE QUANTITY STATED

Since the writing only has to indicate that the parties agreed, it need not state every term of their deal. But one term is essential: quantity. **The Code will enforce the contract only up to the quantity of goods stated in the writing.** This is logical, since a court can surmise other terms, such as price, based on market conditions. Buyer agrees to purchase pencils from Seller. The market value of the pencils is easy to determine, but a court would have no way of knowing whether Buyer meant to purchase 1,000 pencils or 100,000; the quantity must be stated.

EXCEPTIONS

In the following three sets of circumstances, the UCC Statute of Frauds is "turned off."

Merchant Exception. This is a major change from the common law. **When two merchants make an oral contract, and one sends a confirming memo to the other within a reasonable time, and the memo is sufficiently definite that it could be enforced against the sender herself, then the memo is also valid against the merchant who receives it, unless he objects within 10 days.** Laura, a tire wholesaler, signs and sends a memo to Scott, a retailer, saying, "Confm yr order today—500 tires cat #886—cat price." Scott realizes he can get the tires cheaper elsewhere and ignores the memo. Big mistake. Both parties are merchants, and Laura's memo is sufficient to bind her. So it also satisfies the Statute of Frauds *against Scott,* unless he objects within 10 days.

Specialty Goods Exception. If a buyer orders goods that are to be specially manufactured for the buyer and are not suitable for sale to others in the ordinary course of the seller's business, then a verbal agreement is enforceable even if it exceeds $500.

Judicial Admission Exception. If a defendant admits in his pleading, testimony, or otherwise in court that a contract for sale was made, then the contract he admitted to is enforceable against him.

The following case examines all three of these exceptions in the context of an agreement to buy carpet and tile. When the Supreme Court of Virginia issued its ruling, one company was floored.

Code Provisions Discussed in This Case

Issue	Relevant Code Section
1. Is there a confirmatory memo?	UCC 2-201(2)
2. Has the buyer ordered specialty goods?	UCC 2-201(3)(a)
3. Did the buyer admit in its testimony that an agreement existed?	UCC 2-201(3)(b)

© Cengage Learning

DELTA STAR, INC. V. MICHAEL'S CARPET WORLD

276 Va. 524
Supreme Court of Virginia, 2008

Facts: Ivan Tepper, CEO of Delta Star, visited the Michael's Carpet World showroom to view flooring options for a lobby entryway, his office, and his executive assistant's office. Tommy Martin, Michael's sales manager, helped Tepper select carpet and tile from the samples displayed and gave him price quotes. For the entryway, Tepper chose carpet; for the two offices, he selected a tile that, although on showroom display, had never before been sold by Michael's. (After all, it was named Michael's *Carpet* World for a reason.) Tepper verbally agreed to the materials and the prices and directed Martin to make further arrangements with his executive assistant, Donna Nash.

Martin measured the three spaces and faxed Nash a purchase order that read, "Carpet for entrance to lobby, $832.22." Michael's installed the entryway carpet and Delta Star paid the $832.22. Nash then authorized Martin to order the tile for the two offices. When the materials arrived, Nash told Martin to install the tile in her office, but sought to cancel the tile for Tepper's office. Michael's sued.

At trial, Delta Star argued that it never had an enforceable contract with Michael's for the office tiles because the agreement was not in writing as required by the UCC's Statute of Frauds for the sale of goods over $500. Michael's contended that the tile contract did not require a writing to be enforceable because: (1) The specialty goods exception applied, since Michael's ordered that particular tile for the first time, and (2) the judicial admission exception applied, since Nash had testified that she tried to cancel the order and, as Michael's argued, "you can't cancel something unless you're admitting that you got a contract and you want to cancel it." The court agreed with Michael's and awarded $2,565 in damages. Delta Star appealed.

Issue: *Did the specialty goods and judicial admission exceptions to the UCC's Statute of Frauds rule apply?*

Decision: No, neither exception applied. The verbal contract was not enforceable. Reversed.

Reasoning: Tepper and Martin entered into a verbal agreement for the sale and installation of flooring in three different areas. One of the three—the entryway carpet—was confirmed in writing by a purchase order, which only served as confirmation for that specific portion of the transaction. When Delta Star attempted to cancel Tepper's office tile installation, the question became whether that tile purchase was enforceable, even if not in writing.

The trial court concluded that the specialty goods exception applied because the tiles were specially manufactured goods, which Michael's could not resell. The court misapplied the exception. Tepper chose the tiles from among samples displayed in Michael's showroom. The fact that Michael's had never sold these particular tiles before did not mean they were specially made. In fact, the tiles were not altered in any way for Delta Star, and were suitable for sale to others in Michael's ordinary course of business, which was, after all, the sale of flooring. Michael's sold the tile to Delta Star and it could certainly sell it again to someone else. Therefore, the specialty goods exception did not apply.

The trial court also held that the judicial admission exception applied because Nash's testimony referenced the purchase and installation of Tepper's flooring and her attempt to cancel it. A review of Nash's trial testimony reveals that she stated that Delta Star "didn't want to act on the estimate" and that Delta Star "hadn't agreed to order the flooring for Tepper's office yet." Therefore, Nash did not admit the existence of a contract and the judicial admission exception also did not apply.

Because the agreement for Tepper's tiles had not been confirmed in writing and neither exception applied, the contract was not enforceable.

19-3c Added Terms: §2-207

Under the common law's mirror image rule, when one party makes an offer, the offeree must accept those exact terms. If the offeree adds or alters any terms, the acceptance is ineffective and the offeree's response becomes a counteroffer. In one of its most significant modifications of contract law, the UCC changes that result. **Under §2-207, an acceptance that adds or alters terms will often create a contract.** The Code has made this change in response to *battles of the form*. Every day, corporations buy and sell millions of dollars of goods using pre-printed forms. The vast majority of all contracts involve such documents. Typically, the buyer places an order using a pre-printed form, and the seller acknowledges with its own pre-printed acceptance form. Because each form contains language favorable to the party sending it, the two documents rarely agree. The Code's drafters concluded that the law must cope with real practices.

We discuss §2-207 in detail in Chapter 10 and summarize it here only to emphasize how it works with other UCC provisions. The section is confusing, and a diagram helps. For a schematic look at UCC §2-207, see Exhibit 19.1.

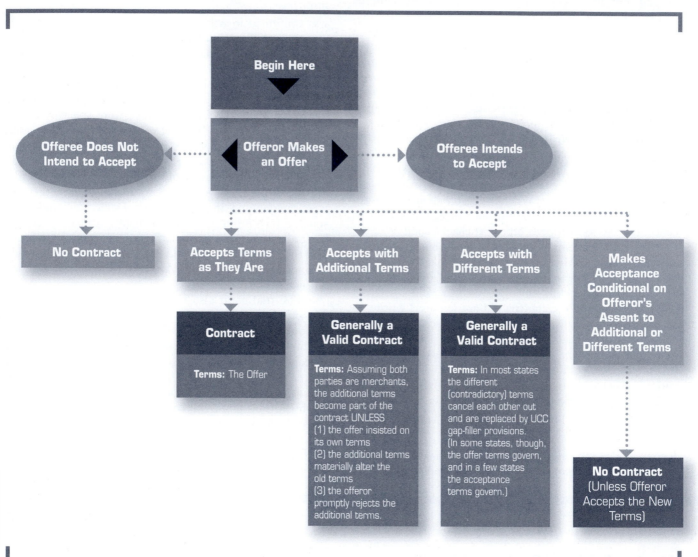

EXHIBIT 19.1 | A Schematic Look at UCC §2-207

INTENTION

The parties must still *intend* to create a contract. Section 2-207 is full of exceptions, but there is no change in this basic requirement of contract law. If the differing forms indicate that the parties never reached agreement, there is no contract.

ADDITIONAL OR DIFFERENT TERMS

An offeree may include a new term in his acceptance and still create a binding deal. Suppose Breeder writes to Pet Shop, offering to sell 100 guinea pigs at $2 each. Pet Shop faxes a memo saying, "We agree to buy 100 g.p. We get credit for any unhealthy pig." Pet Shop has added a new term, concerning unhealthy pigs, but the parties *have* created a binding contract because the writings show they intended an agreement. Now the court must decide what the terms of the contract are, since there is some discrepancy. The first step is to decide whether the new language is an *additional term* or a *different term*.

Additional Terms   **Additional terms** are those that raise issues not covered in the offer. The "unhealthy pig" issue is an additional term because the offer said nothing about it. When both parties are merchants, additional terms generally become part of the bargain. Pet Shop's insistence on credit for sick guinea pigs is binding on Breeder. In three circumstances, however, additional terms *do not* bind the parties:

> **Additional terms**
> Terms that introduce issues not covered in the offer.

- If the original offer *insisted on its own terms*. If Breeder offered the pets for sale "on these and no other terms," Pet Shop's additional language would not become part of their deal.

- If the additional terms *materially alter* the offer. Pet Shop's new language about credit for unhealthy animals is fairly uncontroversial. But suppose Pet Shop wrote back, "Breeder is liable for any illness of any animal in Pet Shop within 90 days of shipment of guinea pigs." Breeder would potentially have to pay for a $500 iguana with pneumonia or a $6,000 parrot with gout. This is a material alteration of the bargain and is not part of the contract.

- If the offeror *promptly objects* to the new terms. If Breeder received Pet Shop's fax and immediately called up to say "No credit for unhealthy pigs," then Pet Shop's additional term is not part of their deal.

In all other circumstances, additional terms do become part of an agreement between merchants.

Different Terms   **Different terms are terms that contradict those in the offer**. Suppose Brilliant Corp. orders 1,500 cellular phones from Makem Co., for use by Brilliant's sales force. Brilliant places the order using a pre-printed form stating that the product is fully warranted for normal use and that seller is liable for compensatory and consequential damages. This means, for example, that Makem could be liable for lost profits if a salesman's phone fails during a lucrative sales pitch. Makem responds with its own memo stating that in the event of defective phones, Makem is liable only to repair or replace, *and is not liable for consequential damages, lost profits, or any other damages.*

Makem's acceptance has included a *different* term because its language contradicts the offer. Almost all courts would agree that the parties intended to reach an agreement and therefore the contract is enforceable. The question is, what are its terms? Is the full warranty of the offer included, or the very limited warranty of the acceptance? The majority of states hold that **different terms cancel each other out**. Neither party's language goes into the contract. But what then *are* the terms of the deal?

If the evidence indicates that the parties had orally agreed on the issue disputed in the forms, then the courts will ignore the contradictory writings and enforce the oral contract. **If there is no clear oral agreement, the Code supplies its own terms, called gap-fillers,** which cover prices, delivery dates and places, warranties, and other subjects. In the cellular phone case, the contradicting warranty provisions cancel each other out. The parties had not orally agreed on a warranty, so a court would enforce the Code's gap-filler warranty, which does permit recovery of compensatory and consequential damages. Therefore, Makem *would* be liable for lost profits. We outline most of the gap-filler terms in Chapter 10. Warranty provisions are analyzed in greater detail in Chapter 20.

In the following case, the Rhode Island Supreme Court seeks the fairest method of sorting out conflicting terms.

Code Provisions Discussed in This Case

Issue	Relevant Code Section
1. Which are the terms of this agreement?	UCC §2-207: *Additional* terms generally but not always become part of the bargain. *Different* terms generally cancel each other out.
2. What is the Code's provision concerning delivery?	UCC §2-309: The time for shipment or delivery if not agreed upon is a reasonable time.
3. What is a "reasonable" delivery time?	UCC §1-204: A "reasonable" time depends on the nature, purpose, and circumstances of the action.

© Cengage Learning

SUPERIOR BOILER WORKS, INC. v. R. J. SANDERS, INC.

711 A.2d 628
Supreme Court of Rhode Island, 1998

CASE SUMMARY

Facts: R. J. Sanders, Inc., had a contract with the federal government to install the heating system at a federal prison camp. The company negotiated with Superior Boiler Works to purchase three large commercial units. On March 27, Superior sent a proposal to Sanders, offering to sell three boilers for a total of $156,000 and estimating time of delivery at four weeks. The parties exchanged further documents and held various discussions. Finally, on July 20, Sanders sent a "purchase order" for three boilers, agreeing to pay $145,827 and stating "Date required: 4 Weeks," that is, August 20. On August 6, Superior sent a "sales order," agreeing to sell the three boilers at that price, but providing a shipping date of October 1. This later delivery date forced Sanders to rent temporary boilers at a cost of $45,315. On October 1, Superior shipped the boilers, which arrived on October 5.

Sanders sent a check in the amount of $100,000, claiming that Superior had delivered the boilers late and deducting the cost of its rental equipment. Superior sued for the additional $45,000 and moved for summary judgment, which the trial court granted. Sanders appealed, claiming that the contract had required Superior to deliver the boilers within four weeks.

Issue: *Did Superior's October delivery breach the contract?*

Decision: No, Superior did not breach the contract. Affirmed.

Reasoning: Sanders's amended purchase order of July 20 and Superior's August 6 response agree on the specifications and price of the boilers. Although the documents disagree on time of delivery, they still create a contract because both parties *intended* to be bound. The time of delivery should be settled under UCC Section 2-207 (2).

Courts in other states rule in a variety of ways when faced with terms that differ. Rhode Island adopts the "knock-out" rule: Conflicting contract terms knock each other out, leaving a hole to be filled by the Code's gap-filler provision. It is true that this may result in a contract provision that neither party wants; however, each side may protect against this by insisting that agreement be made on its own terms.

Section 2-309 states that if the parties do not agree on the time for delivery, it should be a *reasonable* time. Normally, it is for the factfinder to determine reasonableness from all of the circumstances surrounding the transaction, including the parties' earlier deals, standard trade usage, and so on. See UCC Section 1-204 (2). In this case, though, all of the evidence demonstrates that, measured by industry standards, Superior's performance was reasonable.

EXAM Strategy

Question: Martin, a diamond wholesaler, writes Serge, a jewelry retailer, offering to sell 75 specified diamonds for $2 million. Martin's offer sheet specifies the price, quantity, date of delivery, and other key terms. The sheet also states, "Offer is made on these terms and no other." Serge sends Martin his own purchase order, naming the diamonds, price, and so forth, but adding a clause requiring any disputes to be settled by a diamond-industry arbitrator. In the diamond industry, arbitration by such a person is standard. Martin does not object to the arbitration clause. Martin delivers the gems but Serge refuses to pay the full price, claiming that many of the stones are of inferior quality. Martin sues for the balance due, but Serge insists that any dispute must be settled by arbitration. May Martin litigate, or must he arbitrate the case?

Strategy: Under the common law, there might not be a contract between these parties, because Serge added a new term. However, this agreement concerns the sale of goods, meaning that the UCC governs. Under UCC §2-207, when both parties are merchants (as they are here), additional terms become part of the contract except in three instances. Review those three instances, and apply them here.

Result: Additional terms become part of the agreement unless the original offeror insisted on its own terms, the new term materially alters the offer, or the offeror promptly rejects the new term. Martin's offer insisted on its own terms and Serge's arbitration clause does not become part of the agreement. Martin may litigate his dispute.

19-3d Open Terms: §§2-305 and 2-306

OPEN PRICES

Under §2-305, the parties may conclude a contract even though they have not settled the price. Again, this is a change from the common law, which required certainty of such an important contract term. Under the Code, if the parties have not stated one, **the price is a reasonable price at the time of delivery.** A court will use market value and other comparable sales to determine what a reasonable price would have been. If the contract permits the buyer or seller to *determine* the price during contract performance, §2-305 requires that she do so in good faith, as the following case demonstrates.

Code Provisions Discussed in This Case

Issue	Relevant Code Sections
1. May the parties form a binding agreement without specifying the price?	UCC §2-305(1): The parties may conclude a contract even though they have not settled the price.
2. May a contract permit one party to settle the price?	UCC §2-305(2): "A price to be fixed by the seller or by the buyer" requires that it be fixed in good faith.
3. What does *good faith* mean?	UCC §§1-201(19), 1-203, and 2-103: For *non-merchants,* good faith means honesty in fact. For a *merchant,* good faith means honesty in fact *plus* the exercise of reasonable commercial standards of fair dealing.

© Cengage Learning

MATHIS V. EXXON CORPORATION

302 F.3d 448
Fifth Circuit Court of Appeals, 2002

CASE SUMMARY

Facts: Exxon marketed gasoline to retailers in three ways. *Franchisees* (who owned local gas stations) were required to purchase a minimum number of gallons per month. Exxon set the price each month, known as the dealer tank wagon price (DTW). *Jobbers* (distributors who could resell to dealers) paid the "rack price," which was generally lower than the DTW. *Company-operated retail stores* (CORS) paid nothing because Exxon owned them.

A group of 54 Texas franchisees sued, claiming that Exxon set their gasoline prices artificially high. The plaintiffs alleged that Exxon wanted to drive them out of business and replace their franchises with more profitable CORS. The evidence indicated that the franchisees' DTW was consistently higher than the rack price paid by jobbers. Many plaintiffs testified that their franchises had become unprofitable. One study showed that 62 percent of franchisees in Corpus Christi, Texas, were selling gas below the price they paid for it. Plaintiffs' expert testified that 75 percent of their competitors could buy gasoline at a lower price.

The plaintiffs argued that this evidence demonstrated that Exxon set the prices in bad faith. The jury agreed, awarding the plaintiffs $5.7 million, plus $2.3 million in attorney's fees. Exxon appealed.

Issue: *Did Exxon set the prices in bad faith?*

Decision: Yes, Exxon set the prices in bad faith. Affirmed.

Reasoning: The UCC rejects the notion that a seller may fix any price it wants. When a contract permits a seller to set the price, it must do so in good faith. These franchisees allege bad faith. Lawsuits like this are rare because a mere allegation of bad faith is unpersuasive. Here, though, the plaintiffs offered considerable evidence of Exxon's bad faith.

There was testimony and documentation indicating that Exxon planned to replace many of its franchises with CORS. The plaintiffs also showed that the DTW price was higher than the rack price, and that Exxon prevented franchisees from purchasing gas from jobbers. Because of the unnaturally high price that franchisees were forced to pay for their gas, many of their dealerships were unprofitable and uncompetitive.

An Exxon document stated the company's "marketing strategy is to reduce Dealer stores." Another company paper indicated that Exxon wanted to reduce dealer stores in Houston from 95 to 45. Exxon's regional director acknowledged that the company made greater profits from CORS than from franchises. CORS with convenience stores were the most profitable and were considered the wave of the future. The number of dealer stations declined steadily. Even though Exxon was moving to replace independent dealers with CORS, it never made that position clear to its franchisees.

There was more than enough evidence to support the jury's conclusion that Exxon set its prices in bad faith.

EXAM Strategy

Facts: Coffee Retailer sends a form to Cupper, ordering 100 cartons of specified coffee cups to be delivered the first of each month for six months. The order form says nothing about price. For three months, Cupper delivers on time and sends an invoice, which Retailer pays. On the fourth month, Cupper's invoice is 8 percent higher than before. Retailer refuses to pay the increase and informs Cupper that it will accept no more deliveries. Cupper sues. Retailer claims there was no enforceable contract. Cupper says there was a bargain and that it has the right to determine the price. Who is right?

Strategy: Retailer's offer included no price. Under the common law, the absence of such an essential term would mean there was no contract. However, these are goods, and under the UCC the parties can make an enforceable deal without specifying the price. This is a valid contract. The companies may, if they choose, permit one party to determine the price. Did they do so here? If so, is Cupper's conduct reasonable? If the parties did not allow one side to set the price, how would a court do so?

Result: This contract neither stated a price nor allowed one party to determine it. That means that the price is a reasonable one at the time of delivery. A court will use market value, and any comparable sales, to determine the price.

OUTPUT AND REQUIREMENTS CONTRACTS

Under §2-306, an output contract obligates the seller to sell all of his output to the buyer, who agrees to accept it. Suppose Joel has a small plant in which he manufactures large plants; that is, handcrafted artificial flowers and trees, made of silk and other expensive materials. Joel is not sure how many he can produce in a year, but wants a guaranteed market. He makes an output contract with Yolanda, in which he promises to sell the entire output of his plant, and she agrees to buy it all.

A requirements contract is the reverse, obligating a buyer to purchase all his needed goods from the seller. Joel might sign a requirements contract with Worm Express, agreeing to buy from Worm all the silk he needs. Both output and requirements contracts are valid under the Code, although they create certain problems. By definition, the exact quantity of goods is not specified. But then how much may one party demand? Is there any upper or lower limit?

The UCC requires that the parties in an output or requirements contract make their demands in good faith. For example, in a requirements contract, a buyer may not suddenly increase her demand far beyond what the parties expected merely because there has been a market change. Suppose the price of silk skyrockets. Joel's requirements contract obligates Worm Express to sell him all the silk he needs. Could Joel demand 10 times the silk he had anticipated, knowing he could resell it at a big profit to other manufacturers? No. That would be bad faith. Come on, Joel, play by the rules.

May the buyer *reduce* his demand far below what the parties anticipated? Yes, as long as he makes the reduction in good faith.

The following case involves several issues, including a claim that an output contract existed. Some contracts are meticulously written by veteran lawyers who use deliberate and precise legal terms in every part of the agreement. Of course, agreements are not always done so carefully. See what sense you can make of the "Weaner Pig Purchase Agreement."

Code Provisions Discussed in This Case	
Issue	**Relevant Code Section**
1. Which law governs this agreement?	UCC 2-102
2. Is there a writing sufficient to indicate a contract?	UCC 2-201
3. Was an output contract formed?	UCC 2-306

© Cengage Learning

You Be the Judge

LOHMAN V. WAGNER

862 A.2d 1042
Court of Special Appeals of Maryland, 2004

Facts: Legal research can take you in odd directions. Today, for example, we learn that a "weaner pig" is a very young pig that has just been weaned from its mother. You must raise and sell a lot of them to make a living. Farmers who raise pigs to full size need to sell fewer animals to get by.

Farmer Charles Lohman talked extensively with John Wagner about raising weaner pigs for a new "pork network" that Wagner, the owner of Swine Services, was thinking of putting together. Lohman eventually decided to join Wagner and convert his pig farm to one that specialized in raising weaner pigs. He needed to borrow money to remodel his farm, and he needed to convince his bankers that, if they loaned him the necessary money, he would be in a reasonable position to repay them.

He told Wagner that he "would need something to show his banker." Wagner faxed over a document with several blanks entitled "Weaner Pig Purchase Agreement." It said, in part, "PRODUCER agrees to supply ____ weaner pigs weekly." When he received the fax, Lohman wrote "300" in the blank. After showing the fax to his banker, Lohman was able to secure his loan. He never sent Wagner a copy of the document with the blank filled in.

For awhile, everyone was happy. Lohman shipped weaner pigs to Wagner and was paid $28 each for them. But eventually, problems arose. The price Wagner offered for weaner pigs dropped to $18, and Wagner never assembled the promised pork network, which Lohman argued would have helped to boost prices. Lohman sued Wagner for breach of contract.

The trial court found that the agreement did not meet the UCC's requirement that a quantity term be included, that it was unenforceable, and that Lohman was entitled to nothing. Lohman appealed.

You Be the Judge: *Does Lohman have an enforceable agreement with Wagner?*

Argument for Lohman: Your honor, I'm not a ham, and I won't "boar" you with a long story. Our arguments, briefly stated, are these.

First, the UCC's Statute of Frauds, and its requirement that a quantity term be included, should not apply. This agreement is essentially one for services, and not for goods. My client furnishes housing for weaner pigs, labors to raise them, and ships them to the defendant. His services are the largest part of this contract.

Even if this contract is deemed to be a sale of goods, there is a quantity term included in the Weaner Pig Purchase Agreement—300. The number was entered by my client as a good-faith estimate of the number of animals he could produce.

In any event, UCC 2-306 does not require a quantity term in this case. This agreement was an output contract. Lohman sold every weaner pig he produced to Wagner, and Wagner accepted and paid for them. Output contracts, by definition, do not include specific quantity terms; they merely obligate a seller to sell all of his output to the buyer.

This case amounts to nothing more or less than a greedy man trying to reap what he did not sow and to use legal technicalities to hog all the profits for himself.

Argument for Wagner: My counterpart has managed to make several nifty pig-related references in his argument, but nevertheless, no contract exists. The UCC does apply to this agreement, because pigs are clearly goods. Most products require some labor to assemble and bring to market. Someone "labored" to make my shoes, my necktie, and my pen. But all are goods.

In a UCC contract, a quantity must be written by the defendants, but here the "300" was written by the plaintiff. It was never communicated to my client. He never agreed to it, or even had a chance to review it. The same holds true for the claim that this is an output contract. My client never agreed to buy all the pigs that Lohman produced.

My opponent is grasping at straws. Which pigs eat. I think. Get it? Oh, forget it …

19-3e Modification

Another way in which the UCC is pro-contract and pro-business is in its treatment of contract modifications. If two sides have a contract and seek to make changes, are the changes enforceable?

Example 1. Being the best at almost anything pays well, and soccer is no exception. Cristiano Ronaldo's contract with Real Madrid runs through 2015 and averages a whopping $20 million per season. Assume that this year, he leads Real to the fabled treble—a La Liga championship, a victory in the Copa del Rey, and a win in the Champions League. Afterward, the club offers him a raise to $28 million per season through 2015, and Ronaldo accepts. If Spanish law is the same as American law, does the team have a legal obligation to pay the extra millions? No.

This is a services contract, and not a sale of goods. Therefore, common law principles would apply, and they require new consideration for contract modifications to stand. Since Ronaldo did not agree to play any additional seasons or give any other new value to the team, no consideration exists.

We hate to leave out fans of Spain's other big club, so for the next example, we will pay our 70 euros for a ticket on the AVE train and settle in for a three-hour, 500-kilometer trip eastward to Barcelona.

Example 2. FC Barcelona is planning "Lionel Messi Bobblehead Day," and the team orders 10,000 units for the occasion. Unfortunately, the boat carrying the shipment from China is boarded by Somali pirates, who are, it turns out, Barça supporters. The entire shipment is stolen, and the headlines read, TRADE HOBBLED! PIRATES GOBBLE BOBBLES!

The manufacturer calls the team and asks for a three-week extension on the original delivery deadline. The team is very understanding, agrees to the delay, and reschedules the promotion for a later game. Is this modification which extends the delivery deadline now a valid part of the contract? Yes.

In §2-209, the UCC does away with the consideration requirement for changes to contracts, so long as both sides agree to the modification. In this example, no consideration exists to support the extended deadline because the manufacturer gets all the benefit, and the team gets nothing. But, that does not create a problem in enforcing the new deal.

Parties make a contract attempting to control their futures. But one party's certainty can be undercut by the ease with which the other party may obtain a modification. Section 2-209 acknowledges this tension by enabling the parties to limit changes. The UCC allows the parties to modify some contracts orally, but **they may agree to prohibit oral modifications and insist that all modifications be in writing and signed. Between merchants, such a clause is valid. But if either party is *not* a merchant, such a clause is valid only if the non-merchant *separately* signs it.**

Once again the Code gives greater protection to non-merchants than to merchants. Two merchants may agree, as part of their bargain, that any future modifications will be valid only if written and signed. But this limitation on modifications is not valid against a non-merchant unless she separately signs the limiting clause itself. Suppose a furniture retailer orders 200 beds from a manufacturer. The retailer's order form requires any modifications to be in writing. The manufacturer initials the retailer's form at the bottom. The parties have a valid agreement and no oral modifications will be enforced. But suppose the retailer sells a bed to a customer. The sales form also bars oral modifications. That prohibition is void unless the customer separately signs it.

EXAM Strategy

Question: Dale turns 18. For his birthday, he gets $500 cash and his grandmother's ancient station wagon. And yes, it is the kind with wood paneling on the side. Dale cannot do much about how the car looks, but he decides that he can at least make it sound awesome. So, he immediately takes the car to Big Mike's Custom Stereo.

At Big Mike's, Dale makes a verbal agreement to buy an amplifier and two Rockford Fosgate speakers and to have them installed at a cost of $499. The amp and speakers come to $420, and the installation charge is $79. He decides to have them installed while he waits.

After an hour, a clerk finds him and says, "Hey, man, we're out of stock on those speakers. But I can get you some Alpines right now—same size, same price, just as loud." Dale is eager to drive out with a new system, and agrees to the speaker substitution. Moments later, Dale finds the clerk and says, "Wait, I'm not sure about all of this. I don't think I want to buy any of it after all." Can Dale get his money back, or is he stuck with his purchases?

Strategy: Under UCC principles, a contract is considered to be for the sale of goods if the value of the items far exceeds the cost of the labor (installation), and the contract's predominant purpose is a sale of goods. The UCC Statute of Frauds does not apply to a transaction under $500. A contract can be modified without consideration.

Result: The UCC governs this contract because the speakers are much more expensive than the labor. The contract does not have to be in writing because it is for less than $500. The agreement to use Alpine speakers rather than Rockford Fosgates is enforceable, even without consideration for the change. Dale will have to live with the deal, including the Alpine speakers.[4]

---

[4]Bonus point from Chapter 13 material: Since this is Dale's 18th birthday, if he were even one day younger, he could back out of this deal on the grounds that he is a minor and has formed a voidable agreement.

The following table concludes this chapter with an illustration of the Code's impact on the common law.

Selected Code Provisions That Change the Common Law				
Issue	**Common Law Rule**	**UCC Sec.**	**UCC Rule**	**Example**
Contract formation	Offer must be followed by acceptance that shows meeting of the minds on all important terms.	§2-204 and §2-305	Contract can be made in any manner sufficient to show agreement; moment of making not critical; one or more terms, including the price, may be left open.	Tilly writes Meg, "I need a new van for my delivery company." Meg delivers a van and Tilly starts to use it. Under the common law, there is no contract, because no price was ever mentioned; under the UCC, the writing plus the conduct show an intention to contract (2-204). The price is a *reasonable* one (2-305).
Writing requirement	All essential terms must be in writing.	§2-201	Any writing is sufficient if it indicates a contract; terms may be omitted or misstated; "merchant" exception can create a contract enforceable against a party who receives the writing and does nothing within 10 days.	Douglas, a car dealer, signs and sends to Michael, another dealer, a memo saying, "Confirming our deal for your blue Rolls." Michael reads it but ignores it; 10 days later Douglas has satisfied the Statute of Frauds under the UCC's merchant exception.
Added terms in acceptance	An acceptance that adds or changes any term is a counteroffer.	§2-207	Additional or different terms are not necessarily counteroffers; their presence does not prevent a contract from being formed, and in some cases the new terms will become a part of the bargain.	Roberts sends a pre-printed form to Julia, offering to buy 25 computers and stating a price; Julia responds with her own pre-printed form, accepting the offer but adding a term that balances unpaid after 30 days incur a finance charge. The additional term is not a counteroffer; there is a valid contract; and the finance charge is part of the bargain.
Modification	A modification is valid only if supported by new consideration.	§2-209	A modification needs no consideration to be binding.	Martin, a computer manufacturer, agrees to sell Steve, a retailer, 500 computers at a specified price, including delivery. The next day Martin learns that his delivery costs have gone up 20 percent; he calls Steve, who faxes a note agreeing to pay 15 percent extra. Under the common law, the modification would be void; under the Code, it is enforceable.

© Cengage Learning

Chapter Conclusion

The Uniform Commercial Code (UCC) enables parties to create a contract quickly. While this can be helpful in a fast-paced business world, it also places responsibility on executives. Informal conversations may cause at least one party to conclude that it has a binding agreement—and the law may agree.

EXAM REVIEW

1. **UNIFORM COMMERCIAL CODE**   The Code is designed to modernize commercial law and make it uniform throughout the country. (pp. 428–429)

2. **SALE OF GOODS**   Article 2 applies to the sale of goods, which are movable things other than money and investment securities. (p. 426)

EXAM Strategy

Question: While shopping at his local mall, Fred buys an iPad for $499, a barbecue grill for $509, and then pays $25 to have his watchband cleaned. Which of Fred's transactions are governed by Article 2 of the UCC?

Strategy: To answer this question, you must identify the transactions that amount to a sale of goods. Land and buildings are not goods. Neither are money and securities, but other moveable physical objects are. Also, be sure not to confuse the question "Does Article 2 apply?" with the question "Does this agreement need to be in writing?"

3. **LEASING**   Article 2A governs the leasing of goods. (p. 426)

4. **MIXED CONTRACTS**   In a mixed contract involving goods and services, the UCC applies if the predominant purpose is the sale of goods. (p. 429)

5. **MERCHANTS**   A merchant is someone who routinely deals in the particular goods involved, or who appears to have special knowledge or skill in those goods, or who uses agents with special knowledge or skill. The UCC frequently holds a merchant to a higher standard of conduct than a non-merchant. (p. 429)

6. **GOOD FAITH**   The UCC imposes a duty of good faith in the performance of all contracts. (p. 429)

7. **UNCONSCIONABILITY**   A contract is unconscionable if it is shockingly one-sided and fundamentally unfair. A court is much likelier to use unconscionability to protect a consumer than a corporation. (p. 429)

Question: Jim Dan, Inc., owned a golf course that had trouble with crabgrass. Jim Dan bought 20 bags of Scotts Pro Turf Goosegrass/Crabgrass Control for $835 and applied it to the greens. The Pro Turf caused over $36,000 in damage to the greens. Jim Dan sued Scotts. Scotts defended by claiming that it sold the Pro Turf with a clearly written, easy-to-read disclaimer that stated that in the event of damage, the buyer's only remedy would be a refund of the purchase price. Jim Dan, Inc., argued that the clause was unconscionable. Please rule.

Strategy: There are two steps to deciding an issue of unconscionability. First, does the contract involve a consumer, or is this an agreement between two businesses? Second, is the agreement shockingly one-sided?

8. **FORMATION**   UCC §2-204 permits the parties to form a contract in any manner that shows agreement. (p. 430)

9. **WRITING**   For the sale of goods worth $500 or more, UCC §2-201 requires some writing that indicates an agreement. Terms may be omitted or misstated, but the contract will be enforced only to the extent of the quantity stated. (pp. 431–432)

Question: To satisfy the UCC Statute of Frauds regarding the sale of goods, which of the following must generally be in writing?

(a) Designation of the parties as buyer and seller

(b) Delivery terms

(c) Quantity of the goods

(d) Warranties to be made

Strategy: Okay, this may be overkill. But the question illustrates two basic points of UCC law: First, the Code allows a great deal of flexibility in the formation of contracts. Second, there is one term for which no flexibility is allowed. Make sure you know which it is.

10. **MERCHANT'S EXCEPTION**   When two merchants make an oral contract, and one sends a confirming memo to the other within a reasonable time, and the memo is sufficiently definite that it could be enforced against the sender herself, then the merchant who receives it will also be bound unless he objects within 10 days. (p. 432)

11. **ADDITIONAL TERMS**   UCC §2-207 governs an acceptance that does not "mirror" the offer. *Additional terms* usually, but not always, become part of the contract. *Different terms* contradict a term in the offer. When that happens, most courts reject both parties' proposals and rely on gap-filler terms. (p. 435)

Question: Cookie Co. offered to sell Distrib Markets 20,000 pounds of cookies at $1.00 per pound, subject to certain specified terms for delivery. Distrib replied in writing as follows: "We accept your offer for 20,000 pounds of cookies at $1.00 per pound, weighing scale to have valid city certificate." Under the UCC:

(a) A contract was formed between the parties.

(b) A contract will be formed only if Cookie agrees to the weighing scale requirement.

(c) No contract was formed because Distrib included the weighing scale requirement in its reply.

(d) No contract was formed because Distrib's reply was a counteroffer.

Strategy: Distrib's reply included a new term. That means it is governed by UCC §2-207. Is the new term an additional term or a different term? An additional term goes beyond what the offeror stated. Additional terms become a part of the contract except in three specified instances. A different term contradicts one made by the offeror. Different terms generally cancel each other out.

12. **PRICE**   Under UCC §2-305 a contract is enforceable even if the price is not stated. In such cases the price must be reasonable. (pp. 437–438)

13. **MODIFICATION**   UCC §2-209 permits contracts to be modified even if there is no consideration. The parties may prohibit oral modifications, but such a clause is ineffective against a non-merchant unless she signed it. (pp. 441–442)

2. Result: The purchases of the iPad and the barbecue grill are covered by Article 2 of the UCC. Both agreements involve goods; $500 is a figure that is relevant to whether the Statute of Frauds applies to the agreements, but it is not material to the threshold question of whether Article 2 applies in the first place. All sales of goods, from pencils to Ferarris, fall under Article 2.

The watch cleaning is a service, and not a sale of goods. It is not governed by Article 2.

7. Result: This is a bargain between two businesses, and courts rarely find clauses in such agreements unconscionable. The assumption is that sophisticated businesspeople understand what they are getting into and are able to protect themselves. If Jim Dan could run a golf course, the company was sophisticated enough to understand the simple disclaimer in this contract. Scotts wins.

9. Result: (c). The contract will be enforced only to the extent of the quantity stated.

11. Result: The "valid city certificate" phrase raises a new issue; it does not contradict anything in Cookie's offer. That means it is an additional term, and becomes part of the deal unless Cookie insisted on its own terms, the additional term materially alters the offer, or Cookie promptly rejects it. Cookie did not insist on its terms, this is a minor addition, and Cookie never rejected it. The new term is part of a valid contract and the answer is (a).

MULTIPLE-CHOICE QUESTIONS

1. For a contract governed by the UCC sales article, which one of the following statements is correct?

   (a) Merchants and non-merchants are treated alike.

   (b) The contract may involve the sale of any type of personal property.

   (c) The obligations of the parties to the contract must be performed in good faith.

   (d) The contract must involve the sale of goods for a price of $500 or more.

2. Which of the following transactions is *not* governed by Article 2 of the UCC?

   (a) Purchasing an automobile for $35,000

   (b) Leasing an automobile worth $35,000

   (c) Purchasing a stereo worth $501

   (d) Purchasing a stereo worth $499

3. Fred assembles computers in his garage and sells them. He makes an agreement with Alpha Company under which Alpha will deliver 100 keyboards. The agreement does not specify when payment is due. Which of the following is true?

   (a) Fred has no obligation to pay, because there was no "meeting of the minds" and no contract was formed.

   (b) Fred must pay within 10 days of making the agreement.

   (c) Fred must pay within 10 days of accepting the keyboards.

   (d) Fred must pay within a commercially reasonable time.

4. Under the UCC Statute of Frauds, a contract must be signed by the_____ to count as being "in writing." Also, the_____ of the goods must be written.

   (a) plaintiff; price

   (b) plaintiff; quantity

   (c) defendant; price

   (d) defendant; quantity

5. Assume that a contract is modified. New consideration must be present for the modification to be binding if the deal is governed by which of the following?

   (a) The common law

   (b) The UCC

   (c) Both (a) and (b)

   (d) Neither (a) nor (b)

ESSAY QUESTIONS

1. The Massachusetts Bay Transit Authority (MBTA) awarded the Perini Corp. a large contract to rehabilitate a section of railroad tracks. The work involved undercutting the existing track, removing the ballast and foundation, rebuilding the track, and disposing of the old material. Perini solicited an offer from Atlantic Track & Turnout Co. for Atlantic to buy whatever salvageable material Perini removed. Perini estimated the quantity of salvageable material that would be available. Atlantic offered to purchase "all available" material over the course of Perini's deal with the MBTA, and Perini accepted. But three months into the project, the MBTA ran short of money and told Perini to stop the undercutting part of the project. That was the work that made Perini its profit, so Perini requested that the MBTA terminate the agreement, which the agency did. By that point Perini had delivered to Atlantic only about 15 percent of the salvageable material that it had estimated. Atlantic sued. What kind of contract do the parties have? Who should win and why?

2. Hasbro used to manufacture a toy called "Wonder World Aquarium." The toy included a powder that, when mixed with water, formed a gel that filled a plastic aquarium. Children could then place plastic fish in the aquarium and create underwater scenes. Cloud Corporation supplied the powder to Hasbro. The toy sold poorly, and Hasbro's need for the powder diminished.

   The two companies discussed changing the powder's formula. Cloud believed the conversation amounted to an indication that Hasbro would continue to buy powder, so it produced large quantities. Although it did not receive an order from Hasbro, Cloud sent an order acknowledgment for 9.5 million packets to Hasbro. Hasbro made no objection to it.

   Did the order acknowledgment create an enforceable agreement? What specific facts determine your answer?

3. Nina owns a used car lot. She signs and sends a fax to Seth, a used car wholesaler who has a huge lot of cars in the same city. The fax says, "Confirming our agrmt—I pick any 15 cars fr yr lot—30% below blue book." Seth reads the fax, laughs, and throws it away. Two weeks later, Nina arrives and demands to purchase 15 of Seth's cars. Is he obligated to sell?

4. The Brugger Corp. owned a farm, operated by Jason Weimer, who acted as the company's business agent. Tri-Circle, Inc., was a farm equipment company. On behalf of Brugger, Weimer offered to buy from Tri-Circle certain equipment for use on the farm. Tri-Circle accepted the offer, using a pre-printed form. The form included a finance charge for late payment. Weimer's offer had said nothing about finance charges, but he made no objection to the new term. Tri-Circle supplied the farm equipment but later alleged that Brugger had refused to pay for $12,000 worth of the supplies. Tri-Circle sued. In deciding whether Tri-Circle was entitled to finance charges, the court first inquired whether Brugger, Weimer, and Tri-Circle were merchants. Why did it look into that issue? *Were* they merchants?

5. **YOU BE THE JUDGE WRITING PROBLEM** Brewster manufactured plastic bottles. Dial made personal care products at many plants around the country, including one in Salem, Virginia. The companies agreed that Dial would purchase from Brewster all of the plastic bottles it needed for its Salem factory. Dial estimated its requirements for one year at 7,850,000 bottles, but added a clause stating that "quantities are estimated only and do not bind Dial to purchase any minimum quantity." A few

months later, Dial concluded that its Salem plant was unprofitable. The company closed the factory and notified Brewster that it would buy no bottles at all. Brewster sued. Did Dial have the right to reduce its orders to zero? **Argument for Brewster:** The parties had a clear contract for a massive number of bottles. Dial knew that this contract was extremely important to Brewster. Although Dial had some right to adjust its orders, it had no right to reduce them to zero. **Argument for Dial:** The issue is whether Dial acted in good faith. It did. The company had a legitimate reason for closing the factory—it was losing money—and with no factory it certainly did not need any bottles.

DISCUSSION QUESTIONS

Apply the following facts to the next two questions.

The publication of the original UCC in 1952 sparked an expansion of the Statute of Frauds in the United States to cover sales of goods of $500 or more. At about the same time (in 1954), the British Parliament repealed its longstanding Statute of Frauds as applied to sales of goods. Some have argued that we should scrap UCC §2-201 on the grounds that it encourages misdealing as much as it prevents fraud. Consider the following two hypotheticals:

(In the United States) Johnny is looking at a used Chevy Tahoe. He knows that the $7,000 price is a good one, but he wants to go online and see if he can find an even better deal. In the 20 minutes he has been with the car's current owner, the owner has received three phone calls about the car. Johnny wants to make sure that no one else buys the car while he is thinking the deal over, so he makes a verbal agreement to buy the car and shakes the seller's hand. He knows that because of the Statute of Frauds and the fact that nothing is in writing, he does not yet have any enforceable obligation to buy the car.

(In the United Kingdom) Nigel sells used Peugeots in Liverpool. When he senses interest from customers, he aggressively badgers them until they verbally commit to buy. If the customers later get cold feet and try to back out of the deal, he holds them to the verbal contracts. Because there is no longer a UCC-style Statute of Frauds in Britain, the buyers are stuck.

1. Rate the degree to which you believe Johnny and Nigel acted wrongfully. Did one behave more wrongfully than the other? If so, which one, and why?

2. Do you think that the UCC Statute of Frauds as it currently exists is more likely to prevent fraud, or is it more likely to encourage misunderstandings and deception? Why? Overall, is it sensible to require that purchases of big-ticket items be in writing before they are final?

3. The Uniform Commercial Code (UCC) was written by a group of scholars and adopted by elected state legislators. But many contracts that do not involve a sale of goods are still governed by old common law principles that have been created by judges over a period of centuries. Who makes for better lawmakers—judges or legislators? Do you prefer the way in which common law principles or UCC rules were created?

4. Under UCC §2-207, "added terms" in an acceptance can become part of a contract between merchants. Does this seem reasonable to you? Are businesses likely to take advantage of it?

5. This chapter revisits the idea of unconscionability. Courts will sometimes refuse to enforce deals that are, as UCC §2-302 states it, "shocking and fundamentally unfair." Consider the following two cases. In each, an electronics store sells an HDTV with a fair market value of $600 for $1,500.

   (a) Sale #1 is made to Ann. She has a terrible credit score, and is willing to pay $1,500 because the store offers to finance the TV, and she has no other available credit.

   (b) Sale #2 is made to Franklin J. Moneypenny, a very wealthy investment banker, on Christmas Eve. He knows the price is much too high, but he is in a big hurry to finish his last minute shopping.

In both cases, the consumers paid 2.5 times the fair value of the TV. In your opinion, is either transaction unconscionable? If so, why? If not, why not?

CHAPTER 20

OWNERSHIP, RISK, AND WARRANTIES

nuttakit/Shutterstock.com; © picsbyst/Shutterstock.com

He drove his truck fast along the rough country road, hurrying through the shadows of the Cascade Mountains, passing close to the Rogue River. The door panel, freshly painted, read, "Ernest Jenkins, Cattle Buyer." Spinning the wheel hard left, he drove through an impressive gate and under a wooden sign that read, "Double Q Ranch." He knew the ranch by reputation and quickly saw that it was prosperous—a good place for a man like him to do business.

He introduced himself to Kate Vandermeer, the Double Q's business manager, and expressed an interest in buying 300 head of cattle. Vandermeer and the man mounted horses and rode out to inspect the herd. Vandermeer noticed that his boots were brand new and that he rode awkwardly.

He was satisfied with the cattle, so the two bargained, sitting on horseback and looking into the sunset. Vandermeer started at $310,000 and was surprised at how quickly they reached an agreement, at $285,000, a price she considered excellent. They agreed that Vandermeer would deliver the cattle by truck, in one week, in a nearby town. He would pay with a cashier's check and take possession of the cattle and all ownership documents, such as brand inspection certificates and veterinarian's certificates. Back at the ranch, Vandermeer offered him a drink, but he said he had to hurry to another appointment.

The next week, right on schedule, he arrived on Thursday and presented his cashier's check for the full amount. When they had transferred the livestock, Vandermeer suggested they talk over some future business, but he was again in a rush. They shook hands and parted, the man heading due east, fast.

The Double Q's bank sent the cashier's check for collection but learned early the following week that it was forged. Vandermeer called the State Police, who traced the man's movements to the state line. Three weeks later and 1,600 miles east, the FBI located the

> **Vandermeer noticed that his boots were brand new and that he rode awkwardly.**

cattle, with the prominent "QQ" brand, in stockyards in Omaha. Ned Munson had purchased the cattle from the man for $225,000, which he considered a bargain. He had paid with a cashier's check. Ernest Jenkins, of course, had disappeared—literally. The truck's freshly painted door now read, "Ted J. Pringle, Grain Merchant," and it was parked a long, long way from Omaha.

20-1 LEGAL INTEREST

Who owns the cows? The Double Q wanted its cattle back or $285,000. If Munson was foolish enough to pay money to a thief, that was not the ranch's problem. But Ned Munson claimed the cows were his. He had paid a fair price to a man who appeared to own them. If Vandermeer was so foolish as to give up the cattle to a con artist, let the ranch suffer the consequences. The Double Q sued. Both parties to this lawsuit are unhappy, but fortunately for us, they have illustrated the theme for our chapter: When two parties claim a conflicting legal interest in particular goods, *who wins?* Who obtains the law's protection? These are disputes over *conflicting interests in goods*.

An interest is a legal right in something. More than one party can have an interest in particular goods. Suppose you lease a new car from a dealer, agreeing to pay $400 per month for three years. Several parties will have legal interests in the car. The dealer still *owns* the car—interest number one. At the end of three years, the dealer gets it back. For three years, you have the *use* of the car—interest number two. You may use the car for all normal purposes, and you are obligated to make monthly payments. Your payments go to a finance agency, which has made an arrangement with the dealer to obtain the right to your $400 monthly payment. The finance agency has a *security interest* in the car—interest number three. If you fail to pay on time, the finance company has the right to repossess your car. If you take the car to a garage for maintenance, the garage has *temporary possession* of the car—interest number four. The garage has the right to keep the car locked up overnight, to work on it, and to test-drive it. Sometimes legal interests clash, and it is those conflicts we look at here.

Often the parties will claim ownership, each arguing that his interest is stronger than the other's. But in this chapter, we also consider cases where each party argues that the *other* one owns the goods. Suppose a seller manufactures products for a buyer, but while the goods are being shipped, they are destroyed in a fire. The seller may argue that it no longer owned the goods, and the fire is the buyer's misfortune. But the buyer will claim it had not yet acquired the items.

In other cases, a *third party* will be involved. You pay $30,000 cash to buy a new car and expect to pick it up in three days. But the day before you arrive, the dealer's bank seizes all of the cars on the lot, claiming the dealer has defaulted on loans. Now the fight over legal interest is between you and the bank, with the dealer a relatively passive observer.

In the cattle case, three parties had a legal interest in the goods. The Double Q ranch originally had valid **title** to the cattle, meaning the normal rights of ownership. Ernest Jenkins, the con artist, acquired a lesser interest. His contract with Double Q was fraudulent because Jenkins intended to cheat the ranch. Nonetheless, he did have an agreement. He obtained **voidable title**, meaning limited rights in the goods, inferior to those of the owner.[1] Finally, Ned Munson makes a claim to the cattle based on his payment and his possession of the cows and all documents.

The court will use various sections of the Uniform Commercial Code (UCC) to determine who keeps the cows and who ultimately bears the loss. Ned Munson should win the cattle. He was acting in good faith and a commercially reasonable manner when he

Voidable title

Limited rights in goods, inferior to those of the owner.

---

[1]We discuss voidability in detail in Chapter 13, on capacity and consent.

bought the cows from a man who appeared to be a lawful cattle buyer. The Double Q must bear the loss. If, however, the Double Q can convince a court that Munson acted irresponsibly because he had specific grounds for suspecting Jenkins, the court might order Munson to pay for the cattle.[2]

20-2 IDENTIFICATION, TITLE, AND INSURABLE INTEREST

Historically, courts settled disputes about legal interest by looking at one thing: title. But the drafters of the UCC concluded that "title" was too abstract an answer for the assorted practical questions that arose. It sometimes could be hard to prove exactly who did have title, and it made no sense to settle a wide variety of business problems with one legal idea. Today, title is only one of several issues that a court will use to resolve conflicting interests in goods. *Identification* and *insurable interest* have become more important, and title has diminished in significance. We can begin to understand all three doctrines if we examine how title passes from seller to buyer.

20-2a Existence and Identification

Title in goods can pass from one person to another only if the goods exist and have been identified to the contract.

EXISTENCE

Goods must exist before title can pass.[3] Although most goods do exist when people buy and sell them, some have not yet come into being, such as crops to be grown later or goods that have not yet been manufactured. A farmer may contract to sell corn even before it is planted, but title to the corn cannot pass until it actually exists.

IDENTIFICATION

Goods must be identified to the contract before title can pass.[4] This means that the parties must have designated the specific goods being sold. Often, identification is obvious. If Dealer agrees to sell to Buyer a 60-foot yacht with identification number AKX472, the parties have identified the goods. But suppose Paintco agrees to sell Brushworks 1,000 gallons of white base paint at a specified price. Paintco has 25,000 gallons in its warehouse. Title cannot pass until Paintco identifies the specific gallons that will go to Brushworks.

The parties may agree in their contract how and when they will identify the goods.[5] They are free to identify them to the contract in any way they want. Paintco and Brushworks might agree, for example, that within one week of signing the sales agreement, Paintco will mark appropriate gallons. If the gallons are stored 50 to a crate, then Paintco will have a worker stick a "Brushworks" label on 20 crates. Once the label is on, the goods are identified to the contract.

---

[2]For a cattle case that raises these and other issues, see *Rudiger Charolais Ranches v. Van De Graaf Ranches*, 994 F.2d 670, 1993 U.S. App. LEXIS 12412 (9th Cir. 1993).
[3]UCC §2-105(2).
[4]UCC §2-401(1).
[5]UCC §2-501(1).

If the parties do not specify any particular method, identification will occur according to these rules:

- Identification occurs when the parties enter into a contract if the agreement describes specific goods that already exist. If the Dealer agrees to sell a yacht and the parties include the ID number in their contract, the goods are identified (even though the parties never use the term "identify").

- For unborn animals, identification generally takes place when they are conceived; for crops, identification normally happens when they are planted.

- For other goods, identification occurs when the seller marks, ships, or in some other way indicates the *exact* goods that are going to the buyer.[6]

EXAM Strategy

Question: Arielle, an artist, has 25 hand-painted room screens in her studio. She contracts to sell five of them to Retailer for $5,000 each. The contract allows Arielle to choose which five she will sell. Arielle moves five screens from her studio to a warehouse, but a week later, a fire destroys the building and its contents. Two insurance companies dispute whether title to the screens has passed to Retailer. The warehouse insurer claims the goods were identified and title passed; Retailer's insurer says the goods were not identified and title never passed. The contract says nothing about identification. Have the goods been identified?

Strategy: Title cannot pass until the goods have been identified to the contract. Identification can occur in three ways: The parties describe specific goods that already exist; animals are conceived or crops planted; or the seller marks, ships, or otherwise indicates which are going to the buyer. Did any of those things happen?

Result: The parties never described the goods. The goods are neither animals nor crops. However, when Arielle moved five of the screens to the warehouse, she "indicated which goods were going to the buyer." The goods were identified.

20-2b Passing of Title

Once goods exist and are identified to the contract, ownership can pass from one person to another. **Title may pass in any manner on which the parties agree (UCC §2-401).** Once again, the Code allows the parties to control their affairs with commonsense decisions. The parties can agree, for example, that title passes when the goods leave the manufacturer's factory, or when they reach the shipper who will transport them, or at any other time and place. If the parties do not agree on passing title, §2-401 decides. There are three possibilities:

- *When the goods are being moved,* title passes to the buyer when the seller completes whatever transportation it is obligated to do. Suppose Seller is in Milwaukee and Buyer is in Honolulu. The contract requires Seller to deliver the goods to a ship in San Francisco. Title passes when Seller completes its

---

[6]UCC §2-501.

last *contractually required* step. In this example, that happens when the goods reach the ship in San Francisco.

- *When the goods are* not *being moved and a contract calls for delivery of ownership documents,* title passes when the seller delivers these documents to the buyer. Suppose Seller, located in Louisville, has manufactured 5,000 baseball bats, which are stored in a warehouse in San Diego. Under the terms of their contract, Buyer will take possession of the bats at the warehouse. When Seller gives Buyer ownership documents, title passes.

- *When the goods are* not *being moved and the contract does* not *call for delivery of ownership documents,* title passes when the parties form the contract. For example, if the Buyer owns the warehouse where the bats are stored, Buyer needs no documents to take possession; title passes when the parties reach agreement.

20-2c Insurable Interest

Anyone buying or selling expensive goods should make certain that the goods are insured. There are some limits, though, on who may insure goods, and when. As we saw in Chapter 12, a party may insure something such as property or a human life only when she has a legitimate interest in it. If the person buying the policy lacks a real interest in the thing insured, the law regards the policy as a gambling agreement and considers it void.

When does someone have an insurable interest in goods? The UCC gives one answer for buyers and one for sellers. **A buyer obtains an insurable interest when the goods are identified to the contract (UCC §2-501).** Suppose that in January, Grain Broker contracts with Farmer to buy his entire wheat crop. Neither party mentions "identification." In January, the crop is not identified and Broker has no insurable interest. In May, after weeks of breaking the soil, Farmer plants his wheat crop. Once he has planted it, the goods are identified. The Broker now has an insurable interest and purchases insurance. In July, a drought destroys the crop, and the Broker never gets one grain of wheat. The Broker need not worry: His insurance policy will cover his losses.

The seller's insurable interest is different. **The seller retains an insurable interest in goods as long as she has either title to the goods or a security interest in them (UCC §2-501).** "Security interest" refers to cases in which the buyer still owes money for the goods and the seller can repossess the goods if payment is not made. Suppose Flyola Manufacturing sells a small aircraft to WingIt, a dealer, for $300,000. WingIt pays $30,000 cash and agrees to pay interest on the balance until it sells the plane. Flyola has an insurable interest even while the aircraft is in WingIt's showroom and may purchase insurance anytime until WingIt pays off the last dime.

And so, a seller and buyer can have an insurable interest in the same goods simultaneously. Suppose the heavy-metal band Flulike Symptoms hires Inkem Corp., in Minneapolis, to make 25,000 T-shirts with the band's logo, for sale at rock concerts. The parties agree that the T-shirts are identified as soon as the logo is printed, and that title will pass when Inkem delivers the T-shirts to the office of the Symptoms' manager in Kansas City. Inkem obviously has an insurable interest while the company is making the T-shirts and continues to have an interest until it delivers the T-shirts in Kansas City. But the Flulike Symptoms' insurable interest arises the moment their logo is stamped on each shirt, so the Symptoms could insure the goods while they are still stored in Inkem's factory.

In the following case, a car accident leads several insurance companies to dispute who owned the damaged auto. Each company wants to claim that the car belonged to—someone *else*.

Code Provisions Discussed in This Case

Issue	Relevant Code Section
1. Which party had title to the car?	UCC §2-401: Title to goods may pass in any manner on which the parties agree.
2. Did the seller have an insurable interest in the car?	UCC §2-501: The seller retains an insurable interest in the goods as long as it holds title to or a security interest in them.

VALLEY FORGE INSURANCE CO. v. GREAT AMERICAN INSURANCE CO.

1995 Ohio App. LEXIS 3939
Ohio Court of Appeals, 1995

CASE SUMMARY

Facts: On a Friday afternoon, Karl and Linda Kennedy went to John Nolan Ford to buy a new Ford Mustang. The parties signed all necessary documents, including a New Vehicle Buyer's Order, an Agreement to Provide Insurance, and credit applications. The Kennedys made a down payment but could not arrange financing before the dealership closed. John Nolan Ford determined that the Kennedys were creditworthy and allowed them to take the car home for the weekend. That evening, Karl Kennedy permitted his brother-in-law, Cella, to take the car for a drive, along with a passenger named Campbell. Cella wrecked the car, injuring his passenger. Campbell sued, and the question was which insurance company was liable for all of the harm: John Nolan Ford's insurer (Milwaukee Mutual), Cella's insurer (Valley Forge), or Kennedy's insurer (Great American). The trial court ruled that title had never passed to Kennedy and found Milwaukee Mutual liable. The company appealed.

Issue: *Had title passed to Kennedy at the time of the accident?*

Decision: No. Title had not yet passed to Kennedy. Affirmed.

Reasoning: Milwaukee Mutual asserted that the risk of loss passed to the Kennedys when the car was delivered to them. However, the signed contract stated that the buyer acquires "no right, title, or interest" in the automobile until it was delivered and either the full purchase price was paid in cash or satisfactory financing was arranged. At the time of the accident, the Kennedys had neither paid cash nor signed a financing agreement. Title never passed.

Milwaukee also argued that the Kennedys agreed to insure the automobile. The contract, though, did not state when the Kennedys were obligated to obtain insurance. It would be logical for them to do so after they had obtained title. Because the contract was ambiguous on this point, the agreement must be interpreted against the party who wrote it—namely, the automobile dealer. John Nolan Ford still had the risk of loss when the accident occurred.

20-3 IMPERFECT TITLE

20-3a Bona Fide Purchaser

In the chapter opener we saw a scam artist purchase cattle from a respectable ranch and sell them to an honest dealer. The bad guy skipped town, leaving a dispute between two innocent parties. Either the original owner (the ranch) or the buyer (the cattle dealer) must bear the loss. Who loses?

The Question: Who Must Suffer the Loss?

Owner ⟶   Bad Guy ⟶   Buyer

(has valid title)   (obtains goods from Owner and sells)   (buys goods from Bad Guy)

© Cengage Learning

Let's consider a new example, from the beginning. First, we need to know what kind of title Bad Guy obtains: Is it void or voidable? The key is this: Did Bad Guy *take* the item against the will of the owner, or did he fraudulently *trick* the owner into voluntarily handing the item to him?

Abe steals Marvin's BMW in the middle of the night and promptly sells it to Elaine for $35,000 cash. Two weeks later, the police locate the car. When Abe stole it, he obtained void title, which is no title at all. When Bad Guy sells the goods to Buyer, she also gets *no title at all*. Elaine must return the car to Marvin and suffer the $35,000 loss for Abe's theft. This policy makes sense because Marvin has done nothing wrong. If the law permitted Elaine to get valid title, it would encourage theft.

If Bad Guy *attempts to purchase* the goods from Owner using fraud or deception, he obtains **voidable** title, meaning limited rights in the goods, inferior to those of the owner. The owner should be able to recover the goods from Bad Guy (if he can be found), but not from anyone else who ends up with them. Suppose Connie agrees to buy Mark's Jeep. She gives him a check for $20,000 and he signs the vehicle over to her. Connie knows her check will bounce; she has used fraud to obtain the car. As a result, Connie obtains only voidable title. If Mark learns of the deception before Connie sells the car to someone else, he will get his Jeep back.

Unfortunately, Connie is slippery, not stupid. She quickly sells the Jeep to Seth for cash. By the time Connie's check bounces, she is long gone, and Seth has the car. Who keeps the Jeep? Seth wins the car if he is a bona fide purchaser. **A person with voidable title has power to transfer valid title for value to a good faith purchaser, generally called a** *bona fide purchaser* **or** *BFP*.[7]

Seth can prove that he is a bona fide purchaser by showing two things:

- That he gave value for the goods, *and*

- That he acted in good faith.

It is generally easy for purchasers to show that they gave value. The buyer could give cash or a check or could agree to extinguish a debt; that is, to forgive some money that Bad Guy owed. The real issue becomes whether the buyer acted in good faith. If Seth paid a reasonable purchase price and Connie showed him convincing identification and signed over to him all purchase documents, Seth acted in good faith. He keeps the Jeep and Mark loses.

On the other hand, suppose Seth knows the brand-new Jeep is worth more than $28,000. Connie seems in a frantic hurry to sell the car. She cannot produce the car's registration but promises to send it within three days. Connie's conduct, together with the $8,000 discount, would make a reasonable person suspicious. Seth is not acting in good faith and therefore is not a bona fide purchaser. Mark receives the car back, and Seth pays dearly for his automotive lust.

In the following case, German soldiers confiscated property during World War II. What kind of title did they obtain? Could ownership of looted art be passed on to someone else?

---

[7]UCC §2-403(1).

BAKALAR V. VAVRA

619 F.3d 136
Second Circuit Court of Appeals, 2010

Facts: Franz Grunbaum was a Jewish man who lived in Vienna before World War II. In 1938, the Nazis imprisoned him in the Dachau concentration camp, where he died three years later. The Nazis also confiscated his property, which included a valuable drawing by Austrian artist Egon Schiele.

This drawing changed hands several times until it was eventually sold to David Bakalar in 1963. Years later, Grunbaum's heirs, Milos Vavra and Leon Fischer, argued that they were the true owners of the picture, which was worth an estimated $675,000 at that point. The trial court disagreed, finding that Bakalar was the drawing's owner. Vavra and Fischer appealed.

Issue: *If artwork was taken illegally from the original owner, could a subsequent bona fide purchaser rightfully own it?*

Decision: No. A thief cannot pass good title.

Reasoning: New York does not allow a thief to pass good title because this great city does not want to become a marketplace for stolen goods. In other words, the law has long protected the right of the owner whose property has been stolen to recover that property, even if it is in the possession of a bona fide purchaser who acted in good faith. An artwork stolen during World War II still belongs to the original owner, even if there have been subsequent buyers and even if each of those buyers was completely unaware that he was buying stolen goods.

For Bakalar to be judged the rightful owner, he must prove that the Nazis did not steal the drawing from Grunbaum. We are remanding this case the lower court to give Bakalar that opportunity.

20-3b Entrustment

Your old Steinway grand piano needs a complete rebuilding. You hire Fred Showpan, Inc., a company that repairs and sells instruments. Showpan hauls your piano away and promises to return it in perfect shape. Two months later, you are horrified to spot Showpan's showroom boarded up and pasted with bankruptcy notices. Worse still, you learn that Fred sold your beloved instrument to a customer, Frankie List. When you track down List, he claims he paid $18,000 for the piano and likes it just fine. Is he entitled to keep it?

Quite likely he is. Section 2-403(1), the BFP provision we just discussed, would not apply because Showpan did not *purchase* the piano from you. But §2-403(2) does apply. This is the "entrustment" section, and it covers cases in which the owner of goods voluntarily *leaves* them with a merchant, who then sells the goods without permission. According to **UCC §2-403(2), any entrusting to a merchant who deals in goods of that kind gives him power to transfer all rights of the entruster to a buyer in the ordinary course of business (BIOC).**

Entrusting means delivering goods to a merchant or permitting the merchant to retain them.[8] In the piano example, you clearly entrusted goods to a merchant. If you buy a used car from Fast Eddie's and then leave it there for a week while you obtain insurance, you have entrusted it to Eddie.

---

[8]For a discussion of who is and who is not a merchant, see Chapter 19.

DEALS IN GOODS OF THAT KIND

The purpose of the section is to protect innocent buyers who enter a store, see the goods they expect to find, and purchase something, having no idea that the storekeeper is illegally selling the property of others. Shoppers should not have to demand proof of title to everything in the store. Further, if someone has to bear the risk, let it be the person who has entrusted her goods; she is in the best position to investigate the merchant's integrity. But this protection does not extend to a buyer who arrives at a vacuum cleaner store and buys an $80,000 mobile home parked in the lot.

IN THE ORDINARY COURSE OF BUSINESS

Buyer in the ordinary course of business (BIOC)
One who acts in good faith, without knowing that the sale violates the owner's rights.

A **buyer in the ordinary course of business (BIOC)** is one who acts in good faith, without knowing that the sale violates the owner's rights. If Frank List buys your piano assuming that Showpan owns it, he has acted in good faith. If Frank was your neighbor, recognized your instrument, and bought it anyway, he is not buying in the ordinary course of business and must hand over the piano.

Of course, a merchant who violates the owner's rights is liable to that owner. If Showpan were still in business when you discovered your loss, you could sue and recover the value of the piano. The problems arise when the merchant is bankrupt or otherwise unable to reimburse the owner.

EXAM Strategy

Question: Pamela went to University Used Auto and asked if the company had a Lincoln Navigator. University had no such SUV, but a sales representative told Pamela that he would find her one. The representative contacted Royal auto dealership, which sold new and used cars. Royal agreed to supply University with a car, on the understanding that an interested buyer would pay *Royal*, which in turn would give a finder's fee to University. The companies had worked this way in the past. Royal delivered a Navigator as requested. But when the used car company sold the vehicle to Pamela, the company instructed her to pay University directly, which she did. Royal sued Pamela, seeking the car, and the court had to determine whether there had been an entrustment. Royal argued that it never entrusted the Navigator to University because the parties agreed to require payment to Royal.

Strategy: Entrustment means delivering goods to a merchant who routinely deals in such articles.

Result: Royal delivered a used car to a used car dealer. That is entrustment. It is true that both dealers understood that Pamela was to pay Royal—but she did not know that. Entrustment protects good faith buyers, and Pamela wins.

20-4 RISK OF LOSS

Many of the issues we have looked at thus far involve someone doing something wrong. Now we turn to cases where there may be no wrongdoer.

Accidents hurt businesses. When goods are damaged, the law may again need to decide whether it is the seller or buyer who must suffer the loss. In the cases we have seen thus far, the parties were arguing, "It's mine!"—"Like heck it is, it's *mine!*" In risk of loss cases, the parties are generally shouting, "It was yours!"—"No way, dude, it was *yours!*"

Athena, a seafood wholesaler, is gearing up for the Super Bowl, which will bring 150,000 hungry visitors to her city for a week of eating and gabbing. Athena orders 25,000 lobsters from Poseidon's Fishfoods, 500 miles distant, and simultaneously contracts with a dozen local restaurants to resell them. Poseidon loads the lobsters, still kicking, into refrigerated railcars owned by Demeter Trucking. But halfway to the city, the train collides with a prison van. None of the convicts escape, but the lobsters do, hurtling into swamps from which they are never recaptured. Athena loses all of her profits and sues. As luck would have it, Demeter Trucking had foolishly let its insurance lapse. Poseidon claims the goods were out of its hands. Who loses?

The common law answered this problem by looking at which party had title to the goods at the time of loss. But the UCC again rejects the old concept, striving once more for a practical solution. The UCC permits the parties to agree on who bears the risk of loss. **UCC §2-509(4) states that the parties may allocate the risk of loss any way they wish.**

Often the parties will do just that, avoiding arguments and litigation in the event of an accident. As part of her agreement with Poseidon, Athena should have included a one-sentence clause, such as "Seller bears all risk of loss until the lobsters are delivered to Athena's warehouse." So long as the parties make their risk allocation clear, the Code will enforce their terms.

20-4a Shipping Terms

The parties can quickly and easily allocate the risk of loss by using common shipping terms that the Code defines. FOB means free on board; CIF stands for cost, insurance, and freight. By combining these designations with other terms, the parties can specify risk in a few words:

- *FOB place of shipment.* The seller is obligated to put the goods into the possession of the carrier at the place named. The seller bears the expense and risk until they are in the carrier's possession. From that moment onward, the buyer bears the risk.

- *FOB place of destination.* The seller must deliver the goods at the place named and bears the expense *and risk* of shipping.

- *CIF.* The price includes in a lump sum: the cost of the goods and the insurance and freight to the named destination. The risk of loss passes from the seller to the buyer when the seller delivers the goods to the port of shipment.

- *C & F.* This designation is similar to CIF, but the price does not include insurance.

20-4b When the Parties Fail to Allocate the Risk

If the parties fail to specify when the risk passes from seller to buyer, the Code provides the answer. When neither party breached the contract, §2-509 determines the risk; when a party has breached the contract, §2-510 governs. The full analysis of risk is somewhat intricate, so we first supply you with a short version: **When neither party has breached the contract, the risk of loss generally passes from seller to buyer when the seller has transported the goods as far as he is obligated to. When a party has breached, the risk of loss generally lies with that party.**

And now, for the courageous student, the full version of how the UCC allocates the risk of loss when the parties fail to specify it in advance.

WHEN NEITHER PARTY BREACHES

In the example of Athena and Poseidon, both parties did what they were supposed to do, so there was no breach of contract. To settle these cases, we need to know whether the contract obligated the seller to ship the goods or whether the goods were handled in some other way. There are three possibilities: (1) the contract required the seller to ship the goods, or (2) the contract involved a bailment, or (3) other cases.

If the Seller Must Ship the Goods   Most contracts require the seller to arrange shipment of the goods. In a *shipment contract*, the seller must deliver the goods *to a carrier*, which will then transport the goods to the buyer. The carrier might be a trucking company, railroad, airline, or ship, and is generally located near the seller's place of business. **In a shipment contract, the risk passes to the buyer when the seller delivers the goods to the carrier.** Suppose Old Wood, in North Carolina, agrees to sell $100,000 worth of furniture to Pioneer Company, in Anchorage. The contract requires Old Wood to deliver the goods to Great Northern Railroad lines in Chicago. From North Carolina to Chicago, Old Wood bears the risk of loss. If the furniture is damaged, stolen, or destroyed, Old Wood is out of luck. But once the furniture is on board the train in Chicago, the risk of loss passes to Pioneer. If the train derails in Montana and every desk and chair is smashed to kindling, Pioneer must nevertheless pay the full $100,000 to Old Wood.

In a *destination contract*, the seller is responsible for delivering the goods *to the buyer*, and risk passes to the buyer when the goods reach the destination. If the contract required Old Wood to deliver the furniture to Pioneer's warehouse in Anchorage, then Old Wood bears the loss for the entire trip. If the train travels 3,000 miles and then plunges off a bridge in Alaska, 45 feet from its destination, Old Wood picks up the tab.

Bailor

The one who owns goods legally held by another.

Bailee

The one with temporary possession of another's goods.

If There Is a Bailment   Freezem Corp. produces 500 room air conditioners and stores them in Every-Ware's Warehouse. This is a **bailment, meaning that one person or company is legally holding goods for the benefit of another**. Freezem is the **bailor**, the one who owns the goods, and Every-Ware is the **bailee**, the one with temporary possession. Suppose Freezem agrees to sell 300 of its air conditioners to KeepKool Appliances. KeepKool does not need the machines in its store for six months, so it plans to keep them at Every-Ware's until then. But two weeks after Freezem and KeepKool make their deal, Every-Ware burns to the ground. Who bears the loss of the 300 air conditioners? **If the contract requires a bailee to hold the goods for the buyer, the risk passes when the buyer obtains documents entitling her to possession, or when the bailee acknowledges her right to the goods.** If fire broke out in Every-Ware's before KeepKool received any documents enabling it to take the air conditioners away, then the loss would fall on Freezem.

Other Cases   The great majority of contracts involve either shipment by the seller or a bailment. In the remaining cases, if the seller is a *merchant*, risk passes to the buyer on receipt. This means that a merchant is only off the hook if the buyer actually accepts the goods. If the seller is *not a merchant*, risk passes when the seller tenders the goods, meaning that she makes them available to the buyer. The Code is giving more protection to buyers when they deal with a merchant.

WHEN ONE PARTY BREACHES

We now look at how the Code allocates risk when one of the parties *does* breach. Again there are three possibilities: (1) seller breaches and buyer rejects; (2) seller breaches, buyer accepts, but then revokes; or (3) buyer breaches.

Seller Breaches and Buyer Rejects   PlayStore, a sporting goods store, orders 75 canoes from Floataway. PlayStore specifies that the canoes must be 12 feet long, light-weight metal, dark green. Floataway delivers 75 canoes to Truckit, a trucking company. When Truckit's trucks arrive, PlayStore finds that the canoes are the right material and color, but 18 feet long. PlayStore rejects the craft, and Truckit heads back to Floataway. But one of the trucks is hijacked and the 25 canoes it carries are never recovered. Floataway demands its money for the 25 lost canoes. Who loses?

Floataway had delivered **nonconforming goods**; that is, merchandise which differs from that specified in the contract. A buyer has a right to reject such goods. **When the buyer rejects nonconforming goods, the risk of loss remains with the seller until he cures the defect or the buyer decides to accept the goods.** In our example, Floataway must suffer the loss for the stolen canoes. If PlayStore had decided to accept the canoes, even though they were the wrong size, then the risk would have passed to the sports store.

Nonconforming goods
Merchandise that differs from that specified in the contract.

Seller Breaches, Buyer Accepts, but Then Revokes   PlayStore orders 200 tennis rackets from High Strung. When the rackets arrive, they seem fine, so the store accepts them. But then a salesperson notices that the grips are loose. Every racket has the same problem. PlayStore returns the rackets to High Strung, but they are destroyed when a blimp crashes into the delivery truck. **When a buyer accepts goods but then rightfully revokes acceptance, the risk remains with the seller to the extent that the buyer's insurance will not cover the loss.** If PlayStore's insurance covers the damaged rackets, there is no problem. If PlayStore's insurance does not cover the loss of goods in transit, High Strung must pay.

Buyer Breaches   One last time. PlayStore orders 60 tents from ExploreMore. About the time the tents leave the factory, PlayStore decides to drop its line of camping goods and specialize in team sports. PlayStore notifies ExploreMore that it wants to explore less and will not pay. The tents are destroyed in a collision involving a prison van and a train carrying lobsters. This time, PlayStore is liable. **When a buyer breaches the contract before taking possession, it assumes the risk of loss to the extent that the seller's insurance is deficient.**

Exhibit 20.1 should clarify.

In the following case, neither party breached, so §2-509 governs.

| **Code Provisions Discussed in This Case** | |
Issue	Relevant Code Section
1. Did the parties create a bailment?	In a bailment, one person legally holds goods for the benefit of another.
2. Which party bore the risk of the horse's death?	UCC §2-509(2): If the contract requires a bailee to hold the goods for the buyer, the risk passes when the buyer obtains documents entitling her to possession, or when the bailee acknowledges her right to the goods.

Start Here

Did the Parties Allocate the Risk in Their Contract?

If the parties have allocated the risk in their contract, that agreement will control and everything on this chart is gloriously irrelevant.

If the parties have *not* allocated the risk of loss, then §2-509 and §2-510 will determine who suffers the loss.

In using the two Code sections to determine the risk, the first question is whether either party has breached the contract.

No Breach (§2-509)
If neither party breaches, there are three possibilities:

1 Contract requires Seller to ship goods by carrier.

a *Shipment Contract* requires Seller to deliver the goods to a carrier.

Risk passes to Buyer when Seller delivers goods to carrier.

b *Destination Contract* requires Seller to deliver goods to a specified destination.

Risk passes to Buyer when carrier tenders goods at the destination.

2 Contract requires a bailee to hold goods for Buyer.

Risk passes to Buyer when she obtains documents entitling her to possession, or when Bailee acknowledges she is entitled to possession.

3 Other cases.

a If Seller *is* a merchant

Risk passes to Buyer on receipt of goods.

b If Seller *is not* a merchant

Risk passes to Buyer on tender of delivery.

Breach (§2-510)
If a party breaches, there are three possibilities:

1 Seller breaches. The goods are nonconforming and the Buyer rightfully rejects them.

Risk remains with the Seller until he cures the defects or the Buyer decides to accept the goods.

2 Seller breaches. The buyer accepts but then revokes his acceptance.

Risk remains with the Seller to the extent that the Buyer's own insurance is deficient.

3 Buyer breaches. Buyer repudiates conforming goods or in some other way breaches the contract before he takes possession of the goods.

Risk passes to the Buyer to the extent that the Seller's insurance is deficient, for a commercially reasonable time.

© Cengage Learning

EXHIBIT 20.1

HARMON v. DUNN

1997 Tenn. App. LEXIS 217
Tennessee Court of Appeals, 1997

CASE SUMMARY

Facts: Bess Harmon owned a two-year-old Tennessee Walking Horse named Phantom Recall. Harmon, who lived in Tennessee, boarded her horse with Steve Dunn at his stables in Florence, Alabama. Dunn cared for Phantom Recall and showed him at equestrian events. Harmon instructed Dunn to sell the horse for $25,000, and Dunn arranged for his friend Scarbrough to buy the colt. On June 30, Dunn delivered Scarbrough's $25,000 check to Harmon, who handed over the horse's certificate of registration and a "transfer of ownership" document. That night at a horse show, Dunn told Scarbrough that he had delivered the check and had the ownership papers in his car. Dunn did not actually give the documents to his friend. Scarbrough knew that Phantom Recall was at Dunn's stable, where Scarbrough had boarded other horses. Sadly, the colt developed colitis and died suddenly, on July 4. Scarbrough stopped payment on his check, and Harmon sued for her money. The trial court found for Harmon, and Scarbrough appealed.

Issue: *Did Scarbrough bear the risk of Phantom Recall's death?*

Decision: Yes. Scarbrough bore the risk of loss. Affirmed.

Reasoning: UCC §2-509(2) governs those cases where there is no breach of contract and the goods are held by a bailee to be delivered without being moved. Dunn was certainly Harmon's bailee. He worked for Harmon, trained Phantom Recall, and transported the horse to various shows. Because the agreement between Scarbrough and Harmon did not require Phantom Recall to be moved anywhere for delivery, this section of the Code applies. Under UCC §2-509(2), the risk of loss passes to the buyer:

(a) On his receipt of a negotiable document of title covering the goods, or

(b) On acknowledgment by the bailee of the buyer's right to possession of the goods.

Scarbrough argued that he did not bear the risk of the horse's loss because he never received physical possession of the ownership documents. But Scarbrough obtained control of the horse when Dunn told him that he, as bailee, had the transfer papers—four days before the horse's death. He did not receive the ownership documents then, but the papers were already in Dunn's hands, and all parties knew it. Because nothing prevented Scarbrough from exercising complete ownership of Phantom Recall as of that date, he also acquired the risk of loss. Unfortunately for Scarbrough, he was left with nothing but the phantom of Phantom Recall.

20-5 WARRANTIES

The *Harmon* case illustrates what happens when an accident destroys the goods sold and neither party is at fault. But what if Harmon had guaranteed Scarbrough a healthy horse and delivered a sick one? The UCC also addresses this issue in its warranty provisions. A **warranty** is a promise that goods will meet certain standards. Normally a manufacturer or a seller gives a warranty and a buyer relies on it. A warranty might be explicit and written: "The manufacturer warrants that the light bulbs in this package will illuminate for 2,000 hours." Or a warranty could be oral: "Don't worry, this machine can harvest any size of wheat crop ever planted in the state."

Sometimes a manufacturer offers a warranty as a means of attracting buyers: "We provide the finest bumper-to-bumper warranty in the automobile industry." Other times, *the law itself* imposes a warranty on goods, requiring the manufacturer to meet certain standards whether it wants to or not. We will first consider express warranties.

Warranty
A contractual assurance that goods will meet certain standards.

20-6 EXPRESS WARRANTIES

Express warranty
One that the seller creates with his words or actions.

An **express warranty** is one that the seller creates with his words or actions.[9] Whenever a seller *clearly indicates* to a buyer that the goods being sold will meet certain standards, she has created an express warranty. For example, if the sales clerk for a paint store tells a professional house painter that "this exterior paint will not fade for three years, even in direct sunlight," that is an express warranty and the store is bound by it. Or, if the clerk gives the painter a brochure that makes the same promise, the store is again bound by its express warranty. On the other hand, if the salesperson merely says, "I know you're going to be happy with this product," there is no warranty because the promise is too vague. The UCC establishes that the seller may create an express warranty in three ways: (1) with an affirmation of fact or a promise; (2) with a description of the goods; or (3) with a sample or model. In addition, the buyer must demonstrate that what the seller said or did was part of the *basis of the bargain*.

20-6a Affirmation of Fact or Promise

Any affirmation of fact—or any promise—can create an express warranty.[10] An affirmation of fact is simply a statement about the nature or quality of the goods, such as "this scaffolding is made from the highest grade of steel available at any price" or "this car will accelerate from 0 to 60 in 5.3 seconds." A promise can include phrases such as, "we guarantee you that this air conditioning system will cool your building to 72 degrees, regardless of the outdoor temperature."

A common problem in cases of express warranty is to separate true affirmations of fact from mere sales puffery or seller's opinion, which creates no express warranty.

A statement is more likely to be an affirmation of fact if:

- *It is specific and can be proven true or false.* Suppose the brochures of a home builder promise to meet "the strictest building codes." Since there is a code on file, the builder's work can be compared to it, and his promise is binding.

- *It is written.* An oral promise *can* create an express warranty. But promises in brochures are more likely to be taken seriously. Statements in a *written contract* are the likeliest of all to create a binding warranty.

- *Defects are not obvious.* If a used car salesman tells you that a car is rust-free when the driver's door is pockmarked with rust, you should not take the statement seriously—since a court will not, either.

- *Seller has greater expertise.* If the seller knows more than the buyer, his statements will be more influential with buyer and court alike. If your architect assures you that the new porch will be warm in winter, the law recognizes that you will naturally rely on her expertise.

20-6b Description of Goods

Any description of the goods can create an express warranty.[11] The statement can be oral or written. A description might be a label on a bag of seed, referring to the seed as a particular variety of tomato; it could be a tag on airplane parts, assuring the buyer that the goods have met safety tests. Wherever the words appear, if they describe the goods as having particular characteristics or qualities, the seller has probably created an express warranty.

---

[9]UCC §2-313.
[10]UCC §2-313(1)(a).
[11]UCC §2-313(1)(b).

20-6c Sample or Model

Any sample or model can create an express warranty.[12] A sample can be a very effective way of demonstrating the quality of goods to a customer. However, a seller who uses a sample is generally warranting that the merchandise sold will be just as good.

20-6d Basis of Bargain

The seller's conduct must have been part of the basis of the bargain. To prove an express warranty, a buyer must demonstrate that the two parties *included the statements or acts in their bargain*. Some courts have interpreted this to mean that the buyer must have *relied* on the seller's statements. There is logic to this position. For example, suppose a sales brochure makes certain assurances about the quality of goods, but the buyer never sees the brochure until she files suit. Should the seller be held to an express warranty? Some courts would rule that the seller is not liable for breach of warranty.

Other courts, however, have ruled that a seller's statement can be part of the basis of the bargain even when the buyer has not clearly relied on it. These courts are declaring that a seller who chooses to make statements about his goods will be held to them *unless the seller can convince a court that he should not be liable.* This is a policy decision, taken by many courts, to give the buyer the benefit of the doubt since the seller is in the best position to control what he says.

20-7 IMPLIED WARRANTIES

Sean decides to plow driveways during the winter. Emily sells him a snowplow and installs it on his truck, but she makes no promises about its performance. When winter arrives, Sean has plenty of business, but he finds that the plow cannot be raised or lowered whenever the temperature falls below 40 degrees. He demands a refund from Emily, but she declines, saying, "I never said that thing would work in the winter. Tough luck." Is she off the hook? No. It is true she made no express warranties. But many sales are covered by implied warranties.

Implied warranties are those created by the Uniform Commercial Code itself, not by any act or statement of the seller. The Code's drafters concluded that goods should generally meet certain standards of quality, regardless of what the seller did or did not say. So the UCC creates both an implied warranty of merchantability and an implied warranty of fitness.

20-7a Implied Warranty of Merchantability

This is the most important warranty in the UCC. Buyers, whether individual consumers or billion-dollar corporations, are more likely to rely on this than any other section, and sellers must understand it thoroughly when they market goods. **Unless excluded or modified, a warranty that the goods shall be merchantable is implied in a contract for their sale if the seller is a merchant with respect to goods of that kind. Merchantable** means that the goods are fit for the ordinary purposes for which they are sold.[13] This rule contains several important principles:

Merchantable
Means that the goods are fit for the ordinary purposes for which they are sold.

- *Unless excluded or modified* means that the seller does have a chance to escape this warranty.

- *Merchantability* requires that goods be fit for their normal purposes. To be merchantable, a ladder must be able to rest securely against a building and support someone who is climbing it. The ladder need not be serviceable as a boat ramp.

---

[12]UCC §2-313(1)(c).
[13]UCC §2-314(1).

- *Implied* means that the law itself imposes this liability on the seller even if it is not written down.

- A *merchant with respect to goods of that kind* means that the seller is someone who routinely deals in these goods or holds himself out as having special knowledge about these goods. If it is selling vehicles, a car dealer is acting as a merchant. An accountant who sells his used car by listing it online is not a merchant.

Dacor Corp. manufactured and sold scuba diving equipment. Dacor ordered air hoses from Sierra Precision, specifying the exact size and couplings so that the hose would fit tightly and safely into Dacor's oxygen units. Within about one year, customers returned a dozen Dacor units, complaining that the hose connections had cracked or sheared and were unusable. Dacor recalled 16,000 units and refit them with safe hoses, at a cost of more than $136,000. Dacor sued Sierra, claiming a breach of the implied warranty of merchantability. The Illinois court ruled that Sierra was a merchant with respect to scuba hoses because it routinely manufactured and sold them. Further, the court ruled that since use of the faulty hose assemblies under water would be life-threatening, they were clearly not fit for the purpose for which they were sold—which was, after all, scuba diving! The court ordered Sierra to pay the cost of Dacor's recall.[14]

The scuba equipment was not merchantable because a properly made scuba hose should never crack under normal use. But what if the product being sold is food, and the food contains something that is harmful—yet quite normal?

GOODMAN V. WENCO FOODS, INC.

333N.C. 1, 423 S.E.2d 444, 1992 N.C. LEXIS 671
Supreme Court of North Carolina, 1992

CASE SUMMARY

Facts: Fred Goodman and a friend stopped for lunch at a Wendy's restaurant in Hillsborough, North Carolina. Goodman had eaten about half of his double hamburger when he bit down and felt immediate pain in his lower jaw. He took from his mouth a triangular piece of cow bone, about one-sixteenth to one-quarter inch thick and one-half inch long, along with several pieces of his teeth. Goodman's pain was intense, and his dental repairs took months.

The restaurant purchased all of its meat from Greensboro Meat Supply Company (GMSC). Wendy's required its meat to be chopped and "free from bone or cartilage in excess of 1/8 inch in any dimension." GMSC beef was inspected continuously by state regulators and was certified by the United States Department of Agriculture (USDA). The USDA considered any bone fragment less than three-quarters of an inch long to be "insignificant."

Goodman sued, claiming a breach of the implied warranty of merchantability. The trial court dismissed the claim, ruling that the bone was natural to the food and that the hamburger was therefore fit for its ordinary purpose. The appeals court reversed this, holding that a hamburger could be unfit even if the bone occurred naturally. Wendy's appealed to the state's highest court.

Issue: *Was the hamburger unfit for its ordinary purpose because it contained a harmful but natural bone?*

Decision: Yes. Even if the harmful bone occurred naturally, the hamburger could be unfit for its ordinary purpose. Affirmed.

Reasoning: When an object in food harms a consumer, the injured person may recover even if the substance occurred naturally, provided that a reasonable consumer would not expect to encounter it. A triangular, one-half-inch bone shaving may be inherent to a cut of beef, but

---

[14]*Dacor Corp. v. Sierra Precision*, 1993 U.S. Dist. LEXIS 8009 (N.D. Ill. 1993).

whether a reasonable consumer would anticipate it is normally a question for the jury.

Wendy's hamburgers need not be perfect, but they must be fit for their intended purpose. It is difficult to imagine how a consumer could guard against bone particles, short of removing the hamburger from its bun, breaking it apart, and inspecting its small components.

Wendy's argued that because its meat complied with federal and state standards, the hamburgers were merchantable as a matter of law. However, while compliance with legal standards is evidence for the juries to consider, it does not ensure merchantability. A jury could still conclude that a bone this size in hamburger meat was reasonably unforeseeable and that an injured consumer was entitled to compensation.

20-7b Implied Warranty of Fitness for a Particular Purpose

The other warranty that the UCC imposes on sellers is the implied warranty of fitness for a particular purpose. This cumbersome name is often shortened and referred to as simply the *warranty of fitness.* **Where the seller at the time of contracting *knows* about a particular purpose for which the buyer wants the goods, and knows that the buyer is relying on the seller's skill or judgment, there is (unless excluded or modified) an implied warranty that the goods shall be fit for the purpose.**[15] Here are the key points:

- *Particular purpose.* The seller must know about some *special* use that the buyer plans for the goods. For example, if a lumber salesman knows that a builder is purchasing lumber to construct houses in a swamp, the UCC implies a warranty that the lumber will withstand water.

- *Seller's skill.* The buyer must be depending upon the seller's skill or judgment in selecting the product, and the seller must know it. Suppose the builder says to the lumber salesman, "I need four-by-eights that I will be using to build a house in the swamp. What do you have that will do the job?" The builder's reliance is obvious, and the warranty is established. By contrast, suppose that an experienced Alaskan sled driver offers to buy your three huskies, telling you she plans to use them to pull sleds. She has the experience and you do not, and if the dogs refuse to pull more than a one-pound can of dog food, you have probably not breached the implied warranty of fitness.

- *Exclusion or modification.* Once again, the seller is allowed to modify or exclude any warranty of fitness.

20-7c Warranty of Title

Strapped for cash, Maggie steals her boyfriend's rusty Chevy and sells it to Paul for $2,500. As we saw earlier in this chapter, Maggie gets no valid title by her theft, and therefore Paul receives no title either. When the boyfriend finds his car parked at a nightclub, he notifies the police and gets his wheels back. Poor Paul is out of pocket $2,500 and has no car to show for it. That clearly is unjust, and the UCC provides Paul with a remedy: **The seller of goods warrants that her title is valid and that the goods are free of any security interest that the buyer knows nothing about unless the seller has clearly excluded or modified this warranty.**[16] Once again, the Code is imposing a warranty on any seller except those who explicitly exclude or modify it. When Maggie sells the car to Paul, she warrants her valid title to the car and simultaneously breaches that warranty since she obviously has no title. If he can find her, Paul will win a lawsuit against Maggie for $2,500.

---

[15]UCC §2-315.
[16]UCC §2-312(1).

20-8 DISCLAIMERS AND DEFENSES

There are several limitations on warranties. A seller may disclaim *warranties*, meaning that he eliminates express or implied warranties covering the goods. Or the seller may limit the buyer's *remedy*, which means that even if there is a breach of warranty, the buyer still may have only a very limited chance to recover against the seller.

20-8a Disclaimers

Disclaimer
A statement that a particular warranty does not apply.

A **disclaimer** is a statement that a particular warranty *does not* apply. The Code permits the seller to disclaim most warranties.

ORAL EXPRESS WARRANTIES

Under the Code, a seller may disclaim an oral express warranty. Suppose Traffic Co. wants to buy a helicopter from HeliCorp for use in reporting commuter traffic. HeliCorp's salesman tells Traffic Co., "Don't worry, you can fly this bird day and night for six months with nothing more than a fuel stop." HeliCorp's contract may disclaim the oral warranty. The contract could say, "HeliCorp's entire warranty is printed below. Any statements made by any agent or salesperson are disclaimed and form no part of this contract." That disclaimer is valid. If the helicopter requires routine servicing between flights, HeliCorp has not breached an oral warranty.

WRITTEN EXPRESS WARRANTIES

This is the one type of warranty that is almost impossible to disclaim. If a seller includes an express warranty in the *sales contract*, any disclaimer is definitely invalid. Suppose HeliCorp sells an industrial helicopter for use in hauling building equipment. The sales contract describes the aircraft as "operable to 14,000 feet." Later, in the contract, a limited warranty disclaims "any other warranties or statements that appear in this document or in any other document." That disclaimer is invalid and does not cancel the assurance that the helicopter can operate to 14,000 feet. The Code will not permit a seller to take contradictory positions in a document. The goal is simply to be fair, and the UCC assumes that it is confusing and unjust for a seller to say one thing to help close a deal and the opposite to limit its losses.[17]

What if the express written statement is in a different document, such as a sales brochure? The disclaimer is void if it would *unfairly surprise* the buyer. Assume, again, that HeliCorp promises a helicopter that requires no routine maintenance for six months, but this time, the promise appears in a sales brochure that Traffic Co. reads and relies on. If HeliCorp attempts to disclaim the written warranty, it will probably fail. Most people take written information seriously, and courts usually find that consumers would be unfairly surprised if a company tried to go back on promises made in a sales brochure.

IMPLIED WARRANTIES

A seller may disclaim the implied warranty of merchantability provided he *actually mentions the word* merchantability *and makes the disclaimer conspicuous*. Courts demand to see the specific word *merchantability* in the disclaimer to be sure the buyer realized she was giving up this fundamental protection. If the word is there, and the disclaimer is conspicuous enough that the buyer should have seen it, she has forfeited the warranty. A seller may disclaim the implied warranty of fitness with any language that is clear and conspicuous.

To make life easier, the UCC permits a seller to disclaim *all* implied warranties by conspicuously stating that the goods are sold "as is" or "with all faults." Notice the tension

---

[17]UCC §2-316(1).

between this provision and the one just discussed. A seller who wants to disclaim *only* the warranty of merchantability must explicitly mention that term; but a seller wishing to exclude *all* implied warranties may do so with a short expression, such as "sold as is."

Many states, though, prohibit a seller from disclaiming implied warranties in the sale of consumer goods. In these states, if a home furnishings store sells a bunk bed to a consumer, and the top bunk tips out the window on the first night, the seller is liable. Even if the sales contract clearly stated "no warranties of merchantability," the court would reject the clause and find that the seller breached the implied warranty of merchantability.

EXAM Strategy

Question: Marcos's backyard pool, which measured 35 feet by 18 feet, needed a new filter. A sales brochure stated, "This filter will keep any normal backyard pool, up to 50 feet by 25, clean and healthy all summer for a minimum of 5 years." Marcos signed a sales contract, which included this disclaimer: "The filter will work to normal industry standards. This is the only warranty. No other statements, written or oral, apply. Pools vary widely, and the Seller cannot guarantee any specific level of performance or cleanliness. Buyer agrees to this disclaimer." The filter failed to keep Marcos's pool clean, and he sued for breach of warranty. Who should win?

Strategy: Sellers are often able to disclaim oral warranties, but written warranties are difficult to disclaim. Here, the initial promise and the disclaimer were in different documents. Does that change the outcome? Finally, Marcos was a consumer. Courts treat consumers differently from corporate buyers.

Result: It is difficult or impossible for sellers to disclaim written warranties, even if the promise and disclaimer are in different documents. A disclaimer that would unfairly surprise the buyer is void. Marcos relied on the sales brochure—as the company intended—and the seller will probably lose. Furthermore, most states give extra protection to consumers, knowing that they are less sophisticated buyers. A court is likely to find in favor of Marcos based on the seller's express warranty, as well as the implied warranties of merchantability and fitness.

20-8b Remedy Limitations

Simon Aerials, Inc., manufactured boomlifts, the huge cranes used to construct multistoried buildings. Simon agreed to design and build eight unusually large machines for Logan Equipment Corp. Simon delivered the boomlifts late, and they functioned poorly. Logan requested dozens of repairs and modifications, which Simon attempted to accomplish over many months, but the equipment never worked well. Logan gave up and sued for $7.5 million, representing the profits it expected to make from renting the machines and the damage to its reputation. Logan clearly had suffered major losses, and it recovered—nothing. How could that be?

Simon had negotiated a **limitation of remedy** clause, by which the parties may limit or exclude the normal remedies permitted under the UCC.[18] These important rights are entirely distinct from disclaimers. A disclaimer limits the seller's warranties and thus affects whether the seller has breached her contract in the first place. A remedy limitation, by

---

[18]UCC §2-719. A few states prohibit remedy limitations, but most permit them.

contrast, states that if a party *does* breach its warranty, the injured party will not get all of the damages the Code normally allows.

In its contract, Simon had agreed to repair or replace any defective boomlifts, but that was all. The agreement said that if a boomlift was defective, and Logan lost business, profits, and reputation, Simon was not liable. The court upheld the remedy limitation. Since Simon had repeatedly attempted to repair and redesign the defective machines, it had done everything it promised to do. Logan got nothing.[19]

We compare disclaimers and remedy limitations in the table below.

Comparison of Disclaimers and Remedy Limitations

Code Section	Purpose	Setting	Contract Language	Result
Disclaimers: UCC §2-316	Limits warranties, whether express or implied. This section will determine *whether there has been a breach.*	Seller sells Buyer a used "tire shredding machine." UCC §2-314 implies a warranty of merchantability, meaning that the machine will be good for its ordinary purpose, which is shredding tires in a commercial recycling business.	Seller includes in the contract a clause stating that the tire shredder is sold "as is." Under §2-316, this phrase excludes all implied warranties, meaning that the implied warranty of merchantability will NOT apply here.	One tire goes through the machine, the tire emerges completely intact, and the machine falls to pieces. *Result:* Seller has NOT breached the contract, and Buyer gets no damages.
Remedy limitations: UCC §2-719	Limits the remedies available *when one party has breached* the contract.	Seller sells Buyer 10,000 computer circuit boards at $200 each, which Buyer uses in its laptops.	Seller requires a clause limiting Buyer's remedies to "replace or repair." If the boards fail, Seller will replace or repair them for free. But Buyer is permitted NO OTHER REMEDY. Buyer may not seek consequential damages, which would include lost profits and injured reputation.	All of the boards malfunction, and Buyer's customers are angry *at Buyer*. Buyer must take the computers back, losing all of its expected profits and also suffering a serious loss of reputation in the high-tech world. Seller IS in breach of the contract and must repair or replace all circuit boards at its expense. But Seller owes NOTHING for Buyer's lost profits or injured reputation.

© Cengage Learning

20-8c Privity

When two parties contract, they are *in privity*. If Lance buys a chainsaw from the local hardware store, he is in privity with the store. But Lance has no privity with Kwiksaw, the manufacturer of the chainsaw. Under traditional contract law, a plaintiff injured by a breach of contract could sue only a defendant with whom he had privity. This rule hurt consumers because the local retailer might have lacked assets to compensate for serious injuries.

---

[19]*Logan Equipment Corp. v. Simon Aerials, Inc.*, 736 F. Supp. 1188, 1990 U.S. Dist. LEXIS 5720 (D. Mass. 1990).

Today, privity is gradually disappearing as a defense. Various states are approaching the issue in different ways, so there is no single rule. We can, however, highlight the trends.

PERSONAL INJURY

Where a product causes a personal injury, most states permit a warranty lawsuit even without privity. If the chain on Lance's power saw flies off and slashes his arm, he has suffered a personal injury. Of course, he may sue the store, with which he has privity. But he will want to sue the manufacturer, which has more money. In the majority of states, he will be able to sue the manufacturer for breach of warranty even though he had no privity with it. (Note that Lance is sure to make other claims against the manufacturer, including *negligence* and *strict liability*, both discussed in Chapter 6.)

ECONOMIC LOSS DOCTRINE

If the buyer suffers only economic loss, privity may still be required to bring a suit for breach of warranty. If the buyer is a *business*, the majority of states require privity. Fab-Rik makes fabric for furniture and drapes, which it sells to various wholesalers. Siddown makes sofas. Siddown buys Fab-Rik fabric from a wholesaler and, after installing it on 200 sofas, finds the material defective. Siddown may sue the wholesaler but, in most states, will be unable to sue Fab-Rik for breach of any warranties. There was no privity.

By contrast, when the buyer is a *consumer*, more states will permit a suit against the manufacturer, even without privity. Lance, the consumer, buys his power saw to landscape his property. This time, the saw malfunctions without injuring him, but Lance must buy a replacement saw for considerably more money. Many states—but not all—will permit him to recover his losses from Kwiksaw, the manufacturer, on the theory that Kwiksaw intends its product to reach consumers and is in the best position to control losses.

In the following case, a jailhouse tragedy prompts a product liability suit.

Economic loss doctrine
When an injury is purely economic, and arises from a contract made by two businesses, the injured party may only sue under the UCC.

REED v. CITY OF CHICAGO

263 F.Supp.2d 1123
United States District Court for the Northern District of Illinois, 2003

CASE SUMMARY

Facts: J.C. Reed was arrested and brought to Chicago's Fifth District Police Station. Police were allegedly aware that he was suicidal, having seen him slash his wrists earlier. They removed his clothing and dressed him in a paper isolation gown. Sadly, Reed used the gown to hang himself.

Reed's mother, on his behalf, sued the police (for failing to monitor a suicidal inmate) and also Cypress Medical Products, the manufacturer of the isolation gown. The claim was that the gown should have been made of material that would tear if someone attempted to hang himself with it.

Cypress moved to dismiss the suit, claiming that Reed had no privity with the company.

Issue: *Could Reed maintain a lawsuit against Cypress despite lack of privity?*

Decision: Yes. Privity was not required. Reed could have sued Cypress.

Reasoning: Historically, a plaintiff lost a breach of warranty suit if he lacked privity with the defendant. However, UCC §2-318 now extends an express or implied warranty to any injured person who is in the family or household of the buyer, or who is a guest in the home, if it is reasonable to expect that he might use the goods or be affected by a breach of warranty. What is more, Illinois decisions have expanded the class of potential plaintiffs beyond those mentioned in §2-318.

Most of the successful suits have arisen in employment cases. For example, a plaintiff was injured using a bandsaw that his employer had purchased. The court held that the worker was a third party beneficiary of the sales contract and that his safety was part of the basis of the bargain made by the employer. The employee could sue the manufacturer. By contrast, in a case not related to employment, a court refused to allow a warranty claim by a university football player injured because of a defective helmet that the school had purchased.

The facts of this case indicate that the class of plaintiffs who can sue for breach of warranty must be expanded to include injured parties such as Reed. The only users of the gowns that Cypress manufactures will be potentially suicidal detainees. Their safety was necessarily part of the bargain between seller and buyer, whether expressed or implied. If such a detainee is not covered by the warranty, no one will be. A detainee covered by the warranty must be able to enforce it.

Cypress's motion to dismiss was denied.

20-8d Buyer's Misuse

Misuse by the buyer will generally preclude a warranty claim.[20] Common sense tells us that the seller only warrants its goods if they are properly used. Lord & Taylor warranted that its false eyelashes would function well and cause no harm. But when Ms. Caldwell applied them, they severely irritated one eye. She sued, but the store prevailed. Why? Caldwell applied the eyelashes improperly, getting the glue into one eye. On her other eye, she used the product correctly and suffered no harm. Her misuse proved painful to her eye—and fatal to her lawsuit.

Chapter Conclusion

Bad things happen. Deals fall through. Purchased goods disappear. Products injure. Unfortunately, people often fail to consider these possibilities when making a contract. In that case, the UCC steps in with default rules that address critical issues in commercial transactions, such as when an insurable interest exists, the risk of loss shifts, and warranties are made. But these default rules will not always be in a party's best interest. The good news is that the UCC gives buyers and sellers the freedom to change its default settings. Businesspeople who understand the UCC can tailor the rules to their own advantage. Armed with this chapter's information, they will know how and when to alter the UCC's rules to suit their business purposes and protect themselves if and when bad things *do* happen.

EXAM REVIEW

1. **INTEREST AND TITLE**   An *interest* is a legal right in something. *Title* means the normal rights of ownership. (pp. 451–452)

2. **IDENTIFICATION**   Goods must *exist* and be *identified* to the contract before title can pass. The parties may agree in their contract how and when they will identify goods; if they do not specify, the Code stipulates when it happens. The parties may

---

[20]Some courts characterize the misuse as "comparative negligence" or "contributory negligence" or "failure of proximate cause." These tort terms are discussed in Chapter 6, dealing with negligence and strict liability. For our purposes here, though, it is enough to understand that misuse generally precludes a warranty claim.

also state when title passes, and once again, if they do not, the Code provides rules. (pp. 452–453)

3. **INSURABLE INTEREST**   A buyer obtains an *insurable interest* when the goods are identified to the contract. A seller retains an insurable interest in goods as long as she has either title or a security interest in them. (pp. 454–455)

4. **VOID AND VOIDABLE TITLE**   *Void title* is no title at all. *Voidable title* means limited rights in the goods, inferior to those of the owner. A person with voidable title has power to transfer good title to a *bona fide purchaser (BFP)*; that is, someone who purchases in good faith, for value. (pp. 455–456)

5. **ENTRUSTING**   Any *entrusting* of goods to a merchant who deals in goods of that kind gives him the power to transfer all rights of the entruster to a buyer in the ordinary course of business. (pp. 457–458)

6. **BIOC**   A buyer in the ordinary course of business generally takes goods free and clear of any security interest. (p. 458)

7. **RISK OF LOSS**   In their contract, the parties may allocate the *risk of loss* any way they wish. If they fail to do so, the Code provides several steps to determine who pays for any damage. When neither party has breached, the risk of loss generally passes from seller to buyer when the seller has transported the goods as far as he is obligated to. When a party has breached, the risk of loss generally lies with the party that has breached. (pp. 458–463)

8. **EXPRESS WARRANTY**   Seller can create an express warranty with any affirmation or promise, with any description of the goods, or with any sample or model, provided the words or sample is part of the basis of the bargain. (pp. 464–465)

9. **IMPLIED WARRANTY OF MERCHANTABILITY**   With certain exceptions, the Code implies a warranty that the goods will be fit for their ordinary purpose. (pp. 465–466)

10. **IMPLIED WARRANTY OF FITNESS FOR A PARTICULAR PURPOSE**   With some exceptions, the Code implies a warranty that the goods are fit for the buyer's special purpose, provided that the seller knows of that purpose when the contract is made and knows of the buyer's reliance. (p. 467)

MULTIPLE-CHOICE QUESTIONS

1. **CPA QUESTION**   On Monday, Wolfe paid Aston Co., a furniture retailer, $500 for a table. On Thursday, Aston notified Wolfe that the table was ready to be picked up. On Saturday, while Aston was still in possession of the table, it was destroyed in a fire. Who bears the loss of the table?

   (a) Wolfe, because Wolfe had title to the table at the time of loss

   (b) Aston, unless Wolfe is a merchant

   (c) Wolfe, unless Aston breached the contract

   (d) Aston, because Wolfe had not yet taken possession of the table

2. Sheri signs a contract with Farmer Charlie on February 1. Under the deal, she will pay $25,000 for Charlie's entire pumpkin crop on October 1. Charlie plants pumpkin seeds on March 1, and they begin to sprout on April 1. When are the pumpkins identified?

(a) February 1

(b) March 1

(c) April 1

(d) October 1

3. Sam obtains a Patek Philippe watch from Greg by fraud. It has a retail price of $10,000. He sells it to Melissa for $9,000. She believes he owns the watch. Melissa _____ a bona fide purchaser. Sam disappears. If Greg discovers that she has the watch and demands that it be returned, Melissa _____ have to give the watch to Greg.

(a) is; will

(b) is; will not

(c) is not; will

(d) is not; will not

4. CPA QUESTION Vick bought a used boat from Ocean Marina that disclaimed "any and all warranties." Ocean was unaware the boat had been stolen from Kidd. Vick surrendered it to Kidd when confronted with proof of the theft. Vick sued Ocean. Who prevails?

(a) Vick, because the implied warranty of title has been breached

(b) Vick, because a merchant cannot disclaim implied warranties

(c) Ocean, because of the disclaimer of warranties

(d) Ocean, because Vick surrendered the boat to Kidd

5. CPA QUESTION Which of the following conditions must be met for an implied warranty of fitness for a particular purpose to arise?

I. The warranty must be in writing.

II. The seller must know that the buyer was relying on the seller in selecting the goods.

(a) I only

(b) II only

(c) Both I and II

(d) Neither I nor II

Essay Questions

1. Franklin Miller operated Miller Seed Co. in Pea Ridge, Arkansas. He bought, processed, and sold fescue seed, which is used for growing pasture and fodder grass. Farmers brought seed to Miller, who would normally clean, bag, and store it. In some cases, the farmers authorized Miller to sell the seed, in some cases not. Miller mixed together the seed that was for sale with the seed in storage so that a customer could not see any difference between them. Miller defaulted on a $380,000 loan from the First State Bank of Purdy. First State attempted to seize all of the seed in the store.

Tony Havelka, a farmer, protested that his 490,000 pounds of seed was merely in storage and not subject to First State's claim. Who is entitled to the seed?

2. Universal Consolidated Cos. contracted with China Metallurgical Import and Export Corp. (CMIEC) to provide CMIEC with new and used equipment for a cold rolling steel mill. Universal then contracted with Pittsburgh Industrial Furnace Co. (Pifcom) to engineer and build much of the equipment. The contract required Pifcom to deliver the finished equipment to a trucking company, which would then transport it to Universal. Pifcom delivered the goods to the trucking company as scheduled. But before all of the goods reached Universal, CMIEC notified Universal it was canceling the deal. Universal, in turn, notified Pifcom to stop work, but all goods had been delivered to the shipper and ultimately reached Universal. Pifcom claimed that it retained title to the goods, but Universal claimed that title had passed to it. Who is right?

3. **YOU BE THE JUDGE WRITING PROBLEM** Construction Helicopters paid Heli-Dyne Systems $315,000 for three helicopters that were in Argentina. Two were ready to fly, and one was disassembled for routine maintenance. The contract said nothing about risk of loss (the parties could have saved a lot of money by reading this chapter). Heli-Dyne arranged for an Argentine company to oversee their loading on board the freight ship *Lynx*. The two helicopters and 25 crates containing the disassembled craft were properly loaded, but when the ship arrived in Miami, only 7 of the crates appeared. Heli-Dyne refused to supply more parts, and Construction sued. Who bears the loss? **Argument for Construction:** Construction had no control over the goods until they reached Miami. Although we do not know exactly what happened to the crates, we know the one party that had *nothing* to do with the loss: Construction. The company should not pay for damage it never caused. **Argument for Heli-Dyne:** Because the contract failed to specify risk of loss, it is a shipment contract. In such an agreement, risk of loss passes to the buyer when the seller delivers the goods to a carrier. Heli-Dyne delivered the goods and has no further responsibility.

4. Leighton Industries needed steel pipe to build furnaces for a customer. Leighton sent Callier Steel an order for a certain quantity of "A 106 Grade B" steel. Callier confirmed the order and created a contract by sending an invoice to Leighton, stating that it would send "A 106 Grade B" steel, as ordered. Callier delivered the steel, and Leighton built the furnaces, but they leaked badly and required rebuilding. Tests demonstrated that the steel was not in fact "A 106 Grade B," but an inferior steel. Leighton sued. Who wins?

5. Boboli Co. wanted to promote its "California-style" pizza, which it sold in supermarkets. The company contracted with Highland Group, Inc., to produce 2 million recipe brochures, which would be inserted in the carton when the freshly baked pizza was still very hot. Highland contracted with Comark Merchandising to print the brochures. But when Comark asked for details concerning the pizza, the carton, and so forth, Highland refused to supply the information. Comark printed the first lot of 72,000 brochures, which Highland delivered to Boboli. Unfortunately, the hot bread caused the ink to run, and customers opening the carton often found red or blue splotches on their pizzas. Highland refused to accept additional brochures, and Comark sued for breach of contract. Highland defended by claiming that Comark had breached its warranty of merchantability. Please comment.

Discussion Questions

1. In the *Bakalar* case, do you agree with the court's decision? Should the heirs get a chance to recover the drawing that was stolen from their ancestor? Or should Bakalar, who has owned the drawing for 50 years and knew nothing about its origin, be able to keep ownership?

2. Imagine that your laptop gets a virus, and you take it to a local computer repair shop. The shop sells your computer to Heidi. Under the entrustment rules in the UCC, Heidi is a buyer in the ordinary course of business. And so, even if you find Heidi and demand that she return your laptop, *she gets to keep it*. Is this fair? Does the law give too much protection to purchasers in this situation, and not enough to victims?

3. You are about to move, and you take your furniture to a consignment shop. The shop's creditors seize everything in the store, including your furniture.

You demand that the creditors give back your stuff, but under UCC §2-326, *they do not have to*. Is this fair? Should the law change?

4. A seller can disclaim all implied warranties by stating that goods are sold "as is" (or by using other, more specific language). Is this fair? The UCC's implied warranties seem reasonable—that goods are fit for their normal purposes, for example. Should it be so easy for sellers to escape their obligations?

5. After learning more about implied warranties and disclaimers, would you ever buy an item sold "as is"? Imagine a car salesman who offers you a car for $8,000, but who also says that he can knock the price down to $6,500 if you will buy the car "as is." If you live in a state that does not give consumers special protections, which deal would be more appealing?

CHAPTER 21

PERFORMANCE AND REMEDIES

nuttakit/Shutterstock.com; © picsbyst/Shutterstock.com

Was it a 1930s roadster? A drag racing car from the 1950s? Both. When the Plymouth Prowler first hit the road, with its motorcycle-styled front fenders and low-slung hot rod body, it was nearly impossible to get your hands on one. Dealers were swamped with orders, but they did not know if they would receive a single car from the manufacturer.

Donald Hessler wanted a Prowler—and he was a determined man. Hessler went to Crystal Lake Chrysler-Plymouth, met with its owner, Gary Rosenberg, and signed an agreement to buy a Prowler anytime during the next year for $5,000 over the manufacturer's list price. Three months later, Rosenberg revealed that the list price would be $39,000. However, the car dealer also entered into a contract to sell a Prowler to another customer for $50,000.

The next time they spoke, Rosenberg told Hessler that Crystal Lake would not be allotted any Prowlers. The eager buyer, though, responded that a Chrysler representative had told him Crystal Lake would receive at least one car. Rosenberg was furious with a customer who had "gone behind his back" to contact Chrysler, and said he would not sell Hessler a car, even if he did receive one.

> **Donald Hessler wanted a Prowler—and he was a determined man.**

Hessler telephoned 38 Chrysler dealers, but none would promise him a car. One month later, at a promotional event for the car, he saw a new Prowler—with Crystal Lake's name on it! He located Rosenberg, offered to buy the car on the spot—and was again rebuffed. Frustrated and angry, but still determined, Hessler somehow found a Prowler later the same day from another dealer, and bought it—for $77,706.

Ecstatic with his new car, Hessler drove straight to court, where he sued Crystal Lake. Was Rosenberg within his rights, refusing to sell a car to Hessler? Was the customer entitled to compensation for spending so much more on the coveted auto? These are typical issues of contract performance under the Uniform Commercial Code. We look at the issue in this chapter, along with principles of *remedy*. When Hessler bought a car elsewhere, he was *covering*. Did he act reasonably in spending almost $40,000 above list price? You will have to wait a few pages to find out, but we promise to give you the answer before anyone else gets it.

21-1 OBLIGATION ON ALL PARTIES: GOOD FAITH

Surely it is a good idea to begin this final chapter on sale of goods issues in good faith.

The R. G. Ray Corp. needed T-bolts to use in automobile parts it was manufacturing for the Garrett Co. Ray contracted for Maynard Manufacturing to deliver 57,000 T-bolts and provided Maynard with detailed specifications. The contract stated that Ray would be the "final judge" of whether the T-bolts conformed to its specifications and that Ray had the right to return any or all non-conforming bolts. **Conforming goods satisfy the contract terms. Non-conforming goods do not.**[1]

Unfortunately, Ray rejected the 57,000 bolts and sued, demanding every penny it had paid as well as additional damages for its lost business with Garrett. Ray moved for summary judgment, pointing out that the contract explicitly allowed it to judge the bolts, to reject any it found unsatisfactory, and to cancel the contract. The court acknowledged that the contract did give Ray these one-sided powers, yet it denied summary judgment. There was still an issue of *good faith*.

The UCC requires *good faith* in the performance and enforcement of every contract. Good faith means honesty in fact. Between merchants, it also means the use of reasonable commercial standards of fair dealing.[2] So Ray's right to reject the T-bolts was not absolute. There was some evidence that Ray had lost its contract with Garrett for reasons having nothing to do with Maynard's T-bolts. If that was true, and Ray had rejected the T-bolts simply because it no longer needed them, then Ray acted in bad faith and would be fully liable on the contract. The court ruled that Maynard should have its day in court to prove bad faith.[3]

21-2 SELLER'S RIGHTS AND OBLIGATIONS

The seller's primary obligation is to deliver conforming goods to the buyer.[4] But because a buyer might not be willing or able to accept delivery, the UCC demands only that the seller make a reasonable *attempt* at delivery. **The seller must *tender* the goods, which means to make conforming goods available to the buyer.**[5] Normally, the contract will state where and when the seller is obligated to tender delivery. For example, the parties may agree that Manufacturer is to tender 1,000 printers at a certain warehouse on July 3. If Manufacturer makes the printers available on that date, Buyer is obligated to pick them up then and there and is in breach if it fails to do so.

Although a seller must always tender delivery, that does not mean a seller always transports the goods. Sometimes the contract will require the buyer to collect the goods.

---

[1]UCC §2-106(2).
[2]UCC §§1-203, 2-103(1)(b).
[3]*R. G. Ray Corp. v. Maynard Manufacturing Co.*, 1993 U.S. Dist. LEXIS 15754 (N.D. Ill. 1993).
[4]UCC §2-301.
[5]UCC §2-503.

Regardless of where delivery is being made, however, the seller must (1) make the goods available at a reasonable time, (2) keep the goods available for a reasonable period, and (3) deliver to the buyer any documents that it needs to take possession. And as we have said, the seller is expected to deliver *conforming* goods, which brings us to the next rule.

21-2a Perfect Tender Rule

Under the perfect tender rule, the buyer may reject the goods if they fail *in any respect* to conform to the contract.[6]

Stanley and Joan Jakowski agreed to buy a new Camaro automobile from Carole Chevrolet. The contract stated that Carole would apply a polymer undercoating. The Jakowskis paid in full for the car, but the next day, they informed Carole that the car lacked the undercoating. Carole acknowledged the defect and promised to apply the undercoating, but before it could do so, a thief stole the car. The Jakowskis demanded their money back, but Carole refused, saying that the risk of loss had passed to the Jakowskis when Carole tendered delivery. The Jakowskis sued, claiming that they had rejected the Camaro as non-conforming. Carole responded that this was absurd: The car was perfect in every respect except for the very minor undercoating, which Carole had promised to fix promptly. Carole Chevrolet lost the case because of the perfect tender rule.

The New Jersey court found that the defect was minor but said that "despite seller's assertion to the contrary, the degree of their nonconformity is irrelevant in assessing the buyer's right to reject them…. [N]o particular quantum of nonconformity is required." The Jakowskis had lawfully rejected non-conforming goods, and Carole Chevrolet was forced to pay them the full value of the missing car.[7]

21-2b Restrictions on the Perfect Tender Rule

The UCC includes sections that limit the perfect tender rule's effect. Indeed, courts often apply the limitations more enthusiastically than the rule itself, and so while perfect tender is the law, it must be understood in the context of other provisions. We will look at the most common ways that the law undercuts the perfect tender rule. In doing so, we will see the typically flexible approach that the Code takes to a business transaction.

USAGE OF TRADE, COURSE OF DEALING, AND COURSE OF PERFORMANCE

The Uniform Commercial Code takes the commonsense view that a contract for the sale of goods does not exist in a vacuum. It requires courts to consider three things when they apply the perfect tender rule.

"Usage of trade" means any practice that members of an industry *expect* to be part of their dealings.[8] The perfect tender rule may not permit a buyer to reject goods with minor flaws. For example, the textile industry interprets the phrase "first-quality fabric" to permit a limited number of flaws in most materials. If a seller delivers 1,000 bolts of fabric and 5 of them have minor defects, the seller has *not* violated the perfect tender rule.

The course of dealing between the two parties may also limit the rule. **The term *course of dealing* refers to previous commercial transactions between the *same parties*.**[9] The UCC requires that a current contract be interpreted in the light of any past dealings that have

---

[6]UCC §2-601.
[7]*Jakowski v. Carole Chevrolet, Inc.*, 180 N.J. Super. 122, 433 A.2d 841, 1981 N.J. Super. LEXIS 635 (N.J. Super. Ct. 1981).
[8]UCC §1-205(2).
[9]UCC §1-205(1).

created reasonable expectations. Suppose a buyer orders 20,000 board feet of "highest-grade pine" from a lumber company, just as it has in each of the three previous years. In the earlier deliveries, the buyer accepted the lumber even though 1 or 2 percent was not the highest grade. That course of dealing will probably control the present contract, and the buyer will not be permitted suddenly to reject an entire shipment because 1 percent is a lower grade of pine. Such a tender is not "perfect," but it would be good enough.

The course of performance has the same effect on contract interpretation. **The term** *course of performance* **refers to the history of dealings between the parties** *in a single contract,* **and thus assumes that it is the kind of contract demanding an ongoing relationship.**[10] Suppose a newspaper company signs a deal to purchase 5 tons of newsprint from a paper company every week for a year, and the contract also specifies the grade of paper to be delivered. If, during the first three months, the newspaper company routinely accepts paper containing a small number of flaws, that course of performance will control the contract. During the final month, the newspaper may not suddenly reject the type of paper it had earlier accepted.

PARTIES' AGREEMENT

The parties may also choose to limit the effect of the perfect tender rule *themselves* by drafting a contract that *permits* imperfection in the goods. In some industries, this practice is routine. For example, contracts requiring the seller to design or engineer goods especially for the buyer will generally state a level of performance that the equipment must meet. If the goods meet the level described, the buyer has no right to reject, even if the product has some flaws.

CURE

A basic goal of the UCC is a fully performed contract that leaves both parties satisfied. The seller's right to *cure* helps achieve this goal. **When the buyer rejects nonconforming goods, the seller has the right to cure by delivering conforming goods before the contract deadline.**[11] LightCo is obligated to deliver 10,000 specially manufactured bulbs to Burnout Corp. by September 15. LightCo delivers the bulbs on August 20, and on August 25, Burnout notifies the seller that the bulbs do not meet contract specifications. If LightCo promptly notifies Burnout that it intends to cure and then delivers conforming lightbulbs on September 15, it has fulfilled its contract obligations and Burnout must accept the goods. The seller may even cure *after the contract deadline* if the seller (1) reasonably believed the original goods were acceptable and (2) promptly notified the buyer of his intent to cure within a reasonable time. This gives the seller a second chance to replace defective goods. Suppose Chip Co. delivers 25,000 computer chips to Assembler one day before the contract deadline, and two days later, Assembler notifies Chip that the goods are defective. If Chip had tested the chips thoroughly before they left its factory and reasonably believed they met contract specifications, then Chip may cure by promptly notifying Assembler that it will supply conforming goods within a *reasonable* period. Thus, even if the conforming chips arrive two weeks after the contract deadline, Chip will have cured unless Assembler can show that the delay caused it serious harm.

What if a shipment of goods has several nonconformities and the seller offers to fix *some* of the problems? The following case addresses the issue.

---

[10]UCC §2-208(1).
[11]UCC §2-508.

ZION TEMPLE FIRST PENTECOSTAL CHURCH OF CINCINNATI, OHIO, INC. V. BRIGHTER DAY BOOKSTORE & GIFTS & MURPHY CAP & GOWN CO.

2004 WL 23150323
Court of Appeals of Ohio, 2004

CASE SUMMARY

Facts: Zion Temple First Pentecostal Church needed new choir robes. Brighter Day Bookstore was a retailer that sold robes manufactured by Murphy Cap & Gown. Rosalind Bush of Brighter Day showed Glenda Evans of Zion a Murphy robe and a sample board of various Murphy fabrics and colors. A disclaimer on the board said, "all shades subject to dye lot variations." Evans ordered choir robes and overlays in colors and fabrics that she selected.

Murphy then sent sample swatches to Brighter Day, stating they were cut from the actual cloth that would be used for the Zion robes. Bush called Evans to see if she wished to see the swatches, but Evans declined, saying she trusted Bush's judgment. Bush told Murphy to proceed with the order.

When Brighter Day delivered the robes to Zion, Evans and other church members found many faults. They did not like the color or material, which they considered very different from the board sample. The sleeves had been attached facing the wrong way. And on the overlays, the Velcro and tags were visible.

Zion complained to Murphy. The manufacturer offered to repair the sleeves, but Zion declined the offer because of the other problems. Zion returned the robes. When it failed to get its money back, Zion filed suit against both Brighter Day and Murphy.

Zion claimed Murphy breached its warranty by delivering goods that differed from the sample board, and had the sleeve and overlay problems. Because Brighter Day failed to answer Zion's complaint, the court issued a judgment against the retailer (which had certainly seen brighter days). But then trial court gave summary judgment for Murphy, and Zion appealed.

Issues: *Did Murphy breach its warranty? Did Zion afford Murphy a chance to cure?*

Decision: Murphy breached its warranty by sending robes with the wrong sleeves. It is unclear whether Murphy offered to cure all the problems and whether Zion afforded the company an adequate chance to remedy them. Remanded to the trial court.

Reasoning: Brighter Day showed Glenda Evans a typical Murphy robe and offered her actual fabric swatches before going forward with the order. These two samples became part of the contract, creating express warranties from Murphy to Zion. As to the color and feel of the fabric, the delivered robes in fact conformed to the contract samples the company had sent. Zion had no right to reject the robes based on either of those qualities.

However, there were other problems with the garments. The sleeves clearly did not match the pictures in the catalog. Zion also claimed that Velcro was visible on the reversible overlays, and that tags could be seen when the overlays were reversed. The sample robe that Glenda Evans inspected had no such problems. The one acknowledged defect (sleeves) and two alleged problems (tags and Velcro) gave Zion the right to reject the goods, and the church promptly did so.

At that point, Murphy had a right to cure within a reasonable time. The company indicated its willingness to remedy the defective sleeves, but it said nothing about curing the problems concerning the tags and the Velcro.

The court did not have enough information to determine whether the delivered robes were nonconforming when compared to the sample robe and whether Zion gave Murphy fair time to cure. These were critical facts and for that reason, summary judgment for Murphy was reversed and the case was remanded to the trial court.

EXAM Strategy

Question: Xuberant Inc., orders 2000 wristwatches from Timely Co. The watches, with Xuberant's logo on the face, are to be delivered by September 15 so that Xuberant can give them away at its September 25 sales convention. Timely tests the watches and is satisfied they work. But when Xuberant receives them, on September 15, the company rejects them because its name is misspelled. Timely offers to correct the error and deliver the new watches by September 22, but Xuberant refuses and sues. Likely outcome?

Strategy: Timely has delivered nonconforming goods, and Xuberant is entitled to reject them. However, the seller has the right to cure by delivering conforming goods before the contract deadline. Timely is offering to deliver shortly after the deadline. Is it entitled to do so?

Result: If the seller reasonably believed the goods were conforming, it may cure within a reasonable time after the deadline. If the court believes that Timely's spelling error was unreasonable, the company has no right to cure. However, a basic goal of the code is a fully performed contract. A court is likely to declare that the error was excusable and the new delivery date adequate for Xuberant's purpose. Timely will probably win.

SUBSTANTIAL IMPAIRMENT

Sometimes the UCC holds buyers to a higher standard and makes it more difficult to refuse goods. Perfect tender is the usual rule, but in two circumstances, a buyer who claims goods are non-conforming must show that the defects *substantially impair* their value. This standard applies: (1) if the buyer is revoking acceptance of goods or (2) if the buyer is rejecting an installment.

For example, a buyer who initially *accepts* a dozen cement mixers but *later* discovers problems with their engines may revoke his acceptance only by showing that the defects have caused him serious problems. Similarly, if a contract requires a buyer to accept one shipment of diesel fuel each month for two years, the buyer may reject one monthly installment only if the problem with the fuel substantially lowers its value.

DESTRUCTION OF THE GOODS

A farmer contracts to sell 250,000 pounds of sunflower seeds to a broker. The contract describes the 125 acres that the farmer will plant to grow the sunflowers. He plants his crop on time, but a drought destroys most of the plants and he is able to deliver only 75,000 pounds. Is the farmer liable for the seeds he could not deliver? No. Is the broker required to accept the smaller crop? No. **If identified goods are *totally* destroyed before risk passes to the buyer, the contract is void. If identified goods are *partially* destroyed, the buyer may choose whether to accept the goods at a reduced price or void the contract.**[12]

The crop of sunflowers was identified to the contract when the farmer planted it. When a drought destroyed most of the crop, the contract became voidable. The buyer had the right to accept the smaller crop, at a reduced price, or to reject the crop entirely. The farmer is not liable for the shortfall because the destruction was not his fault.[13]

---

[12]UCC §2-613. Identification of goods is discussed in Chapter 20, on ownership, risk, and warranties.
[13]Based on *Red River Commodities, Inc. v. Eidsness*, 459 N.W.2d 805, 1990 N.D. LEXIS 159 (N.D. 1990).

COMMERCIAL IMPRACTICABILITY

Commercial impracticability means that a supervening event excuses performance of a contract, if the event was *not* within the parties' contemplation when they made the agreement.[14] An event is "supervening" if it interrupts the normal course of business and dominates performance of the contract. But a supervening event will excuse performance only if neither party had thought there was a serious chance it would happen.

Harris RF Systems was an American company that manufactured radio equipment. Svenska, a Swedish corporation, bought Harris radio systems and sold them in many countries, including Iran. One contract required Harris to ship a large quantity of spare radio parts, which Svenska would pay $600,000 for and then resell in Iran. Harris attempted to ship the parts to Svenska, but U.S. Customs seized the goods, and the U.S. Department of Defense notified Harris that it believed the parts would be of military value to Iran.

The Defense Department acknowledged that technically, Harris was licensed to ship the goods, but it made two things clear: First, that it would litigate rather than permit the goods to reach Iran; and second, that if Harris attempted to complete the sale in Iran, the department would place all of Harris's future radio shipments on a Munitions List, making it difficult to ship them anywhere in the world. Svenska, on the other hand, pointed out that it had binding contracts to deliver the radio parts to various customers in Iran. If the parts were not forthcoming, Svenska would hold Harris liable for all of its losses. Harris attempted to reach a satisfactory compromise with all parties but failed and eventually agreed not to ship the parts overseas.

Svenska sued. Harris defended, relying on commercial impracticability. Harris persuaded the court that neither party had foreseen the government's intervention and that both parties realized it would be virtually impossible to export goods the Defense Department was determined to block. The court dismissed Svenska's suit.[15]

Sellers offer many excuses to avoid contracts. In the following case, you decide whether the seller's problem was "within the parties' contemplation" when they made the agreement.

---

[14]UCC §2-615.

[15]*Harriscom Svenska AB v. Harris Corp.*, 1990 U.S. Dist. LEXIS 20006 (W.D.N.Y. 1990).

You Be the Judge

Facts: United Aluminum Corporation (UAC) manufactured aluminum coil. For many years, Linde supplied UAC with the nitrogen it needed for its manufacturing processes. The companies signed a long-term contract in 1997, which said, in part:

> Linde agrees that at UAC's sole option, UAC may extend the term of this Agreement for a maximum of five years commencing upon August 31, 2008.

> The contract also called for a price of $0.23 per unit of nitrogen.

UNITED ALUMINUM CORPORATION v. LINDE, INC.

2009 U.S. Dist. LEXIS 74259
United States District Court for the District of Connecticut, 2009

In 2007, UAC sent Linde a letter which stated, in part, "UAC intends to exercise its option to extend the term for an additional five years from September 1, 2008 to August 31, 2013."

Linde replied that the price of nitrogen had risen significantly over the life of the contract and that it would have to increase prices by 38 percent.

UAC sued, seeking the right to continue buying nitrogen from Linde at $0.23 per unit. Linde defended on the grounds of commercial impracticability.

You Be the Judge: *Should Linde be discharged on the grounds of commercial impracticability?*

Argument for Linde: Your honor, our industry has seen substantial increases in costs since 1997. The price of nitrogen is much higher, but that is just the tip of the iceberg. We must pay our workers more, our property taxes have increased, and, because of the rising price of gasoline, our transportation costs are much higher.

We did not anticipate these increases when we made the original agreement. At that time, costs in our industry had been fairly stable for many years. We have small margins even under ideal circumstances. To continue selling at 1997 prices forces us to operate at a substantial loss. Our request for a 38 percent price increase is reasonable.

It is commercially impracticable for use to ship nitrogen for another five years at the prices quoted in the original contract.

Argument for UAC: The Uniform Commercial Code does not allow for a claim of commercial impracticability every time prices increase. It allows such a claim only in the case of an event that was not in the parties' contemplation when they made an agreement.

In some exceptional circumstances, excusing performance is entirely reasonable. But nothing unusual or unforeseeable has happened here. Nitrogen prices have gone up. But over a decade, the price of nearly everything increases. Gasoline, groceries, cable television—the list goes on. Surely Linde knew that price increases were possible.

We made the original contract because Linde offered us long-term stability on the price of nitrogen. Without that part of the bargain, we would likely have sought another supplier. It is not right to allow Linde to back out of its clear contractual obligations.

The accompanying chart outlines the seller's obligations.

Basic Obligation: The seller's basic obligation is to deliver conforming goods. **The perfect tender rule permits the buyer to reject the goods if they are in any way non-conforming.** But many Code provisions limit the harshness of the perfect tender rule.

Limitation on Seller's Obligation	Code Provision	Effect on Seller's Obligations
Good faith	§1-201(19) and §2-103(1)(b)	Prohibits the buyer from using the perfect tender rule as a way out of a contract that has become unprofitable.
Course of dealing, usage of trade, and course of performance	§1-205(1), §1-205(2), and §2-208	If applicable, will limit the buyer's right to reject for relatively routine defects.
The parties' agreement	§2-106	May describe tolerances for imperfections in the goods.
Cure	§2-508	Allows the seller to replace defective goods with conforming goods, if time permits.
Revocation of acceptance	§2-608	A buyer who has accepted goods may later revoke them only if she can show that the defects *substantially impair* its value.
Installment contracts	§2-612	A buyer may reject an installment only if the defects *substantially impair* its value.
Destruction of goods	§2-613	If goods identified to the contract are destroyed, the contract is void.
Commercial impracticability	§2-615	A supervening event excuses performance of a impracticability contract, if the event was not within the parties' contemplation when they made the agreement.

© Cengage Learning

21-3 Buyer's Rights and Obligations

The buyer's primary obligation is to accept conforming goods and pay for them.[16] The buyer must also provide adequate facilities to receive the goods.[17] For example, if the contract requires the seller to deliver to the buyer's warehouse, and the parties anticipate that delivery will be by rail, then the buyer must have facilities for unloading railcars at its warehouse.

21-3a Inspection and Acceptance

The buyer generally has the right to inspect the goods before paying or accepting.[18] If the contract is silent on this issue, the buyer may inspect. Typically, a buyer will insist on this right, but contracts can be created which do *not* give the parties a right to inspect—for example, a contract allowing shipment C.O.D., which means "cash on delivery." In that case, the buyer must pay upon receipt and do her inspecting later.

Along with the right of inspection comes the obligation to do it within a reasonable time and to notify the seller promptly if the buyer intends to reject the goods. **The buyer accepts goods** if (1) after a reasonable opportunity to inspect, she indicates to the seller that the goods are conforming or that she will accept them in spite of non-conformity; or (2) she has had a reasonable opportunity to inspect the goods and has *not rejected them*; or (3) she performs some act indicating that she now owns the goods, such as altering or reselling them.[19]

Partial Acceptance

A buyer has the right to accept some goods while rejecting others if the goods can be divided into *commercial units*. Such a unit is any grouping of goods that the industry normally treats as a whole. For example, one truckload of gravel would be a commercial unit. If the contract called for 100 truckloads of gravel, a buyer could accept 10 that conformed to contract specifications while rejecting 90 that did not.

Revocation

As we mentioned earlier, a buyer has a limited right to revoke acceptance of goods. **A buyer may revoke acceptance but only if the non-conformity *substantially impairs* the value of the goods and only if she had a legitimate reason for the initial acceptance.**[20] This means the perfect tender rule does *not* apply: A buyer in this situation may not revoke because of minor defects. Further, the buyer must show that she had a good reason for accepting the goods originally. Acceptable reasons would include defects that were not visible on inspection or defects that the seller promised but failed to cure.

Rejection

The buyer may reject non-conforming goods by notifying the seller within a reasonable time.[21] Huntsville Hospital purchased electrocardiogram equipment from Mortara Instrument for $155,000. The equipment failed to work properly, and the hospital notified Mortara within a reasonable time that it was rejecting. The hospital asked Mortara to pick up the equipment and refund the full purchase price, but Mortara did neither. When the hospital sued, Mortara claimed that the hospital should have returned the equipment to Mortara and that its failure left it liable for the full cost. The court of appeals was unpersuaded and gave judgment for the

[16]UCC §2-301.
[17]UCC §2-503(1)(b).
[18]UCC §2-513.
[19]UCC §2-606.
[20]UCC §§2-607, 608.
[21]UCC §§2-601, 602.

hospital, declaring that the hospital's only obligation was to notify the seller of a rejection and hold the goods for the seller to collect.[22]

The rule is different in the case of an installment contract. An **installment contract** is one that *requires* goods to be delivered in *separate lots*. If Bus Co. contracts for Oil Co. to deliver 5,000 gallons of gasoline every week for one year, that is an installment contract. **A buyer may reject a non-conforming installment but only if it *substantially impairs* the value of that installment and cannot be cured.**[23] The perfect tender rule does not apply. Bus Co. has no right to reject an installment containing 4,900 gallons of gasoline because the minor shortfall does not impair the shipment's substantial value. On the other hand, if Oil Co. delivered gasoline with lead in it, Bus Co. could reject it since Bus Co. would be legally prohibited from using the gas. (Remember, though, that Oil Co., like all sellers, has the right to cure.)

The following case deals with rejection and revocation. Have a peek inside the trailer, but mind the slippery puddles.

Installment contract
A contract that requires goods to be delivered in separate lots.

LILE V. KIESEL

871 N.E. 2d 995
Indiana Court of Appeals, 2007

CASE SUMMARY

Facts: Edward and Kelly Kiesel bought a new pull-behind trailer from James Lile, the owner of Lile's Trailer Sales. That same day, the couple took their new trailer on its first outing. Because this was a camping trip, it rained all night, and in the morning, the Kiesels noticed water inside the trailer, near the door. The next time it rained, Edward noticed more water pooling in various parts of the trailer. A week later, Edward brought the trailer in for repairs.

Lile repaired the roof, using new silicone. However, a week later the trailer again leaked, and Kelly reported this to Lile, demanding a full refund. Lile refused a refund but offered to seal any leaks, replace interior walls, and sand and paint the exterior. The Kiesels instead took the trailer to a different auto body shop, where the owner said that extensive interior rust indicated the trailer had leaked longer than the Kiesels owned it. The Kiesels sued. Lile claimed that the Kiesels had accepted the vehicle and unfairly refused repairs. The trial court awarded the Kiesels the full price of the trailer, and Lile appealed.

Issue: *Were the Kiesels entitled to the trailer's purchase price?*

Decision: Yes, they were entitled to the full purchase price. Affirmed.

Reasoning: The Kiesels lost their right to *reject* the trailer when they accepted it. But under the UCC, a buyer may *revoke* an acceptance if non-conforming goods have a substantial problem that cannot easily be discovered.

The leaks and subsequent water damage substantially reduced the value of the trailer. The plaintiffs could not have discovered them by making a reasonable inspection prior to the sale.

Lile argues that the Kiesels acted in bad faith when they declined his offer to make repairs. But the UCC only gives sellers a right to cure defects when buyers reject goods. The Kiesels accepted the trailer. *They did not reject it—they revoked their acceptance.* Lile therefore has no right to cure.

The Kiesels are entitled to a refund of the trailer's price.

---

[22]*Huntsville Hospital v. Mortara Instrument*, 57 F.3d 1043, 1995 U.S. App. LEXIS 16925 (11th Cir. 1995).
[23]UCC §2-612.

21-4 SELLER'S REMEDIES

When a buyer breaches a contract, the UCC provides the seller with a variety of potential remedies. Exactly which ones are available depends upon who has the goods (buyer or seller) and what steps the seller took after the buyer breached. The seller can always **cancel the contract**. She may also be able to:

- stop delivery of the goods,
- identify goods to the contract,
- resell and recover damages,
- obtain damages for non-acceptance, or
- obtain the contract price.

21-4a Stop Delivery

Sometimes a buyer breaches before the seller has delivered the goods (for example, by failing to make a payment due under the contract or perhaps by repudiating the contract). A party **repudiates** when it indicates that it will not perform, which it can do either by its conduct or by failing to answer a written demand for assurances that it intends to perform.

Repudiation
A party's indication that it will not perform its contractual obligations.

    If a buyer breaches, **the seller may refuse to deliver the goods.**[24] If, when the buyer breaches, the seller has already placed the goods in the hands of a carrier (such as UPS), the seller may instruct the carrier not to deliver the goods, provided the shipment is at least a carload or larger.

21-4b Identify Goods to the Contract

If the seller has not yet identified goods to the contract when the buyer breaches, he may do so as soon as he learns of the breach.[25] Suppose an electronics manufacturer, with 5,000 Blu-ray players in its warehouse, learns that a retailer refuses to pay for the 800 units it contracted to buy. The manufacturer may now attach a label to 800 units in its warehouse, identifying them to the contract. This will help it recover damages when it resells the identified goods or uses one of the other remedies described below.

21-4c Resale

A seller may resell goods that the buyer has refused to accept, provided she does it reasonably. **If the resale is commercially reasonable, the seller may recover the difference between the resale price and contract price, plus incidental damages, minus expenses saved.**[26]

    Incidental damages are expenses the seller incurs in holding the goods and reselling them—costs such as storage, shipping, and advertising for resale. The seller must deduct expenses saved by the breach. For example, if the contract required the seller to ship heavy machinery from Detroit to San Diego, and the buyer's breach enables the seller to sell its goods in Detroit, the seller must deduct from its claimed losses the transportation costs that it saved.

---

[24]UCC §2-705.
[25]UCC §2-704.
[26]UCC §2-706.

A seller who acts in a commercially reasonable manner is entitled to the following damages:

Contract price (the price Seller expected from the original contract)
− the resale price (the money Seller got at resale)
+ incidental damages (storage, advertising, etc.)
− expenses saved
= Seller's damages

© Cengage Learning

A seller is also permitted to resell goods privately; that is, by simply negotiating a deal with another party. But if the seller does so, she must first give the buyer reasonable notice of the private resale.

EXAM Strategy

Question: Fork manufactures forklift trucks. Fork agrees to sell 10 trucks, for $30,000 each, to McKnife. Fork will store the trucks in a warehouse near McKnife for 3 months, when the buyer will collect them. Storage will cost Fork $2,000 per month. A week after signing the deal, before Fork has moved the trucks to the warehouse, McKnife notifies Fork it cannot pay for the trucks. Fork spends $2,000 advertising the machines and sells them for $25,000 each in a commercially reasonable manner. Fork then sues McKnife. Fork will win—but how much?

Strategy: Apply the formula outlined above.

Result: Fork is entitled to:

	The contract price	$300,000
−	the resale price	250,000
+	incidental damages	2,000
−	expenses saved	6,000
=	Fork's damages	46,000

21-4d Damages for Non-Acceptance

A seller who does not resell, or who resells unreasonably, may recover the difference between the original contract price and the market value of the goods at the time of delivery.[27] Oilko agrees to sell Refinery 100,000 barrels of oil for $100 per barrel, to be delivered on November 1. Oilko tenders the oil on November 1 but Refinery refuses to accept it. Three months later, on February 20, Oilko resells the oil to another purchaser for $92 per barrel and sues Refinery for $800,000 (the difference between its contract price and what it finally obtained), plus the cost of storage. Will Oilko win? No. Oilko's resale was unreasonable. Because there is a ready market for oil, Oilko should have resold immediately. Because

---

[27]UCC §2-708.

Oilko acted unreasonably, it will not obtain damages under the Code's resale provision. Oilko will be forced to base its damages on market value.

Often this remedy will be less valuable to the seller than resale damages. Suppose that on November 1, the market value of Oilko's oil was $99 per barrel. Oilko's contract with Refinery was actually worth only $1 per barrel to Oilko—the amount by which its contract price exceeded the market value. That is all that Oilko will get in court.[28] A seller with a reasonable chance to resell should be certain to do it.

The following chart compares resale and non-acceptance damages:

Resale Damages §2-706		Non-Acceptance Damages §2-708	
Contract price	$10,000,000	Contract price	$10,000,000
Resale price	- 9,200,000	Market value of goods	9,900,000
	$ 800,000		$100,000

© Cengage Learning

21-4e Action for the Price

The seller may recover the contract price if (1) the buyer has already accepted the goods *or* (2) the seller's goods are conforming and the seller is unable to resell after a reasonable effort.[29] Royal Jones was a company that constructed rendering plants—factories that use sophisticated equipment to extract valuable minerals from otherwise useless material. Royal Jones contracted for First Thermal to construct three rendering tanks, at a cost of $64,350. First Thermal built the tanks to Royal Jones's specifications, but Royal Jones never accepted or paid for them, and First Thermal sued. Royal Jones argued that First Thermal deserved no money because it had not attempted to resell the goods, but the court awarded the full contract price, stating:

> First Thermal proved that any effort at resale would have been unavailing because these were the only rendering tanks First Thermal ever made, the tanks were manufactured according to Royal Jones's specifications, First Thermal had no other customers to which it could resell the tanks, and it was unaware how the tanks could have been marketed for resale.[30]

Resale is normally the safest route for an injured seller to recover the maximum amount, but when it is unrealistic, as in the *First Thermal* case, a lawsuit for the full price is appropriate.

All of the seller's remedies are summarized in the chapter review at the end of the chapter. We now move on to the buyer's remedies.

21-5 BUYER'S REMEDIES

The buyer, too, has a variety of potential remedies. If a seller fails to deliver goods, repudiates, or if the buyer rightfully rejects the goods, the buyer is entitled to **cancel the contract.** She may also **recover money paid** to the seller, assuming she has not received the goods. In addition, she may be entitled to:

---

[28]Based on *Baii Banking Corp. v. Atlantic Richfield Co.*, 1993 U.S. Dist. LEXIS 14107 (S.D.N.Y. 1993).
[29]UCC §2-709.
[30]*Royal Jones & Associates, Inc. v. First Thermal Systems, Inc.*, 566 So. 2d 853, 1990 Fla. App. LEXIS 6596 (Fla. Ct. App. 1990).

- incidental and consequential damages,

- specific performance,

- cover,

- damages for non-delivery,

- accept the non-conforming goods and seek damages, or

- liquidated damages.

21-5a Incidental Damages and Consequential Damages

An injured buyer is generally entitled to incidental *and* consequential damages. Incidental damages for buyers include such costs as advertising for replacements, sending buyers to obtain new goods, and shipping the replacement goods. **Consequential damages**, or losses that are caused by a breach, can be much more extensive and may include lost profits caused by the seller's failure to deliver.

A buyer, however, only gets consequential damages for harm that was *unavoidable*. Suppose Wholesaler has a contract to sell 10,000 rosebushes at $10 per bush to FloraMora. Wholesaler contracts to buy 10,000 rosebushes from Growem at $6 per bush, but Growem fails to deliver. Wholesaler in fact could obtain comparable roses at $8 per bush but fails to do so and loses the chance to sell to FloraMora. Wholesaler sues Growem, seeking the $4-per-bush profit it would have made on the FloraMora deal. The company will receive only $2 per bush, representing the difference between its contract price and the market value of the plants. Wholesaler will be denied the additional $2 per bush.

In the following case, the court decided whether *future* profits may be too speculative to award as consequential damages.

Consequential damages
Losses caused by the breach of contract

SMITH V. PENBRIDGE ASSOCIATES, INC.

440 Pa. Super. 410, 655 A.2d 1015, 1995 Pa. Super. LEXIS 574
Superior Court of Pennsylvania, 1995

CASE SUMMARY

Facts: Donna and Alan Smith wanted to raise emus, which are flightless Australian birds that look like ostriches. The creatures produce rapidly in almost any terrain and are sold for their meat, which is high in protein and low in fat, and for their oil, leather, and feathers. The Smiths paid Tomie Clark, the manager of Penbridge Farms, $4,000 as a down payment for "Andrew" and "Rachel," which the

farm called a "proven breeder pair." Since it is impossible to discern an emu's gender by looking, the Smiths asked Clark several times if the two birds were male and female, and he assured them that the pair had successfully produced chicks the previous breeding season.

The Smiths placed the prospective lovebirds in the same pen, but the breeding season passed without a hint of romance. Donna Smith noticed that both birds were grunting, something that only male emus do. She phoned Penbridge Farms, which advised her to "vent sex" the animals, a manual procedure used to determine gender. Donna performed this agreeable task and learned that Andrew and Rachel were both gentlemen. The would-be breeders asked for their money back, but Penbridge refused, so the Smiths flew into court. The trial judge awarded the couple $105,215, representing lost profits from their anticipated chicks. Penbridge appealed, arguing that a buyer cannot count her chicks before they have hatched.

Issue: *Did the trial court err by awarding lost profits?*

Decision: No. The Smiths were entitled to lost profits. Affirmed.

Reasoning: Penbridge argued that the evidence was too speculative to award consequential damages for lost profits. The company claimed that since breeding emus is a new business, there are no reliable data from which to project profits. However, §2-715(2) of the UCC permits consequential damages for any loss resulting from requirements that the seller knew about at the time of contracting, if the loss could not be prevented by cover.

The "proven breeder pair" had supposedly produced 16 chicks the previous season. The trial court found that the value of a 3-month-old emu chick produced that year was $5,000. The court then calculated incidental and consequential damages at $90,000, based on conservative estimations of chick production. This was a reasonable approach. Although the amount is not absolutely certain, the breaching party should not escape liability merely because damages cannot be calculated with perfect accuracy.

21-5b Specific Performance

If the contract goods are rare or unique, the buyer may be allowed *specific performance*, which means a court order requiring the seller to deliver those particular goods.[31] This remedy is most common when the goods are one-of-a-kind. Suppose Gallery agreed to sell to Trisha an original Corot painting for $120,000 but then refused to perform (because another buyer offered more money). Trisha can obtain specific performance because the painting cannot be replaced: The court will order Gallery to deliver the work. By contrast, a car rental company stymied by a dealer's refusal to sell 500 new Ford Mustangs will not obtain specific performance since the rental company can simply buy the same cars from another dealer and sue for the difference.

21-5c Cover

If the seller breaches, the buyer may "cover" by reasonably obtaining substitute goods; it may then obtain the difference between the contract price and its cover price, plus incidental and consequential damages, minus expenses saved.[32] Casein, a protein derived from milk, is used to make cheese and to process many other foods. Erie Casein Co. contracted with Anric Corp. to supply several hundred thousand pounds of casein for about $1 per pound. Half was to be delivered in March of the first year and the other half in March of the second year. By May of the first year, Anric had not finished its first delivery because it was having difficulty obtaining the casein, but Erie told Anric to keep trying. Anric delivered some of the casein later the same year, but by March of the second year was forced to admit it could not meet the second delivery. Anric suggested that it might be able to obtain more casein in the autumn of that second year.

Erie waited until August of the second year, but it finally obtained its casein elsewhere at a price of $1.45 per pound. Erie sued Anric for the extra money it had paid, about $66,000. Anric argued that Erie had no right to the difference because Erie had waited until the price of casein was sky-high before obtaining substitute goods.

---

[31]UCC §2-716.
[32]UCC §2-712.

The court found for Erie. Even though the company might have covered a year earlier, when the price was much lower, it was reasonable for the buyer to wait because Anric indicated it might be able to supply the goods later. Erie had acted in good faith, and when it ultimately covered, it did so at the best price it could find. An injured buyer does not have to do a perfect job of covering, only a reasonable job, and Erie got its full $66,000.[33]

Note that an injured buyer may also be awarded consequential damages, which we discuss below. Finally, if covering saves expense, the savings are deducted from any damages.

> # An injured buyer does not have to do a perfect job of covering, only a reasonable job.

We hope that you recall Donald Hessler, whom we met in the chapter opener. We last saw him circling the courthouse in his Plymouth Prowler, anxiously awaiting the outcome of his suit against the dealership that promised him the same car for a lot less money. It has been a long wait; you and Donald deserve an answer.

HESSLER v. CRYSTAL LAKE CHRYSLER-PLYMOUTH, INC.

Ill.App.3d 1010, 788 N.E.2d 405, 273 Ill.Dec. 96
Appellate Court of Illinois, 2003

CASE SUMMARY

Facts: The facts are provided in the chapter opener. The trial court awarded Hessler $29,853, representing the difference between his contract with Crystal Lake and the sum he ultimately spent purchasing a new Prowler. Crystal Lake appealed, arguing that Hessler covered unreasonably.

Issue: *Did Hessler cover reasonably?*

Decision: Yes, Hessler covered reasonably. Affirmed.

Reasoning: Crystal Lake contracted to deliver a Prowler to Hessler as quickly as possible. But shortly thereafter, the company told Hessler—repeatedly— that it would not in fact sell him a car. In doing so, Crystal Lake breached the contract.

The dealer argues that the trial court damages were excessive, claiming that Hessler covered unreasonably. The company contends that, after it refused to sell Hessler a car, the buyer should have re-contacted the 38 dealers that he had called in September.

Instead, the same day that Hessler learned he would not obtain a car from Crystal Lake, he visited another dealer and bought a Prowler for about $40,000 above list price.

Comment 2 to §2-712 of the UCC provides, in relevant part:

> The test of proper cover is whether at the time and place the buyer acted in good faith and in a reasonable manner, and it is immaterial that hindsight may later prove that the method of cover used was not the cheapest and most effective.

The lower court heard testimony from both parties about the Prowler's limited supply. It also heard the plaintiff's testimony about his unsuccessful efforts to obtain a car one month earlier. The court concluded that Hessler ultimately paid the "best price" available and had covered reasonably. The evidence supports that finding, and the judgment is affirmed.

---

[33] *Erie Casein Co. v. Anric Corp.*, 217 Ill. App. 3d 602, 577 N.E.2d 892, 1991 Ill. App. LEXIS 1429 (Ill. App. Ct. 1991).

Devil's Advocate It is fine for a buyer to cover, but Hessler's conduct is absurd. He bought a car for nearly *double* the contract price. A buyer's behavior must be reasonable, and no court should reward conduct that is clearly obsessive. This purchase was not required by business or financial pressures. We have here a man who believes he is entitled to whatever he wants. If Hessler decides he must have a Prowler *at any price,* then in fairness he should be the one to *pay* that price.

21-5d Non-Delivery

In some cases, the buyer does not cover, or fails to cover *reasonably,* leaving it with damages for non-delivery. **The measure of damages for non-delivery is the difference between the market price at the time the buyer learns of the breach and the contract price, plus incidental and consequential damages, minus expenses saved.**[34] Suppose that in the case described above, Erie had not covered but simply filed suit against Anric. Instead of its $66,000, Erie would have obtained the difference between its contract price with Anric and the market value on the date of breach. That market price was probably only a few pennies higher than the contract price, and Erie would have obtained less than $10,000.

21-5e Acceptance of Non-Conforming Goods

A buyer will sometimes accept non-conforming goods from the seller, either because no alternative is available or because the buyer expects to obtain some compensation for the defects. **Where the buyer has accepted goods but notified the seller that they are non-conforming, he may recover damages for the difference between the goods as promised and as delivered, plus incidental and consequential damages.**[35]

21-5f Liquidated Damages

Liquidated damages are those that the parties agree, at the time of contracting, will compensate the injured party. **They are enforceable, but only in an amount that is reasonable in light of the harm, the difficulties of proving actual loss, and the absence of other remedies.**[36] A clause that establishes unreasonably large or unreasonably small liquidated damages is void. Courts only enforce a liquidated damages clause if it would have been difficult to estimate actual damages when the parties reached the agreement.

Liquidated damages
Damages to which the parties agree at the time of contracting.

Cessna Aircraft agreed to build a "Citation V" business jet and sell it to Aero Consulting for $3,995,000. Cessna's contract required Aero to pay an initial deposit of $125,000, a second deposit of $300,000 six months prior to delivery, and the balance upon delivery. The contract also stated that if Aero failed to pay the balance due, Cessna would keep all deposited monies by way of liquidated damages.

Aero made both deposits, and Cessna built the plane and tendered it to Aero, but Aero refused to pay the full balance due. Cessna notified Aero that it would keep the $425,000 deposited. When Aero sued, seeking a return of the deposits, the issue was whether this liquidated damage was fair. The court concluded that it was. At the time Cessna entered into the deal, it was difficult to estimate actual damages in the event of Aero's breach. The long period required to build a jet aircraft and the uncertainties about supply and demand in

---

[34]UCC §2-713.
[35]UCC §2-714.
[36]UCC §2-718.

the marketplace meant that neither party could say for sure how much Cessna would lose should Aero breach. Further, the liquidated damage here was about 10 percent of the total cost, not an unreasonably high figure. Cessna kept the money (and the plane).[37]

EXAM Strategy

Question: You have a red wine problem. Your California vineyard has strong sales throughout the United States, and it is time to expand into Europe. To penetrate foreign markets, you offer your product at steep discounts to a Swiss importer. Your intent is that the importer will sell your wine inexpensively to retailers, so that low prices will entice consumers. The danger, though, is that the importer will return the wine to the United States and undersell your own product in an established market, taking advantage of your advertising and infuriating established dealers. Such a resale could occur before your wine ever left the country. What can you do to keep this problem from fermenting?

Strategy: A liquidated damages clause can put teeth into your plan to sell the wine to overseas consumers. You might specify substantial compensation if any of your exported wine finds its way back home. However, an overly aggressive clause will be declared a penalty—and void. How can you avoid such a disaster?

Result: Liquidated damages are enforceable in an amount that is reasonable in light of the harm and the difficulties of proving actual loss. Your clause may certainly compensate you for lost goodwill among domestic retailers and for harm to your efforts at establishing the brand in Europe. Make *good faith* estimates of those losses— if the clause gives you too much compensation, a court may void it altogether. Lost profits per case sold in the United States are probably easy to calculate and should *not* be part of the liquidated damages clause.

Chapter Conclusion

The drafters of the UCC intended the law to reflect contemporary commercial practices but also to require a satisfactory level of sensible, ethical behavior. For example, the Code allows numerous exceptions to the perfect tender rule so that a buyer may not pounce on minor defects in goods to avoid a contract that has become financially burdensome. Similarly, a seller forced to resell his goods must do so in a commercially reasonable manner. Good faith and common sense are the hallmarks of contract performance and remedies.

EXAM REVIEW

1. **GOOD FAITH** The Code requires good faith in the performance and enforcement of every contract. (p. 478)

2. **CONFORMING GOODS** Conforming goods are those that satisfy the contract terms; non-conforming goods fail to do so. (p. 478)

---

[37]*Aero Consulting Corp. v. Cessna Aircraft Co.*, 867 F. Supp. 1480, 1994 U.S. Dist. LEXIS 16668 (D. Kan. 1994).

3. **TENDER** The seller must tender the goods, which means make conforming goods available to the buyer. The perfect tender rule permits a buyer to reject goods that are non-conforming in any respect, although there are numerous exceptions. (p. 478)

4. **USAGE OF TRADE** Usage of trade, course of dealing, and course of performance may enable a seller to satisfy the perfect tender rule even though there are some defects in the goods. (pp. 479–480)

5. **CURE** When the buyer rejects non-conforming goods, the seller has the right to cure by delivering conforming goods before the contract deadline. (pp. 480–481)

EXAM Strategy

Question: Allied Semi-Conductors International agreed to buy 50,000 computer chips from Pulsar, for a total price of $365,750. Pulsar delivered the chips, which Allied then sold to Apple Computer. But at least 35,000 of the chips proved defective, so Apple returned them to Allied, which sent them back to Pulsar. Pulsar agreed to replace any defective chips, but only after Allied, at its expense, tested each chip and established the defect. Allied rejected this procedure and sued. Who wins?

Strategy: The chips were non-conforming goods, and Allied was entitled to reject them. Pulsar, in turn, had a right to cure the defects; that is, to solve the problem that it created. Did Pulsar offer to cure? (See the "Result" at the end of this section.)

6. **DESTRUCTION OF THE GOODS** If identified goods are destroyed before risk passes to the buyer, the contract is void. (p. 482)

EXAM Strategy

CPA Question: Under a contract governed by the UCC sales article, which of the following statements is correct?

(a) Unless both the seller and the buyer are merchants, neither party is obligated to perform the contract in good faith.

(b) The contract will not be enforceable if it fails to expressly specify a time and a place for delivery of the goods.

(c) The seller may be excused from performance if the goods are accidentally destroyed before the risk of loss passes to the buyer.

(d) If the price of the goods is less than $500, the goods need not be identified to the contract for title to pass to the buyer.

Strategy: (a) Sounds unlikely. Remind yourself which contracts must be performed in good faith. (b) As we learned in Chapter 19, the Code permits open terms. What are they? (c) Review the rules on destruction of the goods. (d) Goods must be identified to the contract before title can pass. Is there an exception for goods under $500? (See the "Result" at the end of this section.)

7. **COMMERCIAL IMPRACTICABILITY**   Under commercial impracticability, a supervening event excuses performance if it was not within the parties' contemplation when they made the contract. (pp. 483–484)

8. **INSPECTION**   The buyer generally has the right to inspect goods before paying or accepting. If the buyer does not reject goods within a reasonable time after inspecting them, she may be deemed to have accepted them. (pp. 485–486)

EXAM Strategy

CPA Question: Smith contracted in writing to sell Peters a used personal computer for $600. The contract did not specifically address the time for payment, place of delivery, or Peters's right to inspect the computer. Which of the following statements is correct?

(a) Smith is obligated to deliver the computer to Peters's home.

(b) Peters is entitled to inspect the computer before paying for it.

(c) Peters may not pay for the computer using a personal check unless Smith agrees.

(d) Smith is not entitled to payment until 30 days after Peters receives the computer.

Strategy: This question should be no problem. Three of the four possible answers offer rules that appear *nowhere* in the Code. (a) There is no reference in the Code to "home delivery" of goods. (b) The buyer has the right to inspect goods before paying or accepting, unless the contract specifies otherwise. (c) Nowhere does the UCC prohibit payment by check. (d) You have never read in the Code any presumption of a 30-day delay in payment—so do not imagine one. (See the "Result" at the end of this section.)

9. **REVOCATION**   A buyer may revoke his acceptance of non-conforming goods, but only if the defects substantially impair the value of the goods. (p. 485)

10. **REJECTION**   A buyer may reject non-conforming goods by notifying the seller within a reasonable time. (pp. 486–486)

The following chart summarizes the contrasting remedies available to the two parties.

Seller's Remedies	Issue	Buyer's Remedies
§2-705: The seller generally may stop delivery, whether it was to be done by the seller herself or a carrier.	Delivery	§2-716: Specific performance: buyer may obtain specific performance only if the goods are unique.
§2-706: Resale: If the resale is made in good faith and a commercially reasonable manner, the seller may recover	When the injured party makes an	§2-712: Cover: The buyer may purchase alternate goods and obtain the difference in price, plus incidental and

the difference between the resale price and the contract price, plus incidental costs, minus savings.	alternate contract	consequential damages, minus expenses saved.
§2-708: Non-acceptance: The measure of damages for non-acceptance is the time and place of tender and the contract price (plus incidental damages minus expenses saved).	When the goods have not changed hands	§2-713: Non-delivery: If the seller fails to deliver, the buyer's damages are the difference between the market price at the time he learned of the breach and the contract price (plus incidental and consequential damages, minus expenses saved).
§2-709: The seller may sue for the price.	When the buyer has accepted the goods	§2-714: A buyer who has accepted non-conforming goods and notified the seller may recover damages for resulting losses.
§§2-706, 2-708, 2-709, and 2-710: The seller is entitled to incidental damages but not consequential damages.	Incidental and consequential damages	§2-715: The buyer is entitled to incidental and consequential damages.

LIQUIDATED DAMAGES
§2-718: Either party may obtain liquidated damages but only in an amount that is reasonable at the time of the contract.

5. Result: Pulsar never offered a true cure. When the seller delivers defective goods and wishes to cure, it must take all steps—at its expense—to fix the problem. Pulsar could cure only by delivering, at its expense and in a timely manner, 50,000 conforming chips. Pulsar failed to cure, and Allied recovers the entire purchase price.

6. Result: Answer (a) is wrong because all contracts must be performed in good faith. Answer (b) is wrong because a contract with open terms is enforceable. Answer (c) is right because it correctly states the rule on destruction of goods. Answer (d) is wrong because title never passes unless the goods were identified to the contract.

8. Result: Answer (b) is correct. Peters is entitled to inspect the computer unless the contract states otherwise, which it did not.

MULTIPLE-CHOICE QUESTIONS

1. **CPA QUESTION** Cara Fabricating Co. and Taso Corp. agreed orally that Taso would custom-manufacture a compressor for Cara at a price of $120,000. After Taso completed the work at a cost of $90,000, Cara notified Taso that the compressor was no longer needed. Taso is holding the compressor and has requested payment from Cara. Taso has been unable to resell the compressor for any price. Taso incurred storage fees of $2,000. If Cara refuses to pay Taso and Taso sues Cara, the most Taso will be entitled to recover is:

   (a) $92,000

   (b) $105,000

   (c) $120,000

   (d) $122,000

2. **CPA QUESTION** On February 15, Mazur Corp. contracted to sell 1,000 bushels of wheat to Good Bread, Inc., at $6 per bushel, with delivery to be made on June 23. On June 1, Good advised Mazur that it would not accept or pay for the wheat. On June 2, Mazur sold the wheat to another customer at the market price of $5 per bushel. Mazur had advised Good that it intended to resell the wheat. Which of the following statements is correct?

   (a) Mazur can successfully sue Good for the difference between the resale price and the contract price.

   (b) Mazur can resell the wheat only after June 23.

   (c) Good can retract its anticipatory breach at any time before June 23.

   (d) Good can successfully sue Mazur for specific performance.

3. Under the UCC, to tender delivery, a seller must:

   (a) make the goods available at a reasonable time

   (b) keep the goods available for a reasonable period

   (c) deliver to the buyer any documents that it needs to take possession

   (d) All of the above

   (e) None of the above

4. Blackburn FC (go Rovers!) orders 10,000 soccer jerseys from Alpha Co. to sell in its stadium store. They are to be delivered on July 10. When they arrive early on July 2, Blackburn is disappointed because the collars, which are supposed to be white, are blue. Blackburn notifies Alpha of the error. Alpha says that it wants a chance to "make it right." If Alpha delivers another shipment of 10,000 conforming jerseys on July 10, Blackburn…

   (a) absolutely must accept the new shipment

   (b) must accept the new shipment if Alpha offers a reasonable discount

   (c) must accept the new shipment if it has suffered no measureable losses

   (d) may accept the new shipment, but has the option to reject it

5. Assume that a year has passed, and Blackburn FC once again orders 10,000 soccer jerseys from Alpha, to be delivered on July 10. This time, nonconforming jerseys are delivered on July 10. Alpha thoroughly inspected the shirts before shipping and had no reason to spot the error. When Blackburn notifies Alpha of the problem, Alpha says that it intends to cure the defect. If Blackburn cannot show that it will suffer any serious harm, does the UCC require Blackburn to give Alpha a chance to cure this time?

(a) No, because the contract's deadline has passed.

(b) Yes, it must give Alpha until July 17 to cure.

(c) Yes, it must give Alpha until July 20 to cure.

(d) Yes, it must give Alpha a reasonable amount of time to cure.

ESSAY QUESTIONS

1. Jewell-Rung was a Canadian corporation that imported and sold men's clothing wholesale. Haddad was a New York corporation that manufactured and sold men's clothing under the "Lakeland" label. The companies agreed that Haddad would sell 2,325 Lakeland garments to Jewell-Rung for $250,000. Jewell-Rung began to take orders for the garments from its Canadian customers. Jewell-Rung had orders for about 372 garments when it learned that Haddad planned to allow another company, Olympic, the exclusive Canadian right to manufacture and sell Lakeland garments. Jewell-Rung sued Haddad for its lost profits. Haddad moved for summary judgment, claiming that Jewell-Rung could not recover lost profits because it had not covered. Is Haddad right? If so, why might Jewell-Rung not have covered?

2. Mastercraft Boat manufactured boats and often used instrument panels and electrical systems assembled or manufactured by Ace Industries. Typically, Ace would order electrical instruments and other parts and assemble them to specifications that Mastercraft provided. Mastercraft decided to work with a different assembler, M & G Electronics, so it terminated its relationship with Ace. Mastercraft then requested that Ace deliver all of the remaining instruments and other parts that it had purchased for use in Mastercraft boats. Ace delivered the inventory to Mastercraft, which inspected it and kept some of the items, but returned others to Ace, stating that the shipment had been unauthorized. Later, Mastercraft requested that Ace deliver the remaining parts (which Mastercraft had sent back to Ace) to M & G, which Ace did. Mastercraft then refused to pay for these parts, claiming that they were non-conforming. Is Ace entitled to its money for the parts?

3. Lewis River Golf, Inc., grew and sold sod. It bought seed from defendant, O. M. Scott & Sons, under an express warranty. But the sod grown from the Scott seeds developed weeds, a breach of Scott's warranty. Several of Lewis River's customers sued, unhappy with the weeds in their grass. Lewis River lost most of its customers, cut back its production from 275 acres to 45 acres, and destroyed all remaining sod grown from Scott's seeds. Eventually, Lewis River sold its business at a large loss. A jury awarded Lewis River $1,026,800, largely for lost profits and loss of goodwill. Scott appealed, claiming that a plaintiff may not recover for lost profits and goodwill. Comment.

4. The AM/PM Franchise association was a group of 150 owners of ARCO Mini-Market franchises in Pennsylvania and New York. Each owner had an agreement to operate a gas station and mini-market, obtaining all gasoline, food, and other products from ARCO. The association sued, claiming that ARCO had experimented with its formula for unleaded gasoline, using oxinol, and that the poor-quality gas had caused serious engine problems and a steep drop in customers. The association demanded (1) lost profits for gasoline sales, (2) lost profits for food and other items, and (3) loss of goodwill. The trial court dismissed the case, ruling that the plaintiff's claims were too speculative, and the association appealed. Please rule.

5. **YOU BE THE JUDGE WRITING PROBLEM** Clark Oil agreed to sell Amerada Hess several hundred thousand barrels of oil at $24 each by January 31, with the sulfur content not to exceed 1 percent. On January 26, Clark tendered oil from various ships. Most of the oil met specifications, but a small amount contained excess sulfur. Hess rejected all of the oil. Clark recirculated the oil, meaning that it blended the high-sulfur oil with the rest, and it notified Amerada that it could deliver 100 percent of the oil, as specified, by January 31. Hess did not respond. On January 30, Clark offered to replace the oil with an entirely new shipment, due to arrive February 1. Hess rejected the offer. On February 6, Clark retendered the original oil, all of which met contract terms, and Hess rejected it. Clark sold the oil elsewhere for $17.75 per barrel and filed suit. Is Clark entitled to damages? **Argument for Clark:** A seller is entitled to cure any defects. Clark did so in good faith and offered all of the oil by the contract deadline. Clark went even further, offering an entirely new shipment of oil. Hess acted in bad faith, seeking to obtain cheaper oil. Clark is entitled to the difference between the contract price and its resale price. **Argument for Hess:** Hess was entitled to conforming goods, and Clark failed to deliver. Under the perfect tender rule, that is the end of the discussion. Hess had the right to reject non-conforming goods, and it promptly did so. Hess chose not to deal further with Clark because it had lost confidence in Clark's ability to perform.

DISCUSSION QUESTIONS

1. **ETHICS** Laura and Bruce Trethewey hired Basement Waterproofing Nationwide, Inc. (BWNI) to waterproof the walls in their basement for a fee of $2,500. BWNI's contract stated: "BWNI will service any seepage in the areas waterproofed at no additional cost to the customer. All labor and materials will be at the company's expense. Liability for any damage shall be limited to the total price paid for this contract." The material that BWNI used to waterproof the Tretheweys' walls swelled and caused large cracks to open in the walls. Water poured into the basement, and the Tretheweys ultimately spent $38,000 to repair the damage. They sued, claiming negligence and breach of warranty, but BWNI claimed its liability was limited to $2,500. Please rule. Apart from the legal ruling, comment on ethics. BWNI wanted to protect itself against unlimited damage claims. Is this a legitimate way to do it? Is this how BWNI would wish to be treated itself? If you think BWNI *did* behave ethically, what advice would you have for consumers who hire home improvement companies? If you believe the company did *not* behave ethically, imagine that you are a BWNI executive, charged with drafting a standard contract for customers. How would you protect your company's interests while still acting in a way you consider moral?

2. Consider the UCC's exceptions to the perfect tender rule: usage of trade, course of dealing, and course of performance. Do these all seem reasonable, or are they too lenient on sellers who deliver non-conforming goods?

3. Are the UCC's rules related to cure sensible? If a seller ships goods that are not what you ordered, should you (in many circumstances) be *required* to give them a chance to make it right?

4. The opening scenario presented the true story of a man who paid a great deal of money for a Plymouth Prowler. Do you agree with the court's decision to award him nearly $30,000 in damages? Or do you agree with the Devil's Advocate feature and think that he was overcompensated for foolish spending?

5. Review the section "Damages for Non-Acceptance." In that section's example, Refinery refused Oilko's shipment on November 1, when the oil was worth $99 per barrel. Oilko waited three months to resell the oil, and at that time, it received only $92 per barrel. In such a case, the UCC allows Oilko to receive only $1 per barrel in damages rather than the $8-per-barrel reduction in price it actually received. Is this fair? Would it be more sensible to allow a company like Oilko to receive $8 per barrel in damages?

nuttakit/Shutterstock.com; © picsbyst/Shutterstock.com

NEGOTIABLE INSTRUMENTS

When Calvin was in love with Leann, he kept lending her small amounts of money, which eventually added up to $500. Then Calvin saw a photo on Facebook of Leann and Hugh hooking up. After a huge fight, Calvin demanded that Leann pay him what she owed. She said she had no cash, so she wrote and signed an IOU that said, "I am giving Calvin five hundred dollars."

But still Leann did not pay! And more photos appeared on Hugh's timeline! Fed up, Calvin took Leann to small claims court, where he discovered that the paper was not enforceable because Leann had not actually *promised* to pay him. He was out of luck.

Calvin tracked Leann down (at Hugh's apartment) and persuaded her to write him a check for five hundred dollars. But he did not notice until he tried to deposit the check that Leann never signed it. The bank refused the check.

Calvin felt that he had learned a costly lesson on negotiable instruments, but his education was about to get a lot more expensive. He answered his phone one day to hear a gruff voice demanding that he pay the $2,000 Leann owed on a car she had bought last year. Calvin had forgotten that he had agreed to do Leann a favor and co-sign the note on the car. Calvin got indignant and shouted, "You have to go after Leann first! I can give you her address." Calvin was wrong. When he signed the note, he became an accommodation party and was every bit as liable as Leann, even though he had never even ridden in the car. As the poem says, "A sadder and wiser man he rose the morrow morn."

> **After a huge fight, Calvin demanded that Leann pay him what she owed.**

22-1 COMMERCIAL PAPER

The law of commercial paper is important to anyone who borrows money or writes checks (or takes the CPA exam). In early human history, people lived on whatever they could hunt, grow, or make for themselves. Imagine what your life would be like if you had to subsist only on what you could make yourself. Over time, people improved their standard of living by bartering for goods and services they could not make themselves. But traders needed a method for keeping account of who owed how much to whom. That was the role of currency. Many items have been used for currency over the years, including silver, gold, copper, and cowrie shells. These currencies have two disadvantages—they are easy to steal and difficult to carry.

Paper currency weighs less than gold or silver, but it is even easier to steal. As a result, money had to be kept in a safe place, and banks developed to meet that need. However, money in a vault is not very useful unless it can be readily spent. Society needed a system for transferring paper funds easily. Commercial paper is that system.

22-2 TYPES OF NEGOTIABLE INSTRUMENTS

There are two kinds of commercial paper: negotiable and non-negotiable instruments. Article 3 of the Uniform Commercial Code (UCC) covers only negotiable instruments; non-negotiable instruments are governed by ordinary contract law. There are also two categories of negotiable instruments: notes and drafts.

A **note** (also called a **promissory note**) is your promise that you will pay money. A promissory note is used in virtually every loan transaction, whether the borrower is buying a multimillion dollar company or a television set. For example, when you borrow money from AutoLoans to buy a car, you will sign a note promising to repay the money. You are the **maker** because you are the one who has made the promise. AutoLoans is the **payee** because it expects to be paid.

A **draft** is an order directing someone else to pay money for you. A **check** is the most common form of a draft—it is an order telling a bank to pay money. In a draft, three people are involved: The **drawer** orders the **drawee** to pay money to the **payee**. Now before you slam the book shut in despair, let us sort out the players. Suppose that Danica Patrick wins the Daytona 500. NASCAR writes her a check for $1,500,000.

This check is simply an order by NASCAR (the drawer) to its bank (the drawee) to pay money to Patrick (the payee). The terms make sense if you remember that, when you take money out of your account, you *draw* it out. Therefore, when you write a check, you are the draw*er* and the bank is the draw*ee*. The person to whom you make out the check is being paid, so she is called the payee.

The following table illustrates the difference between notes and drafts. Even courts sometimes confuse the terms *drawer* (the person who signs a check) and *maker* (someone who signs a promissory note). **Issuer** is an all-purpose term that means both maker and drawer.

Note

A promise that you will pay money. Also called a *promissory note*.

Maker

The issuer of a promissory note.

Payee

Someone who is owed money under the terms of an instrument.

Draft

The drawer of this instrument orders someone else to pay money.

Check

The most common form of a draft, it is an order telling a bank to pay money.

Drawer

The person who issues a draft.

Drawee

The one ordered by the drawer to pay money to the payee. In the case of a check, the bank is the drawee.

Issuer

The maker of a promissory note or the drawer of a draft.

PROMISSORY NOTE

1,000.00 florins   Verona

16 . 2 . 1595

On or before the fifteenth day of April in the Year of Our Lord, 1595, the undersigned promises to pay to the order of Juliet, daughter of the house of Capulet, in Verona, the sum of 1,000 florins, with interest from the date hereof at five percent per annum, until paid.

                                                            Romeo
_____

In this note, Romeo is the maker and Juliet is the payee.

© Cengage Learning

	Who Pays	Who Plays
Note	You make a promise that you will pay.	Two people are involved: maker and payee.
Draft	You order someone else to pay.	Three people are involved: drawer, drawee, and payee.

22-3 THE FUNDAMENTAL "RULE" OF COMMERCIAL PAPER

The possessor of a piece of commercial paper has an unconditional right to be paid, so long as (1) the paper is *negotiable*; (2) it has been *negotiated* to the possessor; (3) the possessor is a *holder in due course*; and (4) the issuer cannot claim a valid defense.

22-3a Negotiable

To work as a substitute for money, commercial paper must be freely transferable in the marketplace, just as money is. In other words, it must be *negotiable*.

The possessor of *non-negotiable* commercial paper has the same rights—no more, no less—as the person who made the original contract. With non-negotiable commercial paper, the transferee's rights are *conditional* because they depend upon the rights of the original party to the contract. If, for some reason, the original party loses his right to be paid, so does the transferee. The value of non-negotiable commercial paper is greatly reduced because the transferee cannot be absolutely sure what his rights are or whether he will be paid at all.

Checklist

☑ Negotiable
☐ Negotiated
☐ Holder in Due Course
☐ No Valid Defenses

© Cengage Learning

Suppose that Krystal buys a used car from the Trustie Car Lot for her business, Krystal Rocks. She cannot afford to pay the full $15,000 right now, but she is willing to sign a note promising to pay later. So long as Trustie keeps the note, Krystal's obligation to pay is contingent upon the validity of the underlying contract. If, for example, the car is defective, then Krystal might not be liable to Trustie for the full amount of the note. Trustie, however, does not want to keep the note. He needs the cash *now* so that he can buy more cars to sell to other customers. Reggie's Finance Co. is happy to buy Krystal's promissory note from Trustie, but the price Reggie is willing to pay depends upon whether her note is negotiable.

If Krystal's promissory note is non-negotiable, Reggie gets exactly the same rights that Trustie had. As the saying goes, he steps into Trustie's shoes. Suppose that Trustie tampered with the odometer and, as a result, Krystal's car is worth only $12,000. If, under contract law, she owes Trustie only $12,000, then that is all she has to pay Reggie, even though the note *says* $15,000.

The possessor of *negotiable* commercial paper has *more* rights than the person who made the original contract. With negotiable commercial paper, the transferee's rights are *unconditional*. He is entitled to be paid the full amount of the note, regardless of the relationship between the original parties. If Krystal's promissory note is a negotiable instrument, she must pay the full amount to whoever has possession of it, no matter what complaints she might have against Trustie.

Exhibit 22.1 illustrates the difference between negotiable and non-negotiable commercial paper.

EXHIBIT 22.1   The Difference between Non-Negotiable and Negotiable Paper

Because negotiable instruments are more valuable than non-negotiable ones, it is important for buyers and sellers to be able to tell, easily and accurately, if an instrument is indeed negotiable. To be negotiable:

1. **The instrument must be in *writing*.**

2. **The instrument must be *signed* by the maker or drawer.**

3. **The instrument must contain an *unconditional promise* or order *to pay*.** If Krystal's promissory note says, "I will pay $15,000 as long as the car is still in working order," it is not negotiable because it is making a conditional promise. The instrument must also contain a promise or order to pay. It is not enough simply to say, "Krystal owes Trustie $15,000." She has to indicate that she owes the money and also that she intends to pay it. "Krystal promises to pay Trustie $15,000" would work.

4. **The instrument must state a *definite amount* of money that is clear "within its four corners."** "I promise to pay Trustie one-third of my profits this year" would not work, because the amount is unclear. If Krystal's note says, "I promise to pay $15,000 worth of diamonds," it is not negotiable because it does not state a definite amount of *money*.

5. **The instrument must be payable on *demand* or at a *definite time*.** A demand instrument is one that must be paid whenever the holder requests payment. If an instrument is undated, it is treated as a demand instrument and is negotiable. An instrument can be negotiable even if it will not be paid until sometime in the future, provided that the payment date can be determined when the document is made. A graduate of a well-known prep school wrote a generous check to his alma mater, but for payment date he put, "The day the headmaster is fired." This check is not negotiable because it is payable neither on demand nor at a definite time.

Order paper
An instrument that includes the words "pay to the order of" or their equivalent.

6. **The instrument must be payable to *order* or to *bearer*. Order paper** must include the words "Pay to the order of" someone. By including the word "order," the maker is indicating that the instrument is not limited to only one person. "Pay to the order of Trustie Car Lot" means that the money will be paid to Trustie *or to anyone Trustie*

designates. If the note is made out "To bearer," it is **bearer paper** and can be redeemed by *any* holder in due course. "To cash" is the equivalent of "to bearer."

> **Bearer paper**
> A note is bearer paper if it is made out "to bearer" or "to cash." It can be redeemed by any holder in due course.

The rules for checks are different from other negotiable instruments. If properly filled out, checks are negotiable. And sometimes they are negotiable even if not completed correctly. Most checks are preprinted with the words "Pay to the order of," but sometimes people inadvertently cross out "order of." Even so, the check is still negotiable. Checks are frequently received by consumers who, sadly, have not completed a course on business law. The drafters of the UCC did not think it fair to penalize them when the drawer of the check was the one who made the mistake.

EXAM Strategy

Question: Sam had a checking account at Piggy Bank. Piggy sent him special checks that he could use to draw down a line of credit. When he used these checks, Piggy did not take money out of his account; instead it treated the checks as loans and charged him interest. Piggy then sold these used checks to Wolfe. Were the checks negotiable instruments?

Strategy: When faced with a question about negotiability, begin by looking at the list of six requirements. In this case, there is no reason to doubt that the checks are in writing, signed by the issuer, with an unconditional promise to pay to order at a definite time. But do the checks state a definite amount of money? Can the holder "look at the four corners of the check" and determine how much Sam owes?

Result: Sam was supposed to pay Piggy the face amount of the check plus interest. Wolfe does not know the amount of the interest unless he reads the loan agreement. Therefore, the checks are not negotiable.

INTERPRETATION OF AMBIGUITIES

Perhaps you have noticed that people sometimes make mistakes. Although the UCC establishes simple and precise rules for creating negotiable instruments, people do not always follow these rules to the letter. So the UCC has created rules that help to resolve uncertainty and supply missing terms.

Notice anything odd about the check pictured here? Is it for $1,500 or $15,000? When the terms in a negotiable instrument contradict each other, three rules apply:

- Words take precedence over numbers.
- Handwritten terms prevail over typed and printed terms.
- Typed terms win over printed terms.

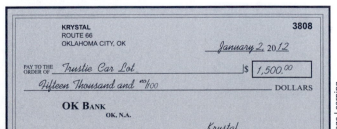

According to these rules, Krystal's check is for $15,000 because, in a conflict between words and numbers, words win.

In the following case, the amount of the check was not completely clear. Was it a negotiable instrument?

You Be the Judge

Facts: Christina Blasco ran out of money. She went to the Money Services Center (MSC) and borrowed $500. To repay the loan, she gave MSC a check for $587.50, which it promised not to cash for two weeks. This kind of transaction is called a "payday loan" because it is made to someone who needs money to tide over until the next paycheck. (Note that in this case, Blasco was paying 17.5 percent interest for a two-week loan, which is an annual compounded interest rate of 6,500 percent. This is the dark side of payday loans: Interest rates are often exorbitant.)

Before MSC could cash the check, Blasco filed for bankruptcy protection. Although MSC knew about Blasco's filing, it deposited the check. It is illegal for creditors to collect debts after a bankruptcy filing, except that creditors are entitled to payment on negotiable instruments.

Ordinarily checks are negotiable instruments, but only if they are for a definite amount. This check had a wrinkle: The numerical amount of the check was $587.50 but the amount in words was written as "five eighty-seven and 50/100 dollars." Did the words mean "five hundred eighty-seven" or "five thousand eighty-seven" or perhaps "five million eighty-seven"? Was the check negotiable despite this ambiguity?

You Be the Judge: *Was this check a negotiable instrument? Was it for a definite amount?*

BLASCO V. MONEY SERVICES CENTER

2006 Bankr. LEXIS 2899
United States Bankruptcy Court
for the Northern District of Alabama, 2006

Argument for Blasco: For a check to be negotiable, two rules apply:

1. The check must state a definite amount of money, which is clear within its four corners.

2. If there is a contradiction between the words and numbers, words take precedence over numbers.

Words prevail over numbers, which means that the check is for "five eighty-seven and 50/100 dollars." This amount is not definite. A holder cannot be sure of the precise amount of the check. Therefore the check is not a negotiable instrument, and MSC had no right to submit it for payment.

Argument for MSC: Blasco is right about the two rules. However, she is wrong in their interpretation. If there is a contradiction between the words and numbers, words take precedence over numbers. In this case, there was no contradiction. The words were ambiguous but they did not contradict the numbers. If the words had said "five thousand eighty-seven," that would have been a contradiction. Instead, the numbers simply clarified the words. Even someone who was a stranger to this transaction could safely figure out the amount of the check. Therefore, it is negotiable.

Checklist

☐ Negotiable
☑ Negotiated
☐ Holder in Due Course
☐ No Valid Defenses

© Cengage Learning

Negotiation

An instrument has been transferred to the holder by someone other than the issuer.

22-3b Negotiated

Negotiation means that an instrument has been transferred to the holder by someone *other than the issuer*. If the issuer has transferred the instrument to the holder, then it has not been negotiated and the issuer can refuse to pay the holder if there was some flaw in the underlying contract. Thus, if Jake gives Madison a promissory note for $2,000 in payment for a new computer, but the computer crashes and burns the first week, Jake has the right to refuse to pay the note. Jake was the issuer and the note was not negotiated. But if, before the computer self-destructs, Madison indorses and transfers the note to Kayla, then Jake is liable to Kayla for the full amount of the note, regardless of his claims against Madison.

To be negotiated, order paper must first be *indorsed* and then *delivered* to the transferee. Bearer paper must simply be *delivered* to the transferee; no indorsement is required.[1]

An indorsement is the signature of a payee. Tess writes a rent check for $475 to her landlord, Larnell. If Larnell signs the back of the check and delivers it to Patty, he has met the two requirements for negotiating order paper: indorsement and delivery. (Note that, for indorsements, a signature is sufficient. Larnell need not write, "pay to" or "pay to the order of.") If Larnell delivers the check to Patty but forgets to sign it, the check has not been indorsed and therefore cannot be negotiated—it has no value to Patty.

Indorsement
The signature of a payee.

EXAM Strategy

Question: Antoine makes a check out to cash and delivers it to Barley. He writes on the back, "Pay to the order of Charlotte." She signs her name. Is this check bearer paper or order paper? Has it been negotiated?

Strategy: "To cash" is the equivalent of "to bearer," so a check made out to cash is bearer paper. Whenever a negotiable instrument is transferred, it is important to ask if the instrument has been properly negotiated. To be negotiated, order paper must be indorsed and delivered; bearer paper need only be delivered, but in both cases by someone other than the issuer.

Result: This check changes back and forth between order and bearer paper, depending on what the indorsement says. When Antoine makes out a check to cash, it is bearer paper. When he gives it to Barley, it is not negotiated because he is the issuer. When Barley writes on the back "Pay to the order of Charlotte," it becomes order paper. When he gives it to Charlotte, it is properly negotiated because he is not the issuer and he has both indorsed the check and transferred it to her. When she signs it, the check becomes bearer paper. And so on it could go forever.

22-3c Holder in Due Course

A holder in due course has an automatic right to receive payment for a negotiable instrument (unless the issuer can claim a valid defense). If the possessor of an instrument is just a holder, not a holder in due course, then his right to payment is no better than the rights of the person from whom he obtained the instrument. If, for example, the issuer has a valid claim against the payee, then the holder may also lose his right to be paid, because he inherits whatever claims and defenses arise out of that contract. Clearly, then, holder in due course status dramatically increases the value of an instrument because it enhances the probability of being paid.

Checklist

☐ Negotiable
☐ Negotiated
☑ Holder in Due Course
☐ No Valid Defenses

© Cengage Learning

REQUIREMENTS FOR BEING A HOLDER IN DUE COURSE

A holder in due course is a *holder* who has given *value* for the instrument, in *good faith*, and *without notice* of outstanding claims or other defects.

Holder in due course
Someone who has given value for an instrument, in good faith, without notice of outstanding claims or other defenses.

---

[1]§3-201. The UCC spells the word "indorsed." Outside the UCC, the word is more commonly spelled "endorsed."

Holder

For order paper, anyone in possession of the instrument if it is payable to or indorsed to her. For bearer paper, anyone in possession.

Value

The holder has already done something in exchange for the instrument.

Holder   For order paper, a **holder** is anyone in possession of the instrument if it is payable to or indorsed to her. For bearer paper, a **holder** is anyone in possession. Tristesse gives Felix a check payable to him. Because Felix owes his mother money, he indorses the check and delivers it to her. This is a valid negotiation because Felix has both indorsed the check (which is order paper) and delivered it. Therefore, Felix's mother is a holder.

Value   A holder in due course must give value for an instrument. **Value** means that the holder has *already* done something in exchange for the instrument. Felix's mother has already loaned him money, so she has given value.

Good Faith   There are two tests to determine if a holder acquired an instrument in good faith. The holder must meet *both* these tests:

- *Subjective Test*. Did the holder *believe* the transaction was honest in fact?

- *Objective Test*. Did the transaction *appear* to be commercially reasonable?

In the following case, the plaintiff passed the subjective test, but failed the objective one.

BUCKEYE CHECK CASHING, INC. v. CAMP

159 Ohio App. 3d 784; 825 N.E.2d 644; 2005 Ohio App. LEXIS 929
Court of Appeals of Ohio, 2005

CASE SUMMARY

Facts: On October 12, Shawn Sheth and James Camp agreed that Camp would provide services to Sheth by October 15. In payment, Sheth gave Camp a check for $1,300 that was postdated October 15. On October 13, Camp sold the check to Buckeye Check Cashing for $1,261.31. On October 14, fearing that Camp would violate the contract, Sheth stopped payment on the check. That same day, Buckeye deposited the check with its bank, believing that the check would reach Sheth's bank on October 15. Buckeye was unaware of the stop payment order. Sheth's bank refused to pay the check. Buckeye filed suit against Sheth.

The trial court ruled that because Buckeye was a holder in due course, the check was valid and Sheth had to pay Buckeye. Sheth appealed.

Issues: *Was Buckeye a holder in due course? Must Sheth pay Buckeye?*

Decision: Sheth is not required to pay Buckeye because the company was not a holder in due course.

Reasoning: To be a holder in due course, Buckeye must have acted in good faith when it bought Sheth's check. In determining good faith, we apply two standards:

1. A subjective test, also called the "pure heart and empty head doctrine." The holder meets this test if he subjectively believed he was negotiating an instrument in good faith. In the absence of obviously fraudulent behavior, an innocent party is assumed to have acted in good faith.

2. An objective test, which requires the observance of reasonable commercial standards of fair dealing.

Check cashing is unlicensed and unregulated in Ohio. Thus, there are no concrete commercial standards by which check-cashing businesses must operate. Buckeye argued that its own internal operating policies did not require that it verify the availability of funds, and apparently the company did not have any guidelines for the acceptance of postdated checks.

Under the purely subjective test, it is clear that Buckeye accepted the check in good faith. But Buckeye fails the objective test because it did not act in a commercially reasonable manner. A postdated check is an obvious sign of trouble, and Buckeye should have realized that there was at least some possibility that the instrument was invalid. Therefore, it should have taken reasonable steps to verify the check before cashing it.

Notice of Outstanding Claims or Other Defects   In certain circumstances, a holder is on notice that an instrument has an outstanding claim or other defect:

1. **The instrument is overdue.** An instrument is overdue the day after its due date. At that point, the recipient ought to wonder why no one has bothered to collect the money owed. A check is overdue 90 days after its date. Any other demand instrument is overdue (1) the day after a request for payment is made or (2) a reasonable time after the instrument was issued.

2. **The instrument is dishonored.** To dishonor an instrument is to refuse to pay it. For example, once a check has been stamped "Insufficient Funds" by the bank, it has been dishonored, and no one who obtains it afterward can be a holder in due course.

3. **The instrument is altered, forged, or incomplete.** Anyone who knows that an instrument has been altered or forged cannot be a holder in due course. Suppose Joe wrote a check to Tony for $200. While showing the check to Liza, Tony cackles to himself and says, "Can you believe what that goof did? Look, he left the line blank after the words 'two hundred.'" Taking his pen out with a flourish, Tony changes the zeroes to nines and adds the words "ninety-nine." He then indorses the check over to Liza, who is definitely not a holder in due course.

4. **The holder has notice of certain claims or disputes.** No one can qualify as a holder in due course if she is on notice that (1) someone else has a claim to the instrument or (2) there is a dispute between the original parties to the instrument. Matt hires Sheila to put aluminum siding on his house. In payment, he gives her a $15,000 promissory note with the due date left blank. They agree that the note will not be due until 60 days after completion of the work. Despite the agreement, Sheila fills in the date immediately and sells the note to Rupert at American Finance Corp., who has bought many similar notes from Sheila. Rupert knows that the note is not supposed to be due until after the work is finished. Usually, before he buys a note from her, he demands a signed document from the home owner certifying that the work is complete. Also, he lives near Matt and can see that Matt's house is only half finished. Rupert is not a holder in due course because he has reason to suspect there is a dispute between Sheila and Matt.

22-3d Defenses against a Holder in Due Course

Negotiable instruments are meant to be a close substitute for money, and, as a general rule, holders expect to be paid. **However, the issuer of a negotiable instrument is not required to pay if:**

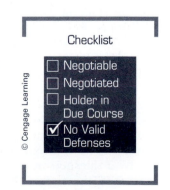

- His signature on the instrument was forged.

- After signing the instrument, his debts were discharged in bankruptcy.

- He was a minor (typically under age 18) at the time he signed the instrument.

- The amount of the instrument was altered after he signed it. (If he left the instrument blank, however, he is liable for any amounts later filled in.)

- He signed the instrument under duress, while mentally incapacitated, or as part of an illegal transaction.

- He was tricked into signing the instrument without knowing what it was and without any reasonable way to find out.

22-3e Consumer Exception

The most common use for negotiable instruments is in consumer transactions. A consumer pays for a refrigerator by giving the store a promissory note. The store promptly sells the note to a finance company. Even if the refrigerator is defective, under Article 3 the consumer must pay full value on the note because the finance company is a holder in due course. However, some states require promissory notes given by a consumer to carry the words "consumer paper." Notes with this legend are non-negotiable.

Consumer credit contract
A contract in which a consumer borrows money from a lender to purchase goods and services from a seller who is affiliated with the lender.

Meanwhile, the Federal Trade Commission (FTC) has special rules for consumer credit contracts. A **consumer credit contract** is one in which a consumer borrows money from a lender to purchase goods and services from a seller who is affiliated with the lender. If Sears loans money to Gerald to buy a high definition television at Sears, that is a consumer credit contract. It is not a consumer credit contract if Gerald borrows money from his cousin Vinnie to buy the television from Sears. The FTC requires all promissory notes in consumer credit contracts to contain the following language:

NOTICE
ANY HOLDER OF THIS CONSUMER CREDIT CONTRACT IS SUBJECT TO ALL CLAIMS AND DEFENSES WHICH THE DEBTOR COULD ASSERT AGAINST THE SELLER OF GOODS OR SERVICES OBTAINED WITH THE PROCEEDS HEREOF.

No one can be a holder in due course of an instrument with this language. If the language is omitted from a consumer note, it is possible to be a holder in due course, but the seller is subject to a fine.

In the following case, consumers found that a home improvement contract, far from improving their home, almost caused them to lose it.

ANTUNA V. NESCOR, INC.

2002 Conn. Super. LEXIS 1003
Superior Court of Connecticut, 2002

CASE SUMMARY

Facts: NESCOR was, in theory, a home improvement company. One of its salespeople signed a contract with the Antunas to install vinyl siding and windows on their house. The contract contained the required FTC language: "Any holder of this consumer credit contract is subject to all claims and defenses which the debtor could assert against the Seller of the goods or services pursuant hereto or with the proceeds hereof." NESCOR assigned this contract to The Money Store (TMS).

Under Connecticut law, a home improvement contract is invalid and unenforceable if it is entered into by a salesperson or contractor who has not registered with the state. The NESCOR salesperson was unregistered.

Unhappy with NESCOR's work, the Antunas stopped making payments under the contract. TMS filed suit, seeking to foreclose on their house. The Antunas moved for summary judgment, arguing that TMS could not enforce the contract because it was not a holder in due course.

Issue: *Was TMS a holder in due course? Does it have the right to foreclose on the Antunas' home?*

Decision: TMS had no right to foreclose because it was not a holder in due course.

Reasoning: Because the NESCOR salesperson was not registered, state law gave the Antunas the right to invalidate the home improvement contract with NESCOR. The FTC language explicitly gave the Antunas the right to assert against TMS whatever defenses they had against NESCOR. Accordingly, because the home improvement contract was invalid, neither NESCOR nor TMS could benefit from it. TMS may not enforce the consumer credit contract by foreclosing on the Antunas' house.

22-4 LIABILITY FOR NEGOTIABLE INSTRUMENTS

Thus far in this chapter, you have learned that the possessor of a piece of commercial paper has an unconditional right to be paid, so long as (1) the paper is *negotiable*; (2) it has been *negotiated* to the possessor; (3) the possessor is a *holder in due course*; and (4) the issuer cannot claim a valid defense.

The life of a negotiable instrument, however, is more complicated than this simple statement indicates. Not everyone who signs a negotiable instrument is an issuer, and not everyone who presents an instrument for payment is a holder in due course. This section focuses on the liability of these extra players: non-issuers who sign an instrument and non-holders who receive payment. The liability of someone who has signed an instrument is called **signature liability.** The liability of someone who receives payment on an instrument is called **warranty liability.**

Signature liability
The liability of someone who signs an instrument.

Warranty liability
The liability of someone who receives payment on an instrument.

22-4a Primary versus Secondary Liability

A number of different people may be liable on the same negotiable instrument, but some are *primarily* liable, others are only *secondarily* liable. Someone with **primary liability** is unconditionally liable—he must pay unless he has a valid defense. Those with **secondary liability** only pay if the person with primary liability does not. The holder of an instrument must first ask for payment from those who are primarily liable before making demand against anyone who is only secondarily liable.

22-5 SIGNATURE LIABILITY

Virtually everyone who signs an instrument is potentially liable for it, but the liability depends upon the capacity in which it was signed. The maker of a note, for example, has different liability from an indorser. Capacity can sometimes be difficult to determine if the signature is not labeled—"maker," "indorser," etc. In the absence of a label, courts generally look at the location of the signature. Someone who signs a check or a note in the lower right-hand corner is presumed to be an issuer. If a drawee bank signs on the face of a check, it is an acceptor. Someone who signs on the back of an instrument is considered to be an indorser.

22-5a Maker

The maker of a note is *primarily* liable. He has promised to pay, and pay he must, unless he has a valid defense.[2] If two makers sign a note, they are both **jointly and severally** liable. The holder can demand full payment from either or partial payment from both. Suppose that Shane offers to buy Marilyn's bookstore in return for a $20,000 promissory note. Because Shane has no assets, Marilyn insists that his supplier, Alexis, also sign the note as co-maker. Once Alexis signs the note, Marilyn has the right to demand full payment from either her or Shane.

22-5b Drawer

The drawer of a check has *secondary* liability. He is not liable until he has received notice that the bank has dishonored the check. Although the bank pays the check with the drawer's funds, the drawer is secondarily liable in the sense that he does not have to write

---

[2]For example, if the maker goes bankrupt, he does not have to pay the note because bankruptcy is a defense even against a holder in due course.

a new check or give cash to the holder unless the bank dishonors the original check. Suppose that Shane writes a $10,000 check to pay Casey for new inventory. Casey is nervous, and before he can get to the bank to deposit the check, he calls Shane seven times to ask whether the check is good. He even asks Shane for payment in cash instead of by check. Shane finally snarls at Casey, "Just go cash the check and get off my back, will you?" At this point, Casey has no recourse against Shane because Shane is only secondarily liable.

Sadly, however, Casey's fears are realized. When he presents the check to the bank teller, she informs him that Shane's account is overdrawn. Casey snatches the check off the counter and hurries over to Shane's shop. It makes no difference that Casey forgot to let the teller stamp "Insufficient Funds" on the check— notice of dishonor can be made orally. Once the bank has refused to pay, the check has been dishonored. Casey has informed Shane, who must now pay the $10,000.

Anne Elliot	0912
Kellynch, N.Y.	
	August 27, 2012
PAY TO THE ORDER OF *Frederick Wentworth*	$ 15,000.00
Fifteen Thousand and 00/100	DOLLARS
TSN Savings Bank	
MEMO *real estate*	*Anne Elliot*
010110562 766 72467 3967	

Anne Elliot is only secondarily liable, but no one is primarily liable until the bank accepts the check.

22-5c Drawee

The **drawee** is the bank on which a check is drawn. Since the draw*er* of a check is only secondarily liable, logically you might expect the drawee bank to be primarily liable. That is not the case, however. When a drawer signs a check, the instrument enters a kind of limbo. **The bank is not liable to the holder and owes no damages to the holder for refusing to pay the check.** The bank may be liable to the *drawer* for violating their checking account agreement, but this contract does not extend to the holder of the check.

When a holder presents a check, the bank can do one of the following:

- Pay the check. In this case, the holder has no complaints.

- Dishonor the check. In this case, the holder must pursue remedies against the *drawer*.

What if Casey is afraid to take a check from Shane? After all, even if Shane has enough money in his account at the moment, it may be gone by the time Casey deposits the check and his bank presents it for payment. To protect himself, Casey can insist that Shane give him a certified check or a cashier's check. A **certified check** is one that the issuer's bank has signed (typically on the front), indicating its acceptance of the check. The bank is then referred to as an **acceptor** and becomes primarily liable. A **cashier's check** is drawn on the bank itself and is a promise that the bank will pay out of its own funds. In either case, Casey is sure to be paid so long as the bank stays solvent. To protect itself once it issues either check, Shane's bank will immediately remove that money from his account.

These rules are precise and must be followed to the letter. In the following example, the court pointed out that the real estate lawyer had been "bamboozled." The MacNabs purchased a piece of property from Richard Harrington's client. The couple came to the closing with an uncertified check drawn on their Merrill Lynch cash management account for $150,000. Harrington called Merrill Lynch and spoke with a Ms. Ruark, who told him there were sufficient funds in the MacNabs' account to cover the check and that she would put a hold on the account in the amount of the check. She also sent the following fax to Harrington: "This letter is to verify that the funds are available in the Merrill Lynch account. There is a pend on the funds for the check that was given you." In fact, the MacNabs' account did not contain sufficient *cleared* funds to cover the check, which bounced. After paying off the McNabs,

Certified check

A check the issuer's bank has signed, indicating its acceptance of the check.

Acceptor

A bank (or other drawee) that accepts a check (or other draft), thereby becoming primarily liable on it.

Cashier's check

A check drawn on the bank itself. It is a promise that the bank will pay out of its own funds.

© Cengage Learning

Harrington sought recovery from Merrill Lynch. But Merrill Lynch was not liable because it had not *signed* the check. An oral certification is invalid.[3]

22-5d Indorser

An **indorser** is anyone, other than an issuer or acceptor, who signs an instrument. Shane gives Hannah a check to pay her for installing new shelves in his bookstore. On the back of Shane's check, Hannah writes, "Pay to Christian," signs her name, and then gives the check to Christian in payment for back rent. Underneath Hannah's name, Christian signs his own name and gives the check to Trustie Car Lot as a deposit on his new Prius. Hannah and Christian are both indorsers. This is the chain of ownership:

Indorser
Anyone, other than an issuer or acceptor, who signs an instrument.

Shane (issuer)   **Hannah** (indorser)   **Christian** (indorser)   **Trustie** (holder)

© Cengage Learning

Indorsers are *secondarily* liable; they must pay if the issuer does not. But indorsers are only liable to those who come *after* them in the chain of ownership, not to those who held the instrument beforehand. If Shane refuses to pay Trustie, the auto dealership can demand payment from Christian or Hannah. If Christian pays Trustie, Christian can then demand payment from Hannah. If, however, Hannah pays Trustie, she has no right to go after Christian because he is not liable to a previous indorser.

There are some exceptions to this rule. **Indorsers are not liable if:**

1. They write the words "without recourse" next to their signature on the instrument,

2. A bank certifies the check,

3. The check is presented for payment more than 30 days after the indorsement, or

4. The check is dishonored and the indorser is not notified within 30 days.

22-5e Accommodation Party

An **accommodation party** is someone—other than an issuer, acceptor, or indorser—who adds her signature to an instrument for the purpose of being liable on it. The accommodation party typically receives no direct benefit from the instrument but is acting for the benefit of the **accommodated party.** Shane wants to buy a truck from the Trustie Car Lot. Trustie, however, will not accept a promissory note from Shane unless his father, Walter, also signs it. Shane has no assets, but Walter is wealthy. When Walter signs, he becomes an accommodation party to Shane, who is the accommodated party. The accommodation party can sign for an issuer, acceptor, or indorser. Anyone who signs an instrument is deemed to be an accommodation party unless it is clear that he is an issuer, acceptor, or indorser.

Accommodation party
Someone other than an issuer, acceptor, or indorser, who adds her signature to an instrument for the purpose of being liable on it.

Accommodated party
Someone who receives a benefit from an accommodation party.

---

[3]*Harrington v. McNab*, 163 F. Supp. 2d 583 (Fed. Dt. Ct., MD, 2001).

An accommodation party has the same liability to the holder as the person for whom he signed. The holder can make a claim directly against the accommodation party without first demanding payment from the accommodated party. Walter is liable to Trustie, whether or not Trustie first demands payment from Shane. If forced to pay Trustie, Walter can try to recover from Shane.

In an earlier example, Shane's supplier, Alexis, had signed a note as co-maker. What is the difference between a co-maker and an accommodation party? The co-maker is liable both to the holder and to the other co-maker. The accommodation party is liable only to the holder, not to the other maker. If Shane pays the note on which Alexis is co-maker, then Alexis is liable to him for half the payment. But if Shane pays the note on which Walter is the accommodation party, Walter has no liability to Shane.

22-6 WARRANTY LIABILITY

Warranty liability rules apply when someone receives payment on an instrument that has been forged, altered, or stolen.

22-6a Basic Rules of Warranty Liability

1. **The wrongdoer is always liable.** If a forger signs someone else's name to an instrument, that signature counts as the forger's, not as that of the person whose name she signed. The forger is liable for the value of the instrument, plus any other expenses or lost interest that subsequent parties may experience because of the forgery. If Hope signs David's name on one of his checks, Hope is liable, but not David. Although this is a sensible rule, the problem is that forgers are difficult to catch and, even when found, often do not have the money to pay what they owe.

2. **The drawee bank is liable if it pays a check on which the *drawer's* name is forged. The bank can recover from the payee only if the payee had reason to suspect the forgery.** If a bank cashes David's forged check, it must reimburse him whether or not it ever recovers from Hope. Suppose that Hope forged the check to pay for a new tattoo. If Gus, the owner of the tattoo parlor, deposits the check and the bank pays it, the bank can only recover from Gus if he had reason to suspect the forgery. Perhaps Gus did suspect because "David" was the name on the check and Hope does not look much like a David.

   Why hold the bank liable for something that is not its fault? In theory, the bank has David's signature on file and can determine that Hope's version does not match. As the saying goes, the drawee bank must know the drawer's signature as a mother knows her own child. Such a rule may have been appropriate in an era when people went to their neighborhood bank to cash checks and a teller would indeed recognize dear Miss Plotkin's signature. In this day and age, most checks—especially those for small amounts—are handled by machine, so perhaps this rule makes less sense. Nonetheless, the rule stands.

3. **In any other case of wrongdoing, a person who first acquires an instrument from a wrongdoer is ultimately liable to anyone else who pays value for it.** These rules are based on the provisions in Article 3 of the UCC that establish transfer and presentment warranties.

22-6b Transfer Warranties

When someone transfers an instrument, she warrants that:

- She is a holder of the instrument—in other words, she is a legitimate owner,

- All signatures are authentic and authorized,

- The instrument has not been altered,

- No defense can be asserted against her, and

- As far as she knows, the issuer is solvent.

When someone transfers an instrument, she promises that it is valid. The wrongdoer—the person who created the defective instrument in the first place—is always liable, but if he does not pay what he owes, the person who took it from him is liable in his place. She may not be that much at fault, but she is more at fault than any of the other innocent people who paid good value for the instrument.

Suppose that Annie writes a check for $100 to pay for a fancy dinner at Barbara's Bistro. Cecelia steals the check from Barbara's cash register, indorses Barbara's name, and uses the check to buy a leather jacket from Deirdre. In her turn, Deirdre takes the check home and indorses it over to her condominium association to pay her monthly service fee. Barbara notices the check is gone and asks Annie to stop payment on it. Once payment is stopped, the condominium association cannot cash the check. Who is liable to whom? The chain of ownership looks like this:

Annie   **Barbara**   **Cecelia (the culprit)**   **Deirdre**   **Condominium Association**

© Cengage Learning

Cecelia is the wrongdoer and, of course, she is liable. Unfortunately, she is currently studying at the University of the Azores and refuses to return to the United States. The condominium association makes a claim against Deirdre. When she transferred the check, she warranted that all the signatures were authentic and authorized, but that was not true because Barbara's signature was forged. (Deirdre should have asked Cecelia for identification.) Deirdre cannot make a claim against Annie or Barbara because neither of them violated their transfer warranties—all the signatures at that point were authentic and authorized.

There are a few additional wrinkles to the transfer warranty rules:

- Transfer warranties flow to all subsequent holders in good faith who have indorsed the instrument. If the condominium association indorses the check over to its maintenance company, Deirdre is liable to the condo association when the maintenance company makes a claim against it.

- If the instrument is *bearer* paper, the transfer warranties extend only to the first transferee. If Annie had made her check out to cash, it would have been bearer paper, and her transfer warranties would have extended only to Barbara. If Barbara transfers the check to Hannah, Barbara's transfer warranties extend to Hannah; Annie's do not.

- If a warranty claim is not made within 30 days of discovering the breach, damages are reduced by the amount of harm that the delay caused. Suppose that the condominium association waits two months to tell Deirdre the check is invalid. Cecelia has been into Deirdre's store several times to try on matching leather pants. By the time Deirdre finds out the check is bad, Cecelia has again left town. Deirdre may not be liable on the check at all because the delay has prevented her from making a claim against Cecelia.

- Transfer warranties apply only if the instrument has been transferred for consideration. Suppose Deirdre gives the check to an employee, Emily, as a birthday present. When the check turns out to be worthless, Emily has no claim against Deirdre.

The following sad case illustrates how important transfer warranties are and how easy it is, even for a careful person, to be conned. Think about what Quimby could have done to protect himself.

You Be the Judge

QUIMBY v. BANK OF AMERICA

2009 U.S. Dist. LEXIS 98575
United States District Court
for the District of Oregon, 2009

Facts: Steve Szabo, a Venezuelan resident, had a checking account with the Bank of America in Palm Beach Gardens, Florida. Someone with an internet address in Nigeria hacked into Szabo's accounts online, called customer service to change the telephone number listed on his account, and ordered blank checks.

Someone then wrote a check on Szabo's account for $120,000 to pay for an investment in Freddie Quimby's gold mine. On February 20, Quimby presented the check for payment at the Bank of America's branch in Osburn, Idaho. At Quimby's request, the branch manager verified through Bank of America's records that Szabo's account had sufficient funds to cover the check. The branch manager also called the telephone number in Szabo's account records and spoke to someone claiming to be Szabo who confirmed that the check was valid.

Quimby endorsed the check to the bank and received in return a cashier's check for $120,000, which he deposited to his account at Bank of America in Baker City, Oregon. [You remember that a cashier's check is a check drawn on the bank itself.] "Szabo" then contacted Quimby, stating that he had changed his mind about the gold mine investment and asking Quimby to return the funds. On February 22, Quimby wired $111,000.00 from his account with Bank of America to an account in Hong Kong. Those funds disappeared and Bank of America has been unable to reclaim them.

On March 3, the real Szabo reported to the Bank that his signature on the Quimby check was a forgery. The Bank repaid Szabo and then filed suit against Quimby, seeking repayment on the cashier's check it had issued to him, with interest. The Bank argued that Quimby had violated his transfer warranties when he endorsed the forged check to it.

You Be the Judge: *Did Quimby violate his transfer warranties? Is he liable to the Bank of America for $120,000?*

Argument for the Bank: When Quimby endorsed the check to the Bank, he warranted that all signatures were authentic and authorized. That was not true—the signature was a forgery and the check was invalid. Moreover, he only waited two days before wiring the funds. If he had waited longer, the fraud might have been discovered in time.

The Bank had to refund $120,000 to Szabo. Quimby must repay the Bank.

Argument for Quimby: This whole problem is the Bank's fault. Let us count the ways: The Bank (1) permitted a thief to hack into Szabo's account; (2) issued blank checks to the thief; (3) assured Quimby that there were good funds to pay the check; (4) issued a cashier's check to Quimby; and (5) wired funds to Hong Kong that it cannot trace.

In short, the Bank was repeatedly negligent and now it seeks recovery from Quimby, who did all he could to ensure that the check was valid. That is unfair and preposterous.

22-6c Comparison of Signature Liability and Transfer Warranties

Transfer warranties fill in holes left by the signature liability rules:

- A forged signature is invalid and therefore creates no signature liability on the part of the person whose name was signed. However, someone who receives a forged instrument may recover under transfer warranty rules, which provide that anyone who transfers a forged instrument is liable for it.

- The signature liability rules do not apply to the transfer of bearer paper. Bearer paper can be negotiated simply by delivery; no indorsement is required. No signature means no signature liability (for anyone other than the issuer—who is the only person actually signing the instrument). Transfer warranties apply to each transfer of bearer paper (although the transferor of bearer paper is liable only to the person to whom he gives the instrument, not to any transferees further down the line).

22-6d Presentment Warranties

Transfer warranties impose liability on anyone who sells a negotiable instrument, such as Deirdre. **Presentment warranties** apply to someone who demands payment for an instrument from the maker, drawee, or anyone else liable on it. Thus, if the condominium association cashes Annie's check, it is subject to presentment warranties because it is demanding payment from her bank, the drawee. In a sense, transfer warranties apply to all transfers *away* from the issuer; presentment warranties apply when the instrument *returns* to the maker or drawee for payment. As a general rule, payment on an instrument is final, and the payer has no right to a refund, unless the presentment warranties are violated.

Anyone who presents a *check* for payment warrants that:

- She is a holder,
- The check has not been altered, and
- She has no reason to believe the drawer's signature is forged.

If any of these promises is untrue, the bank has a right to demand a refund from the presenter. Suppose that Adam writes a $500 check to pay Bruce for repairing his motorcycle. Bruce changes the amount of the check to $1,500 and indorses it over to Chip as payment for an oil bill. When Chip deposits the check, the bank credits his account for $1,500 and deducts the same amount from Adam's account. When Adam discovers the alteration, the bank credits his account for $1,000. Chip violated his *presentment* warranties when he deposited an altered check (even though he did not *know* it was altered). Although Chip was not at fault, he must still reimburse the bank for $1,000. But Chip is not without recourse—Bruce violated his *transfer* warranties to Chip (by transferring an altered check). Bruce must repay the $1,000. Chip loses out only if he cannot make Bruce pay.

The presentment warranty rules for a promissory note are different from those for a check. **Anyone who presents a *promissory note* for payment makes only one warranty—that he is a holder of the instrument.** Someone presenting a note does not need to warrant that the note is unaltered or the maker's signature is authentic because a note is presented for payment to the issuer himself. The issuer presumably remembers the amount of the note and whether he signed it. Suppose Adam gives a promissory note to Bruce to pay for a new motorcycle. If Bruce increases the note from $5,000 to $10,000 before he presents it for payment in six months' time, Adam will almost certainly realize the note has been changed and refuse to pay it.

The presenter of a note warrants that she is a holder, that is, that the instrument was payable to or indorsed to her. But if the signature was forged, subsequent owners are not holders because the instrument was not, in fact, payable to or indorsed to her. Thus, anyone who presents a note with a forged signature is violating the presentment warranties. Suppose that Bruce is totally honest and does not alter the note, but Chip steals it and forges Bruce's indorsement before passing the note on to Donald, who presents it to Adam for payment. Donald has violated his *presentment* warranties because he is not a holder. Adam can refuse to pay him. For his part, Donald can claim repayment from Chip who violated his *transfer* warranties by passing on a note with a forged signature.

EXAM Strategy

Question: Hillary owed Evan $500. She gave Evan's roommate John a check made out to Evan. John indorsed the check to Mike by signing Evan's name. Mike deposited the check in his account at the Amstel Bank. Amstel removed $500 from Hillary's account. Are John and Mike liable on this check?

Strategy: Whenever an instrument goes astray, begin by asking which warranties have been violated and by whom.

Result: Transfer warranties apply to all transfers *away* from the issuer; presentment warranties apply when the instrument *returns* to the maker or drawee for payment. John violated transfer warranties because Evan's signature is neither authentic nor authorized. When Mike deposited the check, he violated presentment warranties. He is not a holder because this check was not properly indorsed to Mike.

> ... he forged her indorsement and deposited the check in his own account without telling her.

22-7 OTHER LIABILITY RULES

This section contains other UCC rules that establish liability for wrongdoing on instruments.

22-7a Conversion Liability

Conversion means that (1) someone has stolen an instrument or (2) a bank has paid a check that has a forged indorsement. The rightful owner of the instrument can recover from either the thief or the bank.

Conversion
Means that (1) someone has stolen an instrument or (2) a bank has paid a check that has a forged indorsement.

For example, Glenn Altman was a lawyer representing Barbara Kirchoff. He settled her case for $12,000, but when he received the check, he forged her indorsement and deposited the check in his own account without telling her. He gave her the money four months later, but by then she had discovered his dishonesty. What claims do the various parties have?

Kirchoff has a claim against the bank because it paid a check with a forged indorsement. If the bank pays Kirchoff, then it can recover from Altman because he violated his presentment warranties. Note, however, that Kirchoff could not sue Altman for violating presentment warranties because he had not presented the check to her for payment. Nor could she sue him for violating transfer warranties because he had not transferred the check *to* her. To the contrary, he had transferred the check *away* from her.

Kirchoff does have a claim against Altman for conversion because he stole the check from her. What about the issuer of the check—can it also sue Altman for conversion? No, an action for conversion cannot be brought by an issuer because the check technically belongs to the payee (Kirchoff). The issuer can bring a claim only against the bank that pays the forged check.

22-7b Impostor Rule

If someone issues an instrument to an impostor, then any indorsement in the name of the payee is valid as long as the person (a bank, say) who pays the instrument does not know of the fraud. A teenager knocks on your door one afternoon. He tells you he is selling magazine subscriptions to pay for a school trip to Washington, D.C. After signing up for *Career* and *Popular Accounting*, you make out a check to "Family Magazine Subscriptions." Unfortunately, the boy does not represent Family Magazine at all. He does cash the check, however, by forging an indorsement for the magazine company. Is the bank liable for cashing the fraudulent check?

No. The teenager was an impostor—he said he represented the magazine company, but he did not. If anyone indorses the check in the name of the payee (Family Magazine Subscriptions), you must pay the check and the bank is not liable. Does this rule seem harsh? Maybe, but you were in the best position to determine if the teenager really worked for the magazine company. You were more at fault than the bank, and you must pay. Of course, the teenager would be liable to you, if you could ever find him.

22-7c Fictitious Payee Rule

If someone issues an instrument to a person who does not exist, then any indorsement in the name of the payee is valid as long as the person (a bank, say) who pays the instrument does not know of the fraud. The *impostor* rule applies if you give a check with a real name to the wrong person. The *fictitious payee* rule applies if you write a check to someone who does not exist. This type of fraud can be very difficult to prevent. Even a large law firm was stung. Dennis Masellis, the manager of payroll for Baker & McKenzie's New York office stole more than $7 million from the firm by creating fictitious employees and then depositing their salaries in his own account.

22-7d Employee Indorsement Rule

If an employee with responsibility for issuing instruments forges a check or other instrument, then any indorsement in the name of the payee, or a similar name, is valid as long as the person (a bank, say) who pays the instrument does not know of the fraud. A dishonest employee, especially one with the authority to issue checks, has the opportunity to steal a great deal of money. The employer cannot shift blame (and liability) onto the bank that unknowingly cashes the forged checks because the employer was more to blame—it not only hired the thief, it failed to supervise him carefully.

Dennis M. Hartotunian had a major gambling problem—he owed nearly $10 million. Unfortunately, he was also the controller and accountant for the Aesar Group. Over the course of three years, he wrote himself 154 checks worth $9.24 million. Any check for more than $500 required the signature of Aesar's general manager, but Hartotunian forged it. After an internal audit revealed that millions were missing, company officers asked to talk with Hartotunian. When he heard they were coming, he walked out and never came back.

It is always a bad sign when the company controller disappears. If an employee is generally authorized to prepare or sign checks, then the bank is not liable on checks that the employee forges. Hartotunian was clearly covered by this rule because he was the company controller. If he had been a mailroom employee without authority to sign checks, the bank would have been liable.

22-7e Negligence

Regardless of the impostor rule, the fictitious payee rule, and the employee indorsement rule (the "three rules"), **anyone who behaves negligently in creating or paying an unauthorized instrument is liable to an innocent third party.** If two people are negligent, they share the loss according to their negligence. Here are two examples:

- **Anyone who is careless in paying an unauthorized instrument is liable, despite the three rules.** Suppose that the boy selling bogus magazine subscriptions goes into the bank and indorses the check: "Family Magazine Subscriptions, by Butch McGraw." The teller peers over her counter and sees a 13-year-old boy standing there with torn jeans and a baseball cap on backwards. She may be negligent if she cashes the check without asking for further identification.

- **Anyone who is careless in allowing a forged or altered instrument to be created is also liable, whether or not he has violated one of the three rules.** The classic case establishing this rule is more than 200 years old. In it, a businessman who was going abroad signed five checks and gave them to his wife with instructions that they were to be used for business expenses. A clerk in the company helpfully showed the missus how to fill out the checks, carefully instructing her to leave a blank space in front of the number. The clerk used this space to add a "3" in front of a "50" and then cashed the £350 check. The court held that the drawee bank was not liable because, "If Young, instead of leaving the check with a female, had left it with a man of business, he would have guarded against fraud in the mode of filling it up."[4] Today, we hiss at the sexist sentiment, but it illustrates the point. Anyone who carelessly creates a situation that facilitates the forgery or alteration of an instrument cannot recover against a party who pays the instrument in good faith.

EXAM Strategy

Question: Jonathan is the head of payroll at Yearbook. He issues checks to his sister, Elizabeth, who happens *not* to work for Yearbook. She does, however, deposit the checks into her bank account. A teller at the bank knows that Elizabeth does not work for Yearbook, but he deposits the checks for her without raising any questions. Is the bank liable for the fraudulent checks?

Strategy: Whenever fraudulent checks are signed by an authorized employee, you will naturally think first of the Employee Indorsement Rule. However, it is important to remember that the bank's negligence overrides the Employee Indorsement Rule.

Result: If the bank were not negligent then, under the Employee Indorsement Rule, it would not be liable because Jonathan was authorized to sign checks. However, because the bank was negligent in paying the checks, it must share the loss with Yearbook. The amount each would have to pay depends upon their share of the blame.

---

[4]*Young v. Grote*, 4 Bing. 253 (Common Pleas), quoted in Douglas J. Whaley, *Problems and Materials on Payment Law* (Boston: Little, Brown & Co., 1995), p. 253.

Chapter Conclusion

It is never wise to play an important game without understanding the rules. As you can see from the cases in this chapter, real harm can come to those who do not know the rules of negotiable instruments.

EXAM REVIEW

1. **NEGOTIABILITY**   The possessor of non-negotiable commercial paper has the same rights—no more, no less—as the person who made the original contract. The possessor of negotiable commercial paper has more rights than the person who made the original contract. (p. 503)

2. **THE FUNDAMENTAL RULE OF COMMERCIAL PAPER**   The possessor of a piece of commercial paper has an unconditional right to be paid, as long as:

   - The paper is negotiable;

   - It has been negotiated to the possessor;

   - The possessor is a holder in due course; and

   - The issuer cannot claim a valid defense. (p. 503)

3. **REQUIREMENTS FOR NEGOTIABILITY**   To be negotiable, an instrument must:

   - Be in writing;

   - Be signed by the maker or drawer;

   - Contain an unconditional promise or order to pay;

   - State a definite amount of money which is clear "within its four corners";

   - Be payable on demand or at a definite time; and

   - Be payable to order or to bearer. (pp. 503–505)

4. **AMBIGUITY**   When the terms in a negotiable instrument contradict each other, three rules apply:

   - Words take precedence over numbers.

   - Handwritten terms prevail over typed and printed terms.

   - Typed terms win over printed terms. (pp. 505–506)

5. **NEGOTIATION**   An instrument has been transferred to the holder by someone other than the issuer. To be negotiated, order paper must first be indorsed and then delivered to the transferee. Bearer paper must simply be delivered to the transferee; no indorsement is required. (pp. 506–507)

6. **HOLDER IN DUE COURSE**   A holder in due course has an automatic right to receive payment for a negotiable instrument (unless the issuer can claim a valid defense). A holder in due course is a holder who has given value for the instrument, in good faith, without notice of outstanding claims or other defects. (p. 507)

EXAM Strategy

Question: After Irene fell behind on her mortgage payments, she answered an advertisement from Best Financial Consultants offering attractive refinancing opportunities. During a meeting at a McDonald's restaurant, a Best representative told her that the company would arrange for a complete refinancing of her home, pay off two of her creditors, and give her an additional $5,000 in spending money. Irene would only have to pay Best $4,000. Irene signed a blank promissory note that was filled in later by Best representatives for $14,986.61. Best did not fulfill its promises to Irene, but within two weeks, it sold the note to Robin for just under $14,000. Irene refused to pay the note, alleging that Robin was not a holder in due course. Is Irene liable to Robin?

Strategy: Whenever a question asks if someone is a holder in due course, begin by reviewing the requirements. Is this person a *holder* who has given *value* for the instrument, in *good faith*, *without notice* of outstanding claims or other defects? (See the "Results" at the end of this section.)

7. **DEFENSES**   The issuer of a negotiable instrument is not required to pay if:

- His signature was forged.

- After signing the instrument, his debts were discharged in bankruptcy.

- He was a minor at the time he signed the instrument.

- The amount of the instrument was altered after he signed it.

- He signed the instrument under duress, while mentally incapacitated, or as part of an illegal transaction.

- He was tricked into signing the instrument without knowing what it was and without any reasonable way to find out. (p. 509)

8. **CONSUMER EXCEPTION**   The Federal Trade Commission requires all promissory notes in consumer credit contracts to contain language preventing any subsequent holder from being a holder in due course. (p. 510)

EXAM Strategy

Question: Gina purchased a Chrysler car with a 70,000-mile warranty. She signed a loan contract with the dealer to pay for the car in monthly installments. The dealer sold the contract to the Chrysler Credit Corp. Soon, the car developed a tendency to accelerate abruptly and without warning. Two Chrysler dealers were unable to correct the problem. Gina filed suit against Chrysler Credit Corp., but the company refused to rescind the loan contract. The company argued that, as a holder in due course on the note, it was entitled to be paid regardless of any defects in the car. How would you decide this case if you were the judge?

Strategy: Whenever consumers are involved, consider the possibility that there is a consumer credit contract. The plaintiff in this case is a consumer who borrowed money from a lender to purchase goods from a seller who is affiliated with the lender (both seller and lender are owned by Chrysler). Thus the contract is a consumer credit contract. (See the "Results" at the end of this section.)

9. **PRIMARY V. SECONDARY LIABILITY** Someone who is primarily liable on a negotiable instrument must pay unless he has a valid defense. Those with secondary liability only pay if the person with primary liability does not. (p. 511)

10. **PRIMARY SIGNATURE LIABILITY** The maker of a note is primarily liable. (p. 511)

11. **SECONDARY SIGNATURE LIABILITY**

   a. The drawer of a check has secondary liability: He is not liable until he has received notice that the bank has dishonored the check.

   b. Indorsers of a note are secondarily liable; they must pay if the issuer does not. But an indorser is only liable to those who come after him in the chain of ownership, not to those who held the instrument before he did. (pp. 511–512)

12. **SIGNATURE LIABILITY FOR AN ACCOMMODATION PARTY** The accommodation party signs an instrument to benefit the accommodated party. By signing the instrument, an accommodation party agrees to be liable on it, whether or not she directly benefits from it. She has the same liability as the person for whom she signed. (pp. 513–514)

EXAM Strategy

Question: Jean borrowed $6,000 from a bank. As part of the loan process, she executed a note to the bank. Her son's widow, Kathy, signed as an accommodation party. The bank issued a check payable to "Kathy *and* Jean." Somehow this check was altered to read "Kathy *or* Jean." Jean cashed the check and spent the proceeds. The bank sought recovery from Kathy, who refused to pay, arguing (1) the bank had to go after Jean first, and (2) her contract with the bank was unenforceable because she had not received any consideration—all of the proceeds of the loan had gone to Jean.

Strategy: An accommodation party is primarily liable; therefore the bank has no obligation to go after Kathy first. An accommodation party is liable whether or not she received any benefit from the loan.

13. **WARRANTY LIABILITY**   The basic rules of warranty liability are as follows:

- The wrongdoer is always liable.

- The drawee bank is responsible if it pays a check on which the drawer's name is forged.

- In any other case of wrongdoing, a person who initially acquires an instrument from a wrongdoer is ultimately liable to anyone else who pays value for it. (p. 514)

14. **TRANSFER WARRANTIES**   When someone transfers an instrument, she warrants that:

- She is a holder of the instrument,

- All signatures are authentic and authorized,

- The instrument has not been altered,

- No defense can be asserted against her, and

- As far as she knows, the issuer is solvent. (pp. 515–516)

15. **PRESENTMENT WARRANTIES FOR A CHECK**   Anyone who presents a check for payment warrants that:

- She is a holder,

- The check has not been altered, and

- She has no reason to believe the drawer's signature is forged. (pp. 517–518)

16. **PRESENTMENT WARRANTIES FOR A NOTE**   The presenter of a note only warrants that he is a holder. (p. 517)

17. **CONVERSION**   Conversion means that (1) someone has stolen an instrument or (2) a bank has paid a check that has a forged indorsement. (pp. 518–519)

18. **IMPOSTOR RULE**   If someone issues an instrument to an impostor, then any indorsement in the name of the payee is valid as long as the person who pays the instrument is ignorant of the fraud. (p. 519)

19. **FICTITIOUS PAYEE RULE**   If someone issues an instrument to a person who does not exist, then any indorsement in the name of the payee is valid as long as the person who pays the instrument does not know of the fraud. (p. 519)

20. **EMPLOYEE INDORSEMENT RULE**   If an employee with responsibility for issuing instruments forges a check or other instrument, then any indorsement in the name of the payee is valid as long as the person who pays the instrument is ignorant of the fraud. (p. 519)

21. **LIABILITY FOR NEGLIGENCE**   Anyone who behaves negligently in creating or paying an unauthorized instrument is liable to an innocent third party. (p. 520)

6. Result: In this case, Robin is a holder who has given value. Did she act in good faith? We don't know if she actually *believed* the transaction was honest, but the court held that the transaction did not *appear* to be commercially reasonable because Robin's profit was so high. Thus, Robin was not a holder in due course, and Irene was not liable to her.

8. Result: Chrysler Credit was not a holder in due course. Therefore, it is subject to any defenses Gina might have against the dealer, including that the car was defective.

12. Result: Kathy is liable, even though she received no benefit from the loan.

MULTIPLE-CHOICE QUESTIONS

1. Which of the following statements are true?

   (a) A draft is always a check.

   (b) A check is always a draft.

   (c) A note must involve at least three people.

   (d) All of the above.

2. Which of the following standards are *required* for negotiability?

   (a) The instrument must be signed by the payee.

   (b) The instrument must be payable on demand.

   (c) The instrument must be payable to order.

   (d) None of the above.

3. Marla is not a holder in due course if she takes an instrument:

   (a) believing that the underlying contract was honest, although it turned out to be dishonest.

   (b) that is a consumer credit contract.

   (c) that appeared commercially reasonable when made but turned out to be dishonest.

   (d) All of the above.

4. CPA QUESTION   In order to negotiate bearer paper, one must:

   (a) indorse the paper.

   (b) indorse and deliver the paper with consideration.

   (c) deliver the paper.

   (d) deliver and indorse the paper.

5. What is the difference between a co-maker and an accommodation party?

   (a) A co-maker is liable both to the holder and the other co-maker, while an accommodation party is liable only to the holder.

   (b) A co-maker is liable to subsequent indorsers, while an accommodation party is not.

   (c) A co-maker is liable only to the other co-maker, while the accommodation party is liable to the holder.

   (d) A co-maker is not liable once a bank certifies a check, while an accommodation party is still liable even after certification.

ESSAY QUESTIONS

1. Duncan Properties, Inc., agrees to buy a car from Shifty for $25,000. The company issues a promissory note in payment. The car that Duncan bought is defective. If Shifty still has the note, does Duncan have to pay it?

2. Shifty sells that note to Honest Abe for $22,000. Does Duncan have to pay Abe?

3. Kay signed a promissory note for $220,000 that was payable to Investments, Inc. The company then indorsed the note over to its lawyers to pay past and future legal fees. Were the lawyers holders in due course?

4. Shelby wrote the following check to Dana. When is it payable, and for how much?

5. Railroad issued a check to Parris which somehow came to be in Eddy's possession. Eddy indorsed the check "Railroad Eddy" and deposited it in his own account at Bank. Parris sued Bank, alleging that it was liable to him for having paid the check over an unauthorized indorsement. Is Bank liable to Parris? On what theory?

6. Sidney entered into a contract for $35,000 with MacDonald Roofing Co., Inc., to reroof his building. Sidney made his initial payment by writing a check for $17,500 payable to "MacDonald Roofing Company, Inc., and Friendly Supply Company." MacDonald took the check to Friendly and requested an indorsement, which Friendly provided. When MacDonald failed to complete the roofing work, Sidney filed suit for damages against Friendly. Sidney argued that Friendly was liable as an indorser. Do you agree?

7. Using her company's check-signing machine, Doris forged $150,000 of checks on the account of her employer, Winkie, Inc. One of Doris's jobs at the company was to prepare checks for the company president, Zach, to sign. He did not (1) look at the sequence of check numbers; (2) examine the monthly account statements; or (3) reconcile company records with bank statements. Winkie's bank, as a matter of policy, did not check indorsements on checks with a face value of less than $1,000. By accident, it paid a forged check that had not even been indorsed. Is the bank liable to Winkie for the forged checks?

8. **ETHICS** When Steven was killed in an automobile accident, his wife, Debra, received $60,000 in life insurance benefits. She decided she needed a fresh start, so she sold her house in Bunkie and moved to Sulphur, Louisiana. Before she left, though, she signed several blank checks and gave them to her mother-in-law, Helen, with instructions to use them to pay off the remaining debt on Debra's mobile home. Instead, Helen used one of the checks to withdraw $50,000 from the account for her own personal use, not to pay off the debt. When Debra discovered the theft, she sued the bank for having paid an unauthorized check. How would you rule in this case? Debra has suffered a grievous loss—her husband died tragically in an automobile accident. She trusted her mother-in-law and counted on her help. Should the bank show compassion? If the bank made good on the forged checks, how great would be the injury to the bank's shareholders compared with the harm to Debra if she loses this entire sum?

DISCUSSION QUESTIONS

1. In the *Buckeye* case, the court ruled that Buckeye was not a holder in due course and the check was not valid because Buckeye should have checked with Sheth's bank before buying the check. Would this remedy have worked? What could Buckeye have done to protect itself?

2. In the *Antuna* case, the Antunas were foolish to sign an agreement with an unlicensed contractor to install aluminum siding. There is no evidence that TMS was acting in bad faith. Why should it suffer for the Antunas' mistake? What could TMS have done to protect itself?

3. Recall the *Quimby* case. This type of fraud is increasingly common. What could Quimby have done to protect himself?

4. Catherine suffered serious physical injuries in an automobile accident and became acutely depressed as a result. One morning, she received a check for $17,400 in settlement of her claims arising out of the accident. She indorsed the check and placed it on the kitchen table. She then called Robert, her longtime roommate, to tell him the check had arrived. That afternoon, she jumped from the roof of her apartment building, killing herself. The police found the check and a note from her, stating that she was giving it to Robert. Had Catherine negotiated the check to Robert?

5. Banks are liable for forged checks except in the case of the three rules (Imposter Rule, Fictitious Payee Rule, and the Employee Indorsement Rule). Do you think this is the proper allocation of liability? Why should banks be liable for forged checks, in this era of automated check machines? Alternatively, could you argue that the three rules provide too much protection to banks?

CHAPTER 23

SECURED TRANSACTIONS

nuttakit/Shutterstock.com; © picsbyst/Shutterstock.com

To: Allison@credit-help-for-all.com
From: Sam12345@yahoo.com
Hi Allison:
Look, this just doesn't make any sense. When I got out of school, I paid a guy $18,000 for my Jeep. I made every payment on my loan —*every one*—for over two years. I paid out over 9,000 bucks for that thing. Then I got laid off and I missed a few payments, and the bank repossessed the car. And O.K., fair enough, I can see why they have to do that.

So they auctioned off the Jeep and somebody else owns it. But now the bank's lawyer called me and said I still owe $5,000. What is that, a joke? I owe money for a Jeep I don't even have anymore? That can't be right. I look forward to your advice.

Sam

> I owe money for a Jeep I don't even have anymore?

To: Sam12345@yahoo.com
From: Allison@credit-help-for-all.com
Dear Sam,

I am sympathetic with your story, but unfortunately the bank is entitled to its money. Here is how the law sees your plight. When you bought the Jeep, you signed two documents: a note, in which you promised to pay the full balance owed, and a security agreement, which said that if you stopped making payments, the bank could repossess the vehicle and sell it.

There are two problems. First, even after two years of writing checks, you might still have owed about $10,000 (because of interest). Second, cars depreciate quickly. Your $18,000 vehicle probably had a market value of about $8,000 thirty months later. The security agreement allowed the bank to sell the Jeep at auction, where prices are still lower. Your car evidently fetched about $5,000. That leaves a deficiency of $5,000—for which you are legally responsible, regardless of who is driving the car.

I hope you have a good weekend.
Allison

23-1 ARTICLE 9: TERMS AND SCOPE

We can sympathize with Sam, but the bank is entitled to its money. The buyer and the bank entered into a secured transaction, meaning that one party gave credit to another, demanding in return an assurance of repayment. Whether a used-car lot sells a car on credit for $18,000 or a bank takes collateral for a $600 million corporate loan, the parties have created a secured transaction.

Article 9 of the Uniform Commercial Code (UCC) governs secured transactions in personal property. It is essential to understand the basics of this law because we live and work in a world economy based on credit. Gravity may cause the earth to spin, but it is secured transactions that keep the commercial world going 'round. The quantity of disputes tells us how important this law is: About *one-half* of all UCC lawsuits involve Article 9.

This part of the Code employs terms not used elsewhere, so we must lead off with some definitions.

23-1a Article 9 Vocabulary

- **Fixtures** are goods that have become attached to real estate. For example, heating ducts are *goods* when a company manufactures them and also when it sells them to a retailer. But when a contractor installs the ducts in a new house, they become *fixtures*.

- **Security interest** means an interest in personal property or fixtures that secures the performance of some *obligation*. If an automobile dealer sells you a new car on credit and retains a security interest in the car, it means she is keeping legal rights *in your car*, including the right to drive it away if you fall behind in your payments. Usually, your obligation is to pay money, such as the money due on the new car. Occasionally, the obligation is to perform some other action, but in this chapter, we concentrate on the payment of money because that is what security interests are generally designed to ensure.

- **Secured party** is the person or company that holds the security interest. The automobile dealer who sells you a car on credit is the secured party.

- **Collateral** is the property subject to a security interest. When a dealer sells you a new car and keeps a security interest, the vehicle is the collateral.

- **Debtor and obligor.** For our purposes, **debtor** refers to a person who has some *original* ownership interest in the collateral. Having a security interest in the collateral does *not* make one a debtor. If Alice borrows money from a bank and uses her Mercedes as collateral, she is the debtor because she owns the car. **Obligor** means a person who must repay money, or perform some other task.

Throughout this chapter, the obligor and debtor will generally be the same person, but not always. When Alice borrows money from a bank and uses her Mercedes as collateral, she is the obligor, because she must repay the loan; as we know, Alice is also the debtor. However, suppose that Toby borrows money from a bank and provides no collateral; Jake co-signs the loan as a favor to Toby, using his Steinway piano as collateral. *Jake* is the only debtor, because he owns the piano. *Both parties* are obligors, because both have agreed to repay the loan.

- **Security agreement** is the contract in which the debtor gives a security interest to the secured party. This agreement protects the secured party's rights in the collateral.

- **Default** occurs when the debtor fails to pay money that is due, for example, on a loan or for a purchase made on credit. Default also includes other failures by the debtor, such as failing to keep the collateral insured.

Fixtures
Goods that have become attached to real estate.

Secured party
A person or company that holds a security interest.

Collateral
Property that is subject to a security interest.

Debtor
A person who has original ownership interest in the collateral.

Obligor
A person who must repay money or perform some other task to satisfy a debt.

Security agreement
A contract in which the debtor gives a security interest to the secured party.

- **Repossession** occurs when the secured party takes back collateral because the debtor has defaulted. Typically, the secured party will demand that the debtor deliver the collateral; if the debtor fails to do so, the secured party may find the collateral and take it.

- **Perfection** is a series of steps the secured party must take to protect its rights in the collateral against people other than the debtor. This is important because if the debtor cannot pay his debts, several creditors may attempt to seize the collateral, but only one may actually obtain it. To perfect its rights in the collateral, the secured party will typically file specific papers with a state agency.

- **Financing statement** is a document that the secured party files to give the general public notice that it has a secured interest in the collateral.

- **Record** refers to information written on paper or stored in an electronic or other medium.

- **Authenticate** means to sign a document or to use any symbol or encryption method that identifies the person and clearly indicates she is adopting the record as her own. You authenticate a security agreement when you sign papers at an auto dealership, for example. A corporation electronically authenticates a loan agreement by using the Internet to transmit an encrypted signature.

AN EXAMPLE

Here is an example using the terms just discussed. A medical equipment company manufactures a CAT scan machine and sells it to a clinic for $2 million, taking $500,000 cash and the clinic's promise to pay the rest over five years. The clinic simultaneously authenticates a security agreement, giving the manufacturer a security interest in the CAT scanner. If the clinic fails to make its payments, the manufacturer can repossess the machine. The manufacturer then electronically files a financing statement with an appropriate state agency. This *perfects* the manufacturer's rights, meaning that its security interest in the CAT scanner is now valid against all the world. If the clinic goes bankrupt and many creditors try to seize its assets, the manufacturer has first claim to the CAT scan machine. Exhibit 23.1 illustrates this transaction.

The clinic's bankruptcy is of great importance. When a debtor has money to pay all of its debts, there are no concerns about security interests. But what if there is not enough money to go around? A creditor insists on a security interest to protect itself in the event the debtor *cannot* pay all of its debts. The secured party intends (1) to give itself a legal interest in specific property of the debtor and (2) to establish a priority claim in that property, ahead of other creditors. In this chapter, we look at a variety of issues that arise in secured transactions.

23-1b Scope of Article 9

Article 9 applies to any transaction intended to create a security interest in personal property or fixtures.

TYPES OF COLLATERAL

The personal property used as collateral may be goods, such as cars or jewelry, but it may also be a variety of other things:

- **Instruments.** Drafts, checks, certificates of deposit, and notes may all be used as collateral, as may stocks, bonds, and other securities.

- **Investment property**, which refers primarily to securities and related rights.

- **Documents of title.** These are papers used by an owner of goods who ships or stores them. The documents are the owner's proof that he owns goods no longer in his possession. For example, an owner sending goods by truck will obtain a *bill of lading*, a receipt indicating where the goods will be shipped and who gets them when they

EXHIBIT 23.1   A simple security agreement:
[1] The manufacturer sells a CAT scan machine to a clinic, taking $500,000 and the clinic's promise to pay the balance over five years.
[2] The clinic simultaneously authenticates a security agreement.
[3] The manufacturer perfects by electronically filing a financing statement.

arrive. Similarly, a *warehouse receipt* is the owner's receipt for goods stored at a warehouse. The owner may use these and other similar documents of title as collateral.

- **Account** means a right to receive payment for goods sold or leased. This includes, for example, accounts receivable, indicating various buyers owe a merchant money for goods they have already received. The category now includes health-insurance receivables.

- **Deposit accounts.** Article 9 now covers security interests in deposit accounts (money placed in banks).

- **Commercial tort claims.** An organization that has filed a tort suit may use its claim as collateral. Personal injuries to *individuals* are not covered by this article.

- **General intangibles.** This is a residual category, designed to include many kinds of collateral that do not appear elsewhere on the list, such as copyrights, patents, trademarks, goodwill, and the right to payment of some loans.

- **Chattel paper.** This is a record that indicates two things: (1) An obligor owes money and (2) a secured party has a security interest in specific goods. Chattel paper most commonly occurs in a consumer sale on credit. If a dealer sells an air conditioner to a customer, who agrees in writing to make monthly payments and also agrees that the dealer has a security interest in the air conditioner, that agreement is chattel paper. The same chattel paper may be collateral for a second security interest. The dealer who sells the air conditioner could use the chattel paper to obtain a loan. If the dealer gives the chattel paper to a bank as collateral for the loan, the bank has a security interest *in the chattel paper*, while the dealer continues to have a security interest *in the air conditioner*. **Electronic chattel paper** is the same thing, except that it is an electronic record rather than a written one.

- **Goods** means movable things, including fixtures, crops, and manufactured homes. For purposes of secured transactions, the Code divides goods into additional categories. In some cases, the rights of the parties will depend upon what category the goods fall into. These are the key categories:

  - *Consumer goods* are those used primarily for personal, family, or household purposes.

  - *Farm products* are crops, livestock, or supplies used directly in farming operations (as opposed to the business aspects of farming).

  - *Inventory* consists of goods held by someone for sale or lease, such as all of the beds and chairs in a furniture store.

  - *Equipment* refers to things used in running a business, such as the desks, telephones, and computers needed to operate a retail store.

SOFTWARE

Article 9 takes into account the increasingly important role that computer software plays in all business. The Code distinguishes *software* from *goods*, and this becomes important when competing creditors are fighting over both a computer system and the software inside it. A program embedded in a computer counts as goods *if* it is customarily considered part of those goods *or* if, by purchasing the goods, the owner acquires the right to use the program. A program that does *not* meet those criteria is termed *software*, and will be treated differently for some purposes.

In sum, Article 9 applies anytime the parties intended to create a security interest in any of the items listed above.

23-2 ATTACHMENT OF A SECURITY INTEREST

Attachment

A three-step process that creates an enforceable security interest.

Attachment is a vital step in a secured transaction. This means that the secured party has taken all of the following steps to create an enforceable security interest:

- The two parties made a security agreement, and either the debtor has *authenticated a security agreement* describing the collateral *or* the secured party has obtained *possession* or *control*;

- The secured party has given value to obtain the security agreement; and

- The debtor has rights in the collateral.[1]

---

[1]UCC §9-203.

23-2a Agreement

Without an agreement, there can be no security interest. Generally, the agreement will be in writing and signed by the debtor or electronically recorded and authenticated by the debtor. The agreement must reasonably identify the collateral. A description of collateral by *type* is often acceptable. For example, a security agreement may properly describe the collateral as "all equipment in the store at 123 Periwinkle Street."[2] In a security agreement for consumer goods, however, a description by type is *not* sufficient, and more specificity is required.

A security agreement at a minimum might:

- State that Happy Homes, Inc., and Martha agree that Martha is buying an Arctic Co. refrigerator and identify the exact unit by its serial number;

- Give the price, the down payment, the monthly payments, and interest rate;

- State that because Happy Homes is selling Martha the refrigerator on credit, it has a security interest in the refrigerator; and

- Provide that if Martha defaults on her payments, Happy Homes is entitled to repossess the refrigerator.

An actual security agreement will add many details, such as Martha's obligation to keep the refrigerator in good condition and to deliver it to the store if she defaults; a precise definition of "default"; and how Happy Homes may go about repossessing if Martha defaults and fails to return the refrigerator.

23-2b Control and Possession

In many cases, the security agreement need not be in writing if the parties have an oral agreement and the secured party has either **control** or **possession**. For many kinds of collateral, it is safer for the secured party actually to take the item than to rely upon a security agreement. The rules follow.

CONTROL

For deposit accounts, electronic chattel paper and certain other collateral, the security interest attaches if the secured party has *control*. The UCC specifies exactly what the secured party must do to obtain control for each type of collateral. In a general sense, *control means that the secured party has certain exclusive rights to dispose of the collateral.*

- **Deposit account (in a bank).** The secured party has control if it is itself the bank holding the deposit or if the debtor has authorized the bank to dispose of funds according to the secured party's instructions.

- **Electronic chattel paper.** A secured party has control of electronic chattel paper when it possesses the only authoritative copy of it, and the record(s) designate the secured party as the assignee. This means that the parties have agreed on an electronic method to verify the uniqueness of the record, so that any copies of the electronic original are clearly recognizable as reproductions.

- **Investment property and letter-of-credit rights.** The Code specifies analogous methods of controlling investment properties and letter-of-credit rights.[3]

---

[2]A security agreement may not use a super-generic term such as "all of Smith's personal property." We will see later that, by contrast, such a super-generic description is legally adequate in a *financing statement*.

[3]*Control* is described in the following sections: 9-104 (deposit accounts), 9-105 (electronic chattel paper), 9-106 (investment property), and 9-107 (letter-of-credit rights).

POSSESSION

For most other forms of collateral, including goods, securities, and most other items, a security interest attaches if the secured party has *possession*. For example, if you loan your neighbor $175,000 and he gives you a Winslow Homer watercolor as collateral, you have an attached security interest in the painting once it is in your possession. It would still be wise to put the agreement in writing, to be certain both parties understand all terms and can prove them if necessary, but the writing is not legally required.

The following case is typical of Article 9 disputes in that it was fought out in bankruptcy court. A debtor claimed to have a security interest in property owned by a bankrupt company. Had the parties made a security agreement?

In Re CFLC, Inc.

209 B.R. 508, 1997 Bankr. LEXIS 821
United States Bankruptcy Appellate Panel of the Ninth Circuit, 1997

CASE SUMMARY

Facts: Expeditors was a freight company that supervised importing and exporting for Everex Systems, Inc. Expeditors negotiated rates and services for its client and frequently had possession of Everex's goods. During a 17-month period, Expeditors sent over 300 invoices to Everex. Each invoice stated that the customer either had to accept all of the invoice's terms or to pay cash, receiving no work on credit. One of those terms gave Expeditors a general lien on all of the customer's property in its possession. In other words, if the customer failed to pay a bill, Expeditors claimed the right to retain the goods, auction them, and keep enough of the proceeds to pay its overdue bills.

Everex filed for bankruptcy. Expeditors expedited its way into the court proceedings, claiming the right to sell Everex's goods, worth about $81,000. The trial judge rejected the claim, ruling that Expeditors lacked a valid security interest. Expeditors appealed.

Issue: *Did Expeditors have a security interest in Everex's goods?*

Decision: No. Expeditors had no security interest in the goods. Affirmed.

Reasoning: Expeditors and Everex never explicitly agreed to create a security interest. Expeditors did send many invoices with terms that the company wished to be part of a general agreement. However, repetitively mailing such documents does not make a security agreement. Everex said nothing about the invoice terms and did nothing to indicate that it agreed to a lien on its goods. All Everex did was pay the invoices.

If the parties had reached an initial agreement, then the invoices might be evidence of a continuing security interest. Without such a clear agreement, though, there is no security interest.

EXAM Strategy

Question: Hector needs money to keep his business afloat. He asks his uncle for a $1 million loan. The uncle agrees, but he insists that his nephew grant him a security interest in Hector's splendid gold clarinet, worth over $2 million. Hector agrees. The uncle prepares a handwritten document summarizing the agreement and asks his nephew to sign it. Hector hands the clarinet to his uncle and receives his money, but he forgets to sign the document. Has a security agreement attached?

Strategy: Attachment occurs if the parties made a security agreement and there was authentication or possession; the secured party has given value; and the debtor had rights in the collateral.

Result: Hector agreed to give his uncle a security interest in the instrument. He never authenticated (signed) the agreement, but the uncle did take possession of the clarinet. The uncle gave Hector $1 million, and Hector owned the instrument. Yes, the security interest attached.

23-2c Value

For the security interest to attach, the secured party must give value. Usually, the value will be apparent. If a bank loans $400 million to an airline, that money is the value, and the bank, therefore, may obtain a security interest in the planes that the airline is buying. If a store sells a living room set to a customer for a small down payment and two years of monthly payments, the value given is the furniture.

FUTURE VALUE

The parties may also agree that some of the value will be given in the future. For example, a finance company might extend a $5 million line of credit to a retail store, even though the store initially takes only $1 million of the money. The remaining credit is available whenever the store needs it to purchase inventory. The Uniform Commercial Code considers the entire $5 million line of credit to be value.[4]

23-2d Debtor Rights in the Collateral

The debtor can grant a security interest in goods only if he has some legal right to those goods himself. Typically, the debtor owns the goods. But a debtor may also give a security interest if he is leasing the goods or even if he is a bailee, meaning that he is lawfully holding them for someone else. Suppose Importer receives a shipment of scallops on behalf of Seafood Wholesaler. Wholesaler asks Importer to hold the scallops for three days as a favor, and to keep a customer happy, Importer agrees. Importer then arranges a $150,000 loan from a bank, using the scallops as collateral. Although Importer has acted unethically, it does have *some right* in the collateral—the right to hold them for three days. That is enough to satisfy this rule.

By contrast, suppose Railroad is transporting 10 carloads of cattle on behalf of Walter, the owner. A devious Meat Dealer uses forged documents to trick Railroad into believing that Meat Dealer is entitled to the animals. Meat Dealer trucks the cattle away and uses them to obtain a bank loan, giving the bank a security interest in the animals. That "security interest" has never attached and is invalid because Dealer had *no* legal interest in the cattle. When Walter, the rightful owner, locates his cattle, he may take them back. The bank can only hope to find the deceitful Dealer, who in fact has probably disappeared.

Once the security interest has attached to the collateral, the secured party is protected against the debtor. If the debtor fails to pay, the secured party may repossess the collateral.

23-2e Attachment to Future Property

The security agreement may specify that the security interest attaches to personal property that the debtor does not yet possess but might obtain in the future.

---

[4]UCC §9-204(c).

AFTER-ACQUIRED PROPERTY

After-acquired property
Items that the debtor obtains after the parties have made their security agreement.

After-acquired property refers to items that the debtor obtains after the parties have made their security agreement. **The parties may agree that the security interest attaches to after-acquired property.**[5] Basil is starting a catering business, but owns only a beat-up car. He borrows $55,000 from the Pesto Bank, which takes a security interest in the car. But Pesto also insists on an after-acquired clause. When Basil purchases a commercial stove, cooking equipment, and freezer, Pesto's security interest attaches to each item as Basil acquires it.

PROCEEDS

Proceeds are whatever is obtained by a debtor who sells the collateral or otherwise disposes of it. **The secured party *automatically* obtains a security interest in the *proceeds* of the collateral, unless the security agreement states otherwise.**[6] Suppose the Pesto Bank obtains a security interest in Basil's $4,000 freezer. Basil then decides he needs a larger model and sells the original freezer to his neighbor for $3,000. The $3,000 cash is proceeds, in which Pesto automatically obtains a security interest.

23-3 PERFECTION

23-3a Nothing Less than Perfection

Once the security interest has attached to the collateral, the secured party is protected against *the debtor*, but it may not be protected against *anyone else*. Pesto Bank loaned money to Basil and has a security interest in all of his property. If Basil defaults on his loan, Pesto may insist he deliver the goods to the bank. If he fails to do that, the bank can seize the collateral. But Pesto's security interest is valid only against Basil; if a third person claims some interest in the goods, the bank may never get them. For example, Basil might have taken out *another* loan, from his friend Olive, and used the same property as collateral. Olive knew nothing about the bank's original loan. To protect itself against Olive, and all other parties, the bank must *perfect* its interest.

There are several kinds of perfection:

- Perfection by filing
- Perfection by possession
- Perfection of consumer goods
- Perfection of movable collateral and fixtures

In some cases, the secured party will have a choice of which method to use; in other cases, only one method works.

23-3b Perfection by Filing

Financing statement
A statement that gives the names of all parties, describes the collateral, and outlines the security interest.

The most common way to perfect an interest is by filing a financing statement with one or more state agencies. A **financing statement** gives the names of all parties, describes the collateral, and outlines the security interest, enabling any interested person to learn about it. Suppose the Pesto Bank obtains a security interest in Basil's catering equipment and then perfects by filing with the Secretary of State. When Basil asks his friend Olive for a loan, she

---

[5]UCC §9-204(a).
[6]UCC §9-203(f).

has the opportunity to check the records to see if anyone already has a security interest in the catering equipment. If Olive's search uncovers Basil's previous security agreement, she will realize it would be unwise to make the loan. If Basil were to default, the collateral would go straight to Pesto Bank, leaving Olive empty-handed. See Exhibit 23.2.

EXHIBIT 23.2   The Pesto Bank:
[1] Loans money to Basil and
[2] Takes a security interest in his equipment.
Later, when Olive:
[3] Considers loaning Basil money, she will
[4] Check to see if any other creditors already have a security interest in his goods.

Article 9 prescribes one form to be used nationwide for financing statements.[7] The financing form is available online at many websites. Remember that the filing may be done on paper or electronically.

---

[7]UCC §9-521.

If the collateral is either *accounts* or *general intangibles*, filing is the *only* way to perfect. Suppose Nester uses his copyright in a screenplay as collateral for a loan. The bank that gives him the loan may perfect *only* by filing.

The most common problems that arise in filing cases are (1) whether the financing statement contained enough information to put other people on notice of the security interest and (2) whether the secured party filed the papers in the right place.

CONTENTS OF THE FINANCING STATEMENT

A financing statement is sufficient if it provides the name of the debtor, the name of the secured party, and an indication of the collateral.[8]

The name of the debtor is critical because that is what an interested person will use to search among the millions of other financing statements on file. Faulty descriptions of the debtor's name have led to thousands of disputes and untold years of litigation, as subsequent creditors have failed to locate any record of an earlier claim on the debtor's property. In response, the UCC is now very precise about what name must be used. If the debtor is a "registered organization," such as a corporation, limited partnership, or limited liability company, the official registered name of the company is the only one acceptable. If the debtor is a person or an unregistered organization (such as a club), then the *correct* name is required. Trade names are not sufficient.

Because misnamed debtors have created so much conflict, the Code now offers a straightforward test: A financing statement is effective if a computer search run under the debtor's correct name produces it. That is true even if the financing statement used the *incorrect* name. If the search does not reveal the document, then the financing statement is ineffective as a matter of law. The burden is on the secured party to file accurately, not on the searcher to seek out erroneous filings.[9]

The collateral must be described reasonably so that another party contemplating a loan to the debtor will understand which property is already secured. A financing statement could properly state that it applies to "all inventory in the debtor's Houston warehouse." If the debtor has given a security interest in everything he owns, then it is sufficient to state simply that the financing statement covers "all assets" or "all personal property."

The filing must be done by the debtor's last name. But which name is the last? The answer is not always entirely straightforward, as the following case indicates. Did the court get it right?

CORONA FRUITS & VEGGIES, INC. v. FROZSUN FOODS, INC.

143 Cal. App. 4th 319, 48 Cal. Rptr. 3d 868
California Court of Appeals, 2006

CASE SUMMARY

Facts: Corona Fruits & Veggies (Corona) leased farmland to a strawberry farmer named Armando Munoz Juarez. He signed the lease, "Armando Munoz." Corona advanced money for payroll and farm production expenses. The company filed a UCC-1 financing statement, claiming a security interest in the strawberry crop. The financing

---

[8]UCC §9-502(a).
[9]UCC §9-506(c).

statement listed the debtor's name as "Armando Munoz." Six months later, Armando Munoz Juarez contracted with Frozsun Foods, Inc., to sell processed strawberries. Frozsun advanced money and filed a financing statement listing the debtor's name as "Armando Juarez."

By the next year, the strawberry farmer owed Corona $230,000 and Frozsun $19,600. When he was unable to make payments on Corona's loan, the company repossessed the farmland. And, while it may sound a bit … lame … it also repossessed the strawberries.

Both Corona and Frozsun claimed the proceeds of the crop. The trial court awarded the money to Frozsun, finding that Corona had filed its financing statement under the wrong last name and therefore had failed to perfect its security interest in the strawberry crop. Corona appealed.

Issue: *Did Corona correctly file its financing statement?*

Decision: No, Corona did not correctly file. Judgment affirmed.

Reasoning: Because UCC-1 financing statements are indexed by last name, it is essential that a creditor use the correct surname. This debtor's true last name was "Juarez," not "Munoz." Corona's own business records, receipts, and checks all refer to him as "Juarez," as do his green card and photo ID.

The record indicates that Frozsun's agent conducted a "Juarez" debtor name search and did not discover appellants' UCC-1 financing statement. The secured party, not the debtor or uninvolved third parties, has the duty of ensuring proper filing and indexing of the notice.

Corona contends that since the debtor is from Mexico, we should follow the traditions of that country, where the surname is formed by listing the father's name, then the mother's. But the strawberries were planted in California, not Mexico. This is where the debt arose and the UCC-1 was filed. The state cannot organize a filing system that will accommodate naming practices in all foreign countries.

Corona failed to file properly, and its security interest never perfected.

Article 9—2010 Amendments In 2010, the authors of the UCC—the Uniform Law Commission (ULC), also known as the National Conference of Commissioners on Uniform State Laws—created a set of Amendments to Article 9. Remember that the ULC has no power to make law. Once it creates a set of model rules, it is up to the states to decide whether or not to enact the proposals.

At the time of this writing, all but twelve states have adopted the changes to Article 9 as law, and it appears likely that the others will adopt the changes soon.

While most of these changes are so technical as to be beyond the scope of this chapter, one of the Amendments addresses the issue of what name must appear on a financing statement. Under the 2010 Amendments, states require that for individuals, the name on a financing statement be the same as that *on a person's driver's license*. If a state also issues official identification cards from a driver's license office to non-drivers, then the name on such an ID card will be acceptable. If a person has neither kind of state ID card, then her surname and first personal name will be required to perfect by filing.

Debtor's Signature Notice one important item that is *not* required on a financing statement: the debtor's signature. The drafters of the UCC have greatly facilitated electronic filing by eliminating the old requirement that a debtor sign. Does this allow a secured party to create any financing statement it wishes? No. The debtor must have entered into a valid security agreement before the secured party is entitled to file any financing statement. Of course, there is the possibility of a fraudulent filing, but the drafters reasoned that the efficiency achieved far outweighs the danger of occasional fraud.

PLACE OF FILING

The United States is a big country, and potential creditors do not want to stagger from one end of it to the other to learn whether particular collateral is already secured elsewhere. Article 9 specifies *where* a secured party must file. These provisions may vary from state to state, so it is essential to check local law because a misfiled record accomplishes nothing. The general rules are as follows.

A secured party must file **in the state of the debtor's location**. An *individual* is located at his principal residence. If Luigi, the debtor, lives in Maryland, works in Virginia, and has a vacation home in Florida, a secured party must file in Maryland. An organization that has only one place of business is located in that state. If the organization has more than one place of business, it is considered to be located at its chief executive office.[10]

Article 9 prescribes central filing within the state for most types of collateral. For *goods*, the central location will typically be the Secretary of State's office, although a state may designate some other office if it wishes. For *fixtures*, the secured party generally has a choice between filing in the same central office that is used for goods (which, again, is usually the Secretary of State's office), or filing in the local *county* office that would be used to file real estate mortgages.[11]

DURATION OF FILING

Once a financing statement has been filed, it is effective for five years.[12] After five years, the statement will expire and leave the secured party unprotected, unless she files a continuation statement within six months prior to expiration. The continuation statement is valid for an additional five years, and if necessary, a secured party may continue to file one periodically, forever.[13]

23-3c Perfection by Possession or Control

For most types of collateral, in addition to filing, a secured party generally may perfect by possession or control. So if the collateral is a diamond brooch or 1,000 shares of stock, a bank may perfect its security interest by holding the items until the loan is paid off. When the debtor gives collateral to the secured party, it is often called a **pledge**: The debtor pledges her goods to secure her performance, and the secured party (sometimes called the **pledgee**) takes the goods to perfect its interest.

Pledge

A secured transaction in which a debtor gives collateral to the secured party.

POSSESSION

When may a party use possession? Whenever the collateral is goods, negotiable documents, instruments, money, chattel paper that is tangible (as opposed to electronic), or most securities.[14]

Perfection by possession has some advantages. First, notice to other parties is very effective. No reasonable finance company assumes that it can obtain a security interest in a Super Bowl championship ring when *another creditor* already holds the ring. Second, possession enables the creditor to ensure that the collateral will not be damaged during the life of the security interest. A bank that loans money based on a rare painting may worry about the painting's condition, but it knows the painting is safe if it is locked up in the bank's vault. Third, if the debtor defaults, a secured party has no difficulties repossessing goods that it already holds.

Of course, for some collateral, possession is impractical. If a consumer buys a new yacht on credit, the seller can hardly expect to perfect its security interest by possession. The buyer would become edgy sailing the boat around the dealer's parking lot. In such a case, the secured party must perfect by filing.

---

[10]UCC §9-307.
[11]UCC §9-501.
[12]The exception to this is for a manufactured home, where it lasts 30 years.
[13]UCC §9-515.
[14]UCC §9-313.

MANDATORY POSSESSION

A party *must* perfect a security interest in *money* by taking possession.[15] Money is easy to transfer, and one $100 bill is the same as another, so only possession will do. Suppose Ed's Real Estate claims that Jennifer, a former employee, has opened her own realty business in violation of their noncompete agreement. Jennifer promises to move her business to another city within 90 days, and Ed agrees not to sue. To secure Jennifer's promise to move, Ed takes a security interest in $50,000 cash. If she fails to move on time, he is entitled to the money. To perfect that interest, Ed must take possession of the money and hold it until Jennifer is out of town.

CONTROL

A security interest in investment property, deposit accounts, letter-of-credit rights, and electronic chattel paper may be perfected by control.[16] We have described control above, in the section on attachment. In general, *control means that the secured party has certain exclusive rights to dispose of the collateral.* Recall, for example, that a secured party which is a bank has control of any deposit account located in that bank.

Mandatory Control   **Security interests in deposit accounts and letter-of-credit rights may be perfected *only* by control.**[17] Once again, filing would be ineffectual with forms of collateral so easily moved, and the UCC will grant perfection only to a secured party that has control.

CARE OF THE COLLATERAL

Possession and control give several advantages to the secured party, but also one important duty: **A secured party must use reasonable care in the custody and preservation of collateral in her possession or control.**[18] If the collateral is something tangible, such as a painting, the secured party must take reasonable steps to ensure that it is safe from harm.

What does "reasonable care" mean when the collateral is something as volatile as shares of stock?

LAYNE V. BANK ONE

395 F.3d 271
Sixth Circuit Court of Appeals, 2005

CASE SUMMARY

Facts: Charles E. Johnson was the founder and CEO of PurchasePro.com, Inc., and Geoff Layne was its marketing director. When their internet stock went public, both officers suddenly owned shares worth millions of dollars. To increase his liquidity, Johnson took out a loan for $2.8 million from Bank One, and Layne borrowed $3.25 million. Each secured the loan with shares of PurchasePro stock.

The loan agreement required a loan-to-value (LTV) ratio of 50 percent, meaning that the value of the shares had to be at least double the outstanding loan balance. If the value of the shares sank below the required level, the two men could either pay off some of the loan or offer additional security. If the two borrowers failed to remedy the problem, the bank was entitled (but not obligated) to sell the shares. Johnson secured his loan with $6.9 million worth of PurchasePro stock.

In February, internet stocks suddenly plummeted, and both loans immediately exceeded their LTV ratio.

---

[15]UCC §9-312(b)(3).
[16]UCC §9-314(a).
[17]UCC §9-312(b)(1).
[18]UCC §9-207.

Johnson and Layne spoke with the bank several times, stating that they would offer additional collateral. During March and April, more calls went back and forth, with the debtors occasionally suggesting that the collateral be sold, while at other times agreeing to provide more security. Finally, in July, over a four-day period, the bank sold Johnson's PurchasePro shares for $524,757, less than 10 percent of its original worth.

Johnson and Layne both filed suit against Bank One, claiming that it failed to exercise reasonable care of the collateral. The trial court gave judgment for the bank, and the plaintiffs appealed.

Issue: *Did the bank exercise reasonable care of the shares?*

Decision: Yes, the bank exercised reasonable care. Judgment affirmed.

Reasoning: A secured party must take reasonable care to preserve the value of collateral such as stock. However, the comment to §9-207 states that the secured party is not liable for a drop in the value of pledged instruments, including shares, even if timely action might have prevented the decline. It is the borrower who decides to buy stock, not the lender. A secured party merely accepts the shares as collateral, and it does not itself invest in the issuing firm. The stock market is notoriously volatile. Requiring a secured party to sell shares held as collateral to avoid losses would shift the investment risk from borrower to lender.

If the borrower is concerned with the decline in share value, it is his responsibility to act, using other assets to reduce the outstanding loan, substituting different collateral for the stock, or selling the pledged shares himself and paying off the loan.

23-3d Perfection of Consumer Goods

The UCC gives special treatment to security interests in most consumer goods. Merchants sell a vast amount of consumer goods on credit. They cannot file a financing statement for every bed, television, and stereo for which a consumer owes money. Yet perfecting by possession is also impossible since the consumer expects to take the goods home. To understand the UCC's treatment of these transactions, we need to know two terms. The first is *consumer goods*, which as we saw earlier means goods used primarily for personal, family, or household purposes. The second term is *purchase money security interest*.

Purchase money security interest (PMSI)

An interest taken by the person who sells the collateral or advances money so the debtor can buy it.

A **purchase money security interest (PMSI)** is one taken by the person who sells the collateral or by the person who advances money so the debtor can buy the collateral.[19] Assume the Gobroke Home Center sells Marion a $5,000 stereo system. The sales document requires a payment of $500 down and $50 per month for the next three centuries, and gives Gobroke a security interest in the system. Because the security interest was "taken by the seller," the document is a PMSI. It would also be a PMSI if a bank had loaned Marion the money to buy the system and the document gave the bank a security interest.

But aren't all security interests PMSIs? No, many are not. Suppose a bank loans a retail company $800,000 and takes a security interest in the store's present inventory. That is not a PMSI since the store did not use the $800,000 to purchase the collateral.

What must Gobroke Home Center do to perfect its security interest? Nothing. **A PMSI in *consumer goods* perfects *automatically*, without filing.**[20] Marion's new stereo is clearly consumer goods because she will use it only in her home. Gobroke's security interest is a PMSI, so the interest has perfected automatically. (See Exhibit 23.3.)

---

[19]UCC §9-103.
[20]UCC §9-309(1).

| EXHIBIT 23.3 | A purchase money security interest can arise in either of two ways. In the first example, a store sells a stereo to a consumer on credit; the consumer in turn signs a PMSI, giving the store a security interest in the stereo. In the second example, the consumer buys the stereo with money loaned from a bank; the consumer signs a PMSI giving the *bank* a security interest in the stereo. |

© Cengage Learning

EXAM Strategy

Question: Winona owns a tropical fish store. To buy a spectacular new aquarium, she borrows $25,000 from her sister, Pauline, and signs an agreement giving Pauline a security interest in the tank. Pauline never files the security agreement. Winona's business goes belly up, and both Pauline and other creditors angle to repossess the tank. Does Pauline have a perfected interest in the tank?

Strategy: Generally, a creditor obtains a perfected security interest by filing or possession. However, a PMSI in consumer goods perfects automatically, without filing. Was Pauline's security agreement a PMSI? Was the fish tank a consumer good?

Result: A PMSI is one taken by the person who sells the collateral or advances money for its purchase. Pauline advanced the money for Winona to buy the tank, so Pauline does have a PMSI, but she has a problem, because PMSIs perfect automatically only for *consumer goods*. Consumer goods are those used primarily for personal, family, or household purposes, and so this was not a consumer purchase. Pauline failed to perfect and is unprotected against other creditors.

23-3e Perfection of Movable Collateral and Fixtures

The rules for perfection are slightly different for security interests in movable goods, such as cars and boats, and in fixtures. We look briefly at each.

MOVABLE GOODS GENERALLY

Goods that are easily moved create problems for creditors. Suppose a bank in Colorado loans Dorothy money, takes a security interest in her Degas sculpture, and perfects its interest in the proper state offices in Colorado. But then Dorothy moves to Ohio and uses the same collateral for another loan. A lender in Ohio will never discover the security interest perfected in Colorado. If Dorothy defaults, who gets the sculpture?

For most collateral, when the *debtor moves* to a new state, a security interest from the old state remains perfected for four months; when the *collateral is transferred* to a new state, the security interest remains perfected for one year.[21] If the secured party reperfects in the new state within the time limits mentioned, the security interest remains valid until it would normally expire. If the secured party fails to re-perfect in the new state, the security interest lapses. Suppose Dorothy takes her Degas into Ohio on February 10 and on March 5 uses it as collateral for a new loan. The original Colorado bank still has a valid security interest in the sculpture and may seize the art if Dorothy defaults. But if Dorothy applies for her new loan on October 10, and the Colorado bank has failed to re-perfect, the Colorado bank has lost its protection.

MOTOR VEHICLES AND THE LIKE

The UCC's provisions about perfecting generally do not apply to motor vehicles, trailers, mobile homes, boats, or farm tractors.[22] Because all of these are so numerous and so mobile, filing may be ineffective and possession is impossible. As a result, almost all states have created special laws to deal with this problem. Anyone offering or taking a security interest in any of these goods must consult local law.

---

[21]UCC §9-316(a).
[22]UCC §9-311(a)(2).

State title laws generally require that a security interest in an automobile be noted directly on the vehicle's certificate of title. A driver needs a certificate of title to obtain registration plates, so the law presumes that the certificate will stay with the car. By requiring that the security interest be noted on the certificate, the law gives the best possible notice to anyone thinking of buying the car or accepting it as collateral. Generally, if a buyer or lender examines the certificate and finds no security interest, he may accept the vehicle for sale, or as collateral, and take it free of any interest. In most states, the same requirement applies to boats.

FIXTURES

Fixtures, you recall, are goods that have become attached to real estate. A security interest may be created in goods that *are* fixtures and may continue in goods that *become* fixtures; however, the UCC does not permit a security interest in ordinary building materials, such as lumber and concrete, once they become part of a construction project.

The primary disputes in these cases are between a creditor holding a security interest in a fixture, such as a furnace, and another creditor with rights in the real estate, such as a bank holding a mortgage on the house. The issues are complex, involving local real property law, and we cannot undertake here a thorough explanation of them. However, we can highlight the issues that arise so that you can anticipate the potential problems. Common disputes concern:

- The status of the personal property when the security interest was created (was it still goods, or had it already been attached to real estate and become a fixture?);

- The status of the real estate (does the debtor *also* have a legal interest in the *real property?*);

- The type of perfection (which was recorded first, the security interest in the fixture or the real estate? does the secured party hold a PMSI?); and

- The physical status of the fixture (can it be removed without damaging the real estate?).[23]

Any creditor who considers accepting collateral that might become a fixture must anticipate these problems and clarify with the debtor exactly what she plans to do with the goods. Armed with that information, the creditor should consult local law on fixtures and make an appropriate security agreement (or just refuse to accept the fixture as collateral).

23-4 PROTECTION OF BUYERS

Generally, once a security interest is perfected, it remains effective regardless of whether the collateral is sold, exchanged, or transferred in some other way. Bubba's Bus Co. needs money to meet its payroll, so it borrows $150,000 from Francine's Finance Co., which takes a security interest in Bubba's 180 buses and perfects its interest. Bubba, still short of cash, sells 30 of his buses to Antelope Transit. But even that money is not enough to keep Bubba solvent: He defaults on his loan to Francine and goes into bankruptcy. Francine pounces on Bubba's buses. May she repossess the 30 that Antelope now operates? Yes. The security interest continued in the buses even after Antelope purchased them, and Francine can whisk them away. (Antelope has a valid claim against Bubba for the value of the buses, but the claim may prove fruitless, since Bubba is now bankrupt.)

---

[23]UCC §9-334.

There are some exceptions to this rule. The Code gives a few kinds of buyers special protection.

23-4a Buyers in Ordinary Course of Business

Buyer in ordinary course of business (BIOC)

Someone who buys goods in good faith from a seller who routinely deals in such goods.

As we saw in Chapter 20, a **buyer in ordinary course of business (BIOC)** is someone who buys goods in good faith from a seller who routinely deals in such goods.[24] For example, Plato's Garden Supply purchases 500 hemlocks from Socrates' Farm, a grower. Plato is a BIOC: He is buying in good faith, and Socrates routinely deals in hemlocks. This is an important status because a BIOC is generally *not affected* by security interests in the goods. However, if Plato *actually realized* that the sale violated another party's rights in the goods, there would be no good faith. If Plato knew that Socrates was bankrupt and had agreed with a creditor not to sell any of his inventory, Plato would not achieve BIOC status.

A buyer in ordinary course of business takes the goods free of a security interest created by its seller even though the security interest is perfected.[25] Suppose that, a month before Plato made his purchase, Socrates borrowed $200,000 from the Athenian Bank. Athenian took a security interest in all of Socrates' trees and perfected by filing. Then Plato purchased his 500 hemlocks. If Socrates defaults on the loan, Athenian will have *no right* to repossess the 500 trees that are now at the Garden Supply. Plato took them free and clear. (Of course, Athenian can still attempt to repossess other trees from Socrates.)

The BIOC exception is designed to encourage ordinary commerce. A buyer making routine purchases should not be forced to perform a financing check before buying. But the rule, efficient though it may be, creates its own problems. A creditor may extend a large sum of money to a merchant based on collateral, such as inventory, only to discover that by the time the merchant defaults the collateral has been sold to BIOCs.

EXAM Strategy

Question: Troy owns an art gallery specializing in Greek artifacts. To modernize the gallery, Troy borrows $150,000 from the Sparta Bank, which takes a security interest in his entire inventory. Sparta promptly perfects. A month later, Troy sells Helen an Athenian warrior's helmet for $675,000. Helen does not bother to perform a financing check, and she is unaware of Sparta's security interest. Troy soon goes bankrupt, and Sparta attempts to seize all of the inventory, including the helmet. Sparta proves that a routine financing check would have revealed its interest. Who wins the helmet?

Strategy: A creditor perfects a security interest to ensure that it is protected against the entire world. However, exceptions leave the secured party unprotected in certain cases, including those of consumers. Analyze this case using that exception.

Result: A BIOC takes the goods free of a security interest created by his seller. Helen acted in good faith, buying from a dealer who routinely dealt in such goods. And it was Troy, Helen's seller, who created the security interest. Helen takes the helmet free of the bank's security interest, despite the fact that it was perfected.

---

[24]UCC §1-201(9).

[25]UCC §9-320(a). In fact, the buyer takes free of the security interest *even if the buyer knew of it*. Yet a BIOC, by definition, must be acting in good faith. Is this a contradiction? No. Plato might know that a third party has a security interest in Socrates' crops yet not realize that his purchase violates the third party's rights. Generally, for example, a security interest will permit a retailer to sell consumer goods, the presumption being that part of the proceeds will go to the secured party. A BIOC cannot be expected to determine what a retailer plans to do with the money he is paid.

Because the BIOC exception undercuts the basic protection given to a secured party, the courts interpret it narrowly. BIOC status is available only if the *seller* created the security interest. Oftentimes, a buyer will purchase goods that have a security interest created by someone other than the seller. If that happens, the buyer is not a BIOC. However, should that rule be strictly enforced even when the results are harsh? You make the call.

You Be the Judge

CONSECO FINANCE SERVICING CORP. v. LEE

2004 WL 1243417
Court of Appeals of Texas, 2004

Facts: Lila Williams purchased a new Roadtrek 200 motor home from New World R.V., Inc. She paid about $14,000 down and financed $63,000, giving a security interest to New World. The RV company assigned its security interest to Conseco Finance, which perfected. Two years later, Williams returned the vehicle to New World (the record does not indicate why), and New World sold the RV to Robert and Ann Lee for $42,800. A year later, Williams defaulted on her payments to Conseco.

The Lees sued Conseco, claiming to be BIOCs and asking for a court declaration that they had sole title to the Roadtrek. Conseco counterclaimed, seeking title based on its perfected security interest. The trial court ruled that the Lees were BIOCs, with full rights to the vehicle. Conseco appealed.

You Be the Judge: *Were the Lees BIOCs?*

Argument for Conseco: Under UCC §9-319, a buyer in ordinary course takes free of a security interest *created by the buyer's seller*. The buyers were the Lees. The seller was New World. New World did not create the security interest—Lila Williams did. There is no security interest created by New World. The security interest held by Conseco was created by someone else (Williams) and is not affected by the Lees' status as BIOC. The law is clear and Conseco is entitled to the Roadtrek.

Argument for the Lees: Conseco weaves a clever argument, but let's look at what they are really saying. Two honest buyers, acting in perfect good faith, can walk into an RV dealership, spend $42,000 for a used vehicle, and end up with—nothing. Conseco claims it is entitled to an RV that the Lees paid for because someone that the Lees have never dealt with, never even heard of, gave *to this RV seller* a security interest which the seller, years earlier, passed on to a finance company. Conseco's argument defies common sense and the goals of Article 9.

Rebuttal from Conseco: The best part of the Lees' argument is the emotional appeal; the worst part is that it does not reflect the law. Yes, $42,000 is a lot of money. That is why a reasonable buyer is careful to do business with conscientious, ethical sellers. New World knew that Williams financed the RV and knew who held the security interest, but never bothered to check on the status of the payments. If the Lees have suffered wrongdoing, it is at the hands of an irresponsible seller—the company they chose to work with, the company from whom they must seek relief.

Rebuttal from the Lees: The purpose of the UCC is to make dealing fair and commerce work; one of its methods is to get away from obscure, technical arguments. Conseco's suggestion would demolish the used-car industry. What buyers will ever pay serious money—*any* money— for a used vehicle, knowing that thousands of dollars later, the car might be towed out of their driveway by a finance company they never heard of?

23-4b Buyers of Consumer Goods

Another exception exists to protect buyers of consumer goods who do not realize that the item they are buying has a security interest in it. This exception tends to apply to relatively casual purchases, such as those between friends. Typically, the pattern is that one purchaser buys consumer goods on credit and then resells. The original purchaser is considered a debtor-seller since she still owes money but is now selling to a second buyer. **In the case of consumer goods purchased from a debtor-seller, a buyer takes free of a security interest if he**

is not aware of the security interest, he pays value for the goods, he is buying for his own family or household use, and the second party has not yet filed a financing statement.[26]

Here is how this exception works. Charles Lau used a Sears credit card to buy a 46-inch TV, a sleeper sofa, love seat, entertainment center, diamond ring, gold chain, and microwave. He had the items delivered to the house of his girlfriend, Teresa Rierman, because he did not want his father to know he had been using the credit card (we cannot imagine why). Lau later sold the items to Rierman's family and then (wait for it) defaulted on his payments to Sears and declared bankruptcy. Sears attempted to repossess its merchandise, but the Riermans claimed they were innocent buyers. The court ruled that if the Riermans could show that they knew nothing about Sears's security interest in the goods, they could keep the goods.[27]

This rule may be confusing because earlier, we discussed the automatic perfection of a security interest in consumer goods. When Sears sold the merchandise to Lau, it took a purchase money security interest in consumer goods. That interest perfected automatically (without filing) and was valid against *almost* everyone. Suppose Lau had used the furniture as collateral to obtain a bank loan. Sears would have retained its perfected security interest in the goods, and when Lau defaulted, Sears could have repossessed everything, leaving the bank with no collateral and no money.

The one person that Sears's perfect security interest could not defeat, however, was a buyer purchasing for *personal use without knowledge of the security interest*—in other words, the Riermans. Assuming the Riermans knew nothing of the security interest, they win. If Sears considers this type of loss important, it must, in the future, protect itself by filing a financing statement. Taking this extra step will leave Sears protected against everyone. Then, if a buyer defaults, Sears can pull the sofa out from under any purchaser.

23-4c Buyers of Chattel Paper, Instruments, and Documents

We have seen that debtors often use chattel paper, instruments, or documents as collateral. Because each of these is so easily transferred, Article 9 gives buyers special protection. **A buyer who purchases chattel paper or an instrument in the ordinary course of her business and then takes possession generally takes free of any security interest.**[28]

Suppose Tele-Maker sells 500 televisions to Retailer on credit, keeping a security interest in the televisions and the proceeds. The proceeds are any money or paper that Retailer earns from selling the sets. Retailer sells 300 of the sets to customers, most of whom pay on credit. The customers sign chattel paper, promising to pay for the sets over time (and giving Retailer a security interest in the sets). All of this chattel paper is proceeds, so Tele-Maker has a perfected security interest in it. The chattel paper is worth about $150,000 if all of the customers pay in full. But Retailer wants money now, so Retailer sells its chattel paper to Financer, who pays $120,000 cash for it. Next, Retailer defaults on its obligation to pay Tele-Maker for the sets. Tele-Maker cannot repossess the televisions because each customer was a BIOC (buyer in ordinary course of business) and took the goods free of any security interest. So Tele-Maker attempts to repossess the *chattel paper*. Will it succeed? No. The buyer of chattel paper takes it free of a perfected security interest. See Exhibit 23.4.

---

[26]UCC §9-320.
[27]*In re Lau*, 140 B.R. 172, 1992 Bankr. LEXIS 671 (N.D. Ohio 1992).
[28]UCC §9-330(a)(b)(d).

© Cengage Learning

EXHIBIT 23.4   The buyer of chattel paper takes it free of a perfected security interest. In this case, Tele-Maker (1) sells 500 units to Retailer on credit, keeping (2) a security interest in the televisions and the proceeds. Retailer (3) sells the sets to customers who (4) sign chattel paper. Retailer (5) sells the chattel paper to Financer and then defaults on its obligations to Tele-Maker.

OTHER PAPER

Similar rules apply for holders in due course of instruments and for purchasers of securities and documents of title. Those parties obtain special rights, described in Articles 3, 7, and 8 of the UCC. The details of those rules are beyond the scope of this chapter, but once again, the lesson for any lender is simple: A security interest is safest when the collateral is in your vault. If you do not take possession of the paper, you may lose it to an innocent buyer.[29]

23-4d Liens

Law student Paul King got a costly lesson when his $28.09 check for an oil change bounced and the repo man snatched his prized Corvette. The bill for the car's return: $644. King was a third-year law student, working part time in a private firm in Houston. He had just walked in from lunch when coworkers told him his car was being towed.

---

[29]UCC §9-331.

"I thought they were joking," King said. They were not. King saw a tow truck backing up to his car and hurried out to speak with the workers. They advised him that Texas law authorized them to pick up his car to satisfy a lien for work done to the car. King hurried inside to telephone the company that had performed the oil change. Unable to make a deal on the phone, he ran back outside and found—no car.

King phoned Harris County Repossession to see about getting his car back. That's easy, they told him. But you owe some fees: $28.09 for the oil change, $20 for the returned check, $25 for the legal notice in the newspapers, $21.24 per day for storage—plus, of course, the $550 repossession fee.[30]

Lien
A security interest created by law, rather than by agreement.

Is that legal? Probably. The service station had a lien on the car. A **lien** is a security interest created by law (rather than by agreement). State and federal law both allow parties to assert a lien against a debtor under prescribed conditions. For example, a state may claim a lien based on unpaid taxes; the state is giving notice to the world that it may seize the debtor's property and sell it. A company may claim a lien based on work performed by the debtor.

To understand the difference between a lien and a security interest, assume that when Paul King bought his Corvette, he made a down payment and signed a security agreement to ensure future payments. *His agreement* gave the dealer a security interest in the sports car. Later, when he paid for an oil change, his check bounced. *State law* gave the service station a lien on the auto, meaning the right to hold the car if it is in the garage and to seize the auto if it is elsewhere. Because automobile repossessions provide such a graphic view of secured transactions, we will return to the subject later in the chapter. In this case, the oil company had an **artisan's lien**, meaning a security interest in personal property created when a worker makes some improvement to the property. A car mechanic, a computer repairman, and a furniture restorer all create artisan's liens. A **mechanic's lien** is similar and is created when a worker improves real property. A carpenter who puts an addition on a kitchen and a painter who paints the kitchen's interior both have a mechanic's lien on the house. The owner of an apartment may obtain a **landlord's lien** in a tenant's personal property if the tenant fails to pay the rent. These security interests vary from state to state, so an affected person must consult local law. Because liens are the creation of statutes rather than agreements, Article 9 generally does not apply. The one aspect of liens that Article 9 does govern is priority between lienholders and other secured parties, which we examine in the following section. In Paul King's case, the repair shop certainly had a valid lien on his car, even though the amount in question was small. The company's method of *collecting* on its lien is more debatable. King admitted that the company had telephoned him and given him a chance to pay for the bounced check. Some courts would hold that the repair shop had done all it was required to do, but others might rule that it should have shown more patience and avoided running up the bill.

Artisan's lien
A security interest in personal property.

Mechanic's lien
A security created when a worker improves real property.

Landlord's lien
A security interest created by law to secure the payment of rent.

23-5 PRIORITIES AMONG CREDITORS

What happens when two creditors have a security interest in the same collateral? The party who has **priority** in the collateral gets it. Typically, the debtor lacks assets to pay everyone, so all creditors struggle to be the first in line. After the first creditor has repossessed the collateral, sold it, and taken enough of the proceeds to pay off his debt, there may be nothing left for anyone else. Who gets priority? There are three principal rules.

---

[30]Rad Sallee and James T. Campbell, "Repo Men Hitch Up Big Fee to Car," *Houston Chronicle*, October 15, 1991, §A, p. 21. Copyright 1991 Houston Chronicle Publishing Company. Reproduced with permission of Houston Chronicle Publishing Company via Copyright Clearance Center.

The first rule is easy: **A party with a perfected security interest takes priority over a party with an unperfected interest**.[31] This, of course, is the whole point of perfecting: to ensure that your security interest gets priority over everyone else's. On August 15, Meredith's Market, an antique store, borrows $100,000 from the Happy Bank, which takes a security interest in all of Meredith's inventory. Happy Bank does not perfect. On September 15, Meredith uses the same collateral to borrow $50,000 from the Suspicion Bank, which files a financing statement the same day. On October 15, as if on cue, Meredith files for bankruptcy and stops paying both creditors. Suspicion wins because it holds a perfected interest, whereas the Happy Bank holds merely an unperfected interest.

The second rule: **If neither secured party has perfected, the first interest to attach gets priority**.[32] Suppose that Suspicion Bank and Happy Bank had both failed to perfect. In that case, Happy Bank would have the first claim to Meredith's inventory since Happy's interest *attached* first.

And the third rule follows logically: **Between perfected security interests, the first to file or perfect wins**.[33] Diminishing Perspective, a railroad, borrows $75 million from the First Bank, which takes a security interest in Diminishing's railroad cars and immediately perfects by filing. Two months later, Diminishing borrows $100 million from Second Bank, which takes a security interest in the same collateral and also files. When Diminishing arrives, on schedule, in bankruptcy court, both banks will race to seize the rolling stock. First Bank gets the railcars because it perfected first.

March 1:	April 2:	May 3:	The Winner:
First Bank loans money and perfects its security interest by filing a financing statement.	Second Bank loans money and perfects its security interest by filing a financing statement.	Diminishing goes bankrupt, and both banks attempt to take the rolling stock.	First Bank, because it perfected first.

The general rules of priority are quite straightforward; however, you will not be surprised to learn that there are some exceptions.

23-5a Filing versus Control or Possession

Recall that a secured party *may* use either filing or control to perfect its security interest in deposit accounts, investment property, and letter-of-credit rights. Which method *should* the secured party use? Control. **For these three types of collateral, a secured party who has control wins over a party who merely filed.**[34] Early Bank obtains a security interest in Lionel's investment property and perfects by filing. Nine months later, Late Bank obtains a security interest in the same property and perfects by taking control. Late Bank wins.

Similarly, a secured party may perfect its interest in an *instrument* either by filing or possession. Once again, possession is the better idea: **Between competing secured parties, the one who possesses wins, even over one who filed earlier.**[35]

---

[31] UCC §9-322(a)(2).
[32] UCC §9-322(a)(3).
[33] UCC §9-322(a)(1).
[34] UCC §§9-327, 9-328, 9-329. If more than one creditor has control of the same collateral, the security interests rank according to the time of obtaining control.
[35] UCC §9-330(d).

23-5b Priority Involving a Purchase Money Security Interest

You may recall that a purchase money security interest (PMSI) is a security interest taken by the seller of the collateral or by a lender whose loan enables the debtor to buy the collateral. A PMSI can be created only in goods, fixtures, and software. On November 1, Manufacturer sells a specially built lathe to Tool Shop for $80,000 and takes a security interest in the lathe. The parties have created a PMSI. Parties holding a PMSI often take priority over other perfected security interests in the same goods, even if the other security interest was perfected first. How can the conflict arise? Suppose that on February 1, Tool Shop had borrowed $100,000 from the Gargoyle Bank, giving Gargoyle a security interest in after-acquired property. When the lathe arrives at the Tool Shop on November 1, Gargoyle's security interest attaches to it. But Manufacturer has a PMSI in the lathe, hence the conflict.

Inventory

Goods that a seller is holding for sale or lease in the ordinary course of its business.

We need to examine PMSIs involving inventory and those involving noninventory. **Inventory** means goods that the seller is holding for sale or lease in the ordinary course of its business. The furniture in a furniture store is inventory; the store's computer, telephones, and filing cabinets are not.

PMSI IN INVENTORY

A PMSI in inventory takes priority over a conflicting perfected security interest (even one perfected earlier), if two conditions are met:

- Before filing its PMSI, the secured party must check for earlier security interests and, if there are any, must notify the holder of that interest concerning the new PMSI; and

- The secured party must then perfect its PMSI (normally by filing) *before* the debtor receives the inventory.[36]

If the holder of the PMSI has met both of these conditions, its PMSI takes priority over any security interests filed earlier, as illustrated in the following chart.

1. February 1: Coltrane Bank loans Monk's Jazz Store $90,000, taking a security interest in all after-acquired property, including inventory.	**2. March 2:** Monk offers to buy 10 saxophones from Webster's Supply for $3,000 each.	**3. March 3:** Webster checks the financing records and learns that Coltrane Bank has a security interest in all of Monk's after-acquired property.	**4. March 4:** Webster notifies Coltrane Bank that he is selling 10 saxophones to Monk for $30,000 and is taking a PMSI in the instruments, which Webster carefully describes.
5. March 4: Webster files a financing statement indicating a PMSI in the 10 saxophones.	**6. March 5:** Webster sells the 10 saxophones to Monk.	**7. September:** Monk goes bankrupt.	**8. The Winner:** Webster. His PMSI in inventory takes priority over Coltrane's earlier interest.

PMSI IN NONINVENTORY COLLATERAL

PMSIs are often given for noninventory goods. When Tool Shop bought the lathe, in the example above, the company gave a PMSI to the seller. The bank simultaneously obtained a security interest in the same lathe, based on its after-acquired property interest. Who wins?

---

[36]UCC §9-324(b)(c).

A PMSI in collateral other than inventory takes priority over a conflicting security interest if the PMSI is perfected at the time the debtor receives the collateral or within 20 days after he receives it.[37] As long as Computer Co. perfects (by filing) within 20 days of delivering the computer, its PMSI takes priority over the bank's earlier security interest. Manufacturer may repossess the machine, and the bank may never get a dime back.

Again, we must note that the PMSI exception undercuts the ability of a creditor to rely on its perfected security interest. As a result, courts insist that a party asserting the PMSI exception demonstrate that it has complied with every requirement. In the following case, the creditor just got in under the wire.

In Re Roser

613 F.3d 1240; 2010 U.S. App. LEXIS 14817
Tenth Circuit Court of Appeals, 2010

CASE SUMMARY

Facts: Robert Roser obtained a loan from Sovereign Bank, which he promptly used to buy a car. Nineteen days later, Sovereign filed a lien with the state of Colorado. The bank expected that with a perfected interest, it would have priority over everyone else.

Unknown to Sovereign Bank, Roser had declared bankruptcy only 12 days after he purchased the car. Later, the bankruptcy trustee argued that he had priority over Sovereign because the bankruptcy filing happened *before Sovereign perfected* its security interest. When the court found for the trustee, Sovereign Bank appealed.

Issue: *Did Sovereign Bank, a PMSI holder, obtain priority over the bankruptcy trustee?*

Decision: Yes, the PMSI holder obtained priority.

Reasoning: On the day that Roser entered bankruptcy, Sovereign Bank had not filed its financing statement, which means that its security interest was not yet perfected. Ordinarily, a bankruptcy trustee would take priority over all security interests that are unperfected on the day that a debtor files a bankruptcy petition. However, there is an exception to this rule: If the creditor files a financing statement for a PMSI within 20 days after the debtor receives the collateral, that security interest is deemed to have been perfected as of the date of the debtor receives the collateral, not the day on which the financing statement was filed. In this case, the bank filed within that 20-day grace period, so its security interest took priority over the bankruptcy trustee.

Reversed and remanded.

23-6 Default and Termination

We have reached the end of the line. Either the debtor has defaulted or it has performed its obligations and may terminate the security agreement.

23-6a Default

The parties define "default" in their security agreement. **Generally, a debtor defaults when he fails to make payments due or enters bankruptcy proceedings.** The parties can agree that other acts will constitute default, such as the debtor's failure to maintain insurance on the collateral. When a debtor defaults, the secured party has two principal options: (1) It may

---

[37]UCC §9-324(a).

take possession of the collateral, or (2) it may file suit against the debtor for the money owed. The secured party does not have to choose between these two remedies; it may try one remedy, such as repossession, and if that fails, attempt the other.[38]

TAKING POSSESSION OF THE COLLATERAL

When the debtor defaults, the secured party may take possession of the collateral.[39] How does the secured party accomplish this? In either of two ways: The secured party may act on its own, without any court order, and simply take the collateral, provided this can be done *without a breach of the peace*. Otherwise, the secured party must file suit against the debtor and request that the court *order* the debtor to deliver the collateral.

Suppose a consumer bought a refrigerator on credit and defaulted. The security agreement may require the consumer to make the collateral available in a reasonable time and manner, such as by emptying the refrigerator of all food and having it ready for a carrier to take away. When the refrigerator is ready, the retailer can haul it away. What if the consumer refuses to cooperate? May the retailer break into the consumer's house to take the collateral? No. Breaking into a house is a clear breach of the peace and violates Article 9.

Secured parties often repossess automobiles without the debtor's cooperation. Typically, the security agreement will state that, in the event of default, the secured party has a right to take possession of the car and drive it away. As we saw earlier, the secured party could be the seller or it could be a mechanic with an artisan's lien on the car.

DISPOSITION OF THE COLLATERAL

Once the secured party has obtained possession of the collateral, it has two choices. The secured party may (1) dispose of the collateral or (2) retain the collateral as full satisfaction of the debt.

Disposal of the Collateral   **A secured party may sell, lease, or otherwise dispose of the collateral in any commercially reasonable manner.**[40] Typically, the secured party will sell the collateral in either a private or a public sale. First, however, the debtor must receive *reasonable notice* of the time and place of the sale so that she may bid on the collateral. The higher the price that the secured party gets for the collateral, the lower the balance still owed by the debtor. Giving the debtor notice of the sale and a chance to bid ensures that the collateral will not be sold for an unreasonably low price.

Suppose Bank loans $65,000 to Farmer to purchase a tractor. While still owing $40,000, Farmer defaults. Bank takes possession of the tractor and then notifies Farmer that it intends to sell the tractor at an auction. Farmer has the right to attend and bid on the tractor.

When the secured party has sold the collateral, it applies the proceeds of the sale: first, to its expenses in repossessing and selling the collateral, and second, to the debt.[41] Assume Bank sold the tractor for $35,000 and that the process of repossessing and selling the tractor cost $5,000. Bank applies the remaining $30,000 to the debt.

Deficiency or Surplus   The sale of the tractor yielded $30,000 to be applied to the debt, which was $40,000. The disposition has left a **deficiency**; that is, insufficient funds to pay off the debt. **The debtor is liable for any deficiency.** So the bank will sue the farmer for the remaining $10,000. On the other hand, sometimes the sale of the collateral yields a **surplus**; that is, a sum greater than the debt. In that case, the secured party must pay the surplus to the debtor.[42]

Deficiency

Having insufficient funds to pay off a debt.

Surplus

A sum of money greater than the debt incurred.

---

[38] UCC §9-601(a)(b)(c).
[39] UCC §9-609.
[40] UCC §9-610.
[41] UCC §9-615(a).
[42] UCC §9-615(d).

When a secured party disposes of collateral in a *commercially unreasonable* manner, then a deficiency or surplus claim may be adjusted based on the sum that *should* have been obtained.[43] Suppose that Seller, who is owed $300,000, repossesses 500 bedroom sets from a hotel and, without giving proper notice, quickly sells them for a net amount of $200,000. Seller sues for the $100,000 deficiency. If a court determines that a properly announced sale would have netted $250,000, Seller is only entitled to a deficiency judgment of $50,000. Similarly, if the collateral is sold *to the secured party* or someone related, and the price obtained is significantly below what would be expected, then any deficiency or surplus must be calculated on what the sale would normally have brought. This protects the debtor from a sale in which the secured party has followed all formalities but ended up owning the goods for a suspiciously low price.[44]

Acceptance of Collateral   In many cases, the secured party has the option to satisfy the debt simply by keeping the collateral. **Acceptance** refers to a secured party's retention of the collateral as full or partial satisfaction of the debt. *Partial satisfaction* means that the debtor will still owe some deficiency to the secured party. This is how the system works.[45]

A secured party who wishes to accept the collateral must notify the debtor. If the debtor agrees in an authenticated record, then the secured party may keep the collateral as full *or* partial satisfaction of the debt. If the debtor does not respond within 20 days, the secured party may still accept the collateral as *full* satisfaction, but *not* as partial satisfaction. In other words, the debtor's silence does not give the secured party the right to keep the goods and still sue for more money.

Suppose the buyer of a $13 million yacht, *Icarus,* has defaulted, and the retailer has repossessed the boat. The firm may decide the boat is worth more than the debt, so it notifies the buyer that it plans to keep *Icarus*. If the buyer does not object, the retailer automatically owns the boat after 20 days.

If the buyer promptly objects to acceptance, the retailer must then dispose of *Icarus* as described above, typically by sale. Why would a debtor object? Because she believes the boat is worth more than the debt. The debtor anticipates that a sale will create a surplus.

Consumers receive additional protection. A secured party may not accept collateral that is consumer goods if the debtor has possession of the goods *or* if the debtor has paid 60 percent of the purchase price. If Maud has defaulted on an oven that is in her kitchen, the Gobroke retail store may be entitled to repossess the oven, but the company must then dispose of the goods (sell the oven) and apply the proceeds to Maud's debt. Similarly, if Ernest is paying for his $10,000 television set in a "layaway" plan, with Gobroke warehousing the goods until the full price is paid, the store may not accept the television once Ernest has paid $6,000. Finally, a secured party is never permitted to accept consumer goods in partial satisfaction.[46]

Right of Redemption   Up to the time the secured party disposes of the collateral, the debtor has the right to **redeem** it, that is, to pay the full value of the debt. If the debtor redeems, she obtains the collateral back. Sylvia borrows $25,000 from the bank and pledges a ruby necklace as collateral. She defaults, still owing $9,000, and the bank notifies her that it will sell the necklace. If Sylvia pays the full $9,000 before the sale occurs, plus any expenses the bank has incurred in arranging the sale, she receives her necklace back.[47]

Acceptance
Retention of the collateral by a secured party as full or partial satisfaction of a debt.

Redeem
To pay the full value of a debt to get the collateral back.

---

[43] UCC §9-626(a)(3).
[44] UCC §§9-615(f), 9-626(a)(5).
[45] UCC §9-620.
[46] UCC §9-620(a)(3), (e), (g).
[47] UCC §9-623.

PROCEEDING TO JUDGMENT

Occasionally, the secured party will prefer to ignore its rights in the collateral and simply sue the debtor. **A secured party may sue the debtor for the full debt.**[48] Why would a creditor, having gone to so much effort to perfect its security interest, ignore that interest and simply file a lawsuit? The collateral may have decreased in value and be insufficient to cover the debt. Suppose a bank loaned $300,000 to a debtor to buy a rare baseball cap worn by Babe Ruth in a World Series game. The debtor defaults, owing $190,000. The bank discovers that the cap is now worth only $110,000. It is true that the bank could sell the cap and sue for the deficiency. But the sale will take time, and the outcome is uncertain. Suppose the bank knows that the debtor has recently paid cash for a $2 million house. The bank may promptly file suit for the full $190,000. The bank will ask the court to freeze the debtor's bank account and legally hold the house until the suit is resolved. The bank expects to prove the debt quickly—the loan documents are clear, and the amount of debt is easily calculated. It will obtain its $190,000 without ever donning the cap. Of course, the bank has the option of doing both things simultaneously: It may slap on the cap and a lawsuit all at once.

23-6b Termination

Finally, we need to look at what happens when a debtor *does not* default, but pays the full debt. (You are forgiven if you have forgotten that things sometimes work out smoothly.) Once that happens, the secured party must complete a **termination statement**, a document indicating that it no longer claims a security interest in the collateral.[49]

Termination statement
A document indicating that a secured party no longer claims a security interest in the collateral.

For a consumer debt, the secured party must file the termination statement in every place that it filed a financing statement. The secured party must do this within one month from the date the debt is fully paid, or within 20 days of a demand from the consumer, whichever comes first. For other transactions, the secured party must, within 20 days, either file the termination statement or send it to the secured party so that he may file it himself. In both cases, the goal is the same: to notify all interested parties that the debt is extinguished.

Chapter Conclusion

Secured transactions are essential to modern commerce. Billions of dollars' worth of goods are sold on credit annually, and creditors normally demand an assurance of payment. A secured party that understands Article 9 and follows its provisions to the letter should be well protected. A company that operates in ignorance of Article 9 invites disaster because others may obtain superior rights in the goods, leaving the "secured" party with no money, no security—and no sympathy from the courts.

EXAM REVIEW

1. **ARTICLE 9**   Article 9 applies to any transaction intended to create a security interest in personal property or fixtures. (pp. 529–532)

---

[48]UCC §9-601(a).
[49]UCC §9-513.

2. ATTACHMENT   Attachment means that (1) the two parties made a security agreement *and* either the debtor has *authenticated a security agreement* describing the collateral *or* the secured party has obtained *possession* or *control*; and (2) the secured party gave value in order to get the security agreement; and (3) the debtor has rights in the collateral. (pp. 532–536)

3. AFTER-ACQUIRED PROPERTY   A security interest may attach to after-acquired property. (p. 536)

4. PERFECTION   Attachment protects against the debtor. Perfection of a security interest protects the secured party against parties other than the debtor. (pp. 536–545)

5. FILING   Filing is the most common way to perfect. For many forms of collateral, the secured party may also perfect by obtaining either possession or control. (pp. 536–540)

6. PMSI   A purchase money security interest (PMSI) is one taken by the person who sells the collateral or advances money so the debtor can buy the collateral. (p. 542)

7. PMSI PERFECTION   A PMSI in consumer goods perfects automatically, without filing. (p. 542)

EXAM Strategy

Question: John and Clara Lockovich bought a 22-foot Chaparrel Villian II boat from Greene County Yacht Club for $32,500. They paid $6,000 cash and borrowed the rest of the purchase price from Gallatin National Bank, which took a security interest in the boat. Gallatin filed a financing statement in Greene County, Pennsylvania, where the bank was located. But Pennsylvania law requires financing statements to be filed in the county of the debtor's residence, and the Lockoviches lived in Allegheny County. The Lockoviches soon washed up in bankruptcy court. Other creditors demanded that the boat be sold, claiming that Gallatin's security interest had been filed in the wrong place. Who wins?

Strategy: Gallatin National Bank obtained a special kind of security interest in the boat. Identify that type of interest. What special rights does this give to the bank? (See the "Result" at the end of this section.)

---

8. BIOC   A buyer in ordinary course of business (BIOC) takes the goods free of a security interest created by his seller even though the security interest is perfected. (pp. 546–547)

9. CHATTEL PAPER   A buyer who purchases chattel paper or an instrument in good faith in the ordinary course of his business and then obtains possession or control generally takes free of any security interest. (p. 548)

10. PRIORITY   Priority among secured parties is generally as follows: (1) A party with a perfected security interest takes priority over a party with an unperfected interest. (2) If neither secured party has perfected, the first interest to attach gets priority. (3) Between perfected security interests, the first to file or perfect wins. (pp. 550–553)

EXAM Strategy

Question: Barwell, Inc., sold McMann Golf Ball Co. a "preformer," a machine that makes golf balls, for $55,000. Barwell delivered the machine on February 20. McMann paid $3,000 down, the remainder to be paid over several years, and signed an agreement giving Barwell a security interest in the preformer. Barwell did not perfect its interest. On March 1, McMann borrowed $350,000 from First of America Bank, giving the bank a security interest in McMann's present and after-acquired property. First of America perfected by filing on March 2. McMann, of course, became insolvent, and both Barwell and the bank attempted to repossess the preformer. Who gets it?

Strategy: Two parties have a valid security interest in this machine. When that happens, there is a three-step process to determine which party gets priority. Apply it. (See the "Result" at the end of this section.)

11. **PMSI AND PRIORITY**   A PMSI may take priority over a conflicting perfected security interest (even one perfected earlier) if the holder of the PMSI meets certain conditions. (p. 552)

12. **CONTROL OR POSSESSION**   For deposit accounts, investment property, letter-of-credit rights, and instruments, a secured party who obtains control or possession takes priority over one who merely filed. (p. 551)

13. **DEFAULT**   When the debtor defaults, the secured party may take possession of the collateral on its own, without a court order, if it can do so without a breach of the peace. (pp. 553–556)

14. **DISPOSAL OF COLLATERAL**   A secured party may sell, lease, or otherwise dispose of the collateral in any commercially reasonable way; in many cases, it may accept the collateral in full or partial satisfaction of the debt. The secured party may also ignore the collateral and sue the debtor for the full debt. (p. 554)

EXAM Strategy

Question: Jerry Payne owed the First State Bank of Pflugerville $342,000. The loan was secured by a 9.25-carat diamond ring. The bank claimed a default on the loan and, without notifying Payne, sold the ring. But the proceeds did not pay off the full debt, and the bank sued Payne for the deficiency. Is Payne liable for the deficiency?

Strategy: A secured party may dispose of the collateral in any commercially reasonable way. What must the secured party do to ensure commercial reasonableness? (See the "Result" at the end of this section.)

15. **TERMINATION**   When the debtor pays the full debt, the secured party must complete a termination statement, notifying the public that it no longer claims a security interest in the collateral. (p. 556)

7. Result: Gallatin advanced the money that the Lockoviches used to buy the boat, meaning the bank obtained a PMSI. A PMSI in consumer goods perfects automatically, without filing. The boat was a consumer good. Gallatin's security interest perfected without any filing at all, and so the bank wins.

10. Result: This question is resolved by the first of those three steps. A party with a perfected security interest takes priority over a party with an unperfected interest. The bank wins because its perfected security interest takes priority over Barwell's unperfected interest.

14. Result: The secured party must give the debtor notice of the time and place of the sale. This ensures that the debtor may bid on the collateral, preventing an unreasonably low sales price. The bank failed to give such notice, and so it lost its right to the deficiency.

MULTIPLE-CHOICE QUESTIONS

1. **CPA QUESTION** Under the UCC Secured Transactions Article, which of the following actions will best perfect a security interest in a negotiable instrument against any other party?

   (a) Filing a security agreement

   (b) Taking possession of the instrument

   (c) Perfecting by attachment

   (d) Obtaining a duly executed financing statement

2. **CPA QUESTION** Under the UCC's Article on Secured Transactions, perfection of a security interest by a creditor provides added protection against other parties in the event the debtor does not pay its debts. Which of the following parties is not affected by perfection of a security interest?

   (a) Other prospective creditors of the debtor

   (b) The trustee in a bankruptcy case

   (c) A buyer in ordinary course of business

   (d) A subsequent personal injury judgment creditor

3. **CPA QUESTION** Mars, Inc., manufactures and sells VCRs on credit directly to wholesalers, retailers, and consumers. Mars can perfect its security interest in the VCRs it sells without having to file a financing statement or take possession of the VCRs if the sale is made to which of the following:

   (a) Retailers

   (b) Wholesalers that sell to distributors for resale

   (c) Consumers

   (d) Wholesalers that sell to buyers in ordinary course of business

4. When Michelle buys a laptop, she pays an extra fee so that the computer arrives at her door with the latest version of Microsoft Word pre-installed. Under Article 9, the word processing program is considered:

   (a) "goods"

   (b) "services"

   (c) "software"

   (d) none of the above

5. Alpha perfects its security interest by properly filing a financing statement on January 1, 2010. Alpha files a continuation statement on September 1, 2014. It files another continuation statement on September 1, 2018. When will Alpha's financing statement expire?

   (a) January 1, 2015

   (b) September 1, 2019

   (c) September 1, 2023

   (d) Never

ESSAY QUESTIONS

1. Eugene Ables ran an excavation company. He borrowed $500,000 from the Highland Park State Bank. Ables signed a note promising to repay the money and an agreement giving Highland a security interest in all of his equipment, including after-acquired equipment. Several years later, Ables agreed with Patricia Myers to purchase a Bantam Backhoe from her for $16,000, which he would repay at the rate of $100 per month, while he used the machine. Ables later defaulted on his note to Highland, and the bank attempted to take the backhoe. Myers and Ables contended that the bank had no right to take the backhoe. Was the backhoe covered by Highland's security interest? Did Ables have sufficient rights in the backhoe for the bank's security interest to attach?

2. The Copper King Inn, Inc., had money problems. It borrowed $62,500 from two of its officers, Noonan and Patterson, but that did not suffice to keep the inn going. So Noonan, on behalf of Copper King, arranged for the inn to borrow $100,000 from Northwest Capital, an investment company that worked closely with Noonan in other ventures. Copper King signed an agreement giving Patterson, Noonan, and Northwest a security interest in the inn's furniture and equipment. But the financing statement that the parties filed made no mention of Northwest. Copper King went bankrupt. Northwest attempted to seize assets, but other creditors objected. Is Northwest entitled to Copper King's furniture and equipment?

3. Sears sold a lawn tractor to Cosmo Fiscante for $1,481. Fiscante paid with his personal credit card. Sears kept a valid security interest in the lawnmower but did not perfect. Fiscante had the machine delivered to his business, Trackers Raceway Park, the only place he ever used the machine. When Fiscante was unable to meet his obligations, various creditors attempted to seize the lawnmower. Sears argued that because it had a purchase money security interest (PMSI) in the lawnmower, its interest had perfected automatically. Is Sears correct?

4. The state of Kentucky filed a tax lien against Panbowl Energy, claiming unpaid taxes. Six months later, Panbowl bought a powerful drill from Whayne Supply, making a down payment of $11,500 and signing a security agreement for the remaining debt of $220,000. Whayne

perfected the next day. Panbowl defaulted. Whayne sold the drill for $58,000, leaving a deficiency of just over $100,000. The state filed suit, seeking the $58,000 proceeds. The trial court gave summary judgment to the state, and Whayne appealed. Who gets the $58,000?

5. **YOU BE THE JUDGE WRITING PROBLEM** Dupont Feed bought and sold agricultural products. Dupont borrowed $300,000 from Wells Fargo Bank and gave Wells Fargo a security interest in all inventory, including after-acquired inventory. Wells Fargo perfected its interest by filing on June 17, 1982. Later, Dupont borrowed $150,000 from the Rushville National Bank and used the money to buy fertilizer. Dupont gave a PMSI to Rushville in the amount of $150,000. Rushville filed its financing statement in February 1984 at the County Recorder's office—the wrong place to file a financing statement for inventory. Then Dupont took possession of the fertilizer, and finally, in December 1984, Rushville filed correctly, with the Indiana Secretary of State. Dupont defaulted on both loans. Rushville seized the fertilizer, and Wells Fargo sued, claiming that it had perfected first. Rushville asserted that it had a PMSI, which took priority over an earlier-filed security interest. Does Rushville's PMSI take priority over Wells Fargo? (Go slowly, the rules are very technical.) **Argument for Rushville:** It is black-letter law that PMSIs take priority over virtually everything, including interests perfected earlier. We are not fools at Rushville: We would not loan $150,000 to buy inventory if our security interest in that inventory was instantly inferior to someone else's. **Argument for Wells Fargo:** A PMSI in inventory gets priority only if the secured party perfects before the debtor receives the collateral. When Dupont obtained the fertilizer, Rushville had not perfected because it had filed in the wrong office. It only perfected long after Dupont bought the inventory; thus, Rushville's PMSI does not get priority.

DISCUSSION QUESTIONS

1. **ETHICS** The Dannemans bought a Kodak copier worth over $40,000. Kodak arranged financing by GECC and assigned its rights to that company. Although the Dannemans thought they had purchased the copier on credit, the papers described the deal as a lease. The Dannemans had constant problems with the machine and stopped making payments. GECC repossessed the machine and, without notifying the Dannemans, sold it back to Kodak for $12,500, leaving a deficiency of $39,927. GECC sued the Dannemans for that amount. The Dannemans argued that the deal was not a lease, but a sale on credit. Why does it matter whether the parties had a sale or a lease? Is GECC entitled to its money? Finally, comment on the ethics. Why did the Dannemans not understand the papers they had signed? Who is responsible for that? Are you satisfied with the ethical conduct of the Dannemans? Kodak? GECC?

2. In the opening scenario, the bank demanded $5,000 from poor Sam for his Jeep that had been repossessed and sold to someone else. As we have seen, Article 9 gives the bank the right to demand this payment. But is that fair? Should Article 9 change so that a person like Sam does not have to pay? Or is the law reasonable now?

3. After reading this chapter, will your behavior as a consumer change? Are there any types of transactions that you might be more inclined to avoid?

4. After reading this chapter, will your future behavior as a businessperson change? What specific steps will you be most careful to take to protect your interests?

5. A perfected security interest is far from perfect. We examined several exceptions to normal perfection rules involving BIOCs, consumer goods, and so on. Are the exceptions reasonable? Should the UCC change to give the holder of a perfected interest absolute rights against absolutely everyone else?

CHAPTER 24

BANKRUPTCY

Three bankruptcy stories:

1. Tim's account: "First, there was Christmas. Was I really not going to buy my eight-year-old the Xbox he'd been begging for? Then my daughter's basketball team qualified for the nationals at Disney World. She's a talented player, and if she sticks with it, maybe she'll get a college scholarship. The kids had never been to Disney World. How could we say no? Then my car died. And I didn't get a bonus this year. Next thing you know, we had $27,000 in credit card debt. Then we had some uninsured medical bills. We were seriously underwater. There was just no way we could pay all that money back."

nuttakit/Shutterstock.com; © picsbyst/Shutterstock.com

> We were seriously underwater. There was just no way we could pay all that money back.

2. Kristen was a talented gardener and had always loved flowers. Sometimes she did the flowers for friends' weddings. When the guy who owned the local flower shop wanted to retire, it seemed a great opportunity to buy the business. She had lots of good ideas for improving it. First, she renovated the space so that people could hold parties there. She hired staff to keep the shop open longer hours. Everything went really well. Then the recession hit, and people cut back on nonessentials like flowers. How could she pay her loans?

3. General Motors (GM), once a symbol of American business, filed for bankruptcy in 2009. At the time, its liabilities were $90 billion more than its assets. It also had 325,000 employees and even more stakeholders: retired employees, car owners, suppliers, investors, and communities in which it operated and its employees lived and paid taxes. GM emerged from bankruptcy 40 days later with fewer brands, factories, and workers, but ready to do business. The next year, the company was profitable.

Bankruptcy law always has been and always will be controversial. Typically, in other countries, the goal of bankruptcy law was to protect creditors and punish debtors, even sending debtors to prison. Indeed, many of America's first settlers fled England to escape debtors' prison. As if to compensate for Europe's harsh regimes, American bankruptcy laws were traditionally more lenient toward debtors.[1]

The General Motors example illustrates the good news about American bankruptcy. It is efficient (40 days!) and effective at reviving ailing companies. Everyone—investors, employees, the country—benefits from GM's survival. And although Kristen's flower shop did not survive, bankruptcy laws will protect her so that she is not afraid to try entrepreneurship again.[2] New businesses fail more often than not, but they are nonetheless important engines of growth for our country. We all benefit from the jobs they create and the taxes they pay.

Tim represents the bad news in bankruptcy laws. Unfortunately, he is often the type of person who first comes to mind when people think about bankrupts. And people do not like Tim very much. They think: Why should he be rewarded for his irresponsibility, when I get stuck paying all my bills? But a more difficult bankruptcy process will probably not discourage Tim. He is the kind of guy who cares a lot about current pleasures and little about future pain. No matter what bankruptcy laws we have, he will not say no to Disney World. Should the laws become too onerous, businesses will fail, entrepreneurs will be discouraged, and the Tims of the world will continue to spend more than they should.

But maybe America has too much of a good thing. This nation has the highest bankruptcy rate in the world. In a recent year, there was one bankruptcy filing for every 200 Americans.[3] Clearly, bankruptcy laws play a vital role in our economy. They have the potential to resuscitate failing companies while encouraging entrepreneurship. At the same time, it is important not to enable irresponsible spendthrifts. Do American bankruptcy laws reach the right balance?

24-1 Overview of the Bankruptcy Code

The federal Bankruptcy Code (the Code) is divided into eight chapters. All chapters except one have odd numbers. Chapters 1, 3, and 5 are administrative rules that generally apply to all types of bankruptcy proceedings. These chapters, for example, define terms and establish the rules of the bankruptcy court. Chapters 7, 9, 11, 12, and 13 are substantive rules for different types of bankruptcies. All of these substantive chapters have one of two objectives—rehabilitation or liquidation.

24-1a Rehabilitation

The objective of Chapters 11 and 13 is to rehabilitate the debtor. Many debtors can return to financial health provided they have the time and breathing space to work out their problems. These chapters hold creditors at bay while the debtor develops a payment plan. In return for retaining some of their assets, debtors typically promise to pay creditors a portion of their future earnings.

---

[1]Bankruptcy law was so important to the drafters of the Constitution that they specifically listed it as one of the subjects that Congress had the right to regulate (Article 1, section 8).

[2]See, for example, Seung-Hyun Lee, Yasuhiro Yamakawa, Mike W. Peng, and Jay B. Barney, "How do bankruptcy laws affect entrepreneurship development around the world?" in the *Journal of Business Venturing*, JBV-05559, 2010.

[3]Some of these filings are by businesses, although that percentage is small. In the last 15 years, more than 95 percent of all bankruptcy filings have been by consumers.

24-1b Liquidation

Straight bankruptcy

Also known as *liquidation*, this form of bankruptcy mandates that the bankrupt's assets be distributed to creditors but the debtor has no obligation to share future earnings.

When debtors are unable to develop a feasible plan for rehabilitation under Chapter 11 or 13, Chapter 7 provides for liquidation (also known as a **straight bankruptcy).** Most of the debtor's assets are distributed to creditors, but the debtor has no obligation to share future earnings.

24-1c Chapter Description

The following options are available under the Bankruptcy Code:

Number	Topic	Description
Chapter 7	Liquidation	The bankrupt's assets are sold to pay creditors. If the debtor owns a business, it terminates. The creditors have no right to the debtor's future earnings.
Chapter 11	Reorganization	This chapter is designed for businesses and wealthy individuals. Businesses continue in operation, and creditors receive a portion of the debtor's current assets and future earnings.
Chapter 13	Consumer reorganization	Chapter 13 offers reorganization for the typical consumer. Creditors usually receive a portion of the individual's current assets and future earnings.

© Cengage Learning

Debtors are sometimes eligible to file under more than one chapter. No choice is irrevocable because both debtors and creditors have the right to ask the court to convert a case from one chapter to another at any time during the proceedings. For example, if creditors have asked for liquidation under Chapter 7, a bankrupt consumer may request rehabilitation under Chapter 13.

24-1d Goals

The Bankruptcy Code has three primary goals:

- **To preserve as much of the debtor's property as possible.** In keeping with this goal, the Code requires debtors to disclose all of their assets and prohibits them from transferring assets immediately before a bankruptcy filing.

- **To divide the debtor's assets fairly between the debtor and creditors.** On the one hand, creditors are entitled to payment. On the other hand, debtors are often so deeply in debt that full payment is virtually impossible in any reasonable period of time. The Code tries to balance the creditors' right to be paid with the debtors' desire to get on with their lives, unburdened by prior debts.

- **To divide the debtor's assets fairly among creditors.** Creditors rarely receive all they are owed, but at least they are treated fairly, according to established rules. Creditors do not benefit from simply being the first to file or from any other gamesmanship.

24-2 CHAPTER 7 LIQUIDATION

All bankruptcy cases proceed in a roughly similar pattern, regardless of chapter. We use Chapter 7 as a template to illustrate common features of all bankruptcy cases. Later on, the discussions of the other chapters will indicate how they differ from Chapter 7.

24-2a Filing a Petition

Any individual, partnership, corporation, or other business organization that lives, conducts business, or owns property in the United States can file under the Code. (Chapter 13, however, is available only to individuals.) The traditional term for someone who could not pay his debts was "bankrupt," but the Code uses the term **"debtor"** instead. We use both terms interchangeably.

A case begins with the filing of a bankruptcy petition in federal district court. The district court typically refers bankruptcy cases to a specialized bankruptcy judge. Either party can appeal the decision of the bankruptcy judge back to the district court and, from there, to the federal appeals court.

Debtors may go willingly into the bankruptcy process by filing a **voluntary petition,** or they may be dragged into court by creditors who file an **involuntary petition.** Originally, when the goal of bankruptcy laws was to protect creditors, voluntary petitions did not exist; all petitions were involuntary. Because the bankruptcy process is now viewed as being favorable to debtors, the vast majority of bankruptcy filings in this country are voluntary petitions.

VOLUNTARY PETITION

Any debtor (whether a business or an individual) has the right to file for bankruptcy. It is not necessary that the debtor's liabilities exceed assets. Debtors sometimes file a bankruptcy petition because cash flow is so tight they cannot pay their debts, even though they are not technically insolvent. However, *individuals* must meet two requirements before filing:

- Within 180 days before the filing, an individual debtor must undergo credit counseling with an approved agency.

- Individual debtors may only file under Chapter 7 if they earn less than the median income in their state or they cannot afford to pay back at least $7,475 over five years.[4] Generally, all other debtors must file under Chapter 11 or Chapter 13. (These Chapters require the bankrupt to repay some debt.)

The voluntary petition must include the following documents:

Document	Description
Petition	Begins the case. Easy to fill out, it requires checking a few boxes and typing in little more than name, address, and Social Security number.
List of Creditors	The names and addresses of all creditors.
Schedule of Assets and Liabilities	A list of the debtor's assets and debts.
Claim of Exemptions	A list of all assets that the debtor is entitled to keep.
Schedule of Income and Expenditures	The debtor's job, income, and expenses.
Statement of Financial Affairs	A summary of the debtor's financial history and current financial condition. In particular, the debtor must list any recent payments to creditors and any other property held by someone else for the debtor.

© Cengage Learning

Debtor
Someone who cannot pay his debts and files for protection under the Bankruptcy Code. Also known as **bankrupt**.

Voluntary petition
Filed by a debtor to initiate a bankruptcy case.

Involuntary petition
Filed by creditors to initiate a bankruptcy case.

---

[4]In some circumstances, debtors with income higher than $7,475 may still be eligible to file under Chapter 7, but the formula is highly complex and more than most readers want to know. The formula is available at 11 USC §707(b)(2)(A). Also, you can google "bapcpa means test" and then click on the Department of Justice website. The dollar amounts are updated every three years. You can find them by googling "federal register bankruptcy revision of dollar amounts."

INVOLUNTARY PETITION

Creditors may force a debtor into bankruptcy by filing an involuntary petition. The creditors' goal is to preserve as much of the debtor's assets as possible and to ensure that all creditors receive a fair share. Naturally, the Code sets strict limits—debtors cannot be forced into bankruptcy every time they miss a credit card payment. **An involuntary petition must meet all of the following requirements:**

- The debtor must owe at least $15,325 in unsecured claims to the creditors who file.[5]

- If the debtor has at least 12 creditors, 3 or more must sign the petition. If the debtor has fewer than 12 creditors, any one of them may file a petition.

- The creditors must allege either that a custodian for the debtor's property has been appointed in the prior 120 days or that the debtor has generally not been paying debts that are due.

What does "a custodian for the debtor's property" mean? *State* laws sometimes permit the appointment of a custodian to protect a debtor's assets. The Code allows creditors to pull a case out from under state law and into federal bankruptcy court by filing an involuntary petition. In the event that a debtor objects to an involuntary petition, the bankruptcy court must hold a trial to determine whether the creditors have met the Code's requirements.

Once a voluntary petition is filed or an involuntary petition approved, the bankruptcy court issues an **order for relief.** This order is an official acknowledgment that the debtor is under the jurisdiction of the court, and it is, in a sense, the start of the whole bankruptcy process. An involuntary debtor must now make all the filings that accompany a voluntary petition.

Order for relief

An official acknowledgment that a debtor is under the jurisdiction of the bankruptcy court.

24-2b Trustee

The trustee is responsible for gathering the bankrupt's assets and dividing them among creditors. This is a critical role in a bankruptcy case. Trustees are typically lawyers or CPAs, but any generally competent person can serve. Creditors have the right to elect the trustee, but often they do not bother. If the creditors do not elect a trustee, then the **U.S. Trustee** appoints one. Each region of the country has a U.S. Trustee selected by the U.S. attorney general. Besides appointing trustees as necessary, this U.S. Trustee oversees the administration of bankruptcy law in the region.

U.S. Trustee

Oversees the administration of bankruptcy law in a region.

24-2c Creditors

After the court issues an order for relief, the U.S. Trustee calls a meeting of all of the creditors. At the meeting, the bankrupt must answer (under oath) any question the creditors pose about his financial situation. If the creditors want to elect a trustee, they do so at this meeting.

After the meeting of creditors, unsecured creditors must submit a **proof of claim.** This document is a simple form stating the name of the creditor and the amount of the claim. The trustee and the debtor also have the right to file on behalf of a creditor. But if a claim is

Proof of claim

A form stating the name of an unsecured creditor and the amount of the claim against the debtor.

---

[5]In Chapter 23, on secured transactions, we discuss the difference between secured and unsecured claims at some length. A secured claim is one in which the creditor has the right to foreclose on a specific piece of the debtor's property (known as collateral) if the debtor fails to pay the debt when due. For example, if Lee borrows money from GMAC Finance to buy a car, the company has the right to repossess the car if Lee fails to repay the loan. GMAC's loan is secured. An unsecured loan has no collateral. If the debtor fails to repay, the creditor can make a general claim against the debtor but has no right to foreclose on a particular item of the debtor's property.

not filed, the creditor loses any right to be paid. The trustee, debtor, or any creditor can object to a claim on the grounds that the debtor does not really owe that money. The court then holds a hearing to determine the validity of the claim.

Secured creditors do not file proofs of claim unless the claim exceeds the value of their collateral. In this case, they are unsecured creditors for the excess amount and must file a proof of claim for it. Suppose that Deborah borrows $750,000 from Morton in return for a mortgage on her house. If she does not repay the debt, he can foreclose. Unfortunately, property values plummet, and by the time Deborah files a voluntary petition in bankruptcy, the house is worth only $500,000. Morton is a secured creditor for $500,000 and need file no proof of claim for that amount. But he is an unsecured creditor for $250,000 and will lose his right to this excess amount unless he files a proof of claim for it.

24-2d Automatic Stay

A fox chased by hounds has no time to make rational long-term decisions. What that fox needs is a safe burrow. Similarly, it is difficult for debtors to make sound financial decisions when hounded night and day by creditors shouting, "Pay me! Pay me!" The Code is designed to give debtors enough breathing space to sort out their affairs sensibly. An automatic stay is a safe burrow for the bankrupt. It goes into effect as soon as the petition is filed. An **automatic stay** prohibits creditors from collecting debts that the bankrupt incurred before the petition was filed. Creditors may not sue a bankrupt to obtain payment, nor may they take other steps, outside of court, to pressure the debtor for payment. The following case illustrates how persistent creditors can be.

> **Automatic stay**
>
> Prohibits creditors from collecting debts that the bankrupt incurred before the petition was filed.

JACKSON v. HOLIDAY FURNITURE

309 B.R. 33, 2004 Bankr. LEXIS 548
United States Bankruptcy Court for the Western District of Missouri, 2004

CASE SUMMARY

Facts: In April, Cora and Frank Jackson purchased a recliner chair on credit from Dan Holiday Furniture. They made payments until November. That month, they filed for protection under the Bankruptcy Code. Dan Holiday received a notice of the bankruptcy. This notice stated that the store must stop all efforts to collect on the Jacksons' debt.

Despite this notice, a Dan Holiday collector telephoned the Jacksons' house ten times between November 15 and December 1 and left a card in their door threatening repossession of the chair. On December 1, Frank—without Cora's knowledge—went to Dan Holiday to pay the $230 owed for November and December. He told the store owner about the bankruptcy filing, but allegedly added that he and his wife wanted to continue making payments directly to Dan Holiday.

In early January, employees at Dan Holiday learned that Frank had died the month before. Nevertheless, after Cora failed to make the payment for the month of January, a collector telephoned her house twenty-six times between January 14 and February 19. The store owner's sister left the following message on Cora's answering machine:

Hello. This is Judy over at Dan Holiday Furniture. And this is the last time I am going to call you. If you do not call me, I will be at your house. And I expect you to call me today. If there is a problem, I need to speak to you about it. You need to call me. We need to get this thing going. You are a January and February payment behind. And if you think you are going to get away with it, you've got another thing coming.

When Cora returned home on February 18, she found seven bright yellow slips of paper in her door jamb stating that a Dan Holiday truck had stopped by to repossess her furniture. The cards read:

OUR TRUCK was here to **REPOSSESS** Your furniture [*sic*]. 241-6933 Dan Holiday Furn. & Appl. Co.

The threat to send a truck was merely a ruse designed to frighten Cora. In truth, Dan Holiday did not really want the recliner back. The owner just wanted to talk directly with Cora about making payments.

Also on February 18, Dan Holiday sent Cora a letter stating that she had 24 hours to bring her account current or else **"Repossession** Will Be Made and **Legal Action Will Be**

Taken." That same day, Cora's bankruptcy attorney contacted Dan Holiday. Thereafter all collection activity ceased.

Issues: *Did Dan Holiday violate the automatic stay provisions of the Bankruptcy Code? What is the penalty for a violation?*

Decision: Dan Holiday was in violation of the Bankruptcy Code. The court awarded the Jacksons their actual damages, attorneys' fees, court costs, and punitive damages.

Reasoning: Anyone injured by a creditor who violates the automatic stay provisions is entitled to recover both actual damages (including court costs and attorneys' fees) as well as punitive damages where appropriate. In this case, the court awarded actual damages of $230, because that is how much Dan Holiday coerced from Frank Jackson on December 1. The Court also awarded the Jacksons their attorneys' fees and court costs in the amount of $1,142.42.

In addition, the Jacksons were entitled to punitive damages because Dan Holiday intentionally and flagrantly violated the automatic stay provision. Dan Holiday's conduct was remarkably bad—employees called the Jackson household no fewer than twenty-six times in January and February.

It was not clear how much the punitive damages should be because there was no evidence presented at trial about how much Dan Holiday could afford. The court was only aware that Dan Holiday was a family-owned business that had been in existence for fifty-two years. It seemed likely that it was a relatively small business. Therefore, the Court assessed a penalty of $100 for each illegal contact with the Jacksons after December 1, when it was crystal clear that Dan Holiday knew about the Jacksons' bankruptcy filing. Under this calculation, punitive damages totaled $2,800. The court believed that this penalty would be enough to sting the pocketbook of Dan Holiday and impress upon the company, its owners, and employees the importance of complying with the provisions of the Bankruptcy Code.

24-2e Bankruptcy Estate

Bankruptcy estate

The new legal entity created when a debtor files a bankruptcy petition. The debtor's existing assets pass into the estate.

The filing of the bankruptcy petition creates a new legal entity separate from the debtor—the **bankruptcy estate.** All of the bankrupt's assets pass to the estate except exempt property and new property that the debtor acquires after the petition is filed.

EXEMPT PROPERTY

Unpaid creditors may be angry, but generally they do not want the debtor to starve to death. **The Code permits *individual* debtors (but not organizations) to keep some property for themselves.** This exempt property saves the debtor from destitution during the bankruptcy process and provides the foundation for a new life once the process is over.

In this one area of bankruptcy law, the Code defers to state law. Although the Code lists various types of exempt property, it permits states to opt out of the federal system and define a different set of exemptions. A majority of states have indeed opted out of the Code, and for their residents, the Code exemptions are irrelevant. Alternatively, some states allow the debtor to choose between state or federal exemptions.

Under the *federal* Code, a debtor is allowed to exempt only $22,975 of the value of her home. If the house is worth more than that, the trustee sells it and returns $22,975 of the proceeds to the debtor. Most *states* exempt items such as the debtor's home, household goods, cars, work tools, disability and pension benefits, alimony, and health aids. Indeed, some states set no limit on the value of exempt property. Both Florida and Texas, for example, permit debtors to keep homes of unlimited value and a certain amount of land. (Texas also allows debtors to hang on to two firearms; athletic and sporting equipment; two horses, mules or donkeys and a saddle, blanket, and bridle for each; up to a total value of $60,000 per family.) Not surprisingly, these generous exemptions sometimes lead to abuses. Therefore, the Code provides that debtors can take advantage of state exemptions only if they have lived in that state for two years prior to the bankruptcy. And they can exempt only $155,675 of any house that was acquired during the 40 months before the bankruptcy.

VOIDABLE PREFERENCES

A major goal of the bankruptcy system is to divide the debtor's assets fairly among creditors. It would not be fair, or in keeping with this goal, if debtors were permitted to pay off some of their creditors immediately before filing a bankruptcy petition. These transfers are called **preferences** because they give unfair preferential treatment to some creditors. The trustee has the right to void such preferences.

Preferences can take two forms: payments and liens. A *payment* simply means that the debtor gives a creditor cash that would otherwise end up in the bankruptcy estate. A *lien* means a security interest in the debtor's property. In bankruptcy proceedings, secured creditors are more likely to be paid than unsecured creditors. If the debtor grants a security interest in specific property, he vaults that creditor out of the great unwashed mass of unsecured creditors and into the elite company of secured creditors. If it happens immediately before the petition is filed, it is unfair to other unsecured creditors.

The trustee can void any transfer (whether payment or lien) that meets all of the following requirements:

- The transfer was to a creditor of the bankrupt.

- It was to pay an existing debt.

- The creditor received more from the transfer than she would have received during the bankruptcy process.

- The debtor's liabilities exceeded assets at the time of the transfer.

- The transfer took place in the 90-day period before the filing of the petition.

In addition, the trustee can void a transfer to an insider that occurs in the *year* preceding the filing of the petition. **Insiders** are family members of an individual, officers and directors of a corporation, or partners of a partnership.

FRAUDULENT TRANSFERS

Suppose that a debtor sees bankruptcy approaching across the horizon like a tornado. He knows that, once the storm hits and he files a petition, everything he owns except a few items of exempt property will become part of the bankruptcy estate. Before that happens, he may be tempted to give some of his property to friends or family to shelter it from the tornado. If he succumbs to temptation, however, he is committing a fraudulent transfer.

A transfer is fraudulent if it is made within the year before a petition is filed and its purpose is to hinder, delay, or defraud creditors. The trustee can void any fraudulent transfer. The debtor has committed a crime and may be prosecuted.

Not all payments by a debtor prior to filing are considered voidable preferences or fraudulent transfers. **A trustee cannot void pre-petition payments made *in the ordinary course.*** In a business context, that means a trustee cannot void payments from, say, a grocery store to its regular cookie supplier. For consumers, the trustee cannot void payments below $650 or other routine payments, say, to the electric or water company. In these situations, the bankrupt is clearly not trying to cheat creditors. Even the insolvent are allowed to shower with the lights on.

Preferences
When a debtor unfairly pays creditors immediately before filing a bankruptcy petition.

Insider
Family members of an individual debtor, officers and directors of a corporation, or partners of a partnership.

> Even the insolvent are allowed to shower with the lights on.

EXAM Strategy

Question: Eddie and Lola appeared to be happily married. But then Eddie's business failed, and he owed millions. Suddenly, Lola announced that she wanted a divorce. Eddie immediately agreed to transfer all of the couple's remaining assets to her as part of the divorce settlement. Are you suspicious? Is there a problem?

Strategy: Was this a voidable preference or a fraudulent transfer? What difference does it make?

Result: In a voidable preference, the debtor makes an unfair transfer to a creditor. In a fraudulent transfer, the bankrupt's goal is to hold on to assets himself. In a case similar to this one, the court ruled that the transfer was fraudulent because Eddie intended to shield his assets from all creditors.

24-2f Payment of Claims

Imagine a crowded delicatessen on a Saturday evening. People are pushing and shoving because they know there is not enough food for everyone; some customers will go home hungry. The delicatessen could simply serve whoever pushes to the front of the line, or it could establish a number system to ensure that the most deserving customers are served first—longtime patrons or those who called ahead. The Code has, in essence, adopted a number system to prevent a free-for-all fight over the bankrupt's assets. Indeed, one of the Code's primary goals is to ensure that creditors are paid in the proper order, not according to who pushes to the front of the line.

All claims are placed in one of three classes: (1) secured claims, (2) priority claims, and (3) unsecured claims. The second class—priority claims—has seven subcategories; the third class—unsecured claims—has three. **The trustee pays the bankruptcy estate to the various classes of claims in order of rank.** A higher class is paid in full before the next class receives any payment at all. In the case of *priority* claims, each *subcategory* is paid in order, with the higher subcategory receiving full payment before the next subcategory receives anything. If there are not enough funds to pay an entire subcategory, all claimants in that group receive a *pro rata* share. The rule is different for unsecured claims. All categories of *unsecured* claims are treated the same, and if there are not enough funds to pay the *entire* class, everyone in the class shares *pro rata*. If, for example, there is only enough money to pay 10 percent of the claims owing to unsecured creditors, then each creditor receives 10 percent of her claim. In bankruptcy parlance, this is referred to as "getting 10 cents on the dollar." The debtor is entitled to any funds remaining after all claims have been paid. The payment order is shown in Exhibit 24.1.

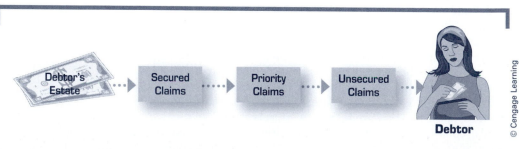

EXHIBIT 24.1   Payment Order

SECURED CLAIMS

Creditors whose loans are secured by specific collateral are paid first. Secured claims are fundamentally different from all other claims because they are paid by selling a specific asset, not out of the general funds of the estate. Sometimes, however, collateral is not valuable enough to pay off the entire secured debt. In this case, the creditor must wait in line with the unsecured creditors for the balance. Deborah (whom we met earlier in the section entitled "Creditors") borrowed $750,000 from Morton, secured by a mortgage on her house. By the time she files a voluntary petition, the house is worth only $500,000. Morton is a secured creditor for $500,000 and is paid that amount as soon as the trustee sells the house. But Morton is an unsecured creditor for $250,000 and will only receive this amount if the estate has enough funds to pay the unsecured creditors.

PRIORITY CLAIMS

There are seven subcategories of priority claims. Each category is paid in order, with the first group receiving full payment before the next group receives anything.

- *Alimony and child support.* The trustee must first pay any claims for alimony and child support. However, if the trustee is administering assets that could pay these support claims, then the trustee's fees are paid first.

- *Administrative expenses.* These include fees to the trustee, lawyers, and accountants.

- *Gap expenses.* If creditors file an involuntary petition, the debtor will continue to operate her business until the order for relief. Any expenses she incurs in the ordinary course of her business during this so-called **gap period** are paid now.

- *Payments to employees.* The trustee now pays back wages to the debtor's employees for work performed during the 180 days prior to the date of the petition. The trustee, however, can pay no more than $12,475 to each employee. Any other wages become unsecured claims.

- *Employee benefit plans.* The trustee pays what the debtor owes to employee pension, health, or life insurance plans for work performed during the 180 days prior to the date of the petition. The total payment for wages and benefits under this and the prior paragraph cannot exceed $12,475 times the number of employees.

- *Consumer deposits.* Any individual who has put down a deposit with the bankrupt for consumer goods is entitled to a refund of up to $2,775. If Stewart puts down a $3,000 deposit on a Miata sports car, he is entitled to a refund of $2,775 when the Trustie Car Lot goes bankrupt.

- *Taxes.* The trustee pays the debtor's income taxes for the three years prior to filing and property taxes for one prior year.

- *Intoxication injuries.* The trustee next pays the claims of anyone injured by a bankrupt who was driving a vehicle while drunk or on drugs.

Gap period
The period between the time that a creditor files an involuntary petition and the court issues the order for relief.

UNSECURED CLAIMS

Last, and frequently very much least, the trustee pays unsecured claims. All three of these unsecured subcategories have an equal claim and must be paid together.

- *Secured claims that exceed the value of the available collateral.* If funds permit, the trustee pays Morton the $250,000 that his collateral did not cover.

- *Priority* claims *that exceed the priority limits.* The trustee now pays employees, Stewart, and the tax authorities who were not paid in full the first time around because their claims exceeded the priority limits.

- *All other unsecured claims.* Unsecured creditors have now reached the delicatessen counter. They can only hope that some food remains.

24-2g Discharge

Filing a bankruptcy petition is embarrassing, time-consuming, and disruptive. It can affect the debtor's credit rating for years, making the simplest car loan a challenge. To encourage debtors to file for bankruptcy despite the pain involved, the Code offers a powerful incentive: the **fresh start.** Once a bankruptcy estate has been distributed to creditors, they cannot make a claim against the debtor for money owed before the filing, *whether or not they actually received any payment.* These pre-petition debts are **discharged.** All is forgiven, if not forgotten.

Discharge is an essential part of bankruptcy law. Without it, debtors would have little incentive to take part. To avoid abuses, however, the Code limits both the type of debts that can be discharged and the circumstances under which discharge can take place. In addition, an individual debtor must complete an approved course on financial management before receiving a discharge.

DEBTS THAT CANNOT BE DISCHARGED

The following debts are *never* discharged, and the debtor remains liable in full until they are paid:

- Income taxes for the three years prior to filing and property taxes for the prior year.

- Money obtained fraudulently. Kenneth Smith ran a home repair business that fleeced senior citizens by making unnecessary repairs. Three months after he was found liable for fraud, he filed a voluntary petition in bankruptcy. The court held that his liability on the fraud claim could not be discharged.[6]

- Any loan of more than $650 that a consumer uses to purchase luxury goods within 90 days before the order for relief is granted.

- Cash advances on a credit card totaling more than $925 that an individual debtor takes out within 70 days before the order for relief.

- Debts omitted from the Schedule of Assets and Liabilities that the debtor filed with the petition, if the creditor did not know about the bankruptcy and therefore did not file a proof of claim.

- Money that the debtor stole or obtained through a violation of fiduciary duty.

- Money owed for alimony or child support.

- Debts stemming from intentional and malicious injury.

- Fines and penalties owed to the government.

- Liability for injuries caused by the debtor while operating a vehicle under the influence of drugs or alcohol. (Yet another reason why friends don't let friends drive drunk.)

- Liability for breach of duty to a bank. During the 1980s, a record number of savings and loans failed because their officers had made too many risky loans

---

[6]*In re Smith*, 848 F.2d 813, 1988 U.S. App. LEXIS 8037 (7th Cir. 1988).

(in some cases to friends and family). This provision, added to the Code in 1990, was designed to prevent these officers from declaring bankruptcy to avoid their liability to bank shareholders.

- Debts stemming from a violation of securities laws.

- Student loans can be discharged only if repayment would cause undue hardship. As the following case illustrates, proving undue hardship is difficult.

IN RE STERN

288 B.R. 36; 2002 Bankr. LEXIS 1609
United States Bankruptcy Court for the Northern District of New York, 2002

CASE SUMMARY

Facts: James Stern took out student loans to attend Bates College and Syracuse College of Law. Afterwards, he had difficulty finding a job as a lawyer, so he opened his own practice. His annual income averaged $17,000, while his wife's earnings averaged $18,000.

Stern was sued for malpractice. Although he won the case, his malpractice premiums increased so much that he could no longer afford the insurance. Believing that his debt and default on his student loans made him unemployable as a lawyer, he moved with his wife to her native country, France. Unfortunately, he did not speak French and, therefore, could not obtain a job, even as a street sweeper. His wife's total income over six months in France was $2,200. Even more unfortunately, their expenses in France were higher than in the United States.

After paying back $27,000, Stern still owed $147,000 in student loans: $56,000 in principal and $91,000 in interest. Stern calculated that paying his debt would cost $1,167 per month over 30 years. He asked the court to discharge these student loans on grounds of undue hardship. As he put it, "I'm never going to be able to get a house, I'm never going to be able to have a car, and I won't you know, I want to have kids. I want to be responsible, and I can't—I can't possibly pay this amount and have a life, not with what I expect I'll be able to earn."

Issue: *Is Stern entitled to a discharge of his student loans?*

Decision: The court did not allow the discharge of these loans.

Reasoning: Educational loans are different from most business loans because they are made without security or cosigners. The lender must rely for repayment solely on the debtor's income (which presumably will increase as a result of the education). These loans are, in a sense, a mortgage on the student's future.

Although Stern has a J.D., he is not required to practice law. However, he must use his education to earn an income that will permit repayment of his loans.

Stern has not only failed to maximize his income, he has also failed to minimize his expenses. He moved to France where his expenses are higher, but he cannot even get a job as a street sweeper because he does not speak French.

Instead of repaying his loans, Stern would like to be able to buy a house or raise children. These desires, while understandable, do not constitute an undue hardship that warrants even a partial discharge. To obtain a discharge, Stern must prove more than his present inability to pay his student loans. He must also show that his current financial hardship is likely to be long term.

While Stern and his wife have experienced some bumps in the road, their future is under their control. They are young and healthy and have a good education. Indeed, the student loans permitted Stern to obtain an education that opens job opportunities not available to others who could not afford such an education.

CIRCUMSTANCES THAT PREVENT DEBTS FROM BEING DISCHARGED

Apart from identifying the *kinds* of debts that cannot be discharged, the Code also prohibits the discharge of debts under the following *circumstances:*

- **Business organizations.** Under Chapter 7 (but *not* the other Chapters), only the debts of individuals can be discharged, not those of business organizations. Once its assets have been distributed, the organization must cease operation. If it continues in business, it is responsible for all pre-petition debts. Shortly after E. G. Sprinkler Corp. entered into an agreement with its union employees, it filed for bankruptcy under Chapter 7. Its debts were discharged, and the company began operation again. A court ordered it to pay its obligations to the employees because, once the company resumed business, it was responsible for all of its pre-filing debts.[7]

- **Revocation.** A court can revoke a discharge within one year if it discovers the debtor engaged in fraud or concealment.

- **Dishonesty or bad faith behavior.** The court may deny discharge altogether if the debtor has, for example, made fraudulent transfers, hidden assets, falsified records, disobeyed court orders, refused to testify, or otherwise acted in bad faith. For instance, a court denied discharge under Chapter 7 to a couple who failed to list 15 pounds of marijuana on their Schedule of Assets and Liabilities. The court was unsympathetic to their arguments that a listing of this asset might have caused larger problems than merely being in debt.[8]

- **Repeated filings for bankruptcy.** Congress feared that some debtors, attracted by the lure of a fresh start, would make a habit of bankruptcy. Therefore, a debtor who has received a discharge under Chapter 7 or 11 cannot receive another discharge under Chapter 7 for at least eight years after the prior filing. And a debtor who received a prior discharge under Chapter 13 cannot in most cases receive one under Chapter 7 for at least six years.

Ethics   Banks and credit card companies lobbied Congress hard for the prohibition against repeated bankruptcy filings. They argued that irresponsible consumers run up debt and then blithely walk away. You might think that, if this were true, lenders would avoid customers with a history of bankruptcy. Research indicates, though, that lenders actually *target* those consumers, repeatedly sending them offers to borrow money. The reason is simple: These consumers are much more likely to take cash advances, which carry very high interest rates. And this is one audience that *must* repay its loans for the simple reason that these borrowers cannot obtain a discharge again anytime soon.[9] Is this strategy ethical?

---

[7]*In re Goodman*, 873 F.2d 598, 1989 U.S. App. LEXIS 5472 (2d Cir. 1989).
[8]*In re Tripp*, 224 B.R. 95, 1998 Bankr. LEXIS 1108 (1998).
[9]See Katherine M. Porter, "Bankrupt Profits: The Credit Industry's Business Model for Postbankruptcy Lending," University of Iowa Legal Studies Research Paper No. 07–26, *Iowa Law Review*, Vol. 94, 2008. This paper is available by googling "ssrn katherine porter bankrupt profits."

EXAM Strategy

Question: Someone stole a truck full of cigarettes. Zeke found the vehicle abandoned at a truck stop. Not being a thoughtful fellow, he took the truck and sold it with its cargo. Although Tobacco Company never found out who stole the truck originally, it did discover Zeke's role. A court ordered Zeke to pay Tobacco $50,000. He also owed his wife $25,000 in child support. Unfortunately, he only had $20,000 in assets. After he files for bankruptcy, who will get paid what?

Strategy: There are two issues: the order in which the debts are paid and whether they will be discharged.

Result: Child support is a priority claim, so that will be paid first. In a similar case, the court refused to discharge the claim over the theft of the truck, ruling that that was an intentional and malicious injury. Nor will a court discharge the child support claim. So Zeke will be on the hook for both debts, but the child support must be paid first.

REAFFIRMATION

Sometimes debtors are willing to **reaffirm** a debt, meaning they promise to pay even after discharge. They may want to reaffirm a secured debt to avoid losing the collateral. For example, a debtor who has taken out a loan secured by a car may reaffirm that debt so that the finance company will not repossess it. Sometimes debtors reaffirm because they feel guilty or want to maintain a good relationship with the creditor. They may have borrowed from a family member or an important supplier. Because discharge is a fundamental pillar of the bankruptcy process, creditors are not permitted to unfairly pressure the bankrupt. To be valid, the reaffirmation must:

Reaffirm
To promise to pay a debt even after it is discharged.

- Not violate common law standards for fraud, duress, or unconscionability. If creditors force a bankrupt into reaffirming a debt, the reaffirmation is invalid.

- Have been filed in court before the discharge is granted.

- Include the detailed disclosure statement required by the statute (§524).

- Be approved by the court if the debtor is not represented by an attorney or if, as a result of the reaffirmed debt, the bankrupt's expenses exceed his income.

   In the following case, the debtor sought to reaffirm the loan on his truck. He may have been afraid that if he did not, the lender would repossess it, leaving him stranded. It is hard to get around Dallas without a car. Should the court permit the reaffirmation?

In Re Grisham

436 B.R. 896; 2010 Bankr. LEXIS 2907
United States Bankruptcy Court for the Northern District of Texas, 2010

CASE SUMMARY

Facts: William Grisham owned a Dodge truck. When he filed for bankruptcy, the vehicle was worth $16,000, but he owed $17,500 on it. The monthly payments were $400. In addition, Grisham owed $200,000 in non-dischargeable debt and $70,000 in unsecured loans.

Grisham sought to reaffirm the truck loan. Should the court allow him to do so?

Issue: *Would reaffirmation of this debt create an undue hardship for the debtor?*

Decision: The court did not approve the reaffirmation.

Reasoning: The debtor's expenses are $1,100 a month higher than his income. He owns no real estate and is living rent-free with a relative. The truck is worth less than he owes on it. The debtor also has enormous non-dischargeable debts. While the monthly payments on the vehicle are not eye-popping, they are nonetheless unduly burdensome for him.

The whole point of a bankruptcy filing is to obtain a fresh start. It is about belt-tightening and shedding past bad habits. Too often, bankrupts do not understand this principle and instead want to go forward in a manner that will impair their fresh start and perpetuate bad habits from the past.

The court presumes that the debtor wants to reaffirm the debt to prevent the lender from repossessing the truck. But the debtor never explained why he especially needed this vehicle. The time has come simply to say "good riddance" to it.

The court will not stamp its seal of approval on the debtor's reaffirmation of the debt. To do so would create a hardship on this debtor and does not otherwise seem justified.

24-3 Chapter 11 Reorganization

For a business, the goal of a Chapter 7 bankruptcy is euthanasia—putting it out of its misery by shutting it down and distributing its assets to creditors. Chapter 11 has a much more complicated and ambitious goal—resuscitating a business so that it can ultimately emerge as a viable economic concern, as General Motors did. Keeping a business in operation benefits virtually all company stakeholders: employees, customers, creditors, shareholders, and the community.

Both individuals and businesses can use Chapter 11. Businesses usually prefer Chapter 11 over Chapter 7 because Chapter 11 does not require them to dissolve at the end, as Chapter 7 does. The threat of death creates a powerful incentive to try rehabilitation under Chapter 11. Individuals, however, tend to prefer Chapter 13 because it is easier and cheaper for them.

A Chapter 11 proceeding follows many of the same steps as Chapter 7: a petition (either voluntary or involuntary), order for relief, meeting of creditors, proofs of claim, and an automatic stay. There are, however, some significant differences.

24-3a Debtor in Possession

Debtor in possession
The debtor acts as trustee in a Chapter 11 bankruptcy.

Chapter 11 does not require a trustee. The bankrupt is called the **debtor in possession** and, in essence, acts as trustee. The debtor in possession has two jobs: to operate the business and to develop a plan of reorganization. A trustee is chosen only if the debtor is incompetent or uncooperative. In that case, the creditors can elect the trustee, but if they do not choose to do so, the U.S. Trustee appoints one.

24-3b Creditors' Committee

In a Chapter 11 case, the creditors' committee is important because typically there is no neutral trustee to watch over their interests. The committee generally protects the interests of its constituency and may play a role in developing the plan of reorganization. Moreover, the Code requires the committee to communicate diligently with all creditors. The U.S. Trustee typically appoints the seven largest *un*secured creditors to the committee. However, the court may require the U.S. Trustee to appoint some small-business creditors as well. Secured creditors do not serve because their interests require less protection. If the debtor is a corporation, the U.S. Trustee may also appoint a committee of shareholders. The Code refers to the **claims** of creditors and the **interests** of shareholders.

24-3c Plan of Reorganization

Once the bankruptcy petition is filed, an automatic stay goes into effect to provide the debtor with temporary relief from creditors. The next stage is to develop a plan of reorganization that provides for the payment of debts and the continuation of the business. For the first 120 days (which the court can extend up to 18 months), the debtor has the exclusive right to propose a plan. If the debtor fails to file a plan, or if the court rejects it, then creditors and shareholders can develop their own plan.

24-3d Confirmation of the Plan

Anyone who proposes a plan of reorganization must also prepare a **disclosure statement** to be mailed out with the plan. The purpose of this statement is to provide creditors and shareholders with enough information to make an informed judgment. The statement describes the company's business, explains the plan, calculates the company's liquidation value, and assesses the likelihood that the debtor can be rehabilitated. The court must approve a disclosure statement before it is sent to creditors and shareholders.

All the creditors and shareholders have the right to vote on the plan of reorganization. In preparation for the vote, each creditor and shareholder is assigned to a class. Everyone in a class has similar claims or interests. Chapter 11 classifies claims in the same way as Chapter 7: (1) secured claims, (2) priority claims, and (3) unsecured claims. Each secured claim is usually in its own class because each one is secured by different collateral. Shareholders are also divided into classes depending upon their interests. For example, holders of preferred stock are in a different class from common shareholders.

Creditors and shareholders receive a ballot with their disclosure statement to vote for or against the plan of reorganization. After the vote, the bankruptcy court holds a **confirmation hearing** to determine whether it should accept the plan. **The court will approve a plan if a majority *of each class* votes in favor of it *and* if the "yes" votes hold at least two-thirds of the total debt in that class.**

Even if some classes vote against the plan, the court can still confirm it under what is called a **cramdown** (as in "the plan is crammed down the creditors' throats"). The court will not impose a cramdown unless, in its view, the plan is feasible and fair. If the court rejects the plan of reorganization, the creditors must develop a new one. In the following case, the court did impose a cramdown.

Cramdown
The bankruptcy court confirms a plan of reorganization despite a negative vote from one or more classes of creditors and/or shareholders.

In Re Fox

2000 Bankr. LEXIS 1713
United States Bankruptcy Court, District of Kansas, 2000

CASE SUMMARY

Facts: Donald Fox founded Midland Fumigant, Inc., a company in the business of fumigating stored wheat, corn, and other grain. In a prior case, a competitor, United Phosphorus, Ltd., obtained a verdict of $2 million against Midland and Fox for fraud.

Unable to pay the judgment, Fox filed a voluntary petition under Chapter 11 of the Bankruptcy Code. His plan of reorganization envisioned that he would use revenues from Midland to pay off his creditors in full over five years, with interest. To ensure that the plan of reorganization was feasible, Fox hired CPA Kirk W. Wiesner to analyze Midland's financial statements and prepare projections of its income and expenses. Wiesner also reviewed Midland's operations, business, products, and the industry. He concluded that the plan's projections were conservative and could easily be met.

Midland had six classes of creditors. All of the classes accepted the plan, except the two classes in which United was a member. The bankruptcy judge noted that United had an incentive to oppose Midland's reorganization because this industry was highly competitive and, if Midland were to cease operations, United would be able to raise its prices substantially.

Issue: *Was Fox's plan of reorganization feasible and fair? Should the court impose a cramdown?*

Decision: Fox's plan of reorganization was feasible and fair. The court did impose a cramdown.

Reasoning: Fox proposed a Plan that paid all creditors in full, with interest. United, the only creditor to object, was to be paid in full within sixteen months.

Fox's goal under the Plan—to keep his business in operation—is consistent with the purposes of the Code. But the Code's objective is also to prevent visionary plans that promise creditors and shareholders more than the debtor can possibly achieve. United contends that Fox's Plan is not feasible because its financial projections are unrealistic. United's fears, however, are not supported by the evidence. An expert witness, Kirk Wiesner, analyzed Midland's financial statements and determined that Midland would have sufficient income and cash flow to comply with the Plan. The court finds Wiesner a reliable witness because his projections in the past have been conservative.

The Plan has a reasonable chance of success and is not likely to result in liquidation or further financial reorganization. Moreover, the U.S. Trustee has filed a statement in support of confirmation. Therefore, debtor's Plan is confirmed over the objection of United and over the dissenting votes of two classes of creditors.

24-3e Discharge

A confirmed plan of reorganization is binding on the debtor, creditors, and shareholders. **The debtor now owns the assets in the bankruptcy estate, free of all obligations except those listed in the plan.** Under a typical plan of reorganization, the debtor gives some current assets to creditors and also promises to pay them a portion of future earnings. In contrast, the Chapter 7 debtor typically relinquishes all assets (except exempt property) to creditors but then has no obligation to turn over future income. Exhibit 24.2 illustrates the steps in a Chapter 11 bankruptcy.

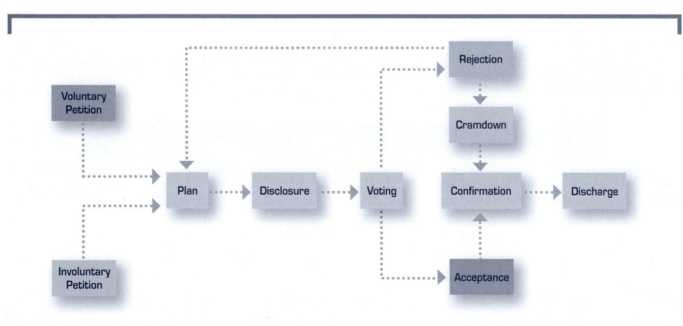

© Cengage Learning

EXHIBIT 24.2   The Steps in a Chapter 11 Bankruptcy

24-3f Small-Business Bankruptcy

Out of concern that the lengthy procedure in Chapter 11 was harming the creditors of small businesses, in 2005 Congress included provisions designed to speed up the process for businesses with less than $2 million in debt. After the order for relief, the bankrupt has the exclusive right to file a plan for 180 days. Both a plan and a disclosure statement must be filed within 300 days. The court must confirm or reject the plan within 45 days after its filing. If these deadlines are not met, the case can be converted to Chapter 7 or dismissed.

24-4 CHAPTER 13 CONSUMER REORGANIZATIONS

The purpose of Chapter 13 **is to rehabilitate an individual debtor.** It is not available at all to businesses or to individuals with more than $383,175 in unsecured debts or $1,149,525 in secured debts. Under Chapter 13, the bankrupt consumer typically keeps most of her assets in exchange for a promise to repay some of her debts using future income. Therefore, to be eligible, the debtor must have a regular source of income. Individuals usually choose this chapter because it is easier and cheaper than Chapters 7 and 11. Consequently, more money is retained for both creditors and debtor.

As you read at the beginning of the chapter, debtors can convert from one chapter to another as they wish. In the following case, the trustees objected to a conversion. The case went all the way to the Supreme Court, which split 5–4. How would you have voted?

You Be the Judge

MARRAMA V. CITIZENS BANK OF MASSACHUSETTS

549 U.S. 365; 127 S. Ct. 1105; 2007 U.S. LEXIS 2651
Supreme Court of the United States, 2007

Facts: When Robert Marrama filed a voluntary petition under Chapter 7, he lied. Although he disclosed that he was the sole beneficiary of a trust that owned a house in Maine, he listed its value as zero. Marrama also denied that he had transferred any property during the prior year. Neither statement was true: The Maine property was valuable (how many houses are worth zero?), and he had given it for free to the trust seven months prior to filing for bankruptcy protection. Marrama also lied when he claimed that he was not entitled to a tax refund. In fact, he knew that a check for $8,700 from the Internal Revenue Service was in the mail.

Once Marrama found out that the bankruptcy trustees were going after the Maine property, he filed a notice to convert his Chapter 7 bankruptcy to Chapter 13. The trustee and creditors objected. They contended that because Marrama had acted in bad faith when he tried to conceal the Maine property from his creditors, he should not be permitted to convert. The bankruptcy court and the appeals court agreed. The Supreme Court granted *certiorari*.

You Be The Judge: *Can a bankruptcy court refuse to allow a debtor to convert from Chapter 7 to Chapter 13?*

Argument for Marrama: Under the Bankruptcy Code, a Chapter 7 debtor may convert a case, with only two restrictions. First, the bankrupt can convert only once. Second, the debtor must meet the conditions that would have been required for him to file under the new chapter in the first place. Nothing in the Code suggests that a bankruptcy judge has the right to prohibit a conversion because of the debtor's bad faith.

If a debtor acts in bad faith, the court has other remedies: It can convert the case back to a Chapter 7 liquidation; it can refuse to approve the plan of payment; or it can charge the debtor with perjury. That is the law, whether the trustee and creditors like it or not.

Argument for the Bankruptcy Trustee: A bankruptcy court has the unquestioned right to dismiss a Chapter 13 petition if the debtor demonstrates bad faith. There seems no logical reason why a court would have the right to dismiss a case for bad faith but not the right to prohibit a filing under Chapter 13 to begin with. In both cases, the court is simply saying that the individual does not qualify as a debtor under Chapter 13. That individual is not a member of the class of honest but unfortunate debtors whom the bankruptcy laws were enacted to protect.

EXAM Strategy

Question: Why did Marrama first file under Chapter 7 and then try to switch to Chapter 13 after he was caught lying?

Strategy: This question is a good test of your understanding of the advantages and disadvantages of the different chapters. For help in answering this question, you might want to look at the chart at the end of the chapter. Remember that Chapter 7 is a liquidation provision—it takes more of the bankrupt's money upfront but then discharges his debts and gives him a fresh start for the future. Chapter 13 does not take as many assets during the bankruptcy process but may attach all the debtor's disposable income for the next five years.

Result: Marrama filed under Chapter 7 in the hope that he could hold on to his house while all his debts were discharged. Once that plan failed, he tried to switch to Chapter 13 in the hope that he could keep the house and give up his disposable income instead. This case illustrates the different emphases of Chapters 7 and 13.

A bankruptcy under Chapter 13 generally follows the same course as Chapter 11: The debtor files a petition, creditors submit proofs of claim, the court imposes an automatic stay, the debtor files a plan, and the court confirms the plan. But there are some differences.

24-4a Beginning a Chapter 13 Case

To initiate a Chapter 13 case, the debtor must file a voluntary petition. **Creditors cannot use an involuntary petition to force a debtor into** Chapter 13. In all Chapter 13 cases, the U.S. Trustee appoints a trustee to supervise the debtor, although the debtor remains in possession of the bankruptcy estate. The trustee also serves as a central clearinghouse for the debtor's payments to creditors. The debtor pays the trustee who, in turn, transmits these funds to creditors. For this service, the trustee is allowed up to 10 percent of the payments.

24-4b Plan of Payment

The debtor must file a plan of payment within 15 days after filing the voluntary petition. Only the debtor can file a plan; the creditors have no right to file their own version. Under the plan, the debtor must (1) commit some future earnings to pay off debts, (2) promise to pay all secured and priority claims in full, and (3) treat all remaining classes equally. If the plan does not provide for the debtor to pay off creditors in full, then all of the debtor's disposable income for the next five years must go to creditors.

Within 30 days after filing the plan of payment, the debtor must begin making payments to the trustee under the plan. The trustee holds these payments until the plan is confirmed and then transmits them to creditors. The debtor continues to make payments to the trustee until the plan has been fully implemented. If the plan is rejected, the trustee returns the payments to the debtor.

Only the bankruptcy court has the authority to confirm or reject a plan of payment. Creditors have no right to vote on it. However, to confirm a plan, the court must ensure that:

- The creditors have the opportunity to voice their objections at a hearing;

- All of the unsecured creditors receive at least as much as they would have if the bankruptcy estate had been liquidated under Chapter 7;

- The plan is feasible and the bankrupt will be able to make the promised payments;

- The plan does not extend beyond three years without good reason and in no event lasts longer than five years; and

- The debtor is acting in good faith, making a reasonable effort to pay obligations.

24-4c Discharge

Once confirmed, a plan is binding on all creditors whether they like it or not. **The debtor is washed clean of all pre-petition debts except those provided for in the plan, but, unlike Chapter 7, the debts are not *permanently* discharged.** If the debtor violates the plan, all of the debts are revived, and the court may either dismiss the case or convert it to a liquidation proceeding under Chapter 7. The debts become permanently discharged only when the bankrupt fully complies with the plan.

Note, however, that any debtor who has received a discharge under Chapter 7 or 11 within the prior four years, or under Chapter 13 within the prior two years, is not eligible under Chapter 13.

If the debtor's circumstances change, the debtor, the trustee, or unsecured creditors can ask the court to modify the plan. Most such requests come from debtors whose income has declined. However, if the debtor's income rises, the creditors or the trustee can ask that payments increase, too.

Chapter Conclusion

Whenever an individual or organization incurs more debts than it can pay in a timely fashion, everyone loses. The debtor loses control of his assets and the creditors lose money. Bankruptcy laws cannot create assets where there are none (or not enough), but they can ensure that the debtor's assets, however limited, are fairly divided between the debtor and creditors. Any bankruptcy system that accomplishes this goal must be deemed a success. Is the U.S. Bankruptcy Code fair?

Exam Review

This chart sets out the important elements of each bankruptcy chapter.

	Chapter 7	Chapter 11	Chapter 13
Objective	Liquidation	Reorganization	Consumer reorganization
Who May Use It	Individual or organization	Individual or organization	Individual
Type of Petition	Voluntary or involuntary	Voluntary or involuntary	Only voluntary
Administration of Bankruptcy Estate	Trustee	Debtor in possession (trustee selected only if debtor is unable to serve)	Trustee
Selection of Trustee	Creditors have right to elect trustee; otherwise, U.S. Trustee makes appointment	Usually no trustee	Appointed by U.S. Trustee
Participation in Formulation of Plan	No plan is filed	Both creditors and debtor can propose plans	Only debtor can propose a plan
Creditor Approval of Plan	Creditors do not vote	Creditors vote on plan, but court may approve plan without the creditors' support	Creditors do not vote on plan
Impact on Debtor's Post-petition Income	Not affected; debtor keeps all future earnings	Must contribute toward payment of pre-petition debts	Must contribute toward payment of pre-petition debts

© Cengage Learning

EXAM Strategy

1. Question: Mark Milbank's custom furniture business was unsuccessful, so he repeatedly borrowed money from his wife and her father. He promised that the loans would enable him to spend more time with his family. Instead, he spent more time in bed with his next-door neighbor. After the divorce, his ex-wife and her father demanded repayment of the loans. Milbank filed for protection under Chapter 13. What could his ex-wife and her father do to help their chances of being repaid?

Strategy: First ask yourself what kind of creditor they are: secured or unsecured. Then think about what creditors can do to get special treatment. (See the "Result" at the end of this section.)

EXAM Strategy

2. After a jury ordered actor Kim Basinger to pay $8 million for violating a movie contract, she filed for bankruptcy protection, claiming $5 million in assets and $11 million in liabilities. Under which Chapter should she file? Why?

Strategy: Look at the requirements for each Chapter. Was Basinger eligible for Chapter 13? What would be the advantages and disadvantages of Chapters 7 and 11? (See the "Result" at the end of this section.)

1. Result: The father and the ex-wife were unsecured creditors who, as a class, come last on the priority list. The court granted their request not to discharge their loans on the grounds that Milbank had acted in bad faith.

2. Result: Basinger was not eligible to file under Chapter 13 because she had debts of $11 million. She first filed under Chapter 11 in an effort to retain some of her assets, but then her creditors would not approve her plan of reorganization, so she converted to liquidation under Chapter 7.

MULTIPLE-CHOICE QUESTIONS

1. **CPA QUESTION** A voluntary petition filed under the liquidation provisions of Chapter 7 of the federal Bankruptcy Code:

   (a) is not available to a corporation unless it has previously filed a petition under the reorganization provisions of Chapter 11 of the Code.

   (b) automatically stays collection actions against the debtor **except** by secured creditors.

   (c) will be dismissed unless the debtor has 12 or more unsecured creditors whose claims total at least $5,000.

   (d) does **not** require the debtor to show that the debtor's liabilities exceed the fair market value of assets.

2. **CPA QUESTION** Decal Corp. incurred substantial operating losses for the past three years. Unable to meet its current obligations, Decal filed a petition of reorganization under Chapter 11 of the federal Bankruptcy Code. Which of the following statements is correct?

   (a) A creditors' committee, if appointed, will consist of unsecured creditors.

   (b) The court must appoint a trustee to manage Decal's affairs.

   (c) Decal may continue in business only with the approval of a trustee.

   (d) The creditors' committee must select a trustee to manage Decal's affairs.

3. **CPA QUESTION** Unger owes a total of $150,000 to eight unsecured creditors and one fully secured creditor. Quincy is one of the unsecured creditors and is owed $32,000. Quincy has filed a petition against Unger under the liquidation provisions of Chapter 7 of the federal Bankruptcy Code. Unger has been unable to pay debts as they become due. Unger's liabilities exceed Unger's assets. Unger has filed papers opposing the bankruptcy petition. Which of the following statements regarding Quincy's petition is correct?

   (a) It will be dismissed because the secured creditor failed to join in the filing of the petition.

   (b) It will be dismissed because three unsecured creditors must join in the filing of the petition.

   (c) It will be granted because Unger's liabilities exceed Unger's assets.

   (d) It will be granted because Unger is unable to pay Unger's debts as they become due.

4. Dale is in bankruptcy proceedings under Chapter 13. Which of the following statements is true?

   (a) His debtors must have filed an involuntary petition.

   (b) His unsecured creditors will be worse off than if he had filed under Chapter 7.

   (c) All of his debts are discharged as soon as the court approves his plan.

   (d) His creditors have an opportunity to voice objections to his plan.

5. Grass Co. is in bankruptcy proceedings under Chapter 11. _____ serves as trustee. In the case of _____ the court can approve a plan of reorganization over the objections of the creditors.

   (a) The debtor in possession; a cramdown

   (b) A person appointed by the U.S. Trustee; fraud

   (c) The head of the creditors' committee; reaffirmation

   (d) The U.S. Trustee; voidable preference

ESSAY QUESTIONS

1. James, the owner of an auto parts store, told his employee, Rickey, to clean and paint some tires in the basement. Highly flammable gasoline fumes accumulated in the poorly ventilated space. James threw a firecracker into the basement as a joke, intending only to startle Rickey. Sparks from the firecracker caused an explosion and fire that severely burned him. Rickey filed a personal injury suit against James for $1 million. Is this debt dischargeable under Chapter 7?

2. Mary Price went for a consultation about a surgical procedure to remove abdominal fat. When Robert Britton met with her, he wore a name tag that identified him as a doctor, and was addressed as "doctor" by the nurse. Britton then examined Price, touching her stomach and showing her where the incision would be made. But Britton was the office manager, not a doctor. Although a doctor actually performed the surgery on Price, Britton was present. It turned out that the doctor left a tube in Price's body at the site of the incision. The area became infected, requiring corrective surgery. A jury awarded Price $275,000 in damages in a suit against Britton. He subsequently filed a Chapter 7 bankruptcy petition. Is this judgment dischargeable in bankruptcy court?

3. **YOU BE THE JUDGE WRITING PROBLEM** Lydia D'Ettore received a degree in computer programming at the DeVry Institute of Technology, with a grade point average of 2.51. To finance her education, she borrowed $20,516.52 from a federal student loan program. After graduation, she could not find a job in her field, so she went to work as a clerk at an annual salary of $12,500. D'Ettore and her daughter lived with her parents free of charge. After setting aside $50 a month in savings and paying bills that included $233 for a new car (a Suzuki Samurai) and $50 for jewelry from Zales, her disposable income was $125 per month. D'Ettore asked the bankruptcy court to discharge the debts she owed DeVry for her education. Did the debts to the DeVry Institute impose an undue hardship on D'Ettore? **Argument for D'Ettore:** Lydia D'Ettore lives at home with her parents. Even so, her disposable income is a meager $125 a month. She would have to spend every single penny of her disposable income for nearly 15 years to pay back her $20,500 debt to DeVry. That would be an undue hardship. **Argument for the Creditors:** The U.S. government guaranteed D'Ettore's loan. Therefore, if the court discharges it, the American taxpayer will have to pay the bill. Why should taxpayers subsidize an irresponsible student? D'Ettore must also stop buying new cars and jewelry. And why should the government pay her debts while she saves money every month?

4. Dr. Ibrahim Khan caused an automobile accident in which a fellow physician, Dolly Yusufji, became a quadriplegic. Khan signed a contract for the lifetime support of Yusufji. When he refused to make payments under the contract, she sued him and obtained a judgment for $1,205,400. Khan filed a Chapter 11 petition. At the time of the bankruptcy hearing, five years after the accident, Khan had not paid Yusufji anything. She was dependent on a motorized wheelchair; he drove a Rolls-Royce. Is Khan's debt dischargeable under Chapter 11?

5. After filing for bankruptcy, Yvonne Brown sought permission of the court to reaffirm a $6,000 debt to her credit union. The debt was unsecured, and she was under no obligation to pay it. The credit union had published the following notice in its newsletter:

> If you are thinking about filing bankruptcy, THINK about the long-term implications. This action, filing bankruptcy, closes the door on TOMORROW. Having no credit means no ability to purchase cars, houses, credit cards. Look into the future—no loans for the education of your children.

Should the court approve Brown's reaffirmation?

Discussion Questions

1. **ETHICS** On November 5, Hawes, Inc., a small subcontractor, opened an account with Basic Corp., a supplier of construction materials. Hawes promised to pay its bills within 30 days of purchase. Although Hawes purchased a substantial quantity of goods on credit from Basic, it made few payments on the accounts until the following March, when it paid Basic over $21,000. On May 14, Hawes filed a voluntary petition under Chapter 7. Does the bankruptcy trustee have a right to recover this payment? Is it fair to Hawes's other creditors if Basic is allowed to keep the $21,000 payment?

2. Look on the web for your state's rules on exempt property. Compared with other states and the federal government, is your state generous or stingy with exemptions? In considering a new bankruptcy statute, Congress struggled mightily over whether or not to permit state exemptions at all. Is it fair for exemptions to vary by state? Why should someone in one state fare better than his or her neighbor across the state line?

3. Some states permit debtors an unlimited exemption on their homes. Is it fair for bankrupts to be allowed to keep multimillion dollar homes while their creditors remain unpaid? But other states allow as little as $5,000. Should bankrupts be thrown out on the street? What amount is fair?

4. What about the rules regarding repeated bankruptcy filings? Debtors cannot obtain a discharge under Chapter 7 within eight years of a prior filing. Under Chapter 13, no discharge is available within four years of a prior Chapter 7 or 11 filing and within two years of a prior Chapter 13 filing. Are these rules too onerous, too lenient, or just right?

5. A bankrupt who owns a house has the option of either paying the mortgage or losing his home. The only advantage of bankruptcy is that his debt to the bank is discharged. The U.S. House of Representatives passed a bill permitting a bankruptcy judge to adjust the terms of mortgages to aid debtors in holding onto their houses. Proponents argued that this change in the law would reduce foreclosures and stabilize the national housing market. Opponents said that it was not fair to reward homeowners for being irresponsible. How would you vote if you were in the Senate?

6. In the *Grisham* case, the debtor had virtually no income but owed about $200,000 in debts that could not be discharged. What kind of fresh start is that? Should limits be placed on the total debt that cannot be discharged? Is the list of non-dischargeable debts appropriate?

CHAPTER 25

AGENCY LAW

nuttakit/Shutterstock.com; © picsbyst/Shutterstock.com

The good news is that Mac's parents gave him a car when he went off to college. (An SUV, which he called "the Tank.") The bad news is that his friends were constantly borrowing it. And you know how these things go.

One night, James borrowed the Tank to drive a friend to the airport. On the way home, he rear-ended a Mini Cooper at a stoplight. Although there was no damage to the Tank, the Mini was totaled. Then Peter borrowed the Tank to drive to work. While at work, he and Teddy went out to buy pizza for the office. When Peter hit a curb, the airbag deployed and broke Teddy's nose. So Mac had to take the Tank to the repair shop. While the car was there overnight, one of the repair people got drunk, took the SUV out for a joy ride, and banged it up. Who is liable for all this damage?

The Mini Cooper: Mac is liable only if James was acting as his agent. But in this case, James was not doing Mac any favors, so he was not his agent. If, on the other hand, James had agreed to pick up some food for Mac, then Mac would be liable for the accident.

Teddy's nose: Mac is clearly not liable because Peter was not his agent. What about Peter's employer? If Peter was acting within the scope of his employment, his employer would be liable. Was buying pizza for the office within this scope? Probably.

The joy ride: The repair shop owner is liable even though the drunk worker was clearly violating company policy. He was on duty at the time, and it is the garage owner's fault for hiring such an unreliable worker.

> **The good news is that Mac's parents gave him a car when he went off to college. The bad news is that his friends were constantly borrowing it.**

Thus far, this book has primarily dealt with issues of individual responsibility: What happens if you knock someone down or *you* sign an agreement? Agency law, on the other hand, is concerned with your responsibility for the actions of others. What happens if your agent assaults someone or signs a contract in your name? Agency law presents a significant trade-off: If you do everything yourself, you have control over the result. But the size and scope of your business (and your life) will be severely limited. Once you hire other people, you can accomplish a great deal more, but your risks increase immensely. Your agents may violate your instructions, and still you could be liable for what they have done. Although it might be safer to do everything yourself, that is not a practical decision for most business owners (or most people). The alternative is to hire carefully and to limit the risks as much as possible by understanding the law of agency.

25-1 CREATING AN AGENCY RELATIONSHIP

Let us begin with two important definitions:

- **Principal:** A person who has someone else acting for him.

- **Agent:** A person who acts for someone else.

Principals have substantial liability for the actions of their agents.[1] Therefore, disputes about whether an agency relationship exists are not mere legal quibbles but important issues with potentially profound financial consequences.

In an agency relationship, someone (the agent) agrees to perform a task for, and under the control of, someone else (the principal). **To create an agency relationship, there must be:**

- a **principal** and

- an **agent**

- who mutually **consent** that the agent will act on behalf of the principal and

- be subject to the principal's **control**,

- thereby creating a **fiduciary** relationship.

25-1a Consent

To establish consent, the principal must ask the agent to do something, and the agent must agree. In the most straightforward example, you ask a neighbor to walk your dog, and she agrees. Matters were more complicated, however, when Steven James met some friends one evening at a restaurant. During the two hours he was there, he drank four to six beers. (It is probably a bad sign that he cannot remember how many.) From then on, one misfortune piled upon another. After leaving the restaurant at about 7:00 p.m., James sped down a highway and crashed into a car that had stalled on the road, thereby killing the driver. James told the police at the scene that he had not seen the parked car (another bad sign). Evidently, James's lawyer was not as perceptive as the police in recognizing drunkenness. In a misguided attempt to help his client, James's lawyer took him to the local hospital for a blood test. Unfortunately, the test confirmed that James had indeed been drunk at the time of the accident.

Principal

In an agency relationship, the person for whom an agent is acting.

Agent

In an agency relationship, the person who is acting on behalf of a principal.

---

[1]The word "principal" is always used when referring to a person. It is not to be confused with the word "principle," which refers to a fundamental idea.

The attorney knew that if this evidence was admitted at trial, his client would soon be receiving free room and board from the Massachusetts Department of Corrections. So at trial, the lawyer argued that the blood test was protected by the client-attorney privilege because the hospital had been his agent and therefore a member of the defense team. The court disagreed, however, holding that the hospital employees were not agents for the lawyer because they had not consented to act in that role.

The court upheld James's conviction of murder in the first degree by reason of extreme atrocity or cruelty.[2]

25-1b Control

Principals are liable for the acts of their agents because they exercise control over the agents. If principals direct their agents to commit an act, it seems fair to hold the principal liable when that act causes harm. How would you apply that rule to the following situation?

William Stanford was an employee of the Agency for International Development. While on his way home to Pakistan to spend the holidays with his family, his plane was hijacked and taken to Iran, where he was killed. Stanford had originally purchased a ticket on Northwest Airlines but had traded it for a seat on Kuwait Airways (KA). The airlines had an agreement permitting passengers to exchange tickets from one to the other. Stanford's widow sued Northwest on the theory that KA was Northwest's agent. The court found, however, that no agency relationship existed because Northwest had no control over KA.[3] Northwest did not tell KA how to fly planes or handle terrorists; therefore, it should not be liable when KA made fatal errors. Not only must an agent and principal consent to an agency relationship, but the principal also must have control over the agent.

25-1c Fiduciary Relationship

In a **fiduciary relationship**, a trustee acts for the benefit of the beneficiary, always putting the interests of the beneficiary before his own. A fiduciary relationship is a special relationship with high standards. The beneficiary places special confidence in the fiduciary who, in turn, is obligated to act in good faith and candor, putting his own needs second. The purpose of a fiduciary relationship is for one person to benefit another. **Agents have a fiduciary duty to their principals.**

All three elements—consent, control, and a fiduciary duty—are necessary to create an agency relationship. In some relationships, for example, there might be a *fiduciary duty* but no *control*. A trustee of a trust must act for the benefit of the beneficiaries, but the beneficiaries have no right to control the trustee. Therefore, a trustee is not an agent of the beneficiaries. *Consent* is present in every contractual relationship, but that does not necessarily mean that the two parties are agent and principal. If Horace sells his car to Lily, they both expect to benefit under the contract, but neither has a *fiduciary duty* to the other and neither *controls* the other, so there is no agency relationship.

> **Fiduciary relationship**
> A trustee acts for the benefit of the beneficiary, always putting the interests of the beneficiary before his own.

25-1d Elements Not Required for an Agency Relationship

Consent, control, and a fiduciary relationship are necessary to establish an agency relationship. The following elements are *not* required:

- **A Written Agreement.** In most cases, an agency agreement does not have to be in writing. An oral understanding is valid, except in one circumstance—the **equal dignities rule**. According to this rule, if an agent is empowered to enter into a contract

> **Equal dignities rule**
> If an agent is empowered to enter into a contract that must be in writing, then the appointment of the agent must also be written.

---

[2]*Commonwealth v. James*, 427 Mass. 312, 693 N.E.2nd 148, 1998 Mass. LEXIS 175. (S.J.C. MA, 1998).
[3]*Stanford v. Kuwait Airways Corp.*, 648 F. Supp. 1158, 1986 U.S. Dist. LEXIS 18880 (S.D.N.Y. 1986).

that must be in writing, then the appointment of the agent must also be written. For example, under the statute of frauds, a contract for the sale of land is unenforceable unless in writing, so the agency agreement to sell land must also be in writing.

- **A Formal Agreement.** The principal and agent need not agree formally that they have an agency relationship. They do not even have to think the word "agent." So long as they act like an agent and a principal, the law will treat them as such.

- **Compensation.** An agency relationship need not meet all the standards of contract law. For example, a contract is not valid without consideration, but an agency agreement is valid *even if the agent is not paid.*

25-2 DUTIES OF AGENTS TO PRINCIPALS

Agents owe a fiduciary duty to their principals. There are four elements to this duty.

25-2a Duty of Loyalty

An agent has a fiduciary duty to act loyally for the principal's benefit in all matters connected with the agency relationship.[4] The agent has an obligation to put the principal first, to strive to accomplish the principal's goals. As the following case illustrates, this duty applies to all employees, no matter how lowly.

OTSUKA V. POLO RALPH LAUREN CORPORATION

2007 U.S. DIST. LEXIS 86523
United States District Court for the Northern District of California, 2007

CASE SUMMARY

Facts: Justin Kiser and Germania worked together at a Ralph Lauren Polo store in San Francisco. After she left the job, he let her buy clothing using merchandise credits made out to nonexistent people. He also let her use his employee discount. Not surprisingly, both of these activities were against store policies. Polo sued Kiser, alleging that he had violated his duty of loyalty.

Kiser filed a motion to dismiss on the grounds that he was such a low-level employee that he did not owe a duty of loyalty to Polo.

Issue: *Do all employees owe a duty of loyalty to their employer?*

Decision: Yes, all employees owe a duty of loyalty.

Reasoning: The cases cited by Polo to support its claim involved higher-level employees than Kiser, who was simply a clerk in a Polo store. No matter—the Restatement (Third) of Agency clearly states that all employees are agents and owe a duty of loyalty to their employers. All employees must put their employer's interests first.

The various components of the duty of loyalty follow.

---

[4]Restatement (Third) of Agency §8.01.

OUTSIDE BENEFITS

An agent may not receive profits unless the principal knows and approves. Suppose that Hope is an employee of the agency Big Egos and Talents, Inc. (BEAT). She has been representing Will Smith in his latest movie negotiations.[5] Smith often drives her to meetings in his new Maybach. He is so thrilled that she has arranged for him to star in the new movie *Little Men* that he buys her a Maybach. Can Hope keep this generous gift? Only with BEAT's permission. She must tell BEAT about the Maybach; the company may then take the vehicle itself or allow her to keep it.

CONFIDENTIAL INFORMATION

The ability to keep secrets is important in any relationship, but especially a fiduciary relationship. Agents can neither disclose nor use for their own benefit any confidential information they acquire during their agency. As the following case shows, this duty continues even after the agency relationship ends.

To listen to the two songs involved in this case, google "benedict copyright."

ABKCO MUSIC, INC. V. HARRISONGS MUSIC, LTD.

722 F.2d 988, 1983 U.S. App. LEXIS 15562
United States Court of Appeals for the Second Circuit, 1983

CASE SUMMARY

Facts: Bright Tunes Music Corp. (Bright Tunes) owned the copyright to the song "He's So Fine." The company sued George Harrison, a Beatle, alleging that the Harrison composition "My Sweet Lord" copied "He's So Fine." At the time the suit was filed, Allen B. Klein handled the business affairs of the Beatles.

Klein (representing Harrison) met with the president of Bright Tunes to discuss possible settlement of the copyright lawsuit. Klein suggested that Harrison might be interested in purchasing the copyright to "He's So Fine." Shortly thereafter, Klein's management contract with the Beatles expired. Without telling Harrison, Klein began negotiating with Bright Tunes to purchase the copyright to "He's So Fine" for himself. To advance these negotiations, Klein gave Bright Tunes information about royalty income for "My Sweet Lord"—information that he had gained as Harrison's agent.

The trial judge in the copyright case ultimately found that Harrison had infringed the copyright on "He's So Fine" and assessed damages of $1,599,987. After the trial, Klein purchased the "He's So Fine" copyright from Bright Tunes and with it, the right to recover from Harrison for the breach of copyright.

Issue: *Did Klein violate his fiduciary duty to Harrison by using confidential information after the agency relationship terminated?*

Decision: Klein did violate his fiduciary duty to Harrison.

Reasoning: While serving as Harrison's agent, Klein learned confidential information about royalty income for "My Sweet Lord." An agent has a duty not to use confidential information to compete against his principal. This duty continues even after the agency relationship ends. A former agent does have the right to compete against his principal using general business knowledge or publicly available information. However, the information that Klein passed on to Bright Tunes was not publicly available.

Although some years separated Klein's attempt to buy the copyright for Harrison and his later purchase for himself, Klein was still under a duty to Harrison. Klein's conduct did not meet the standard required of him as a former fiduciary.

---

[5]Do not be confused by the fact that Hope works as an agent for movie stars. As an employee of BEAT, her duty is to the company. She is an agent of BEAT, and BEAT works for the celebrities.

Ethics   Klein was angry that the Beatles had failed to renew his management contract. Was it reasonable for him to think that he owed no duty to the principal who had fired him? Why kind of world would it be if everyone acted like Klein? Why would George Harrison prefer to owe money to Bright Tunes rather than to Klein?

COMPETITION WITH THE PRINCIPAL

Agents are not allowed to compete with their principal in any matter within the scope of the agency business. If Allen Klein had purchased the "He's So Fine" copyright while he was George Harrison's agent, he would have committed an additional sin against the agency relationship. Owning song rights was clearly part of the agency business, so Klein could not make such purchases without Harrison's consent. Once the agency relationship ends, however, so does the rule against competition. Klein was entitled to buy the "He's So Fine" copyright after the agency relationship ended (so long as he did not use confidential information).

CONFLICT OF INTEREST BETWEEN TWO PRINCIPALS

Unless otherwise agreed, an agent may not act for two principals whose interests conflict. Suppose Travis represents both director Steven Spielberg and actor Amy Adams. Spielberg is casting the title role in his new movie, *Nancy Drew: Girl Detective*, a role that Adams covets. Travis cannot represent these two clients when they are negotiating with each other unless they both know about the conflict and agree to ignore it. The following example illustrates the dangers of acting for two principals at once.

EXAM Strategy

Question: The Sisters of Charity was an order of nuns in New Jersey. Faced with growing health care and retirement costs, they decided to sell off a piece of property. The nuns soon found, however, that the world is not always a charitable place. They agreed to sell the land to Linpro for nearly $10 million. But before the deal closed, Linpro signed a contract to resell the property to Sammis for $34 million. So, you say, the sisters made a bad deal. There is no law against that. But it turned out that the nuns' law firm also represented Linpro. Their lawyer at the firm, Peter Berkley, never told the sisters about the deal between Linpro and Sammis. Was that the charitable—or legal—thing to do?

Strategy: Always begin by asking if there is an agency relationship. Was there consent, control, and a fiduciary relationship? *Consent:* Berkley had agreed to work for the nuns. *Control:* They told him what he was to do—sell the land. The purpose of a *fiduciary relationship* is for one person to benefit another. The point of the nuns' relationship with Berkley is for him to help them. Once you know there is an agency relationship, then ask if the agent has violated his duty of loyalty.

Result: You know that an agent is not permitted to act for two principals whose interests conflict. Here, Berkley is working for the nuns, who want the highest possible price for their land, and Linpro, who wants the lowest price. Berkley has violated his duty of loyalty.

SECRETLY DEALING WITH THE PRINCIPAL

If a principal hires an agent to arrange a transaction, the agent may not become a party to the transaction without the principal's permission. Matt Damon became an overnight sensation after starring in the movie *Good Will Hunting*. Suppose that he hired Trang to read scripts for him. Unbeknownst to Damon, Trang has written her own script, which she thinks would be ideal for him. She may not sell it to him without revealing that she wrote it herself. Damon may be perfectly happy to buy Trang's script, but he has the right, as her principal, to know that she is the person selling it.

APPROPRIATE BEHAVIOR

An agent may not engage in inappropriate behavior that reflects badly on the principal. This rule applies even to *off-duty* conduct. For example, a coed trio of flight attendants went wild at a hotel bar in London. They kissed and caressed each other, showed off their underwear, and poured alcohol down their trousers. The airline fired two of the employees and gave a warning letter to the third.

25-2b Other Duties of an Agent

Before Taylor left for a five-week trip to England, he hired Angie to rent his vacation house. Angie never got around to listing his house on the Multiple Listing Service used by all the area brokers, nor did she post it on the web herself, but when the Fords contacted her looking for rental housing, she did show them Taylor's place. They offered to rent it for $750 per month.

Angie called Taylor in England to tell him. He responded that he would not accept less than $850 a month, which Angie thought the Fords would be willing to pay. He told Angie to call back if there was any problem. The Fords decided that they would go no higher than $800 a month. Although Taylor had told Angie that he could not receive text messages in England, she texted him the Fords' counteroffer. Taylor never received it, so he never responded. When the Fords pressed Angie for an answer, she said she could not get in touch with Taylor. Not until Taylor returned home did he learn that the Fords had rented another house. Did Angie violate any of the duties that agents owe to their principals?

DUTY TO OBEY INSTRUCTIONS

An agent must obey her principal's instructions unless the principal directs her to behave illegally or unethically. Taylor instructed Angie to call him if the Fords rejected the offer. When Angie failed to do so, she violated her duty to obey instructions. If, however, Taylor had asked her to say that the house's basement was dry when in fact it looked like a swamp every spring, Angie would be under no obligation to follow those illegal instructions.

DUTY OF CARE

An agent has a duty to act with reasonable care. In other words, an agent must act as a reasonable person would, under the circumstances. A reasonable person would not have texted Taylor while he was in England.

Under some circumstances, an agent is held to a higher—or lower—standard than usual. **An agent with special skills is held to a higher standard because she is expected to use those skills.** A trained real estate agent should know enough to post all listings on the web.

But suppose Taylor had asked his neighbor, Jed, to help him sell the house. Jed is not a trained real estate agent, and he is not being paid, which makes him a **gratuitous agent**. A gratuitous agent is held to a lower standard because he is doing his principal a favor and, as the old saying goes, you get what you pay for—up to a point. **Gratuitous agents are liable if they commit *gross* negligence, but not *ordinary* negligence.** If Jed, as a gratuitous agent, texted Taylor an important message because he forgot that Taylor could not receive these

Gratuitous agent
An agent who is not paid by the principal.

messages in England, he would not be liable for that ordinary negligence. But if Taylor had, just that day, sent Jed an email complaining that he could not get any text messages, Jed would be liable for gross negligence and a violation of his duty.

DUTY TO PROVIDE INFORMATION

An agent has a duty to provide the principal with all information in her possession that she has reason to believe the principal wants to know. She also has a duty to provide accurate information. Angie knew that the Fords had counteroffered for $800 a month. She had a duty to pass this information on to Taylor.

EXAM Strategy

Question: Jonah tells his friend Derek that he would like to go parasailing. Derek is very enthusiastic and suggests that they try an outfit called Wind Beneath Your Wings because he has heard good things about it. Derek offers to arrange everything. He makes a reservation, puts the $600 fee on his credit card, and picks Jonah up to drive him to the Wings location. What a friend! But the day does not turn out as Jonah had hoped. While he is soaring up in the air over the Pacific Ocean, his sail springs a leak, he goes plummeting into the sea and breaks both legs. During his recuperation in the hospital, he learns that Wings is unlicensed. He also sees an ad for Wings offering parasailing for only $350. And Derek is listed in the ad as one of the company's owners. Is Derek an agent for Jonah? Has he violated his fiduciary responsibility?

Strategy: There are three issues to consider in answering this question: (1) Was there an agency relationship? This requires consent, control, and a fiduciary relationship. (2) Is anything missing—does it matter if the agent is unpaid or the contract is not in writing? (3) Has the agent fulfilled his duties?

Result: There is an agency relationship: Derek had agreed to help Jonah; it was Jonah who set the goal for the relationship (parasailing); the purpose of this relationship is for one person to benefit another. It does not matter if Derek was not paid or the agreement not written. Derek has violated his duty to exercise due care. He should not have taken Jonah to an unlicensed company. He has also violated his duty to provide information: He should have told Jonah the true cost for the lessons and also revealed that he was a principal of the company. And he violated his duty of loyalty when he worked for two principals whose interests were in conflict.

25-2c Principal's Remedies When the Agent Breaches a Duty

A principal has three potential remedies when an agent breaches her duty:

- The principal can recover from the agent any **damages** the breach has caused. Thus, if Taylor can rent his house for only $600 a month instead of the $800 the Fords offered, Angie would be liable for $2,400—$200 a month for one year.

- If an agent breaches the duty of loyalty, he must turn over to the principal any **profits** he has earned as a result of his wrongdoing. Thus, after Klein violated his duty of loyalty to Harrison, he forfeited profits he would have earned from the copyright of "He's So Fine."

- If the agent has violated her duty of loyalty, the principal may **rescind** the transaction. When Trang sold a script to her principal, Matt Damon, without telling him that she was the author, she violated her duty of loyalty. Damon could rescind the contract to buy the script.[6]

25-3 DUTIES OF PRINCIPALS TO AGENTS

In a typical agency relationship, the agent agrees to perform tasks for the principal, and the principal agrees to pay the agent. The range of tasks undertaken by an agent is limited only by the imagination of the principal. Because the agent's job can be so varied, the law needs to define an agent's duties carefully. The role of the principal, on the other hand, is typically less complicated—often little more than paying the agent as required by the agreement. Thus, the law enumerates fewer duties for the principal. Primarily, the principal must reimburse the agent for reasonable expenses and cooperate with the agent in performing agency tasks. The respective duties of agents and principals can be summarized as follows:

Duties of Agents to Principals	Duty of Principals to Agents
Duty of loyalty	Duty to compensate as provided by the agreement
Duty to obey instructions	Duty to reimburse for reasonable expenses
Duty of care	Duty to cooperate
Duty to provide information	

© Cengage Learning

As a general rule, the principal must indemnify (i.e., reimburse) the agent for any expenses she has reasonably incurred. These reimbursable expenses fall into three categories:

- **A principal must indemnify an agent for any expenses or damages reasonably incurred in carrying out his agency responsibilities.** For example, Peace Baptist Church of Birmingham, Alabama, asked its pastor to buy land for a new church. He paid part of the purchase price out of his own pocket, but the church refused to reimburse him. Although the pastor lost in church, he won in court.[7]

- **A principal must indemnify an agent for tort claims brought by a third party if the principal authorized the agent's behavior and the agent did not realize he was committing a tort.** Marisa owns all the apartment buildings on Elm Street, except one. She hires Rajiv to manage the units and tells him that, under the terms of the leases, she has the right to ask guests to leave if a party becomes too rowdy. But she forgets to tell Rajiv that she does not own one of the buildings, which happens to house a college sorority. One night, when the sorority is having a rambunctious party, Rajiv hustles over and starts ejecting the noisy guests. The sorority is furious and sues Rajiv for trespass. If the sorority wins its suit against Rajiv, Marisa would have to pay the judgment, plus Rajiv's attorney's fees, because she had told him to quell noisy parties and he did not realize he was trespassing.

---

[6]A principal can rescind his contract with an agent who has violated her duty, but, as we shall see later in the chapter, the principal might not be able to rescind a contract with a third party when the agent misbehaves.

[7]*Lauderdale v. Peace Baptist Church of Birmingham*, 246 Ala. 178, 19 So. 2d 538, 1944 Ala. LEXIS 508 (S. Ct. AL, 1944).

- **The principal must indemnify the agent for any liability she incurs from third parties as a result of entering into a contract on the principal's behalf, including attorney's fees and reasonable settlements.** An agent signed a contract to buy cucumbers for Vlasic Food Products Co. to use in making pickles. When the first shipment of cucumbers arrived, Vlasic inspectors found them unsuitable and directed the agent to refuse the shipment. The agent found himself in a pickle when the cucumber farmer sued. The agent notified Vlasic, but the company refused to defend him. He settled the claim himself and, in turn, sued Vlasic. The court ordered Vlasic to reimburse the agent because he had notified them of the suit and had acted reasonably and in good faith.[8]

25-3a Duty to Cooperate

Principals have a duty to cooperate with their agent:

- **The principal must furnish the agent with the opportunity to work.** If Lewis agrees to serve as Ida's real estate agent in selling her house, Ida must allow Lewis access to the house. It is unlikely that Lewis will be able to sell the house without taking anyone inside.

- **The principal cannot unreasonably interfere with the agent's ability to accomplish his task.** Ida allows Lewis to show the house, but she refuses to clean it and then makes disparaging comments to prospective purchasers. "I really get tired of living in such a dark, dreary house," she says. "And the neighborhood children are vicious thugs." This behavior would constitute unreasonable interference with an agent.

- **The principal must perform her part of the contract.** Once the agent has successfully completed the task, the principal must pay him, even if the principal has changed her mind and no longer wants the agent to perform. Ida is a 78-year-old widow who has lived alone for many years in a house that she loves. Her asking price is outrageously high. But lo and behold, Lewis finds a couple happy to pay Ida's price. There is only one problem. Ida does not really want to sell. She put her house on the market because she enjoys showing it to all the folks who move to town. She rejects the offer. Now there is a second problem. The contract provided that Lewis would find a willing buyer at the asking price. Because he has done so, Ida must pay his real estate commission even if she does not want to sell her house.

25-4 TERMINATING AN AGENCY RELATIONSHIP

Either the agent or the principal can terminate the agency relationship at any time. In addition, the relationship terminates automatically if the principal or agent no longer can perform their required duties or a change in circumstances renders the agency relationship pointless.

25-4a Termination by Agent or Principal

The two parties—principal and agent—have three choices in terminating their relationship:

- **Term Agreement.** If the principal and agent agree in advance how long their relationship will last, they have a term agreement. For example:

---

[8]*Long v. Vlasic Food Products Co.*, 439 F.2d 229, 1971 U.S. App. LEXIS 11455 (4th Cir. 1971).

- **Time.** Alexandra hires Boris to help her add to her collection of guitars previously owned by rock stars. If they agree that the relationship will last two years, they have a term agreement.

- **Achieving a Purpose.** The principal and agent can agree that the agency relationship will terminate when the principal's goals have been achieved. Alexandra and Boris might agree that their relationship will end when Alexandra has purchased 10 guitars.

- **Mutual Agreement.** No matter what the principal and agent agree at the start, they can always change their minds later on, so long as the change is mutual. If Boris and Alexandra originally agree to a two-year term, but Boris decides he wants to go back to business school and Alexandra runs out of money after only one year, they can decide together to terminate the agency.

- **Agency at Will.** If they make no agreement in advance about the term of the agreement, either principal or agent can terminate at any time.

- **Wrongful Termination.** An agency relationship is a personal relationship. Hiring an agent is not like buying a book. You might not care which copy of the book you buy, but you do care which agent you hire. If an agency relationship is not working out, the courts will not force the agent and principal to stay together. **Either party always has the** *power* **to walk out. They may not, however, have the** *right*. If one party's departure from the agency relationship violates the agreement and causes harm to the other party, the wrongful party must pay damages. Nonetheless, he will be permitted to leave. If Boris has agreed to work for Alexandra for two years but he wants to leave after one, he can leave, provided he pays Alexandra the cost of hiring and training a replacement.

If the agent is a **gratuitous** agent (i.e., is not being paid), he has both the power and the right to quit any time he wants, regardless of the agency agreement. If Boris is doing this job for Alexandra as a favor, he will not owe her damages when he stops work.

25-4b Principal or Agent Can No Longer Perform Required Duties

If the principal or the agent is unable to perform the duties required under the agency agreement, the agreement terminates.

- **If either the agent or the principal fails to obtain (or keep) a license necessary to perform duties under the agency agreement, the agreement ends.** Caleb hires Allegra to represent him in a lawsuit. If she is disbarred, their agency agreement terminates because the agent is no longer allowed in court. Alternatively, if Emil hires Bess to work in his gun shop, their agency relationship terminates when he loses his license to sell firearms.

- **The bankruptcy of the agent or the principal terminates an agency relationship only if it affects their ability to perform.** Bankruptcy rarely interferes with an agent's responsibilities. After all, there is generally no reason why an agent cannot continue to act for the principal whether the agent is rich or poor. If Lewis, the real estate agent, becomes bankrupt, he can continue to represent Ida or anyone else who wants to sell a house. The bankruptcy of a principal is different, however, because after filing for bankruptcy, the principal loses control of his assets. A bankrupt principal may be unable to pay the agent or honor contracts that the agent enters into on his behalf. Therefore, the bankruptcy of a principal is more likely to terminate an agency relationship.

- **An agency relationship terminates upon the death or incapacity of either the principal or the agent.** Agency is a personal relationship, and when the principal dies, the agent cannot act on behalf of a nonexistent person.[9] Of course, a nonexistent person cannot act either, so the relationship also terminates when the agent dies. Incapacity has the same legal effect because either the principal or the agent is at least temporarily unable to act.

- **If the agent violates her duty of loyalty, the agency agreement automatically terminates.** Agents are appointed to represent the principal's interest; if they fail to do so, there is no point to the relationship. Louisa is negotiating a military procurement contract on behalf of her employer, Missiles R Us, Inc. In the midst of these negotiations, she becomes very friendly with Sam, the government negotiator. One night over drinks, she tells Sam what Missiles' real costs are on the project and the lowest bid it could possibly make. By passing on this confidential information, Louisa has violated her duty of loyalty, and her agency relationship terminates.

25-4c Change in Circumstances

After the agency agreement is negotiated, circumstances may change. If these changes are significant enough to undermine the purpose of the agreement, the relationship ends automatically. Andrew hires Melissa to sell his country farm for $100,000. Shortly thereafter, the largest oil reserve in North America is discovered nearby. The farm is now worth 10 times Andrew's asking price. Melissa's authority terminates automatically.

Other changes in circumstance that affect an agency agreement are:

- **Change of Law.** If the agent's responsibilities become illegal, the agency agreement terminates. Oscar has hired Marta to ship him succulent avocados from California's Imperial Valley. Before she sends the shipment, Mediterranean fruit flies are discovered, and all fruits and vegetables in California are quarantined. The agency agreement terminates because it is now illegal to ship the California avocados.

- **Loss or Destruction of Subject Matter.** Andrew hired Damian to sell his Palm Beach condominium, but before Damian could even measure the living room, Andrew's creditors attached the condo. Damian is no longer authorized to sell the real estate because Andrew has "lost" the subject matter of his agency agreement with Damian.

25-4d Effect of Termination

Once an agency relationship ends, the agent no longer has the authority to act for the principal. If she continues to act, she is liable to the principal for any damages he incurs as a result. The Mediterranean fruit fly quarantine ended Marta's agency. If she sends Oscar the avocados anyway and he is fined for possession of a fruit fly, Marta must pay the fine.

The agent loses her authority to act, but some of the duties of both the principal and agent continue even after the relationship ends:

- **Principal's Duty to Indemnify Agent.** Oscar must reimburse Marta for expenses she incurred before the agency ended. If Marta accumulated mileage on her car during her search for the perfect avocado, Oscar must pay her for gasoline and depreciation. But he owes her nothing for her expenses after the agency relationship ends.

- **Confidential Information.** Remember the "He's So Fine" case earlier in the chapter? George Harrison's agent used confidential information to negotiate on his own behalf the purchase of the "He's So Fine" copyright. An agent is not entitled to use confidential information even after the agency relationship terminates.

---

[9]Restatement (Third) of Agency §§3.05, 3.06, 3.07, and 3.08.

25-5 LIABILITY

Thus far, this chapter has dealt with the relationship between principals and agents. Although an agent can dramatically increase his principal's ability to accomplish her goals, an agency relationship also dramatically increases the risk of legal liability to third parties. A principal may be liable in tort for any harm the agent causes and also liable in contract for agreements that the agent signs. Indeed, once a principal hires an agent, she may be liable to third parties for his acts, even if he disobeys instructions. Agents may also find themselves liable to third parties.

25-6 PRINCIPAL'S LIABILITY FOR CONTRACTS

Many agents are hired for the primary purpose of entering into contracts on behalf of their principals. Salespeople, for example, may do little other than sign on the dotted line. Most of the time, the principal wants to be liable on these contracts. But even if the principal is unhappy (because, say, the agent has disobeyed orders), the principal generally cannot rescind contracts entered into by the agent. After all, if someone is going to be penalized, it should be the principal who hired the disobedient agent, not the innocent third party.

The principal is liable for the acts of an agent if (1) *the agent had authority,* **or (2) the principal** *ratifies* **the acts of the agent.**

To say that the principal is "liable for the acts" of the agent means that the principal is as responsible as if he had performed the acts himself. It also means that the principal is liable for statements the agent makes to a third party. Thus, when a lawyer lied on an application for malpractice insurance, the insurance company was allowed to void the policy for the entire law firm. It was as if the firm had lied. In addition, the principal is deemed to know any information that the agent knows or should know.

25-6a Authority

A principal is bound by the acts of an agent if the agent has authority. There are three types of authority: express, implied, and apparent. Express and implied authority are categories of actual authority because the agent is truly authorized to act for the principal. In apparent authority, the principal is liable for the agent's actions even though the agent was *not* authorized.

EXPRESS AUTHORITY

The principal grants **express authority** by words or conduct that, reasonably interpreted, cause the agent to believe the principal desires her to act on the principal's account.[10] In other words, the principal asks the agent to do something and the agent does it. Craig calls his stockbroker, Alice, and asks her to buy 100 shares of Banshee Corp. for his account. She has *express authority* to carry out this transaction.

IMPLIED AUTHORITY

Unless otherwise agreed, authority to conduct a transaction includes authority to do acts that are reasonably necessary to accomplish it.[11] The principal does not have to micromanage the agent. David has recently inherited a house from his grandmother. He hires Nell to auction

---

[10]Restatement (Third) of Agency §2.01.
[11]Restatement (Third) of Agency §2.02.

off the house and its contents. She hires an auctioneer, advertises the event, rents a tent, and generally does everything necessary to conduct a successful auction. After withholding her expenses, she sends the tidy balance to David. Totally outraged, he calls her on the phone, "How dare you hire an auctioneer and rent a tent? I never gave you permission! I absolutely *refuse* to pay these expenses!"

David is wrong. A principal almost never gives an agent absolutely complete instructions. Unless some authority is implied, David would have had to say, "Open the car door, get in, put the key in the ignition, drive to the store, buy stickers, mark an auction number on each sticker ..." and so forth. To solve this problem, the law assumes that the agent has authority to do anything that is reasonably necessary to accomplish her task.

Apparent Authority

A principal can be liable for the acts of an agent who is not, in fact, acting with authority if the *principal's* conduct causes a third party reasonably to believe that the agent is authorized.[12] In the case of *express* and *implied* authority, the principal has authorized the agent to act. Apparent authority is different: The principal has *not* authorized the agent, but has done something to make an innocent third party *believe* the agent is authorized. As a result, the principal is every bit as liable to the third party as if the agent did have authority.

For example, Zbigniew Lambo and Scott Kennedy were brokers at Paulson Investment Co., a stock brokerage firm in Oregon. The two men violated securities laws by selling unregistered stock, which ultimately proved to be worthless. Kennedy and Lambo were liable, but they were unable to repay the money. Either Paulson or its customers would end up bearing the loss. What is the fair result? The law takes the view that the principal is liable, not the third party, because the principal, by word or deed, allowed the third party to believe that the agent was acting on the principal's behalf. The principal could have prevented the third party from losing money.

Although the two brokers did not have *express* or *implied* authority to sell the stock (Paulson had not authorized them to break the law), the company was nonetheless liable on the grounds that the brokers had *apparent* authority. Paulson had sent letters to its customers notifying them when it hired Kennedy. The two brokers made sales presentations at Paulson's offices. The company had never told customers that the two men were not authorized to sell this worthless stock.[13] Thus the agents *appeared* to have authority, even though they did not. Of course, Paulson had the right to recover from Kennedy and Lambo, if it could ever compel them to pay.

Remember that the issue in apparent authority is always what the *principal* has done to make the *third party* believe that the *agent* has authority. Suppose that Kennedy and Lambo never worked for Paulson but, on their own, printed up Paulson stationery. The company would not be liable for the stock the two men sold because it had never done or said anything that would reasonably make a third party believe that the men were its agents.

25-6b Ratification

If a person accepts the benefit of an unauthorized transaction or fails to repudiate it, then he is as bound by the act as if he had originally authorized it. He has *ratified* the act.[14] Many of the cases in agency law involve instances in which one person acts *without* authority for another. To avoid liability, the alleged principal shows that he had not authorized the task at issue. But sometimes after the fact, the principal decides that he approves of what the agent has done even though it was not authorized at the time. The law would be perverse if it did not permit the principal, under those circumstances, to agree to the deal the agent has made.

---

[12]Restatement (Third) of Agency §2.03.
[13]*Badger v. Paulson Investment Co.*, 311 Ore. 14, 803 P.2d 1178, 1991 Ore. LEXIS 7 (S. Ct. OR, 1991).
[14]Restatement (Third) of Agency §4.01.

The law is not perverse, but it is careful. Even if an agent acts without authority, the principal can decide later to be bound by her actions so long as these requirements are met:

- The "agent" indicates to the third party that she is acting for a principal.

- The "principal" knows all the material facts of the transaction.

- The "principal" accepts the benefit of the whole transaction, not just part.

- The third party does not withdraw from the contract before ratification.

A night clerk at the St. Regis Hotel in Detroit, Michigan, was brutally murdered in the course of a robbery. A few days later, the *Detroit News* reported that the St. Regis management had offered a $1,000 reward for any information leading to the arrest and conviction of the killer. Two days after the article appeared, Robert Jackson turned in the man who was subsequently convicted of the crime. But then it was Jackson's turn to be robbed—the hotel refused to pay the reward on the grounds that the manager who had made the offer had no authority. Jackson still had one weapon left: He convinced the court that the hotel had ratified the offer. One of the hotel's owners admitted he read the *Detroit News*. The court concluded that if someone reads a newspaper, he is sure to read any articles about a business he owns; therefore, the owner must have been aware of the offer. He accepted the benefit of the offer by failing to revoke it publicly by, say, announcing to the press that the reward was invalid. This failure to revoke constituted a ratification, and the hotel was liable.[15]

25-6c Subagents

Many of the examples in this chapter involve a single agent acting for a principal. Real life is often more complex. Daniel, the owner of a restaurant, hires Michaela to manage it. She in turn hires chefs, waiters, and dishwashers. Daniel has never even met the restaurant help, yet they are also his agents, albeit a special category called **subagent**. Michaela is called an **intermediary agent**—someone who hires subagents for the principal.

As a general rule, an agent has no authority to delegate her tasks to another unless the principal authorizes her to do so. But when an agent is authorized to hire a subagent, the principal is as liable for the acts of the subagent as he is for the acts of a regular agent. Daniel authorizes Michaela to hire a restaurant staff, so she hires Lydia to serve as produce buyer. When Lydia buys food for the restaurant, Daniel must pay the bill.

25-7 AGENT'S LIABILITY FOR CONTRACTS

The agent's liability on a contract depends upon how much the third party knows about the principal. Disclosure is the agent's best protection against liability.

25-7a Fully Disclosed Principal

An agent is not liable for any contracts she makes on behalf of a *fully* disclosed principal. A principal is fully disclosed if the third party knows of his *existence* and his *identity*. Augusta acts as agent for Parker when he buys Tracey's prize-winning show horse. Augusta and Tracey both grew up in posh Grosse Pointe, Michigan, where they attended the same elite schools. Tracey does not know Parker, but she figures any friend of Augusta's must be OK. She figures wrong—Parker is a charming deadbeat. He injures Tracey's horse, fails to pay the full contract price, and promptly disappears. Tracey angrily demands that Augusta make

---

[15]*Jackson v. Goodman*, 69 Mich. App. 225, 244 N.W.2d 423, 1976 Mich. App., LEXIS 741 (Mich. Ct. App., 1976).

good on Parker's debt. Unfortunately for Tracey, Parker was a fully disclosed principal—Tracey knew of his *existence* and his *identity*. Although Tracey partly relied on Augusta's good character when contracting with Parker, Augusta is not liable because Tracey knew who the principal was and could have (should have) investigated him. Augusta did not promise anything herself, and Tracey's only recourse is against the principal, Parker (wherever he may be).

To avoid liability when signing a contract on behalf of a principal, an agent must clearly state that she is an agent and also must identify the principal. Augusta should sign a contract on behalf of her principal, Parker, as follows: "Augusta, as agent for Parker" or "Parker, by Augusta, Agent."

25-7b Unidentified Principal

In the case of an *unidentified* principal, the third party can recover from either the agent or the principal. (An unidentified principal is also sometimes called a "partially disclosed principal.") A principal is unidentified if the third party knew of his *existence* but not his *identity*. Suppose that, when approaching Tracey about the horse, Augusta simply says, "I have a friend who is interested in buying your champion." Any friend of Augusta's is a friend of Tracey's—or so Tracey thinks. Parker is an unidentified principal because Tracey knows only that he exists, not who he is. She cannot investigate his creditworthiness because she does not know his name. Tracey relies solely on what she is able to learn from the agent, Augusta. Both Augusta and Parker are liable to Tracey. (They are jointly and severally liable, which means that Tracey can recover from either or both of them. However, she cannot recover more than the total she is owed: If her damages are $100,000, she can recover that amount from either Augusta or Parker, or partial amounts from both, but in no event more than $100,000.)

25-7c Undisclosed Principal

In the case of an *undisclosed* principal, the third party can recover from either the agent or the principal. A principal is undisclosed if the third party did not know of his existence. Suppose that Augusta simply asks to buy the horse herself, without mentioning that she is purchasing it for Parker. In this case, Parker is an undisclosed principal because Tracey does not know that Augusta is acting for someone else. Both Parker and Augusta are jointly and severally liable. As Exhibit 25.1 illustrates, the principal is always liable, but the agent is not unless the principal's identity is a mystery.

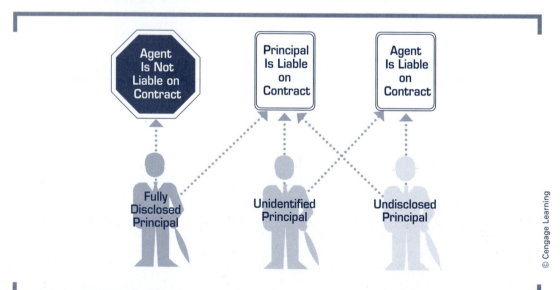

| EXHIBIT 25.1 | Liability of Principal and Agent |

© Cengage Learning

In some ways, the concept of an undisclosed principal violates principles of contract law. If Tracey does not even know that Parker exists, how can they have an agreement or a meeting of the minds? Is such an arrangement fair to Tracey? No matter—a contract with an undisclosed principal is binding. The following incident illustrates why.

William Zeckendorf was a man with a plan. For years, he had been eyeing a six-block tract of land along New York's East River. It was a wasteland of slums and slaughterhouses, but he could see its potential. The meat packers had refused to sell to him, however, because they knew they would never be permitted to build slaughterhouses in Manhattan again. Finally, he got the phone call he had been waiting for. The companies were willing to sell—at more than three times the market price of surrounding land. Undeterred, Zeckendorf immediately put down a $1 million deposit. But to make his investment worthwhile, he needed to buy the neighboring property—once the slaughterhouses were gone, the other land would be much more valuable. Zeckendorf was well known as a wealthy developer; he had begun his business career managing the Astor family's real estate holdings. If he personally tried to negotiate the purchase of the surrounding land, word would soon get out that he wanted to put together a large parcel. Prices would skyrocket, and the project would become too costly. So he hired agents to purchase the land for him. To conceal his involvement further, he went to South America for a month. When he returned, his agents had completed 75 different purchases, and he owned 18 acres of land.

> **Without the cooperation of agency law, the UN headquarters would not be in New York today.**

Shortly afterwards, the United Nations (UN) began seeking a site for its headquarters. President Truman favored Boston, Philadelphia, or a location in the Midwest. The UN committee suggested Greenwich or Stamford, Connecticut. But John D. Rockefeller settled the question once and for all. He purchased Zeckendorf's land and donated it to the UN (netting Zeckendorf a 25 percent profit). Without the cooperation of agency law, the UN headquarters would not be in New York today.

Because of concerns about fair play, there are some exceptions to the rule on undisclosed principals. **A third party is not bound to the contract with an undisclosed principal if (1) the contract specifically provides that the third party is not bound to anyone other than the agent, or (2) the agent lies about the principal because she knows the third party would refuse to contract with him.** Suppose that a large university is buying up land in an impoverished area near its campus. An owner of a house there wants to make sure that if he sells to the university, he gets a higher price than if he sells to an individual with more limited resources. A cagey property owner, when approached by one of the university's agents, could ask for a clause in the contract providing that the agent was not representing someone else. If the agent told the truth, the owner could demand a higher price. If the agent lied, then the owner could rescind the contract when the truth emerged.

25-7d Unauthorized Agent

Thus far in this section, we have been discussing an agent's liability to a third party for a transaction that was authorized by the principal. Sometimes, however, agents act without the authority of a principal. **If the agent has no authority (express, implied, or apparent), the principal is not liable to the third party, and the agent is.** Suppose that Augusta agrees to sell Parker's horse to Tracey. Unfortunately, Parker has never met Augusta and has certainly not authorized this transaction. Augusta is hoping that she can persuade him to sell, but Parker refuses. Augusta, but not Parker, is liable to Tracey for breach of contract.

25-8 Principal's Liability for Torts

An employer is liable for a tort committed by its employee acting within the scope of employment or acting with authority.[16] This principle of liability is called ***respondeat superior****,* which is a Latin phrase that means "let the master answer." Under the theory of *respondeat superior,* the employer (i.e., the principal) is liable for misbehavior by the employee (i.e., the agent) whether or not the employer was at fault. Indeed, the employer is liable even if he *forbade* or tried to *prevent* the employee from misbehaving. Thus, a company could be liable for the damage a worker causes while driving and talking on her cell phone, even if she is violating company policy at the time. This sounds like a harsh rule. The logic is that, because the principal controls the agent, he should be able to *prevent* misbehavior. If he cannot prevent it, at least he can *insure* against the risks. Furthermore, the principal may have deeper pockets than the agent or the injured third party and thus be better able to *afford* the cost of the agent's misbehavior.

To apply the principle of *respondeat superior,* it is important to understand each part of the rule.

25-8a Employee

There are two kinds of agents: (1) *employees* and (2) *independent contractors.* **A principal *may be* liable for the torts of an employee but generally is *not* liable for the torts of an independent contractor.** Because of this rule, the distinction between an employee and an independent contractor is important.

Employee or Independent Contractor?

The more control the principal has over an agent, the more likely that the agent will be considered an employee. Therefore, when determining if agents are employees or independent contractors, courts consider whether:

- The principal supervises details of the work.

- The principal supplies the tools and place of work.

- The agents work full time for the principal.

- The agents receive a salary or hourly wages, not a fixed price for the job.

- The work is part of the regular business of the principal.

- The principal and agents believe they have an employer-employee relationship.

- The principal is in business.[17]

Suppose, for example, that Mutt and Jeff work 40 hours a week at Swansong Media preparing food for the company's onsite dining room. They earn a weekly salary. Swansong provides food, utensils, and kitchen. This year, however, Swansong decides to go all out for its holiday party, so it hires FiFi LaBelle to prepare special food. She buys the food, prepares it in her own kitchen, and delivers it to the company in time for the party. She is an independent contractor, while Mutt and Jeff are employees.

Negligent Hiring

Principals prefer agents to be considered independent contractors, not employees, because, as a general rule, principals are not liable for the torts of an independent contractor. There is, however, one exception to this rule: **The principal is liable for the torts of an independent**

---

[16]Restatement (Third) of Agency §7.07.
[17]Ibid.

contractor *if* the principal has been negligent in hiring or supervising her. Remember that, under *respondeat superior*, the principal is liable *without fault* for the torts of employees. The case of independent contractors is different: The principal is liable only if he was *at fault* by being careless in his hiring or supervising.

Exhibit 25.2 illustrates the difference in liability between an employee and an independent contractor.

Principal

Controls agent

Employee

Principal may be liable for Employee's torts, even if Principal was not negligent

Does not control agent

Independent Contractor

Principal is not liable for torts of an Independent Contractor unless Principal was negligent in hiring or supervising

© Cengage Learning

EXHIBIT 25.2   Liability of Principal

25-8b Scope of Employment

Principals are liable only for torts that an employee commits within the *scope of employment*. If an employee leaves a pool of water on the floor of a store and a customer slips and falls, the employer is liable. But if the same employee leaves water on his own kitchen floor and a friend falls, the employer is not liable because the employee is not acting within the scope of employment. An employee is acting within the scope of employment if the act:

- Is one that employees are generally responsible for
- Takes place during hours that the employee is generally employed
- Is part of the principal's business
- Is similar to the one the principal authorized
- Is one for which the principal supplied the tools; and
- Is not seriously criminal.

Scope of employment cases raise two major issues: authorization and abandonment.

AUTHORIZATION

In authorization cases, the agent is clearly working for the principal but commits an act that the principal has not authorized. Although Jane has often told the driver of her delivery van not to speed, Hank ignores her instructions and plows into Bernadette. At the time of the accident, he is working for Jane, delivering flowers for her shop, but his act is not authorized. **An act is within the scope of employment, even if expressly forbidden, if it is of the same general nature as that authorized or if it is incidental to the conduct authorized.** Hank was authorized to drive the van, but not to speed. However, his speeding was of the same general nature as the authorized act, so Jane is liable to Bernadette.

ABANDONMENT

The second major issue in a *scope of employment* case involves abandonment. **The principal is liable for the actions of the employee that occur while the employee is at work, but not for actions that occur after the employee has abandoned the principal's business.** Although the rule sounds straightforward, the difficulty lies in determining whether the employee has in fact abandoned the principal's business. The employer is liable if the employee is simply on a *detour* from company business, but the employer is not liable if the employee is off on a *frolic of his own.* Suppose that Hank, the delivery van driver, speeds during his afternoon commute home. An employee is generally not acting within the scope of his employment when he commutes to and from work, so his principal, Jane, is not liable. Or suppose that, while on the way to a delivery, he stops to view his favorite movie classic, *Dead on Arrival.* Unable to see in the darkened theater, he knocks Anna down, causing grave harm. Jane is not liable because Hank's visit to the movies is outside the scope of his employment. On the other hand, if Hank stops at the Burger Box drive-in window en route to making a delivery, Jane is liable when he crashes into Anna on the way out of the parking lot because this time, he is simply making a detour.

Was the employee in the following case acting within the scope of his employment while driving to work? You be the judge.

You Be the Judge

Facts: Staff Sergeant William E. Dreyer was a recruiter for the United States Marine Corps. Driving to work one morning at 6:40 a.m., in a government-owned car, he struck and killed 12-year-old Justin Zankel. The child's parents sued the federal government, claiming that it was liable for Dreyer's actions because he had been acting within the scope of his employment at the time of the accident.

The Marine Corps had provided Dreyer with a car to drive while on government business, but he was not permitted to use this car while commuting to and from home unless he had specific authorization from his boss, Major Michael Sherman. However, Sherman was flexible in giving authorization and even permitted his soldiers simply to

ZANKEL V. UNITED STATES OF AMERICA

2008 U.S. Dist. LEXIS 23655
United States District Court for the Western District of Pennsylvania, 2008

leave a message on his voicemail. Indeed, he had denied only about a dozen such requests over a three-year period.

Each month, Dreyer was expected to meet specific quotas for the number of contracts signed and recruits shipped to basic training. However, despite working 16 to 18 hours every day of the week, Dreyer had not met his recruiting quotas for months. Sherman had formally reprimanded him and increased his target for the following month.

On the day before the accident, Dreyer left home at 6:30 a.m., driving his own car. At the office, he switched to a government car and worked until 10:45 p.m. He then discovered that his personal car would not start. He did not want to call Sherman that late, so he drove his government car home without permission. He believed that, had he called, Sherman would have said it was OK.

Dreyer arrived home at midnight. He was under orders to attend an early-morning training session the next day. So he awoke early and left home at 6:35 a.m. At 6:40 a.m., his car hit Justin Zankel.

You Be the Judge: *Was Dreyer within the scope of employment when he killed Zankel?*

Argument for the Zankels: At the time of the accident, Dreyer was driving a government vehicle. Although he had not requested permission to drive the car, if he had done so, permission certainly would have been granted.

Moreover, even if Dreyer was not authorized to drive the Marine Corps car, the government is still liable because his activity was of the same general nature as that authorized and it was incidental to the conduct authorized. Driving the car was part of Dreyer's work. Indeed, he could not perform his job

without it. In addition, Dreyer was on the road early so that he could attend a required training session. He was exhausted from trying to reach impossible goals. The Marine Corps must bear responsibility for this tragic accident.

Argument for United States: The government had a clear policy stating that recruiters were not authorized to drive a government car without first requesting permission. Dreyer had not done so. Therefore, he was not authorized to drive the government car at the time of the accident.

Moreover, it is well established that an employee commuting to and from work is not within the scope of employment. If Dreyer had been driving from one recruiting event to another, that would be a different story. But on the day of the accident, he had not yet started work for the Marine Corps, and therefore the government is not liable.

25-8c Intentional Torts

A principal is *not* liable for the *intentional* torts of an employee unless (1) the employee intended to serve some purpose of the employer; or (2) the employer was negligent in hiring or supervising this employee. During an NBA basketball game, Kobe pushes LeBron into some chairs under the basket to prevent him from scoring a breakaway layup. Kobe's team is liable for his actions because he was motivated, at least in part, by a desire to help his team. But if Kobe hits LeBron in the parking lot after the playoffs are over, Kobe's team is *not* liable because he is no longer motivated by a desire to help the team. His motivation now is personal revenge or frustration.

In the following case, a priest did wrong. Was he serving some purpose of the Church? Was the Church liable for his criminal acts?

DOE v. LIBERATORE

478 F. Supp. 2d 742; 2007 U.S. Dist. LEXIS 19067
United States District Court for the Middle District of Pennsylvania, 2007

CASE SUMMARY

Facts: A number of priests wrote to James Timlin, the Bishop of Scranton, warning him that Father Albert Liberatore was engaging in a sexual relationship with one of his male students. Bishop Timlin transferred Liberatore from the school to a parish church.

Fourteen year-old John Doe was a member of Liberatore's parish. Liberatore befriended Doe, taking him on outings and giving him expensive gifts. Doe routinely slept in Liberatore's bed. A number of priests told Bishop Timlin

that they feared Liberatore was sexually abusing Doe. One witness reported that she had seen Doe put his hand down Liberatore's pants. Eventually, Doe himself told a priest that he was being sexually abused. The priest instructed Doe to forgive Liberatore and not to tell other people because it would ruin Doe's life and the lives of others.

Only after Liberatore pleaded guilty to multiple counts of sexual abuse did the Church dismiss him from the priesthood. Doe filed suit against the Church and Bishop Timlin, alleging that they were liable for the torts committed by Liberatore. The defendants filed a motion to dismiss.

Issues: *Was Liberatore acting within the scope of his employment? Were the defendants liable for his criminal acts?*

Decision: The priest's sexual misconduct was not within the scope of his employment. Nevertheless, the defendants could be liable on the grounds of negligent supervision.

Reasoning: Liberatore's sexual abuse of a child was not within the scope of his employment as a priest. In no way did it serve the purposes of the Church or Bishop Timlin. Therefore, the Court granted summary judgment for the defendants on this issue.

However, an employer owes a duty to exercise reasonable care in hiring and supervising employees. The defendants are not negligent for *hiring* the priest at the beginning because at that point, there was no evidence he would sexually abuse children, but a jury could certainly conclude that both the Church and the Bishop had been negligent in *supervising* Liberatore.

25-8d Physical or Nonphysical Harm

In the case of *physical* torts, a principal is liable for the negligent conduct of a employee that occurs within the scope of employment. The rule for *nonphysical* torts (i.e., torts that harm only reputation, feelings, or wallet) is different. **Nonphysical torts are treated more like a contract claim, and the principal is liable if the employee acted with express, implied, or apparent authority.**[18] For example, suppose that Dwayne buys a house insurance policy from Andy, who is an agent of the Balls of Fire Insurance Company. Andy throws away Dwayne's policy and pockets his premiums. When Dwayne's house burns down, Balls of Fire is liable because Andy was acting with apparent authority.

EXAM Strategy

Question: Daisy was the founder of an Internet start-up company. Jay was her driver. One day, after he had dropped her at a board meeting, he went to the car wash. There, he told an attractive woman that he worked for a money management firm. She gave him money to invest. On the way out of the car wash, he was so excited that he hit another customer's expensive car. Who is liable for Jay's misdeeds?

Strategy: In determining a principal's liability, begin by figuring out whether the agent has committed a physical or nonphysical tort. Remember that the principal is liable for physical torts within the scope of employment, but for nonphysical torts, she is liable only if the employee acted with authority.

Result: In this case, Daisy is liable for the damage to the car because that was a physical tort within the scope of employment. But she is not liable for the investment money because Jay did not have authority (express, implied, or apparent) to take those funds.

---

[18]Restatement (Third) of Agency §7.08.

25-9 AGENT'S LIABILITY FOR TORTS

The focus of the prior section was on the *principal's* liability for the agent's torts. But it is important to remember that **agents are always liable for their own torts.** Agents who commit torts are personally responsible, whether or not their principal is also liable. Even if the tort was committed to benefit the principal, the agent is still liable. So the sailor who got into a fistfight while rousting a shipmate from bed is liable even though he thought he was acting for the benefit of his principal.

This rule makes obvious sense. If the agent were not liable, he would have little incentive to be careful. Imagine Hank driving his delivery van for Jane. If he were not personally liable for his own torts, he might think, "If I drive fast enough, I can make it through that light even though it just turned red. And if I don't, what the heck, it'll be Jane's problem, not mine." Agents, as a rule, may have fewer assets than their principal, but it is important that their personal assets be at risk in the event of their negligent behavior.

If the agent and principal are *both* liable, which does the injured third party sue? The principal and the agent are *jointly and severally liable*, which means, as we have seen, that the injured third party can sue either one or both, as she chooses. If she recovers from the principal, he can sue the agent.

Chapter Conclusion

When students enroll in a business law course, they fully expect to learn about torts and contracts, corporations and partnerships. They probably do not think much about agency law; many of them have not even heard the term before. Yet it is an area of the law that affects us all because each of us has been and will continue to be both an agent and a principal many times in our lives.

EXAM REVIEW

1. **CREATING AN AGENCY RELATIONSHIP**   A principal and an agent mutually consent that the agent will act on behalf of the principal and be subject to the principal's control, thereby creating a fiduciary relationship. (pp. 588–590)

2. **ELEMENTS NOT REQUIRED**   An agency relationship can exist without either a written agreement, a formal agreement, or compensation. (pp. 589–590)

3. **AN AGENT'S DUTIES TO THE PRINCIPAL**   An agent owes these duties to the principal: duty of loyalty, duty to obey instructions, duty of care, and duty to provide information. (pp. 590–595)

4. **THE PRINCIPAL'S REMEDIES IN THE EVENT OF A BREACH**   The principal has three potential remedies when the agent breaches her duty: recovery of damages the breach has caused, recovery of any profits earned by the agent from the breach, and rescission of any transaction with the agent. (pp. 594–595)

5. **THE PRINCIPAL'S DUTIES TO THE AGENT**   The principal has three duties to the agent: to compensate as provided by the agreement, to reimburse legitimate expenses, and to cooperate with the agent. (pp. 595–596)

6. **POWER AND RIGHT TO TERMINATE**   Both the agent and the principal have the power to terminate an agency relationship, but they may not have the right. If the termination violates the agency agreement and causes harm to the other party, the wrongful party must pay damages. (pp. 596–598)

7. **AUTOMATIC TERMINATION**   An agency relationship automatically terminates if the principal or agent no longer can perform the required duties or if a change in circumstances renders the agency relationship pointless. (p. 596)

8. **A PRINCIPAL'S LIABILITY FOR CONTRACTS**   A principal is liable for the contracts of the agent if the agent has express, implied, or apparent authority. (pp. 599–601)

9. **EXPRESS AUTHORITY**   The principal grants express authority by words or conduct that, reasonably interpreted, cause the agent to believe that the principal desires her to act on the principal's account. (p. 599)

10. **IMPLIED AUTHORITY**   Implied authority includes authority to do acts that are incidental to a transaction, usually accompany it, or are reasonably necessary to accomplish it. (pp. 599–600)

11. **APPARENT AUTHORITY**   Apparent authority means that a principal is liable for the acts of an agent who is not, in fact, acting with authority if the principal's conduct causes a third party reasonably to believe that the agent is authorized. (p. 600**)**

EXAM Strategy

Question: Dr. James Leonard wrote Dr. Edward Jacobson to offer him the position of chief of audiology at Jefferson Medical College in Philadelphia. In the letter, Leonard stated that this appointment would have to be approved by the promotion and appointment committee. Jacobson believed that the appointment committee acted only as a "rubber stamp," affirming whatever recommendation Leonard made. Jacobson accepted Leonard's offer and proceeded to sell his house and quit his job in Colorado. You can guess what happened next. Two weeks later, Leonard sent Jacobson another letter, rescinding his offer because of opposition from the appointment committee. Did Leonard have apparent authority?

Strategy: In cases of apparent authority, begin by asking what the principal did to make the third party believe that the agent was authorized. What did the Medical College do? (See the "Result" at the end of this section.)

12. **AN AGENT'S LIABILITY FOR A CONTRACT**   An agent is not liable for any contract she makes on behalf of a fully disclosed principal. The principal is liable. In the case of a unidentified or undisclosed principal, both the agent and the principal are liable on the contract. (pp. 601–603)

13. **A PRINCIPAL'S LIABILITY FOR TORTS**   An employer is liable for a tort committed by its employee acting within the scope of employment or acting with authority. (pp. 604–608)

Question: While drunk, the driver of a subway car plows into the back of the car ahead of him, killing a passenger. It was against the rules for the driver to be drunk. Is the subway authority liable for the negligence of its employee?

Strategy: With a tort case, always determine first if the agents are employees or independent contractors. This worker was an employee. Then ask if the employee was acting within the scope of employment. Yes, he was driving a subway car, which is what he was hired to do. Does it matter than he had violated subway rules? No, his violation of the rules does not eliminate his principal's liability. (See the "Results" at the end of this section.)

14. **INDEPENDENT CONTRACTOR**   The principal is liable for the physical torts of an independent contractor only if the principal has been negligent in hiring or supervising him. (p. 604)

15. **INTENTIONAL TORTS**   A principal is not liable for the intentional torts of an employee unless (1) the employee intended to serve some purpose of the employer; or (2) the employer was negligent in hiring or supervising the employee. (pp. 607–608)

Question: What if the subway driver mentioned above had stabbed a passenger?

Strategy: In the case of an intentional tort, the principal is liable only if the agent was intending to serve some purpose of the employer or the employer was negligent in hiring or supervising him. (See the "Results" at the end of this section.)

16. **NONPHYSICAL TORTS**   A principal is liable only for the nonphysical torts of an employee who is acting with express, implied, or apparent authority. (p. 608)

17. **AGENT'S LIABILITY FOR TORTS**   Agents are always liable for their own torts. (p. 609)

<u>11. Result:</u>   No. Indeed, Leonard had told Jacobson that he did not have authority. If Jacobson chose to believe otherwise, that was his problem.

<u>13. Result:</u>   The subway authority is liable.

<u>15. Result:</u>   When he stabbed a passenger, the driver was not serving the purpose of the employer, so the subway authority would not be liable. There was no evidence that the subway authority had been negligent in its hiring or supervising of employees.

MULTIPLE-CHOICE QUESTIONS

1. At Business University, semester enrollment begins at midnight on April 1. Jasper asked his roommate, Alonso, to register him for an important required course as a favor. Alonso agreed to do so but then overslept. As a result, Jasper could not enroll in the required course he needed to graduate and had to stay in school for an additional semester. Is Alonso liable to Jasper?

   (a) No, because an agency agreement is invalid unless the agent receives payment.

   (b) No, because Alonso was not grossly negligent.

   (c) No, because the cost of the extra semester is unreasonably high.

   (d) Yes, because Alonso disobeyed his instructions.

2. Finn learns that, despite his stellar record, he is being paid less than other salespeople at Barry Co., so he decides to start his own company. During his last month on the Barry payroll, he tells all of his clients about his new business. He also tells them that Barry is a great company, but his fees will be lower. After he opens the doors of his new business, most of his former clients move with him. Is Finn liable to Barry?

   (a) No, because he has not been disloyal to Barry—he praised the company.

   (b) No, because Barry was underpaying him.

   (c) No, because his clients have the right to hire whichever company they choose.

   (d) Yes, Finn has violated his duty of loyalty to Barry.

3. Kurt asked his car mechanic, Quinn, for help in buying a used car. Quinn recommends a Ford Focus that she has been taking care of its whole life. Quinn was working for the seller. Which of the following statements is true?

   (a) Quinn must pay Kurt the amount of money she received from the Ford's prior owner.

   (b) After buying the car, Kurt finds out that it needs $1,000 in repairs. He can recover that amount from Quinn, but only if Quinn knew about the needed repairs before Kurt bought the car.

   (c) Kurt cannot recover anything because Quinn had no obligation to reveal her relationship with the car's seller.

   (d) Kurt cannot recover anything because he had not paid Quinn for her help.

4. Figgins is the dean of a college. He appointed Sue as acting dean while he was out of the country and posted an announcement on the college website announcing that she was authorized to act in his place. He also told Sue privately that she did not have the right to make admissions decisions. While Figgins was gone, Sue overruled the admissions committee to admit the child of a wealthy alumnus. Does the child have the right to attend this college?

   (a) No, because Sue was not authorized to admit him.

   (b) No, because Figgins did not ratify Sue's decision.

   (c) Yes, because Figgins was a fully disclosed principal.

   (d) Yes, because Sue had apparent authority.

5. **CPA QUESTION** A principal will not be liable to a third party for a tort committed by an agent:

    (a) unless the principal instructed the agent to commit the tort.

    (b) unless the tort was committed within the scope of the agency relationship.

    (c) if the agency agreement limits the principal's liability for the agent's tort.

    (d) if the tort is also regarded as a criminal act.

6. **CPA QUESTION** Cox engaged Datz as her agent. It was mutually agreed that Datz would not disclose that he was acting as Cox's agent. Instead, he was to deal with prospective customers as if he were a principal acting on his own behalf. This he did and made several contracts for Cox. Assuming Cox, Datz, or the customer seeks to avoid liability on one of the contracts involved, which of the following statements is correct?

    (a) Cox must ratify the Datz contracts to be held liable.

    (b) Datz has no liability once he discloses that Cox was the real principal.

    (c) The third party can avoid liability because he believed he was dealing with Datz as a principal.

    (d) The third party may choose to hold either Datz or Cox liable.

Essay Questions

1. An elementary school custodian hit a child who wrote graffiti on the wall. Is the school district liable for this intentional tort by its employee?

2. What if the custodian hit one of the schoolchildren for calling him a name? Is the school district liable?

3. A soldier was drinking at a training seminar. Although he was told to leave his car at the seminar, he disobeyed orders and drove to a military club. On the way to the club, he was involved in an accident. Is the military liable for the damage he caused?

4. One afternoon while visiting friends, tennis star Vitas Gerulaitis fell asleep in their pool house. A mechanic had improperly installed the swimming pool heater, which leaked carbon monoxide fumes into the house where he slept, killing him. His mother filed suit against the owners of the estate. On what theory would they be liable?

5. **YOU BE THE JUDGE WRITING PROBLEM** Sarah went to an auction at Christie's to bid on a tapestry for her employer, Fine Arts Gallery. The good news is that she purchased a Dufy tapestry for $77,000. The bad news is that it was not the one her employer had told her to buy. In the excitement of the auction, she forgot her instructions. Fine Art refused to pay, and Christie's filed suit. Is Fine Arts liable for the unauthorized act of its agent? **Argument for Christie's:** Christie's cannot possibly ascertain in each case the exact nature of a bidder's authority. Whether or not Sarah had actual authority, she certainly had apparent authority, and Fine Arts is liable. **Argument for Fine Arts:** Sarah was not authorized to purchase the Dufy tapestry, and therefore Christie's must recover from her, not Fine Arts.

DISCUSSION QUESTIONS

1. **ETHICS** Mercedes has just begun work at Photobook.com. What a great place to work! Although the salary is not high, the company has fabulous perks. The dining room provides great food from 7 a.m. to midnight, five days a week. There is also a free laundry and dry-cleaning service. Mercedes's social life has never been better. She invites her friends over for Photobook meals and has their laundry done for free. And because her job requires her to be online all the time, she has plenty of opportunity to stay in touch with her friends by g-chatting, tweeting, and checking Facebook updates. She is, however, shocked that one of her colleagues takes paper home from the office for his children to use at home. Are these employees behaving ethically?

2. Kevin was the manager of a radio station, WABC. A competing station lured him away. In his last month on the job at WABC, he notified two key on-air personalities that if they were to leave the station, he would not hold them to their noncompete agreements. What can WABC do?

3. Jesse worked as a buyer for the Vegetable Co. Rachel offered to sell Jesse 10 tons of tomatoes for the account of Vegetable. Jesse accepted the offer. Later, Jesse discovered that Rachel was an agent for Sylvester Co. Who is liable on this contract?

4. The Pharmaceutical Association holds an annual convention. At the convention, Brittany, who was president of the association, told Luke that Research Corp. had a promising new cancer vaccine. Luke was so excited that he chartered a plane to fly to Research's headquarters. On the way, the plane crashed and Luke was killed. Is the Pharmaceutical Association liable for Luke's death?

5. Betsy has a two-year contract as a producer at Jackson Movie Studios. She produces a remake of the movie *Footloose*. Unfortunately, it bombs, and Jackson is so furious that he fires her on the weekend the movie opens. Does he have the power to do this?

Employment, Business Organizations and Property

CHAPTER 26

EMPLOYMENT AND LABOR LAW

nuttakit/Shutterstock.com; © Steve Allen/Brand X Pictures/Jupiter Images

"On the killing beds you were apt to be covered with blood, and it would freeze solid; if you leaned against a pillar, you would freeze to that, and if you put your hand upon the blade of your knife, you would run a chance of leaving your skin on it. The men would tie up their feet in newspapers and old sacks, and these would be soaked in blood and frozen, and then soaked again, and so on, until by nighttime a man would be walking on great lumps the size of the feet of an elephant. Now and then, when the bosses were not looking, you would see them plunging their feet and ankles into the steaming hot carcass of the steer. … The cruelest thing of all was that nearly all of them—all of those who used knives—were unable to wear gloves, and their arms would be white with frost and their hands would grow numb, and then of course there would be accidents."[1]

> [… you would see them plunging their feet and ankles into the steaming hot carcass of the steer.]

[1] From Upton Sinclair, *The Jungle* (New York: Bantam Books, 1981), p. 80, a 1906 novel about the meat-packing industry.

26-1 INTRODUCTION

For most of history, the concept of career planning was unknown. By and large, people were born into their jobs. Whatever their parents had been—landowner, soldier, farmer, servant, merchant, or beggar—they became, too. People not only knew their place, they also understood the rights and obligations inherent in each position. The landowner had the right to receive labor from his tenants, but he also cared for them if they fell ill. Certainly, there were abuses, but at a time when people held religious convictions about their position in life and workers had few expectations that their lives would be better than their parents', the role of law was limited.

The primary English law of employment simply established that, in the absence of a contract, an employee was hired for a year at a time. This rule was designed to prevent injustice in a farming society. If an employee worked through harvest time, the landowner could not fire him in the unproductive winter. Conversely, a worker could not stay the winter and then leave for greener pastures in the spring.

In the eighteenth and nineteenth centuries, the Industrial Revolution profoundly altered the employment relationship. Many workers left the farms and villages for large factories in the city. Bosses no longer knew their workers personally, so they felt little responsibility toward them. The old laws that had suited an agrarian economy with stable relationships did not fit the new employment conditions. Instead of duties and responsibilities, courts emphasized the freedom to contract. Since employees could quit their factory jobs whenever they wanted, it seemed only fair for employers to have the same freedom to fire a worker. That was indeed the rule adopted by the courts: Unless workers had an explicit employment contract, they were employees at will. **An *employee at will* could be fired for a good reason, a bad reason, or no reason at all.** For nearly a century, this was the basic common law rule of employment. A court explained the rule this way:

> Precisely as may the employee cease labor at his whim or pleasure, and, whatever be his reason, good, bad, or indifferent, leave no one a legal right to complain; so, upon the other hand, may the employer discharge, and, whatever be his reason, good, bad, or indifferent, no one has suffered a legal wrong.[2]

However evenhanded this common law rule of employment may have sounded in theory, in practice, it could lead to harsh results. The lives of factory workers were grim. It was not as if they could simply pack up and leave; conditions were no better elsewhere. Courts and legislatures gradually began to recognize that individual workers were generally unable to negotiate fair contracts with powerful employers. Since the beginning of the twentieth century, employment law has changed dramatically. Now, the employment relationship is more strictly regulated by statutes and by the common law.

Note well, though: **In the absence of a specific legal exception, the rule in the United States is *still* that an employee at will can be fired for any reason.** But today there are several important exceptions to this rule. Many of the statutes discussed in this chapter and the next were passed by Congress and therefore apply nationally. The common law, however, comes from state courts and only applies locally. We will look at a sampling of cases that illustrates national trends, even though the law may not be the same in every state.

This chapter covers five topics in employment law: (1) employment security, (2) privacy in the workplace, (3) safety issues, (4) financial protection, and (5) labor law. Chapter 27 covers employment discrimination.

---

[2]*Union Labor Hospital Assn. v. Vance Redwood Lumber Co.*, 112 P.886, 888, 1910 Cal. LEXIS 417 (Cal., 1910).

26-2 EMPLOYMENT SECURITY

26-2a Family and Medical Leave Act

The Family and Medical Leave Act (FMLA) guarantees both men and women up to 12 weeks of *unpaid* leave each year for childbirth, adoption, or a serious health condition of their own or in their immediate family. This statute defines an immediate family member as a spouse, child, or parent—but not a sibling, grandchild, or in-law. An employee who takes a leave must be allowed to return to the same or an equivalent job with the same pay and benefits. The FMLA applies only to companies with at least 50 workers and to employees who have been with the company full time for at least a year.

Here are some examples of what counts as a "serious health condition" under this statute:

- Any health issue that requires hospitalization.

- A condition that requires more than one visit to a health care provider. The visits may be spread out over as long as a year.

- A condition that requires only one visit to a health care provider, but which also requires a course of treatment such as physical therapy or prescription medication.

Thus, the FMLA would apply in the case of a heart attack, ongoing kidney dialysis, and an ear infection that required antibiotics. It would generally not cover food poisoning that did not require hospitalization, the common cold, or a sprained ankle.

Kevin Knussman was the first person to win a lawsuit under the FMLA. While a Maryland state trooper, he requested eight weeks of leave to care for his pregnant wife, who was suffering severe complications. His boss granted only two weeks. After Knussman's daughter was born, his boss again denied leave, saying that "God made women to have babies." Knussman ultimately recovered $40,000.[3]

In many FMLA lawsuits, a worker claims that he or she was fired in retaliation for taking leave, while the employer argues that the termination was for some other reason. The following case illustrates this dynamic.

PETERSON v. EXIDE TECHNOLOGIES

2012 U.S. App. LEXIS 7139
Tenth Circuit Court of Appeals, 2012

Facts: Exide Technologies repeatedly warned Robert Peterson that he was driving forklifts too fast and violating other safety rules. After he was injured in a forklift crash, Exide granted him FMLA leave for 10 days while he recovered.

Peterson's manager fired him during the leave for "flagrant violations of safety rules." Peterson sued, claiming that he was terminated in retaliation for exercising his right to take FMLA leave. The lower court granted summary judgment to Exide, and Peterson appealed.

Issue: *Was Peterson fired in retaliation for taking FMLA leave?*

Decision: No, Peterson was fired for violating safety rules. The grant of summary judgment is affirmed.

Reasoning: The FMLA prohibits an employer from retaliating against a worker for exercising his rights under the statute. The analysis of such a claim requires three steps:

---

[3]Eyal Press, "Family-Leave Values," *New York Times*, July 29, 2007.

1. the worker must present evidence of retaliation

2. the company then has to show a legitimate reason for the firing

3. the worker must provide evidence that the company's reason was just a pretext.

Peterson was fired while on FMLA leave. That fact is evidence of retaliation. But Exide presented a legitimate reason for the firing. Photographs of the damage caused by the forklift crash indicated that Peterson had been driving fast and recklessly. Such conduct was a dangerous violation of the company's policies. Moreover, Peterson had a history of such unsafe behavior.

The burden was then on Peterson to show that this reason was simply an excuse. He argued that the accident had been too minor to justify his firing. It is not at all clear that the accident was minor. But, in any event, Exide had the right to fire employees even for minor safety violations. And when a worker has a history of unsafe behavior, a minor accident could well be the last straw.

In short, Peterson did not meet the requirements of the statute to show that the company retaliated against him for exercising his FMLA rights.

Ethics   Although the FMLA offers important protections, the United States is the only wealthy country that does not provide mandatory *paid* maternity leave. Should Congress modify the FMLA to require some period of paid leave for new mothers? If so, for how long? A few weeks while they recuperate from childbirth? Or a few months to care for the newborn? What about paternity leave, which many countries require? And how about workers who take FMLA leave to deal with a serious illness? Should they be paid?

26-2b Health Insurance

Companies are *not* required to provide their employees with health insurance. However, current legislation specifies that, starting in 2015, employers who have more than 50 full-time employees must pay a penalty if they do not provide basic health insurance. In addition, company insurance policies must now cover employees' children up to the age of 26.

Losing your job does not mean that you must also give up your health insurance—at least not right away. Under the Consolidated Omnibus Budget Reconciliation Act (COBRA), **former employees must be allowed to continue their health insurance for 18 months after being terminated from their job.** The catch is that employees must pay for it themselves, up to 102 percent of the cost. (The extra 2 percent covers administrative expenses.) COBRA applies to any company with 20 or more workers.

26-2c Common Law Protections

The employment-at-will doctrine was created by the courts. Because that rule has sometimes led to grossly unfair results, the courts have now created a major exception to the rule—**wrongful discharge.**

WRONGFUL DISCHARGE: VIOLATING PUBLIC POLICY

Olga Monge was a schoolteacher in her native Costa Rica. After moving to New Hampshire, she attended college in the evenings to earn U.S. teaching credentials. At night, she worked at the Beebe Rubber Co. During the day, she cared for her husband and three children. When she applied for a better job at her plant, the foreman offered to promote her if she would be "nice" and go out on a date with him. When she refused, he assigned her to a

Wrongful discharge
An employer may not fire a worker for a reason that violates basic social rights, duties or responsibilities.

lower-wage job, took away her overtime, made her clean the washrooms, and generally ridiculed her. Finally, she collapsed at work, and he fired her.[4]

Imagine that you are one of the judges who decided this case. Olga Monge has been treated abominably, but she was an employee at will and, as you well know, could be fired for any reason. But how can you let the foreman get away with this despicable behavior? The New Hampshire Supreme Court decided that even an employee at will has some rights:

> We hold that a termination by the employer of a contract of employment at will which is motivated by bad faith or malice or based on retaliation is not in the best interest of the economic system or the public good and constitutes a breach of the employment contract.[5]

The *Monge* case illustrates the concept of wrongful discharge, which **prohibits an employer from firing a worker for certain particularly *bad reasons*.**

How do the courts define a "bad reason"? It is a reason that violates public policy. Unfortunately, this **public policy rule** is easier to name than it is to define because its definition and application vary from state to state. **In essence, the public policy rule prohibits an employer from firing a worker for a reason that violates basic social rights, duties, or responsibilities.** Almost every employee who has ever been fired feels that a horrible injustice has been done. The difficulty, from the courts' perspective, is to distinguish those cases of dismissal that are offensive enough to affront the community at large from those that outrage only the employee. The courts have primarily applied the public policy rule when an employee refuses to violate the law, performs a legal duty, exercises a legal right, or supports basic societal values.

Refusing to Violate the Law

Larry Downs went to Duke Hospital for surgery on his cleft palate. When he came out of the operating room, the doctor instructed a nurse, Marie Sides, to give Downs enough anesthetic to immobilize him. Sides refused because she thought the anesthetic was wrong for this patient. The doctor angrily administered the anesthetic himself. Shortly thereafter, Downs stopped breathing. Before the doctors could resuscitate him, he suffered permanent brain damage. When Downs's family sued the hospital, Sides was called to testify. A number of Duke doctors told her that she would be "in trouble" if she testified. She did testify, and after three months of harassment, she was fired. When she sued Duke University, the court held:

> It would be obnoxious to the interests of the state and contrary to public policy and sound morality to allow an employer to discharge any employee, whether the employment be for a designated or unspecified duration, on the ground that the employee declined to commit perjury, an act specifically enjoined by statute. To hold otherwise would be without reason and contrary to the spirit of the law.[6]

As a general rule, employees may not be discharged for refusing to break the law. For example, courts have protected employees who refused to participate in an illegal price-fixing scheme, falsify pollution control records required by state law, pollute navigable waters in violation of federal law, or assist a supervisor in stealing from customers.[7]

---

[4]*Monge v. Beebe*, 114 N.H. 130, 316 A.2d 549, 1974 N.H. LEXIS 223 (NH S. Ct., 1974).

[5]*Id*. at 133.

[6]*Sides v. Duke University*, 74 N.C. App. 331, 328 S.E.2d 818, 1985 N.C. App. LEXIS 3501 (N.C. Ct. App. 1985).

[7]*Tameny v. Atlantic Richfield Co.*, 27 Cal. 3d 167, 610 P.2d 1330, 1980 Cal. LEXIS 171 (1980); *Trombetta v. Detroit*, T. & I. R., 81 Mich. App. 489, 265 N.W.2d 385, 1978 Mich. App. LEXIS 2153 (Mich. Ct. App. 1978); *Sabine Pilot Service, Inc. v. Hauck*, 28 Tex. Sup. J. 339, 687 S.W.2d 733, 1985 Tex. LEXIS 755 (1985); *Vermillion v. AAA Pro Moving & Storage*, 146 Ariz. 215, 704 P.2d 1360, 1985 Ariz. App. LEXIS 592 (Ariz. Ct. App. 1985).

Performing a Legal Duty   Courts have consistently held that an employee may not be fired for serving on a jury. Employers sometimes have difficulty replacing employees who are called up for jury duty and, therefore, prefer that their workers find some excuse for not serving. But jury duty is an important civic obligation that employers are not permitted to undermine.

Exercising a Legal Right   As a general rule, an employer may not discharge a worker for exercising a legal right if that right supports public policy. Dorothy Frampton injured her arm while working at the Central Indiana Gas Co. Her employer (and its insurance company) paid her medical expenses and her salary during the four months she was unable to work. When she discovered that she also qualified for benefits under the state's workers' compensation plan, she filed a claim and received payment. One month later, the company fired her without giving a reason. In her suit against the gas company, the court held:

> The [Workers' Compensation] Act creates a duty in the employer to compensate employees for work-related injuries and a right in the employee to receive such compensation. If employers are permitted to penalize employees for filing workmen's compensation claims, a most important public policy will be undermined. Employees will not file claims for justly deserved compensation—opting, instead, to continue their employment without incident. The end result, of course, is that the employer is effectively relieved of his obligation.[8]

Supporting Societal Values   Courts are sometimes willing to protect employees who do the right thing, even if they violate the boss's orders. Kevin Gardner had just parked his armored truck in front of a bank in Spokane, Washington, when he saw a man with a knife chase the manager out of the bank. While running past the truck, the manager looked directly at Gardner and yelled, "Help me, help me." Gardner got out of his truck and locked the door. By then, the suspect had grabbed another woman, put his knife to her throat, and dragged her into the bank. Gardner followed them in, tackled the suspect, and disarmed him. The rescued woman hailed Gardner as a hero, but his employer fired him for violating a "fundamental" company rule that prohibited drivers from leaving their armored trucks unattended. However, the court held for Gardner on the grounds that, although he had no affirmative legal duty to intervene in such a situation, society values and encourages voluntary rescuers when a life is in danger.[9] This issue is, however, one on which the courts are divided. Not all would have made the same decision.

In the following case, two employees objected when their company supplied defective human tissue for transplantation into live patients. Should the court protect them from termination?

KOZLOSKI V. AMERICAN TISSUE SERVICES FOUNDATION

2006 U.S. Dist. LEXIS 95435
United States District Court for the District of Minnesota, 2006

CASE SUMMARY

Facts: American Tissue Services Foundation (ATSF) was in the business of supplying human tissue from cadavers for transplantation into live patients. Mike Slack, an employee of ATSF, revealed to his boss that he had falsified a donor medical record and changed the donor's blood type on the form. This falsification was not only dangerous to recipients of the tissue, it violated Food and Drug Administration (FDA) regulations. Slack was fired and the infractions were reported to the FDA, as required by law.

---

[8]*Frampton v. Central Indiana Gas Co.*, 260 Ind. 249, 297 N.E.2d 425, 1973 Ind. LEXIS 522 (1973).
[9]*Gardner v. Loomis Armored, Inc.*, 913 P.2d 377, 1996 Wash. LEXIS 109 (1996).

It turned out, however, that Slack was the foster child of the company's chairman. And, in this case, (foster) blood was thicker than water. The chairman not only hired Slack at another company as a quality assurance specialist (believe it or not), but he fired Slack's boss and the two men who had reported the problem to the FDA. The men filed suit against ATSF for wrongful discharge, but the company filed a motion to dismiss on the grounds that the public policy doctrine in Minnesota applied only to employees who had refused to violate the law.

Issues: *Does the public policy doctrine in Minnesota apply only to employees who refuse to violate the law? Do the plaintiffs have the right to proceed with their lawsuit?*

Decision: The wrongful discharge doctrine also applies to situations in which an employee is fired for a reason that clearly violates public policy. The defendants may proceed with their lawsuit.

Reasoning: These plaintiffs were fired because they reported to their employer and the FDA their concerns that human tissue was wrongly labeled. This wrongdoing not only created grave risks for the recipients it also violated federal law. ATSF alleges that under Minnesota law, employees can bring a wrongful discharge claim only if they were fired for refusing to violate the law. This reading of the law is incorrect. Wrongful discharge also applies when the termination is for a reason that *clearly* violates public policy. This termination meets that standard. The safe use of human tissue in live patients is *clearly* a matter of public safety and, therefore, public policy.

CONTRACT LAW

Traditionally, many employers (and employees) thought that only a formal, signed document qualified as an employment contract. Increasingly, however, courts have been willing to enforce an employer's more casual promises, whether written or oral. Sometimes courts have also been willing to *imply* contract terms in the absence of an *express* agreement.

Truth in Hiring   **Oral promises made during the hiring process can be enforceable, even if not approved by the company's top executives.** When the Tanana Valley Medical-Surgical Group, Inc., hired James Eales as a physician's assistant, it promised him that so long as he did his job, he could stay there until retirement age. Six years later, the company fired him without cause. The Alaska Supreme Court held that the clinic's promise was enforceable.[10]

Employee Handbooks   The employee handbook at Blue Cross & Blue Shield stated that employees could be fired only for just cause and then only after warnings, notice, a hearing, and other procedures. Charles Toussaint was fired summarily five years after he joined the company. Although this decision was ultimately reviewed by the personnel department, company president, and chairman of the board of trustees, Toussaint was not given the benefit of all of the procedures in the handbook. The court held that **an employee handbook creates a contract.**[11]

Covenant of Good Faith and Fair Dealing   A covenant of good faith and fair dealing prohibits one party to a contract from interfering with the other's right to benefit under the contract. All parties are expected to behave in a fair, decent, and reasonable manner. **In almost all states, courts will imply a covenant of good faith and fair dealing in an at-will employment relationship.** These cases, however, have all arisen in situations in which an employer fires a worker to avoid paying promised income or benefits.

---

[10]*Eales v. Tanana Valley Medical-Surgical Group, Inc.,* 663 P.2d 958, 1983 Alas. LEXIS 430 (Alaska 1983).

[11]*Toussaint v. Blue Cross & Blue Shield,* 408 Mich. 579, 292 N.W.2d 880, 1980 Mich. LEXIS 227 (1980).

When Forrest Fleming went to work for Parametric Technology Corp., the company promised him valuable stock options if he met his sales goals. He would not be able to *exercise* the options (i.e., purchase the stock), however, until several years after they were granted, and then only if he was still employed by the company. During his four years with Parametric, Fleming received options to purchase about 18,000 shares for a price as low as 25 cents each. The shares ultimately traded in the market for as much as $50. Although Fleming exercised some options, the company fired him three months before he became eligible to purchase an additional 1,000 shares. The jury awarded him $1.6 million in damages. Although Parametric had not violated the explicit terms of the option agreement, the jury believed it had violated the covenant of good faith and fair dealing by firing Fleming to prevent him from exercising his remaining options.[12]

TORT LAW

Workers have successfully sued their employers under the following tort theories.

Defamation **Employers may be liable for defamation when they give false and unfavorable references about a former employee.** In his job as a bartender at the Capitol Grille restaurant, Christopher Kane often flirted with customers. After he was fired from his job, his ex-boss claimed that Kane had been "fired from every job he ever had for sexual misconduct." In fact, Kane had never been fired before. He recovered $300,000 in damages for this defamation.

More than half of the states, however, recognize a qualified privilege for employers who give references about former employees. A **qualified privilege** means that employers are liable only for false statements that they know to be false or that are primarily motivated by ill will. After Becky Chambers left her job at American Trans Air, Inc., she discovered that her former boss was telling anyone who called for a reference that Chambers "does not work good with other people," is a "troublemaker," and "would not be a good person to rehire." Chambers was unable, however, to present compelling evidence that her boss had been primarily motivated by ill will. Neither Trans Air nor the boss was held liable for these statements because they were protected by the qualified privilege.[13]

Even if the employer wins, a trial is an expensive and time-consuming undertaking. Not surprisingly, companies are leery about offering any references for former employees. The company gains little benefit from giving an honest evaluation and may suffer substantial liability. As a matter of policy, many companies instruct their managers to reveal only a person's salary and dates of employment and not to offer an opinion on job performance.

On the flip side, do employers have any obligation to warn about risky workers? **Generally, courts have held that employers do *not* have a legal obligation to disclose information about former employees.** For example, while Jeffrey St. Clair worked at the St. Joseph Nursing Home, he was disciplined 24 times for actions ranging from extreme violence to drug and alcohol use. When he applied for a job with Maintenance Management Corp., St. Joseph refused to give any information other than St. Clair's dates of employment. After he savagely murdered a security guard at his new job, the guard's family sued, but the court dismissed the case.[14]

In some recent cases, however, courts have held that, when a former worker is potentially dangerous, employers do have an obligation to disclose this information. For example, officials from two junior high schools gave Robert Gadams glowing letters of recommendation without mentioning that he had been fired for inappropriate sexual conduct with students. While an assistant principal at a new school, he molested a 13-year-old. Her parents sued the

Qualified privilege
Employers who give references are liable only for false statements that they know to be false or that are primarily motivated by ill will.

---

[12]*Fleming v. Parametric Tech. Corp.*, 1999 U.S. App. LEXIS 14864.

[13]*Chambers v. American Trans Air, Inc.*, 577 N.E.2d 612, 1991 Ind. App. LEXIS 1413 (Ind. Ct. App. 1991).

[14]*Moore v. St. Joseph Nursing Home, Inc.*, 184 Mich. App. 766, 459 N.W.2d 100, 1990 Mich. App. LEXIS 285 (Mich. Ct. App. 1990).

former employers. The court held that the writer of a letter of recommendation owes to third parties (in this case, the student) "a duty not to misrepresent the facts in describing the qualifications and character of a former employee, if making these misrepresentations would present a substantial, foreseeable risk of physical injury to the third persons."[15] As a result of cases such as this, it makes sense to disclose past violent behavior.

To assist employers who are asked for references, Lehigh economist Robert Thornton has written "The Lexicon of Intentional Ambiguous Recommendations" (LIAR). For a candidate with interpersonal problems, he suggests saying, "I am pleased to say that this person is a former colleague of mine." For a candidate with drug or alcohol problems, there are several possibilities: "She was always high in my opinion," "We remember the hours she spent working with us as happy hours," or "I would say that her real talent is getting wasted at her current job."[16]

Ethics   All joking aside, what if someone calls you to check references on a former employee who had a drinking problem? The job is driving a van for junior high school sports teams. What is the manager's ethical obligation in this situation? Many managers say that, in the case of a serious problem such as alcoholism, sexual harassment, or drug use, they will find a way to communicate that an employee is unsuitable. What if the ex-employee says she is reformed? Aren't people entitled to a second chance? Is it right to risk a defamation suit against your company to protect others from harm?

Intentional Infliction of Emotional Distress   **Employers who condone cruel treatment of their workers may face liability under the tort of intentional infliction of emotional distress.** For example, when a 57-year-old social-work manager at Yale–New Haven Hospital was fired, she was forced to place her personal belongings in a plastic bag and was escorted out the door by security guards in full view of gaping coworkers. A supervisor told her that she would be arrested for trespassing if she returned. A jury awarded her $105,000.

26-2d Whistleblowing

No one likes to be accused of wrongdoing even if (or, perhaps, especially if) the accusations are true. **This is exactly what whistleblowers do: They are employees who disclose illegal behavior on the part of their employer.** Not surprisingly, some companies, when faced with such an accusation by an employee, prefer to shoot the messenger. Rather than fixing the reported problem, they retaliate against the informer. Here is one such story.

Although FMC Corp. sold 9,000 Bradley Fighting Vehicles to the U.S. Army, there had been doubts about the Bradley from the beginning. It was designed to ferry soldiers across rivers, but prototypes leaked badly when driven into water. Testing supervisor Henry Boisvert refused to sign a report stating that the Bradley functioned well, and FMC fired him. A jury ultimately agreed with his version of events and awarded him $171 million.

The law on whistleblowers varies across the country. As a general rule, however, whistleblowers are protected in the following situations:

- **The False Claims Act.** Boisvert recovered under the federal False Claims Act, a statute that permits lawsuits against anyone who defrauds the government. The recovery is shared by the government (who receives 75 percent to 85 percent) and the whistleblower (who gets the rest). The Act prohibits employers from firing workers who file suit under the statute.

---

[15]*Randi W. v. Muroc Joint Unified School District*, 14 Cal. 4th 1066, 929 P.2d 582, 1997 Cal. LEXIS 10 (1997), modified, 14 Cal. 4th 1282c, 97 Cal. Daily Op. Service 1439.
[16]Robert J. Thornton, *Lexicon of Intentionally Ambiguous Recommendations*, Barnes and Noble Books, 2005.

- **The Dodd-Frank Wall Street Reform and Consumer Protection Act.** Anyone who provides information to the government about violations of securities or commodities laws is entitled to a payout of from 10 to 30 percent of whatever award the government receives, provided that the award tops $1 million. If a company retaliates against tipsters, they are entitled to reinstatement, double back pay, and attorney's fees. The whistleblowing provision is intended to encourage tips to the government, but companies fear it may also discourage employees from reporting wrongdoing to corporate compliance offices—why report a problem to your own company for free when you could get paid a lot of money to report it to the government?

- **Sarbanes-Oxley Act of 2002.** This act protects employees of publicly traded companies who provide evidence of fraud to investigators (whether in or outside the company). A successful plaintiff is entitled to reinstatement, back pay, and attorney's fees.

- **Constitutional protection for government employees.** Employees of federal, state, and local governments have a right to free speech under the United States Constitution. Therefore, the government cannot retaliate against public employees who blow the whistle if the employee is speaking out on a matter of *public concern*. For example, a New York City social worker complained on TV that the city child welfare agency was not adequately protecting children from horrible abuse. When the city suspended the social worker from her job, she sued. The court ruled that the government has the right to prohibit some employee speech, but if the employee speaks on matters of public concern, the government bears the burden of justifying any retaliation. In this case, the court held for the social worker.[17]

- **Statutory protection for federal employees.** The Civil Service Reform Act and the Whistleblower Protection Act prevent retaliation against federal employees who report wrongdoing. They also permit the award of back pay and attorney's fees to the whistleblower. This statute was used to prevent the National Park Service from disciplining two managers who wrote a report expressing concern over development in Yellowstone National Park.

- **State laws.** The good news is that all 50 states have laws that protect whistleblowers from retaliation by their employers. The bad news is that the scope of this protection varies greatly from state to state. Most courts, however, prohibit the discharge of employees who report illegal activity. For example, a Connecticut court held a company liable when it fired a quality control director who reported to his boss that some products had failed quality tests.[18]

EXAM Strategy

Question: When Shiloh interviewed for a sales job at a medical supply company, the interviewer promised that she could work exclusively selling medical devices and would not have to be involved in the sale of drugs. Once she began work (as an employee at will), Shiloh discovered that the sales force was organized around regions, not products, so she had to sell both devices and drugs. When she complained to her boss over lunch in the employee lunchroom, he said in a loud voice, "You are a big girl now—it's time you learned that you don't always get what you want." That afternoon, she was fired. Does she have a valid claim against the company?

---

[17]*Harman v. City of New York*, 140 F.3d 111, 1998 U.S. App. LEXIS 5567 (2d Cir. 1998).
[18]*Smith v. Calgon Carbon Corp.*, 917 F.2d 1338, 1990 U.S. App. LEXIS 19193 (3rd Cir. 1990).

Strategy: We know that Shiloh is an employee at will. We also know that she is not protected by any statute we have studied. What about the *common law?* Shiloh has had two key interactions with the company—being hired and being fired. What protections does the common law provide during the hiring process? The employer's promises are enforceable. Here, the company is liable because the interviewer clearly made a promise that the company did not keep. What about the way in which Shiloh was fired? Is it intentional infliction of emotional distress? Was this treatment cruel? Probably not cruel enough to constitute intentional infliction of emotional distress.

Result: The company is liable to Shiloh for making false promises to her during the hiring process, but not for the manner in which she was fired.

26-3 Privacy in the Workplace

Upon opening the country's first moving assembly line in the early 1900s, Henry Ford issued a booklet, "Helpful Hints and Advice to Employees," that warned against drinking, gambling, borrowing money, taking in boarders, and practicing poor hygiene. Ford also created a department of 100 investigators for door-to-door checks on his employees' drinking habits, sexual practices, and housekeeping skills.

The right to hire, fire, and make an honest profit is enshrined in American tradition. But so is the right to privacy. Justice Louis D. Brandeis called it the "right to be let alone—the most comprehensive of rights and the right most valued by civilized men." Workers are entitled under the common law to a **reasonable expectation of privacy.** Thus, employers no longer have the right to conduct home inspections, even if, say, looking for items that the worker might have stolen from the company.

However, in the absence of a specific law to the contrary, employers *do* have the right to fire workers for off-duty conduct. Employees have been fired or disciplined for such extracurricular activities as taking part in dangerous sports (such as sky-diving), dating coworkers, smoking, or even having high cholesterol. But some governments have passed statutes that change this common law rule. These statutes take two forms: (1) general lifestyle statutes and (2) laws that protect specific behavior.

26-3a Lifestyle Laws

A few states, such as California, have passed so-called lifestyle laws that protect the right of employees to engage in any *lawful* activity or use any *lawful* product when off duty. Thus, if California residents sky-dive while smoking a cigarette, they may lose their lives, but not their jobs.

About half the states and the federal government have passed laws that protect *particular* off-duty conduct, such as smoking or use of legal drugs.

Smoking

Smokers tend to take more sick days and have higher healthcare expenses than other employees. Indeed, the federal government estimates that it costs an extra $3,400 a year to employ a worker who smokes. As a result, several thousand employers, including Union Pacific and Alaska Airlines, simply refuse to hire those who light up. Such a policy is legal unless state law prohibits it.

Massachusetts is a state that does not specifically protect smokers from employment discrimination. But in the following case, the plaintiff argued that his employer's actions violated his privacy rights. Does his argument have merit? You be the judge.

You Be the Judge

Facts: Scotts Lawnservice refused to hire tobacco users. It also tested all employees for both illegal drugs and nicotine.

Scotts offered Rodrigues a job "contingent upon successful completion of a pre-hire screening which includes a nicotine test." Rodrigues voluntarily submitted a urine sample and started work.

Shortly thereafter, a Scotts supervisor saw a pack of cigarettes on Rodrigues's dashboard and issued a warning. Two weeks later, when Rodrigues's test came back positive for nicotine, he was fired. He sued, claiming a violation of his privacy rights. Massachusetts law states: "A person shall have a right against unreasonable, substantial, or serious interference with his privacy."

You Be the Judge: *Did Scotts' enforcement of its anti-tobacco policy violate Rodrigues's privacy rights?*

Argument for Rodrigues: Under Massachusetts law, people have the right to be free from unreasonable interference with their privacy. Thus employers are limited in how much they can interfere in their employees' personal lives. For Scotts to require a test that reveals what Rodrigues has

RODRIGUES V. SCOTTS LAWNSERVICE

639 F. Supp. 2d 131
United States District Court for the District of Massachusetts, 2009

been doing at home or in his car is a clear violation of these privacy rights. Smoking outside of work has nothing to do with Rodrigues's job performance.

We would have no argument with Scotts if the company prohibited employees from smoking *while on duty*. But a policy that disallows tobacco use at *any* time goes too far. Tobacco is a legal substance, and it is unreasonable for a private business to ban what the government does not.

Argument for Scotts: There is nothing private about smoking. Smokers typically light up in their cars and in public places. They purchase cigarettes openly. Rodrigues had a pack of cigarettes in his truck while at work. A person loses his right to privacy if he does not attempt to keep information private. Rodrigues made no effort to keep his tobacco use secret.

Scotts has a legitimate interest in hiring workers who do not use tobacco. It is seeking a healthy workforce with high productivity and low health care costs. No law, including the Massachusetts privacy statute, prohibits the company's anti-tobacco policy.

Some workers have also claimed that nicotine addiction is a disability under the Americans with Disabilities Act (ADA; see Chapter 27 for more information about that statute), but so far, courts have been skeptical that Congress intended ADA coverage for the roughly 60 million Americans who smoke.[19] Several amendments to the ADA passed in 2008 could provide more protection for smokers, but the courts have not yet decided such a case.

ALCOHOL AND DRUG USE

Private Employers   Under *federal* law, *private* employers are permitted to test job applicants and workers for alcohol and *illegal* drugs. They may sanction workers who fail the test, even if the drug or alcohol use was off duty. *State* laws on drug testing vary widely.

Although employers were traditionally most concerned about illegal drugs, they now also worry about *legal* use of prescription drugs such as Xanax and Oxycodone because these medications may cause impairment. In one study, workers drug-tested after accidents in the workplace were four times more likely to have opiates in their system than job applicants. However, the Equal Employment Opportunity Commission (EEOC), the federal agency charged with enforcing federal employment laws, prohibits testing for prescription drugs unless a worker seems impaired. The EEOC filed suit against a company that randomly tested for legal use of prescription drugs, and a jury awarded substantial damages to the employees.[20]

---

[19]See *Brashear v. Simms*, 138 F.Supp.2d 693 (D.Md. 2001).
[20]*Bates v. Dura Auto Sys Inc.*, 2011 U.S. Dist. LEXIS 97469 (M.D. Tenn 2011).

Government Employers   Governments are sometimes allowed to conduct drug and alcohol tests of their employees. Public safety workers, such as police and firefighters, can be randomly tested for illegal drugs, and they may also be required to report legal drug use that could compromise their ability to perform their jobs. If their drug use (legal or not) is a threat to public safety, they may be suspended or fired from their jobs. Other government employees, whose work does not involve public safety, can be tested only if they show signs of impairment.

POLYGRAPH TESTS

A polygraph exam is a type of lie detector test. Under the Employee Polygraph Protection Act of 1988, employers may not require, or even *suggest*, that an employee or job candidate submit to a polygraph test *except in the following cases*:

- An employee who is part of an "ongoing investigation" into crimes that have already occurred,

- An applicant applying for a government job, or

- An applicant for a job in public transport or banking, or at pharmaceutical firms that deal with controlled substances.

If an employer requires a polygraph test, it must give advance written notice of when the test will be given and advise workers that they are entitled to legal counsel. A private employer may not fire or discriminate against an employee who fails a polygraph exam unless it also finds supporting evidence that the worker has done something wrong.

Ethics   By law, there are few situations in which private employers may require polygraph tests. What would be the advantages and disadvantages of requiring polygraph tests? Should there be different rules for job applicants, as opposed to employees?

ELECTRONIC MONITORING OF THE WORKPLACE

Technological advances in communications have raised a host of new privacy issues. Many companies monitor employee use of electronic equipment in the workplace: telephone calls, voicemail, email, and Internet usage. **The Electronic Communications Privacy Act of 1986 (ECPA) permits employers to monitor workers' telephone calls and email messages if (1) the employee consents, (2) the monitoring occurs in the ordinary course of business, or (3) in the case of email, the employer provides the email system.** However, bosses may not disclose any private information revealed by the monitoring.

Sending personal emails through a company server is dangerous. In one case, a court permitted an employer to fire two workers who exchanged (they claimed) joking emails threatening violence to sales managers even though the company had an explicit policy stating that emails were confidential and would not be intercepted or used against an employee.[21] Over 75 percent of U.S. firms monitor their employees' computer usage. About one third of companies have fired a worker over inappropriate email or Internet use.

A few courts have carved out narrow rights for employees. For example, a New Jersey court recently held that unless company policy explicitly informs workers otherwise, the company does not have the right to monitor a personal, password-protected, web-based

---

[21]*Smyth v. Pillsbury*, 914 F. Supp. 97, 1996 U.S. Dist. LEXIS 776 (Fed. Dist. Ct., 1996).

email account.[22] But unless you enjoy the prospect of engaging in years of litigation to clarify this issue, it is still good advice to consider all email you send through a company server to be public.

SOCIAL MEDIA

Social media are the newest challenge facing both employers and workers. On the one hand, employers may find themselves liable for statements that their workers make electronically. For example, Cisco Systems Inc., has settled two lawsuits brought against the company for statements made by a company lawyer on his blog. Not surprisingly, employers have fired workers who posted inappropriate information in cyberspace. But companies may find themselves liable for violations of employee privacy if a boss reads workers' Facebook or MySpace pages. A high school teacher in Georgia sued her school district after she was forced to resign because of vacation photos on Facebook that showed her holding a glass of wine.

And privacy rights aside, some workers have discovered a new way to fight back. The National Labor Relations Act (NLRA; discussed later in this chapter) gives employees the right to discuss wages, hours, and working conditions. So when American Medical Response fired an employee for making negative comments about her boss on Facebook, the National Labor Relations Board (NLRB) filed a complaint against the company. American Medical Response settled the complaint by promising it would not fire or discipline workers for discussing wages, hours, and working conditions. But in some similar cases, the NLRB has deemed online rants against employers to be mere venting, not a genuine discussion of their jobs, which means that these employees could be fired for their hostile postings.

In short, the law is evolving, subtle, and varies by state, so employees at will should err on the side of caution and remember that the law often does not protect their electronic lives from employer prying. They should consider anything they publish on the Internet to be public.

As for companies, it makes sense to establish policies providing that:

1. Employees should never reveal their company's name on a blog or social website such as Facebook.

2. In addition, all employees' personal blogs must contain a disclaimer that "All postings on this blog are my opinion and not those of my employer, who has neither vetted nor approved them." The blogger should not reveal the company's name.

3. Blog comments should never be offensive, impolite, or reflect badly on the employer. Nor should they reveal confidential or proprietary information.

4. Supervisors have the right to read and take action based on most kinds of electronic information posted by an employee.

IMMIGRATION

Because of discrimination laws, employers should not ask about an applicant's country of origin, but they are permitted to inquire if the person is authorized to work in the United States. If the applicant says, "Yes," the interviewer cannot ask for evidence until the person is hired. At that point, the employer must complete an I-9 form—Employment Eligibility Verification—within three days. This form lists the acceptable documents that can be used for verification. Employees have the right to present whichever documents they want from the list of acceptable items. The employer may not ask for some other document. The I-9 forms must be kept for three years after the worker is hired or one year after termination.

---

[22]*Stengart v. Loving Care Agency, Inc.*, 201 N.J. 300, 2010 N.J. LEXIS 241 (S.Ct. NJ, 2010).

EXAM Strategy

Question: To ensure that its employees did not use illegal drugs in or outside the workplace, Marvel Grocery Store required all employees to take a polygraph exam. Moreover, managers began to screen the company email system for drug references. Jagger was fired for refusing to take the polygraph test. Jonathan was dismissed when a search of his email revealed that he had used cocaine during the prior weekend. Has the company acted legally?

Strategy: First: As employees at will, are Jagger and Jonathan protected by a statute? The Employee Polygraph Protection Act permits employers to require a polygraph test as part of ongoing investigations into crimes that have occurred. Here, Marvel has no reason to believe that a crime occurred, so it cannot require a polygraph test.

   Second: What about Jonathan's cocaine use? The ECPA permits Marvel to monitor email messages on its own system. But can the company fire Jonathan for illegal off-duty conduct? Some statutes protect employees for *legal* behavior outside the workplace, but no state protects employees for behavior that violates the law.

Result: The company is liable to Jagger for requiring him to take the polygraph exam, but not to Jonathan for monitoring his email or firing him for illegal drug use.

26-4 WORKPLACE SAFETY

In 1970, Congress passed the Occupational Safety and Health Act (OSHA) to ensure safe working conditions. Under OSHA:

- Employers must comply with specific health and safety standards. For example, health care personnel who work with blood are not permitted to eat or drink in areas where the blood is kept. Protective clothing—gloves, gowns, and laboratory coats—must be impermeable to blood.

- Employers are under a general obligation to keep their workplace "free from recognized hazards that are causing or are likely to cause death or serious physical harm" to employees.

- Employers must keep records of all workplace injuries and accidents.

- The Occupational Safety and Health Administration (which is also known as OSHA) may inspect workplaces to ensure that they are safe. OSHA may assess fines for violations and order employers to correct unsafe conditions.

   OSHA has done a lot to make the American workplace safer. In 1900, roughly 35,000 workers died at work. A century later, the workforce had grown five times larger, but the number of annual deaths had fallen to about 5,500.

26-5 FINANCIAL PROTECTION

Congress and the states have enacted laws designed to provide employees with a measure of financial security. All of the laws in this section were created by statute, not by the courts.

26-5a Fair Labor Standards Act: Minimum Wage, Overtime, and Child Labor

Passed in 1938, the Fair Labor Standards Act (FLSA) regulates wages and limits child labor nationally. It provides that hourly workers must be paid a minimum wage of $7.25 per hour, plus time and a half for any hours over 40 in one week. These wage provisions do not apply to salaried workers, such as managerial, administrative, or professional staff. More than half the states set a higher minimum wage, so it is important to check state guidelines as well.

Today, the biggest issue that employers face under the FLSA is: "What counts as work, and how do you keep track of it?" What if a worker answers email during lunch or takes a phone call on the train ride home? Although these activities count as work, how can the employer keep track of it? Carla Bird, an assistant at Oprah Winfrey's production company, submitted timesheets showing 800 hours of overtime in 17 weeks. She said she had worked 12 or 13 hours a day, seven days a week, for four months. The company paid her $32,000 in overtime.[23] If employees work all the time, or even if they are just on call, they are entitled to be paid for those hours.

The FLSA also prohibits "oppressive child labor," which means that children under fourteen may work only in agriculture and entertainment. Fourteen-and fifteen-year-olds are permitted to work *limited* hours after school in nonhazardous jobs. Sixteen-and seventeen-year-olds may work *unlimited* hours in nonhazardous jobs.

26-5b Workers' Compensation

Workers' compensation statutes ensure that employees receive payment for injuries incurred at work. Before workers' comp, injured employees could recover damages only if they sued their employer. It is the brave (or carefree) worker who is willing to risk a suit against his own boss. Lawsuits poison the atmosphere at work. Moreover, employers frequently won these suits by claiming that (1) the injured worker was contributorily negligent, (2) a fellow employee had caused the accident, or (3) the injured worker had assumed the risk of injury. As a result, seriously injured workers (or their families) often had no recourse against the employer.

Workers' comp statutes provide a fixed, certain recovery to the injured employee, no matter who was at fault for the accident. In return, employees are not permitted to sue their employers for negligence. The amounts allowed (for medical expenses and lost wages) under workers' comp statutes are often less than a worker might recover in court, but the injured employee trades the certainty of some recovery for the higher risk of rolling the dice at trial. Payments are approved by an administrative board that conducts an informal hearing into each claim.

26-5c Social Security

The federal social security system began in 1935, during the depths of the Great Depression, to provide a basic safety net for the elderly, ill, and unemployed. **Currently, the social security system pays benefits to workers who are retired, disabled, or temporarily unemployed and to the spouses and children of disabled or deceased workers.** It also provides medical insurance to the retired and disabled. The social security program is financed through a tax on wages that is paid by employers, employees, and the self-employed.

Although the social security system has done much to reduce poverty among the elderly, many worry that it cannot survive in its current form. The system was designed to be "pay as you go"; that is, when workers pay taxes, the proceeds do not go into a savings account for their retirement, but instead are used to pay benefits to current retirees. In 1940,

---

[23]Lisa Belkin, "O.T. Isn't as Simple as Telling Time," *New York Times*, September 20, 2007.

there were 40 workers for each retiree; currently, there are 3.3. As a result, the system now pays out more in benefits each year than it receives in tax revenues. By 2025, when the last baby boomers retire, there will be only 2 workers to support each retiree—a prohibitive burden. No wonder younger workers are often cautioned not to count on social security when making their retirement plans.

The Federal Unemployment Tax Act (FUTA) is the part of the social security system that provides support to the unemployed. FUTA establishes some national standards, but states are free to set their own benefit levels and payment schedules. A worker who quits voluntarily or is fired for just cause is ineligible for benefits. While receiving payments, she must make a good-faith effort to look for other employment.

26-5d Pension Benefits

In 1974, Congress passed the Employee Retirement Income Security Act (ERISA) to protect workers covered by private pension plans. Under ERISA, employers are not required to establish pension plans, but if they do, they must follow these federal rules. The law was aimed, in particular, at protecting benefits of retired workers if their companies subsequently go bankrupt. The statute also prohibits risky investments by pension plans. In addition, the statute sets rules on the vesting of benefits. (An employer cannot cancel *vested* benefits; *nonvested* benefits are forfeited when the employee leaves.) Before ERISA, retirement benefits at some companies did not vest until the employee retired—if he quit or was fired before retirement, even after years of service, he lost his pension. Under current law, employee benefits normally must vest within five years of employment.

26-6 LABOR LAW AND COLLECTIVE BARGAINING

The opening scenario of this chapter provides a graphic example of how painful (literally) working conditions could be. Indeed, during the nineteenth and early twentieth centuries, as industrialization spread across the United States, many workers found their employment environment unbearable. Seeking better pay and improved working conditions, some began to band together into unions. But in this era, American courts regarded any coordinated effort by workers as a criminal conspiracy. Courts convicted workers merely for the *act of joining together*, even if no strike took place. A company could usually obtain an immediate injunction merely by alleging that a strike *might* cause harm. Courts were so quick to issue injunctions that most companies became immune to union efforts. But with the economic collapse of 1929 and the vast suffering of the Great Depression, public sympathy shifted to the workers. Congress responded with two landmark statutes.

26-6a Key Pro-Union Statutes

Norris-LaGuardia Act
Prohibits federal court injunctions in nonviolent labor disputes.

National Labor Relations Act (NLRA)
Ensures the right of workers to form unions and encourages management and unions to bargain collectively and productively.

In 1932, Congress passed the **Norris-LaGuardia Act** which prohibited federal court injunctions in nonviolent labor disputes. No longer could management stop a strike merely by mentioning the word "strike." By taking away the injunction remedy, Congress was declaring that workers should be permitted to organize unions and to use their collective power to achieve legitimate economic ends. The statute led to explosive growth in union membership.

In 1935, Congress passed the Wagner Act, generally known as the **National Labor Relations Act (NLRA).** This is the most important of all labor laws. A fundamental aim of the NLRA is the establishment and maintenance of industrial peace, to preserve the flow of commerce. The NLRA ensures the right of workers to form unions and encourages management and unions to bargain collectively and productively. For our purposes, §§7 and 8 of the NLRA are the most important.

Section 7 guarantees employees the right to organize and join unions, bargain collectively through representatives of their own choosing, and engage in other concerted activities. This is the cornerstone of union power. With the enactment of the NLRA, Congress put an end to any notion that unions were inherently illegal by explicitly recognizing that workers could join together, bargain as a group, and use their collective power to seek better conditions.

Section 8 prohibits employers from engaging in the following unfair labor practices (ULPs):

- Interfering with union organizing efforts,

- Dominating or interfering with any union,

- Discriminating against a union member, or

- Refusing to bargain collectively with a union.

The NLRA also established the **National Labor Relations Board (NLRB)** to administer and interpret the statute and to adjudicate labor cases. For example, when a union charges that an employer has committed a ULP—say, by refusing to bargain—the claim goes first to the NLRB.

National Labor Relations Board (NLRB)

Administers and interprets the NLRA and adjudicates labor cases.

26-6b Labor Unions Today

Organized labor is in flux in the United States. In the 1950s, about 1 in 4 workers belonged to a union. Today, only about 1 in 8, or 15 million total U.S. workers, are union members. Employers point to this figure with satisfaction and claim that it shows that unions have failed their memberships. In an increasingly high-tech, service-oriented economy, employers argue, there is no place for organized labor. Union supporters respond that although the country has shed many old factories, workers have not benefited. Throughout the last 20 years, they assert, compensation for executives has soared into the stratosphere while wages for the average worker, in real dollars, have fallen.

Unions continue to attract political attention. For example, legislators in Wisconsin voted to strip most collective bargaining rights from schoolteachers and other state government workers. Public employees are five times more likely to be union members than private sector workers, but they are generally not protected by the NLRA. Instead, state labor laws apply, which tend to provide less protection than federal statutes.

Crowds of as many as 100,000 gathered in Madison, Wisconsin, to protest the proposed legislation, but it passed nonetheless. Commentators on the left forecast significant political consequences for the Wisconsin lawmakers, while editorialists on the right predicted that many states would soon follow the Wisconsin model.

Although overall membership is down, unions still matter.

26-6c Organizing a Union

EXCLUSIVITY

Management is generally opposed—sometimes fiercely opposed—to any union organizing effort. The fight can become ugly, and all because of one principle: *exclusivity*.

Under §9 of the NLRA, a validly recognized union is the *exclusive* representative of the employees. This means that the union represents all of the designated employees, regardless of whether a particular worker *wants* to be represented. The company may not bargain directly with any employee in the group, nor with any other organization representing the designated employees.

However, a union may not exercise power any way it likes: Along with a union's exclusive bargaining power goes a duty of fair representation, which requires that a union treat all members fairly, impartially, and in good faith. A union may not favor some members over others, nor may a union discriminate against a member based on characteristics such as race or gender.

ORGANIZING: STAGES

A union organizing effort generally involves the following pattern.

Campaign   Union organizers talk—or attempt to talk—with employees and interest them in forming a union. The organizers may be employees of the company, who simply chat with fellow workers about unsatisfactory conditions; or a union may send nonemployees of the company to hand out union leaflets to workers as they arrive and depart from work.

Authorization Cards   Union organizers ask workers to sign authorization cards, which state that the particular worker requests the specified union to act as her sole bargaining representative.

If a union obtains authorization cards from a sizable percentage of workers, it seeks **recognition** as the exclusive representative for the bargaining unit. The union may ask the employer to recognize it as the bargaining representative, but most of the time, employers refuse to recognize the union voluntarily.

Petition   Assuming that the employer does not voluntarily recognize a union, the union generally petitions the NLRB for an election. It must submit to the NLRB regional office authorization cards signed by at least 30 percent of the workers. The regional office verifies whether there are enough valid cards to warrant an election and looks closely at the proposed bargaining unit to make sure that it is appropriate. If the regional director determines that the union has identified an appropriate bargaining unit and has enough valid cards, it orders an election.

Election   The NLRB closely supervises the election to ensure fairness. All members of the proposed bargaining unit vote on whether they want the union to represent them. If more than 50 percent of the workers vote for the union, the NLRB designates that union as the exclusive representative of all members of the bargaining unit. When unions hold representation elections in private corporations, they win about half the time.

The "Card-Check" Debate   Before becoming president, then–U.S. senator Barack Obama co-introduced a bill called the Employee Free Choice Act. This bill provides that when more than 50 percent of workers sign an authorization card, the NLRB must immediately designate that union as the exclusive representative of all members in the bargaining unit *without an election*.

Supporters argue that, if a majority of workers return authorization cards, an election is unnecessary and only gives companies an opportunity to intimidate workers. Those who dislike the bill argue that workers may feel bullied into signing an authorization card and should always have the right to a final vote by secret ballot.

The bill has generated much debate but has not passed Congress at the time of this writing.

ORGANIZING: ACTIONS

The NLRA guarantees employees the right to talk among themselves about forming a union, to hand out literature, and ultimately to join a union.[24] Workers may urge other employees to sign authorization cards and may vigorously push their cause. When employees hand out leaflets, the employer generally may not limit the content, so long as it is somewhat related to union activity.

---

[24]NLRA §7.

There are, of course, limits to what union organizers may do. The statute permits an employer to restrict organizing discussions if they interfere with discipline or production. A worker on a moving assembly line has no right to walk away from his task to talk with other employees about organizing a union; these discussions must be left until lunch or some other break time.[25]

May the employer speak out against a union organizing drive? Yes. Management is entitled to communicate to the employees why it believes a union will be harmful to the company. But the employer's efforts must be limited to explanation and advocacy. **The employer may vigorously present anti-union views to its employees but may not use either threats or promises of benefits to defeat a union drive.**[26]

EXAM Strategy

Question: We Haul is a trucking company. The Teamsters Union is attempting to organize the drivers. Workers who favor a union have been using the lunchroom to hand out petitions and urge other drivers to sign authorization cards. The company posts a notice in the lunchroom: "No Union Discussions. Many employees do not want unions discussed in the lunchroom. Out of respect for them, we are prohibiting further union efforts in this lunchroom." Comment.

Strategy: The NLRA guarantees employees the right to talk among themselves about forming a union and to hand out literature. Union workers may vigorously push their cause. Management is entitled to communicate to the employees why it believes a union will be harmful to the company, but the employer's efforts must be limited to explanation and advocacy.

Result: We Haul has violated the NLRA. The company has the right to urge employees not to join the union. However, it is not entitled to block the union from its organizing campaign. Even assuming the company is correct that some employees do not want unions discussed, it has no right to prohibit such advocacy.

26-6d Collective Bargaining

Once a union is formed, a company must then bargain with it toward the goal of creating a new contract, which is called a **collective bargaining agreement (CBA).**

The NLRA *permits* the parties to bargain almost any subject they wish, but it only *requires* them to bargain certain issues. **Mandatory subjects include wages, hours, and other terms and conditions of employment.** Courts generally also find these subjects to be mandatory: benefits, order of layoffs and recalls, production quotas, work rules (such as safety practices), retirement benefits, and onsite food service and prices. An employer may not *unilaterally* make changes in conditions of employment without first bargaining with the union.

Both the union and the employer must bargain in good faith. However, they are *not* obligated to reach an agreement. In the end, this means that the two sides must meet with open minds and make a reasonable effort to reach a contract. In the following case, the Supreme Court examined the requirements of bargaining in good faith.

Collective bargaining agreement (CBA)
A contract between a union and management.

---

[25] *NLRB v. Babcock & Wilcox Co.*, 351 U.S. 105, 76 S. Ct. 679, 1956 U.S. LEXIS 1721 (1956).
[26] *NLRB v. Gissel Packing Co.*, 395 U.S. 575, 89 S. Ct. 1918, 1969 U.S. LEXIS 3172 (1969).

Landmark Case

NLRB v. TRUITT MANUFACTURING CO.

351 U.S. 149
United States Supreme Court, 1956

Facts: A union representing workers at Truitt Manufacturing Company requested a raise of 10 cents per hour for all members. In offering an increase of only 2.5 cents per hour, the company argued that a larger raise would bankrupt the company. The union demanded to examine Truitt's books, and when the company refused, the union complained to the NLRB.

The NLRB determined that the company had failed to bargain in good faith and ordered it to allow union representatives to examine its finances. A court of appeals found no unfair labor practice and refused to enforce the Board's order. The Supreme Court granted *certiorari*.

Issue: *Did the company refuse to bargain in good faith? Does the union have the right to examine the company's finances?*

Decision: Yes, the company committed an unfair labor practice by refusing to bargain in good faith. The union has the right to examine its finances.

Reasoning: The NLRA does not force employers and unions to reach agreement, but it does require both sides to exert every reasonable effort to achieve this goal.

Good-faith bargaining necessarily requires that both sides make honest claims. In this case, the company's ability to afford raises was a crucial issue. In the past, unions have sometimes abandoned their requests for raises or even accepted reductions if the company's financial condition required it. In any event, if an argument is important enough to make in the give and take of bargaining, it is important enough to require some proof of its accuracy.

26-6e Concerted Action

Concerted action

Tactics taken by union members to gain bargaining advantage.

Concerted action refers to any tactics that union members take in unison to gain some bargaining advantage. It is this power that gives a union strength. **The NLRA guarantees the right of employees to engage in concerted action for mutual aid or protection.**[27] The most common forms of concerted action are strikes and picketing.

STRIKES

The NLRA guarantees employees the right to strike, but with some limitations.[28] A union has a guaranteed right to call a strike if the parties are unable to reach a CBA. A union may call a strike to exert economic pressure on management, to protest a ULP, or to preserve work that the employer is considering sending elsewhere. Note that the right to strike can be waived. Management will generally insist that the CBA

No-strike clause

A clause in a CBA that prohibits the union from striking while the CBA is in force.

include a **no-strike clause,** which prohibits the union from striking while the CBA is in force. A strike is illegal in several other situations as well; here, we mention the most important.

Cooling-Off Period   Before striking to terminate or modify a CBA, a union must give management 60 days' notice. Suppose a union contract expires July 1. The two sides attempt to bargain a new contract, but progress is slow. The union may strike as an economic weapon,

[27]NLRA §7.
[28]NLRA §13.

but it must notify management of its intention to do so *and then must wait* 60 *days*. This cooling-off period is designed to give both sides a chance to reassess negotiations and to decide whether some additional compromise would be wiser than enduring a strike.

Statutory Prohibition   Many states have outlawed strikes by public employees. In some states, the prohibition applies to selected employees, such as firefighters or teachers. In other states, all public employees are barred from striking, whether or not they have a contract. The purpose of these statutes is to ensure that unions do not use the public health or welfare as a weapon to secure an unfair bargaining advantage. However, even employees subject to such a rule may find other tactics to press their cause.

Violent Strikes   The NLRA prohibits violent strikes. Violence does sometimes occur on the picket line when union members attempt to prevent other workers from entering the job site. Or a union may stage a **sit-down strike**, in which members stop working but remain at their job posts, physically blocking replacement workers from taking their places. Any such action is illegal.

> **Sit-down strike**
>
> Union members stop working but remain at their job posts, physically blocking replacement workers from taking their places.

Partial Strikes   A partial strike occurs when employees stop working temporarily, then resume, then stop again, and so forth. This tactic is particularly disruptive because management cannot bring in replacement workers. A union may either walk off the job or stay on it, but it may not alternate.

REPLACEMENT WORKERS

When employees go on strike, management generally wants to replace them to keep the company operating. When replacement workers begin to cross a union picket line, tempers are certain to explode, and entire communities may feel the repercussions. Are replacement workers legal? Yes. **Management has the right to hire replacement workers during a strike.** May the employer offer the replacement workers *permanent* jobs, or must the company give union members their jobs back when the strike is over? It depends on the type of strike.

After an *economic strike,* **an employer may not discriminate against a striker, but the employer is *not* obligated to lay off a replacement worker to give a striker his job back.** An economic strike is one intended to gain wages or benefits. When a union bargains for a pay raise but fails to get it and walks off the job, that is an economic strike. During such a strike, an employer may hire permanent replacement workers. When the strike is over, the company has no obligation to lay off the replacement workers to make room for the strikers. However, if the company does hire more workers, it may not discriminate against the strikers.

After a *unfair labor practices (ULP) strike,* **a union member is entitled to her job back, even if that means the employer must lay off a replacement worker.** Suppose that management refuses to bargain in good faith by claiming poverty, without producing records to substantiate its claim. The union strikes. Management's refusal to bargain was a ULP, and the strike is a ULP strike. When it ends, the striking workers must get their jobs back.

PICKETING

Picketing the employer's workplace in support of a strike is generally lawful. Striking workers are permitted to establish picket lines at the employer's job site and to urge all others—employees, replacement workers, and customers—not to cross the line. But the picketers are not permitted to use physical force to *prevent* anyone from crossing the line. The company may terminate violent picketers and permanently replace them, regardless of the nature of the strike.

> The workers have bargained with management for weeks, and discussions have turned belligerent. ... as 150 employees arrive for work, they are amazed to find the company's gate locked and armed guards standing on the other side.

LOCKOUTS

The workers have bargained with management for weeks, and discussions have turned belligerent. It is 6:00 a.m., the start of another day at the factory. But as 150 employees arrive for work, they are amazed to find the company's gate locked and armed guards standing on the other side. In a so-called lockout, management prohibits workers from entering the premises and earning their paychecks. Most lockouts are legal.

Chapter Conclusion

Since the first time one person hired another, there has been tension in the workplace. The law attempts to balance the right of a boss to run a business with the right of a worker to fair treatment. Other countries balance these rights differently. For instance, Japan, Great Britain, France, Germany, and Canada all require employers to show just cause before terminating workers. Indeed, the United States guarantees its workers fewer rights than virtually any other industrialized nation. On the one hand, being mistreated at work or fired can be a terrible, life-altering experience; but on the other, companies that cannot lay off unproductive employees are less likely to add to their workforce, which may be one reason that Europe tends to have a higher unemployment rate than the United States. Although American bosses are not insulated from minimum standards of fairness, reasonable behavior, and compliance with important policies, they still have great freedom to manage their employees.

EXAM REVIEW

1. **TRADITIONAL COMMON LAW RULE**   The traditional common law rule of employment provided that an employee at will could be fired for a good reason, a bad reason, or no reason at all. (p. 617)

2. **FMLA**   The Family and Medical Leave Act guarantees workers up to 12 weeks of unpaid leave each year for childbirth, adoption, a serious health condition of their own or in their immediate family. (pp. 618–619)

3. **HEALTH INSURANCE**   Starting in 2015, employers who have more than 50 full-time employees must pay a penalty if they do not provide basic health insurance. Under the Consolidated Omnibus Budget Reconciliation Act, former employees must be allowed to continue their health insurance for 18 months after being terminated from their job, but they must pay for it themselves. (p. 619)

4. **WRONGFUL DISCHARGE AND PUBLIC POLICY**   An employer who fires a worker for certain bad reasons may be liable under a theory of wrongful discharge. Generally, an employee may not be fired for refusing to violate the law, performing a legal duty, exercising a legal right, or supporting basic societal values. (pp. 619–622)

EXAM Strategy

Question: When Theodore Staats went to his company's "Council of Honor Convention," he was accompanied by a woman who was not his wife, although he told everyone she was. The company fired him. Staats alleged that his termination violated public policy because it infringed upon his freedom of association. He also alleged that he had been fired because he was too successful—his commissions were so high, he outearned even the highest-paid officer of the company. Has Staat's employer violated public policy?

Strategy: Is Staats protected by a statute? No. Is he being asked to break the law? No. Is he trying to perform a legal duty? No. Is he being denied a legal right? (See the "Result" at the end of this section.)

5. **PROMISES MADE DURING THE HIRING PROCESS**   Promises made during the hiring process may be enforceable, even if not approved by the company's top executives. An employee handbook may also create a contract. (pp.622–623)

EXAM Strategy

Question: When Phil McConkey interviewed for a job as an insurance agent with Alexander & Alexander, the company did not tell him that it was engaged in secret negotiations to merge with Aon. When the merger went through soon thereafter, Aon fired McConkey. Was Alexander liable for not telling McConkey about the possible merger?

Strategy: Was McConkey protected by a statute? No. Did the company make any promises to him during the hiring process? (See the "Result" at the end of this section.)

6. **COVENANT OF GOOD FAITH AND FAIR DEALING**   In almost all states, courts will imply this covenant in an at-will employment relationship. (pp. 622–623)

7. **DEFAMATION**   Employers may be liable for defamation if they give false and unfavorable references. (pp. 623–624)

8. **WHISTLEBLOWERS**   Whistleblowers receive some protection under both federal and state laws. (pp. 624–626)

9. **EMPLOYEE PRIVACY**   An employer may not violate a worker's reasonable expectation of privacy. However, unless a state has passed a statute to the contrary, employers may monitor many types of off-duty conduct (even legal activities such as smoking). Most states permit private employers to administer alcohol and drug tests, and employers are generally free to monitor employees' email and social media pages. But many employers are restricted by the Employee Polygraph Protection Act if they wish to administer polygraph exams. (p. 629)

10. **OSHA**   The goal of the Occupational Safety and Health Act is to ensure safe conditions in the workplace. (p. 630)

11. **WORKERS' COMPENSATION**   Workers' compensation statutes ensure that employees receive payment for injuries incurred at work. (p. 631)

12. **SOCIAL SECURITY**   The social security system pays benefits to workers who are retired, disabled, or temporarily unemployed and to the spouses and children of disabled or deceased workers. (pp. 631–632)

13. **ERISA**   The Employee Retirement Income Security Act regulates private pension plans. (p. 632)

14. **RIGHT TO ORGANIZE**   Section 7 of the National Labor Relations Act (NLRA) guarantees employees the right to organize and join unions, bargain collectively, and engage in other concerted activities. Section 8 of the NLRA makes it a ULP for an employer to interfere with union organizing, discriminate against a union member, or refuse to bargain collectively. (p. 633)

15. **DISCRIMINATION**   Section 8 of the NLRA makes it a ULP for a union to interfere with employees who are exercising their rights under §7, to encourage an employer to discriminate against an employee because of a labor dispute, or to refuse to bargain collectively. (p. 633)

16. **EXCLUSIVITY**   Section 9 of the NLRA makes a validly recognized union the *exclusive* representative of the employees. Along with exclusivity comes a duty of fair representation, which requires that a union treat all members fairly, impartially, and in good faith. (pp. 633–634)

17. **EMPLOYER OPPOSITION**   During a union organizing campaign, an employer may vigorously present anti-union views to its employees, but it may not use threats or promises of benefits to defeat the union effort. (p. 635)

EXAM Strategy

Question: Power, Inc., which operated a coal mine, suffered financial losses and had to lay off employees. The United Mine Workers of America (UMWA) began an organizing drive. Power's general manager warned miners that if the company was unionized, it would be shut down. An office manager told one of the miners that the company would get rid of union supporters. Shortly before the election was to take place, Power laid off 13 employees, all of whom had signed union cards. A low-seniority employee who had not signed a union card was not laid off. The union claimed that Power had committed ULPs. Comment.

Strategy: Section 7 of the NLRA guarantees employees the right to organize. An employer may vigorously advocate against a union organizing campaign. However, §8 makes it a ULP to interfere with union organizing or discriminate against a union member. (See the "Result" at the end of this section.)

18. **BARGAINING**   The employer and the union *must* bargain over wages, hours, and other terms and conditions of employment. They *may* bargain other subjects, but neither side may insist on doing so. The union and the employer must bargain in good faith, but they are not obligated to reach an agreement. (pp. 635–636)

19. **STRIKES**   The NLRA guarantees employees the right to strike, with some limitations. After an *economic* strike, an employer is not obligated to lay off replacement workers to give a striker her job back, but it may not discriminate against a striker when filling job openings. After a ULP strike, the striking worker must get her job back. (pp. 636–637)

20. **LOCKOUTS**   Most lockouts are legal. (p. 638)

4. **Result:**   The court held that freedom of association is an important social right and should be protected. However, being fired for bringing a lover to an employer's convention is not a threat to public policy. Nor is discharge for being too successful.

5. **Result:**   The court held that when Alexander hired him, it was making an implied promise that he would not be fired immediately. The company was liable for not having revealed the merger negotiations.

17. **Result:**   Each of the acts described was a ULP. Threatening layoffs or company closure are classic examples of ULPs. Laying off those who had signed union cards, but not those who refused, was clear discrimination. In this case, the NLRB found the violations so extreme that it certified the union without an election and issued an order to bargain.

MULTIPLE-CHOICE QUESTIONS

1. Brook moved from Denver to San Francisco to take a job with an advertising agency. His employment contract stated that he was "at will and could be terminated at any time." After 28 months with the company, he was fired without explanation. Which of the following statements is true?

   (a) His contract implied that he could only be fired for cause.

   (b) Because he had a contract, he was not an employee at will.

   (c) He could only be fired for a good reason.

   (d) He could be fired for any reason.

   (e) He could be fired for any reason except a bad reason.

2. **CPA QUESTION**   An unemployed CPA generally would receive unemployment compensation benefits if the CPA:

   (a) was fired as a result of the employer's business reversals.

   (b) refused to accept a job as an accountant while receiving extended benefits.

   (c) was fired for embezzling from a client.

   (d) left work voluntarily without good cause.

3. During a job interview with Venetia, Jack reveals that he and his wife are expecting twins. Venetia asks him if he is planning to take a leave once the babies are born. When Jack admits that he would like to take a month off work, he can see her face fall. She ultimately decides not to hire him because of the twins. Which of the following statements are true?

   (a) Venetia has violated the FMLA.

   (b) Venetia has violated COBRA.

   (c) Both (a) and (b)

   (d) None of the above

4. Which of the following statutes defines ULPs and ensures workers' right to form a union?

   (a) The Norris-LaGuardia Act

   (b) The National Labor Relations Act

   (c) Both (a) and (b)

   (d) None of the above

5. Alpha Company's workers go on strike. The company hires replacement workers so that it can continue to operate its business. When the strike ends, Alpha must rehire the original workers if the strike was over

   (a) wages

   (b) a ULP

   (c) both (a) and (b)

   (d) none of the above

Essay Questions

1. Debra Agis worked as a waitress in a Ground Round restaurant. The manager informed the waitresses that "there was some stealing going on." Until he found out who was doing it, he intended to fire all the waitresses in alphabetical order, starting with the letter "A." Dionne then fired Agis. Does she have a valid claim against her employer?

2. **YOU BE THE JUDGE WRITING PROBLEM** FedEx gave Marcie Dutschmann an employment handbook stating that (1) she was an at-will employee, (2) the handbook did not create any contractual rights, and (3) employees who were fired had the right to a termination hearing. The company fired Dutschmann, claiming that she had falsified delivery records. She said that FedEx was retaliating against her because she had complained of sexual harassment. FedEx refused her request for a termination hearing. Did the employee handbook create an implied contract guaranteeing Dutschmann a hearing? **Argument for FedEx:** The handbook could not have been clearer—it did not create a contract. Dutschmann is an employee at will and is not entitled to a hearing. **Argument for Dutschmann:** FedEx intended that employees would rely on the handbook. The company used promises of a hearing to attract and retain good employees. Dutschmann was entitled to a hearing.

3. Triec, Inc., is a small electrical contracting company in Springfield, Ohio, owned by its executives, Yeazell, Jones, and Heaton. Employees contacted the International Brotherhood of Electrical Workers, which began an organizing drive, and 6 of the 11 employees in the bargaining unit signed authorization cards. The company declined to recognize the union, which petitioned the NLRB to schedule an election. The company then granted several new benefits for all workers, including higher wages, paid vacations, and other measures. When the election was held, only 2 of the 11 bargaining unit members voted for the union. Did the company violate the NLRA?

4. Q-1 Motor Express was an interstate trucking company. When a union attempted to organize Q-1's drivers, it met heavy resistance. A supervisor told one driver that if he knew what was good for him, he would stay away from the union organizer. The company president told another employee that he had the right to fire everybody, close the company, and then rehire new drivers after 72 hours. He made numerous other threats to workers and their families. Based on the extreme nature of the company's opposition, what exceptional remedy did the union seek before the NLRB?

5. Billy comes down with chicken pox and is sent home from school. His mother takes him to a pediatrician. The doctor tells her, "Well … he should be fine in about a week. Bed rest is all he really needs—and plenty of fluids." Billy's mother calls her employer and requests FMLA leave to take care of Billy for the next few days. Must the employer grant the leave? Why or why not?

DISCUSSION QUESTIONS

1. When Walton Weiner interviewed for a job with McGraw-Hill, Inc., he was assured that the company would not terminate an employee without "just cause." Weiner also signed a contract specifying that his employment would be subject to the provisions of McGraw-Hill's handbook. The handbook said, "[The] company will resort to dismissal for just and sufficient cause only, and only after all practical steps toward rehabilitation or salvage of the employee have been taken and failed. However, if the welfare of the company indicates that dismissal is necessary, then that decision is arrived at and is carried out forthrightly." After eight years, Weiner was fired suddenly for "lack of application." Does Weiner have a valid claim against McGraw-Hill?

2. Some companies now require all job applicants to provide their Facebook login information so that the potential employer can learn more about them. Is this behavior ethical on the part of an employer?

3. Should employers be allowed to fire smokers? Nicotine is highly addictive and many smokers begin as teenagers, when they may not fully understand the consequences of their decisions. As Mark Twain, who began smoking at 12, famously said, "Giving up smoking is the easiest thing in the world. I know because I've done it thousands of times."

4. Union membership has fallen steadily in recent decades, in part because many unionized manufacturing jobs have been shipped overseas. Do you believe that unions will make a comeback in new industries? Would you prefer to be a member of a union if you had a choice? Why or why not?

5. Would you personally be less likely to apply for a job if you were required to first pass a polygraph exam? What if you were required to pass a drug test? For legal or illegal drugs? Would you be less likely to apply because you thought the company was too intrusive or because you want the right to use these substances? What if the company required you to quit smoking or chewing tobacco?

CHAPTER 27

EMPLOYMENT DISCRIMINATION

nuttakit/Shutterstock.com; Steve Allen/Brand X Pictures/Jupiter Images

Imagine that you are on the hiring committee of a top San Francisco law firm. You come across a resume from a candidate who grew up on an isolated ranch in Arizona. Raised in a house without electricity or running water, he had worked alongside the ranch hands his entire childhood. At the age of 16, he left home for Stanford University, and from there had gone on to Stanford Law School, where he finished third in his class. You think to yourself, "This sounds like a real American success story. A great combination of grit and intelligence." But without hesitation, you toss the resume into the wastebasket.

> But without hesitation, you toss the resume into the wastebasket.

This is a true story. Indeed, there was a candidate with these credentials who was unable to find a job in any San Francisco law firm. The only jobs on offer were as a secretary, because this candidate was a woman—Sandra Day O'Connor, who went on to become one of the most influential lawyers of her era and the first woman justice on the Supreme Court of the United States. When she graduated from law school, women and minorities had limited job options, and not just in the legal profession. Before 1960, you might never see a female or African American doctor, engineer, police officer, or firefighter. What a terrible waste of resources—so many talented people unable to use their abilities.

27-1 INTRODUCTION

This chapter is the story of how the United States has travelled the long and bumpy road toward equality of opportunity in the workplace. This story begins after the Civil War, when a torn and bleeding country sought to protect the rights of freed slaves and undo the terrible harm of a century of slavery. The country began by ratifying three Constitutional amendments: The Thirteenth prohibits slavery, the Fourteenth guarantees due process of law and equal protection under the law, and the Fifteenth prohibits restrictions on the right to vote because of race or color. In addition, Congress passed the Civil Rights Act of 1866, which provided that all people born in the United States (except Native Americans) were citizens of the United States and had the same rights as white citizens.[1]

However, in response to these laws, many states passed (and the Supreme Court upheld) statutes that made these protections worthless. The most notorious case was *Plessy v. Ferguson*, in which the Supreme Court upheld the constitutionality of a Louisiana law that prohibited blacks from riding in railroad cars reserved for whites. Blacks were provided with "separate but equal" cars.[2]

Not until 1954, almost a century after the Civil War, did the Supreme Court reverse its *Plessy* decision. In the landmark case *Brown v. Board of Education*, the high court ruled that "separate but equal" policies were unconstitutional.[3] In particular, it prohibited segregated public schools. However, many school districts were slow to apply the case, and even ten years later, segregated public schools still existed. Nonetheless, *Brown* inspired a generation of civil rights leaders such as Martin Luther King, Jr. and Rosa Parks, who led protests, boycotts, and voter registration drives.

These actions inspired Congress to pass the Civil Rights Act of 1964. Title VII of this Act prohibits certain types of employment discrimination and is the focus of this chapter. However, the statute was even more far-reaching because it prohibited a broad range of discrimination: in, for example, education, voting, and public accommodations (such as hotels, restaurants, and movie theaters).

We begin now with a review of constitutional provisions that prohibit discrimination in the workplace and follow with a discussion of the major federal anti-discrimination statutes: the Civil Rights Act of 1866, Title VII of the Civil Rights Act of 1964, the Equal Pay Act, the Pregnancy Discrimination Act, the Age Discrimination in Employment Act, the Rehabilitation Act of 1973, the Americans with Disabilities Act, and the Genetic Information Nondiscrimination Act.

---

[1] 42 USC 21 §1981.
[2] 163 U.S. 537 (S. Ct. 1896).
[3] 347 U.S. 483 (S. Ct. 1954).

27-2 THE UNITED STATES CONSTITUTION

The Fifth Amendment to the Constitution prohibits the *federal government* from depriving individuals of "life, liberty, or property" without due process of law. The Fourteenth Amendment prohibits *state governments* from violating an individual's right to due process and equal protection. The courts have interpreted these provisions to prohibit employment discrimination by federal, state, and local governments.

27-3 CIVIL RIGHTS ACT OF 1866

As we have seen, the Civil Rights Act of 1866 was meant to provide freed slaves with the same rights as white citizens. It has been interpreted to prohibit *racial* discrimination in both private and public employment (except it does not apply to the federal government). As we will see later in the Enforcement section of this chapter, it offers plaintiffs some significant advantages over Title VII.

27-4 TITLE VII OF THE CIVIL RIGHTS ACT OF 1964

Under Title VII of the Civil Rights Act of 1964, it is illegal for employers with 15 or more employees to discriminate on the basis of race, color, religion, sex, or national origin. Discrimination under Title VII applies to every aspect of the employment process, from job ads to postemployment references, and includes hiring, firing, promoting, placement, wages, benefits, and working conditions of anyone who is in one or more of the so-called protected categories under the statute.

27-4a Prohibited Activities

There are four types of illegal activity under this statute: disparate treatment, disparate impact, hostile environment, and retaliation. All of these activities are illegal if used against anyone in a protected category.

DISPARATE TREATMENT

To prove a disparate treatment case, the plaintiff must show that she was *treated* less favorably than others because of her sex, race, color, religion, or national origin. Note that the burden of proof is on the plaintiff: She must prove that the employer *intentionally* discriminated, but this motive can be inferred from the mere fact of differences in treatment. The required steps in a disparate treatment case are:

Step 1. The plaintiff presents evidence that:

- He belongs to a protected category under Title VII.

- He was treated differently from other similar people who are not protected under Title VII.

   If the plaintiff can show these facts, he has made a ***prima facie*** case. The plaintiff is not required to prove discrimination; he need only create a *presumption* that discrimination occurred.

Prima facie

From the Latin, meaning "from its first appearance," something that appears to be true upon a first look.

Suppose that Louisa applies for a job coaching a boys' high school hockey team. She was an All-American hockey star in college. Although Louisa is obviously qualified for the job, Harry, the school principal, rejects her and continues to interview other people. This is not *proof* of discrimination because Harry may have a perfectly good, nondiscriminatory explanation. However, his behavior *could have been* motivated by discrimination.

Step 2. The defendant must present evidence that its decision was based on *legitimate*, *nondiscriminatory* reasons. Harry might say, for example, that he wanted someone with prior coaching experience. Although Louisa is clearly a great player, she has never coached before.

Step 3. To win, the plaintiff must now prove that the employer intentionally discriminated. She may do so either by showing that (1) the reasons offered were simply a *pretext* or (2) that a discriminatory intent is more likely than not. Louisa might show that Harry had recently hired a male tennis coach who had no prior coaching experience (pretext), or Harry's assistant might testify that Harry said, "No way I'm going to put a woman on the ice with those guys." If she can present evidence such as this, Louisa wins.

In the following case, was the bartender treated differently because of her sex? You be the judge.

You Be the Judge

JESPERSEN V. HARRAH'S

444 F.3D 1104, 2006 U.S. APP. LEXIS 9307
United States Court of Appeals
for the Ninth Circuit, 2006

Facts: Darlene Jespersen was a bartender at the sports bar in Harrah's Casino in Reno, Nevada. She was an outstanding employee, frequently praised by both her supervisors and customers.

After Jespersen had been at Harrah's for almost 20 years, the casino implemented a program that required bartenders to be "well groomed, appealing to the eye." More explicitly, for men:

- Hair must not extend below top of shirt collar. Ponytails are prohibited.

- Hands and fingernails must be clean and nails neatly trimmed at all times.

- No colored polish is permitted.

- Eye and facial makeup is not permitted.

- Shoes will be solid black leather or leather type with rubber (non-skid) soles.

The rules for women were:

- Hair must be teased, curled, or styled. Hair must be worn down at all times, no exceptions.

- Nail polish can be clear, white, pink, or red color only. No exotic nail art or length.

- Shoes will be solid black leather or leather type with rubber (non-skid) soles.

- Makeup (foundation/concealer and/or face powder, as well as blush and mascara) must be worn and applied neatly in complimentary colors, and lip color must be worn at all times.

An expert was brought in to show the employees (both male and female) how to dress. The workers were then photographed and told that they must look like the photographs every day at work.

Jespersen tried wearing makeup for a short period of time but then refused to do so. She did not like the feel of it and also believed that this new appearance interfered with her ability to deal with unruly, intoxicated guests because it "took away [her] credibility as an individual and as a person."

After Harrah's fired Jespersen, she sued under Title VII. The district court granted Harrah's motion for summary judgment. Jespersen appealed.

You Be the Judge: *Did Harrah's requirement that women wear makeup violate Title VII?*

Argument for Jespersen: Jespersen refused to wear makeup to work because the cost—in time, money, and personal dignity—was too high.

Employers are free to adopt different appearance standards for each sex, but these standards may not impose a greater burden on one sex than the other. Men were not required to wear makeup, but women were. That difference meant a savings for men of hundreds of dollars and hours of time.[4] Harrah's did not have the right to fire Jespersen for violating a rule that applies only to women, with no equivalent for men. **Argument for Harrah's:** Employers are permitted to impose different appearance rules on women than on men so long as the overall burden on employees is the same. For example, it is not discriminatory to require men to wear their hair short. On balance, Harrah's rules did not impose a heavier burden on women than on men.

DISPARATE IMPACT

Disparate impact applies if the employer has a rule that, *on its face*, is not discriminatory, but *in practice* excludes too many people in a protected category. Unlike disparate treatment, in a disparate impact case, the plaintiff does not have to prove *intentional* discrimination. The following landmark case established the principle of disparate impact. (You have already seen this case in Chapter 4, but it is important enough to study a second time.)

Landmark Case

GRIGGS V. DUKE POWER CO.
401 U.S. 424, 91 S. Ct. 849, 1971 U.S. LEXIS 134
United States Supreme Court, 1971

CASE SUMMARY

Facts: Before Title VII, Duke Power would hire black employees only in the Labor department, where the highest pay was less than the lowest earnings in the other departments. After Title VII, the company required all new hires for jobs in the desirable departments to have a high school education or satisfactory scores on two tests that measured intelligence and mechanical ability. Neither test gauged the ability to perform a particular job. The pass rate for whites was much higher than for blacks and whites were also more likely than blacks to have a high school diploma. The new policy did not apply to the (exclusively white) employees who were already working in the preferred departments. These "unqualified" whites all performed their jobs satisfactorily.

Black employees sued Duke Power, alleging that this hiring policy violated Title VII.

Issue: *Does a policy violate Title VII if it has the effect of discriminating, even though the intent was not discriminatory?*

Decision: Yes, a policy violates Title VII if it has a discriminatory impact, regardless of intent.

Reasoning: Under Title VII, employers may establish job requirements that exclude more blacks than whites, but only if the requirements are *necessary* to do that *particular* work. In this case, there was no evidence that either a high school diploma or the two tests bore any relationship to the job in question. Indeed, white employees without any of these qualifications had been doing the jobs well for years and had even been promoted.

Whether or not Duke Power intended to discriminate is irrelevant. Title VII is concerned with the *consequences* of an employer's practices, not its motivation. The burden is on the employer to show that all job requirements have an important relationship to the work in question. Any tests must measure the person for the job and not the person in the abstract.

---

[4]See, for example, Michael Kinsley, "Making Up Is Hard to Do," *The Washington Post*, March 26, 2008.

The steps in a disparate impact case are:

Step 1. The plaintiff must present a *prima facie* case. The plaintiff is not required to prove discrimination; he need only show a disparate impact—that the employment practice in question excludes a disproportionate number of people in a protected group (women and minorities, for instance). In the *Griggs* case, a far higher percentage of whites than blacks passed the tests required for a job in one of the good departments. The Equal Employment Opportunity Commission (EEOC) defines a disparate impact as one in which the pass rate for a protected category is less than 80 percent of that for others. (As we will see, the EEOC is the federal agency charged with enforcing most discrimination statutes.)

Step 2. The defendant must offer some evidence that the employment practice was a *job-related business necessity*. Duke Power would have to show that the tests predicted job performance.

Step 3. To win, the plaintiff must now prove either that the employer's reason is a *pretext* or that other, *less discriminatory*, rules would achieve the same results. The plaintiffs in *Griggs* showed that the tests were not a job-related business necessity—after all, whites who had not passed any of these tests performed the jobs well. Duke Power could no longer use them as a hiring screen. If the power company wanted to use tests, it would have to find some that measured an employee's ability to perform particular jobs.

Hiring tests remain controversial. For example, New Haven, Connecticut, used an exam to determine which firefighters to promote. When twice as many whites as blacks passed the test, black firefighters threatened to sue on the grounds that the exams were discriminatory. But the city could not win for losing—when it decided to discard the test results, the white firefighters (and one Hispanic) who had done well on the test sued, alleging that the city was now discriminating against them.[5] Ultimately, the Supreme Court ruled against the city, holding that an employer cannot discard test results unless it first clearly shows that it would have lost a disparate impact case. In this case, ruled the court, New Haven could not make this showing because, indeed, the tests *were* valid and the city would have *won* a disparate impact lawsuit. The court reached this decision despite the fact that the test in question consisted of written multiple-choice questions, which are generally thought to be a less useful gauge in employment decisions than actually requiring candidates to perform necessary tasks. In short, the mere existence of a disparate impact does not mean that an employment practice violates the law.

HOSTILE WORK ENVIRONMENT

Employers violate Title VII if they permit a work environment that is so hostile toward people in a protected category that it affects their ability to work. This rule applies whether the hostility is based on race, color, religion, sex, or national origin. (As we shall see, this rule also applies to those treated badly because of pregnancy, age, or disability.) This concept of hostile environment first arose in the context of sexual harassment.

Sexual Harassment When Professor Anita Hill accused Supreme Court nominee Clarence Thomas of sexually harassing her, people across the country were glued to their televisions, watching the Senate hearings on her charges. Thomas was ultimately confirmed to the Supreme Court, but "sexual harassment" became a household phrase. The number of cases—and the size of the damage awards—skyrocketed.

> Everyone has heard of sexual harassment, but few people know exactly what it is.

---

[5] *Ricci v. DeStefano*, 129 S. Ct. 2658, 2009 U.S. LEXIS 4945 (S. Ct. 2009).

Everyone has heard of sexual harassment, but few people know exactly what it is. Men fear that a casual comment or glance will be met with career-ruining charges; women claim that men "just don't get it." So what is sexual harassment anyway? **Sexual harassment involves unwelcome sexual advances, requests for sexual favors, and other verbal or physical conduct of a sexual nature which are so severe and pervasive that they interfere with an employee's ability to work.** There are two categories: (1) *quid pro quo* and (2) hostile work environment.

Named for a Latin phrase that means "one thing in return for another," *quid pro quo* harassment occurs if any aspect of a job is made contingent upon sexual activity. In other words, when a banker says to an assistant, "You can be promoted to teller if you sleep with me," that is *quid pro quo* sexual harassment. As for hostile environment, courts have found that offensive jokes, intrusive comments about clothes or body parts, and public displays of pornographic pictures can create a hostile environment.

Text messages have become a new frontier in sexual harassment—so-called *textual harassment*. In behavior that can only make you ask, "What were they thinking?" bosses have sent wildly inappropriate text messages to their subordinates—in some cases offering promotions in return for sex—that provide clear evidence of wrongdoing. News flash: Text messages can be recovered, and juries can read. "She said, he said" cases are a lot harder to win than "She said, he texted."

In the following case, the Supreme Court defined the standard for a hostile work environment.

TERESA HARRIS V. FORKLIFT SYSTEMS, INC.

510 U.S. 17, 114 S. Ct. 367, 1993 U.S. LEXIS 7155
United States Supreme Court, 1993

CASE SUMMARY

Facts: Teresa Harris was a manager at Forklift Systems; Charles Hardy was its president. Hardy frequently made inappropriate sexual comments to Harris and other women at the company. For example, he said to Harris, in the presence of others, "You're a woman, what do you know?" and "We need a man as the rental manager." He called her "a dumb ass woman" and suggested that the two of them "go to the Holiday Inn to negotiate her raise." He also asked Harris and other female employees to get coins from his front pants pocket. He insisted that Harris and other women pick up objects he had thrown on the ground. When Harris complained to Hardy, he apologized and claimed he was only joking. A month later, while Harris was arranging a deal with one of Forklift's customers, he asked her, in front of other employees, "What did you do, promise the guy some sex Saturday night?"

Harris sued Forklift, claiming that Hardy had created an abusive work environment. The federal trial court ruled against Harris on the grounds that, while Hardy's comments might offend a reasonable woman, they were not severe enough to have a serious impact on Harris's psychological well-being. The

appeals court confirmed, and the Supreme Court granted *certiorari*.

Issue: *To be a violation of Title VII, must sexual harassment seriously affect the employee's psychological well-being?*

Decision: No, a hostile or abusive environment violates Title VII, whether or not the plaintiff suffered psychological injury.

Reasoning: Title VII is not limited to economic or tangible discrimination. A workplace loaded with intimidation, ridicule, and insult creates an abusive environment that violates Title VII.

Merely uttering a swear word or two is not a violation because a reasonable person would not find that hostile or abusive. But Title VII does come into play before the victim has a nervous breakdown. An abusive environment that does not seriously affect employees' psychological well-being, nonetheless, may detract from their job performance and keep them from advancing in their careers. If the environment would reasonably be perceived, and is perceived, as hostile or abusive, Title VII does not require it also to be psychologically injurious.

Same-Sex Harassment   Suppose that one man makes unwelcome sexual overtures to another man in the workplace. The Supreme Court ruled that same-sex harassment is also a violation of Title VII.[6]

Employer Liability for Sexual Harassment   Employees who commit sexual harassment are liable for their own misdeeds. But is their company also liable? The Supreme Court has held that:

- The company is liable if it knew or should have known about the conduct and failed to stop it.

- Even if the company was unaware of the misbehavior, it is nonetheless liable if the victimized employee suffered a "tangible employment action" such as firing, demotion, or reassignment.

- If the company was unaware of the behavior and the victimized employee did not suffer a tangible employment action, the company is still liable unless it can prove that (1) it used reasonable care to prevent and correct sexually harassing behavior, and (2) the employee unreasonably failed to take advantage of the complaint procedure or other preventive opportunities provided by the company.[7]

Corning Consumer Products Co. provides a set of practical guidelines for eliminating sexual harassment. It asks employees to apply four tests in determining whether their behavior violates Title VII:

- Would you say or do this in front of your spouse or parents?

- What about in front of a colleague of the opposite sex?

- Would you like your behavior reported in your local newspaper?

- Does it need to be said or done at all?

Hostile Environment Based on Race   When African American Brenda Chaney worked at the Plainfield nursing home, one of its patients refused to allow people of color to enter her room. In addition, Chaney's coworkers called her racial slurs.

The court ruled that the nursing home had violated Title VII by permitting a hostile work environment.[8]

Hostile Environment Based on Color   Title VII prohibits discrimination based on both race and color. Although many people assume that they are essentially the same, that is not necessarily the case. For example, Dwight Burch alleged that his coworkers at an Applebee's restaurant created a hostile work environment when they called him hateful names because of his dark skin color. These colleagues were also African American but were lighter-skinned. While denying any wrongdoing, Applebee's settled the case by paying Burch $40,000 and agreeing to conduct antidiscrimination training.

Hostile Environment Based on National Origin   Title VII also prohibits a hostile environment based on national origin. While working at Steel Technologies, Inc., Tony Cerros was promoted several times. So what was the problem? Coworkers and supervisors called him "brown boy," "spic," "wetback," "Julio," and "Javier" (although those were not his names). They also told him that "if it ain't white, it ain't right," and "Go Back to Mexico" was written

---

[6]*Oncale v. Sundowner Offshore Services, Inc.*, 523 U.S. 75 (S. Ct. 1998).
[7]*Burlington Industries, Inc. v. Ellerth*, 524 U.S. 742, 118 S. Ct. 2257, 1998 U.S. LEXIS 4217 (1998); *Faragher v. Boca Raton*, 524 U.S. 775, 118 S. Ct. 2275, 1998 U.S. LEXIS 4216 (1998).
[8]*Chaney v. Plainfield Healthcare Ctr.*, 612 F.3d 908 (7th Cir. 2010).

on the bathroom wall. Although the company removed the bathroom graffiti, it did not investigate Cerros's complaints until he filed suit. At that point, it determined that Cerros had not been discriminated against. The trial court agreed because Cerros had, after all, been promoted. However, the appeals court overturned the decision, finding for Cerros on the grounds that he had suffered a hostile work environment, which is in itself a violation of Title VII, even if there is no evidence of adverse employment actions.[9]

RETALIATION

Title VII also prohibits employers from retaliating against workers who oppose discrimination, bring a claim under the statute, or take part in an investigation or hearing. Retaliation means that the employer has done something that would deter a reasonable worker from complaining about discrimination. For example, a company was found liable when it demoted a woman who complained about sexual harassment by her boss.[10] Research indicates that retaliation occurs in as many as 60 percent of discrimination cases.

Title VII prohibits disparate treatment, disparate impact, hostile environment, and retaliation when used against any of the categories protected by Title VII—race, color, religion, sex, and national origin. Now we look at particular rules that apply to only some of these categories.

27-4b Religion

Employers cannot discriminate against a worker because of his religious beliefs. In addition, employers must make reasonable accommodation for a worker's religious practices unless the request would cause undue hardship for the business. A common issue involves employees who cannot work on their Sabbath. This refusal might be an "undue hardship" if there are no other employees who could perform that work on those days. What would you do in the following cases if you were the boss?

1. A Christian says he cannot work at Walmart on Sundays—his Sabbath. It also happens to be one of the store's busiest days.

2. A Jewish police officer wants to wear a beard and yarmulke as part of his religious observance. Facial hair and headgear are banned by the force.

3. Muslim workers at a meat-packing plant want to pray at sundown, but specific break times were specified in the labor contract and sundown changes from day to day. The workers begin to take bathroom breaks at sundown, stopping work on the production line.

Disputes such as these are on the rise and are not easy to handle fairly. In the end, Walmart fired the Christian, but when he sued on the grounds of religious discrimination, the company settled the case. A judge ruled that the police officer could keep his beard because the force allowed other employees with medical conditions to wear facial hair, but the head covering had to go. The boss at the meat-packing plant fired the Muslim employees who left their posts to pray.

27-4c Sex

Title VII has had an enormous impact on the American workplace—half of all workers are now women. But women are still underrepresented at the top of the employment ladder, as CEOs, partners in law and consulting firms, or department heads in hospitals. On average, women working full time earn only 80 percent as much as male coworkers, even after accounting for occupation, industry, race, marital status, and job tenure. Although there are

---

[9]*Cerros v. Steel Techs, Inc.*, 288 F.3d 1040 (7th Cir. 2002).
[10]*Burlington Northern v. White*, 126 S.Ct. 2405 (S.Ct. 2006).

undoubtedly many reasons for this inequality, such as women taking time out of work to care for children, gender discrimination also seems to play a role. For example, male CFOs in public companies earn 16 percent ($215,000) more than female CFOs, even after controlling for age, time in the job, company size, and market capitalization.[11]

What does discrimination on the basis of sex mean? In a landmark case that defined this provision of Title VII, the Supreme Court ruled that "gender must be irrelevant to employment decisions."[12] In this case, the accounting firm Price Waterhouse had refused to promote Ann Hopkins to partner. Of the 88 people who came up for partner that year, she was the only woman. She was not only a high performer, she was also the most successful in bringing in business. The problem? She was "sometimes overly aggressive, unduly harsh, difficult to work with, and impatient with staff." Partners commented that she was macho, overcompensated for being a woman, and needed to take a course at charm school. They were opposed to her use of profanity because it was a "lady using foul language." A partner explicitly told her that she should "walk more femininely, talk more femininely, dress more femininely, wear makeup, have her hair styled, and wear jewelry." In ruling in her favor, the Supreme Court held that Title VII forbids sex stereotyping. The opinion said, "An employer who objects to aggressiveness in women but whose positions require this trait places women in an intolerable and impermissible catch-22: out of a job if they behave aggressively and out of a job if they do not. Title VII lifts women out of this bind."

27-4d Family Responsibility Discrimination

Suppose that you are in charge of hiring at your company. You receive applications from four people: a mother, a father, a childless woman, and a childless man. All have equivalent qualifications. Which one would you hire? In studies, participants repeatedly rank mothers as less qualified than other employees and fathers as most desirable, even when their credentials are exactly the same.

Is parenthood a protected category under Title VII? Increasingly, courts have held that it is. For example, after Dawn Gallina, an associate at the Mintz, Levin law firm, revealed to her boss that she had a young child, he began to treat her differently from her male colleagues and spoke to her "about the commitment differential between men and women." The court ruled that her belief of illegal discrimination was reasonable.[13] The EEOC has issued guidelines indicating that stereotypes are not a legitimate basis for personnel decisions and may violate Title VII.

27-4e Sexual Orientation

Neither Title VII nor any other *federal* statute protects against discrimination based on sexual orientation (being gay). However, President Bill Clinton did sign an executive order prohibiting discrimination based on sexual orientation in federal training and education programs.[14] In addition, almost half the states and hundreds of cities have statutes that prohibit discrimination based on sexual orientation.

27-4f Gender Identity

David Schroer was in the Army for 25 years, including a stint tracking terrorists. The Library of Congress offered him a job as a specialist in terrorism. (Who knew that libraries needed terrorism specialists?) However, when he revealed that he was in the process of becoming *Diane* Schroer, the Library of Congress withdrew the offer. As you can guess, he sued under Title VII.

---

[11]*http://www3.cfo.com/article/2012/4/compensation_gmi-gender-gap-gofoernance-metrics.*
[12]*Price Waterhouse v. Hopkins*, 490 U.S. 228 (S. Ct. 1989).
[13]*Gallina v. Mintz, Levin*, 2005 U.S. App. LEXIS 1710 (4th Cir. 2005).
[14]Executive Order 13160.

Traditionally, courts took the view that sex under Title VII applied only to how people were born, not what they chose to become. Employers could and did fire workers for changing sex. However, a federal court found the Library of Congress in violation of Title VII for withdrawing Schroer's offer.[15] And the EEOC recently ruled that discriminating against someone for being transgender is a violation of Title VII. In addition, almost one-quarter of the states and hundreds of cities prohibit gender identity discrimination.

27-4g Defenses to Charges of Discrimination

Under Title VII, the defendant has four possible defenses.

MERIT

A defendant is not liable if he shows that the person he favored was the most qualified. Test results, education, or productivity can all be used to demonstrate merit, provided they relate to the job in question. Harry can show that he hired Bruce for a coaching job instead of Louisa because Bruce has a master's degree in physical education and seven years of coaching experience. On the other hand, the fact that Bruce scored higher on the National Latin Exam in the eighth grade is not a good reason to hire him over Louisa.

SENIORITY

Many companies use seniority as an important factor in determining everything from compensation to layoffs. While such systems offer many advantages—they encourage a commitment to the company, an incentive to learn job-specific skills, and a willingness to train other workers without fear of losing one's job—they also tend to perpetuate prior discriminatory practices. If historic trends result in black employees having less seniority, they will also be paid less and laid off more. However, a seniority system violates Title VII only if it was designed with the *intention* to discriminate. **A legitimate seniority system is legal even if it perpetuates past discrimination.** Suppose that Harry has always chosen the most senior assistant coach to take over as head coach when a vacancy occurs. Because the majority of the senior assistant coaches are male, most of the head coaches are, too. Such a system does not violate Title VII.

BONA FIDE OCCUPATIONAL QUALIFICATION (BFOQ)

Bona fide occupational qualification (BFOQ)

An employer is permitted to establish discriminatory job requirements if they are essential to the position in question.

An employer is permitted to establish discriminatory job requirements if they are *essential* to the position in question. The business must show that it cannot fulfill its primary function unless it discriminates. Such a requirement is called a **bona fide occupational qualification (BFOQ).** (Note that only religion, sex, or national origin can be a BFOQ—never race or color.)

Catholic schools may, if they choose, refuse to hire non-Catholic teachers; clothing companies may refuse to hire men to model women's attire. Generally, however, courts are not sympathetic to claims of BFOQ. They have almost always rejected BFOQ claims that are based on customer preference. For example, an employer violated the law when it refused to appoint a woman to a position as vice president of international operations because of its fear that men in other countries might not want to work with her.[16]

However, the courts recognize three situations in which employers may consider customer preference:

- Safety: The Supreme Court ruled that a maximum security men's prison could refuse to hire women correctional officers. If a woman wanted to risk her life, that was her

---

[15]*Schroer v. Billington*, 577 F. Supp. 2d 293, 2008 U.S. Dist. LEXIS 71358, (U.S. Dt. Ct. 2008).
[16]*Fernandez v. Wynn Oil Co.*, 653 F.2d 1273, (9th Cir. 1981).

choice, but the Court feared that an attack on her would threaten the safety of both male guards and inmates.[17]

- Privacy: An employer may refuse to hire women to work in a men's bathroom, and vice versa.

- Authenticity: An employer may refuse to hire a man for a woman's role in a movie. In addition, a court ruled that Disney could fire an Asian man from the Norwegian exhibit at its Epcot international theme park, not because he was Asian, but because he was not culturally authentic. He did not have first-hand knowledge of Norwegian culture and did not speak Norwegian.[18]

AFFIRMATIVE ACTION

The goal of affirmative action programs is to remedy the effects of past discrimination. How people feel about affirmative action tends to be a function of how they define the term. Most people are opposed to quotas, but at the same time, they support outreach and recruitment efforts aimed at women and disadvantaged minorities.

Affirmative action is not required by Title VII, nor is it prohibited. Affirmative action programs have three different sources.

Litigation   Courts have the power under Title VII to order affirmative action to remedy the effects of past discrimination.

Voluntary Action   Employers can *voluntarily* introduce an affirmative action plan to remedy the effects of past practices or to achieve (but not to maintain) equitable representation of minorities and women, provided that the plan is not too unfair to majority members.[19] For example, in the university and community college system in Nevada, only 1 percent of the faculty were black (and roughly 25 percent were female). In response, the university instituted a policy that permitted any department that hired a minority candidate to also hire an additional candidate of any race. Although Yvette Farmer was one of three finalists for a job in the sociology department, it hired a black African male without even granting her an interview. The Court ruled that the university's affirmative action plan was legal.[20]

Government Contracts   In 1965, President Lyndon Johnson signed Executive Order 11246, which prohibits discrimination by federal contractors. This order had a profound impact on the American workplace because one-third of all workers are employed by companies that do business with the federal government. If an employer found that women or minorities were underrepresented in its workplace, it was required to establish goals and timetables to correct the deficiency.

In 1995, however, the Supreme Court dramatically limited the extent to which the government can *require* contractors to establish affirmative action programs. The Court ruled that, under the Fourteenth Amendment to the Constitution, these programs are permissible only if they serve a "compelling governmental interest" and are "narrowly tailored" so that they minimize the harm to white males.[21] This case led to a sharp decrease in the number of federal contracts awarded to companies owned by women and minorities.

---

[17]*Dothard v. Rawlinson*, 433 U.S. 321, (S. Ct. 1977).
[18]*Gupta v. Walt Disney World Co.*, 256 Fed. Appx. 279 (11th Cir. 2007).
[19]*In United Steelworkers of America v. Weber*, 443 US 193 (S. Ct. 1979).
[20]*University and Community College System of Nevada v. Farmer*, 113 Nev. 90 (S. Ct. Nev. 1997).
[21]*Adarand Constructors, Inc. v. Pena*, 515 U.S. 200, 115 S. Ct. 2097, 1995 U.S. LEXIS 4037 (S. Ct. 1995).

27-5 EQUAL PAY ACT OF 1963

Under the Equal Pay Act, an employee may not be paid at a lesser rate than employees of the opposite sex for equal work. "Equal work" means tasks that require equal skill, effort, and responsibility under similar working conditions. For example, Corning Glass Works paid the inspectors on its night shift, who were all male, significantly more than the day inspectors who performed the same tasks but were female. After it allowed women to work at night, it equalized wages on the two shifts but grandfathered in the men who had been on the night shift and continued to pay them higher wages. The Supreme Court ruled that this practice violated the Equal Pay Act, on the grounds that:

- The term "working conditions" meant physical surroundings, not time of day.

- Men were paid more not because they worked at night, but because they would not work at the low rates paid to women.

- Grandfathering in the men at higher wages perpetuated the discrimination.[22]

If the employee proves that she is not being paid equally, the employer will be found liable unless the pay difference is based on merit, productivity, seniority, or some factor other than sex. A "factor other than sex" includes prior wages, training, profitability, performance in an interview, and value to the company. For example, female agents sued Allstate Insurance Co. because its salary for new agents was based, in part, on prior salary. The women argued that this system was unfair because it perpetuated the historic wage differences between men and women. The court, however, held for Allstate.[23]

27-6 PREGNANCY DISCRIMINATION ACT

Under the Pregnancy Discrimination Act, an employer may not fire, refuse to hire, or fail to promote a woman because she is pregnant. An employer also violates this statute if the work environment is so hostile towards a pregnant woman that it affects her ability to do her job. And an employer must treat pregnancy and childbirth as any other temporary disability. If, for example, employees are allowed paid time off from work for other medical disabilities, women must also be allowed a paid maternity leave.

The Pregnancy Discrimination Act also protects a woman's right to terminate a pregnancy. An employer cannot fire a woman for having an abortion.[24]

27-7 AGE DISCRIMINATION IN EMPLOYMENT ACT

During the last decade, the number of workers over the age of 65 has doubled and the number of age discrimination cases has also increased dramatically. Under the Age Discrimination in Employment Act (ADEA), an employer with 20 or more workers may not fire, refuse to hire, fail to promote, or otherwise reduce a person's employment opportunities because he is 40 or older. Nor may an employer require workers to retire at a certain age.

---

[22]*Corning Glass Works v. Brennan*, 417 U.S. 188 (S. Ct. 1974).
[23]*Kouba v. Allstate Insurance Co.*, 691 F.2d 873, 1982 U.S. App. LEXIS 24479 (9th Cir. 1982).
[24]*Doe v. C.A.R.S Protection Plus, Inc.*, 527 F.3d 358 (3rd Cir. 2008).

(This retirement rule does not apply to police and top-level corporate executives.) The goal of the statute is to counteract stereotypes about the abilities of older workers. A plaintiff in an age discrimination case can show discrimination in three ways: disparate treatment, disparate impact, and hostile work environment.

27-7a Disparate Treatment

In a disparate treatment claim, the plaintiff must show that the employer intentionally discriminated against him because of his age, or enacted a policy that intentionally treated employees differently because of their age. Proof of intent involves obvious statements and behavior or more subtle circumstantial evidence.

Under the ADEA, a disparate treatment case requires three steps.

Step 1. The plaintiff must show that:

- He is 40 or older.

- He suffered an adverse employment action.

- He was qualified for the job for which he was fired or not hired.

- He was replaced by a younger person.

Step 2. The employer must present evidence that its decision was based on legitimate, nondiscriminatory reasons.

Step 3. The plaintiff must now show that the employer's reasons are a pretext and, in fact, the employer intentionally discriminated. Note that the standard of proof is tougher in an age discrimination case than in Title VII litigation. Under the ADEA, the plaintiff must show that *but for* his age, the employer would not have taken the action it did. In other words, to win a case, the plaintiff must show that age was not just one factor, it was the *deciding* factor. For example, when Jack Gross was 54 years old, his employer transferred most of his responsibilities to a younger woman and "reassigned" him to a different job. Whatever the terminology used, this move was effectively a demotion. Evidence at trial indicated that age may have been one factor in his employer's decision, but there were other reasons as well. The Supreme Court ruled for the employer, on the grounds that Gross had not shown that age was the "but-for" cause of the disputed decision.[25] This case makes the road steeper for ADEA plaintiffs.

What protection does the ADEA provide? In passing this statute, Congress was particularly concerned about employers who relied on unfavorable stereotypes rather than job performance. The following case illustrates this issue.

REID v. GOOGLE, INC.

50 Cal. 4th 512, 2010 Cal. LEXIS 7544
Supreme Court of California, 2010

CASE SUMMARY

Facts: Google's vice-president of engineering, Wayne Rosing (aged 55), hired Brian Reid (52) as director of operations and director of engineering. At the time, the top executives at Google were CEO Eric Schmidt (47), vice-president of engineering operations Urs Hölzle (38), and founders Sergey Brin (28) and Larry Page (29).

During his two years at Google, Reid's only written performance review stated that he had consistently met

---

[25]*Gross v. FBL Financial Services, Inc.*, 129 S. Ct. 2343; 2009 U.S. LEXIS 4535 (S. Ct., 2009).

expectations. The comments indicated that Reid had an extraordinarily broad range of knowledge, an aptitude and orientation towards operational and IT issues, an excellent attitude, and that he projected confidence when dealing with fast-changing situations, was very intelligent and creative, and was a terrific problem solver. The review also commented that "Adapting to Google culture is the primary task. Right or wrong, Google is simply different: Younger contributors, inexperienced first line managers, and the super fast pace are just a few examples of the environment."

According to Reid, even as he received a positive review, Hölzle and other employees made derogatory age-related remarks such as his ideas were "obsolete," "ancient," and "too old to matter," that he was "slow," "fuzzy," "sluggish," and "lethargic," an "old man," an "old guy," and an "old fuddy-duddy," and that he did not "display a sense of urgency" and "lacked energy."

Nineteen months after Reid joined Google, he was fired. Google says it was because of his poor performance. Reid alleges he was told it was based on a lack of "cultural fit."

Reid sued Google for age discrimination. The trial court granted Google's motion for summary judgment on the grounds that Reid did not have sufficient evidence of discrimination. He appealed.

Issues: *Did Reid have enough evidence of age discrimination to warrant a trial? Should the summary judgment motion be granted?*

Decision: The trial court was overruled and summary judgment denied.

Reasoning: Google argued that the trial court should have ignored the ageist comments about Reid because they were "stray remarks," made neither by decision-makers nor during the decision process. But stray remarks may be relevant, circumstantial evidence of discrimination. The jury should decide how relevant.

An ageist remark, in and of itself, does not prove discrimination. But when combined with other testimony, it may provide enough evidence to find liability.

27-7b Disparate Impact

Disparate impact claims arise when an employer's actions do not explicitly discriminate, but nonetheless have an adverse impact on people aged 40 or over. Here, too, the standards are different under the ADEA from those under Title VII. Under the ADEA:

Step 1. The plaintiffs must present a *prima facie* case that the employment practice in question excludes a disproportionate number of people 40 and older.

Step 2. The employer wins if it can show that the discriminatory decision was based on a "reasonable factor other than age."

One reasonable factor other than age is cost. As a general rule, people in their 60s earn 50 percent more than workers in their early 30s. The older folks are more efficient, but not 50 percent more. So sometimes companies fire older workers because they are paid more, receive higher pension benefits, or generally cost more (e.g., higher healthcare expenses). Courts have supported these decisions, holding that an employer is entitled to prefer *lower-paid* workers even if that preference results in the company also choosing *younger* workers. As the court put it in one case, "An action based on price differentials represents the very quintessence of a legitimate business decision."[26] Indeed, economists argue that the U.S. economy's strength is based at least in part on its flexibility—an American employer can hire workers without fear of being stuck with them until retirement. Thus, for example, Circuit City Stores fired 8 percent of its employees because they could be replaced with people who would work for less. The fired workers were more experienced—and older. This action was legal under the ADEA.

27-7c Hostile Work Environment

Diane Kassner (age 79) and Marsha Reiffe (61) worked for 2nd Avenue Delicatessen. They filed suit under the ADEA, alleging that their boss and coworkers made comments to them about their age, such as "Drop dead," "Retire early," "Take off all of that makeup," and

---

[26]*Marks v. Loral Corp.*, 57 Cal. App. 4th 30, 1997 Cal. App. LEXIS 611 (Cal. Ct. App., 1997).

"Take off your wig." In addition, their boss pressured the two women to retire and pointed to the front of the restaurant and said, "There's the door." But the two women were never fired.

The court ruled that the ADEA prohibits a hostile work environment based on age. A workplace is considered hostile if a reasonable person would find that intimidation, ridicule, and insult based on age are pervasive.[27] In short, this case, combined with the *Google* case, indicate that it is wise to avoid any comments about an employee's age.

27-7d Bona Fide Occupational Qualification

As is the case under Title VII, age is rarely a BFOQ. To set a maximum age, the employer must show that:

- The age limit is reasonably necessary to the essence of the business; and either

- Virtually everyone that age is unqualified for the job, or

- Age is the only way an employer can determine who is qualified.

Although some courts have held that age can be a BFOQ in cases where public safety is at issue, such as for pilots and bus drivers, the EEOC is not always in agreement. In short, the BFOQ defense is very limited in ADEA cases.

EXAM Strategy

Question: Solapere ran a job ad on Monster.com, which said that the company would only consider hiring people who either had a job or had been unemployed for less than six months. The average length of unemployment in the United States at that time was nine months, which meant that such a policy eliminated millions of job applicants. Did this ad violate federal law?

Strategy: Solapere was not intentionally discriminating against anyone, thus no disparate treatment claim. What about a disparate impact claim? Did this policy exclude too many people in a protected category? The unemployed are not a protected category under Title VII, but this policy might have had an impact on groups that are protected.

Result: Older people and some minority groups have higher unemployment rates than other workers. Therefore, this practice could violate both Title VII and the ADEA unless Solapere could show that it was a job-related business necessity. Could it be a job-related business necessity?

27-8 DISCRIMINATION ON THE BASIS OF DISABILITY

27-8a The Rehabilitation Act of 1973

The Rehabilitation Act of 1973 prohibits discrimination on the basis of disability by the executive branch of the federal government, federal contractors, and entities that receive federal funds. It also requires these organizations to develop affirmative action plans for the

---

[27]*Kassner v. 2nd Ave. Delicatessen, Inc.*, 496 F.3d 229, (2nd Cir. 2007).

hiring, placement, and promotion of the disabled. The same legal standards apply to both this statute and the Americans with Disabilities Act, discussed next. Cases interpreting one statute also apply to the other.

27-8b Americans with Disabilities Act

The Americans with Disabilities Act (ADA) prohibits employers with 15 or more workers from discriminating on the basis of disability.

DISABILITY

A **disabled person** is:

- Someone with a physical or mental impairment that substantially limits a major life activity or the operation of a major bodily function, or

- Someone who is regarded as having such an impairment.

Major life activities include the following tasks: caring for oneself, performing manual tasks, seeing, hearing, eating, sleeping, walking, standing, lifting, bending, speaking, breathing, learning, reading, concentrating, thinking, communicating, and working. Major bodily functions include functions of the immune system, normal cell growth, digestive, bowel, bladder, neurological, brain, respiratory, circulatory, endocrine, and reproductive functions. The ADA applies to *recovered* drug addicts but not to the *current* use of drugs, sexual disorders, pyromania, exhibitionism, or compulsive gambling. Although the ADA protects alcoholics who can meet the definition of disabled, employers can nonetheless fire alcoholics if their drinking adversely affects job performance.

Suppose an employee has a disabling illness, but one that can be successfully treated. The employee is still considered to be disabled, even if the illness is well controlled. Thus, someone with diabetes is disabled, even if the illness is managed so well that it does not interfere with major life activities. There is one important exception—someone whose vision is normal when wearing glasses or contact lenses is not disabled for purposes of the ADA.

This description of the ADA reflects changes Congress made to the statute in 2008. It expanded the definition of "disability" as the term had been interpreted by the Supreme Court. The following case is one of the first by a circuit court of appeals to interpret the amended ADA. As you can see, despite Congress's intent to expand the scope of the statute, the appeals court did not support the plaintiff's claim. Indeed, by upholding a grant of summary judgment, it prevented her from even presenting her case to a jury.

ALLEN v. SOUTHCREST HOSPITAL

2011 U.S. App. LEXIS 25488
United States Court of Appeals for the Tenth Circuit, 2011

Facts: After some years as a medical assistant at SouthCrest Hospital, Alethia Allen requested a transfer to work for a different physician in the same hospital. Unfortunately, Allen found her new job to be much more stressful than the old one. Indeed, it was so stressful that she began suffering severe migraine headaches several times a week. Prior to this new job, she had only had one migraine headache in her life.

Ultimately, Allen resigned because of the migraines. The hospital asked that she stay on to cover for some assistants who were on vacation. Allen agreed to do so and then decided she did not want to quit after all. But before the hospital made a decision about whether she could stay, she left work one day to seek treatment for a migraine at the emergency room. That night, the doctors in her practice decided she could not continue in her job. After leaving SouthCrest, her migraines stopped.

Allen filed suit against SouthCrest for violating the ADA. During discovery, she testified that on most days, she could care for herself and go to work, but that on days on which she took the migraine medication, she would come home from work and immediately "crash and burn." In other words, she could not care for herself but instead would go straight to bed.

The trial court granted SouthCrest's motion for summary judgment. Allen appealed.

Issue: *Did Allen have a disability that interfered with one or more major life activities?*

Decision: No, Allen failed to show that her disability interfered with any major life activities.

Reasoning: Allen alleged that taking migraine medication interfered with her ability to care for herself in the evenings, which is a major life activity. But even the average person sometimes goes to bed early and is unable to care for herself when asleep. Allen had to show how much worse off she was than the average person who sometimes comes home from work exhausted. Furthermore, Ms. Allen needed to show: how much earlier she went to bed on migraine days, which activities she could not perform, how long she slept, and whether she could complete in the morning the activities she had failed to do the night before.

Ms. Allen also alleged that her migraines interfered with her ability to work, which is certainly a major life activity. However, she had to show that she was unable to perform a general class of jobs for which she had appropriate training and skills, not one single specific job.

ACCOMMODATING THE DISABLED WORKER

Once it is established that a worker is disabled, employers may not discriminate on the basis of disability so long as the worker can, with *reasonable accommodation*, perform the *essential functions* of the job. An accommodation is not reasonable if it would create *undue hardship* for the employer. Let's look at those terms more closely.

Reasonable Accommodation   To meet this standard, employers are expected to:

- Make facilities accessible,

- Permit part-time schedules,

- Acquire or modify equipment, and

- Assign a disabled person to an open position that he can perform. (Note that the employer is not required to create a new job or find a perfect position, just a reasonable one.)

Essential Functions of the Job   A juvenile corrections officer was hit by a baseball that fractured her wrist. Nine months after returning to her job, she was assigned to the night shift, where the only other officer was a newcomer. Concerned that her wrist was not strong enough for her to restrain some of the children in the facility on her own, she asked to be paired with an experienced officer. Her employer fired her on the grounds that she could not perform the essential functions of the job. But the court ruled that since she had been working successfully as an officer during the day, clearly she could perform the essential functions.[28]

Undue Hardship   What constitutes undue hardship is the subject of much litigation. Many courts hold that employers may use cost-benefit analysis—they are not required to make an expensive accommodation that provides little benefit. Nor are they required to provide identical working conditions for all employees. For example, a woman who was wheelchair-bound asked her employer to lower the sink in the kitchenettes that were being built in her building. Otherwise, she would have to use the bathroom sink, which she felt segregated and stigmatized

---

[28]*Leuzinger v. County of Lake*, 2007 U.S. Dist. LEXIS 35955 (N.D. CA 2007).

her. The cost to lower the kitchen sinks ranged from as much as $2,000 (to do all the sinks in the building) to as little as $150 (for just the sink on her floor). The court ruled that the employer had no obligation to provide identical conditions and that it had already made a reasonable accommodation by lowering the sink in the bathroom. Although the employer could, in theory, afford this request, it did not have an obligation to spend so much money for so little benefit.[29]

MEDICAL EXAMS

Employers interact with workers at three key stages: applying, entering (after hiring but before the job starts), and working. The ADA sets different standards for medical exams at these three stages:

- **With applicants,** an employer generally may not require a medical exam or ask about disabilities, except that the interviewer may ask:
  - whether an applicant can perform the work (provided that the same question is asked of all applicants);
  - the applicant to demonstrate how he would perform the job; and
  - (in the event that a disability is obvious) what accommodation the applicant would need.

- **With entering employees,** the company may require a medical test and make it a condition of employment, but the test must be:
  - Required of all employees, whether or not they are disabled; and
  - Treated as a confidential medical record (except in the case of managers who need to know).

- **With existing employees,** an employer may require medical exams or discuss any suspected disability, but only to determine if a worker is still able to perform the existing functions of her job.

RELATIONSHIP WITH A DISABLED PERSON

An employer may not discriminate against someone because of his *relationship* with a disabled person. For example, an employer cannot refuse to hire an applicant because he has a disabled child or a spouse with cancer.

MENTAL DISABILITIES

Under EEOC rules, physical and mental disabilities are to be treated the same. Physical ailments such as diabetes and deafness may sometimes be easier to diagnose, but psychological disabilities are also covered by the ADA. Among other accommodations, the EEOC rules indicate that employers should be willing to put up barriers to isolate people who have difficulty concentrating, provide detailed day-to-day feedback to those who need greater structure in performing their jobs, or allow workers on antidepressants to come to work later if they are groggy in the morning.

DISPARATE TREATMENT AND DISPARATE IMPACT

Both disparate treatment and disparate impact claims are valid under the ADA. The steps in a disparate *treatment* case are:

Step 1. The plaintiff must offer *prima facie* evidence that the employer discriminated because of his disability.

Step 2. The employer must then offer a legitimate, nondiscriminatory reason for its action.

---

[29]*Vande Zande v. Wisconsin Department of Administration*, 44 F.3d 538 (7th Cir. 1995).

Step 3. To win, the plaintiff must now prove that the employer intentionally discriminated. She may do so either by showing that (1) the reasons offered were simply a *pretext* or (2) that a discriminatory intent is more likely than not.

To win a disparate *impact* case, the plaintiff must show that a policy that *looks* neutral falls more harshly on a protected group and cannot be justified by business necessity.

The following Exam Strategy illustrates how disparate treatment and disparate impact are applied in an ADA case and also demonstrates the importance of choosing the correct theory.

EXAM Strategy

Question: Hughes Missile Systems fired Joel Hernandez because he tested positive for cocaine, which, not surprisingly, was a violation of workplace rules. He, however, had no hard feelings, and two years later, he reapplied for a job at Hughes. At the time, he provided evidence that he was clean. However, the company rejected his application because it had a policy against hiring anyone who had been fired for cause. Did the company violate the ADA?

Strategy: Under the ADA, it is legal to discriminate against a drug user, but not against a recovered drug addict. To win a disparate *treatment* case, Hernandez had to show that Hughes's excuse for not rehiring him was just a pretext and its decision was really motivated by an intent to discriminate based on his disability. To win a disparate *impact* claim, Hernandez had to show that the no-rehire policy affected disabled people more than others and that it was not justified by business necessity. Could he prove either of these claims?

Result: The Supreme Court ruled that Hernandez could not prove his disparate treatment claim because its no-rehire rule was legitimate and not just a pretext for discrimination. And because Hernandez had not raised the issue of disparate impact in the lower courts, the Supreme Court refused to consider it. So he lost his case.[30]

HOSTILE WORK ENVIRONMENT

An employee may bring a claim under the ADA if she is subjected to a hostile work environment because of her disability. For example, Sandra Flowers's boss fired her eight months after finding out that she was HIV-positive. During that eight months, Flowers's entire work environment changed. Before, Flowers and her boss had been friends who went out together for lunch, drinks, and the movies. Afterward, the socializing stopped, the boss began monitoring Flowers's phone calls, and then subjected her to four "random" drug tests in one week. A jury found that Flowers's termination was not based on her disability, but that her boss had nonetheless created a hostile work environment by unreasonably interfering with Flowers's ability to work.[31]

While lauding the ADA's objectives, many managers have been apprehensive about its impact on the workplace. Most acknowledge, however, that society is better off if every member has the opportunity to work. And as advocates for the disabled point out, we are all, at best, only temporarily able-bodied. Even with the ADA, only 35 percent of the disabled population who are of working age are employed, whereas 78 percent of able-bodied people have jobs.

---

[30]*Raytheon Co. v. Hernandez*, 540 U.S. 44 (S. Ct. 2003).
[31]*Flowers v. S. Reg'l Physician Servs*, 247 F.3d 229 (5th Cir. 2001).

27-9 GENETIC INFORMATION NONDISCRIMINATION ACT

Suppose you want to promote someone to CFO, but you know that his father and brothers both died young of prostate cancer. Is it legal to consider that information in making a decision? Not since Congress passed the Genetic Information Nondiscrimination Act (GINA). Under this statute, employers with 15 or more workers may not require genetic testing or discriminate against workers because of their genetic makeup. Nor may health insurers use such information to decide coverage or premiums. Thus, neither employers nor health insurers may require you to provide your family medical history—who has died of cancer or heart disease, for instance. And if they find this information out from another source (such as a newspaper obituary), they may not use it in making an employment decision.

27-10 ENFORCEMENT

Employment laws provide plaintiffs with different enforcement options.

27-10a Constitutional Claims

People bringing a claim under the Constitution must file suit on their own.

27-10b The Civil Rights Act of 1866

For plaintiffs alleging racial discrimination, the Civil Rights Act of 1866 offers substantial advantages over Title VII:

- A four-year statute of limitations

- Unlimited compensatory and punitive damages (which, in one case, amounted to $7 million)[32]

- Applicability to all employers, not just those with 15 or more employees

However, this statute is not enforced by the EEOC, which means that the plaintiff is on his own when it comes to negotiating with or filing suit against an employer.

27-10c The Rehabilitation Act of 1973

This statute is enforced by the EEOC (for claims against the executive branch of the federal government), the Department of Labor (for claims against federal contractors), and the Department of Justice (for claims against entities that receive federal funds).

27-10d Other Statutory Claims

The EEOC is the federal agency responsible for enforcing Title VII, the Equal Pay Act, the Pregnancy Discrimination Act, the ADEA, the ADA, and GINA.

Before a plaintiff can bring suit under one of these statutes, she must first file a complaint with the EEOC. Generally the plaintiff must file within 180 days of the wrongdoing.[33] But if

---

[32]*Edwards v. MBTA*. After the verdict, the case settled.
[33]This is the case unless he resides in a state with an appropriate state agency, in which case he has 300 days.

the plaintiff is alleging that she was paid less than she should have been, each paycheck she receives starts the statute of limitations all over again. After it receives a filing, the EEOC conducts an investigation and also attempts to mediate the dispute. If it determines that discrimination has occurred, it will typically file suit on behalf of the plaintiff. This arrangement is favorable for the plaintiff because the government pays the legal bill. If the EEOC decides *not* to bring the case, or does not make a decision within six months, it issues a right to sue letter, and the plaintiff may proceed on her own in court within 90 days. Under the ADEA, a plaintiff may bring suit 60 days after filing a charge with the EEOC. Many states also have their own version of the EEOC.

Remedies available to the successful plaintiff include hiring, reinstatement, retroactive seniority, back pay, front pay (to compensate for future lost wages), and reasonable attorney's fees. Under Title VII and the ADA, plaintiffs are also entitled to compensatory and punitive damages up to $300,000, but only in certain disparate treatment cases, not disparate impact suits. Compensatory damages include future monetary losses, mental anguish, loss of enjoyment of life, and damage to reputation. Punitive damages are available if the defendant acted with malice or reckless indifference to the plaintiff's rights. Under the ADEA, plaintiffs can recover compensatory damages but are eligible for punitive damages only in the case of "willful" violations; that is, knowing or reckless disregard of the law. In the case of willful violations, the damage award is typically doubled.

Two trends, however, have reduced employees' chances of taking home substantial damages. Concerned about a rise in discrimination lawsuits, employers now often require new hires to agree in advance to arbitrate, not litigate, any future employment claims. The Supreme Court has upheld the enforceability of mandatory arbitration provisions.[34] Employees sometimes receive worse results in the arbitrator's office than in the courtroom, because some arbitrators seem to favor repeat customers (such as management) over one-time users (such as employees). In addition, discovery is more limited in arbitration than in court, which means that the plaintiff may not be able to make the strongest case. Also, arbitration awards are usually not disclosed publicly, so employers have less incentive to avoid misbehavior.

But even if a case does go to trial, plaintiffs in job discrimination cases have a much worse track record than other types of plaintiffs—they win less often at trial, and they lose more often on appeal. As a result, the number of discrimination cases in the federal courts has declined.[35]

Every applicant feels slightly apprehensive before a job interview, but interviewers are also nervous—fearing that every question is a potential land mine of liability. Most interviewers (and students who have read this chapter) would know better than Delta Airlines interviewers who allegedly asked applicants about their sexual orientation, birth control methods, and abortion history. The following list provides guidelines for interviewers.

Don't Even Consider Asking	Go Ahead and Ask
Can you perform this function with or without reasonable accommodation?	Would you need reasonable accommodation in this job?
How many days were you sick last year?	How many days were you absent from work last year?
What medications are you currently taking?	Are you currently using drugs illegally?
Where were you born? Are you a United States citizen?	Are you authorized to work in the United States?

---

[34]*Gilmer v. Interstate/Johnson Lane Corp.*, 500 U.S. 20 (S. Ct. 1991).

[35]Kevin M. Clermont and Stewart J. Schwab, *Employment Discrimination Plaintiffs in Federal Court: From Bad to Worse?* 3 Harv. l. & Pol'y Rev. 103 (2009).

How old are you?	What work experience have you had?
How tall are you? How much do you weigh?	Could you carry a 100-pound weight, as required by this job?
When did you graduate from college?	Where did you go to college?
How did you learn this language?	What languages do you speak and write fluently?
Have you ever been arrested?	Have you ever been convicted of a crime that would affect the performance of this job?
Do you plan to have children? How old are your children? What method of birth control do you use?	Can you work weekends? Travel extensively? Would you be willing to relocate?
What is your corrected vision?	Do you have 20/20 corrected vision?
Are you a man or a woman? Are you single or married? What does your spouse do? What will happen if your spouse is transferred? What clubs, societies, or lodges do you belong to?	Talk about the weather instead!

© Cengage Learning

The most common gaffe on the part of interviewers? Asking women about their child-care arrangements. That question assumes the woman is responsible for child care.

Chapter Conclusion

As adults, we spend more time working than in any other single activity. A job that we love can permeate our lives with satisfaction and even joy. Work that bores or bedevils us may shorten our lives. We have devoted two chapters to employment law precisely because work *is* so important in our lives. Now you know both your rights as a worker and your obligations as an employer. We hope that when you have other people's lives in your hands, you will treat them as you would wish to be treated.

EXAM REVIEW

1. **CONSTITUTION** The U.S. Constitution prohibits employment discrimination by federal, state, and local governments. (p. 646)

2. **THE CIVIL RIGHTS ACT OF 1866** The Civil Rights Act of 1866 prohibits racial discrimination in both private and public employment (except it does not apply to the federal government). (p. 646)

3. **TITLE VII** Under Title VII of the Civil Rights Act of 1964, it is illegal for employers with 15 or more workers to discriminate on the basis of race, color, religion, sex, or national origin. (pp. 646–655)

4. **TYPES OF DISCRIMINATION**   There are four types of prohibited activities under Title VII: disparate treatment, disparate impact, hostile environment, and retaliation. (p. 646)

5. **DISPARATE TREATMENT**   To prove a disparate treatment case, the plaintiff must show that she was *treated* less favorably than others because of her sex, race, color, religion, or national origin. (pp. 646–647)

6. **DISPARATE IMPACT**   Disparate impact applies if the employer has a rule that, *on its face*, is not discriminatory, but *in practice* excludes too many people in a protected group and the test is not a job-related business necessity. (pp. 648–649)

7. **HOSTILE WORK ENVIRONMENT**   Employers violate Title VII if they permit a work environment that is so hostile towards people in a protected category that it affects their ability to work. (pp. 649–652)

8. **RETALIATION**   Title VII also prohibits employers from retaliating against workers who oppose discrimination, bring a claim under the statute, or take part in an investigation or hearing. (p. 652)

9. **RELIGION**   Employers cannot discriminate against a worker because of his religious beliefs. In addition, employers must make reasonable accommodation for a worker's religious practices unless the request would cause undue hardship for the business. (p. 652)

10. **DEFENSES**   Under Title VII, the defendant has four possible defenses: merit, seniority, bona fide occupational qualification (BFOQ), and affirmative action. (pp. 654–655)

11. **BONA FIDE OCCUPATIONAL QUALIFICATION**   Under the BFOQ standard, an employer is permitted to establish discriminatory job requirements if they are essential to the position in question. (pp. 654–655)

EXAM Strategy

Question: When Southwest Airlines first started, it refused to hire male flight attendants because its strategy was to court its (mostly male) customers by promoting an image of "feminine spirit, fun, and sex appeal." Its ads featured women in provocative uniforms serving "love bites" (almonds) and "love potions" (cocktails). Its ticketing system featured a "quickie machine" to provide "instant gratification." Is this refusal to hire men a violation of Title VII?

Strategy: Southwest argued that its "Love" campaign was an essential marketing tool. Was being a woman a BFOQ? Remember that the courts have almost always rejected BFOQ claims that are based on customer preference. (See the "Result" at the end of this section.)

12. **EQUAL PAY ACT**   Under the Equal Pay Act, an employee may not be paid at a lesser rate than employees of the opposite sex for equal work. (p. 656)

13. **PREGNANCY DISCRIMINATION ACT**   Under the Pregnancy Discrimination Act, an employer may not fire, refuse to hire, or fail to promote a

woman because she is pregnant or because she has had an abortion. An employer must also treat pregnancy as it would any other temporary disability. (p. 656)

14. **AGE DISCRIMINATION IN EMPLOYMENT ACT**   Under the ADEA, an employer with 20 or more workers may not fire, refuse to hire, fail to promote, or otherwise reduce a person's employment opportunities because he is 40 or older. (pp. 656–659)

Question: Kathy was over 40 when SFI refused to hire her as an insurance agent. It claimed that it had not hired her because she did not have sales experience, but the job ad had not specified that sales experience was required. It turned out that when SFI hired agents from outside the company, it was much more likely to hire people under 40. But when promoting from within, it was much more likely to promote people over 40. Did SFI violate the ADEA when it refused to hire Kathy?

Strategy: An ADEA case involves a three-step analysis. In Step 1, Kathy has shown that she is older than 40, suffered an adverse employment action, was qualified for the job, and a younger person actually got the job. In Step 2, SFI has to show that its decision was based on a legitimate reason. No sales experience is a good reason. In Step 3, Kathy must prove that her age was the deciding factor. (See the "Result" at the end of this section.)

15. **REHABILITATION ACT**   The Rehabilitation Act of 1973 prohibits discrimination on the basis of disability by the federal government, federal contractors, and all entities that receive federal funds. (pp. 659–660)

16. **AMERICANS WITH DISABILITIES ACT**   The ADA prohibits employers with 15 or more workers from discriminating on the basis of disability. (pp. 660–663)

17. **DISABILITY**   A disabled person is:
    - Someone with a physical or mental impairment that substantially limits a major life activity or the operation of a major bodily function, or
    - Someone who is regarded as having such an impairment. (pp. 660–661)

18. **TREATMENT OF DISABLED WORKERS**   Once it is established that a worker is disabled, employers may not discriminate on the basis of disability so long as she can, with reasonable accommodation, perform the essential function of the job. An accommodation is not reasonable if it would create undue hardship for the employer. (pp. 661–662)

Question: When Thomas Lussier filled out a Postal Service employment application, he did not reveal that he had twice pleaded guilty to charges of disorderly conduct. Lussier suffered from Post-Traumatic Stress Disorder (PTSD) acquired during military service. Because of this disorder, he sometimes had panic attacks that required him to leave meetings. He was also a recovered alcoholic and drug user. During his stint with the Postal Service, he had some personality conflicts with other employees. Once, another employee hit him. He also had one episode of "erratic emotional behavior and verbal outburst." In the meantime, a postal employee in Ridgewood, New Jersey, killed four colleagues. The postmaster general encouraged all supervisors to identify workers who had dangerous propensities. Lussier's boss discovered that he had lied on his employment application about the disorderly conduct charges and fired him. Is the Postal Service in violation of the law?

Strategy: Was Lussier disabled under the ADA? He had a mental impairment (PTSD) that substantially limited a major life activity. Could Lussier, with reasonable accommodation, perform his job? Yes. Was his firing illegal? (See the "Result" at the end of this section.)

19. GENETIC INFORMATION NONDISCRIMINATION ACT Under GINA, employers with 15 or more workers may not require genetic testing or discriminate against workers because of their genetic makeup. (p. 664)

11. Result: Safety, privacy, and authenticity are three situations in which customer preference can be a BFOQ. None of these issues was a factor in this case. The court ruled against Southwest on the grounds that it was "not a business where vicarious sex entertainment is the primary service provided." [36]

14. Result: In the absence of specific comments about age, it is very difficult to show that age is the deciding factor. Kathy is likely to lose her case.

18. Result: The court held that the Postal Service was in violation of the law because Lussier had been dismissed solely as a result of his disability. Clearly, he could perform his job with reasonable accommodation.

MULTIPLE-CHOICE QUESTIONS

1. Gregg Young, the CEO of BJY Inc., insisted on calling Mamdouh El-Hakem "Manny" or "Hank" even when El-Hakem asked him not to. El-Hakem was of Arab heritage. Young argued that a "Western" name would increase El-Hakem's chances for success and would be more acceptable to BJY's clientele. Does this behavior violate the law?

   (a) Yes, Young violated Title VII by discriminating against El-Hakem on the basis of his national origin.

   (b) Yes, Young was creating a hostile work environment.

   (c) Both (a) and (b)

   (d) No, Manny is just a nickname. No harm was intended and, indeed, no harm resulted.

   (e) No, because customers did prefer a Western name.

---

[36]*Wilson v. Southwest Airlines*, 517 F. Supp 292 (N.D. Tex, 1981).

2. The CEO of BankTwo realized that not one single officer of the bank was female or minority. He announced that henceforth, the bank would only hire people in these two groups until they made up at least 30 percent of the officers. Is this plan legal?

    (a) Yes, voluntary affirmative action plans are always legal.

    (b) Yes, because fewer than 20 percent of the officers are female or minority.

    (c) No, to be legal, the goal of an affirmative action plan cannot be greater than 20 percent female or minority.

    (d) No, the plan is too unfair to white men, who have no chance of being hired for a long time.

3. When Allain University was looking for a diversity officer, it decided it would only hire a person of color. Is this decision legal?

    (a) Yes, color is a BFOQ for this position.

    (b) No, color is never a BFOQ, but race could be.

    (c) No, neither race nor color can be a BFOQ.

    (d) No, race and color can be a BFOQ, but is not in this situation. A person does not have to be a member of a minority group to promote diversity.

4. Ralph has worked as a model builder at Snowdrop Architects for 30 years. The firm replaces him with Charlotte, who is 24 and willing to work for much less than Ralph's salary. The firm never offered to let him stay for less pay. When he left, one of the partners told him, "Frankly, it's not a bad thing to have a cute young person working with the clients." Which of the following statements is true?

    (a) Snowdrop is liable because it had an obligation to offer Ralph the lower salary before firing him.

    (b) Snowdrop is liable because it is illegal to replace an older worker with a younger one just to save money.

    (c) Snowdrop is liable because age was a factor in Ralph's firing.

    (d) Snowdrop is liable under Title VII because it replaced an old man with a young woman.

    (e) Snowdrop is not liable because age was not the deciding factor in Ralph's firing.

5. During chemotherapy for bone cancer, a delivery person is exhausted, nauseous, and weak. He has asked permission to come in later, work a shorter day, and limit his lifting to 10 pounds. Delivery people typically carry packages of up to 70 pounds. Does Vulcan, his employer, have the right to fire him?

    (a) Vulcan must create a new position so that the employee can do something else.

    (b) Vulcan must transfer the employee to another position, but only if one is vacant and he is able to perform it.

    (c) Vulcan can fire the man because none of his major life activities has been affected.

    (d) Vulcan can fire the man because he cannot perform the essential functions of his job.

    (e) Vulcan can fire him because he is not disabled—once the chemotherapy treatments end, he will feel fine again.

ESSAY QUESTIONS

1. Disney World and Abercrombie & Fitch both fired female employees who insisted upon wearing a Muslim headscarf because such apparel violated the companies' appearance policies. Can these employers make reasonable accommodation for this religious practice? Abercrombie also fired a salesperson who converted to a Christian religion that forbade her from showing skin. When she showed up for work in an ankle-length skirt, her manager told her she had to either wear jeans or short skirts with leggings, but she refused. Did Abercrombie violate Title VII in this case?

2. In the 2008 recession, Roger lost his job as a comptroller. Desperate for work after a year of unemployment, he began to apply for any accounting job at any company. But no one would hire him because he was "over-qualified and over-experienced." He repeatedly explained that he was eager to fill the job that was available. Have these companies that refused to hire Roger violated the ADEA?

3. More than 90 percent of employers conduct criminal background checks, and many of these automatically exclude any job applicant with a criminal record. Is this practice a violation of the law?

4. The Lillie Rubin boutique in Phoenix would hire only women to work in sales because fittings and alterations took place in the dressing room or immediately outside. The customers were buying expensive clothes and demanded a male-free dressing area. Has the Lillie Rubin store violated Title VII? What would its defense be?

5. FedEx refused to promote José Rodriguez to a supervisor's position because of his accent and "how he speaks." Is FedEx in violation of the law?

DISCUSSION QUESTIONS

1. In the *Griggs* disparate impact case, Duke Power based employment decisions on written tests. Why do employers use these types of tests? When are they appropriate in the hiring or promotion process?

2. In disparate *treatment* cases, the plaintiff must show that the defendant intentionally discriminated, but not in disparate *impact* cases. Is it fair to hold employers liable when they have not engaged in intentional wrongdoing?

3. Generally, the BFOQ defense does not apply to customer preference. But recently, some clients have been pressuring their law firms to staff their

cases with female and minority lawyers. If a firm does so, would the BFOQ defense be valid? Should it be?

4. Pam Huber worked at Wal-Mart as a grocery order filler, earning $13 an hour. While on the job, she suffered a permanent injury to her right arm and hand. Both she and Wal-Mart agreed that she was disabled under the ADA. As a reasonable accommodation, she asked for a job as a router, which was then vacant. Although she was qualified for that job, she was not the most qualified. Wal-Mart filled the job with the most qualified person. It offered Huber a position as a janitor at $6.20 per hour. Did Wal-Mart violate the ADA?

5. **ETHICS** Mary Ann Singleton was the librarian at a maximum-security prison located in Tazewell County, Virginia. About four times a week, Gene Shinault, assistant warden for operations, persistently complimented Singleton and stared at her breasts when he spoke to her. On one occasion, he measured the length of her skirt to judge its compliance with the prison's dress code and told her that it looked "real good"; constantly told her how attractive he found her; made references to his physical fitness, considering his advanced age; asked Singleton if he made her nervous (she answered "yes"); and repeatedly remarked to Singleton that if he had a wife as attractive as Singleton, he would not permit her to work in a prison facility around so many inmates. Shinault told Singleton's supervisor in her presence, "Look at her. I bet you have to spank her every day." The supervisor then laughed and said, "No. I probably should, but I don't." Shinault replied, "Well, I know I would." Shinault also had a security camera installed in her office in a way that permitted him to observe her as she worked. Singleton reported this behavior to her supervisor, who simply responded, "Boys will be boys." Did Shinault sexually harass Singleton? Whether or not Shinault violated the law, what *ethical* obligation did Singleton's supervisor have to protect her from this type of behavior?

6. Ronald Lockhart, who was deaf, worked for FedEx as a package handler. Although fluent in American Sign Language, he could not read lips. After 9/11, the company held meetings to talk about security issues. Lockhart complained to the EEOC that he could not understand these discussions. FedEx fired him. Has FedEx violated the law?

nuttakit/Shutterstock.com; Steve Allen/Brand X Pictures/Jupiter Images

STARTING A BUSINESS: LLCS AND OTHER OPTIONS

Jeffrey Horning was stuck in purgatory, with two business partners he loathed and no way out.

Poor Jeffrey Horning. If only he had understood business law. Horning owned a thriving construction company which operated as a corporation—Horning Construction Company, Inc. To lighten his crushing workload, he decided to bring in two partners to handle more day-to-day responsibility. It seemed a good idea at the time.

Horning transferred the business to Horning Construction, LLC and then gave one-third ownership each to two trusted employees, Klimowski and Holdsworth. But Horning did not pay enough attention to the legal formalities—the new LLC had no operating agreement.

Nothing worked out as he had planned. The two men did not take on extra work. Horning's relationship with them went from bad to worse, with the parties bickering over every petty detail and each man trying to sabotage the others. It got to the point that Klimowski sent Horning a letter full of foul language. At his wit's end, Horning proposed that the LLC buy out his share of the business. Klimowski and Holdsworth refused. Really frustrated, Horning asked a court to dissolve the business on the grounds that Klimowski despised him, Holdsworth resented him, and neither of them trusted him. In his view, it was their goal "to make my remaining time with Horning, LLC so unbearable that I will relent and give them for a pittance the remainder of the company for which they have paid nothing to date."

Although the court was sympathetic, it refused to help. Because Horning, LLC did not have an operating agreement that provided for a buyout, it had to depend upon the LLC statute, which only permitted dissolution "whenever it is not reasonably practicable to carry on the business." Unfortunately, Horning, LLC was very successful, grossing over $25 million annually. Jeffrey Horning was stuck in purgatory, with two business partners he loathed and no way out.[1]

Every business, no matter how large, was at one point little more than a gleam in an entrepreneur's eye. The goal of the law is to balance the rights, duties, and liabilities of entrepreneurs, managers, investors, and customers. Time and again in these next chapters, we will see that legal issues can have as profound an impact on the success of a company as any business decision. The law affects virtually every aspect of business. Wise (and successful) entrepreneurs know how to use the law to their advantage. Think of the grief Jeffrey Horning could have saved himself if he had understood the implications of the LLC statute.

To begin, entrepreneurs must select a form of organization. The correct choice can reduce taxes, liability, and conflict while facilitating outside investment. If entrepreneurs do not make a choice for themselves, the law will automatically select a (potentially undesirable) default option.

28-1 SOLE PROPRIETORSHIPS

Sole proprietorship
An unincorporated business owned by one person.

Sole proprietorships are the most common form of business, so we begin there. A **sole proprietorship** is an unincorporated business owned by one person. For example, Linda runs ExSciTe (which stands for Excellence in Science Teaching), a company that helps teachers prepare hands-on science experiments in the classroom using such basic items as vinegar, lemon juice, and red cabbage.

If an individual runs a business without taking any formal steps to create an organization, she automatically has a sole proprietorship. It is, if you will, the default option. She is not required to hire a lawyer or register with the government. The company is not even required to file a separate tax return—because the business is a *flow-through* tax entity. In other words, Linda must pay *personal* income tax on the profits, but the *business* itself does not pay income taxes. A very few states, and some cities and towns, require sole proprietors to obtain a business license. And states generally require sole proprietors to register their business name if it is different from their own. Linda, for example, would file a "d/b/a" or "doing business as" certificate for ExSciTe.

Sole proprietorships have some serious disadvantages. First, the owner of the business is responsible for all of the business's debts. If ExSciTe cannot pay its suppliers or if a student is injured by an exploding cabbage, Linda is *personally* liable. She may have to sell her house and car to pay the debt. Second, the owner of a sole proprietorship has limited options for financing her business. Debt is generally her only source of working capital because she has no stock or memberships to sell. If someone else brings in capital and helps with the management of the business, then it is a partnership, not a sole proprietorship. For this reason, sole proprietorships work best for small businesses without large capital needs.

---

[1]*In the Matter of Jeffrey M. Horning*, 816 N.Y.S.2d 877; 2006 N.Y. Misc. LEXIS 555.

28-2 CORPORATIONS

Corporations are the dominant form of organization for a simple reason—they have been around for a long time and, as a result, they are numerous and the law that regulates them is well developed.

The concept of a corporation is very old indeed—it began with the Greeks and spread from them through the Romans into English law. At the beginning, however, corporations were viewed with deep suspicion. A British jurist commented that they had "neither bodies to be punished nor souls to be condemned." And what were shareholders doing that they needed limited liability? Why did they have to cower behind a corporate shield? For this reason, shareholders originally had to obtain special permission to form a corporation. In England, corporations could be created only by special charter from the monarch or, later, from Parliament. But with the advent of the Industrial Revolution, large-scale manufacturing enterprises needed huge amounts of capital from investors who were not involved in management and did not want to be personally liable for the debts of an organization that they were not managing. In 1811, New York became the first jurisdiction in the United States to permit routine incorporation.[2]

Despite the initial suspicion with which corporations were viewed, economists now suggest that this form of organization, combined with technological advances such as double-entry bookkeeping and stockmarkets, provided the West with an enormous economic advantage. In particular, corporations permitted the investment of outside capital and were more likely than partnerships to survive the death of their founders. In short, corporations permitted the development of large, enduring businesses.

28-2a Corporations in General

As is the case for all forms of organization, corporations have their advantages and disadvantages.

LIMITED LIABILITY

If a business flops and cannot pay its bills, shareholders lose their investment in the company but not their other assets. Likewise, if an employee is in an accident while driving a company van, the business is liable for any harm to the other driver, but its shareholders are not personally liable. Be aware, however, that limited liability does not protect against all debts. Individuals are always responsible for their *own* acts. Suppose that the careless employee who caused the accident was also a company shareholder. Both he and the company would be liable. If the company did not pay the judgment, the employee would have to, from his personal assets. **A corporation protects managers and investors from personal liability for the debts of the corporation and the actions of others, but not against liability for their *own negligence (or other torts and crimes)*.**

TRANSFERABILITY OF INTERESTS

Corporations provide flexibility for enterprises small (with one owner) and large (with thousands of shareholders). As we will see, partnership interests are not transferable without the permission of the other partners, whereas corporate stock can be bought and sold easily.

DURATION

When a sole proprietor dies, legally so does the business. But corporations have perpetual existence: They can continue without their founders.

---

[2]An Act Relative to Incorporation for Manufacturing Purpose, 1811 N.Y. Laws, ch. 67, §111.

LOGISTICS

Corporations require substantial expense and effort to create and operate. The cost of establishing a corporation includes legal and filing fees, not to mention the cost of the annual filings that states require. Corporations must also hold meetings for both shareholders and directors. Minutes of these meetings must be kept indefinitely in the company minute book.

TAXES

Because corporations are taxable entities, they must pay taxes and file returns. This is a simple sentence that requires a complex explanation. Originally, there were only three ways to do business: as a sole proprietorship, a partnership, or a corporation. The sole proprietor pays taxes on all the business's profits. A partnership is not, as we say, a taxable entity, which means it does not pay taxes itself. All income and losses are passed through to the partners and reported on their personal income tax returns. Corporations, by contrast, are taxable entities and pay income tax on their profits. Shareholders must then pay tax on dividends from the corporation. Thus a dollar is taxed only once before it ends up in a partner's bank account, but twice before it is deposited by a shareholder.

Exhibit 28.1 compares the single taxation of partnerships with the double taxation of corporations. Suppose, as shown in the exhibit, that a corporation and a partnership each receives $10,000 in additional income. The corporation pays tax at a top rate of 35 percent.[3]

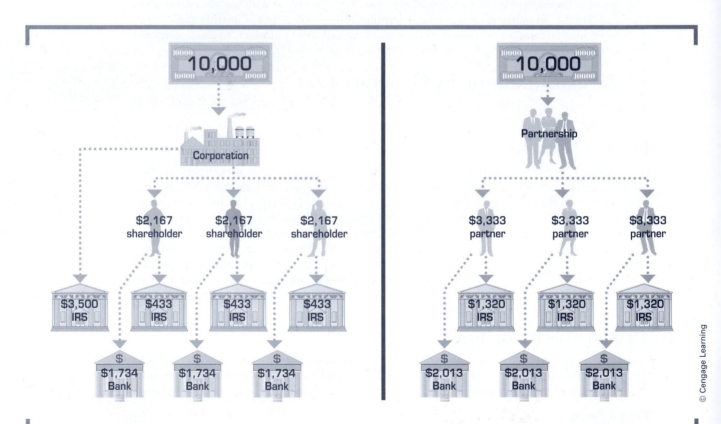

© Cengage Learning

| EXHIBIT 28.1 | Partners pay less in taxes than shareholders. |

[3]This is the federal tax rate; most states also levy a corporate tax.

Thus the corporation pays $3,500 of the $10,000 in tax. The corporation pays out the remaining $6,500 as a dividend of $2,167 to each of its three shareholders. Then the shareholders are taxed at the special dividend rate of 20 percent, which means they each pay a tax of $433. They are each left with $1,734. Of the initial $10,000, almost 48 percent ($4,799) has gone to the Internal Revenue Service (IRS).

Compare the corporation to a partnership. The partnership itself pays no taxes, so it can pass on $3,333 to each of its partners. At a 39.6 percent individual rate, each partner pays an income tax of $1,320. As partners, they pocket $2,013, which is $279 more than they could keep as shareholders. Of the partnership's initial $10,000, 39.6 percent ($3,960) has gone to the IRS, compared with the corporation's 48 percent.

One further tax issue. Corporations are created and regulated by state law but must pay both federal and state taxes. Federal law gives favorable tax treatment to some small corporations, which it calls "S corporations." Many states also treat small corporations differently but call them "close corporations." Federal tax law and state corporation statutes are completely independent. Thus, an organization could be a close corporation under state law and not qualify as an S corporation or, conversely, could be an S corporation under federal law but may or may not be a close corporation for state purposes. Exhibit 28.2 illustrates the difference between state corporate law and federal taxation of corporations.

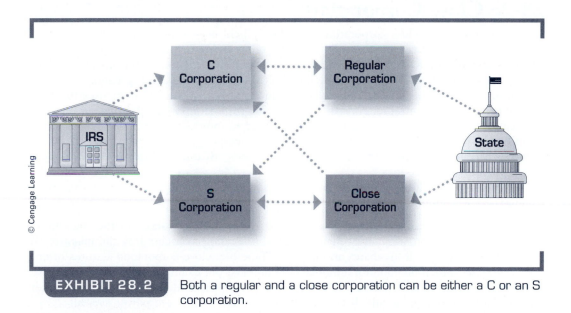

© Cengage Learning

| EXHIBIT 28.2 | Both a regular and a close corporation can be either a C or an S corporation. |

28-2b S Corporations

Although entrepreneurs are often optimistic about the likely success of their new enterprise, in truth, the majority of new businesses lose money in their early years. Congress created S corporations (aka "S corps") to encourage entrepreneurship by offering tax breaks. The name "S corporation" comes from the provision of the Internal Revenue Code that created this form of organization.[4] **Shareholders of S corps have both the limited liability of**

---

[4] 26 U.S.C. §1361.

a corporation and the tax status of a partnership. Like a partnership, an S corp is not a taxable entity—all the company's profits and losses pass through to the shareholders, who pay tax at their individual rates. It avoids the double taxation of a regular corporation (called a "C corporation"). If, as is often the case, the startup loses money, investors can deduct these losses against their other income.

S corps *do* face some major restrictions:

- There can be only one class of stock (although voting rights can vary within the class).

- There can be no more than 100 shareholders.

- Shareholders must be individuals, estates, charities, pension funds, or trusts, not partnerships or corporations.

- Shareholders must be citizens or residents of the United States, not nonresident aliens.

- All shareholders must agree that the company should be an S corporation.

Although *most* states follow the federal lead on S corporations, a small number require these companies to pay state corporate tax.

28-2c Close Corporations

Close corporation

A company whose stock is not publicly traded. Also known as a *closely held corporation*.

Originally, the terms **close corporation** and **closely held corporation** referred simply to a company whose stock was not publicly traded (in other words, a "privately held" company). Most close corporations are small, although some privately held corporations, such as Hallmark Cards, Inc., and Mars, Inc. (maker of M&Ms and Snickers candy bars), are huge. Beginning in New York in 1948, some states amended their corporation statutes to make special provisions for entrepreneurs. In some cases, a corporation must affirmatively elect to be treated as a close corporation; in others, any corporation can take advantage of these special provisions. Now when lawyers refer to "close corporations," they usually mean not merely a privately held company, but one that has taken advantage of the close corporation provisions of its state code.

Although the provisions of close corporation statutes vary from state to state, they tend to have certain common themes:

- **Protection of minority shareholders.** As there is no public market for the stock of a close corporation, a minority shareholder who is being mistreated by the majority cannot simply sell his shares and depart. Therefore, close corporation statutes often provide some protection for minority shareholders. For example, the charter of a close corporation could require a unanimous vote of all shareholders to choose officers, set salaries, or pay dividends. It could grant each shareholder veto power over all important corporate decisions.

- **Transfer restrictions.** The shareholders of a close corporation often need to work closely together in the management of the company. Therefore, statutes typically permit the corporation to require that a shareholder first offer shares to the other owners before selling them to an outsider. In that way, the remaining shareholders have some control over who their new co-owners will be.

- **Flexibility.** Close corporations can typically operate without a board of directors, a formal set of bylaws, or annual shareholder meetings.

- **Dispute resolution.** The shareholders are allowed to agree in advance that any one of them can dissolve the corporation if some particular event occurs or, if they choose, for any reason at all. If the shareholders are in a stalemate, the problem can be solved by dissolving the corporation. Even without such an agreement, a shareholder can ask a court to dissolve a close corporation if the other owners behave "oppressively" or "unfairly."

EXAM Strategy

Question: Consider these two entrepreneurs: Judith formed a corporation to publish a newsletter that will not generate substantial revenues. Drexel operated his construction and remodeling business as a sole proprietorship. Were these forms of organization right for these businesses?

Strategy: Prepare a list of the advantages and disadvantages of each form of organization. Sole proprietorships are best for businesses without substantial capital needs. Corporations can raise capital but are expensive to operate.

Result: Judith would be better off with a sole proprietorship—her revenues will not support the expenses of a corporation. Also, her debts are likely to be small, so she will not need the limited liability of a corporation. And no matter what her form of organization, she would be personally liable for any negligent acts she commits, so a corporation would not provide any additional protection. But for Drexel, a sole proprietorship could be disastrous because his construction company will have substantial expenses and a large number of employees. If an employee causes an injury, Drexel might be personally liable. And if his business fails, the court would liquidate his personal assets. He would be better off with a form of organization that limits his liability, such as a corporation or a limited liability company.

28-3 LIMITED LIABILITY COMPANIES

An LLC offers the limited liability of a corporation and the tax status of a partnership.

Limited liability companies (LLCs) are a relatively new form of organization. Wyoming passed the first LLC statute in 1977, but most states did not follow suit until after 1991. An LLC is an extremely useful form of organization increasingly favored by entrepreneurs. It is not, however, as simple as it perhaps should be. Owing to a complex history that involves painful interaction between IRS regulations and state laws (the details of which we will spare you), the specific provisions of state laws vary greatly. An effort to remedy this confusion—the Uniform Limited Liability Company Act—has not at this point been widely accepted. Indeed, it was so heavily criticized that it was revised, but the revised statute has been adopted by relatively few states. Thus, we can discuss only general trends in state laws. Before forming an LLC, you should review carefully the laws in your particular state.

LIMITED LIABILITY

Members are not personally liable for the debts of the company. They risk only their investment, as if they were shareholders of a corporation. Are the members of the LLC liable in the following case? You be the judge.

You Be the Judge

RIDGAWAY V. SILK

2004 Conn . Super. LEXIS 548
Superior Court of Connecticut, 2004

Facts: Norman Costello and Robert Giordano were members of Silk, LLC, which owned a bar and adult entertainment nightclub in Groton, Connecticut, called Silk Stockings. Anthony Sulls went drinking there one night—and drinking heavily. Although he was obviously drunk, employees at Silk Stockings continued to serve him. Costello and Giordano were working there that night. They both greeted customers (who numbered in the hundreds), supervised employees, and performed "other PR work." When Sulls left the nightclub at 1:45 a.m. with two friends, he drove off the highway at high speed, killing himself and one of his passengers, William Ridgaway, Jr.

Ridgaway's estate sued Costello and Giordano personally. The defendants filed a motion for summary judgment seeking dismissal of the complaint.

You Be the Judge: *Are Costello and Giordano personally liable to Ridgaway's estate?*

Argument for Costello and Giordano: The defendants did not own Silk Stockings; they were simply members of an LLC that owned the nightclub. The whole point of an LLC is to protect members against personal liability. The assets of Silk, LLC, are at risk, but not the personal assets of Costello and Giordano.

Argument for Ridgaway's Estate: The defendants are not liable for being members of Silk, LLC; they are liable for their own misdeeds as employees of the LLC. They were both present at Silk Stockings on the night in question, meeting and greeting customers and supervising employees. It is possible that they might actually have served drinks to Sulls, but in any event, they did not adequately supervise and train their employees to prevent them from serving alcohol to someone who was clearly drunk. The world would be an intolerable place to live if employees were free to be as careless as they wished, knowing that they were not liable because they were members of an LLC.

TAX STATUS

As in a partnership, income flows through the company to the individual members, avoiding the double taxation of a corporation.

FORMATION

To organize an LLC, you must have a charter and you should have an operating agreement. The charter is short, containing basic information such as name and address. It must be filed with the Secretary of State in the jurisdiction in which it is being formed. An operating agreement sets out the rights and obligations of the owners, who are called "members." If an LLC does not adopt its own operating agreement, LLC statutes provide a default option. However, these standardized provisions may not be what members would choose if they thought about it. Therefore, it is often better for an LLC to prepare its own personalized operating agreement. The Horning case that began this chapter illustrates one of the many things that can go wrong when an LLC does not have an operating agreement.

On this issue, corporations have an advantage over LLCs. Corporations are so familiar that the standard documents (such as a charter, bylaws, and shareholder agreement) are well established and widely available. Lawyers can form a corporation easily, and the Internet offers a host of free forms. This is not the case with LLCs. As yet, the law is so unsettled that standard forms may be dangerous, while customized forms can be expensive. The following case illustrates the importance of a well-drafted operating agreement.

WYOMING.COM, LLC V. LIEBERMAN

2005 WY 42; 109 P.3d 883; 2005 Wyo. LEXIS 48
Supreme Court of Wyoming, 2005

CASE SUMMARY

Facts: Lieberman was a member of an LLC called Wyoming.com. After he withdrew, he and the other members disagreed about what his membership was worth. Wyoming.com filed a lawsuit asking the court to determine the financial rights and obligations of the parties, if any, upon the withdrawal of a member.

The Supreme Court of Wyoming reached a decision that may have sounded logical but left Lieberman in a sad twilight zone—neither in nor out of the LLC. The court ruled that Lieberman still owned part of the business despite his withdrawal as a member.

So far, so good. But neither the LLC statute nor the company's operating agreement required the LLC to pay a member the value of his share. In other words, Lieberman was still an owner, but he was not entitled to any payment for his ownership. Not quite understanding the implications of this ruling, Lieberman filed a motion seeking financial information about the company. The original trial court denied the request on the theory that, since Lieberman had no rights to a payout, the company had no obligation to give him financial data.

Issue: *Did Lieberman have a right to any financial data about Wyoming.com?*

Decision: Wyoming.com had no obligation to provide Lieberman with financial data about the company.

Reasoning: The court in the prior Lieberman case ruled that Lieberman was not entitled to any payment from Wyoming.com. Thus, there was no point in requiring the company to give him financial information. He still owned a share of the company, but he had no further rights.

FLEXIBILITY

Unlike S corporations, LLCs can have members that are corporations, partnerships, or nonresident aliens. LLCs can also have different classes of stock. Unlike corporations, LLCs are not required to hold annual meetings or maintain a minute book.

TRANSFERABILITY OF INTERESTS

Unless the operating agreement provides otherwise, the members of the LLC must obtain the unanimous permission of the remaining members before transferring their ownership rights. This is yet another reason to have an operating agreement.

LLCs cannot issue stock options, which is potentially a serious problem because options may be an essential lure in attracting and retaining top talent.

DURATION

It used to be that LLCs automatically dissolved upon the withdrawal of a member (owing to, for example, death, resignation, or bankruptcy). The current trend in state laws, however, is to permit an LLC to continue in operation even after a member withdraws.

GOING PUBLIC

Once an LLC goes public, it loses its favorable tax status and is taxed as a corporation, not a partnership.[5] Thus, there is no advantage to using the LLC form of organization for a publicly traded company. And there are some disadvantages: Unlike corporations, publicly traded LLCs do not enjoy a well-established set of statutory and case law that is relatively consistent across the many states. For this reason, privately held companies that begin as LLCs usually change to corporations when they go public.

---

[5]26 U.S.C. §7704.

It is worth noting, too, that because of securities laws, it is important for an LLC to have an operating agreement that permits managers the right to convert the LLC into a corporation at the time of a public offering without the consent of the members.[6]

CHANGING FORMS

Some companies that are now corporations might prefer to be LLCs. However, the IRS would consider this change to be a sale of the corporate assets and would levy a tax on the value of these assets. For this reason, few corporations have made the change. However, switching from a partnership to an LLC or from an LLC to a corporation is not considered a sale and does not have the same adverse tax impact.

PIERCING THE LLC VEIL

It has long been the case that, if corporate shareholders do not comply with the technicalities of the law, they may be held personally liable for the debts of the corporation (an issue that is discussed in more depth in Chapter 29). As the following case illustrates, members of an LLC can also be held liable under the same circumstances.

BLD PRODUCTS, LTD. V. TECHNICAL PLASTICS OF OREGON, LLC

2006 U.S. Dist. LEXIS 89874
United States District Court for the District of Oregon, 2006

CASE SUMMARY

Facts: Mark Hardie was the sole member of Technical Plastics of Oregon, LLC (TPO). He operated the business out of an office in his home. Hardie regularly used TPO's accounts to pay such expenses as landscaping and housecleaning. TPO also paid some of Hardie's personal credit card bills, loan payments on his Ford truck, the cost of constructing a deck on his house, his stepson's college bills, and the expenses of family vacations to Disneyland. At the same time, Hardie deposited cash advances from his personal credit cards into the TPO checking account. Hardie did not take a salary from TPO. When TPO filed for bankruptcy, it owed BLD Products approximately $120,000.

In some cases, a court will "pierce the veil" of a corporation and hold its shareholders personally liable for the debts of the business. BLD argued that the same doctrine should apply to LLCs and the court should hold Hardie personally liable for TPO's debts.

Issues: *Does the doctrine of "piercing the veil" apply to LLCs? Is Hardie personally liable for TPO's debts?*

Decision: Yes, an LLC's veil can be pierced. Hardie is personally liable for TPO's debts.

Reasoning: An LLC's veil can be pierced if the following three tests are met:

1. The member (that is, Hardie) controlled the LLC;
2. The member engaged in improper conduct; and
3. As a result of that improper conduct, the plaintiff was unable to collect on a debt against the insolvent LLC.

Hardie, as the sole member and manager of TPO, clearly controlled the company. In addition, he engaged in improper conduct when he paid his personal expenses from the TPO business account. These amounts were more than occasional dips into petty cash—they indicated a disregard of TPO's separate LLC identity. Moreover, he did not keep records of these personal payments.

It is not clear whether Hardie's improper conduct prevented BLD from collecting its entire $120,000 debt. A jury will have to determine the amount that Hardie owes BLD.

---

[6]In this way, under Rule 144 members can include the time during which they owned interests in the LLC when calculating their holding period for stock.

LEGAL UNCERTAINTY

As we have observed, LLCs are a relatively new form of organization without a consistent and widely developed body of law. As a result, members of an LLC may find themselves in the unhappy position of litigating issues of law which, although well established for corporations, are not yet clear for LLCs. Win or lose, lawsuits are expensive in both time and money.

An important area of legal uncertainty involves managers' duties to the members of the organization. For example, it is not clear in many jurisdictions if managers of an LLC have a legal obligation to act in the best interest of members. Delaware courts have recently ruled that an LLC's managers do have a fiduciary duty to its members unless the operating agreement provides otherwise. (In that state, an operating agreement can limit any duty except the requirement of good faith and fair dealing.) However, this uncertainty means that, before becoming a member of an LLC, it is important to understand both state law and the terms of the operating agreement.

Furthermore, when managers of a corporation violate their duty to the organization by, say, approving a merger without sufficient investigation, shareholders are allowed to bring a so-called **derivative lawsuit** in the name of the corporation against the managers. This right was established by common law. It is unclear, however, if members of an LLC have the same right, especially in a state such as New York where the LLC statute does not explicitly authorize derivative lawsuits. The following case resolves this issue, but only for New York State.

Derivative lawsuit
Litigation brought in the name of the corporation against its managers or some other third party.

TZOLIS V. WOLFF

884 N.E.2d 1005; 855 N.Y.S.2d 6; 2008 N.Y. LEXIS 226
Court of Appeals of New York, 2008

Facts: Soterios Tzolis owned 25 percent of Smith Pennington Property Co. LLC, which owned a Manhattan hotel. Herbert Wolff managed the LLC. Tzolis alleged that Wolff first leased and then sold the hotel to family and friends at a price below market value. Tzolis filed a derivative suit against Wolff on the grounds that the man had violated his duties to the LLC.

The trial court ruled that members of an LLC had no right to bring a derivative action because the LLC statute had not explicitly permitted such suits. Tzolis appealed.

Issue: *Do members of an LLC have the right to bring a derivative suit against managers of the company?*

Decision: Yes, at least in New York State, members of an LLC may bring a derivative suit against the managers of an LLC.

Reasoning: The New York corporation statute did not authorize derivative lawsuits. But in 1832, a New York court decreed that shareholders could bring derivative suits against corporate managers. The court said that to allow managers to escape liability for wrong-doing would be an "intolerable grievance."

The same principle applies to LLCs. If managers violate their duty, the victims must be able to recover damages. We can create this right for members of an LLC just as the court did in 1832 for corporate shareholders.

In its reasoning, this court relied on corporate law precedents. However, in a recent case also involving derivative actions, a Delaware court did not follow that approach. The Delaware LLC statute clearly provides that *members* can bring derivative actions. That bit of clarity is helpful. But what about *creditors* of an LLC? We know that creditors of a *corporation* have that right. Does the same rule apply to LLCs?

In the case in question, the board of JetDirect Aviation LLC approved four major acquisitions, all the while knowing that its financials were inaccurate. The company ultimately went bankrupt and, thus, was unable to repay a $34 million loan to CML. The lender filed a derivative action against JetDirect's careless board members. But, much to everyone's surprise, two Delaware courts ruled that CML could *not* bring a derivative action because the Delaware LLC statute had not explicitly authorized such lawsuits. CML was simply out of luck. The lower court observed, "[T]here is nothing absurd about different legal principles applying to corporations and LLCs."

CML would not necessarily agree. And the lower court itself acknowledged that commentators had all assumed that such suits were permitted. It turned out they were wrong. This result may make lenders less willing to finance LLCs and therefore render LLCs a less-desirable form of organization.[7] In short, many issues of law that are well established for corporations still reside in foggy territory when it comes to LLCs.

CHOICES: LLC V. CORPORATION

When starting a business, which form makes the most sense—LLC or corporation? The tax status of an LLC is a major advantage over a corporation. Although an S corporation has the same tax status as an LLC, it also has all the annoying rules about classes of stock and number of shareholders. Once an LLC is established, it does not have as many housekeeping rules as corporations—it does not, for example, have to make annual filings or hold annual meetings. However, the LLC is not right for everyone. If done properly, an LLC is more expensive to set up than a corporation because it needs to have a thoughtfully crafted operating agreement. Also, venture capitalists almost always refuse to invest in LLCs, preferring C corporations instead. There are four reasons for this preference: (1) arcane tax issues; (2) C corporations are easier to merge, sell, or take public; (3) corporations can issue stock options; and (4) the general legal uncertainty involving LLCs.

EXAM Strategy

Question: Hortense and Gus are each starting a business. Hortense's business is an Internet startup. Gus will be opening a yarn store. Hortense needs millions of dollars in venture capital and expects to go public soon. Gus has borrowed $10,000 from his girlfriend, which he hopes to pay back soon. Should either of these businesses organize as an LLC?

Strategy: Sole proprietorships may be best for businesses without substantial capital needs and without significant liability issues. Corporations are best for businesses that will need substantial outside capital and expect to go public shortly.

Result: An LLC is not the best choice for either of these businesses. Venture capitalists will insist that Hortense's business be a corporation, especially if it is going public soon. A yarn store has few liability issues, and Gus does not expect to have any outside investors. Hence, a sole proprietorship would be more appropriate for Gus's business.

---

[7] *CML V, LLC v. Bax*, 2011 Del. LEXIS 480 (S. Ct. Del, 2011).

28-4 SOCIALLY CONSCIOUS ORGANIZATIONS

More than a dozen states now permit the formation of socially conscious business organizations. These hybrids are called **flexible-purpose organizations, benefit corporations (B corporations), low-profit limited liability companies (L3Cs)**, and **community interest companies (CICs)**. To form this type of organization, a business must pledge to behave in a socially responsible manner as it pursues profits. Note that these businesses are *not* nonprofits. Instead, they focus on the triple bottom line: "people, planet, and profits." Such businesses consider the interests of their stakeholders (employees, suppliers, customers, and creditors), the community, and the environment, in addition to investors. Company directors are not required to maximize shareholder returns but may instead trade off some profitability in the interests of social responsibility.

To become a socially conscious organization, typically two-thirds of the investors must first give their approval. Then, in the case of Benefit corporations, the company has to obtain certification from an independent third party, such as B Lab. Socially conscious organizations must also prepare regular reports that include an assessment of their societal and environmental impact. At the moment, these organizations do not receive favorable tax treatment, but some advocates are pushing Congress to change the tax code.

Businesses that have taken advantage of these new laws include King Arthur Flour Company, Patagonia, and Seventh Generation. Proponents praise this explicit opportunity to combine profitability and a social conscience. Critics caution, however, that much uncertainty remains. How will a board of directors make decisions? How will it decide, for example, what is more important—being kind to employees or to the environment? The rules are so vague that shareholders will have virtually no right to challenge board decisions because management can always say its goal was to promote the public benefit. Any new form of organization brings with it some legal uncertainty and, as a result, almost inevitable litigation.

28-5 GENERAL PARTNERSHIPS

A **partnership** is an unincorporated association of two or more co-owners who carry on a business for profit.[8] Each co-owner is called a *general partner*.

> **Partnership**
> An unincorporated association of two or more co-owners who operate a business for profit.

Traditionally, partnerships were regulated by common law, but a lack of consistency among the states became troublesome as interstate commerce grew. To solve this problem, the National Conference of Commissioners on Uniform State Laws proposed the Uniform Partnership Act (UPA) in 1914. Since then, there have been several revisions, the most recent coming in 1997. More than two-thirds of the states have now passed the latest revision, so we base our discussion on that version of the law.

TAXES

As we have seen above, partnerships are not a taxable entity, which means that profits flow through to the owners.

---

[8]Uniform Partnership Act §6(1).

LIABILITY

Each partner is personally liable for the debts of the enterprise, whether or not she caused them. Thus, a partner is liable for any injury that another partner or an employee causes while on partnership business as well as for any contract signed on behalf of the partnership. This form of organization can be particularly risky if the group of owners is large and the partners do not know each other.

Daniel Matter knows firsthand about the risks of a partnership. A former partner in the accounting firm Pannell Kerr Foster, he thought he had heard the last of the firm when he resigned his partnership. He was wrong. *Seven years later*, he and 260 other former partners of the California firm were served with a 78-page lawsuit seeking $24 million in damages. The lawsuit alleged that Pannell Kerr had been negligent in preparing financial reports for a bankrupt Tennessee savings and loan. Although Daniel Matter had never worked for that particular client, he was potentially liable because he had been a partner when the audit was done. At age 53, Matter feared losing everything he owned.

> ## At age 53, Matter feared losing everything he owned.

MANAGEMENT

The management of a partnership can be a significant challenge.

Management Rights   Unless the partnership agrees otherwise, partners share both profits and losses equally, and each partner has an equal right to manage the business.[9] In a large partnership, with hundreds of partners, too many cooks can definitely spoil the firm's profitability. That is why large partnerships are almost always run by one or a few partners who are designated as managing partners or members of the executive committee. Some firms are run almost dictatorially by the partner who brings in the most business (called a "rainmaker"). Nonetheless, even in relatively autocratic firms, the atmosphere tends to be less hierarchical than in a corporation, where employees are accustomed to the concept of having a boss. Whatever the reality, partners by and large like to think of themselves as being the equal of every other partner.

Management Duties   Partners have a *fiduciary duty* to the partnership. This duty means that:

- *Partners are liable to the partnership for gross negligence or intentional misconduct.*

- *Partners cannot compete with the partnership.* Each partner must turn over to the partnership all earnings from any activity that is related to the partnership's business. Thus, law firms would typically expect a partner to turn over any fees he earned as a director of a company, but he could keep the royalties he earned from his novel on scuba diving.

- *A partner may not take an opportunity away from the partnership unless the other partners consent.* If the partnership wants to buy a private plane and a partner hears of one for sale that she wants to buy herself, she must give the partnership an opportunity to buy it before she does.

- *If a partner engages in a conflict of interest, he must turn over to the partnership any profits he earned from that activity.* In the following case, one partner bought partnership property secretly. Is that a conflict of interest?

---

[9]Partnerships have the right to change internal management rules, but they cannot alter the rules governing their relationship with outsiders (such as the rules on liability).

MARSH V. GENTRY

642 S.W.2d 574, 1982 KY. LEXIS 315
Supreme Court of Kentucky, 1982

CASE SUMMARY

Facts: Tom Gentry and John Marsh were partners in a business that bought and sold racehorses. The partnership paid $155,000 for Champagne Woman, who subsequently had a foal named Excitable Lady. The partners decided to sell Champagne Woman at the annual Keeneland auction, the world's premier thoroughbred horse auction. On the day of the auction, Gentry decided to bid on the horse personally, without telling Marsh. Gentry bought Champagne Woman for $135,000. Later, he told Marsh that someone from California had approached him about buying Excitable Lady. Marsh agreed to the sale. Although he repeatedly asked Gentry the name of the purchaser, Gentry refused to tell him. Not until 11 months later, when Excitable Lady won a race at Churchill Downs, did Marsh learn that Gentry had been the purchaser. Marsh became the Excitable Man.

Issue: *Did Gentry violate his fiduciary duty when he bought partnership property without telling his partner?*

Decision: Yes, Gentry violated his fiduciary duty to his partner.

Reasoning: Kentucky partnership law required Gentry to make full disclosure to his partner before buying partnership property. Although Gentry did not know that he would be the winning bidder at auction, he had an obligation to tell Marsh that he intended to bid.

As for the private sale, although Marsh had agreed to the price, he still had a right to know that his partner was the offeror. He would certainly have looked more carefully at an offer from a partner than from an unknown third party. Indeed, Marsh said later that he would not have agreed to either sale if he had known Gentry was the purchaser.

Gentry claims that partners frequently place secret bids at auctions of partnership property. Whether or not this is true, such behavior violates the law and is unacceptable. Partners owe each other a high degree of good faith.

TRANSFER OF OWNERSHIP

Financing a partnership may be difficult because the firm cannot sell shares as a corporation does. The capital needs of the partnership must be provided by contributions from partners or by borrowing. Likewise, a partner only has the right to transfer the *value* of her partnership interest, not the interest itself. She cannot, for example, transfer the right to participate in firm management. Take the case of Evan and his mother. She is a partner in the immensely profitable McBain Consulting firm. She dies, leaving him an orphan with no siblings. He overcomes his grief as best he can and goes to her office on the next Monday to take over her job and her partnership. Imagine his surprise when her partners tell him that, as her sole heir, he can inherit the *value* of her partnership but he has no right to be a partner. He is out on the sidewalk within the hour. The partners have promised him a check in the mail.

FORMATION

Given the disadvantages, why does anyone do business as a partnership? A partnership has an important advantage over a sole proprietorship—partners. Sole proprietors are on their own; partners have colleagues to help them and, equally important, to supply capital for the business. Sole proprietorships sometimes turn into partnerships for exactly this reason.

In addition, partnerships are easy to form. Although a partnership *should* have a written agreement, it is perfectly legal without one. In fact, nothing is required in the way of forms or filings or agreements. **If two or more people do business together, sharing management, profits and losses, they have a partnership, whether they know it or not, and are subject to all the rules of partnership law.**

For example, Kevin and Brenda formed an electrical contracting business. The business did so well that Kevin's first wife, Cynthia, asked the court to increase his child support payments. Kevin argued that, because he and Brenda were partners, he was entitled to only half of the business's profits. Therefore, his child support should not be increased.

Cynthia claimed that Kevin and Brenda were not partners because Kevin had reported all the income from the business on his personal tax return, while Brenda had reported none. Kevin had even put "sole proprietorship" in bold letters on the top of his return. No written partnership agreement existed. Kevin and Brenda never informed their accountant that they were a partnership. When Kevin answered interrogatories for Cynthia's lawsuit, he stated that he was the sole owner and that Brenda worked for him. Nonetheless, the court held that Brenda and Kevin were partners because Brenda helped manage the business and shared in its profits.[10]

Partnership by Estoppel   Brenda and Kevin wanted to be partners so that they could share the *profits* of their business. In *partnership by estoppel*, non-partners are treated as if they were actually partners and are forced to share *liability*. **A partnership by estoppel exists if:**

- Participants tell other people that they are partners (even though they are not), or they allow other people to say, without contradiction, that they are partners;

- A third party relies on this assertion; and

- The third party suffers harm.

For example, an obstetrician by the name of Dr. William Martin was held liable under a theory of partnership by estoppel because (1) he told a patient that he and Dr. John Maceluch were partners (although they were not); (2) in reliance on this statement, a patient made appointments to see Dr. Maceluch; and (3) she was harmed by Dr. Maceluch's malpractice. He refused to come to the hospital when she was in labor and, as a result, her child was born with brain damage. Although Dr. Martin was out of the country at the time, he was as liable as if he had committed the malpractice himself.[11]

TERMINATION

Dissociation
When a partner quits a partnership.

When a partner quits, that event is called a **dissociation**. A dissociation is a fork in the road: The partnership can either buy out the departing partner(s) and continue in business, or wind up the business and terminate the partnership. Most large firms provide in their partnership agreement that, upon dissociation, the business continues.

28-6 LIMITED LIABILITY PARTNERSHIPS

A limited liability partnership (LLP) is a type of general partnership that most states now permit. There is a very important distinction, however, between LLPs and general partnerships: In an LLP, the partners are not liable for the debts of the partnership.[12] They are, naturally, liable for their own misdeeds, just as if they were a member of an LLC or a shareholder of a corporation.

To form an LLP, the partners must file a statement of qualification with state officials. LLPs must also file annual reports. The other attributes of a partnership remain the same. Thus, an LLP is not a taxable entity, and it has the right to choose its duration (i.e., it can, but does not have to, survive the dissociation of a member).

[10]*In Re Marriage of Cynthia Hassiepen*, 269 Ill. App. 3d 559, 646 N.E.2d 1348, 1995 Ill. App. LEXIS 101.
[11]*Haught v. Maceluch*, 681 F.2d 290, 1982 U.S. App. LEXIS 17123 (5th Cir. 1982).
[12]UPA §306(c).

Although an LLP can be much more advantageous for partners than a general partnership, it is absolutely crucial to comply with all the technicalities of the LLP statute. Otherwise, partners lose protection against personal liability. Note the sad result for Michael Gaus and John West, who formed a Texas LLP. Unfortunately, they did not renew the LLP registration each year, as the statute required. Four years after its initial registration, the partnership entered into a lease. When the partners ultimately stopped paying rent and abandoned the premises, they were both were held personally liable for the rent because the LLP registration had expired. As the court pointed out, the statute did not contain a "substantial compliance" section, nor did it contain a grace period for filing a renewal application. In short, close only counts in horseshoes and hand grenades, not in LLPs.

28-7 LIMITED PARTNERSHIPS AND LIMITED LIABILITY LIMITED PARTNERSHIPS

Although limited partnerships and limited liability limited partnerships sound confusingly similar to limited liability partnerships and general partnerships, like many siblings, they operate very differently. And truth to tell, limited partnerships and limited liability limited partnerships are relatively rare—they are generally used only for estate planning purposes (usually, to reduce estate taxes) and for highly sophisticated investment vehicles. You should be aware of their existence, but you may not see them very often in your business life. Here are the major features:

STRUCTURE

Limited partnerships must have at least one *limited* partner and one *general* partner.

LIABILITY

Limited partners are not *personally* liable, but general partners are. Like corporate shareholders, limited partners risk only their investment in the partnership (which is called their "capital contribution"). In contrast, general partners of a limited partnership are personally liable for the debts of the organization.

However, the revised version of the Uniform Limited Partnership Act permits a limited partnership, in its certificate of formation and partnership agreement, simply to declare itself a *limited liability* limited partnership.[13] **In a limited liability limited partnership, the general partner is not personally liable for the debts of the partnership.** This provision effectively removes the major disadvantage of limited partnerships. Although, at this writing, fewer than half the states have actually passed the revised version of the Uniform Limited Partnership Act, this revision would seem to indicate the trend for the future.

TAXES

Limited partnerships are not taxable entities. Income is taxed only once before landing in a partner's pocket.

FORMATION

The general partners must file a certificate of limited partnership with their Secretary of State. Although most limited partnerships do have a partnership agreement, it is not required.

---

[13]ULPA §102(9).

Exam Review

	Separate Taxable Entity	Personal Liability for Owners	Ease of Formation	Transferable Interests (Easily Bought and Sold)	Perpetual Existence	Other Features
Sole Proprietorship	No	Yes	Very easy	No, can only sell entire business	No	
Corporation	Yes	No	Difficult	Yes	Yes	
Close Corporation	Yes, for C corporation No, for S corporation	No	Difficult	Transfer restrictions	Yes	Protection of minority shareholders. No board of directors required
S Corporation	No	No	Difficult	Transfer restrictions	Yes	Only 100 shareholders. Only one class of stock. Shareholders must be individuals, estates, trusts, charities, or pension funds and be citizens or residents of the United States. All shareholders must agree to S status
Limited Liability Company	No	No	Difficult	Yes, if the operating agreement permits	Varies by state, but generally, yes	No limit on the number of shareholders, the number of classes of stock, or the type of shareholder
General Partnership	No	Yes	Easy	No	Depends on the partnership agreement	Management can be difficult
Limited Liability Partnership	No	No	Difficult	No	Depends on the partnership agreement	
Limited Partnership	No	Yes, for general partner No, for limited partners	Difficult	Yes (for limited partners), if partnership agreement permits	Yes	
Limited Liability Limited Partnership	No	No	Difficult	Yes (for limited partners), if partnership agreement permits	Yes	
Professional Corporation	Yes	No	Difficult	Shareholders must all be members of same profession	Yes, as long as it has shareholders	Complex tax issues
Joint Venture	No	Yes	Easy	No	No	Partnership for a limited purpose
Franchise	All these issues depend on the form of organization chosen by participants.					Established business. Name recognition. Management assistance. Loss of control. Fees may be high

MULTIPLE-CHOICE QUESTIONS

1. A sole proprietorship:
   (a) must file a tax return.
   (b) requires no formal steps for its creation.
   (c) must register with the Secretary of State.
   (d) may sell stock.
   (e) provides limited liability to the owner.

EXAM Strategy

2. CPA QUESTION Assuming all other requirements are met, a corporation may elect to be treated as an S corporation under the Internal Revenue Code if it has:

   (a) both common and preferred stockholders.
   (b) a partnership as a stockholder.
   (c) 100 or fewer stockholders
   (d) the consent of a majority of the stockholders.

   Strategy: Review the list of requirements for an S corporation. (See the "Result" at the end of this section.)

3. A limited liability company:
   (a) is regulated by a well-established body of law.
   (b) pays taxes on its income.
   (c) may issue stock options.
   (d) must register with state authorities.
   (e) protects the owners from personal liability for their own misdeeds.

4. **CPA QUESTION** A joint venture is a(n):
   (a) association limited to no more than two persons in business for profit.
   (b) enterprise of numerous co-owners in a nonprofit undertaking.
   (c) corporate enterprise for a single undertaking of limited duration.
   (d) association of persons engaged as co-owners in a single undertaking for profit.

5. A limited liability partnership:
   (a) has ownership interests that cannot be transferred.
   (b) protects the partners from liability for the debts of the partnership.
   (c) must pay taxes on its income.
   (d) requires no formal steps for its creation.
   (e) permits a limited number of partners.

6. **CPA QUESTION** Cobb, Inc., a partner in TLC Partnership, assigns its partnership interest to Bean, who is not made a partner. After the assignment, Bean asserts the right to   (1) participate in the management of TLC and (2) take Cobb's share of TLC's partnership profits. Bean is correct as to which of these rights?

(a) 1 only

(b) 2 only

(c) 1 and 2

(d) Neither 1 nor 2

2. Result: An S corporation can have only one class of stock. A partnership cannot be a stockholder, and all the shareholders must consent to S corporation status. (c) is the correct answer.

Essay Questions

1. Question: Alan Dershowitz, a law professor famous for his wealthy clients (O. J. Simpson, among others), joined with other lawyers to open a kosher delicatessen, Maven's Court. Dershowitz met with greater success at the bar than in the kitchen—the deli failed after barely a year in business. One supplier sued for overdue bills. What form of organization would have been the best choice for Maven's Court?

Strategy: A sole proprietorship would not have worked because there was more than one owner. A partnership would have been a disaster because of unlimited liability. They could have met all the requirements of an S corporation or an LLC. (See the "Result" at the end of this section.)

2. Question: Mrs. Meadows opened a biscuit shop called The Biscuit Bakery. The business was not incorporated. Whenever she ordered supplies, she was careful to sign the contract in the name of the business, not personally: the Biscuit Bakery by Daisy Meadows. Unfortunately, she had no money to pay her flour bill. When the vendor threatened to sue her, Mrs. Meadows told him that he could only sue the business because all the contracts were in the business's name. Will Mrs. Meadows lose her dough?

Strategy: The first step is to figure out what type of organization her business is. Then recall what liability protection that organization offers. (See the "Result" at the end of this section.)

EXAM Strategy

EXAM Strategy

3. **YOU BE THE JUDGE WRITING PROBLEM** Cellwave was a limited partnership that applied to the Federal Communications Commission (FCC) for a license to operate cellular telephone systems. After the FCC awarded the license, it discovered that, although all the limited partners had signed the limited partnership agreement, Cellwave had never filed its limited partnership certificate with the Secretary of State in Delaware. The FCC dismissed Cellwave's application on the grounds that the partnership did not exist when the application was filed. Did the FCC have the right to dismiss Cellwave's application? **Argument for Cellwave:** The limited partnership was effectively in existence as soon as the limited partners signed the agreement. The Secretary of State could not refuse to accept the certificate for filing; that was a mere formality. **Argument for the FCC:** When Cellwave applied for a license, it did not exist legally. Formalities matter.

4. Kristine bought a Rocky Mountain Chocolate Factory franchise. Her franchise agreement required her to purchase a cash register that cost $3,000, with an annual maintenance fee of $773. The agreement also provided that Rocky Mountain could change to a more expensive system. Within a few months after signing the agreement, Kristine learned that she would have to buy a new cash register that cost $20,000, with annual maintenance fees of $2,000. Does Kristine have to buy this new cash register? Did Rocky Mountain act in bad faith?

5. What is the difference between close corporations and S corporations?

6. Pedro and Juan have a business selling ties with fraternity insignia. Pedro finds out that an online shirt business is for sale. It sounds like a great idea—customers send in their measurements and get back a custom-made shirt at a price no higher than off-the-rack shirts at the local department store. Does Pedro have to let Juan in on the great opportunity?

---

1. Result: Maven's Court would have chosen an LLC or an S corporation.

2. Result: The Biscuit Bakery was a sole proprietorship. No matter how Mrs. Meadows signed the contracts, she is still personally liable for the debts of the business.

Discussion Questions

1. **ETHICS** Lee McNeely told Hardee's officials that he was interested in purchasing multiple restaurants in Arkansas. A Hardee's officer assured him that any of the company-owned stores in Arkansas would be available for purchase. However, the company urged him to open a new store in Maumelle and sent him a letter estimating first-year sales at around $800,000. McNeely built the Maumelle restaurant, but gross sales the first year were only $508,000. When McNeely asked to buy an existing restaurant, a Hardee's officer refused, informing him that Hardee's rarely sold company-owned restaurants. The disclosure document contained no misstatements, but McNeely brought suit alleging fraud in the sale of the Maumelle franchise. Does McNeely have a valid claim against Hardee's? Apart from the legal issues, did Hardee's officers behave ethically? What Life Principles were they applying?

2. Leonard, an attorney, was negligent in his representation of Anthony. In settlement of Anthony's claim against him, Leonard signed a promissory note for $10,400 on behalf of his law firm, an LLC. When the law firm did not pay, Anthony filed suit against Leonard personally for payment of the note. Is a member personally liable for the debt of an LLC that was caused by his own negligence?

3. Think of a business concept that would be appropriate for each of the following: a sole proprietorship, a corporation, and a limited liability company.

4. As you will see in Chapter 29, Facebook began life as a corporation, not an LLC. Why did the founder, Mark Zuckerberg, make that decision?

5. Corporations developed to encourage investors to contribute the capital needed to create large-scale manufacturing enterprises. But LLCs are often start-ups or other small businesses. Why do their members deserve limited liability? And is it fair that LLCs do not have to pay income taxes?

nuttakit/Shutterstock.com; Steve Allen/Brand X Pictures/Jupiter Images

CORPORATIONS

On July 26, 2004, Mark Zuckerberg signed a Certificate of Incorporation for his company, which he called TheFacebook, Inc. At 11:34 a.m. on July 29, 2004, that Certificate was filed with the Secretary of State for Delaware, and TheFacebook began its life as a corporation. Zuckerberg had started this social networking Internet site the previous February in his dorm room at Harvard. By December of 2004, TheFacebook had almost 1 million users. Less than two years later, the company was estimated to be worth between $750 million and $2 billion. Since then, TheFacebook has been valued at more than $100 billion. As Zuckerberg built his company, what did he need to know about the law?

Most of the country's largest businesses, and many of its small ones, are corporations. In this chapter, you will learn how to form a corporation. You will also learn about the rights and responsibilities of corporate managers and shareholders.

Zuckerberg started TheFacebook in his dorm room at Harvard. Within 10 months, it had almost 1 million users.

29-1 PROMOTER'S LIABILITY

Promoter

Someone who organizes a corporation.

Adopt

Agree to be bound by the terms of a contract.

Novation

A new contract with different parties.

Someone who organizes a corporation is called a **promoter.** It is his idea; he raises the capital, hires the lawyers, calls the shots. Mark Zuckerberg was TheFacebook's promoter.

This role can carry some risk. **A promoter is personally liable on any contract he signs before the corporation is formed.** After formation, the corporation can **adopt** the contract, in which case, both it and the promoter are liable. The promoter can get off the hook personally only if the other party agrees to a **novation**—that is, a new contract with the corporation alone.

EXAM Strategy

Question: Dr. Warfield hired Wolfe, a young carpenter, to build his house. A week or so after they signed the contract, Wolfe filed Articles of Incorporation for Wolfe Construction, Inc. Warfield wrote checks to the corporation, which it cashed. Unfortunately, the work on the house was shoddy. The architect said he did not know whether to try to salvage the house or just blow it up. Warfield sued Wolfe and Wolfe Construction, Inc. for damages. Wolfe argued that if he was liable as a promoter, then the corporation must be absolved and that, conversely, if the corporation was held liable, he, as an individual, must not be. Who is liable to Warfield?

Strategy: Wolfe's argument is wrong—Warfield does not have to choose between suing him individually or suing the corporation. He can sue both.

Result: Wolfe is personally liable on any contract he signed before the corporation is filed, no matter whose name is on the contract. The corporation is liable only if it adopts the contract. Did it do so here? The fact that the corporation cashed checks that were made out to it means that the corporation is also liable. So Warfield can sue both Wolfe and the corporation.

29-2 INCORPORATION PROCESS

There is no federal corporation code, which means that a company can incorporate only under state, not federal, law. No matter where a company actually does business, it may incorporate in any state. This decision is important because the organization must live by the laws of whichever state it chooses for incorporation. To encourage similarity among state corporation statutes, the American Bar Association drafted the Model Business Corporation Act (the Model Act) as a guide. Many states do use the Model Act as a guide, although Delaware does not. Therefore, in this chapter we will give examples from both the Model Act and Delaware. Why Delaware? Despite its small size, it has a disproportionate influence on corporate law. More than half of all public companies have incorporated there, including 60 percent of Fortune 500 companies.

29-2a Where to Incorporate?

Domestic corporation

A corporation is a domestic corporation in the state in which it was formed.

Foreign corporation

A corporation formed in another state.

A company is called a **domestic corporation** in the state where it incorporates and a **foreign corporation** everywhere else. Companies generally incorporate either in the state where they do most of their business or in Delaware. They typically must pay filing fees and franchise taxes in their state of incorporation, plus in any state in which they do business. To avoid this double set of fees, a business that will be operating primarily in one state would probably select that state for incorporation rather than Delaware. But if a company is going to do business in several states, it might consider choosing Delaware, which offers several advantages:

- **Laws that Favor Management.** For example, if the shareholders want to take a vote in writing instead of holding a meeting, many other states require the vote to be unanimous; Delaware requires only a majority to agree. The Delaware legislature also tries to keep up-to-date by changing its code to reflect new developments in corporate law.

- **An Efficient Court System.** Delaware has a special court (called "Chancery Court") that hears nothing but business cases and has judges who are experts in corporate law.

- **An Established Body of Precedent.** Because so many businesses incorporate in the state, its courts hear a vast number of corporate cases, creating a large body of precedent. Thus, lawyers feel they can more easily predict the outcome of a case in Delaware than in a state where few corporate disputes are tried.

29-2b The Charter

Once a company has decided *where* to incorporate, the next step is to prepare and file the charter. The mechanics are easy: Simply download the form and mail or fax it to the Secretary of State. (Some jurisdictions also require that it be filed in a county office.) But do not let this easy process fool you; the incorporation document needs to be completed with some care. The corporate charter defines the corporation, including everything from the company's name to the number of shares it will issue.

States use different terms to refer to a charter; some call it the "articles of incorporation," others use "articles of organization," and still others say "certificate" instead of "articles." All these terms mean the same thing. Similarly, some states use the term "shareholders," and others use "stockholders"; they are both the same.

Name

The Model Act imposes two requirements in selecting a name. First, all corporations must use one of the following words in their name: "corporation," "incorporated," "company," or "limited." Delaware also accepts some additional terms, such as "association" or "institute." Second, under both the Model Act and Delaware law, a new corporate name must be different from that of any corporation, limited liability company, or limited partnership that already exists in that state. If your name is Freddy DuPont, you cannot name your corporation "Freddy DuPont, Inc.," because Delaware already has a company named E. I. DuPont de Nemours & Company. It does not matter that Freddy DuPont is your real name or that the existing company is a large chemical business, whereas you want to open a game arcade. The names are too similar. Zuckerberg chose "TheFacebook" because that was what Harvard students called their freshman directory.

Address and Registered Agent

A company must have an official address in the state in which it is incorporated so that the Secretary of State knows where to contact it and so that anyone who wants to sue the corporation can serve the complaint in-state. Because most companies incorporated in Delaware do not actually have an office there, they hire a registered agent to serve as their official presence in the state.

INCORPORATOR

The incorporator signs the charter and delivers it to the Secretary of State. Incorporators are not required to buy stock, nor do they necessarily have any future relationship with the company. Oftentimes, the lawyer who forms the corporation serves as its incorporator. If no lawyer is involved, typically the promoter is also the incorporator. That is what happened with TheFacebook—Mark Zuckerberg served as incorporator.

PURPOSE

The corporation is required to give its purpose for existence. Most companies use a very broad purpose clause such as TheFacebook's:

> The purpose of the Corporation is to engage in any lawful act or activity for which corporations may be organized under the General Corporation Law of Delaware.

STOCK

The charter must provide three items of information about the company's stock.

Par Value   The concept of par value was designed to protect investors. Originally, par value was supposed to be close to market price. A company could not *issue* stock at a price less than par, which meant that it could not sell to insiders at a sweetheart price well below market value. (Once the stock was issued, it could be traded at any price.) In modern times, par value does not relate to market value; it is usually some nominal figure such as 1¢ or $1 per share. Companies may also issue stock with no par value. TheFacebook stock has a par value of $0.0001 per share.

Number of Shares   Before stock can be sold, it must first be authorized in the charter. The corporation can authorize as many shares as the incorporators choose, but the more shares, the higher the filing fee. After incorporation, a company can add authorized shares by simply amending its charter and paying the additional fee. TheFacebook charter authorizes the creation of 10,000,000 shares.

Stock that has been authorized but not yet sold is called **authorized and unissued**. Stock that has been sold is termed **authorized and issued** or **outstanding**. Stock that the company has sold but later bought back is **treasury stock**.

Authorized and unissued
Stock that has been authorized, but not yet sold.

Authorized and issued
Stock that has been authorized and sold; another word for it is *outstanding*.

Treasury stock
Stock that a company has sold, but later bought back.

Classes of stock
Categories of stock with different rights.

Series
Sub-categories of stock.

Classes and Series   Different shareholders often make different contributions to a company. Some may be involved in management, whereas others may simply contribute financially. Early investors may feel that they are entitled to more control than those who come along later (and who perhaps take less risk). Corporate structure can be infinitely flexible in defining the rights of these various shareholders. Stock can be divided into categories called **classes**, and these classes can be further divided into subcategories called **series**. All stock in a series has the same rights, and all series in a class are fundamentally the same, except for minor distinctions. For example, in a class of preferred stock, all shareholders may be entitled to a dividend, but the amount of the dividend may vary by series. Different classes of stock, however, may have very different rights—a class of preferred stock is different from a class of common stock. Exhibit 29.1 illustrates the concept of class and series.

Defining the rights of a class or series of stock is like baking a cake—the stock can contain virtually any combination of the following ingredients (although the result may not be to everyone's taste):

- **Dividend Rights.** The charter establishes whether the shareholder is entitled to dividends and, if so, in what amount.

- **Voting Rights.** Shareholders are usually entitled to elect directors and vote on charter amendments, among other issues, but these rights can vary among different series and classes of stock. When Ford Motor Co. went public in 1956, it issued Class B

EXHIBIT 29.1   An Illustration of Classes and Series of Stock

common stock to members of the Ford family. This class of stock holds about 40 percent of the voting power and, thereby, effectively controls the company. Not surprisingly, the chairman of the company has often been named "Ford." TheFacebook amended its charter to create two classes of stock with different voting rights, presumably so that Zuckerberg could maintain control when the company went public.

- **Liquidation Rights**. The charter specifies the order in which classes of stockholders will be paid upon dissolution of the company.

These are the ingredients for any class or series of stock. Some stock comes prepackaged like a cake mix. "Preferred" and "common" stock are two classic types. The Model Act does not use these terms, but many states still do.

Owners of *preferred stock* have preference on dividends and also, typically, in liquidation. If a class of preferred stock is entitled to dividends, then it must receive its dividends before common stockholders are paid theirs. If holders of **cumulative preferred stock** miss their dividend one year, common shareholders cannot receive a dividend until the cumulative preferred shareholders have been paid all that they are owed, no matter how long that takes. Alternatively, holders of *non*-**cumulative preferred stock** lose an annual dividend for good if the company cannot afford it in the year it is due. When a company dissolves, preferred stockholders typically have the right to receive their share of corporate assets before common shareholders.

***Common* stock is last in line for any corporate payouts, including dividends and liquidation payments.** If the company is liquidated, creditors of the company and preferred shareholders are paid before common shareholders. Exhibit 29.2 illustrates the order of payment for dividends.

Venture capitalists (professional investors who are in the business of financing companies) often choose a type of stock called **participating preferred stock**, which permits them to have their cake and eat it too. Upon liquidation of the company, these shareholders are paid first, receiving whatever they paid for the stock plus accrued dividends. Then they are treated as if they had converted their preferred shares into common stock, so they also share the rest of the proceeds with common shareholders.

Preferred stock
The owners of preferred stock have preference on dividends and also, typically, in liquidation.

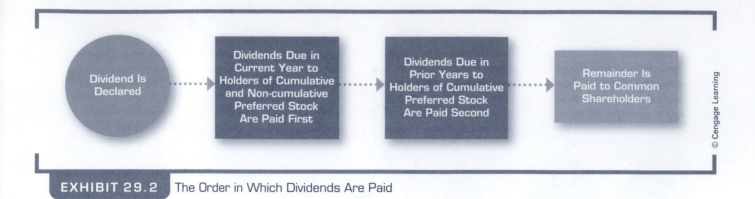

EXHIBIT 29.2   The Order in Which Dividends Are Paid

29-3 AFTER INCORPORATION

29-3a Directors and Officers

Written consent

Instead of holding a meeting, participants may sign a document approving certain actions.

Once the corporation is organized, the incorporators elect the first set of directors. Thereafter, shareholders elect directors. Under the Model Act, a corporation is required to have at least one director, unless (1) all the shareholders sign an agreement that eliminates the board, or (2) the corporation has 50 or fewer shareholders. To elect directors, the shareholders may hold a meeting, or, in the more typical case for a small company, they elect directors by written consent. A typical **written consent** looks like this:

Classic American Novels, Inc.

Written Consent

The undersigned shareholders of Classic American Novels, Inc., a corporation organized and existing under the General Corporation Law of the State of Wherever, hereby agree that the following action shall be taken with full force and effect as if voted at a validly called and held meeting of the shareholders of the corporation:

> Agreed: That the following people are elected to serve as directors for one year, or until their successors have been duly elected and qualified:

Herman Melville
Louisa May Alcott
Mark Twain

Dated: _____   Signed: _____
                                                                       Willa Cather
Dated:_____   Signed: _____
                                                                       Nathaniel Hawthorne
Dated: _____   Signed: _____
                                                                       Harriet Beecher Stowe

---

Once the incorporators or shareholders have chosen the directors, the directors must elect the officers of the corporation. They can use a consent form if they wish. The Model Act is flexible. It simply requires a corporation to have whatever officers are described in the

EXHIBIT 29.3   The Election Process in Corporations

bylaws. The same person can hold more than one office. Exhibit 29.3 illustrates the election process in corporations.

The written consents and any records of actual meetings are kept in a **minute book**, which is the official record of the corporation. Entrepreneurs sometimes feel they are too busy to bother with all these details, but if a corporation is ever sold, the lawyers for the buyers will *insist* on a well-organized and complete minute book. In one case, a company that was seeking a $100,000 bank loan could not find all its minutes. The company had to merge itself into a newly created corporation so it could start fresh with a new set of corporate records. The company spent $10,000 on this task, a large chunk out of the $100,000 loan.

29-3b Bylaws

The **bylaws** list all the "housekeeping" details for the corporation. For example, bylaws set the date of the annual shareholders' meeting, define what a **quorum** is (i.e., what percentage of stock must be represented for a meeting to count), indicate how many directors there will be, give titles to officers, and establish the fiscal (i.e., tax) year of the corporation.

29-3c Issuing Debt

Most startup companies begin with some combination of equity and debt. Equity (i.e., stock) is described in the charter; debt is not. Authorizing debt is often one of the first steps a new company takes. There are several types of debt:

- **Bonds** are long-term debt secured by company assets. If the company is unable to pay the debt, creditors have a right to specific assets, such as accounts receivable or inventory.

- **Debentures** are long-term *unsecured* debt. If the company cannot meet its obligations, the debenture holders are paid after bondholders but before stockholders.

- **Notes** are short-term debt, typically payable within five years. They may be either secured or unsecured.

29-4 DEATH OF THE CORPORATION

Sometimes, business ideas are not successful and the corporation fails. This death can be voluntary (the shareholders elect to terminate the corporation) or forced (by court order). Sometimes, a court takes a step that is much more damaging to shareholders than simply dissolving the corporation—it removes the shareholders' limited liability.

Minute book
The official record of a corporation.

Bylaws
A document that specifies the organizational rules of a corporation or other organization, such as the date of the annual meeting and the required number of directors.

Quorum
The percentage of stock that must be represented for a meeting to count.

Bonds
Long-term secured debt.

Debentures
Long-term unsecured debt.

Notes
When issued by a company, short-term debt, typically payable within five years.

29-4a Piercing the Corporate Veil

Pierce the corporate veil
A court holds shareholders personally liable for the debts of the corporation.

One of the major purposes of a corporation is to protect its owners—the shareholders—from personal liability for the debts of the organization. Sometimes, however, a court will **pierce the corporate veil**; that is, the court will hold shareholders personally liable for the debts of the corporation. Courts generally pierce a corporate veil in four circumstances:

- **Failure to Observe Formalities.** If an organization does not act like a corporation, it will not be treated like one. It must, for example, hold required shareholders' and directors' meetings (or sign consents), keep a minute book as a record of these meetings, and make all the required state filings. In addition, officers must be careful to sign all corporate documents with a corporate title, not as an individual. An officer should sign like this:

Classic American Novels, Inc.

By: *Stephen Crane*

Stephen Crane, President

- **Commingling of Assets.** Nothing makes a court more willing to pierce a corporate veil than evidence that shareholders have mixed their assets with those of the corporation. Sometimes, for example, shareholders may use corporate assets to pay their personal debts. If shareholders commingle assets, it is genuinely difficult for creditors to determine which assets belong to whom. This confusion is generally resolved in favor of the creditors—all assets are deemed to belong to the corporation.

- **Inadequate Capitalization.** If the founders of a corporation do not raise enough capital (either through debt or equity) to give the business a fighting chance of paying its debts, courts may require shareholders to pay corporate obligations. Therefore, if the corporation does not have sufficient capital, it needs to buy insurance, particularly to protect against tort liability. Judges are likelier to hold shareholders liable if the alternative is to send an injured tort victim away empty-handed. For example, Oriental Fireworks Co. had hundreds of thousands of dollars in annual sales, but only $13,000 in assets. The company did not bother to obtain any liability insurance, keep a minute book, or defend lawsuits. There was no need because the company had no money. But then a court pierced the corporate veil and found the owner of the company personally liable.[1]

- **Fraud.** If fraud is committed in the name of a corporation, victims can make a claim against the personal assets of the shareholders who profited from the fraud.

The following case is a good example of when a court should pierce the corporate veil.

BROOKS V. BECKER

2005 VA. CIR. LEXIS 13
Circuit Court Of Fairfax County, Virginia, 2005

CASE SUMMARY

Facts: Ronald Becker was the sole shareholder, officer, and director of Becker Interiors. Becker and his companion, Robert LaPointe, used approximately $300,000 of Becker Interiors' funds to renovate their residence, pay their personal credit card bills, and invest in another company of which Becker was president. Becker sold a corporate car for $73,700 and deposited those funds into his personal account, along with the corporation's income tax refund check of $12,850. Becker Interiors supervised the major renovation of a house in McLean, Virginia. The

---

[1] *Rice v. Oriental Fireworks Co.*, 75 Or. App. 627, 707 P.2d 1250, 1985 Ore. App. LEXIS 3928.

company hired Stephen Brooks as a subcontractor on the project. When the company refused to pay Brooks, he filed suit, winning a judgment against the company for $54,597.09. But it turned out that Becker Interiors had no assets.

Brooks then sued Ronald Becker in an attempt to pierce the corporate veil and hold Becker personally liable for the debts of the corporation.

Issues: *Can Brooks pierce the corporate veil? Is Becker personally liable for the debts of the corporation?*

Decision: The court allowed Brooks to pierce the corporate veil. Becker was held personally liable for the debts of Becker Interiors, Inc.

Reasoning: Courts are extremely reluctant to pierce a corporate veil and hold shareholders personally liable. Indeed, courts will take this extraordinary step only when necessary to promote justice, such as, for example, when a shareholder uses the corporation to evade personal debts,

perpetrate fraud or a crime, commit an injustice, or gain an unfair advantage. To hold a shareholder liable, the boundaries between the shareholder and the corporation must be so confused that, in effect, the business does not exist separately and to pretend that it does is unjust to the plaintiff.

In this case, the extraordinary remedy of piercing the corporate veil should be granted. Becker knowingly violated his duties as an officer, director, and shareholder of Becker Interiors by treating the corporation as his personal piggy bank. He testified that renovations to his personal residence were legitimate corporate expenses because he used the house as a showcase for his work. The court did not find this testimony credible. Nor did the court believe that Becker acted on his accountant's advice when he commingled personal and corporation funds. The court more easily believed his later testimony that his accountant was "mystified" by this commingling of funds.

The court orders Becker to pay Brooks $54,597.09.

29-4b Termination

Terminating a corporation is a three-step process:

- **Vote.** The directors recommend to the shareholders that the corporation be dissolved, and a majority of the shareholders agree.

- **Filing.** The corporation files "Articles of Dissolution" with the Secretary of State.

- **Winding Up.** The officers of the corporation pay its debts and distribute the remaining property to shareholders. When the winding up is completed, the corporation ceases to exist.

The Secretary of State may dissolve a corporation that violates state law by, for example, failing to pay the required annual fees. Indeed, many corporations, particularly small ones, do not bother with the formal dissolution process. They simply cease paying their annual fees and let the Secretary of State act. A court may dissolve a corporation if it is insolvent or if its directors and shareholders cannot resolve conflict over how the corporation should be managed.

29-5 THE ROLE OF CORPORATE MANAGEMENT

As business grows, entrepreneurs face new challenges. One of the most important is attracting outside investors—people with money but without the knowledge or desire to manage the enterprise. How can shareholders protect their interests in an organization without being involved in management themselves? They elect directors to manage for them. Directors set policy and then appoint officers to implement corporate goals. The

Model Act describes the directors' role thus: "All corporate powers shall be exercised by or under the authority of, and the business and affairs of the corporation managed by or under the direction of, its board of directors...."

As managers of the corporation, directors have important responsibilities to shareholders and also to **stakeholders,** such as employees, customers, creditors, suppliers, and neighbors. However, the interests of these various groups often conflict. In the first decade of the twenty-first century, the world faced two financial crises that were caused, in part, by corporate executives who engaged in high-risk activities that left them wealthy, but their shareholders with nothing. Because of abuses by managers that, in some cases, included outright fraud, Congress and other regulators tried to rebalance the power among managers and shareholders. Part of their goal was to enhance shareholder oversight of the companies they own. The rest of this chapter is about this balance of rights and responsibilities.

Managers have a fiduciary duty to act in the best interests of the corporation's shareholders. Because shareholders are primarily concerned about their return on investment, managers must *maximize shareholder value,* which means providing shareholders with the highest possible financial return from dividends and stock price. However, reality is more complicated than this simple rule indicates. It is often difficult to determine which strategy will best maximize shareholder value. And what about stakeholders? A number of states have adopted statutes that permit directors to take into account the interests of stakeholders as well as stockholders. The Indiana Code, for example, permits directors to consider "both the short term and long term best interests of the corporation, taking into account, and weighing as the directors deem appropriate, the effects thereof on the corporation's shareholders and the other corporate constituent groups...."[2] The next section looks more closely at directors' responsibilities to their various constituencies.

Stakeholders

Anyone who is affected by the activities of a corporation, such as a shareholder, employee, customer, creditor, supplier, or neighbor.

29-6 THE BUSINESS JUDGMENT RULE

Business judgment rule

A legal rule that protects managers from liability and their decisions from court interference.

Officers and directors have a fiduciary duty to act in the best interests of their stockholders, but under the **business judgment rule,** the courts allow managers great leeway in carrying out this responsibility. The business judgment rule is a common law concept that has achieved national acceptance. It is a fundamental principle of corporate law. To be protected by the business judgment rule, managers must act in good faith:

Duty of Loyalty	1. Without a conflict of interest
Duty of Care	2. With the care that an ordinarily prudent person would take in a similar situation and 3. In a manner they reasonably believe to be in the best interests of the corporation

The business judgment rule is two shields in one: It protects both the manager and her decisions. **If managers comply with the business judgment rule, a court will not hold them personally liable for any harm their decisions cause the company, nor will the court rescind their decisions.**

---

[2]Indiana Code §23-1-35-1.

The business judgment rule accomplishes three goals:

- **It permits directors to do their job.** If directors were afraid they would be liable for every decision that led to a loss, they would never make a decision, or at least not a risky one.

- **It keeps judges out of corporate management.** Without the business judgment rule, judges would be tempted, if not required, to second-guess managers' decisions.

- **It encourages directors to serve.** No one in his right mind would serve as a director if he knew that every decision was open to attack in the courtroom.

Analysis of the business judgment rule is divided into two parts. The obligation of a manager to act without a conflict of interest is called the **duty of loyalty**. The requirements that a manager act with care and in the best interests of the corporation are referred to as the duty of care.

Duty of loyalty
The obligation of a manager to act without a conflict of interest.

29-6a Duty of Loyalty

The duty of loyalty prohibits managers from making a decision that benefits them at the expense of the corporation.

SELF-DEALING

Self-dealing means that a manager makes a decision benefiting either himself or another company with which he has a relationship. While working at the Blue Moon restaurant, Zeke signs a contract on behalf of the restaurant to purchase bread from Rising Sun Bakery. Unbeknownst to anyone at Blue Moon, he is a part owner of Rising Sun. Zeke has engaged in self-dealing, which is a violation of the duty of loyalty.

Once a manager engages in self-dealing, the business judgment rule no longer applies. This does not mean the manager is automatically liable to the corporation or that his decision is automatically void. All it means is that the court will no longer presume that the transaction was acceptable. Instead, the court will scrutinize the deal more carefully. A self-dealing transaction is valid in any one of the following situations:

- **The disinterested members of the board of directors approve the transaction.** Disinterested directors are those who do not themselves benefit from the transaction.

- **The disinterested shareholders approve it.** The transaction is valid if the shareholders who do not benefit from it are willing to approve it.

- **The transaction was entirely fair to the corporation.** In determining fairness, the courts will consider the impact of the transaction on the corporation and whether the price was reasonable.

Although the business judgment rule did not protect Zeke, he would still not be liable if he sought permission first, or if a court found that he was buying great bread at an excellent price. Exhibit 29.4 illustrates the rules on self-dealing.

29-6b Corporate Opportunity

The self-dealing rules prevent managers from forcing their companies into unfair deals. The corporate opportunity doctrine is the reverse—it prohibits managers from excluding their company from favorable deals. **Managers are in violation of the corporate opportunity doctrine if they compete against the corporation without its consent.**

Long ago, Charles Guth was president of Loft, Inc., which operated a chain of candy stores. These stores sold Coca-Cola. Guth purchased the Pepsi-Cola Company personally, without offering the opportunity to Loft. A Delaware court found that Guth had violated the corporate

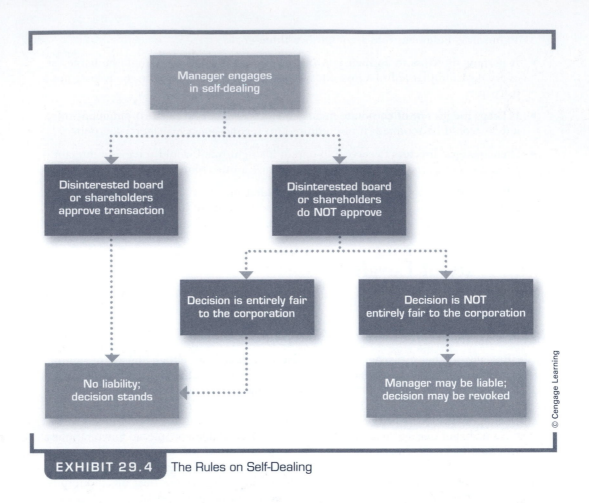

EXHIBIT 29.4   The Rules on Self-Dealing

opportunity doctrine and ordered him to transfer all his shares in Pepsi to Loft.[3] That was in 1939, and Pepsi-Cola was bankrupt; today, PepsiCo, Inc. is worth more than $100 billion.

In the following case, the manager felt that he had a good reason for taking a corporate opportunity. Unfortunately, the court disagreed.

ANDERSON V. BELLINO

265 Neb. 577, 658 N.W.2d 645, 2003 LEXIS 49
Supreme Court Of Nebraska, 2003

CASE SUMMARY

Facts: Richard Bellino and Robert Anderson formed LaVista Lottery, Inc. to operate a restaurant, lounge, and keno game in LaVista, Nevada.[4] They each owned 50 percent of the stock of Lottery, and both were officers and directors. During the next nine years, Lottery grossed more than $100 million. Bellino and Anderson each received over $4 million in salary and dividends.

---

[3]*Guth v. Loft*, 5 A.2d 503, 23 Del. Ch. 255, 1939 Del. LEXIS 13 (Del. 1939).
[4]Keno is a game of chance similar to bingo except that in keno the players choose the numbers on their ticket.

Although Bellino and Anderson were both involved in Lottery, Bellino spent more time, in part because of his personal relationship with Lottery's lounge manager. During this period, Bellino did not complain to Anderson about his lack of involvement in Lottery, and Anderson never refused to do anything that Bellino asked him to do.

Resentful of Anderson's work ethic, Bellino set up a meeting with LaVista's city administrator. Until that meeting, the city had been satisfied with Lottery's performance. But after the meeting, the administrator recommended to the city council that the keno contract be put up for competitive bid. Bellino incorporated LaVista Keno, Inc., to bid on the contract.

Bellino wrote to Anderson complaining that he (Bellino) was doing too much work for Lottery at too little pay. (Evidently, $4 million is not as much as it used to be.) Therefore, Bellino intended to resign from Lottery and bid on the city contract himself. Anderson offered to do more work or whatever Bellino wanted, but Bellino refused any effort at reconciliation. He then submitted a bid on behalf of Keno. At the time he submitted the bid, he was still an officer of Lottery, as well as a director and a 50 percent shareholder. Anderson also bid on the contract on behalf of Lottery. The city awarded the new contract to Keno.

Anderson and Lottery filed suit against Bellino and Keno, alleging that they had usurped a corporate opportunity. The lower court found for Anderson and Lottery. It ordered Bellino to pay $644,992.63 but provided that Bellino could receive a credit of $172,514.63 against the judgment if Bellino transferred the stock of Keno to Lottery and persuaded the city to relicense the keno contract from Keno to Lottery.

Issues: *Did Bellino usurp a corporate opportunity? Is he liable to Lottery?*

Decision: Affirmed. Bellino usurped a corporate opportunity. He must comply with the lower court's order to pay Lottery.

Reasoning: Bellino argued that the corporate opportunity was simply the right to bid on the keno contract. But that is not true—the opportunity was the keno contract itself. The right to bid was simply a preliminary step toward obtaining the opportunity.

Because an officer or director has a fiduciary obligation, he must always act in good faith in his dealings with the corporation. He is liable if he causes harm to the corporation or deprives it of business.

By winning the keno contract, Bellino deprived Lottery of its only business. He should never have bid on the contract himself.

EXAM Strategy

Question: Otto signed a lease with Landlord on a storefront in Georgetown, D.C. He convinced his nephew Nick to start a furniture store in the space. Otto and Nick formed a corporation to operate the store. Otto owned 51 percent and Nick 49 percent of the company's stock. Otto signed a lease between himself and the store at a price that was 20 percent higher than the rent Otto was paying Landlord. Otto purchased a warehouse and then rented it to the corporation at a fair-market rent. Nick sued, alleging that the two leases were not valid. Were they?

Strategy: If the business judgment rule applies, the court will not second-guess a corporate action. But here, the manager engaged in self-dealing, so the business judgment rule is not applicable.

Result: Otto violated the duty of loyalty twice. The lease for the storefront was self-dealing—it directly benefited him. When he purchased the warehouse, he took a corporate opportunity that he should have offered first to the company. He is personally liable for any damages to the corporation. The company also has the right to cancel both leases and to purchase the warehouse from him.

29-6c Duty of Care

In addition to the *duty of loyalty*, managers also owe a *duty of care*. **The duty of care requires officers and directors to act in the best interests of the corporation and to use the same care that an ordinarily prudent person would take in a similar situation.**

RATIONAL BUSINESS PURPOSE

Courts generally agree in principle that directors and officers are liable for decisions that have no rational business purpose. In practice, however, these same courts have been extremely supportive of managerial decisions, looking hard to find some justification. For years, the Chicago Cubs baseball team was the only major American professional sports team to play in a stadium without lights. A shareholder sued on the grounds that the Cubs' revenues were peanuts and crackerjacks compared with those generated by teams that played at night. In their defense, the Cubs argued that a large night crowd would cause the neighborhood to deteriorate, depressing the value of Wrigley Field (which the Cubs did not own). The court rooted for the home team and found that the Cubs' excuse was a "rational purpose" and a legitimate exercise of the business judgment rule.[5]

LEGALITY

Courts are generally unsympathetic to managers who engage in illegal behavior, even if their goal is to help the company. For example, the managing director of an amusement park in New York State used corporate funds to purchase the silence of people who threatened to complain that the park was illegally operating on Sunday. The court ordered the director to repay the money he had spent on bribes, even though the company had earned large profits on Sundays.[6]

INFORMED DECISION

Generally, courts will protect managers who make an *informed* decision, even if the decision ultimately harms the company. Making an informed decision means carefully investigating the facts. However, even if the decision is uninformed, the directors will not be held liable if the decision was entirely fair to the shareholders.

Exhibit 29.5 provides an overview of the duty of care.

EXAM Strategy

Question: You are the CEO of a software company. You will allow your engineers to create software only for Apple computers, not for PCs, because you think Apple is cooler. Some of your shareholders disagree with this policy. Is your decision protected by the business judgment rule?

Strategy: Remember that you owe a duty of care to the corporation. This means that you must have a rational business purpose for your decision.

Result: The courts are very generous in defining a rational business purpose. They would probably uphold your decision so long as it was not in some way personally benefiting you—for example, so long as you were not a major shareholder of Apple.

---

[5]*Shlensky v. Wrigley*, 95 Ill. App. 2d 173, 237 N.E.2d 776, 1968 Ill. App. LEXIS 1107 (Ill. App. Ct. 1968).
[6]*Roth v. Robertson*, 64 Misc. 343, 118 N.Y.S. 351, 1909 N.Y. Misc. LEXIS 279 (N.Y. 1909).

EXHIBIT 29.5   The Duty of Care

29-7 THE ROLE OF SHAREHOLDERS

We have explored the duties and responsibilities of directors and managers. In this section, we look at shareholders' rights—what control do they exercise over the enterprises they own?

The topic of shareholder rights is contentious. As pointed out earlier, in this century, we have already experienced two financial meltdowns—one at the beginning of the 2000s and one at the end—that starkly revealed the different incentives faced by shareholders and managers. Too often, managers earned exorbitant compensation from highly risky short-term decisions that in the longer run left shareholders holding an empty bag. If CEOs made a risky decision that paid off, they profited enormously. If the decision failed, they might be fired, but they would still get to keep all the generous compensation they had received. On the way out the door, many also got severance payments that left them wealthy beyond most people's dreams. For example, in the two years before the investment banks Bear Stearns Companies, Inc., and Lehman Brothers Holdings, Inc., failed, their top five executives took home $1.4 billion and $1 billion, respectively, even as their shareholders were left with nothing.

Even worse, investigations after the fact revealed that too many managers had gamed compensation plans, stacked their boards with friends, and ignored shareholder interests. Compliant boards had been little more than rubber stamps, approving whatever the officers wanted. In anger and frustration, shareholders, Congress, the Securities and Exchange Commission (SEC), and stock exchanges undertook an unprecedented effort to rebalance corporate power. Yet these changes are little more than a shot in the dark, without compelling evidence that they will enhance financial stability or improve shareholder results.

A note before we begin: At one time, corporate stock was primarily owned by individuals. But now institutional investors—pension plans, mutual funds, insurance companies, banks, foundations, and university endowments—own more than 50 percent of all shares publicly traded in the United States. Institutional investors, with enormous sums to invest, have little choice but to buy the stock of large companies. If they are unhappy with management, it is difficult for them to do the "Wall Street walk"—that is, sell their shares—because a sale of their large stock holdings would depress the market price. And where would they invest the proceeds? Institutional investors cannot profit simply by trading shares among themselves. For better or worse, the fate of fund managers hangs on the success of these large companies.

29-7a Rights of Shareholders

Shareholders have neither the right nor the obligation to manage the day-to-day business of the enterprise. If you own stock in Starbucks Corp., your share of stock plus $7.62 entitles you to a cup of Grande Vanilla Latte, the same as everyone else. By the same token, if the pipes freeze and the local Starbucks store floods, the manager has no right to call you, as a shareholder, to help clean up the mess. What rights do shareholders have?

RIGHT TO INFORMATION

Shareholders have the right to obtain certain information about the company they own, but the extent of this right depends on whether the organization is publicly or privately held. (A private corporation's stock is not publicly traded.) All corporations are regulated by state law, but publicly traded enterprises must also meet SEC standards, which require much more extensive information.

Under the Model Act, **shareholders acting in good faith and with a proper purpose have the right to inspect and copy the corporation's minute book, accounting records, and shareholder lists.** A proper purpose is one that aids the shareholder in managing and protecting her investment. If, for example, Celeste is convinced that the directors of Devil Desserts, Inc., are mismanaging the company, she might demand a list of other shareholders so that she can ask them to join her in a lawsuit. This purpose is proper—although the company may not like it—and the company is required to give her the list. If, however, Celeste wants to use the shareholder list as a potential source for her new online business selling exercise equipment, the company could legitimately turn her down.

RIGHT TO VOTE

A corporation must have at least one class of stock with voting rights.

Shareholder Meetings   Although not all states require public companies to hold an annual meeting of shareholders, the New York Stock Exchange (NYSE) and NASDAQ require companies listed with them to do so. Thus, **annual shareholder meetings are the norm for publicly traded companies.**

Companies whose stock is not publicly traded can either hold an annual meeting or use written consents from their shareholders. In addition, under the Model Act, shareholders owning at least 10 percent of the company's stock and the board of directors each have the right to call a *special* meeting to vote on an emergency issue that cannot wait until the next annual meeting—for example, to conclude a merger or sell off substantial assets.

Everyone who owns stock on the record date must be sent notice of a meeting, whether it is an annual or special meeting. The record date can be any day that is no more than 70 days before the meeting. The votes taken at a shareholder meeting are not valid unless a quorum is present, meaning that shareholders owning a certain percentage of the shares are represented, either in person or by proxy.

Companies are permitted to hold shareholder meetings online rather than in person. Many companies do both—conducting a live meeting with virtual access. In 2010, Symantec Corporation became the first Fortune 500 company to eliminate the in-person meeting and hold a virtual-only version. Unfortunately, the company used this opportunity to limit rather than expand access. It broadcast only in audio, not video, which meant that participants had no opportunity to read body language or even realize that three directors were absent. In the question-and-answer period, management read and answered only two questions from shareholders and provided no opportunity for follow-up questions. Nor did they reveal who had asked the questions, or even what questions they had chosen not to answer.

Ethics

Symantec's actions in holding a virtual shareholder meeting were legal. If you had been a shareholder and had attended the meeting in cyberspace, would you have been satisfied with the company's virtual format? Did Symantec do the right thing?

Proxies Shareholders who do not wish to attend a shareholders' meeting may appoint someone else to vote for them. Confusingly, both this person and the document the shareholder signs to appoint the substitute voter are called a **proxy**. Under SEC rules, companies are not required to solicit proxies, but virtually all of them do because the NYSE and NASDAQ require it, and in addition, that is the only practical way to obtain a quorum. Along with the proxy, the company must also give shareholders a **proxy statement** and an **annual report**. The proxy statement provides information on everything from management compensation to a list of directors who miss too many meetings. The annual report contains detailed financial data.

Shareholder Proposals Shareholders who oppose a particular company policy may use the proxy process to challenge that policy. **Under SEC rules, any shareholder who has continuously owned for one year at least 1 percent of the company or $2,000 of stock can require that one proposal be placed in the company's proxy statement to be voted on at the shareholder meeting.** Most of these proposals involve issues of corporate governance (e.g., permitting secret ballots), executive compensation (e.g., "say on pay"), social issues (e.g., healthcare reform) or environmental policy (e.g., greenhouse gases). Prior to 1985, only two proposals had been approved—ever. Recently, 37 percent of the corporate governance proposals passed, but less than 5 percent of the others.

Note, however, that even if shareholders approve a proposal, the company may not implement it. Resolutions are binding on a company only if they are within the narrow realm of shareholder power. For example, because shareholders have the right to amend company bylaws, such proposals are binding. But, a shareholder vote that requires the board to take a specific action is not binding because shareholders have no legal right to manage the company. Thus, even though the SEC requires companies to allow a vote on proposals about succession planning, the board still does not have to develop a succession plan, even if a majority of shareholders vote in favor. Most proposals are nonbinding, and companies implement less than half of those that their shareholders approve.

Frustrated at this unresponsive behavior by boards, shareholders have begun to withhold their vote from any director who fails to support a successful shareholder proposal. However, even this threat has not yet had a significant impact on board responsiveness to shareholder proposals.

Ironically, companies sometimes implement shareholder proposals that have not received support from a majority of the shareholders. The pressure of shareholder proposals is credited with inducing many American companies to withdraw from South Africa in protest against its apartheid regime. Other companies implement shareholder proposals without even putting them up for a vote. Indeed, a substantial number of shareholder proposals are now withdrawn before a vote because the company is willing to negotiate and

Proxy
The person whom a shareholder appoints to vote for her at a meeting of the corporation. Also, the document a shareholder signs appointing this substitute voter.

Proxy statement
Before its annual meeting, a public company provides a document to shareholders that contains information about the corporation.

Annual report
A document that the SEC requires public companies to provide to their shareholders each year. It contains financial data.

accommodate. For instance, Colgate-Palmolive Co. agreed to a proposal by institutional investors to permit secret ballots at shareholder meetings.

ELECTION AND REMOVAL OF DIRECTORS

The process of electing directors to the board of a publicly traded company is different from what most people think. Shareholders do *not* have the right to use the company's proxy statement to propose nominees for director. Instead, the nominating committee of the board of directors produces a slate of directors, with one name per opening. Typically, the names are approved by the CEO. This slate is then placed in the proxy statement and sent to shareholders, whose only choice is to vote in favor of a nominee or to withhold their vote (i.e., not vote at all). If shareholders want to vote for someone who was not selected by the company, they have to nominate their own slate, prepare and distribute a proxy statement to other shareholders, and then communicate why their slate is superior, all the while fighting against the company's almost unlimited financial resources. This process is complex, expensive, and disruptive to the company. Not surprisingly, only a few shareholder groups undertake this effort each year. Recent research does indicate, however, that companies with a director elected through proxy contests outperform their peers over both the short and long term.[7]

Plurality voting
To be elected, a candidate only needs to receive more votes than her opponent, not a majority of the votes cast.

This traditional corporate voting method is called **plurality voting**. A successful candidate does not need to receive a majority vote—he must simply receive more than any competitor. Since typically there are no competitors, one vote is sufficient (and that vote could be his own). Even if a large number of shareholders withhold their votes, the nominee may be embarrassed, but so long as he receives that one vote, he is elected. Thus, for example, in the waning years of Michael Eisner's rule at Disney Enterprises Inc., shareholders withheld 43 percent of their votes from him. But that vote of no confidence did not cause the board to fire him, nor did he immediately resign. Congress, other regulators, and major shareholders are now reforming corporate democracy in an effort to rebalance the relationship between managers and shareholders.

Majority Voting Systems   Because of pressure from shareholder activists, 79 percent of the S&P 500 (which consists of large companies) now refuse to seat a director if fewer than half of the shares that vote tick off her name on the ballot. However, of smaller companies—those in the Russell 3000 index—three-quarters still permit plurality voting, where one vote is often sufficient to insure election.[8]

Independent Directors   Congress began its reform effort by passing the Sarbanes-Oxley Act (SOX), which applies to all publicly traded corporations in the United States, as well as to all foreign companies listed on a U.S. stock exchange. Among other provisions, SOX stipulates that **all members of a board's audit committee must be independent, and at least one of these members must be a financial expert.** Independent directors are those who are not employees *of the company* and, therefore, presumably not in the pocket of the CEO. **Likewise, the NYSE and NASDAQ require that, for companies listed on these exchanges,**

- Independent directors must comprise a majority of the board;

- They must meet regularly on their own, without inside directors;

---

[7]The Investor Responsibility Research Center Institute. See *http://www.irrcinstitute.org/pdf/PR_5_25_09.pdf.*
[8]The S&P 500 is composed of 500 leading companies in the most important U.S. industries, while the Russell 3000 is made up of the largest 3,000 companies in the United States, representing 98 percent of the investable U.S. equity market.

- Only independent directors can serve on audit, compensation, or nominating committees;

- Audit committees must have at least three directors who are financially literate.

The effectiveness of these reforms is uncertain. One study found that 45 percent of directors who are technically "independent" have friendship ties to the CEO. And even independent directors are often financially beholden to the CEO. At a minimum, the CEO is more likely to fire them from their lucrative directorship than shareholders are, so their incentives are often more aligned with the CEO. Some commentators even argue that because independent directors do not work full time for the company, they know *less* about what is really going on and have to rely *more* on company executives.

What happens to independent directors who fail to carry out their watchdog responsibilities? Unless they personally committed fraud, the answer is: not much. After all, if the SEC were aggressive about going after independent directors, few people would be willing to serve in that role. Even if they are sued, the corporation or its insurance company usually pays the damages.

Shareholder Activists   Proxy advisors, such as Institutional Shareholder Services, Inc. (ISS), are a new development in corporate democracy. They advise institutional investors on how to vote their shares. Proxy advisors and hedge funds (who often have substantial stock holdings) wield significant power. ISS alone can affect up to 20 to 40 percent of the vote at a company. Corporate managers argue that it is too much power because (1) activists may well have an agenda that is contrary to that of other shareholders, and (2) they tend to support corporate governance initiatives without proof of effectiveness.

In any event, boards have become more responsive to the demands of shareholder activists and, as a result, are more likely to replace executives who perform badly, either in their corporate or personal lives. For example, the board of Hewlett-Packard fired CEO Mark Hurd for a combination of reasons that included his fudging of expense reports to hide his relationship with someone who accused him of sexual harassment, and, perhaps worst of all, bad press.

Proxy Access   By a 3–2 vote of the commissioners, the SEC approved proxy access rules that required companies to include in their proxy material the names of board nominees selected by large shareholders (i.e., those who had owned 3 percent of the company for three years). But when business groups sued the SEC to prevent implementation, a federal appeals court invalidated the proxy access rule on the grounds that the SEC had not followed required procedures in adopting it. The SEC elected not to appeal this decision.[9] However, proxy access survives in a weakened form: The SEC permits shareholders to make proposals that, if approved, would change company bylaws to require proxy access. This two-step process is more complicated, and less likely to succeed, than the one-step version the SEC originally proposed. Also, such proposals are binding on the company only if state law permits. Such a proposal could be binding in Delaware.

The effectiveness of this rule change is uncertain. At this stage, it has not altered the reality that for most companies, shareholders have little say on board nominations.

COMPENSATION FOR OFFICERS AND DIRECTORS—THE PROBLEM

As we have seen, a CEO has significant influence over the selection process for the company's board of directors. So directors have an incentive to keep the CEO happy. As a result, between 2001 and 2003, public companies spent 9.8 percent of their net income on compensation for top executives. In 1975, the top 100 CEOs earned 39 times as much as the average worker. By 2005, that ratio was over 300. See Exhibit 29.6 for an illustration of this trend. Here are some examples of executive compensation that particularly agitated shareholders:

---

[9]*Business Roundtable v. SEC*, 2011 U.S. App. LEXIS 14988 (D.C. Cir. 2011).

- Michael Eisner was the head of Walt Disney Corporation for 20 years. At the beginning of his tenure, the company did very well and few complained when he was exceedingly well paid. But for the final *13 years,* he earned $800 million while the stock performed worse than government bonds (a low-risk, low-return investment).

- The CEO of Fannie Mae earned $90 million during a time when the company's accounting system was so flawed that it overstated its earnings by $11 billion.

- Executives whose companies survived the 2008 financial crisis only because of taxpayer bailouts still received enormous bonuses. For example, taxpayers spent $180 billion to save American International Group (AIG), Inc., even as the company awarded bonuses of $165 million.

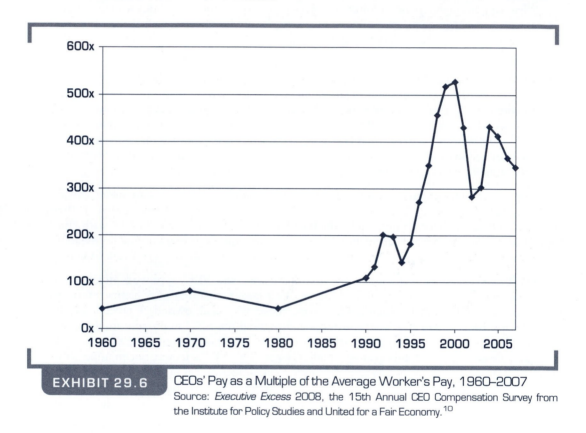

EXHIBIT 29.6   CEOs' Pay as a Multiple of the Average Worker's Pay, 1960–2007
Source: *Executive Excess* 2008, the 15th Annual CEO Compensation Survey from the Institute for Policy Studies and United for a Fair Economy.[10]

To many investors, sky-high executive salaries have become the symbol of all that is wrong with corporate governance. In many companies, salaries are the least of the compensation. Executives also received:

Stock Options   Concerned about escalating executive salaries, shareholder activists began advocating "pay-for-performance" plans. The theory was that if executives received stock options instead of cash salaries, their incentives would be more closely aligned with those of shareholders. It was a good theory, but in practice, it did not work as intended.

Stock options became a "heads, I win; tails, you lose" game. When stock prices soared in a bull market, options became unexpectedly valuable. In some cases, managers were

[10]Prepared by Professor G. William Miller, University of California at Santa Cruz, *http:llsociology.ucsc. edul whorulesamericalpowerlwealth.html.*

richly rewarded even when their company had underperformed the (rising) market. However, when stock prices fell, boards lowered the price of the options.

Also, companies played games with options. After the 9/11 terrorist attack, the stock market was closed for four days. When it reopened, stocks took a bigger plunge than they had in any week since Nazi Germany invaded France at the beginning of World War II. In what appeared to be an unseemly exploitation of a national tragedy, 186 companies granted stock options to 511 executives during those few weeks. That is more than twice the number of companies that usually issued stock options in September.[11] These grants were legal, at least; not so the backdated options that more than 2,000 companies appear to have issued their executives. In granting these options, companies claimed that they had been issued on an earlier date when the stock price was lower. This practice is fraud.

Termination, Retirement Plans, and Death Benefits   Most public companies provide their top executives with generous termination payments, no matter how they leave their jobs. Indeed, many CEO employment contracts provide that the employee is entitled to severance pay unless fired for committing a particular type of felony. Dying also pays. For example, Nabor Industries Ltd. agreed to pay its 78-year-old CEO $263 million when he dies. The CEO of the Shaw Group was entitled to $17 million if he does not compete with the company after he dies. (Yes, you read that right—he was paid not to compete after his death.)

Lavish Perks   Executives had long received perks such as country club memberships and cars, but the roster of options expanded. One of the most popular perks is use of the corporate jet. One study found a high correlation between the use of the company plane and membership in far-flung golf clubs. Unfortunately, the correlation is inverse: The more companies spend on private jets, the worse their stock performs.

Why has executive pay become so lavish?

Directors, not Shareholders, Set Executive Compensation   Directors set the CEO's compensation, but shareholders are the ones who pay the money. People tend to spend someone else's money more generously than their own. Also, directors and the CEO are often friends. Imagine if you got to decide how much your friend could spend dining out, knowing that someone else, whom you had never met, would have to pay the bill. It would be easy to be generous.

Shareholders Bear the Risk   Once again, executive compensation is a "Heads I win, tails you lose" game. As we discussed earlier in the chapter, if CEOs make a risky decision that pays off, they typically profit enormously. But even if the decision turns out badly, they are often well paid anyway. For example, Randall Stephenson, the CEO of AT&T, proposed that his company buy T-Mobile USA. A clever idea, except that the purchase violated the antitrust guidelines of the Justice Department. The risk that the government would not approve the deal was well known. Nonetheless, Stephenson promised that AT&T would pay T-Mobile $4.2 *billion* if the deal fell apart. The government did indeed object, the deal was scuttled, and AT&T had to make the enormous payment to T-Mobile. In response, the AT&T board imposed a punishment on Stephenson that was so harsh it made headlines: His compensation was reduced by $2.08 million to *only* $18.7 million. That was the penalty for losing $4.2 billion of shareholder money.

Benchmarking Games   Compensation is rarely linked closely to individual performance, but instead to overall industry or stock market performance, which is defined in a way to favor executives. Two-thirds of the largest 1,000 U.S. companies report that they

---

[11]Charles Forelle, James Bandler, and Mark Maremont, "Executive Pay: The 9/11 Factor," *The Wall Street Journal,* July, 15, 2006, p. A1.

performed better than their peers.[12] That is, in part, because benchmarks can be manipulated. For example, Tootsie Roll Industries Inc., with $500 million in sales, benchmarked against Kraft Foods Inc., with $42.2 billion in earnings. Indeed, every company Tootsie Roll benchmarked against had higher revenues.

Campbell Soup used one set of benchmark companies to determine executive compensation, but another set to evaluate its total shareholder return. In all fairness, it seems that Campbell's ought to be consistent—presumably only one set of companies is the right comparison group.

The CEO Gets All the Credit   Compensation committees sometimes act as if the CEO (and maybe a few other top executives) are solely responsible for a company's success. Although there is much talk about "pay for performance," the reality is that luck can be as important a determinant of executive compensation as good performance.[13] After James Kilts became CEO of Gillette Co., the stock price went up 61 percent. He had added $20 billion in shareholder value, and therefore, to many it seemed only fair when he was rewarded with a $153 million payout when Procter & Gamble bought the company. Or was it? About half the increase in Gillette revenues during the time that Kilts was running the show were attributable to currency fluctuations. A cheaper dollar increased revenue overseas. If the dollar had moved in the opposite direction, there might not have been any increase in revenue.

The Busier the Directors, the Higher the Executive Pay   Generally, executives are more likely to be overpaid if directors serve on many boards. These directors may be too busy to pay attention to such details. Also, trophy directors may be afraid that if they offend a chief executive at one company, word will get around, jeopardizing their position on other boards.

Most Executives Are Above Average   Of course, not everyone can be above average, but most directors believe that their executives are. No one wants to admit to hiring incompetents. Suppose that you are on a company's compensation committee and have data about industry averages. If your executives are above average in performance, you should pay them above-average salaries. If they are not above average, you should fire them, which few boards want to do, except in the face of disaster. If *you* raise salaries, the industry average also rises. The next company that sets compensation has an even higher bar to jump. For example, Colgate-Palmolive awarded 2 million stock options to its CEO on the understanding that he would receive no further grants for five years. Three years later, however, when consultants found that the CEO's compensation had fallen below the median, the company immediately awarded him an additional 2.6 million options.

Compensation Consultants Often Have Conflicts of Interest   Many companies hire compensation consultants to offer advice on executive pay. These same consultants may also provide other services to the company—such as human resource management—for which the fees can be substantial. The consultants have every incentive to suggest generous packages. In any event, it is not their money.

To make matters even worse for shareholders, lavish compensation does not appear to improve a business's success. A study of the 58 companies that were most generous to their CEOs found that, on average, these companies significantly underperformed both the market generally and their industry in particular.[14]

---

[12]Kevin J. Murphy, "Politics, Economics and Executive Compensation," reported in Lucian Bebchuk and Jesse Fried, *Pay Without Performance*, Harvard University Press, 2004, p. 71.

[13]See, for example, Marianne Bertrand and Sendhil Mullainathan, "Are CEOs Rewarded for Luck? The Ones Without Principals Are," *The Quarterly Journal of Economics*, August 2001.

[14]Reed Abelson, "Who Profits If the Boss Is Overfed?" *New York Times*, June 20, 1999, Business Section, p. 9.

Corporate executives are not the only people to earn fabulous salaries. Some athletes earn more even than CEOs. What is the difference between athletes and executives (besides a hook shot)? Athletes' salaries are negotiated at arm's length with the team owner who will actually be paying the bill. This negotiation process means that (1) athletes' pay is not camouflaged; (2) they do not receive enormous severance packages on their way out the door; and (3) their retirement pay is modest.[15] Also, an athlete's performance is transparent and easy to measure.

COMPENSATION FOR OFFICERS AND DIRECTORS—A SOLUTION?

The federal government has begun to respond to these compensation issues.

Proxy Rules   The SEC began this process by amending its proxy rules to require more information about executive compensation. A proxy statement must now include a summary table setting out the full amount of compensation for the five highest-earning executives. The company must explain, for example, why option grants were approved and how much retirement benefits are worth. Companies must also disclose if the pay package increases the risk of large losses. The goal of this provision is to discourage companies from offering pay plans that reward executives for taking excessive risks.

Sarbanes-Oxley   Under SOX:

- A company cannot make personal loans to its directors or officers.

- If a company has to restate its earnings, its CEO and CFO must reimburse the company for any bonus or profits they received from selling company stock within a year of the release of the flawed financials. This is a so-called claw-back provision.

Dodd-Frank   In 2010, Congress passed the Dodd-Frank Wall Street Reform and Consumer Protection Act. Dodd-Frank:

- Requires that compensation committees for all companies listed on a stock exchange must be composed solely of independent directors.

- Strengthens the claw-back provisions of SOX and extends it to three years.

- Requires "say on pay." At least once every three years, companies must take a *nonbinding* shareholder vote on executive compensation (i.e., for executive officers, but not for directors). In 2010, for the first time ever, shareholders voted against an executive pay plan—54 percent of Motorola's shareholders opposed CEO Sanjay Jha's compensation. The board had promised him 3 percent of the company if the plan to split Motorola in two succeeded, or a guaranteed payment if it did not. This vote was nonbinding, and the company made no concrete promises to respond.

- At least once every six years, companies must take a *nonbinding* shareholder vote on how often to hold the say-on-pay vote—once a year, every two years, or every three years.

- In the event of a merger or sale of all company assets, shareholders have the right to a *nonbinding* vote on so-called golden parachutes—special payments to executives that result from the transaction.

- Companies must disclose the relationship between financial performance and the executive compensation they actually paid.

- Companies must disclose the CEO's compensation and the median compensation of all other company employees, as well as the ratio of these two numbers.

---

[15]Some of the material in this section on executive compensation is drawn from Lucian Bebchuk and Jesse Fried, *Pay Without Performance*, Harvard University Press, 2004.

Even with these new protections in place, shareholder influence over executive compensation is far from guaranteed. Note that the shareholder resolutions are nonbinding. And there is little shareholders can do to challenge executive compensation in the courts. To be successful, shareholders must prove that the board violated the business judgment rule, either by making a decision that was *grossly uninformed* or by setting an amount so high that it had *no relation* to the value of the services performed and was really a gift. As the following case indicates, courts tend to be unsympathetic to this line of argument.

BREHM V. EISNER

2006 Del. LEXIS 307
Supreme Court of Delaware, 2006

CASE SUMMARY

Facts: Michael Ovitz founded Creative Artists Agency, the premier talent agency in Hollywood. As a partner at this firm, he earned between $20 and $25 million per year. He was also a long-time friend of Michael Eisner, who recommended that Disney hire him as president. Upon the advice of Graef Crystal, a compensation consultant, the board approved Ovitz's contract.

After 14 months, all parties agreed that the experiment had failed, so Ovitz left Disney—but not empty-handed. Under his contract, he was entitled to $130 million in severance pay.

Shareholders of Disney sued the board, alleging that it had violated the business judgment rule by failing to exercise due care.

Issues: *Did Disney directors violate the business judgment rule?*

Decision: No, the board complied with the business judgment rule.

Reasoning: The board's choice of Graef Crystal as a compensation advisor was reasonable. He was well known and highly regarded in this field. Once the board had hired him, it was reasonable to rely on his advice. It is true that the behavior of the board did not meet a "best practices" standard—it could have done a more thorough job of understanding the contract. But the business judgment rule does not require best practices. Its purpose is to protect directors who act in good faith and the board did meet that standard. Moreover, the contract had a rational business purpose: to induce Ovitz to leave Creative Artists Agency and join Disney. For these two reasons, the board did not breach its duty of care.

Emerging Growth Companies   In an effort to encourage investment in growth companies, Congress passed the Jumpstart Our Business Startups Act (the JOBS Act) in 2012. Under this statute, the Dodd-Frank rules about say-on-pay and the disclosure of executive compensation do not apply to emerging growth companies (EGCs). An EGC is one for which all the following statements are true:

- It has annual gross revenues of less than $1 billion (indexed for inflation).

- Its stock has been publicly traded for less than five years.

- It has issued less than $700 million in publicly traded stock.

- It has issued less than $1 billion in convertible debt in a three-year period.

FUNDAMENTAL CORPORATE CHANGES

A corporation must seek shareholder approval before undergoing any of the following fundamental changes: a merger, a sale of major assets, dissolution of the corporation, or an amendment to the charter.

RIGHT TO DISSENT

Because a private corporation does not have publicly traded stock, its shareholders may not have an easy way to sell their holdings. Therefore, if a private corporation decides to undertake a fundamental change, the Model Act and many state laws require the company to buy back the stock of any shareholders who object. This process is referred to as **dissenters' rights**, and the company must pay "fair value" for the stock. Fundamental changes include a merger or a sale of most of the company's assets.

Dissenters' rights
A privately held company must buy back the stock of any shareholder who objects to a fundamental change.

RIGHT TO PROTECTION FROM OTHER SHAREHOLDERS

Anyone who owns enough stock to control a corporation has a fiduciary duty to minority shareholders. (Minority shareholders are those with less than a controlling interest.) The courts have long recognized that minority shareholders are entitled to extra protection because it is easy (perhaps even natural) for controlling shareholders to take advantage of them.

　　Although craigslist and eBay are both Internet companies, they have little in common (other than a lowercase first letter). What obligations do they owe each other? You be the judge.

You Be the Judge

eBay Domestic Holdings, Inc. v. Newmark

2010 Del. Ch. LEXIS 187
Court of Chancery of Delaware, 2010

Facts: craigslist, Inc., owned the most popular website in the country for classified ads. It had just two shareholders—Craig Newmark and Jim Buckmaster—and only 34 employees. Rather than trying to maximize its profits or expand its business, craigslist focused instead on enhancing its user community (by, for example, offering free ads). eBay, Inc. was a publicly traded company that operated online auction sites worldwide. It employed over 16,000 people. Its primary focus was increasing profitability and market share.

　　eBay decided to buy 28.4 percent of craigslist's shares, with the goal of ultimately acquiring the company or, failing that, learning the "secret sauce" of craigslist's success. Under the explicit terms of the deal, it had the right to compete with craigslist. Newmark and Buckmaster said that if eBay was able to offer customers a better experience, then it should be allowed to do so.

　　When eBay realized that the two men would never sell craigslist to them, at least in this lifetime, it launched a competing classifieds website at www.Kijiji.com. In this process, it used nonpublic information about craigslist that it garnered from its relationship with the company.

When the two men found out about this "betrayal," they demanded that eBay sell back its craigslist stock. eBay refused.

　　Newmark and Buckmaster, in their role as directors of craigslist, responded by prohibiting eBay from buying more shares of craigslist or selling its existing shares to anyone other than themselves. In response, eBay filed suit, alleging that the two men had violated the company's fiduciary rights to eBay as a minority shareholder.

You Be the Judge: *Did Newmark and Buckmaster violate their fiduciary duty to the minority shareholder?*

Argument for Newmark and Buckmaster: eBay has deliberately harmed craigslist by competing against it. And it used confidential information to do so! eBay does not deserve minority protection.

　　eBay has never grasped that craigslist's success is largely due to its unique corporate culture. The best way to protect shareholders is to prevent eBay (or any other shareholder, for that matter) from undermining all that makes craigslist exceptional. The only way to achieve this goal is to prohibit eBay from buying more stock or selling what they already own to someone who could be even worse.

Argument for eBay: Controlling stockholders are fiduciaries of the minority stockholders and must maximize the value of their investment. Instead, Newmark and Buckmaster have deliberately resisted making a profit. They talk a lot about culture. Offering free ads may be an essential component of a successful online classifieds venture, but it is a sales tactic, not a culture.

Also, Newmark and Buckmaster are majority shareholders. They can keep the company the way it is for their entire lives, if they so desire, as long as they hold onto their own shares. But their goal now is to keep craigslist the same forever, even after their deaths. Essentially, Newmark and Buckmaster regret the deal they made with eBay, and have decided that craigslist should be an eternal testament to their greatness, unchanging forever. That may be their personal preference, but it is not a legitimate corporate purpose.

29-8 ENFORCING SHAREHOLDER RIGHTS

Shareholders in serious conflict with management have two different mechanisms for enforcing their rights: a derivative lawsuit or a direct lawsuit.

29-8a Derivative Lawsuits

A derivative lawsuit is brought by *shareholders* **to remedy a wrong that has been committed against the** *corporation.* The suit is brought in the name of the corporation, and all proceeds of the litigation go to the corporation because it was the *company* that was harmed. Any injury to the shareholders was indirect, affecting only the value of their stock. Thus, only the corporation can bring suit in this situation.

Often in a derivative suit, the alleged wrong was committed by a corporate insider—either an officer or director. But the board has to approve the litigation. How can shareholders force the board to sue itself or some other insider? They have to make demand on the board, meaning they have to ask the board to bring suit. Boards have the right to turn down such a demand, and that is exactly what they generally do.

There is only one hope for shareholders: They have the right to file suit on behalf of the corporation without first seeking the approval of the board if *demand would be* futile. **Demand is considered to be futile if the directors violated the duty of care or the duty of loyalty that are required by the business judgment rule.** Showing a violation of the business judgment rule is, in essence, the only successful way to bring a derivative action.

In the *Brehm v. Eisner* case earlier in this chapter, shareholders of Disney wanted to sue the board of directors over Michael Ovitz's severance pay. But the shareholders had no right to sue *on their own behalf* because it was the corporation that had been damaged. Any harm to the shareholders was indirect, through the value of their shares in the company. As a result, shareholders had to bring a derivative action, *on behalf of the corporation.* They made demand on the board. But, of course, the board did not want to sue itself. And as you have seen, the court decided that the decision to pay Michael Ovitz $130 million did not violate the business judgment rule. Thus, the shareholders were denied their attempt to bring a derivative lawsuit.

To take another example, shareholders wanted to sue directors of eBay, Inc. who had personally received virtually guaranteed profits from initial public offerings run by investment bank Goldman Sachs even as they were hiring Goldman to do work for eBay. The court held that the directors had had a conflict of interest that violated the business judgment rule. Therefore, the shareholders could bring suit against them in the name of the corporation without their permission.[16]

---

[16]*In re eBay, Inc. Shareholder Litigation,* 2004 Del. Ch. LEXIS 4, (Del. 2004).

If shareholders are permitted to proceed with their derivative action, all damages go to the corporation; the individual shareholders benefit only to the extent that the settlement causes their stock to rise in value. Litigation is tremendously expensive. How can shareholders afford to sue if they do not receive the damages? A corporation that loses a derivative suit must pay the legal fees of the victorious shareholders. (Losing shareholders are generally not required to pay the corporation's legal fees.) Most derivative lawsuits are brought by lawyers who seek out shareholders, persuade them to sue, and then collect a good part of any settlement. Without this incentive, few shareholders would bring derivative suits, and much corporate wrongdoing would go unchallenged. But this incentive system also means that some meritless suits are brought.

29-8b Direct Lawsuits

Shareholders are permitted to sue the corporation directly only if their own rights have been harmed. If, for example, the corporation denies shareholders the right to inspect its books and records or to hold a shareholder meeting, they may sue in their own names and keep any damages awarded. The corporation is not required to pay the shareholders' legal fees; winning shareholders can use part of any damage award for this purpose.

Chapter Conclusion

In corporations, shareholders without management skills complement managers without capital. Although this separation between management and owners makes great economic sense and has contributed significantly to the rise of the American economy, it also creates complex legal issues. How can shareholders ensure that the corporation will operate in their best interest? How can managers make tough decisions without being second-guessed by shareholders? Balancing the interests of managers and shareholders is a complex problem the law has struggled to resolve, without completely satisfying either side.

EXAM REVIEW

1. **PROMOTERS**   Promoters are personally liable for contracts they sign before the corporation is formed unless the corporation and the third party agree to a novation. (p. 700)

EXAM Strategy

Question: Ajouelo signed an employment contract with Wilkerson. The contract stated: "Whatever company, partnership, or corporation that Wilkerson may form for the purpose of manufacturing shall succeed Wilkerson and exercise the rights and assume all of Wilkerson's obligations as fixed by this contract." Two months later, Wilkerson formed Auto-Soler Co. Ajouelo entered into a new contract with Auto-Soler providing that the company was liable for Wilkerson's obligations under the old contract. Neither Wilkerson nor the company ever paid Ajouelo. He sued Wilkerson personally. Does Wilkerson have any obligations to Ajouelo?

Strategy: A promoter is not liable for a contract he signed on behalf of a yet-to-be-formed corporation if the third party (in this case, Wilkinson) agrees to a novation. (See the "Result" at the end of this section.)

2. **STATE OF INCORPORATION**   Companies generally incorporate in the state in which they will be doing business. However, if they intend to operate in several states, they may choose to incorporate in a jurisdiction known for its favorable corporate laws, such as Delaware. (pp. 700–701)

3. **THE CHARTER**   A corporate charter must generally include the company's name, address, registered agent, purpose, and a description of its stock. (pp. 701–703)

4. **PIERCING THE CORPORATE VEIL**   A court may, under certain circumstances, pierce the corporate veil and hold shareholders personally liable for the debts of the corporation. (pp. 706–707)

5. **TERMINATION**   Termination of a corporation is a three-step process requiring a shareholder vote, the filing of "Articles of Dissolution," and the winding up of the enterprise's business. (p. 707)

6. **FIDUCIARY DUTY**   Officers and directors have a fiduciary duty to act in the best interests of the shareholders of the corporation. Therefore, managers must maximize shareholder value. (p. 708)

7. **BUSINESS JUDGMENT RULE**   If managers comply with the business judgment rule, a court will not hold them personally liable for any harm their decisions cause the company, nor will the court rescind their decisions. The business judgment rule has two parts: the duty of care and the duty of loyalty. (pp. 708–712)

8. **DUTY OF LOYALTY**   Under the duty of loyalty, managers may not enter into an agreement on behalf of their corporation that benefits them personally, unless the disinterested directors or shareholders have first approved it. If the manager does not seek the necessary approval, the business judgment rule no longer applies, and the manager will be liable unless the transaction was entirely fair to the corporation. (p. 709)

9. **CORPORATE OPPORTUNITY**   Under the duty of loyalty, managers may not take advantage of an opportunity that rightfully belongs to the corporation. (pp. 709–711)

EXAM Strategy

Question: Vern owned 32 percent of Coast Oyster Co. and served as president and director. Coast was struggling to pay its debts, so Vern suggested that the company sell some of its oyster beds to Keypoint Co. After the sale, officers at Coast discovered that Vern owned 50 percent of Keypoint. They demanded that he give the Keypoint stock to Coast. Did Vern violate his duty to Coast?

Strategy: Here, Vern has violated the duty of loyalty not once, but twice. (See the "Result" at the end of this section.)

10. **DUTY OF CARE**   Under the duty of care, managers must make honest, informed decisions that have a rational business purpose. (p. 712)

11. **PROXIES**   Virtually all publicly held companies solicit proxies from their shareholders. A proxy authorizes someone else to vote in place of the shareholder at a company meeting. (p. 715)

12. **SHAREHOLDER PROPOSALS**   Under certain circumstances, public companies must include shareholder proposals in the proxy statement. (pp. 715–716)

13. **INDEPENDENT DIRECTORS**   Under SOX, all members of a board's audit committee must be independent. For companies listed on the NYSE or NASDAQ, independent directors must comprise a majority of the board, and only independent directors can serve on audit, compensation, or nominating committees. (pp. 716–717)

14. **EXECUTIVE COMPENSATION**

   • Under SOX, a company cannot make personal loans to its directors or officers. If a company has to restate its earnings, its CEO and CFO must reimburse the company for any bonus or profits they received from selling company stock within a year of the release of the flawed financials.

   • Dodd-Frank requires shareholder "say on pay." In addition, companies must disclose the CEO's compensation and the median compensation of all other company employees, as well as the ratio of these two numbers.

   • Under the JOBS Act of 2012, the Dodd-Frank rules about say-on-pay and disclosure of executive compensation do not apply to emerging growth companies. (pp. 717–722)

15. **DISSENTERS' RIGHTS**   A shareholder of a privately held company who objects to a fundamental change in the corporation can insist that her shares be bought back at fair value. (p. 723)

16. **MINORITY SHAREHOLDERS**   Controlling shareholders have a fiduciary duty to minority shareholders. (pp. 723–724)

17. **DERIVATIVE LAWSUITS**   A derivative lawsuit is brought by shareholders to remedy a wrong to the corporation. The suit is brought in the name of the corporation, and all proceeds of the litigation go to the corporation. (pp. 724–725)

18. **DIRECT LAWSUITS**   Shareholders are permitted to sue the corporation directly only if their own rights have been harmed. (p. 725)

EXAM Strategy

Question: Daniel Cowin was a minority shareholder of a public company that developed real estate in Washington, D.C. He alleged numerous instances of corporate mismanagement, fraud, self-dealing, and breach of fiduciary duty by the board of directors. He sought damages for the diminished value of his stock. Could Cowin bring this suit as a direct action, or must it be a derivative suit?

Strategy: If the wrong was to the corporation, then Cowin must bring a derivative lawsuit. He can only bring a direct action if the harm was to him personally. (See the "Result" at the end of this section.)

1. Result: Wilkerson may have had an ethical obligation to Ajouelo, but not a legal one. The court held that the second contract was a novation, which ended Wilkerson's obligations under the first contract.

9. Result: If the shareholders and directors did not know of Vern's interest in Keypoint, they could not evaluate the contract properly. Vern should have told them. Also, by purchasing stock in Keypoint, Vern took a corporate opportunity. He had to turn over any profits he had earned on the transaction, as well as his stock in Keypoint.

18. Result: The court ruled that the injury had fallen equally on all the shareholders, and therefore Cowin could only bring a derivative suit.

MULTIPLE-CHOICE QUESTIONS

1. **CPA QUESTION** Generally, a corporation's articles of incorporation must include all of the following except:
   (a) the name of the corporation's registered agent.
   (b) the name of each incorporator.
   (c) the number of authorized shares.
   (d) the quorum requirements.

2. **CPA QUESTION** A corporate stockholder is entitled to which of the following rights?
   (a) Elect officers.
   (b) Receive annual dividends.
   (c) Approve dissolution.
   (d) Prevent corporate borrowing.

3. Participating preferred stockholders:
   (a) only receive payment after other preferred shareholders have been paid.
   (b) only receive payment after common shareholders have been paid.
   (c) are treated like both a preferred shareholder and a common shareholder.
   (d) receive all their payments before all other shareholders.

4. If a manager engages in self-dealing, which of the following answers will NOT protect him from a finding that he violated the business judgment rule?
   (a) The disinterested members of the board approved the transaction.
   (b) The transaction was of minor importance to the company.
   (c) The disinterested shareholders approved the transaction.
   (d) The transaction was entirely fair to the corporation.

5. The duty of care:

   (a) is not a requirement of the business judgment rule.

   (b) protects directors who make an uninformed decision if it was entirely fair to the company.

   (c) protects a decision that has a rational business purpose, even if the activity was illegal.

   (d) will not protect directors who make a decision that harms the company.

6. The president of R. Hoe & Co., Inc., refused to call a special meeting of the shareholders although 55 percent of them requested it. One purpose of the meeting was to reinstate the former president. Do shareholders have the right to make these two requests?

   (a) Yes to both.

   (b) No to both.

   (c) The shareholders have the right to call a meeting, but not to reinstate the president.

   (d) The shareholders have the right to reinstate the president, but not to call a meeting.

7. Under SOX and Dodd-Frank:

   (a) companies are prohibited from making personal loans to directors and officers.

   (b) if a company restates its earnings, the five top executives must reimburse the company for any income they have received during that period.

   (c) all directors must be independent.

   (d) shareholders have the right to strike down golden parachutes.

Essay Questions

1. Michael incorporated Erin Homes, Inc., to manufacture mobile homes. He issued himself a stock certificate for 100 shares for which he made no payment. He and his wife served as officers and directors of the organization, but, during the eight years of its existence, the corporation held only one meeting. Erin always had its own checking account, and all proceeds from the sales of mobile homes were deposited there. It filed federal income tax returns each year, using its own federal identification number. John and Thelma paid $17,500 to purchase a mobile home from Erin, but the company never delivered it to them. John and Thelma sued Erin Homes and Michael, individually. Should the court "pierce the corporate veil" and hold Michael personally liable?

2. **YOU BE THE JUDGE WRITING PROBLEM** Asher Hyman and Stephen Stahl formed a corporation named Ampersand to produce plays. Both men were employed by the corporation. After producing one play, Stahl decided to write *Phillys Beat*, focusing on the history of rock and roll in Philadelphia. As the play went into production, however, the two men quarreled over Hyman's repeated absences from work and the company's serious financial difficulties. Stahl resigned from Ampersand and formed another corporation to produce the play. Did the opportunity to produce

Phillys Beat belong to Ampersand? **Argument for Stahl:** Ampersand was formed for the purpose of producing plays, not writing them. When Stahl wrote *Phillys Beat*, he was not competing against Ampersand. **Argument for Hyman:** Ampersand was in the business of producing plays, and it wanted *Phillys Beat*.

3. Angelica is planning to start a home security business in McGehee, Arkansas. She plans to start modestly but hopes to expand her business within 5 years to neighboring towns and, perhaps, within 10 years to neighboring states. Her inclination is to incorporate her business in Delaware. Is her inclination correct?

4. Eve bought defective ball bearings from Saginaw Corp. Alfred was the sole shareholder of the company and also its landlord. After Alfred sold all of Saginaw's assets, he withheld enough money to cover the rent that Saginaw owed him. As a result, Saginaw had no money to pay Eve. Does Eve have a claim against Alfred?

5. Congressional Airlines was highly profitable operating flights between Washington, D.C., and New York City. The directors approved a plan to offer flights from Washington to Boston. This decision turned out to be a major mistake, and the airline ultimately went bankrupt. Under what circumstances would shareholders be successful in bringing suit against the directors?

DISCUSSION QUESTIONS

1. States compete for lucrative corporate filing fees by passing statutes that favor management. One proposed solution to this problem would be a federal system of corporate registration. Is this a good idea? What are the impediments to such as system?

2. Ford Motor Co. and Facebook have both created dual classes of stock so that the founders can continue to control their company even after it goes public. Should corporate laws permit this? Should some shareholders be more equal than others? If the founders want to control a company, why shouldn't they buy enough regular stock to do so? It is one thing for Mark Zuckerberg to maintain control of Facebook, but should his *grandchildren* also have the right to control the company?

3. **ETHICS** Edgar Bronfman, Jr., dropped out of high school to go to Hollywood and write songs and produce movies. Eventually, he left Hollywood to work in the family business—the Bronfmans owned 36 percent of Seagram Co., a liquor and beverage conglomerate. Promoted to president of the company at the age of 32, Bronfman seized a second chance to live his dream. Seagram received 70 percent of its earnings from its 24 percent ownership of DuPont Co. Bronfman sold this stock at less than market value to purchase (at an inflated price) 80 percent of MCA, a movie and music company that had been a financial disaster for its prior owners. Some observers thought Bronfman had gone Hollywood; others that he had gone crazy. After the deal was announced, the price of Seagram shares fell 18 percent. Was there anything Seagram shareholders could have done to prevent what to them was not a dream but a nightmare? Apart from legal issues, was Bronfman's decision ethical? What ethical obligations did he owe Seagram's shareholders?

4. Pfizer Inc. paid $2.3 billion to settle civil and criminal charges alleging that it had illegally marketed 13 of its most important drugs. This settlement made history, but not in a good way. It was both the largest criminal fine and the largest settlement of civil health care fraud charges ever paid. Shareholders filed a derivative suit against the Pfizer board and top executives. Defendants responded with a motion to dismiss on the grounds that shareholders had not made demand on the board. Is demand necessary?

5. **ETHICS** After a recent annual meeting, Cisco Systems reported the results of the votes on both management and shareholder proposals. The company reported the results of its own proposals as a simple ratio of those in favor divided by the total number of votes cast. But for shareholder proposals, it reported the percentage as a ratio of those in favor divided by all outstanding shares. As a result, it reported the favorable vote for one shareholder proposal as 19 percent when, in fact, 34 percent of the votes cast supported this proposal. Is Cisco behaving ethically?

CHAPTER 30

GOVERNMENT REGULATION: SECURITIES AND ANTITRUST

nuttakit/Shutterstock.com; Steve Allen/Brand X Pictures/Jupiter Images

Sandy is a director of a public company. He tells his girlfriend, Carly, that the company is about to receive a takeover offer. Sandy does not buy any stock himself, but Carly does. When the offer is announced, the stock zooms up in price and Carly makes a tidy profit.

Steve and Joe coach college wrestling teams that are in the same conference, and have very tight budgets. Both men are also about to hire an assistant coach. One day at a meet, Steve suggests to Joe that they each agree to limit their new coach's salary to $52,000. That way, neither of them will break their budget and they might even have more money to give for athletic scholarships. Joe thinks this is a great plan and agrees on the spot.

> **Each of these people is about to find out, in a very unpleasant way, about government regulation.**

Each of these people is about to find out, in a very unpleasant way, about government regulation. Sandy and Carly have violated securities laws on insider trading. Steve and Joe have engaged in price fixing that is illegal under antitrust laws.

The moral of the story? It is important to be familiar with the most crucial government regulations. Ignorance can not only harm your business but also lead to fines and even imprisonment. (Insider trading and price fixing are two common paths to prison for white-collar workers.)

30-1 SECURITIES LAWS

There are two major securities laws: the Securities Act of 1933 (the 1933 Act) and the Securities Exchange Act of 1934 (the 1934 Act).

30-1a What Is a Security?

Both the 1933 and the 1934 Acts regulate securities. **A security is any transaction in which the buyer (1) invests money in a common enterprise and (2) expects to earn a profit predominantly from the efforts of others.**

This definition covers investments that are not necessarily called *securities*. Besides the obvious stocks, bonds, or notes, the definition of security can even include items such as orange trees. W. J. Howey Co. owned large citrus groves in Florida. It sold these trees to investors, most of whom were from out of state and knew nothing about farming. Purchasers were expected to hire someone to take care of their trees. Someone like Howey-in-the-Hills, Inc., a related company that just happened to be in the service business. Customers were free to hire any service company, but 85 percent of the acreage was covered by service contracts with Howey-in-the-Hills. The court held that Howey was selling a security (no matter how orange or tart), because the purchaser was investing in a common enterprise (the orange grove) expecting to earn a profit from Howey's farm work.

Other courts have interpreted the term *security* to include animal breeding arrangements (chinchillas, silver foxes, or beavers, take your pick); condominium purchases in which the developer promises the owner a certain level of income from rentals; and even investments in whiskey.

30-1b Securities Act of 1933

The 1933 Act requires that, before offering or selling securities in a public offering, the issuer must register the securities with the Securities and Exchange Commission (SEC). An **issuer** is the company that sells the stock initially.

It is important to remember that **when an issuer registers securities, the SEC does not investigate the quality of the offering.** Permission from the SEC to sell securities does not mean that the company has a good product or will be successful. SEC approval simply means that, on the surface, the company has provided all required information about itself and its major products. For example, the Green Bay Packers football team sold an offering of stock to finance stadium improvements. The prospectus admitted:

> IT IS VIRTUALLY IMPOSSIBLE that any investor will ever make a profit on the stock purchase. The company will pay no dividends, and the shares cannot be sold.

This does not sound like a stock you want in your retirement fund; on the other hand, the SEC does not prevent Green Bay from selling it, or you from buying it, so long as the company has revealed what the risks are.

Issuer
A company that sells its own stock.

LIABILITY

Under the 1933 Act, the seller of a security is liable for making any material misstatement or omission, either oral or written, in connection with the offer or sale of a security. Anyone who issues fraudulent securities is in violation of the 1933 Act, whether or not the securities are registered. Both the SEC and any purchasers of the stock can sue the issuer. In addition, the Justice Department can bring criminal charges against anyone who willfully violates this statute.

PUBLIC OFFERINGS

A company's first public sale of securities is called an **initial public offering** or an **IPO.** Any subsequent public sale is called a **secondary offering.**

Initial public offering (IPO)
A company's first public sale of securities.

Secondary offering
Any public sale of securities by a company after the initial public offering.

registration statement
A document that notifies the SEC that a sale of securities is pending and discloses information to prospective purchasers.

Registration Statement   To make a public offering, the company must file a registration statement with the SEC. The **registration statement** has two purposes: to notify the SEC that a sale of securities is pending and to disclose information of interest to prospective purchasers. The registration statement must include detailed information about the issuer and its business, a description of the stock, the proposed use of the proceeds from the offering, and two years of audited balance sheets and income statements. Preparing a registration statement is neither quick nor inexpensive—it can cost as much as $8 million for an IPO.

Prospectus
A document that is part of the registration statement. It must be provided to all investors before they purchase stock.

Prospectus   Typically, buyers never see the registration statement; they are given the **prospectus** instead. (The prospectus is part of the registration statement that is sent to the SEC.) The prospectus includes all of the important disclosures about the company, while the registration statement includes additional information that is of interest to the SEC but not to the typical investor, such as the names and addresses of the lawyers for the issuer and underwriter. **All investors must receive a copy of the prospectus before purchasing stock.**

Sales Effort   Even before the final registration statement and prospectus are completed, the investment bank representing the issuer begins its sales effort. It cannot actually make sales during this period, but it can solicit offers. The SEC closely regulates an issuer's sales effort to ensure that it does not hype the stock by making public statements about the company before the stock is sold. For example, the SEC delayed an offering of stock by Google, Inc., after *Playboy* magazine published an interview with its founders.

Comment letter
A document from the SEC listing required changes in the registration statement.

Going Effective   Once the SEC finishes its review of the registration statement, it sends the issuer a **comment letter**, listing required changes. An issuer almost always has to amend the registration statement at least once, and sometimes more than once. Remember that the SEC does not assess the *value* of the stock or the *merit* of the investment. Its role is to ensure that the company has disclosed enough information to enable investors to make an informed decision. After the SEC has approved a final registration statement (which includes, of course, the final prospectus), the issuer and underwriter agree on a price for the stock and the date to **go effective**, that is, to begin the sale.

Go effective
The securities registration is complete and the company may begin the sale of its stock.

Registering securities with the SEC for a public offering is very time-consuming and expensive, but the 1933 Act also permits issuers to sell stock in a private offering, which is much simpler (and cheaper).

PRIVATE OFFERINGS

Private offering
A sale of securities that, under the 1933 Act, is not considered a public offering because of the limited number of investors or the small amount of money raised.

Regulation D   Under the 1933 Act, an issuer is not required to register securities that are sold in a private offering, that is, an offering with a relatively small number of investors or a limited amount of money involved. Tens of thousands of these offerings take place each year, compared with only about 130 IPOs.

Regulation D
The most common and important type of private offering.

The most common and important type of private offering is under **Regulation D** (often referred to as "Reg D"). Half of all Reg D offerings take in less than $1 million but more than twice as much capital is raised each year under this private method than in public offerings. Reg D provides a number of different options, the most popular of which is Rule 506. Under Rule 506, a company may sell an unlimited amount of stock, subject to the following restrictions:

Accredited investors
Institutions (such as banks and insurance companies) or wealthy individuals (with a net worth of more than $1 million or an annual income of more than $200,000).

- The issuer can sell to an unlimited number of accredited investors, but to only 35 unaccredited investors. **Accredited investors** are institutions (such as banks and insurance companies) or wealthy individuals (with a net worth of more than $1 million, not counting their homes, or an annual income of more than $200,000).

- If the issuer sells to unaccredited investors, it may not advertise the stock publicly. But if it limits sales to accredited investors, it may advertise publicly.

- It need not provide information to accredited investors but must make disclosure to unaccredited investors, including a certified balance sheet.

- Stock purchased under this rule is restricted (which means that it cannot be sold for a year).

- One further wrinkle: If an unaccredited purchaser is unsophisticated, he must have a **purchaser representative** to help him evaluate the investment.

Purchaser representative
Someone who has enough knowledge and experience in financial matters to evaluate the merits and risks of an investment.

Crowdfunding   Congress recently passed the Jumpstart Our Business Startups (JOBS) Act, which permits privately held companies to sell up to $1 million in securities in any 12-month period, provided that they do all of the following:

- Make a filing with the SEC and provide appropriate disclosure to the purchaser at the time of purchase, and then annually;

- Limit investments as follows:

  ○ Investors with income or net worth that is less than $100,000 can invest no more than the maximum of $2,000 or 5 percent of their income or net worth.

  ○ Investors with income or net worth that is equal to or greater than $100,000 can invest no more than the maximum of $100,000 or 10 percent of their income or net worth.[1]

- Sell the securities through an approved intermediary, that is, a broker or a so-called funding portal (e.g., a website) that is registered with the SEC;

- Take steps (as determined by the SEC) to reduce the risk of fraud; and

- Prohibit the stock from being resold for one year (except to accredited investors or family members).

- Not advertise the offering (except to tell investors about the approved intermediary);

- Not offer investment advice or pay anyone to sell their securities.

30-1c Securities Exchange Act of 1934

REGISTRATION

Most buyers do not purchase new securities from the issuer in an IPO. Rather, they buy stock that is publicly traded in the open market. This stock is, in a sense, secondhand because other people—perhaps many others—have already owned it. The purpose of the 1934 Act is to provide investors with ongoing information about public companies (i.e., companies with publicly traded stock).

Under the 1934 Act, an issuer must register with the SEC if (1) it completes a public offering under the 1933 Act, or (2) its securities are traded on a national exchange (such as the New York Stock Exchange), or (3) it has at least 2,000 shareholders (with a maximum of 500 unaccredited investors) *and* total assets that exceed $10 million.

The 1934 Act requires public companies to file the following documents:

- **Annual reports** on Form 10-K, containing audited financial statements, a detailed analysis of the company's performance, and information about officers and directors. A public company must also deliver its annual report to shareholders.

---

[1]Note that these provisions are inconsistent. An investor whose income is $50,000 but whose net worth is $150,000 falls into both categories.

- **Quarterly reports** on Form 10-Q, which are less detailed than 10-Ks and contain unaudited financials.

- **Form 8-K** to report any significant developments, such as a change in control, the resignation of a director over a policy dispute, or a change in auditing firms.

In response to corporate scandals, Congress passed the Sarbanes-Oxley Act of 2002. This statute requires each company's CEO and CFO to certify that:

- The information in the quarterly and annual reports is true,

- The company has effective internal controls, and

- The officers have informed the company's audit committee and its auditors of any concerns that they have about the internal control system.

LIABILITY

Section 10(b) (and Rule 10b-5) prohibit fraud in connection with the purchase and sale of any security, whether or not the security is registered under the 1934 Act. Under these rules, anyone who fails to disclose material information or makes incomplete or inaccurate disclosure is liable, so long as the statement or omission was made willfully, knowingly, or recklessly. **Material** means that the information was important enough to affect an investor's decision. An example of fraud: An accounting firm that certified financials in a company's annual report, knowing that it had not in fact adequately audited the firm's books, would be liable under §10(b).

Both the 1933 Act and the 1934 Act specify that misstatements and omissions create liability only if they are material. In the following case, a unanimous Supreme Court provided guidance on what "material" means.

Material
Important enough to affect an investor's decision.

MATRIXX INITIATIVES, INC. v. SIRACUSANO

2011 U.S. LEXIS 2416
Supreme Court of the United States, 2011

CASE SUMMARY

Facts: Zicam Cold Remedy was a nasal spray (or gel) that accounted for 70 percent of Matrixx's sales revenue. Its active ingredient was zinc gluconate. Matrixx began receiving reports that some Zicam users had developed anosmia (i.e., they had lost their sense of smell). The company learned for the first time that some studies had linked the use of zinc sulfate to the loss of smell.

Matrixx then found out that two doctors were planning to make a presentation at a conference about patients who had developed anosmia after Zicam use. Matrixx sent them a letter warning them that they did not have permission to use the name of Matrixx or its products. The doctors deleted references to Zicam.

Nine people filed suit against Matrixx, alleging that Zicam had damaged their sense of smell. Matrixx then issued statements that Zicam was poised for growth and that revenues would increase by more than 80 percent. In its 10-Q

filing with the SEC, Matrixx warned of the potential "material adverse effect" that could result from product liability claims, "whether or not proven to be valid." It did not disclose, however, that plaintiffs had already sued Matrixx.

After the Food and Drug Administration (FDA) announced that it was investigating Zicam, Matrixx's stock price fell. The company issued a press release stating that there are many causes for anosmia, including the common cold, but Zicam was not one of them.

The day after this press release, Matrixx stock price bounced back. Shortly thereafter, however, the TV show *Good Morning America* reported that more than a dozen patients had suffered from anosmia after using Zicam and that some had filed lawsuits against Matrixx. The company's stock price plummeted.

A group of shareholders filed suit, alleging that Matrixx had violated §10(b) and Rule 10b-5. The trial court granted Matrixx's motion to dismiss on the grounds that, without a statistical correlation between the use of Zicam and anosmia, the reported incidents were not material. The Court of Appeals reversed. The Supreme Court granted *certiorari*.

Issues: *Did Matrixx violate §10(b) and Rule 10b-5?*

Decision: Yes, Matrixx was in violation.

Reasoning: Information is material if a reasonable investor would view it to be significant. The FDA sometimes takes action on a product even if the available evidence merely *suggests* but does not *prove* that it causes harm. The FDA does not require statistical correlation; it considers other data as well. If this other information matters to the FDA, then it will also be important to investors.

However, reports of adverse events are common with all pharmaceuticals, and companies are not required to report each and every one of these events to investors. Something more is needed, but that something is less than statistical correlation.

In this case, the "total mix" of information reported by the company was misleading. Matrixx told investors that revenues were going to rise substantially even though it had information that created a significant risk to its leading product. That combination—knowledge of adverse events and an upbeat revenue prediction—created an obligation to report these potential concerns.

Ethics   Matrixx learned that its products were potentially causing a loss of smell, which is no minor matter. People with anosmia cannot properly taste food, so they often lose interest in eating, which can lead to malnutrition and depression. Was it ethical for the company to prohibit doctors from presenting information about Zicam at a conference? Did the company have an ethical obligation to alert the public to this issue? Which concern takes priority—shareholders or the public?

30-1d Short-Swing Trading—Section 16

Section 16 of the 1934 Act was designed to prevent corporate insiders—officers, directors, and shareholders who own more than 10 percent of the company—from taking unfair advantage of privileged information to manipulate the market.

Section 16 takes a two-pronged approach:

- First, insiders must *report* their trades within two business days.

- Second, insiders must *turn over to the corporation* any profits they make from the purchase and sale or sale and purchase of company securities in a *six-month period*. Section 16 is a strict liability provision. It applies even if the insider did not actually take advantage of secret information or try to manipulate the market; if she bought and sold or sold and bought stock in a six-month period, she is liable for any profits she earned.

Suppose that Manuela buys 20,000 shares of her company's stock in June at $10 a share. In September, her (uninsured) winter house in Florida is destroyed by a hurricane. To raise money for rebuilding, she sells the stock at $12 per share, making a profit of $40,000. But she has violated §16 and must turn over the profit to her company.

30-1e Insider Trading

Insider trading is immensely tempting. Anyone with reliable secret information can earn millions of dollars overnight. The downside? Insider trading is a crime punishable by fines and imprisonment. The guilty party may also be forced to turn over to the SEC three times the profit made. For example, Raj Rajaratnam, the billionaire head of a hedge fund, was recently sentenced to 11 years in prison and ordered to pay $63.8 million to the government.

These are the rules on insider trading:

- *Fiduciaries.* Any corporate insider who trades while in possession of nonpublic material information in violation of his fiduciary duty to his company is liable under Rule 10b-5. Corporate insiders include board members, major shareholders, employees, and so-called temporary insiders, such as lawyers and investment bankers who are doing deals for the company. Examples:

  - If the director of research for MediSearch knows that the company will shortly announce a major breakthrough in the treatment of AIDS and then buys stock in the company before the information is public, she is guilty of insider trading.

  - Suppose, however, that while looking in a Dumpster, Harry finds correspondence that reveals MediSearch's new discovery. He then buys MediSearch stock, which promptly quadruples in value. Harry will be dining at the Ritz, not in the Dumpster nor in federal prison, because he has no fiduciary duty to MediSearch.

- *Misappropriation.* So far we have been discussing fiduciaries with a *direct* relationship to the company whose stock was traded. But people with a more remote connection may also be liable. **Anyone (1) with material, non-public information, (2) who breaches a fiduciary duty to the *source of the information* (3) by revealing or trading on it, is liable for insider trading.** This rule applies even if the person does not work for the company whose stock was traded. For example:

  - James O'Hagan was a lawyer in a firm that represented a company attempting to take over Pillsbury Co. Although O'Hagan did not work on the case, he heard about it and then bought stock in Pillsbury. After the takeover attempt was publicly announced, O'Hagan sold his stock in Pillsbury at a profit of more than $4.3 million.[2] Although Hagan's firm did not represent Pillsbury, the Supreme Court ruled that O'Hagan had violated insider trading laws. While it was true that he had no fiduciary duty to Pillsbury, he did owe one to his law firm, which was the source of the information. According to the court, what he had done was the same thing as embezzlement.[3]

- *Tippers.* What about people who do not trade themselves but pass on information to someone who does? Anyone who reveals material nonpublic information in violation of his fiduciary duty is liable if (1) he knows the information was confidential and (2) he expected some personal gain. Personal gain is loosely defined. Essentially, any gift to a friend counts as personal gain. For example:

  - W. Paul Thayer was a corporate director, deputy secretary of defense, and former fighter pilot ace who gave stock tips to his girlfriend in lieu of paying her rent. That counted as personal gain, and he spent a year and a half in prison.

- *Tippees.* **Those who receive tips—tippees—are liable for trading on inside information,** even if they do not have a fiduciary relationship to the company, so long as (1) they know the information is confidential; (2) they know it came from an insider who was violating his fiduciary duty; and (3) the insider expected some personal gain. For example:

  - Barry Switzer, then head football coach at the University of Oklahoma, went to a track meet to see his son compete. While sunbathing on the bleachers, he overheard someone talking about a company that was going to be acquired. Switzer bought the stock, but was acquitted of insider trading charges because the insider had not breached his fiduciary duty. He had not tipped anyone on purpose—he had simply been careless. Also, Switzer did not know

---

[2]O'Hagan used the profits that he gained through this trading to conceal his previous embezzlement of client funds. There is a moral here.

[3]521 U.S. 642, 117 S. Ct. 2199, 1997 U.S. LEXIS 4033.

that the insider was breaching a fiduciary duty, and the insider expected no personal gain from releasing the information.[4]

- *Takeovers.* **Rule 14e-3 prohibits trading on inside information during a tender offer if the trader knows the information was obtained from either the bidder or the target company.** The trader or tipper need not have violated a fiduciary duty.

- *Advanced Planning.* **Under Rule 10b5-1, an insider can avoid insider trading charges if she commits in advance to a plan to sell securities.** Thus, if an insider knows that she will want to sell stock to pay a child's college tuition, she can establish such a sales plan in advance. She will then not be liable for the sales, no matter what inside information she knows. But, she *must* sell according to the plan, despite any change in circumstances.

In the following case, two employees were not *told* specific information, but they made an educated guess. Have they violated insider trading rules?

SECURITIES AND EXCHANGE COMMISSION V. STEFFES

2011 U.S. Dist. LEXIS 85496
United States District Court for the Northern District of Illinois

CASE SUMMARY

Facts: Florida East Coast Industries, Inc. (East Coast), was a publicly traded company that operated a freight railroad between Jacksonville and Miami. As a vice president, Gary Griffiths's job was to oversee maintenance of the railcars. He was married to the sister of his high school friend, Rex Steffes. He had helped Rex's son Cliff obtain a job driving trains for East Coast.

The CFO of East Coast asked Griffiths to prepare an inventory of all the rolling stock the company owned and to arrange trips among its rail yards in a special railroad car reserved for visitors. Griffiths also heard that a large number of men in suits had been touring the company's rail yards. Yard employees began asking Griffiths whether East Coast would be sold and whether they would lose their jobs. Indeed, it turned out that East Coast's Board of Directors had secretly hired an investment bank to sell the company.

During this period, Griffiths, Rex and Cliff called each other repeatedly. After the calls, Rex made various purchases of East Coast stock, although his broker advised against buying so many shares of one company. Rex ultimately spent a total of $1.14 million on East Coast stock. Also, Cliff purchased the first call options of his life, spending $15,015 on East Coast.[5] After the company was sold, both Rex and Cliff made substantial profits.

The SEC filed suit, alleging that Griffiths, Rex, and Cliff had violated §10(b) and Rule 10b-5. The men filed a motion to dismiss.

Issue: *Did the defendants engage in illegal insider trading?*

Decision: Yes, Griffiths, Rex and Cliff were liable for insider trading.

Reasoning: This case is atypical in that Griffiths was not told directly about the merger but instead figured it out himself. Although no one particular piece of information—such as the fact that men in suits were touring rail yards—was itself crucial, his ultimate conclusion that a sale was about to take place was material, nonpublic information.

Although phone calls among family member are not themselves illegal or even suspicious, the fact that Rex bought stock shortly after each of these calls created a reasonable inference that Griffiths tipped Rex. The SEC was entitled to prove its case through circumstantial evidence.

Although Griffiths himself did not buy East Coast stock, he was nonetheless liable, too. He violated his fiduciary duty by passing on this material nonpublic information. He may not have directly benefited from the trades but it is well established that the concept of gain is a broad one and includes a gift of confidential information to a relative or friend.

---

[4]*SEC v. Switzer*, 590 F. Supp. 756, 1984 U.S. Dist. LEXIS 15303 (W.D. Okla. 1984).
[5]Call options are the right to purchase stock of a company at a specific price for a specific period of time. A buyer purchases a call option in the expectation that the stock price will go up.

EXAM STRATEGY

Question: Paul was an investment banker who sometimes bragged about deals he was working on. One night, he told a bartender, Ryanne, about an upcoming deal. Ryanne bought stock in the company Paul had mentioned. Both were prosecuted for insider trading. Ryanne was acquitted but Paul was convicted, even though Ryanne was the one who made money. How is that possible?

Strategy: Note that there are different standards for tippers and tippees.

Result: Paul is liable if he knew the information was confidential and he expected some personal gain. A gift counts as personal gain. (The courts have an expansive definition of gifts—practically anything counts. Here, the information could be interpreted as a tip to the bartender.) Ryanne would not be liable unless she knew the information was confidential and had come from an insider who was violating his fiduciary duty.

Why is insider trading a crime? Who is harmed? Insider trading is illegal because:

- It offends our fundamental sense of fairness. No one wants to be in a poker game with marked cards.

- Investors will lose confidence in the market if they feel that insiders have an unfair advantage.

- Investment banks typically "make a market" in stocks, meaning that they hold extra shares so that orders can be filled smoothly. These marketmakers expect to earn a certain profit, but inside traders skim some of it off. So marketmakers simply raise the commission they charge. As a result, everyone who buys and sells stock pays a slightly higher price.

30-1f Blue Sky Laws

Blue sky laws
State securities laws.

Currently, all states and the District of Columbia also regulate the sale of securities. These state statutes are called **blue sky laws** (because crooks were willing to sell naive investors a "piece of the great blue sky"). However, under the National Securities Markets Improvement Act (NSMIA) of 1996, states may not regulate offerings of securities that are:

- Traded on a national exchange,

- Exempt under Rule 506, or

- Sold to a qualified purchaser.[6]

Any securities offerings not covered by the NSMIA must comply with state securities laws.

30-2 ANTITRUST LAW

Antitrust legislation
Laws aimed at preventing extreme concentrations of economic power and promoting competition.

Congress passed the Sherman Act in 1890 to prevent extreme concentrations of economic power and promote competition. Because this statute was aimed at the Standard Oil Trust, which then controlled the oil industry throughout the country, it was termed **antitrust** legislation.

---

[6]The SEC was supposed to define this term in 1996, but has not yet done so.

Violations of the antitrust laws are divided into two categories: *per se* and **rule of reason**. *Per se* violations are automatic. Defendants charged with this type of violation cannot defend themselves by saying, "But the impact wasn't so bad" or "No one was hurt." The court will not listen to excuses, and violators may be sent to prison.

Rule of reason violations, on the other hand, are illegal only if they have an anticompetitive impact on the market. For example, mergers are illegal only if they harm competition in their industry. Those who commit rule of reason violations are not sent to prison.

Both the Justice Department and the Federal Trade Commission (FTC) have authority to enforce the antitrust laws. In addition to the government, anyone injured by an antitrust violation has the right to sue for damages. The United States is unusual in this regard—in most other countries, only the government is able to sue antitrust violators. A successful plaintiff can recover treble (i.e., triple) damages from the defendant.

> **Per se**
> An automatic breach of antitrust laws.
>
> **Rule of reason**
> An action that breaches antitrust laws only if it has an anticompetitive impact.

30-2a The Sherman Act

PRICE-FIXING

Section 1 of the Sherman Act prohibits all agreements "in restraint of trade." The most common—and one of the most serious—violations of this provision involves horizontal price-fixing. **When competitors agree on the prices at which they will buy or sell products, their price-fixing is a *per se* violation of §1 of the Sherman Act.**

In the following Landmark Case, the defendants argued that price-fixing was wrong only if the prices were *unfair*. Did the Supreme Court agree?

Landmark Case

UNITED STATES V. TRENTON POTTERIES COMPANY

273 U.S. 392; 1927 U.S. LEXIS 975
Supreme Court of the United States, 1927

CASE SUMMARY

Facts: This case involved dirty doings in the bathroom fixture business. The federal government alleged that 23 of the corporations that manufactured these fixtures had agreed on the prices they would charge their customers. The defendants argued that they had not violated the law because their prices had been reasonable.

They were found guilty at trial, but the appeals court overturned their convictions. The Supreme Court granted *certiorari*.

Issue: *Is price-fixing legal so long as the prices are reasonable?*

Decision: Price-fixing is a *per se* violation, even if the prices are reasonable.

Reasoning: The goal of the Sherman Act is to promote competition, but price-fixing automatically eliminates one form of it. Indeed, the power to fix prices is the power to control a market, an outcome that the Sherman Act prohibits.

Moreover, even if the prices were fair when set, the reasonable price today may, through economic and business changes, become the unreasonable price of tomorrow. And it would be wrong to require the government to prove that prices are unreasonable, especially because economists may not be able to agree.

For these reasons, the judgment of the appeals court was reversed.

The Supreme Court has referred to this type of collusion as "the supreme evil of antitrust," and it has been illegal for the better part of a century.[7] But it never seems to go away. Samsung Electronics Co. paid a $300 million fine for having conspired to fix prices of computer chips. Other companies engaged in this conspiracy paid $346 million in fines. These penalties were topped by F. Hoffmann-La Roche, which paid $500 million for conspiring to fix the prices of vitamins. Executives went to prison for their roles in these conspiracies.

Resale Price Maintenance

Resale price maintenance (RPM), also called *vertical price fixing*, means the manufacturer sets the *minimum* prices that retailers may charge. In other words, it prevents retailers from discounting. Why does the manufacturer even care? After all, once the retailer purchases the item, the manufacturer has made its profit. The only way the manufacturer makes more money is to raise its wholesale price, not the retail price. RPM guarantees a profit margin for the retailer.

Manufacturers care about retail prices because pricing affects the product's image with consumers. Armani men's suits sell for around $2,000. What conclusion do you draw about the quality of those suits? Would your opinion change if you saw Armani suits being sold for less? You can understand that Armani might want to prohibit retailers from lowering the prices on its suits. Consumer advocates contend, however, that manufacturers such as Armani are simply protecting dealers from competition. Discounting may or may not harm products, but, they insist, RPM certainly hurts consumers.

In 1911, the Supreme Court ruled that RPM was a *per se* violation of §1 of the Sherman Act.[8] However, what the Supreme Court giveth, it can also taketh away. In 2007, the Supreme Court overruled itself and held that RPM is a rule of reason violation. The following case explains why.

Leegin Creative Leather Products, Inc. v. PSKS, Inc.

551 U.S. 877, 127 S. Ct. 2705, 2007 U.S. LEXIS 8668
Supreme Court of the United States, 2007

Case Summary

Facts: Leegin manufactured belts and other women's fashion accessories under the brand name "Brighton." It sold these products only to small boutiques and specialty stores. Sales of the Brighton brand accounted for about half the profits at Kay's Kloset, a boutique in Lewisville, Texas.

Leegin decided it would no longer sell to retailers who discounted Brighton prices. It wanted to ensure that stores could afford to offer excellent service. It was also concerned that discounting harmed Brighton's image. Despite warnings from Leegin, Kay's Kloset persisted in marking down Brighton products by 20 percent. So Leegin cut the store off.

Kay's sued Leegin, alleging that RPM was a *per se* rule violation of the law. The trial court found for Kay's and entered judgment against Leegin for almost $4 million. The Court of Appeals affirmed. The Supreme Court granted *certiorari*. On appeal, Leegin did not dispute that it had entered into RPM agreements with retailers. Rather, it contended that the rule of reason should apply to those agreements.

Issue: *Is resale price maintenance a **per se** or **rule of reason** violation of the Sherman Act?*

Decision: RPM is a rule of reason violation.

---

[7]*Verizon Communs., Inc. v. Trinko, LLP,* 540 U.S. 398 (S. Ct. 2004).
[8]*Dr. Miles Medical Co. v. John D. Park & Sons,* 220 U.S. 373 (1911).

Reasoning: To be a *per se* violation, an activity must not only be anticompetitive, it must also lack any redeeming virtue. Recent research indicates that resale price maintenance may offer some benefits:

- *Retailers can provide better service.* Without RPM, consumers might go *look* at a product at the retailer who hires experienced sales help or offers product demonstrations, but then go *buy* the item from a discounter who provides none of these services. In short order, the upscale retailer will either go out of business or cut back on service and consumers will have fewer options.

- *If retailers do not have to compete with others who sell the same brand, they can focus instead on competing against other brands.* For example, retailers selling the same brand may pool their marketing dollars to have greater impact.

It is worth noting, though, that RPM can have an anticompetitive effect. A manufacturer with market power could, for example, use resale price maintenance to give retailers an incentive not to sell the products of smaller rivals. Courts must be diligent in recognizing and preventing any RPM that has an anticompetitive impact.

VERTICAL MAXIMUM PRICE FIXING

In the case of resale price maintenance, the manufacturer sets the *minimum* prices its distributors can charge. Vertical maximum price fixing (when a manufacturer sets *maximum* prices), is also a rule of reason violation of §1 of the Sherman Act. The defendant is liable only if the price fixing harms competition. (You remember that, by contrast, all *horizontal* price fixing is a *per se* violation.)

When State Oil Co. leased a gas station to Barkat Khan, it set a maximum price that Khan could charge for gas. Khan sued State Oil, but the Supreme Court ruled in favor of the oil company on the grounds that cutting prices to increase business is the very essence of competition and, furthermore, low prices benefit consumers.[9]

MONOPOLIZATION

Under §2 of the Sherman Act, it is illegal to monopolize or attempt to monopolize a market. To monopolize means to acquire control over a market in the wrong way. *Having* a monopoly is legal unless it is *gained* or *maintained* by using wrongful tactics.

> Possessing a monopoly is not necessarily illegal; using *"bad acts"* to acquire or maintain one is.

To determine if a defendant has illegally monopolized, we must ask three questions:

- **What is the market?** If buyers view two products as close substitutes, then the items are in the same market. For example, imagine that your company sells soft drinks in Smallville. These drinks have unusual food flavors—steak and cheese, among others. For some reason, you are the only company in that area who sells food-flavored soft drinks, so, by definition, you control 100 percent of the market. But is that the *relevant* market? Perhaps the relevant market is flavored drinks or soft drinks or all beverages. The question economists ask is: How high can your prices rise before your buyers will switch to a different product? (This concept is called *cross-elasticity of demand*.) If a price increase from $2 to $2.20 a bottle causes many of your customers to buy Coke instead, it is clear you are part of a larger market. However, if you could raise your price to $5 per bottle and still hold on to many of your customers, then you might well be in your own market.

---

[9]*State Oil Co. v. Khan*, 522 U.S. 3, 1997 U.S. LEXIS 6705 (1997).

- **Does the company control the market?** No matter what its market share, a company does not have a monopoly unless it can exclude competitors or control prices. For example, the Justice Department sued a movie theater chain that possessed a 93 percent share of the box office in Las Vegas. But the court ruled against the Justice Department because the chain's market share decreased to 75 percent within three years. This decline indicated that the company did not control the market and that barriers to entry were low.[10]

- **How did the company acquire or maintain its control?** If the law prohibited the mere possession of a monopoly, it might discourage companies from producing excellent products or offering low prices. So possessing a monopoly is not necessarily illegal; using *"bad acts"* to acquire or maintain one is. For example, Microsoft insisted that computer manufacturers who wanted to install the Windows operating system on *any* computer had to purchase a license for *every* machine they made. This requirement meant that a manufacturer would not even consider offering consumers another operating system because it had already paid for Microsoft's on all of its machines. The Justice Department ordered Microsoft to halt this arrangement.

Predatory pricing is another example of a bad act.

PREDATORY PRICING

Predatory pricing occurs when a company lowers its prices below cost to drive competitors out of business. Once the predator has the market to itself, it raises prices to make up lost profits—and more besides. Typically, the goal of a predatory pricing scheme is either to win control of a market or to maintain it. Therefore, it is illegal under §2 of the Sherman Act. **To win a predatory pricing case, the plaintiff must prove three elements:**

- The defendant is selling its products *below cost*.

- The defendant *intends* that the plaintiff go out of business.

- If the plaintiff does go out of business, the defendant will be able to earn sufficient profits to *recover* its prior losses.

The classic example of predatory pricing is a large grocery store that comes into a small town offering exceptionally low prices that are subsidized by profits from its other branches. Once all the "Ma and Pa" corner groceries go out of business, MegaGrocery raises its prices to much higher levels.

Predatory pricing cases can be difficult to win. For example, it is hard for Ma and Pa to prove that MegaGrocery intended for them to go out of business. It is also difficult for Ma and Pa to show that MegaGrocery will be able to make up all its lost profits once the corner grocery is out of the way. They need to prove, for example, that no other grocery chain will come to town. It is difficult to prove a negative proposition like that, especially in the grocery business, where barriers to entry are low.

In recent times, plaintiffs have not had much success with predatory pricing suits. For example, Liggett began selling generic cigarettes 30 percent below the price of branded cigarettes. Brown & Williamson retaliated by introducing its own generics at an even lower price. Liggett sued, claiming that Brown's prices were below cost. The Supreme Court agreed that Brown was not only selling below cost, but also intended to harm Liggett. Brown still won the case, however, because there was no evidence that it would be able to recover its losses from the below-cost pricing. If Brown raised its prices, other competitors would come back into the market.[11]

---

[10]*United States v. Syufy Enterprises*, 903 F.2d 659, 1990 U.S. App. LEXIS 7396, (9th Cir., 1990).
[11]*Brooke Group Ltd. v. Brown & Williamson Tobacco Corp.*, 509 U.S. 209, 1993 U.S. LEXIS 4245 (1993).

30-2b The Clayton Act

MERGERS

The Clayton Act prohibits mergers that are anticompetitive. Companies with substantial assets must notify the Federal Trade Commission (FTC) before undertaking a merger. This notification gives the government an opportunity to prevent a merger ahead of time, rather than trying to untangle one after the fact.[12]

Horizontal Mergers.   A horizontal merger involves companies that compete in the same market. In determining whether to permit a merger, the government and the courts consider how the merger will affect competition and consumers. Thus the government cleared a merger between aircraft giants Boeing and McDonnell Douglas, which together had a virtual monopoly on the American aircraft business. But the aircraft market is global, and American companies faced severe competition from Europe's Airbus consortium. Therefore, the government believed that the merger would not harm competition.

Conversely, the FTC blocked the merger of office supply giants Staples, Inc., and Office Depot. Nationally, these two retailers controlled only 4 percent of the market for office supplies. But rather than focusing on national market share, the FTC looked instead on the ability to control prices *locally*. The agency found that, when both stores operated in the same market, prices were significantly lower than when only one store was present. Thus, a box of file folders cost $1.72 in Orlando, Florida (where both stores competed), and $4.17 in nearby Leesburg (where Office Depot had a monopoly). In the FTC's view, if the two stores combined, they would have had enough power in local markets to raise prices and harm consumers.

The following landmark case illustrates how the courts analyze merger cases.

Landmark Case

UNITED STATES V. WASTE MANAGEMENT, INC.

743 F.2d 976, 1984 U.S. App. LEXIS 18843
United States Court of Appeals for the Second Circuit, 1984

CASE SUMMARY

Facts: Waste Management, Inc. (WMI) acquired Texas Industrial Disposal, Inc. (TIDI). Both companies were in the trash collection business. In Dallas, their combined market share was 48.8 percent. The trial court held that the merger was illegal and ordered WMI to divest itself of TIDI.

Issue: *Did WMI violate the Clayton Act by acquiring TIDI?*

Decision: No, this merger was not an antitrust violation.

Reasoning: A large market share creates a presumption of monopoly power but the parties can rebut that presumption by showing that the merger does not have an anticompetitive impact.

Although WMI's acquisition of TIDI led to a nearly 50 percent market share, WMI nonetheless made a compelling argument that it was not able to exercise monopoly power. In Dallas, competitors could easily enter the waste hauling business. Thus, if WMI raised

---

[12]Under a statutory amendment called Hart-Scott-Rodino, a transaction must be reported if it involves assets of $70.9 million or higher, or if one party has assets or net revenues of $141.8 million or higher and the other party has at least $14.2 million in assets or net revenues. The FTC adjusts these figures annually for inflation.

prices, new firms could enter the market, driving prices down. Indeed, over the previous 10 years, a number of companies had started in the commercial trash collection business. A person could simply acquire a truck, a few containers, drive the truck himself, and operate out of his home. This individual's success would depend on his personal initiative, and whether he had the desire and energy to provide a high level of service.

Because barriers to entry were low, WMI's 48.8 percent market share did not accurately reflect future market power. Thus, the merger did not substantially lessen competition in the relevant market and was not a violation of the Clayton Act.

In short, traditionally market *share* was the most important factor in evaluating mergers. As *Waste Management* indicates, however, courts are now more concerned about market *power*.

Vertical Mergers A vertical merger involves companies at different stages of the production process—for example, when a producer of a final good acquires a supplier, or vice versa. If Staples bought a paper manufacturer, that would be a vertical merger. This type of merger can also be anticompetitive, especially if it reduces entry into a market by locking up an important supplier or a top distributor. However, the Justice Department's guidelines provide that it will challenge vertical mergers only if they are likely to increase entry barriers in a concentrated market.

TYING ARRANGEMENTS

A tying arrangement is an agreement to sell a product on the condition that the buyer also purchases a different (or tied) product. A tying arrangement is illegal under the Clayton Act if:

- The two products are clearly separate,
- The seller requires the buyer to purchase the two products together,
- The seller has significant power in the market for the tying product, and
- The seller is shutting out a significant part of the market for the tied product.

Tying product

In a tying arrangement, the product offered for sale on the condition that another product be purchased as well.

Tied product

In a tying arrangement, the product that a buyer must purchase as the condition for being allowed to buy another product.

Six movie distributors refused to sell individual films to television stations. Instead, they insisted that a station buy an entire package of movies. To obtain classics such as *Treasure of the Sierra Madre* and *Casablanca* (the **tying product**), the station also had to purchase such forgettable films as *Gorilla Man* and *Tugboat Annie Sails Again* (the **tied product**).[13] The distributors engaged in an illegal tying arrangement. These are the questions that the court asked:

- *Are the two products clearly separate?* A left and right shoe are not separate products, and a seller can legally require that they be purchased together. *Gorilla Man*, on the other hand, is a separate product from *Casablanca*.

- *Is the seller requiring the buyer to purchase the two products together?* Yes, that is the whole point of these "package deals."

- *Does the seller have significant power in the market for the tying product?* In this case, the tying products are the classic movies. Since they are copyrighted, no one else can show them without the distributor's permission. The six distributors controlled a great many classic movies. So, yes, they do have significant market power.

[13]*United States v. Loew's Inc.*, 371 U.S. 38, 1962 U.S. LEXIS 2332 (1962).

- *Is the seller shutting out a significant part of the market for the tied product?* In this case, the tied products are the undesirable films like *Tugboat Annie Sails Again*. Television stations forced to take the unwanted films did not buy "B" movies from other distributors. These other distributors were effectively foreclosed from a substantial part of the market.

EXAM Strategy

Question: Two medical supply companies in the San Francisco area provide oxygen to homes of patients. The companies are owned by the doctors who prescribe the oxygen. These doctors make up 60 percent of the lung specialists in the area. Does this arrangement create an antitrust problem?

Strategy: Does the seller have significant power in the market for the tying product (lung patients)? Is it shutting out a significant part of the market for the tied product (oxygen)?

Result: The FTC charged the doctors with an illegal tying arrangement. Because the doctors effectively controlled such a high percentage of the patients needing the service, other oxygen companies could not enter the market.

30-2c The Robinson-Patman Act

Under the Robinson-Patman Act (RPA), it is illegal to charge different prices to different purchasers if:

- The items are the same, and
- The price discrimination lessens competition.

However, it is legal to charge a lower price to a particular buyer if:

- The costs of serving this buyer are lower, or
- The seller is simply meeting competition.

Congress passed the RPA in 1936 to prevent large chains from driving small, local stores out of business. Owners of these Ma and Pa stores complained that the large chains could sell goods cheaper because suppliers charged them lower prices. As a result of the RPA, managers who would otherwise like to develop different pricing strategies for specific customers or regions may hesitate to do so for fear of violating this statute. In reality, however, they have little to fear.

Under the RPA, a plaintiff must prove both that price discrimination occurred and that it lessened competition. It is perfectly permissible, for example, for a supplier to sell at a different price to its Texas and California distributors, or to its health care and educational distributors, so long as the distributors are not in competition with each other.

The RPA also permits price variations that are based on differences in cost. Thus, Kosmo's Kitchen would be perfectly within its legal rights to sell its frozen cheese enchiladas to Giant at a lower price than to Corner Grocery if Kosmo's costs are lower to do so. Giant often buys shipments the size of railroad containers, which cost less to deliver than smaller boxes.

Chapter Conclusion

In this chapter, you have learned about some of the important government regulations that affect business. They can have a profound impact on your business—and on your life.

EXAM REVIEW

1. **SECURITY**   A security is any transaction in which the buyer (1) invests money in a common enterprise and (2) expects to earn a profit predominantly from the efforts of others. (p. 733)

EXAM Strategy

Question: As a pitcher for the Cleveland Indians farm team, Randy Newsom had dreams of glory, but a paycheck that was a nightmare—$8,000 for the season. Newsom came up with a clever solution: He set up a website that offered fans the opportunity to buy a share of his future. For only $20, the buyer was entitled to .002 percent of his career pay. Any problems with this plan?

Strategy: Remember that even orange trees can be securities. (See the "Result" at the end of this section.)

---

2. **THE 1933 ACT**   The 1933 Act requires that, before offering or selling securities in a public offering, the issuer must register the securities with the Securities and Exchange Commission (SEC). (pp. 733–735)

3. **PROSPECTUS**   All investors must receive a copy of the prospectus before purchasing stock in a public offering. (p. 734)

4. **PRIVATE OFFERING**   Under the 1933 Act, an issuer is not required to register securities that are sold in a private offering, but the issuer may have to meet certain disclosure requirements. (pp. 734–735)

5. **REGULATION D**   The most common and important type of private offering is under Regulation D. It permits issuers to sell stock to a small number of investors and for a limited amount of money. (pp. 734–735)

6. **THE 1934 ACT**   The 1934 Act requires public companies to make regular filings with the SEC, including annual reports, quarterly reports, and Form 8-Ks. (pp. 735–737)

7. **REGISTRATION**   Under the 1934 Act, an issuer must register with the SEC if (1) it completes a public offering under the 1933 Act, or (2) its securities are traded on a national exchange (such as the New York Stock Exchange), or (3) it has at least 2,000 shareholders (with a maximum of 500 unaccredited investors) *and* total assets that exceed $10 million. (pp. 735–736)

8. **SARBANES-OXLEY**   Sarbanes-Oxley requires each company's CEO and CFO to certify that the information in the quarterly and annual reports is true. (p. 736)

9. **SECTION 16**   Insiders must report their trades in company stock within two business days. They must turn over to the corporation any profits they make from the purchase and sale or sale and purchase of company securities in a six-month period. (p. 737)

Question: You are the president of Turbocharge, Inc., a publicly traded company. You have been buying stock recently because you think the company's product—a more efficient hybrid engine—is very promising. One day, you show up at work and find your desk in the hallway. The CEO has fired you. In a huff, you sell all your company stock. The only silver lining to your cloud is that you make a large profit. Or is this a silver lining?

Strategy: You can be in violation of Section 16 even if you did not have any inside information when you trade. (See the "Result" at the end of this section.)

10. **INSIDER TRADING:**

- Any corporate insider who *trades* while in possession of nonpublic material information in violation of his fiduciary duty to his company is liable.

- Anyone (1) with material, non-public information, (2) who breaches a fiduciary duty to the *source of the information* (3) by revealing or trading on it, is liable.

- Anyone who *reveals* material nonpublic information in violation of his fiduciary duty is liable if (1) he knows the information was confidential and (2) he expected some personal gain.

- Those who receive tips—*tippees*—are liable for trading on inside information, even if they do not have a fiduciary relationship to the company, so long as (1) they know the information is confidential; (2) they know it came from an insider who was violating his fiduciary duty; and (3) the insider expected some personal gain.

- Rule 14e-3 prohibits trading on inside information during a *tender offer* if the trader knows the information was obtained from either the bidder or the target company.

11. **THE NSMIA**   The National Securities Markets Improvement Act prohibits states from regulating securities offerings that are:

- traded on a national exchange,

- exempt under Rule 506, or

- sold to "qualified purchasers." (p. 740)

12. **BLUE SKY LAWS**   State securities statutes are called blue sky laws. (p. 740)

13. **PRICE-FIXING**   When competitors agree on the prices at which they will buy or sell products, their price-fixing is a *per se* violation of Section 1 of the Sherman Act. (pp. 741–742)

14. **RPM**   Resale price maintenance means the manufacturer sets minimum prices that retailers may charge. It is a rule of reason violation of Section 1 of the Sherman Act. (pp. 742–743)

15. **VERTICAL MAXIMUM PRICE FIXING**   An arrangement whereby a manufacturer sets maximum prices is a rule of reason violation of §1 of the Sherman Act and, therefore, illegal only if it has an anticompetitive effect. (p.743)

16. **MONOPOLIZATION**   Under §2 of the Sherman Act, it is illegal to monopolize or attempt to monopolize a market. *Having* a monopoly is legal unless it is *gained* or *maintained* by using wrongful tactics. To determine if a company is guilty of monopolization, ask three questions:

- What is the market?

- Does the company control the market?

- How did the company acquire or maintain its control? (pp. 743–744)

EXAM Strategy

Question: BAR/BRI was the largest bar review company in the country, with branches in 45 states. Barpassers was a much smaller company located only in Arizona and California. BAR/BRI distributed pamphlets on campuses that falsely suggested Barpassers was near bankruptcy. Enrollments in Barpassers' courses dropped, and the company was forced to postpone plans for expansion. Did Barpassers have an antitrust claim against BAR/BRI?

Strategy: It did not matter if BAR/BRI *had* a monopoly. These "bad acts" could have helped the company *acquire* one. (See the"Result" at the end of this section.)

17. **PREDATORY PRICING**   Predatory pricing occurs when a company lowers its prices below cost to drive competitors out of business. (p. 744)

18. **THE CLAYTON ACT**   The Clayton Act prohibits mergers that are anticompetitive. (pp. 745–747)

19. **TYING ARRANGEMENTS**   A tying arrangement is an agreement to sell a product on the condition that the buyer also purchases a different (or tied) product. Certain tying arrangements are illegal under the Clayton Act. (pp. 746–747)

20. **RPA**   Under the Robinson-Patman Act, it is illegal to charge different prices to different purchasers if the items are the same and the price discrimination lessens competition. (p. 747)

1. Result: Newsom was selling securities: Buyers were investing in him, hoping that they could earn a profit from his efforts. He needed to comply with the provisions of the 1933 Act.

9. Result: You are in violation of §16. Even though you acted without any bad intent, you must turn over all your profits to the company.

16. Result: A jury found that BAR/BRI had violated §2 of the Sherman Act by attempting to create an illegal monopoly. The jury ordered BAR/BRI to pay Barpassers more than $3 million, plus attorney's fees.

MULTIPLE-CHOICE QUESTIONS

1. Under Regulation D, an issuer:

(a) May not sell to 1,000 accredited investors

(b) May not sell to 27 unaccredited investors

(c) Must make disclosure to accredited investors

(d) Must make disclosure to unaccredited investors

(e) May only sell $1 million worth of stock

2. Which of the following statements is *not* true about a public offering?

(a) The issuer files a registration statement with the SEC.

(b) The issuer files a prospectus with the SEC.

(c) Company officers may make public statements about the offering before the stock is sold.

(d) Company officers may make public statements about the offering after the stock is sold.

(e) The issuer may solicit offers for the stock before the effective date.

3. To have an illegal monopoly, a company must: (I) Control the market (II) Maintain its control improperly (III) Have a market share greater than 50 percent

(a) I, II, and III

(b) I and II

(c) II and III

(d) I and III

(e) Neither I, II, nor III

4. Lloyd sold car floor mats to Mercedes dealerships. Then Mercedes began to include floor mats as standard equipment. Mercedes has a 10 percent share of the luxury car market.

(a) Mercedes has created an illegal tying arrangement because floor mats and cars are separate products.

(b) Mercedes has not created an illegal tying arrangement because it does not have significant power in the luxury car market.

(c) Mercedes has not created an illegal tying arrangement because it is not tying the two products together.

(d) Mercedes has created an illegal tying arrangement because it controls the market in floor mats for its cars.

5. Mike is director of sales for his company. He negotiates prices with Paige and Lauren, who work for two of his biggest customers. Paige tells him that she can buy the same product cheaper elsewhere. He cuts the price for her, but not for his other customers. At the same time, he develops a crush on Lauren, so offers to sell her the product at a lower price. In subsequent months, these two customers come to dominate the market. Which statement is correct?

(a) Mike can charge whatever price he wants to any customer.

(b) Mike must charge all his customers the same price.

(c) The price cut to Paige, but not Lauren, is legal.

(d) The price cut to Lauren, but not Paige, is legal.

(e) Mike is not required to charge all his customers the same price, but neither of these price cuts is legal.

ESSAY QUESTIONS

1. Jonah bought 12 paintings from Theo's Art Gallery, at a total cost of $1 million. Theo told Jonah that the paintings were a safe investment that could only go up in value. The gallery permitted any purchaser to trade in a painting for any other artwork the gallery owned. In the trade-in, the purchaser would get credit for the amount of the original painting and then pay the difference if the new painting was worth more. When Jonah's paintings did not increase in value, he sued Theo for a violation of the securities laws. Were these paintings securities?

2. You are in line at the movie theater when you overhear a stranger say: "The FDA has just approved Hernstrom's new painkiller. When the announcement is made on Monday, Hernstrom stock will take off." Have you violated the law if you buy stock in the company before the announcement on Monday?

3. In New York City, 50 bakeries agreed to raise the retail price of bread. All the association's members printed the new price on their bread sleeves. Are the bakeries in violation of the antitrust laws?

4. Suppose that Disney insists that retailers cannot sell DVDs of *Brave* for less than $16.99. The company threatens to cut off any retailers who discount that price. But stores would like to use these movies as a loss leader, selling them at a very low price to lure customers. Is it legal for Disney to cut off retailers who discount prices?

5. Reserve Supply Corp., a cooperative of 379 lumber dealers, charged that Owens-Corning Fiberglass Corp. violated the Robinson-Patman Act by selling at lower prices to Reserve's competitors. Owens-Corning had granted lower prices to a number of Reserve's competitors to meet, but not beat, the prices of other insulation manufacturers. Is Owens-Corning in violation of the Robinson-Patman Act?

DISCUSSION QUESTIONS

1. Federal security laws are based on the assumption that investors are knowledgeable enough to assess the quality of a stock, so long as the issuer provides adequate disclosure. Is this assumption reasonable, or should securities laws provide greater protection to investors?

2. **ETHICS** David Sokol worked at Berkshire Hathaway for legendary investor Warren Buffett, who is renowned not only for his investment skills but also his ethics. Bankers suggested to both Sokol and the CEO of Lubrizol that the company might be a good buy for Berkshire. Sokol then found out that the CEO of Lubrizol planned to ask his board for permission to approach Berkshire about a possible acquisition. Sokol purchased $10 million worth of Lubrizol stock before recommending Lubrizol to Buffett. Sokol mentioned to Buffett "in passing" that he owned shares of Lubrizol. Buffett did not ask any questions about the timing or amount of Sokol's purchases. Sokol made a $3 million profit when Berkshire acquired Lubrizol. Did Sokol violate insider trading laws? Did he behave ethically? What about Buffett?

3. The SEC believes that anyone in possession of nonpublic material information about a company should be required to disclose it before trading on the stock of that enterprise. Instead, the courts have developed a more complex set of rules. Do you agree with the SEC or the courts on this issue?

4. Resale price maintenance used to be a *per se* violation of the antitrust laws, but now it is a rule of reason violation. Will this change in the law lead to higher or lower prices for consumers? Will it provide other benefits for consumers? Do you agree with the Supreme Court's decision?

5. **ETHICS** Clarice, a young woman with a mental disability, brought a malpractice suit against a doctor at the Medical Center. As a result, the Medical Center refused to treat her on a nonemergency basis. Clarice then went to another local clinic, which was later acquired by the Medical Center. Because the new clinic also refused to treat her, Clarice had to seek medical treatment in another town 40 miles away. Has the Medical Center violated the antitrust laws? Was is it ethical to deny treatment to a patient?

CHAPTER 31

CONSUMER PROTECTION

nuttakit/Shutterstock.com; Steve Allen/Brand X Pictures/Jupiter Images

Three women signed up for a lesson at the Arthur Murray dance studio in Washington, D.C. Expecting a session of quiet fun, they instead found themselves in a nightmare of humiliation and coercion:

- "First of all, I did not want the [additional] lesson, and I think it was unpleasant because I had three, maybe four, people, as I say, pressuring me to buy something by a certain time, and I do recall asking that I be let to think, let me think it over, and I was told that the contest would end at 6 o'clock or something to that effect and if I did not sign by a certain time, it would be too late. I think we got under the deadline by maybe a minute or two. If I had been given time to think, I would not have signed that contract."

> I remember I started crying and couldn't stop crying. All I thought of was getting out of there.

- "I tried to say no and get out of it and I got very, very upset because I got frightened at paying out all that money and having nothing to fall back on. I remember I started crying and couldn't stop crying. All I thought of was getting out of there. So finally after I don't know how much time, Mr. Mara said, well, I could sign up for 250 hours, which was half the 500 Club, which would amount to $4,300. So I finally signed it. After that, I tried to raise the money from the bank and found I couldn't get a loan for that amount and I didn't have any savings and I had to get a bank loan to pay for it. That was when I went back and asked him to cancel that contract. But Mr. Mara said that he couldn't cancel it."

- "I did not wish to join the carnival, and while it was only an additional $55, I had no desire to join. [My instructor] asked everyone in the room to sit down in a circle around me and he stood me up in that circle, in the middle of the circle, and said, 'Everybody, I want you to look at this woman here who is too cheap to join the carnival. I just want you to look at a woman like that. Isn't it awful?'"

Because of abuses such as these, the Federal Trade Commission (FTC) ordered the Arthur Murray dance studio to halt its high-pressure sales techniques, limit each contract to no more than $1,500 in dance lessons, and permit all contracts to be canceled within seven days.[1]

31-1 INTRODUCTION

Years ago, consumers typically dealt with merchants they knew well. A dance instructor in a small town would not stay in business long if he tormented his elderly, vulnerable clients. As the population grew and cities expanded, however, merchants became less and less subject to community pressure. The law has supplemented, if not replaced, these informal policing mechanisms. Both Congress and the states have passed statutes that protect consumers from the unscrupulous. But the legal system is generally too slow and expensive to handle small cases. The women who fell into the web of Arthur Murray had neither the wealth nor the energy to sue the studio themselves. To aid consumers such as these, Congress empowered federal agencies to enforce consumer laws.

31-1a Federal Trade Commission

Congress created the FTC in 1915 to regulate business. Although its original focus was on antitrust law, it now regulates a wide range of business activities that affect consumers—everything from advertising to consumer loans to warranties to debt collection practices. The FTC has several options for enforcing the law:

- **Voluntary Compliance.** When the FTC determines that a business has violated the law, it first asks the offender to sign a voluntary compliance affidavit promising to stop the prohibited activity.

- **Administrative Hearings and Appeals.** If the company refuses to stop voluntarily, the FTC takes the case to an administrative law judge (ALJ) within the agency. The violator may settle the case at this point by signing a **consent order.** If the case proceeds to a hearing, the ALJ has the right to issue a **cease and desist order,** commanding the violator to stop the offending activity. The FTC issued a cease and desist order against the Arthur Murray dance studio. A defendant can appeal such an order to the five Commissioners of the FTC, from there to a federal appeals court, and ultimately to the United States Supreme Court. Both the Commissioners and the Fifth Circuit Court of Appeals confirmed the cease and desist order against Arthur Murray. The case never reached the Supreme Court.

- **Penalties.** The FTC can impose a fine for each violation of a voluntary compliance affidavit, a consent order, a cease and desist order, an FTC rule, or a cease and desist order issued against *someone else*. For example, the Arthur Murray studio could be liable for violating an FTC cease and desist order prohibiting high-pressure sales by the Fred Astaire studio. In addition, the FTC can file suit in federal court asking for damages on behalf of an injured consumer if (1) the defendant has violated FTC rules and (2) a reasonable person would have known under the circumstances that the conduct was dishonest or fraudulent.

---

[1]*In re Arthur Murray Studio of Washington, Inc.,* 78 F.T.C. 401, 1971 FTC LEXIS 75 (1971).

31-1b Consumer Financial Protection Bureau

In 2010, Congress created the Consumer Financial Protection Bureau (CFPB) to regulate consumer financial products and services, including mortgages, credit cards, and private student loans. (It does not have the authority to regulate car loans.) Among its goals is to clarify and simplify the terms of credit cards, checking accounts, and mortgage disclosure forms.

Already, the CFPB has proposed rules that would require banks to clearly reveal overdraft fees on checking accounts, announced its intent to closely supervise credit reporting agencies, and obtained a $210 million settlement from Capital One for deceptive marketing of credit cards.

31-2 SALES

Section 5 of the Federal Trade Commission Act (FTC Act) prohibits "unfair and deceptive acts or practices."

31-2a Deceptive Acts or Practices

Many deceptive acts or practices involve advertisements. **Under the FTC Act, an advertisement is deceptive if it contains an important misrepresentation or omission that is likely to mislead a reasonable consumer.** A company advertised that a pain-relief ointment called "Aspercreme" provided "the strong relief of aspirin right where you hurt." From this ad and the name of the product, do you assume that the ointment contains aspirin? Are you a reasonable consumer? Consumers surveyed in a shopping mall believed the product contained aspirin. In fact, it does not. The FTC required the company to disclose that there is no aspirin in Aspercreme.[2]

In another example, Nestlé sold a drink called Boost Kid Essentials, which contained probiotics, good bacteria that aid digestion and fight bad germs. But Nestlé went further than that in its ads, claiming that Boost would prevent children from getting sick or missing school. How could any parent resist that drink? Only Nestlé had no evidence for these claims. In a settlement with the FTC, Nestlé agreed not to make any claims for which it did not have scientific evidence.

In the following case, the court discussed the type of scientific evidence required to support health claims.

FEDERAL TRADE COMMISSION v. DIRECT MARKETING CONCEPTS, INC.

624 F.3d 1; 2010 U.S. App. LEXIS 21743
United States Court of Appeals for the First Circuit, 2010

CASE SUMMARY

Facts: Direct Marketing Concepts, Inc., broadcast an infomercial for Coral Calcium that featured a spokesperson named Robert Barefoot. In the ad, his claims were as bare as his feet. He asserted that these pills could cure virtually all diseases, including heart disease, cancer, lupus, multiple sclerosis, and Parkinson's. To bolster these claims, Barefoot cited unspecified articles from prominent medical journals. During an 18-month period, this infomercial generated $54 million in sales.

---

[2]*In re Thompson Medical Co., Inc.*, 104 F.T.C. 648, 1984 FTC LEXIS 6 (1984).

The FTC filed suit against the company and Barefoot, alleging that the infomercials were deceptive. The trial court granted the FTC's motion for summary judgment, ruling that the infomercials were misleading as a matter of law and, therefore, there was no need for a trial. The defendants appealed.

Issue: *Were the infomercials misleading as a matter of law?*

Decision: Yes, the infomercials were misleading and no trial was needed.

Reasoning: To make claims such as these, the defendants needed to have had some scientific evidence. But medical experts for the FTC testified that there was no evidence that calcium cures any of the diseases listed in the infomercial. Nor have there ever been any articles in serious medical journals that would support such claims.

The only evidence for these infomercials was excerpts from Barefoot's books, his deposition testimony, and some popular science and pseudoscientific articles, which included references to magazines such as *Reader's Digest*. But none of these sources (other than his own writings) supported Barefoot's claims. Therefore, the defendants engaged in deceptive advertising as a matter of law.

In their defense, Barefoot and the company claimed that the statements were nothing but puffery and that the disclaimers in the ads were sufficient to defeat an action for deceptive advertising. However, specific and measurable claims are not puffery. And the only disclaimer was the notice that the ads were paid advertising. Disclaimers are not effective unless they leave consumers with an accurate impression of the product being advertised. That was not the case here.

31-2b Unfair Practices

The FTC Act also prohibits unfair acts or practices. **The Commission considers a practice to be *unfair* if it meets all of the following three tests:**

- *It causes a substantial consumer injury.* This can mean physical or financial injury. A furnace repair company that dismantled home furnaces for "inspection" and then refused to reassemble them until the consumers agreed to buy services or replacement parts had caused a substantial consumer injury.

- *The harm of the injury outweighs any countervailing benefit.* A pharmaceutical company sold a sunburn remedy without conducting adequate tests to ensure that it worked. The expense of these tests would have forced the company to raise the product's price. The company had demonstrated that the product was safe, and there was evidence in the medical literature that the ingredients when used in other products were effective. The FTC determined that, although the company was technically in violation of its rules, the benefit to consumers of a cheaper product more than outweighed the risk of injury to them.

- *The consumer could not reasonably avoid the injury.* The FTC is particularly vigilant in protecting susceptible consumers—such as the elderly or the ill—who are less able to avoid injury. For instance, the Commission looks especially carefully at those who offer a cure for cancer, as the defendants did in the *Direct Marketing* case.

   In addition, the FTC may decide that a practice is unfair simply because it violates public policy, even if it does not meet these three tests. The Commission refused to allow a mailorder company to file collection suits in states far from where the defendants lived because the practice was unfair, whether or not it met the three tests.

31-2c Additional Sales Rules

Bait-and-Switch

FTC rules prohibit bait-and-switch advertisements: A merchant may not advertise a product and then disparage it to consumers in an effort to sell a different (more expensive) item.

Seven websites based in Brooklyn, New York, such as Best Price Photo and 86th Street Photo, engaged in a classic bait-and-switch operation. They advertised products at a much lower price than competitors. That was the **bait**—an alluring offer that sounds almost too good to be true. Of course, it is. Once a customer placed an order, the company tried to sell an upgraded product at a much higher price. That is the **switch**. The real purpose of the advertisement was simply to find customers who were interested in buying. If customers refused the new item, they would be told that the original product was backordered, and the sale was cancelled. If customers agreed to buy the more expensive product, it would turn out to be of poor quality. But the company would not allow returns—either the return fees would be high or the "customer service" department would refuse to answer the phone.

Bait-and-switch
A practice where sellers advertise products that are not generally available but are being used to draw interested parties in so that they will buy other products.

Merchandise Bought by Mail, by Telephone, or Online

Many consumers buy virtually everything—food, clothing, furnishings—online. **The FTC has established the following rules for this type of merchandise:**

- Sellers must ship an item within the time stated or, if no time is given, within 30 days after receipt of the order.

- If a company cannot ship the product when promised, it must send the customer a notice with the new shipping date and an opportunity to cancel. If the new shipping date is within 30 days of the one originally promised and the customer does not cancel, the order is still valid.

- If the company cannot ship by the second shipment date, it must send the customer another notice. This time, however, the company must cancel the order unless the customer returns the notice, indicating that he still wants the item.

Staples, Inc., violated these FTC rules when it told customers that they were viewing "real-time" inventory and that products would be delivered in one day, even on weekends. In fact, the website was not updated in real time, one-day delivery only applied to customers who lived within 20 miles of a Staples store, and it never happened on weekends. The company paid a fine of $850,000 to settle these charges.

Telemarketing

It used to be that telemarketers would practically ruin dinner hour in the United States with their relentless phone calls. But now, FTC rules prohibit telemarketers from calling any telephone number listed on its do-not-call registry. You can register your home and cell phone numbers with the FTC online at **http://www.donotcall.gov** or by telephone at (888) 382-1222. FTC rules also prohibit telemarketers from blocking their names and telephone numbers on Caller ID systems.

What is even more annoying than telemarketing calls from a live person? Robocalls (prerecorded commercial telemarketing calls) from a machine. Such calls are illegal unless the telemarketer obtains written permission from the person being called. You can file a complaint by calling (877) FTC-HELP or by going to the **ftc.gov** website. Exempted from this ban are informational calls (cancellations of a flight or a school day), debt collection calls (as long as they are not trying to sell anything), political messages, charitable outreach, and health care messages.

UNORDERED MERCHANDISE

Under §5 of the FTC Act, anyone who receives unordered merchandise in the mail can treat it as a gift. She can use it, throw it away, or do whatever else she wants with it.

There you are, watching an infomercial for Anushka products, guaranteed to fight that scourge of modern life—cellulite! Rushing to your phone, you place an order. The Anushka cosmetics arrive, but for some odd reason, the cellulite remains. A month later, another bottle arrives, like magic, in the mail. The magic spell is broken, however, when you get your credit card bill and see that, without your authorization, the company has charged you for the new supply of Anushka. Is this a hot new marketing technique? Not exactly. The FTC ordered the company to cease and desist this unfair and deceptive practice. The company improperly billed its customers, said the FTC, and should have notified them that they were free to treat the unauthorized products as a gift, to use or throw out as they wished.[3]

DOOR-TO-DOOR SALES

Consumers at home need special protection from unscrupulous salespeople. In a store, customers can simply walk out, but at home, they may feel trapped. Under the FTC door-to-door rules, **a salesperson is required to notify the buyer that she has the right to cancel the transaction prior to midnight of the third business day thereafter.** This notice must be given both orally and in writing; the actual cancellation must be in writing. The seller must return the buyer's money within 10 days.

EXAM Strategy

Question: Mantra Films sold "Girls Gone Wild" DVDs on the Internet. When customers ordered one DVD, the company would enroll them automatically in a "continuity program" and send them unordered DVDs each month on a "negative-option" basis, charging consumers' credit cards for each DVD until consumers took action to stop the shipments. Is Mantra's marketing plan legal?

Strategy: Review the various sales regulations—more than one is involved in this case.

Result: This marketing plan was deceptive because customers were not told that they would be enrolled in the continuity program. Also, Mantra could not legally bill for the unordered DVDs. Under the unordered merchandise rule, consumers had the right to treat them as gifts.

31-3 CONSUMER CREDIT

Historically, the practice of charging interest on loans was banned by most countries and by three of the most prominent religions—Christianity, Islam, and Judaism. As the European economy developed, however, moneylending became essential. To compromise, governments began to permit interest charges but limited the maximum rate.

Even in modern times, many states limit the maximum interest rate a lender may charge consumers. (Although, usury laws typically do not apply to credit card debt, mortgages, consumer leases, or commercial loans.) The penalty for violating usury statutes varies among the states. Depending upon the jurisdiction, the lender may forfeit (1) the interest above the usury limit, (2) all of the interest, or (3) all of the loan and the interest.

---

[3] *In the Matter of Synchronal Corp.*, 116 F.T.C. 1189, 1993 FTC LEXIS 280 (1993).

31-3a Truth in Lending Act—General Provisions

To avoid the penalties of usury laws, lenders found many creative methods to disguise the real interest rate from the authorities. In the process, they also hid it from borrowers. Many consumers had no idea what interest rate they were really paying. Congress passed the Truth in Lending Act (TILA) with the simple goal of ensuring that when consumers borrowed money, they understood the terms and costs of the loan. Note that TILA does *not* regulate the actual interest rates or the terms of a loan; that responsibility is left to the states. TILA simply requires lenders to *disclose* the terms of a loan in an understandable and complete manner.

APPLICABILITY

TILA applies to a transaction only if all of the following tests are met:

- *It is a consumer loan.* That means a loan to an individual for personal, family, or household purposes, not a loan to a business.

- *The loan has a finance charge or will be repaid in more than four installments.* Sometimes finance charges masquerade as installment plans. Boris can pay for his 3D TV in six monthly installments of $400 each, or he can pay $1,800 cash up front. If he chooses the installment plan, he is effectively paying a finance charge of $600. That is why TILA applies to loans with more than four installments.

- *The loan is for less than $53,000, is secured by a mortgage on real estate, or is a private education loan.*[4]

- *The loan is made by someone in the business of offering credit.* If Boris borrows from his friend to buy the TV, TILA does not apply.

DISCLOSURE

In all loans regulated by TILA:

- *The disclosure must be clear and in meaningful sequence.* For example, a finance company made all the necessary disclosures, but it violated TILA nonetheless because it scattered the required terms throughout the loan document, intermixed with confusing provisions that were not required by TILA.[5] A loan document should not be a scavenger hunt.

- *The lender must disclose the finance charge.* The finance charge is the amount, in dollars, the consumer will pay in interest and fees over the life of the loan. It is important for consumers to know this amount because otherwise, they may not understand the real cost of the loan. Of course, the longer the loan, the higher the finance charge. Someone who borrows $5,000 for 10 years at 10 percent annual interest will pay $500 each year for 10 years, for a total finance charge of $5,000—equal to the principal borrowed. In 30-year mortgages, the finance charge will typically exceed the amount of the principal.

- *The creditor must also disclose the annual percentage rate (APR).* This number is the actual rate of interest the consumer pays on an annual basis. Without this disclosure, it would be easy in a short-term loan to disguise a very high APR because the finance charge is low. Boris borrows $5 for lunch from his employer's credit union. Under the terms of the loan, he must repay $6 the following week. His finance charge is only $1, but his APR is astronomical—20 percent per week—which is over 1,000 percent for a year.

---

[4]This amount adjusts every December 31, to reflect inflation.
[5]*Allen v. Beneficial Fin. Co. of Gary*, 531 F.2d 797, 1976 U.S. App. LEXIS 12935 (7th Cir. 1976).

All TILA loans must meet these three requirements. TILA requires additional disclosure for two types of loans: open-end credit (discussed later in the chapter) and closed-end credit.

Closed-end Credit In a closed-end transaction, the loan is a fixed amount and the borrower knows the payment schedule in advance. Boris enters into a closed-end transaction when he buys a $30,000 car and agrees to make specified monthly payments over five years. Before a consumer enters into a closed-end transaction, the lender must disclose:

- The cash price;
- The total down payment;
- The amount financed;
- An itemized list of all other charges;
- The number, amount, and due dates of payments;
- The total amount of payments;
- Late payment charges;
- Penalties for prepaying the loan; and
- The lender's security interest in the item purchased.

Enforcement The FTC generally has the right to enforce TILA. In addition, consumers who have been injured by any violation (except for the advertising provisions) have the right to file suit.

31-3b Home Loans

MORTGAGE LOANS

TILA prohibits unfair, abusive, or deceptive home mortgage lending practices. In what seems like an exercise in stating the obvious, TILA (as amended by the Dodd-Frank Wall Street Reform and Consumer Protection Act):

- Requires lenders to make a good-faith effort to determine whether a borrower can afford to repay the loan,
- Prohibits lenders from coercing or bribing an appraiser into misstating a home's value, and
- Bans prepayment penalties on adjustable rate mortgages.

TILA also regulates so-called **subprime loans** (also known as **higher-priced mortgage loans).** These are loans that have an above-market interest rate because they involve high-risk borrowers.[6] For subprime loans, a lender:

Subprime loans
A loan that has an above-market interest rate because the borrower is high-risk.

- Must collect property taxes and homeowners insurance for all first mortgages.
- May not make loans that have balloon payments (very large payments at the end).
- May not charge excessive late fees.

---

[6]In the official definition, subprime loans (also referred to as higher-priced loans) are first mortgages that have an APR 1.5 percentage points or more above the average prime offer rate or second mortgages that have an APR 3.5 percentage points or more above that index.

Home Equity Loans

Scam artists sometimes prey upon the elderly, who are vulnerable to pressure, and upon the poor, who may not have access to conventional financing. These swindlers offer home equity loans, secured by a second mortgage, to finance fraudulent repairs. (There are, of course, many legitimate lenders in the home equity business.) The following news report shows scam artists at work:

> Mack and Jacqueline Moon of East Baltimore hired a home improvement contractor to install a dropped ceiling, paneling, and cabinets in the unfinished basement of their rowhouse. The couple was determined not to put a second mortgage on their house, anticipating they would need backup money to pay medical expenses for their 10-year-old daughter, who had lupus. They signed the contract a few days later after a second salesman assured them, "We were able to work it out, and you don't have to worry about a mortgage." The Moons were never given copies of the loan documents nor told of the 17 percent interest rate. A year later, when they tried to use their home's equity to pay medical bills for their daughter, who had since died, they discovered they had given a second mortgage to the lender without knowing it.[7]

In response to such scams, Congress amended TILA to provide additional consumer safeguards for certain home equity installment loans. If a home equity installment loan:

- Has an APR (interest rate) that is more than 10 percentage points higher than Treasury securities, or

- The consumer must pay fees and points at closing that are higher than 8 percent of the total loan amount, then,

- At least three business days before the loan closing, the lender must notify the consumer that (1) he does not have to go through with the loan (even if he has signed the loan agreement) and (2) he could lose his house if he fails to make payments, and

- Loans that are for less than five years may not contain balloon payments (that is, a payment at the end that is more than twice the regular monthly payment).

Rescission

This change in the law came too late to help the Moons, but they found relief in a different TILA provision. Under TILA, consumers have the right to rescind a mortgage for up to three business days after the signing (including Saturdays). However, if the lender does not comply with the disclosure provisions of TILA, the consumer can rescind for up to three *years* from the date of the mortgage.

The Moons were able to rescind the loan because the lender had not made adequate disclosure. This right of rescission does *not* apply to a *first* mortgage used to finance a house purchase or to any refinancing with the consumer's existing lender. (Note that some states have passed, and others are considering, predatory lending laws that more strictly regulate loans with high fees or interest rates.)

The table below summarizes the major provisions of TILA that we have discussed so far.

[7]Lorraine Mirabella, "With Hopes of Improving Their Homes, Many Owners Fall Prey to Loan Scams." Copyright 1994 by Baltimore Sun Company. Reproduced by permission of Baltimore Sun Company via Copyright Clearance Center.

TILA applies to a transaction only if:	It is a consumer loan.
	The loan has a finance charge or will be repaid in more than four installments.
	The loan is for less than $53,000, is secured by a mortgage on real estate, or is a private education loan.
	The loan is made by someone in the business of offering credit.
In all loans regulated by TILA:	The disclosure must be clear and in meaningful sequence.
	The lender must disclose the finance charge and the APR.
For regular mortgage loans:	Lenders must verify the borrowers' ability to repay the loan. Lenders may not coerce or bribe an appraiser into misstating a home's value. Lenders cannot charge prepayment penalties on adjustable rate mortgages.
For subprime mortgage loans:	Loans with balloon payments are prohibited.
	Late fees are limited.

© Cengage Learning

31-3c Credit Cards

Credit and debit cards are extremely important to most consumers, so lately they have come under increased scrutiny from Congress and the regulatory agencies.

DISCLOSURE

TILA establishes disclosure rules for credit cards, which it calls **open-end credit.** This is a credit transaction in which the lender makes a *series* of loans that the consumer can repay at once or in installments. These rules apply to all consumer credit cards, such as VISA or MasterCard, which permit installment payments, and even to those, such as American Express, that require the full balance to be paid each month.

In any advertisement or solicitation, the lender must disclose:

- Credit terms.

- In the case of a *teaser rate*, it must clearly disclose that the rate is introductory, when it expires, and the permanent rate that will replace it.

Before establishing an open-end credit account, the lender must disclose to the consumer:

- When a finance charge will be imposed, and

- How the finance charge will be calculated (for example, whether it will be based on the account balance at the beginning of the billing cycle, the end, or somewhere in between).

In each monthly statement, the lender must disclose:

- The amount owed at the beginning of the billing cycle (the previous balance);

- Amounts and dates of all purchases, credits, and payments;

- Finance charges and late fees;

- The date by which a bill must be paid to avoid these charges; and

- Either the consequences of making the monthly minimum payment or a toll-free number that can be used to obtain such information.

Open-end credit

A lender makes a series of loans that the consumer can repay at once or in installments.

REGULATION OF CREDIT CARD DEBT

Credit Card Act of 2009   During the economic crisis that began in 2008, many consumers struggled to pay their credit card bills. In response, Congress increased oversight of credit card companies by passing the Credit Card Act of 2009. Under the new rules, these companies:

- Cannot increase the interest rate, fees, or charges on balances a consumer has already run up unless she is more than 60 days late in making the minimum payment.

- Must give 45 days' notice before increasing a card's annual percentage rate (APR) or making any other significant change in credit terms (which gives the consumer a chance to pay off the bill ahead of the increase).

- Must re-evaluate any rate increase every six months, and then, if a decrease is warranted, it must occur within 45 days after the evaluation.

- Must give notice of the consumer's right to cancel a card and pay off the debt once the APR is changed.

- Cannot charge interest on fees or on a bill that is paid on time or during a grace period.

- Cannot charge late payment fees of more than $25 (unless one of the consumer's last six payments was late, in which case the fee may be up to $35 or the company can show that its costs justify a higher fee).

- Cannot charge late fees that are greater than the minimum payment owed.

- Cannot charge more than one fee per event, such as a single late payment.

- Must mail the bill at least 21 days before the due date, disclose what the due date is, and set the same due date each month.

- Cannot set due dates on weekends or in the middle of the day. If the payment arrives by 5 p.m. on the day it is due, or if it arrives on the weekend after a Friday due date, it is on time.

- Must warn consumers about the impact of making minimum-only payments.

- Must apply any payments to whichever debt on the card has the highest interest rate (say, a cash advance rather than a new purchase).

- Must offer consumers the right to set a fixed credit limit. Consumers cannot be charged a fee if the company accepts charges above that limit unless the consumer has agreed to the fee.

- Cannot issue credit cards to people under 21 unless the young person has income or the application is co-signed by someone who can afford to pay the bills, such as a parent or spouse. The co-signer must also approve any increase in the credit limit.

Ethics   Each of the rules in the previous section was aimed at eliminating existing practices. Looking at this list, would you judge any of these practices to be unethical? Banks argue that they will have to replace this lost income by charging other fees for, say, maintaining a basic checking account. What Life Principles should bankers apply when they set fees?

LIABILITY

Stolen Cards   Your wallet is missing, and with it your cash, your driver's license, a photo of your dog, a Groupon, and—oh, no!—all your credit cards! It is a disaster, to be sure. But it could have been worse. There was a time when you would have been responsible for every charge a thief rang up. **Now, under TILA, you are liable only for the first $50 in charges the thief makes before you notify the credit card company.** If you call the company before any charges are made, you have no liability at all. But if, by the time you contact the company, a speedy robber has completely furnished her apartment on your card, you are still liable only for $50. Of course, if you carry a wallet full of cards, $50 for each one can add up to a sizable total. If the thief steals just your credit card number, but not the card itself, you are not liable for any unauthorized charges.

Disputes with Merchants   You use your credit card to buy a new tablet computer at ShadyComputers, but when you take it out of the box, it will not even turn on. You have a major $600 problem. But all is not lost. **In the event of a dispute between a customer and a merchant, the credit card company cannot bill the customer if** (1) she makes a good faith effort to resolve the dispute, (2) the dispute is for more than $50, and (3) the merchant is in the same state where she lives or is within 100 miles of her house.

What happens if the merchant and the consumer cannot resolve their dispute, or if the merchant is not in the same state as the consumer? Clearly, credit card companies do not want to be caught in the middle between consumer and merchant. In practice, they now require all merchants to sign a contract specifying that, in the event of a dispute between the merchant and a customer, the credit card company has the right to charge back the merchant's account. If a customer seems to have a reasonable claim against a merchant, the credit card company will typically transfer the credit it has given the merchant back to the customer's account. Of course, the merchant can try to sue the customer for any money owed.

Disputes with the Credit Card Company   The Fair Credit Billing Act (FCBA) provides additional protection for credit card holders (and for holders of so-called **revolving charge accounts**—such as those from stores). Is there anyone in America who has not sometime or other discovered an error in a credit card bill? Before Congress passed the FCBA in 1975, a dispute with a credit card company often deteriorated into an avalanche of threatening form letters that ignored any response from the hapless cardholder.

Under the FCBA:

- If, within 60 days of receipt of a bill, a consumer writes to a credit card company to complain about the bill, the company must acknowledge receipt of the complaint within 30 days.

- Within two billing cycles (but no more than 90 days), the credit card company must investigate the complaint and respond:

  ○ In the case of an error, by correcting the mistake and notifying the consumer

  ○ If there is no error, by writing to the consumer with an explanation

- Whether or not there was a mistake, if the consumer requests it, the credit card company must supply documentary evidence to support its position—for example, copies of the bill signed by the consumer or evidence that the package actually arrived.

- The credit card company cannot try to collect the disputed debt or close or suspend the account until it has responded to the consumer complaint.

- The credit card company cannot report to credit agencies that the consumer has an unpaid bill until 10 days after the response. If the consumer still disputes the charge, the credit card company may report the amount to a credit agency but must disclose that it is disputed.

In the following case, American Express made a big mistake picking on a law professor. The court's opinion was written by Abner J. Mikva, a highly regarded judge on the federal appeals court. He was clearly exasperated by American Express's arguments and used strong language to reprimand the company—and the lower court. Since Judge Mikva had served in Congress, he could speak with some authority about Congress's approach to consumer legislation.

GRAY V. AMERICAN EXPRESS CO.

743 F.2d 10, 240 U.S. App. D.C. 10, 1984 U.S. App. LEXIS 19033
United States Court of Appeals for the District of Columbia Circuit, 1984

CASE SUMMARY

Facts: In December, Oscar Gray used his American Express credit card to buy airline tickets costing $9,312. American Express agreed that Gray could pay for the tickets in 12 monthly installments. In January, Gray paid $3,500 and then in February, an additional $1,156. In March, American Express billed Gray by mistake for the entire remaining balance, which he did not pay. In April, Gray and his wife went out for dinner to celebrate their wedding anniversary. When he tried to pay with his American Express card, the restaurant told him that the credit card company had not only refused to accept the charges for the meal but had instructed the restaurant to confiscate and destroy the card. While still at the restaurant, Gray spoke on the telephone to an American Express employee, who informed him, "Your account is canceled as of now."

Gray wrote to American Express, pointing out the error. For more than a year, the company failed to respond to Gray or to investigate his claim. It then turned the bill over to a collection agency. Gray sued American Express for violating the Fair Credit Billing Act. The trial court granted summary judgment to American Express and dismissed the complaint on the grounds that Gray had waived his rights under the Act.

Issue: *Was American Express liable to Gray for violating the FCBA?*

Decision: Yes, American Express violated the FCBA.

Reasoning: The FCBA provides that, during an on-going dispute between a credit card company and a consumer, the company cannot close the consumer's account simply for failure to pay the disputed amount. American Express argued, however, that the statute did not apply in this case because its standard credit card contract, which Gray signed, gave the company the right to revoke his card at any time without cause and without notice.

It is true that Gray signed this lopsided contract. However, the whole point of consumer law is to even out bargaining power between companies and consumers. To allow a consumer to waive his rights in this way would make the statute meaningless. A court should not assume that Congress has passed a nonsensical statute.

31-3d Debit Cards

LIABILITY

Check cards
Another name for a debit card.

So your wallet is missing, and with it your *debit* card. No problem, right—it is just like a credit card? Wrong. Debit cards look and feel like credit cards, but legally they are a different plastic altogether. Debit cards work like checks (which is why they are also called **check cards**). When you use your debit card, the bank deducts money directly from your account, which means there is no bill to pay at the end of the month (and no interest charges on unpaid bills). That is the good news.

The bad news is that your liability for a stolen debit card is much greater. If you report the loss before anyone uses your card, you are not liable for any unauthorized withdrawals. If you report the theft within two days of discovering it, the bank will make good on all losses above $50. If you wait until after two days, your bank will only replace stolen funds above $500. After 60 days of receipt of your bank statement, all losses are yours: The bank will not repay any stolen funds. If an unauthorized transfer takes place using just your number, not your card, then you are not liable at all as long as you report the loss within 60 days of receiving the bank statement showing the loss. After 60 days, however, you are liable for the full amount.

FEES

Many people like to use debit cards to help keep track of their spending and to avoid paying the interest rates on credit cards. However, traditionally there was a large downside to debit cards: Banks would charge a flat fee of $20 to $30 *each time* cardholders overdrew their bank account, no matter how small the overdraft. A customer could easily be charged $150 in overdraft fees on $50 worth of overdrafts. Suppose that someone makes a $20 overdraft that he repays in two weeks, but in the meantime, he incurs a $27 fee. In that case, he has paid an interest rate of 3,520 percent.

> ## Debit cards look and feel like credit cards, but legally they are a different plastic altogether.

Under new rules, though, banks are not allowed to overdraw an account and charge the fee unless the consumer signs up for an overdraft plan. Of course, this rule means that consumers who do not "opt in" to the overdraft plan will not be allowed to overdraw their account, no matter how desperate they are. (The same rule applies to ATM withdrawals.)

31-3e Credit Reports

ACCURACY OF CREDIT REPORTS

Gossip and rumor can cause great harm. Bad enough when whispered behind one's back, worse yet when placed in files and distributed to potential creditors. Most adults rely on credit—to acquire a house, credit cards, overdraft privileges at the bank, or even obtain a job or rent an apartment. A sullied credit report makes life immensely more difficult. A number of statutes, including the Fair Credit Reporting Act (FCRA), the Fair and Accurate Credit Transactions Act (FACTA), and Dodd-Frank regulate credit reports.

Consumer reporting agencies are businesses that supply consumer reports to third parties. A **consumer report** is any communication about a consumer's creditworthiness, character, general reputation, or lifestyle that is considered as a factor in establishing credit, obtaining insurance, securing a job, acquiring a government license, or for any other *legitimate business* need. **Under the FCRA:**

- A consumer reporting agency cannot report obsolete information. Ordinary credit information is obsolete after seven years, bankruptcies after 10 years. (But if a consumer is applying for more than $150,000 of credit or life insurance, or for a job that pays more than $75,000 a year, then there is no time limit.)

- **Investigative reports** that discuss character, reputation, or lifestyle become obsolete in three *months*. An investigative report cannot be ordered without first informing the consumer.

Consumer reporting agency
A business that supplies consumer reports to third parties.

Investigative reports
Reports that discuss character, reputation, or lifestyle. They become obsolete in three months.

- A consumer reporting agency cannot report medical information without the consumer's permission.

- An employer cannot request a consumer report on any current or potential employee without the employee's permission. An employer cannot take action because of information in the consumer report without first giving the current or potential employee a copy of the report and a description of the employee's rights under this statute.

- Anyone who makes an adverse decision against a consumer because of a credit report must reveal the name and address of the reporting agency that supplied the information. An "adverse decision" includes denying credit or charging higher rates.

- Upon request from a consumer, a reporting agency must disclose all information in his file, the source of the information (except for investigative reports), the name of anyone to whom a report has been sent in the prior year (two years for employment purposes), and the name of anyone who has requested a report in the prior year.

- If a consumer tells an agency that some of the information in his file is incorrect, the agency must both investigate and forward the data to the information provider. The information provider must investigate and report the results to the agency. If the data are inaccurate, the information provider must so notify all national credit agencies. The consumer also has the right to give the agency a short report telling his side of the story. The agency must then include the consumer's statement with any credit reports it supplies and also, at the consumer's request, send the statement to anyone who has received a report within six months (or two years for employment purposes).

EXAM Strategy

Question: Edo applied for insurance with Geico. In calculating his premium, Geico looked at his credit history and his financial circumstances. It did not offer him the best possible premium, but this was because of his current finances, not his credit history. Was this an "adverse decision" under the FCRA, and was Geico required to notify him?

Strategy: Review the requirements of the FCRA. An adverse decision means that Edo was worse off because of a bad credit report.

Result: Edo's premium was based on his *current* situation, not his credit history. Therefore, Geico did not have to notify Edo of an adverse decision because his premium would have been the same even if his credit report had been neutral.

ACCESS TO CREDIT REPORTS AND CREDIT SCORES

Under FACTA, consumers are entitled by law to one free credit report every year from each of the three major reporting agencies: Equifax, Experian, and TransUnion. You can order these reports at https://www.annualcreditreport.com. Consumer advocates recommend that you check your credit reports every year to make sure they are accurate and that no one else has been obtaining credit in your name. If you find any errors, notify the agency in writing and warn it that failing to make corrections is a violation of the law. (Note, though, that many websites with similar names *pretend* to offer a free credit report but instead enroll customers in paid programs to monitor their credit reports. Be sure to go to the right website.)

Although your credit report is valuable information, you do not know how creditors will evaluate it. For that, you need to know your credit score (usually called a FICO score).[8] This number (which ranges between 300 and 850) is based on your credit report and is supposed to predict your ability to pay your bills. However, it is not automatically included as part of your credit report. But now, under Dodd-Frank, anyone who penalizes you because of your score has to give it to you for free, as well as information about how your score compares with others.

IDENTITY THEFT

In identity theft, a fraudster steals the victim's personal information, such as social security number, credit card information, or mother's maiden name, and uses it to obtain credit or goods in the victim's name and otherwise wreak havoc in the victim's life. One goal of FACTA was to reduce identity theft. Therefore, in addition to your right to a free credit report each year, FACTA also created the National Fraud Alert System, which permits consumers who fear they may be the victim of identity theft to place an alert in their credit files, warning financial institutions to investigate carefully before issuing any new credit. It also requires credit bureaus to share information about identity theft.

A fraud alert does not prevent identity theft—culprits may still be able to open a new account or obtain a credit card. Therefore, many states permit a "security freeze," which prohibits any access to a consumer's credit report. Once an account is frozen, no one, including the consumer, can obtain a new line of credit. The downside is that to obtain new credit, the consumer must pay a fee to thaw the account.

Also, under the Gramm-Leach-Bliley Privacy Act of 1999, banks, other financial institutions, and consumer reporting agencies must notify a consumer (1) before disclosing any personal information to a third party or (2) if there has been unauthorized access to the consumer's sensitive personal information.[9] The company cannot disclose private information if the consumer *opts out* (that is, denies permission).

31-3f Debt Collection

Have you ever fallen behind on your car payments? That is hardly a crime—but in the past, debt collectors might have *treated* you as a criminal. They might have threatened to arrest you. Or they might have changed the password on your cell phone account and obtained your cell phone records so that they could pose as a police officer and call your friends, relatives, and past employers to tell them there was an arrest warrant out for you, even if this was not true.

It is bad enough to be hassled over a debt that one does, in fact, owe, but many times, consumers are threatened and harangued for debts that are not legitimate. Indeed, this author has had such an experience: A hospital billed the wrong insurance company and then notified her (at the wrong address) when the insurance company did not pay. When she failed to pay a bill she had never received and did not owe, the hospital turned it over to a collector who, in violation of state law, called her to yell, harangue, and threaten. In the end, all was resolved (she is, after all, a lawyer aware of her rights), but the experience was terribly unpleasant. Typically, companies sell their consumer debts for pennies on the dollar to collection agencies that are not overly scrupulous in ascertaining whether the debt is legitimate. Hoping for a little help from Washington? In a recent year, the FTC received 66,000 complaints about debt collectors, yet it brought enforcement action against only 10 companies.

---

[8]It is called a FICO score because it was developed by the Fair Isaac Corporation.
[9]15 U.S.C. §6801.

The Fair Debt Collection Practices Act (FDCPA) is designed to protect consumers from abusive debt collection efforts. This statute provides that a collector must, within five days of contacting a debtor, send the debtor a written notice containing the amount of the debt, the name of the creditor to whom the debt is owed, and a statement that if the debtor disputes the debt (in writing), the collector will cease all collection efforts until it has sent evidence of the debt. **Also, under the FDCPA, collectors may not:**

- Call or write a debtor who has notified the collector in writing that he wishes no further contact,

- Call or write a debtor who is represented by an attorney,

- Call a debtor before 8:00 a.m. or after 9:00 p.m.,

- Threaten a debtor or use obscene or abusive language,

- Call or visit the debtor at work if the debtor's employer prohibits such contact,

- Imply that they are attorneys or government representatives when they are not, or use a false name,

- Threaten to arrest consumers who do not pay their debts,

- Make other false or deceptive threats—that is, threats that would be illegal if carried out or which the collector has no intention of doing—such as suing the debtor or seizing property,

- Contact acquaintances of the debtor for any reason other than to locate the debtor (and then only once), or

- Tell acquaintances that the consumer is in debt.

Of course, these rules do not prevent the collector from filing suit against the debtor.

In the event of a violation of the FDCPA, the debtor is entitled to damages, court costs, and attorney's fees. The FTC also has authority to enforce the Act.

In the following case, a collection agency skates close to the edge. Does it go too far?

You Be the Judge

BROWN V. CARD SERVICE CENTER

464 F.3d 450; 2006 U.S. App. LEXIS 24579
United States Court of Appeals for the Third Circuit, 2006

Facts: Card Service Center (CSC) sent Elizabeth Brown a collection letter demanding payment of a delinquent credit card balance of $1,874. The letter said:

"You are requested to contact the Recovery Unit of the Card Service Center…to discuss your account. Refusal to cooperate could result in a legal suit being filed for collection of the account.

You now have five (5) days to make arrangements for payment of this account. Failure on your part to cooperate could result in our forwarding this account to our attorney with directions to continue collection efforts."

Brown did not contact CSC within five days, and CSC did nothing other than send her more collection letters.

Brown filed suit, alleging that CSC had violated the FDCPA. She alleged that the letter was deceptive because the company never had any intention of carrying out its threats. The district court granted CSC's motion to dismiss. Brown appealed.

Issue: *Did CSC's letter violate the FDCPA?*

Argument for Brown: CSC's letter indicated that there were two options: a lawsuit or referral to an attorney. Neither happened, and CSC knew when it sent the letter that neither would happen. This letter was an empty threat, plain and simple—exactly the type of behavior the FDCPA prohibits. It is deceptive for CSC to assert that it *could* take an action that it had no intention of taking and has never or very rarely taken before.

It is possible that a sophisticated debtor would realize that CSC had no intention of filing suit against Brown, but the point of the FCDPA is to protect all consumers, even those who are unsophisticated. As Supreme Court Justice Hugo Black observed, our laws "are made to protect the trusting as well as the suspicious."

Argument for CSC: The letter said "could," not "will." It did not imply that legal action was imminent, only that it was possible. This was not a threat, it was a statement of fact—CSC could file suit if it wanted. That was an option available to CSC, whether or not the company elected to pursue it.

31-3g Equal Credit Opportunity Act

The Equal Credit Opportunity Act (ECOA) prohibits any creditor from discriminating against a borrower because of race, color, religion, national origin, sex, marital status, age (as long as the borrower is old enough to enter into a legal contract), or because the borrower is receiving welfare. A lender must respond to a credit application within 30 days. If a lender rejects an application, it must either tell the applicant why or notify him that he has the right to a written explanation of the reasons for this adverse action.

As an example of the types of abuses that the ECOA is designed to prevent, consider the plight of this African American couple. Florence and Joe made an offer to buy a new home at the Meadowood housing development near Tampa. The developer accepted their offer, contingent upon their obtaining a mortgage. When the couple filed an application with Rancho Mortgage and Investment Corp., they were surprised by the hostility of Rancho's loan processor. She requested information they had already supplied and repeatedly questioned them about whether they intended to occupy the house, which was about 80 miles from their jobs. Florence and Joe insisted they wanted to live near their son and daughter-in-law and escape city crime. Rancho turned down their mortgage, refusing to give either an oral or a written explanation. The house was sold to another buyer.

Joe and Florence didn't get mad, they got even. They sued under the ECOA. Rancho was ordered to pay damages to the couple.[10]

As the following case illustrates, the ECOA protects against a broad range of wrongdoing.

TREADWAY v. GATEWAY CHEVROLET OLDSMOBILE INC.

362 F.3d 971; 2004 U.S. App. LEXIS 6325
United States Court of Appeals for the Seventh Circuit, 2004

CASE SUMMARY

Facts: Gateway Chevrolet Oldsmobile, a car dealership, sent an unsolicited letter to Tonja Treadway notifying her that she was "pre-approved" for the financing to purchase a car. Gateway did not provide financing itself; instead, it arranged loans through banks or finance companies.

Treadway called the dealer to say that she was interested in purchasing a used car. With her permission, Gateway obtained her credit report. Based on this report, the dealer determined that Treadway was not eligible for financing. This was not surprising, given that Gateway

---

[10]Robert J. Bruss, "Home Buyers Sue Mortgage Lender for Racial Discrimination," *Tampa Tribune*, November 5, 1994, p. 3.

had purchased Treadway's name from a list of people who had recently filed for bankruptcy.

Instead of applying for a loan on behalf of Treadway, Gateway told her that it had found a bank that would finance her transaction, but only if she purchased a new car and provided a co-signer. Treadway agreed to purchase a new car and came up with Pearlie Smith, her godmother, to serve as a co-signer.

Concerned as it was with customer convenience, Gateway had an agent deliver papers directly to Smith's house to be signed immediately. If Smith had read the papers before she signed them (which of course you would always do), she might have realized that she had committed herself to be the sole purchaser and owner of the car. But she had no idea that she was the owner until she began receiving bills on the car loan. After Treadway made the first payment on behalf of Smith, both women refused to pay more—Smith, because she did not want a new car; Treadway, because the car was not hers. The car was repossessed, but the financing company continued to demand payment.

It turned out that Gateway was running a scam. The dealership would lure desperate prospects off the bankruptcy rolls and into the showroom with promises of financing for a used car, and then sell a new car to their "co-signer" (who was, in fact, the sole signer). Instead of selling a used car to Tonja Treadway, Gateway sold a new car to Pearlie Smith.

Treadway filed suit against Gateway, alleging that it had violated the ECOA by not notifying her that it had rejected her application.

Issue: *Did Gateway violate the ECOA?*

Decision: Yes, Gateway was in violation because it did not tell Treadway that it had rejected her application.

Reasoning: The ECOA requires any lender who rejects a loan application to tell the applicant the reason or notify her that she has the right to a written explanation.

By deciding not to send Treadway's application to *any* lender, Gateway effectively rejected it. But because Gateway did not tell customers that it had done the rejecting, they naturally assumed that a bank or other lender had turned them down. If the dealership's role is secret, it has no accountability—it can discriminate against any and all without getting caught. Gateway could simply throw the credit report of every minority applicant in the "circular file" and none would be the wiser.

31-3h Consumer Leasing Act

If you, like many other consumers, lease a car rather than buy it, you are protected under the Consumer Leasing Act (CLA). The CLA does not apply to any lease for more than $50,000 or to the rental of real property—that is, to house or apartment leases.

Before a lease is signed, a lessor must disclose the following in writing:

- All required payments, including deposits, down payments, taxes, and license fees,

- The number and amount of each monthly payment and how payments are calculated,

- Balloon payments (that is, payments due at the end of the lease),

- Required insurance payments,

- Annual mileage allowance,

- The total amount the consumer will have paid by the end of the lease,

- Available warranties,

- Maintenance requirements and a description of the lessor's wear and use standards,

- Penalties for late payments,

- The consumer's right to purchase the leased property, and at what price,

- The consumer's right to terminate a lease early, and

- Any penalties for early termination.

EXAM Strategy

Question: Clyde goes into a Tesla dealership to investigate buying an electric sports car. He does not look as if he can afford a six-figure purchase, so the sales staff orders a credit report on him. After all, no point in wasting their time. Do they have the right to order a report on Clyde? Which consumer statute applies?

Strategy: The FCRA regulates the issuance of consumer reports. These reports can be used only for a legitimate business need.

Result: A car dealership cannot obtain a consumer report on someone who simply asks general questions about prices and financing or who wants to test-drive a car; nor can the dealer order a report to use in negotiations. However, a dealer has the right to a report that is needed to arrange financing requested by the consumer or to verify a buyer's creditworthiness when he presents a personal check to pay for the vehicle.

31-4 Magnuson-Moss Warranty Act

When Senator Frank E. Moss sponsored the Magnuson-Moss Warranty Act, this is how he explained the need for such a statute:

> [W]arranties have for many years confused, misled, and frequently angered American consumers.... Consumer anger is expected when purchasers of consumer products discover that their warranty may cover a 25-cent part but not the $100 labor charge, or that there is full coverage on a piano so long as it is shipped at the purchaser's expense to the factory.... There is a growing need to generate consumer understanding by clearly and conspicuously disclosing the terms and conditions of the warranty and by telling the consumer what to do if his guaranteed product becomes defective or malfunctions.[11]

The Magnuson-Moss Warranty Act does not require manufacturers or sellers to provide a warranty on their products. **The Act does require any supplier that offers a written warranty on a consumer product that costs more than $15 to disclose the terms of the warranty in simple, understandable language *before the sale*.** This statute applies only to written warranties on goods (not services) sold to consumers. It does cover sales by catalog or on the Internet. Required disclosure includes the following:

- The name and address of the person the consumer should contact to obtain warranty service,
- The parts that are covered and those that are not,
- What services the warrantor will provide, at whose expense, and for what period of time, and
- A statement of what the consumer must do and what expenses he must pay.

Although suppliers are not required to offer a warranty, if they do offer one, they must indicate whether it is *full* or *limited*. Under a **full warranty,** the warrantor must promise to fix a defective product for a reasonable time without charge. If, after a reasonable number of efforts to fix the defective product, it still does not work, the consumer must have the right to a refund or a replacement without charge; but the warrantor is not required to cover damage caused by the consumer's unreasonable use.

---

[11]Quoted in David G. Epstein and Steve H. Nickles, *Consumer Law* (Eagan, Minn.: West, 1981).

31-5 CONSUMER PRODUCT SAFETY

In 1969, the federal government estimated that consumer products caused 30,000 deaths, 110,000 disabling injuries, and 20 million trips to the doctor. Toys were among the worst offenders, injuring 700,000 children a year. Children were cut by Etch-a-Sketch glass panels, choked by Zulu gun darts, and burned by Little Lady toy ovens. Although injured consumers had the right to seek damages under tort law, the goal of the Consumer Product Safety Act of 1972 (CPSA) was to prevent injuries in the first place. This act created the Consumer Product Safety Commission (CPSC) to evaluate consumer products and develop safety standards. Manufacturers must report all potentially hazardous product defects within 24 hours of discovery. The Commission can impose civil and criminal penalties on those who violate its standards. Individuals have the right to sue under the CPSA for damages, including attorney's fees, from anyone who knowingly violates a consumer product safety rule. You can find out about product recalls or file a report on an unsafe product at the Commission's website (**http://www.cpsc.gov**) or at **saferproducts.gov**.

Ethics   Imagine that you are Robert Eckert, chairman and CEO of Mattel, Inc. Your company has sold millions of Jeep Wrangler Power Wheels. These toys are designed for children as young as two years old. You have just been notified that 150 of the cars have caught on fire, while thousands of others have overheated. In some cases, these toys have burned so fiercely that they have caught their garages on fire, endangering all of the home's occupants. You know that under CPSC rules, you are required to report toy defects within 24 hours. You also know that making the required report could have a significant impact on Mattel's profitability. What would you do?

Mattel decided to figure out what the problem was before reporting anything to the CPSC. In the end, it delayed months. Eckert was quoted as saying that the law was unreasonable and the company would not follow it.[12]

Is Mattel's stance ethical? What would Mill and Kant think? What Life Principle is the CEO applying?

Chapter Conclusion

Virtually no one will go through life without reading an advertisement, ordering online, borrowing money, acquiring a credit report, or using a consumer product. It is important to know your rights.

EXAM REVIEW

1. **UNFAIR PRACTICES**   The Federal Trade Commission (FTC) prohibits "unfair and deceptive acts or practices." A practice is unfair if it violates public policy or if it meets the following three tests:

---

[12]Based on an article by Nicholas Casey and Andy Pasztor, "Safety Agency, Mattel Clash Over Disclosures," *The Wall Street Journal*, September 4, 2007, p. A1.

- It causes a substantial consumer injury.

- The harm of the injury outweighs any countervailing benefit.

- The consumer could not reasonably avoid the injury. (p. 757)

2. **DECEPTIVE ADVERTISEMENTS**   The FTC considers an advertisement to be deceptive if it contains an important misrepresentation or omission that is likely to mislead a reasonable consumer. (pp. 756–757)

3. **BAIT-AND-SWITCH**   FTC rules prohibit bait-and-switch advertisements. A merchant may not advertise a product and then disparage it to consumers in an effort to sell a different item. (p. 758)

4. **MERCHANDISE BOUGHT BY MAIL, BY TELEPHONE, OR ONLINE**   Under FTC rules for this type of merchandise, sellers must ship an item within the time stated or, if no time is given, within 30 days after receipt of the order. (p. 758)

5. **DO-NOT-CALL REGISTRY**   The FTC prohibits telemarketers from calling telephone numbers listed on its do-not-call registry. Telemarketers may not make robocalls unless they have obtained written permission from the person being called. (p. 758)

6. **UNORDERED MERCHANDISE**   Consumers may keep as a gift any unordered merchandise that they receive in the mail. (p. 759)

7. **DOOR-TO-DOOR RULES**   Under the FTC door-to-door rules, a salesperson is required to notify the buyer that she has the right to cancel the transaction prior to midnight of the third business day thereafter. (p. 759)

8. **TILA DISCLOSURE**   In all loans regulated by the Truth in Lending Act, the disclosure must be clear and in meaningful sequence. The lender must disclose the finance charge and the annual percentage rate. (pp. 760–761)

9. **MORTGAGES**   Lenders must make a good faith effort to determine whether a borrower can afford to repay the loan. They may not coerce or bribe an appraiser into misstating a home's value. Nor may they charge prepayment penalties on adjustable rate mortgages. (p. 761)

10. **SUBPRIME LOANS**   For subprime loans, a lender:

- May not make loans with balloon payments.

- Is limited in the late fees it may charge. (p. 761)

11. **HOME EQUITY LOANS**   In the case of a high-rate home equity loan, the lender must notify the consumer at least three business days before the closing that he does not have to go through with the loan (even if he has signed the loan agreement) and (2) he could lose his house if he fails to make payments. If the duration of a high-rate home equity loan is less than five years, it may not contain balloon payments. (p. 762)

12. **RESCINDING A MORTGAGE**   Under TILA, consumers have the right to rescind a mortgage (other than a first mortgage) for three business days after the signing if the lender is not the same as for the first mortgage. If the lender does not comply with the disclosure provisions of TILA, the consumer may rescind for up to three years from the date of the mortgage. (pp. 762–763)

EXAM Strategy

Question: In August, Ethel went to First American Mortgage and Loan Association of Virginia (the Bank) to sign a second mortgage on her home. Her first mortgage was with a different bank. She left the closing without a copy of the required TILA disclosure forms. Ethel defaulted on her loan payments, and, the following May, the Bank began foreclosure proceedings on her house. In June, she notified the Bank that she wished to rescind the loan. Does Ethel have a right to rescind the loan 10 months after it was made?

Strategy: In questions about mortgages, it is important to notice if the question involves a first or subsequent mortgage because the rules are different. Also, it matters whether the bank is the same for both mortgages. (See the "Result" at the end of this section.)

13. **CREDIT V. DEBIT CARDS**   Under TILA, a *credit* card holder is liable only for the first $50 in unauthorized charges made before the credit card company is notified that the card was stolen. If, however, you wait more than two days to report the loss of a *debit* card, your bank will reimburse you only for losses in excess of $500. If you fail to report the lost debit card within 60 days of receipt of your bank statement, the bank is not liable at all. (pp. 765–767)

14. **CREDIT CARD DEBT**   Credit card companies cannot increase the interest rate, fees, or charges on balances unless the consumer is more than 60 days late in making the minimum payment, nor can they charge interest or fees on a bill that is paid on time or during the grace period. Credit card companies must give 45 days' notice before increasing a card's APR. (p. 764)

15. **CREDIT CARD DISPUTE**   In the event of a dispute between a customer and a merchant, the credit card company cannot bill the customer if:

    • She makes a good faith effort to resolve the dispute,

    • The dispute is for more than $50, and

    • The merchant is in the same state where she lives or is within 100 miles of her house. (p. 765)

16. **MORE CREDIT CARD DISPUTES**   Under the Fair Credit Billing Act, a credit card company must promptly investigate and respond to any consumer complaints about a credit card bill. (pp. 765–766)

17. **DEBIT CARD FEES**   Banks may not overdraw an account and charge an overdraft fee unless the consumer signs up for an overdraft plan. (p. 767)

18. **CREDIT REPORTS**   Under the Fair Credit Reporting Act:

- A consumer report can be used only for a legitimate business need,

- A consumer reporting agency cannot report obsolete information,

- An employer cannot request a consumer report on any current or potential employee without the employee's permission, and

- Anyone who makes an adverse decision against a consumer because of a credit report must reveal the name and address of the reporting agency that supplied the negative information. (pp. 767–769)

19. **ACCESS TO CREDIT REPORTS AND CREDIT SCORES**   The Fair and Accurate Credit Transactions Act permits consumers to obtain one free credit report every year from each of the three major reporting agencies. Also, anyone who penalizes a consumer because of her credit score must give it to her at no charge. (pp. 768–769)

20. **DEBT COLLECTION**   Under the Fair Debt Collection Practices Act, a debt collector may not harass or abuse debtors. (pp. 769–771)

21. **ECOA**   The Equal Credit Opportunity Act prohibits any creditor from discriminating against a borrower on the basis of race, color, religion, national origin, sex, marital status, age, or because the borrower is receiving welfare. (pp. 771–772)

EXAM Strategy

Question: Kathleen, a single woman, applied for an Exxon credit card. Exxon rejected her application without giving any specific reason and without providing the name of the credit bureau it had used. When Kathleen asked for a reason for the rejection, she was told that the credit bureau did not have enough information about her to establish creditworthiness. In fact, Exxon had denied her credit application because she did not have a major credit card or a savings account, she had been employed for only one year, and she had no dependents. Did Exxon violate the law?

Strategy: Exxon violated two laws. Review the statutes in the "Consumer Credit" section of the chapter. (See the "Result" at the end of this section.)

22. **CONSUMER LEASING ACT**   This statute applies to any lease up to $50,000 (except for real property). The lessor is required to make certain disclosures before the lease is signed. (p. 772)

23. **WARRANTIES**   The Magnuson-Moss Warranty Act requires any supplier that offers a written warranty on a consumer product costing more than $15 to disclose the terms of the warranty in simple and readily understandable language before the sale. (p. 773)

24. **CONSUMER PRODUCT SAFETY**   The Consumer Product Safety Commission evaluates consumer products and develops safety standards. (p. 774)

EXAM Strategy

Question: Joel was two years old and his brother, Joshua, was three when their father left both children asleep in the rear seat of his automobile while visiting a friend. A cigarette lighter was on the dashboard of the car. After awaking, Joshua began playing with the lighter and set fire to Joel's diaper. Do the parents have a claim against the manufacturer of the lighter under the Consumer Product Safety Act?

Strategy: The CPSA regulates unsafe products. Was the cigarette lighter unsafe? (See the "Result" at the end of this section.)

12. Result: Ethel entered into a second mortgage that was not from the same bank as her first mortgage. Therefore, under TILA, Ethel had an automatic right to rescind for three business days. However, because the lender did not give the required forms to her at the closing, she could rescind for up to three years.

21. Result: The court held that Exxon violated both the Fair Credit Reporting Act (FCRA) and the Equal Credit Opportunity Act (ECOA). The FCRA requires Exxon to tell Kathleen the name of the credit bureau that it used. Under the ECOA, Exxon was required to tell Kathleen the real reasons for the credit denial.

24. Result: The court held that the plaintiff did not have a claim because there was no evidence that the manufacturer had knowingly violated a consumer product safety rule.

MULTIPLE-CHOICE QUESTIONS

1. Dell advertised that a computer came with particular software. In fact, the software was not available for several months. Instead, Dell sent customers a coupon for the software "when available." What did Dell do wrong?

I.   Failed to offer buyers the opportunity to cancel their orders

II. Did not automatically cancel the orders

III. Did not ship the software within 30 days

(a) I and II
(b) I, II, and III
(c) I and III
(d) II and III

2.

> GET ENOUGH BROADLOOM TO CARPET ANY AREA OF YOUR
> HOME OR APARTMENT UP TO 150 SQUARE FEET CUT,
> MEASURED, AND READY FOR INSTALLATION FOR ONLY $77.
> GET 100% DUPONT CONTINUOUS FILAMENT NYLON PILE
> BROADLOOM.
> CALL COLLECT

When customers called the number provided, New Rapids Carpet Center, Inc., sent salespeople to visit them at home to sell them carpet that was not as advertised—it was not continuous filament nylon pile broadloom, and the price was not $77. What set of rules has New Rapids violated?

(a) Unordered merchandise

(b) Consumer Product Safety Act

(c) Bait-and-switch

(d) Fair Credit Reporting Act

3. Which of the following laws set limits on interest rates?

(a) State usury laws

(b) TILA and state usury laws

(c) TILA

(d) None; there are no limits on interest rates

4. Companies must obtain permission from a consumer before charging for overdrafts on:

(a) debit cards

(b) credit cards

(c) neither

(d) both

5. You notice a charge on your credit card bill of $149.99 for a kayak. This seems very strange to you because you have not purchased a kayak. What do you need to do to avoid having to pay this charge?

(a) Call the store

(b) Call the credit card company

(c) Write the store

(d) Write the credit card company

Essay Questions

1. YOU BE THE JUDGE WRITING PROBLEM Process cheese food slices must contain at least 51 percent natural cheese. Imitation cheese slices, by contrast, contain little or no natural cheese and consist primarily of water, vegetable oil, flavoring, and fortifying agents. Kraft, Inc., makes Kraft Singles, which are individually wrapped process cheese food slices. When Kraft began losing market share to imitation slices that were advertised as both less expensive and equally nutritious as Singles, Kraft responded with a series of advertisements informing consumers that Kraft Singles cost more than imitation slices because they are made from 5 ounces of milk. Kraft does use 5 ounces of milk in making each Kraft Single, but 30 percent of the calcium contained in the milk is lost during processing. Imitation slices contain the same amount of calcium as Kraft Singles. Are the Kraft advertisements deceptive?

Argument for Kraft: This statement is completely true—Kraft does use 5 ounces of milk in each Kraft Single. The FTC is assuming that the only value of milk is the calcium. In fact, people might prefer having milk rather than vegetable oil, regardless of the calcium. **Argument for the FTC:** It is deceptive to advertise more milk if the calcium is the same after all the processing.

2. Josephine was a 60-year-old widow who suffered from high blood pressure and epilepsy. A bill collector from Collections Accounts Terminal, Inc., called her and demanded that she pay $56 she owed to Cabrini Hospital. She told him that Medicare was supposed to pay the bill. Shortly thereafter, Josephine received a letter from Collections that stated:

> You have shown that you are unwilling to work out a friendly settlement with us to clear the above debt. Our field investigator has now been instructed to make an investigation in your neighborhood and to personally call on your employer. The immediate payment of the full amount, or a personal visit to this office, will spare you this embarrassment.

Has Collections violated the law?

3. Thomas worked at a Sherwin-Williams paint store that James managed. Thomas and James had a falling out when, according to Thomas, "a relationship began to bloom between Thomas and one of the young female employees, the one James was obsessed with." After Thomas quit, James claimed that Thomas owed the store $121. Sherwin-Williams reported this information to the Chilton credit reporting agency. Thomas sent a letter to Chilton disputing the accuracy of the Sherwin-Williams charges. Chilton contacted James who confirmed that Thomas still owed the money. Chilton failed to note in Thomas's file that a dispute was pending. Thereafter, two of Thomas's requests for credit cards were denied. Have James and Chilton violated the Fair Credit Reporting Act?

4. In October, Renie Guimond discovered that her credit report at TransUnion incorrectly stated that she was married, used the name "Ruth Guimond," and had a credit card from Saks Fifth Avenue. After she reported the errors, TransUnion wrote her in November to say that it had removed this information. However, in March, TransUnion again published the erroneous information. The following October, TransUnion finally removed the incorrect information from her file. Guimond was never denied credit because of these mistakes. Is TransUnion liable for violating the Fair Credit Reporting Act?

5. Thomas Waldock purchased a used BMW 320i from Universal Motors, Inc. It was warranted "to be free of defects in materials or workmanship for a period of three years or 36,000 miles, whichever occurs first." Within the warranty period, the car's engine failed, and upon examination, it was found to be extensively damaged. Universal denied warranty coverage because it concluded that Waldock damaged the engine by over-revving it. Waldock vehemently disputed BMW's contention. He claimed that, while the car was being driven at a low speed, the engine emitted a gear-crunching noise, ceased operation, and would not restart. Is Universal in violation of the law?

6. **ETHICS** After TNT Motor Express hired Joseph Bruce Drury as a truck driver, it ordered a background check from Robert Arden & Associates. TNT provided Drury's social security number and date of birth, but not his middle name. Arden discovered that a Joseph *Thomas* Drury, who coincidentally had the same birth date as Joseph *Bruce* Drury, had served a prison sentence for drunk driving. Not knowing that it had the wrong Drury, Arden reported this information to TNT, which promptly fired Drury. When he asked why, the TNT executive refused to tell him. Did TNT violate the law? Whether or not TNT was in violation, did its executives behave ethically? Who would have been harmed or helped if TNT managers had informed Drury of the Arden report?

DISCUSSION QUESTIONS

1. Should employers use credit checks as part of the hiring process? On one hand, each year employers suffer losses of $55 million because of workplace violence, while retailers lose $30 *billion* a year from employee theft. Those who commit fraud are often living above their means. On the other hand, there is no evidence that workers with poor credit reports are more likely to be violent, steal from their employers, or quit their jobs. And refusing to hire someone with a low credit score may simply be kicking him when he is down. What would you do if you were an employer?

2. The fee on a debit card overdraft can be as high or higher than the amount taken out. Instead of overdrawing their accounts, consumers would be much better off either not spending the money, using a credit card, or paying cash. Typically, the people most likely to sign up for overdraft "protection" are those who can least afford it— they have maxed out their credit cards and used up any home equity. Is it ethical for a bank to offer an overdraft plan?

3. Look at the section entitled "Credit Card Act of 2009" on p. 764. All of these activities used to be legal. Which ones were unethical?

4. Go to youtube.com and search for "free credit reports." Watch the advertisements for **freecreditreport.com**. Although the characters repeat the word, "free" over and over, in fact the reports are not free unless the consumer signs up for the paid credit monitoring service. At the end of the ad, a voice quickly says, "Offer applies with enrollment in Triple Advantage." Are these ads deceptive under FTC rules? Are they ethical according to your Life Principles?

5. Advertisements for Listerine mouthwash claimed that it was as effective as flossing in preventing tooth plaque and gum disease. This statement was true, but only if the flossing was done incorrectly. In fact, many consumers do floss incorrectly. However, if flossing is done right, it is more effective against plaque and gum disease than Listerine. Is this advertisement deceptive?

CHAPTER 32

CYBERLAW

nuttakit/Shutterstock.com; Steve Allen/Brand X Pictures/Jupiter Images

Garrett always said that his computer was his best friend. He was online all the time, g-chatting with his friends, listening to music, doing research for his courses, and, okay, maybe playing a few games now and again. Occasionally, the computer could be annoying. It would crash once in a while, trashing part of a paper before he saved it. And there was the time that a copy of an email he sent Lizzie complaining about Caroline somehow ended up in Caroline's inbox. He was pretty irritated when the White Sox tickets he bought in an online auction turned out to be for a Little League team. And he was tired of all the spam advertising pornographic websites. But these things happen and, despite the petty annoyances, his computer was an important part of his life.

Then one day, Garrett received a panicked text message from a teammate on his college wrestling squad telling him to click on a certain website pronto to see someone they knew. Garrett eagerly clicked on the website and discovered, to his horror, that he was featured—in the nude. The website was selling DVDs showing him and other members of the wrestling team in the locker room in various states of undress. Other DVDs, from other locker and shower rooms, were for sale, too, showing football players and wrestlers from dozens of universities. The DVDs had titles like "Straight Off the Mat" and "Voyeur Time." No longer trusting technology, Garrett pulled on his running shoes and dashed over to the office of his business law professor for help figuring out what his rights were.

> **Garrett eagerly clicked on the website and discovered, to his horror, that he was featured—in the nude.**

Computers and the Internet—cyberspace—together comprise one of the great technological developments of modern times.[1] And its importance and impact continue to grow. Beginning in December 2010, the world watched the "Arab Spring"—popular uprisings throughout the Middle East that brought down governments in Tunisia, Egypt, and Libya, and challenged leaders throughout the area. These movements were organized and fueled by the Internet. In response, threatened governments fought back by trying to limit access to the Internet generally and social media sites in particular. In Syria, police demanded the Facebook passwords of suspected protest organizers. Meanwhile, in England, a different type of protest challenged a court ruling. A married soccer player obtained an injunction prohibiting newspapers from revealing his alleged affair, and even the existence of the injunction. Within days, Ryan Giggs and his affair was one of the top topics on Twitter.

Cyberspace is a disruptive technology which can both fight repression and undermine legitimate laws. It has brought change to every aspect of our lives—how we make friends, buy things, obtain news, campaign for election, start revolutions, challenge the status quo.

Inevitably, new technologies create the need for new law. In the thirteenth century, England was one of the first countries to develop passable roads. Like the Internet, these roadways greatly enhanced communication, creating social and business opportunities, but also enabled new crimes. Good roads meant that bad guys could sneak out of town without paying their bills. Parliament responded with laws to facilitate the collection of out-of-town debts. Similarly, while the Internet has opened up enormous opportunities in both our business and personal lives, it has also created the need for new laws, both to pave the way for these opportunities and to limit their dangers.

The process of lawmaking never stops. Judges sit and legislatures meet—all in an effort to create better rules and a better society. However, in an established area of law, such as contracts, the basic structure changes little. Cyberlaw is different because it is still very much in its infancy. Not only are new laws being created almost daily, but whole areas of regulation are, as yet, unpaved roads. Although the process of rule making has progressed well, much debate still surrounds cyberspace law, and much work remains to be done. This chapter focuses on the existing rules and also discusses the areas of regulation that are still incomplete and being debated.

Cyberlaw affects many areas of our lives. This chapter, however, deals with issues that are unique to the cyberworld, such as online privacy, spam, and cybercrimes.

Before beginning the chapter in earnest, let's return briefly to Garrett, the wrestler. What recourse does Garrett have for his Internet injuries? The nude video incident happened at Illinois State University and seven other colleges. Approximately 30 athletes filed suit against GTE and PSINet for selling the films online, but the two web hosts were found not to be liable under the Communications Decency Act because they had not produced the films themselves—they had simply permitted the sale of someone else's content. What about Garrett's other computer injuries? Lizzie was not being a good friend, but it was perfectly legal for her to forward Garrett's email to Caroline. The seller of the White Sox tickets violated both federal and state fraud statutes. The federal CAN-SPAM Act regulates spam—unsolicited commercial email—but a lawsuit is a slow and awkward tool for killing such a flourishing weed.

---

[1]The term "Internet" means "the international computer network of both Federal and non-Federal interoperable packet switched data networks," according to 47 U.S. §230 (f)(1). It began in the 1960s as a project to link military contractors and universities. Now, it is a giant network that connects smaller groups of linked computer networks. The World Wide Web was created in 1991 by Tim Berners-Lee as a subnetwork of the Internet. It is a decentralized collection of documents containing text, pictures, and sound. Users can move from document to document using links that form a "web" of information.

32-1 PRIVACY

The Internet has vastly increased our ability to communicate quickly and widely. In the pre-Internet era, setting up a meeting required days of phone tag. Intraoffice memos were typed, photocopied, and then hand-delivered by messengers. Catalog orders were sent via regular mail, a slow, inefficient, and costly method. As wonderful as cybercommunication can be, though, it is not without its dangers.

32-1a Tracking Tools

Consumers enter the most personal data—credit card numbers, bank account information, lists of friends, medical data, product preferences—on the Internet. Because our interactions with a computer often take place in isolation (sitting alone at home, at work, or in a cafe), the experience *feels* private. It is anything but. In effect, the Internet provides a very large window through which the government, employers, businesses, and criminals can find out more than they should about you and your money, habits, beliefs, and health. Even email has its dangers: Who has not been embarrassed by an email that ended up in the wrong mailbox?

The most troubling aspect of these Internet privacy issues is that consumers are often unaware of who has access to what personal information, how it is being used, and with what consequences. As a result, a privacy discussion seems abstract. But the reality is that the Internet provides many opportunities for good guys and bad to secretly gather information for their own purposes, both good and bad.

It used to be that marketers geared their ads to specific websites, but now they target individual consumers. The 50 most popular websites in America (which account for 40 percent of all page views) install thousands of tracking tools on the computers of people who visit their sites. Called "behavioral targeting," these tools not only collect data on *all* the websites someone visits, they also record keystrokes to keep track of whatever information the consumer has entered online. These tools are placed on computers without notice or warning to the consumer. In a recent report, Dictionary.com was the worst offender, placing over 200 tools on the computers of unaware visitors. On the other hand, Wikipedia.org is one highly popular site that installs none.[2] To take another example of privacy issues, as part of its Street View program that provides photographs of streets around the world, Google (accidentally, it says) captured data from home Wi-Fi networks.

Once the trackers have gathered financial, health, and other personal information, they sell it to data-gathering companies that build profiles which, while technically anonymous, can include so much personal information that it is possible to identify individuals. How many times have you revealed your ZIP code, birth date, and gender on the Internet? Those three pieces of information are usually enough to identify an individual's name and address. The profiles are then sold to advertisers on stock market–like exchanges. Now that cell phones have GPS tracking devices and readers use electronic books, where you have been and what you are reading are also available. In a recent Dilbert cartoon, the boss refers to a smart phone as an "employee locator device."

Suppose, for example, that you look online at puppies in shelters. You may find that the next time you go to your gmail account, there will be dog ads. One company markets a databank with the names of 150 million registered voters. Anyone can buy a list of voters that is sliced and diced however they want (say, Republicans between the ages of 45 and 60 with Hispanic surnames and incomes greater than $50,000 who live in Kansas City). Puppy ads seem harmless, or even beneficial, but if marketers can put together a databank of Hispanic Republican voters, they can also find out who has visited a website for recovering

---

[2]Julia Angwin and Tom McGinty, "Sites Feed Personal Details to New Tracking Industry," *The Wall Street Journal*, July 30, 2010.

alcoholics or unrecovered gamblers or Nazi sympathizers. Or who uses antidepressants or reads socialist writings. Do you want all this information available to anyone who is willing to pay for it? What if employers buy information about job candidates so that they can refuse to hire someone with health issues?

In short, Internet users are inadvertently providing intensely personal data to unknown people for unknown uses. The problem is likely to grow. The newest web language, HTML5, permits tracking software to store larger amounts of data. Also, software developers have created tracking tools that are harder to delete. Every browser uses a different deletion system, which makes life even more complicated for the concerned consumer.

Many commentators argue that without significant changes in the law, our privacy will be obliterated. But, so far, consumers have been relatively unconcerned. They tend to be unaware of the dangers, and they appreciate the benefits—for example, tracking software can be used to store passwords so that when you log on to Amazon.com, the site recognizes you and lets you in without your having to enter your email address and password. Consumers can also benefit from targeted advertisements—long-distance runners may like seeing ads for running shoes, not cigarettes. Industry representatives argue that without the revenue from ads, many Internet sites would not be free to consumers. As a result, privacy on the Internet is very much like the weather—everyone talks about it, but (so far) no one has done much about it. But this you should believe: Highly personal information about *you* has been collected without your knowledge or approval.

32-1b Regulation of Online Privacy

There is a wide range of possible sources of laws and regulations to protect online privacy, but they are in an early, and relatively ineffective, stage of development.

SELF-REGULATION

In an effort to forestall government regulation, several marketing trade groups issued their own report, "Self-Regulatory Principles for Online Behavioral Advertising." These principles require websites that use tracking tools to provide notice of data collection that is "clear, prominent, and conveniently located." In addition, the websites must permit consumers to opt out of tracking with only a few clicks. However, we have been unable to find a single website that complies with these principles, even among the companies that sponsored the report.

Members of Congress have filed many bills to regulate online privacy. So intense, however, is the debate between industry and consumer advocates that no consensus—and little law—has emerged. There is, however, some applicable government regulation.

THE FIRST AMENDMENT

How would you like to be called a cockroach, mega-scumbag, and crook in front of thousands of people? Or be accused of having a fake medical degree, fat thighs, and poor hygiene? What would you think if your ex-wife told 55,000 people that your insensitivity made her so sick she was throwing up every day? **The First Amendment to the Constitution protects free speech,** and that includes these postings—and worse—which have appeared on Internet message boards and blogs. As upsetting as they may be, they are protected as free speech under the First Amendment so long as the poster is not violating some other law. In these cases, the plaintiffs argued that the statements were defamatory but the courts disagreed, ruling that they were simply opinions.

Explaining its ruling in one of the cases, the court said:

> Users [of the Internet] are able to engage freely in informal debate and criticism, leading many to substitute gossip for accurate reporting and often to adopt a provocative, even combative tone. Hyperbole and exaggeration are common, and "venting" is at least as common as careful and

considered argumentation. Some commentators have likened cyberspace to a frontier society free from the conventions and constraints that limit discourse in the real world.

It hardly need be said that this [court does not] condone [these] rude and childish posts; indeed, [the] intemperate, insulting, and often disgusting remarks understandably offended plaintiff and possibly many other readers. Nevertheless, the fact that society may find speech offensive is not a sufficient reason for suppressing it. Indeed, if it is the speaker's opinion that gives offense, that consequence is a reason for according it constitutional protection.[3]

In the following case, a teacher received hostile emails. Should the First Amendment protect the anonymous person who sent them?

You Be the Judge

JUZWIAK V. JOHN/JANE DOE

415 N.J. Super. 442; 2 A.3d 428;
2010 N.J. Super. LEXIS 154
Superior Court of New Jersey, Appellate Division, 2010

Facts: Juzwiak was a tenured teacher at Hightstown High School in New Jersey. He received three emails from someone who signed himself "Josh," with the address, "Josh Hartnett jharthat@yahoo.com." The teacher did not know anyone of that name. These emails said:

1. Subject line: "Hopefully you will be gone permanently"

   Text: "We are all praying for that. Josh"

2. Subject line: "I hear Friday is 'D' day for you"

   Text: "I certainly hope so. You don't deserve to be allowed to teach anymore. Not just in Hightstown but anywhere. If Hightstown bids you farewell I will make it my lifes [sic] work to ensure that wherever you look for work they know what you have done."

3. Subject line: "Mr. Juzwiak in the Hightstown/East Windsor School System."

   Text: It has been brought to my attention and I am sure many of you know that Mr. J is reapplying for his position as a teacher in this town. It has further been pointed out that certain people are soliciting supporters for him. This is tantamount to supporting the devil himself. I am not asking anyone to speak out against Mr. J but I urge you to then be silent as we can not continue to allow the children of this school system nor the parents to be subjected to his evil ways. Thank you. Josh

It seems that this third email was sent to other people, but it was not clear to whom.

Because Juzwiak did not know who "Josh" was, he filed a complaint against "John/Jane Doe," seeking damages for intentional infliction of emotional distress. As part of the lawsuit, he served a subpoena on Yahoo!, asking it to reveal "Josh's" identity. When Yahoo! notified "Josh" of the lawsuit, he asked the court to quash the subpoena.

In a court hearing, Juzwiak testified that the threatening emails had severely disrupted his life, causing deep anger and depression, as well as insomnia that had impaired his ability to concentrate and function effectively. In addition, this emotional stress had exacerbated his back problems and caused him to lose 20 pounds. Although he had already been taking antidepressants, a psychiatrist prescribed four additional drugs for depression, anxiety, and insomnia, which were not effective in reducing his symptoms. Juzwiak also stated that he had thoughts of hurting himself and the entire episode had consumed his life for several months.

When the trial court refused to issue the subpoena against Yahoo!, Juzwiak appealed.

You Be the Judge: *Should the trial court have issued the subpoena? Which interest is more important: "Josh's" First Amendment right to free speech or Juzwiak's protection from harassing emails?*

Argument for "Josh": Free speech is the first, and most important, right in the Bill of Rights. To ensure a vibrant marketplace of ideas, the First Amendment protects not

---

[3]*Krinsky v. Doe*, 6159 Cal. App. 4th 1154, 2008 Cal. App. LEXIS 180.

only open but also anonymous speech. Sometimes speakers must be allowed to withhold their identities to protect themselves from harassment and persecution.

Nothing in these messages was a realistic threat to the teacher's safety. "Hopefully you will be gone permanently" could easily mean "Hope you will move out of town." Juzwiak reported these emails to the police, but they took no action. Presumably they would have done so if there had been any real threat.

Nor did these emails constitute an intentional infliction of emotional distress. They were not so extreme and outrageous as to be utterly intolerable in a civilized community. "Josh" did not accuse Juzwiak of vile or criminal acts. The language was not obscene or profane. In short, if Juzwiak is going to teach high school, he needs to develop a thicker skin and a better sense of humor.

Argument for Juzwiak: The right to speak anonymously is not absolute. "Josh" requires protection from harassment? That is an absurd argument.

These emails contained death threats: "Hopefully you will be gone permanently" and "I hear Friday is 'D' day for you." Juzwiak was frightened enough to go to the police. He suffered serious physical and emotional harm. These emails are not entitled to the protection of the First Amendment.

Furthermore, the emails constituted intentional infliction of emotional distress. They were extreme and outrageous conduct designed to cause harm. They achieved their goal.

In balancing the rights in this case, why would the court protect "Josh," who has set out to cause harm, over the innocent teacher?

THE FOURTH AMENDMENT

The Fourth Amendment to the Constitution prohibits unreasonable searches and seizures by the government. In enforcing this provision of the Constitution, the courts ask: Did the person being searched have a legitimate expectation of privacy in the place searched or the item seized? If yes, then the government must obtain a warrant from a court before conducting the search. (For more on this topic, investigate Chapter 7, on crime.) The Fourth Amendment applies to computers.

The architecture professor in the following case would have benefited from a course in business law, and perhaps in computer science, too.

UNITED STATES OF AMERICA V. ANGEVINE

281 F.3d 1130, 2002 U.S. App. LEXIS 2746
United States Court of Appeals for the Tenth Circuit, 2002

CASE SUMMARY

Facts: Professor Eric Angevine taught architecture at Oklahoma State University. The university provided him with a computer that was linked to the university network, and through it to the Internet. Professor Angevine used this computer to download more than 3,000 pornographic images of young boys. After viewing the images and printing some of them, he deleted the files. Tipped off by Professor Angevine's wife, police officers seized the computer and turned it over to a police computer expert, who retrieved the pornographic files that the professor had deleted. The police had not obtained a search warrant.

The Oklahoma State University computer policy states that:

- The contents of all storage media owned or stored on university computing facilities are the property of the university.

- Employees cannot use university computers to access obscene material.

- The university reserves the right to view or scan any file or software stored on a computer or passing through the network, and will do so periodically to audit the use of university resources. The university cannot guarantee confidentiality of stored data.

- System administrators keep logs of file names that may indicate why a particular data file is being erased, when it was erased, and what user identification has erased it.

The trial court held that federal agents did not need a warrant to search Professor Angevine's office computer because he had no expectation of privacy. He was sentenced to 51 months in prison for "knowing possession of child pornography." The professor appealed.

Issue: *Did Professor Angevine have a reasonable expectation of privacy in his office computer?*

Decision: No, Professor Angevine did not have a reasonable expectation of privacy.

Reasoning: The university reserved the right to monitor Internet use by employees. The university's computer policy explicitly cautions computer users that information flowing through the university network is not confidential, either in transit or in storage on a computer. As a result, employees cannot have a reasonable expectation of privacy for downloaded data.

Professor Angevine made a careless effort to protect his privacy. Although he did attempt to erase the pornography, the university computer policy warned that system administrators kept logs recording when and by whom files were deleted. In any event, having transmitted pornographic data through a monitored university network, Professor Angevine could not create a reasonable expectation of privacy merely by deleting the files.

This case involved someone who transmitted information through an electronic system owned by his employer. What happens if a suspect in a crime sends emails through a system that he personally pays for? Does he have a reasonable expectation of privacy? The following case answers these questions.

UNITED STATES OF AMERICA V. WARSHAK

631 F.3d 266; 2010 U.S. App. LEXIS 25415
United States Court of Appeals for the Sixth Circuit, 2010

CASE SUMMARY

Facts: Steven Warshak sold Enzyte, a supplement that promised to increase masculine endowment. As is the case with all such products, Enzyte was a fraud. Advertisements quoted surveys that had never been conducted and doctors who did not exist. As a result, customers typically did not buy the product a second time. Warshak had a solution to this problem—an auto-ship program. A man would order a free sample, providing his credit card to pay for the shipping. Warshak's company would then automatically send him more product, and, of course, charge his credit card.

Without obtaining a search warrant first, a federal prosecutor asked Warshak's Internet service provider (ISP) for copies of his emails. Based on the evidence contained in these 25,000 emails, Warshak was convicted of mail, wire, and bank fraud and sentenced to 25 years in prison. He appealed on the grounds that the government had violated the Fourth Amendment by obtaining his emails without a search warrant. He argued that he had a reasonable expectation of privacy in these emails.

Issue: *Did Warshak have a reasonable expectation of privacy in his emails?*

Decision: Yes, his expectation of privacy was reasonable.

Reasoning: Clearly, Warshak thought his emails were private, or he would not have made so many incriminating statements in them. Most people would not display so much dirty laundry in plain view.

However, the defendant has to show not only that he had an expectation of privacy, but also that it was reasonable. Given how significant email is to most of us, this question is very important. People are always sending sensitive and intimate information to friends, family, and colleagues around the world. Sweet nothings, business plans, online purchases, and medical information are transferred with the click of a mouse. *Account* is an apt word to use for email because it does provide an account of its owner's life.

The Fourth Amendment must keep pace with technological progress, or its guarantees will wither and perish. The law requires the police to obtain a warrant before they read a letter at the post office or listen to a private telephone call. An ISP is the functional equivalent of a post office or a telephone company. It only stands to reason that the government should not be able to force a commercial ISP to turn over the contents of a subscriber's emails without first obtaining a warrant. Warshak's expectation of privacy was reasonable.

As the *Warshak* court observes, electronic communications—email, text messages, instant messaging—have for many people taken the place of letters and telephone calls. So it is important to know your privacy rights. **Although the courts are feeling their way in this new territory, at this writing, for criminal cases:**

1. If your employer has a reasonably articulated policy notifying you that it has the right to access and read electronic communications on a system that it provides, then you do not have a reasonable expectation of privacy when using that system. The police need not obtain a search warrant before reading your messages.

2. You do have a reasonable right to privacy on a system that you provide for yourself, so the police must obtain a search warrant before accessing these messages.

Note that both of these Fourth Amendment cases involve criminal defendants. However, Fourth Amendment protections also apply to *government* workers in civil cases. For example, when a police officer persistently exceeded his monthly quota of text messages, his superior accessed these communications to determine if they were work-related. It turned out that they were mostly sexually suggestive texts sent to the married officer's mistress. After the officer was disciplined, he filed suit alleging that the department had violated his Fourth Amendment rights. The Supreme Court held that a government employer has the right to review its employee's electronic communications for a work-related purpose, if the search was "justified at its inception" and if "the measures adopted are reasonably related to the objectives of the search and not excessively intrusive in light of the circumstances giving rise to the search."[4]

THE FEDERAL TRADE COMMISSION (FTC)

Section 5 of the FTC Act prohibits unfair and deceptive acts or practices. The FTC applies this statute to online privacy policies. It does not require websites to have a privacy policy, but if they do have one, they must comply with it, and it cannot be deceptive. For example, Sears paid consumers who visited sears.com and kmart.com websites $10 to become members of the "My SHC Community" and participate in "exciting, engaging, and on-going interactions—always on your terms and always by your choice." As part of this process, consumers downloaded "research" software that tracked their online browsing. Only at the end of a lengthy user agreement did Sears reveal the full extent of the data collected, that it could include the contents of shopping carts, online bank statements, drug prescription records, DVD rental records, and some personal email information. In a consent decree with the FTC, Sears agreed to stop collecting data from consumers who downloaded the software and to destroy all data it had previously collected.

The FTC also brought action against Twitter after hackers gained access through its administrative system to Twitter accounts. Twitter had allowed any employee access to the administrative system, which was protected by an easy-to-guess password. The hackers reset passwords and sent fake tweets. For example, an unauthorized person sent a tweet from President-elect Barack Obama's Twitter account offering free gasoline to users who took an Internet poll (which seems benign compared with what the hacker could have said, but still not a good situation). The FTC found that Twitter had engaged in deceptive acts because its (lack of) security practices had violated the company's promise to users that it would protect their information from unauthorized access. As part of the settlement, Twitter agreed to strengthen its security practices.

In addition to cases the FTC has brought against individual companies, it also issued a report entitled "Self-Regulatory Principles for Online Behavioral Advertising." As the name

---

[4]*City of Ontario v. Quon*, 130 S. Ct. 2619; 2010 U.S. LEXIS 4972 (S. Ct. 2010).

implies, these rules are voluntary. They provide that companies should clearly disclose the information that they collect and also offer consumers an easy-to-use, easy-to-find method for opting out. However, we have not found a website that complies with this policy. The FTC has been working on a binding privacy policy for years, with no result yet.

One more cyberlaw issue: Imagine that you are reading a blog that favorably reviews a new Microsoft product. Before clicking on the Buy button, would you want to know that Microsoft had given the blogger a free computer? The FTC thinks you should. Under FTC rules, bloggers face fines as high as $1,000 if they do not disclose all compensation they receive (either in cash or free products) for writing product reviews. Moreover, celebrities must disclose their relationships with advertisers when making endorsements outside of traditional ads, such as on talk shows or in social media.

ELECTRONIC COMMUNICATIONS PRIVACY ACT OF 1986

The Electronic Communications Privacy Act of 1986 (ECPA) is a federal statute that prohibits unauthorized interception of, access to, or disclosure of wire and electronic communications. The definition of electronic communication includes email and transmissions from pagers and cell phones. Violators are subject to both criminal and civil penalties. An action does not violate the ECPA if it is unintentional or if either party consents. Also, the USA Patriot Act, passed after the September 11 attacks, has broadened the *government's* right to monitor electronic communications.

Under the ECPA:

1. **Any intended recipient of an electronic communication has the right to disclose it.** Thus, if you sound off in an email to a friend about your boss, the (erstwhile) friend may legally forward that email to the boss or anyone else.

2. **Internet service providers (ISPs) are generally prohibited from disclosing electronic messages to anyone other than the addressee,** unless this disclosure is necessary for the performance of their service or for the protection of their own rights or property.

3. **An employer has the right to monitor workers' electronic communications if (1) the employee consents, (2) the monitoring occurs in the ordinary course of business, or (3) in the case of email, if the employer provides the computer system.**[5] Note that an employer has the right to monitor electronic communication even if it does not relate to work activities.

One lesson from the ECPA: Email is not private, and it is dangerous. Although the *Warshak* court ruled that defendants have an expectation of privacy in emails they have sent over a system that they provide for themselves, that simply means the police must first obtain a search warrant before accessing emails, which is not that difficult. To get a search warrant, the police just need probable cause that they will find evidence of a crime in the place to be searched.

The majority of employers monitor their employees' email. In the event of litigation, the opposing party can access all emails—even messages that have in theory been deleted. Many people who should have known better have been caught in the email trap. Merrill Lynch stock analyst Henry Blodget praised stocks to the public even as he was referring to them in emails as a "piece of s***." He has been banned for life from the securities industry. Then there was Harry Stonecipher, the CEO of Boeing, who sent explicit emails to the employee with whom he was having an extramarital affair. When copies of the emails were sent to the board of directors, he was fired. In the following case, two important principles are at stake. Which one should win?

---

[5]The ECPA provides that, under certain circumstances, the police can access email without a warrant, but the *Warshak* court declared that provision unconstitutional.

You Be the Judge

SCOTT V. BETH ISRAEL MEDICAL CENTER INC.

847 N.Y.S.2d 436; 2007 N.Y. Misc. LEXIS 7114
Supreme Court of New York, 2007

Facts: Beth Israel Medical Center (BI)'s email policy stated:

All information and documents created, received, saved, or sent on the Medical Center's computer or communications systems are the property of the Medical Center. Employees have no personal privacy right in any material created, received, saved, or sent using Medical Center communication or computer systems. The Medical Center reserves the right to access and disclose such material at any time without prior notice.

Dr. Norman Scott was head of the orthopedics department at BI. His contract with the hospital provided for $14 million in severance pay if he was fired without cause. BI did fire him, and the question was whether it was for cause or not. In preparation for a lawsuit against BI, Scott used the hospital's computer system to send emails to his lawyer. Each of these emails included the following notice:

This message is intended only for the use of the Addressee and may contain information that is privileged and confidential. If you are not the intended recipient, you are hereby notified that any dissemination of this communication is strictly prohibited. If you have received this communication in error, please erase all copies of the message and its attachments and notify us immediately.

BI obtained copies of all of Scott's emails. It notified him that it had copies of the emails to his lawyer. No one at BI had read the emails yet, but they intended to do so. Communications between a client and lawyer are generally protected, but a client waives this privilege if he publicly discloses the information. When Scott requested that the emails be returned to him unread, BI refused. Scott filed a motion seeking the return of the documents.

You Be the Judge: *Did Scott have a right to privacy in emails he sent to his lawyer using the BI system?*

Argument for Scott: Despite BI's policy, all the emails Scott sent asserted that they were confidential. That should be enough to protect them. The attorney-client privilege is a foundation of our legal system. It is absolutely crucial for justice that clients be able to communicate with their lawyers in confidence. In a test between a core principle such as attorney-client privilege and a private entity's email policy, the privilege must win. The hospital should not be allowed to read Scott's emails.

Argument for BI: Scott was aware of BI's policy and knew that emails were the property of the hospital. Therefore, when he sent the emails, he was disclosing them publicly. If the communications were that important, he should have made a greater effort to protect them. BI has the right to read them.

CHILDREN'S ONLINE PRIVACY PROTECTION ACT OF 1998

The Children's Online Privacy Protection Act of 1998 (COPPA) prohibits Internet operators from collecting information from children under 13 without parental permission. It also requires sites to disclose how they will use any information they acquire. Enforcement is in the hands of the FTC. The website for Mrs. Fields cookies offered birthday coupons for free cookies to children under 13. Although the company did not share information with outsiders, it did collect personal information without parental consent from 84,000 children. This information included names, home addresses, and birth dates. Mrs. Fields paid a penalty of $100,000 and agreed not to violate the law again.

STATE REGULATION

Some states have passed their own online privacy laws. To take some examples, the California Online Privacy Act of 2003 requires any website that collects personal information from California residents to post a privacy policy conspicuously and then abide by its terms. (Further, the California state constitution confers the right to privacy.) Connecticut, Nebraska, and Pennsylvania also regulate online privacy policies.

Two states, Minnesota and Nevada, require ISPs to obtain their customers' consent before providing information about them. Connecticut and Delaware require employers to notify their workers before monitoring emails or Internet usage.

EUROPEAN LAW

The European Convention on Human Rights declares, "Everyone has the right to respect for his private and family life, his home, and his correspondence." The European Union's e-Privacy Directive requires an opt-in system, under which tracking tools cannot be used unless the consumer is told how the tools will be used and then specifically grants permission for their use. However, this directive may be interpreted to mean that consumers have granted permission for tracking tools if they fail to change the default privacy settings on their web browsers. At this writing, European nations are just beginning to implement the e-Privacy Directive, so it may be some time before the impact of these rules is clear.

In theory, even companies outside Europe will have to comply with European rules if they interact with European customers. Recently, European agencies insisted that Google, Microsoft, and Yahoo! enhance their protection of users' search histories; and a court in Italy held that Google had violated that country's privacy laws by posting a video of students bullying an autistic boy. Stay tuned.

SPYWARE

Spyware

A computer program that enters a user's computer without permission and monitors and reports the user's activities.

Is your computer running sluggishly? Does it crash frequently? Has the home page on your web browser suddenly changed without your consent? Is there a program in your systems tray that you do not recognize? You might have **spyware** on your computer. Spyware is a computer program that enters a user's computer without permission and monitors and reports the user's activities.

Congress has considered legislation to control spyware but has not taken final action. California has enacted the Consumer Protection Against Computer Spyware Act, which makes spyware illegal.

32-2 SPAM

Spam is officially known as *unsolicited commercial email (UCE)* or *unsolicited bulk email (UBE)*. Whatever it is called, it is one of the most annoying aspects of email. It has been estimated that 90 percent of email is spam. And roughly half of these messages were fraudulent—either in content (promoting a scam) or in packaging (the headers or return address are false). Aside from the annoyance factor, bulk email adds to the cost of connecting to the Internet as ISPs increase server capacity to handle the millions of spam emails.

The Controlling the Assault of Non-Solicited Pornography and Marketing Act (CAN-SPAM) is a federal statute that does not prohibit spam but instead regulates it. This statute applies to virtually all promotional emails, whether or not the sender has a preexisting relationship with the recipient. Under this statute, commercial email:

- May not have deceptive headings (From, To, Reply To, Subject),

- Must offer an opt-out system permitting the recipient to unsubscribe (and must honor those requests promptly),

- Must clearly indicate that the email is an advertisement,

- Must provide a valid physical return address (not a post office box), and

- Must clearly indicate the nature of pornographic messages.

A company can avoid these requirements by obtaining advance permission from the recipients.

CAN-SPAM seems to have had little impact on the quantity of spam (although it has made opt-out provisions more common in legitimate commercial emails). More effective have been the tools developed by online security firms and governments that prevent as much as 98 percent of spam from reaching your email inbox.

But spammers have found other outlets. They post messages in the comment sections of websites and on social media sites such as Facebook and Twitter. Their goal is to entice you to click on a link that takes you to a website that sells foolproof "investments" or that simply steals bank information from your computer. If that link seems to come from a Facebook friend or someone whom you follow on Twitter, it seems more reliable. A recent study found that 8 percent of links sent via Twitter are fraudulent, but they are 20 times more likely to be clicked than those in spam email.[6]

EXAM Strategy

Question: Cruise.com operated a website selling cruise vacations. It sent unsolicited email advertisements—dubbed "E-deals"—to prospective customers. Eleven of these "E-deals" went to inbox@webguy.net. Each message offered the recipient an opportunity to be removed from the mailing list by clicking on a line of text or by writing to a specific postal address. Has Cruise.com violated the CAN-SPAM Act?

Strategy: Remember that this Act does not prohibit all unsolicited emails.

Result: Cruise.com was not in violation because it offered the recipients a way to unsubscribe. Also, it provided a valid physical return address.

32-3 INTERNET SERVICE PROVIDERS AND WEB HOSTS: COMMUNICATIONS DECENCY ACT OF 1996

ISPs are companies, such as Earthlink, that provide connection to the Internet. Web hosts post web pages on the Internet. Both play important roles in cyberspace. As the legal structure that supports the Internet develops, so have legal issues involving these players.

The Internet is an enormously powerful tool for disseminating information. But what if some of this information happens to be false or in violation of our privacy rights? Is an ISP liable for transmitting it to the world? In 1995, a trial judge in New York held that an ISP, Prodigy Services Company, was potentially liable for defamatory statements that an unidentified person posted on one of its bulletin boards.[7] The message alleged that the president of an investment bank had committed "criminal and fraudulent acts." It was not only a false statement—it was posted on the most widely read financial online bulletin board in the country. Although one can only feel sympathy for the target of this slur, the decision nonetheless alarmed many observers who argued that there was no way ISPs could review every piece of information that hurtles through their portals. The next year, Congress overruled the Prodigy case by passing the Communications Decency Act of 1996 (CDA).[8]

---

[6]"Long life spam," *The Economist*, November 20, 2010, p. 67.
[7]*Stratton Oakmont, Inc. v. Prodigy Services Company*, 1995 N.Y. Misc. LEXIS 229.
[8]47 U.S.C. 230.

Under the CDA, ISPs and web hosts are not liable for information that is provided by someone else. Only content providers are liable. The following case lays out the arguments in favor of the CDA, but also illustrates some of the costs of the statute (and of the Internet).

CARAFANO V. METROSPLASH.COM, INC.[9]

339 F.3d 1119, 2003 U.S. App. LEXIS 16548
United States Court of Appeals for the Ninth Circuit, 2003

CASE SUMMARY

Facts: Matchmaker.com is an Internet dating service that permits members to post profiles of themselves and to view the profiles of other members. Before posting is allowed, Matchmaker reviews photos for inappropriate material but does not examine written profiles.

Christianne Carafano is an actor who uses the stage name Chase Masterson. She has appeared in numerous films and television shows, such as *Star Trek: Deep Space Nine* and *General Hospital.* Without her knowledge or consent, someone in Berlin posted a profile of her in the Los Angeles section of Matchmaker. In answer to the question "Main source of current events?" the person posting the profile put "*Playboy Playgirl*" and for "Why did you call?" responded "Looking for a one-night stand." In addition, the essays indicated that she was looking for a "hard and dominant" man with "a strong sexual appetite" and that she "liked sort of being controlled by a man, in and out of bed." Pictures of the actor, taken off the Internet, were included with the profile. The profile also provided her home address and an email address, which, when contacted, produced an automatic email reply stating, "You think you are the right one? Proof it !!" [*sic*], and providing Carafano's home address and telephone number.

Unaware of the improper posting, Carafano began receiving sexually explicit messages on her home voice mail, as well as a sexually explicit fax that threatened her and her son. She received numerous phone calls, letters, and email from male fans expressing concern that she had given out her address and phone number (but simultaneously indicating an interest in meeting her). Feeling unsafe, Carafano and her son stayed in hotels or away from Los Angeles for several months.

One Saturday a week or two after the profile was first posted, Carafano's assistant, Siouxzan Perry, learned of the false profile through a message from "Jeff." Acting on Carafano's instructions, Perry contacted Matchmaker, demanding that the profile be removed immediately. The Matchmaker employee did not remove it then because Perry herself had not posted it, but on Monday morning, the company blocked the profile from public view, and then deleted it the following day.

Carafano filed suit against Matchmaker alleging invasion of privacy, misappropriation of the right of publicity, defamation, and negligence. The district court rejected Matchmaker's argument for immunity under the CDA on the grounds that the company provided part of the profile content.

Issue: *Did the CDA protect Matchmaker from liability?*

Decision: Yes, the CDA protected Matchmaker from liability for the postings.

Reasoning: Under the CDA, Internet publishers are not liable for false or defamatory material if someone else provided the information. In this way, Internet publishers are different from print, television, and radio publishers.

Interactive computer services have millions of users. It would be impossible for these services to screen each of their millions of postings. If they were liable for content, they might choose to severely limit the number and type of messages. To avoid any restriction on free speech, Congress chose to protect computer services from liability if someone else provided the content.

The fact that some of the content in Carafano's fake profile was provided in response to Matchmaker's questionnaire does not make the company liable. The answers to the questions were provided exclusively by the user. No profile has any content until a user actively creates it. In this case, Carafano's home address and the email address that revealed her phone number were transmitted unaltered to profile viewers. Thus, Matchmaker did not play a significant role in creating, developing, or transforming the relevant information.

Despite the serious and utterly deplorable consequences in this case, the CDA protects Matchmaker from liability.

---

[9]Matchmaker.com, Inc., changed its legal name to Metrosplash.com, Inc., but continued to do business as Matchmaker.com.

Note that the CDA does not protect web hosts or ISPs that engage in wrongdoing. For example, Bright Builders, Inc, hosted copycatclubs.com, a website that, as you might guess, sold counterfeit golf clubs. The court held that Bright Builders was liable despite the CDA because it participated in the design, building, marketing, and support of copycatclubs.com. It even helped locate the counterfeit clubs that the website sold.[10] Ultimately, a jury returned a verdict of $110,150 against Bright Builders.

Also, the CDA does not protect web hosts and ISPs from contract liability. For example, after Cynthia Barnes broke up with her boyfriend, he created a profile of her on a Yahoo! website. He then spitefully posted nude photos of the two of them taken without her knowledge, together with her addresses and phone numbers at home and at work. He also suggested that she was interested in sex with random strangers. Many men were willing to oblige. For months, Yahoo! did not even respond to Barnes's request to remove the profile. Not until a TV show prepared to run a story about the incident did the company's director of communications contact Barnes to promise that the profile would be removed immediately.

Still Yahoo! took no action until two months later, when Barnes sued. The appeals court ruled that Barnes could bring a contract claim against Yahoo! under a theory of promissory estoppel—that she had relied on the company's promise.[11]

EXAM Strategy

Question: Someone posted an anonymous review on TripAdvisor.com alleging that the owner of a restaurant had entertained a prostitute there. The allegation was false. TripAdvisor refused to investigate or remove the review. Does the restaurant owner have a valid claim against the website?

Strategy: Remember that web hosts are liable only if they have engaged in wrongdoing.

Result: As a web host, TripAdvisor is not liable for content. It would be liable only if it promised to take down the review and then did not.

32-4 CRIME ON THE INTERNET

Despite its great benefits, the Internet has also opened new frontiers in crime for the dishonest and unscrupulous.

32-4a Hacking

During the 2008 presidential campaign, college student David Kernell guessed vice-presidential nominee Sarah Palin's email password, accessed her personal Yahoo! account, and published the content of some of her emails. To many, his actions seemed like an amusing prank. The joke turned out not to be so funny when Kernell was sentenced to one year in prison.

Gaining unauthorized access to a computer system is called **hacking**. It is a major crime. The Federal Bureau of Investigation ranks cybercrime as its third-highest priority, right behind terrorism and spying. The Pentagon reports that hackers make more than 250,000

Hacking
Gaining unauthorized access to a computer system.

---

[10]*Roger Cleveland Golf Co. v. Price*, 2010 U.S. Dist. LEXIS 128044.
[11]*Barnes v. Yahoo!, Inc.*, 510 F.3d 1096 (9th Cir., 2008). Promissory estoppel is discussed at greater length in Chapter 9.

attempts annually on its computers. The goal of hackers is varied; some do it for little more than the thrill of the challenge. The objective for other hackers may be espionage, extortion, theft of credit card information, or revenge for perceived slights. Kernell hoped to prevent Palin from being elected vice president.

Hacking is a crime under the federal Computer Fraud and Abuse Act of 1986 (CFAA).[12] This statute applies to any computer, cell phone, iPod, iPad, or other gadget attached to the Internet. **The CFAA prohibits:**

> # The FBI ranks cybercrime as its third-highest priority, right behind terrorism and spying.

- Accessing a computer without authorization and obtaining information from it,

- Computer espionage,

- Theft of financial information,

- Theft of information from the U.S. government,

- Theft from a computer,

- Computer fraud,

- Intentional, reckless, and negligent damage to a computer,

- Trafficking in computer passwords, and

- Computer extortion.

The CFAA also provides for civil remedies so that someone who has been harmed by a hacker can personally recover damages from the wrongdoer. Employers have begun to use the CFAA to bring civil cases against former employees who take company information with them when they go to work for a competitor. At this writing, the courts are inconsistent on the issue of whether such an activity constitutes "unauthorized access" and is, therefore, a violation of the CFAA. Also, database owners sometimes claim that an unauthorized user who "shares" the login credentials of a legitimate purchaser has violated the CFAA. Because the courts have split on these issues, the outcome of such a case depends on geography.[13]

There are two problems with the CFAA. First, while the statute prohibits the use of a virus to harm a computer, it does not ban the creation of viruses that someone else could use for hacking. Thus, it is legal for websites to sell source code for viruses—codes that even beginners can use destructively.

Second, the CFAA applies only to U.S. criminals. Because the Internet is truly international, cybercriminals do not always fall within the jurisdiction of American laws. For example, a computer virus called ILOVEYOU caused an estimated $1 billion worth of damage worldwide. Although the perpetrator would have been subject to prosecution under the CFAA in the United States, he lived in the Philippines, which did not have laws prohibiting cybercrime. Nor could the suspect be extradited to the United States because the extradition treaty only applied if both nations had the same law. The Philippines ultimately dropped all charges against the suspect.

---

[12]18 U.S.C. §1030.

[13]See, for example, *Int'l Airport Centers LLC v. Citrin*, 440 F 3d 418 (7th Cir., 2006); *Lasco Foods, Inc. v. Hall & Shaw Sales*, 600 F. Supp. 2d 1045 (E. Dist. Mo, 2009); *Orbit One Communications Inc. v. Numerex Corp.*, 692 F. Supp. 2d 313 (S.D.N.Y. 2010); *State Analysis Inc. v. American Financial Services Assoc.*, 621 F. Supp. 2d 309 (E.D. Va., 2009); and *AtPac Inc. v. Aptitude Solutions Inc.*, 130 F. Supp. 2d 1114, (E.D. CA, 2010).

32-4b Fraud

Fraud is a growth business on the Internet. The Internet's anonymity and speed facilitate this crime, and computers help criminals identify and contact victims. Common scams include advance fee scams,[14] the sale of merchandise that is either defective or nonexistent, the so-called Nigerian letter scam,[15] billing for services that are touted as "free," fake scholarship search services, romance fraud (you meet someone online who wants to visit you but needs money for travel expenses), and credit card scams (for a fee, you can get a credit card, even with a poor credit rating). One of the new scams involves overpayment. You are renting out a house, selling a pet, or accepting a job, and "by accident," you are sent too much money. You wire the excess back, only to find out that the initial check or funds transfer was no good.

Fraud is the deception of another person for the purpose of obtaining money or property from him. It can be prosecuted under state law or the Computer Fraud and Abuse Act. In addition, federal mail and wire fraud statutes prohibit the use of mail or wire communication in furtherance of a fraudulent scheme.[16] The FTC can bring civil cases under §5 of the FTC Act. (Chapter 7, on crime, discusses fraud.)

Auctions

Internet auctions are the number one source of consumer complaints about online fraud. Wrongdoers either sell goods they do not own, provide defective goods, or offer fakes. In a recent case (which will not reduce the amount of auction fraud) a court held that eBay, the Internet auction site, was not liable to Tiffany & Company for the counterfeit Tiffany products sold on the site. The jewelry company had sued after discovering that most items advertised on eBay as Tiffany products were, in fact, fakes. The court held that eBay's only legal obligation was to remove products once told that they were counterfeit.[17]

Shilling is an increasingly popular online auction fraud. **Shilling means that a seller either bids on his own goods or agrees to cross-bid with a group of other sellers.** Shilling is prohibited because the owner drives up the price of his own item by bidding on it. Thus, for example, Kenneth Walton, a San Francisco lawyer, put up for auction on eBay an abstract painting purportedly by famous artist Richard Diebenkorn. A bidder offered $135,805 before eBay withdrew the item in response to charges that Walton had placed a bid on the painting himself and had also engaged in cross-bidding with a group of other eBay users. Although Walton claimed that he had placed the bids for friends, he ultimately pleaded guilty to charges of federal wire and mail fraud. He was sentenced to almost four years in prison and paid nearly $100,000 in restitution to those who overpaid for the items he bid on.

To date, eBay has generally responded to shillers by suspending them. Shillers are also subject to suit under general anti-fraud statutes. In addition, some states explicitly prohibit shilling.[18]

> **Shilling**
> When a seller at auction either bids on his own goods or agrees to cross-bid with a group of other sellers.

---

[14]As in, "If you are willing to pay a fee in advance, then you will have access to (pick your choice) favorable financing, lottery winnings from overseas, attractive investment opportunities that will make you rich."

[15]Victims receive an email from someone alleging to be a Nigerian government official who has stolen money from the government. He needs some place safe to park the money for a short time. The official promises that, if the victim will permit her account to be used for this purpose, she will be allowed to keep a percentage of the stolen money. Instead, of course, once the "official" has the victim's bank information, he cleans out the account.

[16]U.S.C. §§1341–1346.

[17]*Tiffany Inc. v. eBay, Inc.*, 600 F.3d 93, 2010 U.S. App. LEXIS 6135 (2nd Cir., 2010) and, on remand, 2010 U.S. Dist. LEXIS 96596 (S.D.N.Y, 2010).

[18]For example, New Mexico law provides that "It shall be unlawful to employ shills or puffers at any such auction sale or to offer or to make or to procure to be offered or made any false bid or offer any false bid to buy or pretend to buy any article sold or offered for sale." N.M. Stat. §61-16-14.

IDENTITY THEFT

Identity theft is one of the scariest crimes against property. Thieves steal the victim's social security number and other personal information such as bank account numbers and mother's maiden name, which they use to obtain loans and credit cards. The money owed is never repaid, leaving victims to prove that they were not responsible for the debts. The thieves may even commit (additional) crimes under their new identities. Meanwhile, the victim may find himself unable to obtain a credit card, loan, or job. One victim spent several nights in jail after he was arrested for a crime that his alter ego had committed.

Although identity fraud existed before computers, the Internet has made it much easier. For example, consumer activists were able to purchase the social security numbers of the director of the CIA, the Attorney General of the United States, and other top administration officials. The cost? Only $26 each. No surprise, then, that 8 million Americans are victims of this crime each year.

A number of federal statutes deal with identity theft or its consequences. **The Identity Theft and Assumption Deterrence Act of 1998 prohibits the use of false identification to commit fraud or other crimes, and it also permits the victim to seek restitution in court.**[19] The Truth in Lending Act limits liability on a stolen credit card to $50. The Social Security Protection Act of 2010 prohibits government agencies from printing social security numbers on checks.

A number of states have also passed identity theft statutes. Almost every state now requires companies to notify consumers when their personal information has been stolen. Many states also restrict the use and disclosure of social security numbers.

What can you do to prevent the theft of your identity?

1. Check your credit reports at least once a year. (Consumers are entitled by law to one free credit report every year from each of the three major reporting agencies. You can order these reports at https://www.annualcreditreport.com.)

2. Place a freeze on your credit report so that anyone who is about to issue a loan or credit card will double-check with you first.

3. If you suspect that your identity has been stolen, contact the FTC at 811-IDTHEFT, 811-438-4338, or google "ftc identity theft" to get to the FTC's identity theft site. Also, file a police report immediately and keep a copy to show creditors. Notify the three credit agencies.

PHISHING

Have you ever received an instant message from a Facebook friend saying, "Hey, what's up?" with a link to an IQ test? This instant message is not from a friend, but rather from a fraudster hoping to lure you into revealing your personal information. In this case, people who clicked on the link were told that they had to provide their cell phone number to get the test results. Next thing they knew, they had been signed up for some expensive cell phone service. This scam is part of one of the most rapidly growing areas of Internet fraud: **phishing. In this crime, a fraudster sends a message directing the recipient to enter personal information on a website that is an illegal imitation of a legitimate site.**

In a traditional phishing scam, large numbers of generic emails are sprayed over the Internet asking millions of people to log on to, say, a fake bank site. But the latest development—called **spear phishing**—involves personalized messages sent from someone the victim knows. For example, your sister asks for your social security number so she can add you as a beneficiary to her life insurance policy. In reality, this email has

Phishing

A fraudster sends a message directing the recipient to enter personal information on a website that is an illegal imitation of a legitimate site.

---

[19]18 U.S. §1028.

come from a fraudster who hacked into your sister's Facebook account to gain access to her lists of friends and family.[20] Even "Like" buttons can be "clickjacked" to take unwary users to bogus sites.

Prosecutors can bring criminal charges against phishers for fraud. The companies whose websites have been copied can sue these criminals for fraud, trademark infringement, false advertising, and cybersquatting (discussed further in Chapter 33, on intellectual property).

No reputable company will ask customers to respond to an email with personal information. When in doubt, close the suspicious email, relaunch your web browser, and then go to the company's main website. If the legitimate company needs information from you, it will so indicate on the site.

EXAM Strategy

Question: TruePrint sent emails to thousands of consumers, advertising its business card service. The subject line said, "FREE GIFT!" Consumers who opened the email, were then asked to click on a link, which led to a web page that asked for personal information. After filling in the information and clicking a "Continue" button, they landed on a second web page. In the fine print at the bottom of this page was the following statement: "Printing is free. Pay only for shipping and processing. Please see our Free Offer Details for more information." Finally, at the end of the process on the next web page, consumers learned that shipping the free gift would cost $5.61, payable by credit card or check. The email did not make any reference to TruePrint. Has TruePrint violated the law?

Strategy: Indeed, TruePrint has violated two laws.

Result: First, it has advertised a "free gift" when, in fact, the gift costs $5.61. That is fraud. Second, it has violated the CAN-SPAM act because the subject line of the email is untrue—the gift is not free. It has further violated CAN-SPAM by its failure to provide TruePrint's valid physical return address.

Chapter Conclusion

The Internet has changed our lives in ways that were inconceivable a generation ago, and the law is rushing to catch up. Courts will apply some old laws in new ways, and, as legislators, regulators and courts learn from experience, new laws will be enacted.

Inevitably, the law of cyberspace will become increasingly international. What does Europe accomplish by regulating Internet privacy if its citizens spend a good portion of their time on American websites? What will the FTC do if scam artists or spammers operate offshore? Effective regulation of cyberspace will require cooperation among nations and between government and industry.

---

[20]To prevent your Facebook account from being hijacked, be careful when accessing it over a public network (such as in a hotel or airport), where fraudsters might be able to capture your password. If you text "otp" to 32665, you will receive a password that can be used only once (a "one-time password"). Fraudsters thus cannot use this password to access your account.

EXAM REVIEW

1. **THE FIRST AMENDMENT** The First Amendment to the Constitution protects speech on the Internet so long as the speech does not violate some other law. (pp. 785–787)

2. **THE FOURTH AMENDMENT** The Fourth Amendment to the Constitution prohibits unreasonable searches and seizures by the government. This provision applies to computers. (pp. 787–789)

3. **REASONABLE EXPECTATION OF PRIVACY** Under criminal law, if your employer has a reasonably articulated policy notifying you that it has the right to access and read electronic communications on a system that it provides, then you do not have a reasonable expectation of privacy when using that system. You do have a reasonable right to privacy on a system that you provide for yourself. (pp. 788–789)

EXAM Strategy

Question: Three travel agents use fictitious accounts to steal millions of frequent flyer miles. Must the police obtain a warrant before searching their email accounts?

Strategy: The answer depends on what type of email account the agents used. (See the "Result" at the end of this section.)

4. **THE FTC ACT** Section 5 of the FTC Act prohibits unfair and deceptive practices. The FTC does not require websites to have a privacy policy, but if they do have one, it cannot be deceptive, and they must comply with it. (pp. 789–790)

5. **THE ECPA** The Electronic Communications Privacy Act of 1986 is a federal statute that prohibits unauthorized interception or disclosure of wire and electronic communications. However, it permits an employer to monitor workers' electronic communications if (1) the employee consents, (2) the monitoring occurs in the ordinary course of business, or (3) the employer provides the computer system (in the case of email). (pp. 790–791)

6. **COPPA** The Children's Online Privacy Protection Act of 1998 prohibits Internet operators from collecting information from children under 13 without parental permission. It also requires sites to disclose how they will use any information they acquire. (p. 791)

7. **E-PRIVACY DIRECTIVE** The European Union's e-Privacy Directive requires an opt-in system under which tracking tools cannot be used unless the consumer is told how the tools will be used and then specifically grants permission for their use. (p. 792)

8. **CAN-SPAM** The Controlling the Assault of Non-Solicited Pornography and Marketing Act (CAN-SPAM) is a federal statute that does not prohibit spam but instead regulates it. Under this statute, commercial email:

- May not have deceptive headings (From, To, Reply To, Subject),

- Must offer an opt-out system permitting the recipient to unsubscribe (and must honor those requests promptly),

- Must clearly indicate that the email is an advertisement,

- Must provide a valid physical return address (not a post office box), and

- Must clearly indicate the nature of pornographic messages. (pp. 792–793)

9. **THE CDA**   Under the Communications Decency Act of 1996, ISPs and web hosts are not liable for information that is provided by someone else. (pp. 793–795)

EXAM Strategy

Question: Ton Cremers was the director of security at Amsterdam's famous Rijksmuseum and the operator of the Museum Security Network (the Network) website. Robert Smith, a handyman working for Ellen Batzel in North Carolina, sent an email to the Network alleging that Batzel was the granddaughter of Heinrich Himmler (one of Hitler's henchmen) and that she had art that Himmler had stolen. These allegations were completely untrue. Cremers posted Smith's email on the Network's website and sent it to the Network's subscribers. Cremers exercised some editorial discretion in choosing which emails to send to subscribers, generally omitting any that were unrelated to stolen art. Is Cremers liable to Batzel for the harm that this inaccurate information caused?

Strategy: Cremers is liable only if he is a content provider. (See the "Result" at the end of this section.)

10. **THE CFAA**   Hacking is a crime under the federal Computer Fraud and Abuse Act of 1986. The CFAA prohibits:

- Accessing a computer without authorization and obtaining information from it,

- Computer espionage,

- Theft of financial information,

- Theft of information from the U.S. government,

- Theft from a computer,

- Computer fraud,

- Intentional, reckless, and negligent damage to a computer,

- Trafficking in computer passwords, and

- Computer extortion. (p. 796)

EXAM Strategy

Question: To demonstrate the inadequacies of existing computer security systems, Cornell student Robert Morris created a computer virus. His plan, however, went awry, as plans sometimes do. He thought his virus would be relatively harmless, but it ran amok, crashing scores of computers at universities, military sites, and medical research sites. Has he committed a crime, or is he liable only for civil penalties? Does it matter that he did not intend to cause damage?

Strategy: Review the provisions of the CFAA. (See the "Result" at the end of this section.)

11. **FRAUD**   Fraud is the deception of another person for the purpose of obtaining money or property from him. (pp. 797–799)

12. **IDENTITY THEFT**   The Identity Theft and Assumption Deterrence Act of 1998 prohibits the use of false identification to commit fraud or other crimes. (p. 798)

---

3. Result: If their employer owns the email system, the agents have no expectation of privacy, and the police do not need a search warrant. If, however, they are sending emails over a system they are paying for themselves, then the police do need a warrant.

9. Result: The court found that Cremers was not liable under the CDA.

10. Result: Morris was convicted of a crime under the CFAA. He intended to trespass on a computer, so it did not matter that he had no intent to cause harm.

MULTIPLE-CHOICE QUESTIONS

1. Beth sent fraudulent emails through both her account at work and her personal account at home. Although Beth had never read her employer's handbook, it said the company had the right to access work emails. The police _____ obtain a search warrant before reading her work emails. They _____ obtain a search warrant before reading the emails from her personal account.

   (a) need to, need to
   (b) need not, need not
   (c) need to, need not
   (d) need not, need to

2. Because Blaine Blogger reviews movies on his blog, cinemas allow him in for free. Nellie Newspaper Reporter also gets free admission to movies. Blaine _____ disclose on his blog that he receives free tickets. Nellie _____ disclose in her articles that she receives free tickets.

   (a) must, must
   (b) need not, need not
   (c) must, need not
   (d) need not, must

3. An employer has the right to monitor workers' electronic communications if:
   (a) the employee consents
   (b) the monitoring occurs in the ordinary course of business
   (c) the employer provides the computer system
   (d) all of the above
   (e) none of the above

4. Spiro Spammer sends millions of emails a day asking people to donate to his college tuition fund. Oddly enough, many people do. Everything in the emails is accurate (including his 1.9 GPA). Which of the following statements is true?

    (a) Spiro has violated the CAN-SPAM Act because he has sent unsolicited commercial emails

    (b) Spiro has violated the CAN-SPAM Act if he has not offered recipients an opportunity to unsubscribe

    (c) Spiro has violated the CAN-SPAM Act because he is asking for money

    (d) Spiro has violated the CAN-SPAM Act unless the recipients have granted permission to him to send these emails

5. Sushila suspects that her boyfriend is being unfaithful. While he is asleep, she takes his iPod out from under his pillow and goes through all his playlists. Then she finds what she has been looking for: Plum's Playlist. It is full of romantic songs. Sushila sends Plum an email that says, "You are the most evil person in the universe!" Which law has Sushila violated?

    (a) The First Amendment

    (b) The CDA

    (c) The ECPA

    (d) The CFAA

    (e) None

ESSAY QUESTIONS

1. **ETHICS** Chitika, Inc., provided online tracking tools on websites. When consumers clicked the "opt-out" button, indicating that they did not want to be tracked, they were not—for 10 days. After that, the software would resume tracking. Is there a legal problem with Chitika's system? An ethical problem? What Life Principles were operating here?

2. **YOU BE THE JUDGE WRITING PROBLEM** Jerome Schneider wrote several books on how to avoid taxes. These books were sold on Amazon.com. Amazon permits visitors to post comments about items for sale. Amazon's policy suggests that these comments should be civil (e.g., no profanity or spiteful remarks). The comments about Schneider's books were not so kind. One person alleged Schneider was a felon. When Schneider complained, an Amazon representative agreed that some of the postings violated its guidelines and promised that they would be removed within one to two business days. Two days later, the posting had not been removed. Schneider filed suit. **Argument for Schneider:** Amazon has editorial discretion over the posted comments. It both establishes guidelines and then monitors the comments to ensure that they comply with the guidelines. These activities make Amazon an information content provider, not protected by the Communications Decency Act. Also, Amazon violated its promise to take down the content. **Argument for Amazon:** The right to edit material is not the same thing as creating the material in the first place.

3. Over the course of 10 months, Joseph Melle sent more than 60 million unsolicited email advertisements to AOL members. What charges could be brought against him? Would you need more information before deciding?

4. What can you do to protect your privacy online? Draw up a concrete list of steps that you might reasonably consider. Are there some actions that you would not be willing to take because they are not worth it to you?

5. Craig Hare offered computers and related equipment for sale on various Internet auction websites. He accepted payment but not responsibility—he never shipped the goods. Which government agencies might bring charges against him?

DISCUSSION QUESTIONS

1. Marina Stengart used her company laptop to communicate with her lawyer via her personal, password-protected, web-based email account. The company's policy stated:

   > E-mail and voice mail messages, internet use and communication, and computer files are considered part of the company's business and client records. Such communications are not to be considered private or personal to any individual employee. Occasional personal use is permitted; however, the system should not be used to solicit for outside business ventures, charitable organizations, or for any political or religious purpose, unless authorized by the Director of Human Resources.

   After she filed an employment lawsuit against her employer, the company hired an expert to access her emails that had been automatically stored on the laptop. Are these emails protected by the attorney-client privilege? How does this case differ from *Scott v. Beth Israel* earlier in the chapter?

2. Roommates.com operated a website designed to match people renting spare rooms with those looking for a place to live. Before subscribers could search listings or post housing opportunities on Roommate's website, they had to create profiles, a process that required them to answer a series of questions that included the subscriber's sex, sexual orientation, and whether he would bring children to a household. The site also encouraged subscribers to provide "Additional Comments," describing themselves and their desired roommate in an open-ended essay. Here are some typical ads:

   - "I am not looking for Muslims."

   - "Not acceptable: freaks, geeks, prostitutes (male or female), druggies, pet cobras, drama queens, or mortgage brokers."

   - "Must be a black gay male!"

   - We are 3 Christian females who Love our Lord Jesus Christ…. We have weekly bible studies and bi-weekly times of fellowship."

   Many of the ads violated the Fair Housing Act. Is Roommates.com liable?

3. **ETHICS** Matt Drudge published a report on his website (http://www.drudgereport.com) that White House aide Sidney Blumenthal "has a spousal abuse past that has been effectively covered up There are court records of Blumenthal's violence against his wife." The *Drudge Report* is an electronic publication focusing on Hollywood and Washington gossip. AOL paid Drudge $3,000 a month to make the *Drudge Report* available to AOL subscribers. Drudge emailed his reports to AOL, which then posted them. Before posting, however, AOL had the right to edit content. Drudge ultimately retracted his allegations against Blumenthal, who sued AOL. He alleged that under the Communications Decency Act of 1996, AOL was a "content provider" because it paid Drudge and edited what he wrote. Do you agree? Putting liability aside, what moral obligation did AOL have to its members? To Blumenthal? Should AOL be liable for content it bought and provided to its members?

4. Lori Drew created a fake MySpace profile, pretending to be a teenage boy. Through that boy's identity, she bullied 13-year-old Megan Meier. The girl killed herself shortly after receiving a message saying, "The world would be a better place without you." MySpace requires all users to agree to its terms of service which require "truthful and accurate" information. Has Drew violated the CFAA?

5. Tracking tools provide benefits to consumers but they also carry risks. Should Congress regulate them? If so, what should the law provide?

INTELLECTUAL PROPERTY

Cooper is a producer at a small indie film company in Los Angeles. He puts together packages that have a script, a director, and actors. He then finds investors who pay to make the movie and distributors who purchase the right to release it in cinemas, on TV, and on DVD. (Although most people think that box office results are what count, the reality is that, historically, over half of most movies' revenue came from home entertainment options such as DVD rentals and sales.)

Cooper is pretty excited about two packages he has put together: One stars established actor Robert de Niro, and the other features an up-and-coming director working with movie star Clive Owen. But his excitement has turned to disappointment—shockingly, he cannot find anyone willing to invest in either movie. Cooper hears the same thing from everyone: "DVD sales are way down, so we know we won't get the payback we used to. We can't afford to invest in as many movies."

On a flight to New York in search of investors, Cooper finds himself sitting next to a man who is watching a movie on his computer. Cooper knows this movie has not even been released to DVD yet. Clearly, the man has downloaded it from an illegal website. Cooper slowly crushes the plastic cup in his hand. What's wrong with that guy? Doesn't he know that movies cost money to make? Doesn't he realize people like him are killing an industry?

> On a flight to New York in search of investors, Cooper finds himself sitting next to a man who is watching a movie on his computer.... Clearly, the man has downloaded it from an illegal website.

33-1 INTRODUCTION

For much of history, land was the most valuable form of property. It was the primary source of wealth and social status. Today, intellectual property is a major source of wealth. New ideas—for manufacturing processes, software, apps, medicines, books—bring both affluence and influence.

Although both can be valuable assets, land and intellectual property are fundamentally different. The value of land lies in the owner's right to exclude, to prevent others from entering it. Intellectual property, however, has little economic value unless others use it. This ability to share intellectual property is both good news and bad. On the one hand, the owner can produce and sell unlimited copies of, say, software, but on the other hand, the owner has no easy way to determine if someone is using the program for free. The high cost of developing intellectual property, combined with the low cost of reproducing it, makes it particularly vulnerable to theft.

Because intellectual property is nonexclusive, many people see no problem with using it for free. But when consumers take intellectual property—movies, songs, and books—without paying for it, they ensure that fewer of these items will be produced.

Some commentators suggest that the United States has been a technological leader partly because its laws have always provided strong protection for intellectual property. The Constitution provided for patent and copyright protection early in the country's history.

The conflict between those who have intellectual property and those who want to use it has taken on a global dimension. Developing countries argue that American intellectual property laws increase the price of medicines, such as AIDS drugs and vaccines, that could save more lives if only they were cheaper and, therefore, more readily available. "Patents kill" is their slogan. The United States responds that without patent protection, there would be no innovation, no miracle drugs.

But even U.S. drug companies admit that patents can sometimes stifle innovation. The pharmaceutical company Bristol-Meyers Squibb says that it cannot conduct research on many cancer-fighting drugs because of patents held by its competitors. Information technology firms make a similar complaint. In a study of the American semiconductor business, researchers found that more patents did not necessarily mean more innovation. Instead, some companies were simply more aggressive about patenting every possible aspect of their research. Nor was there any evidence that innovation increased as patent rights were enhanced.

The role of intellectual property law is to balance the rights of those who create intellectual property and those who use it. And as this chapter reveals, such a balancing act is no easy feat.

33-2 PATENTS

Patent
A grant by the government permitting the inventor exclusive use of an invention for a specified period.

A **patent** is a grant by the government permitting the inventor exclusive use of an invention for 20 years from the date of filing (or 14 years from the date of issuance in the case of design patents). During this period, no one may make, use, or sell the invention without permission. In return, the inventor publicly discloses information about the invention that anyone can use upon expiration of the patent.

33-2a Types of Patents

There are three types of patents: utility patents, design patents, and plant patents.

UTILITY PATENT

Whenever people use the word "patent" by itself, they are referring to a utility patent. This type of patent is available to those who invent (or significantly improve) any of the following:

Type of Invention	Example
Mechanical invention	A hydraulic jack used to lift heavy aircraft
Electrical invention	A prewired, portable wall panel for use in large, open-plan offices
Chemical invention	The chemical 2-chloroethylphosphonic acid used as a plant growth regulator
Process	A method for applying a chemical compound to an established plant such as rice in order to inhibit the growth of weeds selectively; the application can be patented separately from the actual chemical
Machine	A device that enables a helicopter pilot to control all flight functions (pitch, roll, and heave) with one hand
Composition of matter	A sludge used as an explosive at construction sites; the patent specifies the water content, the density, and the types of solids contained in the mixture

© Cengage Learning

What about an electronic signal? Is that patentable? An inventor filed a patent application for a method of encoding additional information on electronic signals emitted from digital audio files. The process was very useful, but the court ruled that it was not patentable because the signal is not a mechanical, electrical, or chemical invention, a process, a machine, or the composition of matter.[1]

A patent is not available solely for an idea, but only for its tangible application. Thus patents are not available for laws of nature, scientific principles, mathematical algorithms, mental processes, intellectual concepts, or formulas such as $a^2 + b^2 = c^2$.

Business Method Patents In recent years, so-called "business method patents" have been controversial. These patents involve a particular way of doing business that often includes data processing or mathematical calculations. Business method patents have been particularly common in e-commerce. For example, Amazon.com patented its One-Click method of instant ordering. The company then obtained an injunction to prevent barnesandnoble.com from using its Express Lane service that was similar to One-Click. The judge directed barnesandnoble.com to add another step to its ordering process. The Patent and Trademark Office (PTO) affirmed the Amazon patent, which will expire in 2017.

Facebook has been granted a patent on a process that "dynamically provides a news feed about a user of a social network." Most social media sites, such as LinkedIn, Twitter, and Flickr, use some version of this technology. Two important issues are unknown: the exact scope of the patent and how aggressive Facebook will be in enforcing it.

It would be very helpful if the courts provided more clarity—and certainty—about the scope and enforceability of business method patents. In a recent case, *Bilski v. Kappos*, the Supreme Court ruled that business methods are *generally* patentable, even as it held that the *particular* patent in the case (a method for hedging risk in commodities trading) was too abstract to be acceptable.[2] In the same case, the Supreme Court encouraged lower courts to

---

[1]*In re Nuijten*, 500 F.3d 1346; 2007 U.S. App. LEXIS 22426.
[2]2010 U.S. LEXIS 5521 (S. Ct. 2010).

narrow the scope of business method patents, but did not offer guidance as to what these limits should be. As a result, inventors continue to apply for business method patents while waiting for lower courts to develop standards that meet the approval of the Supreme Court.

As a first step in this direction, a federal appeals court recently struck down a patent that covered a process for verifying credit card information over the Internet. This process determined which credit card numbers were linked with Internet Protocol (IP) or email addresses that had a high incidence of fraud. The court ruled that the patent simply covered a mental process and was, therefore, invalid.[3]

Congress also passed the America Invents Act (AIA). Under this statute, anyone who has been charged with infringement of certain *financial service* business method patents has the right (from 2012 to 2020) to challenge the validity of that patent.

Patents on Living Organisms In 1980, the Supreme Court ruled that living organisms could be patented.[4] That case involved genetically engineered bacteria that was used to treat oil spills. The bacteria could be patented because it was (1) manufactured, (2) different from anything found in nature, and (3) useful.

As a result of this ruling, the PTO began issuing patents on human genetic material (although it issued a policy statement that it would not patent human beings). A total of 20 percent of all genes were patented, and the companies that owned these patents were valued at billions of dollars. However, in 2013, the Supreme Court ruled that ordinary DNA could not be patented, although synthesized (i.e., altered) DNA could be.[5]

DESIGN PATENT

A design patent protects the appearance, not the function, of a useful item. It is granted to anyone who invents a new, original, and ornamental design for an article. For example, Braun, Inc., patented the look of its handheld electric blenders. Design patents last 14 years from the date of issuance, not 20 years from the date of filing.

PLANT PATENT

Anyone who creates a new type of plant can patent it, provided that the inventor is able to reproduce it asexually—through grafting, for instance, rather than by planting its seeds. For example, one company patented its unique heather plant.

33-2b Requirements for a Patent

To receive a patent, an invention must be:

- **Novel.** An invention is not patentable if it has already been (1) patented, (2) described in a printed publication, (3) in public use, (4) for sale, or (5) otherwise available to the public anywhere in the world. For example, an inventor discovered a new use for existing chemical compounds but was not permitted to patent it because the compounds had already been described in prior publications, though the new uses had not.[6] Note, however, that a disclosure does not count under this provision if it was made by the inventor in the year prior to filing the application.

- **Nonobvious.** An invention is not patentable if it is obvious to a person with ordinary skill in that particular area. An inventor was not allowed to patent a waterflush system designed to remove cow manure from the floor of a barn because it was obvious.[7]

---

[3]*CyberSource Corp. v. Retail Decisions, Inc.*, 654 F.3d 1366 (Fed. Cir. 2011).
[4]*Diamond v. Chakrabarty*, 447 U.S. 303 (S. Ct. 1980).
[5]*Association for Molecular Pathology v. Myriad Genetics*, 2013 U.S. Lexis 4540 (S. Ct. 2013).
[6]*In re Schoenwald*, 964 F.2d 1122, 1992 U.S. App. LEXIS 10181 (Fed. Cir. 1992).
[7]*Sakraida v. Ag Pro, Inc.*, 425 U.S. 273, 96 S. Ct. 1532, 1976 U.S. LEXIS 146 (1976).

- **Useful.** To be patented, an invention must be useful. It need not necessarily be commercially valuable, but it must have some current use. Being merely of scientific interest is not enough. Thus, a company was denied a patent for a novel process for making steroids because they had no therapeutic value.[8]

EXAM Strategy

Question: In 1572, during the reign of Queen Elizabeth I of England, a patent application was filed for a knife with a bone handle rather than a wooden one. Would this patent be granted under current U.S. law?

Strategy: Was a bone handle novel, nonobvious, and useful?

Result: It was useful—no splinters from a bone handle. It was novel—no one had ever done it before. But the patent was denied because it was obvious.

33-2c Patent Application and Issuance

To obtain a patent, the inventor must file a complex application with the PTO. If a patent examiner determines that the application meets all legal requirements, the PTO will issue the patent. If an examiner denies a patent application for any reason, the inventor can appeal that decision to the Patent Trial and Appeal Board in the PTO and from there to the Court of Appeals for the Federal Circuit in Washington.[9]

During the patent application process, third parties have the right to submit evidence that the invention is not novel. For the nine months after a patent has been granted, third parties have a broad right to challenge its validity in the PTO (without having to go to court). Thereafter, a patent may still be challenged, but the grounds are limited to evidence of a prior patent or publication.

PRIORITY BETWEEN TWO INVENTORS

When two people invent the same product, who is entitled to a patent—the first to invent or the first to file an application? Until 2013, the person who invented and put the invention into practice had priority over the first filer. But the AIA changed the law so that, beginning in 2013, the first person to *file* a patent application has priority. The AIA brought the United States into conformity with most of the rest of the world.

PRIOR SALE

An inventor must apply for a patent within one year of selling the product commercially anywhere in the world. The purpose of this rule is to encourage prompt disclosure of inventions. It prevents someone from inventing a product, selling it for years, and then obtaining a 20-year monopoly with a patent.

---

[8]*Brenner v. Manson*, 383 U.S. 519, 86 S. Ct. 1033, 1966 U.S. LEXIS 2907 (1966).
[9]Recall from Chapter 3 that the Court of Appeals for the Federal Circuit is the 13th United States Court of Appeals. It hears appeals from specialized trial courts.

PROVISIONAL PATENT APPLICATION

Inventors who are unable to assess the market value of their ideas sometimes hesitate to file a patent application because the process is expensive and cumbersome. A successful application can cost tens of thousands of dollars because the PTO charges a separate fee for each step of the process. Thus, for example, an inventor must pay a fee each time a patent examiner raises a legitimate question that requires an amendment to the application. Even if the examiner is wrong, the applicant may have to pay a fee even to file a disagreement. Thus, an inventor may struggle to raise sufficient funds to pay for the patent process. However, the AIA now permits the PTO to charge lower fees to individuals or small entities.

Provisional patent application

A simpler, shorter filing that provides protection for an invention for one year.

In addition, the PTO permits inventors to make a simpler, shorter filing called a **provisional patent application (PPA)**. This application provides a provable date of filing. Once filed, the application sits dormant for a year, giving the inventors an opportunity to show their ideas to potential investors without incurring the full expense of a patent application. PPA protection lasts only one year. To maintain protection after that time, the inventor must file a nonprovisional patent application.

DURATION OF A PATENT

Patents are valid for 20 years from the date of *filing* the application (except design patents, which are valid for 14 years from date of *issuance*). In the last 15 years, the number of patent applications has increased from 950 a *day* to 2,000. And the typical patent application is longer and more complicated. As a result, more than 1 million applications are now pending. Approval of a patent can take anywhere from 3 to 6 years from the date of filing. These delays mean that patent holders effectively receive much less than 20 years of protection (although in the case of exceptional delays, it is possible to request an extension). They also threaten the ability of American inventors to attract investors, monetize their inventions, and compete with foreign businesses.

As permitted under the AIA, the PTO has set up a Track One system that permits inventors to buy their way to the head of the line by paying an additional fee of $4,800 (for large companies) and $2,400 (for small). Track One applications are supposed to be decided within one year. Only 10,000 Track One applications will be accepted in any given year.

INFRINGEMENT

A patent holder has the exclusive right to use the invention during the term of the patent. A holder can prohibit others from using any product that is substantially the same, license the product to others for a fee, and recover damages from anyone who uses the product without permission.

PATENT TROLLS

As we have seen, the patent office must deal with a growing caseload. As a result, the examiners typically spend less than 25 hours reviewing each application. Applicants are not required to demonstrate that the invention is novel, and often the examiner neither knows nor has the time to research the issue. Thus, patents are sometimes issued for inventions that are not really new.

Patent trolls

Someone who buys a portfolio of patents for the purpose of making patent infringement claims.

Traditionally, this issue was not that important because companies with overlapping patents did not litigate who the real inventor was. They were too busy developing products to sell. But then came **patent trolls**. They do not make or market products—they simply buy portfolios of patents for the purpose of bringing patent infringement claims against companies already using the technology. Typically, patent trolls request an injunction to prevent the use of the technology during litigation, potentially harming a multimillion-dollar product over a patent worth much less. Because the trolls are not using the technology themselves, they do not have to worry about a cross-injunction preventing them from using it. Oftentimes, patent trolls are simply hoping that even legitimate users will pay them to go away. In a recent report, the FTC found that these practices "can deter innovation by raising costs and risks without making a technological contribution."[10] In response to criticism, patent trolls argue that they are encouraging innovation by making patents more valuable.

Some hedge funds have entered the patent troll business. In addition, a company owned by Paul Allen, one of Microsoft's founders, recently began filing suit against companies that are using technology that his research lab allegedly invented prior to 2005. These suits have been filed against most of the major players in Silicon Valley—Apple, eBay, Facebook, Google, and Netflix—for their use of technology that improves users' online experience. (Such as suggestions for related reading and pop-up ads or stock quotes.) The technology at issue is key to these companies.

Ethics   Is the patent troll business ethical? Under what circumstances would you be willing to engage in this practice? Paul Allen is wealthy beyond most people's dreams. Why would he be involved in this litigation? What is your Life Principle in this case?

INTERNATIONAL PATENT TREATIES

About half of all patent applications are filed in more than one country. This process used to be a logistical nightmare because almost every country had its own unique filing procedures and standards. Companies were reluctant to develop products based on technology that they were not sure they actually owned. Several treaties now facilitate this process, although it is still not the one-stop (or one-click) effort that inventors desire. These treaties were drafted by the World Intellectual Property Organization (WIPO) of the United Nations.

The Paris Convention for the Protection of Industrial Property (Paris Convention) requires each member country to grant to citizens of other member countries the same rights under patent law as its own citizens enjoy. Thus, the patent office in each member country must accept and recognize all patent and trademark applications filed with it by anyone who lives in any member country. For example, the French patent office cannot refuse to accept an application from an American, so long as the American has complied with French law. Under this treaty, inventors who file in one country have up to one year to file elsewhere and still maintain patent protection.

The Patent Law Treaty requires that countries use the same standards for the form and content of patent applications (whether submitted on paper or electronically). This treaty reduces the procedural conflicts over issues such as translations and fees.

The **Patent Cooperation Treaty** (PCT) is a step toward providing more coordinated patent review across many countries. Inventors who pay a fee and file a so-called PCT patent application are granted patent protection in the 143 PCT countries for up to 30 months. During this time, they can decide how many countries they actually want to file in. (Inventors have one year of protection under the Paris Convention; this treaty grants an additional 18 months.)

---

[10]U.S. Fed. Trade Comm'n, *The Evolving IP Marketplace: Aligning Patent Notice and Remedies with Competition* (March 7, 2011).

Once a PCT application is filed, one of the major patent offices prepares an "international search report" and issues a nonbinding opinion on whether the invention is patentable. This report, while nonbinding, helps applicants assess the patentability of their inventions and provides persuasive evidence to national patent offices. Inventors who wish to proceed internationally must then have the report translated and file it with applications and fees in whichever countries they want a patent.

The United States PTO has bilateral agreements with 16 other patent offices under a so-called **Patent Prosecution Highway**. Under this system, once a patent is approved by one country, it goes to the head of the line for patent examination in the other country.

In addition to these treaties, any country that joins the World Trade Organization (WTO) must agree to trade-related aspects of intellectual property rights (TRIPS). This agreement does not create an international patent system, but it does require all participants to meet minimum standards for the protection of intellectual property. How individual countries achieve that goal is left to them.

Finally, the European Union is in the process of developing a single European patent that would require only one application.

33-3 COPYRIGHTS

The holder of a copyright owns the *particular tangible expression* of an idea, but not the underlying idea or method of operation. Abner Doubleday could have copyrighted a book setting out his particular version of the rules of baseball, but he could not have copyrighted the rules themselves, nor could he have required players to pay him a royalty. Similarly, the inventor of double-entry bookkeeping could copyright a pamphlet explaining his system, but not the system itself.

Unlike patents, the ideas underlying copyrighted material need not be novel. For example, three movies—*Like Father Like Son*, *Vice Versa*, and *Freaky Friday*—are about a parent and child who switch bodies. The movies all have the same plot, but there is no copyright violation because their *expressions* of the basic idea are different.

The Copyright Act protects literature, music, drama, choreography, pictures, sculpture, movies, recordings, architectural works, and computer databases, and computer programs "to the extent that they incorporate authorship in the programmer's expression of original ideas, as distinguished from the ideas themselves."

A work is copyrighted *automatically* once it is in tangible form. For example, once a songwriter puts notes on paper, the work is copyrighted without further ado. But if she whistles a happy tune without writing it down, the song is not copyrighted, and anyone else can use it without permission. Registration with the Copyright Office of the Library of Congress is necessary only if the holder wishes to bring suit to enforce the copyright. Although authors still routinely place the copyright symbol (©) on their works, such a precaution is not necessary in the United States. However, some lawyers still recommend using the copyright symbol because other countries recognize it. Also, the penalties for intentional copyright infringement are heavier than for unintentional violations, and the presence of a copyright notice is evidence that the infringer's actions were intentional.

In the following case, you can imagine the author's frustration when a celebrity stole her thunder and her sales by writing a book on the very same topic. But did the celebrity violate copyright law? This case also anticipates our discussion of trademarks.

LAPINE V. SEINFELD

375 Fed. Appx. 81; 2010 U.S. App. LEXIS 8778
United States Court of Appeals for the Second Circuit, 2010

CASE SUMMARY

Facts: Missy Chase Lapine wrote a book called *The Sneaky Chef: Simple Strategies for Hiding Healthy Foods in Kids' Favorite Meals*, which was about how to disguise vegetables so that children would eat them. Her strategy was to add pureed vegetables to food that children like, such as macaroni and cheese. (We are not making this up.) Four months later, Jessica Seinfeld, the wife of comedian Jerry Seinfeld, published a book entitled *Deceptively Delicious: Simple Secrets to Get Your Kids Eating Good Food*, which featured recipes involving pureed vegetables in (guess what?) macaroni and cheese and other kid-friendly foods.

Lapine filed suit against Seinfeld, alleging violation of her copyright in *The Sneaky Chef*.

Issue: *Did Seinfeld violate Lapine's copyright in* The Sneaky Chef?

Decision: No, Seinfeld did not infringe on Lapine's copyright.

Reasoning: While it is true that the two books have a similar subject matter, no one can copyright the *idea* of

secretly putting vegetable purees in children's food. It is a fundamental principle of our copyright doctrine that ideas, concepts, and processes are not protected from copying.

As for the *expression* of the ideas in Lapine's work, it is true that the two books take a vaguely similar approach, including their titles, illustrations, health advice, recipes, and language about children's healthy eating. But any book with this subject matter would be likely to do the same. These features follow naturally from the work's theme rather than from the author's creativity.

In any event, the total concept and feel of the two books is different. *Deceptively Delicious* lacks an extensive discussion of child behavior, food philosophy, and parenting. Its recipes are simpler. And it uses brighter colors and more photographs than *The Sneaky Chef*.

In short, Lapine cannot copyright the *idea* of the book. And because the books look so different, it is clear that Seinfeld has not stolen the *expression* of Lapine's idea.

33-3a Copyright Term

More than 300 years ago, on April 10, 1710, Queen Anne of England approved the first copyright statute. Called the Statute of Anne, it provided copyright protection for 14 years, which could be extended by another 14 years if the copyright owner was still alive when the first term expired. Many credit the Statute of Anne with greatly expanding the burst of intellectual activity that we now refer to as the Enlightenment.

American law adopted these same time limits, which stayed in effect until the twentieth century. Since then, copyright holders have fought aggressively to lengthen the copyright period. These efforts have been led by the Walt Disney Company, which wants to protect its rights in Mickey Mouse. Today, a copyright is valid until 70 years after the death of the work's only or last living author, or, in the case of works owned by a corporation, the copyright lasts 95 years from publication or 120 years from creation, whichever is shorter. Once a copyright expires, anyone may use the material. Mark Twain died in 1910, so anyone may now publish *Tom Sawyer* without permission and without paying a copyright fee.

33-3b Infringement

Anyone who uses copyrighted material without permission is violating the Copyright Act. **To prove a violation, the plaintiff must present evidence that the work was original** and that either:

- The infringer actually copied the work, or
- The infringer had access to the original and the two works are substantially similar.

A court may (1) prohibit the infringer from committing further violations, (2) order destruction of the infringing material, and (3) require the infringer to pay damages, profits earned, and attorney's fees. Damages can be substantial. In a recent case, a jury ordered SAP to pay Oracle $1.3 *billion* for copyright infringement of Oracle's software.

33-3c First Sale Doctrine

Suppose you buy a CD that, in the end, you do not like. Under the **first sale doctrine,** you have the legal right to sell that CD. **The first sale doctrine permits a person who owns a lawfully made copy of a copyrighted work to sell or otherwise dispose of the copy.** Note, however, that the first sale doctrine does not permit the owner to *make a copy and sell it*. If you listen to a CD and then decide to sell it, that is legal. But it is not legal to copy the CD onto your iPod and then sell the original or any copy of it.

33-3d Fair Use

Fair use doctrine

Permits limited use of copyrighted material without permission of the author for purposes such as criticism, comment, news reporting, scholarship, or research.

Because the period of copyright protection is so long, it has become even more important to uphold the exceptions to the law. Bear in mind that the point of copyright laws is to encourage creative work. A writer who can control, and profit from, artistic work will be inclined to produce more. If enforced oppressively, however, the copyright laws could stifle creativity by denying access to copyrighted work. The **fair use doctrine** permits limited use of copyrighted material without permission of the author for purposes such as criticism, comment, news reporting, scholarship, or research. Courts generally do not permit a use that will decrease revenues from the original work by, say, competing with it. A reviewer is permitted, for example, to quote from a book without the author's permission, but could not reproduce so much that the review was competing with the book itself.

Fair use has become a highly controversial issue in this age of the Internet. For example, Universal Music demanded that YouTube remove a home video of a toddler dancing to a Prince song. A director making a documentary on torture was denied permission to use a short clip showing torture on the TV show *24*. Then J. K. Rowling, the author of the *Harry Potter* series of books, sued to prevent the publication of the *Harry Potter Lexicon*, an unauthorized reference guide to the books that contained direct quotations, paraphrases, and plot summaries. The court ruled that although such a guide can be fair use, this one was not because the author had copied too much of Rowling's distinctive original language.[11]

Also under the fair use doctrine, faculty members are permitted to distribute copyrighted materials to students, so long as the materials are brief and the teacher's action is spontaneous. If, over his breakfast coffee one morning, Professor Learned spots a terrific article in *Mad Magazine* that perfectly illustrates a point he intends to make in class that day, the fair use doctrine permits him to distribute it to his class. However, under a misinterpretation of the fair use doctrine, some faculty had been in the habit of routinely preparing lengthy course packets of copyrighted material without permission of the authors. In *Basic Books, Inc. v. Kinkos Graphic Corp.*,[12] a federal court held that this practice violated the copyright laws because the material was more than one short passage and because it was sold to students. Now, when professors put together course packets, they (or the copy shop) must obtain permission and pay a royalty for the use of copyrighted material. Likewise, it is illegal for students to make photocopies of a classmate's course packet or textbook.

---

[11]*Warner Bros. Entertainment Inc. v. RDR Books*, 575 F. Supp. 2d 513; 2008 U.S. Dist. LEXIS 67771 (S.D.N.Y., 2008).

[12]758 F. Supp. 1522, 1991 U.S. Dist. LEXIS 3804 (S.D.N.Y. 1991). A federal appeals court reached the same result in *Princeton University Press v. Michigan Document Services, Inc.*, 99 F.3d 1381, 1996 U.S. App. LEXIS 29132 (6th Cir. 1996).

PARODY

Parody has a long history in the United States—some of our most cherished songs have been based on parodies. Before Francis Scott Key wrote the words to "The Star-Spangled Banner," other lyrics that mocked colonial governors had been set to the same music. (The tune was well known as a drinking song.)

Because of the political and social commentary that is inherent in many parodies, courts have long granted them special respect. In a case involving a 2 Live Crew parody of the song "Pretty Woman," the Supreme Court decided in favor of 2 Live Crew, holding that **parody is a fair use of copyrighted material so long as the use of the original is not excessive.**[13] The parody may copy enough to remind the audience of the original work, but not so much that the parody harms the market for the original.

The following email exchange between Richard Saperstein, a movie producer, and Tom Strickler, a talent agent, which zapped around Hollywood, illustrates the importance of the 2 Live Crew case (to which Strickler refers).

> I wish you good luck on your journey to deny our First Amendment rights.

[From Saperstein to Strickler:]
Tom–
Please give me a call about a spec script Elia Infascelli-Smith has gone out with called $40,000 MAN. As you know, along with Universal, we control the rights to SIX MILLION DOLLAR MAN. My understanding is this spec includes characters we own.
Best—Richard

[Strickler's response:]
Richard:
Good news. As you may know, The United States Supreme Court has affirmed the right of Parody as an unassailable First Amendment Right. This has enabled you to make movies like *Scream* and *Scary Movie*, in which you parody many films which Dimension does not own or control.

The script is a parody, and if you have any problems, I suggest you hire a Constitutional lawyer and file a brief with the US Supreme Court. This will be an uphill battle—the court voted 9 to 0 when this last hit the docket and those stubborn justices all believe in Stare Decisis.

And if you succeed at the Supreme Court—you will have to stop making *Scream* and *Scary Movie*.

This will take about 5 to 7 years … and lawyers are an expensive breed, but I wish you good luck on your journey to deny our First Amendment rights.
All the best,
Tom

33-3e Digital Music and Movies

One of the major challenges for legal institutions in regulating copyrights is simply that modern intellectual property is so easy to copy. Many consumers are in the habit of violating the law by downloading copyrighted material—music, movies, and books—for free. They seem to believe that if it is easy to steal something, then the theft is somehow acceptable. In one survey of adolescents aged 12 to 17, 75 percent agreed with the statement, "file-sharing is so easy to do, it's unrealistic to expect people not to do it."[14]

---

[13] *Campbell v. Acuff-Rose Music, Inc.*, 510 U.S. 569, 114 S. Ct. 1164, 1994 U.S. LEXIS 2052 (1994).
[14] http://pewinternet.orgjReports/2009/9-The-State-of-Music-Online-Ten-Years-After-Napster/The-State-of-Music-Online-Ten-Years-Afer-Napster.aspx?view=all#footnote25 or google "pew 10 years after napster."

The entertainment world used to turn a blind eye, but illegal downloading is threatening the viability of recording companies, movie studios, and publishers. The statistics are compelling: In 2008, 40 *billion* songs were downloaded illegally, which is as much as 95 percent of all downloaded music! In the first decade of this century, music sales at American record labels declined by 58 percent. Without profitable record labels, who will find and promote new stars? As we saw in the opening scenario, which is a true story, this type of theft is having a profound effect on entertainment and publishing. But it is not just "big companies" that suffer—it is also the artists, musicians, actors, and writers, most of whom are not wealthy rock stars.

Government and industry are striking back. The Prioritizing Resources and Organization for Intellectual Property Act (Pro-IP) permits law enforcement officials to confiscate any equipment used to steal copyrighted material. In addition, the Recording Industry Association of America (RIAA) developed a strategy of aggressively suing those who download music illegally. Then a coalition of entertainment businesses sued two companies that distributed the software used by many consumers to violate copyright law. So important was this issue that the Supreme Court waded into these murky waters.

METRO-GOLDWYN-MAYER STUDIOS, INC. v. GROKSTER, LTD.

545 U.S. 913, 2005 U.S. LEXIS 5212
Supreme Court of the United States, 2005

CASE SUMMARY

Facts: Grokster, Ltd., and StreamCast Networks, Inc., distributed free software that allowed computer users to share electronic files through peer-to-peer networks, so called because users' computers communicated directly with each other, not through central servers. The Grokster and Stream-Cast software could be used for legal purposes. Indeed, peer-to-peer networks were utilized by universities, government agencies, corporations, libraries, and individuals, among others. Even the briefs in this very case could be downloaded legally with the StreamCast software.

Nonetheless, nearly 90 percent of the files available for download through Grokster or StreamCast were copyrighted. Billions of files were shared each month—the probable scope of copyright infringement was staggering. The two companies even encouraged the illegal uses of their software. For example, the chief technology officer of StreamCast said that "the goal is to get in trouble with the law and get sued. It's the best way to get in the news."

A group of copyright holders (MGM and others) sued Grokster and StreamCast alleging that they were violating the copyright law by knowingly and intentionally distributing their software to users who would reproduce and distribute copyrighted works illegally. Both parties moved for summary judgment. The trial court held for Grokster and StreamCast; the appeals court affirmed. The Supreme Court granted *certiorari*.

Issue: *Were Grokster and StreamCast violating copyright law?*

Decision: Yes, Grokster and StreamCast did violate copyright law.

Reasoning: This case presents a trade-off between protecting artistic expression and inhibiting technological innovation. It is important not to discourage the development of technologies that could have both lawful and unlawful potential. Accordingly, mere knowledge that a product could be used to infringe copyrights is not enough to create liability. But when users can use Grokster software to copy songs or movies easily, they develop a disdain for copyright protection. If a product is widely used to commit infringement, copyright holders may not be able to enforce their rights effectively unless they go against the distributor of the copying device. To balance these competing interests, we hold that distributors are liable only if they deliberately encourage copyright violation.

Grokster distributed an electronic newsletter containing links to articles promoting its software's ability to access popular copyrighted music. Both Grokster and StreamCast helped customers locate and play copyrighted materials. Neither company attempted to develop filtering tools or other mechanisms to reduce the illegal use of their software. The amount of infringement was gigantic.

These companies made money by selling advertisements that were sent to the screens of computers using their software. The more the software was used, the more ads they could send out and the greater their advertising revenue became. The success of the defendant's business model hinged on high-volume use that infringed copyrights. The unlawful objective is unmistakable.

Anyone who distributes a product or software and then promotes its use for the purpose of infringing copyrights is liable for the resulting acts of infringement by third parties.

THE NO ELECTRONIC THEFT ACT

Enacted in 1997, the **No Electronic Theft Act** is intended to deter the downloading of copyrighted material. It provides for criminal penalties for the reproduction or distribution of copyrighted material that has a retail value greater than $1,000, even if the offender has no profit motive. Thus, for instance, if a student photocopied for 10 of her friends a textbook that is worth $150, she could be subject to criminal penalties, including a prison term of one year. Originally, the Justice Department did not enforce this statute, but it has now begun to do so, particularly against those who set up networks to trade games, movies, and music.

THE FAMILY ENTERTAINMENT AND COPYRIGHT ACT

Under the **Family Entertainment and Copyright Act,** it is a criminal offense to use a camcorder to film a movie in the theater. This statute also establishes criminal penalties for willful copyright infringement that involves distributing software, music, or film on a computer network.

THE DIGITAL MILLENNIUM COPYRIGHT ACT

The good news is that Mary Schmich wrote an influential article in the *Chicago Tribune.* The bad news is that people deleted her name, attributed the article to Kurt Vonnegut, and sent it around the world via email. Tom Tomorrow's cartoon was syndicated to 100 newspapers, but by the time the last papers received it, the cartoon had already gone zapping around cyberspace. Because his name had been deleted from the original, some editors thought he had plagiarized it.

In response to such incidents, Congress passed the **Digital Millennium Copyright Act** (DMCA), which provides that:

- **It is illegal to delete copyright information, such as the name of the author or the title of the article.** It is also illegal to distribute false copyright information. Thus, anyone who emailed Schmich's article without her name on it, or who claimed it was his own work, would be violating the law.

- **It is illegal to circumvent encryption or scrambling devices that protect copyrighted works.** For example, some software programs are designed so that they can only be copied once. Anyone who overrides this protective device to make another copy is violating the law. (The statute does permit purchasers of copyrighted software to make one backup copy.) If you buy a Disney DVD that prevents you from fast-forwarding through commercials, you are violating the DMCA if you figure out how to do it anyway.

- **It is illegal to distribute tools and technologies used to circumvent encryption devices.** If you tell others how to fast-forward through the Disney commercials, you have violated the statute.

- **Online service providers (OSPs) are not liable for posting copyrighted material so long as they are unaware that the material is illegal and they remove it promptly after receiving notice that it violates copyright law.** This type of provision is called a *safe harbor*.

EXAM Strategy

Question: Many of the videos posted on YouTube are copyrighted material, including thousands of hours of shows owned by Viacom, such as *The Colbert Report* and *The Daily Show*. Viacom sued YouTube for violating its copyrights. Among the evidence Viacom presented was an email from one YouTube founder to another, saying, "… please stop putting stolen videos on the site. We're going to have a tough time defending the fact that we're not liable for the copyrighted material on the site because we didn't put it up when one of the co-founders is blatantly stealing content from other sites and trying to get everyone to see it."[15] YouTube presented evidence that it had responded within one day to Viacom's "takedown notice." Is YouTube liable?

Strategy: Viacom argued that YouTube was well aware that much of its content was illegal. YouTube responded that it met the requirements of the safe harbor provision.

Result: The court found for YouTube. General awareness that many postings infringed copyrights did not impose a duty for YouTube to monitor its videos. Its only requirement was to respond when notified of infringement. YouTube did just that in this case.[16]

33-3f International Copyright Treaties

The Berne Convention requires member countries to provide automatic copyright protection to any works created in another member country. The protection does not expire until 50 years after the death of the author.[17] The WIPO Copyright Treaty and the WIPO Performances and Phonograms Treaty add computer programs, movies, and music to the list of copyrightable materials.

In 2004, Congress enacted a law that permits the president to appoint a copyright law enforcement officer charged with the responsibility for stopping copyright infringement overseas. Also, for the first time, Congress funded the National Intellectual Property Law Enforcement Coordination Council, which was established to protect American intellectual property internationally.

33-4 TRADEMARKS

Trademark

Any combination of words and symbols that a business uses to identify its products or services and distinguish them from others.

A **trademark** is any combination of words and symbols that a business uses to identify its products or services and distinguish them from others. Trademarks are important to both consumers and businesses. Consumers use trademarks to distinguish between competing products. People who

---

[15]Quoted in "Federal Judge Hands Google Victory in Viacom's $1 Billion Suit Over YouTube Content" by Michael Liedtke on Law.com, June 24, 2010.

[16]*Viacom Int'l, Inc. v. YouTube, Inc.*, 718 F. Supp. 2d 514 (S.D.N.Y., 2010).

[17]Under U.S. law, copyrights last 70 years. The United States must grant works created in other signatory countries a copyright that lasts either 50 years or the length of time granted in that country, whichever is longer, but in no case longer than 70 years.

feel that Nike shoes fit their feet best can rely on the Nike trademark to know they are buying the shoe they want. A business with a high-quality product can use a trademark to develop a loyal base of customers who are able to distinguish its product from another.

33-4a Types of Marks

There are four different types of marks:

- **Trademarks** are affixed to *goods* in interstate commerce.

- **Service marks** are used to identify *services*, not products. Fitness First, Burger King, and Weight Watchers are service marks. In this chapter, the terms "trademark" and "mark" are used to refer to both trademarks and service marks.

- **Certification marks** are words or symbols used by a person or organization to attest that products and services produced by others meet certain standards. The Good Housekeeping Seal of Approval means that the Good Housekeeping organization has determined that a product meets its standards.

- **Collective marks** are used to identify members of an organization. The Lions Club, the Girl Scouts of America, and the Masons are examples of collective marks.

33-4b Ownership and Registration

Under common law, the first person to use a mark in trade owns it. Registration with the federal government is not necessary. However, under the federal Lanham Act, the owner of a mark may register it on the Lanham Act Principal Register. A trademark owner may use the symbol ™ at any time, even before registering it, but not until the mark is registered can the symbol ® be placed next to it. Registration has several advantages:

- Even if a mark has been used in only one or two states, registration makes it valid nationally.

- Registration notifies the public that a mark is in use because anyone who applies for registration first searches the Public Register to ensure that no one else has rights to the mark.

- Five years after registration, a mark becomes virtually incontestable because most challenges are barred.

- The damages available under the Lanham Act are higher than under common law.

- The holder of a registered trademark generally has the right to use it as an Internet domain name.

Under the Lanham Act, the owner files an application with the PTO. The PTO will accept an application only if the owner has already used the mark attached to a product in interstate commerce or promises to use the mark within six months after the filing. In addition, the applicant must be the *first* to use the mark in interstate commerce. Initially, the trademark is valid for 10 years, but the owner can renew it for an unlimited number of 10-year terms as long as the mark is still in use.

33-4c Valid Trademarks

Words (Reebok), symbols (Microsoft's flying window logo), phrases (Nike's "Just do it"), shapes (Apple's iPod), sounds (NBC's three chimes), colors (Owens Corning's pink insulation), and even scents (plumeria blossoms on sewing thread) can be trademarked. **To be** valid, **a trademark must be distinctive**—that is, the mark must clearly distinguish one product from another. There are five basic categories of distinctive marks:

- **Fanciful marks** are made-up words such as Kodak or Saucony.

- **Arbitrary marks** use existing words that do *not* describe the product—Prince tennis racquets, for example. No one really thinks that these racquets are designed by or for royalty.

- **Suggestive marks** *indirectly* describe the product's function. "Greyhound" implies that the bus line is swift, and "Coppertone" suggests what customers will look like after applying the product.

- Marks with **secondary meaning** cannot, by themselves, be trademarked unless they have been used for so long that they are now associated with the product in the public's mind. When a film company released a movie called *Ape*, it used as an illustration a picture that looked like a scene from *King Kong*—a gigantic gorilla astride the World Trade Center in New York City. The court held that the movie posters of *King Kong* had acquired a secondary meaning in the mind of the public, so the *Ape* producers were forced to change their poster.[18]

- **Trade dress** is the image and overall appearance of a business or product. It may include size, shape, color, or texture. The Supreme Court held that a Mexican restaurant was entitled to protection under the Lanham Act for the shape and general appearance of the exterior of its building as well as the decor, menu, servers' uniforms, and other features reflecting the total image of the restaurant.[19]

The following categories *cannot* be trademarked:

- **Similar to an existing mark.** To avoid confusion, the PTO will not grant a trademark that is similar to one already in existence on a similar product. Once the PTO had granted a trademark for "Pledge" furniture polish, it refused to trademark "Promise" for the same product. "Chat noir" and "black cat" were also too similar because one is simply a translation of the other. Houghton-Mifflin Co. successfully sued to prevent a punk rock band from calling itself Furious George because the name is too similar to Curious George, the star of a series of children's books.

- **Generic trademarks.** No one is permitted to trademark an item's ordinary name— "shoe" or "book," for example. Sometimes, however, a word begins as a trademark and later becomes a generic name. Zipper, escalator, aspirin, linoleum, thermos, yoyo, band-aid, ping-pong, and nylon all started out as trademarks but became generic. Once a name is generic, the owner loses the trademark because the name can no longer be used to distinguish one product from another—all products are called the same thing. That is why Xerox Corp. encourages people to say, "I'll photocopy this document," rather than "I'll xerox it." Jeep, Rollerblade, and TiVo are names that began as trademarks and may now be generic. What about "app store"? Microsoft has sued Apple, disputing its right to trademark this term. Meanwhile, Facebook has trademarked, "face," "book," "like," "wall," and "poke." The goal is not to prevent consumers from using these terms but rather to warn off other companies.

- **Descriptive marks.** Words cannot be trademarked if they simply describe the product—such as "low-fat," "green," or "crunchy." Descriptive words can, however, be trademarked if they do *not* describe that particular product because they then

---

[18]*Paramount Pictures Corp. v. Worldwide Entertainment Corp.*, 2 Media L. Rep. 1311, 195 U.S.P.Q. (BNA) 539, 1977 U.S. Dist. LEXIS 17931 (S.D.N.Y., 1977).
[19]*Two Pesos, Inc. v. Taco Cabana, Inc.*, 505 U.S. 763, 112 S. Ct. 2753, 1992 U.S. LEXIS 4533 (1992).

become distinctive rather than descriptive. "Blue Diamond" is an acceptable trademark for nuts so long as the nuts are neither blue nor diamond-shaped.

- **Names.** The PTO generally will not grant a trademark in a surname because other people are already using it and have the right to continue. No one could register "Jefferson" as a trademark. However, a surname can be used as part of a longer title—"Jefferson Home Tours," for instance. Similarly, no one can register a geographical name such as "Boston" unless it is also associated with another word, such as "Boston Ale."

- **Deceptive marks.** The PTO will not register a mark that is deceptive. It refused to register a trademark with the words "National Collection and Credit Control" and an eagle superimposed on a map of the United States because this trademark gave the false impression that the organization was an official government agency.

- **Scandalous or immoral trademarks.** The PTO refused to register a mark that featured a nude man and woman embracing. In upholding the PTO's decision, the court was unsympathetic to arguments that this was the perfect trademark for a newsletter on sex.[20] This author once had a client who wanted to apply for a trademark for marijuana: "Sweet Mary Jane, she never lets you down." However, the client was unwilling to admit to affixing the name to his product and shipping it in interstate commerce. Now, medical marijuana is legal in 18 states but the PTO refuses to register marijuana trademarks.

33-4d Infringement

To win an infringement suit, the trademark owner must show that the defendant's trademark is likely to deceive customers about who has made the goods or provided the services. In the *Seinfeld* case, the court ruled there was no trademark infringement because consumers would not be confused by the names or covers of the two books.

In the event of infringement, the rightful owner is entitled to (1) an injunction prohibiting further violations, (2) destruction of the infringing material, (3) up to three times actual damages, (4) any profits the infringer earned on the product, and (5) attorney's fees.

What about a perfume for dogs? Would a reasonable consumer confuse Pucci with Gucci, Bono Sports with Ralph Lauren Polo Sports, or Miss Claybone for Liz Claiborne? None of these companies challenged the parody use of their names for a dog perfume. But Tommy Hilfiger Licensing, Inc. did not see the humor in the name Timmy Holedigger. The court, however, advised Hilfiger "to chill," pointing out that there was no evidence of actual confusion.[21] On the other hand, auction website eBay did prevent a seller of perfumes from using the name Perfumebay. The court ruled that the use of "ebay" confused consumers.[22]

The following case raises an issue of confusion in cyberspace. Once again, the Internet is challenging intellectual property laws that were not conceived with this technology in mind.

---

[20]*In re McGinley*, 660 F.2d 481, 211 U.S.P.Q. (BNA) 668, 1981 CCPA LEXIS 177 (C.C.P.A., 1981).

[21]*Tommy Hilfiger Licensing, Inc. v. Nature Labs*, LLC, 221 F. Supp. 2d 410; 2002 U.S. Dist. LEXIS 14841 (2002).

[22]*Perfumebay.com Inc. v. eBay Inc.*, 506 F.3d 1165, 2007 U.S. App. LEXIS 25726.

You Be the Judge

NETWORK AUTOMATION, INC. v. ADVANCED SYSTEMS CONCEPTS, INC.

2011 U.S. App. LEXIS 4488
United States Court of Appeals for the Ninth Circuit, 2011

Facts: Network Automation and Advanced Systems Concepts both sold job scheduling and management software, and both advertised on the Internet. Network sold its software under the trademarked name AutoMate, while Systems used the trademark ActiveBatch. Customers paid between $995 and $10,995 to use these software programs.

Google AdWords is a program that sells "keywords," which are search terms that trigger the display of a sponsor's advertisement. When a user enters a keyword, Google displays the links generated by its own algorithm in the main part of the page, along with advertisements in a separate "Sponsored Links" section next to or above the objective results. Multiple advertisers can purchase the same keyword.

Although ActiveBatch was Systems's trademark, Network purchased it as a keyword. This purchase meant that anyone who googled "ActiveBatch" would see a web page where the top results were links to Systems' own website and various articles about the product. But in the "Sponsored Sites" section of the page, users would see the following ad:

Job Scheduler

Windows Job Scheduling + Much More. Easy to Deploy, Scalable. D/L Trial www.NetworkAutomation.com

Sometimes, they would also see an equivalent ad for Systems' software—the real ActiveBatch.

Systems alleged that this use of ActiveBatch was a violation of its trademark on the word. The trial court issued an injunction prohibiting Network's purchase of the Google keyword. Network appealed.

You Be the Judge: *Has Network violated Systems's trademark by purchasing it as a Google keyword?*

Argument for Systems: Network and Systems are direct competitors. Their two products—AutoMate and ActiveBatch—perform the same functions and are both advertised on the Internet. Network is deliberately confusing customers about whose product ActiveBatch really is.

When consumers use the Internet, they tend not to read carefully—they just click away. Few customers analyze the web address of an ad to make sure they are going to the right website. Indeed, customers may not even be aware of who owns ActiveBatch. The Network ad certainly does not reveal that Systems owns this software. Customers could easily assume that whatever web address comes up belongs to the rightful owner.

When customers search for a generic term, they know that they will encounter links from a variety of sources, but when they look for a trade name, their expectation is that they will only be linked to that specific product. For this reason, the use of another company's trade name can create tremendous confusion.

Network has bought the right to use Systems's trademark as a ruse to fool potential customers. This subterfuge is exactly the sort of behavior that trademark laws are designed to prevent.

Argument for Network: Today, most consumers are sophisticated about the Internet. They skip from site to site, ready to hit the Back button whenever they are not satisfied with a site's contents. They fully expect to find some sites that are not what they imagine based on a glance at the domain name or search engine summary. Consumers do not form any firm expectations about the sponsorship of a website until they have seen the landing page—if then.

Even if Systems's arguments were true for consumer purchases, the typical customer for this software is a sophisticated businessperson buying an expensive product. These purchasers are likely to be very careful and will not be confused by Google ads. Also, they will probably understand the mechanics of Internet search engines and the nature of sponsored links.

In the end, Network's intent was not to confuse consumers but rather to allow them to compare its product to ActiveBatch. That goal is a completely appropriate use of a trademark.

33-4e Federal Trademark Dilution Act of 1995

Before Congress passed the Federal Trademark Dilution Act of 1995 (FTDA), a trademark owner could win an infringement lawsuit only by proving that consumers would be deceived about who had really made the product. **This statute prevents others from using a trademark in a way that** (1) **dilutes its value, even though consumers are not confused about the origin of the product; or** (2) **tarnishes it by association with unwholesome goods or services.** For example, Barbie's Playhouse was an adult entertainment website with a font and colors similar to those used by Mattel for its copyrighted Barbie doll. Also, the doll at the bottom of the website looked like a Barbie doll. The court found that Barbie's Playhouse had violated the FTDA.[23]

33-4f Domain Names

Over 130 million Internet addresses, known as *domain names*, are currently active, so it is often difficult to find a distinctive name for a new business. Domain names can be immensely valuable as they are an important component of doing business. Suppose you want to buy a new pair of jeans. Without thinking twice, you type in http://www.jcrew.com and there you are, ready to order. What if that address took you to a different site altogether, say, the personal site of one Jackie Crew? The store might lose out on a sale. Companies not only want to own their own domain name, they want to prevent complaint sites such as http://www.untied.com (about United Airlines), http://www.ihatestarbucks.com, or the always popular variation on the "sucks" theme, such as http://macdonaldssucks.com. Generic domain names can be valuable, too. Shopping.com paid $750,000 to acquire its domain name from the previous (lucky) owner.

CYBERSQUATTING

Who has the right to a domain name? In the beginning, the National Science Foundation, which maintained the Internet, granted Network Solutions, Inc. (NSI), a private company, the right to allocate domain names. NSI charged no fee for domain names and the rule was "first come, first served." Then so-called cybersquatters began to register domain names, not to use, but to sell to others. Someone, for example, tried to sell the name "Bill Gates" for $1 million.

In response to complaints, NSI began suspending any domain name that was challenged by the holder of a registered trademark. For instance, NSI would not allow Princeton Review to keep kaplan.com, which Princeton had acquired simply to inconvenience its arch rival in the test preparation business. Congress then passed the **Anticybersquatting Consumer Protection Act (ACPA), which permits both trademark owners and famous people to sue anyone who registers their name as a domain name in "bad faith."** The rightful owner of a trademark is entitled to damages of up to $100,000. Verizon was awarded damages of $33.15 million against OnlineNIC Inc., which had registered 663 domain names that were confusingly similar to Verizon trademarks.

ICANN

As both the value and the number of domain names soared, the U.S. government transferred management of the Internet, including the allocation of names, to a private, nonprofit, international organization, the Internet Corporation for Assigned Names and Numbers (ICANN). Disputes over domain names can be decided by arbitration under ICANN's Uniform Domain Name Dispute Resolution Policy (UDRP) rather than by litigation under the ACPA. For example, Jay Leno used the ICANN process to win a cybersquatting case against someone who was using thejaylenoshow.com to attract viewers to his own real estate website.

---

[23]*Mattel, Inc. v. Jcom, Inc.*, 1998 U.S. Dist. LEXIS 16195.

To bring a UDRP case, the complainant (i.e., the plaintiff) must allege that:

- The domain name creates confusion because it is similar to a registered trademark.

- The respondent (i.e., the defendant) has no legitimate reason to use the domain name.

- The respondent registered the domain name in bad faith. If the respondent is a competitor of the complainant and has acquired the domain name to disrupt the complainant's business (à la Princeton Review), that is evidence of bad faith. So is an attempt by the respondent to sell the name to the complainant.

If the complainant wins, it is entitled either to take over the domain name or to cancel it. For example, in a dispute over wal-martsucks.com, the WIPO arbitrator ordered that the name be transferred to Walmart. The respondent had demonstrated his bad faith by attempting to sell the name for $530,000. In a similar case, however, the WIPO arbitrator found for a respondent who had registered Wallmartcanadasucks.com. In this case, the respondent had not tried to sell the name and was using the website to criticize Walmart. As the arbitrator stated in his opinion, "Posting defamatory material on a website would not justify revocation of a domain name. The Policy should not be used to shut down robust debate and criticism." Either party has the option before or after an ICANN arbitration to litigate the issue in court.

At this writing, the courts have also held that criticism sites do not violate the ACPA so long as they do not have a bad faith intent to make a profit. The sites do not violate trademark law unless they create consumer confusion.[24]

THEFT OF DOMAIN NAME

In this crowded world, few people are the first to do anything. David Goncalves achieved this distinction in an unfortunate way—he became the first person in the United States to be convicted of stealing a domain name. After hacking into the files of a domain name registrar, he transferred to himself ownership of P2P.com. He then sold this name for $111,211 to professional basketball player Mark Madsen, who was running a business that bought and sold domain names. P2P could be a valuable name for someone who wanted to operate a peer-to-peer network. Goncalves was convicted under a state fraud statute as well as the Computer Fraud and Abuse Act (which we discussed in Chapter 32, on cyberlaw).

TRADEMARKING A DOMAIN NAME

Our discussion thus far has been about registering a trademark as a domain name. Sometimes businesses want to do the opposite—trademark a domain name. The PTO will issue such a trademark only for services offered via the Internet. Thus, it trademarked "eBay" for "on-line trading services in which seller posts items to be auctioned and bidding is done electronically." The PTO will not trademark a domain name that is merely an address and does not identify the service provided.

33-4g International Trademark Treaties

Under the **Paris Convention**, if someone registers a trademark in one country, then he has a grace period of six months, during which he can file in any other country using the same original filing date. Under the **Madrid Agreement**, any trademark registered with the international registry is valid in all signatory countries. (The United States is a signatory.)

---

[24]See, for example, *Career Agents Network, Inc. v. careeragentsnetwork.biz*, 2010 U.S. Dist. LEXIS 17263 (E.D.MI, 2010).

The **Trademark Law Treaty** simplifies and harmonizes the process of applying for trademarks around the world. Now, a U.S. firm seeking international trademark protection need only file one application, in English, with the PTO, which sends the application to the WIPO, which transmits it to each country in which the applicant would like trademark protection.

EXAM Strategy

Question: Jerry Falwell was a nationally known Baptist minister. You can read about him on falwell.com. You can also read about him at fallwell.com—a site critical of his views on homosexuality. This site has a disclaimer indicating that it is not affiliated with Reverend Falwell. The minister sued fallwell.com, alleging a violation of trademark law and the anticybersquatting statute. Was there a violation?

Strategy: To win a trademark claim, the reverend had to show that there was some confusion between the two sites. To win the cybersquatting claim, he had to show bad faith on the part of fallwell.com.

Result: The reverend lost on both counts. The court ruled that there was no confusion—fallwell.com had a clear disclaimer. Also, there was no indication of bad faith. The court was reluctant to censor political commentary.

33-5 TRADE SECRETS

What do the formulas for Coke and motor oil have in common with computer circuitry, a machine for making adhesive tape, and a procedure for applying hair dye? They are all trade secrets. **A trade secret is a formula, device, process, method, or compilation of information that, when used in business, gives the owner an advantage over competitors who do not know it.** In determining if information is a trade secret, courts consider:

- How difficult (and expensive) was the information to obtain? Was it readily available from other sources?

- Does the information create an important competitive advantage?

- Did the company make a reasonable effort to protect it?

It has been estimated that the theft of trade secrets costs U.S. businesses $100 billion a year. In response, most states have now adopted the **Uniform Trade Secrets Act (UTSA).** Anyone who misappropriates a trade secret is liable to the owner for (1) actual damages, (2) unjust enrichment, or (3) a reasonable royalty. If the misappropriation was willful or malicious, the court may award attorney's fees and double damages. A jury awarded Avery Dennison Corp. $40 million in damages from a competitor that had misappropriated secret information about the adhesives used in self-stick stamps.

Although a company can patent some types of trade secrets, it may be reluctant to do so because patent registration requires that the formula be disclosed publicly. In addition, patent protection expires after 20 years. Some types of trade secrets cannot be patented—such as customer lists, business plans, and marketing strategies.

The following case deals with a typical issue: How much information can employees take with them when they start their own, competing business?

Trade secret
A formula, device, process, method, or compilation of information that, when used in business, gives the owner an advantage over competitors.

POLLACK V. SKINSMART DERMATOLOGY AND AESTHETIC CENTER P.C.

2004 Pa. Dist. & Cnty. Dec. LEXIS 214
Common Pleas Court of Philadelphia County, Pennsylvania, 2004

CASE SUMMARY

Facts: Dr. Andrew Pollack owned the Philadelphia Institute of Dermatology (PID), a dermatology practice. Drs. Toby Shawe and Samy Badawy worked for PID as independent contractors, receiving a certain percentage of the revenues from each patient they treated. Natalie Wilson was Dr. Pollack's medical assistant.

Pollack tentatively agreed to sell the practice to Shawe and Badawy. But instead of buying his practice, the two doctors decided to start their own, which they called Skinsmart. They executed a lease for the Skinsmart office space, offered Wilson a job, and instructed PID staff members to make copies of their appointment books and printouts of the patient list. Then they abruptly resigned from PID. Wilson called PID patients to reschedule procedures at Skinsmart. The two doctors also called patients and sent out a mailing to patients and referring physicians to tell them about Skinsmart.

Pollack filed suit, alleging that the two doctors had misappropriated trade secrets.

Issue: *Did Shawe and Badawy misappropriate trade secrets from PID?*

Decision: Yes, the two doctors did misappropriate trade secrets.

Reasoning: The right to protect trade secrets must be balanced against the right of individuals to pursue whatever occupation they choose. For this reason, secrets will only be protected if they are the particular information of the employer, not general secrets of the trade. Pollack must also demonstrate that the trade secrets had value and importance to his business and that he either discovered or owned the secrets.

Against this backdrop, it is clear the patient list is a trade secret, worthy of protection. Patient information is confidential and is not known to anyone outside the practice. Pollack relied upon the patient list as the core component of his practice. For this reason, it is valuable. He made substantial effort to compile the list over a number of years. It contained 20,000 names with related information. He spent money on computers, software, and employees to keep and maintain the list.

He also sought to protect the secrecy of the information. Within PID's offices, the information was not universally known or accessible. Not every staff member, including the practicing physicians, could pull the records. Wilson did not have access to them, and the doctors relied on other PID employees to access the patient list.

Only civil penalties are available under the Uniform Trade Secrets Act. To safeguard national security and maintain the nation's industrial and economic edge, Congress passed the **Economic Espionage Act of 1996, which makes it a criminal offense to steal (or attempt to steal) trade secrets for the benefit of someone other than the owner, including for the benefit of any foreign government.** Xiaodong Sheldon Meng was convicted of violating this statute after he was caught stealing computer code used in military weapons. He had committed the theft on behalf of the government of China. Meng was sentenced to 24 months in prison. Timothy Kissane received the same sentence for stealing computer source code from an employer. He planned to sell it to the company's competitors.

Chapter Conclusion

Intellectual property takes many different forms. It can be an Internet domain name, a software program, a cartoon character, a formula for motor oil, or a process for making drugs. Because of its great variety, intellectual property can be difficult to protect. Yet, for many individuals and companies, intellectual property is the most valuable asset they will ever own. As its economic value increases, so does the need to understand the rules of intellectual property law.

EXAM REVIEW

	Patent	Copyright	Trademark	Trade Secrets
Protects:	Mechanical, electrical, chemical inventions; processes; machines; composition of matter; designs; plants	The tangible expression of an idea, but not the idea itself	Words and symbols that a business uses to identify its products or services	A formula, device, process, method, or compilation of information that, when used in business, gives the owner an advantage over competitors who do not know it
Requirements for Legal Protection:	Application approved by PTO	An item is automatically copyrighted once it is in tangible form	Use is the only requirement; registration is not necessary but does offer some benefits	Must be kept confidential
Duration:	20 years after the application is filed (14 years from date of issuance for a design patent)	70 years after the death of the work's only or last living author or, for a corporation, 95 years from publication or 120 years from creation	Valid for 10 years but the owner can renew for an unlimited number of terms as long as the mark is still being used	As long as it is kept confidential

MULTIPLE-CHOICE QUESTIONS

1. Thomas's English muffins wanted to protect the method by which it makes muffins with air pockets—what it calls "nooks and crannies." What would be the best way to achieve this goal?

   (a) Patent

   (b) Copyright

   (c) Trademark

   (d) Trade secret

   (e) This method cannot be protected.

2. VitaminWater has become such a success that other companies are also now selling similar (but not identical) flavored colored water. Some competitors bottle their drinks in a similar bell-shaped bottle with a two-toned label that has a horizontal color band. What is the best infringement claim for VitaminWater to make against these competitors?

   (a) Patent

   (b) Copyright

   (c) Trademark

   (d) Trade secret

   (e) There is no good claim.

3. Faber-Castell began manufacturing pencils in 1761. Although pencils and erasers had both existed for some time, the company did not begin putting erasers on the ends of its pencils until the 1870s. The company was sued by an inventor who had previously patented this idea. The case went to the Supreme Court. Who won the case?

   (a) The patent holder, because no one had ever put an eraser on a pencil before.

   (b) The patent holder, because the PTO had approved his patent.

   (c) Faber-Castell, because the pencil with an eraser was not novel.

   (d) Faber-Castell, because the pencil with an eraser was not useful.

4. If you buy a DVD, you have the legal right to:

   (a) watch it as many times as you want and then give it away.

   (b) copy it to your computer and then give it to a friend.

   (c) copy it to your computer and sell it on eBay.

   (d) all of the above.

   (e) (a) and (b) only.

5. A couple thought of a clever name for an automobile. They wanted to protect this name so that they could ultimately sell it to a car manufacturer. What would be the best method to achieve this goal?

   (a) Patent

   (b) Copyright

   (c) Trademark

   (d) Trade secret

   (e) This name cannot be protected.

ESSAY QUESTIONS

1. In the documentary movie *Expelled: No Intelligence Allowed,* there was a 15-second clip of "Imagine," a song by John Lennon. The purpose of the scene was to criticize the song's message. His wife and sons, who held the copyright, sued to block this use of the song. Under what theory did the movie makers argue that they had the right to use this music? Did they win?

2. **ETHICS** After Edward Miller left his job as a salesperson at the New England Insurance Agency, Inc., he took some of his New England customers to his new employer. At New England, the customer lists had been kept in file cabinets. Although the company did not restrict access to these files, it claimed there was a "You do not peruse my files and I do not peruse yours" understanding. The lists were not marked "confidential" or "not to be disclosed." Did Miller steal New England's trade secrets? Whether or not he violated the law, was it ethical for him to use this information at his new job? What is your Life Principle?

3. Rebecca Reyher wrote (and copyrighted) a children's book entitled *My Mother Is the Most Beautiful Woman in the World.* The story was based on a Russian folk tale told to her by her own mother. Years later, the children's TV show *Sesame Street* televised a skit entitled "The Most Beautiful Woman in the World." The *Sesame Street* version took place in a different locale and had fewer frills, but the sequence of events in both stories was identical. Has *Sesame Street* infringed Reyher's copyright?

4. Roger Schlafly applied for a patent for two prime numbers. (A prime number cannot be evenly divided by any number other than itself and 1. Examples of primes are 2, 3, 5, 7, 11, and 13.) Schlafly's numbers are a bit longer—one is 150 digits, the other is 300. His numbers, when used together, can help perform the type of mathematical operation necessary for exchanging coded messages by computer. Should the PTO issue this patent?

5. Frank B. McMahon wrote one of the first psychology textbooks to feature a light, easily readable style. He also included many colloquialisms and examples that appealed to a youthful student market. Charles G. Morris wrote a psychology textbook that copied McMahon's style. Has Morris infringed McMahon's copyright?

6. Victoria's Secret, a well-known lingerie company, found out that a man named Victor Moseley was running a small store in Kentucky named "Victor's Little Secret." Moseley's shop sold clocks, patches, temporary tattoos, stuffed animals, coffee mugs, leather biker wallets, Zippo lighters, diet formula, jigsaw puzzles, handcuffs, hosiery, greeting cards, incense burners, car air fresheners, sunglasses, jewelry, candles, and adult novelties. Women's lingerie represented about 5 percent of its sales. Does Victoria's Secret have a valid intellectual property claim?

EXAM Strategy

7. **Question:** DatagraphiX manufactured and sold computer graphics equipment that allowed users to transfer large volumes of information directly from computers to microfilm. Customers were required to keep maintenance documentation on site for the DatagraphiX service personnel. The service manual carried this legend: "No other use, direct or indirect, of this document or of any information derived there from is authorized. No copies of any part of this document shall be

made without written approval by DatagraphiX." In addition, on every page of the maintenance manual, the company placed warnings that the information was proprietary and not to be duplicated. Frederick J. Lennen left DatagraphiX to start his own company that serviced DatagraphiX equipment. Can DatagraphiX prevent Lennen from using its manuals?

Strategy: With trade secrets, the key is that the owner has made a reasonable effort to protect them. (See the "Result" at the end of this section.)

EXAM Strategy

8. Question: "Hey, Paula," a pop hit that spent months on the music charts, was back on the radio 30 years later, but in a form the song's author never intended. Talk-show host Rush Limbaugh played a version with the same music as the original but with lyrics that made fun of President Bill Clinton's alleged sexual misconduct with Paula Jones. Has Limbaugh violated the author's copyright?

Strategy: Although this example may look like a copyright violation, it falls under an exception. (See the "Result" at the end of this section.)

EXAM Strategy

9. Question: Research Corp. applied for a patent for a so-called halftoning technique that uses a mathematical formula to enable monitors and printers with limited color options to simulate a wider range of colors. Is this technique patentable?

Strategy: Are these inventors attempting to patent a mathematical algorithm or formula? (See the "Result" at the end of this section.)

7. Result: The court held that these manuals were DatagraphiX's trade secrets.

8. Result: Parody (especially about politics!) is a fair use of copyrighted material so long as use of the original is not excessive.

9. Result: The trial court ruled that this patent application was invalid because it was too abstract. But the appellate court overruled, holding that, although the patent used mathematical algorithms, the inventors were patenting the process not the algorithms. It upheld the patent.[25]

---

[25] *Research Corporation Technologies, Inc. v. Microsoft Corporation,* 627 F.3d 859; 2010 U.S. App. LEXIS 24984; 97 U.S.P.Q.2D (BNA) 1274 (Fed. Cir. 2010).

DISCUSSION QUESTIONS

1. **ETHICS** Virtually any TV show, movie, or song can be downloaded for free on the Internet. Most of this material is copyrighted and was very expensive to produce. Most of it is also available for a fee through such legitimate sites such as iTunes. What is your ethical obligation? Should you pay $1.99 to download an episode of *American Idol* from iTunes or take it for free from an illegal site? What is your Life Principle?

2. For much of history, the copyright term was limited to 28 years. Now it is as long as 120 years. What is a fair copyright term? Some commentators argue that because so much intellectual property is stolen, owners need longer protection. Do you agree with this argument?

3. Do you agree with the court that the band Furious George violated the copyright of Curious George?

4. Should Amazon be able to patent the One-Click method of ordering? What about Facebook's patent on a process that "dynamically provides a news feed about a user of a social network"? Were these inventions really novel and nonobvious?

   What should the standard be for business method patents?

5. Fredrik Colting wrote a book entitled *60 Years Later: Coming Through the Rye*, a riff on J. D. Salinger's famous *Catcher in the Rye*. Colting's book imagined how Salinger's protagonist, Holden Caulfield, would view life as a 76-year old. Alice Randall wrote a novel entitled *The Wind Done Gone*, which retells the Civil War novel *Gone with the Wind* from the perspective of Scarlett O'Hara's (imagined) black half-sister. Both Colting and Randall were sued and both alleged fair use. Should they win?

6. The Susan G. Komen breast cancer charity trademarked the term "for the cure." It has brought suit against other charities that use the term, as in "run for the cure" or "kites for the cure." It also sues charities that use the same shade of pink that it has long used on its ribbons. Should Komen be able to trademark "for the cure" and the color pink?

7. Should a wildflower garden be eligible for intellectual property protection?

CHAPTER 34

REAL AND PERSONAL PROPERTY

"My only child is a no-good thief," Riley murmurs sadly to his visitors. "He has always treated me contemptuously. Now he's been sentenced to five years for stealing from a children's charity. He is my only heir, but why should I leave him everything?"

Riley continues talking to his three guests: a bishop, a rabbi, and Earnest, a Boy Scout leader. "I have $500,000 in stocks and bonds in my bank deposit box. Tomorrow morning, I'm going to go down to the bank, take out all the papers, and hand them over to the Boy Scouts so that other kids won't turn out so bad." Everyone applauds his generosity, and they photograph Riley and Earnest shaking hands. But the following morning, on his way to the bank, Riley is struck by an ambulance and killed. A dispute arises over the money. The three witnesses assure the court that Riley was on his way to give the money to the Boy Scouts. From prison, the ne'er-do-well son demands the money as Riley's sole heir. Who wins? Property law holds the answer.

In this chapter, we will examine personal property. In the section on gifts, we learn that Riley's no-good son gets the money. Riley intended to give the stocks and bonds to the Boy Scouts the following day, but he never completed a valid gift because he failed to *deliver* the papers.

But first, we will take a look at real property and landlord-tenant law.

> My only child is a no-good thief. He is my only heir, but why should I leave him everything?

nuttakit/Shutterstock.com; Steve Allen/Brand X Pictures/Jupiter Images

34-1 NATURE OF REAL PROPERTY

Property falls into three categories: real, personal, and intellectual. Real property consists of the following:

- **Land.** Land is the most common and important form of real property. In England, land was historically the greatest source of wealth and social status, far more important than industrial or commercial enterprises. As a result, the law of real property has been of paramount importance for nearly 1,000 years, developing very gradually to reflect changing conditions. Some real property terms sound medieval for the simple reason that they are medieval. By contrast, the common law of torts and contracts is comparatively new.

    Real property usually also includes anything underground (subsurface rights), and some amount of airspace above land (air rights).

- **Buildings.** Buildings are real property. Houses, office buildings, apartment complexes, and factories all fall in this category.

- **Plant life.** Plant life growing on land is real property whether the plants are naturally occurring, such as trees, or cultivated crops. When a landowner sells his property, plant life is automatically included in the sale unless the parties agree otherwise. A landowner may also sell the plant life separately if he wishes. A sale of the plant life alone, without the land, is a sale of goods. (Goods, as you may recall, are movable things.) If Douglas agrees to sell all of the fir trees on his property, this sale of goods will be governed by the Uniform Commercial Code (UCC), regardless of whether Douglas or the buyer is obligated to cut the trees.[1]

- **Fixtures.** Fixtures are goods that have become attached to real property. A house (which is real property) contains many fixtures. The furnace and heating ducts were goods when they were manufactured and when they were sold to the builder because they were movable. But when the builder attached them to the house, the items became fixtures. By contrast, neither the refrigerator nor the grand piano is a fixture.

When an owner sells real property, the buyer normally obtains the fixtures unless the parties specify otherwise. Sometimes it is difficult to determine whether something is a fixture. The general rule is this: **An object is a fixture if a reasonable person would consider the item to be a permanent part of the property.**

For many, beef is a dietary fixture. But is the cattle scale in the following case a fixture?

FREEMAN v. BARRS

237 S.W.3d 285
Missouri Court of Appeals, 2007

CASE SUMMARY

Facts: Mary Ann Barrs paid $3.5 million to Francis Freeman for 4,000 acres of ranch land, including a covered "pole-barn," which had open sides, a large cattle scale, and an enclosed veterinarian's office. The parties used a form contract, which stated that all fixtures were included with the sale. The document offered space for the parties to specify items that were included or excluded with the sale, but neither party listed the cattle scale as either in or out of the deal. After the agreement went through, Barrs and Freeman got into a beef over who owned the scale.

[1] UCC §2-107(2).

The trial judge grilled numerous witnesses and ultimately weighed in on the side of Barrs, declaring the scale a fixture that belonged to the real estate. Broiling, Freeman appealed.

Issue: *Was the cattle scale a fixture?*

Decision: Yes, the scale was a fixture. Affirmed.

Reasoning: The scale's maker testified that it was designed to be portable. It would only take him an hour to cut away a welded metal fence and then fifteen minutes to move the scale itself.

On the other hand, the scale weighs 6,500 pounds. It is inside a covered barn that also includes a vet's office. To install the scale, a fence and gates within the barn had to be cut. There were concrete ramps and fencing around the scale to direct cattle onto it. The fence posts were set in concrete. No one had moved the scale since its installation.

A 6,500-pound scale placed inside a structure on a specially sized concrete pad and surrounded by metal pole fencing is annexed to the real estate. The scale was a fixture, and was included in the sale of the real estate.

34-2 ESTATES IN REAL PROPERTY

Use and ownership of real estate can take many different legal forms. A person may own property outright, having the unrestricted use of the land and an unlimited right to sell it. Such a person owns a **fee simple absolute**. However, someone may also own a lesser interest in real property. The different rights that someone can hold in real property are known as **estates** or **interests.** Both terms simply indicate specified rights in property.

Fee simple absolute
Full ownership privileges in a property.

34-2a Concurrent Estates

Concurrent estates
Two or more people owning property at the same time.

When two or more people own real property at the same time, they have **concurrent estates**. The most common forms of concurrent estates are tenancy in common, joint tenancy, and tenancy by the entirety.

TENANCY IN COMMON

Tenancy in common
Two or more people holding equal interest in a property, but with no right of survivorship.

The most common form of concurrent estate is **tenancy in common**. Suppose Patricia owns a house. Patricia agrees to sell her house to Quincy and Rebecca. When she **conveys** the deed (that is, transfers the deed) "to Quincy and Rebecca," those two now have a tenancy in common. This kind of estate can also be created in a will. If Patricia had died still owning the house, and left it in her will to "Sam and Tracy," then Sam and Tracy would have a tenancy in common. Tenancy in common is the "default setting" when multiple people acquire property. Co-owners are automatically considered tenants in common unless another type of interest (joint tenancy, tenancy by the entirety) is specified.

A tenancy in common might have 2 owners, or 22, or any number. The tenants in common do not own a particular section of the property; they own an equal interest in the entire property. Quincy and Rebecca each own a 50 percent interest in the entire house.

Any co-tenant may convey her interest in the property to another person. Thus, if Rebecca moves 1,000 miles away, she may sell her 50 percent interest in the house to Sidney. Further, when a co-tenant dies, her interest in the property passes to her heirs, along with all of her other assets.

Partition   Since any tenant in common has the power to convey her interest, some people may find themselves sharing ownership with others they do not know or, worse, dislike. What to do? Partition, or division of the property among the co-tenants. Any co-tenant is entitled to demand partition of the property. If the various co-tenants cannot agree on a fair division, a co-tenant may request a court to do it. **All co-tenants have an absolute right to partition.**

A court will normally attempt a **partition by kind**, meaning that it actually divides the land equally among the co-tenants. If three co-tenants own a 300-acre farm and the court can divide the land so that the three sections are of roughly equal value, it will perform a partition in kind, even if one or two of the co-tenants oppose partition. If partition by kind is impossible because there is no fair way to divide the property, the court will order the real estate sold and the proceeds divided equally.

JOINT TENANCY

Joint tenancy is similar to tenancy in common but is used less frequently. The parties, called joint tenants, again own a percentage of the entire property and also have the absolute right of partition. The primary difference is that a **joint tenancy** includes the right of survivorship. This means that when one joint tenant dies, his interest in the property passes to *the surviving joint tenants.* Recall that a tenant in common, by contrast, has the power to leave his interest in the real estate to his heirs. Because a joint tenant cannot leave the property to his heirs, courts do not favor this form of ownership. The law presumes that a concurrent estate is a tenancy in common; a court will interpret an estate as a joint tenancy only if the parties creating it clearly intended that result.

Joint tenancy

Two or more people holding equal interest in a property, with the right of survivorship.

Joint tenancy has one other curious feature. Although joint tenants may not convey their interest by will, they may do so during their lifetime. If Frank and George own vacation property as joint tenants, Frank has the power to sell his interest to Harry. But as soon as he does so, the joint tenancy is **severed**; that is, broken. Harry and George are now tenants in common, and the right of survivorship is destroyed.

But when does a severance officially take place? The answer was of critical importance in the following case.

JACKSON V. ESTATE OF GREEN

771 N.W.2d 675
Supreme Court of Michigan, 2009

CASE SUMMARY

Facts: Green and Jackson owned land as joint tenants. Green filed a petition asking a court to partition the parcels, that is, to sever the joint tenancy, But he died while the partition was still pending.

The lower courts found that because the partition was not complete at the time of Green's death, the land reverted to Jackson.

Green's estate appealed.

Issue: *Did filing for the partition of a joint tenancy terminate survivorship rights?*

Decision: No, filing alone did not terminate the joint tenancy.

Reasoning: The principal characteristic of a joint tenancy is the right of survivorship. That is, when

one joint tenant dies, the surviving owner takes the whole estate. But when a joint tenancy is severed, this right of survivorship is destroyed. Severance occurs if ordered by a court, or if either owner sells his share of the property.

In this case, Green filed for a partition of the parcel, but before the court approved the partition, he died. The question was whether the act of filing alone was enough to undo the joint tenancy.

Sadly for Green's already-grieving heirs, severance takes place at the moment a court enters the final order of partition. No court had entered such an order in this case, so when Green died, his interest automatically went to Jackson. Green's estate lost.

EXAM Strategy

Question: Thomas, age 80, has spent a lifetime accumulating unspoiled land in Oregon. He owns 16,000 acres, which he plans to leave to his five children. He is not so crazy about his grandchildren. Thomas cringes at the problems the grandchildren would cause if some of them inherited an interest in the land and became part-owners along with Thomas's own children. Should Thomas leave his land to his children as tenants in common or joint tenants?

Strategy: When a co-tenant dies, her interest in property passes to her heirs. When a joint tenant dies, his interest in the property passes to the surviving joint tenants.

Result: Thomas is better off leaving the land to his children as joint tenants. That way, when one of his children dies, that child's interest in the land will go to Thomas's surviving children, not to his grandchildren.

Tenancy in Common

Three tenants in common, each owning a 1/3 interest in the entire property.

Alice	Ben	Clem
↓	↓	↓
dies		
↓	↓	↓
Kate	Ben	Clem

Kate inherits and becomes a tenant in common with Ben and Clem

Ben → **sells**

Kate	Larry	Clem

Larry buys and becomes a tenant in common with Kate and Clem

Joint Tenancy

Three joint tenants, each owning a 1/3 interest in the entire property, with right of survivorship.

Doug	Eliza	Fred
↓	↓	↓
dies	Eliza	Fred

Doug's interest passes to Eliza and Fred

Fred → **conveys to**

Fred's conveyance severs his joint tenancy with Eliza

Eliza		George

Eliza and George now have a tenancy in common

© Cengage Learning

EXHIBIT 34.1   The Differences Between Tenancy in Common and Joint Tenancy

TENANCY BY THE ENTIRETY

This form of ownership exists in slightly over half of the states. **The husband and wife each own the entire property, and they both have a right of survivorship.** So when the husband dies, his one-half interest in the property automatically passes to his wife. Neither party has a right to convey his or her interest. If the parties wish to sell their interests, they must do so together. An advantage of this is that no creditor may seize the property based on a debt incurred by only one spouse. If a husband goes bankrupt, creditors may not take his house if he and his wife own it as tenants by the entirety. Divorce terminates a tenancy by the entirety and leaves the two parties as tenants in common.

34-3 NONPOSSESSORY INTERESTS

All of the estates and interests that we have examined thus far focused on one thing: possession of the land. Now we look at interests that *never* involve possession. These interests may be very valuable, even though the holder never lives on the land.

34-3a Easements

The Alabama Power Co. drove a flatbed truck over land owned by Thomas Burgess, damaging the property. The power company did this to reach its power lines and wooden transmission poles. Burgess had never given Alabama Power permission to enter his land, and he sued for the damage that the heavy trucks caused. He recovered—nothing. Alabama Power had an *easement* to use Burgess's land.

An **easement** gives one person the right to enter land belonging to another and make a limited use of it, without taking anything away. Burgess had bought his land from a man named Denton, who years earlier had sold an easement to Alabama Power. The easement gave the power company the right to construct several transmission poles on one section of Denton's land and to use reasonable means to reach the poles. Alabama Power owned that easement forever, and when Burgess bought the land, he took it subject to the easement. Alabama Power drove its trucks across a section of land where the power company had never gone before, and the easement did not explicitly give the company this right. But the court found that the company had no other way to reach its poles, and therefore, the easement allowed this use. Burgess is stuck with his uninvited guest as long as he owns the land.[2]

Easement
The right to enter land belonging to another and make limited use of it.

34-3b Profit

A **profit** gives one person the right to enter land belonging to another and take something away. You own 100 acres of vacation property, and suddenly a mining company informs you that the land contains valuable nickel deposits. You may choose to sell a profit to the mining company, allowing it to enter your land and take away the nickel. You receive cash up front, and the company earns money from the sale of the mineral. The rules about creating and transferring easements apply to profits as well.

Profit
The right to enter land belonging to another and take something from it.

34-3c License

A **license** gives the holder temporary permission to enter another's property. Unlike an easement or profit, a license is a *temporary* right. When you attend a basketball game by buying a ticket, the basketball team that sells you the ticket is the licensor and you are the licensee. You are entitled to enter the licensor's premises, namely the basketball arena, and to remain during the game, though the club can revoke the license if you behave unacceptably, and you must leave when the game is over.

License
The right to enter land belonging to another temporarily.

[2]*Burgess v. Alabama Power Co.*, 658 So. 2d 435, 1995 Ala. LEXIS 119 (Ala. 1995).

34-3d Mortgage

Generally, in order to buy a house, a prospective owner must borrow money. The bank or other lender will require security before it hands over its money, and the most common form of security for a real estate loan is a mortgage. A **mortgage** is a security interest in real property. The homeowner who borrows money is the **mortgagor** because she is *giving* the mortgage to the lender. The lender, in turn, is the **mortgagee**, the party acquiring a security interest. The mortgagee in most cases obtains a **lien** on the house, meaning the right to foreclose on the property if the mortgagor fails to pay back the money borrowed. A mortgagee forecloses by taking legal possession of the property, auctioning it to the highest bidder, and using the proceeds to pay off the loan.

34-4 Land Use Regulation

34-4a Nuisance Law

A nuisance is an unprivileged interference with a person's use and enjoyment of her property. Offensive noise, odors, or smoke often give rise to nuisance claims. Courts typically balance the utility of the act that is causing the problem against the harm done to neighboring property owners. If a suburban homeowner begins to raise pigs in her backyard, the neighbors may find the bouquet offensive; a court will probably issue an **abatement**; that is, an order requiring the homeowner to eliminate the nuisance.

Community members can use the old doctrine of nuisance for more serious problems than pigs. An apartment building in Berkeley, California, became widely known as a drug house, and the neighbors suffered. Here is how two of the neighbors described their lives:

> I have been confronted by the drug dealers, drug customers, and prostitutes that frequent and work around and from 1615–1617 Russell Street. Weekly I have lost many hours of sleep from the cars that burn rubber after each drug buy in the middle of the night.
>
> Because of this illegal activity, my child is unable to use our front yard, and I even have to check the back yard since it has been intruded upon from time to time by people running from the police. He is learning to count by how many gunshots he hears and can't understand why he can't even enjoy our rose garden.

These were but two of the affidavits written by neighbors of a 36-unit building owned by Albert Lew. Month after month neighbors complained to Lew that his tenants were destroying the neighborhood. But Lew refused to evict the drug dealers or take any serious steps to limit the crime. So the neighbors used the law of nuisance to restore their community.

Sixty-six neighbors of the drug house each filed a small claims case against Lew, claiming that he was permitting a nuisance to exist on his property. The neighbors won their small claims cases, but Lew appealed, as he had a right to, for a new trial in Superior Court. A sergeant testified that he had been to the building over 250 times during two years. Residents testified about how frightening life had become. The Superior Court awarded damages of $218,325 to the neighbors, and the court of appeals affirmed the award, holding that neighbors injured by a nuisance may seek an abatement and damages. As Lew discovered, the law of nuisance can be a powerful weapon for creating a better neighborhood.[3]

---

[3]*Lew v. Superior Court*, 20 Cal. App. 4th 866, 1993 Cal. App. LEXIS 1198 (Cal. Ct. App. 1993).

34-4b Zoning

Zoning statutes are state laws that permit local communities to regulate building and land use. The local communities, whether cities, towns, or counties, then pass zoning ordinances that control many aspects of land development. For example, a town's zoning ordinance may divide the community into an industrial zone where factories may be built, a commercial zone in which stores of a certain size are allowed, and several residential zones in which only houses may be constructed. Within the residential zones, there may be further divisions, for example, permitting two-family houses in certain areas and requiring larger lots in others.

An owner prohibited by an ordinance from erecting a certain kind of building, or adding on to his present building, may seek a **variance** from the zoning board, meaning an exception granted for special reasons unique to the property. Whether a board will grant a variance generally depends upon the type of the proposed building, the nature of the community, the reason the owner claims he is harmed by the ordinance, and the reaction of neighbors.

Variance
An exception from zoning laws that is granted by a zoning board for special reasons unique to the property.

Ethics Many people abhor "adult" businesses, such as strip clubs and pornography shops. Urban experts agree that a large number of these concerns in a neighborhood often causes crime to increase and property values to drop. Nonetheless, many people patronize such businesses, which can earn a good profit. Should a city have the right to restrict adult businesses? New York City officials determined that the number of sex shops had grown steadily for two decades and that their presence harmed various neighborhoods. With the support of community groups, the city passed a zoning ordinance that prohibited adult businesses from all residential neighborhoods, from some commercial districts, *and* from being within 500 feet of schools, houses of worship, day-care centers, or other sex shops (to avoid clustering). Owners and patrons of these shops protested, claiming that the city was unfairly denying the public access to a form of entertainment that it obviously desired. Is the New York City zoning ordinance reasonable?

34-4c Eminent Domain

Eminent domain is the power of the government to take private property for public use. A government may need land to construct a highway, airport, university, or public housing. All levels of government—federal, state, and local—have this power. But the Fifth Amendment of the United States Constitution states: "… nor shall private property be taken for public use, without just compensation." The Supreme Court has held that this clause, the Takings Clause, applies not only to the federal government but also to state and local governments. So, although all levels of government have the power to take property, they must pay the owner a fair price.

A "fair price" generally means the reasonable market value of the land. Generally, if the property owner refuses the government's offer, the government will file suit seeking **condemnation** of the land; that is, a court order specifying what compensation is just and awarding title to the government.

A related issue concerns local governments requiring property owners to *dedicate* some of their land to public use in exchange for zoning permission to build or expand on their own property. For example, if a store owner wishes to expand his store, a town might grant zoning permission only if the owner dedicates a different part of his property for use as a public bike path. The Supreme Court has diminished the power of local governments to require such dedication.[4]

Eminent domain
The power of the government to take private property for public use.

---

[4]The Supreme Court's ruling came in *Dolan v. City of Tigard*, 512 U.S. 374, 114 S. Ct. 2309, 1994 U.S. LEXIS 4836 (1994).

34-5 LANDLORD-TENANT LAW

Apartments are certainly a type of real property, and many students are keenly interested in renters' rights. We now turn our attention to landlord-tenant law.

A freehold estate is the right to possess real property and use it in any lawful manner. What we think of as "owning" land is in fact a freehold estate. **When an owner of a freehold estate allows another person temporary, exclusive possession of the property, the parties have created a landlord-tenant relationship.** The freehold owner is the **landlord**, and the person allowed to possess the property is the **tenant**. The landlord has conveyed a **leasehold** interest to the tenant, meaning the right to temporary possession. Courts also use the word *tenancy* to describe the tenant's right to possession.

A leasehold may be commercial or residential. In a commercial tenancy, the owner of a building may rent retail space to a merchant, offices to a business, or industrial space to a manufacturer. When someone rents an apartment or house, he has a residential leasehold.

34-5a Three Legal Areas Combined

Property law influences landlord-tenant cases because the landlord is conveying rights in real property to the tenant. She is also keeping a **reversionary interest** in the property, meaning the right to possess the property when the lease ends. Contract law plays a role because the basic agreement between the landlord and tenant is a contract. A **lease** is a contract that creates a landlord-tenant relationship. And negligence law increasingly determines the liability of landlord and tenant when there is an injury to a person or property. Many states have combined these three legal issues into landlord-tenant statutes.

34-5b Lease

The Statute of Frauds generally requires that a lease be in writing. Some states will enforce an oral lease if it is for a short term, such as one year or less, but even when an oral lease is permitted, it is wiser for the parties to put their agreement in writing because a written lease avoids many misunderstandings. At a minimum, a lease must state the names of the parties, the premises being leased, the duration of the agreement, and the rent. But a well-drafted lease generally includes many provisions, called *covenants* and *conditions*. **A covenant is simply a promise by either the landlord or the tenant to do something or refrain from doing something.** For example, most leases include a covenant concerning the tenant's payment of a security deposit and the landlord's return of the deposit, a covenant describing how the tenant may use the premises, and several covenants about who must maintain and repair the property. Generally, tenants may be fined but not evicted for violating lease covenants. A **condition is similar to a covenant, but it allows for a landlord to evict a tenant if there is a violation.** In many states, conditions in leases must be clearly labeled as "conditions" or "evictable offenses."

34-6 TYPES OF TENANCY

There are four types of tenancy: a tenancy for years, a periodic tenancy, a tenancy at will, and a tenancy at sufferance. The most important feature distinguishing one from the other is how each tenancy terminates. In some cases, a tenancy terminates automatically, while in others, one party must take certain steps to end the agreement.

Landlord
The owner of a freehold estate who allows another person temporarily to live on his property.

Tenant
A person given temporary possession of the landlord's property.

Reversionary interest
The right of an owner (or her heirs) to property upon the death of a life tenant.

Lease
An agreement in which an owner gives a tenant the right to use property.

34-6a Tenancy for Years

Any lease for a stated, fixed period is a **tenancy for years**. If a landlord rents a summer apartment for the months of June, July, and August of next year, that is a tenancy for years. A company that rents retail space in a mall beginning January 1, 2014, and ending December 31, 2020, also has a tenancy for years. A tenancy for years terminates automatically when the agreed period ends.

Tenancy for years
A lease for a stated, fixed period.

34-6b Periodic Tenancy

A **periodic tenancy** is created for a fixed period and then automatically continues for additional periods until either party notifies the other of termination. This is probably the most common variety of tenancy, and the parties may create one in either of two ways. Suppose a landlord agrees to rent you an apartment "from month to month, rent payable on the first." That is a periodic tenancy. The tenancy automatically renews itself every month unless either party gives adequate notice to the other that she wishes to terminate. A periodic tenancy could also be for one-year periods—in which case it automatically renews for an additional year if neither party terminates—or for any other period.

Periodic tenancy
A lease for a fixed period, automatically renewable unless terminated.

34-6c Tenancy at Will

A **tenancy at will** has no fixed duration and may be terminated by either party at any time. Tenancies at will are unusual tenancies.[5] Typically, the agreement is vague, with no specified rental period and with payment, perhaps, to be made in kind. The parties might agree, for example, that a tenant farmer could use a portion of his crop as rent. Since either party can end the agreement at any time, it provides no security for either landlord or tenant.

Tenancy at will
A tenancy with no fixed duration, which may be terminated by either party at any time.

34-6d Tenancy at Sufferance

A **tenancy at sufferance** occurs when a tenant remains on the premises, against the wishes of the landlord, after the expiration of a true tenancy. Thus, a tenancy at sufferance is not a true tenancy because the tenant is staying without the landlord's agreement. The landlord has the option of seeking to evict the tenant or of forcing the tenant to pay a *use and occupancy fee* for as long as she stays.

Tenancy at sufferance
A tenancy that exists without the permission of the landlord, after the expiration of a true tenancy.

34-7 LANDLORD'S DUTIES

34-7a Duty to Deliver Possession

The landlord's first important duty is to deliver possession of the premises at the beginning of the tenancy; that is, to make the rented space available to the tenant. In most cases, this presents no problems and the new tenant moves in. But what happens if the previous tenant has refused to leave when the new tenancy begins? In most states, the landlord is legally required to remove the previous tenant. In some states, it is up to the new tenant either to evict the existing occupant or begin charging him rent.

---

[5]The courts of some states, annoyingly, use the term "tenancy at will" for what are, in reality, periodic tenancies. They do this to bewilder law students and even lawyers, a goal at which they are quite successful. This text uses tenancy at will in its more widely known sense, meaning a tenancy terminable at any time.

34-7b Quiet Enjoyment

All tenants are entitled to quiet enjoyment of the premises, meaning the right to use the property without the interference of the landlord. Most leases expressly state this covenant of quiet enjoyment. And if a lease includes no such covenant, the law implies the right of quiet enjoyment anyway, so all tenants are protected. If a landlord interferes with the tenant's quiet enjoyment, he has breached the lease, entitling the tenant to damages.

The most common interference with quiet enjoyment is an **eviction**, meaning some act that forces the tenant to abandon the premises. Of course, some evictions are legal, as when a tenant fails to pay the rent. But some evictions are illegal. There are two types of eviction: actual and constructive.

ACTUAL EVICTION

If a landlord prevents the tenant from possessing the premises, he has actually evicted her. Suppose a landlord decides that a group of students are "troublemakers." Without going through lawful eviction procedures in court, the landlord simply waits until the students are out of the apartment and changes all the locks. By denying the students access to the premises, the landlord has actually evicted them and has breached their right of quiet enjoyment. He is liable for all expenses they suffer, such as retrieving their possessions, the cost of alternate housing, and moving expenses. In some states, he may be liable for punitive damages for failing to go through proper eviction procedures.

Even a partial eviction is an interference with quiet enjoyment. Suppose Louise rents an apartment with a storage room. If the landlord places his own goods in the storage room, he has partially evicted Louise because a tenant is entitled to the *exclusive* possession of the premises. In all states, Louise would be allowed to deduct from her rent the value of the storage space, and in many states, she would not be obligated to pay any rent for the apartment so long as the landlord continued the partial eviction.

CONSTRUCTIVE EVICTION

If a landlord substantially interferes with the tenant's use and enjoyment of the premises, he has constructively evicted her. Courts construe certain behavior as the equivalent of an eviction. In these cases, the landlord has not actually prevented the tenant from *possessing* the premises but has instead interfered so greatly with her *use and enjoyment* that the law regards the landlord's actions as equivalent to an eviction. Suppose the heating system in an apartment house in Juneau, Alaska, fails during January. The landlord, an avid sled dog racer, tells the tenants he is too busy to fix the problem. If the tenants move out, the landlord has constructively evicted them and is liable for all expenses they suffer.

To claim a constructive eviction, the tenant must vacate the premises. The tenant must also prove that the interference was sufficiently serious and lasted long enough that she was forced to move out. A lack of hot water for two days is not fatal, but lack of any water for two weeks creates a constructive eviction.

34-7c Duty to Maintain Premises

Historically, the common law placed no burden on the landlord to repair and maintain the premises. This made sense because rental property had traditionally been farmland. Buildings, such as a house or barn, were far less important than the land itself, and no one expected the landlord to fix a leaking roof. Today, the vast majority of rental property is used for housing or business purposes. Space in a building is frequently all that a tenant is renting, and the condition of the building is of paramount importance. Most states have changed the common law rule and placed various obligations on the landlord to maintain the property.

In most states, a landlord has a duty to deliver the premises in a habitable condition and a continuing duty to maintain the habitable condition. This duty overlaps with the quiet enjoyment obligation, but it is not identical. The tenant's right to quiet enjoyment focuses primarily on the tenant's *ability to use* the rented property. The landlord's duty to maintain the property focuses on whether the property *meets a particular legal standard*. The required standard may be stated in the lease, created by a state statute, or implied by law.

LEASE

The lease itself generally obligates the landlord to maintain the exterior of any buildings and the common areas. If a lease does not do so, state law may imply the obligation.

BUILDING CODES

Many state and local governments have passed building codes, which mandate minimum standards for commercial and/or residential property. The codes are likely to be stricter for residential property and may demand such things as minimum room size, sufficient hot water, secure locks, proper working kitchens and bathrooms, absence of insects and rodents, and other basics of decent housing. Generally, all rental property must comply with the building code, whether the lease mentions the code or not.

IMPLIED WARRANTY OF HABITABILITY

Students Maria Ivanow, Thomas Tecza, and Kenneth Gearin rented a house from Les and Martha Vanlandingham. The monthly rent was $900. But the roommates failed to pay any rent for the final five months of the tenancy. After they moved out, the Vanlandinghams sued. How much did the landlords recover? Nothing. The landlords had breached the implied warranty of habitability.

The implied warranty of habitability requires that a landlord meet all standards set by the local building code, or that the premises be fit for human habitation. Most states, though not all, *imply* this warranty of habitability, meaning that the landlord must meet this standard whether the lease includes it or not. In some states, the implied warranty means that the premises must at least satisfy the local building code. Other states require property that is "fit for human habitation," which means that a landlord might comply with the building code, yet still fail the implied warranty of habitability if the rental property is unfit to live in.

The Vanlandinghams breached the implied warranty. The students had complained repeatedly about a variety of problems. The washer and dryer, which were included in the lease, frequently failed. A severe roof leak caused water damage in one of the bedrooms. Defective pipes flooded the bathroom. The refrigerator frequently malfunctioned, and the roommates repaired it several times. The basement often flooded, and when it was dry, rats and opossums lived in it. The heat sometimes failed.

In warranty of habitability cases, a court normally considers the severity of the problems and their duration. If the defective conditions seriously interfere with the tenancy, the court declares the implied warranty breached and orders a **rent abatement**; that is, a reduction in the rent owed. The longer the defects continued and the greater their severity, the more the rent is abated. In the case of Maria Ivanow and friends, the court abated the rent 50 percent. The students had already paid more than the abated rent to the landlord, so they owed nothing for the last five months.[6]

---

[6]*Vanlandingham v. Ivanow*, 246 Ill. App. 3d 348, 615 N.E.2d 1361, 1993 Ill. App. LEXIS 985 (Ill. Ct. App. 1993).

DUTY TO RETURN SECURITY DEPOSIT

Most landlords require tenants to pay a security deposit, in case the tenant damages the premises. In many states, a landlord must either return the security deposit soon after the tenant has moved out or notify the tenant of the damage and the cost of the repairs. In addition, landlords are often obligated to credit tenants with interest earned on the deposit. In many states, a landlord who fails to return the deposit in a timely fashion can be forced to pay double or even triple damages to the tenant, a question raised in the following dispute.

MISHKIN V. YOUNG

107 P.3d 393, 2005 WL 452168
Supreme Court of Colorado, 2005

CASE SUMMARY

Facts: A Colorado statute required a landlord either to return a security deposit or provide an accounting of why money was being withheld. The landlord had to do this within 30 days of the tenant's surrender of the property, or up to 60 days if the lease permitted. If the landlord failed to refund the money, the tenant, after giving seven days' notice, could sue for treble damages. The landlord could avoid the treble damages by refunding the deposit within those seven days.

Marc Mishkin leased an apartment from Dean Young, paying a security deposit of $1,625. The lease stated that the deposit would be returned no later than 45 days after the tenant moved out. After Mishkin left, Young did not return the money. Forty-eight days after leaving, Mishkin sent a demand for the deposit, notifying Young that in seven days he would sue for treble damages. Six days later, Young gave Mishkin a statement detailing $1,574.60 worth of property damage, along with a check for $50.40.

Mishkin sued. The trial court ruled that Young was entitled to withhold the money because of the damages. Mishkin appealed. The appellate court ruled that the Colorado statute required the landlord to return the full security deposit within the seven-day period. Young appealed.

Issue: *Did the landlord avoid the treble damages by accounting for the security deposit within seven days of the tenant's notice to sue?*

Decision: No, the landlord could have avoided treble damages during the seven-day period only by refunding the full deposit. Affirmed.

Reasoning: Landlords may withhold security deposits only if they account for all deductions within 30 days. The language in Mishkin's lease legally extended this deadline to 45 days. Young failed to make an accounting within 45 days, and therefore he forfeited the right to retain any portion of Mishkin's security deposit.

The notice period creates only two possibilities. A landlord may refund every penny of a former tenant's security deposit within seven days. If he fails to do so, he is liable to the tenant for treble damages. The law is strict, and it acts as a significant deterrent to landlords who choose to keep deposits wrongfully.

Final Word on Security Deposits   The discussion and case both concerned residential leases, where security deposits are almost inevitable. Note that, in a commercial lease, the tenant may have less statutory protection but more bargaining power. A financially sound company might negotiate a lease with no security deposit or perhaps offer a letter of credit for security instead of cash. The interest saved over several years could be substantial.

34-8 TENANT'S DUTIES

34-8a Duty to Pay Rent

Rent is the compensation the tenant pays the landlord for use of the premises, and paying the rent is the tenant's foremost obligation. The lease normally specifies the amount of rent and when it must be paid. Typically, the landlord requires that rent be paid at the beginning of each rental period, whether that is monthly, annually, or otherwise.

Both parties must be certain they understand whether the rent includes utilities such as heat and hot water. Some states mandate that the landlord pay certain utilities, such as water. Many leases include an **escalator clause**, permitting the landlord to raise the rent during the course of the lease if his expenses increase for specified reasons. For example, a tax escalator clause allows the landlord to raise the rent if his real estate taxes go up. Any escalator clause should state the percentage of the increase that the landlord may pass on to the tenant.

Rent
Compensation paid by a tenant to a landlord.

Escalator clause
A clause in a lease allowing the landlord to raise the rent for specified reasons.

LANDLORD'S REMEDIES FOR NONPAYMENT OF RENT

If the tenant fails to pay rent on time, the landlord has several remedies. She is entitled to apply the security deposit to the unpaid rent. She may also sue the tenant for nonpayment of rent, demanding the unpaid sums, cost of collection, and interest. Finally, the landlord may evict a tenant who has failed to pay rent.

State statutes prescribe the steps a landlord must take to evict a tenant for nonpayment. Typically, the landlord must serve a termination notice on the tenant and wait for a court hearing. At the hearing, the landlord must prove that the tenant has failed to pay rent on time. If the tenant has no excuse for the nonpayment, the court grants an order evicting him. The order authorizes a sheriff to remove the tenant's goods and place them in storage, at the tenant's expense. However, if the tenant was withholding rent because of unlivable conditions, the court may refuse to evict.

EXAM Strategy

Question: Leo rents an apartment from Donna for $900 per month, both parties signing a lease. After six months, Leo complains about defects, including bugs, inadequate heat, and window leaks. He asks Donna to fix the problems, but she responds that the heat is fine and that Leo caused the insects and leaks. Leo begins to send in only $700 for the monthly rent. Donna repeatedly phones Leo, asking for the remaining rent. When he refuses to pay, she waits until he leaves for the day, then has a moving company place his belongings in storage. She changes the locks, making it impossible for him to re-enter. Leo sues. What is the likely outcome?

Strategy: A landlord is entitled to begin proper eviction proceedings against a tenant who has not paid rent. However, the landlord must follow specified steps, including a termination notice and a court hearing. Review the consequences for actual eviction, described in the section "Quiet Enjoyment."

Result: Donna has ignored the legal procedures for evicting a tenant. Instead, she engaged in *actual eviction*, which is quick, and in the short term, effective. However, by breaking the law, Donna has ensured that Leo will win his lawsuit. He is entitled to possession of the apartment, as well as damages for rent he may have been forced to pay elsewhere, injury to his possessions, and the cost of retrieving them. He may receive punitive damages as well. Bad strategy, Donna.

LANDLORD'S DUTY TO MITIGATE

Pickwick & Perkins, Ltd., was a store in the Burlington Square Mall in Burlington, Vermont. Pickwick had a five-year lease but abandoned the space almost two years early and ceased paying rent. The landlord waited approximately eight months before renting the space to a new tenant and then sued, seeking the unpaid rent. Pickwick defended on the grounds that Burlington had failed to **mitigate damages**; that is, to keep its losses to a minimum by promptly seeking another tenant. Burlington argued that it had no legal obligation to mitigate. Burlington's position accurately reflected the common law rule, which permitted the landlord to let the property lie vacant and allow the damages to add up. But the common law evolves over time, and this time, the Vermont Supreme Court changed the rule. The judges pointed out that, historically, a lease was a conveyance of an estate, and property law had never required mitigation. However, the court asserted, a lease is now regarded as both a contract and a conveyance. Under contract law, the nonbreaching party must make a reasonable effort to minimize losses, and that same rule applies, said the court, to a landlord. Burlington lost. The Vermont ruling is typical of current decisions, although some courts still do not require mitigation.[7]

34-8b Duty to Use Premises for Proper Purpose

A lease normally lists what a tenant may do in the premises and prohibits other activities. For example, a residential lease allows the tenant to use the property for normal living purposes, but not for any retail, commercial, or industrial purpose. A commercial lease might allow a tenant to operate a retail clothing store, but not a restaurant. A landlord may evict a tenant who violates the lease by using the premises for prohibited purposes.

A tenant may not use the premises for any illegal activity, such as gambling or selling drugs. The law itself implies this condition in every lease, so a tenant who engages in illegal acts on the leased property is subject to eviction, regardless of whether the lease mentions such conduct.

34-8c Duty Not to Damage Premises

A tenant is liable to the landlord for any significant damage he causes to the property. The tenant is not liable for normal wear and tear. If, however, he knocks a hole in a wall or damages the plumbing, the landlord may collect the cost of repairs, either by using the security deposit or by suing, if necessary. A landlord may also seek to evict a tenant for serious damage to the property.

A tenant is permitted to make reasonable changes in the leased property so that he can use it as intended. Someone leasing an apartment is permitted to hang pictures on the wall. But a tenant leasing commercial space should make certain that the lease specifies the alterations he can make and whether he is obligated to return the premises to their original condition at the end of the lease.

34-8d Duty Not to Disturb Other Tenants

Most leases, commercial and residential, include a covenant that the tenant will not disturb other tenants in the building. A landlord may evict a tenant who unreasonably disturbs others. The test is *reasonableness*. A landlord does not have the right to evict a residential tenant for giving one loud party but may evict a tenant who repeatedly plays loud music late at night and disturbs the quiet enjoyment of other tenants.

---

[7]*O'Brien v. Black*, 162 Vt. 448, 648 A.2d 1374, 1994 Vt. LEXIS 89 (1994).

34-9 INJURIES

You invite a friend to dinner in your rented home, but after the meal, she slips and falls, seriously injuring her back. Are you liable? Is the landlord?

34-9a Tenant's Liability

A tenant is generally liable for injuries occurring within the premises she is leasing, whether that is an apartment, a store, or otherwise. If a tenant permits grease to accumulate on a kitchen floor and a guest slips and falls, the tenant is liable. If a merchant negligently installs display shelving that tips onto a customer, the merchant pays for the harm. Generally, a tenant is not liable for injuries occurring in common areas over which she has no control, such as exterior walkways. If a tenant's dinner guest falls because the building's common stairway has loose steps, the landlord is probably liable.

34-9b Landlord's Liability

COMMON LAW RULES

Historically, the common law held a landlord responsible for injuries on the premises only in a limited number of circumstances, which we will describe. In reading these common law rules, be aware that many states have changed them, dramatically increasing the landlord's liability.

Latent Defects   If the landlord knows of a dangerous condition on the property and realizes the tenant will not notice it, the landlord is liable for any injuries. For example, if a landlord knows that a porch railing is weak and fails to inform the tenant, the landlord is responsible if the tenant plunges off the porch. But notice that, under the common law, if the landlord notifies the tenant of the latent defect, he is no longer liable.

Common Areas   The landlord is usually responsible for maintaining the common areas, and along with this obligation may go liability for torts. As we saw above, if your guest falls downstairs in a common hallway because the stairs were defective, the landlord is probably liable.

Negligent Repairs   Even in areas where the landlord has no duty to make repairs, if he volunteers to do so and does the work badly, he is responsible for any resulting harm.

Public Use   If the premises are to be used for a public purpose, such as a store or office, the landlord is generally obligated to repair any dangerous defects, although the tenant is probably liable as well. The purpose of this stricter rule is to ensure that the general public can safely visit commercial establishments. If a landlord realizes that the plate glass in a store's door is loose, he must promptly repair it or suffer liability for any injuries.

MODERN TREND

Increasingly, state legislatures and courts are discarding the common law classifications described above and holding landlords liable under the normal rules of negligence law. **In many states, a landlord must use reasonable care to maintain safe premises and is liable for foreseeable harm.** For example, the common law rule merely required a landlord to notify a tenant of a latent defect, such as a defective porch railing. Most states now have building codes that require a landlord to maintain structural elements such as railings in safe condition. States further imply a warranty of habitability, which mandates reasonably safe living conditions. So, in many states, a landlord is no longer saved from negligence suits merely by giving notice of defects—he has to fix them.

34-10 PERSONAL PROPERTY

Personal property is all property other than real property. In this section, we look at two important aspects of personal property: gifts and bailments.

34-11 GIFTS

A gift is a voluntary transfer of property from one person to another without any consideration. Recall from Chapter 11 that, for consideration to exist, parties must normally make an exchange. But a gift is a one-way transaction, without anything given in return. The person who gives property away is the *donor*, and the one who receives it is the *donee*.

A gift involves three elements:

- The donor *intends to transfer* ownership of the property to the donee immediately.

- The donor *delivers* the property to the donee.

- The donee *accepts* the property.

If all three elements are met, the donee becomes the legal owner of the property. If the donor later says, "I've changed my mind, give that back!" the donee is free to refuse.

34-11a Intention to Transfer Ownership

The donor must intend to transfer ownership to the property right away, immediately giving up all control of the item. Notice the two important parts of this element. First, the donor's intention must be to *transfer ownership;* that is, to give title to the donee. Merely proving that the owner handed you property does not guarantee that you have received a gift; if the owner only intended that you *use* the item, there is no gift, and she can demand it back.

Second, the donor must also intend the property to transfer *immediately*. A promise to make a gift in the future is unenforceable. Promises about future behavior are governed by contract law, and a contract is unenforceable without consideration. If Sarah hands Lenny the keys to a $600,000 yacht and says, "Lenny, it's yours," then it *is* his, since Sarah intends to transfer ownership right away. But if Sarah says to Max, "Next week, I'm going to give you my yacht," Max has not received a gift because Sarah did not intend an immediate transfer. Neither does Max have an enforceable contract since there is no consideration for Sarah's promise.

A revocable gift is governed by a special rule, and it is actually not a gift at all. Suppose Harold tells his daughter Faith, "The mule is yours from now on, but if you start acting stupid again, I'm taking her back." Harold has retained some control over the animal, which means he has not intended to transfer ownership. There is no gift, and no transfer of ownership. Harold still owns the mule.

When Dominic Tenaglia's automobile broke down, his brother Nick generously offered to give him a replacement car. Nick delivered a Chevrolet to Dominic, and both brothers understood that the car was a gift. Nick wrote "gift" on the car's certificate of title, but he did not immediately give the certificate to Dominic. A week later, while Dominic was driving the Chevrolet, he was involved in an accident. Both brothers had insurance, through different insurers, for cars they owned. The two companies disputed which one was liable for Dominic's accident. The court determined that Nick's company was still liable for any damage caused by the Chevrolet. Nick had presented the car to Dominic but had not relinquished *all* control over it. Ownership of a car is unlike ownership of a computer or a sweater because it requires possession of a certificate of title. Because Nick still had the certificate at the time of the accident, he had the power to take back the Chevrolet whenever he wanted. He had not made a valid gift of the automobile, and Dominic's insurer won the case.[8]

34-11b Delivery

PHYSICAL DELIVERY

The donor must deliver the property to the donee. Generally, this involves physical delivery— a handoff, if you will. If Anna hands Eddie a Rembrandt drawing, saying "I want you to have this forever," she has satisfied the delivery requirement. In the chapter opening, Riley promised to give half a million dollars to the Boy Scouts the following day. But he never delivered the stocks and bonds, so there was no gift. The Boy Scouts received nothing, and all the money became part of Riley's estate, to be inherited by his unworthy son.

CONSTRUCTIVE DELIVERY

Physical delivery is the most common and the surest way to make a gift, but it is not always necessary. **A donor makes constructive delivery by transferring ownership without a physical delivery.** Most courts permit constructive delivery only when physical delivery is impossible or extremely inconvenient. Suppose that Anna wants to give her niece Jen a blimp, which is parked in a hangar at the airport. The blimp will not fit through the doorway of Jen's dorm. Instead of flying the aircraft to the university, Anna may simply deliver to Jen the certificate of title and the keys to the blimp. When she has done that, Jen owns the aircraft.

DELIVERY TO AN AGENT

A donor might deliver the property to an agent, either someone working for him or for the donee. Assume that Randolph says to Mortimer, "Old boy, I should like for you to have my Rolls Royce." If Randolph gives the keys and the title to his own butler, there is no gift. By definition, the agent works for the donor, and thus the donor still has control and ownership of the property. But if the donor delivers the property to the donee's agent, the gift is made. So, if Randolph delivers the car to Mortimer's butler, then Mortimer owns the car.

PROPERTY ALREADY IN DONEE'S POSSESSION

Sometimes a donor decides to give property to a donee who already has possession of it. In that case, no delivery is required, and the donee need only demonstrate that the donor intended to transfer present *ownership*. Larry lends a grand piano to Leslie for the summer. At the end of the summer, Larry announces that she can keep the instrument. So long as Larry clearly intends that Leslie gets ownership of the piano, the gift is completed.

34-11c *Inter Vivos* Gifts and Gifts *Causa Mortis*

A gift can be either *inter vivos* or *causa mortis*. An **inter vivos gift** means a gift made "during life"; that is, when the donor is not under any fear of impending death. The vast majority of gifts are *inter vivos*, involving a healthy donor and donee. Shirley, age 30 and in good health, gives Terry an eraser for his birthday. This is an *inter vivos* gift, which is absolute. The gift becomes final upon delivery, and the donor may *not* revoke it. If Shirley and Terry have a fight the next day, Shirley has no power to erase her eraser gift.

  A gift *causa mortis* is one made in contemplation of approaching death. The gift is valid if the donor dies as expected, but it is revoked if he recovers. Suppose that Lenny's doctors have told him he will probably die of a liver ailment within a month. Lenny calls Jane to his bedside and hands her a fistful of cash, saying, "I'm dying, this money is yours." Jane sheds a tear, then sprints

---

[8]*Motorists Mutual Insurance Co. v. State Farm Mutual Automobile Insurance Co.*, 1990 Ohio App. LEXIS 3027 (Ohio Ct. App. 1990).

to the bank. If Lenny dies of the liver ailment within a few weeks, Jane gets to keep the money. The law permits the gift *causa mortis* to act as a kind of substitute for a will since the donor's delivery of the property clearly indicates his intentions. But note that this kind of gift is revocable. Since a gift *causa mortis* is conditional (upon the donor's death), the donor has the right to revoke it at any time before he dies. If Lenny telephones Jane the next day and says that he has changed his mind, he gets the money back. Further, if the donor recovers and does not die as expected, the gift is automatically revoked.

EXAM Strategy

Question: Julie does good deeds for countless people, and many are deeply grateful. On Monday, Wilson tells Julie, "You are a wonderful person, and I have a present for you. I am giving you this baseball, which was the 500th home run hit by one of the great players of all time." He hands her the ball, which is worth nearly half a million dollars.

Julie's good fortune continues on Tuesday, when another friend, Cassandra, tells Julie, "I only have a few weeks to live. I want you to have this signed first edition of *Ulysses*. It is priceless, and it is yours." The book is worth about $200,000. On Wednesday, Wilson and Cassandra decide they have been foolhardy, and both demand that Julie return the items. Must she do so?

Strategy: Both of these donors are attempting to revoke their gifts. An *inter vivos* gift cannot be revoked, but a gift *causa mortis* can be. To answer the question, you must know what kind of gifts these were.

Result: A gift *causa mortis* is one made in fear of approaching death, and this rule applies to Cassandra. Such a gift is revocable any time before the donor dies, so Cassandra gets her book back. A gift *inter vivos* is one made without any such fear of death. Most gifts fall in this category, and they are irrevocable. Wilson was not anticipating his demise, so his was a gift *inter vivos*. Julie keeps the baseball.

34-11d Acceptance

The donee must accept the gift. This rarely leads to disputes, but if a donee should refuse a gift and then change her mind, she is out of luck. Her repudiation of the donor's offer means there is no gift, and she has no rights in the property.

The following case offers a combination of love, alcohol, and diamonds—always a volatile mix.

You Be the Judge

ALBINGER V. HARRIS
2002 Mont. 118, 2002 WL 1226858
Montana Supreme Court, 2002

Facts: Michelle Harris and Michael Albinger lived together, on and off, for three years. Their roller-coaster relationship was marred by alcohol abuse and violence. When they announced their engagement, Albinger gave Harris a $29,000 diamond ring, but the couple broke off their wedding plans because of emotional and physical turmoil. Harris returned the ring. Later, they reconciled and resumed their marriage plans, and Albinger gave his fiancée the ring again. This cycle repeated several times over the three years. Each time they broke off their relationship, Harris returned the ring to Albinger, and each time they made up, he gave it back to her.

On one occasion, Albinger held a knife over Harris as she lay in bed, threatening to chop off her finger if she did not remove the ring. He beat her and forcibly removed the ring.

Criminal charges were brought but then dropped when, inevitably, the couple reconciled. Another time, Albinger told her to "take the car, the horse, the dog, and the ring and get the hell out." Finally, mercifully, they ended their stormy affair, and Harris moved to Kentucky—keeping the ring.

Albinger sued for the value of the ring. The trial court found that the ring was a conditional gift, made in contemplation of marriage, and ordered Harris to pay its full value. She appealed. The Montana Supreme Court had to decide, in a case of first impression, whether an engagement ring was given in contemplation of marriage. (In Montana, and many states, neither party to a broken engagement may sue for breach of contract.)

You Be the Judge: *Who owns the ring?*

Argument for Harris: The main problem with calling the ring a "conditional gift" is that there is no such thing. The elements of a gift are intent, delivery, and acceptance, and Harris has proved all three. A gift is not a contract, nor is it a loan. Once a gift has been accepted, the donor has no more rights in the property and may not demand its return. Hundreds of years of litigation have resulted in only one exception to this rule—a gift *causa mortis*—and despite some cynical claims to the contrary, marriage is not death.

If this court carves a new exception to the longstanding rule, other unhappy donors will dream up more "conditions" that supposedly entitle them to their property. What is more, to create a special rule for engagement rings would be blatant gender bias because the exception would only benefit men. This court should stick to settled law and permit the recipient of a gift to keep it.

Argument for Albinger: The symbolism of an engagement ring is not exactly news. For decades, Americans have given rings—frequently diamond—in contemplation of marriage. All parties understand why the gift is made and what is expected if the engagement is called off: The ring must be returned. Albinger's *intent*, to focus on one element, was conditional—and Michelle Harris understood that. Each time the couple separated, she gave the ring back. She knew that she could wear this beautiful ring in anticipation of their marriage, but that custom and decency required its return if the wedding was off. She knew it, that is, until greed got the better of her and she fled to Kentucky, attempting to profit at the expense of Albinger's generosity. We are not asking for new law, but for confirmation of what everyone has known for generations: There is no wedding ring when there is no wedding.

The following table distinguishes between a contract and a gift:

A Contract and a Gift Distinguished

A Contract:

Lou: I will pay you $2,000 to paint the house, if you promise to finish by July.	Abby: I agree to paint the house by July 3, for $2,000.

Lou and Abby have a contract. Each promise is consideration in support of the other promise. Lou and Abby can each enforce the other's promise.

A Gift:

Lou hands Phil two opera tickets, saying: I want you to have these two tickets to *Rigoletto*."	Phil says, "Hey, thanks."

This is a valid *inter vivos* gift. Lou intended to transfer ownership immediately and delivered the property to Phil, who now owns the tickets.

Neither Contract nor Gift:

Lou: You're a great guy. Next week, I'm going to give you two tickets to *Rigoletto*.	Jason: Hey, thanks.

There is no gift because Lou did not intend to transfer ownership immediately, and he did not deliver the tickets. There is no contract because Jason has given no consideration to support Lou's promise.

34-12 Bailment

Bailment
The rightful possession of goods by someone who is not the owner, usually by mutual agreement between the bailor and bailee.

A **bailment** is the rightful possession of goods by someone who is not the owner. The one who delivers the goods is the *bailor* and the one in possession is the *bailee*. Bailments are common. Suppose that you are going out of town for the weekend and lend your motorcycle to Stan. You are the bailor, and your friend is the bailee. When you check your suitcase with the airline, you are again the bailor and the airline is the bailee. If you rent a car at your destination, you become the bailee, while the rental agency is the bailor. In each case, someone other than the true owner has rightful, temporary possession of personal property.

Parties generally create a bailment by agreement. In each of the examples above, the parties agreed to the bailment. In two cases, the agreement included payment, which is common but not essential. When you buy your airline ticket, you pay for your ticket, and the price includes the airline's agreement, as bailee, to transport your suitcase. When you rent a car, you pay the bailor for the privilege of using it. By lending your motorcycle, you engage in a bailment without either party paying compensation.

Involuntary bailment
A bailment that occurs without an agreement between the bailor and bailee.

A bailment without any agreement is called a **constructive** or **involuntary bailment**. Suppose that you find a wristwatch in your house that you know belongs to a friend. You are obligated to return the watch to the true owner, and until you do so, you are the bailee, liable for harm to the property. This is called a constructive bailment because, with no agreement between the parties, the law is *construing* a bailment.

34-12a Control

To create a bailment, the bailee must assume physical control of an item with intent to possess. A bailee may be liable for loss or damage to the property, so it is not fair to hold him liable unless he has taken physical control of the goods, intending to possess them.

Disputes about whether someone has taken control often arise in parking lot cases. When a car is damaged or stolen, the lot's owner may try to avoid liability by claiming it lacked control of the parked auto and therefore was not a bailee. If the lot is a "park and lock" facility, where the car's owner retains the key and the lot owner exercises *no control at all*, there is probably no bailment and no liability for damage.

By contrast, when a driver leaves her keys with a parking attendant, the lot clearly is exercising control of the auto, and the parties have created a bailment. The lot is probably liable for loss or damage in that case.

> If you store your furniture in a warehouse, the storage company is your bailee, but it has no right to curl up in your bed.

34-12b Rights of the Bailee

The bailee's primary right is possession of the property. **Anyone who interferes with the bailee's rightful possession is liable to her.** Suppose that, after you lend your motorcycle to Stan, Mel sees Stan park the bike, realizes Stan is not the owner, rides the motorcycle away, and locks it up until you return. Mel is liable to Stan for any damages Stan suffered while deprived of transportation.

Even a bailor is liable if he wrongfully takes back property from a bailee. If a car agency rents Francine a car for a three-day weekend but then repossesses it for use elsewhere, it is liable to her for any damages, even though it owns the car. The bailor must abide by the agreement.

The bailee is typically, though not always, permitted to use the property. Obviously, a customer is permitted to drive a car rented from an agency. When a farmer lends his tractor to a neighbor, the bailee is entitled to use the machine for normal farm purposes. But some bailees have no authority to use the goods. If you store your furniture in a warehouse, the storage company is your bailee, but it has no right to curl up in your bed. The bailee may be entitled to compensation. This depends upon the agreement. If Owner leaves a power boat at the boatyard for repairs, the boatyard, a bailee, is entitled to payment for the work it does. As with any contract, the exact compensation should be clearly agreed upon before any work begins. If there is no agreement, the boatyard will probably receive the reasonable value of its services.

34-12c Duties of the Bailee

The bailee is strictly liable to redeliver the goods on time to the bailor, or to whomever the bailor designates. Strict liability means there are virtually no exceptions. Rudy stores his $6,000 drum set with Melissa's Warehouse while he is on vacation. Blake arrives at the warehouse and shows a forged letter, supposedly from Rudy, granting Blake permission to remove the drums. If Melissa permits Blake to take the drums, she will owe Rudy $6,000, even if the forgery was a high-quality job.

Due Care

The bailee is obligated to exercise due care. **The level of care required depends upon who receives the benefit of the bailment.** There are three possibilities:

- *Sole benefit of bailee.* If the bailment is for the sole benefit of the bailee, the bailee is required to use **extraordinary care** with the property. Generally, in these cases, the bailor lends something for free to the bailee. Since the bailee is paying nothing for the use of the goods, most courts consider her the only one to benefit from the bailment. If your neighbor lends you a power lawn mower, the bailment is probably for your sole benefit. You are liable if you are even slightly inattentive in handling the lawn mower and can expect to pay for virtually any harm done.

- *Mutual benefit.* When the bailment is for the mutual benefit of bailor and bailee, the bailee must use **ordinary care** with the property. Ordinary care is what a reasonably prudent person would use under the circumstances. When you rent a car, you benefit from the use of the car, and the agency profits from the fee you pay. When the airline hauls your suitcase to your destination, both parties benefit. Most bailments benefit both parties, and courts decide the majority of bailment disputes under this standard.

- *Sole benefit of bailor.* When the bailment benefits only the bailor, the bailee must use only **slight care**. This kind of bailment is called a **gratuitous bailment**, and the bailee is liable only for **gross negligence**. Sheila enters a pie-eating contest and asks you to hold her $14,000 diamond engagement ring while she competes. You put the ring in your pocket. Sheila wins the $20 first prize, but the ring has disappeared. This was a gratuitous bailment, and you are not liable to Sheila unless she can prove gross negligence on your part. If the ring dropped from your pocket or was stolen, you are not liable. If you used the ring to play catch with friends, you are liable.

Burden of Proof

In an ordinary negligence case, the plaintiff has the burden of proof to demonstrate that the defendant was negligent and caused the harm alleged. In bailment cases, the burden of proof is reversed. **Once the bailor has proven the existence of a bailment and loss or harm to the goods, a presumption of negligence arises, and the burden shifts to the bailee to prove adequate care.** This is a major change from ordinary negligence cases. Georgina's car is struck by another auto. If Georgina sues for negligence, it is her burden to prove that the defendant was driving unreasonably and caused the harm. By comparison, assume that Georgina rents Chance her sailboat for a month. At the end of the month, Chance announces that the boat is at the bottom of Lake Michigan. If Georgina sues Chance, she only needs to demonstrate that the parties had a bailment and that Chance failed to return the boat. The burden then shifts to Chance to prove that the boat was lost through no fault of his own. If Chance cannot meet that burden, Georgina recovers the full value of the boat.

The following case raises many of the issues in this section. Long before his time as president, Abraham Lincoln was a lawyer who argued more than 150 cases before the Supreme Court of Illinois. The case for Weedman is modeled after the arguments that a young Lincoln actually made.

You Be the Judge

JOHNSON v. WEEDMAN
5 Ill. 495
Supreme Court of Illinois, 1843

Facts: Johnson left his horse with Weedman, paying him to board and feed the animal. Johnson did not grant Weedman permission to ride the horse. Nonetheless, Weedman took the horse for a 15-mile ride.

Later that day, the horse died. However, the trial court found that Weedman had not abused the animal and that the ride had not caused the horse's death. The court did not grant damages to Johnson, and Johnson appealed.

You Be the Judge: *Should Weedman pay for Johnson's dead horse?*

Argument for Johnson: Your honor, Weedman was in possession of my client's horse only to feed him and see to his basic needs. My client did not give him permission to take the horse out of the pasture. Weedman made personal use of my client's property when he took a 15-mile ride that was in no way necessary. The trial court's finding that Weedman did not abuse the horse during the ride is irrelevant. My client must be compensated for the loss of his animal.

Argument for Weedman: My client had a legal right to possession of the horse. Riding the horse was not a substantial abuse of his rights as bailee. The horse was returned to the pasture in good condition. It was not abandoned and was not devalued in any way by the ride. The plaintiff is therefore not entitled to any compensation. The coincidental death of the horse does not change that fact.

34-12d Rights and Duties of the Bailor

The bailor's rights and duties are the reverse of the bailee's. The bailor is entitled to the return of his property on the agreed-upon date. He is also entitled to receive the property in good condition and to recover damages for harm to the property if the bailee failed to use adequate care.

Chapter Conclusion

Real property law is ancient but forceful. Although real property today is not the dominant source of wealth that it was in medieval England, it is still the greatest asset that most people will ever possess—and it is worth understanding.

EXAM REVIEW

1. **REAL PROPERTY; FIXTURES**   Real property includes land, buildings, air and subsurface rights, plant life, and fixtures. A fixture is any good that has become attached to other real property, such as land. (pp. 833–834)

Question: Paul and Shelly Higgins had two wood stoves in their home. Each rested on, but was not attached to, a built-in brick platform. The downstairs wood stove was connected to the chimney flue and was used as part of the main heating system for the house. The upstairs stove, in the master bedroom, was purely decorative. It had no stovepipe connecting it to the chimney. The Higginses sold their house to Jack Everitt, and neither party said anything about the two stoves. Is Everitt entitled to either stove? Both stoves?

Strategy: An object is a fixture if a reasonable person would consider the item to be a permanent part of the property, taking into account attachment, adaptation, and other objective manifestations of permanence. (See the "Result" at the end of this section.)

2. **CONCURRENT ESTATES**   When two or more people own real property at the same time, they have a concurrent estate. In both a tenancy in common and a joint tenancy, all owners have a share in the entire property. The primary difference is that joint tenants have the right of survivorship, meaning that when a joint tenant dies, his interest passes to the other joint tenants. A tenant in common has the power to leave her estate to her heirs. (pp. 834–837)

Question: Howard Geib, Walker McKinney, and John D. McKinney owned two vacation properties as joint tenants with right of survivorship. The parties were not getting along well, and Geib petitioned the court to partition the properties. The trial court ruled that the fairest way to do this was to sell both properties and divide the proceeds. The two McKinneys appealed, claiming that a partition by sale was improper because it would destroy their right of survivorship. Comment.

Strategy: Do joint tenants have a right to partition? Are there any limits on that right? (See the "Result" at the end of this section.)

3. **NONPOSSESSORY INTERESTS**   Some valuable interests in real property do not involve possession. Easements, profits, and licenses grant limited rights to use property owned by someone else. (pp. 837–838)

4. **GOVERNMENT REGULATION**   Nuisance law, zoning ordinances, and eminent domain all permit a government to regulate property and, in some cases, to take it for public use. (pp. 838–839)

5. **LANDLORD-TENANT**   When an owner of a freehold estate allows another person temporary, exclusive possession of the property, the parties have created a landlord-tenant relationship. (p. 840)

6. **TENANCIES**   Any lease for a stated, fixed period is a tenancy for years. A periodic tenancy is created for a fixed period and then automatically continues for additional periods until either party notifies the other of termination. A tenancy at will has no fixed duration and may be terminated by either party at any time. A tenancy at sufferance occurs when a tenant remains, against the wishes of the landlord, after the expiration of a true tenancy. (pp. 840–841)

7. **QUIET ENJOYMENT**   All tenants are entitled to the quiet enjoyment of the premises, without the interference of the landlord. (p. 842)

8. **SECURITY DEPOSITS**   Landlords may require tenants to post a deposit that can be used to pay for repairs if a tenant damages the property. But many landlords fail to promptly return security deposits to tenants who leave no damage behind. In those cases, tenants are often able to sue for as much as three times their security deposit. (p. 844)

9. **RENT**   The tenant is obligated to pay the rent, and the landlord may evict for nonpayment. The modern trend is to require a landlord to mitigate damages caused by a tenant who abandons the premises before the lease expires. (pp. 845–846)

EXAM Strategy

Question: Loren Andreo leased retail space in his shopping plaza to Tropical Isle Pet Shop for five years, at a monthly rent of $2,100. Tropical Isle vacated the premises 18 months early, turned in the key to Andreo, and acknowledged liability for the unpaid rent. Andreo placed a FOR RENT sign in the store window and spoke to a commercial real estate broker about the space. But he did not enter into a formal listing agreement with the broker, or take any other steps to rent the space, for about nine months. With approximately nine months remaining on the unused part of Tropical's lease, Andreo hired a commercial broker to rent the space. He also sued Tropical for 18 months' rent. Comment.

Strategy: When a tenant abandons leased property early, the landlord is obligated to mitigate damages. Did Andreo? (See the "Result" at the end of this section.)

10. **TENANT'S LIABILITY**   A tenant is liable to the landlord for any significant damage he causes to the property. A tenant is also generally liable for injuries occurring within the premises she is leasing. (p. 847)

11. **PERSONAL INJURY**   At common law, a landlord had very limited liability for injuries on the premises, but today, many courts require a landlord to use reasonable care and hold her liable for foreseeable harm. (p. 847)

12. **GIFTS**   A gift is a voluntary transfer of property from one person to another without consideration. The elements of a gift are intention to transfer ownership immediately, delivery, and acceptance. (pp. 848–851)

13. **BAILMENT**   A bailment is the rightful possession of goods by one who is not the owner. The one who delivers the goods is the bailor, and the one in possession is the bailee. To create a bailment, the bailee must assume physical control with intent to possess. (pp. 852–854)

14. **BAILEE'S RIGHTS**   The bailee is always entitled to possess the property, is frequently allowed to use it, and may be entitled to compensation. (pp. 852–853)

15. **BAILEE'S DUTY OF CARE**   The bailee is obligated to exercise due care. The level of care required depends upon who receives the benefit of the bailment: If the bailee is the sole beneficiary, she must use extraordinary care; if the parties mutually benefit, the bailee must use ordinary care; and if the bailor is the sole beneficiary of the bailment, the bailee must use only slight care. (p. 853)

1. Result: A buyer normally takes all fixtures. The downstairs stove was permanently attached to the house and used as part of the heating system. The owner who installed it *intended* that it remain, and it was a fixture; Everitt got it. The upstairs stove was not permanently attached and was not a fixture; the sellers could take it with them.

2. Result: The McKinneys lost. Any co-tenant (including a joint tenant) has an absolute right to partition. Difficulties in partitioning are irrelevant.

9. Result: For about nine months, Andreo made no serious effort to lease the store. The court rejected his rent claim for that period, permitting him to recover unpaid money only for the period he made a genuine effort to lease the space.

MULTIPLE-CHOICE QUESTIONS

1. Quick, Onyx, and Nash were deeded a piece of land as tenants in common. The deed provided that Quick owned one-half the property and Onyx and Nash owned one-quarter each. If Nash dies, the property will be owned as follows:
   (a) Quick 1/2, Onyx 1/2
   (b) Quick 5/8, Onyx 3/8
   (c) Quick 1/3, Onyx 1/3, Nash's heirs 1/3
   (d) Quick 1/2, Onyx 1/4, Nash's heirs 1/4

2. Which of the following forms of tenancy will be created if a tenant stays in possession of leased premises without the landlord's consent, after the tenant's one-year written lease expires?
   (a) Tenancy at will
   (b) Tenancy for years
   (c) Periodic tendency
   (d) Tenancy at sufferance

3. Consider the following:

   I.   A house (value: $150,000)

   II. A giant high-definition television in the house (value: $4,999)

   III. The land that the house sits upon (value: $30,000)

   IV. An old car in the house's garage (value: $5,001) How many of these items are personal property?

    (a) All four of them

    (b) Three of them

    (c) Two of them

    (d) One of them

    (e) None of them

4. Holding out an envelope, Alan says, "Ben, I'm giving you these opera tickets." Without taking the envelope, Ben replies, "Why would I want opera tickets? Loser." Alan leaves, crestfallen. Later that day, a girl whom Ben has liked for some time says, "I sure wish I were going to the opera tonight." Ben scrambles, calls Alan, and says, "Alan, old buddy, I accept your gift of the opera tickets. I'm on my way over to pick them up."

Does Ben have a legal right to the tickets?

(a) Yes, because Alan intended to transfer ownership.

(b) Yes, because offers to give gifts cannot be revoked.

(c) No, because no consideration was given.

(d) No, because Ben did not accept the gift when offered.

5. A tenant renting an apartment under a three-year written lease that does not contain any specific restrictions may be evicted for:

(a) counterfeiting money in the apartment.

(b) keeping a dog in the apartment.

(c) failing to maintain a liability insurance policy on the apartment.

(d) making structural repairs to the apartment.

Essay Questions

1. YOU BE THE JUDGE WRITING PROBLEM Frank Deluca and his son David owned the Sportsman's Pub on Fountain Street in Providence, Rhode Island. The Delucas applied to the city for a license to employ topless dancers in the pub. Did the city have the power to deny the Delucas' request? **Argument for the Delucas:** Our pub is perfectly legal. Further, no law in Rhode Island prohibits topless dancing. We are morally and legally entitled to present this entertainment. The city should not use some phony moralizing to deny customers what they want. **Argument for Providence:** This section of Providence is zoned to prohibit topless dancing, just as it is zoned to bar manufacturing. There are other parts of town where the Delucas can open one of their sleazy clubs if they want to, but we are entitled to deny a permit in this area.

2. Kenmart Realty sued to evict Mr. and Ms. Alghalabio for nonpayment of rent and sought the unpaid monies, totaling several thousand dollars. In defense, the Alghalabios claimed that their apartment was infested with rats. They testified that there were numerous rat holes in the walls of the living room, bedroom, and kitchen, that there were rat droppings all over the apartment, and that on one occasion, they saw their toddler holding a live rat. They testified that the landlord had refused numerous requests to exterminate. Please rule on the landlord's suit.

3. Lisa Preece rented an apartment from Turman Realty, paying a $300 security deposit. Georgia law states: "Any landlord who fails to return any part of a security deposit which is required to be returned to a tenant pursuant to this article shall be liable to the tenant in the amount of three times the sum improperly withheld plus reasonable attorney's fees." When Preece moved out, Turman did not return her security deposit, and she sued for triple damages plus attorney's fees, totaling $1,800. Turman offered evidence that its failure to return the deposit was inadvertent and that it had procedures reasonably designed to avoid such errors. Is Preece entitled to triple damages? Attorney's fees?

4. Ronald Armstead worked for First American Bank as a courier. His duties included making deliveries between the bank's branches in Washington, D.C. Armstead parked the bank's station wagon near the entrance of one branch in violation of a sign saying: NO PARKING—RUSH HOUR ZONE. In the rear luggage section of the station wagon were four locked bank dispatch bags containing checks and other valuable documents. Armstead had received tickets for illegal parking at this spot on five occasions. Shortly after Armstead entered the bank, a tow truck arrived, and its operator prepared to tow the station wagon. Transportation Management, Inc., operated the towing service on behalf of the District of Columbia. Armstead ran out to the vehicle and told the tow truck operator that he was prepared to drive the vehicle away immediately. But the operator drove away with the station wagon in tow. One-and-a-half hours later, a bank employee paid for the car's release, but one dispatch bag, containing documents worth $107,000, was missing. First American sued Transportation Management and the District of Columbia. The defendants sought summary judgment, claiming they *could not* be liable. Were they correct?

5. YOU BE THE JUDGE WRITING PROBLEM Eileen Murphy often cared for her elderly neighbor, Thomas Kenney. He paid her $25 per day for her help and once gave her a bank certificate of deposit worth $25,000. She spent the money. Murphy alleged that shortly before his death, Kenney gave her a large block of shares in three corporations. He called his broker, intending to instruct him to transfer the shares to Murphy's name, but the broker was ill and unavailable. So Kenney told Murphy to write her name on the shares and keep them, which she did. Two weeks later, Kenney died. When Murphy presented the shares to Kenney's broker to transfer ownership to her, the broker refused because Kenney had never endorsed the shares as the law requires—that is, signed them over to Murphy. Was Murphy entitled to the $25,000? To the shares? **Argument for Murphy:** The purpose of the law is to do what a donor intended, and it is obvious that Kenney intended Murphy to have the $25,000 and the shares. Why else would he have given them to her? A greedy estate should not be allowed to interfere with the deceased's intentions. **Argument for the Estate:** Murphy is not entitled to the $25,000 because we have no way of knowing what Kenney's intentions were when he gave her the money. She is not entitled to the shares of stock because Kenney's failure to endorse them over to her meant he never *delivered* them, and that is an essential element of a gift.

DISCUSSION QUESTIONS

1. Is it sensible to distinguish between *inter vivos* gifts and gifts *causa mortis?* Should someone "on his deathbed" be able to change his mind so easily?

2. Donny Delt and Sammy Sigma are students and roommates. They lease a house in a neighborhood near campus. Few students live on the block. The students do not have large parties, but they often have friends over at night. The friends sometimes play high-volume music in their cars and sometimes speak loudly when going to and from their cars. Also, departing late-night guests often leave beer cans and fast-food wrappers in the street.

   Neighbors complain about being awakened in the wee hours of the morning. They are considering filing a nuisance lawsuit against Donny and Sammy. Would such an action be reasonable? Do you think Donny and Sammy are creating a nuisance? If so, why? If not, where is the line—what amount of late-night noise does amount to a nuisance?

3. Imagine that you sign a lease and that you are to move into your new apartment on August 15. When you arrive, the previous tenant has not moved out. In fact, he has no intention of moving out. Should the landlord be in charge of getting rid of the old tenant, or should you have the obligation to evict him?

4. When landlords wrongfully withhold security deposits, they can often be sued for three times the amount of the security deposit. Is this reasonable? Should a landlord have to pay $3,000 for a $1,000 debt? What if you fail to pay a rent on time? Should you have to pay three times the amount of your normal rent? If your answers to these two questions are different, why?

5. In the case of a gratuitous bailment, the bailee is liable only if he is grossly negligent. Is this good policy? If you agree to watch someone's property, shouldn't you be required to be careful even if you are not being paid?

THE CONSTITUTION OF THE UNITED STATES

Preamble

We the People of the United States, in Order to form a more perfect Union, establish Justice, insure domestic Tranquility, provide for the common defense, promote the general Welfare, and secure the Blessings of Liberty to ourselves and our Posterity, do ordain and establish this Constitution for the United States of America.

ARTICLE I

Section 1.

All legislative Powers herein granted shall be vested in a Congress of the United States, which shall consist of a Senate and House of Representatives.

Section 2.

The House of Representatives shall be composed of Members chosen every second Year by the People of the several States, and the Electors in each State shall have the Qualifications requisite for Electors of the most numerous Branch of the State Legislature.

No Person shall be a Representative who shall not have attained to the Age of twenty five Years, and been seven Years a Citizen of the United States, and who shall not, when elected, be an Inhabitant of that State in which he shall be chosen.

Representatives and direct Taxes shall be apportioned among the several States which may be included within this Union, according to their respective Numbers, which shall be determined by adding to the whole Number of free Persons, including those bound to Service for a Term of Years, and excluding Indians not taxed, three fifths of all other Persons. The actual Enumeration shall be made within three Years after the first Meeting of the Congress of the United States, and within every subsequent Term of ten Years, in such Manner as they shall by Law direct. The number of Representatives shall not exceed one for every thirty Thousand, but each State shall have at Least one Representative; and until such enumeration shall be made, the State of New Hampshire shall be entitled to chuse three, Massachusetts eight, Rhode Island and Providence Plantations one, Connecticut five, New-York six, New Jersey four, Pennsylvania eight, Delaware one, Maryland six, Virginia ten, North Carolina five, South Carolina five, and Georgia three.

When vacancies happen in the Representation from any State, the Executive Authority thereof shall issue Writs of Election to fill such vacancies.

The House of Representatives shall chuse their Speaker and other Officers; and shall have the sole Power of Impeachment.

Section 3.

The Senate of the United States shall be composed of two Senators from each State, chosen by the Legislature thereof, for six Years; and each Senator shall have one Vote.

Immediately after they shall be assembled in Consequence of the first Election, they shall be divided as equally as may be into three Classes. The Seats of the Senators of the first Class shall be vacated at the Expiration of the second Year, of the second Class at the Expiration of the fourth Year, and of the third Class at the Expiration of the sixth Year, so that one third may be chosen every second Year; and if Vacancies happen by Resignation or otherwise, during the Recess of the Legislature of any State, the Executive thereof may make temporary Appointments until the next Meeting of the Legislature, which shall then fill such Vacancies.

No Person shall be a Senator who shall not have attained to the Age of thirty Years, and been nine Years a Citizen of the United States, and who shall not, when elected, be an Inhabitant of that State for which he shall be chosen.

The Vice President of the United States shall be President of the Senate, but shall have no Vote, unless they be equally divided.

The Senate shall chuse their other Officers, and also a President pro tempore, in the Absence of the Vice President, or when he shall exercise the Office of President of the United States.

The Senate shall have the sole power to try all Impeachments. When sitting for that Purpose, they shall be an Oath or Affirmation. When the President of the United States is tried, the Chief Justice shall preside: And no Person shall be convicted without the Concurrence of two thirds of the Members present.

Judgment in Cases of Impeachment shall not extend further than to removal from Office, and disqualification to hold and enjoy any Office of honor, Trust or Profit under the United States: but the Party convicted shall nevertheless be liable and subject to Indictment, Trial, Judgment and Punishment, according to Law.

Section 4.

The Times, Places and Manner of holding Elections for Senators and Representatives, shall be prescribed in each State by the Legislature thereof: but the Congress may at any time by Law make or alter such Regulations, except as to the Places of chusing Senators.

The Congress shall assemble at least once in every Year, and such Meeting shall be on the first Monday in December, unless they shall by Law appoint a different Day.

Section 5.

Each House shall be the Judge of the Elections, Returns and Qualifications of its own Members, and a Majority of each shall constitute a Quorum to do Business; but a smaller Number may adjourn from day to day, and may be authorized to compel the Attendance of absent Members, in such Manner, and under such Penalties as each House may provide.

Each House may determine the Rules of its Proceedings, punish its Members for disorderly Behaviour, and, with the Concurrence of two thirds, expel a Member.

Each House shall keep a Journal of its Proceedings, and from time to time publish the same, excepting such Parts as may in their Judgment require Secrecy; and the Yeas and Nays of the Members of either House on any question shall, at the Desire of one fifth of those Present, be entered on the Journal.

Neither House, during the Session of Congress, shall, without the Consent of the other, adjourn for more than three days, nor to any other Place than that in which the two Houses shall be sitting.

Section 6.

The Senators and Representatives shall receive a Compensation for their Services, to be ascertained by Law, and paid out of the Treasury of the United States. They shall in all Cases, except Treason, Felony and Breach of the Peace, be privileged from Arrest during their Attendance at the Session of their respective Houses, and in going to and returning from the same; and for any Speech or Debate in either House, they shall not be questioned in any other Place.

No Senator or Representative shall, during the Time for which he was elected, be appointed to any civil Office under the Authority of the United States, which shall have been created, or the Emoluments whereof shall have been encreased during such time; and no Person holding any Office under the United States, shall be a Member of either House during his Continuance in Office.

Section 7.

All Bills for raising Revenue shall originate in the House of Representatives; but the Senate may propose or concur with Amendments as on other Bills.

Every Bill which shall have passed the House of Representatives and the Senate, shall, before it become a Law, be presented to the President of the United States; If he approve he shall sign it, but if not he shall return it, with his Objections to that House in which it shall have originated, who shall enter the Objections at large on their Journal, and proceed to reconsider it. If after such Reconsideration two thirds of that House shall agree to pass the Bill, it shall be sent, together with the Objections, to the other House, by which it shall likewise be reconsidered, and if approved by two thirds of that House, it shall become a Law. But in all such Cases the Votes of both Houses shall be determined by Yeas and Nays, and the Names of the Persons voting for and against the Bill shall be entered on the Journal of each House respectively. If any Bill shall not be returned by the President within ten Days (Sundays excepted) after it shall have been presented to him, the Same shall be a Law, in like Manner as if he had signed it, unless the Congress by their Adjournment prevent its Return, in which Case it shall not be a Law.

Every Order, Resolution, or Vote to which the Concurrence of the Senate and House of Representatives may be necessary (except on a question of Adjournment) shall be presented to the President of the United States; and before the Same shall take Effect, shall be approved by him, or being disapproved by him, shall be repassed by two thirds of the Senate and House of Representatives, according to the Rules and Limitations prescribed in the Case of a Bill.

Section 8.

The Congress shall have Power to lay and collect Taxes, Duties, Imposts and Excises, to pay the Debts and provide for the common Defence and general Welfare of the United States; but all Duties, Imposts and Excises shall be uniform throughout the United States;

To borrow Money on the credit of the United States;

To regulate Commerce with foreign Nations, and among the several States, and with the Indian Tribes;

To establish an uniform Rule of Naturalization, and uniform Laws on the subject of Bankruptcies throughout the United States;

To coin Money, regulate the Value thereof, and of foreign Coin, and fix the Standard of Weights and Measures;

To provide for the Punishment of counterfeiting the Securities and current Coin of the United States;

To establish Post Offices and post Roads;

To promote the Progress of Science and useful Arts, by securing for limited Times to Authors and Inventors the exclusive Right to their respective Writings and Discoveries;

To constitute Tribunals inferior to the Supreme Court;

To define and punish Piracies and Felonies committed on the high Seas, and Offenses against the Law of Nations;

To declare War, grant Letters of Marque and Reprisal, and make Rules concerning Captures on Land and Water;

To raise and support Armies, but no Appropriation of Money to that Use shall be for a longer Term than two Years;

To provide and maintain a Navy;

To make Rules for the Government and Regulation of the land and naval Forces;

To provide for calling forth the Militia to execute the Laws of the Union, suppress Insurrections and repel Invasions;

To provide for organizing, arming, and disciplining, the Militia, and for governing such Part of them as may be employed in the Service of the United States, reserving to the States respectively, the Appointment of the Officers, and the Authority of training the Militia according to the discipline described by Congress;

To exercise exclusive Legislation in all Cases whatsoever, over such District (not exceeding ten Miles square) as may, by Cession of particular States, and the Acceptance of Congress, become the Seat of the Government of the United States, and to exercise like Authority over all Places purchased by the Consent of the Legislature of the State in which the Same shall be, for the Erection of Forts, Magazines, Arsenals, dock-Yards, and other needful Buildings;—And

To make all Laws which shall be necessary and proper for carrying into Execution the foregoing Powers, and all other Powers vested by this Constitution in the Government of the United States, or in any Department or Officer thereof.

Section 9.

The Migration or Importation of such Persons as any of the States now existing shall think proper to admit, shall not be prohibited by the Congress prior to the Year one thousand eight hundred and eight, but a Tax or Duty may be imposed on such Importation, not exceeding ten dollars for each Person.

The Privilege of the Writ of Habeas Corpus shall not be suspended, unless when in Cases of Rebellion or Invasion the public Safety may require it.

No Bill of Attainder or ex post facto Law shall be passed.

No Capitation, or other direct, Tax shall be laid, unless in Proportion to the Census or Enumeration herein before directed to be taken.

No Tax or Duty shall be laid on Articles exported from any State.

No Preference shall be given by any Regulation of Commerce or Revenue to the Ports of one State over those of another; nor shall Vessels bound to, or from, one State, be obliged to enter, clear, or pay Duties in another.

No Money shall be drawn from the Treasury, but in Consequence of Appropriations made by Laws; and a regular Statement and Account of the Receipts and Expenditures of all public Money shall be published from time to time.

No Title of Nobility shall be granted by the United States: And no Person holding any Office of Profit or Trust under them, shall, without the Consent of the Congress, accept of any present, Emolument, Office, or Title, of any kind whatever, from any King, Prince, or foreign State.

Section 10.

No State shall enter into any Treaty, Alliance, or Confederation; grant Letters of Marque and Reprisal; coin Money; emit Bills of Credit; make any Thing but gold and silver Coin a Tender in Payment of Debts; pass any Bill of Attainder, ex post facto Law, or Law impairing the Obligation of Contracts, or grant any Title of Nobility.

No State shall, without the Consent of the Congress, lay any Imposts or Duties on Imports or Exports, except what may be absolutely necessary for executing its inspection Laws: and the net Produce of all Duties and Imposts, laid by any State on Imports or Exports, shall be for the Use of the Treasury of the United States; and all such Laws shall be subject to the Revision and Controul of the Congress.

No State shall, without the Consent of Congress, lay any Duty of Tonnage, keep Troops, or Ships of War in time of Peace, enter into any Agreement or Compact with another State, or with a foreign Power, or engage in War, unless actually invaded, or in such imminent Danger as will not admit of delay.

ARTICLE II

Section 1.

The executive Power shall be vested in a President of the United States of America. He shall hold his Office during the Term of four Years, and, together with the Vice President, chosen for the same Term, be elected, as follows:

Each State shall appoint, in such Manner as the Legislature thereof may direct, a Number of Electors, equal to the whole Number of Senators and Representatives to which the State may be entitled in the Congress: but no Senator or Representative, or Person holding an Office of Trust or Profit under the United States, shall be appointed an Elector.

The Electors shall meet in their respective States, and vote by Ballot for two Persons, of whom one at least shall not be an Inhabitant of the same State with themselves. And they shall make a list of all the Persons voted for, and of the Number of Votes for each; which List they shall sign and certify, and transmit sealed to the Seat of the Government of the United States, directed to the President of the Senate. The President of the Senate shall, in the presence of the Senate and House of Representatives, open all the Certificates, and the Votes shall be counted. The Person having the greatest Number of Votes shall be the President, if such Number be a Majority of the whole Number of Electors appointed; and if there be more than one who have such Majority, and have an equal Number of Votes, then the House of Representatives shall immediately chuse by Ballot one of them for President; and if no Person have a Majority, then from the five highest on the List the said House shall in like Manner chuse the President. But in chusing the President, the Votes shall be taken by States, the Representation from each State having one Vote; A quorum for this Purpose shall consist of a Member or Members from two thirds of the States, and a Majority of all the States shall be necessary to a Choice. In every Case, after the Choice of the President, the Person having the greatest Number of Votes of the Electors shall be the Vice President. But if there should remain two or more who have equal Votes, the Senate shall chuse from them by Ballot the Vice President.

The Congress may determine the Time of Chusing the Electors, and the Day on which they shall give their Votes; which Day shall be the same throughout the United States.

No Person except a natural born Citizen, or a Citizen of the United States, at the time of the Adoption of this Constitution, shall be eligible to the Office of President; neither shall any Person be eligible to that Office who shall not have attained to the Age of thirty five Years, and been fourteen Years a Resident within the United States.

In Case of the Removal of the President from Office, or of his Death, Resignation, or Inability to discharge the Powers and Duties of the said Office, the Same shall devolve on the Vice President, and the Congress may by Law provide for the Case of Removal, Death, Resignation or Inability, both of the President and Vice President, declaring what Officer shall then act as President, and such Officer shall act accordingly, until the Disability be removed, or a President shall be elected.

The President shall, at stated Times, receive for his Services, a Compensation, which shall neither be encreased nor diminished during the Period for which he shall have been elected, and he shall not receive within that Period any other Emolument from the United States, or any of them.

Before he enter on the Execution of his Office, he shall take the following Oath or Affirmation:—"I do solemnly swear (or affirm) that I will faithfully execute the Office of President of the United States, and will to the best of my Ability, preserve, protect and defend the Constitution of the United States."

Section 2.

The President shall be Commander in Chief of the Army and Navy of the United States, and of the Militia of the several States, when called into the actual Service of the United States; he may require the Opinion, in writing, of the principal Officer in each of the executive Departments, upon any Subject relating to the Duties of their respective Offices, and he shall have Power to grant Reprieves and Pardons for Offenses against the United States, except in Cases of Impeachment.

He shall have Power, by and with the Advice and Consent of the Senate, to make Treaties, providing two thirds of the Senators present concur; and he shall nominate, and by and with the Advice and Consent of the Senate, shall appoint Ambassadors, other public Ministers and Consuls, Judges of the supreme Court, and all other Officers of the United States, whose Appointments are not herein otherwise provided for, and which shall be established by Law: but the Congress may by Law vest the Appointment of such inferior Officers, as they think proper, in the President alone, in the Courts of Law, or in the Heads of Departments.

The President shall have Power to fill up all Vacancies that may happen during the Recess of the Senate, by granting Commissions which shall expire at the End of their next Session.

Section 3.   He shall from time to time give to the Congress Information of the State of the Union, and recommend to their Consideration such Measures as he shall judge necessary and expedient; he may, on extraordinary Occasions, convene both Houses, or either of them, and in Case of Disagreement between them, with Respect to the Time of Adjournment, he may adjourn them to such Time as he shall think proper, he shall receive Ambassadors and other public Ministers; he shall take Care that the Laws be faithfully executed, and shall Commission all the Offices of the United States.

Section 4.   The President, Vice President and all civil Officers of the United States, shall be removed from Office on Impeachment for, and Conviction of, Treason, Bribery, or other high Crimes and Misdemeanors.

ARTICLE III

Section 1.   The judicial Power of the United States, shall be vested in one supreme Court, and in such inferior Courts as the Congress may from time to time ordain and establish. The Judges, both of the supreme and inferior Courts, shall hold their Offices during good Behaviour, and shall, at Times, receive for their Services, a Compensation, which shall not be diminished during their Continuance in Office.

Section 2.   The judicial Power shall extend to all Cases, in Law and Equity, arising under this Constitution, the Laws of the United States, and Treaties made, or which shall be made, under their Authority;—to all Cases affecting Ambassadors, other public Ministers and Consuls;—to all Cases of admiralty and maritime Jurisdiction;—to Controversies to which the United States shall be a Party;—to controversies between two or more States;—between a State and Citizens of another State;—between Citizens of different States;—between Citizens of the same State claiming Lands under Grants of different States; and between a State, or the Citizens thereof, and foreign States, Citizens or Subjects.

In all Cases affecting Ambassadors, other public Ministers and Consuls, and those in which a State shall be Party, the supreme Court shall have original Jurisdiction. In all the other Cases before mentioned, the supreme Court shall have appellate Jurisdiction, both as to Law and Fact, with such Exceptions, and under such Regulations as the Congress shall make.

The Trial of all Crimes, except in Cases of Impeachment, shall be by Jury; and such Trial shall be held in the State where the said Crimes shall have been committed; but when not committed within any State, the Trial shall be at such Place or Places as the Congress may by Law have directed.

Section 3.
Treason against the United States, shall consist only in levying War against them, or in adhering to their Enemies, giving them Aid and Comfort. No Person shall be convicted of Treason unless on the Testimony of two Witnesses to the same overt Act, or on Confession in open Court.

The Congress shall have Power to declare the Punishment of Treason, but no Attainder of Treason shall work Corruption of Blood, or Forfeiture except during the Life of the Person attainted.

ARTICLE IV

Section 1.
Full Faith and Credit shall be given in each State to the public Acts, Records, and judicial Proceedings of every other State. And the Congress may by general Laws prescribe the Manner in which such Acts, Records and Proceedings shall be proved, and the Effect thereof.

Section 2.
The Citizens of each State shall be entitled to all Privileges and Immunities of Citizens in the several States.

A Person charged in any State with Treason, Felony, or other Crime, who shall flee from Justice, and be found in another State, shall on Demand of the executive Authority of the State from which he fled, be delivered up, to be removed to the State having Jurisdiction of the Crime.

No Person held to Service or Labour in one State, under the Laws thereof, escaping into another, shall, in Consequence of any Law or Regulation therein, be discharged from such Service or Labour, but shall be delivered up on Claim of the Party to whom such Service or Labour may be due.

Section 3.
New States may be admitted by the Congress into this Union; but no new State shall be formed or erected within the Jurisdiction of any other State; nor any State be formed by the Junction of two or more States, or Parts of States, without the Consent of the Legislatures of the States concerned as well as the Congress.

The Congress shall have Power to dispose of and make all needful Rules and Regulations respecting the Territory or other Property belonging to the United States; and nothing in this Constitution shall be so construed as to Prejudice any Claims of the United States, or of any particular State.

Section 4.
The United States shall guarantee to every State in this Union a Republican Form of Government, and shall protect each of them against Invasion; and on Application of the Legislature, or of the Executive (when the Legislature cannot be convened) against domestic Violence.

ARTICLE V

The Congress, whenever two thirds of both Houses shall deem it necessary, shall propose Amendments to this Constitution, or, on the Application of the Legislatures of two thirds of the several States, shall call a Convention for proposing Amendments, which, in either Case, shall be valid to all Intents and Purposes, as Part of this Constitution, when ratified by the Legislatures of three fourths of the several States, or by Conventions in three fourths thereof, as the one or the other Mode of Ratification may be proposed by the Congress; Provided that no Amendment which may be made prior to the Year One thousand eight hundred and eight shall in any Manner affect the first and fourth Clauses in the Ninth Section of the first Article; and that no State, without its Consent, shall be deprived of its equal Suffrage in the Senate.

ARTICLE VI

All Debts contracted and Engagements entered into, before the Adoption of this Constitution, shall be as valid against the United States under this Constitution, as under the Confederation.

This Constitution, and the Laws of the United States which shall be made in Pursuance thereof; and all Treaties made, or which shall be made, under the Authority of the United States, shall be the supreme Law of the Land; and the Judges in every State shall be bound thereby, any Thing in the Constitution or Laws of any State to the Contrary notwithstanding.

The Senators and Representatives before mentioned, and the Members of the several State Legislatures, and all executive and judicial Officers, both of the United States and of the Several States, shall be bound by Oath or Affirmation, to support this Constitution; but no religious Test shall ever be required as a Qualification to any Office or public Trust under the United States.

ARTICLE VII

The Ratification of the Conventions of nine States, shall be sufficient for the Establishment of this Constitution between the States so ratifying the Same.

Amendment I [1791].

Congress shall make no law respecting an establishment of religion, or prohibiting the free exercise thereof; or abridging the freedom of speech, or the press; or the right of the people peaceably to assemble, and to petition the Government for a redress of grievances.

Amendment II [1791].

A well regulated Militia, being necessary to the security for a free State, the right of the people to keep and bear Arms, shall not be infringed.

Amendment III [1791].

No Soldier shall, in time of peace be quartered in any house, without the consent of the Owner, nor in time of war, but in a manner to be prescribed by law.

Amendment IV [1791].

The right of the people to be secure in their persons, houses, papers, and effects, against unreasonable searches and seizures, shall not be violated, and no Warrants shall issue, but upon probable cause, supported by Oath or Affirmation, and particularly describing the place to be searched, and the persons or things to be seized.

Amendment V [1791].

No person shall be held to answer for a capital, or otherwise infamous crime, unless on a presentment or indictment of a Grand Jury, except in cases arising in the land or naval forces, or in the Militia, when in actual service in time of War or public danger;

nor shall any person be subject for the same offense to be twice put in jeopardy of life or limb; nor shall be compelled in any criminal case to be a witness against himself, nor be deprived of life, liberty, or property, without due process of law; nor shall private property be taken for public use, without just compensation.

Amendment VI [1791].

In all criminal prosecutions, the accused shall enjoy the right to a speedy and public trial, by an impartial jury of the State and district wherein the crime shall have been committed, which district shall have been previously ascertained by law, and to be informed of the nature and cause of the accusation; to be confronted with the Witnesses against him; to have compulsory process for obtaining witnesses in his favor, and to have the Assistance of counsel for his defence.

Amendment VII [1791].

In suits at common law, where the value in controversy shall exceed twenty dollars, the right of trial by jury shall be preserved, and no fact tried by a jury, shall be otherwise re-examined in any Court of the United States, than according to the rules of the common law.

Amendment VIII [1791].

Excessive bail shall not be required, no excessive fines imposed, nor cruel and unusual punishments inflicted.

Amendment IX [1791].

The enumeration in the Constitution, of certain rights, shall not be construed to deny or disparage others retained by the people.

Amendment X [1791].

The powers not delegated to the United States by the Constitution, nor prohibited by it to the States, are reserved to the States respectively, or to the people.

Amendment XI [1798].

The judicial power of the United States shall not be construed to extend to any suit in law or equity, commenced or prosecuted against one of the United States by Citizens of another State, or by Citizens or Subjects of any Foreign State.

Amendment XII [1804].

The Electors shall meet in their respective states and vote by ballot for President and Vice-President, one of whom, at least, shall not be an inhabitant of the same state with themselves; they shall name in their ballots the person voted for as President, and in distinct ballots the person voted for as Vice-President, and they shall make distinct lists of all persons voted for as President, and of all persons voted for as Vice-President, and of the number of votes for each, which lists they shall sign and certify, and transmit sealed to the seat of the government of the United States, directed to the President of the Senate;—The President of the Senate shall, in the presence of the Senate and House of Representatives, open all the certificates and the votes shall then be counted;—The person having the greatest number of votes for President, shall be the President, if such number be a majority of the whole number of Electors appointed; and if no person have such majority, then from the persons having the highest numbers not exceeding three on the list of those voted for as President, the House of Representatives shall choose immediately, by ballot, the President. But in choosing the President, the votes shall be taken by states, the representation from each state having one vote; a quorum for this purpose shall consist of a member or members from two-thirds of the states, and a majority of all the states shall be necessary to a choice. And if the House of Representatives shall not choose a President whenever the right of choice shall devolve upon them, before the fourth day of March next following, then the Vice-President shall act as President, as in the case of the death or other constitutional disability of the President. The person having the greatest number of votes as Vice-President, shall be the Vice-President, if such number be a majority of the whole number of Electors appointed, and if no person have a majority, then from the two highest numbers on the list, the Senate shall choose the Vice-President; a quorum for the purpose shall consist of two-thirds of the whole number of Senators, and a majority of the whole number shall be necessary to a choice. But no person constitutionally ineligible to the office of President shall be eligible to that of the Vice-President of the United States.

Amendment XIII [1865].

Section 1. Neither slavery nor involuntary servitude, except as a punishment for crime whereof the party shall have been duly convicted, shall exist within the United States, or any place subject to their jurisdiction.

Section 2. Congress shall have power to enforce this article by appropriate legislation.

Amendment XIV [1868].

Section 1. All persons born or naturalized in the United States, and subject to the jurisdiction thereof, are citizens of the United States and of the State wherein they reside. No State shall make or enforce any law which shall abridge the privileges or immunities of citizens of the United States; nor shall any State deprive any person of life, liberty, or property, without due process of law; nor deny to any person within its jurisdiction the equal protection of the laws.

Section 2. Representatives shall be appointed among the several States according to their respective numbers, counting the whole number of persons in each State, excluding Indians not taxed. But when the right to vote at any election for the choice of electors for President and Vice President of the United States, Representatives in Congress, the Executive and Judicial officers of a State, or the members of the Legislature thereof, is denied to any of the male inhabitants of such State, being twenty-one years of age, and citizens of the United States, or in any way abridged, except for participation in rebellion, or other crime, the basis of representation therein shall be reduced in the proportion which the number of such male citizens shall bear the whole number of male citizens twenty-one years of age in such State.

Section 3. No person shall be a Senator or Representative in Congress, or elector of President and Vice President, or hold any office, civil or military, under the United States, or under any State, who, having previously taken an oath, as a member of Congress, or as an officer of the United States, or as a member of any State legislature, or as an executive or judicial officer of any State, to support the Constitution of the United States, shall have engaged in insurrection or rebellion against the same, or given aid or comfort to the enemies thereof. But Congress may by a vote of two-thirds of each House, remove such disability.

Section 4. The validity of the public debt of the United States, authorized by law, including debts incurred for payment of pensions and bounties for services in suppressing insurrection or rebellion, shall not be questioned. But neither the United States nor any State shall assume or pay any debt or obligation incurred in aid of insurrection of rebellion against the United States, or any claim for the loss or emancipation of any slave; but all such debts, obligations and claims shall be held illegal and void.

Section 5. The Congress shall have power to enforce, by appropriate legislation, the provisions of this article.

Amendment XV [1870].

Section 1. The right of citizens of the United States to vote shall not be denied or abridged by the United States or by any State on account of race, color, or previous condition of servitude.

Section 2. The Congress shall have power to enforce this article by appropriate legislation.

Amendment XVI [1913].

The Congress shall have power to lay and collect taxes on incomes, from whatever source derived, without apportionment among the several States, and without regard to any census or enumeration.

Amendment XVII [1913].

The Senate of the United States shall be composed of two Senators from each State, elected by the people thereof, for six years; and each Senator shall have one vote. The electors in each State shall have the qualifications requisite for electors of the most numerous branch of the State legislatures.

When vacancies happen in the representation of any State in the Senate, the executive authority of each State shall issue writs of election to fill such vacancies; *Provided*, That the legislature of any State may empower the executive thereof to make temporary appointments until the people fill the vacancies by election as the legislature may direct.

This amendment shall not be construed as to affect the election or term of any Senator chosen before it becomes valid as part of the Constitution.

Amendment XVIII [1919].

Section 1. After one year from the ratification of this article the manufacture, sale, or transportation of intoxicating liquors within, the importation thereof into, or the exportation thereof from the United States and all territory subject to the jurisdiction thereof for beverage purposes is hereby prohibited.

Section 2. The Congress and the several States shall have concurrent power to enforce this article by appropriate legislation.

Section 3. This article shall be inoperative unless it shall have been ratified as an amendment to the Constitution by the legislatures of the several States, as provided in the Constitution, within seven years from the date of the submission hereof to the States by the Congress.

Amendment XIX [1920].

The right of citizens of the United States to vote shall not be denied or abridged by the United States or by any State on account of sex.

Congress shall have power to enforce this article by appropriate legislation.

Amendment XX [1933].

Section 1. The terms of the President and Vice President shall end at noon on the 20th day of January, and the terms of Senators and Representatives at noon on the 3d day of January, of the years in which such terms would have ended if this article had not been ratified; and the terms of their successors shall then begin.

Section 2. The Congress shall assemble at least once in every year, and such meeting shall begin at noon on the 3d day of January, unless they shall by law appoint a different day.

Section 3. If, at the time fixed for the beginning of the term of the President, the President elect shall have died, the Vice President elect shall become President. If a President shall not have been chosen before the time fixed for the beginning of his term, or if the President elect shall have failed to qualify, then the Vice President elect shall act as President until a President shall have qualified; and the Congress may by law provide for the case wherein neither a President elect nor a Vice President elect shall have qualified, declaring who shall then act as President, or the manner in which one who is to act shall be selected, and such person shall act accordingly until a President or Vice President shall have qualified.

Section 4. The Congress may by law provide for the case of the death of any of the persons from whom the House of Representatives may choose a President whenever the right of choice shall have devolved upon them, and for the case of the death of any of the persons from whom the Senate may choose a Vice President whenever the right of choice shall have devolved upon them.

Section 5. Sections 1 and 2 shall take effect on the 15th day of October following the ratification of this article.

Section 6. This article shall be inoperative unless it shall have been ratified as an amendment to the Constitution by the legislatures of three-fourths of the several States within seven years from the date of its submission.

Amendment XXI [1933].

Section 1. The eighteenth article of amendment to the Constitution of the United States is hereby repealed.

Section 2. The transportation or importation into any State, Territory, or possession of the United States for delivery or use therein of intoxicating liquors, in violation of the laws thereof, is hereby prohibited.

Section 3. This article shall be inoperative unless it shall have been ratified as an amendment to the Constitution by conventions in the several States, as provided in the Constitution, within seven years from the date of the submission hereof to the States by the Congress.

Amendment XXII [1951].

Section 1. No person shall be elected to the office of the President more than twice, and no person who has held the office of President, or acted as President, for more than two years of a term to which some other person was elected President shall be elected to the office of the President more than once. But this Article shall not apply to any person holding the office of President when this Article was proposed by the Congress, and shall not prevent any person who may be holding the office of President, or acting as President, during the term within which this Article becomes operative from holding the office of President, or acting as President during the remainder of such term.

Section 2. This article shall be inoperative unless it shall have been ratified as an amendment to the Constitution by the legislatures of three-fourths of the several States within seven years from the date of its submission to the States by the Congress.

Amendment XXIII [1961].

Section 1. The District constituting the seat of Government of the United States shall appoint in such manner as the Congress may direct:

A number of electors of President and Vice President equal to the whole number of Senators and Representatives in Congress to which the District would be entitled if it were a State, but in no event more than the least populous State; they shall be in addition to those appointed by the States, but they shall be considered, for the purposes of the election of President and Vice President, to be electors appointed by a State; and they shall meet in the District and perform such duties as provided by the twelfth article of amendment.

Section 2. The Congress shall have power to enforce this article by appropriate legislation.

Amendment XXIV [1964].

Section 1. The right of citizens of the United States to vote in any primary or other election for President or Vice President, for electors for President or Vice President, or for Senator or Representative in Congress, shall not be denied or abridged by the United States or any State by reason of failure to pay any poll tax or other tax.

Section 2. The Congress shall have power to enforce this article by appropriate legislation.

Amendment XXV [1967].

Section 1. In case of the removal of the President from office or of his death or resignation, the Vice President shall become President.

Section 2. Whenever there is a vacancy in the office of the Vice President, the President shall nominate a Vice President who shall take office upon confirmation by a majority vote of both Houses of Congress.

Section 3. Whenever the President transmits to the President pro tempore of the Senate and the Speaker of the House of Representatives his written declaration that he is unable to discharge the powers and duties of his office, and until he transmits to them a written declaration to the contrary, such powers and duties shall be discharged by the Vice President as Acting President.

Section 4. Whenever the Vice President and a majority of either the principal officers of the executive departments or of such other body as Congress may by law provide, transmit to the President pro tempore of the Senate and the Speaker of the House of Representatives their written declaration that the President is unable to discharge the powers and duties of his office, the Vice President shall immediately assume the powers and duties of the office as Acting President.

Thereafter, when the President transmits to the President pro tempore of the Senate and the Speaker of the House of Representatives his written declaration that no inability exists, he shall resume the powers and duties of his office unless the Vice President and a majority of either the principal officers of the executive department or of such other body as Congress may by law provide, transmit within four days to the President pro tempore of the Senate and the Speaker of the House of Representatives their written declaration that the President is unable to discharge the powers and duties of his office. Thereupon Congress shall decide the issue, assembling within forty-eight hours for that purpose if not in session. If the Congress, within twenty-one days after receipt of the latter written declaration, or, if Congress is not in session, within twenty-one days after Congress is required to assemble, determines by two-thirds vote of both Houses that the President is unable to discharge the powers and duties of his office, the Vice President shall continue to discharge the same as Acting President; otherwise, the President shall resume the powers and duties of his office.

Amendment XXVI [1971].

Section 1. The right of citizens of the United States, who are eighteen years of age or older, to vote shall not be denied or abridged by the United States or by any State on account of age.

Section 2. The Congress shall have power to enforce this article by appropriate legislation.

Amendment XXVII [1992].

No law, varying the compensation for the services of the Senators and Representatives, shall take effect, until an election of Representatives shall have intervened.

UNIFORM COMMERCIAL CODE (SELECTED PROVISIONS)

ARTICLE I
GENERAL PROVISIONS

PART 1   Short Title, Construction, Application and Subject Matter of the Act

§ 1–101.   Short Title.

This Act shall be known and may be cited as Uniform Commercial Code.

§ 1–102.   Purposes; Rules of Construction; Variation by Agreement.

(1) This Act shall be liberally construed and applied to promote its underlying purposes and policies.

(2) Underlying purposes and policies of this Act are

(a) to simplify, clarify and modernize the law governing commercial transactions;

(b) to permit the continued expansion of commercial practices through custom, usage and agreement of the parties;

(c) to make uniform the law among the various jurisdictions.

(3) The effect of provisions of this Act may be varied by agreement, except as otherwise provided in this Act and except that the obligations of good faith, diligence, reasonableness and care prescribed by this Act may not be disclaimed by agreement but the parties may by agreement determine the standards by which the performance of such obligations is to be measured if such standards are not manifestly unreasonable.

(4) The presence in certain provisions of this Act of the words "unless otherwise agreed" or words of similar import does not imply that the effect of other provisions may not be varied by agreement under subsection (3).

(5) In this Act unless the context otherwise requires

(a) words in the singular number include the plural, and in the plural include the singular;

(b) words of the masculine gender include the feminine and the neuter, and when the sense so indicates words of the neuter gender may refer to any gender.

§ 1–103.   Supplementary General Principles of Law Applicable.

Unless displaced by the particular provisions of this Act, the principles of law and equity, including the law merchant and the law relative to capacity to contract, principal and agent, estoppel, fraud, misrepresentation, duress, coercion, mistake, bankruptcy, or other validating or invalidating cause shall supplement its provisions.

§ 1–104.   Construction Against Implicit Repeal.

This Act being a general act intended as a unified coverage of its subject matter, no part of it shall be deemed to be impliedly repealed by subsequent legislation if such construction can reasonably be avoided.

§ 1–105.   Territorial Application of the Act; Parties' Power to Choose Applicable Law.

(1) Except as provided hereafter in this section, when a transaction bears a reasonable relation to this state and also to another state or nation the parties may agree that the law either of this state or of such other state or nation shall govern their rights and duties. Failing such agreement this Act applies to transactions bearing an appropriate relation to this state.

(2) Where one of the following provisions of this Act specifies the applicable law, that provision governs and a contrary agreement is effective only to the extent permitted by the law (including the conflict of laws rules) so specified:

Rights of creditors against sold goods. Section 2–402.

Applicability of the Article on Leases. Sections 2A–105 and 2A–106.

Applicability of the Article on Bank Deposits and Collections. Section 4–102.

Governing law in the Article on Funds Transfers. Section 4A–507.

Letters of Credit, Section 5–116.

Bulk sales subject to the Article on Bulk Sales. Section 6–103.

Applicability of the Article on Investment Securities. Section 8–106.

Law governing perfection, the effect of perfection or nonperfection, and the priority of security interests and agricultural liens. Sections 9–301 through 9–307.

As amended in 1972, 1987, 1988, 1989, 1994, 1995, and 1999.

§ 1–106. Remedies to Be Liberally Administered.

(1) The remedies provided by this Act shall be liberally administered to the end that the aggrieved party may be put in as good a position as if the other party had fully performed but neither consequential or special nor penal damages may be had except as specifically provided in this Act or by other rule of law.

(2) Any right or obligation declared by this Act is enforceable by action unless the provision declaring it specifies a different and limited effect.

§ 1–107. Waiver or Renunciation of Claim or Right After Breach.

Any claim or right arising out of an alleged breach can be discharged in whole or in part without consideration by a written waiver or renunciation signed and delivered by the aggrieved party.

§ 1–108. Severability.

If any provision or clause of this Act or application thereof to any person or circumstances is held invalid, such invalidity shall not affect other provisions or applications of the Act which can be given effect without the invalid provision or application, and to this end the provisions of this Act are declared to be severable.

§ 1–109. Section Captions.

Section captions are parts of this Act.

PART 2   General Definitions and Principles of Interpretation

§ 1–201. General Definitions.

Subject to additional definitions contained in the subsequent Articles of this Act which are applicable to specific Articles or Parts thereof, and unless the context otherwise requires, in this Act:

(1) "Action" in the sense of a judicial proceeding includes recoupment, counterclaim, set-off, suit in equity and any other proceedings in which rights are determined.

(2) "Aggrieved party" means a party entitled to resort to a remedy.

(3) "Agreement" means the bargain of the parties in fact as found in their language or by implication from other circumstances including course of dealing or usage of trade or course of performance as provided in this Act (Sections 1–205 and 2–208). Whether an agreement has legal consequences is determined by the provisions of this Act, if applicable; otherwise by the law of contracts (Section 1–103). (Compare "Contract".)

(4) "Bank" means any person engaged in the business of banking.

(5) "Bearer" means the person in possession of an instrument, document of title, or certificated security payable to bearer or indorsed in blank.

(6) "Bill of lading" means a document evidencing the receipt of goods for shipment issued by a person engaged in the business of transporting or forwarding goods, and includes an airbill. "Airbill" means a document serving for air transportation as a bill of lading does for marine or rail transportation, and includes an air consignment note or air waybill.

(7) "Branch" includes a separately incorporated foreign branch of a bank.

(8) "Burden of establishing" a fact means the burden of persuading the triers of fact that the existence of the fact is more probable than its non-existence.

(9) "Buyer in ordinary course of business" means a person that buys goods in good faith, without knowledge that the sale violates the rights of another person in the goods, and in the ordinary course from a person, other than a pawnbroker, in the business of selling goods of that kind. A person buys goods in the ordinary course if the sale to the person comports with the usual or customary practices in the kind of business in which the seller is engaged or with the seller's own usual or customary practices. A person that sells oil, gas, or other minerals at the wellhead or minehead is a person in the business of selling goods of that kind. A buyer in ordinary course of business may buy for cash, by exchange of other property, or on secured or unsecured credit, and may acquire goods or documents of title under a pre-existing contract for sale. Only a buyer that takes possession of the goods or has a right to recover the goods from the seller under Article 2 may be a buyer in ordinary course of business. A person that acquires goods in a transfer in bulk or as security for or in total or partial satisfaction of a money debt is not a buyer in ordinary course of business.

(10) "Conspicuous": A term or clause is conspicuous when it is so written that a reasonable person against whom it is to operate ought to have noticed it. A printed heading in capitals (as: NON-NEGOTIABLE BILL OF LADING) is conspicuous. Language in the body of a form is "conspicuous" if it is in larger or other contrasting type or color. But in a telegram any stated term is "conspicuous". Whether a term or clause is "conspicuous" or not is for decision by the court.

(11) "Contract" means the total legal obligation which results from the parties' agreement as affected by this Act and any other applicable rules of law. (Compare "Agreement".)

(12) "Creditor" includes a general creditor, a secured creditor, a lien creditor and any representative of creditors, including an assignee for the benefit of creditors, a trustee in bankruptcy, a receiver in equity and an executor or administrator of an insolvent debtor's or assignor's estate.

(13) "Defendant" includes a person in the position of defendant in a cross-action or counterclaim.

(14) "Delivery" with respect to instruments, documents of title, chattel paper, or certificated securities means voluntary transfer of possession.

(15) "Document of title" includes bill of lading, dock warrant, dock receipt, warehouse receipt or order for the delivery of goods, and also any other document which in the regular course of business or financing is treated as adequately evidencing that the person in possession of it is entitled to receive, hold and dispose of the document and the goods it covers. To be a document of title a document must purport to be issued by or addressed to a bailee and purport to cover goods in the bailee's possession which are either identified or are fungible portions of an identified mass.

(16) "Fault" means wrongful act, omission or breach.

(17) "Fungible" with respect to goods or securities means goods or securities of which any unit is, by nature or usage of trade, the equivalent of any other like unit. Goods which are not fungible shall be deemed fungible for the purposes of this Act to the extent that under a particular agreement or document unlike units are treated as equivalents.

(18) "Genuine" means free of forgery or counterfeiting.

(19) "Good faith" means honesty in fact in the conduct or transaction concerned.

(20) "Holder" with respect to a negotiable instrument, means the person in possession if the instrument is payable to bearer or, in the cases of an instrument payable to an identified person, if the identified person is in possession. "Holder" with respect to a document of title means the person in possession if the goods are deliverable to bearer or to the order of the person in possession.

(21) To "honor" is to pay or to accept and pay, or where a credit so engages to purchase or discount a draft complying with the terms of the credit.

(22) "Insolvency proceedings" includes any assignment for the benefit of creditors or other proceedings intended to liquidate or rehabilitate the estate of the person involved.

(23) A person is "insolvent" who either has ceased to pay his debts in the ordinary course of business or cannot pay his debts as they become due or is insolvent within the meaning of the federal bankruptcy law.

(24) "Money" means a medium of exchange authorized or adopted by a domestic or foreign government and includes a monetary unit of account established by an intergovernmental organization or by agreement between two or more nations.

(25) A person has "notice" of a fact when

(a) he has actual knowledge of it; or

(b) he has received a notice or notification of it; or

(c) from all the facts and circumstances known to him at the time in question he has reason to know that it exists.

A person "knows" or has "knowledge" of a fact when he has actual knowledge of it. "Discover" or "learn" or a word or phrase of similar import refers to knowledge rather than to reason to know. The time and circumstances under which a notice or notification may cease to be effective are not determined by this Act.

(26) A person "notifies" or "gives" a notice or notification to another by taking such steps as may be reasonably required to inform the other in ordinary course whether or not such other actually comes to know of it. A person "receives" a notice or notification when

(a) it comes to his attention; or

(b) it is duly delivered at the place of business through which the contract was made or at any other place held out by him as the place for receipt of such communications.

(27) Notice, knowledge or a notice or notification received by an organization is effective for a particular transaction from the time when it is brought to the attention of the individual conducting that transaction, and in any event from the time when it would have been brought to his attention if the organization had exercised due diligence. An organization exercises due diligence if it maintains reasonable routines for communicating significant information to the person conducting the transaction and there is reasonable compliance with the routines. Due diligence does not require an individual acting for the organization to communicate information unless such communication is part of his regular duties or unless he has reason to know of the transaction and that the transaction would be materially affected by the information.

(28) "Organization" includes a corporation, government or governmental subdivision or agency, business trust, estate, trust, partnership or association, two or more persons having a joint or common interest, or any other legal or commercial entity.

(29) "Party", as distinct from "third party", means a person who has engaged in a transaction or made an agreement within this Act.

(30) "Person" includes an individual or an organization (See Section 1–102).

(31) "Presumption" or "presumed" means that the trier of fact must find the existence of the fact presumed unless and until evidence is introduced which would support a finding of its non-existence.

(32) "Purchase" includes taking by sale, discount, negotiation, mortgage, pledge, lien, issue or re-issue, gift or any other voluntary transaction creating an interest in property.

(33) "Purchaser" means a person who takes by purchase.

(34) "Remedy" means any remedial right to which an aggrieved party is entitled with or without resort to a tribunal.

(35) "Representative" includes an agent, an officer of a corporation or association, and a trustee, executor or administrator of an estate, or any other person empowered to act for another.

(36) "Rights" includes remedies.

(37) "Security interest" means an interest in personal property or fixtures which secures payment or performance of an obligation. The term also includes any interest of a consignor and a buyer of accounts, chattel paper, a payment intangible, or a promissory note in a transaction that is subject to Article 9. The special property interest of a buyer of goods on identification of those goods to a contract for sale under Section 2–401 is not a "security interest", but a buyer may also acquire a "security interest" by complying with Article 9. Except as otherwise provided in Section 2–505, the right of a seller or lessor of goods under Article 2 or 2A to retain or acquire possession of the goods is not a "security interest", but a seller or lessor may also acquire a "security interest" by complying with Article 9. The retention or reservation of title by a seller of goods notwithstanding shipment or delivery to the buyer (Section 2–401) is limited in effect to a reservation of a "security interest".

Whether a transaction creates a lease or security interest is determined by the facts of each case; however, a transaction creates a security interest if the consideration the lessee is to pay the lessor for the right to possession and use of the goods is an obligation for the term of the lease not subject to termination by the lessee, and

(a) the original term of the lease is equal to or greater than the remaining economic life of the goods,

(b) the lessee is bound to renew the lease for the remaining economic life of the goods or is bound to become the owner of the goods,

(c) the lessee has an option to renew the lease for the remaining economic life of the goods for no additional consideration or nominal additional consideration upon compliance with the lease agreement, or

(d) the lessee has an option to become the owner of the goods for no additional consideration or nominal additional consideration upon compliance with the lease agreement.

A transaction does not create a security interest merely because it provides that

(a) the present value of the consideration the lessee is obligated to pay the lessor for the right to possession and use of the goods is substantially equal to or is greater than the fair market value of the goods at the time the lease is entered into,

(b) the lessee assumes risk of loss of the goods, or agrees to pay taxes, insurance, filing, recording, or registration fees, or service or maintenance costs with respect to the goods,

(c) the lessee has an option to renew the lease or to become the owner of the goods,

(d) the lessee has an option to renew the lease for a fixed rent that is equal to or greater than the reasonably predictable fair market rent for the use of the goods for the term of the renewal at the time the option is to be performed, or

(e) the lessee has an option to become the owner of the goods for a fixed price that is equal to or greater than the reasonably predictable fair market value of the goods at the time the option is to be performed.

For purposes of this subsection (37):

(x) Additional consideration is not nominal if (i) when the option to renew the lease is granted to the lessee the rent is stated to be the fair market rent for the use of the goods for the term of the renewal determined at the time the option is to be performed, or (ii) when the option to become the owner of the goods is granted to the lessee the price is stated to be the fair market value of the goods determined at the time the option is to be performed. Additional consideration is nominal if it is less than the lessee's reasonably predictable cost of performing under the lease agreement if the option is not exercised;

(y) "Reasonably predictable" and "remaining economic life of the goods" are to be determined with reference to the facts and circumstances at the time the transaction is entered into; and

(z) "Present value" means the amount as of a date certain of one or more sums payable in the future, discounted to the date certain. The discount is determined by the interest rate specified by the parties if the rate is not manifestly unreasonable at the time the transaction is entered into; otherwise, the discount is determined by a commercially reasonable rate that takes into account the facts and circumstances of each case at the time the transaction was entered into.

(38) "Send" in connection with any writing or notice means to deposit in the mail or deliver for transmission by any other usual means of communication with postage or cost of transmission provided for and properly addressed and in the case of an instrument to an address specified thereon or otherwise agreed, or if there be none to any address reasonable under the circumstances. The receipt of any writing or notice within the time at which it would have arrived if properly sent has the effect of a proper sending.

(39) "Signed" includes any symbol executed or adopted by a party with present intention to authenticate a writing.

(40) "Surety" includes guarantor.

(41) "Telegram" includes a message transmitted by radio, teletype, cable, any mechanical method of transmission, or the like.

(42) "Term" means that portion of an agreement which relates to a particular matter.

(43) "Unauthorized" signature means one made without actual, implied or apparent authority and includes a forgery.

(44) "Value". Except as otherwise provided with respect to negotiable instruments and bank collections (Sections 3–303, 4–210 and 4–211) a person gives "value" for rights if he acquires them

(a) in return for a binding commitment to extend credit or for the extension of immediately available credit whether or not drawn upon and whether or not a chargeback is provided for in the event of difficulties in collection; or

(b) as security for or in total or partial satisfaction of a pre-existing claim; or

(c) by accepting delivery pursuant to a preexisting contract for purchase; or

(d) generally, in return for any consideration sufficient to support a simple contract.

(45) "Warehouse receipt" means a receipt issued by a person engaged in the business of storing goods for hire.

(46) "Written" or "writing" includes printing, typewriting or any other intentional reduction to tangible form.

§ 1–202.   Prima Facie Evidence by Third Party Documents.

A document in due form purporting to be a bill of lading, policy or certificate of insurance, official weigher's or inspector's certificate, consular invoice, or any other document authorized or required by the contract to be issued by a third party shall be prima facie evidence of its own authenticity and genuineness and of the facts stated in the document by the third party.

§ 1–203.   Obligation of Good Faith.

Every contract or duty within this Act imposes an obligation of good faith in its performance or enforcement.

§ 1–204.   Time; Reasonable Time; "Seasonably".

(1) Whenever this Act requires any action to be taken within a reasonable time, any time which is not manifestly unreasonable may be fixed by agreement.

(2) What is a reasonable time for taking any action depends on the nature, purpose and circumstances of such action.

(3) An action is taken "seasonably" when it is taken at or within the time agreed or if no time is agreed at or within a reasonable time.

§ 1–205.   Course of Dealing and Usage of Trade.

(1) A course of dealing is a sequence of previous conduct between the parties to a particular transaction which is fairly to be regarded as establishing a common basis of understanding for interpreting their expressions and other conduct.

(2) A usage of trade is any practice or method of dealing having such regularity of observance in a place, vocation or trade as to justify an expectation that it will be observed with respect to the transaction in question. The existence and scope of such a usage are to be proved as facts. If it is established that such a usage is embodied in a written trade code or similar writing the interpretation of the writing is for the court.

(3) A course of dealing between parties and any usage of trade in the vocation or trade in which they are engaged or of which they are or should be aware give particular meaning to and supplement or qualify terms of an agreement.

(4) The express terms of an agreement and an applicable course of dealing or usage of trade shall be construed wherever reasonable as consistent with each other; but when such construction is unreasonable express terms control both course of dealing and usage of trade and course of dealing controls usage trade.

(5) An applicable usage of trade in the place where any part of performance is to occur shall be used in interpreting the agreement as to that part of the performance.

(6) Evidence of a relevant usage of trade offered by one party is not admissible unless and until he has given the other party such notice as the court finds sufficient to prevent unfair surprise to the latter.

§ 1–206.   Statute of Frauds for Kinds of Personal Property Not Otherwise Covered.

(1) Except in the cases described in subsection (2) of this section a contract for the sale of personal property is not enforceable by way of action or defense beyond five thousand dollars in amount or value of remedy unless there is some writing which indicates that a contract for sale has been made between the parties at a defined or stated price, reasonably identifies the subject matter, and is signed by the party against whom enforcement is sought or by his authorized agent.

(2) Subsection (1) of this section does not apply to contracts for the sale of goods (Section 2–201) nor of securities (Section 8–113) nor to security agreements (Section 9–203).

As amended in 1994.

§ 1–207.   Performance or Acceptance Under Reservation of Rights.

(1) A party who with explicit reservation of rights performs or promises performance or assents to performance in a manner demanded or offered by the other party does not thereby prejudice the rights reserved. Such words as "without prejudice", "under protest" or the like are sufficient.

(2) Subsection (1) does not apply to an accord and satisfaction.

As amended in 1990.

§ 1–208.   Option to Accelerate at Will.

A term providing that one party or his successor in interest may accelerate payment or performance or require collateral or additional collateral "at will" or "when he deems himself insecure" or in words of similar import shall be construed to mean that he shall have power to do so only if he in good faith believes that the prospect of payment or performance is impaired. The burden of establishing lack of good faith is on the party against whom the power has been exercised.

§ 1–209.   Subordinated Obligations.

An obligation may be issued as subordinated to payment of another obligation of the person obligated, or a creditor may subordinate his right to payment of an obligation by agreement with either the person obligated or another creditor of the person obligated. Such a subordination does not create a security interest as against either the common debtor or a subordinated creditor. This section shall be construed as declaring the law as it existed prior to the enactment of this section and not as modifying it. Added 1966.

Note: *This new section is proposed as an optional provision to make it clear that a subordination agreement does not create a security interest unless so intended.*

ARTICLE II
SALES

PART 1   Short Title, General Construction and Subject Matter

§ 2–101.   Short Title.

This Article shall be known and may be cited as Uniform Commercial Code—Sales.

§ 2–102.   Scope; Certain Security and Other Transactions Excluded From This Article.

Unless the context otherwise requires, this Article applies to transactions in goods; it does not apply to any transaction which although in the form of an unconditional contract to sell or present sale is intended to operate only as a security transaction nor does this Article impair or repeal any statute regulating sales to consumers, farmers or other specified classes of buyers.

§ 2–103.   Definitions and Index of Definitions.

(1) In this Article unless the context otherwise requires

  (a) "Buyer" means a person who buys or contracts to buy goods.

  (b) "Good faith" in the case of a merchant means honesty in fact and the observance of reasonable commercial standards of fair dealing in the trade.

  (c) "Receipt" of goods means taking physical possession of them.

  (d) "Seller" means a person who sells or contracts to sell goods.

(2) Other definitions applying to this Article or to specified Parts thereof, and the sections in which they appear are:

"Acceptance". Section 2–606.
"Banker's credit". Section 2–325.
"Between merchants". Section 2–104.
"Cancellation". Section 2–106(4).
"Commercial unit". Section 2–105.
"Confirmed credit". Section 2–325.
"Conforming to contract". Section 2–106.
"Contract for sale". Section 2–106.
"Cover". Section 2–712.
"Entrusting". Section 2–403.
"Financing agency". Section 2–104.
"Future goods". Section 2–105.
"Goods". Section 2–105.
"Identification". Section 2–501.
"Installment contract". Section 2–612.
"Letter of Credit". Section 2–325.
"Lot". Section 2–105
"Merchant". Section 2–104.
"Overseas". Section 2–323.
"Person in position of seller". Section 2–707.
"Present sale". Section 2–106.
"Sale". Section 2–106.
"Sale on approval". Section 2–326.
"Sale or return". Section 2–326.
"Termination". Section 2–106.

(3) The following definitions in other Articles apply to this Article:

"Check". Section 3–104.
"Consignee". Section 7–102.
"Consignor". Section 7–102.
"Consumer goods". Section 9–109.
"Dishonor". Section 3–507.
"Draft". Section 3–104.

(4) In addition Article 1 contains general definitions and principles of construction and interpretation applicable throughout this Article.

As amended in 1994 and 1999.

§ 2–104.   Definitions: "Merchant"; "Between Merchants"; "Financing Agency".

(1) "Merchant" means a person who deals in goods of the kind or otherwise by his occupation holds himself out as having knowledge or skill peculiar to the practices or goods involved in the transaction or to whom such knowledge or skill may be attributed by his employment of an agent or broker or other intermediary who by his occupation holds himself out as having such knowledge or skill.

(2) "Financing agency" means a bank, finance company or other person who in the ordinary course of business makes advances against goods or documents of title or who by arrangement with either the seller or the buyer intervenes in ordinary course to make or collect payment due or claimed under the contract for sale, as by purchasing or paying the seller's draft or making advances against it or by merely taking it for collection whether

or not documents of title accompany the draft. "Financing agency" includes also a bank or other person who similarly intervenes between persons who are in the position of seller and buyer in respect to the goods (Section 2–707).

(3) "Between merchants" means in any transaction with respect to which both parties are chargeable with the knowledge or skill of merchants.

§ 2–105. Definitions: Transferability; "Goods"; "Future" Goods; "Lot"; "Commercial Unit".

(1) "Goods" means all things (including specially manufactured goods) which are movable at the time of identification to the contract for sale other than the money in which the price is to be paid, investment securities (Article 8) and things in action. "Goods" also includes the unborn young of animals and growing crops and other identified things attached to realty as described in the section on goods to be severed from realty (Section 2–107).

(2) Goods must be both existing and identified before any interest in them can pass. Goods which are not both existing and identified are "future" goods. A purported present sale of future goods or of any interest therein operates as a contract to sell.

(3) There may be a sale of a part interest in existing identified goods.

(4) An undivided share in an identified bulk of fungible goods is sufficiently identified to be sold although the quantity of the bulk is not determined. Any agreed proportion of such a bulk or any quantity thereof agreed upon by number, weight or other measure may to the extent of the seller's interest in the bulk be sold to the buyer who then becomes an owner in common.

(5) "Lot" means a parcel or a single article which is the subject matter of a separate sale or delivery, whether or not it is sufficient to perform the contract.

(6) "Commercial unit" means such a unit of goods as by commercial usage is a single whole for purposes of sale and division of which materially impairs its character or value on the market or in use. A commercial unit may be a single article (as a machine) or a set of articles (as a suite of furniture or an assortment of sizes) or a quantity (as a bale, gross, or carload) or any other unit treated in use or in the relevant market as a single whole.

§ 2–106. Definitions: "Contract"; "Agreement"; "Contract for Sale"; "Sale"; "Present Sale"; "Conforming" to Contract; "Termination"; "Cancellation".

(1) In this Article unless the context otherwise requires "contract" and "agreement" are limited to those relating to the present or future sale of goods. "Contract for sale" includes both a present sale of goods and a contract to sell goods at a future time. A "sale" consists in the passing of title from the seller to the buyer for a price (Section 2–401). A "present sale" means a sale which is accomplished by the making of the contract.

(2) Goods or conduct including any part of a performance are "conforming" or conform to the contract when they are in accordance with the obligations under the contract.

(3) "Termination" occurs when either party pursuant to a power created by agreement or law puts an end to the contract otherwise than for its breach. On "termination" all obligations which are still executory on both sides are discharged but any right based on prior breach or performance survives.

(4) "Cancellation" occurs when either party puts an end to the contract for breach by the other and its effect is the same as that of "termination" except that the cancelling party also retains any remedy for breach of the whole contract or any unperformed balance.

§ 2–107. Goods to Be Severed From Realty: Recording.

(1) A contract for the sale of minerals or the like (including oil and gas) or a structure or its materials to be removed from realty is a contract for the sale of goods within this Article if they are to be severed by the seller but until severance a purported present sale thereof which is not effective as a transfer of an interest in land is effective only as a contract to sell.

(2) A contract for the sale apart from the land of growing crops or other things attached to realty and capable of severance without material harm thereto but not described in subsection (1) or of timber to be cut is a contract for the sale of goods within this Article whether the subject matter is to be severed by the buyer or by the seller even though it forms part of the realty at the time of contracting, and the parties can by identification effect a present sale before severance.

(3) The provisions of this section are subject to any third party rights provided by the law relating to realty records, and the contract for sale may be executed and recorded as a document transferring an interest in land and shall then constitute notice to third parties of the buyer's rights under the contract for sale.

As amended in 1972.

PART 2   Form, Formation and Readjustment of Contract

§ 2–201. Formal Requirements; Statute of Frauds.

(1) Except as otherwise provided in this section a contract for the sale of goods for the price of $500 or more is not enforceable by way of action or defense unless there is some writing sufficient to indicate that a contract for sale has been made between the parties and signed by the party against whom enforcement is sought or by his authorized agent or broker. A writing is not insufficient because it omits or incorrectly states a term agreed upon but the contract is not enforceable under this paragraph beyond the quantity of goods shown in such writing.

(2) Between merchants if within a reasonable time a writing in confirmation of the contract and sufficient against the sender is received and the party receiving it has reason to know its contents, it satisfies the requirements of subsection (1) against such party unless written notice of objection to its contents is given within ten days after it is received.

(3) A contract which does not satisfy the requirements of subsection (1) but which is valid in other respects is enforceable

(a) if the goods are to be specially manufactured for the buyer and are not suitable for sale to others in the ordinary course of the seller's business and the seller, before notice of repudiation is received and under circumstances which reasonably indicate that the goods are for the buyer, has made either a substantial beginning of their manufacture or commitments for their procurement; or

(b) if the party against whom enforcement is sought admits in his pleading, testimony or otherwise in court that a contract for sale was made, but the contract is not enforceable under this provision beyond the quantity of goods admitted; or

(c) with respect to goods for which payment has been made and accepted or which have been received and accepted (Sec. 2–606).

§ 2–202.   Final Written Expression: Parol or Extrinsic Evidence.

Terms with respect to which the confirmatory memoranda of the parties agree or which are otherwise set forth in a writing intended by the parties as a final expression of their agreement with respect to such terms as are included therein may not be contradicted by evidence of any prior agreement or of a contemporaneous oral agreement but may be explained or supplemented

(a) by course of dealing or usage of trade (Section 1–205) or by course of performance (Section 2–208); and

(b) by evidence of consistent additional terms unless the court finds the writing to have been intended also as a complete and exclusive statement of the terms of the agreement.

§ 2–203.   Seals Inoperative.

The affixing of a seal to a writing evidencing a contract for sale or an offer to buy or sell goods does not constitute the writing a sealed instrument and the law with respect to sealed instruments does not apply to such a contract or offer.

§ 2–204.   Formation in General.

(1) A contract for sale of goods may be made in any manner sufficient to show agreement, including conduct by both parties which recognizes the existence of such a contract.

(2) An agreement sufficient to constitute a contract for sale may be found even though the moment of its making is undetermined.

(3) Even though one or more terms are left open a contract for sale does not fail for indefiniteness if the parties have intended

to make a contract and there is a reasonably certain basis for giving an appropriate remedy.

§ 2–205.   Firm Offers.

An offer by a merchant to buy or sell goods in a signed writing which by its terms gives assurance that it will be held open is not revocable, for lack of consideration, during the time stated or if no time is stated for a reasonable time, but in no event may such period of irrevocability exceed three months; but any such term of assurance on a form supplied by the offeree must be separately signed by the offeror.

§ 2–206.   Offer and Acceptance in Formation of Contract.

(1) Unless other unambiguously indicated by the language or circumstances

(a) an offer to make a contract shall be construed as inviting acceptance in any manner and by any medium reasonable in the circumstances;

(b) an order or other offer to buy goods for prompt or current shipment shall be construed as inviting acceptance either by a prompt promise to ship or by the prompt or current shipment of conforming or nonconforming goods, but such a shipment of non-conforming goods does not constitute an acceptance if the seller seasonably notifies the buyer that the shipment is offered only as an accommodation to the buyer.

(2) Where the beginning of a requested performance is a reasonable mode of acceptance an offeror who is not notified of acceptance within a reasonable time may treat the offer as having lapsed before acceptance.

§ 2–207.   Additional Terms in Acceptance or Confirmation.

(1) A definite and seasonable expression of acceptance or a written confirmation which is sent within a reasonable time operates as an acceptance even though it states terms additional to or different from those offered or agreed upon, unless acceptance is expressly made conditional on assent to the additional or different terms.

(2) The additional terms are to be construed as proposals for addition to the contract. Between merchants such terms become part of the contract unless:

(a) the offer expressly limits acceptance to the terms of the offer;

(b) they materially alter it; or

(c) notification of objection to them has already been given or is given within a reasonable time after notice of them is received.

(3) Conduct by both parties which recognizes the existence of a contract is sufficient to establish a contract for sale although the writings of the parties do not otherwise establish a contract. In such case the terms of the particular contract consist of those

terms on which the writings of the parties agree, together with any supplementary terms incorporated under any other provisions of this Act.

§ 2–208.   Course of Performance or Practical Construction.

(1) Where the contract for sale involves repeated occasions for performance by either party with knowledge of the nature of the performance and opportunity for objection to it by the other, any course of performance accepted or acquiesced in without objection shall be relevant to determine the meaning of the agreement.

(2) The express terms of the agreement and any such course of performance, as well as any course of dealing and usage of trade, shall be construed whenever reasonable as consistent with each other; but when such construction is unreasonable, express terms shall control course of performance and course of performance shall control both course of dealing and usage of trade (Section 1–205).

(3) Subject to the provisions of the next section on modification and waiver, such course of performance shall be relevant to show a waiver or modification of any term inconsistent with such course of performance.

§ 2–209.   Modification, Rescission and Waiver.

(1) An agreement modifying a contract within this Article needs no consideration to be binding.

(2) A signed agreement which excludes modification or rescission except by a signed writing cannot be otherwise modified or rescinded, but except as between merchants such a requirement on a form supplied by the merchant must be separately signed by the other party.

(3) The requirements of the statute of frauds section of this Article (Section 2–201) must be satisfied if the contract as modified is within its provisions.

(4) Although an attempt at modification or rescission does not satisfy the requirements of subsection (2) or (3) it can operate as a waiver.

(5) A party who has made a waiver affecting an executory portion of the contract may retract the waiver by reasonable notification received by the other party that strict performance will be required of any term waived, unless the retraction would be unjust in view of a material change of position in reliance on the waiver.

§ 2–210.   Delegation of Performance; Assignment of Rights.

(1) A party may perform his duty through a delegate unless otherwise agreed or unless the other party has a substantial interest in having his original promisor perform or control the acts required by the contract. No delegation of performance relieves the party delegating of any duty to perform or any liability for breach.

(2) Except as otherwise provided in Section 9–406, unless otherwise agreed, all rights of either seller or buyer can be assigned except where the assignment would materially change the duty of the other party, or increase materially the burden or risk imposed on him by his contract, or impair materially his chance of obtaining return performance. A right to damages for breach of the whole contract or a right arising out of the assignor's due performance of his entire obligation can be assigned despite agreement otherwise.

(3) The creation, attachment, perfection, or enforcement of a security interest in the seller's interest under a contract is not a transfer that materially changes the duty of or increases materially the burden or risk imposed on the buyer or impairs materially the buyer's chance of obtaining return performance within the purview of subsection (2) unless, and then only to the extent that, enforcement actually results in a delegation of material performance of the seller. Even in that event, the creation, attachment, perfection, and enforcement of the security interest remain effective, but (i) the seller is liable to the buyer for damages caused by the delegation to the extent that the damages could not reasonably by prevented by the buyer, and (ii) a court having jurisdiction may grant other appropriate relief, including cancellation of the contract for sale or an injunction against enforcement of the security interest or consummation of the enforcement.

(4) Unless the circumstances indicate the contrary a prohibition of assignment of "the contract" is to be construed as barring only the delegation to the assignee of the assignor's performance.

(5) An assignment of "the contract" or of "all my rights under the contract" or an assignment in similar general terms is an assignment of rights and unless the language or the circumstances (as in an assignment for security) indicate the contrary, it is a delegation of performance of the duties of the assignor and its acceptance by the assignee constitutes a promise by him to perform those duties. This promise is enforceable by either the assignor or the other party to the original contract.

(6) The other party may treat any assignment which delegates performance as creating reasonable grounds for insecurity and may without prejudice to his rights against the assignor demand assurances from the assignee (Section 2–609).

As amended in 1999.

PART 3   General Obligation and Construction of Contract

§ 2–301.   General Obligations of Parties.

The obligation of the seller is to transfer and deliver and that of the buyer is to accept and pay in accordance with the contract.

§ 2–302.   Unconscionable Contract or Clause.

(1) If the court as a matter of law finds the contract or any clause of the contract to have been unconscionable at the time it was made the court may refuse to enforce the contract, or it may enforce the remainder of the contract without the

unconscionable clause, or it may so limit the application of any unconscionable clause as to avoid any unconscionable result.

(2) When it is claimed or appears to the court that the contract or any clause thereof may be unconscionable the parties shall be afforded a reasonable opportunity to present evidence as to its commercial setting, purpose and effect to aid the court in making the determination.

§ 2–303.   Allocations or Division of Risks.

Where this Article allocates a risk or a burden as between the parties "unless otherwise agreed", the agreement may not only shift the allocation but may also divide the risk or burden.

§ 2–304.   Price Payable in Money, Goods, Realty, or Otherwise.

(1) The price can be made payable in money or otherwise. If it is payable in whole or in part in goods each party is a seller of the goods which he is to transfer.

(2) Even though all or part of the price is payable in an interest in realty the transfer of the goods and the seller's obligations with reference to them are subject to this Article, but not the transfer of the interest in realty or the transferor's obligations in connection therewith.

§ 2–305.   Open Price Term.

(1) The parties if they so intend can conclude a contract for sale even though the price is not settled. In such a case the price is a reasonable price at the time for delivery if

(a) nothing is said as to price; or

(b) the price is left to be agreed by the parties and they fail to agree; or

(c) the price is to be fixed in terms of some agreed market or other standard as set or recorded by a third person or agency and it is not so set or recorded.

(2) A price to be fixed by the seller or by the buyer means a price for him to fix in good faith.

(3) When a price left to be fixed otherwise than by agreement of the parties fails to be fixed through fault of one party the other may at his option treat the contract as cancelled or himself fix a reasonable price.

(4) Where, however, the parties intend not to be bound unless the price be fixed or agreed and it is not fixed or agreed there is no contract. In such a case the buyer must return any goods already received or if unable so to do must pay their reasonable value at the time of delivery and the seller must return any portion of the price paid on account.

§ 2–306.   Output, Requirements and Exclusive Dealings.

(1) A term which measures the quantity by the output of the seller or the requirements of the buyer means such actual output or

requirements as may occur in good faith, except that no quantity unreasonably disproportionate to any stated estimate or in the absence of a stated estimate to any normal or otherwise comparable prior output or requirements may be tendered or demanded.

(2) A lawful agreement by either the seller or the buyer for exclusive dealing in the kind of goods concerned imposes unless otherwise agreed an obligation by the seller to use best efforts to supply the goods and by the buyer to use best efforts to promote their sale.

§ 2–307.   Delivery in Single Lot or Several Lots.

Unless otherwise agreed all goods called for by a contract for sale must be tendered in a single delivery and payment is due only on such tender but where the circumstances give either party the right to make or demand delivery in lots the price if it can be apportioned may be demanded for each lot.

§ 2–308.   Absence of Specified Place for Delivery.

Unless otherwise agreed

(a) the place for delivery of goods is the seller's place of business or if he has none his residence; but

(b) in a contract for sale of identified goods which to the knowledge of the parties at the time of contracting are in some other place, that place is the place for their delivery; and

(c) documents of title may be delivered through customary banking channels.

§ 2–309.   Absence of Specific Time Provisions; Notice of Termination.

(1) The time for shipment or delivery or any other action under a contract if not provided in this Article or agreed upon shall be a reasonable time.

(2) Where the contract provides for successive performances but is indefinite in duration it is valid for a reasonable time but unless otherwise agreed may be terminated at any time by either party.

(3) Termination of a contract by one party except on the happening of an agreed event requires that reasonable notification be received by the other party and an agreement dispensing with notification is invalid if its operation would be unconscionable.

§ 2–310.   Open Time for Payment or Running of Credit; Authority to Ship Under Reservation.

Unless otherwise agreed

(a) payment is due at the time and place at which the buyer is to receive the goods even though the place of shipment is the place of delivery; and

(b) if the seller is authorized to send the goods he may ship them under reservation, and may tender the documents of title, but the buyer may inspect the goods after their arrival before payment is due unless such inspection is inconsistent with the terms of the contract (Section 2–513); and

(c) if delivery is authorized and made by way of documents of title otherwise than by subsection (b) then payment is due at the time and place at which the buyer is to receive the documents regardless of where the goods are to be received; and

(d) where the seller is required or authorized to ship the goods on credit the credit period runs from the time of shipment but post-dating the invoice or delaying its dispatch will correspondingly delay the starting of the credit period.

§ 2–311.   Options and Cooperation Respecting Performance.

(1) An agreement for sale which is otherwise sufficiently definite (subsection (3) of Section 2–204) to be a contract is not made invalid by the fact that it leaves particulars of performance to be specified by one of the parties. Any such specification must be made in good faith and within limits set by commercial reasonableness.

(2) Unless otherwise agreed specifications relating to assortment of the goods are at the buyer's option and except as otherwise provided in subsections (1)(c) and (3) of Section 2–319 specifications or arrangements relating to shipment are at the seller's option.

(3) Where such specification would materially affect the other party's performance but is not seasonably made or where one party's cooperation is necessary to the agreed performance of the other but is not seasonably forthcoming, the other party in addition to all other remedies

(a) is excused for any resulting delay in his own performance; and

(b) may also either proceed to perform in any reasonable manner or after the time for a material part of his own performance treat the failure to specify or to cooperate as a breach by failure to deliver or accept the goods.

§ 2–312.   Warranty of Title and Against Infringement; Buyer's Obligation Against Infringement.

(1) Subject to subsection (2) there is in a contract for sale a warranty by the seller that

(a) the title conveyed shall be good, and its transfer rightful; and

(b) the goods shall be delivered free from any security interest or other lien or encumbrance of which the buyer at the time of contracting has no knowledge.

(2) A warranty under subsection (1) will be excluded or modified only by specific language or by circumstances which give the buyer reason to know that the person selling does not claim title

in himself or that he is purporting to sell only such right or title as he or a third person may have.

(3) Unless otherwise agreed a seller who is a merchant regularly dealing in goods of the kind warrants that the goods shall be delivered free of the rightful claim of any third person by way of infringement or the like but a buyer who furnishes specifications to the seller must hold the seller harmless against any such claim which arises out of compliance with the specifications.

§ 2–313.   Express Warranties by Affirmation, Promise, Description, Sample.

(1) Express warranties by the seller are created as follows:

(a) Any affirmation of fact or promise made by the seller to the buyer which relates to the goods and becomes part of the basis of the bargain creates an express warranty that the goods shall conform to the affirmation or promise.

(b) Any description of the goods which is made part of the basis of the bargain creates an express warranty that the goods shall conform to the description.

(c) Any sample or model which is made part of the basis of the bargain creates an express warranty that the whole of the goods shall conform to the sample or model.

(2) It is not necessary to the creation of an express warranty that the seller use formal words such as "warrant" or "guarantee" or that he have a specific intention to make a warranty, but an affirmation merely of the value of the goods or a statement purporting to be merely the seller's opinion or commendation of the goods does not create a warranty.

§ 2–314.   Implied Warranty: Merchantability; Usage of Trade.

(1) Unless excluded or modified (Section 2–316), a warranty that the goods shall be merchantable is implied in a contract for their sale if the seller is a merchant with respect to goods of that kind. Under this section the serving for value of food or drink to be consumed either on the premises or elsewhere is a sale.

(2) Goods to be merchantable must be at least such as

(a) pass without objection in the trade under the contract description; and

(b) in the case of fungible goods, are of fair average quality within the description; and

(c) are fit for the ordinary purposes for which such goods are used; and

(d) run, within the variations permitted by the agreement, of even kind, quality and quantity within each unit and among all units involved; and

(e) are adequately contained, packaged, and labeled as the agreement may require; and

(f) conform to the promises or affirmations of fact made on the container or label if any.

(3) Unless excluded or modified (Section 2–316) other implied warranties may arise from course of dealing or usage of trade.

§ 2–315.   Implied Warranty: Fitness for Particular Purpose.

Where the seller at the time of contracting has reason to know any particular purpose for which the goods are required and that the buyer is relying on the seller's skill or judgment to select or furnish suitable goods, there is unless excluded or modified under the next section an implied warranty that the goods shall be fit for such purpose.

§ 2–316.   Exclusion or Modification of Warranties.

(1) Words or conduct relevant to the creation of an express warranty and words or conduct tending to negate or limit warranty shall be construed wherever reasonable as consistent with each other; but subject to the provisions of this Article on parol or extrinsic evidence (Section 2–202) negation or limitation is inoperative to the extent that such construction is unreasonable.

(2) Subject to subsection (3), to exclude or modify the implied warranty of merchantability or any part of it the language must mention merchantability and in case of a writing must be conspicuous, and to exclude or modify any implied warranty of fitness the exclusion must be by a writing and conspicuous. Language to exclude all implied warranties of fitness is sufficient if it states, for example, that "There are no warranties which extend beyond the description on the face hereof."

(3) Notwithstanding subsection (2)

(a) unless the circumstances indicate otherwise, all implied warranties are excluded by expressions like "as is", "with all faults" or other language which in common understanding calls the buyer's attention to the exclusion of warranties and makes plain that there is no implied warranty; and

(b) when the buyer before entering into the contract has examined the goods or the sample or model as fully as he desired or has refused to examine the goods there is no implied warranty with regard to defects which an examination ought in the circumstances to have revealed to him; and

(c) an implied warranty can also be excluded or modified by course of dealing or course of performance or usage of trade.

(4) Remedies for breach of warranty can be limited in accordance with the provisions of this Article on liquidation or limitation of damages and on contractual modification of remedy (Sections 2–718 and 2–719).

§ 2–317.   Cumulation and Conflict of Warranties Express or Implied.

Warranties whether express or implied shall be construed as consistent with each other and as cumulative, but if such construction is unreasonable the intention of the parties shall determine which warranty is dominant. In ascertaining that intention the following rules apply:

(a) Exact or technical specifications displace an inconsistent sample or model or general language of description.

(b) A sample from an existing bulk displaces inconsistent general language of description.

(c) Express warranties displace inconsistent implied warranties other than an implied warranty of fitness for a particular purpose.

§ 2–318.   Third Party Beneficiaries of Warranties Express or Implied.

Note: If this Act is introduced in the Congress of the United States this section should be omitted. (States to select one alternative.)

Alternative A   A seller's warranty whether express or implied extends to any natural person who is in the family or household of his buyer or who is a guest in his home if it is reasonable to expect that such person may use, consume or be affected by the goods and who is injured in person by breach of the warranty. A seller may not exclude or limit the operation of this section.

Alternative B   A seller's warranty whether express or implied extends to any natural person who may reasonably be expected to use, consume or be affected by the goods and who is injured in person by breach of the warranty. A seller may not exclude or limit the operation of this section.

Alternative C   A seller's warranty whether express or implied extends to any person who may reasonably be expected to use, consume or be affected by the goods and who is injured by breach of the warranty. A seller may not exclude or limit the operation of this section with respect to injury to the person of an individual to whom the warranty extends.

As amended 1966.

§ 2–319.   F.O.B. and F.A.S. Terms.

(1) Unless otherwise agreed the term F.O.B. (which means "free on board") at a named place, even though used only in connection with the stated price, is a delivery term under which

(a) when the term is F.O.B. the place of shipment, the seller must at that place ship the goods in the manner provided in this Article (Section 2–504) and bear the expense and risk of putting them into the possession of the carrier; or

(b) when the term is F.O.B. the place of destination, the seller must at his own expense and risk transport the goods to that place and there tender delivery of them in the manner provided in this Article (Section 2–503);

(c) when under either (a) or (b) the term is also F.O.B. vessel, car or other vehicle, the seller must in addition at his own expense and risk load the goods on board. If the term is F.O.B. vessel the buyer must name the vessel and in an appropriate case the seller must comply with the provisions of this Article on the form of bill of lading (Section 2–323).

(2) Unless otherwise agreed the term F.A.S. vessel (which means "free alongside") at a named port, even though used only in connection with the stated price, is a delivery term under which the seller must

(a) at his own expense and risk deliver the goods alongside the vessel in the manner usual in that port or on a dock designated and provided by the buyer; and

(b) obtain and tender a receipt for the goods in exchange for which the carrier is under a duty to issue a bill of lading.

(3) Unless otherwise agreed in any case falling within subsection (1)(a) or (c) or subsection (2) the buyer must seasonably give any needed instructions for making delivery, including when the term is F.A.S. or F.O.B. the loading berth of the vessel and in an appropriate case its name and sailing date. The seller may treat the failure of needed instructions as a failure of cooperation under this Article (Section 2–311). He may also at his option move the goods in any reasonable manner preparatory to delivery or shipment.

(4) Under the term F.O.B. vessel or F.A.S. unless otherwise agreed the buyer must make payment against tender of the required documents and the seller may not tender nor the buyer demand delivery of the goods in substitution for the documents.

§ 2–320.   C.I.F. and C. & F. Terms.

(1) The term C.I.F. means that the price includes in a lump sum the cost of the goods and the insurance and freight to the named destination. The term C. & F. or C.F. means that the price so includes cost and freight to the named destination.

(2) Unless otherwise agreed and even though used only in connection with the stated price and destination, the term C.I.F. destination or its equivalent requires the seller at his own expense and risk to

(a) put the goods into the possession of a carrier at the port for shipment and obtain a negotiable bill or bills of lading covering the entire transportation to the named destination; and

(b) load the goods and obtain a receipt from the carrier (which may be contained in the bill of lading) showing that the freight has been paid or provided for; and

(c) obtain a policy or certificate of insurance, including any war risk insurance, of a kind and on terms then current at the port of shipment in the usual amount, in the currency of the contract, shown to cover the same goods covered by the bill of lading and providing for payment of loss to the order of the buyer or for the account of whom it may concern; but the seller may add to the price the amount of the premium for any such war risk insurance; and

(d) prepare an invoice of the goods and procure any other documents required to effect shipment or to comply with the contract; and

(e) forward and tender with commercial promptness all the documents in due form and with any indorsement necessary to perfect the buyer's rights.

(3) Unless otherwise agreed the term C. & F. or its equivalent has the same effect and imposes upon the seller the same obligations and risks as a C.I.F. term except the obligation as to insurance.

(4) Under the term C.I.F. or C. & F. unless otherwise agreed the buyer must make payment against tender of the required documents and the seller may not tender nor the buyer demand delivery of the goods in substitution for the documents.

§ 2–321.   C.I.F. or C. & F.: "Net Landed Weights"; "Payment on Arrival"; Warranty of Condition on Arrival.

Under a contract containing a term C.I.F. or C. & F.

(1) Where the price is based on or is to be adjusted according to "net landed weights", "delivered weights", "out turn" quantity or quality or the like, unless otherwise agreed the seller must reasonably estimate the price. The payment due on tender of the documents called for by the contract is the amount so estimated, but after final adjustment of the price a settlement must be made with commercial promptness.

(2) An agreement described in subsection (1) or any warranty of quality or condition of the goods on arrival places upon the seller the risk of ordinary deterioration, shrinkage and the like in transportation but has no effect on the place or time of identification to the contract for sale or delivery or on the passing of the risk of loss.

(3) Unless otherwise agreed where the contract provides for payment on or after arrival of the goods the seller must before payment allow such preliminary inspection as is feasible; but if the goods are lost delivery of the documents and payment are due when the goods should have arrived.

§ 2–322.   Delivery "Ex-Ship".

(1) Unless otherwise agreed a term for delivery of goods "ex-ship" (which means from the carrying vessel) or in equivalent language is not restricted to a particular ship and requires delivery from a ship which has reached a place at the named port of destination where goods of the kind are usually discharged.

(2) Under such a term unless otherwise agreed

(a) the seller must discharge all liens arising out of the carriage and furnish the buyer with a direction which puts the carrier under a duty to deliver the goods; and

(b) the risk of loss does not pass to the buyer until the goods leave the ship's tackle or are otherwise properly unloaded.

§ 2–323.   Form of Bill of Lading Required in Overseas Shipment; "Overseas".

(1) Where the contract contemplates overseas shipment and contains a term C.I.F. or C. & F. or F.O.B. vessel, the seller unless otherwise agreed must obtain a negotiable bill of lading stating that the goods have been loaded on board or, in the case of a term C.I.F. or C. & F., received for shipment.

(2) Where in a case within subsection (1) a bill of lading has been issued in a set of parts, unless otherwise agreed if the documents are not to be sent from abroad the buyer may demand tender of

the full set; otherwise only one part of the bill of lading need be tendered. Even if the agreement expressly requires a full set

(a) due tender of a single part is acceptable within the provisions of this Article on cure of improper delivery (subsection (1) of Section 2–508); and

(b) even though the full set is demanded, if the documents are sent from abroad the person tendering an incomplete set may nevertheless require payment upon furnishing an indemnity which the buyer in good faith deems adequate.

(3) A shipment by water or by air or a contract contemplating such shipment is "overseas" insofar as by usage of trade or agreement it is subject to the commercial, financing or shipping practices characteristic of international deep water commerce.

§ 2–324.   "No Arrival, No Sale" Term.

Under a term "no arrival, no sale" or terms of like meaning, unless otherwise agreed,

(a) the seller must properly ship conforming goods and if they arrive by any means he must tender them on arrival but he assumes no obligation that the goods will arrive unless he has caused the non-arrival; and

(b) where without fault of the seller the goods are in part lost or have so deteriorated as no longer to conform to the contract or arrive after the contract time, the buyer may proceed as if there had been casualty to identified goods (Section 2–613).

§ 2–325.   "Letter of Credit" Term; "Confirmed Credit".

(1) Failure of the buyer seasonably to furnish an agreed letter of credit is a breach of the contract for sale.

(2) The delivery to seller of a proper letter of credit suspends the buyer's obligation to pay. If the letter of credit is dishonored, the seller may on seasonable notification to the buyer require payment directly from him.

(3) Unless otherwise agreed the term "letter of credit" or "banker's credit" in a contract for sale means an irrevocable credit issued by a financing agency of good repute and, where the shipment is overseas, of good international repute. The term "confirmed credit" means that the credit must also carry the direct obligation of such an agency which does business in the seller's financial market.

§ 2–326.   Sale on Approval and Sale or Return; Rights of Creditors.

(1) Unless otherwise agreed, if delivered goods may be returned by the buyer even though they conform to the contract, the transaction is

(a) a "sale on approval" if the goods are delivered primarily for use, and

(b) a "sale or return" if the goods are delivered primarily for resale.

(2) Goods held on approval are not subject to the claims of the buyer's creditors until acceptance; goods held on sale or return are subject to such claims while in the buyer's possession.

(3) Any "or return" term of a contract for sale is to be treated as a separate contract for sale within the statute of frauds section of this Article (Section 2–201) and as contradicting the sale aspect of the contract within the provisions of this Article or on parol or extrinsic evidence (Section 2–202).

As amended in 1999.

§ 2–327.   Special Incidents of Sale on Approval and Sale or Return.

(1) Under a sale on approval unless otherwise agreed

(a) although the goods are identified to the contract the risk of loss and the title do not pass to the buyer until acceptance; and

(b) use of the goods consistent with the purpose of trial is not acceptance but failure seasonably to notify the seller of election to return the goods is acceptance, and if the goods conform to the contract acceptance of any part is acceptance of the whole; and

(c) after due notification of election to return, the return is at the seller's risk and expense but a merchant buyer must follow any reasonable instructions.

(2) Under a sale or return unless otherwise agreed

(a) the option to return extends to the whole or any commercial unit of the goods while in substantially their original condition, but must be exercised seasonably; and

(b) the return is at the buyer's risk and expense.

§ 2–328.   Sale by Auction.

(1) In a sale by auction if goods are put up in lots each lot is the subject of a separate sale.

(2) A sale by auction is complete when the auctioneer so announces by the fall of the hammer or in other customary manner. Where a bid is made while the hammer is falling in acceptance of a prior bid the auctioneer may in his discretion reopen the bidding or declare the goods sold under the bid on which the hammer was falling.

(3) Such a sale is with reserve unless the goods are in explicit terms put up without reserve. In an auction with reserve the auctioneer may withdraw the goods at any time until he announces completion of the sale. In an auction without reserve, after the auctioneer calls for bids on an article or lot, that article or lot cannot be withdrawn unless no bid is made within a reasonable time. In either case a bidder may retract his bid until the auctioneer's announcement of completion of the sale, but a bidder's retraction does not revive any previous bid.

(4) If the auctioneer knowingly receives a bid on the seller's behalf or the seller makes or procures such as bid, and notice has not been given that liberty for such bidding is reserved, the buyer may at his option avoid the sale or take the goods at the price of the last good faith bid prior to the completion of the sale. This subsection shall not apply to any bid at a forced sale.

PART 4   Title, Creditors and Good Faith Purchasers

§ 2–401.   Passing of Title; Reservation for Security; Limited Application of This Section.

Each provision of this Article with regard to the rights, obligations and remedies of the seller, the buyer, purchasers or other third parties applies irrespective of title to the goods except where the provision refers to such title. Insofar as situations are not covered by the other provisions of this Article and matters concerning title became material the following rules apply:

(1) Title to goods cannot pass under a contract for sale prior to their identification to the contract (Section 2–501), and unless otherwise explicitly agreed the buyer acquires by their identification a special property as limited by this Act. Any retention or reservation by the seller of the title (property) in goods shipped or delivered to the buyer is limited in effect to a reservation of a security interest. Subject to these provisions and to the provisions of the Article on Secured Transactions (Article 9), title to goods passes from the seller to the buyer in any manner and on any conditions explicitly agreed on by the parties.

(2) Unless otherwise explicitly agreed title passes to the buyer at the time and place at which the seller completes his performance with reference to the physical delivery of the goods, despite any reservation of a security interest and even though a document of title is to be delivered at a different time or place; and in particular and despite any reservation of a security interest by the bill of lading

(a) if the contract requires or authorizes the seller to send the goods to the buyer but does not require him to deliver them at destination, title passes to the buyer at the time and place of shipment; but

(b) if the contract requires delivery at destination, title passes on tender there.

(3) Unless otherwise explicitly agreed where delivery is to be made without moving the goods,

(a) if the seller is to deliver a document of title, title passes at the time when and the place where he delivers such documents; or

(b) if the goods are at the time of contracting already identified and no documents are to be delivered, title passes at the time and place of contracting.

(4) A rejection or other refusal by the buyer to receive or retain the goods, whether or not justified, or a justified revocation of acceptance revests title to the goods in the seller. Such revesting occurs by operation of law and is not a "sale".

§ 2–402.   Rights of Seller's Creditors Against Sold Goods.

(1) Except as provided in subsections (2) and (3), rights of unsecured creditors of the seller with respect to goods which have been identified to a contract for sale are subject to the buyer's rights to recover the goods under this Article (Sections 2–502 and 2–716).

(2) A creditor of the seller may treat a sale or an identification of goods to a contract for sale as void if as against him a retention of possession by the seller is fraudulent under any rule of law of the state where the goods are situated, except that retention of possession in good faith and current course of trade by a merchant-seller for a commercially reasonable time after a sale or identification is not fraudulent.

(3) Nothing in this Article shall be deemed to impair the rights of creditors of the seller

(a) under the provisions of the Article on Secured Transactions (Article 9); or

(b) where identification to the contract or delivery is made not in current course of trade but in satisfaction of or as security for a pre-existing claim for money, security or the like and is made under circumstances which under any rule of law of the state where the goods are situated would apart from this Article constitute the transaction a fraudulent transfer or voidable preference.

§ 2–403.   Power to Transfer; Good Faith Purchase of Goods; "Entrusting".

(1) A purchaser of goods acquires all title which his transferor had or had power to transfer except that a purchaser of a limited interest acquires rights only to the extent of the interest purchased. A person with voidable title has power to transfer a good title to a good faith purchaser for value. When goods have been delivered under a transaction of purchase the purchaser has such power even though

(a) the transferor was deceived as to the identity of the purchaser, or

(b) the delivery was in exchange for a check which is later dishonored, or

(c) it was agreed that the transaction was to be a "cash sale", or

(d) the delivery was procured through fraud punishable as larcenous under the criminal law.

(2) Any entrusting of possession of goods to a merchant who deals in goods of that kind gives him power to transfer all rights of the entruster to a buyer in ordinary course of business.

(3) "Entrusting" includes any delivery and any acquiescence in retention of possession regardless of any condition expressed between the parties to the delivery or acquiescence and regardless of whether the procurement of the entrusting or the possessor's disposition of the goods have been such as to be larcenous under the criminal law.

(4) The rights of other purchasers of goods and of lien creditors are governed by the Articles on Secured Transactions (Article 9), Bulk Transfers (Article 6) and Documents of Title (Article 7).

As amended in 1988.

PART 5   Performance

§ 2–501.   Insurable Interest in Goods; Manner of Identification of Goods.

(1) The buyer obtains a special property and an insurable interest in goods by identification of existing goods as goods to which the contract refers even though the goods so identified are non-conforming and he has an option to return or reject them. Such identification can be made at any time and in any manner explicitly agreed to by the parties. In the absence of explicit agreement identification occurs

(a) when the contract is made if it is for the sale of goods already existing and identified;

(b) if the contract is for the sale of future goods other than those described in paragraph (c), when goods are shipped, marked or otherwise designated by the seller as goods to which the contract refers;

(c) when the crops are planted or otherwise become growing crops or the young are conceived if the contract is for the sale of unborn young to be born within twelve months after contracting or for the sale of crops to be harvested within twelve months or the next normal harvest season after contracting whichever is longer.

(2) The seller retains an insurable interest in goods so long as title to or any security interest in the goods remains in him and where the identification is by the seller alone he may until default or insolvency or notification to the buyer that the identification is final substitute other goods for those identified.

(3) Nothing in this section impairs any insurable interest recognized under any other statute or rule of law.

§ 2–502.   Buyer's Right to Goods on Seller's Insolvency.

(1) Subject to subsections (2) and (3) and even though the goods have not been shipped a buyer who has paid a part or all of the price of goods in which he has a special property under the provisions of the immediately preceding section may on making and keeping good a tender of any unpaid portion of their price recover them from the seller if:

(a) in the case of goods bought for personal, family, or household purposes, the seller repudiates or fails to deliver as required by the contract; or

(b) in all cases, the seller becomes insolvent within ten days after receipt of the first installment on their price.

(2) The buyer's right to recover the goods under subsection (1) (a) vests upon acquisition of a special property, even if the seller had not then repudiated or failed to deliver.

(3) If the identification creating his special property has been made by the buyer he acquires the right to recover the goods only if they conform to the contract for sale.

As amended in 1999.

§ 2–503.   Manner of Seller's Tender of Delivery.

(1) Tender of delivery requires that the seller put and hold conforming goods at the buyer's disposition and give the buyer any notification reasonably necessary to enable him to take delivery. The manner, time and place for tender are determined by the agreement and this Article, and in particular

(a) tender must be at a reasonable hour, and if it is of goods they must be kept available for the period reasonably necessary to enable the buyer to take possession; but

(b) unless otherwise agreed the buyer must furnish facilities reasonably suited to the receipt of the goods.

(2) Where the case is within the next section respecting shipment tender requires that the seller comply with its provisions.

(3) Where the seller is required to deliver at a particular destination tender requires that he comply with subsection (1) and also in any appropriate case tender documents as described in subsections (4) and (5) of this section.

(4) Where goods are in the possession of a bailee and are to be delivered without being moved

(a) tender requires that the seller either tender a negotiable document of title covering such goods or procure acknowledgment by the bailee of the buyer's right to possession of the goods; but

(b) tender to the buyer of a non-negotiable document of title or of a written direction to the bailee to deliver is sufficient tender unless the buyer seasonably objects, and receipt by the bailee of notification of the buyer's rights fixes those rights as against the bailee and all third persons; but risk of loss of the goods and of any failure by the bailee to honor the non-negotiable document of title or to obey the direction remains on the seller until the buyer has had a reasonable time to present the document or direction, and a refusal by the bailee to honor the document or to obey the direction defeats the tender.

(5) Where the contract requires the seller to deliver documents

(a) he must tender all such documents in correct form, except as provided in this Article with respect to bills of lading in a set (subsection (2) of Section 2–323); and

(b) tender through customary banking channels is sufficient and dishonor of a draft accompanying the documents constitutes non-acceptance or rejection.

§ 2–504.   Shipment by Seller.

Where the seller is required or authorized to send the goods to the buyer and the contract does not require him to deliver them at a particular destination, then unless otherwise agreed he must

(a) put the goods in the possession of such a carrier and make such a contract for their transportation as may be reasonable having regard to the nature of the goods and other circumstances of the case; and

(b) obtain and promptly deliver or tender in due form any document necessary to enable the buyer to obtain possession of the goods or otherwise required by the agreement or by usage of trade; and

(c) promptly notify the buyer of the shipment.

Failure to notify the buyer under paragraph (c) or to make a proper contract under paragraph (a) is a ground for rejection only if material delay or loss ensues.

§ 2–505.   Seller's Shipment under Reservation.

(1) Where the seller has identified goods to the contract by or before shipment:

(a) his procurement of a negotiable bill of lading to his own order or otherwise reserves in him a security interest in the goods. His procurement of the bill to the order of a financing agency or of the buyer indicates in addition only the seller's expectation of transferring that interest to the person named.

(b) a non-negotiable bill of lading to himself or his nominee reserves possession of the goods as security but except in a case of conditional delivery (subsection (2) of Section 2–507) a non-negotiable bill of lading naming the buyer as consignee reserves no security interest even though the seller retains possession of the bill of lading.

(2) When shipment by the seller with reservation of a security interest is in violation of the contract for sale it constitutes an improper contract for transportation within the preceding section but impairs neither the rights given to the buyer by shipment and identification of the goods to the contract nor the seller's powers as a holder of a negotiable document.

§ 2–506.   Rights of Financing Agency.

(1) A financing agency by paying or purchasing for value a draft which relates to a shipment of goods acquires to the extent of the payment or purchase and in addition to its own rights under the draft and any document of title securing it any rights of the shipper in the goods including the right to stop delivery and the shipper's right to have the draft honored by the buyer.

(2) The right to reimbursement of a financing agency which has in good faith honored or purchased the draft under commitment to or authority from the buyer is not impaired by subsequent discovery of defects with reference to any relevant document which was apparently regular on its face.

§ 2–507.   Effect of Seller's Tender; Delivery on Condition.

(1) Tender of delivery is a condition to the buyer's duty to accept the goods and, unless otherwise agreed, to his duty to pay for them. Tender entitles the seller to acceptance of the goods and to payment according to the contract.

(2) Where payment is due and demanded on the delivery to the buyer of goods or documents of title, his right as against the seller to retain or dispose of them is conditional upon his making the payment due.

§ 2–508.   Cure by Seller of Improper Tender or Delivery; Replacement.

(1) Where any tender or delivery by the seller is rejected because non-conforming and the time for performance has not yet expired, the seller may seasonably notify the buyer of his intention to cure and may then within the contract time make a conforming delivery.

(2) Where the buyer rejects a non-conforming tender which the seller had reasonable grounds to believe would be acceptable with or without money allowance the seller may if he seasonably notifies the buyer have a further reasonable time to substitute a conforming tender.

§ 2–509.   Risk of Loss in the Absence of Breach.

(1) Where the contract requires or authorizes the seller to ship the goods by carrier

(a) if it does not require him to deliver them at a particular destination, the risk of loss passes to the buyer when the goods are duly delivered to the carrier even though the shipment is under reservation (Section 2–505); but

(b) if it does require him to deliver them at a particular destination and the goods are there duly tendered while in the possession of the carrier, the risk of loss passes to the buyer when the goods are there duly so tendered as to enable the buyer to take delivery.

(2) Where the goods are held by a bailee to be delivered without being moved, the risk of loss passes to the buyer

(a) on his receipt of a negotiable document of title covering the goods; or

(b) on acknowledgment by the bailee of the buyer's right to possession of the goods; or

(c) after his receipt of a non-negotiable document of title or other written direction to deliver, as provided in subsection (4) (b) of Section 2–503.

(3) In any case not within subsection (1) or (2), the risk of loss passes to the buyer on his receipt of the goods if the seller is a merchant; otherwise the risk passes to the buyer on tender of delivery.

(4) The provisions of this section are subject to contrary agreement of the parties and to the provisions of this Article on sale on approval (Section 2–327) and on effect of breach on risk of loss (Section 2–510).

§ 2–510.   Effect of Breach on Risk of Loss.

(1) Where a tender or delivery of goods so fails to conform to the contract as to give a right of rejection the risk of their loss remains on the seller until cure or acceptance.

(2) Where the buyer rightfully revokes acceptance he may to the extent of any deficiency in his effective insurance

coverage treat the risk of loss as having rested on the seller from the beginning.

(3) Where the buyer as to conforming goods already identified to the contract for sale repudiates or is otherwise in breach before risk of their loss has passed to him, the seller may to the extent of any deficiency in his effective insurance coverage treat the risk of loss as resting on the buyer for a commercially reasonable time.

§ 2–511.   Tender of Payment by Buyer; Payment by Check.

(1) Unless otherwise agreed tender of payment is a condition to the seller's duty to tender and complete any delivery.

(2) Tender of payment is sufficient when made by any means or in any manner current in the ordinary course of business unless the seller demands payment in legal tender and gives any extension of time reasonably necessary to procure it.

(3) Subject to the provisions of this Act on the effect of an instrument on an obligation (Section 3–310), payment by check is conditional and is defeated as between the parties by dishonor of the check on due presentment.

As amended in 1994.

§ 2–512.   Payment by Buyer Before Inspection.

(1) Where the contract requires payment before inspection non-conformity of the goods does not excuse the buyer from so making payment unless

(a) the non-conformity appears without inspection; or

(b) despite tender of the required documents the circumstances would justify injunction against honor under this Act (Section 5–109(b)).

(2) Payment pursuant to subsection (1) does not constitute an acceptance of goods or impair the buyer's right to inspect or any of his remedies.

As amended in 1995.

§ 2–513.   Buyer's Right to Inspection of Goods.

(1) Unless otherwise agreed and subject to subsection (3), where goods are tendered or delivered or identified to the contract for sale, the buyer has a right before payment or acceptance to inspect them at any reasonable place and time and in any reasonable manner. When the seller is required or authorized to send the goods to the buyer, the inspection may be after their arrival.

(2) Expenses of inspection must be borne by the buyer but may be recovered from the seller if the goods do not conform and are rejected.

(3) Unless otherwise agreed and subject to the provisions of this Article on C.I.F. contracts (subsection (3) of Section 2–321), the buyer is not entitled to inspect the goods before payment of the price when the contract provides

(a) for delivery "C.O.D." or on other like terms; or

(b) for payment against documents of title, except where such payment is due only after the goods are to become available for inspection.

(4) A place or method of inspection fixed by the parties is presumed to be exclusive but unless otherwise expressly agreed it does not postpone identification or shift the place for delivery or for passing the risk of loss. If compliance becomes impossible, inspection shall be as provided in this section unless the place or method fixed was clearly intended as an indispensable condition failure of which avoids the contract.

§ 2–514.   When Documents Deliverable on Acceptance; When on Payment.

Unless otherwise agreed documents against which a draft is drawn are to be delivered to the drawee on acceptance of the draft if it is payable more than three days after presentment; otherwise, only on payment.

§ 2–515.   Preserving Evidence of Goods in Dispute.

In furtherance of the adjustment of any claim or dispute

(a) either party on reasonable notification to the other and for the purpose of ascertaining the facts and preserving evidence has the right to inspect, test and sample the goods including such of them as may be in the possession or control of the other; and

(b) the parties may agree to a third party inspection or survey to determine the conformity or condition of the goods and may agree that the findings shall be binding upon them in any subsequent litigation or adjustment.

PART 6   Breach, Repudiation and Excuse

§ 2–601.   Buyer's Rights on Improper Delivery.

Subject to the provisions of this Article on breach in installment contracts (Section 2–612) and unless otherwise agreed under the sections on contractual limitations of remedy (Sections 2–718 and 2–719), if the goods or the tender of delivery fail in any respect to conform to the contract, the buyer may

(a) reject the whole; or

(b) accept the whole; or

(c) accept any commercial unit or units and reject the rest.

§ 2–602.   Manner and Effect of Rightful Rejection.

(1) Rejection of goods must be within a reasonable time after their delivery or tender. It is ineffective unless the buyer seasonably notifies the seller.

(2) Subject to the provisions of the two following sections on rejected goods (Sections 2–603 and 2–604),

(a) after rejection any exercise of ownership by the buyer with respect to any commercial unit is wrongful as against the seller; and

(b) if the buyer has before rejection taken physical possession of goods in which he does not have a security interest under the provisions of this Article (subsection (3) of Section 2–711), he is under a duty after rejection to hold them with reasonable care at the seller's disposition for a time sufficient to permit the seller to remove them; but

(c) the buyer has no further obligations with regard to goods rightfully rejected.

(3) The seller's rights with respect to goods wrongfully rejected are governed by the provisions of this Article on Seller's remedies in general (Section 2–703).

§ 2–603.   Merchant Buyer's Duties as to Rightfully Rejected Goods.

(1) Subject to any security interest in the buyer (subsection (3) of Section 2–711), when the seller has no agent or place of business at the market of rejection a merchant buyer is under a duty after rejection of goods in his possession or control to follow any reasonable instructions received from the seller with respect to the goods and in the absence of such instructions to make reasonable efforts to sell them for the seller's account if they are perishable or threaten to decline in value speedily. Instructions are not reasonable if on demand indemnity for expenses is not forthcoming.

(2) When the buyer sells goods under subsection (1), he is entitled to reimbursement from the seller or out of the proceeds for reasonable expenses of caring for and selling them, and if the expenses include no selling commission then to such commission as is usual in the trade or if there is none to a reasonable sum not exceeding ten per cent on the gross proceeds.

(3) In complying with this section the buyer is held only to good faith and good faith conduct hereunder is neither acceptance nor conversion nor the basis of an action for damages.

§ 2–604.   Buyer's Options as to Salvage of Rightfully Rejected Goods.

Subject to the provisions of the immediately preceding section on perishables if the seller gives no instructions within a reasonable time after notification of rejection the buyer may store the rejected goods for the seller's account or reship them to him or resell them for the seller's account with reimbursement as provided in the preceding section. Such action is not acceptance or conversion.

§ 2–605.   Waiver of Buyer's Objections by Failure to Particularize.

(1) The buyer's failure to state in connection with rejection a particular defect which is ascertainable by reasonable inspection precludes him from relying on the unstated defect to justify rejection or to establish breach

(a) where the seller could have cured it if stated seasonably; or

(b) between merchants when the seller has after rejection made a request in writing for a full and final written statement of all defects on which the buyer proposes to rely.

(2) Payment against documents made without reservation of rights precludes recovery of the payment for defects apparent on the face of the documents.

§ 2–606.   What Constitutes Acceptance of Goods.

(1) Acceptance of goods occurs when the buyer

(a) after a reasonable opportunity to inspect the goods signifies to the seller that the goods are conforming or that he will take or retain them in spite of their nonconformity; or

(b) fails to make an effective rejection (subsection (1) of Section 2–602), but such acceptance does not occur until the buyer has had a reasonable opportunity to inspect them; or

(c) does any act inconsistent with the seller's ownership; but if such act is wrongful as against the seller it is an acceptance only if ratified by him.

(2) Acceptance of a part of any commercial unit is acceptance of that entire unit.

§ 2–607.   Effect of Acceptance; Notice of Breach; Burden of Establishing Breach After Acceptance; Notice of Claim or Litigation to Person Answerable Over.

(1) The buyer must pay at the contract rate for any goods accepted.

(2) Acceptance of goods by the buyer precludes rejection of the goods accepted and if made with knowledge of a non-conformity cannot be revoked because of it unless the acceptance was on the reasonable assumption that the non-conformity would be seasonably cured but acceptance does not of itself impair any other remedy provided by this Article for non-conformity.

(3) Where a tender has been accepted

(a) the buyer must within a reasonable time after he discovers or should have discovered any breach notify the seller of breach or be barred from any remedy; and

(b) if the claim is one for infringement or the like (subsection (3) of Section 2–312) and the buyer is sued as a result of such a breach he must so notify the seller within a reasonable time after he receives notice of the litigation or be barred from any remedy over for liability established by the litigation.

(4) The burden is on the buyer to establish any breach with respect to the goods accepted.

(5) Where the buyer is sued for breach of a warranty or other obligation for which his seller is answerable over

(a) he may give his seller written notice of the litigation. If the notice states that the seller may come in and defend and that if the seller does not do so he will be bound in any action against him by his buyer by any determination of fact common to the two litigations, then unless the seller after seasonable receipt of the notice does come in and defend he is so bound.

(b) if the claim is one for infringement or the like (subsection (3) of Section 2–312) the original seller may demand in writing that his buyer turn over to him control of the litigation including settlement or else be barred from any remedy over and if he also agrees to bear all expense and to satisfy any adverse judgment, then unless the buyer after seasonable receipt of the demand does turn over control the buyer is so barred.

(6) The provisions of subsections (3), (4) and (5) apply to any obligation of a buyer to hold the seller harmless against infringement or the like (subsection (3) of Section 2–312).

§ 2–608. Revocation of Acceptance in Whole or in Part.

(1) The buyer may revoke his acceptance of a lot or commercial unit whose non-conformity substantially impairs its value to him if he has accepted it

(a) on the reasonable assumption that its nonconformity would be cured and it has not been seasonably cured; or

(b) without discovery of such non-conformity if his acceptance was reasonably induced either by the difficulty of discovery before acceptance or by the seller's assurances.

(2) Revocation of acceptance must occur within a reasonable time after the buyer discovers or should have discovered the ground for it and before any substantial change in condition of the goods which is not caused by their own defects. It is not effective until the buyer notifies the seller of it.

(3) A buyer who so revokes has the same rights and duties with regard to the goods involved as if he had rejected them.

§ 2–609. Right to Adequate Assurance of Performance.

(1) A contract for sale imposes an obligation on each party that the other's expectation of receiving due performance will not be impaired. When reasonable grounds for insecurity arise with respect to the performance of either party the other may in writing demand adequate assurance of due performance and until he receives such assurance may if commercially reasonable suspend any performance for which he has not already received the agreed return.

(2) Between merchants the reasonableness of grounds for insecurity and the adequacy of any assurance offered shall be determined according to commercial standards.

(3) Acceptance of any improper delivery or payment does not prejudice the party's right to demand adequate assurance of future performance.

(4) After receipt of a justified demand failure to provide within a reasonable time not exceeding thirty days such assurance of due performance as is adequate under the circumstances of the particular case is a repudiation of the contract.

§ 2–610. Anticipatory Repudiation.

When either party repudiates the contract with respect to a performance not yet due the loss of which will substantially impair the value of the contract to the other, the aggrieved party may

(a) for a commercially reasonable time await performance by the repudiating party; or

(b) resort to any remedy for breach (Section 2–703 or Section 2–711), even though he has notified the repudiating party that he would await the latter's performance and has urged retraction; and

(c) in either case suspend his own performance or proceed in accordance with the provisions of this Article on the seller's right to identify goods to the contract notwithstanding breach or to salvage unfinished goods (Section 2–704).

§ 2–611. Retraction of Anticipatory Repudiation.

(1) Until the repudiating party's next performance is due he can retract his repudiation unless the aggrieved party has since the repudiation cancelled or materially changed his position or otherwise indicated that he considers the repudiation final.

(2) Retraction may be by any method which clearly indicates to the aggrieved party that the repudiating party intends to perform, but must include any assurance justifiably demanded under the provisions of this Article (Section 2–609).

(3) Retraction reinstates the repudiating party's rights under the contract with due excuse and allowance to the aggrieved party for any delay occasioned by the repudiation.

§ 2–612. "Installment Contract"; Breach.

(1) An "installment contract" is one which requires or authorizes the delivery of goods in separate lots to be separately accepted, even though the contract contains a clause "each delivery is a separate contract" or its equivalent.

(2) The buyer may reject any installment which is non-conforming if the non-conformity substantially impairs the value of that installment and cannot be cured or if the non-conformity is a defect in the required documents; but if the non-conformity does not fall within subsection (3) and the seller gives adequate assurance of its cure the buyer must accept that installment.

(3) Whenever non-conformity or default with respect to one or more installments substantially impairs the value of the whole contract there is a breach of the whole. But the aggrieved party reinstates the contract if he accepts a non-conforming installment without seasonably notifying of cancellation or if he brings an action with respect only to past installments or demands performance as to future installments.

§ 2–613. Casualty to Identified Goods.

Where the contract requires for its performance goods identified when the contract is made, and the goods suffer casualty without fault of either party before the risk of loss passes to the buyer, or in a proper case under a "no arrival, no sale" term (Section 2–324) then

(a) if the loss is total the contract is avoided; and

(b) if the loss is partial or the goods have so deteriorated as no longer to conform to the contract the buyer may nevertheless demand inspection and at his option either treat the contract as voided or accept the goods with due allowance from the contract price for the deterioration or the deficiency in quantity but without further right against the seller.

§ 2–614. Substituted Performance.

(1) Where without fault of either party the agreed berthing, loading, or unloading facilities fail or an agreed type of carrier becomes unavailable or the agreed manner of delivery otherwise becomes commercially impracticable but a commercially reasonable substitute is available, such substitute performance must be tendered and accepted.

(2) If the agreed means or manner of payment fails because of domestic or foreign governmental regulation, the seller may withhold or stop delivery unless the buyer provides a means or manner of payment which is commercially a substantial equivalent. If delivery has already been taken, payment by the means or in the manner provided by the regulation discharges the buyer's obligation unless the regulation is discriminatory, oppressive or predatory.

§ 2–615. Excuse by Failure of Presupposed Conditions.

Except so far as a seller may have assumed a greater obligation and subject to the preceding section on substituted performance:

(a) Delay in delivery or non-delivery in whole or in part by a seller who complies with paragraphs (b) and (c) is not a breach of his duty under a contract for sale if performance as agreed has been made impracticable by the occurrence of a contingency the nonoccurrence of which was a basic assumption on which the contract was made or by compliance in good faith with any applicable foreign or domestic governmental regulation or order whether or not it later proves to be invalid.

(b) Where the causes mentioned in paragraph (a) affect only a part of the seller's capacity to perform, he must allocate production and deliveries among his customers but may at his option include regular customers not then under contract as well as his own requirements for further manufacture. He may so allocate in any manner which is fair and reasonable.

(c) The seller must notify the buyer seasonably that there will be delay or non-delivery and, when allocation is required under paragraph (b), of the estimated quota thus made available for the buyer.

§ 2–616. Procedure on Notice Claiming Excuse.

(1) Where the buyer receives notification of a material or indefinite delay or an allocation justified under the preceding section he may by written notification to the seller as to any delivery concerned, and where the prospective deficiency substantially impairs the value of the whole contract under the provisions of this Article relating to breach of installment contracts (Section 2–612), then also as to the whole,

(a) terminate and thereby discharge any unexecuted portion of the contract; or

(b) modify the contract by agreeing to take his available quota in substitution.

(2) If after receipt of such notification from the seller the buyer fails so to modify the contract within a reasonable time not exceeding thirty days the contract lapses with respect to any deliveries affected.

(3) The provisions of this section may not be negated by agreement except in so far as the seller has assumed a greater obligation under the preceding section.

PART 7   Remedies

§ 2–701. Remedies for Breach of Collateral Contracts Not Impaired.

Remedies for breach of any obligation or promise collateral or ancillary to a contract for sale are not impaired by the provisions of this Article.

§ 2–702. Seller's Remedies on Discovery of Buyer's Insolvency.

(1) Where the seller discovers the buyer to be insolvent he may refuse delivery except for cash including payment for all goods theretofore delivered under the contract, and stop delivery under this Article (Section 2–705).

(2) Where the seller discovers that the buyer has received goods on credit while insolvent he may reclaim the goods upon demand made within ten days after the receipt, but if misrepresentation of solvency has been made to the particular seller in writing within three months before delivery the ten day limitation does not apply. Except as provided in this subsection the seller may not base a right to reclaim goods on the buyer's fraudulent or innocent misrepresentation of solvency or of intent to pay.

(3) The seller's right to reclaim under subsection (2) is subject to the rights of a buyer in ordinary course or other good faith purchaser under this Article (Section 2–403). Successful reclamation of goods excludes all other remedies with respect to them.

§ 2–703. Seller's Remedies in General.

Where the buyer wrongfully rejects or revokes acceptance of goods or fails to make a payment due on or before delivery or repudiates with respect to a part or the whole, then with respect to any goods directly affected and, if the breach is of the whole contract (Section 2–612), then also with respect to the whole undelivered balance, the aggrieved seller may

(a) withhold delivery of such goods;

(b) stop delivery by any bailee as hereafter provided (Section 2–705);

(c) proceed under the next section respecting goods still unidentified to the contract;

(d) resell and recover damages as hereafter provided (Section 2–706);

(e) recover damages for non-acceptance (Section 2–708) or in a proper case the price (Section 2–709);

(f) cancel.

§ 2–704.   Seller's Right to Identify Goods to the Contract Notwithstanding Breach or to Salvage Unfinished Goods.

(1) An aggrieved seller under the preceding section may

(a) identify to the contract conforming goods not already identified if at the time he learned of the breach they are in his possession or control;

(b) treat as the subject of resale goods which have demonstrably been intended for the particular contract even though those goods are unfinished.

(2) Where the goods are unfinished an aggrieved seller may in the exercise of reasonable commercial judgment for the purposes of avoiding loss and of effective realization either complete the manufacture and wholly identify the goods to the contract or cease manufacture and resell for scrap or salvage value or proceed in any other reasonable manner.

§ 2–705.   Seller's Stoppage of Delivery in Transit or Otherwise.

(1) The seller may stop delivery of goods in the possession of a carrier or other bailee when he discovers the buyer to be insolvent (Section 2–702) and may stop delivery of carload, truckload, planeload or larger shipments of express or freight when the buyer repudiates or fails to make a payment due before delivery or if for any other reason the seller has a right to withhold or reclaim the goods.

(2) As against such buyer the seller may stop delivery until

(a) receipt of the goods by the buyer; or

(b) acknowledgment to the buyer by any bailee of the goods except a carrier that the bailee holds the goods for the buyer; or

(c) such acknowledgment to the buyer by a carrier by reshipment or as warehouseman; or

(d) negotiation to the buyer of any negotiable document of title covering the goods.

(3) (a) To stop delivery the seller must so notify as to enable the bailee by reasonable diligence to prevent delivery of the goods.

(b) After such notification the bailee must hold and deliver the goods according to the directions of the seller but the seller is liable to the bailee for any ensuing charges or damages.

(c) If a negotiable document of title has been issued for goods the bailee is not obliged to obey a notification to stop until surrender of the document.

(d) A carrier who has issued a non-negotiable bill of lading is not obliged to obey a notification to stop received from a person other than the consignor.

§ 2–706.   Seller's Resale Including Contract for Resale.

(1) Under the conditions stated in Section 2–703 on seller's remedies, the seller may resell the goods concerned or the undelivered balance thereof. Where the resale is made in good faith and in a commercially reasonable manner the seller may recover the difference between the resale price and the contract price together with any incidental damages allowed under the provisions of this Article (Section 2–710), but less expenses saved in consequence of the buyer's breach.

(2) Except as otherwise provided in subsection (3) or unless otherwise agreed resale may be at public or private sale including sale by way of one or more contracts to sell or of identification to an existing contract of the seller. Sale may be as a unit or in parcels and at any time and place and on any terms but every aspect of the sale including the method, manner, time, place and terms must be commercially reasonable. The resale must be reasonably identified as referring to the broken contract, but it is not necessary that the goods be in existence or that any or all of them have been identified to the contract before the breach.

(3) Where the resale is at private sale the seller must give the buyer reasonable notification of his intention to resell.

(4) Where the resale is at public sale

(a) only identified goods can be sold except where there is a recognized market for a public sale of futures in goods of the kind; and

(b) it must be made at a usual place or market for public sale if one is reasonably available and except in the case of goods which are perishable or threaten to decline in value speedily the seller must give the buyer reasonable notice of the time and place of the resale; and

(c) if the goods are not to be within the view of those attending the sale the notification of sale must state the place where the goods are located and provide for their reasonable inspection by prospective bidders; and

(d) the seller may buy.

(5) A purchaser who buys in good faith at a resale takes the goods free of any rights of the original buyer even though the seller fails to comply with one or more of the requirements of this section.

(6) The seller is not accountable to the buyer for any profit made on any resale. A person in the position of a seller (Section 2–707) or a buyer who has rightfully rejected or justifiably revoked acceptance must account for any excess over the amount of his security interest, as hereinafter defined (subsection (3) of Section 2–711).

§ 2–707.   "Person in the Position of a Seller".

(1) A "person in the position of a seller" includes as against a principal an agent who has paid or become responsible for the price of goods on behalf of his principal or anyone who otherwise holds a security interest or other right in goods similar to that of a seller.

(2) A person in the position of a seller may as provided in this Article withhold or stop delivery (Section 2–705) and resell (Section 2–706) and recover incidental damages (Section 2–710).

§ 2–708.   Seller's Damages for Non-Acceptance or Repudiation.

(1) Subject to subsection (2) and to the provisions of this Article with respect to proof of market price (Section 2–723), the measure of damages for non-acceptance or repudiation by the buyer is the difference between the market price at the time and place for tender and the unpaid contract price together with any incidental damages provided in this Article (Section 2–710), but less expenses saved in consequence of the buyer's breach.

(2) If the measure of damages provided in subsection (1) is inadequate to put the seller in as good a position as performance would have done then the measure of damages is the profit (including reasonable overhead) which the seller would have made from full performance by the buyer, together with any incidental damages provided in this Article (Section 2–710), due allowance for costs reasonably incurred and due credit for payments or proceeds of resale.

§ 2–709.   Action for the Price.

(1) When the buyer fails to pay the price as it becomes due the seller may recover, together with any incidental damages under the next section, the price

(a) of goods accepted or of conforming goods lost or damaged within a commercially reasonable time after risk of their loss has passed to the buyer; and

(b) of goods identified to the contract if the seller is unable after reasonable effort to resell them at a reasonable price or the circumstances reasonably indicate that such effort will be unavailing.

(2) Where the seller sues for the price he must hold for the buyer any goods which have been identified to the contract and are still in his control except that if resale becomes possible he may resell them at any time prior to the collection of the judgment. The net proceeds of any such resale must be credited to the buyer and payment of the judgment entitles him to any goods not resold.

(3) After the buyer has wrongfully rejected or revoked acceptance of the goods or has failed to make a payment due or has repudiated (Section 2–610), a seller who is held not entitled to the price under this section shall nevertheless be awarded damages for non-acceptance under the preceding section.

§ 2–710.   Seller's Incidental Damages.

Incidental damages to an aggrieved seller include any commercially reasonable charges, expenses or commissions incurred in stopping delivery, in the transportation, care and custody of goods after the buyer's breach, in connection with return or resale of the goods or otherwise resulting from the breach.

§ 2–711.   Buyer's Remedies in General; Buyer's Security Interest in Rejected Goods.

(1) Where the seller fails to make delivery or repudiates or the buyer rightfully rejects or justifiably revokes acceptance then with respect to any goods involved, and with respect to the whole if the breach goes to the whole contract (Section 2–612), the buyer may cancel and whether or not he has done so may in addition to recovering so much of the price as has been paid

(a) "cover" and have damages under the next section as to all the goods affected whether or not they have been identified to the contract; or

(b) recover damages for non-delivery as provided in this Article (Section 2–713).

(2) Where the seller fails to deliver or repudiates the buyer may also

(a) if the goods have been identified recover them as provided in this Article (Section 2–502); or

(b) in a proper case obtain specific performance or replevy the goods as provided in this Article (Section 2–716).

(3) On rightful rejection or justifiable revocation of acceptance a buyer has a security interest in goods in his possession or control for any payments made on their price and any expenses reasonably incurred in their inspection, receipt, transportation, care and custody and may hold such goods and resell them in like manner as an aggrieved seller (Section 2–706).

§ 2–712.   "Cover"; Buyer's Procurement of Substitute Goods.

(1) After a breach within the preceding section the buyer may "cover" by making in good faith and without unreasonable delay any reasonable purchase of or contract to purchase goods in substitution for those due from the seller.

(2) The buyer may recover from the seller as damages the difference between the cost of cover and the contract price together with any incidental or consequential damages as hereinafter defined (Section 2–715), but less expenses saved in consequence of the seller's breach.

(3) Failure of the buyer to effect cover within this section does not bar him from any other remedy.

§ 2–713.   Buyer's Damages for Non-Delivery or Repudiation.

(1) Subject to the provisions of this Article with respect to proof of market price (Section 2–723), the measure of damages for non-delivery or repudiation by the seller is the difference between the market price at the time when the buyer learned of the breach and the contract price together with any incidental and consequential damages provided in this Article (Section 2–715), but less expenses saved in consequence of the seller's breach.

(2) Market price is to be determined as of the place for tender or, in cases of rejection after arrival or revocation of acceptance, as of the place of arrival.

§ 2–714.   Buyer's Damages for Breach in Regard to Accepted Goods.

(1) Where the buyer has accepted goods and given notification (subsection (3) of Section 2–607) he may recover as damages for any non-conformity of tender the loss resulting in the ordinary course of events from the seller's breach as determined in any manner which is reasonable.

(2) The measure of damages for breach of warranty is the difference at the time and place of acceptance between the value of the goods accepted and the value they would have had if they had been as warranted, unless special circumstances show proximate damages of a different amount.

(3) In a proper case any incidental and consequential damages under the next section may also be recovered.

§ 2–715.   Buyer's Incidental and Consequential Damages.

(1) Incidental damages resulting from the seller's breach include expenses reasonably incurred in inspection, receipt, transportation and care and custody of goods rightfully rejected, any commercially reasonable charges, expenses or commissions in connection with effecting cover and any other reasonable expense incident to the delay or other breach.

(2) Consequential damages resulting from the seller's breach include

(a) any loss resulting from general or particular requirements and needs of which the seller at the time of contracting had reason to know and which could not reasonably be prevented by cover or otherwise; and

(b) injury to person or property proximately resulting from any breach of warranty.

§ 2–716.   Buyer's Right to Specific Performance or Replevin.

(1) Specific performance may be decreed where the goods are unique or in other proper circumstances.

(2) The decree for specific performance may include such terms and conditions as to payment of the price, damages, or other relief as the court may deem just.

(3) The buyer has a right of replevin for goods identified to the contract if after reasonable effort he is unable to effect cover for such goods or the circumstances reasonably indicate that such effort will be unavailing or if the goods have been shipped under reservation and satisfaction of the security interest in them has been made or tendered. In the case of goods bought for personal, family, or household purposes, the buyer's right of replevin vests upon acquisition of a special property, even if the seller had not then repudiated or failed to deliver.

As amended in 1999.

§ 2–717.   Deduction of Damages From the Price.

The buyer on notifying the seller of his intention to do so may deduct all or any part of the damages resulting from any breach of the contract from any part of the price still due under the same contract.

§ 2–718.   Liquidation or Limitation of Damages; Deposits.

(1) Damages for breach by either party may be liquidated in the agreement but only at an amount which is reasonable in the light of the anticipated or actual harm caused by the breach, the difficulties of proof of loss, and the inconvenience or nonfeasibility of otherwise obtaining an adequate remedy. A term fixing unreasonably large liquidated damages is void as a penalty.

(2) Where the seller justifiably withholds delivery of goods because of the buyer's breach, the buyer is entitled to restitution of any amount by which the sum of his payments exceeds

(a) the amount to which the seller is entitled by virtue of terms liquidating the seller's damages in accordance with subsection (1), or

(b) in the absence of such terms, twenty per cent of the value of the total performance for which the buyer is obligated under the contract or $500, whichever is smaller.

(3) The buyer's right to restitution under subsection (2) is subject to offset to the extent that the seller establishes

(a) a right to recover damages under the provisions of this Article other than subsection (1), and

(b) the amount or value of any benefits received by the buyer directly or indirectly by reason of the contract.

(4) Where a seller has received payment in goods their reasonable value or the proceeds of their resale shall be treated as payments for the purposes of subsection (2); but if the seller has notice of the buyer's breach before reselling goods received in part performance, his resale is subject to the conditions laid down in this Article on resale by an aggrieved seller (Section 2–706).

§ 2–719.   Contractual Modification or Limitation of Remedy.

(1) Subject to the provisions of subsections (2) and (3) of this section and of the preceding section on liquidation and limitation of damages,

(a) the agreement may provide for remedies in addition to or in substitution for those provided in this Article and may limit or alter the measure of damages recoverable under this Article, as by limiting the buyer's remedies to return of the goods and repayment of the price or to repair and replacement of nonconforming goods or parts; and

(b) resort to a remedy as provided is optional unless the remedy is expressly agreed to be exclusive, in which case it is the sole remedy.

(2) Where circumstances cause an exclusive or limited remedy to fail of its essential purpose, remedy may be had as provided in this Act.

(3) Consequential damages may be limited or excluded unless the limitation or exclusion is unconscionable. Limitation of consequential damages for injury to the person in the case of consumer goods is prima facie unconscionable but limitation of damages where the loss is commercial is not.

§ 2–720.   Effect of "Cancellation" or "Rescission" on Claims for Antecedent Breach.

Unless the contrary intention clearly appears, expressions of "cancellation" or "rescission" of the contract or the like shall not be construed as a renunciation or discharge of any claim in damages for an antecedent breach.

§ 2–721.   Remedies for Fraud.

Remedies for material misrepresentation or fraud include all remedies available under this Article for non-fraudulent breach. Neither rescission or a claim for rescission of the contract for sale nor rejection or return of the goods shall bar or be deemed inconsistent with a claim for damages or other remedy.

§ 2–722.   Who Can Sue Third Parties for Injury to Goods.

Where a third party so deals with goods which have been identified to a contract for sale as to cause actionable injury to a party to that contract

(a) a right of action against the third party is in either party to the contract for sale who has title to or a security interest or a special property or an insurable interest in the goods; and if the goods have been destroyed or converted a right of action is also in the party who either bore the risk of loss under the contract for sale or has since the injury assumed that risk as against the other;

(b) if at the time of the injury the party plaintiff did not bear the risk of loss as against the other party to the contract for sale and there is no arrangement between them for disposition of the recovery, his suit or settlement is, subject to his own interest, as a fiduciary for the other party to the contract;

(c) either party may with the consent of the other sue for the benefit of whom it may concern.

§ 2–723.   Proof of Market Price: Time and Place.

(1) If an action based on anticipatory repudiation comes to trial before the time for performance with respect to some or all of the goods, any damages based on market price (Section 2–708 or Section 2–713) shall be determined according to the price of such goods prevailing at the time when the aggrieved party learned of the repudiation.

(2) If evidence of a price prevailing at the times or places described in this Article is not readily available the price prevailing within any reasonable time before or after the time described or at any other place which in commercial judgment or under usage of trade would serve as a reasonable substitute for the one described may be used, making any proper allowance for the cost of transporting the goods to or from such other place.

(3) Evidence of a relevant price prevailing at a time or place other than the one described in this Article offered by one party is not admissible unless and until he has given the other party such notice as the court finds sufficient to prevent unfair surprise.

§ 2–724.   Admissibility of Market Quotations.

Whenever the prevailing price or value of any goods regularly bought and sold in any established commodity market is in issue, reports in official publications or trade journals or in newspapers or periodicals of general circulation published as the reports of such market shall be admissible in evidence. The circumstances of the preparation of such a report may be shown to affect its weight but not its admissibility.

§ 2–725.   Statute of Limitations in Contracts for Sale.

(1) An action for breach of any contract for sale must be commenced within four years after the cause of action has accrued. By the original agreement the parties may reduce the period of limitation to not less than one year but may not extend it.

(2) A cause of action accrues when the breach occurs, regardless of the aggrieved party's lack of knowledge of the breach. A breach of warranty occurs when tender of delivery is made, except that where a warranty explicitly extends to future performance of the goods and discovery of the breach must await the time of such performance the cause of action accrues when the breach is or should have been discovered.

(3) Where an action commenced within the time limited by subsection (1) is so terminated as to leave available a remedy by another action for the same breach such other action may be commenced after the expiration of the time limited and within six months after the termination of the first action unless the termination resulted from voluntary discontinuance or from dismissal for failure or neglect to prosecute.

(4) This section does not alter the law on tolling of the statute of limitations nor does it apply to causes of action which have accrued before this Act becomes effective.

REVISED ARTICLE IX
SECURED TRANSACTIONS

PART 1   General Provisions

[Subpart 1. Short Title, Definitions, and General Concepts]

§ 9–101.   Short Title.

This article may be cited as Uniform Commercial Code—Secured Transactions.

§ 9–102.   Definitions and Index of Definitions.

(a) In this article:

(1) "Accession" means goods that are physically united with other goods in such a manner that the identity of the original goods is not lost.

(2) "Account", except as used in "account for", means a right to payment of a monetary obligation, whether or not earned by performance, (i) for property that has been or is to be sold, leased, licensed, assigned, or otherwise disposed of, (ii) for services rendered or to be rendered, (iii) for a policy of insurance issued or to be issued, (iv) for a secondary obligation incurred or to be incurred, (v) for energy provided or to be provided, (vi) for the use or hire of a vessel under a charter or other contract, (vii) arising out of the use of a credit or charge card or information contained on or for use with the card, or (viii) as winnings in a lottery or other game of chance operated or sponsored by a State, governmental unit of a State, or person licensed or authorized to operate the game by a State or governmental unit of a State. The term includes health-care insurance receivables. The term does not include (i) rights to payment evidenced by chattel paper or an instrument, (ii) commercial tort claims, (iii) deposit accounts, (iv) investment property, (v) letter-of-credit rights or letters of credit, or (vi) rights to payment for money or funds advanced or sold, other than rights arising out of the use of a credit or charge card or information contained on or for use with the card.

(3) "Account debtor" means a person obligated on an account, chattel paper, or general intangible. The term does not include persons obligated to pay a negotiable instrument, even if the instrument constitutes part of chattel paper.

(4) "Accounting", except as used in "accounting for", means a record:

(A) authenticated by a secured party;

(B) indicating the aggregate unpaid secured obligations as of a date not more than 35 days earlier or 35 days later than the date of the record; and

(C) identifying the components of the obligations in reasonable detail.

(5) "Agricultural lien" means an interest, other than a security interest, in farm products:

(A) which secures payment or performance of an obligation for:

(i) goods or services furnished in connection with a debtor's farming operation; or

(ii) rent on real property leased by a debtor in connection with its farming operation;

(B) which is created by statute in favor of a person that:

(i) in the ordinary course of its business furnished goods or services to a debtor in connection with a debtor's farming operation; or

(ii) leased real property to a debtor in connection with the debtor's farming operation; and

(C) whose effectiveness does not depend on the person's possession of the personal property.

(6) "As-extracted collateral" means:

(A) oil, gas, or other minerals that are subject to a security interest that:

(i) is created by a debtor having an interest in the minerals before extraction; and

(ii) attaches to the minerals as extracted; or

(B) accounts arising out of the sale at the wellhead or minehead of oil, gas, or other minerals in which the debtor had an interest before extraction.

(7) "Authenticate" means:

(A) to sign; or

(B) to execute or otherwise adopt a symbol, or encrypt or similarly process a record in whole or in part, with the present intent of the authenticating person to identify the person and adopt or accept a record.

(8) "Bank" means an organization that is engaged in the business of banking. The term includes savings banks, savings and loan associations, credit unions, and trust companies.

(9) "Cash proceeds" means proceeds that are money, checks, deposit accounts, or the like.

(10) "Certificate of title" means a certificate of title with respect to which a statute provides for the security interest in question to be indicated on the certificate as a condition or result of the security interest's obtaining priority over the rights of a lien creditor with respect to the collateral.

(11) "Chattel paper" means a record or records that evidence both a monetary obligation and a security interest in specific goods, a security interest in specific goods and software used in the goods, a security interest in specific goods and license of software used in the goods, a lease of specific goods, or a lease of specific goods and license of software used in the goods. In this paragraph, "monetary obligation" means a monetary obligation secured by the goods or owed under a lease of the goods and includes a monetary obligation with respect to software used in

the goods. The term does not include (i) charters or other contracts involving the use or hire of a vessel or (ii) records that evidence a right to payment arising out of the use of a credit or charge card or information contained on or for use with the card. If a transaction is evidenced by records that include an instrument or series of instruments, the group of records taken together constitutes chattel paper.

(12) "Collateral" means the property subject to a security interest or agricultural lien. The term includes:

(A) proceeds to which a security interest attaches;

(B) accounts, chattel paper, payment intangibles, and promissory notes that have been sold; and

(C) goods that are the subject of a consignment.

(13) "Commercial tort claim" means a claim arising in tort with respect to which:

(A) the claimant is an organization; or

(B) the claimant is an individual and the claim:

(i) arose in the course of the claimant's business or profession; and

(ii) does not include damages arising out of personal injury to or the death of an individual.

(14) "Commodity account" means an account maintained by a commodity intermediary in which a commodity contract is carried for a commodity customer.

(15) "Commodity contract" means a commodity futures contract, an option on a commodity futures contract, a commodity option, or another contract if the contract or option is:

(A) traded on or subject to the rules of a board of trade that has been designated as a contract market for such a contract pursuant to federal commodities laws; or

(B) traded on a foreign commodity board of trade, exchange, or market, and is carried on the books of a commodity intermediary for a commodity customer.

(16) "Commodity customer" means a person for which a commodity intermediary carries a commodity contract on its books.

(17) "Commodity intermediary" means a person that:

(A) is registered as a futures commission merchant under federal commodities law; or

(B) in the ordinary course of its business provides clearance or settlement services for a board of trade that has been designated as a contract market pursuant to federal commodities law.

(18) "Communicate" means:

(A) to send a written or other tangible record;

(B) to transmit a record by any means agreed upon by the persons sending and receiving the record; or

(C) in the case of transmission of a record to or by a filing office, to transmit a record by any means prescribed by filing-office rule.

(19) "Consignee" means a merchant to which goods are delivered in a consignment.

(20) "Consignment" means a transaction, regardless of its form, in which a person delivers goods to a merchant for the purpose of sale and:

(A) the merchant:

(i) deals in goods of that kind under a name other than the name of the person making delivery;

(ii) is not an auctioneer; and

(iii) is not generally known by its creditors to be substantially engaged in selling the goods of others;

(B) with respect to each delivery, the aggregate value of the goods is $1,000 or more at the time of delivery;

(C) the goods are not consumer goods immediately before delivery; and

(D) the transaction does not create a security interest that secures an obligation.

(21) "Consignor" means a person that delivers goods to a consignee in a consignment.

(22) "Consumer debtor" means a debtor in a consumer transaction.

(23) "Consumer goods" means goods that are used or bought for use primarily for personal, family, or household purposes.

(24) "Consumer goods transaction" means a consumer transaction in which:

(A) an individual incurs an obligation primarily for personal, family, or household purposes; and

(B) a security interest in consumer goods secures the obligation.

(25) "Consumer obligor" means an obligor who is an individual and who incurred the obligation as part of a transaction entered into primarily for personal, family, or household purposes.

(26) "Consumer transaction" means a transaction in which (i) an individual incurs an obligation primarily for personal, family, or household purposes, (ii) a security interest secures the obligation, and (iii) the collateral is held or acquired primarily for personal, family, or household purposes. The term includes consumer-goods transactions.

(27) "Continuation statement" means an amendment of a financing statement which:

(A) identifies, by its file number, the initial financing statement to which it relates; and

(B) indicates that it is a continuation statement for, or that it is filed to continue the effectiveness of, the identified financing statement.

(28) "Debtor" means:

(A) a person having an interest, other than a security interest or other lien, in the collateral, whether or not the person is an obligor;

(B) a seller of accounts, chattel paper, payment intangibles, or promissory notes; or

(C) a consignee.

(29) "Deposit account" means a demand, time, savings, passbook, or similar account maintained with a bank. The term does not include investment property or accounts evidenced by an instrument.

(30) "Document" means a document of title or a receipt of the type described in Section 7–201(2).

(31) "Electronic chattel paper" means chattel paper evidenced by a record or records consisting of information stored in an electronic medium.

(32) "Encumbrance" means a right, other than an ownership interest, in real property. The term includes mortgages and other liens on real property.

(33) "Equipment" means goods other than inventory, farm products, or consumer goods.

(34) "Farm products" means goods, other than standing timber, with respect to which the debtor is engaged in a farming operation and which are:

    (A) crops grown, growing, or to be grown, including:

        (i) crops produced on trees, vines, and bushes; and

        (ii) aquatic goods produced in aquacultural operations;

    (B) livestock, born or unborn, including aquatic goods produced in aquacultural operations;

    (C) supplies used or produced in a farming operation; or

    (D) products of crops or livestock in their unmanufactured states.

(35) "Farming operation" means raising, cultivating, propagating, fattening, grazing, or any other farming, livestock, or aquacultural operation.

(36) "File number" means the number assigned to an initial financing statement pursuant to Section 9–519(a).

(37) "Filing office" means an office designated in Section 9–501 as the place to file a financing statement.

(38) "Filing-office rule" means a rule adopted pursuant to Section 9–526.

(39) "Financing statement" means a record or records composed of an initial financing statement and any filed record relating to the initial financing statement.

(40) "Fixture filing" means the filing of a financing statement covering goods that are or are to become fixtures and satisfying Section 9–502(a) and (b). The term includes the filing of a financing statement covering goods of a transmitting utility which are or are to become fixtures.

(41) "Fixtures" means goods that have become so related to particular real property that an interest in them arises under real property law.

(42) "General intangible" means any personal property, including things in action, other than accounts, chattel paper, commercial tort claims, deposit accounts, documents, goods, instruments, investment property, letter-of-credit rights, letters of credit, money, and oil, gas, or other minerals before extraction. The term includes payment intangibles and software.

(43) "Good faith" means honesty in fact and the observance of reasonable commercial standards of fair dealing.

(44) "Goods" means all things that are movable when a security interest attaches. The term includes (i) fixtures, (ii) standing timber that is to be cut and removed under a conveyance or contract for sale, (iii) the unborn young of animals, (iv) crops grown, growing, or to be grown, even if the crops are produced on trees, vines, or bushes, and (v) manufactured homes. The term also includes a computer program embedded in goods and any supporting information provided in connection with a transaction relating to the program if (i) the program is associated with the goods in such a manner that it customarily is considered part of the goods, or (ii) by becoming the owner of the goods, a person acquires a right to use the program in connection with the goods. The term does not include a computer program embedded in goods that consist solely of the medium in which the program is embedded. The term also does not include accounts, chattel paper, commercial tort claims, deposit accounts, documents, general intangibles, instruments, investment property, letter-of-credit rights, letters of credit, money, or oil, gas, or other minerals before extraction.

(45) "Governmental unit" means a subdivision, agency, department, county, parish, municipality, or other unit of the government of the United States, a State, or a foreign country. The term includes an organization having a separate corporate existence if the organization is eligible to issue debt on which interest is exempt from income taxation under the laws of the United States.

(46) "Health-care-insurance receivable" means an interest in or claim under a policy of insurance which is a right to payment of a monetary obligation for health-care goods or servies provided.

(47) "Instrument" means a negotiable instrument or any other writing that evidences a right to the payment of a monetary obligation, is not itself a security agreement or lease, and is of a type that in ordinary course of business is transferred by delivery with any necessary indorsement or assignment. The term does not include (i) investment property, (ii) letters of credit, or (iii) writings that evidence a right to payment arising out of the use of a credit or charge card or information contained on or for use with the card.

(48) "Inventory" means goods, other than farm products, which:

    (A) are leased by a person as lessor;

    (B) are held by a person for sale or lease or to be furnished under a contract of service;

    (C) are furnished by a person under a contract of service; or

    (D) consist of raw materials, work in process, or materials used or consumed in a business.

(49) "Investment property" means a security, whether certificated or uncertificated, security entitlement, securities account, commodity contract, or commodity account.

(50) "Jurisdiction of organization", with respect to a registered organization, means the jurisdiction under whose law the organization is organized.

(51) "Letter-of-credit right" means a right to payment or performance under a letter of credit, whether or not the beneficiary has demanded or is at the time entitled to demand

payment or performance. The term does not include the right of a beneficiary to demand payment or performance under a letter of credit.

(52) "Lien creditor" means:

(A) a creditor that has acquired a lien on the property involved by attachment, levy, or the like;

(B) an assignee for benefit of creditors from the time of assignment;

(C) a trustee in bankruptcy from the date of the filing of the petition; or

(D) a receiver in equity from the time of appointment.

(53) "Manufactured home" means a structure, transportable in one or more sections, which, in the traveling mode, is eight body feet or more in width or 40 body feet or more in length, or, when erected on site, is 320 or more square feet, and which is built on a permanent chassis and designed to be used as a dwelling with or without a permanent foundation when connected to the required utilities, and includes the plumbing, heating, air-conditioning, and electrical systems contained therein. The term includes any structure that meets all of the requirements of this paragraph except the size requirements and with respect to which the manufacturer voluntarily files a certification required by the United States Secretary of Housing and Urban Development and complies with the standards established under Title 42 of the United States Code.

(54) "Manufactured-home transaction" means a secured transaction:

(A) that creates a purchase-money security interest in a manufactured home, other than a manufactured home held as inventory; or

(B) in which a manufactured home, other than a manufactured home held as inventory, is the primary collateral.

(55) "Mortgage" means a consensual interest in real property, including fixtures, which secures payment or performance of an obligation.

(56) "New debtor" means a person that becomes bound as debtor under Section 9–203(d) by a security agreement previously entered into by another person.

(57) "New value" means (i) money, (ii) money's worth in property, services, or new credit, or (iii) release by a transferee of an interest in property previously transferred to the transferee. The term does not include an obligation substituted for another obligation.

(58) "Noncash proceeds" means proceeds other than cash proceeds.

(59) "Obligor" means a person that, with respect to an obligation secured by a security interest in or an agricultural lien on the collateral, (i) owes payment or other performance of the obligation, (ii) has provided property other than the collateral to secure payment or other performance of the obligation, or (iii) is otherwise accountable in whole or in part for payment or other performance of the obligation. The term

does not include issuers or nominated persons under a letter of credit.

(60) "Original debtor", except as used in Section 9–310(c), means a person that, as debtor, entered into a security agreement to which a new debtor has become bound under Section 9–203(d).

(61) "Payment intangible" means a general intangible under which the account debtor's principal obligation is a monetary obligation.

(62) "Person related to", with respect to an individual, means:

(A) the spouse of the individual;

(B) a brother, brother-in-law, sister, or sister-in-law of the individual;

(C) an ancestor or lineal descendant of the individual or the individual's spouse; or

(D) any other relative, by blood or marriage, of the individual or the individual's spouse who shares the same home with the individual.

(63) "Person related to", with respect to an organization, means:

(A) a person directly or indirectly controlling, controlled by, or under common control with the organization;

(B) an officer or director of, or a person performing similar functions with respect to, the organization;

(C) an officer or director of, or a person performing similar functions with respect to, a person described in subparagraph (A);

(D) the spouse of an individual described in subparagraph (A), (B), or (C); or

(E) an individual who is related by blood or marriage to an individual described in subparagraph (A), (B), (C), or (D) and shares the same home with the individual.

(64) "Proceeds", except as used in Section 9–609(b), means the following property:

(A) whatever is acquired upon the sale, lease, license, exchange, or other disposition of collateral;

(B) whatever is collected on, or distributed on account of, collateral;

(C) rights arising out of collateral;

(D) to the extent of the value of collateral, claims arising out of the loss, nonconformity, or interference with the use of, defects or infringement of rights in, or damage to, the collateral; or (E) to the extent of the value of collateral and to the extent payable to the debtor or the secured party, insurance payable by reason of the loss or nonconformity of, defects or infringement of rights in, or damage to, the collateral.

(65) "Promissory note" means an instrument that evidences a promise to pay a monetary obligation, does not evidence an order to pay, and does not contain an acknowledgment by a bank that the bank has received for deposit a sum of money or funds.

(66) "Proposal" means a record authenticated by a secured party which includes the terms on which the secured party is willing to accept collateral in full or partial satisfaction of the obligation it secures pursuant to Sections 9–620, 9–621, and 9–622.

(67) "Public-finance transaction" means a secured transaction in connection with which:

(A) debt securities are issued;

(B) all or a portion of the securities issued have an initial stated maturity of at least 20 years; and

(C) the debtor, obligor, secured party, account debtor or other person obligated on collateral, assignor or assignee of a secured obligation, or assignor or assignee of a security interest is a State or a governmental unit of a State.

(68) "Pursuant to commitment", with respect to an advance made or other value given by a secured party, means pursuant to the secured party's obligation, whether or not a subsequent event of default or other event not within the secured party's control has relieved or may relieve the secured party from its obligation.

(69) "Record", except as used in "for record", "of record", "record or legal title", and "record owner", means information that is inscribed on a tangible medium or which is stored in an electronic or other medium and is retrievable in perceivable form.

(70) "Registered organization" means an organization organized solely under the law of a single State or the United States and as to which the State or the United States must maintain a public record showing the organization to have been organized.

(71) "Secondary obligor" means an obligor to the extent that:

(A) the obligor's obligation is secondary; or

(B) the obligor has a right of recourse with respect to an obligation secured by collateral against the debtor, another obligor, or property of either.

(72) "Secured party" means:

(A) a person in whose favor a security interest is created or provided for under a security agreement, whether or not any obligation to be secured is outstanding;

(B) a person that holds an agricultural lien;

(C) a consignor;

(D) a person to which accounts, chattel paper, payment intangibles, or promissory notes have been sold;

(E) a trustee, indenture trustee, agent, collateral agent, or other representative in whose favor a security interest or agricultural lien is created or provided for; or

(F) a person that holds a security interest arising under Section 2–401, 2–505, 2–711(3), 2A–508(5), 4–210, or 5–118.

(73) "Security agreement" means an agreement that creates or provides for a security interest.

(74) "Send", in connection with a record or notification, means:

(A) to deposit in the mail, deliver for transmission, or transmit by any other usual means of communication, with postage or cost of transmission provided for, addressed to any address reasonable under the circumstances; or

(B) to cause the record or notification to be received within the timce that it would have been received if properly sent under subparagraph (A).

(75) "Software" means a computer program and any supporting information provided in connection with a transaction relating to the program. The term does not include a computer program that is included in the definition of goods.

(76) "State" means a State of the United States, the District of Columbia, Puerto Rico, the United States Virgin Islands, or any territory or insular possession subject to the jurisdiction of the United States.

(77) "Supporting obligation" means a letter-of-credit right or secondary obligation that supports the payment or performance of an account, chattel paper, a document, a general intangible, an instrument, or investment property.

(78) "Tangible chattel paper" means chattel paper evidenced by a record or records consisting of information that is inscribed on a tangible medium.

(79) "Termination statement" means an amendment of a financing statement which:

(A) identifies, by its file number, the initial financing statement to which it relates; and

(B) indicates either that it is a termination statement or that the identified financing statement is no longer effective.

(80) "Transmitting utility" means a person primarily engaged in the business of:

(A) operating a railroad, subway, street railway, or trolley bus;

(B) transmitting communications electrically, electromagnetically, or by light;

(C) transmitting goods by pipeline or sewer; or

(D) transmitting or producing and transmitting electricity, steam, gas, or water.

(b) The following definitions in other articles apply to this article:

"Applicant." Section 5–102

"Beneficiary." Section 5–102

"Broker." Section 8–102

"Certificated security." Section 8–102

"Check." Section 3–104

"Clearing corporation." Section 8–102

"Contract for sale." Section 2–106

"Customer." Section 4–104

"Entitlement holder." Section 8–102

"Financial asset." Section 8–102

"Holder in due course." Section 3–302

"Issuer" (with respect to a letter of credit or letter-of-credit right). Section 5–102

"Issuer" (with respect to a security). Section 8–201

"Lease." Section 2A–103

"Lease agreement." Section 2A–103

"Lease contract." Section 2A–103

"Leasehold interest." Section 2A–103

"Lessee." Section 2A–103

"Lessee in ordinary course of business." Section 2A–103

"Lessor." Section 2A–103

"Lessor's residual interest." Section 2A–103

"Letter of credit." Section 5–102

"Merchant." Section 2–104

"Negotiable instrument." Section 3–104

"Nominated person." Section 5–102

"Note." Section 3–104

"Proceeds of a letter of credit." Section 5–114

"Prove." Section 3–103

"Sale." Section 2–106

"Securities account." Section 8–501

"Securities intermediary." Section 8–102

"Security." Section 8–102

"Security certificate." Section 8–102

"Security entitlement." Section 8–102

"Uncertificated security." Section 8–102

(c) Article 1 contains general definitions and principles of construction and interpretation applicable throughout this article.

Amended in 1999 and 2000.

§ 9–103.   Purchase-Money Security Interest; Application of Payments; Burden of Establishing.

(a) In this section:

(1) "purchase-money collateral" means goods or software that secures a purchase-money obligation incurred with respect to that collateral; and

(2) "purchase-money obligation" means an obligation of an obligor incurred as all or part of the price of the collateral or for value given to enable the debtor to acquire rights in or the use of the collateral if the value is in fact so used.

(b) A security interest in goods is a purchase-money security interest:

(1) to the extent that the goods are purchase-money collateral with respect to that security interest;

(2) if the security interest is in inventory that is or was purchase-money collateral, also to the extent that the security interest secures a purchase-money obligation incurred with respect to other inventory in which the secured party holds or held a purchase-money security interest; and

(3) also to the extent that the security interest secures a purchase-money obligation incurred with respect to software in which the secured party holds or held a purchase-money security interest.

(c) A security interest in software is a purchase-money security interest to the extent that the security interest also secures a purchase-money obligation incurred with respect to goods in which the secured party holds or held a purchase-money security interest if:

(1) the debtor acquired its interest in the software in an integrated transaction in which it acquired an interest in the goods; and

(2) the debtor acquired its interest in the software for the principal purpose of using the software in the goods.

(d) The security interest of a consignor in goods that are the subject of a consignment is a purchase-money security interest in inventory.

(e) In a transaction other than a consumer-goods transaction, if the extent to which a security interest is a purchase-money security interest depends on the application of a payment to a particular obligation, the payment must be applied:

(1) in accordance with any reasonable method of application to which the parties agree;

(2) in the absence of the parties' agreement to a reasonable method, in accordance with any intention of the obligor manifested at or before the time of payment; or

(3) in the absence of an agreement to a reasonable method and a timely manifestation of the obligor's intention, in the following order:

(A) to obligations that are not secured; and

(B) if more than one obligation is secured, to obligations secured by purchase-money security interests in the order in which those obligations were incurred.

(f) In a transaction other than a consumer-goods transaction, a purchase-money security interest does not lose its status as such, even if:

(1) the purchase-money collateral also secures an obligation that is not a purchase-money obligation;

(2) collateral that is not purchase-money collateral also secures the purchase-money obligation; or

(3) the purchase-money obligation has been renewed, refinanced, consolidated, or restructured.

(g) In a transaction other than a consumer-goods transaction, a secured party claiming a purchase-money security interest has the burden of establishing the extent to which the security interest is a purchase-money security interest.

(h) The limitation of the rules in subsections (e), (f), and (g) to transactions other than consumer-goods transactions is intended to leave to the court the determination of the proper rules in consumer-goods transactions. The court may not infer from that limitation the nature of the proper rule in consumer-goods transactions and may continue to apply established approaches.

§ 9–104.   Control of Deposit Account.

(a) A secured party has control of a deposit account if:

(1) the secured party is the bank with which the deposit account is maintained;

(2) the debtor, secured party, and bank have agreed in an authenticated record that the bank will comply with instructions originated by the secured party directing disposition of the funds in the deposit account without further consent by the debtor; or

(3) the secured party becomes the bank's customer with respect to the deposit account.

(b) A secured party that has satisfied subsection (a) has control, even if the debtor retains the right to direct the disposition of funds from the deposit account.

§ 9–105.   Control of Electronic Chattel Paper.

A secured party has control of electronic chattel paper if the record or records comprising the chattel paper are created, stored, and assigned in such a manner that:

(1) a single authoritative copy of the record or records exists which is unique, identifiable and, except as otherwise provided in paragraphs (4), (5), and (6), unalterable;

(2) the authoritative copy identifies the secured party as the assignee of the record or records;

(3) the authoritative copy is communicated to and maintained by the secured party or its designated custodian;

(4) copies or revisions that add or change an identified assignee of the authoritative copy can be made only with the participation of the secured party;

(5) each copy of the authoritative copy and any copy of a copy is readily identifiable as a copy that is not the authoritative copy; and

(6) any revision of the authoritative copy is readily identifiable as an authorized or unauthorized revision.

§ 9–106.   Control of Investment Property.

(a) A person has control of a certificated security, uncertificated security, or security entitlement as provided in Section 8–106.

(b) A secured party has control of a commodity contract if:

(1) the secured party is the commodity intermediary with which the commodity contract is carried; or

(2) the commodity customer, secured party, and commodity intermediary have agreed that the commodity intermediary will apply any value distributed on account of the commodity contract as directed by the secured party without further consent by the commodity customer.

(c) A secured party having control of all security entitlements or commodity contracts carried in a securities account or commodity account has control over the securities account or commodity account.

§ 9–107.   Control of Letter-of-Credit Right.

A secured party has control of a letter-of-credit right to the extent of any right to payment or performance by the issuer or any nominated person if the issuer or nominated person has consented to an assignment of proceeds of the letter of credit under Section 5–114(c) or otherwise applicable law or practice.

§ 9–108.   Sufficiency of Description.

(a) Except as otherwise provided in subsections (c), (d), and (e), a description of personal or real property is sufficient, whether or not it is specific, if it reasonably identifies what is described.

(b) Except as otherwise provided in subsection (d), a description of collateral reasonably identifies the collateral if it identifies the collateral by:

(1) specific listing;

(2) category;

(3) except as otherwise provided in subsection (e), a type of collateral defined in [the Uniform Commercial Code];

(4) quantity;

(5) computational or allocational formula or procedure; or

(6) except as otherwise provided in subsection (c), any other method, if the identity of the collateral is objectively determinable.

(c) A description of collateral as "all the debtor's assets" or "all the debtor's personal property" or using words of similar import does not reasonably identify the collateral.

(d) Except as otherwise provided in subsection (e), a description of a security entitlement, securities account, or commodity account is sufficient if it describes:

(1) the collateral by those terms or as investment property; or

(2) the underlying financial asset or commodity contract.

(e) A description only by type of collateral defined in [the Uniform Commercial Code] is an insufficient description of:

(1) a commercial tort claim; or

(2) in a consumer transaction, consumer goods, a security entitlement, a securities account, or a commodity account.

[Subpart 2. Applicability of Article]

§ 9–109.   Scope.

(a) Except as otherwise provided in subsections (c) and (d), this article applies to:

(1) a transaction, regardless of its form, that creates a security interest in personal property or fixtures by contract;

(2) an agricultural lien;

(3) a sale of accounts, chattel paper, payment intangibles, or promissory notes;

(4) a consignment;

(5) a security interest arising under Section 2–401, 2–505, 2–711 (3), or 2A–508(5), as provided in Section 9–110; and

(6) a security interest arising under Section 4–210 or 5–118.

(b) The application of this article to a security interest in a secured obligation is not affected by the fact that the obligation is itself secured by a transaction or interest to which this article does not apply.

(c) This article does not apply to the extent that:

(1) a statute, regulation, or treaty of the United States preempts this article;

(2) another statute of this State expressly governs the creation, perfection, priority, or enforcement of a security interest created by this State or a governmental unit of this State;

(3) a statute of another State, a foreign country, or a governmental unit of another State or a foreign country, other than a statute generally applicable to security interests, expressly governs creation, perfection, priority, or enforcement of a security interest created by the State, country, or governmental unit; or

(4) the rights of a transferee beneficiary or nominated person under a letter of credit are independent and superior under Section 5–114.

(d) This article does not apply to:

(1) a landlord's lien, other than an agricultural lien;

(2) a lien, other than an agricultural lien, given by statute or other rule of law for services or materials, but Section 9–333 applies with respect to priority of the lien;

(3) an assignment of a claim for wages, salary, or other compensation of an employee;

(4) a sale of accounts, chattel paper, payment intangibles, or promissory notes as part of a sale of the business out of which they arose;

(5) an assignment of accounts, chattel paper, payment intangibles, or promissory notes which is for the purpose of collection only;

(6) an assignment of a right to payment under a contract to an assignee that is also obligated to perform under the contract;

(7) an assignment of a single account, payment intangible, or promissory note to an assignee in full or partial satisfaction of a preexisting indebtedness;

(8) a transfer of an interest in or an assignment of a claim under a policy of insurance, other than an assignment by or to a health-care provider of a health-care-insurance receivable and any subsequent assignment of the right to payment, but Sections 9–315 and 9–322 apply with respect to proceeds and priorities in proceeds;

(9) an assignment of a right represented by a judgment, other than a judgment taken on a right to payment that was collateral;

(10) a right of recoupment or set-off, but:

(A) Section 9–340 applies with respect to the effectiveness of rights of recoupment or set-off against deposit accounts; and

(B) Section 9–404 applies with respect to defenses or claims of an account debtor;

(11) the creation or transfer of an interest in or lien on real property, including a lease or rents thereunder, except to the extent that provision is made for:

(A) liens on real property in Sections 9–203 and 9–308;

(B) fixtures in Section 9–334;

(C) fixture filings in Sections 9–501, 9–502, 9–512, 9–516, and 9–519; and

(D) security agreements covering personal and real property in Section 9–604;

(12) an assignment of a claim arising in tort, other than a commercial tort claim, but Sections 9–315 and 9–322 apply with respect to proceeds and priorities in proceeds; or

(13) an assignment of a deposit account in a consumer transaction, but Sections 9–315 and 9–322 apply with respect to proceeds and priorities in proceeds.

§ 9–110.   Security Interests Arising under Article 2 or 2A.

A security interest arising under Section 2–401, 2–505, 2–711(3), or 2A–508(5) is subject to this article. However, until the debtor obtains possession of the goods:

(1) the security interest is enforceable, even if Section 9–203(b) (3) has not been satisfied;

(2) filing is not required to perfect the security interest;

(3) the rights of the secured party after default by the debtor are governed by Article 2 or 2A; and

(4) the security interest has priority over a conflicting security interest created by the debtor.

PART 2   Effectiveness of Security Agreement; Attachment of Security Interest; Rights of Parties to Security Agreement

[Subpart 1. Effectiveness and Attachment]

§ 9–201.   General Effectiveness of Security Agreement.

(a) Except as otherwise provided in [the Uniform Commercial Code], a security agreement is effective according to its terms between the parties, against purchasers of the collateral, and against creditors.

(b) A transaction subject to this article is subject to any applicable rule of law which establishes a different rule for consumers and [insert reference to (i) any other statute or regulation that regulates the rates, charges, agreements, and practices for loans, credit sales, or other extensions of credit and (ii) any consumer-protection statute or regulation].

(c) In case of conflict between this article and a rule of law, statute, or regulation described in subsection (b), the rule of law, statute, or regulation controls. Failure to comply with a statute or regulation described in subsection (b) has only the effect the statute or regulation specifies.

(d) This article does not:

(1) validate any rate, charge, agreement, or practice that violates a rule of law, statute, or regulation described in subsection (b); or

(2) extend the application of the rule of law, statute, or regulation to a transaction not otherwise subject to it.

§ 9–202.   Title to Collateral Immaterial.

Except as otherwise provided with respect to consignments or sales of accounts, chattel paper, payment intangibles, or promissory notes, the provisions of this article with regard to rights and obligations apply whether title to collateral is in the secured party or the debtor.

§ 9–203.   Attachment and Enforceability of Security Interest; Proceeds; Supporting Obligations; Formal Requisites.

(a) A security interest attaches to collateral when it becomes enforceable against the debtor with respect to the collateral, unless an agreement expressly postpones the time of attachment.

(b) Except as otherwise provided in subsections (c) through (i), a security interest is enforceable against the debtor and third parties with respect to the collateral only if:

(1) value has been given;

(2) the debtor has rights in the collateral or the power to transfer rights in the collateral to a secured party; and

(3) one of the following conditions is met:

(A) the debtor has authenticated a security agreement that provides a description of the collateral and, if the security interest covers timber to be cut, a description of the land concerned;

(B) the collateral is not a certificated security and is in the possession of the secured party under Section 9–313 pursuant to the debtor's security agreement;

(C) the collateral is a certificated security in registered form and the security certificate has been delivered to the secured party under Section 8–301 pursuant to the debtor's security agreement; or

(D) the collateral is deposit accounts, electronic chattel paper, investment property, or letter-of-credit rights, and the secured party has control under Section 9–104, 9–105, 9–106, or 9–107 pursuant to the debtor's security agreement.

(c) Subsection (b) is subject to Section 4–210 on the security interest of a collecting bank, Section 5–118 on the security interest of a letter-of-credit issuer or nominated person, Section 9–110 on a security interest arising under Article 2 or 2A, and Section 9–206 on security interests in investment property.

(d) A person becomes bound as debtor by a security agreement entered into by another person if, by operation of law other than this article or by contract:

(1) the security agreement becomes effective to create a security interest in the person's property; or

(2) the person becomes generally obligated for the obligations of the other person, including the obligation secured under the security agreement, and acquires or succeeds to all or substantially all of the assets of the other person.

(e) If a new debtor becomes bound as debtor by a security agreement entered into by another person:

(1) the agreement satisfies subsection (b)(3) with respect to existing or after-acquired property of the new debtor to the extent the property is described in the agreement; and

(2) another agreement is not necessary to make a security interest in the property enforceable.

(f) The attachment of a security interest in collateral gives the secured party the rights to proceeds provided by Section 9–315 and is also attachment of a security interest in a supporting obligation for the collateral.

(g) The attachment of a security interest in a right to payment or performance secured by a security interest or other lien on personal or real property is also attachment of a security interest in the security interest, mortgage, or other lien.

(h) The attachment of a security interest in a securities account is also attachment of a security interest in the security entitlements carried in the securities account.

(i) The attachment of a security interest in a commodity account is also attachment of a security interest in the commodity contracts carried in the commodity account.

§ 9–204.   After-Acquired Property; Future Advances.

(a) Except as otherwise provided in subsection (b), a security agreement may create or provide for a security interest in after-acquired collateral.

(b) A security interest does not attach under a term constituting an after-acquired property clause to:

(1) consumer goods, other than an accession when given as additional security, unless the debtor acquires rights in them within 10 days after the secured party gives value; or

(2) a commercial tort claim.

(c) A security agreement may provide that collateral secures, or that accounts, chattel paper, payment intangibles, or promissory notes are sold in connection with, future advances or other value, whether or not the advances or value are given pursuant to commitment.

§ 9–205.   Use or Disposition of Collateral Permissible.

(a) A security interest is not invalid or fraudulent against creditors solely because:

(1) the debtor has the right or ability to:

(A) use, commingle, or dispose of all or part of the collateral, including returned or repossessed goods;

(B) collect, compromise, enforce, or otherwise deal with collateral;

(C) accept the return of collateral or make repossessions; or

(D) use, commingle, or dispose of proceeds; or

(2) the secured party fails to require the debtor to account for proceeds or replace collateral.

(b) This section does not relax the requirements of possession if attachment, perfection, or enforcement of a security interest depends upon possession of the collateral by the secured party.

§ 9–206.   Security Interest Arising in Purchase or Delivery of Financial Asset.

(a) A security interest in favor of a securities intermediary attaches to a person's security entitlement if:

(1) the person buys a financial asset through the securities intermediary in a transaction in which the person is obligated to pay the purchase price to the securities intermediary at the time of the purchase; and

(2) the securities intermediary credits the financial asset to the buyer's securities account before the buyer pays the securities intermediary.

(b) The security interest described in subsection (a) secures the person's obligation to pay for the financial asset.

(c) A security interest in favor of a person that delivers a certificated security or other financial asset represented by a writing attaches to the security or other financial asset if:

(1) the security or other financial asset:

(A) in the ordinary course of business is transferred by delivery with any necessary indorsement or assignment; and

(B) is delivered under an agreement between persons in the business of dealing with such securities or financial assets; and

(2) the agreement calls for delivery against payment.

(d) The security interest described in subsection (c) secures the obligation to make payment for the delivery.

[Subpart 2. Rights and Duties]

§ 9–207.   Rights and Duties of Secured Party Having Possession or Control of Collateral.

(a) Except as otherwise provided in subsection (d), a secured party shall use reasonable care in the custody and preservation of collateral in the secured party's possession. In the case of chattel paper or an instrument, reasonable care includes taking necessary steps to preserve rights against prior parties unless otherwise agreed.

(b) Except as otherwise provided in subsection (d), if a secured party has possession of collateral:

(1) reasonable expenses, including the cost of insurance and payment of taxes or other charges, incurred in the custody, preservation, use, or operation of the collateral are chargeable to the debtor and are secured by the collateral;

(2) the risk of accidental loss or damage is on the debtor to the extent of a deficiency in any effective insurance coverage;

(3) the secured party shall keep the collateral identifiable, but fungible collateral may be commingled; and

(4) the secured party may use or operate the collateral:

(A) for the purpose of preserving the collateral or its value;

(B) as permitted by an order of a court having competent jurisdiction; or

(C) except in the case of consumer goods, in the manner and to the extent agreed by the debtor.

(c) Except as otherwise provided in subsection (d), a secured party having possession of collateral or control of collateral under Section 9–104, 9–105, 9–106, or 9–107:

(1) may hold as additional security any proceeds, except money or funds, received from the collateral;

(2) shall apply money or funds received from the collateral to reduce the secured obligation, unless remitted to the debtor; and

(3) may create a security interest in the collateral.

(d) If the secured party is a buyer of accounts, chattel paper, payment intangibles, or promissory notes or a consignor:

(1) subsection (a) does not apply unless the secured party is entitled under an agreement:

(A) to charge back uncollected collateral; or

(B) otherwise to full or limited recourse against the debtor or a secondary obligor based on the nonpayment or other default of an account debtor or other obligor on the collateral; and

(2) subsections (b) and (c) do not apply.

§ 9–208.   Additional Duties of Secured Party Having Control of Collateral.

(a) This section applies to cases in which there is no outstanding secured obligation and the secured party is not committed to make advances, incur obligations, or otherwise give value.

(b) Within 10 days after receiving an authenticated demand by the debtor:

(1) a secured party having control of a deposit account under Section 9–104(a)(2) shall send to the bank with which the deposit account is maintained an authenticated statement that releases the bank from any further obligation to comply with instructions originated by the secured party;

(2) a secured party having control of a deposit account under Section 9–104(a)(3) shall:

(A) pay the debtor the balance on deposit in the deposit account; or

(B) transfer the balance on deposit into a deposit account in the debtor's name;

(3) a secured party, other than a buyer, having control of electronic chattel paper under Section 9–105 shall:

(A) communicate the authoritative copy of the electronic chattel paper to the debtor or its designated custodian;

(B) if the debtor designates a custodian that is the designated custodian with which the authoritative copy of the electronic chattel paper is maintained for the secured party, communicate to the custodian an authenticated record releasing the designated custodian from any further obligation to comply with instructions originated by the secured party and instructing

the custodian to comply with instructions originated by the debtor; and

(C) take appropriate action to enable the debtor or its designated custodian to make copies of or revisions to the authoritative copy which add or change an identified assignee of the authoritative copy without the consent of the secured party;

(4) a secured party having control of investment property under Section 8–106(d)(2) or 9–106(b) shall send to the securities intermediary or commodity intermediary with which the security entitlement or commodity contract is maintained an authenticated record that releases the securities intermediary or commodity intermediary from any further obligation to comply with entitlement orders or directions originated by the secured party; and

(5) a secured party having control of a letter-of-credit right under Section 9–107 shall send to each person having an unfulfilled obligation to pay or deliver proceeds of the letter of credit to the secured party an authenticated release from any further obligation to pay or deliver proceeds of the letter of credit to the secured party.

§ 9–209.   Duties of Secured Party If Account Debtor Has Been Notified of Assignment.

(a) Except as otherwise provided in subsection (c), this section applies if:

(1) there is no outstanding secured obligation; and

(2) the secured party is not committed to make advances, incur obligations, or otherwise give value.

(b) Within 10 days after receiving an authenticated demand by the debtor, a secured party shall send to an account debtor that has received notification of an assignment to the secured party as assignee under Section 9–406(a) an authenticated record that releases the account debtor from any further obligation to the secured party.

(c) This section does not apply to an assignment constituting the sale of an account, chattel paper, or payment intangible.

§ 9–210.   Request for Accounting; Request Regarding List of Collateral or Statement of Account.

(a) In this section:

(1) "Request" means a record of a type described in paragraph (2), (3), or (4).

(2) "Request for an accounting" means a record authenticated by a debtor requesting that the recipient provide an accounting of the unpaid obligations secured by collateral and reasonably identifying the transaction or relationship that is the subject of the request.

(3) "Request regarding a list of collateral" means a record authenticated by a debtor requesting that the recipient approve or correct a list of what the debtor believes to be the collateral securing an obligation and reasonably identifying the transaction or relationship that is the subject of the request.

(4) "Request regarding a statement of account" means a record authenticated by a debtor requesting that the recipient approve or correct a statement indicating what the debtor believes to be the aggregate amount of unpaid obligations secured by collateral as of a specified date and reasonably identifying the transaction or relationship that is the subject of the request.

(b) Subject to subsections (c), (d), (e), and (f), a secured party, other than a buyer of accounts, chattel paper, payment intangibles, or promissory notes or a consignor, shall comply with a request within 14 days after receipt:

(1) in the case of a request for an accounting, by authenticating and sending to the debtor an accounting; and

(2) in the case of a request regarding a list of collateral or a request regarding a statement of account, by authenticating and sending to the debtor an approval or correction.

(c) A secured party that claims a security interest in all of a particular type of collateral owned by the debtor may comply with a request regarding a list of collateral by sending to the debtor an authenticated record including a statement to that effect within 14 days after receipt.

(d) A person that receives a request regarding a list of collateral, claims no interest in the collateral when it receives the request, and claimed an interest in the collateral at an earlier time shall comply with the request within 14 days after receipt by sending to the debtor an authenticated record:

(1) disclaiming any interest in the collateral; and

(2) if known to the recipient, providing the name and mailing address of any assignee of or successor to the recipient's interest in the collateral.

(e) A person that receives a request for an accounting or a request regarding a statement of account, claims no interest in the obligations when it receives the request, and claimed an interest in the obligations at an earlier time shall comply with the request within 14 days after receipt by sending to the debtor an authenticated record:

(1) disclaiming any interest in the obligations; and

(2) if known to the recipient, providing the name and mailing address of any assignee of or successor to the recipient's interest in the obligations.

(f) A debtor is entitled without charge to one response to a request under this section during any six-month period. The secured party may require payment of a charge not exceeding $25 for each additional response.

As amended in 1999.

PART 3   Perfection and Priority

[Subpart 1. Law Governing Perfection and Priority]

§ 9–301.   Law Governing Perfection and Priority of Security Interests.

Except as otherwise provided in Sections 9–303 through 9–306, the following rules determine the law governing perfection, the effect of perfection or nonperfection, and the priority of a security interest in collateral:

(1) Except as otherwise provided in this section, while a debtor is located in a jurisdiction, the local law of that jurisdiction governs perfection, the effect of perfection or nonperfection, and the priority of a security interest in collateral.

(2) While collateral is located in a jurisdiction, the local law of that jurisdiction governs perfection, the effect of perfection or nonperfection, and the priority of a possessory security interest in that collateral.

(3) Except as otherwise provided in paragraph (4), while negotiable documents, goods, instruments, money, or tangible chattel paper is located in a jurisdiction, the local law of that jurisdiction governs:

(A) perfection of a security interest in the goods by filing a fixture filing;

(B) perfection of a security interest in timber to be cut; and

(C) the effect of perfection or nonperfection and the priority of a nonpossessory security interest in the collateral.

(4) The local law of the jurisdiction in which the wellhead or minehead is located governs perfection, the effect of perfection or nonperfection, and the priority of a security interest in as-extracted collateral.

§ 9–302.   Law Governing Perfection and Priority of Agricultural Liens.

While farm products are located in a jurisdiction, the local law of that jurisdiction governs perfection, the effect of perfection or nonperfection, and the priority of an agricultural lien on the farm products.

§ 9–303.   Law Governing Perfection and Priority of Security Interests in Goods Covered by a Certificate of Title.

(a) This section applies to goods covered by a certificate of title, even if there is no other relationship between the jurisdiction under whose certificate of title the goods are covered and the goods or the debtor.

(b) Goods become covered by a certificate of title when a valid application for the certificate of title and the applicable fee are delivered to the appropriate authority. Goods cease to be covered by a certificate of title at the earlier of the time the certificate of title ceases to be effective under the law of the issuing jurisdiction or the time the goods become covered subsequently by a certificate of title issued by another jurisdiction.

(c) The local law of the jurisdiction under whose certificate of title the goods are covered governs perfection, the effect of perfection or nonperfection, and the priority of a security interest in goods covered by a certificate of title from the time the goods become covered by the certificate of title until the goods cease to be covered by the certificate of title.

§ 9–304. Law Governing Perfection and Priority of Security Interests in Deposit Accounts.

(a) The local law of a bank's jurisdiction governs perfection, the effect of perfection or nonperfection, and the priority of a security interest in a deposit account maintained with that bank.

(b) The following rules determine a bank's jurisdiction for purposes of this part:

(1) If an agreement between the bank and the debtor governing the deposit account expressly provides that a particular jurisdiction is the bank's jurisdiction for purposes of this part, this article, or [the Uniform Commercial Code], that jurisdiction is the bank's jurisdiction.

(2) If paragraph (1) does not apply and an agreement between the bank and its customer governing the deposit account expressly provides that the agreement is governed by the law of a particular jurisdiction, that jurisdiction is the bank's jurisdiction.

(3) If neither paragraph (1) nor paragraph (2) applies and an agreement between the bank and its customer governing the deposit account expressly provides that the deposit account is maintained at an office in a particular jurisdiction, that jurisdiction is the bank's jurisdiction.

(4) If none of the preceding paragraphs applies, the bank's jurisdiction is the jurisdiction in which the office identified in an account statement as the office serving the customer's account is located.

(5) If none of the preceding paragraphs applies, the bank's jurisdiction is the jurisdiction in which the chief executive office of the bank is located.

§ 9–305. Law Governing Perfection and Priority of Security Interests in Investment Property.

(a) Except as otherwise provided in subsection (c), the following rules apply:

(1) While a security certificate is located in a jurisdiction, the local law of that jurisdiction governs perfection, the

effect of perfection or nonperfection, and the priority of a security interest in the certificated security represented thereby.

(2) The local law of the issuer's jurisdiction as specified in Section 8–110(d) governs perfection, the effect of perfection or nonperfection, and the priority of a security interest in an uncertificated security.

(3) The local law of the securities intermediary's jurisdiction as specified in Section 8–110(e) governs perfection, the effect of perfection or nonperfection, and the priority of a security interest in a security entitlement or securities account.

(4) The local law of the commodity intermediary's jurisdiction governs perfection, the effect of perfection or nonperfection, and the priority of a security interest in a commodity contract or commodity account.

(b) The following rules determine a commodity intermediary's jurisdiction for purposes of this part:

(1) If an agreement between the commodity intermediary and commodity customer governing the commodity account expressly provides that a particular jurisdiction is the commodity intermediary's jurisdiction for purposes of this part, this article, or [the Uniform Commercial Code], that jurisdiction is the commodity intermediary's jurisdiction.

(2) If paragraph (1) does not apply and an agreement between the commodity intermediary and commodity customer governing the commodity account expressly provides that the agreement is governed by the law of a particular jurisdiction, that jurisdiction is the commodity intermediary's jurisdiction.

(3) If neither paragraph (1) nor paragraph (2) applies and an agreement between the commodity intermediary and commodity customer governing the commodity account expressly provides that the commodity account is maintained at an office in a particular jurisdiction, that jurisdiction is the commodity intermediary's jurisdiction.

(4) If none of the preceding paragraphs applies, the commodity intermediary's jurisdiction is the jurisdiction in which the office identified in an account statement as the office serving the commodity customer's account is located.

(5) If none of the preceding paragraphs applies, the commodity intermediary's jurisdiction is the jurisdiction in which the chief executive office of the commodity intermediary is located.

(c) The local law of the jurisdiction in which the debtor is located governs:

(1) perfection of a security interest in investment property by filing;

(2) automatic perfection of a security interest in investment property created by a broker or securities intermediary; and

(3) automatic perfection of a security interest in a commodity contract or commodity account created by a commodity intermediary.

§ 9–306.   Law Governing Perfection and Priority of Security Interests in Letter-of-Credit Rights.

(a) Subject to subsection (c), the local law of the issuer's jurisdiction or a nominated person's jurisdiction governs perfection, the effect of perfection or nonperfection, and the priority of a security interest in a letter-of-credit right if the issuer's jurisdiction or nominated person's jurisdiction is a State.

(b) For purposes of this part, an issuer's jurisdiction or nominated person's jurisdiction is the jurisdiction whose law governs the liability of the issuer or nominated person with respect to the letter-of-credit right as provided in Section 5–116.

(c) This section does not apply to a security interest that is perfected only under Section 9–308(d).

§ 9–307.   Location of Debtor.

(a) In this section, "place of business" means a place where a debtor conducts its affairs.

(b) Except as otherwise provided in this section, the following rules determine a debtor's location:

(1) A debtor who is an individual is located at the individual's principal residence.

(2) A debtor that is an organization and has only one place of business is located at its place of business.

(3) A debtor that is an organization and has more than one place of business is located at its chief executive office.

(c) Subsection (b) applies only if a debtor's residence, place of business, or chief executive office, as applicable, is located in a jurisdiction whose law generally requires information concerning the existence of a nonpossessory security interest to be made generally available in a filing, recording, or registration system as a condition or result of the security interest's obtaining priority over the rights of a lien creditor with respect to the collateral. If subsection (b) does not apply, the debtor is located in the District of Columbia.

(d) A person that ceases to exist, have a residence, or have a place of business continues to be located in the jurisdiction specified by subsections (b) and (c).

(e) A registered organization that is organized under the law of a State is located in that State.

(f) Except as otherwise provided in subsection (i), a registered organization that is organized under the law of the United Statesand a branch or agency of a bank that is not organized under the law of the United States or a State are located:

(1) in the State that the law of the United States designates, if the law designates a State of location;

(2) in the State that the registered organization, branch, or agency designates, if the law of the United States authorizes the registered organization, branch, or agency to designate its State of location; or

(3) in the District of Columbia, if neither paragraph (1) nor paragraph (2) applies.

(g) A registered organization continues to be located in the jurisdiction specified by subsection (e) or (f) notwithstanding:

(1) the suspension, revocation, forfeiture, or lapse of the registered organization's status as such in its jurisdiction of organization; or

(2) the dissolution, winding up, or cancellation of the existence of the registered organization.

(h) The United States is located in the District of Columbia.

(i) A branch or agency of a bank that is not organized under the law of the United States or a State is located in the State in which the branch or agency is licensed, if all branches and agencies of the bank are licensed in only one State.

(j) A foreign air carrier under the Federal Aviation Act of 1958, as amended, is located at the designated office of the agent upon which service of process may be made on behalf of the carrier.

(k) This section applies only for purposes of this part.

[Subpart 2. Perfection]

§ 9–308.   When Security Interest or Agricultural Lien Is Perfected; Continuity of Perfection.

(a) Except as otherwise provided in this section and Section 9–309, a security interest is perfected if it has attached and all of the applicable requirements for perfection in Sections 9–310 through 9–316 have been satisfied. A security interest is perfected when it attaches if the applicable requirements are satisfied before the security interest attaches.

(b) An agricultural lien is perfected if it has become effective and all of the applicable requirements for perfection in Section 9–310 have been satisfied. An agricultural lien is perfected when it becomes effective if the applicable requirements are satisfied before the agricultural lien becomes effective.

(c) A security interest or agricultural lien is perfected continuously if it is originally perfected by one method under this article and is later perfected by another method under this article, without an intermediate period when it was unperfected.

(d) Perfection of a security interest in collateral also perfects a security interest in a supporting obligation for the collateral.

(e) Perfection of a security interest in a right to payment or performance also perfects a security interest in a security interest, mortgage, or other lien on personal or real property securing the right.

(f) Perfection of a security interest in a securities account also perfects a security interest in the security entitlements carried in the securities account.

(g) Perfection of a security interest in a commodity account also perfects a security interest in the commodity contracts carried in the commodity account.

Legislative Note: Any statute conflicting with subsection (e) must be made expressly subject to that subsection.

§ 9–309. Security Interest Perfected upon Attachment.

The following security interests are perfected when they attach:

(1) a purchase-money security interest in consumer goods, except as otherwise provided in Section 9–311(b) with respect to consumer goods that are subject to a statute or treaty described in Section 9–311(a);

(2) an assignment of accounts or payment intangibles which does not by itself or in conjunction with other assignments to the same assignee transfer a significant part of the assignor's outstanding accounts or payment intangibles;

(3) a sale of a payment intangible;

(4) a sale of a promissory note;

(5) a security interest created by the assignment of a health-care-insurance receivable to the provider of the health-care goods or services;

(6) a security interest arising under Section 2–401, 2–505, 2–711 (3), or 2A–508(5), until the debtor obtains possession of the collateral;

(7) a security interest of a collecting bank arising under Section 4–210;

(8) a security interest of an issuer or nominated person arising under Section 5–118;

(9) a security interest arising in the delivery of a financial asset under Section 9–206(c);

(10) a security interest in investment property created by a broker or securities intermediary;

(11) a security interest in a commodity contract or a commodity account created by a commodity intermediary;

(12) an assignment for the benefit of all creditors of the transferor and subsequent transfers by the assignee thereunder; and

(13) a security interest created by an assignment of a beneficial interest in a decedent's estate; and

(14) a sale by an individual of an account that is a right to payment of winnings in a lottery or other game of chance.

§ 9–310. When Filing Required to Perfect Security Interest or Agricultural Lien; Security Interests and Agricultural Liens to Which Filing Provisions Do Not Apply.

(a) Except as otherwise provided in subsection (b) and Section 9–312(b), a financing statement must be filed to perfect all security interests and agricultural liens.

(b) The filing of a financing statement is not necessary to perfect a security interest:

(1) that is perfected under Section 9–308(d), (e), (f), or (g);

(2) that is perfected under Section 9–309 when it attaches;

(3) in property subject to a statute, regulation, or treaty described in Section 9–311(a);

(4) in goods in possession of a bailee which is perfected under Section 9–312(d)(1) or (2);

(5) in certificated securities, documents, goods, or instruments which is perfected without filing or possession under Section 9–312(e), (f), or (g);

(6) in collateral in the secured party's possession under Section 9–313;

(7) in a certificated security which is perfected by delivery of the security certificate to the secured party under Section 9–313;

(8) in deposit accounts, electronic chattel paper, investment property, or letter-of-credit rights which is perfected by control under Section 9–314;

(9) in proceeds which is perfected under Section 9–315; or

(10) that is perfected under Section 9–316.

(c) If a secured party assigns a perfected security interest or agricultural lien, a filing under this article is not required to continue the perfected status of the security interest against creditors of and transferees from the original debtor.

§ 9–311. Perfection of Security Interests in Property Subject to Certain Statutes, Regulations, and Treaties.

(a) Except as otherwise provided in subsection (d), the filing of a financing statement is not necessary or effective to perfect a security interest in property subject to:

(1) a statute, regulation, or treaty of the United States whose requirements for a security interest's obtaining priority over the rights of a lien creditor with respect to the property preempt Section 9–310(a);

(2) [list any certificate-of-title statute covering automobiles, trailers, mobile homes, boats, farm tractors, or the like, which provides for a security interest to be indicated on the certificate as a condition or result of perfection, and any non-Uniform Commercial Code central filing statute]; or

(3) a certificate-of-title statute of another jurisdiction which provides for a security interest to be indicated on the certificate as a condition or result of the security interest's obtaining priority over the rights of a lien creditor with respect to the property.

(b) Compliance with the requirements of a statute, regulation, or treaty described in subsection (a) for obtaining priority over the rights of a lien creditor is equivalent to the filing of a financing statement under this article. Except as otherwise provided in subsection (d) and Sections 9–313 and 9–316(d) and (e) for goods covered by a certificate of title, a security interest in property subject to a statute, regulation, or treaty described in subsection (a) may be perfected only by compliance with those requirements, and a security interest so perfected remains perfected notwithstanding a change in the use or transfer of possession of the collateral.

(c) Except as otherwise provided in subsection (d) and Section 9–316(d) and (e), duration and renewal of perfection of a security interest perfected by compliance with the requirements prescribed by a statute, regulation, or treaty described in subsection (a) are governed by the statute, regulation, or treaty. In other respects, the security interest is subject to this article.

(d) During any period in which collateral subject to a statute specified in subsection (a)(2) is inventory held for sale or lease by a person or leased by that person as lessor and that person is in the business of selling goods of that kind, this section does not apply to a security interest in that collateral created by that person.

Legislative Note: This Article contemplates that perfection of a security interest in goods covered by a certificate of title occurs upon receipt by appropriate State officials of a properly tendered application for a certificate of title on which the security interest is to be indicated, without a relation back to an earlier time. States whose certificate-of-title statutes provide for perfection at a different time or contain a relation-back provision should amend the statutes accordingly.

§ 9–312. Perfection of Security Interests in Chattel Paper, Deposit Accounts, Documents, Goods Covered by Documents, Instruments, Investment Property, Letter-of-Credit Rights, and Money; Perfection by Permissive Filing; Temporary Perfection without Filing or Transfer of Possession.

(a) A security interest in chattel paper, negotiable documents, instruments, or investment property may be perfected by filing.

(b) Except as otherwise provided in Section 9–315(c) and (d) for proceeds:

(1) a security interest in a deposit account may be perfected only by control under Section 9–314;

(2) and except as otherwise provided in Section 9–308(d), a security interest in a letter-of-credit right may be perfected only by control under Section 9–314; and

(3) a security interest in money may be perfected only by the secured party's taking possession under Section 9–313.

(c) While goods are in the possession of a bailee that has issued a negotiable document covering the goods:

(1) a security interest in the goods may be perfected by perfecting a security interest in the document; and

(2) a security interest perfected in the document has priority over any security interest that becomes perfected in the goods by another method during that time.

(d) While goods are in the possession of a bailee that has issued a nonnegotiable document covering the goods, a security interest in the goods may be perfected by:

(1) issuance of a document in the name of the secured party;

(2) the bailee's receipt of notification of the secured party's interest; or

(3) filing as to the goods.

(e) A security interest in certificated securities, negotiable documents, or instruments is perfected without filing or the taking of possession for a period of 20 days from the time it attaches to the extent that it arises for new value given under an authenticated security agreement.

(f) A perfected security interest in a negotiable document or goods in possession of a bailee, other than one that has issued a negotiable document for the goods, remains perfected for 20 days without filing if the secured party makes available to the debtor the goods or documents representing the goods for the purpose of:

(1) ultimate sale or exchange; or

(2) loading, unloading, storing, shipping, transshipping, manufacturing, processing, or otherwise dealing with them in a manner preliminary to their sale or exchange.

(g) A perfected security interest in a certificated security or instrument remains perfected for 20 days without filing if the secured party delivers the security certificate or instrument to the debtor for the purpose of:

(1) ultimate sale or exchange; or

(2) presentation, collection, enforcement, renewal, or registration of transfer.

(h) After the 20-day period specified in subsection (e), (f), or (g) expires, perfection depends upon compliance with this article.

§ 9–313. When Possession by or Delivery to Secured Party Perfects Security Interest without Filing.

(a) Except as otherwise provided in subsection (b), a secured party may perfect a security interest in negotiable documents, goods, instruments, money, or tangible chattel paper by taking possession of the collateral. A secured party may perfect a security interest in certificated securities by taking delivery of the certificated securities under Section 8–301.

(b) With respect to goods covered by a certificate of title issued by this State, a secured party may perfect a security interest in the goods by taking possession of the goods only in the circumstances described in Section 9–316(d).

(c) With respect to collateral other than certificated securities and goods covered by a document, a secured party takes possession of collateral in the possession of a person other than the debtor, the secured party, or a lessee of the collateral from the debtor in the ordinary course of the debtor's business, when:

(1) the person in possession authenticates a record acknowledging that it holds possession of the collateral for the secured party's benefit; or

(2) the person takes possession of the collateral after having authenticated a record acknowledging that it will hold possession of collateral for the secured party's benefit.

(d) If perfection of a security interest depends upon possession of the collateral by a secured party, perfection occurs no earlier than the time the secured party takes possession and continues only while the secured party retains possession.

(e) A security interest in a certificated security in registered form is perfected by delivery when delivery of the certificated security occurs under Section 8–301 and remains perfected by delivery until the debtor obtains possession of the security certificate.

(f) A person in possession of collateral is not required to acknowledge that it holds possession for a secured party's benefit.

(g) If a person acknowledges that it holds possession for the secured party's benefit:

(1) the acknowledgment is effective under subsection (c) or Section 8–301(a), even if the acknowledgment violates the rights of a debtor; and

(2) unless the person otherwise agrees or law other than this article otherwise provides, the person does not owe any duty to the secured party and is not required to confirm the acknowledgment to another person.

(h) A secured party having possession of collateral does not relinquish possession by delivering the collateral to a person other than the debtor or a lessee of the collateral from the debtor in the ordinary course of the debtor's business if the person was instructed before the delivery or is instructed contemporaneously with the delivery:

(1) to hold possession of the collateral for the secured party's benefit; or

(2) to redeliver the collateral to the secured party.

(i) A secured party does not relinquish possession, even if a delivery under subsection (h) violates the rights of a debtor. A person to which collateral is delivered under subsection (h) does not owe any duty to the secured party and is not required to confirm the delivery to another person unless the person otherwise agrees or law other than this article otherwise provides.

§ 9–314.   Perfection by Control.

(a) A security interest in investment property, deposit accounts, letter-of-credit rights, or electronic chattel paper may be perfected by control of the collateral under Section 9–104, 9–105, 9–106, or 9–107.

(b) A security interest in deposit accounts, electronic chattel paper, or letter-of-credit rights is perfected by control under Section 9–104, 9–105, or 9–107 when the secured party obtains control and remains perfected by control only while the secured party retains control.

(c) A security interest in investment property is perfected by control under Section 9–106 from the time the secured party obtains control and remains perfected by control until:

(1) the secured party does not have control; and

(2) one of the following occurs:

(A) if the collateral is a certificated security, the debtor has or acquires possession of the security certificate;

(B) if the collateral is an uncertificated security, the issuer has registered or registers the debtor as the registered owner; or

(C) if the collateral is a security entitlement, the debtor is or becomes the entitlement holder.

§ 9–315.   Secured Party's Rights on Disposition of Collateral and in Proceeds.

(a) Except as otherwise provided in this article and in Section 2–403(2):

(1) a security interest or agricultural lien continues in collateral notwithstanding sale, lease, license, exchange, or other disposition thereof unless the secured party authorized the disposition free of the security interest or agricultural lien; and

(2) a security interest attaches to any identifiable proceeds of collateral.

(b) Proceeds that are commingled with other property are identifiable proceeds:

(1) if the proceeds are goods, to the extent provided by Section 9–336; and

(2) if the proceeds are not goods, to the extent that the secured party identifies the proceeds by a method of tracing, including

application of equitable principles, that is permitted under law other than this article with respect to commingled property of the type involved.

(c) A security interest in proceeds is a perfected security interest if the security interest in the original collateral was perfected.

(d) A perfected security interest in proceeds becomes unperfected on the 21st day after the security interest attaches to the proceeds unless:

(1) the following conditions are satisfied:

(A) a filed financing statement covers the original collateral;

(B) the proceeds are collateral in which a security interest may be perfected by filing in the office in which the financing statement has been filed; and

(C) the proceeds are not acquired with cash proceeds;

(2) the proceeds are identifiable cash proceeds; or

(3) the security interest in the proceeds is perfected other than under subsection (c) when the security interest attaches to the proceeds or within 20 days thereafter.

(e) If a filed financing statement covers the original collateral, a security interest in proceeds which remains perfected under subsection (d)(1) becomes unperfected at the later of:

(1) when the effectiveness of the filed financing statement lapses under Section 9–515 or is terminated under Section 9–513; or

(2) the 21st day after the security interest attaches to the proceeds.

§ 9–316.   Continued Perfection of Security Interest Following Change in Governing Law.

(a) A security interest perfected pursuant to the law of the jurisdiction designated in Section 9–301(1) or 9–305(c) remains perfected until the earliest of:

(1) the time perfection would have ceased under the law of that jurisdiction;

(2) the expiration of four months after a change of the debtor's location to another jurisdiction; or

(3) the expiration of one year after a transfer of collateral to a person that thereby becomes a debtor and is located in another jurisdiction.

(b) If a security interest described in subsection (a) becomes perfected under the law of the other jurisdiction before the earliest time or event described in that subsection, it remains perfected thereafter. If the security interest does not become perfected under the law of the other jurisdiction before the

earliest time or event, it becomes unperfected and is deemed never to have been perfected as against a purchaser of the collateral for value.

(c) A possessory security interest in collateral, other than goods covered by a certificate of title and as-extracted collateral consisting of goods, remains continuously perfected if:

(1) the collateral is located in one jurisdiction and subject to a security interest perfected under the law of that jurisdiction;

(2) thereafter the collateral is brought into another jurisdiction; and

(3) upon entry into the other jurisdiction, the security interest is perfected under the law of the other jurisdiction.

(d) Except as otherwise provided in subsection (e), a security interest in goods covered by a certificate of title which is perfected by any method under the law of another jurisdiction when the goods become covered by a certificate of title from this State remains perfected until the security interest would have become unperfected under the law of the other jurisdiction had the goods not become so covered.

(e) A security interest described in subsection (d) becomes unperfected as against a purchaser of the goods for value and is deemed never to have been perfected as against a purchaser of the goods for value if the applicable requirements for perfection under Section 9–311(b) or 9–313 are not satisfied before the earlier of:

(1) the time the security interest would have become unperfected under the law of the other jurisdiction had the goods not become covered by a certificate of title from this State; or

(2) the expiration of four months after the goods had become so covered.

(f) A security interest in deposit accounts, letter-of-credit rights, or investment property which is perfected under the law of the bank's jurisdiction, the issuer's jurisdiction, a nominated person's jurisdiction, the securities intermediary's jurisdiction, or the commodity intermediary's jurisdiction, as applicable, remains perfected until the earlier of:

(1) the time the security interest would have become unperfected under the law of that jurisdiction; or

(2) the expiration of four months after a change of the applicable jurisdiction to another jurisdiction.

(g) If a security interest described in subsection (f) becomes perfected under the law of the other jurisdiction before the earlier of the time or the end of the period described in that subsection, it remains perfected thereafter. If the security interest does not become perfected under the law of the other jurisdiction before the earlier of that time or the end of that period, it becomes unperfected and is deemed never to have been perfected as against a purchaser of the collateral for value.

[Subpart 3. Priority]

§ 9–317.   Interests That Take Priority over or Take Free of Security Interest or Agricultural Lien.

(a) A security interest or agricultural lien is subordinate to the rights of:

(1) a person entitled to priority under Section 9–322; and

(2) except as otherwise provided in subsection (e), a person that becomes a lien creditor before the earlier of the time:

(A) the security interest or agricultural lien is perfected; or

(B) one of the conditions specified in Section 9–203(b)(3) is met and a financing statement covering the collateral is filed.

(b) Except as otherwise provided in subsection (e), a buyer, other than a secured party, of tangible chattel paper, documents, goods, instruments, or a security certificate takes free of a security interest or agricultural lien if the buyer gives value and receives delivery of the collateral without knowledge of the security interest or agricultural lien and before it is perfected.

(c) Except as otherwise provided in subsection (e), a lessee of goods takes free of a security interest or agricultural lien if the lessee gives value and receives delivery of the collateral without knowledge of the security interest or agricultural lien and before it is perfected.

(d) A licensee of a general intangible or a buyer, other than a secured party, of accounts, electronic chattel paper, general intangibles, or investment property other than a certificated security takes free of a security interest if the licensee or buyer gives value without knowledge of the security interest and before it is perfected.

(e) Except as otherwise provided in Sections 9–320 and 9–321, if a person files a financing statement with respect to a purchase-money security interest before or within 20 days after the debtor receives delivery of the collateral, the security interest takes priority over the rights of a buyer, lessee, or lien creditor which arise between the time the security interest attaches and the time of filing.

As amended in 2000.

§ 9–318.   No Interest Retained in Right to Payment That Is Sold; Rights and Title of Seller of Account or Chattel Paper with Respect to Creditors and Purchasers.

(a) A debtor that has sold an account, chattel paper, payment intangible, or promissory note does not retain a legal or equitable interest in the collateral sold.

(b) For purposes of determining the rights of creditors of, and purchasers for value of an account or chattel paper from, a debtor that has sold an account or chattel paper, while the buyer's security interest is unperfected, the debtor is deemed to have rights and title to the account or chattel paper identical to those the debtor sold.

§ 9–319.   Rights and Title of Consignee with Respect to Creditors and Purchasers.

(a) Except as otherwise provided in subsection (b), for purposes of determining the rights of creditors of, and purchasers for value of goods from, a consignee, while the goods are in the possession of the consignee, the consignee is deemed to have rights and title to the goods identical to those the consignor had or had power to transfer.

(b) For purposes of determining the rights of a creditor of a consignee, law other than this article determines the rights and title of a consignee while goods are in the consignee's possession if, under this part, a perfected security interest held by the consignor would have priority over the rights of the creditor.

§ 9–320.   Buyer of Goods.

(a) Except as otherwise provided in subsection (e), a buyer in ordinary course of business, other than a person buying farm products from a person engaged in farming operations, takes free of a security interest created by the buyer's seller, even if the security interest is perfected and the buyer knows of its existence.

(b) Except as otherwise provided in subsection (e), a buyer of goods from a person who used or bought the goods for use primarily for personal, family, or household purposes takes free of a security interest, even if perfected, if the buyer buys:

(1) without knowledge of the security interest;

(2) for value;

(3) primarily for the buyer's personal, family, or household purposes; and

(4) before the filing of a financing statement covering the goods.

(c) To the extent that it affects the priority of a security interest over a buyer of goods under subsection (b), the period of effectiveness of a filing made in the jurisdiction in which the seller is located is governed by Section 9–316(a) and (b).

(d) A buyer in ordinary course of business buying oil, gas, or other minerals at the wellhead or minehead or after extraction takes free of an interest arising out of an encumbrance.

(e) Subsections (a) and (b) do not affect a security interest in goods in the possession of the secured party under Section 9–313.

§ 9–321.   Licensee of General Intangible and Lessee of Goods in Ordinary Course of Business.

(a) In this section, "licensee in ordinary course of business" means a person that becomes a licensee of a general intangible in good faith, without knowledge that the license violates the rights of another person in the general intangible, and in the ordinary course from a person in the business of licensing general intangibles of that kind. A person becomes a licensee in the ordinary course if the license to the person comports with the usual or customary practices in the kind of business in which the licensor is engaged or with the licensor's own usual or customary practices.

(b) A licensee in ordinary course of business takes its rights under a nonexclusive license free of a security interest in the general intangible created by the licensor, even if the security interest is perfected and the licensee knows of its existence.

(c) A lessee in ordinary course of business takes its leasehold interest free of a security interest in the goods created by the lessor, even if the security interest is perfected and the lessee knows of its existence.

§ 9–322.   Priorities among Conflicting Security Interests in and Agricultural Liens on Same Collateral.

(a) Except as otherwise provided in this section, priority among conflicting security interests and agricultural liens in the same collateral is determined according to the following rules:

(1) Conflicting perfected security interests and agricultural liens rank according to priority in time of filing or perfection. Priority dates from the earlier of the time a filing covering the collateral is first made or the security interest or agricultural lien is first perfected, if there is no period thereafter when there is neither filing nor perfection.

(2) A perfected security interest or agricultural lien has priority over a conflicting unperfected security interest or agricultural lien.

(3) The first security interest or agricultural lien to attach or become effective has priority if conflicting security interests and agricultural liens are unperfected.

(b) For the purposes of subsection (a)(1):

(1) the time of filing or perfection as to a security interest in collateral is also the time of filing or perfection as to a security interest in proceeds; and

(2) the time of filing or perfection as to a security interest in collateral supported by a supporting obligation is also the time of filing or perfection as to a security interest in the supporting obligation.

(c) Except as otherwise provided in subsection (f), a security interest in collateral which qualifies for priority over a conflicting security interest under Section 9–327, 9–328, 9–329, 9–330, or 9–331 also has priority over a conflicting security interest in:

(1) any supporting obligation for the collateral; and

(2) proceeds of the collateral if:

(A) the security interest in proceeds is perfected;

(B) the proceeds are cash proceeds or of the same type as the collateral; and

(C) in the case of proceeds that are proceeds of proceeds, all intervening proceeds are cash proceeds, proceeds of the same type as the collateral, or an account relating to the collateral.

(d) Subject to subsection (e) and except as otherwise provided in subsection (f), if a security interest in chattel paper, deposit accounts, negotiable documents, instruments, investment property, or letter-of-credit rights is perfected by a method other than filing, conflicting perfected security interests in proceeds of the collateral rank according to priority in time of filing.

(e) Subsection (d) applies only if the proceeds of the collateral are not cash proceeds, chattel paper, negotiable documents, instruments, investment property, or letter-of-credit rights.

(f) Subsections (a) through (e) are subject to:

(1) subsection (g) and the other provisions of this part;

(2) Section 4–210 with respect to a security interest of a collecting bank;

(3) Section 5–118 with respect to a security interest of an issuer or nominated person; and

(4) Section 9–110 with respect to a security interest arising under Article 2 or 2A.

(g) A perfected agricultural lien on collateral has priority over a conflicting security interest in or agricultural lien on the same collateral if the statute creating the agricultural lien so provides.

§ 9–323.   Future Advances.

(a) Except as otherwise provided in subsection (c), for purposes of determining the priority of a perfected security interest under Section 9–322(a)(1), perfection of the security interest dates from the time an advance is made to the extent that the security interest secures an advance that:

(1) is made while the security interest is perfected only:

(A) under Section 9–309 when it attaches; or

(B) temporarily under Section 9–312(e), (f), or (g); and

(2) is not made pursuant to a commitment entered into before or while the security interest is perfected by a method other than under Section 9–309 or 9–312(e), (f), or (g).

(b) Except as otherwise provided in subsection (c), a security interest is subordinate to the rights of a person that becomes a lien creditor to the extent that the security interest secures an advance made more than 45 days after the person becomes a lien creditor unless the advance is made:

(1) without knowledge of the lien; or

(2) pursuant to a commitment entered into without knowledge of the lien.

(c) Subsections (a) and (b) do not apply to a security interest held by a secured party that is a buyer of accounts, chattel paper, payment intangibles, or promissory notes or a consignor.

(d) Except as otherwise provided in subsection (e), a buyer of goods other than a buyer in ordinary course of business takes free of a security interest to the extent that it secures advances made after the earlier of:

(1) the time the secured party acquires knowledge of the buyer's purchase; or

(2) 45 days after the purchase.

(e) Subsection (d) does not apply if the advance is made pursuant to a commitment entered into without knowledge of the buyer's purchase and before the expiration of the 45-day period.

(f) Except as otherwise provided in subsection (g), a lessee of goods, other than a lessee in ordinary course of business, takes the leasehold interest free of a security interest to the extent that it secures advances made after the earlier of:

(1) the time the secured party acquires knowledge of the lease; or

(2) 45 days after the lease contract becomes enforceable.

(g) Subsection (f) does not apply if the advance is made pursuant to a commitment entered into without knowledge of the lease and before the expiration of the 45-day period.

As amended in 1999.

§ 9–324.   Priority of Purchase-Money Security Interests.

(a) Except as otherwise provided in subsection (g), a perfected purchase-money security interest in goods other than inventory or livestock has priority over a conflicting security interest in the same goods, and, except as otherwise provided in Section 9–327, a perfected security interest in its identifiable proceeds also has priority, if the purchase-money security interest is perfected when the debtor receives possession of the collateral or within 20 days thereafter.

(b) Subject to subsection (c) and except as otherwise provided in subsection (g), a perfected purchase-money security interest in inventory has priority over a conflicting security interest in the same inventory, has priority over a conflicting security interest in chattel paper or an instrument constituting proceeds of the inventory and in proceeds of the chattel paper, if so provided in Section 9–330, and, except as otherwise provided in Section 9–327, also has priority in

identifiable cash proceeds of the inventory to the extent the identifiable cash proceeds are received on or before the delivery of the inventory to a buyer, if:

(1) the purchase-money security interest is perfected when the debtor receives possession of the inventory;

(2) the purchase-money secured party sends an authenticated notification to the holder of the conflicting security interest;

(3) the holder of the conflicting security interest receives the notification within five years before the debtor receives possession of the inventory; and

(4) the notification states that the person sending the notification has or expects to acquire a purchase-money security interest in inventory of the debtor and describes the inventory.

(c) Subsections (b)(2) through (4) apply only if the holder of the conflicting security interest had filed a financing statement covering the same types of inventory:

(1) if the purchase-money security interest is perfected by filing, before the date of the filing; or

(2) if the purchase-money security interest is temporarily perfected without filing or possession under Section 9–312(f), before the beginning of the 20-day period thereunder.

(d) Subject to subsection (e) and except as otherwise provided in subsection (g), a perfected purchase-money security interest in livestock that are farm products has priority over a conflicting security interest in the same livestock, and, except as otherwise provided in Section 9–327, a perfected security interest in their identifiable proceeds and identifiable products in their unmanufactured states also has priority, if:

(1) the purchase-money security interest is perfected when the debtor receives possession of the livestock;

(2) the purchase-money secured party sends an authenticated notification to the holder of the conflicting security interest;

(3) the holder of the conflicting security interest receives the notification within six months before the debtor receives possession of the livestock; and

(4) the notification states that the person sending the notification has or expects to acquire a purchase-money security interest in livestock of the debtor and describes the livestock.

(e) Subsections (d)(2) through (4) apply only if the holder of the conflicting security interest had filed a financing statement covering the same types of livestock:

(1) if the purchase-money security interest is perfected by filing, before the date of the filing; or

(2) if the purchase-money security interest is temporarily perfected without filing or possession under Section 9–312(f), before the beginning of the 20-day period thereunder.

(f) Except as otherwise provided in subsection (g), a perfected purchase-money security interest in software has priority over a conflicting security interest in the same collateral, and, except as otherwise provided in Section 9–327, a perfected security interest in its identifiable proceeds also has priority, to the extent that the purchase-money security interest in the goods in which the software was acquired for use has priority in the goods and proceeds of the goods under this section.

(g) If more than one security interest qualifies for priority in the same collateral under subsection (a), (b), (d), or (f):

(1) a security interest securing an obligation incurred as all or part of the price of the collateral has priority over a security interest securing an obligation incurred for value given to enable the debtor to acquire rights in or the use of collateral; and

(2) in all other cases, Section 9–322(a) applies to the qualifying security interests.

§ 9–325.   Priority of Security Interests in Transferred Collateral.

(a) Except as otherwise provided in subsection (b), a security interest created by a debtor is subordinate to a security interest in the same collateral created by another person if:

(1) the debtor acquired the collateral subject to the security interest created by the other person;

(2) the security interest created by the other person was perfected when the debtor acquired the collateral; and

(3) there is no period thereafter when the security interest is unperfected.

(b) Subsection (a) subordinates a security interest only if the security interest:

(1) otherwise would have priority solely under Section 9–322(a) or 9–324; or

(2) arose solely under Section 2–711(3) or 2A–508(5).

§ 9–326.   Priority of Security Interests Created by New Debtor.

(a) Subject to subsection (b), a security interest created by a new debtor which is perfected by a filed financing statement that is effective solely under Section 9–508 in collateral in which a new debtor has or acquires rights is subordinate to a security interest in the same collateral which is perfected other than by a filed financing statement that is effective solely under Section 9–508.

(b) The other provisions of this part determine the priority among conflicting security interests in the same collateral perfected by filed financing statements that are effective solely under Section 9–508. However, if the security agreements to which a new debtor became bound as debtor were not entered into by the same original debtor, the conflicting security interests rank according to priority in time of the new debtor's having become bound.

§ 9–327.   Priority of Security Interests in Deposit Account.

The following rules govern priority among conflicting security interests in the same deposit account:

(1) A security interest held by a secured party having control of the deposit account under Section 9–104 has priority over a conflicting security interest held by a secured party that does not have control.

(2) Except as otherwise provided in paragraphs (3) and (4), security interests perfected by control under Section 9–314 rank according to priority in time of obtaining control.

(3) Except as otherwise provided in paragraph (4), a security interest held by the bank with which the deposit account is maintained has priority over a conflicting security interest held by another secured party.

(4) A security interest perfected by control under Section 9–104 (a)(3) has priority over a security interest held by the bank with which the deposit account is maintained.

§ 9–328.   Priority of Security Interests in Investment Property.

The following rules govern priority among conflicting security interests in the same investment property:

(1) A security interest held by a secured party having control of investment property under Section 9–106 has priority over a security interest held by a secured party that does not have control of the investment property.

(2) Except as otherwise provided in paragraphs (3) and (4), conflicting security interests held by secured parties each of which has control under Section 9–106 rank according to priority in time of:

(A) if the collateral is a security, obtaining control;

(B) if the collateral is a security entitlement carried in a securities account and:

(i) if the secured party obtained control under Section 8–106(d)(1), the secured party's becoming the person for which the securities account is maintained;

(ii) if the secured party obtained control under Section 8–106(d)(2), the securities intermediary's agreement to comply with the secured party's entitlement orders with respect to security entitlements carried or to be carried in the securities account; or

(iii) if the secured party obtained control through another person under Section 8–106(d)(3), the time on which priority would be based under this paragraph if the other person were the secured party; or

(C) if the collateral is a commodity contract carried with a commodity intermediary, the satisfaction of the requirement for control specified in Section 9–106(b)(2) with respect to commodity contracts carried or to be carried with the commodity intermediary.

(3) A security interest held by a securities intermediary in a security entitlement or a securities account maintained with the securities intermediary has priority over a conflicting security interest held by another secured party.

(4) A security interest held by a commodity intermediary in a commodity contract or a commodity account maintained with the commodity intermediary has priority over a conflicting security interest held by another secured party.

(5) A security interest in a certificated security in registered form which is perfected by taking delivery under Section 9–313(a) and not by control under Section 9–314 has priority over a conflicting security interest perfected by a method other than control.

(6) Conflicting security interests created by a broker, securities intermediary, or commodity intermediary which are perfected without control under Section 9–106 rank equally.

(7) In all other cases, priority among conflicting security interests in investment property is governed by Sections 9–322 and 9–323.

§ 9–329.   Priority of Security Interests in Letter-of-Credit Right.

The following rules govern priority among conflicting security interests in the same letter-of-credit right:

(1) A security interest held by a secured party having control of the letter-of-credit right under Section 9–107 has priority to the extent of its control over a conflicting security interest held by a secured party that does not have control.

(2) Security interests perfected by control under Section 9–314 rank according to priority in time of obtaining control.

§ 9–330.   Priority of Purchaser of Chattel Paper or Instrument.

(a) A purchaser of chattel paper has priority over a security interest in the chattel paper which is claimed merely as proceeds of inventory subject to a security interest if:

(1) in good faith and in the ordinary course of the purchaser's business, the purchaser gives new value and takes possession of the chattel paper or obtains control of the chattel paper under Section 9–105; and

(2) the chattel paper does not indicate that it has been assigned to an identified assignee other than the purchaser.

(b) A purchaser of chattel paper has priority over a security interest in the chattel paper which is claimed other than merely as proceeds of inventory subject to a security interest if the purchaser gives new value and takes possession of the chattel paper or obtains control of the chattel paper under Section 9–105 in good faith, in the ordinary course of the purchaser's business, and without knowledge that the purchase violates the rights of the secured party.

(c) Except as otherwise provided in Section 9–327, a purchaser having priority in chattel paper under subsection (a) or (b) also has priority in proceeds of the chattel paper to the extent that:

(1) Section 9–322 provides for priority in the proceeds; or

(2) the proceeds consist of the specific goods covered by the chattel paper or cash proceeds of the specific goods, even if the purchaser's security interest in the proceeds is unperfected.

(d) Except as otherwise provided in Section 9–331(a), a purchaser of an instrument has priority over a security interest in the instrument perfected by a method other than possession if the purchaser gives value and takes possession of the instrument in good faith and without knowledge that the purchase violates the rights of the secured party.

(e) For purposes of subsections (a) and (b), the holder of a purchase-money security interest in inventory gives new value for chattel paper constituting proceeds of the inventory.

(f) For purposes of subsections (b) and (d), if chattel paper or an instrument indicates that it has been assigned to an identified secured party other than the purchaser, a purchaser of the chattel paper or instrument has knowledge that the purchase violates the rights of the secured party.

§ 9–331.   Priority of Rights of Purchasers of Instruments, Documents, and Securities under Other Articles; Priority of Interests in Financial Assets and Security Entitlements under Article 8.

(a) This article does not limit the rights of a holder in due course of a negotiable instrument, a holder to which a negotiable document of title has been duly negotiated, or a protected purchaser of a security. These holders or purchasers take priority over an earlier security interest, even if perfected, to the extent provided in Articles 3, 7, and 8.

(b) This article does not limit the rights of or impose liability on a person to the extent that the person is protected against the assertion of a claim under Article 8.

(c) Filing under this article does not constitute notice of a claim or defense to the holders, or purchasers, or persons described in subsections (a) and (b).

§ 9–332.   Transfer of Money; Transfer of Funds from Deposit Account.

(a) A transferee of money takes the money free of a security interest unless the transferee acts in collusion with the debtor in violating the rights of the secured party.

(b) A transferee of funds from a deposit account takes the funds free of a security interest in the deposit account unless the transferee acts in collusion with the debtor in violating the rights of the secured party.

§ 9–333.   Priority of Certain Liens Arising by Operation of Law.

(a) In this section, "possessory lien" means an interest, other than a security interest or an agricultural lien:

(1) which secures payment or performance of an obligation for services or materials furnished with respect to goods by a person in the ordinary course of the person's business;

(2) which is created by statute or rule of law in favor of the person; and

(3) whose effectiveness depends on the person's possession of the goods.

(b) A possessory lien on goods has priority over a security interest in the goods unless the lien is created by a statute that expressly provides otherwise.

§ 9–334.   Priority of Security Interests in Fixtures and Crops.

(a) A security interest under this article may be created in goods that are fixtures or may continue in goods that become fixtures. A security interest does not exist under this article in ordinary building materials incorporated into an improvement on land.

(b) This article does not prevent creation of an encumbrance upon fixtures under real property law.

(c) In cases not governed by subsections (d) through (h), a security interest in fixtures is subordinate to a conflicting interest of an encumbrancer or owner of the related real property other than the debtor.

(d) Except as otherwise provided in subsection (h), a perfected security interest in fixtures has priority over a conflicting interest of an encumbrancer or owner of the real property if the debtor has an interest of record in or is in possession of the real property and:

(1) the security interest is a purchase-money security interest;

(2) the interest of the encumbrancer or owner arises before the goods become fixtures; and

(3) the security interest is perfected by a fixture filing before the goods become fixtures or within 20 days thereafter.

(e) A perfected security interest in fixtures has priority over a conflicting interest of an encumbrancer or owner of the real property if:

(1) the debtor has an interest of record in the real property or is in possession of the real property and the security interest:

(A) is perfected by a fixture filing before the interest of the encumbrancer or owner is of record; and

(B) has priority over any conflicting interest of a predecessor in title of the encumbrancer or owner;

(2) before the goods become fixtures, the security interest is perfected by any method permitted by this article and the fixtures are readily removable:

(A) factory or office machines;

(B) equipment that is not primarily used or leased for use in the operation of the real property; or

(C) replacements of domestic appliances that are consumer goods;

(3) the conflicting interest is a lien on the real property obtained by legal or equitable proceedings after the security interest was perfected by any method permitted by this article; or

(4) the security interest is:

(A) created in a manufactured home in a manufactured-home transaction; and

(B) perfected pursuant to a statute described in Section 9–311(a)(2).

(f) A security interest in fixtures, whether or not perfected, has priority over a conflicting interest of an encumbrancer or owner of the real property if:

(1) the encumbrancer or owner has, in an authenticated record, consented to the security interest or disclaimed an interest in the goods as fixtures; or

(2) the debtor has a right to remove the goods as against the encumbrancer or owner.

(g) The priority of the security interest under paragraph (f)(2) continues for a reasonable time if the debtor's right to remove the goods as against the encumbrancer or owner terminates.

(h) A mortgage is a construction mortgage to the extent that it secures an obligation incurred for the construction of an improvement on land, including the acquisition cost of the land, if a recorded record of the mortgage so indicates. Except as otherwise provided in subsections (e) and (f), a security interest in fixtures is subordinate to a construction mortgage if a record of the mortgage is recorded before the goods become fixtures and the goods become fixtures before the completion of the construction. A mortgage has this priority to the same extent as a construction mortgage to the extent that it is given to refinance a construction mortgage.

(i) A perfected security interest in crops growing on real property has priority over a conflicting interest of an encumbrancer or owner of the real property if the debtor has an interest of record in or is in possession of the real property.

(j) Subsection (i) prevails over any inconsistent provisions of the following statutes:

[List here any statutes containing provisions inconsistent with subsection (i).]

Legislative Note: States that amend statutes to remove provisions inconsistent with subsection (i) need not enact subsection (j).

§ 9–335. Accessions.

(a) A security interest may be created in an accession and continues in collateral that becomes an accession.

(b) If a security interest is perfected when the collateral becomes an accession, the security interest remains perfected in the collateral.

(c) Except as otherwise provided in subsection (d), the other provisions of this part determine the priority of a security interest in an accession.

(d) A security interest in an accession is subordinate to a security interest in the whole which is perfected by compliance with the requirements of a certificate-of-title statute under Section 9–311(b).

(e) After default, subject to Part 6, a secured party may remove an accession from other goods if the security interest in the accession has priority over the claims of every person having an interest in the whole.

(f) A secured party that removes an accession from other goods under subsection (e) shall promptly reimburse any holder of a security interest or other lien on, or owner of, the whole or of the other goods, other than the debtor, for the cost of repair of any physical injury to the whole or the other goods. The secured party need not reimburse the holder or owner for any diminution in value of the whole or the other goods caused by the absence of the accession removed or by any necessity for replacing it. A person entitled to reimbursement may refuse permission to remove until the secured party gives adequate assurance for the performance of the obligation to reimburse.

§ 9–336. Commingled Goods.

(a) In this section, "commingled goods" means goods that are physically united with other goods in such a manner that their identity is lost in a product or mass.

(b) A security interest does not exist in commingled goods as such. However, a security interest may attach to a product or mass that results when goods become commingled goods.

(c) If collateral becomes commingled goods, a security interest attaches to the product or mass.

(d) If a security interest in collateral is perfected before the collateral becomes commingled goods, the security interest that attaches to the product or mass under subsection (c) is perfected.

(e) Except as otherwise provided in subsection (f), the other provisions of this part determine the priority of a security interest that attaches to the product or mass under subsection (c).

(f) If more than one security interest attaches to the product or mass under subsection (c), the following rules determine priority:

(1) A security interest that is perfected under subsection (d) has priority over a security interest that is unperfected at the time the collateral becomes commingled goods.

(2) If more than one security interest is perfected under subsection (d), the security interests rank equally in proportion to the value of the collateral at the time it became commingled goods.

§ 9–337. Priority of Security Interests in Goods Covered by Certificate of Title.

If, while a security interest in goods is perfected by any method under the law of another jurisdiction, this State issues a certificate of title that does not show that the goods are subject to the security interest or contain a statement that they may be subject to security interests not shown on the certificate:

(1) a buyer of the goods, other than a person in the business of selling goods of that kind, takes free of the security interest if the buyer gives value and receives delivery of the goods after issuance of the certificate and without knowledge of the security interest; and

(2) the security interest is subordinate to a conflicting security interest in the goods that attaches, and is perfected under Section 9–311(b), after issuance of the certificate and without the conflicting secured party's knowledge of the security interest.

§ 9–338. Priority of Security Interest or Agricultural Lien Perfected by Filed Financing Statement Providing Certain Incorrect Information.

If a security interest or agricultural lien is perfected by a filed financing statement providing information described in Section 9–516(b)(5) which is incorrect at the time the financing statement is filed:

(1) the security interest or agricultural lien is subordinate to a conflicting perfected security interest in the collateral to the extent that the holder of the conflicting security interest gives value in reasonable reliance upon the incorrect information; and

(2) a purchaser, other than a secured party, of the collateral takes free of the security interest or agricultural lien to the extent that, in reasonable reliance upon the incorrect information, the purchaser gives value and, in the case of chattel paper, documents, goods, instruments, or a security certificate, receives delivery of the collateral.

§ 9–339. Priority Subject to Subordination.

This article does not preclude subordination by agreement by a person entitled to priority.

[Subpart 4. Rights of Bank]

§ 9–340.   Effectiveness of Right of Recoupment or Set-Off against Deposit Account.

(a) Except as otherwise provided in subsection (c), a bank with which a deposit account is maintained may exercise any right of recoupment or set-off against a secured party that holds a security interest in the deposit account.

(b) Except as otherwise provided in subsection (c), the application of this article to a security interest in a deposit account does not affect a right of recoupment or set-off of the secured party as to a deposit account maintained with the secured party.

(c) The exercise by a bank of a set-off against a deposit account is ineffective against a secured party that holds a security interest in the deposit account which is perfected by control under Section 9–104(a)(3), if the set-off is based on a claim against the debtor.

§ 9–341.   Bank's Rights and Duties with Respect to Deposit Account.

Except as otherwise provided in Section 9–340(c), and unless the bank otherwise agrees in an authenticated record, a bank's rights and duties with respect to a deposit account maintained with the bank are not terminated, suspended, or modified by:

(1) the creation, attachment, or perfection of a security interest in the deposit account;

(2) the bank's knowledge of the security interest; or

(3) the bank's receipt of instructions from the secured party.

§ 9–342.   Bank's Right to Refuse to Enter into or Disclose Existence of Control Agreement.

This article does not require a bank to enter into an agreement of the kind described in Section 9–104(a)(2), even if its customer so requests or directs. A bank that has entered into such an agreement is not required to confirm the existence of the agreement to another person unless requested to do so by its customer.

PART 4   Rights of Third Parties

§ 9–401.   Alienability of Debtor's Rights.

(a) Except as otherwise provided in subsection (b) and Sections 9–406, 9–407, 9–408, and 9–409, whether a debtor's rights in collateral may be voluntarily or involuntarily transferred is governed by law other than this article.

(b) An agreement between the debtor and secured party which prohibits a transfer of the debtor's rights in collateral or makes the transfer a default does not prevent the transfer from taking effect.

§ 9–402.   Secured Party Not Obligated on Contract of Debtor or in Tort.

The existence of a security interest, agricultural lien, or authority given to a debtor to dispose of or use collateral, without more, does not subject a secured party to liability in contract or tort for the debtor's acts or omissions.

§ 9–403.   Agreement Not to Assert Defenses against Assignee.

(a) In this section, "value" has the meaning provided in Section 3–303(a).

(b) Except as otherwise provided in this section, an agreement between an account debtor and an assignor not to assert against an assignee any claim or defense that the account debtor may have against the assignor is enforceable by an assignee that takes an assignment:

(1) for value;

(2) in good faith;

(3) without notice of a claim of a property or possessory right to the property assigned; and

(4) without notice of a defense or claim in recoupment of the type that may be asserted against a person entitled to enforce a negotiable instrument under Section 3–305(a).

(c) Subsection (b) does not apply to defenses of a type that may be asserted against a holder in due course of a negotiable instrument under Section 3–305(b).

(d) In a consumer transaction, if a record evidences the account debtor's obligation, law other than this article requires that the record include a statement to the effect that the rights of an assignee are subject to claims or defenses that the account debtor could assert against the original obligee, and the record does not include such a statement:

(1) the record has the same effect as if the record included such a statement; and

(2) the account debtor may assert against an assignee those claims and defenses that would have been available if the record included such a statement.

(e) This section is subject to law other than this article which establishes a different rule for an account debtor who is an individual and who incurred the obligation primarily for personal, family, or household purposes.

(f) Except as otherwise provided in subsection (d), this section does not displace law other than this article which gives effect to an agreement by an account debtor not to assert a claim or defense against an assignee.

§ 9–404.   Rights Acquired by Assignee; Claims and Defenses against Assignee.

(a) Unless an account debtor has made an enforceable agreement not to assert defenses or claims, and subject to subsections (b) through (e), the rights of an assignee are subject to:

(1) all terms of the agreement between the account debtor and assignor and any defense or claim in recoupment arising from the transaction that gave rise to the contract; and

(2) any other defense or claim of the account debtor against the assignor which accrues before the account debtor receives a notification of the assignment authenticated by the assignor or the assignee.

(b) Subject to subsection (c) and except as otherwise provided in subsection (d), the claim of an account debtor against an assignor may be asserted against an assignee under subsection (a) only to reduce the amount the account debtor owes.

(c) This section is subject to law other than this article which establishes a different rule for an account debtor who is an individual and who incurred the obligation primarily for personal, family, or household purposes.

(d) In a consumer transaction, if a record evidences the account debtor's obligation, law other than this article requires that the record include a statement to the effect that the account debtor's recovery against an assignee with respect to claims and defenses against the assignor may not exceed amounts paid by the account debtor under the record, and the record does not include such a statement, the extent to which a claim of an account debtor against the assignor may be asserted against an assignee is determined as if the record included such a statement.

(e) This section does not apply to an assignment of a health-care-insurance receivable.

§ 9–405.   Modification of Assigned Contract.

(a) A modification of or substitution for an assigned contract is effective against an assignee if made in good faith. The assignee acquires corresponding rights under the modified or substituted contract. The assignment may provide that the modification or substitution is a breach of contract by the assignor. This subsection is subject to subsections (b) through (d).

(b) Subsection (a) applies to the extent that:

(1) the right to payment or a part thereof under an assigned contract has not been fully earned by performance; or

(2) the right to payment or a part thereof has been fully earned by performance and the account debtor has not received notification of the assignment under Section 9–406(a).

(c) This section is subject to law other than this article which establishes a different rule for an account debtor who is

an individual and who incurred the obligation primarily for personal, family, or household purposes.

(d) This section does not apply to an assignment of a health-care-insurance receivable.

§ 9–406.   Discharge of Account Debtor; Notification of Assignment; Identification and Proof of Assignment; Restrictions on Assignment of Accounts, Chattel Paper, Payment Intangibles, and Promissory Notes Ineffective.

(a) Subject to subsections (b) through (i), an account debtor on an account, chattel paper, or a payment intangible may discharge its obligation by paying the assignor until, but not after, the account debtor receives a notification, authenticated by the assignor or the assignee, that the amount due or to become due has been assigned and that payment is to be made to the assignee. After receipt of the notification, the account debtor may discharge its obligation by paying the assignee and may not discharge the obligation by paying the assignor.

(b) Subject to subsection (h), notification is ineffective under subsection (a):

(1) if it does not reasonably identify the rights assigned;

(2) to the extent that an agreement between an account debtor and a seller of a payment intangible limits the account debtor's duty to pay a person other than the seller and the limitation is effective under law other than this article; or

(3) at the option of an account debtor, if the notification notifies the account debtor to make less than the full amount of any installment or other periodic payment to the assignee, even if:

(A) only a portion of the account, chattel paper, or payment intangible has been assigned to that assignee;

(B) a portion has been assigned to another assignee; or

(C) the account debtor knows that the assignment to that assignee is limited.

(c) Subject to subsection (h), if requested by the account debtor, an assignee shall seasonably furnish reasonable proof that the assignment has been made. Unless the assignee complies, the account debtor may discharge its obligation by paying the assignor, even if the account debtor has received a notification under subsection (a).

(d) Except as otherwise provided in subsection (e) and Sections 2A–303 and 9–407, and subject to subsection (h), a term in an agreement between an account debtor and an assignor or in a promissory note is ineffective to the extent that it:

(1) prohibits, restricts, or requires the consent of the account debtor or person obligated on the promissory note to the assignment or transfer of, or the creation, attachment, perfection,

or enforcement of a security interest in, the account, chattel paper, payment intangible, or promissory note; or

(2) provides that the assignment or transfer or the creation, attachment, perfection, or enforcement of the security interest may give rise to a default, breach, right of recoupment, claim, defense, termination, right of termination, or remedy under the account, chattel paper, payment intangible, or promissory note.

(e) Subsection (d) does not apply to the sale of a payment intangible or promissory note.

(f) Except as otherwise provided in Sections 2A–303 and 9–407 and subject to subsections (h) and (i), a rule of law, statute, or regulation that prohibits, restricts, or requires the consent of a government, governmental body or official, or account debtor to the assignment or transfer of, or creation of a security interest in, an account or chattel paper is ineffective to the extent that the rule of law, statute, or regulation:

(1) prohibits, restricts, or requires the consent of the government, governmental body or official, or account debtor to the assignment or transfer of, or the creation, attachment, perfection, or enforcement of a security interest in the account or chattel paper; or

(2) provides that the assignment or transfer or the creation, attachment, perfection, or enforcement of the security interest may give rise to a default, breach, right of recoupment, claim, defense, termination, right of termination, or remedy under the account or chattel paper.

(g) Subject to subsection (h), an account debtor may not waive or vary its option under subsection (b)(3).

(h) This section is subject to law other than this article which establishes a different rule for an account debtor who is an individual and who incurred the obligation primarily for personal, family, or household purposes.

(i) This section does not apply to an assignment of a health-care-insurance receivable.

(j) This section prevails over any inconsistent provisions of the following statutes, rules, and regulations:

[List here any statutes, rules, and regulations containing provisions inconsistent with this section.]

Legislative Note: States that amend statutes, rules, and regulations to remove provisions inconsistent with this section need not enact subsection (j).

As amended in 1999 and 2000.

§ 9–407.   Restrictions on Creation or Enforcement of Security Interest in Leasehold Interest or in Lessor's Residual Interest.

(a) Except as otherwise provided in subsection (b), a term in a lease agreement is ineffective to the extent that it:

(1) prohibits, restricts, or requires the consent of a party to the lease to the assignment or transfer of, or the creation,

attachment, perfection, or enforcement of a security interest in an interest of a party under the lease contract or in the lessor's residual interest in the goods; or

(2) provides that the assignment or transfer or the creation, attachment, perfection, or enforcement of the security interest may give rise to a default, breach, right of recoupment, claim, defense, termination, right of termination, or remedy under the lease.

(b) Except as otherwise provided in Section 2A–303(7), a term described in subsection (a)(2) is effective to the extent that there is:

(1) a transfer by the lessee of the lessee's right of possession or use of the goods in violation of the term; or

(2) a delegation of a material performance of either party to the lease contract in violation of the term.

(c) The creation, attachment, perfection, or enforcement of a security interest in the lessor's interest under the lease contract or the lessor's residual interest in the goods is not a transfer that materially impairs the lessee's prospect of obtaining return performance or materially changes the duty of or materially increases the burden or risk imposed on the lessee within the purview of Section 2A–303(4) unless, and then only to the extent that, enforcement actually results in a delegation of material performance of the lessor.

As amended in 1999.

§ 9–408.   Restrictions on Assignment of Promissory Notes, Health-Care-Insurance Receivables, and Certain General Intangibles Ineffective.

(a) Except as otherwise provided in subsection (b), a term in a promissory note or in an agreement between an account debtor and a debtor which relates to a health-care-insurance receivable or a general intangible, including a contract, permit, license, or franchise, and which term prohibits, restricts, or requires the consent of the person obligated on the promissory note or the account debtor to, the assignment or transfer of, or creation, attachment, or perfection of a security interest in, the promissory note, health-care-insurance receivable, or general intangible, is ineffective to the extent that the term:

(1) would impair the creation, attachment, or perfection of a security interest; or

(2) provides that the assignment or transfer or the creation, attachment, or perfection of the security interest may give rise to a default, breach, right of recoupment, claim, defense, termination, right of termination, or remedy under the promissory note, health-care-insurance receivable, or general intangible.

(b) Subsection (a) applies to a security interest in a payment intangible or promissory note only if the security interest arises out of a sale of the payment intangible or promissory note.

(c) A rule of law, statute, or regulation that prohibits, restricts, or requires the consent of a government, governmental body or official, person obligated on a promissory note, or account debtor to the assignment or transfer of, or creation of a security interest in, a promissory note, health-care-insurance receivable, or general intangible, including a contract, permit, license, or franchise between an account debtor and a debtor, is ineffective to the extent that the rule of law, statute, or regulation:

(1) would impair the creation, attachment, or perfection of a security interest; or

(2) provides that the assignment or transfer or the creation, attachment, or perfection of the security interest may give rise to a default, breach, right of recoupment, claim, defense, termination, right of termination, or remedy under the promissory note, health-care-insurance receivable, or general intangible.

(d) To the extent that a term in a promissory note or in an agreement between an account debtor and a debtor which relates to a health-care-insurance receivable or general intangible or a rule of law, statute, or regulation described in subsection (c) would be effective under law other than this article but is ineffective under subsection (a) or (c), the creation, attachment, or perfection of a security interest in the promissory note, health-care-insurance receivable, or general intangible:

(1) is not enforceable against the person obligated on the promissory note or the account debtor;

(2) does not impose a duty or obligation on the person obligated on the promissory note or the account debtor;

(3) does not require the person obligated on the promissory note or the account debtor to recognize the security interest, pay or render performance to the secured party, or accept payment or performance from the secured party;

(4) does not entitle the secured party to use or assign the debtor's rights under the promissory note, health-care-insurance receivable, or general intangible, including any related information or materials furnished to the debtor in the transaction giving rise to the promissory note, health-care-insurance receivable, or general intangible;

(5) does not entitle the secured party to use, assign, possess, or have access to any trade secrets or confidential information of the person obligated on the promissory note or the account debtor; and

(6) does not entitle the secured party to enforce the security interest in the promissory note, health-care-insurance receivable, or general intangible.

(e) This section prevails over any inconsistent provisions of the following statutes, rules, and regulations:

[List here any statutes, rules, and regulations containing provisions inconsistent with this section.]

Legislative Note: States that amend statutes, rules, and regulations to remove provisions inconsistent with this section need not enact subsection (e).

As amended in 1999.

§ 9–409.   Restrictions on Assignment of Letter-of-Credit Rights Ineffective.

(a) A term in a letter of credit or a rule of law, statute, regulation, custom, or practice applicable to the letter of credit which prohibits, restricts, or requires the consent of an applicant, issuer, or nominated person to a beneficiary's assignment of or creation of a security interest in a letter-of-credit right is ineffective to the extent that the term or rule of law, statute, regulation, custom, or practice:

(1) would impair the creation, attachment, or perfection of a security interest in the letter-of-credit right; or

(2) provides that the assignment or the creation, attachment, or perfection of the security interest may give rise to a default, breach, right of recoupment, claim, defense, termination, right of termination, or remedy under the letter-of-credit right.

(b) To the extent that a term in a letter of credit is ineffective under subsection (a) but would be effective under law other than this article or a custom or practice applicable to the letter of credit, to the transfer of a right to draw or otherwise demand performance under the letter of credit, or to the assignment of a right to proceeds of the letter of credit, the creation, attachment, or perfection of a security interest in the letter-of-credit right:

(1) is not enforceable against the applicant, issuer, nominated person, or transferee beneficiary;

(2) imposes no duties or obligations on the applicant, issuer, nominated person, or transferee beneficiary; and

(3) does not require the applicant, issuer, nominated person, or transferee beneficiary to recognize the security interest, pay or render performance to the secured party, or accept payment or other performance from the secured party.

As amended in 1999.

PART 5   Filing

[Subpart 1. Filing Office; Contents and Effectiveness of Financing Statement]

§ 9–501.   Filing Office.

(a) Except as otherwise provided in subsection (b), if the local law of this State governs perfection of a security interest or agricultural lien, the office in which to file a financing statement to perfect the security interest or agricultural lien is:

(1) the office designated for the filing or recording of a record of a mortgage on the related real property, if:

(A) the collateral is as-extracted collateral or timber to be cut; or

(B) the financing statement is filed as a fixture filing and the collateral is goods that are or are to become fixtures; or

(2) the office of [ ] [or any office duly authorized by [ ]], in all other cases, including a case in which the collateral is goods that are or are to become fixtures and the financing statement is not filed as a fixture filing.

(b) The office in which to file a financing statement to perfect a security interest in collateral, including fixtures, of a transmitting utility is the office of [ ]. The financing statement also constitutes a fixture filing as to the collateral indicated in the financing statement which is or is to become fixtures.

Legislative Note: The State should designate the filing office where the brackets appear. The filing office may be that of a governmental official (e.g., the Secretary of State) or a private party that maintains the State's filing system.

§ 9–502.   Contents of Financing Statement; Record of Mortgage as Financing Statement; Time of Filing Financing Statement.

(a) Subject to subsection (b), a financing statement is sufficient only if it:

(1) provides the name of the debtor;

(2) provides the name of the secured party or a representative of the secured party; and

(3) indicates the collateral covered by the financing statement.

(b) Except as otherwise provided in Section 9–501(b), to be sufficient, a financing statement that covers as-extracted collateral or timber to be cut, or which is filed as a fixture filing and covers goods that are or are to become fixtures, must satisfy subsection (a) and also:

(1) indicate that it covers this type of collateral;

(2) indicate that it is to be filed [for record] in the real property records;

(3) provide a description of the real property to which the collateral is related [sufficient to give constructive notice of a mortgage under the law of this State if the description were contained in a record of the mortgage of the real property]; and

(4) if the debtor does not have an interest of record in the real property, provide the name of a record owner.

(c) A record of a mortgage is effective, from the date of recording, as a financing statement filed as a fixture filing or as a financing statement covering as-extracted collateral or timber to be cut only if:

(1) the record indicates the goods or accounts that it covers;

(2) the goods are or are to become fixtures related to the real property described in the record or the collateral is related to the real property described in the record and is as-extracted collateral or timber to be cut;

(3) the record satisfies the requirements for a financing statement in this section other than an indication that it is to be filed in the real property records; and

(4) the record is [duly] recorded.

(d) A financing statement may be filed before a security agreement is made or a security interest otherwise attaches.

Legislative Note: Language in brackets is optional. Where the State has any special recording system for real property other than the usual grantor-grantee index (as, for instance, a tract system or a title registration or Torrens system) local adaptations of subsection (b) and Section 9–519(d) and (e) may be necessary. See, e.g., Mass. Gen. Laws Chapter 106, Section 9–410.

§ 9–503.   Name of Debtor and Secured Party.

(a) A financing statement sufficiently provides the name of the debtor:

(1) if the debtor is a registered organization, only if the financing statement provides the name of the debtor indicated on the public record of the debtor's jurisdiction of organization which shows the debtor to have been organized;

(2) if the debtor is a decedent's estate, only if the financing statement provides the name of the decedent and indicates that the debtor is an estate;

(3) if the debtor is a trust or a trustee acting with respect to property held in trust, only if the financing statement:

(A) provides the name specified for the trust in its organic documents or, if no name is specified, provides the name of the settlor and additional information sufficient to distinguish the debtor from other trusts having one or more of the same settlors; and

(B) indicates, in the debtor's name or otherwise, that the debtor is a trust or is a trustee acting with respect to property held in trust; and

(4) in other cases:

(A) if the debtor has a name, only if it provides the individual or organizational name of the debtor; and

(B) if the debtor does not have a name, only if it provides the names of the partners, members, associates, or other persons comprising the debtor.

(b) A financing statement that provides the name of the debtor in accordance with subsection (a) is not rendered ineffective by the absence of:

(1) a trade name or other name of the debtor; or

(2) unless required under subsection (a)(4)(B), names of partners, members, associates, or other persons comprising the debtor.

(c) A financing statement that provides only the debtor's trade name does not sufficiently provide the name of the debtor.

(d) Failure to indicate the representative capacity of a secured party or representative of a secured party does not affect the sufficiency of a financing statement.

(e) A financing statement may provide the name of more than one debtor and the name of more than one secured party.

§ 9–504.   Indication of Collateral.

A financing statement sufficiently indicates the collateral that it covers if the financing statement provides:

(1) a description of the collateral pursuant to Section 9–108; or

(2) an indication that the financing statement covers all assets or all personal property.

As amended in 1999.

§ 9–505.   Filing and Compliance with Other Statutes and Treaties for Consignments, Leases, Other Bailments, and Other Transactions.

(a) A consignor, lessor, or other bailor of goods, a licensor, or a buyer of a payment intangible or promissory note may file a financing statement, or may comply with a statute or treaty described in Section 9–311(a), using the terms "consignor", "consignee", "lessor", "lessee", "bailor", "bailee", "licensor", "licensee", "owner", "registered owner", "buyer", "seller", or words of similar import, instead of the terms "secured party" and "debtor".

(b) This part applies to the filing of a financing statement under subsection (a) and, as appropriate, to compliance that is equivalent to filing a financing statement under Section 9–311 (b), but the filing or compliance is not of itself a factor in determining whether the collateral secures an obligation. If it is determined for another reason that the collateral secures an obligation, a security interest held by the consignor, lessor, bailor, licensor, owner, or buyer which attaches to the collateral is perfected by the filing or compliance.

§ 9–506.   Effect of Errors or Omissions.

(a) A financing statement substantially satisfying the requirements of this part is effective, even if it has minor errors or omissions, unless the errors or omissions make the financing statement seriously misleading.

(b) Except as otherwise provided in subsection (c), a financing statement that fails sufficiently to provide the name of the debtor in accordance with Section 9–503(a) is seriously misleading.

(c) If a search of the records of the filing office under the debtor's correct name, using the filing office's standard search logic, if any, would disclose a financing statement that fails sufficiently to provide the name of the debtor in accordance with Section 9–503(a), the name provided does not make the financing statement seriously misleading.

(d) For purposes of Section 9–508(b), the "debtor's correct name" in subsection (c) means the correct name of the new debtor.

§ 9–507.   Effect of Certain Events on Effectiveness of Financing Statement.

(a) A filed financing statement remains effective with respect to collateral that is sold, exchanged, leased, licensed, or otherwise disposed of and in which a security interest or agricultural lien continues, even if the secured party knows of or consents to the disposition.

(b) Except as otherwise provided in subsection (c) and Section 9–508, a financing statement is not rendered ineffective if, after the financing statement is filed, the information provided in the financing statement becomes seriously misleading under Section 9–506.

(c) If a debtor so changes its name that a filed financing statement becomes seriously misleading under Section 9–506:

(1) the financing statement is effective to perfect a security interest in collateral acquired by the debtor before, or within four months after, the change; and

(2) the financing statement is not effective to perfect a security interest in collateral acquired by the debtor more than four months after the change, unless an amendment to the financing statement which renders the financing statement not seriously misleading is filed within four months after the change.

§ 9–508.   Effectiveness of Financing Statement If New Debtor Becomes Bound by Security Agreement.

(a) Except as otherwise provided in this section, a filed financing statement naming an original debtor is effective to perfect a security interest in collateral in which a new debtor has or acquires rights to the extent that the financing statement would have been effective had the original debtor acquired rights in the collateral.

(b) If the difference between the name of the original debtor and that of the new debtor causes a filed financing statement that is effective under subsection (a) to be seriously misleading under Section 9–506:

(1) the financing statement is effective to perfect a security interest in collateral acquired by the new debtor before, and within four months after, the new debtor becomes bound under Section 9B–203(d); and

(2) the financing statement is not effective to perfect a security interest in collateral acquired by the new debtor more than four months after the new debtor becomes bound under Section 9–203(d) unless an initial financing statement providing the name of the new debtor is filed before the expiration of that time.

(c) This section does not apply to collateral as to which a filed financing statement remains effective against the new debtor under Section 9–507(a).

§ 9–509.   Persons Entitled to File a Record.

(a) A person may file an initial financing statement, amendment that adds collateral covered by a financing statement, or amendment that adds a debtor to a financing statement only if:

(1) the debtor authorizes the filing in an authenticated record or pursuant to subsection (b) or (c); or

(2) the person holds an agricultural lien that has become effective at the time of filing and the financing statement covers only collateral in which the person holds an agricultural lien.

(b) By authenticating or becoming bound as debtor by a security agreement, a debtor or new debtor authorizes the filing of an initial financing statement, and an amendment, covering:

(1) the collateral described in the security agreement; and

(2) property that becomes collateral under Section 9–315(a)(2), whether or not the security agreement expressly covers proceeds.

(c) By acquiring collateral in which a security interest or agricultural lien continues under Section 9–315(a)(1), a debtor authorizes the filing of an initial financing statement, and an amendment, covering the collateral and property that becomes collateral under Section 9–315(a)(2).

(d) A person may file an amendment other than an amendment that adds collateral covered by a financing statement or an amendment that adds a debtor to a financing statement only if:

(1) the secured party of record authorizes the filing; or

(2) the amendment is a termination statement for a financing statement as to which the secured party of record has failed to file or send a termination statement as required by Section 9–513(a) or (c), the debtor authorizes the filing, and the termination statement indicates that the debtor authorized it to be filed.

(e) If there is more than one secured party of record for a financing statement, each secured party of record may authorize the filing of an amendment under subsection (d).

As amended in 2000.

§ 9–510.   Effectiveness of Filed Record.

(a) A filed record is effective only to the extent that it was filed by a person that may file it under Section 9–509.

(b) A record authorized by one secured party of record does not affect the financing statement with respect to another secured party of record.

(c) A continuation statement that is not filed within the six-month period prescribed by Section 9–515(d) is ineffective.

§ 9–511.   Secured Party of Record.

(a) A secured party of record with respect to a financing statement is a person whose name is provided as the name of the secured party or a representative of the secured party in an initial financing statement that has been filed. If an initial financing statement is filed under Section 9–514(a), the assignee named in the initial financing statement is the secured party of record with respect to the financing statement.

(b) If an amendment of a financing statement which provides the name of a person as a secured party or a representative of a secured party is filed, the person named in the amendment is a secured party of record. If an amendment is filed under Section 9–514(b), the assignee named in the amendment is a secured party of record.

(c) A person remains a secured party of record until the filing of an amendment of the financing statement which deletes the person.

§ 9–512.   Amendment of Financing Statement.
[Alternative A]

(a) Subject to Section 9–509, a person may add or delete collateral covered by, continue or terminate the effectiveness of, or, subject to subsection (e), otherwise amend the information provided in, a financing statement by filing an amendment that:

(1) identifies, by its file number, the initial financing statement to which the amendment relates; and

(2) if the amendment relates to an initial financing statement filed [or recorded] in a filing office described in Section 9–501(a)(1), provides the information specified in Section 9–502(b).

[Alternative B]

(a) Subject to Section 9–509, a person may add or delete collateral covered by, continue or terminate the effectiveness of, or, subject to subsection (e), otherwise amend the information provided in, a financing statement by filing an amendment that:

(1) identifies, by its file number, the initial financing statement to which the amendment relates; and

(2) if the amendment relates to an initial financing statement filed [or recorded] in a filing office described in Section 9–501(a)(1), provides the date [and time] that the initial financing statement was filed [or recorded] and the information specified in Section 9–502(b).

[End of Alternatives]

(b) Except as otherwise provided in Section 9–515, the filing of an amendment does not extend the period of effectiveness of the financing statement.

(c) A financing statement that is amended by an amendment that adds collateral is effective as to the added collateral only from the date of the filing of the amendment.

(d) A financing statement that is amended by an amendment that adds a debtor is effective as to the added debtor only from the date of the filing of the amendment.

(e) An amendment is ineffective to the extent it:

(1) purports to delete all debtors and fails to provide the name of a debtor to be covered by the financing statement; or

(2) purports to delete all secured parties of record and fails to provide the name of a new secured party of record.

Legislative Note: States whose real-estate filing offices require additional information in amendments and cannot search their records by both the name of the debtor and the file number should enact Alternative B to Sections 9–512(a), 9–518(b), 9–519(f), and 9–522(a).

§ 9–513.   Termination Statement.

(a) A secured party shall cause the secured party of record for a financing statement to file a termination statement for the financing statement if the financing statement covers consumer goods and:

(1) there is no obligation secured by the collateral covered by the financing statement and no commitment to make an advance, incur an obligation, or otherwise give value; or

(2) the debtor did not authorize the filing of the initial financing statement.

(b) To comply with subsection (a), a secured party shall cause the secured party of record to file the termination statement:

(1) within one month after there is no obligation secured by the collateral covered by the financing statement and no commitment to make an advance, incur an obligation, or otherwise give value; or

(2) if earlier, within 20 days after the secured party receives an authenticated demand from a debtor.

(c) In cases not governed by subsection (a), within 20 days after a secured party receives an authenticated demand from a debtor, the secured party shall cause the secured party of record for a financing statement to send to the debtor a termination statement for the financing statement or file the termination statement in the filing office if:

(1) except in the case of a financing statement covering accounts or chattel paper that has been sold or goods that are the subject of a consignment, there is no obligation secured by the collateral covered by the financing statement and no commitment to make an advance, incur an obligation, or otherwise give value;

(2) the financing statement covers accounts or chattel paper that has been sold but as to which the account debtor or other person obligated has discharged its obligation;

(3) the financing statement covers goods that were the subject of a consignment to the debtor but are not in the debtor's possession; or

(4) the debtor did not authorize the filing of the initial financing statement.

(d) Except as otherwise provided in Section 9–510, upon the filing of a termination statement with the filing office, the financing statement to which the termination statement relates ceases to be effective. Except as otherwise provided in Section 9–510, for purposes of Sections 9–519(g), 9–522(a), and 9–523 (c), the filing with the filing office of a termination statement relating to a financing statement that indicates that the debtor is a transmitting utility also causes the effectiveness of the financing statement to lapse.

As amended in 2000.

§ 9–514.   Assignment of Powers of Secured Party of Record.

(a) Except as otherwise provided in subsection (c), an initial financing statement may reflect an assignment of all of the secured party's power to authorize an amendment to the financing statement by providing the name and mailing address of the assignee as the name and address of the secured party.

(b) Except as otherwise provided in subsection (c), a secured party of record may assign of record all or part of its power to authorize an amendment to a financing statement by filing in the filing office an amendment of the financing statement which:

(1) identifies, by its file number, the initial financing statement to which it relates;

(2) provides the name of the assignor; and

(3) provides the name and mailing address of the assignee.

(c) An assignment of record of a security interest in a fixture covered by a record of a mortgage which is effective as a financing statement filed as a fixture filing under Section 9–502(c) may be made only by an assignment of record of the mortgage in the manner provided by law of this State other than [the Uniform Commercial Code].

§ 9–515.   Duration and Effectiveness of Financing Statement; Effect of Lapsed Financing Statement.

(a) Except as otherwise provided in subsections (b), (e), (f), and (g), a filed financing statement is effective for a period of five years after the date of filing.

(b) Except as otherwise provided in subsections (e), (f), and (g), an initial financing statement filed in connection with a public-finance transaction or manufactured-home transaction is effective for a period of 30 years after the date of filing if it indicates that it is filed in connection with a public-finance transaction or manufactured-home transaction.

(c) The effectiveness of a filed financing statement lapses on the expiration of the period of its effectiveness unless before the lapse a continuation statement is filed pursuant to subsection (d). Upon lapse, a financing statement ceases to be effective and any security interest or agricultural lien that was perfected by the financing statement becomes unperfected, unless the security interest is perfected otherwise. If the security interest or agricultural lien becomes unperfected upon lapse, it is deemed never to have been perfected as against a purchaser of the collateral for value.

(d) A continuation statement may be filed only within six months before the expiration of the five-year period specified in subsection (a) or the 30-year period specified in subsection (b), whichever is applicable.

(e) Except as otherwise provided in Section 9–510, upon timely filing of a continuation statement, the effectiveness of the initial financing statement continues for a period of five years commencing on the day on which the financing statement would have become ineffective in the absence of the filing. Upon the expiration of the five-year period, the financing statement lapses in the same manner as provided in subsection (c), unless, before the lapse, another continuation statement is filed pursuant to subsection (d). Succeeding continuation statements may be filed in the same manner to continue the effectiveness of the initial financing statement.

(f) If a debtor is a transmitting utility and a filed financing statement so indicates, the financing statement is effective until a termination statement is filed.

(g) A record of a mortgage that is effective as a financing statement filed as a fixture filing under Section 9–502(c) remains effective as a financing statement filed as a fixture filing until the mortgage is released or satisfied of record or its effectiveness otherwise terminates as to the real property.

§ 9–516. What Constitutes Filing; Effectiveness of Filing.

(a) Except as otherwise provided in subsection (b), communication of a record to a filing office and tender of the filing fee or acceptance of the record by the filing office constitutes filing.

(b) Filing does not occur with respect to a record that a filing office refuses to accept because:

(1) the record is not communicated by a method or medium of communication authorized by the filing office;

(2) an amount equal to or greater than the applicable filing fee is not tendered;

(3) the filing office is unable to index the record because:

(A) in the case of an initial financing statement, the record does not provide a name for the debtor;

(B) in the case of an amendment or correction statement, the record:

(i) does not identify the initial financing statement as required by Section 9–512 or 9–518, as applicable; or

(ii) identifies an initial financing statement whose effectiveness has lapsed under Section 9–515;

(C) in the case of an initial financing statement that provides the name of a debtor identified as an individual or an amendment that provides a name of a debtor identified as an individual which was not previously provided in the financing statement to which the record relates, the record does not identify the debtor's last name; or

(D) in the case of a record filed [or recorded] in the filing office described in Section 9–501(a)(1), the record does not provide a sufficient description of the real property to which it relates;

(4) in the case of an initial financing statement or an amendment that adds a secured party of record, the record does not provide a name and mailing address for the secured party of record;

(5) in the case of an initial financing statement or an amendment that provides a name of a debtor which was not previously provided in the financing statement to which the amendment relates, the record does not:

(A) provide a mailing address for the debtor;

(B) indicate whether the debtor is an individual or an organization; or

(C) if the financing statement indicates that the debtor is an organization, provide:

(i) a type of organization for the debtor;

(ii) a jurisdiction of organization for the debtor; or

(iii) an organizational identification number for the debtor or indicate that the debtor has none;

(6) in the case of an assignment reflected in an initial financing statement under Section 9–514(a) or an amendment filed under Section 9–514(b), the record does not provide a name and mailing address for the assignee; or

(7) in the case of a continuation statement, the record is not filed within the six-month period prescribed by Section 9–515(d).

(c) For purposes of subsection (b):

(1) a record does not provide information if the filing office is unable to read or decipher the information; and

(2) a record that does not indicate that it is an amendment or identify an initial financing statement to which it relates, as required by Section 9–512, 9–514, or 9–518, is an initial financing statement.

(d) A record that is communicated to the filing office with tender of the filing fee, but which the filing office refuses to accept for a reason other than one set forth in subsection (b), is effective as a filed record except as against a purchaser of the collateral which gives value in reasonable reliance upon the absence of the record from the files.

§ 9–517. Effect of Indexing Errors.

The failure of the filing office to index a record correctly does not affect the effectiveness of the filed record.

§ 9–518.   Claim Concerning Inaccurate or Wrongfully Filed Record.

(a) A person may file in the filing office a correction statement with respect to a record indexed there under the person's name if the person believes that the record is inaccurate or was wrongfully filed.

[Alternative A]

(b) A correction statement must:

(1) identify the record to which it relates by the file number assigned to the initial financing statement to which the record relates;

(2) indicate that it is a correction statement; and

(3) provide the basis for the person's belief that the record is inaccurate and indicate the manner in which the person believes the record should be amended to cure any inaccuracy or provide the basis for the person's belief that the record was wrongfully filed.

[Alternative B]

(b) A correction statement must:

(1) identify the record to which it relates by:

(A) the file number assigned to the initial financing statement to which the record relates; and

(B) if the correction statement relates to a record filed [or recorded] in a filing office described in Section 9–501(a)(1), the date [and time] that the initial financing statement was filed [or recorded] and the information specified in Section 9–502(b);

(2) indicate that it is a correction statement; and

(3) provide the basis for the person's belief that the record is inaccurate and indicate the manner in which the person believes the record should be amended to cure any inaccuracy or provide the basis for the person's belief that the record was wrongfully filed.

[End of Alternatives]

(c) The filing of a correction statement does not affect the effectiveness of an initial financing statement or other filed record. *Legislative Note: States whose real-estate filing offices require additional information in amendments and cannot search their records by both the name of the debtor and the file number should enact Alternative B to Sections 9–512(a), 9–518(b), 9–519(f), and 9–522(a).*

[Subpart 2. Duties and Operation of Filing Office]

§ 9–519.   Numbering, Maintaining, and Indexing Records; Communicating Information Provided in Records.

(a) For each record filed in a filing office, the filing office shall:

(1) assign a unique number to the filed record;

(2) create a record that bears the number assigned to the filed record and the date and time of filing;

(3) maintain the filed record for public inspection; and

(4) index the filed record in accordance with subsections (c), (d), and (e).

(b) A file number [assigned after January 1, 2002,] must include a digit that:

(1) is mathematically derived from or related to the other digits of the file number; and

(2) aids the filing office in determining whether a number communicated as the file number includes a single-digit or transpositional error.

(c) Except as otherwise provided in subsections (d) and (e), the filing office shall:

(1) index an initial financing statement according to the name of the debtor and index all filed records relating to the initial financing statement in a manner that associates with one another an initial financing statement and all filed records relating to the initial financing statement; and

(2) index a record that provides a name of a debtor which was not previously provided in the financing statement to which the record relates also according to the name that was not previously provided.

(d) If a financing statement is filed as a fixture filing or covers as-extracted collateral or timber to be cut, [it must be filed for record and] the filing office shall index it:

(1) under the names of the debtor and of each owner of record shown on the financing statement as if they were the mortgagors under a mortgage of the real property described; and

(2) to the extent that the law of this State provides for indexing of records of mortgages under the name of the mortgagee, under the name of the secured party as if the secured party were the mortgagee thereunder, or, if indexing is by description, as if the financing statement were a record of a mortgage of the real property described.

(e) If a financing statement is filed as a fixture filing or covers as-extracted collateral or timber to be cut, the filing office shall index an assignment filed under Section 9–514(a) or an amendment filed under Section 9–514(b):

(1) under the name of the assignor as grantor; and

(2) to the extent that the law of this State provides for indexing a record of the assignment of a mortgage under the name of the assignee, under the name of the assignee.

[Alternative A]

(f) The filing office shall maintain a capability:

(1) to retrieve a record by the name of the debtor and by the file number assigned to the initial financing statement to which the record relates; and

(2) to associate and retrieve with one another an initial financing statement and each filed record relating to the initial financing statement.

[Alternative B]

(f) The filing office shall maintain a capability:
(1) to retrieve a record by the name of the debtor and:

(A) if the filing office is described in Section 9–501(a)(1), by the file number assigned to the initial financing statement to which the record relates and the date [and time] that the record was filed [or recorded]; or

(B) if the filing office is described in Section 9–501(a)(2), by the file number assigned to the initial financing statement to which the record relates; and

(2) to associate and retrieve with one another an initial financing statement and each filed record relating to the initial financing statement.

[End of Alternatives]

(g) The filing office may not remove a debtor's name from the index until one year after the effectiveness of a financing statement naming the debtor lapses under Section 9–515 with respect to all secured parties of record.

(h) The filing office shall perform the acts required by subsections (a) through (e) at the time and in the manner prescribed by filing-office rule, but not later than two business days after the filing office receives the record in question.
[(i) Subsection[s] [(b)] [and] [(h)] do[es] not apply to a filing office described in Section 9–501(a)(1).]

Legislative Notes:

1. States whose filing offices currently assign file numbers that include a verification number, commonly known as a "check digit," or can implement this requirement before the effective date of this Article should omit the bracketed language in subsection (b).

2. In States in which writings will not appear in the real property records and indices unless actually recorded the bracketed language in subsection (d) should be used.

3. States whose real-estate filing offices require additional information in amendments and cannot search their records by both the name of the debtor and the file number should enact Alternative B to Sections 9–512 (a), 9–518(b), 9–519(f), and 9–522(a).

4. A State that elects not to require real-estate filing offices to comply with either or both of subsections (b) and (h) may adopt an applicable variation of subsection (i) and add "Except as otherwise provided in subsection (i)," to the appropriate subsection or subsections.

§ 9–520.   Acceptance and Refusal to Accept Record.

(a) A filing office shall refuse to accept a record for filing for a reason set forth in Section 9–516(b) and may refuse to accept a record for filing only for a reason set forth in Section 9–516(b).

(b) If a filing office refuses to accept a record for filing, it shall communicate to the person that presented the record the fact of and reason for the refusal and the date and time the record would have been filed had the filing office accepted it. The communication must be made at the time and in the

manner prescribed by filing-office rule but [, in the case of a filing office described in Section 9–501(a)(2),] in no event more than two business days after the filing office receives the record.

(c) A filed financing statement satisfying Section 9–502(a) and (b) is effective, even if the filing office is required to refuse to accept it for filing under subsection (a). However, Section 9–338 applies to a filed financing statement providing information described in Section 9–516(b)(5) which is incorrect at the time the financing statement is filed.

(d) If a record communicated to a filing office provides information that relates to more than one debtor, this part applies as to each debtor separately.

Legislative Note: A State that elects not to require real-property filing offices to comply with subsection (b) should include the bracketed language.

§ 9–521.   Uniform Form of Written Financing Statement and Amendment.

(a) A filing office that accepts written records may not refuse to accept a written initial financing statement in the following form and format except for a reason set forth in Section 9–516(b):

[NATIONAL UCC FINANCING STATEMENT (FORM UCC1)(REV. 7/29/98]]

[NATIONAL UCC FINANCING STATEMENT ADDENDUM (FORM UCC1Ad)(REV. 07/29/98]]

(b) A filing office that accepts written records may not refuse to accept a written record in the following form and format except for a reason set forth in Section 9–516(b):

[NATIONAL UCC FINANCING STATEMENT AMENDMENT (FORM UCC3)(REV. 07/29/98]]

[NATIONAL UCC FINANCING STATEMENT AMENDMENT ADDENDUM (FORM UCC3Ad)(REV. 07/29/98]]

§ 9–522.   Maintenance and Destruction of Records.

[Alternative A]

(a) The filing office shall maintain a record of the information provided in a filed financing statement for at least one year after the effectiveness of the financing statement has lapsed under Section 9–515 with respect to all secured parties of record. The record must be retrievable by using the name of the debtor and by using the file number assigned to the initial financing statement to which the record relates.

[Alternative B]

(a) The filing office shall maintain a record of the information provided in a filed financing statement for at least one year after the effectiveness of the financing statement has lapsed under Section 9–515 with respect to all secured parties of record. The record must be retrievable by using the name of the debtor and:

(1) if the record was filed [or recorded] in the filing office described in Section 9–501(a)(1), by using the file number assigned to the initial financing statement to which the record relates and the date [and time] that the record was filed [or recorded]; or

(2) if the record was filed in the filing office described in Section 9–501(a)(2), by using the file number assigned to the initial financing statement to which the record relates.

[End of Alternatives]

(b) Except to the extent that a statute governing disposition of public records provides otherwise, the filing office immediately may destroy any written record evidencing a financing statement. However, if the filing office destroys a written record, it shall maintain another record of the financing statement which complies with subsection (a).

Legislative Note: States whose real-estate filing offices require additional information in amendments and cannot search their records by both the name of the debtor and the file number should enact Alternative B to Sections 9–512(a), 9–518(b), 9–519(f), and 9–522(a).

§ 9–523.   Information from Filing Office; Sale or License of Records.

(a) If a person that files a written record requests an acknowledgment of the filing, the filing office shall send to the person an image of the record showing the number assigned to the record pursuant to Section 9–519(a)(1) and the date and time of the filing of the record. However, if the person furnishes a copy of the record to the filing office, the filing office may instead:

(1) note upon the copy the number assigned to the record pursuant to Section 9–519(a)(1) and the date and time of the filing of the record; and

(2) send the copy to the person.

(b) If a person files a record other than a written record, the filing office shall communicate to the person an acknowledgment that provides:

(1) the information in the record;

(2) the number assigned to the record pursuant to Section 9–519(a)(1); and

(3) the date and time of the filing of the record.

(c) The filing office shall communicate or otherwise make available in a record the following information to any person that requests it:

(1) whether there is on file on a date and time specified by the filing office, but not a date earlier than three business days before the filing office receives the request, any financing statement that:

(A) designates a particular debtor [or, if the request so states, designates a particular debtor at the address specified in the request];

(B) has not lapsed under Section 9–515 with respect to all secured parties of record; and

(C) if the request so states, has lapsed under Section 9–515 and a record of which is maintained by the filing office under Section 9–522(a);

(2) the date and time of filing of each financing statement; and

(3) the information provided in each financing statement.

(d) In complying with its duty under subsection (c), the filing office may communicate information in any medium. However, if requested, the filing office shall communicate information by issuing [its written certificate] [a record that can be admitted into evidence in the courts of this State without extrinsic evidence of its authenticity].

(e) The filing office shall perform the acts required by subsections (a) through (d) at the time and in the manner prescribed by filing-office rule, but not later than two business days after the filing office receives the request.

(f) At least weekly, the [insert appropriate official or governmental agency] [filing office] shall offer to sell or license to the public on a nonexclusive basis, in bulk, copies of all records filed in it under this part, in every medium from time to time available to the filing office.

Legislative Notes:

1. States whose filing office does not offer the additional service of responding to search requests limited to a particular address should omit the bracketed language in subsection (c)(1)(A).

2. A State that elects not to require real-estate filing offices to comply with either or both of subsections (e) and (f) should specify in the appropriate subsection(s) only the filing office described in Section 9–501(a)(2).

§ 9–524.   Delay by Filing Office.

Delay by the filing office beyond a time limit prescribed by this part is excused if:

(1) the delay is caused by interruption of communication or computer facilities, war, emergency conditions, failure of equipment, or other circumstances beyond control of the filing office; and

(2) the filing office exercises reasonable diligence under the circumstances.

§ 9–525.   Fees.

(a) Except as otherwise provided in subsection (e), the fee for filing and indexing a record under this part, other than an initial financing statement of the kind described in subsection (b), is [the amount specified in subsection (c), if applicable, plus]:

(1) $[X] if the record is communicated in writing and consists of one or two pages;

(2) $[2X] if the record is communicated in writing and consists of more than two pages; and

(3) $[1/2X] if the record is communicated by another medium authorized by filing-office rule.

(b) Except as otherwise provided in subsection (e), the fee for filing and indexing an initial financing statement of the following kind is [the amount specified in subsection (c), if applicable, plus]:

(1) $——— if the financing statement indicates that it is filed in connection with a public-finance transaction;

(2) $——— if the financing statement indicates that it is filed in connection with a manufactured-home transaction.

[Alternative A]

(c) The number of names required to be indexed does not affect the amount of the fee in subsections (a) and (b).

[Alternative B]

(c) Except as otherwise provided in subsection (e), if a record is communicated in writing, the fee for each name more than two required to be indexed is $———.

[End of Alternatives]

(a) The fee for responding to a request for information from the filing office, including for [issuing a certificate showing] [communicating] whether there is on file any financing statement naming a particular debtor, is:

(1) $——— if the request is communicated in writing; and

(2) $——— if the request is communicated by another medium authorized by filing-office rule.

(e) This section does not require a fee with respect to a record of a mortgage which is effective as a financing statement filed as a fixture filing or as a financing statement covering as-extracted collateral or timber to be cut under Section 9–502(c). However, the recording and satisfaction fees that otherwise would be applicable to the record of the mortgage apply.

Legislative Notes:

1. To preserve uniformity, a State that places the provisions of this section together with statutes setting fees for other services should do so without modification.

2. A State should enact subsection (c), Alternative A, and omit the bracketed language in subsections (a) and (b) unless its indexing system entails a substantial additional cost when indexing additional names.

As amended in 2000.

§ 9–526. Filing-Office Rules.

(a) The [insert appropriate governmental official or agency] shall adopt and publish rules to implement this article. The filing-office rules must be[:

(1) consistent with this article[; and

(2) adopted and published in accordance with the [insert any applicable state administrative procedure act]].

(b) To keep the filing-office rules and practices of the filing office in harmony with the rules and practices of filing offices in other jurisdictions that enact substantially this part, and to keep the technology used by the filing office compatible with the technology used by filing offices in other jurisdictions that enact substantially this part, the [insert appropriate governmental official or agency], so far as is consistent with the purposes, policies, and provisions of this article, in adopting, amending, and repealing filing-office rules, shall:

(1) consult with filing offices in other jurisdictions that enact substantially this part; and

(2) consult the most recent version of the Model Rules promulgated by the International Association of Corporate Administrators or any successor organization; and

(3) take into consideration the rules and practices of, and the technology used by, filing offices in other jurisdictions that enact substantially this part.

§ 9–527. Duty to Report.

The [insert appropriate governmental official or agency] shall report [annually on or before ———] to the [Governor and Legislature] on the operation of the filing office. The report must contain a statement of the extent to which:

(1) the filing-office rules are not in harmony with the rules of filing offices in other jurisdictions that enact substantially this part and the reasons for these variations; and

(2) the filing-office rules are not in harmony with the most recent version of the Model Rules promulgated by the International Association of Corporate Administrators, or any successor organization, and the reasons for these variations.

PART 6   Default

[Subpart 1. Default and Enforcement of Security Interest]

§ 9–601. Rights after Default; Judicial Enforcement; Consignor or Buyer of Accounts, Chattel Paper, Payment Intangibles, or Promissory Notes.

(a) After default, a secured party has the rights provided in this part and, except as otherwise provided in Section 9–602, those provided by agreement of the parties. A secured party:

(1) may reduce a claim to judgment, foreclose, or otherwise enforce the claim, security interest, or agricultural lien by any available judicial procedure; and

(2) if the collateral is documents, may proceed either as to the documents or as to the goods they cover.

(b) A secured party in possession of collateral or control of collateral under Section 9–104, 9–105, 9–106, or 9–107 has the rights and duties provided in Section 9–207.

(c) The rights under subsections (a) and (b) are cumulative and may be exercised simultaneously.

(d) Except as otherwise provided in subsection (g) and Section 9–605, after default, a debtor and an obligor have the rights provided in this part and by agreement of the parties.

(e) If a secured party has reduced its claim to judgment, the lien of any levy that may be made upon the collateral by virtue of an execution based upon the judgment relates back to the earliest of:

(1) the date of perfection of the security interest or agricultural lien in the collateral;

(2) the date of filing a financing statement covering the collateral; or

(3) any date specified in a statute under which the agricultural lien was created.

(f) A sale pursuant to an execution is a foreclosure of the security interest or agricultural lien by judicial procedure within the meaning of this section. A secured party may purchase at the sale and thereafter hold the collateral free of any other requirements of this article.

(g) Except as otherwise provided in Section 9–607(c), this part imposes no duties upon a secured party that is a consignor or is a buyer of accounts, chattel paper, payment intangibles, or promissory notes.

§ 9–602.   Waiver and Variance of Rights and Duties.

Except as otherwise provided in Section 9–624, to the extent that they give rights to a debtor or obligor and impose duties on a secured party, the debtor or obligor may not waive or vary the rules stated in the following listed sections:

(1) Section 9–207(b)(4)(C), which deals with use and operation of the collateral by the secured party;

(2) Section 9–210, which deals with requests for an accounting and requests concerning a list of collateral and statement of account;

(3) Section 9–607(c), which deals with collection and enforcement of collateral;

(4) Sections 9–608(a) and 9–615(c) to the extent that they deal with application or payment of noncash proceeds of collection, enforcement, or disposition;

(5) Sections 9–608(a) and 9–615(d) to the extent that they require accounting for or payment of surplus proceeds of collateral;

(6) Section 9–609 to the extent that it imposes upon a secured party that takes possession of collateral without judicial process the duty to do so without breach of the peace;

(7) Sections 9–610(b), 9–611, 9–613, and 9–614, which deal with disposition of collateral;

(8) Section 9–615(f), which deals with calculation of a deficiency or surplus when a disposition is made to the secured party, a person related to the secured party, or a secondary obligor;

(9) Section 9–616, which deals with explanation of the calculation of a surplus or deficiency;

(10) Sections 9–620, 9–621, and 9–622, which deal with acceptance of collateral in satisfaction of obligation;

(11) Section 9–623, which deals with redemption of collateral;

(12) Section 9–624, which deals with permissible waivers; and

(13) Sections 9–625 and 9–626, which deal with the secured party's liability for failure to comply with this article.

§ 9–603.   Agreement on Standards Concerning Rights and Duties.

(a) The parties may determine by agreement the standards measuring the fulfillment of the rights of a debtor or obligor and the duties of a secured party under a rule stated in Section 9–602 if the standards are not manifestly unreasonable.

(b) Subsection (a) does not apply to the duty under Section 9–609 to refrain from breaching the peace.

§ 9–604.   Procedure If Security Agreement Covers Real Property or Fixtures.

(a) If a security agreement covers both personal and real property, a secured party may proceed:

(1) under this part as to the personal property without prejudicing any rights with respect to the real property; or

(2) as to both the personal property and the real property in accordance with the rights with respect to the real property, in which case the other provisions of this part do not apply.

(b) Subject to subsection (c), if a security agreement covers goods that are or become fixtures, a secured party may proceed:

(1) under this part; or

(2) in accordance with the rights with respect to real property, in which case the other provisions of this part do not apply.

(c) Subject to the other provisions of this part, if a secured party holding a security interest in fixtures has priority over all owners and encumbrancers of the real property, the secured party, after default, may remove the collateral from the real property.

(d) A secured party that removes collateral shall promptly reimburse any encumbrancer or owner of the real property, other than the debtor, for the cost of repair of any physical injury caused by the removal. The secured party need not reimburse the encumbrancer or owner for any diminution in value of the real property caused by the absence of the goods removed or by any necessity of replacing them. A person entitled to reimbursement may refuse permission to remove until the secured party gives adequate assurance for the performance of the obligation to reimburse.

§ 9–605.   Unknown Debtor or Secondary Obligor.

A secured party does not owe a duty based on its status as secured party:

(1) to a person that is a debtor or obligor, unless the secured party knows:

(A) that the person is a debtor or obligor;

(B) the identity of the person; and

(C) how to communicate with the person; or

(2) to a secured party or lienholder that has filed a financing statement against a person, unless the secured party knows:

(A) that the person is a debtor; and

(B) the identity of the person.

§ 9–606.   Time of Default for Agricultural Lien.

For purposes of this part, a default occurs in connection with an agricultural lien at the time the secured party becomes entitled to enforce the lien in accordance with the statute under which it was created.

§ 9–607.   Collection and Enforcement by Secured Party.

(a) If so agreed, and in any event after default, a secured party:

(1) may notify an account debtor or other person obligated on collateral to make payment or otherwise render performance to or for the benefit of the secured party;

(2) may take any proceeds to which the secured party is entitled under Section 9–315;

(3) may enforce the obligations of an account debtor or other person obligated on collateral and exercise the rights of the debtor with respect to the obligation of the account debtor or other person obligated on collateral to make payment or otherwise render performance to the debtor, and with respect to any property that secures the obligations of the account debtor or other person obligated on the collateral;

(4) if it holds a security interest in a deposit account perfected by control under Section 9–104(a)(1), may apply the balance of the deposit account to the obligation secured by the deposit account; and

(5) if it holds a security interest in a deposit account perfected by control under Section 9–104(a)(2) or (3), may instruct the bank to pay the balance of the deposit account to or for the benefit of the secured party.

(b) If necessary to enable a secured party to exercise under subsection (a)(3) the right of a debtor to enforce a mortgage nonjudicially, the secured party may record in the office in which a record of the mortgage is recorded:

(1) a copy of the security agreement that creates or provides for a security interest in the obligation secured by the mortgage; and

(2) the secured party's sworn affidavit in recordable form stating that:

(A) a default has occurred; and

(B) the secured party is entitled to enforce the mortgage nonjudicially.

(c) A secured party shall proceed in a commercially reasonable manner if the secured party:

(1) undertakes to collect from or enforce an obligation of an account debtor or other person obligated on collateral; and

(2) is entitled to charge back uncollected collateral or otherwise to full or limited recourse against the debtor or a secondary obligor.

(d) A secured party may deduct from the collections made pursuant to subsection (c) reasonable expenses of collection and enforcement, including reasonable attorney's fees and legal expenses incurred by the secured party.

(e) This section does not determine whether an account debtor, bank, or other person obligated on collateral owes a duty to a secured party.

As amended in 2000.

§ 9–608.   Application of Proceeds of Collection or Enforcement; Liability for Deficiency and Right to Surplus.

(a) If a security interest or agricultural lien secures payment or performance of an obligation, the following rules apply:

(1) A secured party shall apply or pay over for application the cash proceeds of collection or enforcement under Section 9–607 in the following order to:

(A) the reasonable expenses of collection and enforcement and, to the extent provided for by agreement and not prohibited by law, reasonable attorney's fees and legal expenses incurred by the secured party;

(B) the satisfaction of obligations secured by the security interest or agricultural lien under which the collection or enforcement is made; and

(C) the satisfaction of obligations secured by any subordinate security interest in or other lien on the collateral subject to the security interest or agricultural lien under which the collection or enforcement is made if the secured party receives an authenticated demand for proceeds before distribution of the proceeds is completed.

(2) If requested by a secured party, a holder of a subordinate security interest or other lien shall furnish reasonable proof of the interest or lien within a reasonable time. Unless the holder complies, the secured party need not comply with the holder's demand under paragraph (1)(C).

(3) A secured party need not apply or pay over for application noncash proceeds of collection and enforcement under Section 9–607 unless the failure to do so would be commercially unreasonable. A secured party that applies or pays over for application noncash proceeds shall do so in a commercially reasonable manner.

(4) A secured party shall account to and pay a debtor for any surplus, and the obligor is liable for any deficiency.

(b) If the underlying transaction is a sale of accounts, chattel paper, payment intangibles, or promissory notes, the debtor is not entitled to any surplus, and the obligor is not liable for any deficiency.

As amended in 2000.

§ 9–609.   Secured Party's Right to Take Possession after Default.

(a) After default, a secured party:

(1) may take possession of the collateral; and

(2) without removal, may render equipment unusable and dispose of collateral on a debtor's premises under Section 9–610.

(b) A secured party may proceed under subsection (a):

(1) pursuant to judicial process; or

(2) without judicial process, if it proceeds without breach of the peace.

(c) If so agreed, and in any event after default, a secured party may require the debtor to assemble the collateral and make it available to the secured party at a place to be designated by the secured party which is reasonably convenient to both parties.

§ 9–610.   Disposition of Collateral after Default.

(a) After default, a secured party may sell, lease, license, or otherwise dispose of any or all of the collateral in its present condition or following any commercially reasonable preparation or processing.

(b) Every aspect of a disposition of collateral, including the method, manner, time, place, and other terms, must be commercially reasonable. If commercially reasonable, a secured party may dispose of collateral by public or private proceedings, by one or more contracts, as a unit or in parcels, and at any time and place and on any terms.

(c) A secured party may purchase collateral:

(1) at a public disposition; or

(2) at a private disposition only if the collateral is of a kind that is customarily sold on a recognized market or the subject of widely distributed standard price quotations.

(d) A contract for sale, lease, license, or other disposition includes the warranties relating to title, possession, quiet enjoyment, and the like which by operation of law accompany a voluntary disposition of property of the kind subject to the contract.

(e) A secured party may disclaim or modify warranties under subsection (d):

(1) in a manner that would be effective to disclaim or modify the warranties in a voluntary disposition of property of the kind subject to the contract of disposition; or

(2) by communicating to the purchaser a record evidencing the contract for disposition and including an express disclaimer or modification of the warranties.

(f) A record is sufficient to disclaim warranties under subsection (e) if it indicates "There is no warranty relating to title, possession, quiet enjoyment, or the like in this disposition" or uses words of similar import.

§ 9–611.   Notification before Disposition of Collateral.

(a) In this section, "notification date" means the earlier of the date on which:

(1) a secured party sends to the debtor and any secondary obligor an authenticated notification of disposition; or

(2) the debtor and any secondary obligor waive the right to notification.

(b) Except as otherwise provided in subsection (d), a secured party that disposes of collateral under Section 9–610 shall send to the persons specified in subsection (c) a reasonable authenticated notification of disposition.

(c) To comply with subsection (b), the secured party shall send an authenticated notification of disposition to:

(1) the debtor;

(2) any secondary obligor; and

(3) if the collateral is other than consumer goods:

(A) any other person from which the secured party has received, before the notification date, an authenticated notification of a claim of an interest in the collateral;

(B) any other secured party or lienholder that, 10 days before the notification date, held a security interest in or other lien on the collateral perfected by the filing of a financing statement that:

(i) identified the collateral;

(ii) was indexed under the debtor's name as of that date; and

(iii) was filed in the office in which to file a financing statement against the debtor covering the collateral as of that date; and

(C) any other secured party that, 10 days before the notification date, held a security interest in the collateral perfected by compliance with a statute, regulation, or treaty described in Section 9–311(a).

(d) Subsection (b) does not apply if the collateral is perishable or threatens to decline speedily in value or is of a type customarily sold on a recognized market.

(e) A secured party complies with the requirement for notification prescribed by subsection (c)(3)(B) if:

(1) not later than 20 days or earlier than 30 days before the notification date, the secured party requests, in a commercially reasonable manner, information concerning financing statements indexed under the debtor's name in the office indicated in subsection (c)(3)(B); and

(2) before the notification date, the secured party:

(A) did not receive a response to the request for information; or

(B) received a response to the request for information and sent an authenticated notification of disposition to each secured party or other lienholder named in that response whose financing statement covered the collateral.

§ 9–612.   Timeliness of Notification before Disposition of Collateral.

(a) Except as otherwise provided in subsection (b), whether a notification is sent within a reasonable time is a question of fact.

(b) In a transaction other than a consumer transaction, a notification of disposition sent after default and 10 days or more before the earliest time of disposition set forth in the notification is sent within a reasonable time before the disposition.

§ 9–613.   Contents and Form of Notification before Disposition of Collateral: General.

Except in a consumer-goods transaction, the following rules apply:

(1) The contents of a notification of disposition are sufficient if the notification:

(A) describes the debtor and the secured party;

(B) describes the collateral that is the subject of the intended disposition;

(C) states the method of intended disposition;

(D) states that the debtor is entitled to an accounting of the unpaid indebtedness and states the charge, if any, for an accounting; and

(E) states the time and place of a public disposition or the time after which any other disposition is to be made.

(2) Whether the contents of a notification that lacks any of the information specified in paragraph (1) are nevertheless sufficient is a question of fact.

(3) The contents of a notification providing substantially the information specified in paragraph (1) are sufficient, even if the notification includes:

(A) information not specified by that paragraph; or

(b) minor errors that are not seriously misleading.

(4) A particular phrasing of the notification is not required.

(5) The following form of notification and the form appearing in Section 9–614(3), when completed, each provides sufficient information:

NOTIFICATION OF DISPOSITION OF COLLATERAL

To: [*Name of debtor, obligor, or other person to which the notification is sent*]

From: [*Name, address, and telephone number of secured party*]

Name of Debtor(s): [*Include only if debtor(s) are not an addressee*]

[*For a public disposition:*]

We will sell [or lease or license, *as applicable*] the [*describe collateral*] [to the highest qualified bidder] in public as follows:

Day and Date: _____

Time: _____

Place: _____

[*For a private disposition:*]

We will sell [or lease or license, *as applicable*] the [*describe collateral*] privately sometime after [*day and date*].

You are entitled to an accounting of the unpaid indebted ness secured by the property that we intend to sell [or lease or license a*s applicable*] [for a charge of $_____]. You may request an accounting by calling us at [*telephone number*].

[End of Form]

As amended in 2000.

§ 9–614.   Contents and Form of Notification before Disposition of Collateral: Consumer-Goods Transaction.

In a consumer-goods transaction, the following rules apply:

(1) A notification of disposition must provide the following information:

(A) the information specified in Section 9–613(1);

(B) a description of any liability for a deficiency of the person to which the notification is sent;

(C) a telephone number from which the amount that must be paid to the secured party to redeem the collateral under Section 9–623 is available; and

(D) a telephone number or mailing address from which additional information concerning the disposition and the obligation secured is available.

(2) A particular phrasing of the notification is not required.

(3) The following form of notification, when completed, provides sufficient information:

[*Name and address of secured party*]

[*Date*]

NOTICE OF OUR PLAN TO SELL PROPERTY

[*Name and address of any obligor who is also a debtor*]

Subject: [*Identification of Transaction*]

We have your [*describe collateral*], because you broke promises in our agreement.

[*For a public disposition:*]

We will sell [*describe collateral*] at public sale. A sale could include a lease or license. The sale will be held as follows:

Date: _____

Time: _____

Place: _____

You may attend the sale and bring bidders if you want.

[*For a private disposition:*]

We will sell [*describe collateral*] at private sale sometime after

[*date*]. A sale could include a lease or license.

The money that we get from the sale (after paying our costs) will reduce the amount you owe. If we get less money than you owe, you [*will or will not, as applicable*] still owe us the difference. If we get more money than you owe, you will get the extra money, unless we must pay it to someone else.

You can get the property back at any time before we sell it by paying us the full amount you owe (not just the past due payments), including our expenses. To learn the exact amount you must pay, call us at [*telephone number*].

If you want us to explain to you in writing how we have figured the amount that you owe us, you may call us at [*telephone number*] [or write us at [*secured party's address*]] and request a written explanation. [We will charge you $_____ for the explanation if we sent you another written explanation of the amount you owe us within the last six months.]

If you need more information about the sale call us at [*telephone number*] [or write us at [*secured party's address*]].

We are sending this notice to the following other people who have an interest in [*describe collateral*] or who owe money under your agreement:

[*Names of all other debtors and obligors, if any*]

[End of Form]

(4) A notification in the form of paragraph (3) is sufficient, even if additional information appears at the end of the form.

(5) A notification in the form of paragraph (3) is sufficient, even if it includes errors in information not required by paragraph (1), unless the error is misleading with respect to rights arising under this article.

(6) If a notification under this section is not in the form of paragraph (3), law other than this article determines the effect of including information not required by paragraph (1).

§ 9–615. Application of Proceeds of Disposition; Liability for Deficiency and Right to Surplus.

(a) A secured party shall apply or pay over for application the cash proceeds of disposition under Section 9–610 in the following order to:

(1) the reasonable expenses of retaking, holding, preparing for disposition, processing, and disposing, and, to the extent provided for by agreement and not prohibited by law, reasonable attorney's fees and legal expenses incurred by the secured party;

(2) the satisfaction of obligations secured by the security interest or agricultural lien under which the disposition is made;

(3) the satisfaction of obligations secured by any subordinate security interest in or other subordinate lien on the collateral if:

(A) the secured party receives from the holder of the subordinate security interest or other lien an authenticated demand for proceeds before distribution of the proceeds is completed; and

(B) in a case in which a consignor has an interest in the collateral, the subordinate security interest or other lien is senior to the interest of the consignor; and

(4) a secured party that is a consignor of the collateral if the secured party receives from the consignor an authenticated demand for proceeds before distribution of the proceeds is completed.

(b) If requested by a secured party, a holder of a subordinate security interest or other lien shall furnish reasonable proof of the interest or lien within a reasonable time. Unless the holder does so, the secured party need not comply with the holder's demand under subsection (a)(3).

(c) A secured party need not apply or pay over for application noncash proceeds of disposition under Section 9–610 unless the failure to do so would be commercially unreasonable. A secured party that applies or pays over for application noncash proceeds shall do so in a commercially reasonable manner.

(d) If the security interest under which a disposition is made secures payment or performance of an obligation, after making the payments and applications required by subsection (a) and permitted by subsection (c):

(1) unless subsection (a)(4) requires the secured party to apply or pay over cash proceeds to a consignor, the secured party shall account to and pay a debtor for any surplus; and

(2) the obligor is liable for any deficiency.

(e) If the underlying transaction is a sale of accounts, chattel paper, payment intangibles, or promissory notes:

(1) the debtor is not entitled to any surplus; and

(2) the obligor is not liable for any deficiency.

(f) The surplus or deficiency following a disposition is calculated based on the amount of proceeds that would have been realized in a disposition complying with this part to a transferee other than the secured party, a person related to the secured party, or a secondary obligor if:

(1) the transferee in the disposition is the secured party, a person related to the secured party, or a secondary obligor; and

(2) the amount of proceeds of the disposition is significantly below the range of proceeds that a complying disposition to a person other than the secured party, a person related to the secured party, or a secondary obligor would have brought.

(g) A secured party that receives cash proceeds of a disposition in good faith and without knowledge that the receipt violates the rights of the holder of a security interest or other lien that is not subordinate to the security interest or agricultural lien under which the disposition is made:

(1) takes the cash proceeds free of the security interest or other lien;

(2) is not obligated to apply the proceeds of the disposition to the satisfaction of obligations secured by the security interest or other lien; and

(3) is not obligated to account to or pay the holder of the security interest or other lien for any surplus.

As amended in 2000.

§ 9–616. Explanation of Calculation of Surplus or Deficiency.

(a) In this section:

(1) "Explanation" means a writing that:

(A) states the amount of the surplus or deficiency;

(B) provides an explanation in accordance with subsection (c) of how the secured party calculated the surplus or deficiency;

(C) states, if applicable, that future debits, credits, charges, including additional credit service charges or interest, rebates, and expenses may affect the amount of the surplus or deficiency; and

(D) provides a telephone number or mailing address from which additional information concerning the transaction is available.

(2) "Request" means a record:

(A) authenticated by a debtor or consumer obligor;

(B) requesting that the recipient provide an explanation; and

(C) sent after disposition of the collateral under Section 9–610.

(b) In a consumer-goods transaction in which the debtor is entitled to a surplus or a consumer obligor is liable for a deficiency under Section 9–615, the secured party shall:

(1) send an explanation to the debtor or consumer obligor, as applicable, after the disposition and:

(A) before or when the secured party accounts to the debtor and pays any surplus or first makes written demand on the consumer obligor after the disposition for payment of the deficiency; and

(B) within 14 days after receipt of a request; or

(2) in the case of a consumer obligor who is liable for a deficiency, within 14 days after receipt of a request, send to the consumer obligor a record waiving the secured party's right to a deficiency.

(c) To comply with subsection (a)(1)(B), a writing must provide the following information in the following order:

(1) the aggregate amount of obligations secured by the security interest under which the disposition was made, and, if the amount reflects a rebate of unearned interest or credit service charge, an indication of that fact, calculated as of a specified date:

(A) if the secured party takes or receives possession of the collateral after default, not more than 35 days before the secured party takes or receives possession; or

(B) if the secured party takes or receives possession of the collateral before default or does not take possession of the collateral, not more than 35 days before the disposition;

(2) the amount of proceeds of the disposition;

(3) the aggregate amount of the obligations after deducting the amount of proceeds;

(4) the amount, in the aggregate or by type, and types of expenses, including expenses of retaking, holding, preparing for disposition, processing, and disposing of the collateral, and attorney's fees secured by the collateral which are known to the secured party and relate to the current disposition;

(5) the amount, in the aggregate or by type, and types of credits, including rebates of interest or credit service charges, to which the obligor is known to be entitled and which are not reflected in the amount in paragraph (1); and

(6) the amount of the surplus or deficiency.

(d) A particular phrasing of the explanation is not required. An explanation complying substantially with the requirements of subsection (a) is sufficient, even if it includes minor errors that are not seriously misleading.

(e) A debtor or consumer obligor is entitled without charge to one response to a request under this section during any six-month period in which the secured party did not send to the debtor or consumer obligor an explanation pursuant to subsection (b)(1). The secured party may require payment of a charge not exceeding $25 for each additional response.

§ 9–617. Rights of Transferee of Collateral.

(a) A secured party's disposition of collateral after default:

(1) transfers to a transferee for value all of the debtor's rights in the collateral;

(2) discharges the security interest under which the disposition is made; and

(3) discharges any subordinate security interest or other subordinate lien [other than liens created under [cite acts or statutes providing for liens, if any, that are not to be discharged]].

(b) A transferee that acts in good faith takes free of the rights and interests described in subsection (a), even if the secured party fails to comply with this article or the requirements of any judicial proceeding.

(c) If a transferee does not take free of the rights and interests described in subsection (a), the transferee takes the collateral subject to:

(1) the debtor's rights in the collateral;

(2) the security interest or agricultural lien under which the disposition is made; and

(3) any other security interest or other lien.

§ 9–618.   Rights and Duties of Certain Secondary Obligors.

(a) A secondary obligor acquires the rights and becomes obligated to perform the duties of the secured party after the secondary obligor:

(1) receives an assignment of a secured obligation from the secured party;

(2) receives a transfer of collateral from the secured party and agrees to accept the rights and assume the duties of the secured party; or

(3) is subrogated to the rights of a secured party with respect to collateral.

(b) An assignment, transfer, or subrogation described in subsection (a):

(1) is not a disposition of collateral under Section 9–610; and

(2) relieves the secured party of further duties under this article.

§ 9–619.   Transfer of Record or Legal Title.

(a) In this section, "transfer statement" means a record authenticated by a secured party stating:

(1) that the debtor has defaulted in connection with an obligation secured by specified collateral;

(2) that the secured party has exercised its post-default remedies with respect to the collateral;

(3) that, by reason of the exercise, a transferee has acquired the rights of the debtor in the collateral; and

(4) the name and mailing address of the secured party, debtor, and transferee.

(b) A transfer statement entitles the transferee to the transfer of record of all rights of the debtor in the collateral specified in the statement in any official filing, recording, registration, or certificate-of-title system covering the collateral. If a transfer statement is presented with the applicable fee and request form to the official or office responsible for maintaining the system, the official or office shall:

(1) accept the transfer statement;

(2) promptly amend its records to reflect the transfer; and

(3) if applicable, issue a new appropriate certificate of title in the name of the transferee.

(c) A transfer of the record or legal title to collateral to a secured party under subsection (b) or otherwise is not of itself a disposition of collateral under this article and does not of itself relieve the secured party of its duties under this article.

§ 9–620.   Acceptance of Collateral in Full or Partial Satisfaction of Obligation; Compulsory Disposition of Collateral.

(a) Except as otherwise provided in subsection (g), a secured party may accept collateral in full or partial satisfaction of the obligation it secures only if:

(1) the debtor consents to the acceptance under subsection (c);

(2) the secured party does not receive, within the time set forth in subsection (d), a notification of objection to the proposal authenticated by:

(A) a person to which the secured party was required to send a proposal under Section 9–621; or

(B) any other person, other than the debtor, holding an interest in the collateral subordinate to the security interest that is the subject of the proposal;

(3) if the collateral is consumer goods, the collateral is not in the possession of the debtor when the debtor consents to the acceptance; and

(4) subsection (e) does not require the secured party to dispose of the collateral or the debtor waives the requirement pursuant to Section 9–624.

(b) A purported or apparent acceptance of collateral under this section is ineffective unless:

(1) the secured party consents to the acceptance in an authenticated record or sends a proposal to the debtor; and

(2) the conditions of subsection (a) are met.

(c) For purposes of this section:

(1) a debtor consents to an acceptance of collateral in partial satisfaction of the obligation it secures only if the debtor agrees to the terms of the acceptance in a record authenticated after default; and

(2) a debtor consents to an acceptance of collateral in full satisfaction of the obligation it secures only if the debtor agrees to the terms of the acceptance in a record authenticated after default or the secured party:

(A) sends to the debtor after default a proposal that is unconditional or subject only to a condition that collateral not in the possession of the secured party be preserved or maintained;

(B) in the proposal, proposes to accept collateral in full satisfaction of the obligation it secures; and

(C) does not receive a notification of objection authenticated by the debtor within 20 days after the proposal is sent.

(d) To be effective under subsection (a)(2), a notification of objection must be received by the secured party:

(1) in the case of a person to which the proposal was sent pursuant to Section 9–621, within 20 days after notification was sent to that person; and

(2) in other cases:

(A) within 20 days after the last notification was sent pursuant to Section 9–621; or

(B) if a notification was not sent, before the debtor consents to the acceptance under subsection (c).

(e) A secured party that has taken possession of collateral shall dispose of the collateral pursuant to Section 9–610 within the time specified in subsection (f) if:

(1) 60 percent of the cash price has been paid in the case of a purchase-money security interest in consumer goods; or

(2) 60 percent of the principal amount of the obligation secured has been paid in the case of a non-purchase-money security interest in consumer goods.

(f) To comply with subsection (e), the secured party shall dispose of the collateral:

(1) within 90 days after taking possession; or

(2) within any longer period to which the debtor and all secondary obligors have agreed in an agreement to that effect entered into and authenticated after default.

(g) In a consumer transaction, a secured party may not accept collateral in partial satisfaction of the obligation it secures.

§ 9–621.   Notification of Proposal to Accept Collateral.

(a) A secured party that desires to accept collateral in full or partial satisfaction of the obligation it secures shall send its proposal to:

(1) any person from which the secured party has received, before the debtor consented to the acceptance, an authenticated notification of a claim of an interest in the collateral;

(2) any other secured party or lienholder that, 10 days before the debtor consented to the acceptance, held a security interest in or other lien on the collateral perfected by the filing of a financing statement that:

(A) identified the collateral;

(B) was indexed under the debtor's name as of that date; and

(C) was filed in the office or offices in which to file a financing statement against the debtor covering the collateral as of that date; and

(3) any other secured party that, 10 days before the debtor consented to the acceptance, held a security interest in the collateral perfected by compliance with a statute, regulation, or treaty described in Section 9–311(a).

(b) A secured party that desires to accept collateral in partial satisfaction of the obligation it secures shall send its proposal to any secondary obligor in addition to the persons described in subsection (a).

§ 9–622.   Effect of Acceptance of Collateral.

(a) A secured party's acceptance of collateral in full or partial satisfaction of the obligation it secures:

(1) discharges the obligation to the extent consented to by the debtor;

(2) transfers to the secured party all of a debtor's rights in the collateral;

(3) discharges the security interest or agricultural lien that is the subject of the debtor's consent and any subordinate security interest or other subordinate lien; and

(4) terminates any other subordinate interest.

(b) A subordinate interest is discharged or terminated under subsection (a), even if the secured party fails to comply with this article.

§ 9–623.   Right to Redeem Collateral.

(a) A debtor, any secondary obligor, or any other secured party or lienholder may redeem collateral.

(b) To redeem collateral, a person shall tender:

(1) fulfillment of all obligations secured by the collateral; and

(2) the reasonable expenses and attorney's fees described in Section 9–615(a)(1).

(c) A redemption may occur at any time before a secured party:

(1) has collected collateral under Section 9–607;

(2) has disposed of collateral or entered into a contract for its disposition under Section 9–610; or

(3) has accepted collateral in full or partial satisfaction of the obligation it secures under Section 9–622.

§ 9–624.   Waiver.

(a) A debtor or secondary obligor may waive the right to notification of disposition of collateral under Section 9–611 only by an agreement to that effect entered into and authenticated after default.

(b) A debtor may waive the right to require disposition of collateral under Section 9–620(e) only by an agreement to that effect entered into and authenticated after default.

(c) Except in a consumer-goods transaction, a debtor or secondary obligor may waive the right to redeem collateral under

Section 9–623 only by an agreement to that effect entered into and authenticated after default.

[Subpart 2. Noncompliance with Article]

§ 9–625.   Remedies for Secured Party's Failure to Comply with Article.

(a) If it is established that a secured party is not proceeding in accordance with this article, a court may order or restrain collection, enforcement, or disposition of collateral on appropriate terms and conditions.

(b) Subject to subsections (c), (d), and (f), a person is liable for damages in the amount of any loss caused by a failure to comply with this article. Loss caused by a failure to comply may include loss resulting from the debtor's inability to obtain, or increased costs of, alternative financing.

(c) Except as otherwise provided in Section 9–628:

(1) a person that, at the time of the failure, was a debtor, was an obligor, or held a security interest in or other lien on the collateral may recover damages under subsection (b) for its loss; and

(2) if the collateral is consumer goods, a person that was a debtor or a secondary obligor at the time a secured party failed to comply with this part may recover for that failure in any event an amount not less than the credit service charge plus 10 percent of the principal amount of the obligation or the time-price differential plus 10 percent of the cash price.

(d) A debtor whose deficiency is eliminated under Section 9–626 may recover damages for the loss of any surplus. However, a debtor or secondary obligor whose deficiency is eliminated or reduced under Section 9–626 may not otherwise recover under subsection (b) for noncompliance with the provisions of this part relating to collection, enforcement, disposition, or acceptance.

(e) In addition to any damages recoverable under subsection (b), the debtor, consumer obligor, or person named as a debtor in a filed record, as applicable, may recover $500 in each case from a person that:

(1) fails to comply with Section 9–208;

(2) fails to comply with Section 9–209;

(3) files a record that the person is not entitled to file under Section 9–509(a);

(4) fails to cause the secured party of record to file or send a termination statement as required by Section 9–513(a) or (c);

(5) fails to comply with Section 9–616(b)(1) and whose failure is part of a pattern, or consistent with a practice, of noncompliance; or

(6) fails to comply with Section 9–616(b)(2).

(f) A debtor or consumer obligor may recover damages under subsection (b) and, in addition, $500 in each case from a person that, without reasonable cause, fails to comply with a request under Section 9–210. A recipient of a request under Section 9–210 which never claimed an interest in the collateral or obligations that are the subject of a request under that section has a reasonable excuse for failure to comply with the request within the meaning of this subsection.

(g) If a secured party fails to comply with a request regarding a list of collateral or a statement of account under Section 9–210, the secured party may claim a security interest only as shown in the list or statement included in the request as against a person that is reasonably misled by the failure.

As amended in 2000.

§ 9–626.   Action in Which Deficiency or Surplus Is in Issue.

(a) In an action arising from a transaction, other than a consumer transaction, in which the amount of a deficiency or surplus is in issue, the following rules apply:

(1) A secured party need not prove compliance with the provisions of this part relating to collection, enforcement, disposition, or acceptance unless the debtor or a secondary obligor places the secured party's compliance in issue.

(2) If the secured party's compliance is placed in issue, the secured party has the burden of establishing that the collection, enforcement, disposition, or acceptance was conducted in accordance with this part.

(3) Except as otherwise provided in Section 9–628, if a secured party fails to prove that the collection, enforcement, disposition, or acceptance was conducted in accordance with the provisions of this part relating to collection, enforcement, disposition, or acceptance, the liability of a debtor or a secondary obligor for a deficiency is limited to an amount by which the sum of the secured obligation, expenses, and attorney's fees exceeds the greater of:

(A) the proceeds of the collection, enforcement, disposition, or acceptance; or

(B) the amount of proceeds that would have been realized had the noncomplying secured party proceeded in accordance with the provisions of this part relating to collection, enforcement, disposition, or acceptance.

(4) For purposes of paragraph (3)(B), the amount of proceeds that would have been realized is equal to the sum of the secured obligation, expenses, and attorney's fees unless the secured party proves that the amount is less than that sum.

(5) If a deficiency or surplus is calculated under Section 9–615 (f), the debtor or obligor has the burden of establishing that the amount of proceeds of the disposition is significantly below the range of prices that a complying disposition to a person other than the secured party, a person related to the secured party, or a secondary obligor would have brought.

(b) The limitation of the rules in subsection (a) to transactions other than consumer transactions is intended to leave to the court the determination of the proper rules in consumer transactions. The court may not infer from that limitation the nature of the proper rule in consumer transactions and may continue to apply established approaches.

§ 9–627.   Determination of Whether Conduct Was Commercially Reasonable.

(a) The fact that a greater amount could have been obtained by a collection, enforcement, disposition, or acceptance at a different time or in a different method from that selected by the secured party is not of itself sufficient to preclude the secured party from establishing that the collection, enforcement, disposition, or acceptance was made in a commercially reasonable manner.

(b) A disposition of collateral is made in a commercially reasonable manner if the disposition is made:

(1) in the usual manner on any recognized market;

(2) at the price current in any recognized market at the time of the disposition; or

(3) otherwise in conformity with reasonable commercial practices among dealers in the type of property that was the subject of the disposition.

(c) A collection, enforcement, disposition, or acceptance is commercially reasonable if it has been approved:

(1) in a judicial proceeding;

(2) by a bona fide creditors' committee;

(3) by a representative of creditors; or

(4) by an assignee for the benefit of creditors.

(d) Approval under subsection (c) need not be obtained, and lack of approval does not mean that the collection, enforcement, disposition, or acceptance is not commercially reasonable.

§ 9–628.   Nonliability and Limitation on Liability of Secured Party; Liability of Secondary Obligor.

(a) Unless a secured party knows that a person is a debtor or obligor, knows the identity of the person, and knows how to communicate with the person:

(1) the secured party is not liable to the person, or to a secured party or lienholder that has filed a financing statement against the person, for failure to comply with this article; and

(2) the secured party's failure to comply with this article does not affect the liability of the person for a deficiency.

(b) A secured party is not liable because of its status as secured party:

(1) to a person that is a debtor or obligor, unless the secured party knows:

(A) that the person is a debtor or obligor;

(B) the identity of the person; and

(C) how to communicate with the person; or

(2) to a secured party or lienholder that has filed a financing statement against a person, unless the secured party knows:

(A) that the person is a debtor; and

(B) the identity of the person.

(c) A secured party is not liable to any person, and a person's liability for a deficiency is not affected, because of any act or omission arising out of the secured party's reasonable belief that a transaction is not a consumer-goods transaction or a consumer transaction or that goods are not consumer goods, if the secured party's belief is based on its reasonable reliance on:

(1) a debtor's representation concerning the purpose for which collateral was to be used, acquired, or held; or

(2) an obligor's representation concerning the purpose for which a secured obligation was incurred.

(d) A secured party is not liable to any person under Section 9–625(c)(2) for its failure to comply with Section 9–616.

(e) A secured party is not liable under Section 9–625(c)(2) more than once with respect to any one secured obligation.

PART 7   Transition

§ 9–701.   Effective Date.

This [Act] takes effect on July 1, 2001.

§ 9–702.   Savings Clause.

(a) Except as otherwise provided in this part, this [Act] applies to a transaction or lien within its scope, even if the transaction or lien was entered into or created before this [Act] takes effect.

(b) Except as otherwise provided in subsection (c) and Sections 9–703 through 9–709:

(1) transactions and liens that were not governed by [former Article 9], were validly entered into or created before this [Act] takes effect, and would be subject to this [Act] if they had been entered into or created after this [Act] takes effect, and the rights, duties, and interests flowing from those transactions and liens remain valid after this [Act] takes effect; and

(2) the transactions and liens may be terminated, completed, consummated, and enforced as required or permitted by this [Act] or by the law that otherwise would apply if this [Act] had not taken effect.

(c) This [Act] does not affect an action, case, or proceeding commenced before this [Act] takes effect.

As amended in 2000.

§ 9–703.   Security Interest Perfected before Effective Date.

(a) A security interest that is enforceable immediately before this [Act] takes effect and would have priority over the rights of a person that becomes a lien creditor at that time is a perfected security interest under this [Act] if, when this [Act] takes effect, the applicable requirements for enforceability and perfection under this [Act] are satisfied without further action.

(b) Except as otherwise provided in Section 9–705, if, immediately before this [Act] takes effect, a security interest is enforceable and would have priority over the rights of a person that becomes a lien creditor at that time, but the applicable requirements for enforceability or perfection under this [Act] are not satisfied when this [Act] takes effect, the security interest:

(1) is a perfected security interest for one year after this [Act] takes effect;

(2) remains enforceable thereafter only if the security interest becomes enforceable under Section 9–203 before the year expires; and

(3) remains perfected thereafter only if the applicable requirements for perfection under this [Act] are satisfied before the year expires.

§ 9–704.   Security Interest Unperfected before Effective Date.

A security interest that is enforceable immediately before this [Act] takes effect but which would be subordinate to the rights of a person that becomes a lien creditor at that time:

(1) remains an enforceable security interest for one year after this [Act] takes effect;

(2) remains enforceable thereafter if the security interest becomes enforceable under Section 9–203 when this [Act] takes effect or within one year thereafter; and

(3) becomes perfected:

(A) without further action, when this [Act] takes effect if the applicable requirements for perfection under this [Act] are satisfied before or at that time; or

(B) when the applicable requirements for perfection are satisfied if the requirements are satisfied after that time.

§ 9–705.   Effectiveness of Action Taken before Effective Date.

(a) If action, other than the filing of a financing statement, is taken before this [Act] takes effect and the action would have resulted in priority of a security interest over the rights of a person that becomes a lien creditor had the security interest become enforceable before this [Act] takes effect, the action is effective to perfect a security interest that attaches under this [Act] within one year after this [Act] takes effect. An attached security interest becomes unperfected one year after this [Act] takes effect unless the security interest becomes a perfected security interest under this [Act] before the expiration of that period.

(b) The filing of a financing statement before this [Act] takes effect is effective to perfect a security interest to the extent the filing would satisfy the applicable requirements for perfection under this [Act].

(c) This [Act] does not render ineffective an effective financing statement that, before this [Act] takes effect, is filed and satisfies the applicable requirements for perfection under the law of the jurisdiction governing perfection as provided in [former Section 9–103]. However, except as otherwise provided in subsections (d) and (e) and Section 9–706, the financing statement ceases to be effective at the earlier of:

(1) the time the financing statement would have ceased to be effective under the law of the jurisdiction in which it is filed; or

(2) June 30, 2006.

(d) The filing of a continuation statement after this [Act] takes effect does not continue the effectiveness of the financing statement filed before this [Act] takes effect. However, upon the timely filing of a continuation statement after this [Act] takes effect and in accordance with the law of the jurisdiction governing perfection as provided in Part 3, the effectiveness of a financing statement filed in the same office in that jurisdiction before this [Act] takes effect continues for the period provided by the law of that jurisdiction.

(e) Subsection (c)(2) applies to a financing statement that, before this [Act] takes effect, is filed against a transmitting utility and satisfies the applicable requirements for perfection under the law of the jurisdiction governing perfection as provided in [former Section 9–103] only to the extent that Part 3 provides that the law of a jurisdiction other than the jurisdiction in which the financing statement is filed governs perfection of a security interest in collateral covered by the financing statement.

(f) A financing statement that includes a financing statement filed before this [Act] takes effect and a continuation statement filed after this [Act] takes effect is effective only to the extent that it satisfies the requirements of Part 5 for an initial financing statement.

§ 9–706.   When Initial Financing Statement Suffices to Continue Effectiveness of Financing Statement.

(a) The filing of an initial financing statement in the office specified in Section 9–501 continues the effectiveness of a financing statement filed before this [Act] takes effect if:

(1) the filing of an initial financing statement in that office would be effective to perfect a security interest under this [Act];

(2) the pre-effective-date financing statement was filed in an office in another State or another office in this State; and

(3) the initial financing statement satisfies subsection (c).

(b) The filing of an initial financing statement under subsection (a) continues the effectiveness of the pre-effective-date financing statement:

(1) if the initial financing statement is filed before this [Act] takes effect, for the period provided in [former Section 9–403] with respect to a financing statement; and

(2) if the initial financing statement is filed after this [Act] takes effect, for the period provided in Section 9–515 with respect to an initial financing statement.

(c) To be effective for purposes of subsection (a), an initial financing statement must:

(1) satisfy the requirements of Part 5 for an initial financing statement;

(2) identify the pre-effective-date financing statement by indicating the office in which the financing statement was filed and providing the dates of filing and file numbers, if any, of the financing statement and of the most recent continuation statement filed with respect to the financing statement; and

(3) indicate that the pre-effective-date financing statement remains effective.

§ 9–707.   Amendment of Pre-Effective-Date Financing Statement.

(a) In this section, "Pre-effective-date financing statement" means a financing statement filed before this [Act] takes effect.

(b) After this [Act] takes effect, a person may add or delete collateral covered by, continue or terminate the effectiveness of, or otherwise amend the information provided in, a pre-effective-date financing statement only in accordance with the law of the jurisdiction governing perfection as provided in Part 3. However, the effectiveness of a pre-effective-date financing statement also may be terminated in accordance with the law of the jurisdiction in which the financing statement is filed.

(c) Except as otherwise provided in subsection (d), if the law of this State governs perfection of a security interest, the information in a pre-effective-date financing statement may be amended after this [Act] takes effect only if:

(1) the pre-effective-date financing statement and an amendment are filed in the office specified in Section 9–501;

(2) an amendment is filed in the office specified in Section 9–501 concurrently with, or after the filing in that office of, an initial financing statement that satisfies Section 9–706(c); or

(3) an initial financing statement that provides the information as amended and satisfies Section 9–706(c) is filed in the office specified in Section 9–501.

(d) If the law of this State governs perfection of a security interest, the effectiveness of a pre-effective-date financing statement may be continued only under Section 9–705(d) and (f) or 9–706.

(e) Whether or not the law of this State governs perfection of a security interest, the effectiveness of a pre-effective-date financing statement filed in this State may be terminated after this [Act] takes effect by filing a termination statement in the office in which the pre-effective-date financing statement is filed, unless an initial financing statement that satisfies Section 9–706(c) has been filed in the office specified by the law of the jurisdiction governing perfection as provided in Part 3 as the office in which to file a financing statement.

As amended in 2000.

§ 9–708.   Persons Entitled to File Initial Financing Statement or Continuation Statement.

A person may file an initial financing statement or a continuation statement under this part if:

(1) the secured party of record authorizes the filing; and

(2) the filing is necessary under this part:

(A) to continue the effectiveness of a financing statement filed before this [Act] takes effect; or

(B) to perfect or continue the perfection of a security interest.

As amended in 2000.

§ 9–709.   Priority.

(a) This [Act] determines the priority of conflicting claims to collateral. However, if the relative priorities of the claims were established before this [Act] takes effect, [former Article 9] determines priority.

(b) For purposes of Section 9–322(a), the priority of a security interest that becomes enforceable under Section 9–203 of this [Act] dates from the time this [Act] takes effect if the security interest is perfected under this [Act] by the filing of a financing statement before this [Act] takes effect which would not have been effective to perfect the security interest under [former Article 9]. This subsection does not apply to conflicting security interests each of which is perfected by the filing of such a financing statement.

A

Abatement An order to the owner of a property to eliminate a nuisance.

Absolute privilege Exists in courtrooms and legislative hearings. Anyone speaking there, such as a witness in a court, can say anything and never be sued for defamation.

Accept To sign a check.

Acceptance Retention of the collateral by a secured party as full or partial satisfaction of a debt.

Accepted check A check that the drawee bank has signed. This signature is a promise that the bank will pay the check out of its own funds.

Accession The use of labor and/or materials to add value to the personal property of another.

Accommodation party Someone who does not benefit from an instrument but agrees to guarantee its payment.

Accord and satisfaction An agreement to settle a debt for less than the sum claimed.

Accounts Any right to receive payment for goods sold or leased, other than rights covered by chattel paper or instruments.

Account party Party that applies for the letter of credit from its bank.

Accredited investor Under the Securities Act of 1933, an accredited investor is an institution (such as a bank or insurance company) or any individual with a net worth of more than $1 million or an annual income of more than $200,000.

Acquit To find the defendant not guilty of the crime for which he was tried.

Act of State doctrine A rule requiring American courts to abstain from cases if a court order would interfere with the ability of the President or Congress to conduct foreign policy.

Actual authority An agent is authorized to act for a principal.

Actus reus The guilty act. The prosecution must show that a criminal defendant committed some proscribed act. In a murder prosecution, taking another person's life is the *actus reus*.

Ad valorem According to the value of the goods.

Additional terms Those terms that raise issues not covered in an offer.

Adhesion contract A standard form contract prepared by one party and presented to the other on a "take it or leave it" basis.

Adjudicate To hold a formal hearing in a disputed matter and issue an official decision.

Administrative law Concerns all agencies, boards, commissions, and other entities created by a federal or state legislature and charged with investigating, regulating, and adjudicating a particular industry or issue.

Administrative law judge An agency employee who acts as an impartial decision-maker.

Administrator A person appointed by the court to oversee the probate process for someone who has died intestate (that is, without a will).

Administratrix A female administrator.

Adverse possession A means of gaining ownership of land belonging to another by entering upon the property, openly and notoriously, and claiming exclusive use of it for a period of years.

Affidavit A written statement signed under oath.

Affirm An appellate court issues a decision upholding the judgment of a lower court.

Affirmative action A plan introduced in a workplace for the purpose of either remedying the effects of past discrimination or achieving equitable representation of minorities and women.

After-acquired property Items that a debtor obtains after making a security agreement with the secured party.

Agent A person who acts for a principal.

Alternative dispute resolution Any method of resolving a legal conflict other than litigation, such as negotiation, arbitration, mediation, mini-trials, and summary jury trials.

Amendment Any addition to a legal document. The constitutional amendments, the first ten of which are known collectively as the Bill of Rights, secure numerous liberties and protections directly for the people.

Annual report Each year, public companies must send their shareholders a document that contains detailed financial data.

Annuity Payment to a beneficiary during his lifetime.

Answer The pleading, filed by the defendant in court and served on the plaintiff, which responds to each allegation in the plaintiff's complaint.

Antitrust laws Make it illegal to destroy competition and capture an entire market.

Apparent authority A situation in which conduct of a principal causes a third party to believe that the principal consents to have an act done on his behalf by a person purporting to act for him when, in fact, that person is not acting for the principal.

Appeals court Any court in a state or federal system that reviews cases that have already been tried.

Appellant The party who appeals a lower court decision to a higher court.

Appellee The party opposing an appeal from a lower court to a higher court.

Arbitration A form of alternative dispute resolution in which the parties hire a neutral third party to hear their respective arguments, receive evidence, and then make a binding decision.

Arson Malicious use of fire or explosives to damage or destroy real estate or personal property.

Artisan's lien A security interest in personal property.

Assault An intentional act that causes the plaintiff to fear an imminent battery.

Assignee The party who receives an assignment of contract rights from a party to the contract.

Assignment The act by which a party transfers contract rights to a third person.

Assignor The party who assigns contract rights to a third person.

Assisted suicide The process of hastening death for a terminally ill patient at the request of this patient.

Attachment A court order seizing property of a party to a civil action, so that there will be sufficient assets available to pay the judgment.

Authorized and unissued stock Stock that has been approved by the corporation's charter but has not yet been sold.

Authorized and issued stock Stock that has been approved by the corporation's charter and subsequently sold.

Automatic stay Prohibits creditors from collecting debts that the bankrupt incurred before the bankruptcy petition was filed.

B

Bailee A person who rightfully possesses goods belonging to another.

Bailment Giving possession and control of personal property to another person.

Bailor One who creates a bailment by delivering goods to another.

Bait and switch A practice where sellers advertise products that are not generally available but are being used to draw interested parties in so that they will buy other products.

Bankrupt Another term for debtor.

Bankruptcy estate The new legal entity created when a debtor files a bankruptcy petition. All of the debtor's existing assets pass into the estate.

Battery The intentional touching of another person in a way that is unwanted or offensive.

Bearer paper An instrument payable "to bearer." Any holder in due course can demand payment.

Beneficiary Party that will be paid by the issuing bank pursuant to a letter of credit.

Best efforts underwriting When the underwriter does not buy the stock but instead acts as the company's agent in selling it.

Beyond a reasonable doubt The government's burden in a criminal prosecution.

Bilateral contract A binding agreement in which each party has made a promise to the other.

Bilateral mistake Occurs when both parties negotiate based on the same factual error.

Bill A proposed statute that has been submitted for consideration to Congress or a state legislature.

Bill of lading A receipt for goods, given by a carrier such as a ship, that minutely describes the merchandise being shipped. A negotiable bill of lading may be transferred to other parties, and entitles any holder to collect the goods.

Bill of Rights The first ten amendments to the Constitution.

Blue sky laws State securities laws.

Bona fide occupational qualification (BFOQ) A job requirement that would otherwise be discriminatory is permitted in situations in which it is *essential* to the position in question.

Bona fide purchaser Someone who buys goods in good faith, for value, typically from a seller who has merely voidable title.

Bonds Long-term debt secured by some of the issuing company's assets.

Brief The written legal argument that an attorney files with an appeal court.

Bulk sale A transfer of most or all of a merchant's assets.

Burden of proof The allocation of which party must prove its case. In a civil case, the plaintiff has the burden of proof to persuade the fact finder of every element of her case. In a criminal case, the government has the burden of proof.

Business judgment rule A common law rule that protects managers from liability if they are acting without a conflict of interest and make informed decisions that have a rational business purpose.

Business trust An unincorporated association run by trustees for the benefit of investors.

Buyer in ordinary course of business (BIOC) Someone who buys goods in good faith from a seller who routinely deals in such goods.

Bylaws A document that specifies the organizational rules of a corporation or other organization, such as the date of the annual meeting and the required number of directors.

C

Cap and trade A market-based system for reducing emissions.

Capacity The legal ability to enter into a contract.

Cashier's check A check that is drawn by a bank on itself.

Certificate of deposit An instrument issued by a bank which promises to repay a deposit, with interest, on a specified date.

Certified check A check that the drawee bank has signed. This signature is a promise that the bank will pay the check out of its own funds.

***Certiorari*, writ of** Formal notice from the United States Supreme Court that it will accept a case for review.

Challenge for cause An attorney's request, during *voir dire*, to excuse a prospective juror because of apparent bias.

Chancery, court of In medieval England, the court originally operated by the Chancellor.

Charging order A court order granting the creditor of a partner the right to receive that partner's share of partnership profits.

Chattel paper Any writing that indicates two things: (1) a debtor owes money and (2) a secured party has a security interest in specific goods. The most common chattel paper is a document indicating a consumer sale on credit.

Check An instrument in which the drawer orders the drawee bank to pay money to the payee.

Chicago School A theory of antitrust law first developed at the University of Chicago. Adherents to this theory believe that antitrust enforcement should focus on promoting efficiency and should not generally be concerned about the size or number of competitors in any market.

CISG *See* Convention on Contracts for the International Sale of Goods (CISG).

Civil law The large body of law concerning the rights and duties between parties. It is distinguished from criminal law, which concerns behavior outlawed by a government.

Claim in recoupment An issuer subtracts (i.e., "sets off") any other claims that he has against the initial payee from the amount that he owes on an instrument.

Class action A method of litigating a civil lawsuit in which one or more plaintiffs (or occasionally defendants) seek to represent an entire group of people with similar claims against a common opponent.

Classification The process by which the Customs Service decides what label to attach to imported merchandise, and therefore what level of tariff to impose.

Classes of stock Categories of stock with different rights.

Close corporation A corporation with a small number of shareholders. Its stock is not publicly traded. Also known as a *closely held corporation*.

Codicil An amendment to a will.

Collateral The property subject to a security interest.

Collateral promise A promise to pay the debt of another person, as a favor to the debtor.

Collective bargaining Contract negotiations between an employer and a union.

Collective bargaining agreement (CBA) A contract between a union and management.

Collective bargaining unit The precisely defined group of employees who are represented by a particular union.

Comity A doctrine that requires a court to abstain from hearing a case out of respect for another court that also has jurisdiction. *International comity* demands that a U.S. court refuse to hear a case in which a foreign court shares jurisdiction if there is a conflict between the laws and if it is more logical for the foreign court to take the case.

Comment letter A document from the SEC listing required changes in the registration statement.

Commerce clause One of the powers granted by Article I, Section 8 of the Constitution, it gives Congress exclusive power to regulate international commerce and concurrent power with the states to regulate domestic commerce.

Commercial impracticability After the creation of a contract, an entirely unforeseen event occurs which makes enforcement of the contract extraordinarily unfair.

Commercial paper Instruments such as checks and promissory notes that contain a promise to pay money. Commercial paper includes both negotiable and non-negotiable instruments.

Commercial speech Communication, such as television advertisements, that has the dominant theme of proposing a commercial transaction.

Common carrier A transportation company that makes its services available on a regular basis to the general public.

Common law Judge-made law, that is, the body of all decisions made by appellate courts over the years.

Common stock Certificates that reflect ownership in a corporation. Owners of this equity security are last in line for corporate payouts such as dividends and liquidation proceeds.

Comparative negligence A rule of tort law that permits a plaintiff to recover even when the defendant can show that the plaintiff's own conduct contributed in some way to her harm.

Compensatory damages The amount of money that the court thinks will restore the plaintiff to the position he was in before the defendant's conduct caused an injury.

Complaint A pleading, filed by the plaintiff, providing a short statement of the claim.

Concerted action Tactics, such as a strike, used by a union to gain a bargaining advantage.

Concurrent estate Two or more people owning property at the same time.

Condition A condition is an event that must occur in order for a party to be obligated under a contract.

Condition precedent A condition that must occur before a particular contract duty arises.

Condition subsequent A condition that must occur after a particular contract duty arises, or the duty will be discharged.

Confiscation Expropriation without adequate compensation of property owned by foreigners.

Conforming goods Items that satisfy the contract terms. If a contract calls for blue sailboats, then green sailboats are non-conforming.

Consent order An agreement entered into by a wrongdoer and an administrative agency (such as the Securities and Exchange Commission or the Federal Trade Commission) in which the wrongdoer agrees not to violate the law in the future.

Consequential damages Those resulting from the unique circumstances of *this injured party*.

Consideration In contract law, something of legal value that has been bargained for and given in exchange by the parties.

Constitution The supreme law of a political entity. The United States Constitution is the highest law in the country.

Consumer Any natural person, that is, not a corporation or business.

Consumer credit contract A contract in which a consumer borrows money from a lender to purchase goods and services from a seller who is affiliated with the lender.

Consumer reporting agency A business that supplies consumer reports to third parties.

Contract A legally enforceable promise or set of promises.

Contract carrier A transportation company that does not make its services available to the general public but engages in continuing agreements with particular customers.

Contributory negligence A rule of tort law that permits a negligent defendant to escape liability if she can demonstrate that the plaintiff's own conduct contributed in any way to the plaintiff's harm.

Control security Stock owned by any officer or director of the issuer, or by any shareholder who holds more than 10 percent of a class of stock of the issuer.

Convention on Contracts for the International Sale of Goods (CISG) A United Nations–sponsored agreement that creates a neutral body of law for sale of goods contracts between companies from different countries.

Conversion (1) A tort committed by taking or using someone else's personal property without his permission. (2) A bank has paid a check that has a forged indorsement.

Cookie A small computer file that identifies the user of a computer. Internet sites typically place cookies on a computer's hard drive to track visitors to their site.

Cooperative A group of individuals or businesses that join together to gain the advantages of volume purchases or sales.

Copyright Under federal law, the holder of a copyright owns a particular expression of an idea, but not the idea itself. This ownership right applies to creative activities such as literature, music, drama, and software.

Corporate social responsibility An organization's obligation to contribute positively to the world around it.

Corporation by estoppel Even if a corporation has not actually been formed, courts will sometimes enforce contracts entered into in the belief that the corporation did indeed exist.

Compliance program A plan to prevent and detect criminal conduct at all levels of the company.

Constructive insider Anyone who has an indirect employment relationship with a company, such as employees of the company's auditors or law firm.

Counter-claim A claim made by the defendant against the plaintiff.

Counteroffer A return offer and a rejection of the original offer.

Cover The buyer's right to obtain substitute goods when a seller has breached a contract.

Cramdown The bankruptcy court confirms a plan of reorganization despite a negative vote from one or more classes of creditors and/or shareholders.

Creditor beneficiary When one party to a contract intends to benefit a third party to whom he owes a debt, that third party is referred to as a creditor beneficiary.

Criminal law Rules that permit a government to punish certain behavior by fine or imprisonment.

Criminal procedure The process of investigating, interrogating, and trying a criminal defendant.

Cross-examine During a hearing, when a lawyer questions an opposing witness.

Cure The seller's right to respond to a buyer's rejection of nonconforming goods; the seller accomplishes this by delivering conforming goods before the contract deadline.

D

Damages (1) The harm that a plaintiff complains of at trial, such as an injury to her person, or money lost because of a contract breach. (2) Money awarded by a trial court for injury suffered.

De facto corporation Occurs when a promoter makes a good faith effort to incorporate (although fails to complete the process entirely) and uses the corporation to conduct business. The state can challenge the validity of the corporation, but a third party cannot.

De jure corporation The promoter of the corporation has substantially complied with the requirements for incorporation, but has made some minor error. No one has the right to challenge the validity of the corporation.

De novo decision The power of an appellate court or appellate agency to make a new decision in a matter under appeal, entirely ignoring the findings and conclusions of the lower court or agency official.

Debentures Long-term, unsecured debt, typically issued by a corporation.

Debtor A person who owes money or some other obligation to another party.

Decedent A person who has died.

Deed A document that proves ownership of property.

Defamation The act of injuring someone's reputation by stating something false about her to a third person. *Libel* is defamation done either in writing or by broadcast. *Slander* is defamation done orally.

Default The failure to perform an obligation, such as the failure to pay money when due.

Default judgment A court order awarding one party everything it requested because the opposing party failed to respond in time.

Default rules Under the Uniform Partnership Act, these rules govern the relationship among the partners unless the partners explicitly make a different agreement.

Defendant The person being sued.

Deficiency Having insufficient funds to pay off a debt.

Definiteness A doctrine holding that a contract will only be enforced if its terms are sufficiently precise that a court can determine what the parties meant.

Delegation The act by which a party to a contract transfers duties to a third person who is not a party to the contract.

Deontological From the Greek word for *obligation*. The duty to do the right thing, regardless of the result.

Deponent The person being questioned in a deposition.

Deposition A form of discovery in which a party's attorney has the right to ask oral questions of the other party or of a witness. Answers are given under oath.

Derivative action A lawsuit brought by shareholders in the name of the corporation to enforce a right of the corporation.

Deterrence Using punishment, such as imprisonment, to discourage criminal behavior.

Devisee Someone who inherits under a will.

Different terms Terms that contradict those in an offer.

Difference principle Rawls' suggestion that society should reward behavior that provides the most benefit to the community as a whole.

Direct examination During a hearing, when a lawyer asks questions of his own witness.

Directed verdict The decision by a court to instruct a jury that it must find in favor of a particular party because, in the judge's opinion, no reasonable person could disagree on the outcome.

Disabled person Someone with a physical or mental impairment that substantially limits a major life activity, or someone who is regarded as having such an impairment.

Disability insurance Replaces the insured's income if he becomes unable to work because of illness or injury.

Disaffirm To give notice to the other party to a contract that the party giving the notice refuses to be bound by the agreement.

Discharge (1) A party to a contract has no more duties. (2) A party to an instrument is released from liability.

Disclaimer A statement that a particular warranty does not apply.

Discovery A stage in litigation, after all pleadings have been served, in which each party seeks as much relevant information as possible about the opposing party's case.

Dishonor An obligor refuses to pay an instrument that is due.

Dismiss To terminate a lawsuit, often on procedural grounds, without reaching the merits of the case.

Dissenters' rights A privately held company must buy back the stock of any shareholder who objects to a fundamental change.

Dissociation A dissociation occurs when a partner leaves a partnership.

Diversity jurisdiction One of the two main types of civil cases that a U.S. district court has the power to hear. It involves a lawsuit between citizens of different states, in which at least one party makes a claim for more than $75,000.

Domestic corporation A corporation is a domestic corporation in the state in which it was formed.

Donee A person who receives a gift.

Donee beneficiary When one party to a contract intends to make a gift to a third party, that third party is referred to as a donee beneficiary.

Donor A person who makes a gift to another.

Double jeopardy A criminal defendant may be prosecuted only once for a particular criminal offense.

Draft The drawer of this instrument orders someone else to pay money. Checks are the most common form of draft. The drawer of a check orders a bank to pay money.

Dram acts Make businesses liable for serving drinks to intoxicated customers who later cause harm.

Drawee The person who pays a draft. In the case of a check, the bank is the drawee.

Drawer The person who issues a draft.

Due diligence An investigation of the registration statement by someone who signs it.

Due Process Clause Part of the Fifth Amendment. *Procedural due process* ensures that before depriving anyone of liberty or property, the government must go through procedures which ensure that the deprivation is fair. *Substantive due process* holds that certain rights, such as privacy, are so fundamental that the government may not eliminate them.

Dumping Selling merchandise at one price in the domestic market and at a cheaper, unfair price in an international market.

Durable power of attorney An instrument that permits an attorney-in-fact to act for a principal. A durable power is effective until the principal revokes it or dies. It continues in effect even if the principal becomes incapacitated.

Duress (1) A criminal defense in which the defendant shows that she committed the wrongful act because a third person threatened her with imminent physical harm. (2) An improper threat made to force another party to enter into a contract.

Duty A tax imposed on imported items.

Duty of care The requirement that a manager act with care and in the best interests of the corporation.

Duty of loyalty The obligation of a manager to act without a conflict of interest.

E

Easement The right to enter land belonging to another and make a limited use of it, without taking anything away.

Economic loss doctrine A common-law rule holding that when an injury is purely economic, and it arises from a contract made between two businesses, the injured party may sue only under the Universal Commercial Code (UCC).

Electronic funds Moneys that are moved between accounts by means of a computer, an ATM, or a wire transfer.

Element A fact that a party to a lawsuit must prove in order to prevail.

Embezzlement Fraudulent conversion of property already in the defendant's possession.

Eminent domain The power of the government to take private property for public use.

Employee at will A worker whose job does not have a specified duration.

Enabling legislation A statute authorizing the creation of a new administrative agency and specifying its powers and duties.

Engagement letter A written contract by which a client hires an accountant.

Entrapment A criminal defense in which the defendant demonstrates that the government induced him to break the law.

Equal dignities rule If an agent is empowered to enter into a contract that must be in writing, then the appointment of the agent must also be written.

Equal Protection Clause Part of the Fourteenth Amendment, it generally requires the government to treat equally situated people the same.

Equity The broad powers of a court to fashion a remedy where justice demands it and no common law remedy exists. An injunction is an example of an equitable remedy.

Error of law A mistake made by a trial judge that concerns a legal issue as opposed to a factual matter. Permitting too many leading questions is a legal error; choosing to believe one witness rather than another is a factual matter.

Escalator clause A lease clause allowing the landlord to raise the rent for specified reasons.

Estate The legal entity that holds title to assets after the owner dies and before the property is distributed.

Estoppel Out of fairness, a person is denied the right to assert a claim.

Ethics The study of how people ought to act.

Ethics decision Any choice that affects people or animals.

Euro The common currency of most EU countries.

Eviction An act that forces a tenant to abandon the property.

Evidence, rules of Law governing the proof offered during a trial or formal hearing. These rules limit the questions that may be asked of witnesses and the introduction of physical objects.

Exclusionary rule In a criminal trial, a ban on the use of evidence obtained in violation of the Constitution.

Exclusive dealing contract A contract in which a distributor or retailer agrees with a supplier not to carry the products of any other supplier.

Exculpatory clause A contract provision that attempts to release one party from liability in the event the other party is injured.

Executed contract A binding agreement in which all parties have fulfilled all obligations.

Executive agency An administrative agency within the executive branch of government.

Executive order An order by a president or governor, having the full force of law.

Executor A person chosen by the decedent to oversee the probate process.

Executory contract A binding agreement in which one or more of the parties has not fulfilled its obligations.

Executrix A female executor.

Exhaustion of remedies A principle of administrative law that no party may appeal an agency action to a court until she has utilized all available appeals within the agency itself.

Expectation interest A remedy in a contract case that puts the injured party in the position he would have been in had both sides fully performed.

Expert witness A witness in a court case who has special training or qualifications to discuss a specific issue, and who is generally permitted to state an opinion.

Export To transport goods or services out of a country.

Express authority Conduct of a principal that, reasonably interpreted, causes the agent to believe that the principal desires him to do a specific act.

Express contract A binding agreement in which the parties explicitly state all important terms.

Express warranty A guarantee, created by the words or actions of the seller, that goods will meet certain standards.

Expropriation A government's seizure of property or companies owned by foreigners.

Extraterritoriality The power of one nation to impose its laws in other countries.

F

Factfinder The one responsible, during a trial, for deciding what occurred, that is, who did what to whom, when, how, and why. It is either the jury or, in a jury-waived case, the judge.

Fair representation, duty of The union's obligation to act on behalf of all members impartially and in good faith.

Fair use doctrine Permits limited use of copyrighted material without permission of the author.

False imprisonment The intentional restraint of another person without reasonable cause and without her consent.

Federal question One of the two main types of civil cases that a U.S. district court has the power to hear. It involves a federal statute or a constitutional provision.

Federal Sentencing Guidelines Detailed rules that judges must follow when sentencing defendants convicted of crimes in federal court.

Federalism A form of national government in which power is shared between one central authority and numerous local authorities.

Fee simple absolute The greatest possible ownership right in real property, including the right to possess, use, and dispose of the property in any lawful manner.

Fee simple defeasible Ownership interest in real property that may terminate upon the occurrence of some limiting event.

Felony The most serious crimes, typically those for which the defendant could be imprisoned for more than a year.

Fiduciary duty An obligation to behave in a trustworthy and confidential fashion toward the object of that duty.

Fiduciary relationship A trustee acts for the benefit of the beneficiary, always putting the interests of the beneficiary before his own.

Financing statement A document that a secured party files to give the general public notice that the secured party has a secured interest in the collateral.

Finding statutes Laws that govern found property. Also known as *estray statutes*.

Firm commitment underwriting The underwriter buys stock from the issuer and sells it to the public.

Firm offer A contract offer that cannot be withdrawn during a stated period.

Fixtures Goods that are attached to real estate.

Forced share The percentage of a decedent's estate that a spouse is entitled to claim under state law. Also known as statutory share.

Foreign corporation A corporation formed in another state.

Foreign Corrupt Practices Act A statute that illegalizes bribes to foreign officials by U.S. individuals or businesses.

Foreign Sovereign Immunity Act (FSIA) A federal statute that protects other nations from suit in courts of the United States, except under specified circumstances.

Formal rulemaking The process whereby an administrative agency notifies the public of a proposed new rule and then permits a formal hearing, with opportunity for evidence and cross-examination, before promulgating the final rule.

Founding Fathers The authors of the U.S. Constitution, who participated in the Constitutional Convention in Philadelphia in 1787.

Framers *See* Founding Fathers.

Franchise An arrangement in which the franchisee buys from a franchiser the right to establish a business using the franchiser's trade name and selling the franchiser's products. Typically the franchiser also trains the franchisee in the proper operation of the business.

Fraud Deception of another person to obtain money or property.

Freedom of Information Act (FOIA) A federal statute giving private citizens and corporations access to many of the documents possessed by an administrative agency.

Freehold estate The present right to possess property and to use it in any lawful manner.

Fresh start After the termination of a bankruptcy case, creditors cannot make a claim against the debtor for money owed before the initial bankruptcy petition was filed.

Frustration of purpose After the creation of a contract, an entirely unforeseen event occurs that eliminates the value of the contract for one of the parties.

Fully disclosed principal If the third party in an agency relationship knows the identity of the principal, that principal is fully disclosed.

Fundamental rights In constitutional law, those rights that are so basic that any governmental interference with them is suspect and likely to be unconstitutional.

G

GAAP Generally accepted accounting principles. Rules set by the Financial Accounting Standards Board to be used in preparing financial statements.

GAAS Generally accepted auditing standards. Rules set by the American Institute of Certified Public Accountants (AICPA) to be used in conducting audits.

Gap-filler provisions Uniform Commercial Code (UCC) rules for supplying missing terms.

Gap period The period between the time that creditors file an involuntary petition and the court issues the order for relief.

GATT *See* General Agreement on Tariffs and Trade.

General Agreement on Tariffs and Trade (GATT) A massive international treaty, negotiated in stages between the 1940s and 1994 and signed by over 130 nations.

General deterrence *See* Deterrence.

General intangibles Potential sources of income such as copyrights, patents, trademarks, goodwill and certain other rights to payment.

General intent The defendant intended to do the prohibited physical action (the *actus reus*).

Gift A voluntary transfer of property from one person to another without consideration.

Gift causa mortis A gift made in contemplation of approaching death.

Go effective The securities registration is complete and the company may begin the sale of its stock.

Goods Anything movable, except for money, securities, and certain legal rights.

Grand jury A group of ordinary citizens that decides whether there is probable cause the defendant committed the crime and should be tried.

Grantee The person who receives property, or some interest in it, from the owner.

Grantor (1) An owner who conveys property, or some interest in it. (2) Someone who creates a trust.

Gratuitous agent An agent who is not paid by the principal.

Gratuitous assignment An assignment made as a gift, for no consideration.

Greenmail If a company is threatened with a hostile takeover, its board of directors may offer to buy the stock of the attacker at an above-market price with the hope that the attacker will take her profits and leave the company alone.

Grievance A formal complaint alleging a contract violation.

Guilty A court's finding that a defendant has committed a crime.

H

Hacking Gaining unauthorized access to a computer system.

Harmless error A ruling made by a trial court which an appeals court determines was legally wrong but not fatal to the decision.

Heir Someone who inherits from a decedent who died intestate (that is, without a will).

Holder For order paper, anyone in possession of the instrument if it is payable to or indorsed to her. For bearer paper, anyone in possession.

Holder in due course Someone who has given value for an instrument, in good faith, without notice of outstanding claims or other defenses.

Holographic will A handwritten will that has not been witnessed.

Horizontal agreement or merger An agreement or merger between two potential competitors.

Hostile takeover An outsider buys a company in the face of opposition from the target company's board of directors.

Hybrid rulemaking A method of administrative agency procedure incorporating some elements of formal and some elements of informal rulemaking, typically involving a limited public hearing with restricted rights of testimony and cross-examination.

I

Identify In sales law, to designate the specific goods that are the subject of a contract.

IFRS "International Financial Reporting Standards" is a new set of international standard accounting rules, used by over 100 countries, currently being proposed for U.S. companies to follow.

Illegal contract An agreement that is void because it violates a statute or public policy.

Illusory promise An apparent promise that is unenforceable because the promisor makes no firm commitment.

Implied authority When a principal directs an agent to undertake a transaction, the agent has the right to do acts that are incidental to it, usually accompany it, or are reasonably necessary to accomplish it.

Implied contract A binding agreement created not by explicit language but by the informal words and conduct of the parties.

Implied warranty Guarantees created by the Uniform Commercial Code and imposed on the seller of goods.

Implied warranty of fitness for a particular purpose If the seller knows that the buyer plans to use the goods for a particular purpose, the seller generally is held to warrant that the goods are in fact fit for that purpose.

Implied warranty of habitability A landlord must meet all standards set by the local building code, or otherwise ensure that the premises are fit for human habitation.

Implied warranty of merchantability Requires that goods must be of at least average, passable quality in the trade.

Import To transport goods or services into a country.

Import ban A prohibition of certain goods.

In camera "In the judge's chambers," meaning that the judge does something out of view of the jury and the public.

In camera inspection A judge's private review of evidence to determine whether it should be provided to the opposing party.

Incidental beneficiary Someone who might have benefited from a contract between two others but has no right to enforce that agreement.

Incidental damages The relatively minor costs, such as storage and advertising, that the injured party suffered when responding to a contract breach.

Incorporator The person who signs a corporate charter.

Indemnification A promise to pay someone else's obligations.

Independent agency An administrative agency outside the executive branch of government, such as the Interstate Commerce Commission.

Independent contractor Someone who undertakes tasks for others and whose work is not closely controlled.

Indictment The government's formal charge that a defendant has committed a crime.

Indorser Anyone, other than the issuer or acceptor, who signs an instrument.

Indorsement The signature of a payee.

Infliction of emotional distress A tort. It can be the *intentional infliction of emotional distress*, meaning that the defendant behaved outrageously and deliberately caused the plaintiff severe psychological injury, or it can be the *negligent infliction of emotional distress*, meaning that the defendant's conduct violated the rules of negligence.

Informal rulemaking The process whereby an administrative agency notifies the public of a proposed new rule and permits comment but is then free to promulgate the final rule without a public hearing.

Initial public offering (IPO) A company's first public sale of securities.

Injunction A court order that a person either do or stop doing something.

Inside directors Members of the board of directors who are also officers of the corporation.

Insider Family members of an individual debtor, officers and directors of a corporation, or partners of a partnership.

Instructions or charge The explanation given by a judge to a jury, outlining the jury's task in deciding a lawsuit and the underlying rules of law the jury should use in reaching its decision.

Instruments Drafts, checks, certificates of deposit and notes.

Insurable interest A person has an insurable interest if she would be harmed by the danger that she has insured against.

Insured A person whose loss is the subject of an insurance policy.

Insurer The person who issues an insurance policy.

Integrated contract A writing that the parties intend as the complete and final expression of their agreement.

Intended beneficiary Someone who may enforce a contract made between two other parties.

Intentional infliction of emotional distress Results from extreme and outrageous conduct that causes serious emotional harm.

Intentional tort An act deliberately performed that violates a legally imposed duty and injures someone.

Inter vivos gift A gift made "during life," that is, when the donor is not under any fear of impending death.

Inter vivos trust A trust established while the grantor is still living.

Interest A legal right in something, such as ownership or a mortgage or a tenancy.

Interference with a contract *See* Tortious interference with a contract.

Interference with a prospective advantage *See* Tortious interference with a prospective advantage.

International comity Requires one court to reject a lawsuit that would more logically be resolved in another nation.

Internet An international computer network that connects smaller groups of linked computer networks.

Interpretive rules A formal statement by an administrative agency expressing its view of what existing statutes or regulations mean.

Interrogatory A form of discovery in which one party sends to an opposing party written questions that must be answered under oath.

Intestate Without a will.

Intrusion A tort if a reasonable person would find the invasion of her private life offensive.

Inventory Goods that the seller is holding for sale or lease in the ordinary course of its business.

Involuntary bailment A bailment that occurs without an agreement between the bailor and bailee.

Invitee Someone who has the right to be on property, such as a customer in a shop.

Issue All direct descendants such as children, grandchildren, and so on.

Issuer The maker of a promissory note or the drawer of a draft.

J

Joint and several liability All members of a group are liable. They can be sued as a group, or any one of them can be sued individually for the full amount owing.

Joint liability All members of a group are liable and must be sued together.

Joint tenancy Two or more people holding equal interest in a property, with the right of survivorship.

Joint venture A partnership for a limited purpose.

Judgment *non obstante veredicto* (JNOV) "Judgment notwithstanding the verdict." A trial judge overturns the verdict of the jury and enters a judgment in favor of the opposing party.

Judgment rate The interest rate that courts use on court-ordered judgments.

Judicial activism The willingness shown by certain courts (and not by others) to decide issues of public policy, such as constitutional questions (free speech, equal protection, etc.) and matters of contract fairness (promissory estoppel, unconscionability, etc.).

Judicial restraint A court's preference to abstain from adjudicating major social issues and to leave such matters to legislatures.

Judicial review The power of the judicial system to examine, interpret, and even nullify actions taken by another branch of government.

Jurisdiction The power of a court to hear a particular dispute, civil or criminal, and to make a binding decision.

Jurisprudence The study of the purposes and philosophies of the law, as opposed to particular provisions of the law.

Justification A criminal defense in which the defendant establishes that he broke the law to avoid a greater harm.

K

Kantian evasion or **palter** A truthful statement that is nonetheless misleading.

Kant's categorical imperative An act is only ethical if it would be acceptable for everyone to do the same thing.

L

Labor-Management Relations Act Designed to curb union abuses.

Landlord The owner of a freehold estate who allows another person to live on his property temporarily.

Larceny Taking personal property with the intention of preventing the owner from ever using it.

Law merchant The body of rules and customs developed by traders and businesspersons throughout Europe from roughly the fifteenth to the eighteenth century.

Lease A contract creating a landlord-tenant relationship.

Legal positivism The legal philosophy holding that law is what the sovereign says it is, regardless of its moral content.

Legal realism The legal philosophy holding that what really influences law is who makes and enforces it, not what is put in writing.

Legal remedy Generally, money damages. It is distinguished from equitable remedy, which includes injunctions and other nonmonetary relief.

Legislative history Used by courts to interpret the meaning of a statute, this is the record of hearings, speeches, and explanations that accompanied a statute as it made its way from newly proposed bill to final law.

Legislative rules Regulations issued by an administrative agency.

Letter of credit A commercial device used to guarantee payment in international trade, usually between parties that have not previously worked together.

Letter of intent A letter that summarizes negotiating progress.

Liability insurance Reimburses the insured for any liability she incurs by accidentally harming someone else.

Libel The act of injuring someone's reputation by stating (in writing or by broadcast) something false about her to a third person.

License To grant permission to another person (1) to make or sell something or (2) to enter on property.

Licensee A person who is on the property of another for her own purposes, but with the owner's permission. A social guest is a typical licensee.

Lien A security interest created by rule of law, often based on labor that the secured party has expended on the collateral.

Life estate An ownership interest in real property entitling the holder to use the property during his lifetime, but which terminates upon his death.

Life insurance Provides for payments to a beneficiary upon the death of the insured.

Life-prospects The opportunities one has at birth, based on one's natural attributes and initial place in society.

Life tenant A person who has the use of a property during his lifetime only.

Limited liability company An organization that has the limited liability of a corporation but is not a taxable entity.

Limited liability limited partnership In a limited liability limited partnership, the general partner is not personally liable for the debts of the partnership.

Limited partnership A partnership with two types of partners: (1) limited partners who have no personal liability for the debts of the enterprise nor any right to manage the business, and (2) general partners who are responsible for management and personally liable for all debts.

Liquidated damages clause A contract clause specifying how much a party must pay upon breach.

Liquidated debt The amount of the indebtedness is not in dispute.

Litigation The process of resolving disputes through formal court proceedings.

Litigator A lawyer who handles court cases.

Living trust A trust established while the grantor is alive. *See inter vivos* trust.

Living will An instrument that permits adults to refuse medical treatment. It can also appoint a health care proxy to make medical decisions for a person who has become incompetent.

Local A regional union that represents workers at a particular company.

Lockout A management tactic, designed to gain a bargaining advantage, in which the company refuses to allow union members to work (and hence deprives them of their pay).

M

Mailbox rule A contract doctrine holding that acceptance is effective upon dispatch, that is, when it is mailed or otherwise taken out of the control of the offeree.

Maker The issuer of a promissory note.

Marital trust A legal entity created for the purpose of reducing a married couple's estate taxes.

Material Important or significant. Information that would affect a person's decision if he knew it.

Mechanic's lien A security created when a worker improves real property.

Mediation The process of using a neutral person to aid in the settlement of a legal dispute. A mediator's decision is non-binding.

Meeting of the minds The parties understood each other and intended to reach an agreement.

Memorandum A document detailing the arguments in support of a motion.

Mens rea Guilty state of mind.

Merchant Someone who routinely deals in the particular goods involved, or who appears to have special knowledge or skill in those goods, or who uses agents with special knowledge or skill in those goods.

Merchantable The goods are fit for the ordinary purposes for which they are used.

Merger An acquisition of one company by another.

Midnight deadline A rule that each bank in the collection process must pass a check along before midnight of the next banking day after it receives the check.

Minor A person under the age of 18.

Minority shareholders Shareholders who do not own enough stock to control their corporation.

Minute book Records of shareholder meetings and directors' meetings are kept in the corporation's minute book.

Mirror image rule A contract doctrine that requires acceptance to be on exactly the same terms as the offer.

Misdemeanor A less serious crime, typically one for which the maximum penalty is incarceration for less than a year, often in a jail, as opposed to a prison.

Misrepresentation A factually incorrect statement made during contract negotiations.

Mitigation One party acts to minimize its losses when the other party breaches a contract.

Modify An appellate court issues an order changing a lower court ruling.

Money laundering Taking the profits of criminal acts and either (1) using the money to promote more crime or (2) attempting to conceal the money's source.

Monopolization A company acquires or maintains a monopoly through the commission of unacceptably aggressive acts. A violation of Section 2 of the Sherman Act.

Mortgage A security interest in real property.

Mortgagee A creditor who obtains a security interest in real property, typically in exchange for money given to the mortgagor to buy the property.

Mortgagor A debtor who gives a mortgage (security interest) in real property to a creditor, typically in exchange for money used to buy the property.

Motion A formal request that a court take some specified step during litigation. A motion to compel discovery is a request that a trial judge order the other party to respond to discovery.

Motion for a protective order A request that the court limit discovery.

Motion to suppress A request that the court exclude evidence because it was obtained in violation of the Constitution.

Multinational enterprise A corporation that is doing business in more than one country simultaneously.

N

NAFTA *See* North American Free Trade Agreement (NAFTA).

National Labor Relations Act (NLRA) Ensures the right of workers to form unions and encourages management and unions to bargain collectively.

National Labor Relations Board (NLRB) The administrative agency charged with overseeing labor law.

Nationalization A government's seizure of property or companies.

Natural law The theory that an unjust law is no law at all, and that a rule is only legitimate if based on an immutable morality.

Negative or dormant aspect of the Commerce Clause The doctrine that prohibits a state from any action that interferes with or discriminates against interstate commerce.

Negligence and strict liability Injuries caused by neglect and oversight rather than by deliberate conduct.

Negligence _per se_ Violation of a standard of care set by statute. Driving while intoxicated is illegal; thus, if a drunk driver injures a pedestrian, he has committed negligence per se.

Negotiable bill of lading A document of title that describes the goods received by the common carrier.

Negotiable instrument A type of commercial paper that is freely transferable.

Negotiation The transfer of an instrument. To be negotiated, order paper must be indorsed and then delivered to the transferee. For bearer paper, no indorsement is required—it must simply be delivered to the transferee.

No-strike clause A clause in a CBA that prohibits the union from striking while the CBA is in force.

Nominal damages A token sum, such as one dollar, given to a plaintiff who demonstrates that the defendant breached the contract but cannot prove serious injury.

Noncompetition agreement A contract in which one party agrees not to compete with another in a stated type of business.

Nonconforming goods Merchandise that differs from that specified in the contract.

Non-point source When pollutants are released simultaneously from more than one source.

Norris-LaGuardia Act Prohibits federal court injunctions in peaceful labor disputes.

North American Free Trade Agreement A commercial association among Canada, the United States, and Mexico designed to eliminate almost all trade barriers.

Note An unconditional, written promise that the maker of the instrument will pay a specific amount of money on demand or at a definite time. When issued by a corporation, a note refers to short-term debt, typically payable within five years.

Notice to quit A landlord's notice terminating a tenancy.

Novation A three-way agreement in which the obligor transfers all rights and duties to a third party.

Nuisance An unprivileged interference with a person's use and enjoyment of property.

Nuncupative will An oral will.

O

Obligee The party to a contract who is entitled to receive performance from the other party.

Obligor The party to a contract who is required to do something for the benefit of the other party.

Obscenity Constitutional law doctrine holding that some works will receive no First Amendment protection because a court determines they depict sexual matters in an offensive way.

Offer In contract law, an act or statement that proposes definite terms and permits the other party to create a contract by accepting those terms.

Offeree The party in contract negotiations who receives the first offer.

Offeror The party in contract negotiations who makes the first offer.

Open-end credit A lender makes a series of loans that the consumer can repay at once or in installments.

Opinion Because it cannot be proven right or wrong, an opinion is generally a valid defense in defamation cases.

Oppression One party uses its superior power to force a contract on the weaker party.

Order for relief An official acknowledgment that a debtor is under the jurisdiction of the bankruptcy court.

Order paper An instrument that includes the words "pay to the order of" or their equivalent.

Output contract An agreement that obligates the seller of goods to sell everything he produces during a stated period to a particular buyer.

Outside directors Members of the board of directors who are not employees of the corporation. Also known as _independent directors_.

Override The power of Congress or a state legislature to pass legislation despite a veto by a president or governor. A congressional override requires a two-thirds vote in each house.

P

Parol evidence Written or oral evidence, outside the language of a contract, offered by one party to clarify interpretation of the agreement.

Parol evidence rule In the case of an integrated contract, neither party may use evidence outside the writing to contradict, vary, or add to its terms.

Part performance An exception to the statute of frauds permitting a buyer of real estate to enforce an oral contract if she paid part of the price, entered the property, and made improvements, with the owner's knowledge.

Partially disclosed principal If the third party in an agency relationship knows that the agent is acting for a principal, but does not know the identity of the principal, that principal is partially disclosed.

Partnership An association of two or more persons to carry on as co-owners of a business for profit.

Partnership at will A partnership that has no fixed duration. A partner has the right to resign from the partnership at any time.

Partnership by estoppel If a person who is not a partner implies that he is a partner or does not object when other people imply it, he is liable as if he really were a partner.

Patent The right to the exclusive use of an invention for 20 years.

Payable on demand The holder of an instrument is entitled to be paid whenever she asks.

Payee Someone who is owed money under the terms of an instrument.

Payment order A transfer money from the issuer's account into the payee's.

Per se An automatic breach of antitrust laws.

Per se violation of an antitrust law An automatic breach. Courts will generally not consider mitigating factors.

Peremptory challenge During *voir dire*, a request by one attorney that a prospective juror be excused for an unstated reason.

Perfect tender rule A rule permitting the buyer to reject goods if they fail in any respect to conform to the contract.

Perfection A series of steps a secured party must take to protect its rights in collateral against people other than the debtor.

Periodic tenancy A lease for a fixed period, automatically renewable unless terminated.

Period for years A lease for a fixed period, automatically renewable unless terminated.

Perpetual trust A trust that lasts forever. Also known as a dynasty trust.

Personal property All property other than real property.

Personally identifiable information (PII) Data that identifies a user of a Web site, such as name and address.

Personal satisfaction contracts Permits the promisee to make a subjective evaluation of the promisor's performance.

Pierce the corporate veil When the court holds shareholders personally liable for the debts of the corporation.

Plain meaning rule In statutory interpretation, the premise that words with an ordinary, everyday significance will be so interpreted, unless there is some apparent reason not to.

Plaintiff The person who is suing.

Plea bargain An agreement in which the defendant pleads guilty to a reduced charge and the prosecution recommends to the judge a relatively lenient sentence.

Pleadings The documents that begin a lawsuit: the complaint, the answer, the counter-claim, and the reply.

Pledge A secured transaction in which a debtor gives collateral to the secured party.

Point source A single producer of pollution.

Political speech Protected unless it is intended and likely to create imminent lawless action.

Positive aspect of the Commerce Clause The power granted to Congress to regulate commerce between the states.

Precedent An earlier case that decided the same legal issue as that presently in dispute, and which therefore will control the outcome of the current case.

Predatory pricing A violation of Section 2 of the Sherman Act in which a company lowers its prices below cost to drive competitors out of business.

Preemption The doctrine, based on the Supremacy Clause, by which any federal statute takes priority whenever (1) a state statute conflicts or (2) there is no conflict but Congress indicated an intention to control the issue involved.

Preference When a debtor unfairly pays creditors immediately before filing a bankruptcy petition.

Preferred stock Owners of preferred stock have a right to receive dividends and liquidation proceeds of the company before common shareholders.

Preponderance of the evidence The level of proof that a plaintiff must meet to prevail in a civil lawsuit. It means that the plaintiff must offer evidence that, in sum, is slightly more persuasive than the defendant's evidence.

Presentment A holder of an instrument makes a demand for payment.

Pretermitted child A child omitted from a parent's will.

Prima facie "At first sight." A fact or conclusion that is presumed to be true unless someone presents evidence to disprove it.

Principal In an agency relationship, the principal is the person for whom the agent is acting.

Privacy Act A federal statute prohibiting federal agencies from divulging to other agencies or organizations information about private citizens.

Private offering A sale of securities that, under the 1933 Act, is not considered a public offering because of the limited number of investors or the small amount of money raised.

Privity The relationship that exists between two parties who make a contract, as opposed to a third party who, though affected by the contract, is not a party to it.

Probable cause In a search and seizure case, it means that the information available indicates that it is more likely than not that a search will uncover particular criminal evidence.

Probate The process of carrying out the terms of a will.

Procedural due process *See* Due Process Clause.

Procedural law The rules establishing how the legal system itself is to operate in a particular kind of case.

Proceeds Anything that a debtor obtains from the sale or disposition of collateral. Normally, the term *proceeds* refers to cash obtained from the sale of the secured property.

Production of documents and things A form of discovery in which one party demands that the other furnish original documents or physical things, relating to the suit, for inspection and copying.

Product liability The potential responsibility that a manufacturer or seller has for injuries caused by defective goods.

Professional corporation A form of organization that permits professionals (such as doctors, lawyers, and accountants) to incorporate. Shareholders are not personally liable for the torts of other shareholders, or for the contract debts of the organization.

Profit The right to enter land belonging to another and take something away, such as minerals or timber.

Promisee The person to whom a promise is made.

Promisor A person who makes a promise.

Promissory estoppel A doctrine in which a court may enforce a promise made by the defendant even when there is no contract, if the defendant knew that the plaintiff was likely to rely on the promise, the plaintiff did in fact rely, and enforcement of it is the only way to avoid injustice.

Promissory note The maker of the instrument promises to pay a specific amount of money.

Promoter The person who creates a corporation by raising capital and undertaking the legal steps necessary for formation.

Promulgate To issue a new rule.

Proof of claim A form stating the name of an unsecured creditor and the amount of the claim against the debtor.

Property insurance Covers physical damage to real estate, personal property, or inventory from causes such as fire, smoke, lightning, wind, riot, vandalism, or theft.

Prosecution The government's attempt to convict a defendant of a crime by charging him, trying the case, and forcing him to defend himself.

Prospectus Under the Securities Act of 1933, an issuer must provide this document to anyone who purchases a security in a public transaction. The prospectus contains detailed information about the issuer and its business, a description of the stock, and audited financial statements.

Protective order A court order limiting one party's discovery.

Provisional patent application A simpler, shorter filing that provides protection for an invention for one year.

Proxy (1) A person whom the shareholder designates to vote in his place. (2) The written form (typically a card) that the shareholder uses to appoint a designated voter.

Proxy statement When a public company seeks proxy votes from its shareholders, it must include a proxy statement. This statement contains information about the company, such as a detailed description of management compensation.

Publicly traded corporation A company that (1) has completed a public offering under the Securities Act of 1933, or (2) has securities traded on a national exchange, or (3) has 500 shareholders and $10 million in assets.

Punitive damages Money awarded at trial not to compensate the plaintiff for harm but to punish the defendant for conduct that the factfinder considers extreme and outrageous.

Purchase money security interest (PMSI) A security interest taken by the person who sells the collateral to the debtor, or by a person who advances money so that the debtor may buy the collateral.

Purchaser representative Someone who has enough knowledge and experience in financial matters to evaluate the merits and risks of an investment.

Q

Qualified privilege When providing a reference about a former employee, an employer is liable for false statements only if he knows them to be false or if he is primarily motivated by ill will between two people who have a legitimate need to exchange information.

Qualifying to do business Registering a corporation in a state in which it is not organized but in which it has an ongoing presence.

Quantum meruit "As much as she deserves." The damages awarded in a quasi-contract case.

Quasi-contract A legal fiction in which, to avoid injustice, the court awards damages as if a contract had existed, although one did not.

Quid pro quo A Latin phrase meaning "this for that." It refers to a form of sexual harassment in which some aspect of a job is made contingent upon sexual activity.

Quiet enjoyment A tenant's right to use property without the interference of the landlord.

Quota A limit on the quantity of a particular good that may enter a nation.

Quorum The number of voters that must be present for a meeting to count.

R

Racketeer Influenced and Corrupt Organizations Act (RICO) A powerful federal statute, originally aimed at organized crime, now used in many criminal prosecutions and civil lawsuits.

Racketeering acts Any of a long list of specified crimes, such as embezzlement, arson, mail fraud, wire fraud, and so forth.

Ratification When someone accepts the benefit of an unauthorized transaction or fails to repudiate it once he has learned of it, he is then bound by it.

Reaffirm To promise to pay a debt even after it is discharged.

Real property Land, together with certain things associated with it, such as buildings, subsurface rights, air rights, plant life and fixtures.

Reasonable doubt The level of proof that the government must meet to convict the defendant in a criminal case. The factfinder must be persuaded to a very high degree of certainty that the defendant did what the government alleges.

Reciprocal dealing agreement An agreement under which Company A will purchase from Company B only if Company B also buys from Company A. These agreements are rule of reason violations of the Sherman Act.

Record Information written on paper or stored in an electronic or other medium.

Record date To vote at a shareholders meeting, a shareholder must own stock on the record date.

Red herring A preliminary prospectus.

Redeem To pay the full value of a debt to get the collateral back.

Reformation The process by which a court rewrites a contract to ensure its accuracy or viability.

Refusal to deal An agreement among competitors that they will not trade with a particular supplier or buyer. Such an agreement is a rule of reason violation of the Sherman Act.

Registration statement A document filed with the Securities and Exchange Commission under the Securities Act of 1933 by an issuer seeking to sell securities in a public transaction.

Regulation D The most common and important type of private offering.

Reliance interest A remedy in a contract case that puts the injured party in the position he would have been in had the parties never entered into a contract.

Remand The power of an appellate court to return a case to a lower court for additional action.

Rent Compensation paid by a tenant to a landlord.

Repatriation of profits The act of bringing profits earned in a foreign country back to a company's home country.

Reply A pleading, filed by the plaintiff in response to a defendant's counter-claim.

Repossession A secured party takes collateral because the debtor has defaulted on payments.

Repudiation An indication made by one contracting party to the other that it will not perform.

Request for admission A form of discovery in which one party demands that the opposing party either admit or deny particular factual or legal allegations.

Requirements contract An agreement that obligates a buyer of specified goods to purchase all of the goods she needs during a stated period from a particular seller.

Res ipsa loquitur A doctrine of tort law holding that the facts may imply negligence when the defendant had exclusive control of the thing that caused the harm, the accident would not normally have occurred without negligence, and the plaintiff played no role in causing the injury.

Resale price maintenance A *per se* violation of the Sherman Act in which a manufacturer enters into an agreement with retailers about the prices they will charge.

Rescind To cancel a contract.

Rescission To "undo" a contract and put the parties where they were before they made their agreement.

Respondeat superior A rule of agency law holding that a principal is liable when a servant acting within the scope of employment commits a tort that causes physical harm to a person or property.

Restitution Restoring an injured party to its original position.

Restitution interest A remedy in a contract case that returns to the injured party a benefit that he has conferred on the other party, which would be unjust to leave with that person.

Restricted security Any stock purchased in a private offering (such as one under Regulation D).

Restricted stock Securities purchased strictly for investment purposes.

Retribution Giving a criminal defendant the punishment he deserves.

Reverse An appellate court issues an order overruling a lower court and granting judgment for the party that had lost in the lower court.

Reverse and remand To nullify the lower decision and return the case for reconsideration or retrial.

Reversion The right of an owner (or her heirs) to property upon the death of a life tenant.

Revocable trust A trust that can be undone or changed at any time.

Revocation The act of disavowing a contract offer, so that the offeree no longer has the power to accept.

Rule of reason violation An action that breaches the antitrust laws only if it has an anticompetitive impact.

Rulemaking The power of an administrative agency to issue regulations.

S

S corporation A corporation that is not a taxable entity.

Sale on approval A transfer in which a buyer takes goods intending to use them herself, but has the right to return the goods to the seller.

Sale or return A transfer in which the buyer takes the goods intending to resell them, but has the right to return the goods to the original owner.

Scienter In a case of securities fraud, the plaintiff must prove that the defendant acted willfully, knowingly, or recklessly.

Secondary boycott Picketing, directed by a union against a company, designed to force that company to stop doing business with the union's employer.

Secondary offering Any public sale of securities by a company after the initial public offering.

Secured party A person or company that holds a security interest.

Security Any purchase in which the buyer invests money in a common enterprise and expects to earn a profit predominantly from the efforts of others.

Security agreement A contract in which the debtor gives a security interest to the secured party.

Security interest An interest in personal property or fixtures that secures the performance of some obligation.

Separation of powers The principle, established by the first three articles of the Constitution, that authority should be divided among the legislative, executive, and judicial branches.

Series Sub-categories of stock.

Servant An agent whose work is closely controlled by the principal.

Service mark A type of trademark used to identify services, not products.

Settlor Someone who creates a trust.

Sexual harassment Unwanted sexual advances, comments or touching, sufficiently severe to violate Title VII of the 1964 Civil Rights Act.

Shilling A seller at auction either bids on his own goods or agrees to cross-bid with a group of other sellers.

Short-swing trading Under Section 16 of the Securities Exchange Act, insiders must turn over to the corporation any profits they make from the purchase and sale or sale and purchase of company securities in a six-month period.

Signatory A person, company, or nation that has signed a legal document, such as a contract, agreement, or treaty.

Signature liability The liability of someone who signs an instrument.

Sight draft An order directing someone else to pay money on demand.

Single recovery principle A rule of tort litigation that requires a plaintiff to claim all damages, present and future, at the time of trial, not afterwards.

Sit-down strike Union members stop working but remain at their job posts, physically blocking replacement workers from taking their places.

Slander *See* Defamation.

Sole proprietorship An unincorporated business owned by a single person.

Sovereign The recognized political power, whom citizens obey.

Sovereign immunity The right of a national government to be free of lawsuits brought in foreign courts.

Spam Unsolicited commercial or bulk e-mail. ("To spam" is to send such e-mail.)

Specific deterrence *See* Deterrence.

Specific performance A contract remedy requiring the breaching party to perform the contract, by conveying land or some unique asset, rather than by paying money damages.

Spyware A computer program that enters a user's computer without permission and monitors and reports the user's activities.

Stakeholder Anyone who is affected by the activities of a corporation, such as employees, customers, creditors, suppliers, shareholders, and neighbors.

Stale check A check presented more than six months after its due date.

Stare decisis "Let the decision stand." A basic principle of the common law, it means that precedent is usually binding.

Statute A law passed by a legislative body, such as Congress.

Statute of frauds This law provides that certain contracts are not enforceable unless in writing.

Statute of limitations A statute that determines the period within which a particular kind of lawsuit must be filed.

Statute of repose A law that places an absolute limit on when a lawsuit may be filed, regardless of when the defect was discovered.

Statutory interpretation A court's power to give meaning to new legislation by clarifying ambiguities, providing limits, and ultimately applying it to a specific fact pattern in litigation.

Straight bankruptcy Also known as liquidation, this form of bankruptcy mandates that the bankrupt's assets be sold to pay creditors but the creditor has no obligation to share future earnings.

Strict liability A tort doctrine holding to a very high standard all those who engage in ultrahazardous activity (e.g., using explosives) or who manufacture certain products.

Strict performance Requires one party to perform its obligations precisely, with no deviation from the contract terms.

Strike The ultimate weapon of a labor union, it occurs when all or most employees of a particular plant or employer walk off the job and refuse to work.

Strike suit A lawsuit without merit that defendants sometimes settle simply to avoid the nuisance of litigation.

Sublease A tenant's transfer of *some* of his legal interest in a property.

Subpoena An order to appear, issued by a court or government body.

Subpoena *duces tecum* An order to produce certain documents or things before a court or government body.

Subprime loan A loan that has an above-market interest rate because the borrower is high-risk.

Subrogated to The bank can substitute for, or take the place of, a party.

Substantial performance The promisor performs contract duties well enough to be entitled to his full contract price, minus the value of any defects.

Substantive due process *See* Due Process Clause.

Substantive law Rules that establish the rights of parties. For example, the prohibition against slander is substantive law, as opposed to procedural law.

Substitute check A paper printout of the electronic version of a check, which is legally the same as the original.

Summary judgment The power of a trial court to terminate a lawsuit before a trial has begun, on the grounds that no essential facts are in dispute.

Supermajority voting Typically, shareholders can approve charter amendments by a majority vote. However, sometimes corporations require more than a majority of shareholders (e.g., 80 percent) to approve certain charter amendments, such as a merger. These provisions are designed to discourage hostile takeovers.

Superseding cause An event that interrupts the chain of causation and relieves a defendant from liability based on her own act.

Supremacy Clause From Article VI of the Constitution, it declares that federal statutes and treaties take priority over any state law, if there is a conflict between the two or, even absent a conflict, if Congress manifests an intent to preempt the field.

Surplus A sum of money greater than the debt incurred.

T

Takings Clause Part of the Fifth Amendment, it ensures that when any governmental unit takes private property for public use, it must compensate the owner.

Tariff A duty imposed on imported goods by the government of the importing nation.

Tenancy at sufferance A tenancy that exists without the permission of the landlord, after the expiration of a true tenancy.

Tenancy at will A tenancy with no fixed duration, which may be terminated by either party at any time.

Tenancy by the entirety A form of joint ownership available only to married couples. If one member of the couple dies, the property goes automatically to the survivor. Creditors cannot attach the property, nor can one owner sell the property without the other's permission.

Tenancy for years A lease for a stated, fixed period.

Tenancy in common Two or more people holding equal interest in a property, but with no right of survivorship.

Tenant A person given temporary possession of the landlord's property.

Tender To make conforming goods available to the buyer.

Tender offer A public offer to buy a block of stock directly from shareholders.

Term partnership When the partners agree in advance on the duration of a partnership.

Termination statement A document indicating that a secured party no longer claims a security interest in the collateral.

Testamentary trust A trust created by the grantor's will.

Testator Someone who dies having executed a will.

Testatrix A female testator.

Third party beneficiary Someone who stands to benefit from a contract to which she is not a party. An *intended* beneficiary may enforce such a contract; an *incidental* beneficiary may not.

Three-Fifths Clause A clause in Article 1, section 2 of the United States Constitution, now void and regarded as racist, which required that for purposes of taxation and representation, a slave should be counted as three-fifths of a person.

Tied product In a tying arrangement, the product that a buyer must purchase as the condition for being allowed to buy another product.

Time draft An order directing someone else to pay money in the future.

Time of the essence clause A clause that generally makes contract dates strictly enforceable.

Tort A civil wrong, committed in violation of a duty that the law imposes.

Tortious interference with a contract A tort in which the defendant deliberately impedes an existing contract between the plaintiff and another entity.

Tortious interference with a prospective advantage A tort in which the defendant deliberately obstructs a developing venture or advantage that the plaintiff has created.

Tracing When an auditor takes an item of original data and tracks it forward to ensure that it has been properly recorded throughout the bookkeeping process.

Trade acceptance A draft drawn by a seller of goods on the buyer and payable to the seller or some third party.

Trade secret A formula, device, process, method, or compilation of information that, when used in business, gives the owner an advantage over competitors who do not know it.

Trademark Any combination of words and symbols that a business uses to identify its products or services and that federal law will protect.

Treasury stock Stock that has been bought back by its issuing corporation.

Trespass A tort committed by intentionally entering land that belongs to someone else, or remaining on the land after being asked to leave.

Trespasser Anyone on a property without consent.

Trial court Any court in a state or federal system that holds formal hearings to determine the facts in a civil or criminal case.

Trust An entity that separates legal and beneficial ownership.

Tying a product In a tying arrangement, the product offered for sale on the condition that another product be purchased as well.

Tying arrangement A violation of the Sherman and Clayton Acts in which a seller requires that two distinct products be purchased together. The seller uses its significant power in the market for the tying product to shut out a substantial part of the market for the tied product.

U

Ultra vires An activity that is not permitted by a corporation's charter.

Ultrahazardous activity Conduct that is lawful yet unusual and much more likely to cause injury than normal commercial activity.

Unconscionable contract An agreement that a court refuses to enforce because it is fundamentally unfair as a result of unequal bargaining power by one party.

Undisclosed principal If a third party in an agency relationship does not know that the agent is acting for a principal, that principal is undisclosed.

Undue influence One party so dominates the thinking of another party to a contract that the dominant party cannot truly consent to the agreement.

Unenforceable agreement An agreement that a court will not enforce.

Unfair labor practice An act, committed by either a union or an employer, that violates the National Labor Relations Act, such as failing to bargain in good faith.

Unilateral contract A binding agreement in which one party has made an offer that the other can accept only by action, not words.

Unilateral mistake Occurs when only one party enters a contract under a mistaken assumption.

Unliquidated debt A claimed debt that is disputed, either because the parties disagree over whether there is in fact a debt or because they disagree over the amount.

U.S. Trustee, The Oversees the administration of bankruptcy law in a region.

Usury Charging interest at a rate that exceeds legal limits.

Utter To pass on an instrument that one knows to be forged.

V

Valid contract An agreement that satisfies all of the law's requirements and is enforceable in court.

Value The holder has *already* done something in exchange for the instrument.

Valuation A process by which the Customs Service determines the fair value of goods being imported, for purposes of imposing a duty.

Variance An exception from zoning laws that is granted by a zoning board for special reasons unique to the property.

Veil of ignorance The rules for society that we would propose if we did not know how lucky we would be in life's lottery.

Verdict The decision of the factfinder in a case.

Vertical agreement or merger An agreement or merger between two companies at different stages of the production process, such as when a company acquires one of its suppliers or distributors.

Veto The power of the president to reject legislation passed by Congress, terminating the bill unless Congress votes by a 2/3 majority to override.

Vouching Auditors choose a transaction listed in a company's books and check backwards for original data to support it.

Void agreement An agreement that neither party may legally enforce, usually because the purpose of the bargain was illegal or because one of the parties lacked capacity to make it.

Voidable contract An agreement that, because of some defect, may be terminated by one party, such as a minor, but not by both parties.

Voidable title Limited rights in goods, inferior to those of the owner.

Voir dire The process of selecting a jury. Attorneys for the parties and the judge may inquire of prospective jurors whether they are biased or incapable of rendering a fair and impartial verdict.

W

Warranty A guarantee that goods will meet certain standards.

Warranty of fitness for a particular purpose An assurance under the Uniform Commercial Code that the goods are fit for the special purpose for which the buyer intends them and of which the seller is aware.

Warranty liability The liability of someone who receives payment on an instrument.

Warranty of merchantability An assurance under the Uniform Commercial Code that the goods are fit for their ordinary purpose.

Whistleblower Someone who discloses wrongful behavior.

Winding up The process whereby the assets of a partnership are sold and the proceeds distributed.

World Trade Organization (WTO) Created by GATT to stimulate international commerce and resolve trade disputes.

World Wide Web A decentralized collection of documents containing text, pictures and sound that is accessible from Internet sites. It is a sub-network of the Internet.

Writ An order from a government compelling someone to do a particular thing.

Writ of certiorari A petition asking the Supreme Court to hear a case.

Written consent Instead of holding a meeting, participants may sign a document approving certain actions.

Wrongful discharge An employer may not fire a worker for a reason that violates basic social rights, duties, or responsibilities.